CODE OF FEDERAL REGULATIONS

Title 12
Banks and Banking

Parts 500 to 599

Revised as of January 1, 2012

Containing a codification of documents
of general applicability and future effect

As of January 1, 2012

Published by the Office of the Federal Register
National Archives and Records Administration
as a Special Edition of the Federal Register

Table of Contents

	Page
Explanation	v

Title 12:

| Chapter V—Office of Thrift Supervision, Department of the Treasury | 3 |

Finding Aids:

Table of CFR Titles and Chapters	567
Alphabetical List of Agencies Appearing in the CFR	587
List of CFR Sections Affected	597

Cite this Code: CFR

To cite the regulations in this volume use title, part and section number. Thus, 12 CFR 500.1 refers to title 12, part 500, section 1.

Explanation

The Code of Federal Regulations is a codification of the general and permanent rules published in the Federal Register by the Executive departments and agencies of the Federal Government. The Code is divided into 50 titles which represent broad areas subject to Federal regulation. Each title is divided into chapters which usually bear the name of the issuing agency. Each chapter is further subdivided into parts covering specific regulatory areas.

Each volume of the Code is revised at least once each calendar year and issued on a quarterly basis approximately as follows:

Title 1 through Title 16..as of January 1
Title 17 through Title 27..as of April 1
Title 28 through Title 41..as of July 1
Title 42 through Title 50..as of October 1

The appropriate revision date is printed on the cover of each volume.

LEGAL STATUS

The contents of the Federal Register are required to be judicially noticed (44 U.S.C. 1507). The Code of Federal Regulations is prima facie evidence of the text of the original documents (44 U.S.C. 1510).

HOW TO USE THE CODE OF FEDERAL REGULATIONS

The Code of Federal Regulations is kept up to date by the individual issues of the Federal Register. These two publications must be used together to determine the latest version of any given rule.

To determine whether a Code volume has been amended since its revision date (in this case, January 1, 2012), consult the "List of CFR Sections Affected (LSA)," which is issued monthly, and the "Cumulative List of Parts Affected," which appears in the Reader Aids section of the daily Federal Register. These two lists will identify the Federal Register page number of the latest amendment of any given rule.

EFFECTIVE AND EXPIRATION DATES

Each volume of the Code contains amendments published in the Federal Register since the last revision of that volume of the Code. Source citations for the regulations are referred to by volume number and page number of the Federal Register and date of publication. Publication dates and effective dates are usually not the same and care must be exercised by the user in determining the actual effective date. In instances where the effective date is beyond the cut-off date for the Code a note has been inserted to reflect the future effective date. In those instances where a regulation published in the Federal Register states a date certain for expiration, an appropriate note will be inserted following the text.

OMB CONTROL NUMBERS

The Paperwork Reduction Act of 1980 (Pub. L. 96–511) requires Federal agencies to display an OMB control number with their information collection request.

Many agencies have begun publishing numerous OMB control numbers as amendments to existing regulations in the CFR. These OMB numbers are placed as close as possible to the applicable recordkeeping or reporting requirements.

OBSOLETE PROVISIONS

Provisions that become obsolete before the revision date stated on the cover of each volume are not carried. Code users may find the text of provisions in effect on a given date in the past by using the appropriate numerical list of sections affected. For the period before April 1, 2001, consult either the List of CFR Sections Affected, 1949–1963, 1964–1972, 1973–1985, or 1986–2000, published in eleven separate volumes. For the period beginning April 1, 2001, a "List of CFR Sections Affected" is published at the end of each CFR volume.

"[RESERVED]" TERMINOLOGY

The term "[Reserved]" is used as a place holder within the Code of Federal Regulations. An agency may add regulatory information at a "[Reserved]" location at any time. Occasionally "[Reserved]" is used editorially to indicate that a portion of the CFR was left vacant and not accidentally dropped due to a printing or computer error.

INCORPORATION BY REFERENCE

What is incorporation by reference? Incorporation by reference was established by statute and allows Federal agencies to meet the requirement to publish regulations in the Federal Register by referring to materials already published elsewhere. For an incorporation to be valid, the Director of the Federal Register must approve it. The legal effect of incorporation by reference is that the material is treated as if it were published in full in the Federal Register (5 U.S.C. 552(a)). This material, like any other properly issued regulation, has the force of law.

What is a proper incorporation by reference? The Director of the Federal Register will approve an incorporation by reference only when the requirements of 1 CFR part 51 are met. Some of the elements on which approval is based are:

(a) The incorporation will substantially reduce the volume of material published in the Federal Register.

(b) The matter incorporated is in fact available to the extent necessary to afford fairness and uniformity in the administrative process.

(c) The incorporating document is drafted and submitted for publication in accordance with 1 CFR part 51.

What if the material incorporated by reference cannot be found? If you have any problem locating or obtaining a copy of material listed as an approved incorporation by reference, please contact the agency that issued the regulation containing that incorporation. If, after contacting the agency, you find the material is not available, please notify the Director of the Federal Register, National Archives and Records Administration, 8601 Adelphi Road, College Park, MD 20740-6001, or call 202-741-6010.

CFR INDEXES AND TABULAR GUIDES

A subject index to the Code of Federal Regulations is contained in a separate volume, revised annually as of January 1, entitled CFR INDEX AND FINDING AIDS. This volume contains the Parallel Table of Authorities and Rules. A list of CFR titles, chapters, subchapters, and parts and an alphabetical list of agencies publishing in the CFR are also included in this volume.

An index to the text of "Title 3—The President" is carried within that volume.

The Federal Register Index is issued monthly in cumulative form. This index is based on a consolidation of the "Contents" entries in the daily Federal Register.

A List of CFR Sections Affected (LSA) is published monthly, keyed to the revision dates of the 50 CFR titles.

REPUBLICATION OF MATERIAL

There are no restrictions on the republication of material appearing in the Code of Federal Regulations.

INQUIRIES

For a legal interpretation or explanation of any regulation in this volume, contact the issuing agency. The issuing agency's name appears at the top of odd-numbered pages.

For inquiries concerning CFR reference assistance, call 202-741-6000 or write to the Director, Office of the Federal Register, National Archives and Records Administration, 8601 Adelphi Road, College Park, MD 20740-6001 or e-mail fedreg.info@nara.gov.

THIS TITLE

Title 12—BANKS AND BANKING is composed of eight volumes. The parts in these volumes are arranged in the following order: Parts 1–199, 200–219, 220–229, 230–299, 300–499, 500–599, part 600–899, and 900–end. The first volume containing parts 1–199 is comprised of chapter I—Comptroller of the Currency, Department of the Treasury. The second, third and fourth volumes containing parts 200–299 are comprised of chapter II—Federal Reserve System. The fifth volume containing parts 300–499 is comprised of chapter III—Federal Deposit Insurance Corporation and chapter IV—Export-Import Bank of the United States. The sixth volume containing parts 500–599 is comprised of chapter V—Office of Thrift Supervision, Department of the Treasury. The seventh volume containing parts 600–899 is comprised of chapter VI—Farm Credit Administration, chapter VII—National Credit Union Administration, chapter VIII—Federal Financing Bank. The eighth volume containing part 900–end is comprised of chapter IX—Federal Housing Finance Board, chapter XI—Federal Financial Institutions Examination Council, chapter XIV—Farm Credit System Insurance Corporation, chapter XV—Department of the Treasury, chapter XVII—Office of Federal Housing Enterprise Oversight, Department of Housing and Urban Development and chapter XVIII—Community Development Financial Institutions Fund, Department of the Treasury. The contents of these volumes represent all of the current regulations codified under this title of the CFR as of January 1, 2012.

For this volume, Bonnie Fritts was Chief Editor. The Code of Federal Regulations publication program is under the direction of Michael L. White, assisted by Ann Worley.

Title 12—Banks and Banking

(This book contains parts 500 to 599)

	Part
CHAPTER V—Office of Thrift Supervision, Department of the Treasury	500

CHAPTER V—OFFICE OF THRIFT SUPERVISION, DEPARTMENT OF THE TREASURY

EDITORIAL NOTE: Nomenclature changes to chapter V appear at 59 FR 18475, Apr. 19, 1994, and 60 FR 66715, Dec. 26, 1995.

Part		Page
500	Agency organization and functions	5
502	Assessments and fees	6
503	Privacy Act	12
505	Freedom of Information Act	14
506	Information collection requirements under the Paperwork Reduction Act	15
507	Restrictions on post-employment activities of senior examiners	16
508	Removals, suspensions, and prohibitions where a crime is charged or proven	17
509	Rules of practice and procedure in adjudicatory proceedings	21
510	Miscellaneous organizational regulations	46
512	Rules for investigative proceedings and formal examination proceedings	51
513	Practice before the Office	53
516	Application processing procedures	60
517	Contracting outreach programs	71
528	Nondiscrimination requirements	72
533	Disclosure and reporting of CRA-related agreements	78
535	Unfair or deceptive acts or practices	90
536	Consumer protection in sales of insurance	93
541	Definitions for regulations affecting Federal savings associations	97
543	Federal mutual savings associations—incorporation, organization, and conversion	99
544	Federal mutual savings associations—charter and bylaws	105
545	Federal savings associations—operations	113
546	Federal mutual savings associations—merger, dissolution, reorganization, and conversion	118
550	Fiduciary powers of savings associations	120

Part		Page
551	Recordkeeping and confirmation requirements for securities transactions	131
552	Federal stock associations—incorporation, organization, and conversion	139
555	Electronic operations	157
557	Deposits	158
558	Possession by conservators and receivers for Federal and State savings associations	160
559	Subordinate organizations	161
560	Lending and investment	168
561	Definitions for regulations affecting all savings associations	191
562	Regulatory reporting standards	197
563	Savings associations—operations	199
563b	Conversions from mutual to stock form	235
563c	Accounting requirements	262
563d	Securities of savings associations	271
563e	Community reinvestment	273
563f	Management official interlocks	295
563g	Securities offerings	300
564	Appraisals	309
565	Prompt corrective action	314
567	Capital	324
568	Security procedures	419
569	Proxies	420
570	Safety and soundness guidelines and compliance procedures	421
571	Fair Credit Reporting	433
572	Loans in areas having special flood hazards	467
573	Privacy of consumer financial information	471
574	Acquisition of control of savings associations	498
575	Mutual holding companies	519
583	Definitions for regulations affecting savings and loan holding companies	541
584	Savings and loan holding companies	544
585	Prohibited service at savings and loan holding companies	551
590	Preemption of State usury laws	554
591	Preemption of State due-on-sale laws	560
592–599	[Reserved]	

PART 500—AGENCY ORGANIZATION AND FUNCTIONS

Subpart A—Functions and Responsibilities of the Director of the Office of Thrift Supervision

Sec.
500.1 General statement and statutory authority.
500.2–500.5 [Reserved]
500.6 General statement concerning gender-related terminology.

Subpart B—General Organization

500.10 The OTS or The Office.

Subpart C—Procedures

500.30 General statement concerning procedures and forms.

AUTHORITY: 12 U.S.C. 1462a, 1463, 1464.

SOURCE: 54 FR 49440, Nov. 30, 1989, unless otherwise noted.

Subpart A—Functions and Responsibilities of the Director of the Office of Thrift Supervision

§ 500.1 General statement and statutory authority.

(a) The Director of the Office of Thrift Supervision (referred to in this chapter as "Director" or "Office") is responsible for the administration and enforcement of the Home Owners' Loan Act of 1933, ("HOLA"), and applicable portions of the Federal Deposit Insurance Act and with respect to savings associations subject to provisions of the foregoing acts and title, the Bank Protection Act of 1968, the Truth in Lending Act, and the Fair Credit Reporting Act.

(b) The Office is authorized under such rules and regulations as it may prescribe to provide for the organization, incorporation, examination, operation, and regulation of Federal savings associations. Under this authority, the Office's functions include, but are not limited to, regulation of the corporate structure of such associations, regulation of the distribution of their earnings, regulation of their lending and other investment powers, acting upon their applications for facility offices (including branch offices, limited facilities, mobile facilities and satellite offices), the regulation of mergers, conversions, and dissolutions involving such associations, the appointment of conservators and receivers for such associations, and the enforcement of laws, regulations, or conditions against such associations or the officers or directors thereof by proceedings under section 5 of the Home Owners' Loan Act of 1933, as amended.

(c) The Office regulates and examines savings associations within the authority conferred by the HOLA and the FDIA and is authorized to enforce applicable laws, regulations, or conditions against savings associations or the officers or directors thereof by proceedings under section 5 of the HOLA and section 8 of the FDIA as amended. The Office also regulates and supervises savings and loan holding companies pursuant to the provisions of section 10 of the HOLA, as amended, and section 8 of the FDIA.

(d) The Office exercises supervisory and regulatory authority over all building and loan or savings and loan associations and similar institutions of or doing business in or maintaining offices in the District of Columbia.

[54 FR 49440, Nov. 30, 1989, as amended at 60 FR 66868, Dec. 27, 1995]

§ 500.2–500.5 [Reserved]

§ 500.6 General statement concerning gender-related terminology.

The statutes administered by the Office and the rules, regulations, policies, practices, publications, directives, and guidelines promulgated pursuant to such statutes that prescribe the course and methods to be followed by the Office that inadvertently use or contain gender-related terminology are to be interpreted as equally applicable to either sex.

Subpart B—General Organization

§ 500.10 The OTS or The Office.

The Office of Thrift Supervision (referred to as "OTS" or "Office") is an

§ 500.30

office of the Department of the Treasury. Its functions are to charter, supervise, regulate and examine Federal savings associations and to supervise, regulate and examine all savings associations. It is directed by a Director, who is appointed by the President and confirmed by the Senate to a five-year term. The Director directs and carries out the mission of the OTS with the assistance of offices reporting directly to him. One of these offices oversees the direct examination and supervision of savings associations by regulatory staff to ensure the safety and soundness of the industry.

[57 FR 14335, Apr. 20, 1992, as amended at 60 FR 66869, Dec. 27, 1995]

Subpart C—Procedures

§ 500.30 General statement concerning procedures and forms.

(a) Rules and procedures of the Office are published in chapter V of title 12 of the Code of Federal Regulations and in supplementary material published in the FEDERAL REGISTER. The statutes administered by the Office and the rules and regulations promulgated pursuant to such statutes prescribe the course and method of the formal procedures to be followed in proceedings of the Office. These are supplemented where practicable by informal procedures designed to aid the public and facilitate the execution of the Office's functions. The informal procedures of the Office consist principally in the rendering of advice and assistance to members of the public dealing with the Office. Opinions expressed by members of the staff do not constitute an official expression of the views of the Office, but do represent views of persons working with the provisions of the statute or regulation involved. The Director may, for good cause and to the extent permitted by statute, waive the applicability of any provision of this chapter.

(b) Information with respect to procedures, forms, and instructions of the Office is available to the public at the headquarters of the Office. Forms of concern to the public consist principally of periodic financial reports and of applications to the Office. The Office may from time to time require the completion by individuals or savings associations of miscellaneous forms, questionnaires, reports, or other papers. In each instance, the individual or savings association is given actual and timely notice of the scope and contents of the papers in question.

[54 FR 49440, Nov. 30, 1989, as amended at 59 FR 53570, Oct. 25, 1994]

PART 502—ASSESSMENTS AND FEES

Sec.
502.5 Who must pay assessments and fees?

Subpart A—Assessments

SAVING ASSOCIATIONS—CALCULATION OF ASSESSMENTS

502.10 How does OTS calculate the semi-annual assessment for savings associations?
502.15 How does OTS determine my size component?
502.20 How does OTS determine my condition component?
502.25 How does OTS determine my complexity component?

SAVINGS AND LOAN HOLDING COMPANIES—CALCULATION OF ASSESSMENTS

502.26 How does OTS calculate the semi-annual assessment for savings and loan holding companies?
502.27 How does OTS determine the risk/complexity component for a savings and loan holding company?
502.28 How does OTS determine the organizational form component for a savings and loan holding company?
502.29 How does OTS determine the condition component for a savings and loan holding company?

PAYMENT OF ASSESSMENTS

502.30 When must I pay my assessment?
502.35 How do I pay my assessment?
502.40 Will OTS refund or prorate my assessment?
502.45 What will happen if I do not pay my assessment on time?

Subpart B—Fees

502.50 What fees does OTS charge?
502.55 Where can I find OTS's fee schedule?
502.60 When will OTS adjust, add, waive, or eliminate a fee?
502.65 When is an application fee due?
502.70 How must I pay an application fee?
502.75 What if I do not pay my fees on time?

AUTHORITY: 12 U.S.C. 1462a, 1463, 1467, 1467a.

SOURCE: 63 FR 65670, Nov. 30, 1998, unless otherwise noted.

Office of Thrift Supervision, Treasury § 502.15

§ 502.5 Who must pay assessments and fees?

(a) *Authority.* Section 9 of the HOLA, 12 U.S.C. 1467, authorizes the Director to charge assessments to recover the costs of examining savings associations and their affiliates, to charge fees to recover the costs of processing applications and other filings, and to charge fees to cover OTS's direct and indirect expenses in regulating savings associations and their affiliates.

(b) *Assessments.* If you are a savings association or a responsible savings and loan holding company, and OTS regulates you on the last day of January or on the last day of July of each year, you must pay a semi-annual assessment due on that day. Subpart A of this part describes OTS's assessment procedures and requirements.

(c) *Fees.* If you make a filing with OTS or use OTS services, the Director may require you to pay a fee to cover the costs of processing your submission or providing those services. The Director may charge a fee for any filing including notices, applications, and securities filings. The Director may charge a fee for any service including publications, seminars, certifications for official copies of agency documents, and records or services requested by other agencies. The Director also assesses fees for examining and investigating savings associations that administer trust assets of $1 billion or less, and savings association affiliates. If OTS incurs extraordinary expenses related to examination, investigation, regulation, or supervision of a savings association or its affiliate, the Director may charge the savings association or the affiliate a fee to fund those expenses. Subpart B of this part describes OTS's fee procedures and requirements.

[63 FR 65670, Nov. 30, 1998, as amended at 67 FR 78151, Dec. 23, 2002; 69 FR 30568, May 28, 2004]

Subpart A—Assessments

SOURCE: 69 FR 30568, May 28, 2004, unless otherwise noted.

SAVINGS ASSOCIATIONS—CALCULATION OF ASSESSMENTS

§ 502.10 How does OTS calculate the semi-annual assessment for savings associations?

(a) If you are a savings association, OTS determines your semi-annual assessment by totaling three components: your size, your condition, and the complexity of your business. OTS determines the amounts of each component under §§ 502.15 through 502.25 of this part.

(b) OTS uses the September 30 Thrift Financial Report to determine amounts due at the January 31 assessment; and the March 31 Thrift Financial Report to determine amounts due at the July 31 assessment. For purposes of §§ 502.10 through 502.25 of this part, total assets are your total assets as reported on Thrift Financial Reports filed with OTS.

§ 502.15 How does OTS determine my size component?

(a) *Chart.* If you are a savings association, OTS uses the following chart to calculate your size component:

If your total assets are: . . .		Your size component is:		
Over—*	But not over—	This amount— Base assessment amount	Plus—Marginal rate	Of assets over—Class floor
Column A	Column B	Column C	Column D	Column E
0	$67 million	C1	D1	0.
$67 million	215 million	C2	D2	$67 million.
215 million	1 billion	C3	D3	215 million.
1 billion	6.03 billion	C4	D4	1 billion.
6.03 billion	18 billion	C5	D5	6.03 billion.
18 billion	35 billion	C6	D6	18 billion.
35 billion		C7	D7	35 billion.

§ 502.20

(b) *Calculation.* To calculate your size component, find the row in Columns A and B that describes your total assets. Reading across in that same row, find your base assessment amount in Column C, your marginal rate in Column D, and your class floor in Column E. Calculate how much your total assets exceed your Column E class floor. Multiply this number by your Column D marginal rate. Add this number to your Column C base assessment amount. The total is your size component. OTS will establish the base assessment amounts and the marginal rates in columns C and D in a Thrift Bulletin.

§ 502.20 How does OTS determine my condition component?

(a) If you are a savings association, OTS uses the following chart to determine your condition component:

If your composite rating is:	Then your condition component is:
1 or 2	Zero.
3	50 percent of your size component.
4 or 5	100 percent of your size component.

(b) For the purposes of this section, OTS uses the most recent composite rating, as defined in 12 CFR part 516, of which you have been notified in writing before an assessment's due date.

§ 502.25 How does OTS determine my complexity component?

If you are a savings association and your portfolio exceeds any of the thresholds in paragraph (a) of this section, OTS will calculate your complexity component according to paragraph (c) of this section. If your portfolio does not exceed any of the thresholds in paragraph (a) of this section, your complexity component is zero.

(a) *Thresholds for complexity component.* OTS uses three separate thresholds in calculating your complexity component. You exceed a threshold if you have more than $1 billion in any of the following:

(1) Trust assets that you administer.

(2) The outstanding principal balances of assets that are covered, fully or partially, by your recourse obligations or direct credit substitutes.

(3) The principal amount of loans that you service for others.

(b) *Assessment rates.* OTS will establish one or more assessment rates for each of the types of activities listed in paragraph (a) of this section. OTS will publish those assessment rates in a Thrift Bulletin.

(c) *Calculation of complexity component.* OTS separately considers each of the thresholds in paragraph (a) of this section in calculating your complexity component. OTS first calculates the amount by which you exceed any of those thresholds. OTS multiplies the amount by which you exceed any thresholds in paragraph (a) of this section by the applicable assessment rate(s) under paragraph (b) of this section. OTS then totals the results. This total is your complexity component.

SAVINGS AND LOAN HOLDING COMPANIES—CALCULATION OF ASSESSMENTS

§ 502.26 How does OTS calculate the semi-annual assessment for savings and loan holding companies?

(a) OTS calculates the semi-annual assessment savings and loan holding companies as follows:

(1) OTS will assess a base assessment amount of $3,500 on responsible savings and loan holding companies. The base assessment amount reflects OTS's estimate of the base costs of conducting on- and off-site supervision of a noncomplex, low risk savings and loan holding company structure. OTS will periodically revise this amount to reflect changes in inflation based on a readily available index. OTS will establish the revised amount of the base assessment in a Thrift Bulletin.

(2) OTS will add three components to the base assessment amount to compute the amount of the semi-annual assessment for responsible savings and loan holding companies: a component based on the risk or complexity of the savings and loan holding company's business, a component based on its organizational form, and a component based on its condition. OTS determines the amount of each component under §§ 502.27 through 502.29 of this part.

(b) For purposes of the semi-annual assessment of savings and loan holding companies:

(1) The *responsible holding company* is the registered holding company at the highest level of ownership in a holding

Office of Thrift Supervision, Treasury § 502.27

company structure, unless OTS designates another savings and loan holding company in the holding company structure. OTS may designate an intermediate-tier holding company if the assessment of this entity would more accurately reflect OTS costs of supervising the holding company structure and:

(i) There are multiple top-tier holding companies in the holding company structure;

(ii) The top-tier holding company is organized outside of the United States, and is subject to the consolidated review of a foreign regulator; or

(iii) Other circumstances indicate that the assessment of the top-tier holding company is inappropriate.

(2) *Total consolidated holding company assets* are the total assets as reported on the Thrift Financial Report, Schedule HC. If Schedule HC is unavailable, OTS will use total assets reported on report H–(b)11. OTS uses information contained in the September 30 Schedule HC or report H–(b)11 to determine amounts due at the January 31 assessment; and the March 31 Schedule HC or report H–(b)11 to determine amounts due at the July 31 assessment.

[69 FR 30568, May 28, 2004, as amended at 74 FR 68665, Dec. 29, 2009]

§ 502.27 How does OTS determine the risk/complexity component for a savings and loan holding company?

(a) OTS computes the risk/complexity component for responsible savings and loan holding companies using schedules that set out charges based on OTS holding company risk/complexity classifications and total consolidated holding company assets. OTS will establish these schedules in a Thrift Bulletin.

(b) For the purposes of this section, the holding company risk/complexity classification is the most recent risk/complexity classification of which OTS notified the savings and loan holding company in writing before an assessment's due date.

(1) OTS classifies holding companies as Category I (low risk, noncomplex holding company); Category II (complex or high risk holding company); or Category III (conglomerate).

(2) The OTS holding company risk/complexity classifications reflect OTS's assessment of a holding company's financial condition, financial independence of the savings association and other affiliates that are regulated financial entities, operational independence of the savings association and other affiliates that are regulated financial entities, reputational risks raised by affiliation with the holding company, and management experience of the holding company, savings association, and affiliates. The OTS holding company risk/complexity classification system is more fully described in the OTS Holding Company Handbook.

(3) A conglomerate is a holding company that: (i) is one of the most complex or highest risk holding companies under the holding company risk/complexity classification system; (ii) is made up of a number of different companies or legal enterprises that offer products from more than one financial sector (e.g., insurance, securities, and banking) or operate in diversified fields; and (iii) generally manages these companies and enterprises along functional lines, rather than as separate legal entities.

(c) OTS uses the following chart to compute the risk/complexity component under this section. OTS will establish the amounts in column C and D in the Thrift Bulletin for each holding company risk/complexity classification. The amounts established for column C and D that are applicable to conglomerates will be three times the amounts established for column C and D for complex or higher risk holding company enterprises of the same asset size.

If your total consolidated assets are . . .		Your risk/complexity component is . . .		
Over . . .	But not over . . .	This amount . . .	Plus—this marginal rate . . .	Of assets over . . .
Column A	Column B	Column C	Column D	Column E
$0	$150 Million	C1	D1	$0
150 Million	250 Million	C2	D2	150 Million

§ 502.28

If your total consolidated assets are . . .		Your risk/complexity component is . . .		
Over . . .	But not over . . .	This amount . . .	Plus—this marginal rate . . .	Of assets over . . .
Column A	Column B	Column C	Column D	Column E
250 Million	500 Million	C3	D3	250 Million
500 Million	1 Billion	C4	D4	500 Million
1 Billion	5 Billion	C5	D5	1 Billion
5 Billion	50 Billion	C6	D6	5 Billion
50 Billion	100 Billion	C7	D7	50 Billion
100 Billion	300 Billion	C8	D8	100 Billion
Over 300 Billion		C9	D9	300 Billion

(d) To compute your risk/complexity component, find the row in the appropriate schedule that describes your total consolidated assets by referring to the amounts in Columns A and B. In that row, calculate how much your total consolidated assets exceed the class floor (Column E); multiply this number by your marginal rate (Column D); and add the product to the amount in Column C. The total is your risk/complexity component.

§ 502.28 How does OTS determine the organizational form component for a savings and loan holding company?

OTS will include an organizational form component if you are a responsible savings and loan holding company that OTS regulates under section 10(l) of the HOLA. OTS will compute your organizational form component by adding the base assessment to your risk/complexity component, and multiplying this amount by 25 percent.

§ 502.29 How does OTS determine the condition component for a savings and loan holding company?

(a) If the most recent examination rating assigned to the responsible savings and loan holding company (or most recent examination rating assigned to any savings and loan holding company in the holding company structure) is a composite rating of 4 or 5, OTS will assess a charge under the condition component. The amount of the condition component is equal to 100 percent of the sum of the base assessment amount, the risk/complexity component, and any organizational form component.

(b) For the purposes of this section, examination ratings are the ratings that OTS assigns under the OTS holding company rating system. OTS uses the most recent rating of which the savings and loan holding company has been notified in writing before an assessment's due date.

[69 FR 30568, May 28, 2004, as amended at 74 FR 68665, Dec. 29, 2009]

PAYMENT OF ASSESSMENTS

§ 502.30 When must I pay my assessment?

OTS will bill you semi-annually for your assessments. Assessments are due January 31 and July 31 of each year, unless that date is a Saturday, Sunday, or Federal holiday. If the due date is a Saturday, Sunday or Federal holiday, your assessment is due on the first day preceding the due date that is not a Saturday, Sunday or Federal holiday. At least seven days before your assessment is due, the Director will mail you a notice that indicates the amount of your assessment, explains how OTS calculated the amount, and specifies when payment is due.

§ 502.35 How do I pay my assessment?

(a) *Savings associations.* (1) If you are a member of a Federal Home Loan Bank that offers demand deposit accounts which permit direct debits, you must maintain a demand deposit account at your Federal Home Loan Bank with sufficient funds to pay your assessment when due. OTS will notify your Federal Home Loan Bank of the amount of your assessment. OTS will debit your account for your assessments.

(2) If paragraph (a)(1) of this section does not apply to you, OTS will directly debit an account you must maintain at your association.

(b) *Savings and loan holding companies.* You may establish an account at

Office of Thrift Supervision, Treasury

§ 502.60

an insured depository institution and authorize OTS to debit the account for your semi-annual assessment. If you do not establish an account and maintain funds in the account sufficient to pay the semi-annual assessment when due, OTS may charge you a fee to cover its administrative costs of collecting and billing your assessment. This fee is in addition to interest on delinquent assessments charged under § 502.45 of this part. OTS will establish the amount of the administrative fee and publish the amount of the fee in a Thrift Bulletin.

§ 502.40 Will OTS refund or prorate my assessment?

(a) OTS will not refund or prorate your assessment, even if you cease to be a savings association or a savings and loan holding company.

(b) If a conservator or receiver has been appointed, you must continue to pay assessments in accordance with this part. OTS will not increase or decrease your assessment based on events that occur after the date of the Thrift Financial Report or H–(b)11 Annual/Current Report upon which your assessment is based.

§ 502.45 What will happen if I do not pay my assessment on time?

(a) Your assessment is delinquent if you do not pay it on the date it is due under § 502.30 of this part. The Director will charge interest on delinquent assessments. Interest will accrue at a rate (that OTS will determine quarterly) equal to 150 percent of the average of the bond-equivalent rates of 13-week Treasury bills auctioned during the calendar quarter preceding the assessment.

(b) If a savings and loan holding company fails to pay an assessment within 60 days of the date it is due under § 502.30 of this part, the Director may assess and collect the assessment with interest from a subsidiary savings association. If a savings and loan holding company controls more than one savings association, the Director may assess and collect the assessment from each savings association as the Director may prescribe.

Subpart B—Fees

§ 502.50 What fees does OTS charge?

(a) The Director assesses fees for examining or investigating savings associations that administer trust assets of $1 billion or less, and saving association affiliates. Because OTS recovers the ordinary costs of examining and investigating savings and loan holding companies through the semi-annual assessment under §§ 502.25 through 502.29 of this part, the Director will not generally charge an examination fee to a savings and loan holding company. "Affiliate" has the meaning in 12 U.S.C. 1462(9), except that, for this part only, "affiliate" does not include any entity that is consolidated with a savings association on the Consolidated Statement of Condition of the Thrift Financial Report.

(b) The Director assesses fees for processing notices, applications, securities filings, and requests, and for providing other services.

[69 FR 30571, May 28, 2004]

§ 502.55 Where can I find OTS's fee schedule?

OTS will periodically publish a schedule of its fees in a Thrift Bulletin. OTS will publish these fees at least 30 days before they are effective.

§ 502.60 When will OTS adjust, add, waive, or eliminate a fee?

Under unusual circumstances, the Director may deem it necessary or appropriate to adjust, add, waive, or eliminate a fee. For example, the Director may:

(a) Reduce any fee to adjust for any inequities, efficiencies, or changed procedures that OTS projects will reduce its applications processing costs but that OTS did not consider in determining its fees;

(b) Reduce or waive any fee if OTS determines that the fee would unduly or unjustifiably discourage particular types of applications or applications for particular categories of transactions;

(c) Add a fee for a new type of application;

(d) Increase a fee for an application that presents unusual or particularly

§ 502.65

complex issues of law or policy or otherwise causes the agency to incur unusually high processing costs; or

(e) Charge a fee to recover extraordinary expenses related to examination, investigation, regulation, or supervision of savings associations or their affiliates.

§ 502.65 When is an application fee due?

(a) You must pay the application fee when you file an application. OTS will not process your application if you do not include the required fee.

(b) If OTS cannot complete its review of your application because the application is materially deficient and it refuses to accept your application for processing, you must pay a new application fee upon filing a revised application.

(c) If a transaction involves multiple applications, you must pay the appropriate fee for each application, unless OTS specifies otherwise by Thrift Bulletin.

§ 502.70 How must I pay an application fee?

You must pay an application fee to the Office of Thrift Supervision. You must include a statement of the fee and how you calculated the fee.

§ 502.75 What if I do not pay my fees on time?

(a) *Interest.* An examination or investigation fee is delinquent if OTS does not receive the fee within 30 days of the date specified in a bill. The Director will charge interest on a delinquent examination or investigation fee. Interest will accrue at a rate (that OTS will determine quarterly) equal to 150 percent of the average of the bond-equivalent rates of 13-week Treasury bills auctioned during the preceding calendar quarter.

(b) *Failure to pay.* If you are a savings association and your holding company, affiliate, or subsidiary fails to pay any fee within 60 days of the date specified in a bill, the Director may assess and collect that fee, with interest, from you. If the holding company, affiliate, or subsidiary is related to more than one savings association, the Director may assess the fee against and collect it from each savings association as the Director may prescribe.

[63 FR 65670, Nov. 30, 1998, as amended at 69 FR 30571, May 28 1, 2004]

PART 503—PRIVACY ACT

Sec.
503.1 Scope and procedures.
503.2 Exemptions of records containing investigatory material compiled for law enforcement purposes.

AUTHORITY: 5 U.S.C. 552a; 12 U.S.C. 1462a, 1463, 1464.

CROSS REFERENCE: See 31 CFR part 1, subpart C.

§ 503.1 Scope and procedures.

(a) *In general.* The Privacy Act regulations of the Department of the Treasury, 31 CFR part 1, subpart C, apply to the Office as a component part of the Department of the Treasury. This part 503 sets forth, for the Office, specific notification and access procedures with respect to particular systems of records, and identifies the officials designated to make the initial determinations with respect to notification and access to records and accountings of disclosures of records. This part 503 also sets forth the specific procedures for requesting amendment of records and identifies the officials designated to make the initial and appellate determinations with respect to requests for amendment of records. It identifies the officials designated to grant extensions of time on appeal, the officials with whom "Statements of Disagreement" may be filed, the official designated to receive service of process and the addresses for delivery of requests, appeals, and service of process. In addition, it references the notice of systems of records and notices of the routine uses of the information in the system required by 5 U.S.C. 552a(e) (4) and (11) and published annually by the Office of the Federal Register in "Privacy Act Issuances."

(b) *Requests for notification and access to records and accountings of disclosures.* Initial determinations under 31 CFR 1.26, whether to grant requests for notification and access to records and accountings of disclosures for the Office,

Office of Thrift Supervision, Treasury § 503.2

will be made by the head of the organizational unit having immediate custody of the records requested or an official designated by this official. This is indicated in the appropriate system notice in "Privacy Act Issuances" published annually by the Office of the Federal Register. Requests for information and specific guidance on where to send requests for records may be mailed or delivered personally to: Privacy Act Request, Manager, Dissemination Branch, Information Management & Services Division, Office of Thrift Supervision, 1700 G Street, NW., Washington, DC 20552.

(c) *Requests for amendment of records.* Initial determinations under 31 CFR 1.27(a) through (d), whether to grant requests to amend records will be made by the head of the organizational unit having immediate custody of the records or the delegate of such official. Requests for amendment should be addressed to: Privacy Act Amendment Request, Manager, Dissemination Branch, Information Management & Services Division, Office of Thrift Supervision, 1700 G Street, NW., Washington, DC 20552.

(d) *Administrative appeal of initial determinations refusing amendment of records.* Appellate determinations refusing amendment of records under 31 CFR 1.27(e) including extensions of time on appeal, with respect to records of the Office will be made by the Director of the Office of Thrift Supervision ("Director") or Chief Counsel or the delegate of the Director or Chief Counsel. Appeals made by mail should be addressed to, or delivered personally to: Privacy Act Amendment Appeal, Deputy Chief Counsel for General Law, Office of Thrift Supervision, 1700 G Street, NW., Washington, DC 20552.

(e) *Statements of disagreement.* "Statements of Disagreement" under 31 CFR 1.27(e)(4)(i) shall be filed with the Deputy Director for Washington Operations at the address indicated in the letter of notification within 35 days of the date of such notification and should be limited to one page.

(f) *Service of process.* Service of process will be received by the Chief Counsel's Office or the delegate of such official and shall be delivered to the following location: Chief Counsel's Office, Office of Thrift Supervision, 1700 G Street, NW., Washington, DC 20552.

(g) *Annual notice of systems of records.* The annual notice of systems of records is published by the Office of the Federal Register, as specified in 5 U.S.C. 552a(f). The publication is entitled "Privacy Act Issuance." Any specific requirements for access, including identification requirements, in addition to the requirements set forth in 31 CFR 1.26 and 1.27 are indicated in the notice for the pertinent system.

[54 FR 49443, Nov. 30, 1989, as amended at 59 FR 18475, Apr. 19, 1994; 64 FR 69184, Dec. 10, 1999]

§ 503.2 **Exemptions of records containing investigatory material compiled for law enforcement purposes.**

(a) *Scope.* The Office has established a system of records, entitled the "Confidential Individual Information System." The purpose of this system is to assist the Office in the accomplishment of its statutory and regulatory responsibilities in connection with supervision of savings associations. This system will be exempt from certain provisions of the Privacy Act of 1974 for the reasons set forth in paragraph (c) of this section.

(b) *Exemptions Under 5 U.S.C. 552a(k)(2).* (1) Pursuant to 5 U.S.C. 552a(k)(2), the head of an agency may issue rules to exempt any system of records within the agency from certain provisions of the Privacy Act of 1974 if the system contains investigatory material compiled for law enforcement purposes.

(2) Provisions of the Privacy Act of 1974 from which exemptions will be made under 5 U.S.C. 552a(k)(2) are as follows:

(i) 5 U.S.C. 552a(c)(3);

(ii) 5 U.S.C. 552a(d)(1), (d)(2), (d)(3), and (d)(4);

(iii) 5 U.S.C. 552a(e)(1);

(iv) 5 U.S.C. 552a(e)(4)(G), (e)(4)(H), and (e)(4)(I); and

(v) 5 U.S.C. 552a(f).

(c) *Reasons for exemptions under 5 U.S.C. 552a(k)(2).* (1) 5 U.S.C. 552a(c)(3) requires that an agency make accountings of disclosures of records available to individuals named in the records at their request. These accountings must state the date, nature, and purpose of

13

each disclosure of a record and the name and address of the recipient. The application of this provision would make known to subjects of an investigation that an investigation is taking place and that they are the subjects of it. Release of such information could result in the alteration or destruction of documentary evidence, improper influencing of witnesses, and reluctance of witnesses to offer information, and could otherwise impede or compromise an investigation.

(2) 5 U.S.C. 552a(d)(1), (d)(2), (d)(3), and (d)(4), (e)(4)(G) and (e)(4)(H), and (f), relate to an individual's right to be notified of the existence of, and the right to examine, records pertaining to such individual. Notifying an individual at the individual's request of the existence of records and allowing the individual to examine an investigative file pertaining to such individual, or granting access to an investigative file, could:

(i) Interfere with investigations and enforcement proceedings;

(ii) Constitute an unwarranted invasion of the personal privacy of others;

(iii) Disclose the identity of confidential sources and reveal confidential information supplied by those sources; or

(iv) Disclose investigative techniques and procedures.

(3) 5 U.S.C. 552a(e)(4)(I) requires the publication of the categories of sources of records in each system. Application of this provision could disclose investigative techniques and procedures and cause sources to refrain from giving such information because of fear of reprisal, or fear of breach of promises of anonymity and confidentiality, thus compromising the agency's ability to conduct investigations and to identify, detect, and apprehend violators.

(4) 5 U.S.C. 552a(e)(1) requires each agency to maintain in its records only information about an individual that is relevant and necessary to accomplish a purpose of the agency required by statute or Executive Order. Limiting the system as described would impede enforcement activities because:

(i) It is not always possible to determine the relevance or necessity of specific information in the early stages of an investigation; and

(ii) In any investigation the Office may obtain information concerning violations of laws other than those within the scope of its jurisdiction. In the interest of effective law enforcement, the Office should retain this information to aid in establishing patterns of criminal activity, and to provide leads for those law enforcement agencies charged with enforcing criminal or civil laws.

(d) *Documents exempted.* Exemptions will be applied only when appropriate under 5 U.S.C. 552a(k).

[55 FR 31371, Aug. 2, 1990]

PART 505—FREEDOM OF INFORMATION ACT

Sec.
505.1 Basis and scope.
505.2 Public Reading Room.
505.3 Requests for records.
505.4 Administrative appeal of initial determination to deny records.
505.5 Delivery of process.

AUTHORITY: 5 U.S.C. 552; 12 U.S.C. 1462a, 1463, 1464.

CROSS REFERENCE: See 31 CFR part 1, subpart A.

§ 505.1 Basis and scope.

(a) This part is issued by the Office of Thrift Supervision ("OTS") as a supplement to the Freedom of Information Act regulations of the Department of the Treasury, 31 CFR part 1, subpart A, which apply to the OTS as a component part of the Department of the Treasury.

(b) This part is issued by the OTS pursuant to the requirement of section 552 of title 5 of the United States Code, which requires every federal agency to publish in the FEDERAL REGISTER the established places at which, the employees from whom, and the methods whereby, the public may obtain information, make submittals on requests, or obtain decisions, and the forms available or the places at which forms and instructions as to the scope and contents of all papers, reports, or examinations may be found. Information about the Public Reading Room is set forth in § 505.2 of this part. Procedures for requests for records are set forth in § 505.3 of this part. Information about administrative appeals is set forth in

§ 505.4 of this part. Provisions relating to delivery of process upon the OTS are set forth in § 505.5 of this part.

[54 FR 49444, Nov. 30, 1989, as amended at 60 FR 66716, Dec. 26, 1995; 66 FR 65819, Dec. 21, 2001]

§ 505.2 Public Reading Room.

OTS will make materials available for review on an ad hoc basis when necessary. Contact the FOIA Office, Office of Thrift Supervision, 1700 G Street, NW., Washington, DC 20552, or you may visit the Public Reading Room at 1700 G Street, NW., by appointment only. (Please identify the materials you would like to inspect, to assist us in serving you.) We schedule appointments on business days between 10 a.m. and 4 p.m. In most cases, appointments will be available the next business day following the date we receive your request.

[66 FR 65819, Dec. 21, 2001, as amended at 67 FR 78151, Dec. 23, 2002]

§ 505.3 Requests for records.

A designated official will make the initial determination under 31 CFR 1.5(g) whether to grant a request for OTS records. Requests may be mailed to: Freedom of Information Act Request, FOIA Office, Office of Thrift Supervision, 1700 G Street, NW., Washington, DC 20552, or marked "FOIA" and delivered in person to the FOIA Office, 1700 G Street, NW., Washington, DC 20552. Requests may also be sent by e-mail or facsimile to the e-mail address and facsimile number in § 505.2 of this part.

[67 FR 78151, Dec. 23, 2002]

§ 505.4 Administrative appeal of initial determination to deny records.

A designated official will make appellate determinations under 31 CFR 1.5(h) with respect to OTS records. Appeals by mail should be addressed to: FOIA Appeals, 1700 G Street, NW., Washington, DC 20552. Appeals may be delivered personally to FOIA Appeals, Office of Thrift Supervision, 1700 G Street, NW., Washington, DC 20552. Appeals may also be sent by e-mail or facsimile to the e-mail address and facsimile number in § 505.2 of this part.

[67 FR 78151, Dec. 23, 2002]

§ 505.5 Delivery of process.

Service of process will be received as set forth in § 510.4 of this chapter.

[54 FR 49444, Nov. 30, 1989]

PART 506—INFORMATION COLLECTION REQUIREMENTS UNDER THE PAPERWORK REDUCTION ACT

AUTHORITY: 44 U.S.C. 3501 *et seq.*

§ 506.1 OMB control numbers assigned pursuant to the Paperwork Reduction Act.

(a) *Purpose.* This part collects and displays the control numbers assigned to information collection requirements contained in regulations of the Office of Thrift Supervision by the Office of Management and Budget (OMB) pursuant to the Paperwork Reduction Act of 1995, Pub. L. 104–13, 109 Stat. 163, and is adopted in compliance with the requirements of 5 CFR 1320.8. Information collection requirements that are not mandated by statute must be assigned control numbers by OMB in order to be enforceable. Respondents/recordkeepers are not required to comply with any collection of information unless it displays a currently valid OMB control number.

(b) *Display.*

12 CFR part or section where identified and described	Current OMB control No.
502.70	1550–0053.
510	1550–0081.
Part 516	1550–0056.
Part 528	1550–0021.
533.4	1550–0105.
533.6	1550–0105.
533.7	1550–0105.
536.40	1550–0106.
543.2	1550–0005.
543.3	1550–0005
543.9	1550–0007.
544.2	1550–0018.
544.5	1550–0018.
544.8	1550–0011.
545.93 and 545.95	1500–0006.
545.96(c)	1550–0011.
546.2	1550–0016.
546.4	1550–0066.
Part 550	1550–0037.
Part 551	1550–0109.
551.50	1550–0109.
551.70 through 551.100	1550–0109.
551.140	1550–0109.
551.150	1550–0109.
552.2–1	1550–0005.
552.2–6	1550–0007.
552.4	1550–0017.
552.5	1550–0018.

Pt. 507

12 CFR part or section where identified and described	Current OMB control No.
552.11	1550–0011.
552.13	1550–0016, 1550–0025.
555.300	1550–0095.
555.310	1550–0095.
557.20	1550–0092.
559.3	1550–0077.
559.11	1550–0077.
559.12	1550–0013.
559.13	1550–0065.
560.1	1550–0078.
560.2	1550–0078.
560.32	1550–0078.
560.35	1550–0078.
560.93(f)	1550–0078.
560.101	1550–0078.
560.170(c)	1550–0078.
560.172	1550–0078.
560.210	1550–0078.
562.1	1550–0011.
562.1(b)	1550–0078.
562.4	1550–0011.
563.1(b)	1550–0011.
563.3	1550–0027.
563.22	1550–0016, 1550–0025.
563.41(c)(3) and (4)	1550–0078
563.43	1550–0075.
563.47(e)	1550–0011.
563.74	1550–0050.
563.76(c)	1550–0011.
563.81	1550–0030.
563.143 through 563.146	1550–0059.
563.170	1550–0078.
563.177	1550–0041.
563.180	1550–0084.
563.180(d)	1550–0003.
563.180(e)	1550–0079.
Part 563b	1550–0014.
Part 563d	1550–0019.
Part 563e	1550–0012.
Part 563f	1550–0051.
Part 563g	1550–0035.
Part 564	1550–0078.
Part 568	1550–0062.
572.6	1550–0088.
572.7	1550–0088.
572.9	1550–0088.
572.10	1550–0088.
Part 573	1550–0103.
574.3(b)	1550–0032.
574.4	1550–0032.
574.5	1550–0032.
574.6	1550–0015.
Part 575	1550–0072.
584.1(f)	1550–0011.
584.2–1	1550–0063.
584.2–2	1550–0063.
584.9	1550–0063.
590.4(h)	1550–0078.

[60 FR 66716, Dec. 26, 1995, as amended by 61 FR 65178, Dec. 11, 1996; 62 FR 54764, Oct. 22, 1997; 62 FR 66261, Dec. 18, 1997; 63 FR 71211, Dec. 24, 1998; 65 FR 78901, Dec. 18, 2000; 66 FR 15017, Mar. 15, 2001; 66 FR 65819, Dec. 21, 2001; 67 FR 76269, Dec. 12, 2002; 67 FR 77916, Dec. 20, 2002; 67 FR 78151, Dec. 23, 2002; 68 FR 75109, Dec. 30, 2003; 69 FR 68246, Nov. 24, 2004; 69 FR 76602, Dec. 22, 2004]

PART 507—RESTRICTIONS ON POST-EMPLOYMENT ACTIVITIES OF SENIOR EXAMINERS

Sec.
507.1 What does this part do?
507.2 Who is a senior examiner?
507.3 What post-employment restrictions apply to senior examiners?
507.4 When will OTS waive the post-employment restrictions?
507.5 What are the penalties for violating the post-employment restrictions?

AUTHORITY: 12 U.S.C. 1462a, 1463 and 1820(k).

SOURCE: 70 FR 69640, Nov. 17, 2005, unless otherwise noted.

§ 507.1 What does this part do?

This part implements section 10(k) of the Federal Deposit Insurance Act (FDIA), which prohibits senior examiners from accepting compensation from certain companies following the termination of their employment. See 12 U.S.C. 1820(k). Except where otherwise provided, the terms used in this part have the meanings given in section 3 of the FDIA (12 U.S.C. 1813).

§ 507.2 Who is a senior examiner?

An individual is a senior examiner for a particular savings association or savings and loan holding company if—

(a) The individual is an officer or employee of OTS (including a special government employee) who has been authorized by OTS to conduct examinations or inspections of savings associations or savings and loan holding companies;

(b) The individual has been assigned continuing, broad and lead responsibility for the examination or inspection of that savings association or savings and loan holding company; and

(c) The individual's responsibilities for examining, inspecting, or supervising that savings association or savings and loan holding company:

(1) Represent a substantial portion of the individual's assigned responsibilities at OTS; and

(2) Require the individual to interact on a routine basis with officers and employees of the savings association, savings and loan holding company, or its affiliates.

§507.3 What post-employment restrictions apply to senior examiners?

(a) *Prohibition.* (1) Senior examiner of savings association. An individual who serves as a senior examiner of a savings association for two or more of the last 12 months of his or her employment with OTS may not, within one year after the termination date of his or her employment with OTS, knowingly accept compensation as an employee, officer, director, or consultant from—

(i) The savings association; or

(ii) A savings and loan holding company, bank holding company, or any other company that controls the savings association.

(2) *Senior examiner of a savings and loan holding company.* An individual who serves as a senior examiner of a savings and loan holding company for two or more of the last 12 months of his or her employment with OTS may not, within one year after the termination date of his or her employment with OTS, knowingly accept compensation as an employee, officer, director, or consultant from—

(i) The savings and loan holding company; or

(ii) Any depository institution that is controlled by the savings and loan holding company.

(b) *Effective date.* The post-employment restrictions in paragraph (a) of this section do not apply to any senior examiner who terminated his employment at OTS before December 17, 2005.

(c) *Definitions.* For the purposes of this section—

(1) *Consultant.* An individual acts as a consultant for a savings association or other company only if he or she directly works on matters for, or on behalf of, the savings association or company.

(2) *Control.* Control has the same meaning given in part 574 of this chapter.

§507.4 When will OTS waive the post-employment restrictions?

The post-employment restriction in §507.3 of this part will not apply to a senior examiner if the Director certifies in writing and on a case-by-case basis that a waiver of the restriction will not affect the integrity of OTS's supervisory program.

§507.5 What are the penalties for violating the post-employment restrictions?

(a) *Penalties.* A senior examiner who violates §507.3 shall, in accordance with 12 U.S.C. 1820(k)(6), be subject to one or both of the following penalties:

(1) An order—

(i) Removing the person from office or prohibiting the person from further participating in the conduct of the affairs of the relevant depository institution, savings and loan holding company, bank holding company or other company for up to five years, and

(ii) Prohibiting the person from participating in the affairs of any insured depository institution for up to five years.

(2) A civil money penalty not to exceed $250,000.

(b) *Scope of prohibition orders.* Any senior examiner who is subject to an order issued under paragraph (a)(1) of this section shall be subject to 12 U.S.C. 1818(e)(6) and (7) in the same manner and to the same extent as a person subject to an order issued under 12 U.S.C. 1818(e).

(c) *Procedures.* 12 U.S.C. 1820(k) describes the procedures that are applicable to actions under paragraph (a) of this section and the appropriate Federal banking agency authorized to take the action, which may be an agency other than OTS. Where OTS is the appropriate Federal banking agency, it will conduct administrative proceedings under 12 CFR part 509.

(d) *Other penalties.* The penalties under this section are not exclusive. A senior examiner who violates the restriction in §507.3 may also be subject to other administrative, civil, or criminal remedy or penalty as provided by law.

PART 508—REMOVALS, SUSPENSIONS, AND PROHIBITIONS WHERE A CRIME IS CHARGED OR PROVEN

Sec.
508.1 Scope.
508.2 Definitions.
508.3 Issuance of Notice or Order.
508.4 Contents and service of the Notice or Order.
508.5 Petition for hearing.

§ 508.1

508.6 Initiation of hearing.
508.7 Conduct of hearings.
508.8 Default.
508.9 Rules of evidence.
508.10 Burden of persuasion.
508.11 Relevant considerations.
508.12 Proposed findings and conclusions and recommended decision.
508.13 Decision of the Office.
508.14 Miscellaneous.

AUTHORITY: 12 U.S.C. 1464, 1818.

SOURCE: 54 FR 49444, Nov. 30, 1989, unless otherwise noted.

§ 508.1 Scope.

The rules in this part apply to hearings, which are exempt from the adjudicative provisions of the Administrative Procedure Act, afforded to any officer, director, or other person participating in the conduct of the affairs of a savings association, affiliate service corporation, savings and loan holding company, or subsidiary of such a holding company, where such person has been suspended or removed from office or prohibited from further participation in the conduct of the affairs of one of the aforementioned entities by a Notice or Order served by the Office upon the grounds set forth in section 8(g) of the Federal Deposit Insurance Act, (12 U.S.C. 1818(g)).

§ 508.2 Definitions.

As used in this part—

(a) The term *Office* means the Office of Thrift Supervision.

(b) The term *Secretary* means the Secretary to the Office and any Assistant or Acting Secretary to the Office.

(c) The term *Notice* means a Notice of Suspension or Notice of Prohibition issued by the Office pursuant to section 8(g) of the Federal Deposit Insurance Act.

(d) The term *Order* means an Order of Removal or Order of Prohibition issued by the Office pursuant to section 8(g) of the Federal Deposit Insurance Act.

(e) The term *association* means a savings association within the meaning of section 2(4) of the Home Owners' Loan Act of 1933, as amended, 12 U.S.C. 1462(4) ("HOLA"), an affiliate service corporation within the meaning of section 8(b)(8) of the Federal Deposit Insurance Act, as amended, 12 U.S.C. 1818(b)(8) ("FDIA"), a savings and loan holding company within the meaning

12 CFR Ch. V (1-1-12 Edition)

of section 10(a)(1)(D) of the HOLA, 12 U.S.C. 1467a(a)(1)(D) and a subsidiary of a savings and loan holding company (other than a savings association) within the meaning of section 10(a)(1)(G) of the Home Owners' Loan Act of 1933.

(f) The term *subject individual* means a person served with a Notice or Order.

(g) The term *petitioner* means a subject individual who has filed a petition for informal hearing under this part.

§ 508.3 Issuance of Notice or Order.

(a) The Office may issue and serve a Notice upon an officer, director, or other person participating in the conduct of the affairs of an association, where the individual is charged in any information, indictment, or complaint with the commission of or participation in a crime involving dishonesty or breach of trust that is punishable by imprisonment for a term exceeding one year under State or Federal law, if the Office, upon due deliberation, determines that continued service or participation by the individual may pose a threat to the interests of the association's depositors or may threaten to impair public confidence in the association. The Notice shall remain in effect until the information, indictment, or complaint is finally disposed of or until terminated by the Office.

(b) The Office may issue and serve an Order upon a subject individual against whom a judgment of conviction, or an agreement to enter a pretrial diversion or other similar program has been rendered, where such judgment is not subject to further appellate review, and the Office, upon the deliberation, has determined that continued service or participation by the subject individual may pose a threat to the interests of the association's depositors or may threaten to impair public confidence in the association.

§ 508.4 Contents and service of the Notice or Order.

(a) The Notice or Order shall set forth the basis and facts in support of the Office's issuance of such Notice or Order, and shall inform the subject individual of his right to a hearing, in accordance with this part, for the purpose of determining whether the Notice or Order should be continued, terminated, or otherwise modified.

(b) The Secretary shall serve a copy of the Notice or Order upon the subject individual and the related association in the manner set forth in §509.11 of this chapter.

(c) Upon receipt of the Notice or Order, the subject individual shall immediately comply with the requirements thereof.

[54 FR 49444, Nov. 30, 1989, as amended at 56 FR 38306, Aug. 12, 1991]

§ 508.5 Petition for hearing.

(a) To obtain a hearing, the subject individual must file two copies of a petition with the Secretary within 30 days of being served with the Notice or Order.

(b) The petition filed under this section shall admit or deny specifically each allegation in the Notice or Order, unless the petitioner is without knowledge or information, in which case the petition shall so state and the statement shall have the effect of a denial. Any allegation not denied shall be deemed to be admitted. When a petitioner intends in good faith to deny only a part of or to qualify an allegation, he shall specify so much of it as is true and shall deny only the remainder.

(c) The petition shall state whether the petitioner is requesting termination or modification of the Notice or Order, and shall state with particularity how the petitioner intends to show that his continued service to or participation in the conduct of the affairs of the association would not, or is not likely to, pose a threat to the interests of the association's depositors or to impair public confidence in the association.

§ 508.6 Initiation of hearing.

(a) Within 10 days of the filing of a petition for hearing, the Office shall notify the petitioner of the time and place fixed for hearing, and it shall designate one or more Office employees to serve as presiding officer.

(b) The hearing shall be scheduled to be held no later than 30 days from the date the petition was filed, unless the time is extended at the request of the petitioner.

(c) A petitioner may appear personally or through counsel, but if represented by counsel, said counsel is required to comply with § 509.6 of this chapter.

(d) A representative(s) of the Office's Office of Enforcement also may attend the hearing and participate therein as a party.

[54 FR 49444, Nov. 30, 1989, as amended at 56 FR 38306, Aug. 12, 1991]

§ 508.7 Conduct of hearings.

(a) Hearings provided by this section are not subject to the adjudicative provisions of the Administrative Procedure Act (5 U.S.C. 554–557). The presiding officer is, however, authorized to exercise all of the powers enumerated in § 509.5 of this chapter.

(b) Witnesses may be presented, within time limits specified by the presiding officer, provided that at least 10 days prior to the hearing date, the party presenting the witnesses furnishes the presiding officer and the opposing party with a list of such witnesses and a summary of the proposed testimony. However, the requirement for furnishing such a witness list and summary of testimony shall not apply to the presentation of rebuttal witnesses. The presiding officer may ask questions of any witness, and each party shall have an opportunity to cross-examine any witness presented by an opposing party.

(c) Upon the request of either the petitioner or a representative of the Office of Enforcement, the record shall remain open for a period of 5 business days following the hearing, during which time the parties may make any additional submissions for the record. Thereafter, the record shall be closed.

(d) Following the introduction of all evidence, the petitioner and the representative of the Office of Enforcement shall have an opportunity for oral argument; however, the parties may jointly waive the right to oral argument, and, in lieu thereof, elect to submit written argument.

(e) All oral testimony and oral argument shall be recorded, and transcripts made available to the petitioner upon payment of the cost thereof. A copy of the transcript shall be sent directly to the presiding officer, who shall have

§ 508.8

authority to correct the record sua sponte or upon the motion of any party.

(f) The parties may, in writing, jointly waive an oral hearing and instead elect a hearing upon a written record in which all evidence and argument would be submitted to the presiding officer in documentary form and statements of individuals would be made by affidavit.

[54 FR 49444, Nov. 30, 1989, as amended at 56 FR 38306, Aug. 12, 1991]

§ 508.8 Default.

If the subject individual fails to file a petition for a hearing, or fails to appear at a hearing, either in person or by attorney, or fails to submit a written argument where oral argument has been waived pursuant to § 508.7(d) or (f) of this part, the Notice shall remain in effect until the information, indictment, or complaint is finally disposed of and the Order shall remain in effect until terminated by the Office.

§ 508.9 Rules of evidence.

(a) Formal rules of evidence shall not apply to a hearing, but the presiding officer may limit the introduction of irrelevant, immaterial, or unduly repetitious evidence.

(b) All matters officially noticed by the presiding officer shall appear on the record.

§ 508.10 Burden of persuasion.

The petitioner has the burden of showing, by a preponderance of the evidence, that his or her continued service to or participation in the conduct of the affairs of the association does not, or is not likely to, pose a threat to the interests of the association's depositors or threaten to impair public confidence in the association.

§ 508.11 Relevant considerations.

(a) In determining whether the petitioner has shown that his or her continued service to or participation in the conduct of the affairs of the association would not, or is not likely to, pose a threat to the interests of the association's depositors or threaten to impair public confidence in the association, in order to decide whether the Notice or Order should be continued, terminated, or otherwise modified, the Office will consider:

(1) The nature and extent of the petitioner's participation in the affairs of the association;

(2) The nature of the offense with which the petitioner has been charged;

(3) The extent of the publicity accorded the indictment and trial; and

(4) Such other relevant factors as may be entered on the record.

(b) When considering a request for the termination or modification of a Notice, the Office will not consider the ultimate guilt or innocence of the petitioner with respect to the criminal charge that is outstanding.

(c) When considering a request for the termination or modification of an Order which has been issued following a final judgment of conviction against a subject individual, the Office will not collaterally review such final judgment of conviction.

§ 508.12 Proposed findings and conclusions and recommended decision.

(a) Within 30 days after completion of oral argument or the submission of written argument where oral argument has been waived, the presiding officer shall file with the Secretary and certify to the Office for decision the entire record of the hearing, which shall include a recommended decision, the Notice or Order, and all other documents filed in connection with the hearing.

(b) The recommended decision shall contain:

(1) A statement of the issue(s) presented,

(2) A statement of findings and conclusions, and the reasons or basis therefor, on all material issues of fact, law, or discretion presented on the record, and

(3) An appropriate recommendation as to whether the suspension, removal, or prohibition should be continued, modified, or terminated.

§ 508.13 Decision of the Office.

(a) Within 30 days after the recommended decision has been certified to the Office, the Office shall issue a final decision.

Office of Thrift Supervision, Treasury

§ 509.1

(b) The Office's final decision shall contain a statement of the basis therefor. The Office may satisfy this requirement where it adopts the recommended decision of the presiding officer upon finding that the recommended decision satisfies the requirements of § 509.38 of this chapter.

(c) The Secretary shall serve upon the petitioner and the representative of the Office of Enforcement a copy of the Office's final decision and the related recommended decision.

[54 FR 49444, Nov. 30, 1989, as amended at 56 FR 38306, Aug. 12, 1991; 59 FR 53570, Oct. 25, 1994]

§ 508.14 Miscellaneous.

The provisions of §§ 509.10, 509.11, and 509.12 of this chapter shall apply to proceedings under this part.

[54 FR 49444, Nov. 30, 1989, as amended at 56 FR 38306, Aug. 12, 1991]

PART 509—RULES OF PRACTICE AND PROCEDURE IN ADJUDICATORY PROCEEDINGS

Subpart A—Uniform Rules of Practice and Procedure

Sec.
509.1 Scope.
509.2 Rules of construction.
509.3 Definitions.
509.4 Authority of Director.
509.5 Authority of the administrative law judge.
509.6 Appearance and practice in adjudicatory proceedings.
509.7 Good faith certification.
509.8 Conflicts of interest.
509.9 Ex parte communications.
509.10 Filing of papers.
509.11 Service of papers.
509.12 Construction of time limits.
509.13 Change of time limits.
509.14 Witness fees and expenses.
509.15 Opportunity for informal settlement.
509.16 Office's right to conduct examination.
509.17 Collateral attacks on adjudicatory proceeding.
509.18 Commencement of proceeding and contents of notice.
509.19 Answer.
509.20 Amended pleadings.
509.21 Failure to appear.
509.22 Consolidation and severance of actions.
509.23 Motions.
509.24 Scope of document discovery.
509.25 Request for document discovery from parties.
509.26 Document subpoenas to nonparties.
509.27 Deposition of witness unavailable for hearing.
509.28 Interlocutory review.
509.29 Summary disposition.
509.30 Partial summary disposition.
509.31 Scheduling and prehearing conferences.
509.32 Prehearing submissions.
509.33 Public hearings.
509.34 Hearing subpoenas.
509.35 Conduct of hearings.
509.36 Evidence.
509.37 Post-hearing filings.
509.38 Recommended decision and filing of record.
509.39 Exceptions to recommended decision.
509.40 Review by the Director.
509.41 Stays pending judicial review.

Subpart B—Local Rules

509.100 Scope.
509.101 Appointment of Office of Financial Institution Adjudication.
509.102 Discovery.
509.103 Civil money penalties.
509.104 Additional procedures.

Subpart C—Special Rules

509.200 Scope.
509.201 Definitions.
509.202 Commencement of proceedings and contents of notice.
509.203 Answer, consequences of failure to answer, and consent.
509.204 Hearing Procedure.

Subpart D—Exemptions under Section 19(e) of the FDIA

509.300 Scope.
509.301 Hearing procedures.

AUTHORITY: 5 U.S.C. 504, 554–557; 12 U.S.C. 1464, 1467, 1467a, 1468, 1817(j), 1818, 1820(k), 1829(e), 3349, 4717; 15 U.S.C. 78(l), 78o–5, 78u–2; 28 U.S.C. 2461 note; 31 U.S.C. 5321; 42 U.S.C. 4012a.

SOURCE: 56 FR 38306, Aug. 12, 1991, unless otherwise noted.

Subpart A—Uniform Rules of Practice and Procedure

§ 509.1 Scope.

This subpart prescribes Uniform Rules of practice and procedure applicable to adjudicatory proceedings as to which hearings on the record are provided for by the following statutory provisions:

§ 509.2

(a) Cease-and-desist proceedings under section 8(b) of the Federal Deposit Insurance Act (FDIA) (12 U.S.C. 1818(b));

(b) Removal and prohibition proceedings under section 8(e) of the FDIA (12 U.S.C. 1818(e));

(c) Change-in-control proceedings under section 7(j)(4) of the FDIA (12 U.S.C. 1817(j)(4)) to determine whether the Office should issue an order to approve or disapprove a person's proposed acquisition of an institution and/or institution holding company;

(d) Proceedings under section 15C(c)(2) of the Securities Exchange Act of 1934 (Exchange Act) (15 U.S.C. 78o–5), to impose sanctions upon any government securities broker or dealer or upon any person associated or seeking to become associated with a government securities broker or dealer for which the Office is the appropriate Office;

(e) Assessment of civil money penalties by the Office against institutions, institution-affiliated parties, and certain other persons for which it is the appropriate Office for any violation of:

(1) Section 5 of the Home Owners' Loan Act (HOLA) or any regulation or order issued thereunder, pursuant to 12 U.S.C. 1464 (d), (s) and (v);

(2) Section 9 of the HOLA or any regulation or order issued thereunder, pursuant to 12 U.S.C. 1467(d);

(3) Section 10 of the HOLA, pursuant to 12 U.S.C. 1467a (i) and (r);

(4) Any provisions of the Change in Bank Control Act, any regulation or order issued thereunder or certain unsafe or unsound practices or breaches of fiduciary duty, pursuant to 12 U.S.C. 1817(j)(16);

(5) Sections 22(h) and 23 of the Federal Reserve Act, or any regulation issued thereunder or certain unsafe or unsound practices or breaches of fiduciary duty, pursuant to 12 U.S.C. 1468;

(6) Certain provisions of the Exchange Act, pursuant to section 21B of the Exchange Act (15 U.S.C. 78u–2);

(7) Section 1120 of Financial Institutions Reform, Recovery and Enforcement Act of 1989 (12 U.S.C. 3349), or any order or regulation issued thereunder;

(8) The terms of any final or temporary order issued or enforceable pursuant to section 8 of the FDIA or of any written agreement executed by the Office, the terms of any conditions imposed in writing by the Office in connection with the grant of an application or request, certain unsafe or unsound practices or breaches of fiduciary duty, or any law or regulation not otherwise provided herein pursuant to 12 U.S.C. 1818(i)(2);

(9) Any provision of law referenced in section 102 of the Flood Disaster Protection Act of 1973 (42 U.S.C. 4012a(f)) or any order or regulation issued thereunder; and

(10) Any provision of law referenced in 31 U.S.C. 5321 or any order or regulation issued thereunder;

(f) Remedial action under section 102 of the Flood Disaster Protection Act of 1973 (42 U.S.C. 4012a(g));

(g) Proceedings under section 10(k) of the FDIA (12 U.S.C. 1820(k)) to impose penalties on senior examiners for violation of post-employment prohibitions; and

(h) This subpart also applies to all other adjudications required by statute to be determined on the record after opportunity for an agency hearing, unless otherwise specifically provided for in the Local Rules.

(i) Subpart D of this part governs hearings on denials of applications for case-by-case exemptions under 12 CFR part 585, which implements section 19(e) of the FDIA.

[56 FR 38306, Aug. 12, 1991, as amended at 56 FR 59866, Nov. 26, 1991; 61 FR 20353, May 6, 1996; 70 FR 69641, Nov. 17, 2005; 72 FR 25955, May 8, 2007]

§ 509.2 Rules of construction.

For purposes of this subpart:

(a) Any term in the singular includes the plural, and the plural includes the singular, if such use would be appropriate;

(b) Any use of a masculine, feminine, or neuter gender encompasses all three, if such use would be appropriate;

(c) The term *counsel* includes a non-attorney representative; and

(d) Unless the context requires otherwise, a party's counsel of record, if any, may, on behalf of that party, take any action required to be taken by the party.

§ 509.3 Definitions.

For purposes of this subpart, unless explicitly stated to the contrary:

(a) *Administrative law judge* means one who presides at an administrative hearing under authority set forth at 5 U.S.C. 556.

(b) *Adjudicatory proceeding* means a proceeding conducted pursuant to these rules and leading to the formulation of a final order other than a regulation.

(c) *Decisional employee* means any member of the Office's or administrative law judge's staff who has not engaged in an investigative or prosecutorial role in a proceeding and who may assist the Office or the administrative law judge, respectively, in preparing orders, recommended decisions, decisions, and other documents under the Uniform Rules.

(d) *Director* means the Director of the Office of Thrift Supervision or his or her designee.

(e) *Enforcement Counsel* means any individual who files a notice of appearance as counsel on behalf of the Office in an adjudicatory proceeding.

(f) *Final order* means an order issued by the Office with or without the consent of the affected institution or the institution-affiliated party, that has become final, without regard to the pendency of any petition for reconsideration or review.

(g) *Institution* includes any savings association as that term is defined in section 3(b) of the FDIA (12 U.S.C. 1813(b)), any savings and loan holding company or any subsidiary thereof whether wholly or partly owned (other than a bank) as those terms are defined in section 10(a) of the HOLA (12 U.S.C. 1467(a)).

(h) *Institution-affiliated party* means any institution-affiliated party as that term is defined in section 3(u) of the FDIA (12 U.S.C. 1813(u)).

(i) *Local Rules* means those rules found in subpart B of this part.

(j) *Office* means the Office of Thrift Supervision in the case of any savings association or any savings and loan holding company, and subsidiary (other than a bank or subsidiary of that bank) of a savings and loan holding company, any service corporation of a savings association, and any subsidiary of such service corporation, whether wholly or partly owned.

(k) *Office of Financial Institution Adjudication* (OFIA) means the executive body charged with overseeing the administration of administrative enforcement proceedings for the Office of the Comptroller of the Currency, the Board of Governors of the Federal Reserve Board, the Federal Deposit Insurance Corporation, the National Credit Union Administration and the Office.

(l) *Party* means the Office and any person named as a party in any notice.

(m) *Person* means an individual, sole proprietor, partnership, corporation, unincorporated association, trust, joint venture, pool, syndicate, agency or other entity or organization, including an institution as defined in paragraph (g) of this section.

(n) *Respondent* means any party other than the Office.

(o) *Uniform Rules* means those rules in subpart A of this part.

(p) *Violation* includes any action (alone or with another or others) for or toward causing, bringing about, participating in, counseling, or aiding or abetting a violation.

§ 509.4 Authority of Director.

The Director may, at any time during the pendency of a proceeding perform, direct the performance of, or waive performance of, any act which could be done or ordered by the administrative law judge.

§ 509.5 Authority of the administrative law judge.

(a) *General rule.* All proceedings governed by this part shall be conducted in accordance with the provisions of chapter 5 of title 5 of the United States Code. The administrative law judge shall have all powers necessary to conduct a proceeding in a fair and impartial manner and to avoid unnecessary delay.

(b) *Powers.* The administrative law judge shall have all powers necessary to conduct the proceeding in accordance with paragraph (a) of this section, including the following powers:

(1) To administer oaths and affirmations;

(2) To issue subpoenas, subpoenas duces tecum, and protective orders, as

§ 509.6

authorized by this part, and to quash or modify any such subpoenas and orders;

(3) To receive relevant evidence and to rule upon the admission of evidence and offers of proof;

(4) To take or cause depositions to be taken as authorized by this subpart;

(5) To regulate the course of the hearing and the conduct of the parties and their counsel;

(6) To hold scheduling and/or prehearing conferences as set forth in § 509.31 of this subpart;

(7) To consider and rule upon all procedural and other motions appropriate in an adjudicatory proceeding, provided that only the Director shall have the power to grant any motion to dismiss the proceeding or to decide any other motion that results in a final determination of the merits of the proceeding;

(8) To prepare and present to the Director a recommended decision as provided herein;

(9) To recuse himself or herself by motion made by a party or on his or her own motion;

(10) To establish time, place and manner limitations on the attendance of the public and the media for any public hearing; and

(11) To do all other things necessary and appropriate to discharge the duties of a presiding officer.

§ 509.6 Appearance and practice in adjudicatory proceedings.

(a) *Appearance before an Office or an administrative law judge*—(1) *By attorneys.* Any member in good standing of the bar of the highest court of any state, commonwealth, possession, territory of the United States, or the District of Columbia may represent others before the Office if such attorney is not currently suspended or debarred from practice before the Office.

(2) *By non-attorneys.* An individual may appear on his or her own behalf; a member of a partnership may represent the partnership; a duly authorized officer, director, or employee of any government unit, agency, institution, corporation or authority may represent that unit, agency, institution, corporation or authority if such officer, director, or employee is not currently sus-

pended or debarred from practice before the Office.

(3) *Notice of appearance.* Any individual acting as counsel on behalf of a party, including the Director, shall file a notice of appearance with OFIA at or before the time that individual submits papers or otherwise appears on behalf of a party in the adjudicatory proceeding. The notice of appearance must include a written declaration that the individual is currently qualified as provided in paragraph (a)(1) or (a)(2) of this section and is authorized to represent the particular party. By filing a notice of appearance on behalf of a party in an adjudicatory proceeding, the counsel agrees and represents that he or she is authorized to accept service on behalf of the represented party and that, in the event of withdrawal from representation, he or she will, if required by the administrative law judge, continue to accept service until new counsel has filed a notice of appearance or until the represented party indicates that he or she will proceed on a *pro se* basis.

(b) *Sanctions.* Dilatory, obstructionist, egregious, contemptuous or contumacious conduct at any phase of any adjudicatory proceeding may be grounds for exclusion or suspension of counsel from the proceeding.

[56 FR 38306, Aug. 12, 1991, as amended at 61 FR 20354, May 6, 1996]

§ 509.7 Good faith certification.

(a) *General requirement.* Every filing or submission of record following the issuance of a notice shall be signed by at least one counsel of record in his or her individual name and shall state that counsel's address and telephone number. A party who acts as his or her own counsel shall sign his or her individual name and state his or her address and telephone number on every filing or submission of record.

(b) *Effect of signature.* (1) The signature of counsel or a party shall constitute a certification that: the counsel or party has read the filing or submission of record; to the best of his or her knowledge, information, and belief formed after reasonable inquiry, the filing or submission of record is well-grounded in fact and is warranted by existing law or a good faith argument for the extension, modification, or reversal of existing law; and the filing or submission of record is not made for any improper purpose, such as to harass or to cause unnecessary delay or needless increase in the cost of litigation.

(2) If a filing or submission of record is not signed, the administrative law judge shall strike the filing or submission of record, unless it is signed promptly after the omission is called to the attention of the pleader or movant.

(c) *Effect of making oral motion or argument.* The act of making any oral motion or oral argument by any counsel or party constitutes a certification that to the best of his or her knowledge, information, and belief formed after reasonable inquiry, his or her statements are well-grounded in fact and are warranted by existing law or a good faith argument for the extension, modification, or reversal of existing law, and are not made for any improper purpose, such as to harass or to cause unnecessary delay or needless increase in the cost of litigation.

§ 509.8 Conflicts of interest.

(a) *Conflict of interest in representation.* No person shall appear as counsel for another person in an adjudicatory proceeding if it reasonably appears that such representation may be materially limited by that counsel's responsibilities to a third person or by the counsel's own interests. The administrative law judge may take corrective measures at any stage of a proceeding to cure a conflict of interest in representation, including the issuance of an order limiting the scope of representation or disqualifying an individual from appearing in a representative capacity for the duration of the proceeding.

(b) *Certification and waiver.* If any person appearing as counsel represents two or more parties to an adjudicatory proceeding or also represents a non-party on a matter relevant to an issue in the proceeding, counsel must certify in writing at the time of filing the notice of appearance required by § 509.6(a):

(1) That the counsel has personally and fully discussed the possibility of conflicts of interest with each such party and non-party; and

(2) That each such party and non-party waives any right it might otherwise have had to assert any known conflicts of interest or to assert any non-material conflicts of interest during the course of the proceeding.

[56 FR 38306, Aug. 12, 1991, as amended at 61 FR 20354, May 6, 1996]

§ 509.9 Ex parte communications.

(a) *Definition*—(1) *Ex parte communication* means any material oral or written communication relevant to the merits of an adjudicatory proceeding that was neither on the record nor on reasonable prior notice to all parties that takes place between:

(i) An interested person outside the Office (including such person's counsel); and

(ii) The administrative law judge handling that proceeding, the Director, or a decisional employee.

(2) *Exception.* A request for status of the proceeding does not constitute an *ex parte* communication.

(b) *Prohibition of ex parte communications.* From the time the notice is issued by the Director until the date that the Director issues the final decision pursuant to § 509.40(c) of this subpart:

(1) No interested person outside the Office shall make or knowingly cause to be made an *ex parte* communication to the Director, the administrative law judge, or a decisional employee; and

(2) The Director, administrative law judge, or decisional employee shall not make or knowingly cause to be made to any interested person outside the Office any *ex parte* communication.

(c) *Procedure upon occurrence of ex parte communication.* If an ex parte communication is received by the administrative law judge, the Director or other person identified in paragraph (a) of this section, that person shall cause all such written communications (or, if the communication is oral, a memorandum stating the substance of the communication) to be placed on the record of the proceeding and served on all parties. All other parties to the proceeding shall have an opportunity, within ten days of receipt of service of

§ 509.10

the ex parte communication to file responses thereto and to recommend any sanctions, in accordance with paragraph (d) of this section, that they believe to be appropriate under the circumstances.

(d) *Sanctions.* Any party or his or her counsel who makes a prohibited ex parte communication, or who encourages or solicits another to make any such communication, may be subject to any appropriate sanction or sanctions imposed by the Director or the administrative law judge including, but not limited to, exclusion from the proceedings and an adverse ruling on the issue which is the subject of the prohibited communication.

(e) *Separation-of-functions.* Except to the extent required for the disposition of *ex parte* matters as authorized by law, the administrative law judge may not consult a person or party on any matter relevant to the merits of the adjudication, unless on notice and opportunity for all parties to participate. An employee or agent engaged in the performance of investigative or prosecuting functions for the Office in a case may not, in that or a factually related case, participate or advise in the decision, recommended decision, or agency review of the recommended decision under § 509.40 of this subpart, except as witness or counsel in public proceedings.

[56 FR 38306, Aug. 12, 1991, as amended at 60 FR 28035, May 30, 1995]

§ 509.10   Filing of papers.

(a) *Filing.* Any papers required to be filed, excluding documents produced in response to a discovery request pursuant to §§ 509.25 and 509.26 of this subpart, shall be filed with the OFIA, except as otherwise provided.

(b) *Manner of filing.* Unless otherwise specified by the Director or the administrative law judge, filing may be accomplished by:

(1) Personal service;

(2) Delivering the papers to a reliable commercial courier service, overnight delivery service, or to the U.S. Post Office for Express Mail delivery;

(3) Mailing the papers by first class, registered, or certified mail; or

(4) Transmission by electronic media, only if expressly authorized, and upon any conditions specified, by the Director or the administrative law judge. All papers filed by electronic media shall also concurrently be filed in accordance with paragraph (c) of this section as to form.

(c) *Formal requirements as to papers filed*—(1) *Form.* All papers filed must set forth the name, address, and telephone number of the counsel or party making the filing and must be accompanied by a certification setting forth when and how service has been made on all other parties. All papers filed must be double-spaced and printed or typewritten on 8½×11 inch paper, and must be clear and legible.

(2) *Signature.* All papers must be dated and signed as provided in § 509.7 of this subpart.

(3) *Caption.* All papers filed must include at the head thereof, or on a title page, the name of the Office and of the filing party, the title and docket number of the proceeding, and the subject of the particular paper.

(4) *Number of copies.* Unless otherwise specified by the Director, or the administrative law judge, an original and one copy of all documents and papers shall be filed, except that only one copy of transcripts of testimony and exhibits shall be filed.

§ 509.11   Service of papers.

(a) *By the parties.* Except as otherwise provided, a party filing papers shall serve a copy upon the counsel of record for all other parties to the proceeding so represented, and upon any party not so represented.

(b) *Method of service.* Except as provided in paragraphs (c)(2) and (d) of this section, a serving party shall use one or more of the following methods of service:

(1) Personal service;

(2) Delivering the papers to a reliable commercial courier service, overnight delivery service, or to the U.S. Post Office for Express Mail delivery;

(3) Mailing the papers by first class, registered, or certified mail; or

(4) Transmission by electronic media, only if the parties mutually agree. Any papers served by electronic media shall also concurrently be served in accordance with the requirements of § 509.10(c) of this subpart as to form.

Office of Thrift Supervision, Treasury § 509.12

(c) *By the Director or the administrative law judge.* (1) All papers required to be served by the Director or the administrative law judge upon a party who has appeared in the proceeding through a counsel of record, shall be served by any means specified in paragraph (b) of this section.

(2) If a party has not appeared in the proceeding in accordance with § 509.6 of this subpart, the Director or the administrative law judge shall make service by any of the following methods:

(i) By personal service;

(ii) If the person to be served is an individual, by delivery to a person of suitable age and discretion at the physical location where the individual resides or works;

(iii) If the person to be served is a corporation or other association, by delivery to an officer, managing or general agent, or to any other agent authorized by appointment or by law to receive service and, if the agent is one authorized by statute to receive service and the statute so requires, by also mailing a copy to the party;

(iv) By registered or certified mail addressed to the person's last known address; or

(v) By any other method reasonably calculated to give actual notice.

(d) *Subpoenas.* Service of a subpoena may be made:

(1) By personal service;

(2) If the person to be served is an individual, by delivery to a person of suitable age and discretion at the physical location where the individual resides or works;

(3) By delivery to an agent, which in the case of a corporation or other association, is delivery to an officer, managing or general agent, or to any other agent authorized by appointment or by law to receive service and, if the agent is one authorized by statute to receive service and the statute so requires, by also mailing a copy to the party;

(4) By registered or certified mail addressed to the person's last known address; or

(5) By any other method reasonably calculated to give actual notice.

(e) *Area of service.* Service in any state, territory, possession of the United States, or the District of Columbia, on any person or company doing business in any state, territory, possession of the United States, or the District of Columbia, or on any person as otherwise provided by law, is effective without regard to the place where the hearing is held, provided that if service is made on a foreign bank in connection with an action or proceeding involving one or more of its branches or agencies located in any state, territory, possession of the United States, or the District of Columbia, service shall be made on at least one branch or agency so involved.

[56 FR 38306, Aug. 12, 1991, as amended at 61 FR 20354, May 6, 1996]

§ 509.12 **Construction of time limits.**

(a) *General rule.* In computing any period of time prescribed by this subpart, the date of the act or event that commences the designated period of time is not included. The last day so computed is included unless it is a Saturday, Sunday, or Federal holiday. When the last day is a Saturday, Sunday, or Federal holiday, the period runs until the end of the next day that is not a Saturday, Sunday, or Federal holiday. Intermediate Saturdays, Sundays, and Federal holidays are included in the computation of time. However, when the time period within which an act is to be performed is ten days or less, not including any additional time allowed for in paragraph (c) of this section, intermediate Saturdays, Sundays, and Federal holidays are not included.

(b) *When papers are deemed to be filed or served.* (1) Filing and service are deemed to be effective:

(i) In the case of personal service or same day commercial courier delivery, upon actual service;

(ii) In the case of overnight commercial delivery service, U.S. Express mail delivery, or first class, registered, or certified mail, upon deposit in or delivery to an appropriate point of collection; or

(iii) In the case of transmission by electronic media, as specified by the authority receiving the filing, in the case of filing, and as agreed among the parties, in the case of service.

(2) The effective filing and service dates specified in paragraph (b)(1) of

§ 509.13

this section may be modified by the Director or administrative law judge in the case of filing or by agreement of the parties in the case of service.

(c) *Calculation of time for service and filing of responsive papers.* Whenever a time limit is measured by a prescribed period from the service of any notice or paper, the applicable time limits are calculated as follows:

(1) If service is made by first class, registered, or certified mail, add three calendar days to the prescribed period;

(2) If service is made by express mail or overnight delivery service, add one calendar day to the prescribed period; or

(3) If service is made by electronic media transmission, add one calendar day to the prescribed period, unless otherwise determined by the Director or the administrative law judge in the case of filing, or by agreement among the parties in the case of service.

[56 FR 38306, Aug. 12, 1991, as amended at 61 FR 20354, May 6, 1996]

§ 509.13 Change of time limits.

Except as otherwise provided by law, the administrative law judge may, for good cause shown, extend the time limits prescribed by the Uniform Rules or any notice or order issued in the proceedings. After the referral of the case to the Director pursuant to § 509.38 of this subpart, the Director may grant extensions of the time limits for good cause shown. Extensions may be granted at the motion of a party or on the Director's or the administrative law judge's own motion after notice and opportunity to respond is afforded all non-moving parties.

§ 509.14 Witness fees and expenses.

Witnesses subpoenaed for testimony or deposition shall be paid the same fees for attendance and mileage as are paid in the United States district courts in proceedings in which the United States is a party, provided that, in the case of a discovery subpoena addressed to a party, no witness fees or mileage need be paid. Fees for witnesses shall be tendered in advance by the party requesting the subpoena, except that fees and mileage need not be tendered in advance where the Office is the party requesting the subpoena. The Office shall not be required to pay any fees to, or expenses of, any witness not subpoenaed by the Office.

§ 509.15 Opportunity for informal settlement.

Any respondent may, at any time in the proceeding, unilaterally submit to Enforcement Counsel written offers or proposals for settlement of a proceeding, without prejudice to the rights of any of the parties. No such offer or proposal shall be made to any Office representative other than Enforcement Counsel. Submission of a written settlement offer does not provide a basis for adjourning or otherwise delaying all or any portion of a proceeding under this part. No settlement offer or proposal, or any subsequent negotiation or resolution, is admissible as evidence in any proceeding.

§ 509.16 Office's right to conduct examination.

Nothing contained in this subpart limits in any manner the right of the Office to conduct any examination, inspection, or visitation of any institution or institution-affiliated party, or the right of the Office to conduct or continue any form of investigation authorized by law.

§ 509.17 Collateral attacks on adjudicatory proceeding.

If an interlocutory appeal or collateral attack is brought in any court concerning all or any part of an adjudicatory proceeding, the challenged adjudicatory proceeding shall continue without regard to the pendency of that court proceeding. No default or other failure to act as directed in the adjudicatory proceeding within the times prescribed in this subpart shall be excused based on the pendency before any court of any interlocutory appeal or collateral attack.

§ 509.18 Commencement of proceeding and contents of notice.

(a) *Commencement of proceeding.* (1)(i) Except for change-in-control proceedings under section 7(j)(4) of the FDIA (12 U.S.C. 1817(j)(4)), a proceeding governed by this subpart is commenced by issuance of a notice by the Director.

Office of Thrift Supervision, Treasury

(ii) The notice must be served by the Director upon the respondent and given to any other appropriate financial institution supervisory authority where required by law.

(iii) The notice must be filed with the OFIA.

(2) Change-in control proceedings under section 7(j)(4) of the FDIA (12 U.S.C. 1817(j)(4)) commence with the issuance of an order by the Director.

(b) *Contents of notice.* The notice must set forth:

(1) The legal authority for the proceeding and for the Office's jurisdiction over the proceeding;

(2) A statement of the matters of fact or law showing that the Office is entitled to relief;

(3) A proposed order or prayer for an order granting the requested relief;

(4) The time, place, and nature of the hearing as required by law or regulation;

(5) The time within which to file an answer as required by law or regulation;

(6) The time within which to request a hearing as required by law or regulation; and

(7) The answer and/or request for a hearing shall be filed with OFIA.

§ 509.19 Answer.

(a) *When.* Within 20 days of service of the notice, respondent shall file an answer as designated in the notice. In a civil money penalty proceeding, respondent shall also file a request for a hearing within 20 days of service of the notice.

(b) *Content of answer.* An answer must specifically respond to each paragraph or allegation of fact contained in the notice and must admit, deny, or state that the party lacks sufficient information to admit or deny each allegation of fact. A statement of lack of information has the effect of a denial. Denials must fairly meet the substance of each allegation of fact denied; general denials are not permitted. When a respondent denies part of an allegation, that part must be denied and the remainder specifically admitted. Any allegation of fact in the notice which is not denied in the answer must be deemed admitted for purposes of the proceeding. A respondent is not required to respond to the portion of a notice that constitutes the prayer for relief or proposed order. The answer must set forth affirmative defenses, if any, asserted by the respondent.

(c) *Default*—(1) *Effect of failure to answer.* Failure of a respondent to file an answer required by this section within the time provided constitutes a waiver of his or her right to appear and contest the allegations in the notice. If no timely answer is filed, Enforcement Counsel may file a motion for entry of an order of default. Upon a finding that no good cause has been shown for the failure to file a timely answer, the administrative law judge shall file with the Director a recommended decision containing the findings and the relief sought in the notice. Any final order issued by the Director based upon a respondent's failure to answer is deemed to be an order issued upon consent.

(2) *Effect of failure to request a hearing in civil money penalty proceedings.* If respondent fails to request a hearing as required by law within the time provided, the notice of assessment constitutes a final and unappealable order.

[56 FR 38306, Aug. 12, 1991, as amended at 65 FR 78901, Dec. 18, 2000]

§ 509.20 Amended pleadings.

(a) *Amendments.* The notice or answer may be amended or supplemented at any stage of the proceeding. The respondent must answer an amended notice within the time remaining for the respondent's answer to the original notice, or within ten days after service of the amended notice, whichever period is longer, unless the Director or administrative law judge orders otherwise for good cause.

(b) *Amendments to conform to the evidence.* When issues not raised in the notice or answer are tried at the hearing by express or implied consent of the parties, they will be treated in all respects as if they had been raised in the notice or answer, and no formal amendments are required. If evidence is objected to at the hearing on the ground that it is not within the issues raised by the notice or answer, the administrative law judge may admit the evidence when admission is likely to assist in adjudicating the merits of the action and the objecting party fails to satisfy the administrative law judge that the admission of such evidence would unfairly prejudice that party's action or defense upon the merits. The administrative law judge may grant a continuance to enable the objecting party to meet such evidence.

[61 FR 20354, May 6, 1996]

§ 509.21 Failure to appear.

Failure of a respondent to appear in person at the hearing or by a duly authorized counsel constitutes a waiver of respondent's right to a hearing and is deemed an admission of the facts as alleged and consent to the relief sought in the notice. Without further proceedings or notice to the respondent, the administrative law judge shall file with the Director a recommended decision containing the findings and the relief sought in the notice.

§ 509.22 Consolidation and severance of actions.

(a) *Consolidation.* (1) On the motion of any party, or on the administrative law judge's own motion, the administrative law judge may consolidate, for some or all purposes, any two or more proceedings, if each such proceeding involves or arises out of the same transaction, occurrence or series of transactions or occurrences, or involves at least one common respondent or a material common question of law or fact, unless such consolidation would cause unreasonable delay or injustice.

(2) In the event of consolidation under paragraph (a)(1) of this section, appropriate adjustment to the prehearing schedule must be made to avoid unnecessary expense, inconvenience, or delay.

(b) *Severance.* The administrative law judge may, upon the motion of any party, sever the proceeding for separate resolution of the matter as to any respondent only if the administrative law judge finds that:

(1) Undue prejudice or injustice to the moving party would result from not severing the proceeding; and

(2) Such undue prejudice or injustice would outweigh the interests of judicial economy and expedition in the complete and final resolution of the proceeding.

§ 509.23 Motions.

(a) *In writing.* (1) Except as otherwise provided herein, an application or request for an order or ruling must be made by written motion.

(2) All written motions must state with particularity the relief sought and must be accompanied by a proposed order.

(3) No oral argument may be held on written motions except as otherwise directed by the administrative law judge. Written memoranda, briefs, affidavits or other relevant material or documents may be filed in support of or in opposition to a motion.

(b) *Oral motions.* A motion may be made orally on the record unless the administrative law judge directs that such motion be reduced to writing.

(c) *Filing of motions.* Motions must be filed with the administrative law judge, but upon the filing of the recommended decision, motions must be filed with the Director.

(d) *Responses.* (1) Except as otherwise provided herein, within ten days after service of any written motion, or within such other period of time as may be established by the administrative law judge or the Director, any party may file a written response to a motion. The administrative law judge shall not rule on any oral or written motion before each party has had an opportunity to file a response.

(2) The failure of a party to oppose a written motion or an oral motion made on the record is deemed a consent by that party to the entry of an order substantially in the form of the order accompanying the motion.

(e) *Dilatory motions.* Frivolous, dilatory or repetitive motions are prohibited. The filing of such motions may form the basis for sanctions.

(f) *Dispositive motions.* Dispositive motions are governed by §§ 509.29 and 509.30 of this subpart.

§ 509.24 Scope of document discovery.

(a) *Limits on discovery.* (1) Subject to the limitations set out in paragraphs (b), (c), and (d) of this section, a party to a proceeding under this subpart may obtain document discovery by serving a written request to produce documents. For purposes of a request to

Office of Thrift Supervision, Treasury § 509.25

produce documents, the term "documents" may be defined to include drawings, graphs, charts, photographs, recordings, data stored in electronic form, and other data compilations from which information can be obtained, or translated, if necessary, by the parties through detection devices into reasonably usable form, as well as written material of all kinds.

(2) Discovery by use of deposition is governed by § 509.102 of this part.

(3) Discovery by use of interrogatories is not permitted.

(b) *Relevance.* A party may obtain document discovery regarding any matter, not privileged, that has material relevance to the merits of the pending action. Any request to produce documents that calls for irrelevant material, that is unreasonable, oppressive, excessive in scope, unduly burdensome, or repetitive of previous requests, or that seeks to obtain privileged documents will be denied or modified. A request is unreasonable, oppressive, excessive in scope or unduly burdensome if, among other things, it fails to include justifiable limitations on the time period covered and the geographic locations to be searched, the time provided to respond in the request is inadequate, or the request calls for copies of documents to be delivered to the requesting party and fails to include the requestor's written agreement to pay in advance for the copying, in accordance with § 509.25 of this subpart.

(c) *Privileged matter.* Privileged documents are not discoverable. Privileges include the attorney-client privilege, work-product privilege, any government's or government agency's deliberative-process privilege, and any other privileges the Constitution, any applicable act of Congress, or the principles of common law provide.

(d) *Time limits.* All discovery, including all responses to discovery requests, shall be completed at least 20 days prior to the date scheduled for the commencement of the hearing, except as provided in the Local Rules. No exceptions to this time limit shall be permitted, unless the administrative law judge finds on the record that good cause exists for waiving the requirements of this paragraph.

[56 FR 38306, Aug. 12, 1991, as amended at 61 FR 20354, May 6, 1996]

§ 509.25 Request for document discovery from parties.

(a) *General rule.* Any party may serve on any other party a request to produce for inspection any discoverable documents that are in the possession, custody, or control of the party upon whom the request is served. The request must identify the documents to be produced either by individual item or by category, and must describe each item and category with reasonable particularity. Documents must be produced as they are kept in the usual course of business or must be organized to correspond with the categories in the request.

(b) *Production or copying.* The request must specify a reasonable time, place, and manner for production and performing any related acts. In lieu of inspecting the documents, the requesting party may specify that all or some of the responsive documents be copied and the copies delivered to the requesting party. If copying of fewer than 250 pages is requested, the party to whom the request is addressed shall bear the cost of copying and shipping charges. If a party requests 250 pages or more of copying, the requesting party shall pay for the copying and shipping charges. Copying charges are the current per-page copying rate imposed under 12 CFR 502.7 for requests under the Freedom of Information Act (5 U.S.C. 552). The party to whom the request is addressed may require payment in advance before producing the documents.

(c) *Obligation to update responses.* A party who has responded to a discovery request with a response that was complete when made is not required to supplement the response to include documents thereafter acquired, unless the responding party learns that:

(1) The response was materially incorrect when made; or

(2) The response, though correct when made, is no longer true and a failure to amend the response is, in substance, a knowing concealment.

§ 509.26

(d) *Motions to limit discovery.* (1) Any party that objects to a discovery request may, within ten days of being served with such request, file a motion in accordance with the provisions of § 509.23 of this subpart to revoke or otherwise limit the request. If an objection is made to only a portion of an item or category in a request, the portion objected to shall be specified. Any objections not made in accordance with this paragraph and § 509.23 of this subpart are waived.

(2) The party who served the request that is the subject of a motion to revoke or limit may file a written response within five days of service of the motion. No other party may file a response.

(e) *Privilege.* At the time other documents are produced, the producing party must reasonably identify all documents withheld on the grounds of privilege and must produce a statement of the basis for the assertion of privilege. When similar documents that are protected by deliberative process, attorney-work-product, or attorney-client privilege are voluminous, these documents may be identified by category instead of by individual document. The administrative law judge retains discretion to determine when the identification by category is insufficient.

(f) *Motions to compel production.* (1) If a party withholds any documents as privileged or fails to comply fully with a discovery request, the requesting party may, within ten days of the assertion of privilege or of the time the failure to comply becomes known to the requesting party, file a motion in accordance with the provisions of § 509.23 of this subpart for the issuance of a subpoena compelling production.

(2) The party who asserted the privilege or failed to comply with the request may file a written response to a motion to compel within five days of service of the motion. No other party may file a response.

(g) *Ruling on motions.* After the time for filing responses pursuant to this section has expired, the administrative law judge shall rule promptly on all motions filed pursuant to this section. If the administrative law judge determines that a discovery request, or any of its terms, calls for irrelevant material, is unreasonable, oppressive, excessive in scope, unduly burdensome, or repetitive of previous requests, or seeks to obtain privileged documents, he or she may deny or modify the request, and may issue appropriate protective orders, upon such conditions as justice may require. The pendency of a motion to strike or limit discovery or to compel production is not a basis for staying or continuing the proceeding, unless otherwise ordered by the administrative law judge. Notwithstanding any other provision in this part, the administrative law judge may not release, or order a party to produce, documents withheld on grounds of privilege if the party has stated to the administrative law judge its intention to file a timely motion for interlocutory review of the administrative law judge's order to produce the documents, and until the motion for interlocutory review has been decided.

(h) *Enforcing discovery subpoenas.* If the administrative law judge issues a subpoena compelling production of documents by a party, the subpoenaing party may, in the event of noncompliance and to the extent authorized by applicable law, apply to any appropriate United States district court for an order requiring compliance with the subpoena. A party's right to seek court enforcement of a subpoena shall not in any manner limit the sanctions that may be imposed by the administrative law judge against a party who fails to produce subpoenaed documents.

[56 FR 38306, Aug. 12, 1991, as amended at 61 FR 20355, May 6, 1996]

§ 509.26 Document subpoenas to nonparties.

(a) *General rules.* (1) Any party may apply to the administrative law judge for the issuance of a document discovery subpoena addressed to any person who is not a party to the proceeding. The application must contain a proposed document subpoena and a brief statement showing the general relevance and reasonableness of the scope of documents sought. The subpoenaing party shall specify a reasonable time, place, and manner for making production in response to the document subpoena.

(2) A party shall only apply for a document subpoena under this section within the time period during which such party could serve a discovery request under § 509.24(d) of this subpart. The party obtaining the document subpoena is responsible for serving it on the subpoenaed person and for serving copies on all parties. Document subpoenas may be served in any state, territory, or possession of the United States, the District of Columbia, or as otherwise provided by law.

(3) The administrative law judge shall promptly issue any document subpoena requested pursuant to this section. If the administrative law judge determines that the application does not set forth a valid basis for the issuance of the subpoena, or that any of its terms are unreasonable, oppressive, excessive in scope, or unduly burdensome, he or she may refuse to issue the subpoena or may issue it in a modified form upon such conditions as may be consistent with the Uniform Rules.

(b) *Motion to quash or modify.* (1) Any person to whom a document subpoena is directed may file a motion to quash or modify such subpoena, accompanied by a statement of the basis for quashing or modifying the subpoena. The movant shall serve the motion on all parties, and any party may respond to such motion within ten days of service of the motion.

(2) Any motion to quash or modify a document subpoena must be filed on the same basis, including the assertion of privilege, upon which a party could object to a discovery request under § 509.25(d) of this subpart, and during the same time limits during which such an objection could be filed.

(c) *Enforcing document subpoenas.* If a subpoenaed person fails to comply with any subpoena issued pursuant to this section or any order of the administrative law judge which directs compliance with all or any portion of a document subpoena, the subpoenaing party or any other aggrieved party may, to the extent authorized by applicable law, apply to an appropriate United States district court for an order requiring compliance with so much of the document subpoena as the administrative law judge has not quashed or modified. A party's right to seek court enforcement of a document subpoena shall in no way limit the sanctions that may be imposed by the administrative law judge on a party who induces a failure to comply with subpoenas issued under this section.

§ 509.27 Deposition of witness unavailable for hearing.

(a) *General rules.* (1) If a witness will not be available for the hearing, a party may apply in accordance with the procedures set forth in paragraph (a)(2) of this section, to the administrative law judge for the issuance of a subpoena, including a subpoena duces tecum, requiring the attendance of the witness at a deposition. The administrative law judge may issue a deposition subpoena under this section upon showing that:

(i) The witness will be unable to attend or may be prevented from attending the hearing because of age, sickness or infirmity, or will otherwise be unavailable;

(ii) The witness' unavailability was not procured or caused by the subpoenaing party;

(iii) The testimony is reasonably expected to be material; and

(iv) Taking the deposition will not result in any undue burden to any other party and will not cause undue delay of the proceeding.

(2) The application must contain a proposed deposition subpoena and a brief statement of the reasons for the issuance of the subpoena. The subpoena must name the witness whose deposition is to be taken and specify the time and place for taking the deposition. A deposition subpoena may require the witness to be deposed at any place within the country in which that witness resides or has a regular place of employment or such other convenient place as the administrative law judge shall fix.

(3) Any requested subpoena that sets forth a valid basis for its issuance must be promptly issued, unless the administrative law judge on his or her own motion, requires a written response or requires attendance at a conference concerning whether the requested subpoena should be issued.

(4) The party obtaining a deposition subpoena is responsible for serving it

§ 509.28

on the witness and for serving copies on all parties. Unless the administrative law judge orders otherwise, no deposition under this section shall be taken on fewer than ten days' notice to the witness and all parties. Deposition subpoenas may be served in any state, territory, possession of the United States, or the District of Columbia, on any person or company doing business in any state, territory, possession of the United States, or the District of Columbia, or as otherwise permitted by law.

(b) *Objections to deposition subpoenas.* (1) The witness and any party who has not had an opportunity to oppose a deposition subpoena issued under this section may file a motion with the administrative law judge to quash or modify the subpoena prior to the time for compliance specified in the subpoena, but not more than ten days after service of the subpoena.

(2) A statement of the basis for the motion to quash or modify a subpoena issued under this section must accompany the motion. The motion must be served on all parties.

(c) *Procedure upon deposition.* (1) Each witness testifying pursuant to a deposition subpoena must be duly sworn, and each party shall have the right to examine the witness. Objections to questions or documents must be in short form, stating the grounds for the objection. Failure to object to questions or documents is not deemed a waiver except where the ground for the objection might have been avoided if the objection had been timely presented. All questions, answers, and objections must be recorded.

(2) Any party may move before the administrative law judge for an order compelling the witness to answer any questions the witness has refused to answer or submit any evidence the witness has refused to submit during the deposition.

(3) The deposition must be subscribed by the witness, unless the parties and the witness, by stipulation, have waived the signing, or the witness is ill, cannot be found, or has refused to sign. If the deposition is not subscribed by the witness, the court reporter taking the deposition shall certify that the transcript is a true and complete transcript of the deposition.

(d) *Enforcing subpoenas.* If a subpoenaed person fails to comply with any order of the administrative law judge which directs compliance with all or any portion of a deposition subpoena under paragraph (b) or (c)(2) of this section, the subpoenaing party or other aggrieved party may, to the extent authorized by applicable law, apply to an appropriate United States district court for an order requiring compliance with the portions of the subpoena that the administrative law judge has ordered enforced. A party's right to seek court enforcement of a deposition subpoena in no way limits the sanctions that may be imposed by the administrative law judge on a party who fails to comply with or procures a failure to comply with, a subpoena issued under this section.

§ 509.28 Interlocutory review.

(a) *General rule.* The Director may review a ruling of the administrative law judge prior to the certification of the record to the Director only in accordance with the procedures set forth in this section and § 509.23 of this subpart.

(b) *Scope of review.* The Director may exercise interlocutory review of a ruling of the administrative law judge if the Director finds that:

(1) The ruling involves a controlling question of law or policy as to which substantial grounds exist for a difference of opinion;

(2) Immediate review of the ruling may materially advance the ultimate termination of the proceeding;

(3) Subsequent modification of the ruling at the conclusion of the proceeding would be an inadequate remedy; or

(4) Subsequent modification of the ruling would cause unusual delay or expense.

(c) *Procedure.* Any request for interlocutory review shall be filed by a party with the administrative law judge within ten days of his or her ruling and shall otherwise comply with § 509.23 of this subpart. Any party may file a response to a request for interlocutory review in accordance with

§ 509.23(d) of this subpart. Upon the expiration of the time for filing all responses, the administrative law judge shall refer the matter to the Director for final disposition.

(d) *Suspension of proceeding.* Neither a request for interlocutory review nor any disposition of such a request by the Director under this section suspends or stays the proceeding unless otherwise ordered by the administrative law judge or the Director.

§ 509.29 Summary disposition.

(a) *In general.* The administrative law judge shall recommend that the Director issue a final order granting a motion for summary disposition if the undisputed pleaded facts, admissions, affidavits, stipulations, documentary evidence, matters as to which official notice may be taken, and any other evidentiary materials properly submitted in connection with a motion for summary disposition show that:

(1) There is no genuine issue as to any material fact; and

(2) The moving party is entitled to a decision in its favor as a matter of law.

(b) *Filing of motions and responses.* (1) Any party who believes that there is no genuine issue of material fact to be determined and that he or she is entitled to a decision as a matter of law may move at any time for summary disposition in its favor of all or any part of the proceeding. Any party, within 20 days after service of such a motion, or within such time period as allowed by the administrative law judge, may file a response to such motion.

(2) A motion for summary disposition must be accompanied by a statement of the material facts as to which the moving party contends there is no genuine issue. Such motion must be supported by documentary evidence, which may take the form of admissions in pleadings, stipulations, depositions, investigatory depositions, transcripts, affidavits and any other evidentiary materials that the moving party contends support his or her position. The motion must also be accompanied by a brief containing the points and authorities in support of the contention of the moving party. Any party opposing a motion for summary disposition must file a statement setting forth those material facts as to which he or she contends a genuine dispute exists. Such opposition must be supported by evidence of the same type as that submitted with the motion for summary disposition and a brief containing the points and authorities in support of the contention that summary disposition would be inappropriate.

(c) *Hearing on motion.* At the request of any party or on his or her own motion, the administrative law judge may hear oral argument on the motion for summary disposition.

(d) *Decision on motion.* Following receipt of a motion for summary disposition and all responses thereto, the administrative law judge shall determine whether the moving party is entitled to summary disposition. If the administrative law judge determines that summary disposition is warranted, the administrative law judge shall submit a recommended decision to that effect to the Director. If the administrative law judge finds that no party is entitled to summary disposition, he or she shall make a ruling denying the motion.

§ 509.30 Partial summary disposition.

If the administrative law judge determines that a party is entitled to summary disposition as to certain claims only, he or she shall defer submitting a recommended decision as to those claims. A hearing on the remaining issues must be ordered. Those claims for which the administrative law judge has determined that summary disposition is warranted will be addressed in the recommended decision filed at the conclusion of the hearing.

§ 509.31 Scheduling and prehearing conferences.

(a) *Scheduling conference.* Within 30 days of service of the notice or order commencing a proceeding or such other time as parties may agree, the administrative law judge shall direct counsel for all parties to meet with him or her in person at a specified time and place prior to the hearing or to confer by telephone for the purpose of scheduling the course and conduct of the proceeding. This meeting or telephone

§ 509.32

conference is called a "scheduling conference." The identification of potential witnesses, the time for and manner of discovery, and the exchange of any prehearing materials including witness lists, statements of issues, stipulations, exhibits and any other materials may also be determined at the scheduling conference.

(b) *Prehearing conferences.* The administrative law judge may, in addition to the scheduling conference, on his or her own motion or at the request of any party, direct counsel for the parties to meet with him or her (in person or by telephone) at a prehearing conference to address any or all of the following:

(1) Simplification and clarification of the issues;

(2) Stipulations, admissions of fact, and the contents, authenticity and admissibility into evidence of documents;

(3) Matters of which official notice may be taken;

(4) Limitation of the number of witnesses;

(5) Summary disposition of any or all issues;

(6) Resolution of discovery issues or disputes;

(7) Amendments to pleadings; and

(8) Such other matters as may aid in the orderly disposition of the proceeding.

(c) *Transcript.* The administrative law judge, in his or her discretion, may require that a scheduling or prehearing conference be recorded by a court reporter. A transcript of the conference and any materials filed, including orders, becomes part of the record of the proceeding. A party may obtain a copy of the transcript at its expense.

(d) *Scheduling or prehearing orders.* At or within a reasonable time following the conclusion of the scheduling conference or any prehearing conference, the administrative law judge shall serve on each party an order setting forth any agreements reached and any procedural determinations made.

[56 FR 38306, Aug. 12, 1991, as amended at 65 FR 78901, Dec. 18, 2000]

§ 509.32 Prehearing submissions.

(a) Within the time set by the administrative law judge, but in no case later than 14 days before the start of the hearing, each party shall serve on every other party, his or her:

(1) Prehearing statement;

(2) Final list of witnesses to be called to testify at the hearing, including name and address of each witness and a short summary of the expected testimony of each witness;

(3) List of the exhibits to be introduced at the hearing along with a copy of each exhibit; and

(4) Stipulations of fact, if any.

(b) *Effect of failure to comply.* No witness may testify and no exhibits may be introduced at the hearing if such witness or exhibit is not listed in the prehearing submissions pursuant to paragraph (a) of this section, except for good cause shown.

§ 509.33 Public hearings.

(a) *General rule.* All hearings shall be open to the public, unless the Director, in the Director's discretion, determines that holding an open hearing would be contrary to the public interest. Within 20 days of service of the notice or, in the case of change-in-control proceedings under section 7(j)(4) of the FDIA (12 U.S.C. 1817(j)(4)), within 20 days from service of the hearing order, any respondent may file with the Director a request for a private hearing, and any party may file a reply to such a request. A party must serve on the administrative law judge a copy of any request or reply the party files with the Director. The form of, and procedure for, these requests and replies are governed by § 509.23 of this subpart. A party's failure to file a request or a reply constitutes a waiver of any objections regarding whether the hearing will be public or private.

(b) *Filing document under seal.* Enforcement Counsel, in his or her discretion, may file any document or part of a document under seal if disclosure of the document would be contrary to the public interest. The administrative law judge shall take all appropriate steps to preserve the confidentiality of such documents or parts thereof, including closing portions of the hearing to the public.

[56 FR 38306, Aug. 12, 1991, as amended at 61 FR 20355, May 6, 1996]

Office of Thrift Supervision, Treasury § 509.35

§ 509.34 Hearing subpoenas.

(a) *Issuance.* (1) Upon application of a party showing general relevance and reasonableness of scope of the testimony or other evidence sought, the administrative law judge may issue a subpoena or a subpoena duces tecum requiring the attendance of a witness at the hearing or the production of documentary or physical evidence at the hearing. The application for a hearing subpoena must also contain a proposed subpoena specifying the attendance of a witness or the production of evidence from any state, territory, or possession of the United States, the District of Columbia, or as otherwise provided by law at any designated place where the hearing is being conducted. The party making the application shall serve a copy of the application and the proposed subpoena on every other party.

(2) A party may apply for a hearing subpoena at any time before the commencement of a hearing. During a hearing, a party may make an application for a subpoena orally on the record before the administrative law judge.

(3) The administrative law judge shall promptly issue any hearing subpoena requested pursuant to this section. If the administrative law judge determines that the application does not set forth a valid basis for the issuance of the subpoena, or that any of its terms are unreasonable, oppressive, excessive in scope, or unduly burdensome, he or she may refuse to issue the subpoena or may issue it in a modified form upon any conditions consistent with this subpart. Upon issuance by the administrative law judge, the party making the application shall serve the subpoena on the person named in the subpoena and on each party.

(b) *Motion to quash or modify.* (1) Any person to whom a hearing subpoena is directed or any party may file a motion to quash or modify the subpoena, accompanied by a statement of the basis for quashing or modifying the subpoena. The movant must serve the motion on each party and on the person named in the subpoena. Any party may respond to the motion within ten days of service of the motion.

(2) Any motion to quash or modify a hearing subpoena must be filed prior to the time specified in the subpoena for compliance, but not more than ten days after the date of service of the subpoena upon the movant.

(c) *Enforcing subpoenas.* If a subpoenaed person fails to comply with any subpoena issued pursuant to this section or any order of the administrative law judge which directs compliance with all or any portion of a document subpoena, the subpoenaing party or any other aggrieved party may seek enforcement of the subpoena pursuant to section § 509.26(c) of this subpart.

[56 FR 38306, Aug. 12, 1991, as amended at 61 FR 20355, May 6, 1996]

§ 509.35 Conduct of hearings.

(a) *General rules.* (1) Hearings shall be conducted so as to provide a fair and expeditious presentation of the relevant disputed issues. Each party has the right to present its case or defense by oral and documentary evidence and to conduct such cross examination as may be required for full disclosure of the facts.

(2) *Order of hearing.* Enforcement Counsel shall present its case-in-chief first, unless otherwise ordered by the administrative law judge, or unless otherwise expressly specified by law or regulation. Enforcement Counsel shall be the first party to present an opening statement and a closing statement, and may make a rebuttal statement after the respondent's closing statement. If there are multiple respondents, respondents may agree among themselves as to their order of presentation of their cases, but if they do not agree the administrative law judge shall fix the order.

(3) *Examination of witnesses.* Only one counsel for each party may conduct an examination of a witness, except that in the case of extensive direct examination, the administrative law judge may permit more than one counsel for the party presenting the witness to conduct the examination. A party may have one counsel conduct the direct examination and another counsel conduct re-direct examination of a witness, or may have one counsel conduct the

§ 509.36

cross examination of a witness and another counsel conduct the re-cross examination of a witness.

(4) *Stipulations.* Unless the administrative law judge directs otherwise, all stipulations of fact and law previously agreed upon by the parties, and all documents, the admissibility of which have been previously stipulated, will be admitted into evidence upon commencement of the hearing.

(b) *Transcript.* The hearing must be recorded and transcribed. The reporter will make the transcript available to any party upon payment by that party to the reporter of the cost of the transcript. The administrative law judge may order the record corrected, either upon motion to correct, upon stipulation of the parties, or following notice to the parties upon the administrative law judge's own motion.

[56 FR 38306, Aug. 12, 1991, as amended at 61 FR 20356, May 6, 1996]

§ 509.36 Evidence.

(a) *Admissibility.* (1) Except as is otherwise set forth in this section, relevant, material, and reliable evidence that is not unduly repetitive is admissible to the fullest extent authorized by the APA and other applicable law.

(2) Evidence that would be admissible under the Federal Rules of Evidence is admissible in a proceeding conducted pursuant to this subpart.

(3) Evidence that would be inadmissible under the Federal Rules of Evidence may not deemed or ruled to be inadmissible in a proceeding conducted pursuant to this subpart if such evidence is relevant, material, reliable and not unduly repetitive.

(b) *Official notice.* (1) Official notice may be taken of any material fact which may be judicially noticed by a United States district court and any material information in the official public records of any Federal or state government agency.

(2) All matters officially noticed by the administrative law judge or Director shall appear on the record.

(3) If official notice is requested or taken of any material fact, the parties, upon timely request, shall be afforded an opportunity to object.

(c) *Documents.* (1) A duplicate copy of a document is admissible to the same extent as the original, unless a genuine issue is raised as to whether the copy is in some material respect not a true and legible copy of the original.

(2) Subject to the requirements of paragraph (a) of this section, any document, including a report of examination, supervisory activity, inspection or visitation, prepared by the appropriate Office or state regulatory agency, is admissible either with or without a sponsoring witness.

(3) Witnesses may use existing or newly created charts, exhibits, calendars, calculations, outlines or other graphic material to summarize, illustrate, or simplify the presentation of testimony. Such materials may, subject to the administrative law judge's discretion, be used with or without being admitted into evidence.

(d) *Objections.* (1) Objections to the admissibility of evidence must be timely made and rulings on all objections must appear on the record.

(2) When an objection to a question or line of questioning propounded to a witness is sustained, the examining counsel may make a specific proffer on the record of what he or she expected to prove by the expected testimony of the witness, either by representation of counsel or by direct interrogation of the witness.

(3) The administrative law judge shall retain rejected exhibits, adequately marked for identification, for the record, and transmit such exhibits to the Director.

(4) Failure to object to admission of evidence or to any ruling constitutes a waiver of the objection.

(e) *Stipulations.* The parties may stipulate as to any relevant matters of fact or the authentication of any relevant documents. Such stipulations must be received in evidence at a hearing, and are binding on the parties with respect to the matters therein stipulated.

(f) *Depositions of unavailable witnesses.* (1) If a witness is unavailable to testify at a hearing, and that witness has testified in a deposition to which all parties in a proceeding had notice and an opportunity to participate, a party may offer as evidence all or any part of the transcript of the deposition, including deposition exhibits, if any.

Office of Thrift Supervision, Treasury § 509.38

(2) Such deposition transcript is admissible to the same extent that testimony would have been admissible had that person testified at the hearing, provided that if a witness refused to answer proper questions during the depositions, the administrative law judge may, on that basis, limit the admissibility of the deposition in any manner that justice requires.

(3) Only those portions of a deposition received in evidence at the hearing constitute a part of the record.

§ 509.37 Post-hearing filings.

(a) *Proposed findings and conclusions and supporting briefs.* (1) Using the same method of service for each party, the administrative law judge shall serve notice upon each party, that the certified transcript, together with all hearing exhibits and exhibits introduced but not admitted into evidence at the hearing, has been filed. Any party may file with the administrative law judge proposed findings of fact, proposed conclusions of law, and a proposed order within 30 days following service of this notice by the administrative law judge or within such longer period as may be ordered by the administrative law judge.

(2) Proposed findings and conclusions must be supported by citation to any relevant authorities and by page references to any relevant portions of the record. A post-hearing brief may be filed in support of proposed findings and conclusions, either as part of the same document or in a separate document. Any party who fails to file timely with the administrative law judge any proposed finding or conclusion is deemed to have waived the right to raise in any subsequent filing or submission any issue not addressed in such party's proposed finding or conclusion.

(b) *Reply briefs.* Reply briefs may be filed within 15 days after the date on which the parties' proposed findings, conclusions, and order are due. Reply briefs must be strictly limited to responding to new matters, issues, or arguments raised in another party's papers. A party who has not filed proposed findings of fact and conclusions of law or a post-hearing brief may not file a reply brief.

(c) *Simultaneous filing required.* The administrative law judge shall not order the filing by any party of any brief or reply brief in advance of the other party's filing of its brief.

[56 FR 38306, Aug. 12, 1991, as amended at 61 FR 20356, May 6, 1996]

§ 509.38 Recommended decision and filing of record.

(a) *Filing of recommended decision and record.* Within 45 days after expiration of the time allowed for filing reply briefs under § 509.37(b) of this subpart, the administrative law judge shall file with and certify to the Director, for decision, the record of the proceeding. The record must include the administrative law judge's recommended decision, recommended findings of fact, recommended conclusions of law, and proposed order; all prehearing and hearing transcripts, exhibits, and rulings; and the motions, briefs, memoranda, and other supporting papers filed in connection with the hearing. The administrative law judge shall serve upon each party the recommended decision, findings, conclusions, and proposed order.

(b) *Filing of index.* At the same time the administrative law judge files with and certifies to the Director for final determination the record of the proceeding, the administrative law judge shall furnish to the Director a certified index of the entire record of the proceeding. The certified index shall include, at a minimum, an entry for each paper, document or motion filed with the administrative law judge in the proceeding, the date of the filing, and the identity of the filer. The certified index shall also include an exhibit index containing, at a minimum, an entry consisting of exhibit number and title or description for: Each exhibit introduced and admitted into evidence at the hearing; each exhibit introduced but not admitted into evidence at the hearing; each exhibit introduced and admitted into evidence after the completion of the hearing; and each exhibit introduced but not admitted into evidence after the completion of the hearing.

[61 FR 20356, May 6, 1996]

§ 509.39 Exceptions to recommended decision.

(a) *Filing exceptions.* Within 30 days after service of the recommended decision, findings, conclusions, and proposed order under § 509.38 of this subpart, a party may file with the Director written exceptions to the administrative law judge's recommended decision, findings, conclusions or proposed order, to the admission or exclusion of evidence, or to the failure of the administrative law judge to make a ruling proposed by a party. A supporting brief may be filed at the time the exceptions are filed, either as part of the same document or in a separate document.

(b) *Effect of failure to file or raise exceptions.* (1) Failure of a party to file exceptions to those matters specified in paragraph (a) of this section within the time prescribed is deemed a waiver of objection thereto.

(2) No exception need be considered by the Director if the party taking exception had an opportunity to raise the same objection, issue, or argument before the administrative law judge and failed to do so.

(c) *Contents.* (1) All exceptions and briefs in support of such exceptions must be confined to the particular matters in, or omissions from, the administrative law judge's recommendations to which that party takes exception.

(2) All exceptions and briefs in support of exceptions must set forth page or paragraph references to the specific parts of the administrative law judge's recommendations to which exception is taken, the page or paragraph references to those portions of the record relied upon to support each exception, and the legal authority relied upon to support each exception.

§ 509.40 Review by the Director.

(a) *Notice of submission to the Director.* When the Director determines that the record in the proceeding is complete, the Director shall serve notice upon the parties that the proceeding has been submitted to the Director for final decision.

(b) *Oral argument before the Director.* Upon the initiative of the Director or on the written request of any party filed with the Director within the time for filing exceptions, the Director may order and hear oral argument on the recommended findings, conclusions, decision, and order of the administrative law judge. A written request by a party must show good cause for oral argument and state reasons why arguments cannot be presented adequately in writing. A denial of a request for oral argument may be set forth in the Director's final decision. Oral argument before the Director must be on the record.

(c) *Director's final decision.* (1) Decisional employees may advise and assist the Director in the consideration and disposition of the case. The final decision of the Director will be based upon review of the entire record of the proceeding, except that the director may limit the issues to be reviewed to those findings and conclusions to which opposing arguments or exceptions have been filed by the parties.

(2) The Director shall render a final decision within 90 days after notification of the parties that the case has been submitted for final decision, or 90 days after oral argument, whichever is later, unless the Director orders that the action or any aspect thereof be remanded to the administrative law judge for further proceedings. Copies of the final decision and order of the Director shall be served upon each party to the proceeding, upon other persons required by statute, and, if directed by the Director or required by statute, upon any appropriate state or Federal supervisory authority.

§ 509.41 Stays pending judicial review.

The commencement of proceedings for judicial review of a final decision and order of the Office may not, unless specifically ordered by the Director or a reviewing court, operate as a stay of any order issued by the Director. The Director may, in its discretion, and on such terms as it finds just, stay the effectiveness of all or any part of its order pending a final decision on a petition for review of the order.

Office of Thrift Supervision, Treasury § 509.102

Subpart B—Local Rules

§ 509.100 Scope.

The rules and procedures in this subpart B shall apply to those proceedings covered by subpart A of this part. In addition, subpart A of this part and this subpart shall apply to adjudicatory proceedings for which hearings on the record are provided for by the following statutory provisions:

(a) Proceedings under section 10(a)(2)(D) of the HOLA (12 U.S.C. 1467a(a)(2)(D)) to determine whether any person directly or indirectly exercises a controlling influence over the management or policies of a savings association or any other company, except to the extent the Director exercises his or her discretion to commence a proceeding of the kind identified in subpart C of this part;

(b) Proceedings under section 10(g)(5)(A) of the HOLA (12 U.S.C. 1467a(g)(5)(A)) to determine whether to terminate certain activities by savings and loan holding companies or to terminate ownership or control of a non-insured savings and loan holding company subsidiary; and

(c) Proceedings under section 15(c)(4) of the Securities and Exchange Act of 1934 (15 U.S.C. 78o(c)(4)) (Exchange Act) to determine whether any association or person subject to the jurisdiction of the Office pursuant to section 12(i) of the Exchange Act (15 U.S.C. 78l(i)) has failed to comply with the provisions of sections 12, 13, 14(a), 14(c), 14(d) or 14(f) of the Exchange Act.

[56 FR 38306, Aug. 12, 1991, as amended at 70 FR 10023, Mar. 2, 2005]

§ 509.101 Appointment of Office of Financial Institution Adjudication.

Unless otherwise directed by the Office, all hearings under subpart A of this part and this subpart shall be conducted by administrative law judges under the direction of the Office of Financial Institution Adjudication, 1700 G Street NW., Washington, DC 20552.

§ 509.102 Discovery.

(a) *In general.* A party may take the deposition of an expert, or of a person, including another party, who has direct knowledge of matters that are non-privileged, relevant and material to the proceeding and where there is a need for the deposition. The deposition of experts shall be limited to those experts who are expected to testify at the hearing.

(b) *Notice.* A party desiring to take a deposition shall give reasonable notice in writing to the deponent and to every other party to the proceeding. The notice must state the time and place for taking the deposition and the name and address of the person to be deposed.

(c) *Time limits.* A party may take depositions at any time after the commencement of the proceeding, but no later than ten days before the scheduled hearing date, except with permission of the administrative law judge for good cause shown.

(d) *Conduct of the deposition.* The witness must be duly sworn, and each party shall have the right to examine the witness with respect to all non-privileged, relevant and material matters of which the witness has factual, direct and personal knowledge. Objections to questions or exhibits shall be in short form, stating the grounds for objection. Failure to object to questions or exhibits is not a waiver except where the grounds for the objection might have been avoided if the objection had been timely presented. The court reporter shall transcribe or otherwise record the witness's testimony, as agreed among the parties.

(e) *Protective orders.* At any time after notice of a deposition has been given, a party may file a motion for the issuance of a protective order. Such protective order may prohibit, terminate, or limit the scope or manner of the taking of a deposition. The administrative law judge shall grant such protective order upon a showing of sufficient grounds, including that the deposition:

(1) Is unreasonable, oppressive, excessive in scope, or unduly burdensome;

(2) Involves privileged, investigative, trial preparation, irrelevant or immaterial matters; or

(3) Is being conducted in bad faith or in such manner as to unreasonably annoy, embarrass, or oppress the deponent.

§ 509.103

(f) *Fees.* Deposition witnesses, including expert witnesses, shall be paid the same expenses in the same manner as are paid witnesses in the district courts of the United States in proceedings in which the United States Government is a party. Expenses in accordance with this paragraph shall be paid by the party seeking to take the deposition.

(g) *Deposition subpoenas*—(1) *Issuance.* At the request of a party, the administrative law judge shall issue a subpoena requiring the attendance of a witness at a deposition. The attendance of a witness may be required from any place in any state or territory that is subject to the jurisdiction of the United States or as otherwise permitted by law.

(2) *Service.* The party requesting the subpoena must serve it on the person named therein or upon that person's counsel, by any of the methods identified in § 509.11(d) of this part. The party serving the subpoena must file proof of service with the administrative law judge.

(3) *Motion to quash.* A person named in the subpoena or a party may file a motion to quash or modify the subpoena. A statement of the reasons for the motion must accompany it and a copy of the motion must be served on the party that requested the subpoena. The motion must be made prior to the time for compliance specified in the subpoena and not more than ten days after the date of service of the subpoena, or if the subpoena is served within 15 days of the hearing, within five days after the date of service.

(4) *Enforcement of deposition subpoena.* Enforcement of a deposition subpoena shall be in accordance with the procedures of § 509.27(d) of this part.

[56 FR 38306, Aug. 12, 1991, as amended at 61 FR 20356, May 6, 1996]

§ 509.103 Civil money penalties.

(a) *Assessment.* In the event of consent, or if upon the record developed at the hearing the Office finds that any of the grounds specified in the notice issued pursuant to § 509.18 of this part have been established, the Office may serve an order of assessment of civil money penalty upon the party concerned. The assessment order shall be effective immediately upon service or upon such other date as may be specified therein and shall remain effective and enforceable until it is stayed, modified, terminated, or set aside by the Office or by a reviewing court.

(b) *Payment.* (1) Civil penalties assessed pursuant to subpart A of this part and this subpart B are payable and to be collected within 60 days after the issuance of the notice of assessment, unless the Office fixes a different time for payment where it determines that the purpose of the civil money penalty would be better served thereby; however, if a party has made a timely request for a hearing to challenge the assessment of the penalty, the party may not be required to pay such penalty until the Office has issued a final order of assessment following the hearing. In such instances, the penalty shall be paid within 60 days of service of such order unless the Office fixes a different time for payment. Notwithstanding the foregoing, the Office may seek to attach the party's assets or to have a receiver appointed to secure payment of the potential civil money penalty or other obligation in advance of the hearing in accordance with section 8(i)(4) of the FDIA (12 U.S.C. 1818(i)(4)).

(2) Checks in payment of civil penalties shall be made payable to the Treasurer of the United States and sent to the Controller's Division of the Office. Upon receipt, the Office shall forward the check to the Treasury of the United States.

(c) *Inflation adjustment.* Under the Federal Civil Monetary Penalties Inflation Adjustment Act of 1990 (28 U.S.C. 2461 note), OTS must adjust for inflation the civil money penalties in statutes that it administers. The following chart displays the adjusted civil money penalties. The amounts in this chart apply to violations that occur after October 27, 2008:

U.S. Code citation	CMP description	New maximum amount
12 U.S.C. 1464(v)(4)	Reports of Condition—1st Tier	$2,200
12 U.S.C. 1464(v)(5)	Reports of Condition—2nd Tier	32,500

Office of Thrift Supervision, Treasury   § 509.104

U.S. Code citation	CMP description	New maximum amount
12 U.S.C. 1464(v)(6)	Reports of Condition—3rd Tier	1,375,000
12 U.S.C. 1467(d)	Refusal to Cooperate in Exam	7,500
12 U.S.C. 1467a(i)(2)	Holding Company Act Violation	32,500
12 U.S.C. 1467a(i)(3)	Holding Company Act Violation	32,500
12 U.S.C. 1467a(r)(1)	Late/Inaccurate Reports—1st Tier	2,200
12 U.S.C. 1467a(r)(2)	Late/Inaccurate Reports—2nd Tier	32,500
12 U.S.C. 1467a(r)(3)	Late/Inaccurate Reports—3rd Tier	1,375,000
12 U.S.C. 1817(j)(16)(A)	Change in Control—1st Tier	7,500
12 U.S.C. 1817(j)(16)(B)	Change in Control—2nd Tier	37,500
12 U.S.C. 1817(j)(16)(C)	Change in Control—3rd Tier	1,375,000
12 U.S.C. 1818(i)(2)(A)	Violation of Law or Unsafe or Unsound Practice—1st Tier	7,500
12 U.S.C. 1818(i)(2)(B)	Violation of Law or Unsafe or Unsound Practice—2nd Tier	37,500
12 U.S.C. 1818(i)(2)(C)	Violation of Law or Unsafe or Unsound Practice—3rd Tier	1,375,000
12 U.S.C. 1820(k)(6)(A)(ii)	Violation of Post Employment Restrictions	275,000
12 U.S.C. 1884	Violation of Security Rules	110
12 U.S.C. 3349(b)	Appraisals Violation—1st Tier	7,500
12 U.S.C. 3349(b)	Appraisals Violation—2nd Tier	37,500
12 U.S.C. 3349(b)	Appraisals Violation—3rd Tier	1,375,000
42 U.S.C. 4012a(f)	Flood Insurance	[1] 385 [2] 135,000

[1] Per day.
[2] Per year.

[56 FR 38306, Aug. 12, 1991, as amended at 65 FR 61262, Oct. 17, 2000; 69 FR 64251, Nov. 4, 2004; 73 FR 63626, Oct. 27, 2008]

§ 509.104 Additional procedures.

(a) *Replies to exceptions.* Replies to written exceptions to the administrative law judge's recommended decision, findings, conclusions or proposed order pursuant to § 509.39 of this part shall be filed within 10 days of the date such written exceptions were required to be filed.

(b) *Motions.* All motions shall be filed with the administrative law judge and an additional copy shall be filed with the Secretary to the Office, who receives adjudicatory filings, ("Secretary"); provided, however, that once the administrative law judge has certified the record to the Director pursuant to § 509.38 of this part, all motions must be filed with the Director, to the attention of the Secretary, within the 10 day period following the filing of exceptions allowed for the filing of replies to exceptions. Responses to such motions filed in a timely manner with the Director, other than motions for oral argument before the Director, shall be allowed pursuant to the procedures at § 509.23(d) of this part. No response is required for the Director to make a determination on a motion for oral argument.

(c) *Authority of administrative law judge.* In addition to the powers listed in § 509.5 of this part, the administrative law judge shall have the authority to deny any dispositive motion and shall follow the procedures set forth for motions for summary disposition at § 509.29 of this part and partial summary disposition at § 509.30 of this part in making determinations on such motions.

(d) *Notification of submission of proceeding to the Director.* Upon the expiration of the time for filing any exceptions, any replies to such exceptions or any motions and any ruling thereon, and after receipt of certified record, the Office shall notify the parties within ten days of the submission of the proceeding to the Director for final determination.

(e) *Extensions of time for final determination.* The Director may, *sua sponte,* extend the time for final determination by signing an order of extension of time within the 90 day time period and notifying the parties of such extension thereafter.

(f) *Service upon the Office.* Service of any document upon the Office shall be made by filing with the Secretary, in addition to the individuals and/or offices designated by the Office in its Notice issued pursuant to § 509.18 of this part, or such other means reasonably suited to provide notice of the person

§ 509.200

and/or office designated to receive filings.

(g) *Filings with the Director.* An additional copy of all materials required or permitted to be filed with or referred to the administrative law judge pursuant to subpart A and B of this part shall be filed with the Secretary. This rule shall not apply to the transcript of testimony and exhibits adduced at the hearing or to proposed exhibits submitted in advance of the hearing pursuant to an order of the administrative law judge under § 509.32 of this part. Materials required or permitted to be filed with or referred to the Director pursuant to subparts A and B of this part shall be filed with the Director, to the attention of the Secretary.

(h) *Presence of cameras and other recording devices.* The use of cameras and other recording devices, other than those used by the court reporter, shall be prohibited and excluded from the proceedings.

[56 FR 38306, Aug. 12, 1991, as amended at 58 FR 4311, Jan. 14, 1993; 61 FR 20356, May 6, 1996]

Subpart C—Special Rules

SOURCE: 70 FR 10023, Mar. 2, 2005, unless otherwise noted.

§ 509.200 Scope.

The rules and procedures in subpart C of this part and those rules and procedures in subparts A and B of this part that are identified in subpart C of this part shall apply to any proceedings under section 10(a)(2)(D) of the HOLA (12 U.S.C. 1467a(a)(2)(D)) to determine for purposes of section 10 of the HOLA, other than subsections (c), (d), (f), (h)(2), (m), (n), (q) and (s), whether any company that owns at least one percent but no more than 10 percent of the outstanding shares of a savings association or savings and loan holding company directly or indirectly exercises a controlling influence over the management or policies of such savings association or savings and loan holding company.

§ 509.201 Definitions.

The definitions contained in § 509.3 of this part shall apply to this subpart.

§ 509.202 Commencement of proceedings and contents of notice.

(a) *Commencement of proceedings.* The Director commences a proceeding by issuing a notice and having it served on the respondent in the manner provided for service by the Director in § 509.11 of this part;

(b) *Contents of notice.* The notice must set forth: (1) The legal authority for the proceeding and for the Office's jurisdiction over the proceeding;

(2) A statement of the matters of fact or law showing the Office is entitled to issue an Order finding, for purposes of section 10 of the HOLA, other than subsections (c), (d), (f), (h)(2), (m), (n), (q) and (s), the respondent to be directly or indirectly exercising a controlling influence over the management or policies of a savings association or savings and loan holding company;

(3) A proposed Order;

(4) A statement that the respondent must file an answer and, if it so desires, request a hearing within 20 days of service of the notice; and

(5) The time and place of the hearing if one is properly requested by the respondent.

§ 509.203 Answer, consequences of failure to answer, and consent.

(a) *Content of answer.* (1) An answer must specifically respond to each paragraph or allegation of fact contained in the notice and must admit, deny, or state that the party lacks sufficient information to admit or deny each allegation of fact. A statement of lack of information has the effect of a denial. Denials must fairly meet the substance of each allegation of fact denied; general denials are not permitted. When a respondent denies part of an allegation, that part must be denied and the remainder specifically admitted. Any allegation of fact in the notice which is not denied in the answer must be deemed admitted for purposes of the proceeding. A respondent is not required to respond to the portion of a notice that constitutes a prayer for relief or proposed Order.

(2) If a respondent does not contest the allegations in a notice, the respondent may file an answer that contains only a statement that the respondent consents to the entry of the

proposed Order. At any time thereafter, the proposed Order may be issued as a final Order.

(b) *Default.* Failure of a respondent to file an answer within the time provided constitutes a waiver of its right to appear and contest the allegations in the notice. If a timely answer is not filed, a default Order may be entered. A respondent that believes that there was good cause for it to not file an answer within the time allowed may request that the Office exercise its discretion to vacate such a default Order. A default Order based upon a respondent's failure to answer is deemed to be a final Order issued upon consent.

§ 509.204 Hearing Procedure.

(a) (1) The Director shall preside at the hearing and enter the final decision of the agency, provided that no party seeks discovery or proffers any oral testimony;

(2) Respondents shall provide two copies of any pleadings and other filings to the Office of the Chief Counsel, Business Transactions Division. The Office of the Chief Counsel, Business Transactions Division shall serve in the manner provided in § 509.11 of this part, each respondent separately represented with a copy of any pleading or other filing made by the Office.

(b) If any party seeks discovery or proffers any oral testimony, the procedures in subparts A and B of this part shall apply from that time until the conclusion of the proceeding.

Subpart D—Exemptions under Section 19(e) of the FDIA

SOURCE: 72 FR 25955, May 8, 2007, unless otherwise noted.

§ 509.300 Scope.

The procedures in this subpart D govern hearings on denials of applications for case-by-case exemptions under 12 CFR part 585. Part 585 implements section 19(e) of the FDIA, which prohibits persons who have been convicted of certain criminal offenses or who have agreed to enter into a pre-trial diversion or similar program in connection with a prosecution for such criminal offenses from occupying various positions with a savings and loan holding company.

§ 509.301 Hearing procedures.

(a) *Hearings.* The following procedures apply to hearings under 12 CFR part 585.

(1) The hearing shall be held in Washington, DC, or at another designated place, before a presiding officer designated by the Director.

(2) An applicant may elect in writing to have the matter determined on the basis of written submissions, rather than an oral hearing.

(3) The parties to the hearing are OTS Enforcement counsel and the applicant.

(4) 12 CFR 509.2, 509.4, 509.6 through 509.12, and 509.16 apply to the hearing.

(5) Discovery is not permitted.

(6) A party may introduce relevant and material documents and make oral argument at the hearing.

(7) At the discretion of the presiding officer, witnesses may be presented within specified time limits, provided that a list of witnesses is furnished to the presiding officer and to all other parties before to the hearing. Witnesses must be sworn, unless otherwise directed by the presiding officer. The presiding officer may ask questions of any witness. Each party may cross-examine any witness presented by the opposing party. OTS will furnish a transcript of the proceedings upon an applicant's request and upon the payment of the costs of the transcript.

(8) The presiding officer has the power to administer oaths and affirmations, to take or cause to be taken depositions of unavailable witnesses, and to issue, revoke, quash, or modify subpoenas and subpoenas duces tecum. If the presentation of witnesses is permitted, the presiding officer may require the attendance of witnesses from any state, territory, or other place subject to the jurisdiction of the United States at any location where the proceeding is being conducted. Witness fees are paid in accordance with 12 CFR 509.14.

(9) Upon the request of a party, the record will remain open for five business days following the hearing for additional submissions to the record.

(10) OTS Enforcement Counsel has the burden of proving a *prima facie* case that a person is prohibited from a position under section 19(e) of the FDIA. The applicant has the burden of proof on all other matters.

(11) The presiding officer must make recommendations to the Director, where possible, within 20 days after the last day for the parties to submit additions to the record.

(12) The presiding officer must forward his or her recommendation to the Director who shall promptly certify the entire record, including the presiding officer's recommendations. The Director's certification will close the record.

(b) *Decision.* After the certification of the record, the Director will notify the parties of his or her decision by issuing an order approving or denying the application.

(1) An approval order will require fidelity bond coverage for the position to the same extent as similar positions with the savings and loan holding company. The approval order may include such other conditions as may be appropriate.

(2) A denial order will include a summary of the relevant factors under 12 CFR 585.120(b).

PART 510—MISCELLANEOUS ORGANIZATIONAL REGULATIONS

Sec.
510.2 Provisions related to regulations of the Office.
510.4 Service of process.
510.5 Release of unpublished OTS information.

AUTHORITY: 12 U.S.C. 1462a, 1463, 1464; Pub. L. 101–410, 104 Stat. 890; Pub. L. 104–134, 110 Stat. 1321–358.

SOURCE: 54 FR 49456, Nov. 30, 1989, unless otherwise noted.

§ 510.2 Provisions related to regulations of the Office.

(a) *Amendments.* The Office expressly reserves the right to amend (including the right to alter or repeal) the regulations set forth in this chapter.

(b) *Waiver or relaxation of regulatory provisions with respect to disaster or emergency areas.* Whenever the President of the United States determines that a major disaster or emergency exists, or declares an area a major disaster or emergency area, the Office may, to the extent not inconsistent with law, by order waive or relax any limitations pertaining to the operations of Federal savings associations and savings associations in any area or areas affected by such disaster or emergency so declared.

(c) *Bar on participation in notice and comment rulemaking by suspended or disbarred persons.* No person who has been suspended or debarred from practice before the Office in accordance with the provisions of part 513 of this chapter may submit to the Office, either directly or on behalf of an interested party, any written documents or petitions otherwise permitted by the Administrative Procedures Act.

[54 FR 49456, Nov. 30, 1989, as amended at 60 FR 66716, Dec. 26, 1995; 70 FR 76675, Dec. 28, 2005]

§ 510.4 Service of process.

(a) *Service of Process.* Service of process may be made upon the Office by delivering a copy of the summons and complaint to the U.S. Attorney for the district in which the action is brought or to an assistant U.S. Attorney or clerical employee designated by the U.S. Attorney in a writing filed with the clerk of the court, and by sending copies of the summons and of the complaint by registered or certified mail to the Attorney General of the United States, Washington, DC, and to the Secretary of the Office.

(b) *Subpoenas.* Any subpoena to obtain information maintained by Office shall be duly issued and served upon the Secretary of the Office of Thrift Supervision, 1700 G Street, NW., Washington, DC, 20552.

§ 510.5 Release of unpublished OTS information.

(a) *Scope.* (1) This section applies to requests by the public for unpublished OTS information, such as requests for records or testimony from parties to lawsuits in which the OTS is not a party.

(2) Unpublished OTS information includes records created or obtained in connection with the OTS's performance of its responsibilities, such as records

concerning supervision, regulation, and examination of savings associations, their holding companies, and affiliates, and records compiled in connection with the OTS's enforcement responsibilities. Unpublished OTS information also includes information that current and former employees, officers, and agents obtained in their official capacities. Examples of unpublished information include:

(i) Information in the memory of a current or former employee, officer, or agent of the OTS (or the Federal Home Loan Bank Board, the predecessor agency of the OTS), by testimony or informal interview, that was acquired in the course of performing official duties or because of the employee's, officer's or agent's official status;

(ii) Reports of examination, supervisory correspondence, internal agency memoranda and investigatory files compiled in connection with an investigation, whether such records are in the possession of the OTS or some other individual or entity; and

(iii) Unpublished OTS records obtained by or in the possession of third parties, including other government agencies.

(3) This section does not apply to:

(i) Requests for records or testimony in proceedings in which the OTS is a party;

(ii) Requests for information by other government agencies, except when specifically provided;

(iii) Requests for records that are required to be disclosed under the Freedom of Information Act, *see* 5 U.S.C. 552, and 31 CFR 1.1–1.6; and

(iv) Requests for a Suspicious Activity Report (SAR), or any information that would reveal the existence of a SAR.

(b) *Purpose.* The purposes of this section are:

(1) To afford an orderly mechanism for the OTS to expeditiously process requests for unpublished OTS information and, where appropriate, for the OTS to assert evidentiary privileges in litigation;

(2) To balance the need for confidentiality of unpublished OTS information with the private party's interest in obtaining disclosure of that information;

(3) To ensure that the time of OTS employees is utilized in the most efficient manner consistent with the OTS's statutory mission;

(4) To prevent undue burdens on the OTS;

(5) To limit the expenditure of the OTS's funds for private purposes; and

(6) To maintain the impartiality of the OTS among private litigants.

(c) *Procedure*—(1) *Requests for records and testimony in general.* A request for unpublished OTS information must be in writing, furnish the caption of the lawsuit if the request arises in the course of litigation, and support the requester's claim that the information sought is highly relevant to the purpose for which it is sought. In demonstrating that the information is highly relevant, the requester must explain in detail how the requested OTS information relates to the issues in the case or the matter.

(i) For requests arising in lawsuits, the submission also must include:

(A) A copy of the complaint or equivalent document in the case and any other pleadings necessary to show relevance;

(B) A description of any prior decisions or pending motions in the case that may bear on the asserted relevance of the information being sought from the OTS; and

(C) The names, addresses and phone numbers of counsel to all other parties in the case.

(ii) In all instances, in addition to demonstrating that the information sought is highly relevant to the purpose for which it is sought, the requester must:

(A) Demonstrate that the information sought is not available from any other source; and

(B) Demonstrate that the need for the information clearly outweighs the need to maintain the confidentiality of the OTS information and the burden on the OTS to produce the information.

(iii) If a request seeks a response in fewer than 30 days, it must include an explanation of why the requester was unable to submit the request earlier and why expediting the request is required.

§ 510.5

(2) *Additional provisions relating to requests for records.* In addition to the requirements of paragraph (c)(1) of this section, the provisions in paragraphs (c)(2)(i) and (c)(2)(ii) of this section apply to requests for disclosure of records.

(i) A request for records must list the categories of records sought and describe the specific information sought, including the relevant time period.

(ii) When the OTS believes that another person has a claim of privilege regarding the information in the records and the records are in the possession or control of that person, such as reports prepared by a savings association's attorneys that are shared with the OTS, the OTS may respond to the request by authorizing that person to release the records pursuant to an appropriate confidentiality order rather than by the OTS releasing the records directly to the requesting party. This will enable the person possessing or controlling the records to argue any issues of privilege to the appropriate court.

(3) *Additional provisions relating to requests for testimony from OTS employees.* In addition to the requirements of paragraph (c)(1) of this section, the provisions in paragraphs (c)(3)(i) through (c)(3)(iv) of this section apply to requests that current or former OTS employees be authorized to give testimony.

(i) The request must specifically describe the substance of the testimony sought and show a compelling need for the testimony. A showing of compelling need should include a demonstration that the requested information is not available from any other source, such as the books and records of other persons or entities, OTS records that have been or might be released, or the testimony of other non-OTS persons, including retained experts.

(ii) OTS employees will not be authorized to provide expert or opinion testimony for private parties.

(iii) The OTS expects litigants to anticipate their need for OTS testimony in sufficient time to request and obtain that testimony in deposition form. A request for testimony at a trial or hearing may not be granted unless the requester shows that properly developed deposition testimony could not be used or would not be adequate at the trial or hearing.

(iv) The OTS shall specify the scope of any authorized testimony and may take steps to ensure that the scope of testimony taken adheres to the scope authorized. Parties to the case who did not join in the request and who wish to question the witness beyond the authorized scope should request expanded authorization pursuant to this regulation. The OTS will attempt to render decisions on such requests in an expedited manner.

(4) *Information available to savings associations, holding companies, state and Federal agencies and requesters.* (i) The regular report of examination of a savings association, savings and loan holding company, or other affiliate of a savings association is made available by the appropriate Regional Office to the entity examined.

(ii) A subsidiary savings association of a savings and loan holding company may reproduce and furnish a copy of its report of examination and related supervisory correspondence of the savings association to its parent holding company(ies) without prior approval of the OTS. A savings and loan holding company may reproduce and furnish a copy of its report of examination and related supervisory correspondence to another affiliated savings and loan holding company that controls the same savings association or its subsidiary savings association(s) without prior approval of the OTS. This paragraph does not require such disclosure by a parent savings and loan holding company or subsidiary savings association.

(iii) Reports of examination and other information relating to state-chartered savings associations and affiliates are made available, upon request, by the OTS to the state governmental authority having general supervision of such state-chartered savings associations.

(iv) Reports of examination and other information may be made available by the OTS to other agencies of the United States, a state agency, or to the Federal Home Loan Banks, for use where necessary in the performance of their official duties.

Office of Thrift Supervision, Treasury §510.5

(v) All reports or other information made available to savings associations, holding companies, affiliates, other governmental agencies or requesters shall remain the property of the OTS and, except as permitted by this section or otherwise by the Director or his delegate, no person, company, agency, or authority to whom the information is made available, or any officer, director, employee or agent thereof, shall disclose any such information except published statistical material that would not disclose the identity of any individual or corporation.

(5) *Where to submit requests.* In all matters covered by this section, notification of the issuance of subpoenas or compulsory process and requests for records or testimony covered by this section must be sent to the OTS at 1700 G Street NW., Washington, DC 20552, to the attention of the Corporate Secretary, and should be labelled "Request for Release of Unpublished Information Under Section 510.5." Requesters may furnish copies of the request or subpoenas simultaneously to the appropriate OTS Regional Office, but the furnishing of such copies does not constitute service on the OTS.

(d) *Consideration of requests*—(1) *In general.* The OTS will generally process requests in the order in which they are received. The OTS will endeavor to respond to requests within 30 days, but this may vary depending on the scope and precision of the request. The OTS will weigh requests for processing in less than 30 days against the burden to the OTS of expedited processing and the unfairness to other parties whose pending requests may be delayed.

(2) *Consultation with requester.* The OTS may consult with the requester to:

(i) Refine and limit the scope of the request so as to reduce the burden and expense on the OTS; or

(ii) Obtain additional information necessary for the OTS to make an informed determination on the request. To the extent necessary to reach an informed determination on the request, the OTS may inquire into the circumstances of the underlying matter and rely on sources of information beyond the requester, including other interested parties.

(3) *Final determinations.* Final determinations on requests will be made by the Director or his delegate. All such determinations are the sole discretion of the Director or his delegate. Requesters will be notified in writing of the disposition of the request.

(4) *Denial of requests.* (i) The OTS may deny requests for records or testimony that seek information that the OTS deems to be:

(A) Not highly relevant;

(B) Privileged;

(C) Available from other sources;

(D) Information that should not be disclosed for reasons that warrant restriction of discovery under the Federal Rules of Civil Procedure (28 U.S.C. appendix); and

(E) Information that should not be disclosed, because such disclosure is prohibited by law.

(ii) The OTS may also deny a records or testimony request when it considers production of the information to be overly burdensome or contrary to the public interest, or where OTS determines that the need for the information does not clearly outweigh the need to maintain the confidentiality of the information, or where the requester seeks testimony and has not shown a compelling need for the testimony.

(5) *Confidentiality Orders and Agreements.* As is set forth in paragraph (f) of this section, the OTS may condition release of information on the entry by the relevant tribunal of an order satisfactory to the OTS or, in a non-litigated matter, the execution of a confidentiality agreement that limits access of third parties to the unpublished OTS information. It shall be the duty of the requesting party to obtain such an order or to execute a confidentiality agreement.

(e) *Parties with access to OTS information; restriction on dissemination*—(1) *Current and former employees.* Except as authorized by this section or as otherwise authorized by the Director or his delegate, no current or former employee, officer or agent of the OTS or a predecessor agency shall disclose or permit the disclosure of any unpublished information of the OTS to anyone (other than an employee, officer or agent of the OTS properly entitled to such information for the performance

§ 510.5

of their official duties), whether by giving out or furnishing such information or a copy thereof or by allowing any person to inspect, examine, or copy such information or copy thereof, or otherwise.

(2) *Duty of person served.* If any person, whether or not a current or former employee, officer or agent of the OTS, has information of the OTS that may not be disclosed under the regulations of the OTS or other applicable law, and in connection therewith is served with a subpoena, order, or other process requiring personal attendance as a witness or production of records or information in any proceeding, that person shall promptly advise the OTS of such service or request for information. Upon such notice the OTS will take appropriate action to advise the court or tribunal that issued the process and the attorney for the party at whose instance the process was issued, if known, of the substance of this section. Such notice to the OTS shall be made by contacting the Litigation Division, Office of Chief Counsel, Office of Thrift Supervision, 1700 G Street NW., Washington, DC 20552. As provided in paragraph (e)(3) of this section, a person so served with process may not disclose OTS information without OTS authorization. To obtain OTS authorization, a request must be sent to the OTS in Washington, DC, in accordance with paragraph (c) of this section.

(3) *Appearance by person served.* Except as the OTS has authorized disclosure of the relevant information, or except as authorized by law, any person who has information of the OTS that may not be disclosed under this section and is required to respond to a subpoena or other legal process shall attend at the time and place therein mentioned and respectfully decline to produce such records or give any testimony with respect thereto, basing such refusal on this part. If, notwithstanding, the court or other body orders the disclosure of such records or the giving of such testimony, the person having such information of the OTS shall continue respectfully to decline to produce such information and shall promptly advise the Litigation Division of the Chief Counsel's Office, Office of Thrift Supervision. Upon such notice the OTS will take appropriate action to advise the court or tribunal which issued the order, of the substance of this section.

(4) *Non-waiver of privilege.* The possession by any entity or individual described in paragraph (c)(4) of this section of OTS records covered by this section shall not waive any privilege of the OTS or the OTS's right to supervise the further dissemination of these records.

(f) *Orders and agreements protecting the confidentiality of unpublished OTS information*—(1) *Records.* Unless otherwise permitted by the OTS, release of records authorized pursuant to this section will be conditioned by the OTS upon entry of an acceptable protective order by the court or administrative tribunal presiding in the particular case, or, in non-litigated matters, upon execution of an acceptable confidentiality agreement. In cases where protective orders have already been entered, the OTS reserves the right to condition approval for release of information upon the inclusion of additional or amended provisions.

(2) *Testimony.* The OTS may condition its authorization of deposition testimony on an agreement of the parties that the transcript of the testimony will be kept under seal, or will be made available only to the parties, the court and the jury, except to the extent that the OTS may allow use of the transcript in related litigation. The party who requested the testimony shall, at its expense, furnish to the OTS a copy of the transcript of testimony of the OTS employee or former employee.

(g) *Limitation of burden on the OTS in connection with released records*—(1) *Authentication for use as evidence.* The OTS will authenticate released records to facilitate their use as evidence. Requesters who require authenticated records should request certified copies at least 30 days prior to the date they will be needed. The request should be sent to the OTS Public Disclosure Branch and shall identify the records, giving the office or record depository where they are located (if known) and include copies of the records and payment of the certification fee.

(2) *Responsibility of litigants to share released records.* The party who has

sought and obtained OTS records has the responsibility of:

(i) Notifying other parties to the case of the release and, after entry of a protective order, providing copies of the records to the other parties who are subject to the protective order; and

(ii) Retrieving any records from the court's file as soon as the records are no longer required by the court and returning them to the OTS. Where a party may be involved in related litigation, the OTS may, upon a request made to it pursuant to this section, authorize such party to transfer the records for use in that related case.

(h) *Fees*—(1) *Fees for records searches, copying and certifications.* Requesters shall be charged fees in accordance with Treasury Department regulations, 31 CFR 1.7. With certain exceptions, the regulations in 31 CFR 1.7 provide for recovery of the full direct costs of searching, reviewing, certifying and duplicating the records sought. An estimate of the statement of charges will be sent to requesters, and fees shall be remitted by check payable to the OTS prior to release of the requested records. Where it deems appropriate, the OTS may contract with commercial copying concerns to copy the records, with the cost billed to the requester.

(2) *Witness fees and allowances.* (i) Litigants whose requests for testimony of current OTS employees are approved shall, upon completion of the testimonial appearance, promptly tender a check payable to the OTS for witness fees and allowances in accordance with 28 U.S.C. 1821.

(ii) All litigants whose requests for testimony of former OTS employees are approved, shall also promptly tender witness fees and allowances to the witness in accordance with 28 U.S.C. 1821.

[54 FR 49456, Nov. 30, 1989, as amended at 60 FR 28031, May 30, 1995; 75 FR 75586, Dec. 3, 2010]

PART 512—RULES FOR INVESTIGATIVE PROCEEDINGS AND FORMAL EXAMINATION PROCEEDINGS

Sec.
512.1 Scope of part.
512.2 Definitions.
512.3 Confidentiality of proceedings.
512.4 Transcripts.
512.5 Rights of witnesses.
512.6 Obstruction of the proceedings.
512.7 Subpoenas.

AUTHORITY: 12 U.S.C. 1462a, 1463, 1464, 1467, 1467a, 1813; 15 U.S.C. 78 *l.*

SOURCE: 54 FR 49457, Nov. 30, 1989, unless otherwise noted.

§ 512.1 Scope of part.

This part prescribes rules of practice and procedure applicable to the conduct of investigative proceedings under section 10(g)(2) of the Home Owners' Loan Act, as amended, 12 U.S.C. 1467a(g)(2) ("HOLA") and to the conduct of formal examination proceedings with respect to savings associations and their affiliates under section 5(d)(1)(B) of the HOLA, as amended, 12 U.S.C. 1464(d)(1)(B) or section 7(j)(15) of the Federal Deposit Insurance Act, as amended, 12 U.S.C. 1817(j)(15) ("FDIA"), section 8(n) of the FDIA, 12 U.S.C. 1818(n), or section 10(c) of the FDIA, 12 U.S.C. 1820(c). This part does not apply to adjudicatory proceedings as to which hearings are required by statute, the rules for which are contained in part 509 of this chapter.

§ 512.2 Definitions.

As used in this part:

(a) *Office* means the Office of Thrift Supervision;

(b) *Investigative proceeding* means an investigation conducted under section 10(g)(2) of the HOLA;

(c) *Formal examination proceeding* means the administration of oaths and affirmations, taking and preserving of testimony, requiring the production of books, papers, correspondence, memoranda, and all other records, the issuance of subpoenas, and all related activities in connection with examination of savings associations and their affiliates conducted pursuant to section 5(d)(1)(B) of the HOLA, section 7(j)(15) of the FDIA, section 8(n) of the FDIA or section 10(c) of the FDIA; and

(d) *Designated representative* means the person or persons empowered by the Office to conduct an investigative proceeding or a formal examination proceeding.

§ 512.3 Confidentiality of proceedings.

All formal examination proceedings shall be private and, unless otherwise ordered by the Office, all investigative proceedings shall also be private. Unless otherwise ordered or permitted by the Office, or required by law, and except as provided in §§ 512.4 and 512.5, the entire record of any investigative proceeding or formal examination proceeding, including the resolution of the Office or its delegate(s) authorizing the proceeding, the transcript of such proceeding, and all documents and information obtained by the designated representative(s) during the course of said proceedings shall be confidential.

§ 512.4 Transcripts.

Transcripts or other recordings, if any, of investigative proceedings or formal examination proceedings shall be prepared solely by an official reporter or by any other person or means authorized by the designated representative. A person who has submitted documentary evidence or given testimony in an investigative proceeding or formal examination proceeding may procure a copy of his own documentary evidence or transcript of his own testimony upon payment of the cost thereof; *provided,* that a person seeking a transcript of his own testimony must file a written request with the Deputy Chief Counsel for Enforcement or the appropriate Regional Counsel for Enforcement stating the reason he desires to procure such transcript, and said persons may for good cause deny such request. In any event, any witness (or his counsel) shall have the right to inspect the transcript of the witness' own testimony.

[54 FR 49457, Nov. 30, 1989, as amended at 60 FR 66717, Dec. 26, 1995]

§ 512.5 Rights of witnesses.

(a) Any person who is compelled or requested to furnish documentary evidence or give testimony at an investigative proceeding or formal examination proceeding shall have the right to examine, upon request, the Office resolution authorizing such proceeding. Copies of such resolution shall be furnished, for their retention, to such persons only with the written approval of the Deputy Chief Counsel for Enforcement or the appropriate Regional Counsel for Enforcement.

(b) Any witness at an investigative proceeding or formal examination proceeding may be accompanied and advised by an attorney personally representing that witness.

(1) Such attorney shall be a member in good standing of the bar of the highest court of any state, Commonwealth, possession, territory, or the District of Columbia, who has not been suspended or debarred from practice by the bar of any such political entity or before the Office in accordance with the provisions of part 513 of this chapter and has not been excluded from the particular investigative proceeding or formal examination proceeding in accordance with paragraph (b)(3) of this section.

(2) Such attorney may advise the witness before, during, and after the taking of his testimony and may briefly question the witness, on the record, at the conclusion of his testimony, for the sole purpose of clarifying any of the answers the witness has given. During the taking of the testimony of a witness, such attorney may make summary notes solely for his use in representing his client. All witnesses shall be sequestered, and, unless permitted in the discretion of the designated representative, no witness or accompanying attorney may be permitted to be present during the taking of testimony of any other witness called in such proceeding. Neither attorney(s) for the association(s) that are the subjects of the investigative proceedings or formal examination proceedings, nor attorneys for any other interested persons, shall have any right to be present during the testimony of any witness not personally being represented by such attorney.

(3) The Office, for good cause, may exclude a particular attorney from further participation in any investigation in which the Office has found the attorney to have engaged in dilatory, obstructionist, egregious, contemptuous or contumacious conduct. The person conducting an investigation may report to the Office instances of apparently dilatory, obstructionist, egregious, contemptuous or contumacious conduct on the part of an attorney.

After due notice to the attorney, the Office may take such action as the circumstances warrant based upon a written record evidencing the conduct of the attorney in that investigation or such other or additional written or oral presentation as the Office may permit or direct.

[54 FR 49457, Nov. 30, 1989, as amended at 60 FR 66717, Dec. 26, 1995]

§ 512.6 Obstruction of the proceedings.

The designated representative shall report to the Office any instances where any witness or counsel has engaged in dilatory, obstructionist, or contumacious conduct or has otherwise violated any provision of this part during the course of an investigative proceeding or formal examination proceeding; and the Office may take such action as the circumstances warrant, including the exclusion of counsel from further participation in such proceeding.

§ 512.7 Subpoenas.

(a) *Service.* Service of a subpoena in connection with any investigative proceeding or formal examination proceeding shall be effected in the following manner:

(1) *Service upon a natural person.* Service of a subpoena upon a natural person may be effected by handing it to such person; by leaving it at his office with the person in charge thereof, or, if there is no one in charge, by leaving it in a conspicuous place therein; by leaving it at his dwelling place or usual place of abode with some person of suitable age and discretion then residing therein; by mailing it to him by registered or certified mail or by an express delivery service at his last known address; or by any method whereby actual notice is given to him.

(2) *Service upon other persons.* When the person to be served is not a natural person, service of the subpoena may be effected by handing the subpoena to a registered agent for service, or to any officer, director, or agent in charge of any office of such person; by mailing it to any such representative by registered or certified mail or by an express delivery service at his last known address; or by any method whereby actual notice is given to such person.

(b) *Motions to quash.* Any person to whom a subpoena is directed may, prior to the time specified therein for compliance, but in no event more than 10 days after the date of service of such subpoena, apply to the Chief Counsel or his designee to quash or modify such subpoena, accompanying such application with a statement of the reasons therefor. The Chief Counsel or his designee, as appropriate, may:

(1) Deny the application;
(2) Quash or revoke the subpoena;
(3) Modify the subpoena; or
(4) Condition the granting of the application on such terms as the Chief Counsel or his designee determines to be just, reasonable, and proper.

(c) *Attendance of witnesses.* Subpoenas issued in connection with an investigative proceeding or formal examination proceeding may require the attendance and/or testimony of witnesses from any State or territory of the United States and the production by such witnesses of documentary or other tangible evidence at any designated place where the proceeding is being (or is to be) conducted. Foreign nationals are subject to such subpoenas if such service is made upon a duly authorized agent located in the United States.

(d) *Witness fees and mileage.* Witnesses summoned in any proceeding under this part shall be paid the same fees and mileage that are paid witnesses in the district courts of the United States. Such fees and mileage need not be tendered when the subpoena is issued on behalf of the Office by any of its designated representatives.

[54 FR 49457, Nov. 30, 1989, as amended at 56 FR 38317, Aug. 12, 1991]

PART 513—PRACTICE BEFORE THE OFFICE

Sec.
513.1 Scope of part.
513.2 Definitions.
513.3 Who may practice.
513.4 Suspension and debarment.
513.5 Reinstatement.
513.6 Duty to file information concerning adverse judicial or administrative action.
513.7 Proceeding under this part.
513.8 Removal, suspension, or debarment of independent public accountants and accounting firms performing audit services.

AUTHORITY: 12 U.S.C. 1462a, 1463, 1464, 1467a, 1813, 1831m, and 15 U.S.C. 78.

SOURCE: 54 FR 49459, Nov. 30, 1989, unless otherwise noted.

§ 513.1 Scope of part.

This part prescribes rules with regard to general practice before the Office on one's own behalf or in a representative capacity and prescribes rules describing the circumstances under which attorneys, accountants, appraisers, or other persons may be suspended or debarred, either temporarily or permanently, from practicing before the Office. In connection with any particular matter, reference also should be made to any special requirements of procedure and practice that may be contained in the particular statute involved or the rules and forms adopted by the Office thereunder, which special requirements are controlling. In addition to any suspension hereunder, a person may be excluded from further participation under this chapter from a rulemaking hearing in accordance with § 510.2, from an adjudicatory proceeding in accordance with § 509.6(a)(1), from a removal hearing in accordance with § 508.3, or from an investigatory proceeding in accordance with § 512.5(b)(2) of this chapter.

[54 FR 49459, Nov. 30, 1989, as amended at 56 FR 38317, Aug. 12, 1991]

§ 513.2 Definitions.

As used in this part:

(a) *Office* means the Office;

(b) The term *Secretary* means the Secretary and any Assistant or Acting Secretary to the Office;

(c) The term *presiding officer* includes the Office, his delegatee or an administrative law judge appointed under section 3105 or detailed pursuant to section 3344 of title 5 of the U.S. Code and, as used in this part, the term shall be construed to refer to whichever of the above-identified individuals presides at a hearing or other proceeding, except as otherwise specified in the text;

(d) The term *attorney* means any person who is a member in good standing of the bar of the highest court of any State, possession, territory, Commonwealth or the District of Columbia; and

(e) The term *practice* means transacting any business with the Office, including:

(1) The representation of another person at any adjudicatory, investigatory, removal or rulemaking proceeding conducted before the Office, a presiding officer or the Office's staff, including those proceedings covered in parts 508, 509, 510, and 512 of this chapter;

(2) The preparation of any statement, opinion, financial statement, appraisal report, audit report, or other document or report by any attorney, accountant, appraiser or other licensed expert which is filed with or submitted to the Office, with such expert's consent or knowledge in connection with any application or other filing with the Office;

(3) A presentation to the Office, a presiding officer or the Office's staff at a conference or meeting relating to an association's or other person's rights, privileges or liabilities under the laws administered by the Office and rules and regulations promulgated thereunder;

(4) Any business correspondence or communication with the Office, a presiding officer or the Office's staff; and

(5) The transaction of any other formal business with the Office on behalf of another, in the capacity of an attorney, accountant, appraiser or other licensed expert.

§ 513.3 Who may practice.

(a) *By non-attorneys.* (1) An individual may appear on his own behalf (pro se); a member of a partnership may represent the partnership; a bona fide and duly authorized officer of a corporation, trust or association may represent the corporation, trust or association; and an officer or employee of a commission, department or political subdivision may represent that commission, department or political subdivision before the Office.

(2) Any accountant, appraiser or other licensed expert may practice before the Office in a professional capacity.

(b) *By attorneys.* Any association or other person may be represented in any proceeding or other matter before the Office by an attorney.

Office of Thrift Supervision, Treasury § 513.4

(c) Any licensed expert or professional transacting business with the Office in a representative capacity may be required to show his authority to act in such capacity.

§ 513.4 Suspension and debarment.

(a) The Office may censure any person practicing before it or may deny, temporarily or permanently, the privilege of any person to practice before it if such person is found by the Office, after notice of and opportunity for hearing in the matter,

(1) Not to possess the requisite qualifications to represent others,

(2) To be lacking in character or professional integrity,

(3) To have engaged in any dilatory, obstructionist, egregious, contemptuous, contumacious or other unethical or improper professional conduct before the Office, or

(4) To have willfully violated, or willfully aided and abetted the violation of, any provision of the laws administered by the Office or the rules and regulations promulgated thereunder.

(b) *Automatic suspension.* (1) Any person who, after being licensed as a professional or expert by any competent authority, has been convicted of a felony, or of a misdemeanor involving moral turpitude, personal dishonesty or breach of trust, shall be suspended forthwith from practicing before the Office.

(2) Any accountant, appraiser or other licensed expert whose license to practice has been revoked in any State, possession, territory, Commonwealth or the District of Columbia, shall be suspended forthwith from practice before the Office.

(3) Any attorney who has been suspended or disbarred by a court of the United States or in any State, possession, territory, Commonwealth or the District of Columbia, shall be suspended forthwith from practicing before the Office.

(4) A conviction (including a judgment or order on a plea of nolo contendere), revocation, suspension or disbarment under paragraphs (b)(1), (b)(2) and (b)(3) of this section shall be deemed to have occurred when the convicting, revoking, suspending or disbarring agency or tribunal enters its judgment or order, regardless of whether an appeal is pending or could be taken.

(5) For purposes of this section, it shall be irrelevant that any attorney, accountant, appraiser or other licensed expert who has been suspended, disbarred or otherwise disqualified from practice before a court or in a jurisdiction continues in professional good standing before other courts or in other jurisdictions.

(c) *Temporary suspension.* (1) The Office, with due regard to the public interest and without preliminary hearing, by order, may temporarily suspend any person from appearing or practicing before it who, on or after June 20, 1984, by name, has been:

(i) Permanently enjoined (whether by consent, default or summary judgment or after trial) by any court of competent jurisdiction or by the Office itself in a final administrative order, by reason of his misconduct in any action brought by the Office based upon violations of, or aiding and abetting the violation of, the Home Owners, Loan Act of 1933, as amended, 12 U.S.C. 1461 *et seq.*, the Federal Deposit Insurance Act, as amended, 12 U.S.C. 1811 *et seq.* or any provision of the Securities Exchange Act of 1934, as amended, 15 U.S.C. 78a, *et seq.*, which is administered by the Office, or of any rule or regulation promulgated thereunder; or

(ii) Found by any court of competent jurisdiction (whether by consent, default, or summary judgment, or after trial) in any action brought by the Office to which he is a party or found by the Office (whether by consent, default, upon summary judgment or after hearing) in any administrative proceeding in which the Office is a complainant and he is a party, to have willfully committed, caused or aided or abetted a violation of any provision of the Home Owners' Loan Act of 1933, as amended, 12 U.S.C. 1461 *et seq.*, the Federal Deposit Insurance Act, as amended, 12 U.S.C. 1811 *et seq.* or any provision of the Securities Exchange Act of 1934, as amended, 15 U.S.C. 78a, *et seq.*, which is administered by the Office, or of any rule or regulation promulgated thereunder.

(2) An order of temporary suspension shall become effective when served by certified or registered mail directed to

§ 513.5

the last known business or residential address of the person involved. No order of temporary suspension shall be entered by the Office pursuant to paragraph (c)(1) of this section more than three months after the final judgment or order entered in a judicial or administrative proceeding described in paragraphs (c)(1)(i) or (c)(1)(ii) of this section has become effective and all review or appeal procedures have been completed or are no longer available.

(3) Any person temporarily suspended from appearing and practicing before the Office in accordance with paragraph (c)(1) of this section may, within 30 days after service upon him of the order of temporary suspension, petition the Office to lift such suspension. If no petition is received by the Office within those 30 days, the suspension shall become permanent.

(4) Within 30 days after the filing of a petition in accordance with paragraph (c)(3) of this section, the Office shall either lift the temporary suspension or set the matter down for hearing at a time and place to be designated by the Office, or both. After opportunity for hearing, the Office may censure the petitioner or may suspend the petitioner from appearing or practicing before the Office temporarily or permanently. In every case in which the temporary suspension has not been lifted, the hearing and any other action taken pursuant to this paragraph (c)(4) shall be expedited by the Office in order to ensure the petitioner's right to address the allegations against him.

(5) In any hearing held on a petition filed in accordance with paragraph (c)(3) of this section, a showing that the petitioner has been enjoined or has been found to have committed, caused or aided or abetted violations as described in paragraph (c)(1) of this section, without more, may be a basis for suspension or debarment; that showing having been made, the burden shall then be on the petitioner to show why he should not be censured or be temporarily or permanently suspended or debarred. A petitioner will not be permitted to contest any findings against him or any admissions made by him in the judicial or administrative proceedings upon which the proposed censure, suspension or debarment is based.

12 CFR Ch. V (1–1–12 Edition)

A petitioner who has consented to the entry of a permanent injunction or order as described in paragraph (c)(1)(i) of this section, without admitting the facts set forth in the complaint, shall nevertheless be presumed for all purposes under this section to have been enjoined or ordered by reason of the misconduct alleged in the complaint.

§ 513.5 Reinstatement.

(a) Any person who is suspended from practicing before the Office under paragraph (a) or (c) of § 513.4 of this part may file an application for reinstatement at any time. Denial of the privilege of practicing before the Office shall continue unless and until the applicant has been reinstated by order of the Office for good cause shown.

(b) Any person suspended under paragraph (b) of § 513.4 shall be reinstated by the Office, upon appropriate application, if all of the grounds for application of the provisions of paragraph (b) of § 513.4 subsequently are removed by a reversal of the conviction or termination of the suspension, disbarment or revocation. An application for reinstatement on any other grounds by any person suspended under paragraph (b) of § 513.4 may be filed at any time. Such application shall state with particularity the relief desired and the grounds therefor and shall include supporting evidence, when available. The applicant shall be accorded an opportunity for an informal hearing in the matter, unless the applicant has waived a hearing in the application and, instead, has elected to have the matter determined on the basis of written submissions. Such hearing shall utilize the procedures established in § 508.3 and paragraph (a) of § 508.7 of this chapter. However, such suspension shall continue unless and until the applicant has been reinstated by order of the Office for good cause shown.

[54 FR 49459, Nov. 30, 1989, as amended at 56 FR 38318, Aug. 12, 1991]

§ 513.6 Duty to file information concerning adverse judicial or administrative action.

Any person appearing or practicing before the Office who has been or is the subject of a conviction, suspension, debarment, license revocation, injunction or other finding of the kind described in §513.4 (b) or (c) of this part in an action not instituted by the Office shall promptly file a copy of the relevant order, judgment or decree with the Secretary to the Office together with any related opinion or statement of the agency or tribunal involved. Any person who fails to so file a copy of the order, judgment or decree within 30 days after the later of June 15, 1984, the entry of the order, judgment or decree, or the date such person initiates practice before the Office, for that reason alone may be disqualified from practicing before the Office until such time as the appropriate filing shall be made, but neither the filing of these documents nor the failure of a person to file them shall in any way impair the operation of any other provision of this part.

§ 513.7 **Proceeding under this part.**

(a) All hearings required or permitted to be held under paragraphs (a) and (c) of § 513.4 of this part shall be held before a presiding officer utilizing the procedures established in the rules of practice and procedure in adjudicatory proceedings under part 509 of this chapter.

(b) All hearings held under this part shall be closed to the public unless the Office on its own motion or upon the request of a party otherwise directs.

(c) Any proceeding brought under any section of this part 513 shall not preclude a proceeding under any other section of this part, or any other part of the Office's regulations.

§ 513.8 **Removal, suspension, or debarment of independent public accountants and accounting firms performing audit services.**

(a) *Scope.* This subpart, which implements section 36(g)(4) of the Federal Deposit Insurance Act (FDIA) (12 U.S.C. 1831m(g)(4)), provides rules and procedures for the removal, suspension, or debarment of independent public accountants and their accounting firms from performing independent audit and attestation services required by section 36 of the FDIA (12 U.S.C. 1831m) for insured savings associations and savings and loan holding companies.

(b) *Definitions.* As used in this section, the following terms have the meaning given below unless the context requires otherwise:

(1) *Accounting firm.* The term *accounting firm* means a corporation, proprietorship, partnership, or other business firm providing audit services.

(2) *Audit services.* The term *audit services* means any service required to be performed by an independent public accountant by section 36 of the FDIA Act and 12 CFR part 363, including attestation services. Audit services include any service performed with respect to a savings and loan holding company of a savings association that is used to satisfy requirements imposed by section 36 or part 363 on that savings association.

(3) *Independent public accountant.* The term *independent public accountant* means any individual who performs or participates in providing audit services.

(c) *Removal, suspension, or debarment of independent public accountants.* The Office may remove, suspend, or debar an independent public accountant from performing audit services for savings associations that are subject to section 36 of the FDIA if, after service of a notice of intention and opportunity for hearing in the matter, the Office finds that the independent public accountant:

(1) Lacks the requisite qualifications to perform audit services;

(2) Has knowingly or recklessly engaged in conduct that results in a violation of applicable professional standards, including those standards and conflicts of interest provisions applicable to independent public accountants through the Sarbanes-Oxley Act of 2002, Pub. L. 107–204, 116 Stat. 745 (2002) (Sarbanes-Oxley Act), and developed by the Public Company Accounting Oversight Board and the Securities and Exchange Commission;

(3) Has engaged in negligent conduct in the form of: (i) A single instance of highly unreasonable conduct that results in a violation of applicable professional standards in circumstances in which an independent public accountant knows, or should know, that heightened scrutiny is warranted; or

§ 513.8

(ii) Repeated instances of unreasonable conduct, each resulting in a violation of applicable professional standards, that indicate a lack of competence to perform audit services;

(4) Has knowingly or recklessly given false or misleading information or knowingly or recklessly participated in any way in the giving of false or misleading information to the Office or any officer or employee of the Office;

(5) Has engaged in, or aided and abetted, a material and knowing or reckless violation of any provision of the Federal banking or securities laws or the rules and regulations thereunder, or any other law;

(6) Has been removed, suspended, or debarred from practice before any federal or state agency regulating the banking, insurance, or securities industries, other than by action listed in paragraph (j) of this section, on grounds relevant to the provision of audit services; or

(7) Is suspended or debarred for cause from practice as an accountant by any duly constituted licensing authority of any state, possession, commonwealth, or the District of Columbia.

(d) *Removal, suspension or debarment of an accounting firm.* If the Office determines that there is good cause for the removal, suspension, or debarment of a member or employee of an accounting firm under paragraph (c) of this section, the Office also may remove, suspend, or debar such firm or one or more offices of such firm. In considering whether to remove, suspend, or debar an accounting firm or office thereof, and the term of any sanction against an accounting firm under this section, the Office may consider, for example:

(1) The gravity, scope, or repetition of the act or failure to act that constitutes good cause for the removal, suspension, or debarment;

(2) The adequacy of, and adherence to, applicable policies, practices, or procedures for the accounting firm's conduct of its business and the performance of audit services;

(3) The selection, training, supervision, and conduct of members or employees of the accounting firm involved in the performance of audit services;

(4) The extent to which managing partners or senior officers of the accounting firm have participated, directly or indirectly through oversight or review, in the act or failure to act; and

(5) The extent to which the accounting firm has, since the occurrence of the act or failure to act, implemented corrective internal controls to prevent its recurrence.

(e) *Remedies.* The remedies provided in this section are in addition to any other remedies the Office may have under any other applicable provisions of law, rule, or regulation.

(f) *Proceedings to remove, suspend, or debar.* (1) The Office may initiate a proceeding to remove, suspend, or debar an independent public accountant or accounting firm from performing audit services by issuing a written notice of intention to take such action that names the individual or firm as a respondent and describes the nature of the conduct that constitutes good cause for such action.

(2) An independent public accountant or accounting firm named as a respondent in the notice issued under paragraph (f)(1) of this section may request a hearing on the allegations in the notice. Hearings conducted under this paragraph shall be conducted in the same manner as other hearings under the Uniform Rules of Practice and Procedure (12 CFR part 509).

(g) *Immediate suspension from performing audit services.* (1) If the Office serves written notice of intention to remove, suspend, or debar an independent public accountant or accounting firm from performing audit services, the Office may, with due regard for the public interest and without preliminary hearing, immediately suspend an independent public accountant or accounting firm from performing audit services for savings associations, if the Office:

(i) Has a reasonable basis to believe that the independent public accountant or accounting firm engaged in conduct (specified in the notice served upon the independent public accountant or accounting firm under paragraph (f) of this section) that would constitute

Office of Thrift Supervision, Treasury § 513.8

grounds for removal, suspension, or debarment under paragraph (c) or (d) of this section;

(ii) Determines that immediate suspension is necessary to avoid immediate harm to an insured depository institution or its depositors or to the depository system as a whole; and

(iii) Serves such independent public accountant or accounting firm with written notice of the immediate suspension.

(2) An immediate suspension notice issued under this paragraph will become effective upon service. Such suspension will remain in effect until the date the Office dismisses the charges contained in the notice of intention, or the effective date of a final order of removal, suspension, or debarment issued by the Office to the independent public accountant or accounting firm.

(h) *Petition to stay.* (1) Any independent public accountant or accounting firm immediately suspended from performing audit services in accordance with paragraph (g) of this section may, within 10 calendar days after service of the notice of immediate suspension, file a petition with the Office for a stay of such suspension. If no petition is filed within 10 calendar days, the immediate suspension shall remain in effect.

(2) Upon receipt of a stay petition, the Office will designate a presiding officer who shall fix a place and time (not more than 10 calendar days after receipt of such petition, unless extended at the request of the petitioner), at which the immediately suspended party may appear, personally or through counsel, to submit written materials and oral argument. Any OTS employee engaged in investigative or prosecuting functions for the OTS in a case may not, in that or a factually related case, serve as a presiding officer or participate or advise in the decision of the presiding officer or of the OTS, except as witness or counsel in the proceeding. In the sole discretion of the presiding officer, upon a specific showing of compelling need, oral testimony of witnesses may also be presented. In hearings held pursuant to this paragraph, there will be no discovery and the provisions of §§ 509.6 through 509.12, 509.16, and 509.21 of the Uniform Rules will apply.

(3) Within 30 calendar days after the hearing, the presiding officer shall issue a decision. The presiding officer will grant a stay upon a demonstration that a substantial likelihood exists of the respondent's success on the issues raised by the notice of intention and that, absent such relief, the respondent will suffer immediate and irreparable injury, loss, or damage. In the absence of such a demonstration, the presiding officer will notify the parties that the immediate suspension will be continued pending the completion of the administrative proceedings pursuant to the notice.

(4) The parties may seek review of the presiding officer's decision by filing a petition for review with the presiding officer within 10 calendar days after service of the decision. Replies must be filed within 10 calendar days after the petition filing date. Upon receipt of a petition for review and any reply, the presiding officer must promptly certify the entire record to the Director. Within 60 calendar days of the presiding officer's certification, the Director shall issue an order notifying the affected party whether or not the immediate suspension should be continued or reinstated. The order shall state the basis of the Director's decision.

(i) *Scope of any order of removal, suspension, or debarment.* (1) Except as provided in paragraph (i)(2), any independent public accountant or accounting firm that has been removed, suspended (including an immediate suspension), or debarred from performing audit services by the Office may not, while such order is in effect, perform audit services for any savings association.

(2) An order of removal, suspension (including an immediate suspension), or debarment may, at the discretion of the Office, be made applicable to a limited number of savings associations or savings and loan holding companies (limited scope order).

(j) *Automatic removal, suspension, and debarment.* (1) An independent public accountant or accounting firm may not perform audit services for a savings association if the independent public accountant or accounting firm:

(i) Is subject to a final order of removal, suspension, or debarment (other than a limited scope order) issued by the Board of Governors of the Federal Reserve System, the Federal Deposit Insurance Corporation, or the Office of the Comptroller of the Currency under section 36 of the FDIA;

(ii) Is subject to a temporary suspension or permanent revocation of registration or a temporary or permanent suspension or bar from further association with any registered public accounting firm issued by the Public Company Accounting Oversight Board or the Securities and Exchange Commission under sections 105(c)(4)(A) or (B) of the Sarbanes-Oxley Act (15 U.S.C. 7215(c)(4)(A) or (B)); or

(iii) Is subject to an order of suspension or denial of the privilege of appearing or practicing before the Securities and Exchange Commission.

(2) Upon written request, the Office, for good cause shown, may grant written permission to an independent public accountant or accounting firm to perform audit services for savings associations. The request must contain a concise statement of action requested. The Office may require the applicant to submit additional information.

(k) *Notice of removal, suspension, or debarment.* (1) Upon issuance of a final order for removal, suspension, or debarment of an independent public accountant or accounting firm from providing audit services, the Office shall make the order publicly available and provide notice of the order to the other Federal banking agencies.

(2) An independent public accountant or accounting firm that provides audit services to a savings association must provide the Office with written notice of:

(i) Any currently effective order or other action described in paragraphs (c)(6) through (c)(7) or paragraphs (j)(1)(ii) through (j)(1)(iii) of this section; and

(ii) Any currently effective action by the Public Company Accounting Oversight Board under sections 105(c)(4)(C) or (G) of the Sarbanes-Oxley Act (15 U.S.C. 7215(c)(4)(C) or (G)).

(3) Written notice required by this paragraph shall be given no later than 15 calendar days following the effective date of an order or action or 15 calendar days before an independent public accountant or accounting firm accepts an engagement to provide audit services, whichever date is earlier.

(1) *Application for reinstatement.* (1) Unless otherwise ordered by the Office, an independent public accountant, accounting firm, or office of a firm that was removed, suspended or debarred under this section may apply for reinstatement in writing at any time. The request shall contain a concise statement of action requested. The Office may require the applicant to submit additional information.

(2) An applicant for reinstatement under paragraph (1)(1) of this section may, in the Office's sole discretion, be afforded a hearing. The independent public accountant or accounting firm shall bear the burden of going forward with an application and the burden of proving the grounds supporting the application. The Office may, in its sole discretion, direct that any reinstatement proceeding be limited to written submissions. The removal, suspension, or debarment shall continue until the Office, for good cause shown, has reinstated the applicant or until, in the case of a suspension, the suspension period has expired. The filing of a petition for reinstatement shall not stay the effectiveness of the removal, suspension, or debarment of an independent public accountant or accounting firm.

[68 FR 48272, Aug. 13, 2003]

PART 516—APPLICATION PROCESSING PROCEDURES

Sec.
516.1 What does this part do?
516.5 Do the same procedures apply to all applications under this part?
516.10 How does OTS compute time periods under this part?

Subpart A—Pre-Filing and Filing Procedures

PRE-FILING PROCEDURES

516.15 Must I meet with OTS before I file my application?
516.20 What information must I include in my draft business plan?

Office of Thrift Supervision, Treasury

§ 516.1

FILING PROCEDURES

516.25 What type of application must I file?
516.30 What information must I provide with my application?
516.35 May I keep portions of my application confidential?
516.40 Where do I file my application?
516.45 What is the filing date of my application?
516.47 How do I amend or supplement my application?

Subpart B—Publication Requirements

516.50 Who must publish a public notice of an application?
516.55 What information must I include in my public notice?
516.60 When must I publish the public notice?
516.70 Where must I publish the public notice?
516.80 What language must I use in my publication?

Subpart C—Comment Procedures

516.100 What does this subpart do?
516.110 Who may submit a written comment?
516.120 What information should a comment include?
516.130 Where are comments filed?
516.140 How long is the comment period?

Subpart D—Meeting Procedures

516.160 What does this subpart do?
516.170 When will OTS conduct a meeting on an application?
516.180 What procedures govern the conduct of the meeting?
516.185 Will OTS approve or disapprove an application at a meeting?
516.190 Will a meeting affect application processing time frames?

Subpart E—OTS Review

EXPEDITED TREATMENT

516.200 If I file a notice under expedited treatment, when may I engage in the proposed activities?

STANDARD TREATMENT

516.210 What will OTS do after I file my application?
516.220 If OTS requests additional information to complete my application, how will it process my application?
516.230 Will OTS conduct an eligibility examination?
516.240 What may OTS require me to do after my application is deemed complete?
516.250 Will OTS require me to publish a new public notice?
516.260 May OTS suspend processing of my application?
516.270 How long is the OTS review period?
516.280 How will I know if my application has been approved?
516.290 What will happen if OTS does not approve or disapprove my application within two calendar years after the filing date?

AUTHORITY: 5 U.S.C. 552, 559; 12 U.S.C. 1462a, 1463, 1464, 2901 et seq.

SOURCE: 57 FR 14336, Apr. 20, 1992, unless otherwise noted.

§ 516.1 What does this part do?

(a) This part explains OTS procedures for processing applications, notices, or filings (applications). Except as provided in paragraph (b) of this section, subparts A and E of this part apply whenever an OTS regulation requires any person (you) to file an application with OTS. Subparts B, C, and D, however, only apply when an OTS regulation incorporates the procedures in the subpart or where otherwise required by OTS.

(b) This part does not apply to any of the following:

(1) An application related to a transaction under section 13(c) or (k) of the Federal Deposit Insurance Act, 12 U.S.C. 1823(c) or (k).

(2) A request for reconsideration, modification, or appeal of a final OTS action.

(3) A request related to litigation, an enforcement proceeding, a supervisory directive or supervisory agreement. Such requests include a request seeking approval under, modification of, or termination of an order issued under part 508 or 509 of this chapter, a supervisory agreement, a supervisory directive, a consent merger agreement or a document negotiated in settlement of an enforcement matter or other litigation, unless an applicable OTS regulation specifically requires an application under this part.

(4) An application filed under an OTS regulation that prescribes other application processing procedures and time frames for the approval of applications.

(c) If an OTS regulation for a specific type of application prescribes some application processing procedures, or time frames, OTS will apply this part to the extent necessary to process the application. For example, if an OTS

§ 516.5

regulation for a specific type of application does not identify time periods for the processing of an application, the time periods in this part apply.

[66 FR 13000, Mar. 2, 2001]

§ 516.5 Do the same procedures apply to all applications under this part?

OTS processes applications under this part using two procedures, expedited treatment and standard treatment. To determine which treatment applies, you may use the following chart:

If * * *	Then OTS will process your application under * * *
(a) The applicable regulation does not specifically state that expedited treatment is available.	Standard treatment.
(b) You are not a savings association	Standard treatment.
(c) Your composite rating is 3, 4, or 5. The composite rating is the composite numeric rating that OTS or the other federal banking regulator assigned to you under the Uniform Financial Institutions Rating System[1] or under a comparable rating system. The composite rating refers to the rating assigned and provided to you, in writing, as a result of the most recent examination.	Standard treatment.
(d) Your Community Reinvestment Act (CRA) rating is Needs to Improve or Substantial Noncompliance. The CRA rating is the Community Reinvestment Act performance rating that OTS or the other federal banking regulator assigned and provided to you, in writing, as a result of the most recent compliance examination. See, for example, § 563e.28 of this chapter.	Standard treatment.
(e) Your compliance rating is 3, 4, or 5. The compliance rating is the numeric rating that OTS or the other federal banking regulator assigned to you under OTS compliance rating system, or a comparable rating system used by the other federal banking regulator. The compliance rating refers to the rating assigned and provided to you, in writing, as a result of the most recent compliance examination.	Standard treatment.
(f) You fail any one of your capital requirements under part 567 of this chapter.	Standard treatment.
(g) OTS has notified you that you are an association in troubled condition.	Standard treatment.
(h) Neither OTS nor any other federal banking regulator has assigned you a composite rating, a CRA rating or a compliance rating.	Standard treatment.
(i) You do not meet any of the criteria listed in paragraphs (a) through (h) of this section.	Expedited treatment.

[1] A savings association may obtain a copy of its composite rating from the appropriate Regional Office.

[66 FR 13000, Mar. 2, 2001]

§ 516.10 How does OTS compute time periods under this part?

In computing time periods under this part, OTS does not include the day of the act or event that commences the time period. When the last day of a time period is a Saturday, Sunday, or Federal holiday, the time period runs until the end of the next day that is not a Saturday, Sunday, or Federal holiday.

[66 FR 13000, Mar. 2, 2001]

Subpart A—Pre-Filing and Filing Procedures

SOURCE: 66 FR 13000, Mar. 2, 2001, unless otherwise noted.

PRE-FILING PROCEDURES

§ 516.15 Must I meet with OTS before I file my application?

(a) *Chart.* To determine whether you must attend a pre-filing meeting before you file an application, please consult the following chart:

If you file * * *	Then * * *
(1) An application for permission to organize a *de novo* federal savings association.	You must meet with OTS before filing your application. You must submit a draft business plan before this meeting.
(2) An application to convert an existing insured depository institution (other than a state-chartered savings association or a state-chartered savings bank) or a credit union to a federal savings association.	You must meet with OTS before filing your application. OTS may require you to submit a draft business plan or other relevant information before this meeting.

Office of Thrift Supervision, Treasury § 516.30

If you file ***	Then ***
(3) An application to acquire control of a savings association.	OTS may require you to meet with OTS before filing your application and may require you to submit a draft business plan or other relevant information before this meeting.

(b) *Contacting the Regional Office.* (1) You must contact the appropriate Regional Office a reasonable time before you file an application described in paragraph (a) of this section. Unless paragraph (a) already requires a pre-filing meeting or a draft business plan, the Regional Office will determine whether it will require a pre-filing meeting, and whether you must submit a business plan or other relevant information before the meeting. The Regional Office will also establish a schedule for any meeting and the submission of any information.

(2) All other applicants are encouraged to contact the appropriate Regional Office to determine whether a pre-filing meeting or the submission of a draft business plan or other relevant information would expedite the application review process.

§ 516.20 What information must I include in my draft business plan?

If you must submit a draft business plan under § 516.15, your plan must:

(a) Clearly and completely describe the savings association's projected operations and activities;

(b) Describe the risks associated with the transaction and the impact of this transaction on any existing activities and operations of the savings association, including financial projections for a minimum of three years;

(c) Identify the majority of the proposed board of directors and the key senior executive officers (as defined in § 563.555 of this chapter) of the savings association and demonstrate that these individuals have the expertise to prudently manage the activities and operations described in the savings association's draft business plan; and

(d) Demonstrate how applicable requirements regarding serving the credit and lending needs in the market areas served by the savings association will be met.

FILING PROCEDURES

§ 516.25 What type of application must I file?

(a) *Expedited treatment.* If you are eligible for expedited treatment under § 516.5, you may file your application in the form of a notice that includes all information required by the applicable substantive regulation. If OTS has designated a form for your notice, you must file that form. Your notice is an application for the purposes of all statutory and regulatory references to "applications."

(b) *Standard treatment.* If you are subject to standard treatment under § 516.5, you must file your application following all applicable substantive regulations and guidelines governing the filing of applications. If OTS has a designated form for your application, you must file that form.

(c) *Waiver requests.* If you want OTS to waive a requirement that you provide certain information with the notice or application, you must include a written waiver request:

(1) Describing the requirement to be waived and

(2) Explaining why the information is not needed to enable OTS to evaluate your notice or application under applicable standards.

§ 516.30 What information must I provide with my application?

(a) *Required information.* You may obtain information about required certifications, other regulations and guidelines affecting particular notices and applications, appropriate forms, and instructions from any OTS Regional Office. You may also obtain forms and instructions on OTS's web page at *www.ots.treas.gov.*

(b) *Captions and exhibits.* You must caption the original application and required copies with the type of filing, and must include all exhibits and other pertinent documents with the original application and all required copies. You are not required to include original signatures on copies if you include a copy of the signed signature page or the copy otherwise indicates that the original was signed.

63

§ 516.35 May I keep portions of my application confidential?

(a) *Confidentiality.* OTS makes submissions under this part available to the public, but may keep portions of your application confidential based on the rules in this section.

(b) *Confidentiality request.* (1) You may request OTS to keep portions of your application confidential. You must submit your request in writing with your application and must explain in detail how your request is consistent with the standards under the Freedom of Information Act (5 U.S.C. 552) and part 505 of this chapter. For example, you should explain how you will be substantially harmed by pubic disclosure of the information. You must separately bind and mark the portions of the application you consider confidential and the portions you consider non-confidential.

(2) OTS will not treat as confidential the portion of your application describing how you plan to meet your Community Reinvestment Act (CRA) objectives. OTS will make information in your CRA plan, including any information incorporated by reference from other parts of your application, available to the public upon request.

(c) *OTS determination on confidentiality.* OTS will determine whether information that you designate as confidential may be withheld from the public under the Freedom of Information Act (5 U.S.C. 552) and part 505 of this chapter. OTS will advise you before it makes information you designate as confidential available to the public.

§ 516.40 Where do I file my application?

(a) *Regional Office.* (1) You must file the original application and the number of copies indicated on the applicable form with the applications filing division of the appropriate OTS Regional Office. You should address the filings to "Attn: Applications Filing Room" at the Regional address listed in paragraph (a)(2) of this section. If the form does not indicate the number of copies you must file or if OTS has not prescribed a form for your application, you must file the original application and two copies.

(2) The addresses of each Regional Office and the states covered by each office are:

Region	Office address	States served
Northeast ...	Office of Thrift Supervision, Harborside Financial Center, Plaza Five, Suite 1600, Jersey City, New Jersey 07311.	Connecticut, Delaware, Maine, Massachusetts, New Hampshire, New Jersey, New York, Pennsylvania, Rhode Island, Vermont, West Virginia.
Southeast ..	Office of Thrift Supervision, 1475 Peachtree Street, NW., Atlanta, Georgia 30309 (Mail Stop: P.O. Box 105217, Atlanta, Georgia 30348–5217).	Alabama, District of Columbia, Florida, Georgia, Kentucky, Maryland, North Carolina, Puerto Rico, South Carolina, Virginia, the Virgin Islands.
Central	Office of Thrift Supervision, 1 South Wacker Drive, Suite 2000, Chicago, Illinois 60606.	Illinois, Indiana, Ohio, Michigan, Wisconsin.
Midwest	Office of Thrift Supervision, 225 E. John Carpenter Freeway, Suite 500, Irving, Texas 75062–2326 (Mail to: P.O. Box 619027, Dallas/Ft. Worth, Texas 75261–9027.	Arkansas, Iowa, Kansas, Louisiana, Mississippi, Missouri Nebraska, Oklahoma, Tennessee, Texas.
West	Office of Thrift Supervision, Pacific Plaza, 2001 Junipero Serra Boulevard, Suite 650, Daly City, California.	Alaska, Arizona, California, Colorado, Guam, Hawaii, Idaho, Montana, Nevada, New Mexico, North Dakota, Northern Mariana Islands, Oregon, South Dakota, Utah, Washington, Wyoming.

(b) *Additional filings with OTS Headquarters.* (1) In addition to filing in the Regional Office, if your application involves a significant issue of law or policy or if an applicable regulation or form directs you to file with OTS Headquarters, you must also file copies of your application with the Applications Filing Room at OTS headquarters, 1700 G Street, NW., Washington, DC 20552. You must file the number of copies indicated on the applicable form. If the form does not indicate the number of copies you must file or if OTS has not prescribed a form for your application, you must file three copies.

(2)(i) You may obtain a list of applications involving significant issues of law or policy at the OTS website at

Office of Thrift Supervision, Treasury

§ 516.60

www.ots.treas.gov or by contacting a Regional Office.

(ii) OTS reserves the right to identify significant issues of law or policy in a particular application. OTS will advise you, in writing, if it makes this determination.

[66 FR 13000, Mar. 2, 2001, as amended at 66 FR 65820, Dec. 21, 2001; 67 FR 78152, Dec. 23, 2002; 69 FR 76602, Dec. 22, 2004; 73 FR 76939, Dec. 18, 2008]

§ 516.45 What is the filing date of my application?

(a) Your application's filing date is the date that you complete all of the following requirements.

(1) You attend a pre-filing meeting and submit a draft business plan or relevant information, if OTS requires you to do so under § 516.15.

(2) You file your application and all required copies with OTS, as described under § 516.40.

(i) If you are required to file with a Regional Office and with OTS Headquarters, you have not filed with OTS until you file with both offices.

(ii) You have not filed with a Regional Office or OTS Headquarters until you file the application and the required number of copies with that office.

(iii) If you file after the close of business established by a Regional Office or OTS Headquarters, you have filed with that office on the next business day.

(3) You pay the applicable fee. You have not paid the fee until you submit the fee to the appropriate Regional Office, or OTS waives the fee. You may pay by check, money order, cashier's check or wire transfer payable to OTS.

(b) OTS may notify you that it has adjusted your application filing date if you fail to meet any applicable publication requirements.

(c) If, after you properly file your application with the Regional Office, OTS determines that a significant issue of law or policy exists under § 516.40(b)(2)(ii), the filing date of your application is the day you filed with the Regional Office. The 30-day review period under §§ 516.200 or 516.210 of this part will restart in its entirety when the Regional Office forwards the appropriate number of copies of your application to OTS Headquarters.

§ 516.47 How do I amend or supplement my application?

To amend or supplement your application, you must file the amendment or supplemental information at the appropriate OTS office(s) along with the number of copies required under § 516.40. Your amendment or supplemental information also must meet the caption and exhibit requirements at § 516.30(b).

Subpart B—Publication Requirements

SOURCE: 62 FR 64143, Dec. 4, 1997, unless otherwise noted.

§ 516.50 Who must publish a public notice of an application?

This subpart applies whenever an OTS regulation requires an applicant ("you") to follow the public notice procedures in this subpart.

§ 516.55 What information must I include in my public notice?

Your public notice must include the following:

(a) Your name and address.

(b) The type of application.

(c) The name of the depository institution(s) that is the subject matter of the application.

(d) A statement indicating that the public may submit comments to the appropriate OTS office(s).

(e) The address of the appropriate OTS offices where the public may submit comments.

(f) The date that the comment period closes.

(g) A statement indicating that the nonconfidential portions of the application are on file in the Regional Office, and are available for public inspection during regular business hours.

(h) Any other information that OTS requires you to publish. You may find the format for various publication notices in the appendix to OTS application processing handbook.

[66 FR 13002, Mar. 2, 2001]

§ 516.60 When must I publish the public notice?

You must publish a public notice of the application no earlier than seven

§ 516.70

days before and no later than the date of filing of the application.

§ 516.70 Where must I publish the public notice?

You must publish the notice in a newspaper having a general circulation in the communities indicated in the following chart:

If you file . . .	You must publish in the following communities . . .
(a) An application for permission to organize under § 543.2 of this chapter, a Bank Merger Act application under 563.22(a) of this chapter, an application to convert to is a federal charter under § 543.8 or § 552.2–6 of this chapter, or an application for a mutual to stock conversion under part 563b of this chapter . . .	The community in which your home office is located.
(b) An application to establish a branch office under § 545.95 of this chapter . . .	The community to be served by the branch office.
(c) An application for the change of permanent location of a home or branch office under § 545.95 of this chapter . . .	The community in which the existing office is located and the community to be served by the new office.
(d) A holding company application or a change of control notice under part 574 of this chapter . . .	The community in which the home office of the savings association whose stock is to be acquired is located and, if applicable, the community in which the home office of the acquiror's largest subsidiary savings association is located.

[69 FR 68246, Nov. 24, 2004]

§ 516.80 What language must I use in my publication?

(a) *English.* You must publish the notice in a newspaper printed in the English language.

(b) *Other than English.* If the OTS determines that the primary language of a significant number of adult residents of the community is a language other than English, the OTS may require that you simultaneously publish additional notice(s) in the community in the appropriate language(s).

Subpart C—Comment Procedures

SOURCE: 62 FR 64144, Dec. 4, 1997, unless otherwise noted.

§ 516.100 What does this subpart do?

This subpart contains the procedures governing the submission of public comments on certain types of applications or notices ("applications") pending before the OTS. It applies whenever a regulation incorporates the procedures in this subpart, or where otherwise required by the OTS.

§ 516.110 Who may submit a written comment?

Any person may submit a written comment supporting or opposing an application.

[62 FR 64144, Dec. 4, 1997, as amended at 66 FR 13003, Mar. 2, 2001]

§ 516.120 What information should a comment include?

(a) A comment should recite relevant facts, including any demographic, economic, or financial data, supporting the commenter's position. A comment opposing an application should also:

(1) Address at least one of the reasons why OTS may deny the application under the relevant statute or regulation;

(2) Recite any relevant facts and supporting data addressing these reasons; and;

(3) Address how the approval of the application could harm the commenter or any community.

(b) A commenter must include any request for a meeting under § 516.170 in its comment. The commenter must describe the nature of the issues or facts to be discussed and the reasons why written submissions are insufficient to

Office of Thrift Supervision, Treasury § 516.190

adequately address these facts or issues.

[66 FR 13003, Mar. 2, 2001, as amended at 69 FR 68247, Nov. 24, 2004]

§ 516.130 Where are comments filed?

A commenter must file with the appropriate OTS Regional Office (See table at § 516.40(a)(2)). The commenter must simultaneously send a copy of the comment to the applicant.

[66 FR 13003, Mar. 2, 2001]

§ 516.140 How long is the comment period?

(a) *General.* Except as provided in paragraph (b) of this section, a commenter must file a written comment with OTS within 30 calendar days after the date of publication of the initial public notice.

(b) *Late-filed comments.* OTS may consider late-filed comments if OTS determines that the comment will assist in the disposition of the application.

[69 FR 68247, Nov. 24, 2004]

Subpart D—Meeting Procedures

SOURCE: 69 FR 68247, Nov. 24, 2004, unless otherwise noted.

§ 516.160 What does this subpart do?

This subpart contains meeting procedures. It applies whenever a regulation incorporates the procedures in this subpart, or when otherwise required by OTS.

§ 516.170 When will OTS conduct a meeting on an application?

(a) OTS will grant a meeting request or conduct a meeting on its own initiative, if it finds that written submissions are insufficient to address facts or issues raised in an application, or otherwise determines that a meeting will benefit the decision-making process. OTS may limit the issues considered at the meeting to issues that OTS decides are relevant or material.

(b) OTS will inform the applicant and all commenters requesting a meeting of its decision to grant or deny a meeting request, or of its decision to conduct a meeting on its own initiative.

(c) If OTS decides to conduct a meeting, OTS will invite the applicant and any commenters requesting a meeting and raising an issue that OTS intends to consider at the meeting. OTS may also invite other interested persons to attend. OTS will inform the participants of the date, time, location, issues to be considered, and format for the meeting a reasonable time before the meeting.

§ 516.180 What procedures govern the conduct of the meeting?

(a) OTS may conduct meetings in any format including, but not limited to, a telephone conference, a face-to-face meeting, or a more formal meeting.

(b) The Administrative Procedure Act (5 U.S.C. 551 *et seq.*), the Federal Rules of Evidence (28 U.S.C. Appendix), the Federal Rules of Civil Procedure (28 U.S.C. Rule 1 *et seq.*) and the OTS Rules of Practice and Procedure in Adjudicatory Proceedings (12 CFR part 509) do not apply to meetings under this section.

§ 516.185 Will OTS approve or disapprove an application at a meeting?

OTS will not approve or deny an application at a meeting under this subpart.

§ 516.190 Will a meeting affect application processing time frames?

If OTS decides to conduct a meeting, it may suspend applicable application processing time frames, including the time frames for deeming an application complete and the applicable approval time frames in subpart E of this part. If OTS suspends applicable application processing time frames, the time period will resume when OTS determines that a record has been developed that sufficiently supports a determination on the issues considered at the meeting.

Subpart E—OTS Review

SOURCE: 66 FR 13003, Mar. 2, 2001, unless otherwise noted.

§ 516.200

EXPEDITED TREATMENT

§ 516.200 If I file a notice under expedited treatment, when may I engage in the proposed activities?

If you are eligible for expedited treatment and you have appropriately filed your notice with OTS, you may engage in the proposed activities upon the expiration of 30 days after the filing date of your notice, unless OTS takes one of the following actions before the expiration of that time period:

(a) OTS notifies you in writing that you must file additional information supplementing your notice. If you are required to file additional information, you may engage in the proposed activities upon the expiration of 30 calendar days after the date you file the additional information, unless OTS takes one of the actions described in paragraphs (b) through (d) of this section before the expiration of that time period;

(b) OTS notifies you in writing that your notice is subject to standard treatment under this subpart. OTS will subject your notice to standard treatment if it raises a supervisory concern, raises a significant issue of law or policy, or requires significant additional information;

(c) OTS notifies you in writing that it is suspending the applicable time frames under § 516.190; or

(d) OTS notifies you that it disapproves your notice.

STANDARD TREATMENT

§ 516.210 What will OTS do after I file my application?

(a) *OTS action.* Within 30 calendar days after the filing date of your application, OTS will take one of the following actions:

If OTS * * *	Then * * *
(1) Notifies you, in writing, that your application is complete * * *.	The applicable review period will begin on the date that OTS deems your application complete.
(2) Notifies you, in writing, that you must submit additional information to complete your application * * *.	You must submit the required additional information under § 516.220.
(3) Notifies you, in writing, that your application is materially deficient * * *.	OTS will not process your application.
(4) Takes no action * * *	Your application is deemed complete. The applicable review period will begin on the day the 30-day time period expires.

(b) *Waiver requests.* If your application includes a request for waiver of an information requirement under § 516.25(b), and OTS has not notified you that you must submit additional information under paragraph (a)(2) of this section, your request for waiver is granted.

§ 516.220 If OTS requests additional information to complete my application, how will it process my application?

(a) You may use the following chart to determine the procedure that applies to your submission of additional information under § 516.210(a)(1):

If, within 30 calendar days after the date of OTS's request for additional information * * *	Then, OTS may * * *.	And * * *.
(1) You file a response to all information requests * * *.	(i) Notify you in writing within 15 days after the filing date of your response that your application is complete * * * applicable to all response that your application is complete * * *.	The applicable review period will begin on the date that OTS deems your application complete.
	(ii) Notify you in writing within 15 calendar days after the filing date of your response that you must submit additional information regarding matters derived from or prompted by information already furnished or any additional information information necessary to resolve the issues presented in your application * * *.	You must respond to the additional information request within the time period required by OTS. OTS will review your response under the procedures described in this section.
	(iii) Notify you in writing within 15 calendar days after the filing date of your response that your application is materially deficient * * *.	OTS will not process your application.

68

Office of Thrift Supervision, Treasury § 516.240

If, within 30 calendar days after the date of OTS's request for additional information * * *	Then, OTS may * * *.	And * * *.
	(iv) Take no action within 15 calendar days after the filing date of your response * * *.	Your application is deemed complete. The applicable review period will begin on the day that the 15-day time period expires.
(2) You request an extension of time to file additional information * * *.	(i) Grant an extension, in writing, specifying the number of days for the extension * * *.	You must fully respond within the extended time period specified by OTS. OTS will review your response under the procedures described under this section.
	(ii) Notify you in writing that your extension request is disapproved * * *.	OTS will not process your application further. You may resubmit the application for processing as a new filing under the applicable regulation.
(3) You fail to respond completely * * *..	(i) Notify you in writing that your application is deemed withdrawn * * *.	OTS will not process your application further. You may resubmit the application for processing as a new filing under the applicable regulation.
	(ii) Notify you, in writing, that your response is incomplete and extend the response period, specifying the number of days for the respond extension * * *.	You must fully respond within the extended time period specified by OTS. OTS will review your response under the procedures described under this section.

(b) OTS may extend the 15-day period referenced in paragraph (a)(1) of this section by up to 15 calendar days, if OTS requires the additional time to review your response. OTS will notify you that it has extended the period before the end of the initial 15-day period and will briefly explain why the extension is necessary.

(c) If your response filed under paragraph (a)(1) of this section includes a request for a waiver of an informational requirement, your request for a waiver is granted if OTS fails to act on it within 15 calendar days after the filing of your response, unless OTS extends the review period under paragraph (b). If OTS extends the review period under paragraph (b), your request is granted if OTS fails to act on it by the end of the extended review period.

[66 FR 13003, Mar. 2, 2001; 67 FR 3264, Jan. 23, 2002]

§ 516.230 Will OTS conduct an eligibility examination?

(a) *Eligibility examination.* OTS may notify you at any time before it deems your application complete that it will conduct an eligibility examination. If OTS decides to conduct an eligibility examination, it will not deem your application complete until it concludes the examination.

(b) *Additional information.* OTS may, as a result of the eligibility examination, notify you that you must submit additional information to complete your application. If so, you must respond to the additional information request within the time period required by OTS. OTS will review your response under the procedures described in § 516.220.

§ 516.240 What may OTS require me to do after my application is deemed complete?

After your application is deemed complete, but before the end of the applicable review period,

(a) OTS may require you to provide additional information if the information is necessary to resolve or clarify the issues presented by your application.

(b) OTS may determine that a major issue of law or a change in circumstances arose after you filed your application, and that the issue or changed circumstances will substantially effect your application. If OTS identifies such an issue or changed circumstances, it may:

(1) Notify you, in writing, that your application is now incomplete and require you to submit additional information to complete the application under the procedures described at § 516.220; and

(2) Require you to publish a new public notice of your application under § 516.250.

§ 516.250 Will OTS require me to publish a new public notice?

(a) If your application was subject to a publication requirement, OTS may require you to publish a new public notice of your application if:

(1) You submitted a revision to the application, you submitted new or additional information, or a major issue of law or a change in circumstances arose after the filing of your application; and

(2) OTS determines that additional comment on these matters is appropriate because of the significance of the new information or circumstances.

(b) OTS will notify you in writing if you must publish a new public notice of your revised application.

(c) If you are required to publish a new public notice of your revised application, you must notify OTS after you publish the new public notice.

§ 516.260 May OTS suspend processing of my application?

(a) *Suspension.* OTS may, at any time, indefinitely suspend processing of your application if:

(1) OTS, another governmental entity, or a self-regulatory trade or professional organization initiates an investigation, examination, or administrative proceeding that is relevant to OTS's evaluation of your application;

(2) You request the suspension or there are other extraordinary circumstances that have a significant impact on the processing of your application.

(b) *Notice.* OTS will promptly notify you, in writing, if it suspends your application.

§ 516.270 How long is the OTS review period?

(a) *General.* The applicable OTS review period is 60 calendar days after the date that your application is deemed complete, unless an applicable OTS regulation specifies a different review period.

(b) *Multiple applications.* If you submit more than one application in connection with a proposed action or if two or more applicants submit related applications, the applicable review period for all applications is the review period for the application with the longest review period, subject to statutory review periods.

(c) *Extensions.* (1) OTS may extend the review period for up to 30 calendar days beyond the period described in paragraph (a) or (b) of this section. OTS must notify you in writing of the extension and the duration of the extension. OTS must issue the written extension before the end of the review period.

(2) OTS may also extend the review period as needed until it acts on the application, if the application presents a significant issue of law or policy that requires additional time to resolve. OTS must notify you in writing of the extension and the general reasons for the extension. OTS must issue the written extension before the end of the review period, including any extension of that period under paragraph (c)(1) of this section. This section applies to applications and notices filed under § 575.3(b) and part 574 of this chapter.

§ 516.280 How will I know if my application has been approved?

(a) *OTS approval or denial.* (1) OTS will approve or deny your application before the expiration of the applicable review period, including any extensions of the review period.

(2) OTS will promptly notify you in writing of its decision to approve or deny your application.

(b) *No OTS action.* If OTS fails to act under paragraph (a)(1) of this section, your application is approved.

§ 516.290 What will happen if OTS does not approve or disapprove my application within two calendar years after the filing date?

(a) *Withdrawal.* If OTS has not approved or denied your pending application within two calendar years after the filing date under § 516.45, OTS will notify you, in writing, that your application is deemed withdrawn unless OTS determines that you are actively pursuing a final OTS determination on your application. You are not actively pursuing a final OTS determination if you have failed to timely take an action required under this part, including filing required additional information, or OTS has suspended processing of your application under § 516.260 based on circumstances that are, in whole or in part, within your control and you have failed to take reasonable steps to resolve these circumstances.

(b) *Effective date.* This section is effective July 1, 2001.

PART 517—CONTRACTING OUTREACH PROGRAMS

Sec.
517.1 Purpose and scope.
517.2 Definitions.
517.3 Policy.
517.4 Oversight and monitoring.
517.5 Outreach.
517.6 Certification.
517.7 Contract award guidelines.

AUTHORITY: 12 U.S.C. 1833(e); 42 U.S.C. 12101 et seq.

SOURCE: 58 FR 33324, June 17, 1993, unless otherwise noted.

§ 517.1 Purpose and scope.

The purpose of the OTS Minority-, Women- and Individuals with Disabilities-Owned Businesses Outreach Program (Outreach Program) is to ensure that firms owned and operated by minorities, women and individuals with disabilities are given the opportunity to participate to the maximum extent possible in all contracts entered into by the OTS. Sections 517.5 through 517.7 of this part apply to all contracting activities, with the exception of contracting for legal services, engaged in by OTS in any of its capacities, for all OTS functions authorized by law. These contracts will typically pertain to services in support of OTS's business operations, such as consulting, programming, auditing, expert witnesses, customized training, relocation services, information systems technology (computer systems, database management, software and office automation), or micrographic services; or in support of its day-to-day operations, such as facilities management, mail and printing services, or procurement of office supplies, furniture and office equipment.

§ 517.2 Definitions.

The definitions included in this part are derived from common usage of these terms. A term in this part includes all those who are commonly understood to be included within that term.

(a) *Minority- and/or women-owned (small and large) businesses and entities owned by minorities and women* means firms at least fifty-one (51) percent owned by individuals who are members of the minority group or women and who are citizens of the United States. In the case of publicly-owned companies, at least fifty-one (51) percent of each class of voting stock must be owned by one or more members of the minority group or by one or more women, who are citizens of the United States. In the case of partnerships, at least fifty-one (51) percent of the partnership interest must be owned by one or more members of the minority group or by one or more women, who are citizens of the United States. Additionally, the management and daily business operations of the firm must be controlled by one or more such individuals.

(b) *Minority* means any Black/African-American; Native American (American Indians, Eskimos, Aleuts and Native Hawaiians); Hispanic American; Asian-Pacific American; or Sub-continent-Asian American.

(c) *Small and large businesses and entities owned by individuals with disabilities* means firms at least fifty-one (51) percent owned by individuals with disabilities who are citizens of the United States. In the case of publicly-owned companies, at least fifty-one (51) percent of each class of voting stock must be owned by individuals with disabilities who are citizens of the United States. In the case of partnerships, at least fifty-one (51) percent of the partnership interest must be owned by individuals with disabilities who are citizens of the United States. Additionally, the management and daily business operations must be controlled by one or more such individuals.

(d) *Disability*, as used in this part, has the same meaning as the term used in section 3 of the Americans With Disabilities Act of 1990, Public Law 101–336, 104 Stat. 327 (42 U.S.C. 12101 et seq).

§ 517.3 Policy.

It is the policy of the OTS that minorities, women and individuals with

§ 517.4

disabilities and entities owned by minorities, women and individuals with disabilities are given the opportunity to participate to the maximum extent possible in all contracts entered into by the OTS.

§ 517.4 Oversight and monitoring.

The Director of OTS shall appoint an Outreach Program Advocate, who shall have primary responsibility for furthering the purposes of the Outreach Program.

§ 517.5 Outreach.

(a) The outreach program advocate shall perform outreach activities and act as liaison between the OTS and the public on outreach program issues.

(b) Outreach activities include the identification and registration of minority-, women-owned (small and large) businesses and entities owned by individuals with disabilities who can provide goods and services utilized by the OTS. This includes distributing information concerning the Outreach Program and providing appropriate registration materials for use by vendors and contractors. Identification will primarily be accomplished by:

(1) Obtaining various lists and directories maintained by other federal, state and local governmental agencies of Outreach Program businesses;

(2) Participating in conventions, seminars and professional meetings oriented towards Outreach Programs;

(3) Conducting seminars, meetings, workshops and various other functions; and

(4) Monitoring proposed purchases and contracts to assure that OTS contracting staff understand and actively promote the Outreach Program.

§ 517.6 Certification.

In order to qualify as an Outreach Program participant, each business or contractor must either:

(a) Self-certify ownership status by filing with the OTS Outreach Program Advocate a completed and signed Solicitation Mailing List Application, Standard Form 129 (SF–129), as prescribed by the Federal Acquisition Regulation (48 CFR part 53);

(b) Self-certify ownership status by filing with the OTS Outreach Program Advocate a completed and signed ABELS Registration/Certification Form, as prescribed by the U.S. Department of Commerce's Minority Business Development Agency and available from the Outreach Program Advocate at the headquarters address of the OTS listed in § 516.40(b) of this chapter.

(c) Submit a valid Outreach Program certification received from a Federal agency, or a designated state or authorized local agency.

[58 FR 33324, June 17, 1993, as amended at 66 FR 13005, Mar. 2, 2001]

§ 517.7 Contract award guidelines.

Contracts for goods or services shall be awarded in accordance with OTS procurement rules and policies (48 CFR chapter 1 and FIRMR, 41 CFR chapter 201). The OTS Outreach Program Advocate shall work to facilitate the maximum participation of minority-, women-owned (small and large) businesses and entities owned by individuals with disabilities in the OTS procurement of goods or services.

PART 528—NONDISCRIMINATION REQUIREMENTS

Sec.
528.1 Definitions.
528.1a Supplementary guidelines.
528.2 Nondiscrimination in lending and other services.
528.2a Nondiscriminatory appraisal and underwriting.
528.3 Nondiscrimination in applications.
528.4 Nondiscriminatory advertising.
528.5 Equal Housing Lender Poster.
528.6 Loan application register.
528.7 Nondiscrimination in employment.
528.8 Complaints.
528.9 Guidelines relating to nondiscrimination in lending.

AUTHORITY: 12 U.S.C. 1464, 2810 et seq., 2901 et seq.; 15 U.S.C. 1691; 42 U.S.C. 1981, 1982, 3601–3619.

SOURCE: 55 FR 1388, Jan. 16, 1990, unless otherwise noted.

§ 528.1 Definitions.

As used in this part 528—

(a) *Application.* For purposes of this part, an application for a loan or other service is as defined in Regulation C, 12 CFR 203.2(b).

(b) *Savings association.* The term "savings association" means any savings association as defined in 12 U.S.C. 1813(b).

(c) *Dwelling.* The term "dwelling" means a residential structure (whether or not it is attached to real property) located in a state of the United States of America, the District of Colombia, or the Commonwealth of Puerto Rico. The term includes an individual condominium unit, cooperative unit, or mobile or manufactured home.

[55 FR 1388, Jan. 16, 1990, as amended at 58 FR 4312, Jan. 14, 1993; 63 FR 71212, Dec. 24, 1998; 71 FR 19811, Apr. 18, 2006]

§ 528.1a **Supplementary guidelines.**

The Office's policy statement found at 12 CFR 528.9 supplements this part and should be read together with this part. Refer also to the HUD Fair Housing regulations at 24 CFR parts 100 *et seq.*, Federal Reserve Regulation B at 12 CFR part 202, and Federal Reserve Regulation C at 12 CFR part 203.

[63 FR 71212, Dec. 24, 1998]

§ 528.2 **Nondiscrimination in lending and other services.**

(a) No savings association may deny a loan or other service, or discriminate in the purchase of loans or securities or discriminate in fixing the amount, interest rate, duration, application procedures, collection or enforcement procedures, or other terms or conditions of such loan or other service on the basis of the age or location of the dwelling, or on the basis of the race, color, religion, sex, handicap, familial status (having one or more children under the age of 18), marital status, age (provided the person has the capacity to contract) or national origin of:

(1) An applicant or joint applicant;

(2) Any person associated with an applicant or joint applicant regarding such loan or other service, or with the purposes of such loan or other service;

(3) The present or prospective owners, lessees, tenants, or occupants of the dwelling(s) for which such loan or other service is to be made or given;

(4) The present or prospective owners, lessees, tenants, or occupants of other dwellings in the vicinity of the dwelling(s) for which such loan or other service is to be made or given.

(b) A savings association shall consider without prejudice the combined income of joint applicants for a loan or other service.

(c) No savings association may discriminate against an applicant for a loan or other service on any prohibited basis (as defined in 12 CFR 202.2(z) and 24 CFR part 100).

NOTE: See also, § 528.9 (b) and (c).

[55 FR 1388, Jan. 16, 1990, as amended at 63 FR 71212, Dec. 24, 1998]

§ 528.2a **Nondiscriminatory appraisal and underwriting.**

(a) *Appraisal.* No savings association may use or rely upon an appraisal of a dwelling which the savings association knows, or reasonably should know, is discriminatory on the basis of the age or location of the dwelling, or is discriminatory per se or in effect under the Fair Housing Act of 1968 or the Equal Credit Opportunity Act.

(b) *Underwriting.* Each savings association shall have clearly written, nondiscriminatory loan underwriting standards, available to the public upon request, at each of its offices. Each association shall, at least annually, review its standards, and business practices implementing them, to ensure equal opportunity in lending

NOTE: See also, § 528.9(b), (c)(6), and (c)(7).

[55 FR 1388, Jan. 16, 1990, as amended at 63 FR 71212, Dec. 24, 1998]

§ 528.3 **Nondiscrimination in applications.**

(a) No savings association may discourage, or refuse to allow, receive, or consider, any application, request, or inquiry regarding a loan or other service, or discriminate in imposing conditions upon, or in processing, any such application, request, or inquiry on the basis of the age or location of the dwelling, or on the basis of the race, color, religion, sex, handicap, familial status (having one or more children under the age of 18), marital status, age (provided the person has the capacity to contract), national origin, or other characteristics prohibited from consideration in § 528.2(c) of this part,

§ 528.4

of the prospective borrower or other person, who:

(1) Makes application for any such loan or other service;

(2) Requests forms or papers to be used to make application for any such loan or other service; or

(3) Inquires about the availability of such loan or other service.

(b) A savings association shall inform each inquirer of his or her right to file a written loan application, and to receive a copy of the association's underwriting standards.

NOTE: See also, § 528.9(a) through (d).

[55 FR 1388, Jan. 16, 1990, as amended at 63 FR 71212, Dec. 24, 1998]

§ 528.4 Nondiscriminatory advertising.

No savings association may directly or indirectly engage in any form of advertising that implies or suggests a policy of discrimination or exclusion in violation of title VIII of the Civil Rights Acts of 1968, the Equal Credit Opportunity Act, or this part 528. Advertisements for any loan for the purpose of purchasing, constructing, improving, repairing, or maintaining a dwelling or any loan secured by a dwelling shall include a facsimile of the following logotype and legend:

EQUAL HOUSING LENDER

[55 FR 1388, Jan. 16, 1990, as amended at 69 FR 68247, Nov. 24, 2004]

§ 528.5 Equal Housing Lender Poster.

(a) Each savings association shall post and maintain one or more Equal Housing Lender Posters, the text of which is prescribed in paragraph (b) of this section, in the lobby of each of its offices in a prominent place or places readily apparent to all persons seeking loans. The poster shall be at least 11 by 14 inches in size, and the text shall be easily legible. It is recommended that savings associations post a Spanish language version of the poster in offices serving areas with a substantial Spanish-speaking population.

(b) The text of the Equal Housing Lender Poster shall be as follows:

EQUAL HOUSING LENDER

We Do Business In Accordance With Federal Fair Lending Laws.

UNDER THE FEDERAL FAIR HOUSING ACT, IT IS ILLEGAL, ON THE BASIS OF RACE, COLOR, NATIONAL ORIGIN, RELIGION, SEX, HANDICAP, OR FAMILIAL STATUS (HAVING CHILDREN UNDER THE AGE OF 18) TO:

[ ]Deny a loan for the purpose of purchasing, constructing, improving, repairing or maintaining a dwelling or to deny any loan secured by a dwelling; or

[ ]Discriminate in fixing the amount, interest rate, duration, application procedures, or other terms or conditions of such a loan or in appraising property.

IF YOU BELIEVE YOU HAVE BEEN DISCRIMINATED AGAINST, YOU SHOULD: SEND A COMPLAINT TO:

Assistant Secretary for Fair Housing and Equal Opportunity, Department of Housing and Urban Development, Washington, DC 20410.

For processing under the Federal Fair Housing Act

AND TO:

Director, Consumer Affairs, Office of Thrift Supervision, Washington, DC 20552.

For processing under Office of Thrift Supervision Regulations.

UNDER THE EQUAL CREDIT OPPORTUNITY ACT, IT IS ILLEGAL TO DISCRIMINATE IN ANY CREDIT TRANSACTION:

[ ]On the basis of race, color, national origin, religion, sex, marital status, or age;

[ ]Because income is from public assistance; or

[ ]Because a right has been exercised under the Consumer Credit Protection Act.

IF YOU BELIEVE YOU HAVE BEEN DISCRIMINATED AGAINST, YOU SHOULD SEND A COMPLAINT TO: Director, Consumer Affairs, Office of Thrift Supervision, Washington, DC 20552.

§ 528.6 Loan application register.

Savings associations and other lenders required to file Home Mortgage Disclosure Act Loan Application Registers with the Office of Thrift Supervision in accordance with 12 CFR part 203 must enter the reason for denial, using the codes provided in 12 CFR part 203, with respect to all loan denials.

[58 FR 4312, Jan. 14, 1993]

§ 528.7 Nondiscrimination in employment.

(a) No savings association shall, because of an individual's race, color, religion, sex, or national origin:

(1) Fail or refuse to hire such individual;

(2) Discharge such individual;

(3) Otherwise discriminate against such individual with respect to such individual's compensation, promotion, or the terms, conditions, or privileges of such individual's employment; or

(4) Discriminate in admission to, or employment in, any program of apprenticeship, training, or retraining, including on-the-job training.

(b) No savings association shall limit, segregate, or classify its employees in any way which would deprive or tend to deprive any individual of employment opportunities or otherwise adversely affect such individual's status as an employee because of such individual's race, color, religion, sex, or national origin.

(c) No savings association shall discriminate against any employee or applicant for employment because such employee or applicant has opposed any employment practice made unlawful by Federal, State, or local law or regulation or because he has in good faith made a charge of such practice or testified, assisted, or participated in any manner in an investigation, proceeding, or hearing of such practice by any lawfully constituted authority.

(d) No savings association shall print or publish or cause to be printed or published any notice or advertisement relating to employment by such savings association indicating any preference, limitation, specification, or discrimination based on race, color, religion, sex, or national origin.

(e) This regulation shall not apply in any case in which the Federal Equal Employment Opportunities law is made inapplicable by the provisions of section 2000e-1 or sections 2000e-2 (e) through (j) of title 42, United States Code.

(f) Any violation of the following laws or regulations by a savings association shall be deemed to be a violation of this part 528:

(1) The Equal Employment Opportunity Act, as amended, 42 U.S.C. 2000e-2000h-2, and Equal Employment Opportunity Commission (EEOC) regulations at 29 CFR part 1600;

(2) The Age Discrimination in Employment Act, 29 U.S.C. 621-633, and EEOC and Department of Labor regulations;

(3) Department of the Treasury regulations at 31 CFR part 12 and Office of Federal Contract Compliance Programs (OFCCP) regulations at 41 CFR part 60;

(4) The Veterans Employment and Readjustment Act of 1972, 38 U.S.C. 2011-2012, and the Vietnam Era Veterans Readjustment Adjustment Assistance Act of 1974, 38 U.S.C. 2021-2026;

(5) The Rehabilitation Act of 1973, 29 U.S.C. 701 et al.; and

(6) The Immigration and Nationality Act, 8 U.S.C. 1324b, and INS regulations at 8 CFR part 274a.

§ 528.8 Complaints.

Complaints regarding discrimination in lending by a savings association shall be referred to the Assistant Secretary for Fair Housing and Equal Opportunity, U.S. Department of Housing and Urban Development, Washington, DC 20410 for processing under the Fair Housing Act, and to the Director, Consumer Affairs, Office of Thrift Supervision, Washington, DC 20552 for processing under Office regulations. Complaints regarding discrimination in employment by a savings association should be referred to the Equal Employment Opportunity Commission, Washington, DC 20506 and a copy, for information only, sent to the Director,

§ 528.9

Consumer Affairs, Office of Thrift Supervision, Washington, DC 20552.

§ 528.9 Guidelines relating to nondiscrimination in lending.

(a) *General.* Fair housing and equal opportunity in home financing is a policy of the United States established by Federal statutes and Presidential orders and proclamations. In furtherance of the Federal civil rights laws and the economical home financing purposes of the statutes administered by the Office, the Office has adopted, in part 528 of this chapter, nondiscrimination regulations that, among other things, prohibit arbitrary refusals to consider loan applications on the basis of the age or location of a dwelling, and prohibit discrimination based on race, color, religion, sex, handicap, familial status (having one or more children under the age of 18), marital status, age (provided the person has the capacity to contract), or national origin in fixing the amount, interest rate, duration, application procedures, collection or enforcement procedures, or other terms or conditions of housing related loans. Such discrimination is also prohibited in the purchase of loans and securities. This section provides supplementary guidelines to aid savings associations in developing and implementing nondiscriminatory lending policies. Each savings association should reexamine its underwriting standards at least annually in order to ensure equal opportunity.

(b) *Loan underwriting standards.* The basic purpose of the Office's nondiscrimination regulations is to require that every applicant be given an equal opportunity to obtain a loan. Each loan applicant's creditworthiness should be evaluated on an individual basis without reference to presumed characteristics of a group. The use of lending standards which have no economic basis and which are discriminatory in effect is a violation of law even in the absence of an actual intent to discriminate. However, a standard which has a discriminatory effect is not necessarily improper if its use achieves a genuine business need which cannot be achieved by means which are not discriminatory in effect or less discriminatory in effect.

(c) *Discriminatory practices*—(1) *Discrimination on the basis of sex or marital status.* The Civil Rights Act of 1968 and the National Housing Act prohibit discrimination in lending on the basis of sex. The Equal Credit Opportunity Act, in addition to this prohibition, forbids discrimination on the basis of marital status. Refusing to lend to, requiring higher standards of creditworthiness of, or imposing different requirements on, members of one sex or individuals of one marital status, is discrimination based on sex or marital status. Loan underwriting decisions must be based on an applicant's credit history and present and reasonably foreseeable economic prospects, rather than on the basis of assumptions regarding comparative differences in creditworthiness between married and unmarried individuals, or between men and women.

(2) *Discrimination on the basis of language.* Requiring fluency in the English language as a prerequisite for obtaining a loan may be a discriminatory practice based on national origin.

(3) *Income of husbands and wives.* A practice of discounting all or part of either spouse's income where spouses apply jointly is a violation of section 527 of the National Housing Act. As with other income, when spouses apply jointly for a loan, the determination as to whether a spouse's income qualifies for credit purposes should depend upon a reasonable evaluation of his or her past, present, and reasonably foreseeable economic circumstances. Information relating to child-bearing intentions of a couple or an individual may not be requested.

(4) *Supplementary income.* Lending standards which consider as effective only the non-overtime income of the primary wage-earner may result in discrimination because they do not take account of variations in employment patterns among individuals and families. The Office favors loan underwriting which reasonably evaluates the credit worthiness of each applicant based on a realistic appraisal of his or her own past, present, and foreseeable economic circumstances. The determination as to whether primary income or additional income qualifies as

effective for credit purposes should depend upon whether such income may reasonably be expected to continue through the early period of the mortgage risk. Automatically discounting other income from bonuses, overtime, or part-time employment, will cause some applicants to be denied financing without a realistic analysis of their credit worthiness. Since statistics show that minority group members and low- and moderate-income families rely more often on such supplemental income, the practice may be racially discriminatory in effect, as well as artificially restrictive of opportunities for home financing.

(5) *Applicant's prior history.* Loan decisions should be based upon a realistic evaluation of all pertinent factors respecting an individual's creditworthiness, without giving undue weight to any one factor. The savings association should, among other things, take into consideration that:

(i) In some instances, past credit difficulties may have resulted from discriminatory practices;

(ii) A policy favoring applicants who previously owned homes may perpetuate prior discrimination;

(iii) A current, stable earnings record may be the most reliable indicator of credit-worthiness, and entitled to more weight than factors such as educational level attained;

(iv) Job or residential changes may indicate upward mobility; and

(v) Preferring applicants who have done business with the lender can perpetuate previous discriminatory policies.

(6) *Income level or racial composition of area.* Refusing to lend or lending on less favorable terms in particular areas because of their racial composition is unlawful. Refusing to lend, or offering less favorable terms (such as interest rate, downpayment, or maturity) to applicants because of the income level in an area can discriminate against minority group persons.

(7) *Age and location factors.* Sections 528.2, 528.2a, and 528.3 of this chapter prohibit loan denials based upon the age or location of a dwelling. These restrictions are intended to prohibit use of unfounded or unsubstantiated assumptions regarding the effect upon loan risk of the age of a dwelling or the physical or economic characteristics of an area. Loan decisions should be based on the present market value of the property offered as security (including consideration of specific improvements to be made by the borrower) and the likelihood that the property will retain an adequate value over the term of the loan. Specific factors which may negatively affect its short-range future value (up to 3–5 years) should be clearly documented. Factors which in some cases may cause the market value of a property to decline are recent zoning changes or a significant number of abandoned homes in the immediate vicinity of the property. However, not all zoning changes will cause a decline in property values, and proximity to abandoned buildings may not affect the market value of a property because of rehabilitation programs or affirmative lending programs, or because the cause of abandonment is unrelated to high risk. Proper underwriting considerations include the condition and utility of the improvements, and various physical factors such as street conditions, amenities such as parks and recreation areas, availability of public utilities and municipal services, and exposure to flooding and land faults. However, arbitrary decisions based on age or location are prohibited, since many older, soundly constructed homes provide housing opportunities which may be precluded by an arbitrary lending policy.

(8) *Fair Housing Act (title VIII, Civil Rights Act of 1968, as amended).* Savings associations must comply with all regulations promulgated by the Department of Housing and Urban Development to implement the Fair Housing Act, found at 24 CFR part 100 et seq., except that they shall use the Equal Housing Lender logo and poster prescribed by Office regulations at 12 CFR 528.4 and 528.5 rather than the Equal Housing Opportunity logo and poster required by 24 CFR parts 109 and 110.

(d) *Marketing practices.* Savings associations should review their advertising and marketing practices to ensure that their services are available without discrimination to the community they serve. Discrimination in lending is not limited to loan decisions and underwriting standards; a savings association does not meet its obligations to the community or implement its equal lending responsibility if its marketing practices and business relationships with developers and real estate brokers improperly restrict its clientele to segments of the community. A review of marketing practices could begin with an examination of an association's loan portfolio and applications to ascertain whether, in view of the demographic characteristics and credit demands of the community in which the institution is located, it is adequately serving the community on a nondiscriminatory basis. The Office will systematically review marketing practices where evidence of discrimination in lending is discovered.

[54 FR 49666, Nov. 30, 1989, as amended at 60 FR 66870, Dec. 27, 1995. Redesignated at 63 FR 71212, Dec. 24, 1998]

PART 533—DISCLOSURE AND REPORTING OF CRA-RELATED AGREEMENTS

Sec.
533.1 Purpose and scope of this part.
533.2 Definition of covered agreement.
533.3 CRA communications.
533.4 Fulfillment of the CRA.
533.5 Related agreements considered a single agreement.
533.6 Disclosure of covered agreements.
533.7 Annual reports.
533.8 Release of information under FOIA.
533.9 Compliance provisions.
533.10 Transition provisions.
533.11 Other definitions and rules of construction used in this part.

AUTHORITY: 12 U.S.C. 1462a, 1463, 1464, 1467a, and 1831y.

SOURCE: 66 FR 2106, Jan. 10, 2001, unless otherwise noted.

§ 533.1 Purpose and scope of this part.

(a) *General.* This part implements section 711 of the Gramm-Leach-Bliley Act (12 U.S.C. 1831y). That section requires any nongovernmental entity or person (NGEP), insured depository institution, or affiliate of an insured depository institution that enters into a covered agreement to—

(1) Make the covered agreement available to the public and the appropriate Federal banking agency; and

(2) File an annual report with the appropriate Federal banking agency concerning the covered agreement.

(b) *Scope of this part.* The provisions of this part apply to—

(1) Savings associations and their subsidiaries;

(2) Savings and loan holding companies;

(3) Affiliates of savings associations and savings and loan holding companies, other than bank holding companies, banks, and subsidiaries of bank holding companies and banks; and

(4) NGEPs that enter into covered agreements with any company listed in paragraphs (b)(1) through (b)(3) of this section.

(c) *Relation to Community Reinvestment Act.* This part does not affect in any way the Community Reinvestment Act of 1977 (CRA) (12 U.S.C. 2901 et seq.), OTS's Community Reinvestment rule (12 CFR Part 563e), or OTS's interpretations or administration of the CRA or Community Reinvestment rule.

(d) *Examples.* (1) The examples in this part are not exclusive. Compliance with an example, to the extent applicable, constitutes compliance with this part.

(2) Examples in a paragraph illustrate only the issue described in the paragraph and do not illustrate any other issues that may arise in this part.

§ 533.2 Definition of covered agreement.

(a) *General definition of covered agreement.* A covered agreement is any contract, arrangement, or understanding that meets all of the following criteria—

(1) The agreement is in writing.

(2) The parties to the agreement include—

(i) One or more insured depository institutions or affiliates of an insured depository institution; and

(ii) One or more NGEPs.

(3) The agreement provides for the insured depository institution or any affiliate to—

(i) Provide to one or more individuals or entities (whether or not parties to the agreement) cash payments, grants, or other consideration (except loans)

Office of Thrift Supervision, Treasury § 533.2

that have an aggregate value of more than $10,000 in any calendar year; or

(ii) Make to one or more individuals or entities (whether or not parties to the agreement) loans that have an aggregate principal amount of more than $50,000 in any calendar year.

(4) The agreement is made pursuant to, or in connection with, the fulfillment of the CRA, as defined in § 533.4 of this part.

(5) The agreement is with a NGEP that has had a CRA communication as described in § 533.3 of this part prior to entering into the agreement.

(b) *Examples concerning written arrangements or understandings*—(1) *Example 1.* A NGEP meets with an insured depository institution and states that the institution needs to make more community development investments in the NGEP's community. The NGEP and insured depository institution do not reach an agreement concerning the community development investments the institution should make in the community, and the parties do not reach any mutual arrangement or understanding. Two weeks later, the institution unilaterally issues a press release announcing that it has established a general goal of making $100 million of community development grants in low- and moderate-income neighborhoods served by the insured depository institution over the next 5 years. The NGEP is not identified in the press release. The press release is not a written arrangement or understanding.

(2) *Example 2.* A NGEP meets with an insured depository institution and states that the institution needs to offer new loan programs in the NGEP's community. The NGEP and the insured depository institution reach a mutual arrangement or understanding that the institution will provide additional loans in the NGEP's community. The institution tells the NGEP that it will issue a press release announcing the program. Later, the insured depository institution issues a press release announcing the loan program. The press release incorporates the key terms of the understanding reached between the NGEP and the insured depository institution. The written press release reflects the mutual arrangement or understanding of the NGEP and the insured depository institution and is, therefore, a written arrangement or understanding.

(3) *Example 3.* An NGEP sends a letter to an insured depository institution requesting that the institution provide a $15,000 grant to the NGEP. The insured depository institution responds in writing and agrees to provide the grant in connection with its annual grant program. The exchange of letters constitutes a written arrangement or understanding.

(c) *Loan agreements that are not covered agreements.* A covered agreement does not include—

(1) Any individual loan that is secured by real estate; or

(2) Any specific contract or commitment for a loan or extension of credit to an individual, business, farm, or other entity, or group of such individuals or entities, if—

(i) The funds are loaned at rates that are not substantially below market rates; and

(ii) The loan application or other loan documentation does not indicate that the borrower intends to or is authorized to use the borrowed funds to make a loan or extension of credit to one or more third parties.

(d) *Examples concerning loan agreements*—(1) *Example 1.* An insured depository institution provides an organization with a $1 million loan that is documented in writing and is secured by real estate owned or to-be-acquired by the organization. The agreement is an individual mortgage loan and is exempt from coverage under paragraph (c)(1) of this section, regardless of the interest rate on the loan or whether the organization intends or is authorized to re-loan the funds to a third party.

(2) *Example 2.* An insured depository institution commits to provide a $500,000 line of credit to a small business that is documented by a written agreement. The loan is made at rates that are within the range of rates offered by the institution to similarly situated small businesses in the market and the loan documentation does not indicate that the small business intends or is authorized to re-lend the

borrowed funds. The agreement is exempt from coverage under paragraph (c)(2) of this section.

(3) *Example 3.* An insured depository institution offers small business loans that are guaranteed by the Small Business Administration (SBA). A small business obtains a $75,000 loan, documented in writing, from the institution under the institution's SBA loan program. The loan documentation does not indicate that the borrower intends or is authorized to re-lend the funds. Although the rate charged on the loan is well below that charged by the institution on commercial loans, the rate is within the range of rates that the institution would charge a similarly situated small business for a similar loan under the SBA loan program. Accordingly, the loan is not made at substantially below market rates and is exempt from coverage under paragraph (c)(2) of this section.

(4) *Example 4.* A bank holding company enters into a written agreement with a community development organization that provides that insured depository institutions owned by the bank holding company will make $250 million in small business loans in the community over the next 5 years. The written agreement is not a specific contract or commitment for a loan or an extension of credit and, thus, is not exempt from coverage under paragraph (c)(2) of this section. Each small business loan made by the insured depository institution pursuant to this general commitment would, however, be exempt from coverage if the loan is made at rates that are not substantially below market rates and the loan documentation does not indicate that the borrower intended or was authorized to re-lend the funds.

(e) *Agreements that include exempt loan agreements.* If an agreement includes a loan, extension of credit or loan commitment that, if documented separately, would be exempt under paragraph (c) of this section, the exempt loan, extension of credit or loan commitment may be excluded for purposes of determining whether the agreement is a covered agreement.

(f) *Determining annual value of agreements that lack schedule of disbursements.* For purposes of paragraph (a)(3) of this section, a multi-year agreement that does not include a schedule for the disbursement of payments, grants, loans or other consideration by the insured depository institution or affiliate, is considered to have a value in the first year of the agreement equal to all payments, grants, loans and other consideration to be provided at any time under the agreement.

§ 533.3 CRA communications.

(a) *Definition of CRA communication.* A CRA communication is any of the following—

(1) Any written or oral comment or testimony provided to a Federal banking agency concerning the adequacy of the performance under the CRA of the insured depository institution, any affiliated insured depository institution, or any CRA affiliate.

(2) Any written comment submitted to the insured depository institution that discusses the adequacy of the performance under the CRA of the institution and must be included in the institution's CRA public file.

(3) Any discussion or other contact with the insured depository institution or any affiliate about—

(i) Providing (or refraining from providing) written or oral comments or testimony to any Federal banking agency concerning the adequacy of the performance under the CRA of the insured depository institution, any affiliated insured depository institution, or any CRA affiliate;

(ii) Providing (or refraining from providing) written comments to the insured depository institution that concern the adequacy of the institution's performance under the CRA and must be included in the institution's CRA public file; or

(iii) The adequacy of the performance under the CRA of the insured depository institution, any affiliated insured depository institution, or any CRA affiliate.

(b) *Discussions or contacts that are not CRA communications*—(1) *Timing of contacts with a Federal banking agency.* An oral or written communication with a Federal banking agency is not a CRA communication if it occurred more than 3 years before the parties entered into the agreement.

Office of Thrift Supervision, Treasury § 533.3

(2) *Timing of contacts with insured depository institutions and affiliates.* A communication with an insured depository institution or affiliate is not a CRA communication if the communication occurred—

(i) More than 3 years before the parties entered into the agreement, in the case of any written communication;

(ii) More than 3 years before the parties entered into the agreement, in the case of any oral communication in which the NGEP discusses providing (or refraining from providing) comments or testimony to a Federal banking agency or written comments that must be included in the institution's CRA public file in connection with a request to, or agreement by, the institution or affiliate to take (or refrain from taking) any action that is in fulfillment of the CRA; or

(iii) More than 1 year before the parties entered into the agreement, in the case of any other oral communication not described in paragraph (b)(2)(ii).

(3) *Knowledge of communication by insured depository institution or affiliate.*
(i) A communication is only a CRA communication under paragraph (a) of this section if the insured depository institution or its affiliate has knowledge of the communication under paragraph (b)(3)(ii) or (b)(3)(iii) of this section.

(ii) *Communication with insured depository institution or affiliate.* An insured depository institution or affiliate has knowledge of a communication by the NGEP to the institution or its affiliate under this paragraph only if one of the following representatives of the insured depository institution or any affiliate has knowledge of the communication—

(A) An employee who approves, directs, authorizes, or negotiates the agreement with the NGEP; or

(B) An employee designated with responsibility for compliance with the CRA or executive officer if the employee or executive officer knows that the institution or affiliate is negotiating, intends to negotiate, or has been informed by the NGEP that it expects to request that the institution or affiliate negotiate an agreement with the NGEP.

(iii) *Other communications.* An insured depository institution or affiliate is deemed to have knowledge of—

(A) Any testimony provided to a Federal banking agency at a public meeting or hearing;

(B) Any comment submitted to a Federal banking agency that is conveyed in writing by the agency to the insured depository institution or affiliate; and

(C) Any written comment submitted to the insured depository institution that must be and is included in the institution's CRA public file.

(4) *Communication where NGEP has knowledge.* A NGEP has a CRA communication with an insured depository institution or affiliate only if any of the following individuals has knowledge of the communication—

(i) A director, employee, or member of the NGEP who approves, directs, authorizes, or negotiates the agreement with the insured depository institution or affiliate;

(ii) A person who functions as an executive officer of the NGEP and who knows that the NGEP is negotiating or intends to negotiate an agreement with the insured depository institution or affiliate; or

(iii) Where the NGEP is an individual, the NGEP.

(c) *Examples of CRA communications*—
(1) *Examples of actions that are CRA communications.* The following are examples of CRA communications. These examples are not exclusive and assume that the communication occurs within the relevant time period as described in paragraph (b)(1) or (b)(2) of this section and the appropriate representatives have knowledge of the communication as specified in paragraphs (b)(3) and (b)(4) of this section.

(i) *Example 1.* A NGEP files a written comment with a Federal banking agency that states than an insured depository institution successfully addresses the credit needs of its community. The written comment is in response to a general request from the agency for comments on an application of the insured depository institution to open a new branch and a copy of the comment is provided to the institution.

§ 533.3

(ii) *Example 2.* A NGEP meets with an executive officer of an insured depository institution and states that the institution must improve its CRA performance.

(iii) *Example 3.* A NGEP meets with an executive officer of an insured depository institution and states that the institution needs to make more mortgage loans in low- and moderate-income neighborhoods in its community.

(iv) *Example 4.* A bank holding company files an application with a Federal banking agency to acquire an insured depository institution. Two weeks later, the NGEP meets with an executive officer of the bank holding company to discuss the adequacy of the performance under the CRA of the target insured depository institution. The insured depository institution was an affiliate of the bank holding company at the time the NGEP met with the target institution. (See § 533.11(a) of this part.) Accordingly, the NGEP had a CRA communication with an affiliate of the bank holding company.

(2) *Examples of actions that are not CRA communications.* The following are examples of actions that are not by themselves CRA communications. These examples are not exclusive.

(i) *Example 1.* A NGEP provides to a Federal banking agency comments or testimony concerning an insured depository institution or affiliate in response to a direct request by the agency for comments or testimony from that NGEP. Direct requests for comments or testimony do not include a general invitation by a Federal banking agency for comments or testimony from the public in connection with a CRA performance evaluation of, or application for a deposit facility (as defined in section 803 of the CRA (12 U.S.C. 2902(3)) by, an insured depository institution or an application by a company to acquire an insured depository institution.

(ii) *Example 2.* A NGEP makes a statement concerning an insured depository institution or affiliate at a widely attended conference or seminar regarding a general topic. A public or private meeting, public hearing, or other meeting regarding one or more specific institutions, affiliates or transactions involving an application for a deposit facility is not considered a widely attended conference or seminar.

(iii) *Example 3.* A NGEP, such as a civil rights group, community group providing housing and other services in low- and moderate-income neighborhoods, veterans organization, community theater group, or youth organization, sends a fundraising letter to insured depository institutions and to other businesses in its community. The letter encourages all businesses in the community to meet their obligation to assist in making the local community a better place to live and work by supporting the fundraising efforts of the NGEP.

(iv) *Example 4.* A NGEP discusses with an insured depository institution or affiliate whether particular loans, services, investments, community development activities, or other activities are generally eligible for consideration by a Federal banking agency under the CRA. The NGEP and insured depository institution or affiliate do not discuss the adequacy of the CRA performance of the insured depository institution or affiliate.

(v) *Example 5.* A NGEP engaged in the sale or purchase of loans in the secondary market sends a general offering circular to financial institutions offering to sell or purchase a portfolio of loans. An insured depository institution that receives the offering circular discusses with the NGEP the types of loans included in the loan pool, whether such loans are generally eligible for consideration under the CRA, and which loans are made to borrowers in the institution's local community. The NGEP and insured depository institution do not discuss the adequacy of the institution's CRA performance.

(d) *Multiparty covered agreements.* (1) A NGEP that is a party to a covered agreement that involves multiple NGEPs is not required to comply with the requirements of this part if—

(i) The NGEP has not had a CRA communication; and

(ii) No representative of the NGEP identified in paragraph (b)(4) of this section has knowledge at the time of the agreement that another NGEP that is a party to the agreement has had a CRA communication.

Office of Thrift Supervision, Treasury § 533.5

(2) An insured depository institution or affiliate that is a party to a covered agreement that involves multiple insured depository institutions or affiliates is not required to comply with the requirements in §§ 533.6 and 533.7 if—

(i) No NGEP that is a party to the agreement has had a CRA communication concerning the insured depository institution or any affiliate; and

(ii) No representative of the insured depository institution or any affiliate identified in paragraph (b)(3) of this section has knowledge at the time of the agreement that an NGEP that is a party to the agreement has had a CRA communication concerning any other insured depository institution or affiliate that is a party to the agreement.

§ 533.4 Fulfillment of the CRA

(a) *List of factors that are in fulfillment of the CRA.* Fulfillment of the CRA, for purposes of this part, means the following list of factors—

(1) *Comments to a Federal banking agency or included in CRA public file.* Providing or refraining from providing written or oral comments or testimony to any Federal banking agency concerning the performance under the CRA of an insured depository institution or CRA affiliate that is a party to the agreement or an affiliate of a party to the agreement or written comments that are required to be included in the CRA public file of any such insured depository institution; or

(2) *Activities given favorable CRA consideration.* Performing any of the following activities if the activity is of the type that is likely to receive favorable consideration by a Federal banking agency in evaluating the performance under the CRA of the insured depository institution that is a party to the agreement or an affiliate of a party to the agreement—

(i) Home-purchase, home-improvement, small business, small farm, community development, and consumer lending, as described in § 563e.22 of this chapter, including loan purchases, loan commitments, and letters of credit;

(ii) Making investments, deposits, or grants, or acquiring membership shares, that have as their primary purpose community development, as described in § 563e.23 of this chapter;

(iii) Delivering retail banking services, as described in § 563.24(d) of this chapter;

(iv) Providing community development services, as described in § 563e.24(e) of this chapter;

(v) In the case of a wholesale or limited-purpose insured depository institution, community development lending, including originating and purchasing loans and making loan commitments and letters of credit, making qualified investments, or providing community development services, as described in § 563e.25(c) of this chapter;

(vi) In the case of a small insured depository institution, any lending or other activity described in § 563e.26(a) of this chapter; or

(vii) In the case of an insured depository institution that is evaluated on the basis of a strategic plan, any element of the strategic plan, as described in § 563e.27(f) of this chapter.

(b) *Agreements relating to activities of CRA affiliates.* An insured depository institution or affiliate that is a party to a covered agreement that concerns any activity described in paragraph (a) of this section of a CRA affiliate must, prior to the time the agreement is entered into, notify each NGEP that is a party to the agreement that the agreement concerns a CRA affiliate.

§ 533.5 Related agreements considered a single agreement.

The following rules must be applied in determining whether an agreement is a covered agreement under § 533.2 of this part.

(a) *Agreements entered into by same parties.* All written agreements to which an insured depository institution or an affiliate of the insured depository institution is a party shall be considered to be a single agreement if the agreements—

(1) Are entered into with the same NGEP;

(2) Were entered into within the same 12-month period; and

(3) Are each in fulfillment of the CRA.

(b) *Substantively related contracts.* All written contracts to which an insured depository institution or an affiliate of the insured depository institution is a party shall be considered to be a single

§ 533.6

agreement, without regard to whether the other parties to the contracts are the same or whether each such contract is in fulfillment of the CRA, if the contracts were negotiated in a coordinated fashion and a NGEP is a party to each contract.

§ 533.6 Disclosure of covered agreements.

(a) *Applicability date.* This section applies only to covered agreements entered into after November 12, 1999.

(b) *Disclosure of covered agreements to the public*—(1) *Disclosure required.* Each NGEP and each insured depository institution or affiliate that enters into a covered agreement must make a copy of the covered agreement available to any individual or entity upon request.

(2) *Nondisclosure of confidential and proprietary information permitted.* In responding to a request for a covered agreement from any individual or entity under paragraph (b)(1) of this section, a NGEP, insured depository institution, or affiliate may withhold from public disclosure confidential or proprietary information that the party believes the relevant supervisory agency could withhold from disclosure under the Freedom of Information Act (5 U.S.C. 552 *et seq.*) (FOIA).

(3) *Information that must be disclosed.* Notwithstanding paragraph (b)(2) of this section, a party must disclose any of the following information that is contained in a covered agreement—

(i) The names and addresses of the parties to the agreement;

(ii) The amount of any payments, fees, loans, or other consideration to be made or provided by any party to the agreement;

(iii) Any description of how the funds or other resources provided under the agreement are to be used;

(iv) The term of the agreement (if the agreement establishes a term); and

(v) Any other information that the relevant supervisory agency determines is not properly exempt from public disclosure.

(4) *Request for review of withheld information.* Any individual or entity may request that the relevant supervisory agency review whether any information in a covered agreement withheld by a party must be disclosed. Any requests for agency review of withheld information must be filed, and will be processed in accordance with, the relevant supervisory agency's rules concerning the availability of information (*see* part 505 of this chapter and the Department of Treasury's rules (31 CFR part 1)).

(5) *Duration of obligation.* The obligation to disclose a covered agreement to the public terminates 12 months after the end of the term of the agreement.

(6) *Reasonable copy and mailing fees.* Each NGEP and each insured depository institution or affiliate may charge an individual or entity that requests a copy of a covered agreement a reasonable fee not to exceed the cost of copying and mailing the agreement.

(7) *Use of CRA public file by insured depository institution or affiliate.* An insured depository institution and any affiliate of an insured depository institution may fulfill its obligation under this paragraph (b) by placing a copy of the covered agreement in the insured depository institution's CRA public file if the institution makes the agreement available in accordance with the procedures set forth in § 563e.43 of this chapter.

(c) *Disclosure by NGEPs of covered agreements to the relevant supervisory agency.* (1) Each NGEP that is a party to a covered agreement must provide the following within 30 days of receiving a request from the relevant supervisory agency—

(i) A complete copy of the agreement; and

(ii) In the event the NGEP proposes the withholding of any information contained in the agreement in accordance with paragraph (b)(2) of this section, a public version of the agreement that excludes such information and an explanation justifying the exclusions. Any public version must include the information described in paragraph (b)(3) of this section.

(2) The obligation to provide a covered agreement to the relevant supervisory agency terminates 12 months after the end of the term of the covered agreement.

(d) *Disclosure by insured depository institution or affiliate of covered agreements to the relevant supervisory agency*—(1) *In general.* Within 60 days of the end of

Office of Thrift Supervision, Treasury § 533.7

each calendar quarter, each insured depository institution and affiliate must provide each relevant supervisory agency with—

(i)(A) A complete copy of each covered agreement entered into by the insured depository institution or affiliate during the calendar quarter; and

(B) In the event the institution or affiliate proposes the withholding of any information contained in the agreement in accordance with paragraph (b)(2) of this section, a public version of the agreement that excludes such information (other than any information described in paragraph (b)(3) of this section) and an explanation justifying the exclusions; or

(ii) A list of all covered agreements entered into by the insured depository institution or affiliate during the calendar quarter that contains—

(A) The name and address of each insured depository institution or affiliate that is a party to the agreement;

(B) The name and address of each NGEP that is a party to the agreement;

(C) The date the agreement was entered into;

(D) The estimated total value of all payments, fees, loans and other consideration to be provided by the institution or any affiliate of the institution under the agreement; and

(E) The date the agreement terminates.

(2) *Prompt filing of covered agreements contained in list required.* (i) If an insured depository institution or affiliate files a list of the covered agreements entered into by the institution or affiliate pursuant to paragraph (d)(1)(ii) of this section, the institution or affiliate must provide any relevant supervisory agency a complete copy and public version of any covered agreement referenced in the list within 7 calendar days of receiving a request from the agency for a copy of the agreement.

(ii) The obligation of an insured depository institution or affiliate to provide a covered agreement to the relevant supervisory agency under this paragraph (d)(2) terminates 36 months after the end of the term of the covered agreement.

(3) *Joint filings.* In the event that 2 or more insured depository institutions or affiliates are parties to a covered agreement, the insured depository institution(s) and affiliate(s) may jointly file the documents required by this paragraph (d) of this section. Any joint filing must identify the insured depository institution(s) and affiliate(s) for whom the filings are being made.

§ 533.7 **Annual reports.**

(a) *Applicability date.* This section applies only to covered agreements entered into on or after May 12, 2000.

(b) *Annual report required.* Each NGEP and each insured depository institution or affiliate that is a party to a covered agreement must file an annual report with each relevant supervisory agency concerning the disbursement, receipt, and uses of funds or other resources under the covered agreement.

(c) *Duration of reporting requirement—* (1) *NGEPs.* A NGEP must file an annual report for a covered agreement for any fiscal year in which the NGEP receives or uses funds or other resources under the agreement.

(2) *Insured depository institutions and affiliates.* An insured depository institution or affiliate must file an annual report for a covered agreement for any fiscal year in which the institution or affiliate—

(i) Provides or receives any payments, fees, or loans under the covered agreement that must be reported under paragraphs (e)(1)(iii) and (e)(1)(iv) of this section; or

(ii) Has data to report on loans, investments, and services provided by a party to the covered agreement under the covered agreement under paragraph (e)(1)(vi) of this section.

(d) *Annual reports filed by NGEP*—(1) *Contents of report.* The annual report filed by a NGEP under this section must include the following—

(i) The name and mailing address of the NGEP filing the report;

(ii) Information sufficient to identify the covered agreement for which the annual report is being filed, such as by providing the names of the parties to the agreement and the date the agreement was entered into or by providing a copy of the agreement;

(iii) The amount of funds or resources received under the covered agreement during the fiscal year; and

§ 533.7

(iv) A detailed, itemized list of how the funds or resources received by the NGEP under the covered agreement were used during the fiscal year, including the total amount used for—
(A) Compensation of officers, directors, and employees;
(B) Administrative expenses;
(C) Travel expenses;
(D) Entertainment expenses;
(E) Payment of consulting and professional fees; and
(F) Other expenses and uses (specify expense or use).

(2) *More detailed reporting of uses of funds or resources permitted*—(i) *In general.* If a NGEP allocated and used funds received under a covered agreement for a specific purpose, the NGEP may fulfill the requirements of paragraph (d)(1)(iv) of this section with respect to such funds by providing—
(A) A brief description of each specific purpose for which the funds or other resources were used; and
(B) The amount of funds or resources used during the fiscal year for each specific purpose.
(ii) *Specific purpose defined.* A NGEP allocates and uses funds for a specific purpose if the NGEP receives and uses the funds for a purpose that is more specific and limited than the categories listed in paragraph (d)(1)(iv) of this section.

(3) *Use of other reports.* The annual report filed by a NGEP may consist of or incorporate a report prepared for any other purpose, such as the Internal Revenue Service Return of Organization Exempt From Income Tax on Form 990, or any other Internal Revenue Service form, state tax form, report to members or shareholders, audited or unaudited financial statements, audit report, or other report, so long as the annual report filed by the NGEP contains all of the information required by this paragraph (d).

(4) *Consolidated reports permitted.* A NGEP that is a party to 2 or more covered agreements may file with each relevant supervisory agency a single consolidated annual report covering all the covered agreements. Any consolidated report must contain all the information required by this paragraph (d). The information reported under paragraphs (d)(1)(iv) and (d)(2) of this section may be reported on an aggregate basis for all covered agreements.

(5) *Examples of annual report requirements for NGEPs*—(i) *Example 1.* A NGEP receives an unrestricted grant of $15,000 under a covered agreement, includes the funds in its general operating budget and uses the funds during its fiscal year. The NGEP's annual report for the fiscal year must provide the name and mailing address of the NGEP, information sufficient to identify the covered agreement, and state that the NGEP received $15,000 during the fiscal year. The report must also indicate the total expenditures made by the NGEP during the fiscal year for compensation, administrative expenses, travel expenses, entertainment expenses, consulting and professional fees, and other expenses and uses. The NGEP's annual report may provide this information by submitting an Internal Revenue Service Form 990 that includes the required information. If the Internal Revenue Service Form does not include information for all of the required categories listed in this part, the NGEP must report the total expenditures in the remaining categories either by providing that information directly or by providing another form or report that includes the required information.

(ii) *Example 2.* An organization receives $15,000 from an insured depository institution under a covered agreement and allocates and uses the $15,000 during the fiscal year to purchase computer equipment to support its functions. The organization's annual report must include the name and address of the organization, information sufficient to identify the agreement, and a statement that the organization received $15,000 during the year. In addition, since the organization allocated and used the funds for a specific purpose that is more narrow and limited than the categories of expenses included in the detailed, itemized list of expenses, the organization would have the option of providing either the total amount it used during the year for each category of expenses included in paragraph (d)(1)(iv) of this section, or a statement that it used the $15,000 to purchase computer equipment and a brief description of the equipment purchased.

Office of Thrift Supervision, Treasury § 533.7

(iii) *Example 3.* A community group receives $50,000 from an insured depository institution under a covered agreement. During its fiscal year, the community group specifically allocates and uses $5,000 of the funds to pay for a particular business trip and uses the remaining $45,000 for general operating expenses. The group's annual report for the fiscal year must include the name and address of the group, information sufficient to identify the agreement, and a statement that the group received $50,000. Because the group did not allocate and use all of the funds for a specific purpose, the group's annual report must provide the total amount of funds it used during the year for each category of expenses included in paragraph (d)(1)(iv) of this section. The group's annual report also could state that it used $5,000 for a particular business trip and include a brief description of the trip.

(iv) *Example 4.* A community development organization is a party to two separate covered agreements with two unaffiliated insured depository institutions. Under each agreement, the organization receives $15,000 during its fiscal year and uses the funds to support its activities during that year. If the organization elects to file a consolidated annual report, the consolidated report must identify the organization and the two covered agreements, state that the organization received $15,000 during the fiscal year under each agreement, and provide the total amount that the organization used during the year for each category of expenses included in paragraph (d)(1)(iv) of this section.

(e) *Annual report filed by insured depository institution or affiliate*—(1) *General.* The annual report filed by an insured depository institution or affiliate must include the following—

(i) The name and principal place of business of the insured depository institution or affiliate filing the report;

(ii) Information sufficient to identify the covered agreement for which the annual report is being filed, such as by providing the names of the parties to the agreement and the date the agreement was entered into or by providing a copy of the agreement;

(iii) The aggregate amount of payments, aggregate amount of fees, and aggregate amount of loans provided by the insured depository institution or affiliate under the covered agreement to any other party to the agreement during the fiscal year;

(iv) The aggregate amount of payments, aggregate amount of fees, and aggregate amount of loans received by the insured depository institution or affiliate under the covered agreement from any other party to the agreement during the fiscal year;

(v) A general description of the terms and conditions of any payments, fees, or loans reported under paragraphs (e)(1)(iii) and (e)(1)(iv) of this section, or, in the event such terms and conditions are set forth—

(A) In the covered agreement, a statement identifying the covered agreement and the date the agreement (or a list identifying the agreement) was filed with the relevant supervisory agency; or

(B) In a previous annual report filed by the insured depository institution or affiliate, a statement identifying the date the report was filed with the relevant supervisory agency; and

(vi) The aggregate amount and number of loans, aggregate amount and number of investments, and aggregate amount of services provided under the covered agreement to any individual or entity not a party to the agreement—

(A) By the insured depository institution or affiliate during its fiscal year; and

(B) By any other party to the agreement, unless such information is not known to the insured depository institution or affiliate filing the report or such information is or will be contained in the annual report filed by another party under this section.

(2) *Consolidated reports permitted*—(i) *Party to multiple agreements.* An insured depository institution or affiliate that is a party to 2 or more covered agreements may file a single consolidated annual report with each relevant supervisory agency concerning all the covered agreements.

(ii) *Affiliated entities party to the same agreement.* An insured depository institution and its affiliates that are parties to the same covered agreement

§ 533.8

may file a single consolidated annual report relating to the agreement with each relevant supervisory agency for the covered agreement.

(iii) *Content of report.* Any consolidated annual report must contain all the information required by this paragraph (e). The amounts and data required to be reported under paragraphs (e)(1)(iv) and (e)(1)(vi) of this section may be reported on an aggregate basis for all covered agreements.

(f) *Time and place of filing*—(1) *General.* Each party must file its annual report with each relevant supervisory agency for the covered agreement no later than six months following the end of the fiscal year covered by the report.

(2) *Alternative method of fulfilling annual reporting requirement for a NGEP.* (i) A NGEP may fulfill the filing requirements of this section by providing the following materials to an insured depository institution or affiliate that is a party to the agreement no later than six months following the end of the NGEP's fiscal year—

(A) A copy of the NGEP's annual report required under paragraph (d) of this section for the fiscal year; and

(B) Written instructions that the insured depository institution or affiliate promptly forward the annual report to the relevant supervisory agency or agencies on behalf of the NGEP.

(ii) An insured depository institution or affiliate that receives an annual report from a NGEP pursuant to paragraph (f)(2)(i) of this section must file the report with the relevant supervisory agency or agencies on behalf of the NGEP within 30 days.

§ 533.8 Release of information under FOIA.

OTS will make covered agreements and annual reports available to the public in accordance with the Freedom of Information Act (5 U.S.C. 552 *et seq.*), OTS's rules (part 505 of this chapter), and the Department of Treasury's rules (31 CFR part 1). A party to a covered agreement may request confidential treatment of proprietary and confidential information in a covered agreement or an annual report under those procedures.

§ 533.9 Compliance provisions.

(a) *Willful failure to comply with disclosure and reporting obligations.* (1) If OTS determines that a NGEP has willfully failed to comply in a material way with §§ 533.6 or 533.7 of this part, OTS will notify the NGEP in writing of that determination and provide the NGEP a period of 90 days (or such longer period as OTS finds to be reasonable under the circumstances) to comply.

(2) If the NGEP does not comply within the time period established by OTS, the agreement shall thereafter be unenforceable by that NGEP by operation of section 48 of the Federal Deposit Insurance Act (12 U.S.C. 1831y).

(3) OTS may assist any insured depository institution or affiliate that is a party to a covered agreement that is unenforceable by a NGEP by operation of section 48 of the Federal Deposit Insurance Act (12 U.S.C. 1831y) in identifying a successor to assume the NGEP's responsibilities under the agreement.

(b) *Diversion of funds.* If a court or other body of competent jurisdiction determines that funds or resources received under a covered agreement have been diverted contrary to the purposes of the covered agreement for an individual's personal financial gain, OTS may take either or both of the following actions—

(1) Order the individual to disgorge the diverted funds or resources received under the agreement;

(2) Prohibit the individual from being a party to any covered agreement for a period not to exceed 10 years.

(c) *Notice and opportunity to respond.* Before making a determination under paragraph (a)(1) of this section, or taking any action under paragraph (b) of this section, OTS will provide written notice and an opportunity to present information to OTS concerning any relevant facts or circumstances relating to the matter.

(d) *Inadvertent or de minimis errors.* Inadvertent or de minimis errors in annual reports or other documents filed with OTS under §§ 533.6 or 533.7 of this part will not subject the reporting party to any penalty.

(e) *Enforcement of provisions in covered agreements.* No provision of this part shall be construed as authorizing OTS

Office of Thrift Supervision, Treasury § 533.11

to enforce the provisions of any covered agreement.

§ 533.10 Transition provisions.

(a) *Disclosure of covered agreements entered into before the effective date of this part.* The following disclosure requirements apply to covered agreements that were entered into after November 12, 1999, and that terminated before April 1, 2001.

(1) *Disclosure to the public.* Each NGEP and each insured depository institution or affiliate that was a party to the agreement must make the agreement available to the public under § 533.6 of this part until at least April 1, 2002.

(2) *Disclosure to the relevant supervisory agency.* (i) Each NGEP that was a party to the agreement must make the agreement available to the relevant supervisory agency under § 533.6 of this part until at least April 1, 2002.

(ii) Each insured depository institution or affiliate that was a party to the agreement must, by June 30, 2001, provide each relevant supervisory agency either—

(A) A copy of the agreement under § 533.6(d)(1)(i) of this part; or

(B) The information described in § 533.6(d)(1)(ii) of this part for each agreement.

(b) *Filing of annual reports that relate to fiscal years ending on or before December 31, 2000.* In the event that a NGEP, insured depository institution or affiliate has any information to report under § 533.7 of this part for a fiscal that ends on or before December 31, 2000, and that concerns a covered agreement entered into between May 12, 2000, and December 31, 2000, the annual report for that fiscal year must be provided, no later than June 30, 2001, to—

(1) Each relevant supervisory agency; or

(2) In the case of a NGEP, to an insured depository institution or affiliate that is a party to the agreement in accordance with § 533.7(f)(2) of this part.

§ 533.11 Other definitions and rules of construction used in this part.

(a) *Affiliate. Affiliate* means—

(1) Any company that controls, is controlled by, or is under common control with another company; and

(2) For the purpose of determining whether an agreement is a covered agreement under § 533.2, an *affiliate* includes any company that would be under common control or merged with another company on consummation of any transaction pending before a Federal banking agency at the time—

(i) The parties enter into the agreement; and

(ii) The NGEP that is a party to the agreement makes a CRA communication, as described in § 533.3 of this part.

(b) *Control. Control* is defined in section 2(a) of the Bank Holding Company Act (12 U.S.C. 1841(a)).

(c) *CRA affiliate.* A *CRA affiliate* of an insured depository institution is any company that is an affiliate of an insured depository institution to the extent, and only to the extent, that the activities of the affiliate were considered by the appropriate Federal banking agency when evaluating the CRA performance of the institution at its most recent CRA examination prior to the agreement. An insured depository institution or affiliate also may designate any company as a CRA affiliate at any time prior to the time a covered agreement is entered into by informing the NGEP that is a party to the agreement of such designation.

(d) *CRA public file. CRA public file* means the public file maintained by an insured depository institution and described in § 563.43 of this chapter.

(e) *Executive officer.* The term *executive officer* has the same meaning as in § 215.2(e)(1) of the Board of Governors of the Federal Reserve's Regulation O (12 CFR 215.2(e)(1)). In applying this definition under this part, the term *savings association* shall be used in place of the term *bank*.

(f) *Federal banking agency; appropriate Federal banking agency.* The terms *Federal banking agency* and *appropriate Federal banking agency* have the same meanings as in section 3 of the Federal Deposit Insurance Act (12 U.S.C. 1813).

(g) *Fiscal year.* (1) The fiscal year for a NGEP that does not have a fiscal year shall be the calendar year.

(2) Any NGEP, insured depository institution, or affiliate that has a fiscal

year may elect to have the calendar year be its fiscal year for purposes of this part.

(h) *Insured depository institution.* Insured depository institution has the same meaning as in section 3 of the Federal Deposit Insurance Act (12 U.S.C. 1813).

(i) *Nongovernmental entity or person or NGEP*—(1) *General.* A *nongovernmental entity or person or NGEP* is any partnership, association, trust, joint venture, joint stock company, corporation, limited liability corporation, company, firm, society, other organization, or individual.

(2) *Exclusions.* A nongovernmental entity or person does not include—

(i) The United States government, a state government, a unit of local government (including a county, city, town, township, parish, village, or other general-purpose subdivision of a state) or an Indian tribe or tribal organization established under Federal, state or Indian tribal law (including the Department of Hawaiian Home Lands), or a department, agency, or instrumentality of any such entity;

(ii) A federally-chartered public corporation that receives Federal funds appropriated specifically for that corporation;

(iii) An insured depository institution or affiliate of an insured depository institution; or

(iv) An officer, director, employee, or representative (acting in his or her capacity as an officer, director, employee, or representative) of an entity listed in paragraphs (i)(2)(i), (i)(2)(ii), or (i)(2)(iii) of this section.

(j) *Party.* The term *party* with respect to a covered agreement means each NGEP and each insured depository institution or affiliate that entered into the agreement.

(k) *Relevant supervisory agency.* The *relevant supervisory agency* for a covered agreement means the appropriate Federal banking agency for—

(1) Each insured depository institution (or subsidiary thereof) that is a party to the covered agreement;

(2) Each insured depository institution (or subsidiary thereof) or CRA affiliate that makes payments or loans or provides services that are subject to the covered agreement; and

(3) Any company (other than an insured depository institution or subsidiary thereof) that is a party to the covered agreement.

(l) *Term of agreement.* An agreement that does not have a fixed termination date is considered to terminate on the last date on which any party to the agreement makes any payment or provides any loan or other resources under the agreement, unless the relevant supervisory agency for the agreement otherwise notifies each party in writing.

PART 535—UNFAIR OR DECEPTIVE ACTS OR PRACTICES

Subpart A—General Provisions

Sec.
535.1 Authority, purpose, and scope.

Subpart B—Consumer Credit Practices

535.11 Definitions.
535.12 Unfair credit contract provisions.
535.13 Unfair or deceptive cosigner practices.
535.14 Unfair late charges.
APPENDIX TO PART 535—OFFICIAL STAFF COMMENTARY

AUTHORITY: 12 U.S.C. 1462a, 1463, 1464; 15 U.S.C. 57a.

SOURCE: 75 FR 23566, May 4, 2010, unless otherwise noted.

Subpart A—General Provisions

§ 535.1 **Authority, purpose and scope.**

(a) *Authority.* This part is issued by OTS under section 18(f) of the Federal Trade Commission Act, 15 U.S.C. 57a(f) (section 202(a) of the Magnuson-Moss Warranty—Federal Trade Commission Improvement Act, Pub. L. 93–637) and the Home Owners' Loan Act, 12 U.S.C. 1461 et seq.

(b) *Purpose.* The purpose of this part is to prohibit unfair or deceptive acts or practices in violation of section 5(a)(1) of the Federal Trade Commission Act, 15 U.S.C. 45(a)(1). Subpart B defines and contains requirements prescribed for the purpose of preventing specific unfair or deceptive acts or practices of savings associations. The prohibitions in subpart B do not limit OTS's authority to enforce the FTC Act with respect to any other unfair or deceptive acts or practices. The purpose of this part is also to prohibit unsafe and unsound practices and protect consumers under the Home Owners' Loan Act, 12 U.S.C. 1461 *et seq.*

(c) *Scope.* This part applies to savings associations and subsidiaries owned in whole or in part by a savings association ("you").

Subpart B—Consumer Credit Practices

§ 535.11 Definitions.

For purposes of this subpart, the following definitions apply:

(a) *Consumer* means a natural person who seeks or acquires goods, services, or money for personal, family, or household purposes, other than for the purchase of real property, and who applies for or is extended *consumer credit.*

(b) *Consumer credit* means credit extended to a natural person for personal, family, or household purposes. It includes consumer loans; educational loans; unsecured loans for real property alteration, repair or improvement, or for the equipping of real property; overdraft loans; and credit cards. It also includes loans secured by liens on real estate and chattel liens secured by mobile homes and leases of personal property to consumers that may be considered the functional equivalent of loans on personal security but only if you rely substantially upon other factors, such as the general credit standing of the borrower, guaranties, or security other than the real estate or mobile home, as the primary security for the loan.

(c) *Earnings* means compensation paid or payable to an individual or for the individual's account for personal services rendered or to be rendered by the individual, whether denominated as wages, salary, commission, bonus, or otherwise, including periodic payments pursuant to a pension, retirement, or disability program.

(d) *Obligation* means an agreement between you and a consumer.

(e) *Person* means an individual, corporation, or other business organization.

§ 535.12 Unfair credit contract provisions.

It is an unfair act or practice for you, directly or indirectly, to enter into a consumer credit obligation that constitutes or contains, or to enforce in a consumer credit obligation you purchased, any of the following provisions:

(a) *Confession of judgment.* A cognovit or confession of judgment (for purposes other than executory process in the State of Louisiana), warrant of attorney, or other waiver of the right to notice and the opportunity to be heard in the event of suit or process thereon.

(b) *Waiver of exemption.* An executory waiver or a limitation of exemption from attachment, execution, or other process on real or personal property held, owned by, or due to the consumer, unless the waiver applies solely to property subject to a security interest executed in connection with the obligation.

(c) *Assignment of wages.* An assignment of wages or other earnings unless:

(1) The assignment by its terms is revocable at the will of the debtor;

(2) The assignment is a payroll deduction plan or preauthorized payment plan, commencing at the time of the transaction, in which the consumer authorizes a series of wage deductions as a method of making each payment; or

(3) The assignment applies only to wages or other earnings already earned at the time of the assignment.

(d) *Security interest in household goods.* A nonpossessory security interest in household goods other than a purchase-money security interest. For purposes of this paragraph, *household goods:*

(1) Means clothing, furniture, appliances, linens, china, crockery, kitchenware, and personal effects of the consumer and the consumer's dependents.

(2) Does not include:

(i) Works of art;

(ii) Electronic entertainment equipment (except one television and one radio);

(iii) Antiques (any item over one hundred years of age, including such items that have been repaired or renovated without changing their original form or character); or

(iv) Jewelry (other than wedding rings).

§ 535.13 Unfair or deceptive cosigner practices.

(a) *Prohibited deception.* It is a deceptive act or practice for you, directly or indirectly in connection with the extension of credit to consumers, to misrepresent the nature or extent of cosigner liability to any person.

(b) *Prohibited unfairness.* It is an unfair act or practice for you, directly or indirectly in connection with the extension of credit to consumers, to obligate a cosigner unless the cosigner is informed, before becoming obligated, of the nature of the cosigner's liability.

(c) *Disclosure requirement*—(1) *Disclosure statement.* A clear and conspicuous statement must be given in writing to the cosigner before becoming obligated. In the case of open-end credit, the disclosure statement must be given to the cosigner before the time that the cosigner becomes obligated for any fees or transactions on the account. The disclosure statement must contain the following statement or one that is substantially similar:

NOTICE OF COSIGNER

You are being asked to guarantee this debt. Think carefully before you do. If the borrower doesn't pay the debt, you will have to. Be sure you can afford to pay if you have to, and that you want to accept this responsibility.

You may have to pay up to the full amount of the debt if the borrower does not pay. You may also have to pay late fees or collection costs, which increase this amount.

The creditor can collect this debt from you without first trying to collect from the borrower. The creditor can use the same collection methods against you that can be used against the borrower, such as suing you, garnishing your wages, etc. If this debt is ever in default, that fact may become a part of your credit record.

(2) *Compliance.* Compliance with paragraph (d)(1) of this section constitutes compliance with the consumer disclosure requirement in paragraph (b) of this section.

(3) *Additional content limitations.* If the notice is a separate document, nothing other than the following items may appear with the notice:

(i) Your name and address;

(ii) An identification of the debt to be cosigned (*e.g.*, a loan identification number);

(iii) The date (of the transaction); and

(iv) The statement, "This notice is not the contract that makes you liable for the debt."

(d) *Cosigner defined.* (1) *Cosigner* means a natural person who assumes liability for the obligation of a consumer without receiving goods, services, or money in return for the obligation, or, in the case of an open-end credit obligation, without receiving the contractual right to obtain extensions of credit under the account.

(2) *Cosigner* includes any person whose signature is requested as a condition to granting credit to a consumer, or as a condition for forbearance on collection of a consumer's obligation that is in default. The term does not include a spouse or other person whose signature is required on a credit obligation to perfect a security interest pursuant to state law.

(3) A person who meets the definition in this paragraph is a *cosigner*, whether or not the person is designated as such on a credit obligation.

§ 535.14 Unfair late charges.

(a) *Prohibition.* In connection with collecting a debt arising out of an extension of credit to a consumer, it is an unfair act or practice for you, directly or indirectly, to levy or collect any delinquency charge on a payment, when the only delinquency is attributable to late fees or ydelinquency charges assessed on earlier installments and the payment is otherwise a full payment for the applicable period and is paid on its due date or within an applicable grace period.

(b) *Collecting a debt defined*—*Collecting a debt* means, for the purposes of this section, any activity, other than the use of judicial process, that is intended to bring about or does bring about repayment of all or part of money due (or alleged to be due) from a consumer.

APPENDIX TO PART 535—OFFICIAL STAFF COMMENTARY

SUBPART A—GENERAL PROVISIONS

Section 535.1 Authority, Purpose, and Scope.

1(c) Scope

1. *Penalties for noncompliance.* Administrative enforcement of the rule for savings associations may involve actions under section 8 of the Federal Deposit Insurance Act (12 U.S.C. 1818), including cease-and-desist orders requiring that actions be taken to remedy violations and civil money penalties.

2. *Application to subsidiaries.* The term "savings association" as used in this Appendix also includes subsidiaries owned in whole or in part by a savings association.

PART 536—CONSUMER PROTECTION IN SALES OF INSURANCE

Sec.
536.10 Purpose and scope.
536.20 Definitions.
536.30 Prohibited practices.
536.40 What you must disclose.
536.50 Where insurance activities may take place.
536.60 Qualification and licensing requirements for insurance sales personnel.

APPENDIX A TO PART 536—CONSUMER GRIEVANCE PROCESS.

AUTHORITY: 12 U.S.C. 1462a, 1463, 1464, 1467a, and 1831x.

SOURCE: 65 FR 75845, Dec. 4, 2000, unless otherwise noted.

§ 536.10 Purpose and scope.

(a) *General rule.* This part establishes consumer protections in connection with retail sales practices, solicitations, advertising, or offers of any insurance product or annuity to a consumer by:

(1) Any savings association; or

(2) Any other person that is engaged in such activities at an office of a savings association or on behalf of a savings association.

(b) *Application to operating subsidiaries.* For purposes of § 559.3(h) of this chapter, an operating subsidiary is subject to this part only to the extent that it sells, solicits, advertises, or offers insurance products or annuities at an office of a savings association or on behalf of a savings association.

§ 536.20 Definitions.

As used in this part:

Affiliate means a company that controls, is controlled by, or is under common control with another company.

Company means any corporation, partnership, business trust, association or similar organization, or any other trust (unless by its terms the trust must terminate within twenty-five years or not later than twenty-one years and ten months after the death of individuals living on the effective date of the trust). It does not include any corporation the majority of the shares of which are owned by the United States or by any State, or a qualified family partnership, as defined in section 2(o)(10) of the Bank Holding Company Act of 1956, as amended (12 U.S.C. 1841(o)(10)).

Consumer means an individual who purchases, applies to purchase, or is solicited to purchase from a covered person insurance products or annuities primarily for personal, family, or household purposes.

Control of a company has the same meaning as in section 3(w)(5) of the Federal Deposit Insurance Act (12 U.S.C. 1813(w)(5)).

Domestic violence means the occurrence of one or more of the following acts by a current or former family member, household member, intimate partner, or caretaker:

(1) Attempting to cause or causing or threatening another person physical harm, severe emotional distress, psychological trauma, rape, or sexual assault;

(2) Engaging in a course of conduct or repeatedly committing acts toward another person, including following the person without proper authority, under circumstances that place the person in reasonable fear of bodily injury or physical harm;

(3) Subjecting another person to false imprisonment; or

(4) Attempting to cause or causing damage to property so as to intimidate or attempt to control the behavior of another person.

Electronic media includes any means for transmitting messages electronically between a covered person and a consumer in a format that allows visual text to be displayed on equipment,

§ 536.30

for example, a personal computer monitor.

Office means the premises of a savings association where retail deposits are accepted from the public.

Subsidiary has the same meaning as in section 3(w)(4) of the Federal Deposit Insurance Act (12 U.S.C. 1813(w)(4)).

You means:

(1) A savings association, as defined in § 561.43 of this chapter; or

(2) Any other person only when the person sells, solicits, advertises, or offers an insurance product or annuity to a consumer at an office of a savings association, or on behalf of a savings association. For purposes of this definition, activities on behalf of a savings association include activities where a person, whether at an office of the savings association or at another location, sells, solicits, advertises, or offers an insurance product or annuity and at least one of the following applies:

(i) The person represents to a consumer that the sale, solicitation, advertisement, or offer of any insurance product or annuity is by or on behalf of the savings association;

(ii) The savings association refers a consumer to a seller of insurance products and annuities and the savings association has a contractual arrangement to receive commissions or fees derived from a sale of an insurance product or annuity resulting from that referral; or

(iii) Documents evidencing the sale, solicitation, advertising, or offer of an insurance product or annuity identify or refer to the savings association.

§ 536.30 Prohibited practices.

(a) *Anticoercion and antitying rules.* You may not engage in any practice that would lead a consumer to believe that an extension of credit, in violation of section 5(q) of the Home Owners' Loan Act (12 U.S.C. 1464(q)), is conditional upon either:

(1) The purchase of an insurance product or annuity from a savings association or any of its affiliates; or

(2) An agreement by the consumer not to obtain, or a prohibition on the consumer from obtaining, an insurance product or annuity from an unaffiliated entity.

(b) *Prohibition on misrepresentations generally.* You may not engage in any practice or use any advertisement at any office of, or on behalf of, a savings association or a subsidiary of a savings association that could mislead any person or otherwise cause a reasonable person to reach an erroneous belief with respect to:

(1) The fact that an insurance product or annuity you or any subsidiary of a savings association sell or offer for sale is not backed by the Federal government or a savings association, or the fact that the insurance product or annuity is not insured by the Federal Deposit Insurance Corporation;

(2) In the case of an insurance product or annuity that involves investment risk, the fact that there is an investment risk, including the potential that principal may be lost and that the product may decline in value; or

(3) In the case of a savings association or subsidiary of a savings association at which insurance products or annuities are sold or offered for sale, the fact that:

(i) The approval of an extension of credit to a consumer by the savings association or subsidiary may not be conditioned on the purchase of an insurance product or annuity by the consumer from the savings association or a subsidiary of a savings association; and

(ii) The consumer is free to purchase the insurance product or annuity from another source.

(c) *Prohibition on domestic violence discrimination.* You may not sell or offer for sale, as principal, agent, or broker, any life or health insurance product if the status of the applicant or insured as a victim of domestic violence or as a provider of services to victims of domestic violence is considered as a criterion in any decision with regard to insurance underwriting, pricing, renewal, or scope of coverage of such product, or with regard to the payment of insurance claims on such product, except as required or expressly permitted under State law.

Office of Thrift Supervision, Treasury § 536.40

§ 536.40 What you must disclose.

(a) *Insurance disclosures.* In connection with the initial purchase of an insurance product or annuity by a consumer from you, you must disclose to the consumer, except to the extent the disclosure would not be accurate, that:

(1) The insurance product or annuity is not a deposit or other obligation of, or guaranteed by, a savings association or an affiliate of a savings association;

(2) The insurance product or annuity is not insured by the Federal Deposit Insurance Corporation (FDIC) or any other agency of the United States, a savings association, or (if applicable) an affiliate of a savings association; and

(3) In the case of an insurance product or annuity that involves an investment risk, there is investment risk associated with the product, including the possible loss of value.

(b) *Credit disclosures.* In the case of an application for credit in connection with which an insurance product or annuity is solicited, offered, or sold, you must disclose that a savings association may not condition an extension of credit on either:

(1) The consumer's purchase of an insurance product or annuity from the savings association or any of its affiliates; or

(2) The consumer's agreement not to obtain, or a prohibition on the consumer from obtaining, an insurance product or annuity from an unaffiliated entity.

(c) *Timing and method of disclosures—*
(1) *In general.* The disclosures required by paragraph (a) of this section must be provided orally and in writing before the completion of the initial sale of an insurance product or annuity to a consumer. The disclosure required by paragraph (b) of this section must be made orally and in writing at the time the consumer applies for an extension of credit in connection with which an insurance product or annuity is solicited, offered, or sold.

(2) *Exception for transactions by mail.* If you conduct an insurance product or annuity sale by mail, you are not required to make the oral disclosures required by paragraph (a) of this section. If you take an application for credit by mail, you are not required to make the oral disclosure required by paragraph (b) of this section.

(3) *Exception for transactions by telephone.* If a sale of an insurance product or annuity is conducted by telephone, you may provide the written disclosures required by paragraph (a) of this section by mail within 3 business days beginning on the first business day after the sale, solicitation, or offer, excluding Sundays and the legal public holidays specified in 5 U.S.C. 6103(a). If you take an application for credit by telephone, you may provide the written disclosure required by paragraph (b) of this section by mail, provided you mail it to the consumer within three days beginning the first business day after the application is taken, excluding Sundays and the legal public holidays specified in 5 U.S.C. 6103(a).

(4) *Electronic form of disclosures.* (i) Subject to the requirements of section 101(c) of the Electronic Signatures in Global and National Commerce Act (12 U.S.C. 7001(c)), you may provide the written disclosures required by paragraph (a) and (b) of this section through electronic media instead of on paper, if the consumer affirmatively consents to receiving the disclosures electronically and if the disclosures are provided in a format that the consumer may retain or obtain later, for example, by printing or storing electronically (such as by downloading).

(ii) You are not required to provide orally any disclosures required by paragraphs (a) or (b) of this section that you provide by electronic media.

(5) *Disclosures must be readily understandable.* The disclosures provided shall be conspicuous, simple, direct, readily understandable, and designed to call attention to the nature and significance of the information provided. For instance, you may use the following disclosures in visual media, such as television broadcasting, ATM screens, billboards, signs, posters and written advertisements and promotional materials, as appropriate and consistent with paragraphs (a) and (b) of this section:

- NOT A DEPOSIT
- NOT FDIC-INSURED
- NOT INSURED BY ANY FEDERAL GOVERNMENT AGENCY

§ 536.50

- NOT GUARANTEED BY THE SAVINGS ASSOCIATION
- MAY GO DOWN IN VALUE

(6) *Disclosures must be meaningful.* (i) You must provide the disclosures required by paragraphs (a) and (b) of this section in a meaningful form. Examples of the types of methods that could call attention to the nature and significance of the information provided include:

(A) A plain-language heading to call attention to the disclosures;

(B) A typeface and type size that are easy to read;

(C) Wide margins and ample line spacing;

(D) Boldface or italics for key words; and

(E) Distinctive type size, style, and graphic devices, such as shading or sidebars, when the disclosures are combined with other information.

(ii) You have not provided the disclosures in a meaningful form if you merely state to the consumer that the required disclosures are available in printed material, but do not provide the printed material when required and do not orally disclose the information to the consumer when required.

(iii) With respect to those disclosures made through electronic media for which paper or oral disclosures are not required, the disclosures are not meaningfully provided if the consumer may bypass the visual text of the disclosures before purchasing an insurance product or annuity.

(7) *Consumer acknowledgment.* You must obtain from the consumer, at the time a consumer receives the disclosures required under paragraphs (a) or (b) of this section, or at the time of the initial purchase by the consumer of an insurance product or annuity, a written acknowledgment by the consumer that the consumer received the disclosures. You may permit a consumer to acknowledge receipt of the disclosures electronically or in paper form. If the disclosures required under paragraphs (a) or (b) of this section are provided in connection with a transaction that is conducted by telephone, you must:

(i) Obtain an oral acknowledgment of receipt of the disclosures and maintain sufficient documentation to show that the acknowledgment was given; and

(ii) Make reasonable efforts to obtain a written acknowledgment from the consumer.

(d) *Advertisements and other promotional material for insurance products or annuities.* The disclosures described in paragraph (a) of this section are required in advertisements and promotional material for insurance products or annuities unless the advertisements and promotional material are of a general nature describing or listing the services or products offered by a savings association.

§ 536.50 Where insurance activities may take place.

(a) *General rule.* A savings association must, to the extent practicable:

(1) Keep the area where the savings association conducts transactions involving insurance products or annuities physically segregated from areas where retail deposits are routinely accepted from the general public;

(2) Identify the areas where insurance product or annuity sales activities occur; and

(3) Clearly delineate and distinguish those areas from the areas where the savings association's retail deposit-taking activities occur.

(b) *Referrals.* Any person who accepts deposits from the public in an area where such transactions are routinely conducted in a savings association may refer a consumer who seeks to purchase an insurance product or annuity to a qualified person who sells that product only if the person making the referral receives no more than a one-time, nominal fee of a fixed dollar amount for each referral that does not depend on whether the referral results in a transaction.

§ 536.60 Qualification and licensing requirements for insurance sales personnel.

A savings association may not permit any person to sell or offer for sale any insurance product or annuity in any part of the savings association's office or on its behalf, unless the person is at all times appropriately qualified and licensed under applicable State insurance licensing standards with regard to the specific products being sold or recommended.

Office of Thrift Supervision, Treasury § 541.15

APPENDIX A TO PART 536—CONSUMER GRIEVANCE PROCESS

Any consumer who believes that any savings association or any other person selling, soliciting, advertising, or offering insurance products or annuities to the consumer at an office of the savings association or on behalf of the savings association has violated the requirements of this part should contact the Director, Consumer Programs, Office of Thrift Supervision, at the following address: 1700 G Street, NW., Washington, DC 20552, or telephone 202–906–6237 or 800–842–6929, or e-mail *consumer.complaint@ots.treas.gov.*

PART 541—DEFINITIONS FOR REGULATIONS AFFECTING FEDERAL SAVINGS ASSOCIATIONS

Sec.
541.1 When do the definitions in this part apply?
541.2 Act.
541.5 Commercial paper.
541.7 Corporate debt security.
541.8 Debit card.
541.10 Dwelling unit.
541.11 Federal savings association.
541.14 Home.
541.15 Improved nonresidential real estate.
541.16 Improved residential real estate.
541.18 Interim Federal savings association.
541.19 Interim state savings association.
541.20 Loans.
541.21 Nonresidential real estate.
541.22 [Reserved]
541.23 Residential real estate.
541.25 Single-family dwelling.
541.26 Surplus.
541.27 Unimproved real estate.
541.28 Withdrawal value of a savings account.

AUTHORITY: 12 U.S.C. 1462a, 1463, 1464.

SOURCE: 54 FR 49480, Nov. 30, 1989, unless otherwise noted.

§ 541.1 When do the definitions in this part apply?

The definitions in this part and in 12 CFR part 561 apply throughout this chapter, unless another definition is specifically provided.

[67 FR 78152, Dec. 23, 2002]

§ 541.2 Act.

The term *Act* means the Home Owners' Loan Act of 1933, as amended.

§ 541.5 Commercial paper.

The term *commercial paper* means any note, draft, or bill of exchange which arises out of a current transaction or the proceeds of which have been or are to be used for current transactions, and which has a maturity at the time of issuance of not exceeding nine months, exclusive of days of grace, or any renewal thereof the maturity of which is likewise limited.

§ 541.7 Corporate debt security.

The term *corporate debt security* means a marketable obligation, evidencing the indebtedness of any corporation in the form of a bond, note and/or debenture which is commonly regarded as a debt security and is not predominantly speculative in nature. A security is marketable if it may be sold with reasonable promptness at a price which corresponds reasonably to its fair value.

§ 541.8 Debit card.

The term *debit card* means a card that enables an accountholder to obtain access to a savings account for the purpose of making withdrawals or of transferring funds to a third party by non-transferable order or authorization.

§ 541.10 Dwelling unit.

The term *dwelling unit* means the unified combination of rooms designed for residential use by one family, other than a single-family dwelling.

§ 541.11 Federal savings association.

The term *Federal savings association* means a Federal savings association or Federal savings bank chartered under section 5(o) of the Act.

§ 541.14 Home.

The term *home* means real estate comprising a single-family dwelling(s) or a dwelling unit(s) for four or fewer families in the aggregate.

§ 541.15 Improved nonresidential real estate.

The term *improved nonresidential real estate* means nonresidential real estate:
(a) Containing a permanent structure(s) constituting at least 25 percent of its value; or
(b) Containing improvements which make it usable by a business or industrial enterprise; or

§ 541.16

(c) Used, or to be used within a reasonable time, for commercial farming, excluding hobby and vacation property.

§ 541.16 Improved residential real estate.

The term *improved residential real estate* means residential real estate containing offsite or other improvements sufficient to make the property ready for primarily residential construction, and real estate in the process of being improved by a building or buildings to be constructed or in the process of construction for primarily residential use.

§ 541.18 Interim Federal savings association.

The term *interim Federal savings association* means a Federal savings association chartered by the Office under section 5 of the Act to facilitate the acquisition of 100 percent of the voting shares of an existing Federal stock savings association or other insured stock savings association by a newly formed company or an existing savings and loan holding company or to facilitate any other transaction the Office may approve.

§ 541.19 Interim state savings association.

The term *interim state savings association* means a savings association, other than a Federal savings association, the accounts of which are insured by the FDIC to facilitate the acquisition of 100 percent of the voting shares of an existing Federal stock savings association or other insured stock savings association by a newly formed company or an existing savings and loan holding company or to facilitate any other transaction the Office may approve.

§ 541.20 Loans.

The term *loans* means obligations and extensions or advances of credit; and any reference to a loan or investment includes an interest in such a loan or investment.

§ 541.21 Nonresidential real estate.

The terms *nonresidential real estate* or *nonresidential real property* mean real estate that is not *residential real estate*, as that term is defined in § 541.23 of this part.

§ 541.22 [Reserved]

§ 541.23 Residential real estate.

The terms *residential real estate* or *residential real property* mean:

(a) Homes (including a dwelling unit in a multi-family residential property such as a condominium or a cooperative);

(b) Combinations of homes and business property (i.e., a home used in part for business);

(c) Other real estate used for primarily residential purposes other than a home (but which may include homes);

(d) Combinations of such real estate and business property involving only minor business use (i.e., where no more than 20 percent of the total appraised value of the real estate is attributable to the business use);

(e) Farm residences and combinations of farm residences and commercial farm real estate;

(f) Property to be improved by the construction of such structures; or

(g) Leasehold interests in the above real estate.

[64 FR 46564, Aug. 26, 1999]

§ 541.25 Single-family dwelling.

The term *single-family dwelling* means a structure designed for residential use by one family, or a unit so designed, whose owner owns, directly or through a non-profit cooperative housing organization, an undivided interest in the underling real estate, including property owned in common with others which contributes to the use and enjoyment of the structure or unit.

[69 FR 76602, Dec. 22, 2004]

§ 541.26 Surplus.

The term *surplus* means undistributed earnings held as unallocated reserves for general corporate use.

§ 541.27 Unimproved real estate.

The term *unimproved real estate* means real estate that will be improved, as defined in § 541.15 or § 541.16 of this part.

§ 541.28 Withdrawal value of a savings account.

The term *withdrawal value of a savings account* means the amount invested in a savings account plus earnings credited thereto, less lawful deductions therefrom.

PART 543—FEDERAL MUTUAL SAVINGS ASSOCIATIONS—INCORPORATION, ORGANIZATION, AND CONVERSION

Sec.
543.1 Corporate title.

ORGANIZATION

543.2 Application for permission to organize.
543.3 "De novo" applications for a Federal savings association charter.
543.5 Issuance of charter.
543.6 Completion of organization.
543.7 Limitations on transaction of business.
543.7-1 Federal savings association created in connection with an association in default or in danger of default.

CONVERSION

543.8 Conversion of depository institutions to Federal mutual charter.
543.9 Application for conversion to Federal mutual charter.
543.10 Organization after conversion.
543.11 Organization plan for governance during first years after issuance of Federal mutual savings bank charter.
543.11-1 Grandfathered authority.
543.14 Continuity of existence.

AUTHORITY: 12 U.S.C. 1462, 1462a, 1463, 1464, 1467a, 2901 *et seq.*

SOURCE: 54 FR 49482, Nov. 30, 1989, unless otherwise noted.

§ 543.1 Corporate title.

(a) *General.* A Federal savings association shall not adopt a title that misrepresents the nature of the institution or the services it offers.

(b) *Title change.* Prior to changing its corporate title, an association must file with the OTS a written notice indicating the intended change. The OTS shall provide to the association a timely written acknowledgment stating when the notice was received. If, within 30 days of receipt of notice, the OTS does not notify the association of its objection on the grounds set forth in paragraph (a) of this section, the association may change its title by amending its charter in accordance with § 544.2(b) or § 552.4 and the amendment provisions of its charter, except that an association chartered as a Federal Savings and Loan Association may change its title to indicate that it is a Federal Savings Bank, and an association chartered as a Federal Savings Bank may change its title to indicate that it is a Federal Savings and Loan Association.

[54 FR 49482, Nov. 30, 1989, as amended at 57 FR 14338, Apr. 20, 1992; 58 FR 4312, Jan. 14, 1993; 61 FR 64015, Dec. 3, 1996]

ORGANIZATION

§ 543.2 Application for permission to organize.

(a) *General.* Recommendations by employees of the OTS regarding applications for permission to organize a Federal savings association are privileged, confidential, and subject to § 510.5 (b) and (c) of this chapter.

(b)–(c) [Reserved]

(d) *Public notice and inspection.* (1) The applicant must publish a public notice of the application to organize in accordance with the procedures specified in subpart B of part 516 of this chapter.

(2) Promptly after publication, the applicant(s) shall transmit copies of each notice and publisher's affidavit of publication in the same manner as the original filing.

(3) The OTS shall give notice of the application to the State official who supervises savings associations in the State in which the new association is to be located.

(4) Any person may inspect the application and all related communications at the Regional Office during regular business hours, unless such information is exempt from public disclosure.

(e) *Submission of comments.* Commenters may submit comments on the application in accordance with the procedures specified in subpart C of part 516 of this chapter.

(f) *Meetings.* OTS may arrange a meeting in accordance with the procedures in subpart D of part 516 of this chapter.

§ 543.3

(g) *Approval.* (1) Factors that will be considered are:

(i) Whether the applicants are persons of good character and responsibility;

(ii) Whether a necessity exists for such association in the community to be served;

(iii) Whether there is a reasonable probability of the association's usefulness and success;

(iv) Whether the association can be established without undue injury to properly conducted existing local thrift and home financing institutions;

(v) Whether the association will perform a role of providing credit for housing consistent with safe and sound operation of a Federal savings association; and

(vi) Whether the factors set forth in § 543.3 are met, in the case of an application that would result in the formation of a *de novo* association, as defined in § 543.3(a).

(2) Approvals of applications will be conditioned on the following:

(i) Receipt by the Office of written confirmation from the Federal Deposit Insurance Corporation that the accounts of the Federal savings association will be insured by the Federal Deposit Insurance Corporation;

(ii) A minimum amount of capital to be paid into the association's accounts prior to commencing business;

(iii) The submission of a statement that—

(A) The applicants have complied in all respects with the Act and these rules and regulations regarding organization of a Federal savings association;

(B) The applicants have incurred no expense in forming the association which is chargeable to it, and no such expense will be incurred;

(C) No funds have been collected on account of the association before the Office's approval;

(D) An organization committee has been created (naming the committee and its officers);

(E) The committee will organize the association and serve as temporary officers of the association until officers are elected by the association's board of directors under § 543.6 of this part; and

(F) No funds will be accepted for deposit by the association until organization has been completed; and

(iv) The satisfaction of any other requirement the Director, or his or her designee, may impose.

(h) *Alternative procedures for interim Federal savings associations.* (1) Applications for permission to organize an interim Federal savings association are not subject to paragraphs (d), (e), (f) or (g)(2) of this section.

(2) Approval of an application for permission to organize an interim Federal savings association shall be conditioned on approval by the Office of an application to merge the interim Federal savings association and an existing insured stock association or on approval by the Office of such other transaction which the interim was chartered to facilitate. In evaluating the application, the Director or his or her designee will consider the purpose for which the association will be organized, the form of any proposed transactions involving the organizing association, the effect of the transactions on existing associations involved in the transactions, and the factors specified in section § 543.2(g)(1) to the extent relevant.

[54 FR 49482, Nov. 30, 1989, as amended at 55 FR 13510, Apr. 11, 1990; 57 FR 14338, Apr. 20, 1992; 62 FR 27180, May 19, 1997; 62 FR 64145, Dec. 4, 1997; 69 FR 68247, Nov. 24, 2004]

§ 543.3 "De novo" applications for a Federal savings association charter.

(a) *Definitions.* For purposes of this section, the term "*de novo* association" means any Federal savings association chartered by the Office, the business of which has not been conducted previously under any charter or conducted in the previous three years in substantially the same form as is proposed by the *de novo* association. A "*de novo* applicant" means any person or persons who apply to establish a *de novo* association.

(b) *Minimum initial capitalization.* (1) A *de novo* association must have at least two million dollars in initial capital stock (stock institutions) or initial pledged savings or cash (mutual institutions), except as provided in paragraph (b)(2) of this section. The minimum initial capitalization is the

Office of Thrift Supervision, Treasury § 543.3

amount of proceeds net of all incurred and anticipated securities issuance expenses, organization expenses, preopening expenses, or any expenses paid (or funds advanced) by organizers that are to be reimbursed from the proceeds of a securities offering. In securities offerings for a *de novo* association, all securities of a particular class in the initial offering shall be sold at the same price.

(2) On a case by case basis, the Director may, for good cause, approve a *de novo* association that has less than two million dollars in initial capital or may require a *de novo* association to have more than two million dollars in initial capital.

(c) *Business and investment plans of de novo associations.* (1) To assist the Office in making the determinations required under section 5(e) of the Home Owners' Loan Act, a *de novo* applicant shall submit a business plan describing, for the first three years of operation of the *de novo* association, the major areas of operation, including:

(i) Lending, leasing and investment activity, including plans for meeting Qualified Thrift Lender requirements;

(ii) Deposit, savings and borrowing activity;

(iii) Interest-rate risk management;

(iv) Internal controls and procedures;

(v) Plans for meeting the credit needs of the proposed *de novo* association's community (including low- and moderate-income neighborhoods);

(vi) Projected statements of condition;

(vii) Projected statements of operations; and

(viii) Any other information requested by the Office.

(2) The business plan shall:

(i) Provide for the continuation or succession of competent management subject to the approval of the Regional Director;

(ii) Provide that any material change in, or deviation from, the business plan must receive the prior approval of the Regional Director;

(iii) Demonstrate the *de novo* association's ability to maintain required minimum regulatory capital under 12 CFR parts 565 and 567 for the duration of the plan.

(d) *Composition of the board of directors.* (1) A majority of a *de novo* association's board of directors must be representative of the state in which the savings association is located. The Office generally will consider a director to be representative of the state if the director resides, works or maintains a place of business in the state in which the savings association is located. If the association is located in a Metropolitan Statistical Area (MSA), Primary Metropolitan Statistical Area (PMSA) or Consolidated Metropolitan Statistical Area (CMSA) that incorporates portions of more than one state, a director will be considered representative of the association's state if he or she resides, works or maintains a place of business in the MSA, PMSA or CMSA in which the association is located.

(2) The *de novo* association's board of directors must be diversified and composed of individuals with varied business and professional experience. In addition, except in the case of a *de novo* association that is wholly-owned by a holding company, no more than one-third of a board of directors may be in closely related businesses. The background of each director must reflect a history of responsibility and personal integrity, and must show a level of competence and experience sufficient to demonstrate that such individual has the ability to direct the policies of the association in a safe and sound manner. Where a *de novo* association is owned by a holding company that does not have substantial independent economic substance, the foregoing standards will be applied to the board of directors of the holding company.

(e) *Management Officials.* Proposed stockholders of ten percent or more of the stock of a *de novo* association will be considered management officials of the association for the purpose of the Office's evaluation of the character and qualifications of the management of the association. In connection with the Office's consideration of an application for permission to organize and subsequent to issuance of a Federal savings association charter to the association by the Office, any individual or group of individuals acting in concert under 12 CFR part 574, who owns or proposes to acquire, directly or indirectly, ten percent or more of the stock of an association subject to this section, shall submit a Biographical and Financial Report, on forms prescribed by the Office, to the Regional Director.

(f) *Supervisory transactions.* This section does not apply to any application for a Federal savings association charter submitted in connection with a transfer or an acquisition of the business or accounts of a savings association if the Office determines that such transfer or acquisition is instituted for supervisory purposes, or in connection with applications for Federal charters for interim *de novo* associations chartered for the purpose of facilitating mergers, holding company reorganizations, or similar transactions.

[62 FR 27180, May 19, 1997; 62 FR 28983, May 29, 1997]

§ 543.5 Issuance of charter.

Approval by the Office of the organization of a Federal savings association or the conversion of an insured association to Federal savings association form shall constitute issuance of a charter and shall be final, provided that the association complies with the procedures set out at § 544.2(a) of this chapter. The charter shall conform with the requirements of § 544.1 of this chapter, the permissible provisions of § 544.2, or other provisions specifically approved by the Office.

§ 543.6 Completion of organization.

(a)(1) *Temporary officers.* When the Office approves an application for permission to organize a Federal savings association, the applicants shall constitute the organization committee and elect a chairperson, vice-chairperson, and a secretary, who shall act as the temporary officers of the association until their successors are duly elected and qualified. The temporary officers may effect compliance with any conditions prescribed by the Office.

(2) *Organization meeting.* Promptly upon receipt of a charter, the temporary officers shall call a meeting of the association's capital subscribers; notice of such meeting shall be mailed to each subscriber at least 5 days before the meeting day. Subscribers who have subscribed for a majority of the association's capital, present in person or by proxy, shall constitute a quorum. At such meeting, directors of the association shall be elected according to the association's charter and bylaws, and any other action permitted by such charter and bylaws may be taken; any such action shall be considered an acceptance by the association of such charter and of such bylaws, which shall be in the form provided in parts 544 and 552 of this chapter.

(b) *First meeting of directors.* Upon election, the association's board of directors shall hold a meeting to elect officers of the association as provided by its charter and bylaws and to take any other action necessary to permit operation of the association in accordance with law, the association's charter and bylaws, and these rules and regulations. When such officers have been bonded under § 563.190 of this chapter, they shall immediately collect the sums due on subscriptions to the association's capital.

(c) *Membership in Federal Home Loan Bank and insurance of accounts.* When a Federal savings association's charter is issued it must promptly qualify as a member of a Federal Home Loan Bank and meet all requirements necessary to obtain insurance of its accounts by the Federal Deposit Insurance Corporation.

(d) *Failure to complete.* Organization of a Federal savings association is completed when the organization meeting and the first meeting of its directors have been held, permanent officers have been bonded, the association holds the cash required to be paid on subscriptions to its capital, if required, Federal Home Loan Bank membership has been obtained and Federal Deposit Insurance Corporation insurance of accounts has been confirmed and any conditions imposed by the Office in connection with approval of the application have been met. If organization is not so completed within six months after issuance of a charter, or within such additional period as the Director or his or her designee may for good cause grant, and in the case of an interim Federal savings association, if a merger, or other transaction facilitated by the existence of an interim association, has not been approved, the charter shall become void and all cash

Office of Thrift Supervision, Treasury § 543.9

collected on subscriptions shall thereupon be returned.

§ 543.7 Limitations on transaction of business.

No person may organize a Federal savings association, collect money from others for such purpose, or represent himself or herself as authorized to do so, and no Federal savings association shall transact any business prior to completion of its organization, except as provided in this part.

§ 543.7-1 Federal savings association created in connection with an association in default or in danger of default.

The preceding sections of this part do not apply to a Federal savings association which is proposed by the Federal Deposit Insurance Corporation or the Resolution Trust Corporation under section 11(c) of the Federal Deposit Insurance Act (12 U.S.C. 1821(c)) or section 21A of the Federal Home Loan Bank Act (12 U.S.C. 1441A), or is otherwise chartered by the Office in connection with an association in default or in danger of default. Incorporation and organization of such associations are complete when the Director or his or her designee so determines.

CONVERSION

§ 543.8 Conversion of depository institutions to Federal mutual charter.

(a) With the approval of the OTS, any depository institution, as defined in § 552.13 of this chapter, that is in mutual form, may convert into a Federal mutual savings association, provided that:

(1) The depository institution, upon conversion, will have its deposits insured by the Federal Deposit Insurance Corporation;

(2) The depository institution, in accomplishing the conversion, complies with all applicable state and federal statutes and regulations, and OTS policies, and obtains all necessary regulatory and member approvals; and

(3) The resulting Federal mutual association conforms, within the time prescribed by the OTS, to the requirements of section 5(c) of the Home Owners' Loan Act.

(b) Recommendations regarding applications for issuance of Federal charters are privileged, confidential and subject to § 510.5 (b) and (c) of this chapter.

[54 FR 49482, Nov. 30, 1989, as amended at 57 FR 14339, Apr. 20, 1992; 60 FR 66717, Dec. 26, 1995; 62 FR 45309, Aug. 27, 1997]

§ 543.9 Application for conversion to Federal mutual charter.

(a)(1) *Filing.* Any depository institution that proposes to convert to a Federal mutual association as provided in § 543.8 must, after approval by its board of directors, file an application on forms obtained from OTS. The applicant must submit any financial statements or other information OTS may require.

(2) *Procedures.* An application for conversion filed under this section is subject to the procedures for organization of a federal mutual association at § 543.2(d) through (f) of this chapter.

(b) *Plan of conversion.* The applicant shall submit with its application a plan of conversion specifying the location of the home office and any branch offices to be maintained by the Federal savings association, and providing for:

(1) Appropriate reserves and surplus for the Federal savings association;

(2) Satisfaction in full or assumption by the Federal savings association of all creditor obligations of the applicant;

(3) Issuance by the Federal savings association of savings accounts to current holders of withdrawable accounts in an amount equalling the value of such accounts; and

(4) If applicable, issuance of additional savings accounts to current holders of nonwithdrawable capital stock of the applicant in an amount equalling the value of their nonwithdrawable capital stock, including the present value of any preference to which such holders are entitled.

(c) *Action on application.* The OTS will consider such application and any information submitted with the application, and may approve the application in accordance with section 5(e) of the Home Owners' Loan Act and § 543.2(g)(1). Converting depository institutions that have been in existence less than three years will be subject to

§ 543.10

all approval criteria and other requirements applicable to *de novo* Federal associations. Approval of an application and issuance by the OTS of a charter will be subject to:

(1) Compliance by the applicant with all conditions prescribed in the approval;

(2) Receipt by the applicant of approval of the plan of conversion by such vote as may be required by the laws of the applicant's jurisdiction to consider such action;

(3) In the case of a converting association the accounts of which are not insured by the Federal Deposit Insurance Corporation, receipt by the OTS of written confirmation from the Federal Deposit Insurance Corporation that the accounts of the converting association will be insured by the Federal Deposit Insurance Corporation; and

(4) Receipt by the OTS of written confirmation from the appropriate Federal Home Loan Bank of approval of the converting institution's application for Federal Home Loan Bank membership, if the institution is not a member.

[54 FR 49482, Nov. 30, 1989, as amended at 55 FR 13510, Apr. 11, 1990; 57 FR 14339, Apr. 20, 1992; 62 FR 45309, Aug. 27, 1997; 66 FR 13005, Mar. 2, 2001]

§ 543.10 Organization after conversion.

Except as provided in § 543.11, after a Federal charter is issued under § 543.9 the association's members shall, after due notice, or upon a valid adjournment of a previous legal meeting, hold a meeting to elect directors and take all other action necessary fully to effect the conversion and operate the association in accordance with law and these rules and regulations. Immediately thereafter the board of directors shall meet, elect officers, and transact any other appropriate business.

§ 543.11 Organization plan for governance during first years after issuance of Federal mutual savings bank charter.

(a) *Organizational meeting.* Except as provided in paragraph (c)(1) of this section, promptly upon receipt of a charter, the officers of a Federal mutual savings bank which, immediately prior to conversion, was a state chartered mutual savings bank, shall call a meeting of the members. Notice for, and conduct of, such meeting shall be in accordance with the bank's Federal charter and bylaws. Business to be conducted at the organizational meeting shall include the election of trustees (who may also be known as a board of directors) and any other matters permitted by the charter and bylaws. Any action taken at such meeting shall be deemed an acceptance of the charter and bylaws approved by the Office pursuant to § 544.1 of this chapter.

(b) *First meeting of trustees.* Upon election or appointment, the board of trustees shall hold a meeting to elect the officers of the bank in accordance with its Federal charter and bylaws, and to take other action necessary to permit the operation of the bank in accordance with the Home Owners' Loan Act of 1933, as amended, the bank's charter and bylaws, these rules and regulations, and orders of the Office.

(c) *Plan for governance of association during first six years after issuance of Federal charter.* (1)(i) An applicant for a Federal mutual savings bank charter may submit a plan which provides that each member of its governing board, *i.e.,* board of trustees, managers, or directors, may continue to serve, provided that within two years of the issuance of a Federal charter at least one-fifth of the members of such board shall have been elected by vote, either in person or by proxy, of the bank's membership as provided in its Federal charter, that within three years of the issuance of its Federal charter at least two-fifths of the members of such board shall have been elected by such a membership vote, that within four years of the issuance of its Federal charter at least three-fifths of the members of such board shall have been elected by such a membership vote, that within five years of the issuance of its Federal charter at least four-fifths of the members of such board shall have been elected by such a membership vote, and that within six years of the issuance of its Federal charter all of the members of such board shall have been elected by such a membership vote.

(ii) The plan:

Office of Thrift Supervision, Treasury

(A) Shall set forth the names of those persons who are being proposed for service on the applicant's governing board after conversion to a Federal charter,

(B) Shall show how trustees not elected by the converted bank's membership will be appointed or otherwise selected, and

(C) Shall provide that no trustees may be appointed or elected to terms of more than three years.

(iii) The plan may provide that

(A) After receipt of its Federal charter the bank will be organized by its existing governing board,

(B) Within the first two years following receipt of its Federal charter, the bank's charter may be amended without a membership vote, provided any such amendment is first approved by a two-thirds vote of its board of trustees and is thereafter approved by the Office, and

(C) The bank's first annual membership meeting need not take place until two years after receipt of its Federal charter.

(2) Except to the extent that the Office approves a plan under this paragraph (c) which is inconsistent with other provisions of this section, a Federal mutual savings bank shall in all respects comply with those other provisions.

[54 FR 49482, Nov. 30, 1989, as amended at 60 FR 66717, Dec. 26, 1995]

§ 543.11-1 Grandfathered authority.

(a) A Federal savings bank formerly chartered or designated as a mutual savings bank under state law may exercise any authority it was authorized to exercise as a mutual savings bank under state law at the time of its conversion from a state mutual savings bank to a Federal or other state charter. Except to the extent such authority may be exercised by Federal savings associations not enjoying grandfathered rights hereunder, such authority may be exercised only to the degree authorized under state law at the time of such conversion. Unless otherwise determined by the Director, an association, in the exercise of grandfathered authority, may continue to follow applicable state laws and regulations in effect at the time of such conversion.

(b) A Federal savings association that acquires, or has acquired, a Federal savings bank by merger or consolidation may itself exercise any grandfathered rights enjoyed by the disappearing institution, whether such rights were obtained directly through conversion or through merger or consolidation. The extent of the grandfathered rights of a Federal savings association that disappeared prior to the effective date of this section shall be determined exclusively pursuant to this section.

(c) This section shall not be construed to prevent the exercise by a Federal savings association enjoying grandfathered rights hereunder of authority that is available under the applicable state law only upon the occurrence of specific preconditions, such as the attainment of a particular future date or specified level of regulatory capital, which have not occurred at the time of conversion from a state mutual savings bank, provided they occur thereafter.

(d) This section shall not be construed to permit the exercise of any particular authority on a more liberal basis than is allowable under the most liberal construction of either state or Federal law or regulation.

§ 543.14 Continuity of existence.

The corporate existence of an association converting under this part shall continue in its successor. Each savings or demand accountholder shall receive a savings account or accounts in the converted association equal in amount to the value of accounts held in the former association.

[54 FR 49482, Nov. 30, 1989, as amended at 61 FR 64015, Dec. 3, 1996]

PART 544—FEDERAL MUTUAL SAVINGS ASSOCIATIONS—CHARTER AND BYLAWS

CHARTER

Sec.
544.1 Federal mutual charter.
544.2 Charter amendments.
544.4 Issuance of charter.

BYLAWS

544.5 Federal mutual savings association bylaws.

§ 544.1

544.6 Effect of subsequent charter or bylaw change.

AVAILABILITY

544.7 In association offices.
544.8 Communication between members of a Federal mutual savings association.

AUTHORITY: 12 U.S.C. 1462, 1462a, 1463, 1464, 1467a, 2901 et seq.

SOURCE: 54 FR 49486, Nov. 30, 1989, unless otherwise noted.

CHARTER

§ 544.1 Federal mutual charter.

A Federal mutual savings association shall have a charter in the following form, which may include any of the additional provisions set forth in § 544.2 of this Part, if such provisions are specifically requested. A charter for a Federal mutual savings bank shall substitute the term "savings bank" for "association." The term "trustee" may be substituted for the term "director." Associations adopting this charter with existing borrower members must grandfather those borrower members who were members as of the date of issuance of the new charter by the Office. Such borrowers shall have one vote for the period of time such borrowings are in existence.

FEDERAL MUTUAL CHARTER

Section 1. Corporate title. The full corporate title of the Federal savings association is _____.

Section 2. Office. The home office shall be located in _____ [city, state].

Section 3. Duration. The duration of the association is perpetual.

Section 4. Purpose and powers. The purpose of the association is to pursue any or all of the lawful objectives of a Federal mutual savings association chartered under section 5 of the Home Owners' Loan Act and to exercise all the express, implied, and incidental powers conferred thereby and by all acts amendatory thereof and supplemental thereto, subject to the Constitution and laws of the United States as they are now in effect, or as they may hereafter be amended, and subject to all lawful and applicable rules, regulations, and orders of the Office of Thrift Supervision ("Office").

Section 5. Capital. The association may raise capital by accepting payments on savings and demand accounts and by any other means authorized by the Office.

Section 6. Members. All holders of the association's savings, demand, or other authorized accounts are members of the association. In the consideration of all questions requiring action by the members of the association, each holder of an account shall be permitted to cast one vote for each $100, or fraction thereof, of the withdrawal value of the member's account. No member, however, shall cast more than 1000 votes. All accounts shall be nonassessable.

Section 7. Directors. The association shall be under the direction of a board of directors. The authorized number of directors shall not be fewer than five nor more than fifteen persons, as fixed in the association's bylaws, except that the number of directors may be decreased to a number less than five or increased to a number greater than fifteen with the prior approval of the Director of the Office or his or her delegate.

Section 8. Capital, surplus, and distribution of earnings. The association shall maintain for the purpose of meeting losses the amount of capital required by section 5 of the Home Owners' Loan Act and by regulations of the Office. The association shall distribute net earnings on its accounts on such basis and in accordance with such terms and conditions as may from time to time be authorized by the Director of the Office: *Provided,* That the association may establish minimum-balance requirements for accounts to be eligible for distribution of earnings.

All holders of accounts of the association shall be entitled to equal distribution of assets, *pro rata* to the value of their accounts, in the event of voluntary or involuntary liquidation, dissolution, or winding up of the association. Moreover, in any such event, or in any other situation in which the priority of such accounts is in controversy, all such accounts shall, to the extent of their withdrawal value, be debts of the association having the same priority as the claims of general creditors of the association not having priority (other than any priority arising or resulting from consensual subordination) over other general creditors of the association.

Section 9. Amendment of charter. Adoption of any preapproved charter amendment shall be effective after such preapproved amendment has been approved by the members at a legal meeting. Any other amendment, addition, change, or repeal of this charter must be approved by the Office prior to approval by the members at a legal meeting, and shall be effective upon filing with the Office in accordance with regulatory procedures.

Attest: _____
   Secretary of the Association
By: _____
   President or Chief Executive Officer of the Association
Attest: _____
   Secretary of the Office of Thrift Supervision
By: _____

Office of Thrift Supervision, Treasury § 544.2

Director of the Office of Thrift Supervision

Effective Date: _____

[54 FR 49486, Nov. 30, 1989, as amended at 61 FR 64015, Dec. 3, 1996]

§ 544.2 Charter amendments.

(a) *General.* In order to adopt a charter amendment, a Federal mutual savings association must comply with the following requirements:

(1) *Board of directors approval.* The board of directors of the association must adopt a resolution proposing the charter amendment that states the text of such amendment;

(2) *Form of filing*—(i) *Application requirement.* If the proposed charter amendment would: render more difficult or discourage a merger, proxy contest, the assumption of control by a mutual account holder of the association, or the removal of incumbent management; or involve a significant issue of law or policy; then, the association shall file the proposed amendment and obtain the prior approval of the OTS.

(ii) *Notice requirement.* If the proposed charter amendment does not involve a provision that would be covered by paragraph (a)(2)(i) of this section and is permissible under all applicable laws, rules and regulations, then the association shall submit the proposed amendment to the OTS, at least 30 days prior to the effective date of the proposed charter amendment.

(b) *Approval.* Any charter amendment filed pursuant to paragraph (a)(2)(ii) of this section shall automatically be approved 30 days from the date of filing of such amendment, provided that the association follows the requirements of its charter in adopting such amendment. This automatic approval does not apply if, prior to the expiration of such 30-day period, the OTS notifies the association that such amendment is rejected or that such amendment is deemed to be filed under the provisions of paragraph (a)(2)(i) of this section. In addition, notwithstanding anything in paragraph (a) of this section to the contrary, the following charter amendments, including the adoption of the Federal mutual charter as set forth in § 544.1 of this part, shall be effective and deemed approved at the time of adoption, if adopted without change and filed with OTS, within 30 days after adoption, provided the association follows the requirements of its charter in adopting such amendments:

(1) *Purpose and powers.* Add a second paragraph to section 4, as follows:

Section 4. Purpose and powers. * * * The association shall have the express power: (i) To act as fiscal agent of the United States when designated for that purpose by the Secretary of the Treasury, under such regulations as the Secretary may prescribe, to perform all such reasonable duties as fiscal agent of the United States as may be required, and to act as agent for any other instrumentality of the United States when designated for that purpose by any such instrumentality; (ii) To sue and be sued, complain and defend in any court of law or equity; (iii) To have a corporate seal, affixed by imprint, facsimile or otherwise; (iv) To appoint officers and agents as its business shall require and allow them suitable compensation; (v) To adopt bylaws not inconsistent with the Constitution or laws of the United States and rules and regulations adopted thereunder and under this Charter; (vi) To raise capital, which shall be unlimited, by accepting payments on savings, demand, or other accounts, as are authorized by rules and regulations made by the Office, and the holders of all such accounts or other accounts as shall, to such extent as may be provided by such rules and regulations, be members of the association and shall have such voting rights and such other rights as are thereby provided; (vii) To issue notes, bonds, debentures, or other obligations, or securities, provided by or under any provision of Federal statute as from time to time is in effect; (viii) To provide for redemption of insured accounts; (ix) To borrow money without limitation and pledge and otherwise encumber any of its assets to secure its debts; (x) To lend and otherwise invest its funds as authorized by statute and the rules and regulations of the Office; (xi) To wind up and dissolve, merge, consolidate, convert, or reorganize; (xii) To purchase, hold, and convey real estate and personalty consistent with its objects, purposes, and powers; (xiii) To mortgage or lease any real estate and personalty and take such property by gift, devise, or bequest; and (xiv) To exercise all powers conferred by law. In addition to the foregoing powers expressly enumerated, this association shall have power to do all things reasonably incident to the accomplishment of its express objects and the performance of its express powers.

(2) *Title change.* A Federal mutual savings association that has complied with § 543.1(b) of this chapter may amend its charter by substituting a new corporate title in section 1.

§ 544.4

(3) *Home office.* A Federal mutual savings association may amend its charter by substituting a new home office in section 2, if it has complied with applicable requirements of § 545.95 of this chapter.

(4) *Maximum number of votes.* A Federal mutual savings association may amend its charter by substituting ____ votes per member in section 6. [Fill in a number from 1 to 1000.]

(c) *Reissuance of charter.* A Federal mutual savings association that has amended its charter may apply to have its charter, including the amendments, reissued by the Office. Such request for reissuance should be filed with the Corporate Secretary at the Washington Headquarters Office at the address listed at § 516.40(b) of this chapter and contain signatures required under § 544.1 of this part, together with such supporting documents as may be needed to demonstrate that the amendments were properly adopted.

[54 FR 49486, Nov. 30, 1989, as amended at 55 FR 13510, Apr. 11, 1990; 57 FR 14339, Apr. 20, 1992; 61 FR 64016, Dec. 3, 1996; 63 FR 46160, Aug. 31, 1998; 66 FR 13005, Mar. 2, 2001; 69 FR 68248, Nov. 24, 2004]

§ 544.4 Issuance of charter.

Issuance by the Office of a charter to a Federal mutual savings association within the meaning of § 543.5 of this chapter constitutes the incorporation of that association by the Office.

BYLAWS

§ 544.5 Federal mutual savings association bylaws.

(a) *General.* A Federal mutual savings association shall operate under bylaws that contain provisions that comply with all requirements specified by the OTS in this section and that are not otherwise inconsistent with the provisions of this section, the association's charter, and all other applicable laws, rules, and regulations *provided that*, a bylaw provision inconsistent with the provisions of this section may be adopted with the approval of the OTS. Bylaws may be adopted, amended or repealed by a majority of the votes cast by the members at a legal meeting or a majority of the association's board of directors. The bylaws for a Federal mutual savings bank shall substitute the term "savings bank" for "association". The term "trustee" may be substituted for the term "director".

(b) The following requirements are applicable to Federal mutual savings associations:

(1) *Annual meetings of members.* An association shall provide for and conduct an annual meeting of its members for the election of directors and at which any other business of the association may be conducted. Such meeting shall be held, as designated by its board of directors, at a location within the state that constitutes the principal place of business of the association, or at any other convenient place the board of directors may designate, and at a date and time within 150 days after the end of the association's fiscal year. At each annual meeting, the officers shall make a full report of the financial condition of the association and of its progress for the preceding year and shall outline a program for the succeeding year.

(2) *Special meetings of members.* Procedures for calling any special meeting of the members and for conducting such a meeting shall be set forth in the bylaws. The subject matter of such special meeting must be established in the notice for such meeting. The board of directors of the association or the holders of 10 percent or more of the voting capital shall be entitled to call a special meeting. For purposes of this section, "voting capital" means FDIC-insured deposits as of the voting record date.

(3) *Notice of meeting of members.* Notice specifying the date, time, and place of the annual or any special meeting and adequately describing any business to be conducted shall be published for two successive weeks immediately prior to the week in which such meeting shall convene in a newspaper of general circulation in the city or county in which the principal place of business of the association is located, or mailed postage prepaid at least 15 days and not more than 45 days prior to the date on which such meeting shall convene to each of its members of record at the last address appearing on the books of the association. A similar notice shall be posted in a conspicuous place in

each of the offices of the association during the 14 days immediately preceding the date on which such meeting shall convene. The bylaws may permit a member to waive in writing any right to receive personal delivery of the notice. When any meeting is adjourned for 30 days or more, notice of the adjournment and reconvening of the meeting shall be given as in the case of the original meeting.

(4) *Fixing of record date.* For the purpose of determining members entitled to notice of or to vote at any meeting of members or any adjournment thereof, or in order to make a determination of members for any other proper purpose, the bylaws shall provide for the fixing of a record date and a method for determining from the books of the association the members entitled to vote. Such date shall be not more than 60 days nor fewer than 10 days prior to the date on which the action, requiring such determination of members, is to be taken. The same determination shall apply to any adjourned meeting.

(5) *Member quorum.* Any number of members present and voting, represented in person or by proxy, at a regular or special meeting of the members shall constitute a quorum. A majority of all votes cast at any meeting of the members shall determine any question, unless otherwise required by regulation. At any adjourned meeting, any business may be transacted that might have been transacted at the meeting as originally called. Members present at a duly constituted meeting may continue to transact business until adjournment.

(6) *Voting by proxy.* Procedures shall be established for voting at any annual or special meeting of the members by proxy pursuant to the rules and regulations of the Office, including the placing of such proxies on file with the secretary of the association, for verification, prior to the convening of such meeting. Proxies may be given telephonically or electronically as long as the holder uses a procedure for verifying the identity of the member. All proxies with a term greater than eleven months or solicited at the expense of the association must run to the board of directors as a whole, or to a committee appointed by a majority of such board.

(7) *Communications between members.* Provisions relating to communications between members shall be consistent with §544.8 of this part. No member, however, shall have the right to inspect or copy any portion of any books or records of a Federal mutual savings association containing:

(i) A list of depositors in or borrowers from such association;

(ii) Their addresses;

(iii) Individual deposit or loan balances or records; or

(iv) Any data from which such information could be reasonably constructed.

(8) *Number of directors, membership.* The bylaws shall set forth a specific number of directors, not a range. The number of directors shall be not fewer than five nor more than fifteen, unless a higher or lower number has been authorized by the Director of the Office or his or her designee. Each director of the association shall be a member of the association. Directors may be elected for periods of one to three years and until their successors are elected and qualified, but if a staggered board is chosen, provision shall be made for the election of approximately one-third or one-half of the board each year, as appropriate. State-chartered savings banks converting to Federal savings banks may include alternative provisions for the election and term of office of directors so long as such provisions are authorized by the Office, and provide for compliance with the standard provisions of this section no later than six years after the conversion to a Federal savings association.

(9) *Meetings of the board.* The board of directors shall determine the place, frequency, time, procedure for notice, which shall be at least 24 hours unless waived by the directors, and waiver of notice for all regular and special meetings. The meetings shall be under the direction of a chairman, appointed annually by the board; or in the absence of the chairman, the meetings shall be under the direction of the president. The board also may permit telephonic participation at meetings. The bylaws may provide for action to be taken

§ 544.5

without a meeting if unanimous written consent is obtained for such action. A majority of the authorized directors shall constitute a quorum for the transaction of business. The act of a majority of the directors present at any meeting at which there is a quorum shall be the act of the board.

(10) *Officers, employees. and agents.* (i) The bylaws shall contain provisions regarding the officers of the association, their functions, duties, and powers. The officers of the association shall consist of a president, one or more vice presidents, a secretary, and a treasurer or comptroller, each of whom shall be elected annually by the board of directors. Such other officers and assistant officers and agents as may be deemed necessary may be elected or appointed by the board of directors or chosen in such other manner as may be prescribed in the bylaws. Any two or more offices may be held by the same person, except the offices of president and secretary.

(ii) All officers and agents of the association, as between themselves and the association, shall have such authority and perform such duties in the management of the association as may be provided in the bylaws, or as may be determined by resolution of the board of directors not inconsistent with the bylaws. In the absence of any such provision, officers shall have such powers and duties as generally pertain to their respective offices. Any officer may be removed by the board of directors with or without cause, but such removal, other than for cause, shall be without prejudice to the contractual rights, if any, of the person so removed.

(iii) Any indemnification provision must provide that any indemnification is subject to applicable Federal law, rules, and regulations.

(11) *Vacancies, resignation or removal of directors.* Members of the association shall elect directors by ballot: Provided, that in the event of a vacancy on the board, the board of directors may, by their affirmative vote, fill such vacancy, even if the remaining directors constitute less than a quorum. A director elected to fill a vacancy shall be elected to serve only until the next election of directors by the members. The bylaws shall set out the procedure for the resignation of a director, which shall be by written notice or by any other procedure established in the bylaws. Directors may be removed only for cause as defined in § 563.39 of this chapter, by a vote of the holders of a majority of the shares then entitled to vote at an election of directors.

(12) *Powers of the board.* The board of directors shall have the power:

(i) By resolution, to appoint from among its members and remove an executive committee and one or more other committees, which committee[s] shall have and may exercise all the powers of the board between the meetings or the board; but no such committee shall have the authority of the board to amend the charter or bylaws, adopt a plan of merger, consolidation, dissolution, or provide for the disposition of all or substantially all the property and assets of the association. Such committee shall not operate to relieve the board, or any member thereof, of any responsibility imposed by law;

(ii) To fix the compensation of directors, officers, and employees; and to remove any officer or employee at any time with or without cause;

(iii) To exercise any and all of the powers of the association not expressly reserved by the charter to the members.

(13) *Nominations for directors.* The bylaws shall provide that nominations for directors may be made at the annual meeting by any member and shall be voted upon, except, however, the bylaws may require that nominations by a member must be submitted to the secretary and then prominently posted in the principal place of business, at least 10 days prior to the date of the annual meeting. However, if such provision is made for prior submission of nominations by a member, then the bylaws must provide for a nominating committee, which, except in the case of a nominee substituted as a result of death or other incapacity, must submit nominations to the secretary and have such nominations similarly posted at least 15 days prior to the date of the annual meeting.

(14) *New business.* The bylaws shall provide procedures for the introduction of new business at the annual meeting. Those provisions may require that such

new business be stated in writing and filed with the secretary prior to the annual meeting at least 30 days prior to the date of the annual meeting.

(15) *Amendment.* Bylaws may include any provision for their amendment that would be consistent with applicable law, rules, and regulations and adequately addresses its subject and purpose.

(i) Amendments shall be effective:

(A) After approval by a majority vote of the authorized board, or by a majority of the vote cast by the members of the association at a legal meeting; and

(B) After receipt of any applicable regulatory approval.

(ii) When an association fails to meet its quorum requirement, solely due to vacancies on the board, the bylaws may be amended by an affirmative vote of a majority of the sitting board.

(16) *Miscellaneous.* The bylaws may also address the subject of age limitations for directors or officers as long as they are consistent with applicable Federal law, rules or regulations, and any other subjects necessary or appropriate for effective operation of the association.

(c) *Form of filing*—(1) *Application requirement.* (i) Any bylaw amendment shall be submitted to the OTS if it would:

(A) Render more difficult or discourage a merger, proxy contest, the assumption of control by a mutual account holder of the association, or the removal of incumbent management;

(B) Involve a significant issue of law or policy, including indemnification, conflicts of interest, and limitations on director or officer liability; or

(C) Be inconsistent with the requirements of this section or with applicable laws, rules, regulations, or the association's charter.

(ii) Applications submitted under paragraph (c)(1)(i) of this section are subject to standard treatment processing procedures at part 516, subparts A and E of this chapter.

(iii) For purposes of this paragraph (c), bylaw provisions that adopt the language of the model or optional bylaws in OTS's Application Processing Handbook, if adopted without change, and filed with OTS within 30 days after adoption, are effective upon adoption.

(2) *Filing requirement.* If the proposed bylaw amendment does not involve a provision that would be covered by paragraph (c)(1) or (c)(3) of this section, then the association shall submit the amendment to the OTS at least 30 days prior to the date the bylaw amendment is to be adopted by the association.

(3) *Corporate governance procedures.* A Federal mutual association may elect to follow the corporate governance procedures of the laws of the state where the main office of the institution is located, provided that such procedures may be elected only to the extent not inconsistent with applicable Federal statutes, regulations, and safety and soundness, and such procedures are not of the type described in paragraph (c)(1) of this section. If this election is selected, a Federal mutual association shall designate in its bylaws the provision or provisions from the body of law selected for its corporate governance procedures, and shall file a copy of such bylaws, which are effective upon adoption, within 30 days after adoption. The submission shall indicate, where not obvious, why the bylaw provisions meet the requirements stated in paragraph (c)(1) of this section.

(d) *Effectiveness.* Any bylaw amendment filed pursuant to paragraph (c)(2) of this section shall automatically be effective 30 days from the date of filing of such amendment, provided that the association follows the requirements of its charter and bylaws in adopting such amendment. This automatic effective date does not apply if, prior to the expiration of such 30-day period, the OTS notifies the association that such amendment is rejected or that such amendment requires an application to be filed pursuant to paragraph (c)(1) of this section.

[54 FR 49486, Nov. 30, 1989, as amended at 55 FR 13511, Apr. 11, 1990; 57 FR 14339, Apr. 20, 1992; 61 FR 64016, Dec. 3, 1996; 62 FR 66262, Dec. 18, 1997; 66 FR 13006, Mar. 2, 2001; 66 FR 15020, Mar. 15, 2001]

§ 544.6 Effect of subsequent charter or bylaw change.

Notwithstanding any subsequent change to its charter or bylaws, the authority of a Federal mutual savings association to engage in any transaction shall be determined only by the association's charter or bylaws then in effect.

AVAILABILITY

§ 544.7 In association offices.

A Federal mutual savings association shall make available to its members at all times in its offices a true copy of its charter and bylaws, including any amendments, and shall deliver such a copy to any member on request.

§ 544.8 Communication between members of a Federal mutual savings association.

(a) *Right of communication with other members.* A member of a Federal mutual savings association has the right to communicate, as prescribed in paragraph (b) of this section, with other members of the Federal savings association regarding any matter related to the Federal savings association's affairs, except for "improper" communications, as defined in paragraph (c) of this section. The association may not defeat that right by redeeming a savings member's savings account in the Federal mutual savings association.

(b) *Member communication procedures.* If a member of a Federal mutual savings association desires to communicate with other members, the following procedures shall be followed:

(1) The member shall give the Federal mutual savings association a written request to communicate;

(2) If the proposed communication is in connection with a meeting of the Federal savings association's members, the request shall be given at least thirty days before the annual meeting or 10 days before a special meeting;

(3) The request shall contain—

(i) The member's full name and address;

(ii) The nature and extent of the member's interest in the Federal savings association at the time the information is given;

(iii) A copy of the proposed communication; and

(iv) If the communication is in connection with a meeting of the members, the date of the meeting;

(4) The Federal savings association shall reply to the request within either—

(i) Fourteen days;
(ii) Ten days, if the communication is in connection with the annual meeting; or
(iii) Three days, if the communication is in connection with a special meeting;

(5) The reply shall provide either—
(i) The number of the Federal savings association's members and the estimated reasonable cost to the Federal savings association of mailing to them the proposed communication; or
(ii) Notification that the Federal savings association has determined not to mail the communication because it is "improper", as defined in paragraph (c) of this section;

(6) After receiving the amount of the estimated costs of mailing and sufficient copies of the communication, the Federal savings association shall mail the communication to all members, by a class of mail specified by the requesting member, either—
(i) Within fourteen days;
(ii) Within seven days, if the communication is in connection with the annual meeting;
(iii) As soon as practicable before the meeting, if the communication is in connection with a special meeting; or
(iv) On a later date specified by the member;

(7) If the Federal savings association refuses to mail the proposed communication, it shall return the requesting member's materials together with a written statement of the specific reasons for refusal, and shall simultaneously send to the Regional Director two copies each of the requesting member's materials, the Federal savings association's written statement, and any other relevant material. The materials shall be sent within:
(i) Fourteen days,
(ii) Ten days if the communication is in connection with the annual meeting, or
(iii) Three days, if the communication is in connection with a special meeting,
after the Federal savings association receives the request for communication.

(c) *Improper communication.* A communication is an "improper communication" if it contains material which:

(1) At the time and in the light of the circumstances under which it is made:

(i) Is false or misleading with respect to any material fact; or

(ii) Omits a material fact necessary to make the statements therein not false or misleading, or necessary to correct a statement in an earlier communication on the same subject which has become false or misleading;

(2) Relates to a personal claim or a personal grievance, or is solicitous of personal gain or business advantage by or on behalf of any party;

(3) Relates to any matter, including a general economic, political, racial, religious, social, or similar cause, that is not significantly related to the business of the Federal savings association or is not within the control of the Federal savings association; or

(4) Directly or indirectly and without expressed factual foundation:

(i) Impugns character, integrity, or personal reputation,

(ii) Makes charges concerning improper, illegal, or immoral conduct, or

(iii) Makes statements impugning the stability and soundness of the Federal savings association.

[54 FR 49492, Nov. 30, 1989, as amended at 60 FR 66717, Dec. 26, 1995. Redesignated at 61 FR 64018, Dec. 3, 1996.]

PART 545—FEDERAL SAVINGS ASSOCIATIONS—OPERATIONS

Sec.
545.1 General authority.
545.2 Federal preemption.
545.16 Public deposits, depositaries, and fiscal agents.
545.17 Funds transfer services.
545.91 Home office.
545.92 Branch offices.
545.93 Application and notice requirements for branch and home offices.
545.95 What processing procedures apply to my home or branch office application or notice?
545.96 Agency office.
545.101 Fiscal agency.
545.121 Indemnification of directors, officers and employees.

AUTHORITY: 12 U.S.C. 1462a, 1463, 1464, 1828.

SOURCE: 54 FR 49492, Nov. 30, 1989, unless otherwise noted.

§ 545.1 General authority.

A Federal savings association may exercise all authority granted it by the Home Owners' Loan Act of 1933 ("Act"), 12 U.S.C. 1464, as amended, and its charter and bylaws, whether or not implemented specifically by Office regulations, subject to the limitations and interpretations contained in this part.

§ 545.2 Federal preemption.

The regulations in this part 545 are promulgated pursuant to the plenary and exclusive authority of the Office to regulate all aspects of the operations of Federal savings associations, as set forth in section 5(a) of the Act. This exercise of the Office's authority is preemptive of any state law purporting to address the subject of the operations of a Federal savings association.

§ 545.16 Public deposits, depositaries, and fiscal agents.

(a) *Definitions.* As used in this section—

(1) *Moneys* includes *monies* and has the meaning it has in applicable state law;

(2) *State law* includes actions by a governmental body which has a charter adopted under the constitution of the state with provisions respecting deposits of public money of that body;

(3) *Surety* means surety under real and/or personal suretyship, and includes guarantor; and

(4) Terms in paragraph (b) of this section have the meanings they have under applicable state law.

(b) *Authority to act as surety for public deposits.* (1) A Federal savings association that is a deposit association may give bond or security for deposit in it of public moneys or investment in it by a governmental unit if required to do so by state law, either as an alternative condition or otherwise, regardless of the amount required. Any bond or security may be given and any substitution or increase thereof may be made under this section at any time.

(2) If state law requires as a condition of such deposit or investment that the Federal savings association or its bond or security, or any combination thereof, be surety for or with respect to other deposits or instruments, whether of that depositor or investor or of any

§ 545.17

other(s), and whether in the Federal savings association or in any other institution(s) having, when the investments or deposits were made, insurance by the Federal Deposit Insurance Corporation, the same shall become, or if the state law is self-executing shall be, such surety.

(c) *Depositaries and fiscal agents.* Subject to regulation of the United States Treasury Department, a Federal savings association may serve as a depositary for Federal taxes, as a Treasury tax and loan depositary, or as a depositary of public money and fiscal agent of the Government or any other instrumentality thereof when designated for that purpose by such instrumentality and approved by the Office, and may satisfy any requirement in connection therewith, including maintaining accounts described in §§ 561.33, 561.52, 561.53, and 561.54 of this chapter; pledging collateral; and performing the services outlined in 31 CFR 202.3(b) or any section that supersedes or amends § 202.3(b).

§ 545.17 Funds transfer services.

A Federal savings association is authorized to transfer, with or without fee, its customers' funds from any account (including a line of credit) of the customer at the Federal savings association or at another financial intermediary to third parties or other accounts of the customer on the customer's order or authorization by any mechanism or device, including cashier's checks, conforming with applicable laws and established commercial practices.

§ 545.91 Home office.

(a) All operations of a Federal savings association ("you") are subject to direction from the home office.

(b) You must notify the appropriate OTS Regional Office if the permanent address of your home office changes, unless you have submitted an application or notice regarding the change under §§ 545.93 and 545.95 of this chapter.

[69 FR 68248, Nov. 24, 2004]

§ 545.92 Branch offices.

(a) *Definition.* A branch office of a Federal savings association ("you") is any office other than your home office, agency office, administrative office, data processing office, or an electronic means or facility under part 555 of this chapter.

(b) *Branching.* Subject to the application and notice requirements at §§ 545.93 and 545.95 of this chapter, you may branch in any State or States of the United States and its territories unless the location would violate:

(1) Section 5(r) of the HOLA (12 U.S.C. 1464(r));

(2) Section 10(e)(3) of the HOLA (12 U.S.C. 1467a(e)(3)); or

(3) Section 13(k)(4) of the FDIA (12 U.S.C. 1823(k)(4)).

(c) *Preemption.* This exercise of OTS authority is preemptive of any State law purporting to address the subject of branching by a Federal savings association.

[69 FR 68248, Nov. 24, 2004]

§ 545.93 Application and notice requirements for branch and home offices.

(a) *Application and notice requirements.* A Federal savings association ("you") must file an application or notice and receive OTS approval or non-objection under § 545.95 before you change the permanent location of, or establish a new, home or branch office, except as provided in this section.

(b) *Exceptions.* You are not required to submit an application or notice and receive OTS approval or non-objection under § 545.95 under the following circumstances:

(1) *Drive-in or pedestrian offices.* You may establish a drive-in or pedestrian office that is located within 500 feet of a public entrance to your existing home or branch office, provided the functions performed at the office are limited to functions that are ordinarily performed at a teller window.

(2) *Short-distance relocation.* You may change the permanent location of an existing home or branch office to a site that is within the market area and short-distance location area of the existing home or branch office. The

Office of Thrift Supervision, Treasury § 545.95

short-distance relocation area of an existing office is the area that is within:

(i) A 1000-foot radius of an existing office that is within a Principal City in a Metropolitan Statistical Area (MSA) designated by the U.S. Department of Commerce;

(ii) A one-mile radius of an existing office that is within an MSA, but is not within a Principal City; or

(iii) A two-mile radius of an existing office that is not in an MSA.

(3) *Highly-rated Federal savings associations.* You may change the permanent location of, or establish a new, branch or home office if you meet all of the following requirements:

(i) You are eligible for expedited treatment under § 516.5 of this chapter. For the purposes of that section, you must meet the capital requirements under part 567 of this chapter before and immediately after you change the location of your home or branch office or establish a new branch office.

(ii) You published a notice of your intent to change the location of your home or branch office or establish a new branch office. To satisfy this publication requirement, you must follow the procedures in subpart B of part 516 of this chapter except that:

(A) Under § 516.55(d) and (e) of this chapter, your public notice must state that the public may submit comments to you and to the appropriate OTS office(s), and must provide addresses for you and for the appropriate OTS office(s) where the public may submit comments;

(B) Section 516.55(g) of this chapter, which addresses public inspections of filings with OTS, does not apply; and

(C) Under § 516.60 of this chapter, you must publish the public notice at least 35 days before you take the proposed action. If you publish a public notice more than 12 months before you take the proposed action, the publication is invalid.

(iii) If you intend to change the location of an existing office, you posted a notice of your intent in a prominent location in the existing office to be relocated. You must post the notice for 30 days from the date of publication of the initial public notice described in paragraph (b)(3)(ii) of this section.

(iv)(A) No person files a comment opposing the proposed action within 30 days after the date of the publication of the proposed notice, or (B) A person files a comment opposing the proposed action and OTS determines that the comment raises issues that are not relevant to the approval standards in § 545.95(b) of this chapter or that OTS action in response to the comment is not required.

(4) *Re-designations of home and branch offices.* You may re-designate an existing branch office as a home office at the same time that you re-designate your existing home office as a branch office.

(c) *Section 5(m) of the HOLA.* If you are incorporated under the laws of, organized in, or do business in the District of Columbia and you satisfy the requirements of paragraph (b) of this section, the Director of OTS has approved your home or branch office changes under section 5(m) of the HOLA.

(d) *Maintenance of branch and home office following conversion, consolidation, purchase of bulk assets, merger, or purchase from receiver.* An existing savings association that converts to a federal savings association may maintain an existing office and a federal savings association may maintain any office acquired through consolidation, purchase of bulk assets, merger or purchase from the receiver of an association, except to the extent that the approval of the conversion, consolidation, merger, or purchase specifies otherwise.

(e) *Prohibition.* You may not file an application or notice (or utilize any exception described in paragraph (b) of this section) to establish a branch office, if you filed an application to merge or otherwise surrender your charter and the application has been pending for less than six months.

[69 FR 68248, Nov. 24, 2004, as amended at 70 FR 51586, Aug. 31, 2005]

§ 545.95 What processing procedures apply to my home or branch office application or notice?

(a) *Processing procedures.* Applications and notices under § 545.93 are subject to expedited or standard treatment under the application processing procedures at part 516 of this chapter.

§ 545.96

(1) *Publication and posting requirements.* (i) You must publish a public notice of your application or notice in accordance with the procedures in subpart B of part 516 of this chapter. Promptly after publication, you must transmit copies of the public notice and the publisher's affidavit to OTS.

(ii) If you propose to change the location of an existing office, you must also post a notice of the application in a prominent location in the office to be relocated. You must post the notice for 30 days from the date of publication of the initial public notice.

(2) *Comment procedures.* Commenters may submit comments on your application or notice in accordance with the procedures in subpart C of part 516 of this chapter.

(3) *Meeting procedures.* OTS may arrange a meeting in accordance with the procedures in subpart D of part 516 of this chapter.

(4) *OTS Review.* OTS will process your application or notice in accordance with the procedures in subpart E of part 516 of this chapter. The applicable review period for applications filed under standard treatment is 30 days rather than the time period specified at § 516.270(a) of this chapter.

(b) *Approval standards.* (1) OTS will approve an application (or not object to a notice), if your overall policies, condition, and operations afford no basis for supervisory objection.

(i) You should meet or exceed minimum capital requirements under part 567 of this chapter and should be at least adequately capitalized as described in § 565.4(b)(2) of this chapter, before and immediately after the proposed action. If you are undercapitalized as described in § 565.4(b)(3), OTS will deny your application (or disapprove your notice), unless the proposed action is otherwise permitted under section 38(e)(4) of the FDIA.

(ii) OTS will evaluate your record of helping to meet the credit needs of your entire community, including low- and moderate-income neighborhoods, under part 563e of this chapter. OTS may:

(A) Deny your application or disapprove your notice based upon this evaluation; or

(B) Impose a condition to the approval of your application (or non-objection to your notice) requiring you to improve specific practices and/or aspects of your performance under part 563e of this chapter. In most cases, a commitment to improve will not be sufficient to overcome a seriously deficient record.

(iii) OTS will review the application or notice under the National Environmental Policy Act (42 U.S.C. 3421 *et seq.*) and the National Historic Preservation Act (16 U.S.C. 470).

(2) In reviewing your application and notice, OTS may consider information available from any source, including any comments submitted by interested parties or views expressed by interested parties at meetings with OTS.

(3) OTS may approve an amendment to your charter in connection with a home office relocation under this section.

(c) *Expiration of OTS approval.* (1) You must open or relocate your office within twelve months of OTS approval of your application (or the date of OTS non-objection to your notice), unless OTS prescribes another time period. OTS may extend the time period if it determines that you are making a good-faith effort to promptly open or relocate the proposed office.

(2) If you do not open or relocate the proposed office within this time period, you must comply with the application and notice requirements of this section before you may open or relocate the proposed office.

[69 FR 68249, Nov. 24, 2004, as amended at 70 FR 51586, Aug. 31, 2005]

§ 545.96 Agency office.

(a) *General.* A Federal savings association may establish or maintain an agency office to engage in one or more of the following activities: (1) Servicing, originating, or approving loans and contracts; (2) managing or selling real estate owned by the Federal savings association; and (3) conducting fiduciary activities or activities ancillary to the association's fiduciary business in compliance with subpart A of part 550 of this chapter.

(b) *Additional services.* A Federal savings association may request, and OTS may approve, any service not listed in paragraph (a) of this section, except for payment on savings accounts.

(c) *Records.* A Federal savings association must maintain records of all business it transacts at an agency office. It must maintain these records at the agency office, and must transmit copies to a home or branch office.

[69 FR 68249, Nov. 24, 2004]

§ 545.101 Fiscal agency.

A Federal savings association designated fiscal agent by the Secretary of the Treasury or with Office approval by another instrumentality of the United States, shall, as such, perform such reasonable duties and exercise only such powers and privileges as the Secretary of the Treasury or such instrumentality may prescribe.

§ 545.121 Indemnification of directors, officers and employees.

A Federal savings association shall indemnify its directors, officers, and employees in accordance with the following requirements:

(a) *Definitions and rules of construction.* (1) Definitions for purposes of this section.

(i) *Action.* The term "action" means any judicial or administrative proceeding, or threatened proceeding, whether civil, criminal, or otherwise, including any appeal or other proceeding for review;

(ii) *Court.* The term "court" includes, without limitation, any court to which or in which any appeal or any proceeding for review is brought.

(iii) *Final judgment.* The term "final judgment" means a judgment, decree, or order which is not appealable or as to which the period for appeal has expired with no appeal taken.

(iv) *Settlement.* The term "settlement" includes entry of a judgment by consent or confession or a plea of guilty or *nolo contendere.*

(2) References in this section to any individual or other person, including any association, shall include legal representatives, successors, and assigns thereof.

(b) *General.* Subject to paragraphs (c) and (g) of this section, a savings association shall indemnify any person against whom an action is brought or threatened because that person is or was a director, officer, or employee of the association, for:

(1) Any amount for which that person becomes liable under a judgment if such action; and

(2) Reasonable costs and expenses, including reasonable attorney's fees, actually paid or incurred by that person in defending or settling such action, or in enforcing his or her rights under this section if he or she attains a favorable judgment in such enforcement action.

(c) *Requirements.* Indemnification shall be made to such period under paragraph (b) of this section only if:

(1) Final judgment on the merits is in his or her favor; or

(2) In case of:

(i) Settlement,

(ii) Final judgment against him or her, or

(iii) Final judgment in his or her favor, other than on the merits, if a majority of the disinterested directors of the savings association determine that he or she was acting in good faith within the scope of his or her employment or authority as he or she could reasonably have perceived it under the circumstances and for a purpose he or she could reasonably have believed under the circumstances was in the best interests of the savings association or its members.

However, no indemnification shall be made unless the association gives the Office at least 60 days' notice of its intention to make such indemnification. Such notice shall state the facts on which the action arose, the terms of any settlement, and any disposition of the action by a court. Such notice, a copy thereof, and a certified copy of the resolution containing the required determination by the board of directors shall be sent to the Regional Director, who shall promptly acknowledge receipt thereof. The notice period shall run from the date of such receipt. No such indemnification shall be made if the OTS advises the association in writing, within such notice period, of his or her objection thereto.

(d) *Insurance.* A savings association may obtain insurance to protect it and its directors, officers, and employees from potential losses arising from claims against any of them for alleged wrongful acts, or wrongful acts, committed in their capacity as directors, officers, or employees. However, no savings association may obtain insurance which provides for payment of losses of any person incurred as a consequence of his or her willful or criminal misconduct.

(e) *Payment of expenses.* If a majority of the directors of a savings association concludes that, in connection with an action, any person ultimately may become entitled to indemnification under this section, the directors may authorize payment of reasonable costs and expenses, including reasonable attorneys' fees, arising from the defense or settlement of such action. Nothing in this paragraph (e) shall prevent the directors of a savings association from imposing such conditions on a payment of expenses as they deem warranted and in the interests of the savings association. Before making advance payment of expenses under this paragraph (e), the savings association shall obtain an agreement that the savings association will be repaid if the person on whose behalf payment is made is later determined not to be entitled to such indemnification.

(f) *Exclusiveness of provisions.* No savings association shall indemnify any person referred to in paragraph (b) of this section or obtain insurance referred to in paragraph (d) of the section other than in accordance with this section. However, an association which has a bylaw in effect relating to indemnification of its personnel shall be governed solely by that bylaw, except that its authority to obtain insurance shall be governed by paragraph (d) of this section.

(g) The indemnification provided for in paragraph (b) of this section is subject to and qualified by 12 U.S.C. 1821(k).

[54 FR 49492, Nov. 30, 1989, as amended at 56 FR 59866, Nov. 26, 1991; 60 FR 66717, Dec. 26, 1995]

PART 546—FEDERAL MUTUAL SAVINGS ASSOCIATIONS—MERGER, DISSOLUTION, REORGANIZATION, AND CONVERSION

Sec.
546.1 Definitions.
546.2 Procedure; effective date.
546.3 Transfer of assets upon merger or consolidation.
546.4 Voluntary dissolution.

AUTHORITY: 12 U.S.C. 1462, 1462a, 1463, 1464, 1467a, 2901 et seq.

SOURCE: 54 FR 49517, Nov. 30, 1989, unless otherwise noted.

§ 546.1 Definitions.

The terms used in §§ 546.2 and 546.3 shall have the same meaning as set forth in §§ 552.13(b) and 563.22(g) of this chapter.

[59 FR 44622, Aug. 30, 1994]

§ 546.2 Procedure; effective date.

(a) A Federal mutual savings association may combine with any depository institution, provided that:

(1) The combination is in compliance with, and receives all approvals required under, any applicable statutes and regulations;

(2) Any resulting Federal savings association meets the requirements for Federal Home Loan Bank membership and insurance of accounts;

(3) Any resulting Federal savings association conforms within the time prescribed by the OTS to the requirements of sections 5(c) and 10(m) of the Home Owners' Loan Act; and

(4) The resulting institution shall be a mutually held savings association, unless:

(i) The transaction involves a supervisory merger;

(ii) The transaction is approved under part 563b of this chapter; or

(iii) The transaction involves a transfer in the context of a mutual holding company reorganization under section 10(o) of the Home Owners' Loan Act.

(b) Each Federal mutual savings association, by a two-thirds vote of its board of directors, shall approve a plan of combination evidenced by a combination agreement. The agreement shall state:

(1) That the combination shall not be effective unless and until the combination receives any necessary approval from the Office pursuant to § 563.22 (a) or (c), or in the case of a transaction requiring a notice pursuant to § 563.22(c), the notice has been filed, and the appropriate period of time has

passed or the OTS has advised the parties that it will not disapprove the transaction;

(2) Which constituent institution is to be the resulting institution;

(3) The name of the resulting institution;

(4) The location of the home office and any other offices of the resulting institution;

(5) The terms and conditions of the combination and the method of effectuation;

(6) Any charter amendments, or the new charter in the combination;

(7) The basis upon which the resulting institution's savings accounts will be issued;

(8) If the Federal mutual savings association is the resulting institution, the number, names, residence addresses, and terms of directors;

(9) The effect upon and assumption of any liquidation account of a disappearing institution by the resulting institution; and

(10) Such other provisions, agreements, or understandings as relate to the combination.

(c) Prior written notification to, notice to, or prior written approval of, the Office pursuant to §563.22 of this chapter is required for every combination. In the case of applications and notices pursuant to 563.22 (a) or (c), the Office shall apply the criteria set out in §563.22 of this chapter and shall impose any conditions it deems necessary or appropriate to ensure compliance with those criteria and the requirements of this chapter.

(d) Where the resulting institution is a Federal mutual savings association, the Office may approve a temporary increase in the number of directors of the resulting institution provided that the association submits a plan for bringing the board of directors into compliance with the requirements of §544.1 of this chapter within a reasonable period of time.

(e) Notwithstanding any other provision of this part, the Office may require that a plan of combination be submitted to the voting members of any of the mutual savings associations that are constituent institutions at a duly called meeting(s), and that the plan, to be effective, be approved by such voting members.

(f) A conservator or receiver for a Federal mutual savings association may combine the association with another insured depository institution without submitting the plan to the association's board of directors or members for their approval.

(g) If a plan of combination provides for a resulting Federal mutual savings association's name or location to be changed, its charter shall be amended accordingly. If the resulting institution is a Federal mutual savings association, the effective date of the combination shall be the date specified in the approval; if the resulting institution is not a Federal savings association, the effective date shall be that prescribed under applicable law. Approval of a merger automatically cancels the Federal charter of a Federal association that is a disappearing institution as of the effective date of merger, and the association shall, on that date, surrender its charter to the Office.

[59 FR 44622, Aug. 30, 1994, as amended at 71 FR 19811, Apr. 18, 2006]

§ 546.3 Transfer of assets upon merger or consolidation.

On the effective date of a merger or consolidation in which the resulting institution is a Federal association, all assets and property of the disappearing institutions shall immediately, without any further act, become the property of the resulting institution to the same extent as they were the property of the disappearing institutions, and the resulting institution shall be a continuation of the entity which absorbed the disappearing institutions. All rights and obligations of the disappearing institutions shall remain unimpaired, and the resulting institution shall, on the effective date of the merger or consolidation, succeed to all those rights and obligations, subject to the Home Owners' Loan Act and other applicable statutes.

[59 FR 44623, Aug. 30, 1994]

§ 546.4 Voluntary dissolution.

A Federal savings association's board of directors may propose a plan for dissolution of the association. The plan may provide for either:

(a) Appointment of the Federal Deposit Insurance Corporation (under section 5 of the Act and section 11 of the Federal Deposit Insurance Act, as amended or section 21A of the Federal Home Loan Bank Act, as amended) as receiver for the purpose of liquidation;

(b) Transfer of all the association's assets to another association or home-financing institutions under Federal or State charter either for cash sufficient to pay all obligations of the association and retire all outstanding accounts or in exchange for that association's payment of all the association's outstanding obligations and issuance of share accounts or other evidence of interest to the association's members on a *pro rata* basis; or

(c) Dissolution in a manner proposed by the directors which they consider best for all concerned.

The plan, and a statement of reasons for proposing dissolution and for proposing the plan, shall be submitted to the OTS for approval. The OTS will approve the plan if the OTS believes dissolution is advisable and the plan best for all concerned, but if the OTS considers the plan inadvisable, the OTS may either make recommendations to the association concerning the plan or disapprove it. When the plan is approved by the association's board of directors and by the OTS, it shall be submitted to the association's members at a duly called meeting and, when approved by a majority of votes cast at that meeting, shall become effective. After dissolution in accordance with the plan, a certificate evidencing dissolution, supported by such evidence as the OTS may require, shall immediately be filed with the OTS. When the OTS receives such evidence satisfactory to the OTS, it will terminate the corporate existence of the dissolved association and the association's charter shall thereby be canceled. A Federal savings association is not required to obtain approval under this section where the Federal savings association transfers all of its assets and liabilities to a bank in a transaction that is subject to § 563.22(b) of this chapter.

[54 FR 49517, Nov. 30, 1989, as amended at 55 FR 13512, Apr. 11, 1990; 57 FR 14342, Apr. 20, 1992; 59 FR 44623, Aug. 30, 1994; 70 FR 76675, Dec. 28, 2005]

PART 550—FIDUCIARY POWERS OF SAVINGS ASSOCIATIONS

Sec.
550.10 What regulations govern the fiduciary operations of savings associations?
550.20 What are fiduciary powers?
550.30 What fiduciary capacities does this part cover?
550.40 When do I have investment discretion?
550.50 What is a fiduciary account?
550.60 What other definitions apply to this part?

Subpart A—Obtaining Fiduciary Powers

550.70 Must I obtain OTS approval or file a notice before I exercise fiduciary powers?
550.80 How do I obtain OTS approval?
550.90 What information must I include in my application?
550.100 What factors may the OTS consider in its review of my application?
550.110 Who will act on my application?
550.120 What action will the OTS take on my application?
550.125 How do I file the notice under § 550.70(c)?

Subpart B—Exercising Fiduciary Powers

550.130 How may I conduct multi-state operations?
550.135 How do I determine which State's laws apply to my operations?
550.136 To what extent do State laws apply to my fiduciary operations?
550.140 Must I adopt and follow written policies and procedures in exercising fiduciary powers?

FIDUCIARY PERSONNEL AND FACILITIES

550.150 Who is responsible for the exercise of fiduciary powers?
550.160 What personnel and facilities may I use to perform fiduciary services?
550.170 May my other departments or affiliates use fiduciary personnel and facilities to perform other services?
550.180 May I perform fiduciary services for, or purchase fiduciary services from, another association or entity?
550.190 Must fiduciary officers and employees be bonded?

Office of Thrift Supervision, Treasury § 550.10

REVIEW OF A FIDUCIARY ACCOUNT

550.200 Must I review a prospective account before I accept it?
550.210 Must I conduct another review of an account after I accept it?
550.220 Are any other account reviews required?

CUSTODY AND CONTROL OF ASSETS

550.230 Who must maintain custody or control of assets in a fiduciary account?
550.240 May I hold investments of a fiduciary account off-premises?
550.250 Must I keep fiduciary assets separate from other assets?

INVESTING FUNDS OF A FIDUCIARY ACCOUNT

550.260 How may I invest funds of a fiduciary account?

FUNDS AWAITING INVESTMENT OR DISTRIBUTION

550.290 What must I do with fiduciary funds awaiting investment or distribution?
550.300 Where may I deposit fiduciary funds awaiting investment or distribution?
550.310 What if the FDIC does not insure the deposits?
550.320 What is acceptable collateral for uninsured deposits?

RESTRICTIONS ON SELF DEALING

550.330 Are there investments in which I may not invest funds of a fiduciary account?
550.340 May I exercise rights to purchase additional stock or fractional shares of my stock or obligations or the stock or obligations of my affiliates?
550.350 May I lend, sell, or transfer assets of a fiduciary account if I have an interest in the transaction?
550.360 May I make a loan to a fiduciary account that is secured by an interest in the assets in the account?
550.370 May I sell assets or lend money between fiduciary accounts?

COMPENSATION, GIFTS, AND BEQUESTS

550.380 May I earn compensation for acting in a fiduciary capacity?
550.390 May my officer or employee retain compensation for acting as a co-fiduciary?
550.400 May my fiduciary officer or employee accept a gift or bequest?

RECORDKEEPING REQUIREMENTS

550.410 What records must I keep?
550.420 How long must I keep these records?
550.430 Must I keep fiduciary records separate and distinct from other records?

AUDIT REQUIREMENTS

550.440 When do I have to audit my fiduciary activities?
550.450 What standards govern the conduct of the audit?
550.460 Who may conduct an audit?
550.470 Who directs the conduct of the audit?
550.480 How do I report the results of the audit?

Subpart C—Depositing Securities With State Authorities

550.490 When must I deposit securities with State authorities?
550.500 How much must I deposit if I administer fiduciary assets in more than one State?
550.510 What must I do if State authorities refuse my deposit?

Subpart D—Terminating Fiduciary Activities

RECEIVERSHIP OR LIQUIDATION

550.520 What happens if I am placed in receivership or voluntary liquidation?

SURRENDER OF FIDUCIARY POWERS

550.530 How do I surrender fiduciary powers?
550.540 When will the OTS terminate my fiduciary powers?
550.550 May I recover my deposit from State authorities?

REVOCATION OF FIDUCIARY POWERS

550.560 When may the OTS revoke my fiduciary powers?
550.570 What procedures govern the revocation?

Subpart E—Activities Exempt From This Part

550.580 When may I conduct fiduciary activities without obtaining OTS approval?
550.590 What standards must I observe when acting in exempt fiduciary capacities?
550.600 How may funds be invested when I act in an exempt fiduciary capacity?
550.610 What disclosures must I make when acting in exempt fiduciary capacities?
550.620 May I receive compensation for acting in exempt fiduciary capacities?

AUTHORITY: 12 U.S.C. 1462a, 1463, 1464.

SOURCE: 62 FR 67703, Dec. 30, 1997, unless otherwise noted.

§ 550.10 What regulations govern the fiduciary operations of savings associations?

(a) *Federal savings associations.* A Federal savings association ("you") must

§ 550.20

conduct its fiduciary operations in accordance with 12 U.S.C. 1464(n) and this part.

(b) *State-chartered savings associations.* (1) A State-chartered savings association must conduct its fiduciary operations in accordance with applicable State law, and must exercise its fiduciary powers in a safe and sound manner. To ensure safe and sound operations, State-chartered savings associations and their subsidiaries should follow the standards for the exercise of fiduciary powers in this part.

(2) The OTS will monitor the fiduciary operations of State-chartered savings associations and their subsidiaries to ensure that those operations are conducted in a safe and sound manner. The OTS may object to practices that deviate materially from the practices described in this part, and may restrict or prohibit activities that threaten the safety and soundness of a State-chartered savings association.

§ 550.20 What are fiduciary powers?

Fiduciary powers are the authority that OTS permits you to exercise under 12 U.S.C. 1464(n).

[67 FR 76298, Dec. 12, 2002]

§ 550.30 What fiduciary capacities does this part cover?

You are subject to this part if you act in a fiduciary capacity, except as described in subpart E of this part. You act in a fiduciary capacity when you act in any of the following capacities:

(a) Trustee.
(b) Executor.
(c) Administrator.
(d) Registrar of stocks and bonds.
(e) Transfer agent.
(f) Assignee.
(g) Receiver.
(h) Guardian or conservator of the estate of a minor, an incompetent person, an absent person, or a person over whose estate a court has taken jurisdiction, other than under bankruptcy or insolvency laws.
(i) A fiduciary in a relationship established under a State law that is substantially similar to the Uniform Gifts to Minors Act or the Uniform Transfers to Minors Act as published by the American Law Institute.

(j) Investment adviser, if you receive a fee for your investment advice.
(k) Any capacity in which you have investment discretion on behalf of another.
(l) Any other similar capacity that the OTS may authorize under 12 U.S.C. 1464(n).

§ 550.40 When do I have investment discretion?

(a) *General.* You have investment discretion when you have, with respect to a fiduciary account, the sole or shared authority to determine what securities or other assets to purchase or sell on behalf of that account. It does not matter whether you have exercised this authority.

(b) *Delegations.* You retain investment discretion if you delegate investment discretion to another. You also have investment discretion if you receive delegated authority to exercise investment discretion from another.

§ 550.50 What is a fiduciary account?

A fiduciary account is an account that you administer acting in a fiduciary capacity.

§ 550.60 What other definitions apply to this part?

Activities ancillary to your fiduciary business include advertising, marketing, or soliciting fiduciary business, contacting existing or potential customers, answering questions and providing information to customers related to their accounts, acting as liaison between you and your customer (for example, forwarding requests for distribution, changes in investment objectives, forms, or funds received from the customer), and inspecting or maintaining custody of fiduciary assets or holding title to real property. This list is illustrative and not comprehensive. Other activities may also be "ancillary activities" for purposes of this definition.

Affiliate has the same meaning as in 12 U.S.C. 221a(b). For purposes of this part, substitute the term "Federal savings association" for the term "member bank" whenever it appears in 12 U.S.C. 221a(b).

Applicable law means the law of a State or other jurisdiction governing your fiduciary relationships, any Federal law governing those relationships, the terms of the instrument governing a fiduciary relationship, and any court order pertaining to the relationship.

Fiduciary activities include accepting a fiduciary appointment, executing fiduciary-related documents, providing investment advice for a fee regarding fiduciary assets, or making discretionary decisions regarding investment or distribution of assets.

Fiduciary officers and employees means the officers and employees of a Federal savings association to whom the board of directors or its designee has assigned functions involving the exercise of the association's fiduciary powers.

[62 FR 67703, Dec. 30, 1997, as amended at 67 FR 76298, Dec. 12, 2002]

Subpart A—Obtaining Fiduciary Powers

§ 550.70 Must I obtain OTS approval or file a notice before I exercise fiduciary powers?

You should refer to the following chart to determine if you must obtain OTS approval or file a notice with OTS before you exercise fiduciary powers. This chart does not apply to activities that are exempt under subpart E of this part.

If you will conduct . . .	Then . . .
(a) Fiduciary activities for the first time and OTS has not previously approved an application that you submitted under this part.	You must obtain prior approval from OTS under §§ 550.80 through 550.120 before you conduct the activities
(b) Fiduciary activities that are materially different from the activities that OTS has previously approved for you, including fiduciary activities that OTS has previously approved for you that you have not exercised for at least five years.	You must obtain prior approval from OTS under §§ 550.80 through 550.120 before you conduct the activities
(c) Fiduciary activities that are not materially different from the activities that OTS has previously approved for you.	You must file a written notice described at § 550.125 if you commence the activities in a new State. You do not need to file a written notice if you commence the activities at a new location in a State where you already conduct these activities.
(d) Activities that are ancillary to your fiduciary business.	You do not have to obtain prior OTS approval or file a notice with OTS.

[67 FR 76298, Dec. 12, 2002; 68 FR 2108, Jan. 15, 2003, as amended at 68 FR 75109, Dec. 30, 2003]

§ 550.80 How do I obtain OTS approval?

You must file an application under part 516, subparts A and E of this chapter.

[66 FR 13006, Mar. 2, 2001]

§ 550.90 What information must I include in my application?

You must describe the fiduciary powers that you or your affiliate will exercise. You must also include information necessary to enable the OTS to make the determinations described in § 550.100.

§ 550.100 What factors may the OTS consider in its review of my application?

The OTS may consider the following factors when reviewing your application:

(a) Your financial condition.

(b) Your capital and whether that capital is sufficient under the circumstances.

(c) Your overall performance.

(d) The fiduciary powers you propose to exercise.

(e) Your proposed supervision of those powers.

(f) The availability of legal counsel.

(g) The needs of the community to be served.

(h) Any other facts or circumstances that the OTS considers proper.

§ 550.110 Who will act on my application?

The Director of OTS may act on any application. The Regional Director may act on an application if it does not raise any significant issues of law or policy on which the OTS has not taken a formal position.

§ 550.120 What action will the OTS take on my application?

The OTS may approve or deny your application. If your application is approved, the OTS may impose conditions to ensure that the requirements of this part are met.

§ 550.125 How do I file the notice under § 550.70(c)?

(a) If you are required to file a notice under § 550.70(c), within ten days after you commence the fiduciary activities in a new State, you must file a written notice that identifies each new State in which you conduct or will conduct fiduciary activities, describe the fiduciary activities that you conduct or will conduct in each new State, and provide sufficient information supporting a conclusion that the activities are permissible in the State.

(b) You must file the notice with the appropriate OTS Regional Office at the address in § 516.40(a) of this chapter.

[67 FR 76299, Dec. 12, 2002]

Subpart B—Exercising Fiduciary Powers

§ 550.130 How may I conduct multistate operations?

(a) *Conducting fiduciary activities in more than one State.* You may conduct fiduciary activities in any State, subject to the application and notice requirements in subpart A of this part.

(b) *Serving customers in more than one State.* When you conduct fiduciary activities in a State:

(1) You may market your fiduciary services to, and act as a fiduciary for, customers located in any State, may act as a fiduciary for relationships that include property located in other States, and may act as a testamentary trustee for a testator located in other States.

(2) You may establish or utilize an office in any State to perform activities that are ancillary to your fiduciary business.

[67 FR 76299, Dec. 12, 2002]

§ 550.135 How do I determine which State's laws apply to my operations?

(a) The State laws that apply to you by virtue of 12 U.S.C. 1464(n) are the laws of the States in which you conduct fiduciary activities. For each individual State, you may conduct fiduciary activities in the capacity of trustee, executor, administrator, guardian, or in any other fiduciary capacity the State permits for its State banks, trust companies, or other corporations that compete with Federal savings associations in the State.

(b) For each fiduciary relationship, the State referred to in 12 U.S.C. 1464(n) is the State in which you conduct fiduciary activities for that relationship.

[67 FR 76299, Dec. 12, 2002]

§ 550.136 To what extent do State laws apply to my fiduciary operations?

(a) *Occupation of field.* To enhance safety and soundness and to enable Federal savings associations to conduct their fiduciary activities in accordance with the best practices of thrift institutions in the United States (by efficiently delivering fiduciary services to the public free from undue regulatory duplication and burden), OTS occupies the field of the regulation of the fiduciary activities of Federal savings associations. In so doing, OTS intends to give Federal savings associations maximum flexibility to exercise their fiduciary powers in accordance with a uniform scheme of Federal regulation. Accordingly, Federal savings associations may exercise fiduciary powers as authorized under Federal law, including this part, without regard to State laws that purport to regulate or otherwise affect their fiduciary activities, except to the extent provided in 12 U.S.C. 1464(n) (State laws regarding scope of fiduciary powers, access to examination reports regarding trust activities, deposits of securities, oaths and affidavits, and capital) or in paragraph (c) of this section. For purposes of this section, "State law" includes any State statute, regulation, ruling, order, or judicial decision.

(b) *Illustrative examples.* Examples of State laws that are preempted by the HOLA and this section include those regarding:

(1) Registration and licensing;

(2) Recordkeeping;

(3) Advertising and marketing;

(4) The ability of a federal savings association conducting fiduciary activities to maintain an action or proceeding in State court; and

(5) Fiduciary-related fees.

(c) *State laws that are not preempted.* State laws of the following types are not preempted to the extent that they only incidentally affect the fiduciary operations of Federal savings associations or are otherwise consistent with the purposes of paragraph (a) of this section:

(1) Contract and commercial law;
(2) Real property law;
(3) Tort law;
(4) Criminal law;
(5) Probate law; and
(6) Any other law that OTS, upon review, finds:
(i) Furthers a vital State interest; and
(ii) Either has only an incidental effect on fiduciary operations or is not otherwise contrary to the purposes expressed in paragraph (a) of this section.

[67 FR 76299, Dec. 12, 2002, as amended at 68 FR 53026, Sept. 9, 2003]

§ 550.140 Must I adopt and follow written policies and procedures in exercising fiduciary powers?

You must adopt and follow written policies and procedures adequate to maintain your fiduciary activities in compliance with applicable law. Among other relevant matters, the policies and procedures should address, where appropriate, the following areas:

(a) Your brokerage placement practices.

(b) Your methods for ensuring that your fiduciary officers and employees do not use material inside information in connection with any decision or recommendation to purchase or sell any security.

(c) Your methods for preventing self-dealing and conflicts of interest.

(d) Your selection and retention of legal counsel who is ready and available to advise you and your fiduciary officers and employees on fiduciary matters.

(e) Your investment of funds held as fiduciary, including short-term investments and the treatment of fiduciary funds awaiting investment or distribution.

FIDUCIARY PERSONNEL AND FACILITIES

§ 550.150 Who is responsible for the exercise of fiduciary powers?

The exercise of your fiduciary powers must be managed by or under the direction of your board of directors. In discharging its responsibilities, the board may assign any function related to the exercise of fiduciary powers to any director, officer, employee, or committee of directors, officers, or employees.

§ 550.160 What personnel and facilities may I use to perform fiduciary services?

You may use your qualified personnel and facilities or an affiliate's qualified personnel and facilities to perform services related to the exercise of fiduciary powers.

§ 550.170 May my other departments or affiliates use fiduciary personnel and facilities to perform other services?

Your other departments or affiliates may use fiduciary officers, employees, and facilities to perform services unrelated to the exercise of fiduciary powers, to the extent not prohibited by applicable law.

§ 550.180 May I perform fiduciary services for, or purchase fiduciary services from, another association or entity?

You may perform services related to the exercise of fiduciary powers for another association or other entity under a written agreement. You may also purchase services related to the exercise of fiduciary powers from another association or other entity under a written agreement.

§ 550.190 Must fiduciary officers and employees be bonded?

You must obtain an adequate bond for all fiduciary officers and employees.

REVIEW OF A FIDUCIARY ACCOUNT

§ 550.200 Must I review a prospective account before I accept it?

Before accepting a prospective fiduciary account, you must review it to determine whether you can properly administer the account.

§ 550.210 Must I conduct another review of an account after I accept it?

After you accept a fiduciary account for which you have investment discretion, you must conduct a prompt review of all assets of the account to evaluate whether they are appropriate, individually and collectively, for the account.

§ 550.220 Are any other account reviews required?

At least once every calendar year, you must conduct a review of all assets of each fiduciary account for which you have investment discretion. In this review, you must evaluate whether the assets are appropriate, individually and collectively, for the account.

CUSTODY AND CONTROL OF ASSETS

§ 550.230 Who must maintain custody or control of assets in a fiduciary account?

You must place assets of fiduciary accounts in the joint custody or control of not fewer than two fiduciary officers or employees designated for that purpose by the board of directors.

§ 550.240 May I hold investments of a fiduciary account off-premises?

You may hold the investments of a fiduciary account off-premises, if this practice is consistent with applicable law, and you maintain adequate safeguards and controls.

§ 550.250 Must I keep fiduciary assets separate from other assets?

You must keep the assets of fiduciary accounts separate from your other assets. You must also keep the assets of each fiduciary account separate from all other accounts, or you must identify the investments as the property of a particular account, except as provided in §§ 550.260.

INVESTING FUNDS OF A FIDUCIARY ACCOUNT

§ 550.260 How may I invest funds of a fiduciary account?

(a) *General.* You must invest funds of a fiduciary account in a manner consistent with applicable law.

(b) *Collective investment funds.* (1) You may invest funds of a fiduciary account in a collective investment fund, including a collective investment fund that you have established. In establishing and administering such funds, you must comply with 12 CFR 9.18.

(2) If you must file a document with the Comptroller of the Currency under 12 CFR 9.18, you must also file that document with the appropriate Regional Office at § 516.40(a) of this chapter. The OTS may review such documents for compliance with this part and other laws and regulations.

(3) "Bank" and "national bank" as used in 12 CFR 9.18 shall be deemed to include a Federal savings association.

[62 FR 67703, Dec. 30, 1997, as amended at 66 FR 13006, Mar. 2, 2001]

FUNDS AWAITING INVESTMENT OR DISTRIBUTION

§ 550.290 What must I do with fiduciary funds awaiting investment or distribution?

If you have investment discretion or discretion over distributions for a fiduciary account which contains funds awaiting investment or distribution, you must ensure that those funds do not remain uninvested and undistributed any longer than is reasonable for the proper management of the account and consistent with applicable law. You also must obtain a rate of return for those funds that is consistent with applicable law.

§ 550.300 Where may I deposit fiduciary funds awaiting investment or distribution?

(a) *Self deposits.* You may deposit funds of a fiduciary account that are awaiting investment or distribution in your other departments, unless prohibited by applicable law.

(b) *Affiliate deposits.* You may also deposit funds of a fiduciary account that are awaiting investment or distribution with an affiliated insured depository institution, unless prohibited by applicable law.

§ 550.310 What if the FDIC does not insure the deposits?

If the FDIC does not insure the entire amount of a self deposit, you must set aside collateral as security. If the FDIC does not insure the entire amount of an affiliate deposit, you or your affiliate must set aside collateral as security. The market value of the collateral must at all times equal or exceed the amount of the uninsured fiduciary funds. You must place the collateral under the control of appropriate fiduciary officers and employees.

[62 FR 67703, Dec. 30, 1997, as amended at 67 FR 76299, Dec. 12, 2002]

§ 550.320 **What is acceptable collateral for uninsured deposits?**

Any of the following is acceptable collateral for self deposits or affiliate deposits under § 550.310:

(a) Direct obligations of the United States, or other obligations fully guaranteed by the United States as to principal and interest.

(b) Readily marketable securities of the classes in which State-chartered corporate fiduciaries are permitted to invest fiduciary funds under applicable State law.

(c) Other readily marketable securities as the OTS may determine.

(d) Surety bonds, to the extent they provide adequate security, unless prohibited by applicable law.

(e) Any other assets that qualify under applicable State law as appropriate security for deposits of fiduciary funds.

RESTRICTIONS ON SELF DEALING

§ 550.330 **Are there investments in which I may not invest funds of a fiduciary account?**

You may not invest funds of a fiduciary account for which you have investment discretion in the following assets, unless authorized by applicable law:

(a) The stock or obligations of, or assets acquired from, you or any of your directors, officers, or employees.

(b) The stock or obligations of, or assets acquired from, your affiliates or any of their directors, officers, or employees.

(c) The stock or obligations of, or assets acquired from, other individuals or organizations if you have an interest in the individual or organization that might affect the exercise of your best judgment.

§ 550.340 **May I exercise rights to purchase additional stock or fractional shares of my stock or obligations or the stock or obligations of my affiliates?**

If the retention of investments in your stock or obligations or the stock or obligations of an affiliate in fiduciary accounts is consistent with applicable law, you may do either of the following:

(a) Exercise rights to purchase additional stock (or securities convertible into additional stock) when these rights are offered *pro rata* to stockholders.

(b) Purchase fractional shares to complement fractional shares acquired through the exercise of rights or through the receipt of a stock dividend resulting in fractional share holdings.

§ 550.350 **May I lend, sell, or transfer assets of a fiduciary account if I have an interest in the transaction?**

(a) *General restriction.* Except as provided in paragraph (b) of this section, you may not lend, sell, or otherwise transfer assets of a fiduciary account for which you have investment discretion to yourself or any of your directors, officers, or employees; to your affiliates or any of their directors, officers, or employees; or to other individuals or organizations with whom you have an interest that might affect the exercise of your best judgment.

(b) *Exceptions*—(1) *Funds for which you have investment discretion.* You may lend, sell or otherwise transfer assets of a fiduciary account for which you have investment discretion to yourself or any of your directors, officers, or employees; to your affiliates or any of their directors, officers, or employees; or to other individuals or organizations with whom you have an interest that might affect the exercise of your best judgment, if you meet one of the following conditions:

(i) The transaction is authorized by applicable law.

(ii) Legal counsel advises you in writing that you have incurred, in your fiduciary capacity, a contingent or potential liability. Upon the sale or transfer of assets, you must reimburse

§ 550.360

the fiduciary account in cash in an amount equal to the greater of book or market value of the assets.

(iii) The transaction is permitted under 12 CFR 9.18(b)(8)(iii) for defaulted fixed-income investments.

(iv) The OTS requires you to do so.

(2) *Funds held as trustee.* You may make loans of funds held in trust to any of your directors, officers, or employees if the funds are held in an employee benefit plan and the loan is made in accordance with the exemptions found at section 408 of the Employee Retirement Income Security Act of 1974 (29 U.S.C. 1108).

§ 550.360 May I make a loan to a fiduciary account that is secured by an interest in the assets of the account?

You may make a loan to a fiduciary account that is secured by an interest in the assets of the account, if the transaction is fair to the account and is not prohibited by applicable law.

§ 550.370 May I sell assets or lend money between fiduciary accounts?

You may sell assets or lend money between fiduciary accounts, if the transaction is fair to both accounts and is not prohibited by applicable law.

COMPENSATION, GIFTS, AND BEQUESTS

§ 550.380 May I earn compensation for acting in a fiduciary capacity?

If the amount of your compensation for acting in a fiduciary capacity is not set or governed by applicable law, you may charge a reasonable fee for your services.

§ 550.390 May my officer or employee retain compensation for acting as a co-fiduciary?

You may not permit your officers or employees to retain any compensation for acting as a co-fiduciary with you in the administration of a fiduciary account, except with the specific approval of your board of directors.

§ 550.400 May my fiduciary officer or employee accept a gift or bequest?

You may not permit any fiduciary officer or employee to accept a bequest or gift of fiduciary assets, unless the bequest or gift is directed or made by a relative of the officer or employee or is specifically approved by your board of directors.

RECORDKEEPING REQUIREMENTS

§ 550.410 What records must I keep?

You must keep adequate records for all fiduciary accounts. For example, you must keep documents on the establishment and termination of each fiduciary account.

§ 550.420 How long must I keep these records?

You must keep fiduciary records for three years after the termination of the account or the termination of any litigation relating to the account, whichever is later.

§ 550.430 Must I keep fiduciary records separate and distinct from other records?

You must keep fiduciary records separate and distinct from your other records.

AUDIT REQUIREMENTS

§ 550.440 When do I have to audit my fiduciary activities?

(a) *Annual Audit.* If you do not use a continuous audit system described in paragraph (b) of this section, then you must arrange for a suitable audit of all significant fiduciary activities at least once during each calendar year.

(b) *Continuous audit.* Instead of an annual audit, you may adopt a continuous audit system. Under a continuous audit system, you must arrange for a discrete audit of each significant fiduciary activity (*i.e.*, on an activity-by-activity basis) at an interval commensurate with the nature and risk of that activity. Some fiduciary activities may receive audits at intervals greater or less than one year, as appropriate.

§ 550.450 What standards govern the conduct of the audit?

Auditors must follow generally accepted standards for attestation engagements and other standards established by the OTS. An audit must ascertain whether your internal control policies and procedures provide reasonable assurance of three things:

Office of Thrift Supervision, Treasury § 550.530

(a) You are administering fiduciary activities in accordance with applicable law.

(b) You are properly safeguarding fiduciary assets.

(c) You are accurately recording transactions in appropriate accounts in a timely manner.

§ 550.460 Who may conduct an audit?

Internal auditors, external auditors, or other qualified persons who are responsible only to the board of directors, may conduct an audit.

§ 550.470 Who directs the conduct of the audit?

Your fiduciary audit committee directs the conduct of the audit. Your fiduciary audit committee may consist of a committee of your directors or an audit committee of an affiliate. There are two restrictions on who may serve on the committee:

(a) Your officers and officers of an affiliate who participate significantly in administering your fiduciary activities may not serve on the audit committee.

(b) A majority of the members of the audit committee may not serve on any committee to which the board of directors has delegated power to manage and control your fiduciary activities.

§ 550.480 How do I report the results of the audit?

(a) *Annual audit.* If you conduct an annual audit, you must note the results of the audit (including significant actions taken as a result of the audit) in the minutes of the board of directors.

(b) *Continuous audit.* If you adopt a continuous audit system, you must note the results of all discrete audits conducted since the last audit report (including significant actions taken as a result of the audits) in the minutes of the board of directors at least once during each calendar year.

Subpart C—Depositing Securities With State Authorities

§ 550.490 When must I deposit securities with State authorities?

You must deposit securities with a State's authorities or, if applicable, a Federal Home Loan Bank under § 550.510, if you meet all of the following:

(a) You are located in the State.

(b) You act as a private or court-appointed trustee.

(c) The law of the State requires corporations acting in a fiduciary capacity to deposit securities with State authorities for the protection of private or court trusts.

§ 550.500 How much must I deposit if I administer fiduciary assets in more than one State?

If you administer fiduciary assets in more than one State, you must compute the amount of deposit required for each State on the basis of fiduciary assets that you administer primarily from offices located in that State.

§ 550.510 What must I do if State authorities refuse my deposit?

If State authorities refuse to accept your deposit under § 550.490, you must deposit the securities with the Federal Home Loan Bank of which you are a member. The Federal Home Loan Bank will hold the securities for the protection of private or court trusts to the same extent as if the securities had been deposited with State authorities.

Subpart D—Terminating Fiduciary Activities

RECEIVERSHIP OR LIQUIDATION

§ 550.520 What happens if I am placed in receivership or voluntary liquidation?

If the OTS appoints a conservator or receiver for you under part 558 of this chapter, or if you place yourself in voluntary liquidation, the receiver, conservator, or liquidating agent must promptly close or transfer all fiduciary accounts to a substitute fiduciary, in accordance with OTS instructions and the orders of the court having jurisdiction.

SURRENDER OF FIDUCIARY POWERS

§ 550.530 How do I surrender fiduciary powers?

If you want to surrender your fiduciary powers, you must file a certified copy of a resolution of your board of directors evidencing that intent. You

§ 550.540

must file the resolution with the appropriate Regional Office at the address listed in § 516.40(a) of this chapter.

[62 FR 66703, Dec. 30, 1997, as amended at 66 FR 13006, Mar. 2, 2001]

§ 550.540 When will the OTS terminate my fiduciary powers?

If, after appropriate investigation, the Regional Director is satisfied that you have been discharged from all fiduciary duties, the Regional Director will issue a written notice indicating that you are no longer authorized to exercise fiduciary powers.

§ 550.550 May I recover my deposit from State authorities?

Upon issuance of the OTS written notice under § 550.540, you may recover any securities deposited with State authorities, or a Federal Home Loan Bank, under subpart C of this part.

REVOCATION OF FIDUCIARY POWERS

§ 550.560 When may the OTS revoke my fiduciary powers?

The OTS may revoke your fiduciary powers if it determines that you have done any of the following:

(a) Exercised those fiduciary powers unlawfully or unsoundly.

(b) Failed to exercise those fiduciary powers for five consecutive years.

(c) Otherwise failed to follow the requirements of this part.

§ 550.570 What procedures govern the revocation?

The procedures for revocation of fiduciary powers are set forth in 12 U.S.C. 1464(n)(10). The OTS will conduct the hearing required under 12 U.S.C. 1464(n)(10)(B) under part 509 of this chapter.

Subpart E—Activities Exempt From This Part

§ 550.580 When may I conduct fiduciary activities without obtaining OTS approval?

Subject to the requirements of this subpart E, you do not need OTS approval under subpart B if you conduct fiduciary activities in the following fiduciary capacities:

(a) Trustee of a trust created or organized in the United States and forming part of a stock bonus, pension, or profit-sharing plan qualifying for specific tax treatment under section 401(d) of the Internal Revenue Code of 1954 (26 U.S.C. 401(d)).

(b) Trustee or custodian of a Individual Retirement Account within the meaning of section 408(a) of the Internal Revenue Code of 1954 (26 U.S.C. 408(a)).

[62 FR 67703, Dec. 30, 1997, as amended at 67 FR 76299, Dec. 12, 2002]

§ 550.590 What standards must I observe when acting in exempt fiduciary capacities?

You must observe principles of sound fiduciary administration, including those related to recordkeeping and segregation of assets.

§ 550.600 How may funds be invested when I act in an exempt fiduciary capacity?

If you act in an exempt fiduciary capacity under § 550.580, the funds of the fiduciary account may be invested only in the following:

(a) Your accounts, deposits, obligations, or securities.

(b) Other assets as the customer may direct, provided you do not exercise any investment discretion and do not directly or indirectly provide any investment advice for the fiduciary account.

[62 FR 67703, Dec. 30, 1997, as amended at 67 FR 76299, Dec. 12, 2002]

§ 550.610 What disclosures must I make when acting in exempt fiduciary capacities?

If you act in an exempt fiduciary capacity under § 550.580 and fiduciary investments are not limited to accounts or deposits insured by the FDIC, you must include the following language in bold type on the first page of any contract documents:

Funds invested pursuant to this agreement are not insured by the Federal Deposit Insurance Corporation ("FDIC") merely because the trustee or custodian is a Federal savings association the accounts of which are covered by such insurance. Only investments in the accounts of a Federal savings association

Office of Thrift Supervision, Treasury § 551.20

are insured by the FDIC, subject to its rules and regulations.

§ 550.620 May I receive compensation for acting in exempt fiduciary capacities?

You may receive reasonable compensation.

PART 551—RECORDKEEPING AND CONFIRMATION REQUIREMENTS FOR SECURITIES TRANSACTIONS

Sec.
551.10 What does this part do?
551.20 Must I comply with this part?
551.30 What requirements apply to all transactions?
551.40 What definitions apply to this part?

Subpart A—Recordkeeping Requirements

551.50 What records must I maintain for securities transactions?
551.60 How must I maintain my records?

Subpart B—Content and Timing of Notice

551.70 What type of notice must I provide when I effect a securities transaction for a customer?
551.80 How do I provide a registered broker-dealer confirmation?
551.90 How do I provide a written notice?
551.100 What are the alternate notice requirements?
551.110 May I provide a notice electronically?
551.120 May I charge a fee for a notice?

Subpart C—Settlement of Securities Transactions

551.130 When must I settle a securities transaction?

Subpart D—Securities Trading Policies and Procedures

551.140 What policies and procedures must I maintain and follow for securities transactions?
551.150 How do my officers and employees file reports of personal securities trading transactions?

AUTHORITY: 12 U.S.C. 1462a, 1463, 1464.

SOURCE: 67 FR 76299, Dec. 12, 2002, unless otherwise noted.

§ 551.10 What does this part do?

This part establishes recordkeeping and confirmation requirements that apply when a savings association ("you") effects certain securities transactions for customers.

§ 551.20 Must I comply with this part?

(a) *General*. Except as provided under paragraph (b) of this section, you must comply with this part when:

(1) You effect a securities transaction for a customer.

(2) You effect a transaction in government securities.

(3) You effect a transaction in municipal securities and are not registered as a municipal securities dealer with the SEC.

(4) You effect a securities transaction as fiduciary. If you are a Federal savings association, you also must comply with 12 CFR part 550 when you effect such a transaction. If you are a State savings association, you must comply with applicable law when you effect such a transaction.

(b) *Exceptions*—(1) *Small number of transactions*. You are not required to comply with § 551.50(b) through (d) (recordkeeping) and § 551.140(a) through (c) (policies and procedures), if you effected an average of fewer than 500 securities transactions per year for customers over the three prior calendar years. You may exclude transactions in government securities when you calculate this average.

(2) *Government securities*. If you effect fewer than 500 government securities brokerage transactions per year, you are not required to comply with § 551.50 (recordkeeping) for those transactions. This exception does not apply to government securities dealer transactions. See 17 CFR 404.4(a).

(3) *Municipal securities*. If you are registered with the SEC as a "municipal securities dealer," as defined in 15 U.S.C. 78c(a)(30) (see 15 U.S.C. 78o-4), you are not required to comply with this part when you conduct municipal securities transactions.

(4) *Foreign branches*. You are not required to comply with this part when you conduct a transaction at your foreign branch.

(5) *Transactions by registered broker-dealers*. You are not required to comply with this part for securities transactions effected by a registered broker-dealer, if the registered broker-dealer directly provides the customer with a

§ 551.30

confirmation. These transactions include a transaction effected by your employee who also acts as an employee of a registered broker-dealer ("dual employee").

§ 551.30 What requirements apply to all transactions?

You must effect all transactions, including transactions excepted under § 551.20, in a safe and sound manner. You must maintain effective systems of records and controls regarding your customers' securities transactions. These systems must clearly and accurately reflect all appropriate information and provide an adequate basis for an audit.

§ 551.40 What definitions apply to this part?

Asset-backed security means a security that is primarily serviced by the cash flows of a discrete pool of receivables or other financial assets, either fixed or revolving, that by their terms convert into cash within a finite time period. *Asset-backed security* includes any rights or other assets designed to ensure the servicing or timely distribution of proceeds to the security holders.

Common or collective investment fund means any fund established under 12 CFR 550.260(b) or 12 CFR 9.18.

Completion of the transaction means:

(1) If the customer purchases a security through or from you, except as provided in paragraph (2) of this definition, the time the customer pays you any part of the purchase price. If payment is made by a bookkeeping entry, the time you make the bookkeeping entry for any part of the purchase price.

(2) If the customer purchases a security through or from you and pays for the security before you request payment or notify the customer that payment is due, the time you deliver the security to or into the account of the customer.

(3) If the customer sells a security through or to you, except as provided in paragraph (4) of this definition, the time the customer delivers the security to you. If you have custody of the security at the time of sale, the time you transfer the security from the customer's account.

(4) If the customer sells a security through or to you and delivers the security to you before you request delivery or notify the customer that delivery is due, the time you pay the customer or pay into the customer's account.

Customer means a person or account, including an agency, trust, estate, guardianship, or other fiduciary account for which you effect a securities transaction. *Customer* does not include a broker or dealer, or you when you: act as a broker or dealer; act as a fiduciary with investment discretion over an account; are a trustee that acts as the shareholder of record for the purchase or sale of securities; or are the issuer of securities that are the subject of the transaction.

Debt security means any security, such as a bond, debenture, note, or any other similar instrument that evidences a liability of the issuer (including any security of this type that is convertible into stock or a similar security). *Debt security* also includes a fractional or participation interest in these debt securities. *Debt security* does not include securities issued by an investment company registered under the Investment Company Act of 1940, 15 U.S.C. 80a-1, et seq.

Government security means:

(1) A security that is a direct obligation of, or an obligation that is guaranteed as to principal and interest by, the United States;

(2) A security that is issued or guaranteed by a corporation in which the United States has a direct or indirect interest if the Secretary of the Treasury has designated the security for exemption as necessary or appropriate in the public interest or for the protection of investors;

(3) A security issued or guaranteed as to principal and interest by a corporation if a statute specifically designates, by name, the corporation's securities as exempt securities within the meaning of the laws administered by the SEC; or

(4) Any put, call, straddle, option, or privilege on a government security described in this definition, other than a put, call, straddle, option, or privilege:

Office of Thrift Supervision, Treasury §551.40

(i) That is traded on one or more national securities exchanges; or

(ii) For which quotations are disseminated through an automated quotation system operated by a registered securities association.

Investment discretion means the same as under 12 CFR 550.40(a).

Investment company plan means any plan under which:

(1) A customer purchases securities issued by an open-end investment company or unit investment trust registered under the Investment Company Act of 1940, making the payments directly to, or made payable to, the registered investment company, or the principal underwriter, custodian, trustee, or other designated agent of the registered investment company; or

(2) A customer sells securities issued by an open-end investment company or unit investment trust registered under the Investment Company Act of 1940 under:

(i) An individual retirement or individual pension plan qualified under the Internal Revenue Code; or

(ii) A contractual or systematic agreement under which the customer purchases at the applicable public offering price, or redeems at the applicable redemption price, securities in specified amounts (calculated in security units or dollars) at specified time intervals, and stating the commissions or charges (or the means of calculating them) that the customer will pay in connection with the purchase.

Municipal security means:

(1) A security that is a direct obligation of, or an obligation guaranteed as to principal or interest by, a State or any political subdivision, or any agency or instrumentality of a State or any political subdivision.

(2) A security that is a direct obligation of, or an obligation guaranteed as to principal or interest by, any municipal corporate instrumentality of one or more States; or

(3) A security that is an industrial development bond, the interest on which is excludable from gross income under section 103(a) of the Code (26 U.S.C. 103(a)).

Periodic plan means a written document that authorizes you to act as agent to purchase or sell for a customer a specific security or securities (other than securities issued by an open end investment company or unit investment trust registered under the Investment Company Act of 1940). The written document must authorize you to purchase or sell in specific amounts (calculated in security units or dollars) or to the extent of dividends and funds available, at specific time intervals, and must set forth the commission or charges to be paid by the customer or the manner of calculating them.

SEC means the Securities and Exchange Commission.

Security means any note, stock, treasury stock, bond, debenture, certificate of interest or participation in any profit-sharing agreement or in any oil, gas, or other mineral royalty or lease, any collateral-trust certificate, preorganization certificate or subscription, transferable share, investment contract, voting-trust certificate, and any put, call, straddle, option, or privilege on any security or group or index of securities (including any interest therein or based on the value thereof), or, in general, any instrument commonly known as a "security"; or any certificate of interest or participation in, temporary or interim certificate for, receipt for, or warrant or right to subscribe to or purchase, any of the foregoing. *Security* does not include currency; any note, draft, bill of exchange, or banker's acceptance which has a maturity at the time of issuance of less than nine months, exclusive of days of grace, or any renewal thereof, the maturity of which is likewise limited; a deposit or share account in a Federal or State chartered depository institution; a loan participation; a letter of credit or other form of bank indebtedness incurred in the ordinary course of business; units of a collective investment fund; interests in a variable amount (master) note of a borrower of prime credit; U.S. Savings Bonds; or any other instrument OTS determines does not constitute a security for purposes of this part.

Sweep account means any prearranged, automatic transfer or sweep of funds above a certain dollar level from a deposit account to purchase a security or securities, or any prearranged, automatic redemption or

§ 551.50

sale of a security or securities when a deposit account drops below a certain level with the proceeds being transferred into a deposit account.

Subpart A—Recordkeeping Requirements

§ 551.50 What records must I maintain for securities transactions?

If you effect securities transactions for customers, you must maintain all of the following records for at least three years:

(a) *Chronological records.* You must maintain an itemized daily record of each purchase and sale of securities in chronological order, including:

(1) The account or customer name for which you effected each transaction;

(2) The name and amount of the securities;

(3) The unit and aggregate purchase or sale price;

(4) The trade date; and

(5) The name or other designation of the registered broker-dealer or other person from whom you purchased the securities or to whom you sold the securities.

(b) *Account records.* You must maintain account records for each customer reflecting:

(1) Purchases and sales of securities;

(2) Receipts and deliveries of securities;

(3) Receipts and disbursements of cash; and

(4) Other debits and credits pertaining to transactions in securities.

(c) *Memorandum (order ticket).* You must make and keep current a memorandum (order ticket) of each order or any other instruction given or received for the purchase or sale of securities (whether executed or not), including:

(1) The account or customer name for which you effected each transaction;

(2) Whether the transaction was a market order, limit order, or subject to special instructions;

(3) The time the trader received the order;

(4) The time the trader placed the order with the registered broker-dealer, or if there was no registered broker-dealer, the time the trader executed or cancelled the order;

(5) The price at which the trader executed the order;

(6) The name of the registered broker-dealer you used.

(d) *Record of registered broker-dealers.* You must maintain a record of all registered broker-dealers that you selected to effect securities transactions and the amount of commissions that you paid or allocated to each registered broker-dealer during each calendar year.

(e) *Notices.* You must maintain a copy of the written notice required under subpart B of this part.

§ 551.60 How must I maintain my records?

(a) You may maintain the records required under § 551.50 in any manner, form, or format that you deem appropriate. However, your records must clearly and accurately reflect the required information and provide an adequate basis for an audit of the information.

(b) You, or the person that maintains and preserves records on your behalf, must:

(1) Arrange and index the records in a way that permits easy location, access, and retrieval of a particular record;

(2) Separately store, for the time required for preservation of the original record, a duplicate copy of the record on any medium allowed by this section;

(3) Provide promptly any of the following that OTS examiners or your directors may request:

(i) A legible, true, and complete copy of the record in the medium and format in which it is stored;

(ii) A legible, true, and complete printout of the record; and

(iii) Means to access, view, and print the records.

(4) In the case of records on electronic storage media, you, or the person that maintains and preserves records for you, must establish procedures:

(i) To maintain, preserve, and reasonably safeguard the records from loss, alteration, or destruction;

(ii) To limit access to the records to properly authorized personnel, your directors, and OTS examiners; and

Office of Thrift Supervision, Treasury § 551.90

(iii) To reasonably ensure that any reproduction of a non-electronic original record on electronic storage media is complete, true, and legible when retrieved.

(c) You may contract with third party service providers to maintain the records.

Subpart B—Content and Timing of Notice

§ 551.70 What type of notice must I provide when I effect a securities transaction for a customer?

If you effect a securities transaction for a customer, you must give or send the customer the registered broker-dealer confirmation described at § 551.80, or the written notice described at § 551.90. For certain types of transactions, you may elect to provide the alternate notices described in § 551.100.

§ 551.80 How do I provide a registered broker-dealer confirmation?

(a) If you elect to satisfy § 551.70 by providing the customer with a registered broker-dealer confirmation, you must provide the confirmation by having the registered broker-dealer send the confirmation directly to the customer or by sending a copy of the registered broker-dealer's confirmation to the customer within one business day after you receive it.

(b) If you have received or will receive remuneration from any source, including the customer, in connection with the transaction, you must provide a statement of the source and amount of the remuneration in addition to the registered broker-dealer confirmation described in paragraph (a) of this section.

§ 551.90 How do I provide a written notice?

If you elect to satisfy § 551.70 by providing the customer a written notice, you must give or send the written notice at or before the completion of the securities transaction. You must include all of the following information in a written notice:

(a) Your name and the customer's name.

(b) The capacity in which you acted (for example, as agent).

(c) The date and time of execution of the securities transaction (or a statement that you will furnish this information within a reasonable time after the customer's written request), and the identity, price, and number of shares or units (or principal amount in the case of debt securities) of the security the customer purchased or sold.

(d) The name of the person from whom you purchased or to whom you sold the security, or a statement that you will furnish this information within a reasonable time after the customer's written request.

(e) The amount of any remuneration that you have received or will receive from the customer in connection with the transaction unless the remuneration paid by the customer is determined under a written agreement, other than on a transaction basis.

(f) The source and amount of any other remuneration you have received or will receive in connection with the transaction. If, in the case of a purchase, you were not participating in a distribution, or in the case of a sale, were not participating in a tender offer, the written notice may state whether you have or will receive any other remuneration and state that you will furnish the source and amount of the other remuneration within a reasonable time after the customer's written request.

(g) That you are not a member of the Securities Investor Protection Corporation, if that is the case. This does not apply to a transaction in shares of a registered open-end investment company or unit investment trust if the customer sends funds or securities directly to, or receives funds or securities directly from, the registered open-end investment company or unit investment trust, its transfer agent, its custodian, or a designated broker or dealer who sends the customer either a confirmation or the written notice in this section.

(h) Additional disclosures. You must provide all of the additional disclosures described in the following chart for transactions involving certain debt securities:

135

§ 551.100

If you effect a transaction involving . . .	You must provide the following additional information in your written notice . . .
(1) A debt security subject to redemption before maturity.	A statement that the issuer may redeem the debt security in whole or in part before maturity, that the redemption could affect the represented yield, and that additional redemption information is available upon request.

(2) A debt security that you effected exclusively on the basis of a dollar price.	(i) The dollar price at which you effected the transaction; and
	(ii) The yield to maturity calculated from the dollar price. You do not have to disclose the yield to maturity if:
	   (A) The issuer may extend the maturity date of the security with a variable interest rate; or
	   (B) The security is an asset-backed security that represents an interest in, or is secured by, a pool of receivables or other financial assets that are subject continuously to prepayment.

(3) A debt security that you effected on basis of yield.	(i) The yield at which the transaction, including the percentage amount and its characterization (e.g., current yield, yield to maturity, or yield to call). If you effected the transaction at yield to call, you must indicate the type of call, the call date, and the call price;
	(ii) The dollar price calculated from that yield; and
	(iii) The yield to maturity and the represented yield, if you effected the transaction on a basis other than yield to maturity and the yield to maturity is lower than the represented yield. You are not required to disclose this information if:
	   (A) The issuer may extend the maturity date of the security with a variable interest rate; or
	   (B) The security is an asset-backed security that represents an interest in, or is secured by, a pool of receivables or other financial assets that are subject continuously to prepayment.

(4) A debt security that is an asset-backed security that represents an interest in, or is secured by, a pool of receivables or other financial assets that are subject continuously to prepayment.	(i) A statement that the actual yield of the asset-backed security may vary according to the rate at which the underlying receivables or other financial assets are prepaid; and (ii) A statement that you will furnish information concerning the factors that affect yield (including at a minimum estimated yield, weighted average life, and the prepayment assumptions underlying yield) upon the customer's written request.
(5) A debt security, other than a government security.	A statement that the security is unrated by a nationally recognized statistical rating organization, if that is the case.

§ 551.100 What are the alternate notice requirements?

You may elect to satisfy § 551.70 by providing the alternate notices described in the following chart for certain types of transactions.

If you effect a securities transaction . . .	Then you may elect to . . .
(a) For or with the account of a customer under a periodic plan, sweep account, or investment company plan.	Give or send to the customer within five business days after the end of each quarterly period a written statement disclosing: (1) Each purchase and redemption that you effected for or with, and each dividend or distribution that you credited to or reinvested for, the customer's account during the period; (2) The date of each transaction; (3) The identity, number, and price of any securities that the customer purchased or redeemed in each transaction; (4) The total number of shares of the securities in the customer's account; (5) Any remuneration that you received or will receive in connection with the transaction; and (6) That you will give or send the registered broker-dealer confirmation described in § 551.80 or the written notice described in § 551.90 within a reasonable time after the customer's written request.
(b) For or with the account of a customer in shares of an open-ended management company registered under the Investment Company Act of 1940 that holds itself out as a money market fund and attempts to maintain a stable net asset value per share.	Give or send to the customer the written statement described at paragraph (a) of this section on a monthly basis. You may not use the alternate notice, however, if you deduct sales loads upon the purchase or redemption of shares in the money market fund.
(c) For an account for which you do not exercise investment discretion, and for which you and the customer have agreed in writing to an arrangement concerning the time and content of the written notice.	Give or send to the customer a written notice at the agreed-upon time and with the agreed-upon content, and include a statement that you will furnish the registered broker-dealer confirmation described in § 551.80 or the written notice described in § 551.90 within a reasonable time after the customer's written request.
(d) For an account for which you exercise investment discretion other than in an agency capacity, excluding common or collective investment funds.	Give or send the registered broker-dealer confirmation described in § 551.80 or the written notice described in § 551.90 within a reasonable time after a written request by the person with the power to terminate the account or, if there is no such person, any person holding a vested beneficial interest in the account.

Office of Thrift Supervision, Treasury

If you effect a securities transaction . . .	Then you may elect to . . .
(e) For an account in which you exercise investment discretion in an agency capacity.	Give or send each customer a written itemized statement specifying the funds and securities in your custody or possession and all debits, credits, and transactions in the customer's account. You must provide this information to the customer not less than once every three months. You must give or send the registered broker-dealer confirmation described in § 551.80 or the written notice described in § 551.90 within a reasonable time after a customer's written request.
(f) For a common or collective investment fund.	(1) Give or send to a customer who invests in the fund a copy of the annual financial report of the fund, or (2) Notify the customer that a copy of the report is available and that you will furnish the report within a reasonable time after a written request by a person to whom a regular periodic accounting would ordinarily be rendered with respect to each participating account.

§ 551.110 May I provide a notice electronically?

You may provide any written notice required under this subpart B electronically. If a customer has a facsimile machine, you may send the notice by facsimile transmission. You may use other electronic communications if:

(a) The parties agree to use electronic instead of hard copy notices;

(b) The parties are able to print or download the notice;

(c) Your electronic communications system cannot automatically delete the electronic notice; and

(d) Both parties are able to receive electronic messages.

§ 551.120 May I charge a fee for a notice?

You may not charge a fee for providing a notice required under this subpart B, except that you may charge a reasonable fee for the notices provided under §§ 551.100(a), (d), and (e).

Subpart C—Settlement of Securities Transactions

§ 551.130 When must I settle a securities transaction?

(a) You may not effect or enter into a contract for the purchase or sale of a security that provides for payment of funds and delivery of securities later than the latest of:

(1) The third business day after the date of the contract. This deadline is no later than the fourth business day after the contract for contracts involving the sale for cash of securities that are priced after 4:30 p.m. Eastern Standard Time on the date the securities are priced and are sold by an issuer to an underwriter under a firm commitment underwritten offering registered under the Securities Act of 1933, 15 U.S.C. 77a, *et seq.*, or are sold by you to an initial purchaser participating in the offering;

(2) Such other time as the SEC specifies by rule (*see* SEC Rule 15c6–1, 17 CFR 240.15c6–1); or

(3) Such time as the parties expressly agree at the time of the transaction. The parties to a contract are deemed to have expressly agreed to an alternate date for payment of funds and delivery of securities at the time of the transaction for a contract for the sale for cash of securities under a firm commitment offering, if the managing underwriter and the issuer have agreed to the date for all securities sold under the offering and the parties to the contract have not expressly agreed to another date for payment of funds and delivery of securities at the time of the transaction.

(b) The deadlines in paragraph (a) of this section do not apply to the purchase or sale of limited partnership interests that are not listed on an exchange or for which quotations are not disseminated through an automated quotation system of a registered securities association.

Subpart D—Securities Trading Policies and Procedures

§ 551.140 What policies and procedures must I maintain and follow for securities transactions?

If you effect securities transactions for customers, you must maintain and follow policies and procedures that meet all of the following requirements:

(a) Your policies and procedures must assign responsibility for the supervision of all officers or employees who:

(1) Transmit orders to, or place orders with, registered broker-dealers;

(2) Execute transactions in securities for customers; or

(3) Process orders for notice or settlement purposes, or perform other back office functions for securities transactions that you effect for customers. Policies and procedures for personnel described in this paragraph (a)(3) must provide supervision and reporting lines that are separate from supervision and reporting lines for personnel described in paragraphs (a)(1) and (2) of this section.

(b) Your policies and procedures must provide for the fair and equitable allocation of securities and prices to accounts when you receive orders for the same security at approximately the same time and you place the orders for execution either individually or in combination.

(c) Your policies and procedures must provide for securities transactions in which you act as agent for the buyer and seller (crossing of buy and sell orders) on a fair and equitable basis to the parties to the transaction, where permissible under applicable law.

(d) Your policies and procedures must require your officers and employees to file the personal securities trading reports described at § 551.150, if the officer or employee:

(1) Makes investment recommendations or decisions for the accounts of customers;

(2) Participates in the determination of these recommendations or decisions; or

(3) In connection with their duties, obtains information concerning which securities you intend to purchase, sell, or recommend for purchase or sale.

§ 551.150 How do my officers and employees file reports of personal securities trading transactions?

An officer or employee described in § 551.140(d) must report all personal transactions in securities made by or on behalf of the officer or employee if he or she has a beneficial interest in the security.

(a) *Contents and filing of report.* The officer or employee must file the report with you no later than 30 calendar days after the end of each calendar quarter. The report must include the following information:

(1) The date of each transaction, the title and number of shares, the interest rate and maturity date (if applicable), and the principal amount of each security involved.

(2) The nature of each transaction (i.e., purchase, sale, or other type of acquisition or disposition).

(3) The price at which each transaction was effected.

(4) The name of the broker, dealer, or other intermediary effecting the transaction.

(5) The date the officer or employee submitted the report.

(b) *Report not required for certain transactions.* Your officer or employee is not required to report a transaction if:

(1) He or she has no direct or indirect influence or control over the account for which the transaction was effected or over the securities held in that account;

(2) The transaction was in shares issued by an open-end investment company registered under the Investment Company Act of 1940;

(3) The transaction was in direct obligations of the government of the United States;

(4) The transaction was in bankers' acceptances, bank certificates of deposit, commercial paper or high quality short term debt instruments, including repurchase agreements; or

(5) The officer or employee had an aggregate amount of purchases and sales of $10,000 or less during the calendar quarter.

Office of Thrift Supervision, Treasury § 552.2-1

(c) *Alternate report.* When you act as an investment adviser to an investment company registered under the Investment Company Act of 1940, an officer or employee that is an "access person" may fulfill his or her reporting requirements under this section by filing with you the "access person" personal securities trading report required by SEC Rule 17j–1(d), 17 CFR 270.17j–1(d).

[67 FR 76299, Dec. 12, 2002, as amended at 72 FR 30474, June 1, 2007]

PART 552—FEDERAL STOCK ASSOCIATIONS—INCORPORATION, ORGANIZATION, AND CONVERSION

Sec.
552.2-1 Procedure for organization of Federal stock association.
552.2-2 Procedures for organization of interim Federal stock association.
552.2-3 Federal stock association created in connection with an association in default or in danger of default.
552.2-6 Conversion from stock form depository institution to Federal stock association.
552.2-7 Conversion to National banking association or State bank.
552.3 Charters for Federal stock associations.
552.4 Charter amendments.
552.5 Bylaws.
552.6 Shareholders.
552.6-1 Board of directors.
552.6-2 Officers.
552.6-3 Certificates for shares and their transfer.
552.6-4 [Reserved]
552.9 [Reserved]
552.10 Annual reports to stockholders.
552.11 Books and records.
552.12 [Reserved]
552.13 Combinations involving Federal stock associations.
552.14 Dissenter and appraisal rights.
552.15 Supervisory combinations.
552.16 Effect of subsequent charter or bylaw change.

AUTHORITY: 12 U.S.C. 1462, 1462a, 1463, 1464, 1467a.

SOURCE: 54 FR 49523, Nov. 30, 1989, unless otherwise noted.

§ 552.2-1 Procedure for organization of Federal stock association.

(a) *Application for permission to organize.* Applications for permission to organize a Federal stock association are subject to this section and to § 543.3 of this chapter. Recommendations by employees of the OTS regarding applications for permission to organize are privileged, confidential, and subject to § 510.5 (b) and (c) of this chapter. The processing of an application under this section shall be subject to the following procedures:

(1) *Publication.* (i) The applicant shall publish a public notice of the application to organize in accordance with the procedures specified in subpart B of part 516 of this chapter.

(ii) Promptly after publication of the public notice, the applicant shall transmit copies of the public notice and publisher's affidavit of publication to the OTS in the same manner as the original filing.

(iii) Any person may inspect the application and all related communications at the Regional Office during regular business hours, unless such information is exempt from public disclosure.

(2) *Notification to interested parties.* The OTS shall give notice of the application to the State official who supervises savings associations in the State in which the new association is to be located.

(3) *Submission of comments.* Commenters may submit comments on the application in accordance with the procedures specified in subpart C of part 516 of this chapter.

(4) *Meetings.* OTS may arrange a meeting in accordance with the procedures in subpart D of part 516 of this chapter.

(b) *Conditions of approval.* The OTS will decide all applications for permission to organize a Federal stock association.

(1) Factors that will be considered on all applications for permission to organize a Federal stock association are:

(i) Whether the applicants are persons of good character and responsibility;

(ii) Whether a necessity exists for such association in the community to be served;

(iii) Whether there is a reasonable probability of the association's usefulness and success;

(iv) Whether the association can be established without undue injury to

§ 552.2–1

properly conducted existing local thrift and home financing institutions; and

(v) Whether the association will perform a role of providing credit for housing consistent with safe and sound operation of a Federal savings association.

(2) [Reserved]

(3) Approvals of applications will be conditioned on the following:

(i) Receipt by the Office of written confirmation from the Federal Deposit Insurance Corporation that the accounts of the association will be insured by the Federal Deposit Insurance Corporation;

(ii) The sale of a minimum amount of fully-paid capital stock of the association prior to commencing business;

(iii) The submission of a statement that:

(A) The applicants have incurred no expense in organization which is chargeable to the association, and that no such expense will be incurred, and

(B) No funds will be accepted for deposit by the association until organization has been completed;

(iv) Compliance with all applicable laws, rules, and regulations; and

(v) The satisfaction of any other requirement or condition the Director or his or her designee may impose.

(c) *Issuance of charter.* Upon approval of an application, the Office shall issue to the association a charter for a Federal stock savings association or for a Federal stock savings bank, as requested by the applicants, which shall be in the form provided in this part. Issuance of the charter shall be subject to the condition subsequent that the organization of the association is completed pursuant to this section.

(d) *Interim board of directors and officers.* Upon approval of the application and the issuance of the charter, the applicants shall constitute the interim board of directors of the association until the board of directors of the association are elected by its stockholders at the organizational meeting required by paragraph (g) of this section, and the interim officers of the association shall be those persons set forth in the application for permission to organize.

(e) *Sale of capital stock.* Upon the issuance of the charter, the association shall proceed to offer and sell its capital stock pursuant to the requirements of part 563g of this chapter.

(f) *Bank membership and insurance of accounts.* Promptly upon the issuance of the charter, a Federal stock association must qualify as a member of the appropriate Federal Home Loan Bank and meet all requirements necessary to obtain insurance of accounts by the Federal Deposit Insurance Corporation.

(g) *Organizational meeting.* Promptly upon the completion of the sale of its capital stock, the association shall provide notice, pursuant to § 552.6(b), of a meeting of its stockholders to elect a board of directors. Immediately following such election, the directors shall meet to elect the officers of the association and to undertake any other action necessary under the charter or bylaws to complete corporate organization.

(h) *Completion of organization.* Organization of a Federal stock association shall be deemed complete for the purposes of this part when:

(1) The association has obtained Federal Home Loan Bank membership and insurance of its accounts from the Federal Deposit Insurance Corporation;

(2) It has completed the sale of and received full payment for its capital stock;

(3) It has complied with all requirements of part 563g of this chapter;

(4) It has held its organizational meeting for the election of directors and all directors have been elected;

(5) Its officers have been elected and bonded; and

(6) It has met the requirements and conditions imposed by the Office in connection with approval of the application.

(i) *Failure of completion.* If organization of a Federal stock association is not completed within six months after the OTS approves the application, or within such additional period as the OTS for good cause may grant, the charter shall become null and void and all subscriptions to capital stock shall be returned.

[54 FR 49523, Nov. 30, 1989, as amended at 57 FR 14342, Apr. 20, 1992; 62 FR 27181, May 19, 1997; 62 FR 64146, Dec. 4, 1997; 69 FR 68249, Nov. 24, 2004]

§ 552.2-2 Procedures for organization of interim Federal stock association.

(a) Applications for permission to organize an interim Federal savings association are not subject to subparts B, C and D of part 516 of this chapter or § 552.2-1(b)(3) of this part.

(b) Approval of an application for permission to organize an interim Federal stock association shall be conditioned upon approval by the Office of an application to merge the interim Federal stock association, or upon approval by the Office of other transaction which the interim was chartered to facilitate. Applications for permission to organize an interim Federal stock association shall be submitted in the same manner as the related filing(s). In evaluating the application, the Office will consider the purpose for which the association will be organized, the form of any proposed transactions involving the association, the effect of the transactions on existing associations involved in the transactions, and the factors specified in § 552.1(b)(1) to the extent relevant.

(c) If a merger or other transaction facilitated by the existence of the interim Federal stock association has not been approved within six months of the approval of the application for permission to organize, unless extended by OTS for good cause shown, the charter shall be void and all subscriptions for capital stock shall be returned.

[54 FR 49523, Nov. 30, 1989, as amended at 55 FR 13513, Apr. 11, 1990; 57 FR 14342, Apr. 20, 1992; 62 FR 64146, Dec. 4, 1997]

§ 552.2-3 Federal stock association created in connection with an association in default or in danger of default.

Sections 552.2-1 and 552.2-2 of this part do not apply to a Federal stock association which is proposed by the Federal Deposit Insurance Corporation, or the Resolution Trust Corporation under section 5(p) of the Home Owner's Loan Act of 1933, section 11(c) of the Federal Deposit Insurance Act, or section 21A of the Federal Home Loan Bank Act, or is otherwise chartered by the Office in connection with an association in default or in danger of default. Incorporation and organization of such associations are complete when and under such conditions as the Director or his or her designee so determines.

§ 552.2-6 Conversion from stock form depository institution to Federal stock association.

(a) With the approval of the Office, any stock depository institution that is, or is eligible to become, a member of a Federal Home Loan Bank, may convert to a Federal stock association, provided that the depository institution, at the time of the conversion, has deposits insured by the Federal Deposit Insurance Corporation, and provided further, that the depository institution, in accomplishing the conversion, complies with all applicable statutes and regulations, including, without limitation, section 5(d) of the Federal Deposit Insurance Act. The resulting Federal stock association must conform within the time prescribed by the OTS to the requirements of section 5(c) of the Home Owners' Loan Act. For purposes of this section, the term "depository institution" shall have the meaning set forth at 12 CFR 552.13(b). An application for conversion filed under this section is subject to the procedures for organization of a federal stock organization at § 552.2-1.

(b) Any and all of the assets and other property (whether real, personal, mixed, tangible or intangible, including choses in action, rights, and credits) of the former stock form depository institution become assets and property of the Federal stock association when the conversion occurs. Similarly, any and all of the obligations and debts of or claims against the former stock form depository institution become obligations and debts of and claims against the Federal stock association when the conversion occurs. In effect, the Federal stock association is the same as the former stock form depository institution with respect to any and all assets, property, claims and debts of or claims against the former stock form depository institution.

[59 FR 44623, Aug. 30, 1994, as amended at 66 FR 13006, Mar. 2, 2001; 66 FR 23154, May 8, 2001]

§ 552.2-7 Conversion to National banking association or State bank.

A Federal stock association may convert to a National banking association or a State bank after filing a notification or application, as appropriate, with the Office in accordance with the applicable provisions of § 563.22(b) of this chapter.

[59 FR 44623, Aug. 30, 1994]

§ 552.3 Charters for Federal stock associations.

The charter of a Federal stock association shall be in the following form, except that an association that has converted from the mutual form pursuant to part 563b of this chapter shall include in its charter a section establishing a liquidation account as required by § 563b.3(c)(13) of this chapter. A charter for a Federal stock savings bank shall substitute the term "savings bank" for "association." Charters may also include any preapproved optional provision contained in § 552.4 of this part.

FEDERAL STOCK CHARTER

Section 1. Corporate title. The full corporate title of the association is ____.

Section 2. Office. The home office shall be located in ____ [city, state].

Section 3. Duration. The duration of the association is perpetual.

Section 4. Purpose and powers. The purpose of the association is to pursue any or all of the lawful objectives of a Federal savings association chartered under section 5 of the Home Owners' Loan Act and to exercise all of the express, implied, and incidental powers conferred thereby and by all acts amendatory thereof and supplemental thereto, subject to the Constitution and laws of the United States as they are now in effect, or as they may hereafter be amended, and subject to all lawful and applicable rules, regulations, and orders of the Office of Thrift Supervision ("Office").

Section 5. Capital stock. The total number of shares of all classes of the capital stock that the association has the authority to issue is ____, all of which shall be common stock of par [or if no par is specified then shares shall have a stated] value of ____ per share. The shares may be issued from time to time as authorized by the board of directors without the approval of its shareholders, except as otherwise provided in this Section 5 or to the extent that such approval is required by governing law, rule, or regulation. The consideration for the issuance of the shares shall be paid in full before their issuance and shall not be less than the par [or stated] value. Neither promissory notes nor future services shall constitute payment or part payment for the issuance of shares of the association. The consideration for the shares shall be cash, tangible or intangible property (to the extent direct investment in such property would be permitted to the association), labor, or services actually performed for the association, or any combination of the foregoing. In the absence of actual fraud in the transaction, the value of such property, labor, or services, as determined by the board of directors of the association, shall be conclusive. Upon payment of such consideration, such shares shall be deemed to be fully paid and nonassessable. In the case of a stock dividend, that part of the retained earnings of the association that is transferred to common stock or paid-in capital accounts upon the issuance of shares as a stock dividend shall be deemed to be the consideration for their issuance.

Except for shares issued in the initial organization of the association or in connection with the conversion of the association from the mutual to stock form of capitalization, no shares of capital stock (including shares issuable upon conversion, exchange, or exercise of other securities) shall be issued, directly or indirectly, to officers, directors, or controlling persons of the association other than as part of a general public offering or as qualifying shares to a director, unless the issuance or the plan under which they would be issued has been approved by a majority of the total votes eligible to be cast at a legal meeting.

The holders of the common stock shall exclusively possess all voting power. Each holder of shares of common stock shall be entitled to one vote for each share held by such holder, except as to the cumulation of votes for the election of directors, unless the charter provides that there shall be no such cumulative voting. Subject to any provision for a liquidation account, in the event of any liquidation, dissolution, or winding up of the association, the holders of the common stock shall be entitled, after payment or provision for payment of all debts and liabilities of the association, to receive the remaining assets of the association available for distribution, in cash or in kind. Each share of common stock shall have the same relative rights as and be identical in all respects with all the other shares of common stock.

Section 6. Preemptive rights. Holders of the capital stock of the association shall not be entitled to preemptive rights with respect to any shares of the association which may be issued.

Section 7. Directors. The association shall be under the direction of a board of directors. The authorized number of directors, as stated in the association's bylaws, shall not be fewer than five nor more than fifteen except when a greater or lesser number is approved by the Director of the Office, or his or her delegate.

Section 8. Amendment of charter. Except as provided in Section 5, no amendment, addition, alteration, change or repeal of this charter shall be made, unless such is proposed by the board of directors of the association, approved by the shareholders by a majority of the votes eligible to be cast at a legal meeting, unless a higher vote is otherwise required, and approved or preapproved by the Office.

Attest: _____
   Secretary of the Association
By: _____
   President or Chief Executive Officer of the Association
Attest: _____
   Secretary of the Office of Thrift Supervision
By: _____
   Director of the Office of Thrift Supervision
Effective Date: _____

[54 FR 49523, Nov. 30, 1989, as amended at 59 FR 53571, Oct. 25, 1994; 61 FR 64018, Dec. 3, 1996]

§ 552.4 Charter amendments.

(a) *General.* In order to adopt a charter amendment, a Federal stock association must comply with the following requirements:

(1) *Board of directors approval.* The board of directors of the association must adopt a resolution proposing the charter amendment that states the text of such amendment.

(2) *Form of filing*—(i) *Application requirement.* If the proposed charter amendment would render more difficult or discourage a merger, tender offer, or proxy contest, the assumption of control by a holder of a block of the association's stock, the removal of incumbent management, or involve a significant issue of law or policy, the association shall file the proposed amendment and shall obtain the prior approval of the OTS; and

(ii) *Notice requirement.* If the proposed charter amendment does not involve a provision that would be covered by paragraph (a)(2)(i) of this section and such amendment is permissible under all applicable laws, rules or regulations, then the association shall submit the proposed amendments to the OTS, at least 30 days prior to the date the proposed charter amendment is to be mailed for consideration by the association's shareholders.

(b) *Approval.* Any charter amendment filed pursuant to paragraph (a)(2)(ii) of this section shall automatically be approved 30 days from the date of filing of such amendment, provided that the association follows the requirements of its charter in adopting such amendment, unless prior to the expiration of such 30-day period the OTS notifies the association that such amendment is rejected or that such amendment is deemed to be filed under the provisions of paragraph (a)(2)(i) of this section. In addition, the following charter amendments, including the adoption of the Federal stock charter as set forth in § 552.3 of this part, shall be approved at the time of adoption, if adopted without change and filed with OTS within 30 days after adoption, provided the association follows the requirements of its charter in adopting such amendments:

(1) *Title change.* A Federal stock association that has complied with § 543.1(b) of this chapter may amend its charter by substituting a new corporate title in section 1.

(2) *Home office.* A Federal savings association may amend its charter by substituting a new home office in section 2, if it has complied with applicable requirements of § 545.95 of this chapter.

(3) *Number of shares of stock and par value.* A Federal stock association may amend Section 5 of its charter to change the number of authorized shares of stock, the number of shares within each class of stock, and the par or stated value of such shares.

(4) *Capital stock.* A Federal stock association may amend its charter by revising Section 5 to read as follows:

Section 5. Capital stock. The total number of shares of all classes of capital stock that the association has the authority to issue is _____, of which _____ shall be common stock of par [or if no par value is specified the stated] value of _____ per share and of which [list the number of each class of preferred and the par or if no par value is specified the stated value per share of each such class]. The shares may be issued from time to time as authorized by the board of directors without further approval of shareholders, except as otherwise provided in this Section 5 or to

§ 552.4

the extent that such approval is required by governing law, rule, or regulation. The consideration for the issuance of the shares shall be paid in full before their issuance and shall not be less than the par [or stated] value. Neither promissory notes nor future services shall constitute payment or part payment for the issuance of shares of the association. The consideration for the shares shall be cash, tangible or intangible property (to the extent direct investment in such property would be permitted), labor, or services actually performed for the association, or any combination of the foregoing. In the absence of actual fraud in the transaction, the value of such property, labor, or services, as determined by the board of directors of the association, shall be conclusive. Upon payment of such consideration, such shares shall be deemed to be fully paid and nonassessable. In the case of a stock dividend, that part of the retained earnings of the association that is transferred to common stock or paid-in capital accounts upon the issuance of shares as a stock dividend shall be deemed to be the consideration for their issuance.

Except for shares issued in the initial organization of the association or in connection with the conversion of the association from the mutual to the stock form of capitalization, no shares of capital stock (including shares issuable upon conversion, exchange, or exercise of other securities) shall be issued, directly or indirectly, to officers, directors, or controlling persons of the association other than as part of a general public offering or as qualifying shares to a director, unless their issuance or the plan under which they would be issued has been approved by a majority of the total votes eligible to be cast at a legal meeting.

Nothing contained in this Section 5 (or in any supplementary sections hereto) shall entitle the holders of any class of a series of capital stock to vote as a separate class or series or to more than one vote per share, except as to the cumulation of votes for the election of directors, unless the charter otherwise provides that there shall be no such cumulative voting: *Provided,* That this restriction on voting separately by class or series shall not apply:

(i) To any provision which would authorize the holders of preferred stock, voting as a class or series, to elect some members of the board of directors, less than a majority thereof, in the event of default in the payment of dividends on any class or series of preferred stock;

(ii) To any provision that would require the holders of preferred stock, voting as a class or series, to approve the merger or consolidation of the association with another corporation or the sale, lease, or conveyance (other than by mortgage or pledge) of properties or business in exchange for securities of a corporation other than the association if the preferred stock is exchanged for securities of such other corporation: *Provided,* That no provision may require such approval for transactions undertaken with the assistance or pursuant to the direction of the Office or the Federal Deposit Insurance Corporation;

(iii) To any amendment which would adversely change the specific terms of any class or series of capital stock as set forth in this Section 5 (or in any supplementary sections hereto), including any amendment which would create or enlarge any class or series ranking prior thereto in rights and preferences. An amendment which increases the number of authorized shares of any class or series of capital stock, or substitutes the surviving association in a merger or consolidation for the association, shall not be considered to be such an adverse change.

A description of the different classes and series (if any) of the association's capital stock and a statement of the designations, and the relative rights, preferences, and limitations of the shares of each class of and series (if any) of capital stock are as follows:

A. *Common stock.* Except as provided in this Section 5 (or in any supplementary sections thereto) the holders of the common stock shall exclusively possess all voting power. Each holder of shares of the common stock shall be entitled to one vote for each share held by each holder, except as to the cumulation of votes for the election of directors, unless the charter otherwise provides that there shall be no such cumulative voting.

Whenever there shall have been paid, or declared and set aside for payment, to the holders of the outstanding shares of any class of stock having preference over the common stock as to the payment of dividends, the full amount of dividends and of sinking fund, retirement fund, or other retirement payments, if any, to which such holders are respectively entitled in preference to the common stock, then dividends may be paid on the common stock and on any class or series of stock entitled to participate therewith as to dividends out of any assets legally available for the payment of dividends.

In the event of any liquidation, dissolution, or winding up of the association, the holders of the common stock (and the holders of any class or series of stock entitled to participate with the common stock in the distribution of assets) shall be entitled to receive, in cash or in kind, the assets of the association available for distribution remaining after: (i) Payment or provision for payment of the association's debts and liabilities; (ii) distributions or provision for distributions in settlement of its liquidation account; and (iii) distributions or provision for distributions to holders of any class or series of stock having preference over the common stock in the liquidation, dissolution, or winding up of the association. Each share of common stock shall have the same relative rights as and be identical in all respects with all the other shares of common stock.

B. *Preferred stock.* The association may provide in supplementary sections to its charter for one or more classes of preferred stock, which shall be separately identified. The shares of any class may be divided into and issued in series, with each series separately designated so as to distinguish the shares thereof from the shares of all other series and classes. The terms of each series shall be set forth in a supplementary section to the charter. All shares of the same class shall be identical except as to the following relative rights and preferences, as to which there may be variations between different series:

(a) The distinctive serial designation and the number of shares constituting such series;

(b) The dividend rate or the amount of dividends to be paid on the shares of such series, whether dividends shall be cumulative and, if so, from which date(s), the payment date(s) for dividends, and the participating or other special rights, if any, with respect to dividends;

(c) The voting powers, full or limited, if any, of shares of such series;

(d) Whether the shares of such series shall be redeemable and, if so, the price(s) at which, and the terms and conditions on which, such shares may be redeemed;

(e) The amount(s) payable upon the shares of such series in the event of voluntary or involuntary liquidation, dissolution, or winding up of the association;

(f) Whether the shares of such series shall be entitled to the benefit of a sinking or retirement fund to be applied to the purchase or redemption of such shares, and if so entitled, the amount of such fund and the manner of its application, including the price(s) at which such shares may be redeemed or purchased through the application of such fund;

(g) Whether the shares of such series shall be convertible into, or exchangeable for, shares of any other class or classes of stock of the association and, if so, the conversion price(s) or the rate(s) of exchange, and the adjustments thereof, if any, at which such conversion or exchange may be made, and any other terms and conditions of such conversion or exchange.

(h) The price or other consideration for which the shares of such series shall be issued; and

(i) Whether the shares of such series which are redeemed or converted shall have the status of authorized but unissued shares of serial preferred stock and whether such shares may be reissued as shares of the same or any other series of serial preferred stock.

Each share of each series of serial preferred stock shall have the same relative rights as and be identical in all respects with all the other shares of the same series.

The board of directors shall have authority to divide, by the adoption of supplementary charter sections, any authorized class of preferred stock into series, and, within the limitations set forth in this section and the remainder of this charter, fix and determine the relative rights and preferences of the shares of any series so established.

Prior to the issuance of any preferred shares of a series established by a supplementary charter section adopted by the board of directors, the association shall file with the Secretary to the Office a dated copy of that supplementary section of this charter established and designating the series and fixing and determining the relative rights and preferences thereof.

(5) *Limitations on subsequent issuances.* A Federal stock association may amend its charter to require shareholder approval of the issuance or reservation of common stock or securities convertible into common stock under circumstances which would require shareholder approval under the rules of the New York or American Stock Exchange if the shares were then listed on the New York or American Stock Exchange.

(6) *Cumulative voting.* A Federal stock association may amend its charter by substituting the following sentence for the second sentence in the third paragraph of Section 5: "Each holder of shares of common stock shall be entitled to one vote for each share held by such holder and there shall be no right to cumulate votes in an election of directors."

(7) [Reserved]

(8) *Anti-takeover provisions following mutual to stock conversion.* Notwithstanding the law of the state in which the association is located, a Federal stock association may amend its charter by renumbering existing sections as appropriate and adding a new section 8 as follows:

Section 8. Certain Provisions Applicable for Five Years. Notwithstanding anything contained in the Association's charter or bylaws to the contrary, for a period of [specify number of years up to five] years from the date of completion of the conversion of the Association from mutual to stock form, the following provisions shall apply:

§ 552.5

A. *Beneficial Ownership Limitation.* No person shall directly or indirectly offer to acquire or acquire the beneficial ownership of more than 10 percent of any class of an equity security of the association. This limitation shall not apply to a transaction in which the association forms a holding company without change in the respective beneficial ownership interests of its stockholders other than pursuant to the exercise of any dissenter and appraisal rights, the purchase of shares by underwriters in connection with a public offering, or the purchase of shares by a tax-qualified employee stock benefit plan which is exempt from the approval requirements under § 574.3(c)(1)(vi) of the Office's regulations.

In the event shares are acquired in violation of this section 8, all shares beneficially owned by any person in excess of 10% shall be considered "excess shares" and shall not be counted as shares entitled to vote and shall not be voted by any person or counted as voting shares in connection with any matters submitted to the stockholders for a vote.

For purposes of this section 8, the following definitions apply:

(1) The term "person" includes an individual, a group acting in concert, a corporation, a partnership, an association, a joint stock company, a trust, an unincorporated organization or similar company, a syndicate or any other group formed for the purpose of acquiring, holding or disposing of the equity securities of the association.

(2) The term "offer" includes every offer to buy or otherwise acquire, solicitation of an offer to sell, tender offer for, or request or invitation for tenders of, a security or interest in a security for value.

(3) The term "acquire" includes every type of acquisition, whether effected by purchase, exchange, operation of law or otherwise.

(4) The term "acting in concert" means (a) knowing participation in a joint activity or conscious parallel action towards a common goal whether or not pursuant to an express agreement, or (b) a combination or pooling of voting or other interests in the securities of an issuer for a common purpose pursuant to any contract, understanding, relationship, agreement or other arrangements, whether written or otherwise.

B. *Cumulative Voting Limitation.* Stockholders shall not be permitted to cumulate their votes for election of directors.

C. *Call for Special Meetings.* Special meetings of stockholders relating to changes in control of the association or amendments to its charter shall be called only upon direction of the board of directors.

(c) *Anti-takeover provisions.* The Office may grant approval to a charter amendment not listed in paragraph (b) of this section regarding the acquisition by any person or persons of its equity securities provided that the association shall file as part of its application for approval an opinion, acceptable to the OTS, of counsel independent from the association that the proposed charter provision would be permitted to be adopted by a corporation chartered by the state in which the principal office of the association is located. Any such provision must be consistent with applicable statutes, regulations, and OTS policies. Further, any such provision that would have the effect of rendering more difficult a change in control of the association and would require for any corporate action (other than the removal of directors) the affirmative vote of a larger percentage of shareholders than is required by this Part, shall not be effective unless adopted by a percentage of shareholder vote at least equal to the highest percentage that would be required to take any action under such provision.

(d) *Reissuance of charter.* A Federal stock association that has amended its charter may apply to have its charter, including the amendments, reissued by the Office. Such requests for reissuance should be filed with the Corporate Secretary at Washington Headquarters Office at the address listed in § 516.40(b) of this chapter, and contain signatures required under § 552.3 of this part, together with such supporting documents as needed to demonstrate that the amendments were properly adopted.

[54 FR 49523, Nov. 30, 1989, as amended at 55 FR 13513, Apr. 11, 1990; 57 FR 14343, Apr. 20, 1992; 59 FR 18476, Apr. 19, 1994; 61 FR 64018, Dec. 3, 1996; 62 FR 66262, Dec. 18, 1997; 66 FR 13006, Mar. 2, 2001; 69 FR 68249, Nov. 24, 2004]

§ 552.5 Bylaws.

(a) *General.* At its first organizational meeting, the board of directors of a Federal stock association shall adopt a set of bylaws for the administration and regulation of its affairs. Bylaws may be adopted, amended or repealed by either a majority of the votes cast by the shareholders at a legal meeting or a majority of the board of directors. The bylaws shall contain sufficient provisions to govern the association in accordance with the requirements of §§ 552.6, 552.6–1, 552.6–2, and 552.6–3 of

Office of Thrift Supervision, Treasury § 552.6

this part and shall not contain any provision that is inconsistent with those sections or with applicable laws, rules, regulations or the association's charter, except that a bylaw provision inconsistent with §§ 552.6, 552.6–1, 552.6–3, and 552.6–4 of this part may be adopted with the approval of the OTS.

(b) *Form of Filing*—(1) *Application requirement.* (i) Any bylaw amendment shall be submitted to the OTS for approval if it would:

(A) Render more difficult or discourage a merger, tender offer, or proxy contest, the assumption of control by a holder of a large block of the association's stock, or the removal of incumbent management; or

(B) Be inconsistent with §§ 552.6, 552.6–1, 552.6–2, and 552.6–3 of this part, with applicable laws, rules, regulations or the association's charter or involve a significant issue of law or policy, including indemnification, conflicts of interest, and limitations on director or officer liability.

(ii) Applications submitted under paragraph (b)(1)(i) of this section are subject to standard treatment processing procedures at part 516, subparts A and E of this chapter.

(iii) Bylaw provisions that adopt the language of the model or optional bylaws in OTS's Application Processing Handbook, if adopted without change, and filed with OTS within 30 days after adoption, are effective upon adoption.

(2) *Filing requirement.* If the proposed bylaw amendment does not involve a provision that would be covered by paragraph (b)(1) or (b)(3) of this section and is permissible under all applicable laws, rules, or regulations, then the association shall submit the amendment to the OTS at least 30 days prior to the date the bylaw amendment is to be adopted by the association.

(3) *Corporate governance procedures.* A Federal stock association may elect to follow the corporate governance procedures of: The laws of the state where the main office of the association is located; the laws of the state where the association's holding company, if any, is incorporated or chartered; Delaware General Corporation law; or The Model Business Corporation Act, provided that such procedures may be elected to the extent not inconsistent with applicable Federal statutes and regulations and safety and soundness, and such procedures are not of the type described in paragraph (b)(1) of this section. If this election is selected, a Federal stock association shall designate in its bylaws the provision or provisions from the body or bodies of law selected for its corporate governance procedures, and shall file a copy of such bylaws, which are effective upon adoption, within 30 days after adoption. The submission shall indicate, where not obvious, why the bylaw provisions meet the requirements stated in paragraph (b)(1) of this section.

(c) *Effectiveness.* Any bylaw amendment filed pursuant to paragraph (b)(2) of this section shall automatically be effective 30 days from the date of filing of such amendment, provided that the association follows the requirements of its charter and bylaws in adopting such amendment, unless prior to the expiration of such 30-day period the OTS notifies the association that such amendment is rejected or that such amendment requires an application to be filed pursuant to paragraph (b)(1) of this section.

(d) *Effect of subsequent charter or bylaw change.* Notwithstanding any subsequent change to its charter or bylaws, the authority of a Federal stock association to engage in any transaction shall be determined only by the association's charter or bylaws then in effect, unless otherwise provided by Federal law or regulation.

[57 FR 14343, Apr. 20, 1992, as amended at 60 FR 66718, Dec. 26, 1995; 61 FR 64019, Dec. 3, 1996; 66 FR 13006, Mar. 2, 2001; 66 FR 15020, Mar. 15, 2001]

§ 552.6 Shareholders.

(a) *Shareholder meetings.* An annual meeting of the shareholders of the association for the election of directors and for the transaction of any other business of the association shall be held annually within 150 days after the end of the association's fiscal year. Unless otherwise provided in the association's charter, special meetings of the shareholders may be called by the board of directors or on the request of the holders of 10 percent or more of the shares entitled to vote at the meeting, or by such other persons as may be

§ 552.6

specified in the bylaws of the association. All annual and special meetings of shareholders shall be held at such place as the board of directors may determine in the state in which the association has its principal place of business, or at any other convenient place the board of directors may designate.

(b) *Notice of shareholder meetings.* Written notice stating the place, day, and hour of the meeting and the purpose or purposes for which the meeting is called shall be delivered not fewer than 20 nor more than 50 days before the date of the meeting, either personally or by mail, by or at the direction of the chairman of the board, the president, the secretary, or the directors, or other persons calling the meeting, to each shareholder of record entitled to vote at such meeting. If mailed, such notice shall be deemed to be delivered when deposited in the mail, addressed to the shareholder at the address appearing on the stock transfer books or records of the association as of the record date prescribed in paragraph (c) of this section, with postage thereon prepaid. When any shareholders' meeting, either annual or special, is adjourned for 30 days or more, notice of the adjourned meeting shall be given as in the case of an original meeting. Notwithstanding anything in this section, however, a Federal stock association that is wholly owned shall not be subject to the shareholder notice requirement.

(c) *Fixing of record date.* For the purpose of determining shareholders entitled to notice of or to vote at any meeting of shareholders or any adjournment thereof, or shareholders entitled to receive payment of any dividend, or in order to make a determination of shareholders for any other proper purpose, the board of directors shall fix in advance a date as the record date for any such determination of shareholders. Such date in any case shall be not more than 60 days and, in case of a meeting of shareholders, not less than 10 days prior to the date on which the particular action, requiring such determination of shareholders, is to be taken. When a determination of shareholders entitled to vote at any meeting of shareholders has been made as provided in this section, such determination shall apply to any adjournment thereof.

(d) *Voting lists.* (1) At least 20 days before each meeting of the shareholders, the officer or agent having charge of the stock transfer books for the shares of the association shall make a complete list of the stockholders of record entitled to vote at such meeting, or any adjournments thereof, arranged in alphabetical order, with the address and the number of shares held by each. This list of shareholders shall be kept on file at the home office of the association and shall be subject to inspection by any shareholder of record or the stockholder's agent during the entire time of the meeting. The original stock transfer book shall constitute *prima facie* evidence of the stockholders entitled to examine such list or transfer books or to vote at any meeting of stockholders. Notwithstanding anything in this section, however, a Federal stock association that is wholly owned shall not be subject to the voting list requirements.

(2) In lieu of making the shareholders list available for inspection by any shareholders as provided in paragraph (d)(1) of this section, the board of directors may perform such acts as required by paragraphs (a) and (b) of Rule 14a–7 of the General Rules and Regulations under the Securities and Exchange Act of 1934 (17 CFR 240.14a–7) as may be duly requested in writing, with respect to any matter which may be properly considered at a meeting of shareholders, by any shareholder who is entitled to vote on such matter and who shall defray the reasonable expenses to be incurred by the association in performance of the act or acts required.

(e) *Shareholder quorum.* A majority of the outstanding shares of the association entitled to vote, represented in person or by proxy, shall constitute a quorum at a meeting of shareholders. The shareholders present at a duly organized meeting may continue to transact business until adjournment, notwithstanding the withdrawal of enough shareholders to leave less than a quorum. If a quorum is present, the affirmative vote of the majority of the shares represented at the meeting and entitled to vote on the subject matter shall be the act of the stockholders,

Office of Thrift Supervision, Treasury   § 552.6-1

unless the vote of a greater number of stockholders voting together or voting by classes is required by law or the charter. Directors, however, are elected by a plurality of the votes cast at an election of directors.

(f) *Shareholder voting*—(1) *Proxies.* Unless otherwise provided in the association's charter, at all meetings of shareholders, a shareholder may vote in person or by proxy executed in writing by the shareholder or by a duly authorized attorney in fact. Proxies may be given telephonically or electronically as long as the holder uses a procedure for verifying the identity of the shareholder. A proxy may designate as holder a corporation, partnership or company as defined in Part 574 of this chapter, or other person. Proxies solicited on behalf of the management shall be voted as directed by the shareholder or, in the absence of such direction, as determined by a majority of the board of directors. No proxy shall be valid more than eleven months from the date of its execution except for a proxy coupled with an interest.

(2) *Shares controlled by association.* Neither treasury shares of its own stock held by the association nor shares held by another corporation, if a majority of the shares entitled to vote for the election of directors of such other corporation are held by the association, shall be voted at any meeting or counted in determining the total number of outstanding shares at any given time for purposes of any meeting.

(g) *Nominations and new business submitted by shareholders.* Nominations for directors and new business submitted by shareholders shall be voted upon at the annual meeting if such nominations or new business are submitted in writing and delivered to the secretary of the association at least five days prior to the date of the annual meeting. Ballots bearing the names of all the persons nominated shall be provided for use at the annual meeting.

(h) *Informal action by stockholders.* If the bylaws of the association so provide, any action required to be taken at a meeting of the stockholders, or any other action that may be taken at a meeting of the stockholders, may be taken without a meeting if consent in writing has been given by all the stockholders entitled to vote with respect to the subject matter.

[54 FR 49523, Nov. 30, 1989, as amended at 59 FR 18476, Apr. 19, 1994; 61 FR 64019, Dec. 3, 1996]

§ 552.6-1 Board of directors.

(a) *General powers and duties.* The business and affairs of the association shall be under the direction of its board of directors. The board of directors shall annually elect a chairman of the board from among its members and shall designate the chairman of the board, when present, to preside at its meeting. Directors need not be stockholders unless the bylaws so require.

(b) *Number and term.* The bylaws shall set forth a specific number of directors, not a range. The number of directors shall be not fewer than five nor more than fifteen, unless a higher or lower number has been authorized by the Director of the Office or his or her delegate. Directors shall be elected for a term of one to three years and until their successors are elected and qualified. If a staggered board is chosen, the directors shall be divided into two or three classes as nearly equal in number as possible and one class shall be elected by ballot annually. In the case of a converting or newly chartered association where all directors shall be elected at the first election of directors, if a staggered board is chosen, the terms shall be staggered in length from one to three years.

(c) *Regular meetings.* A regular meeting of the board of directors shall be held immediately after, and at the same place as, the annual meeting of shareholders. The board of directors shall determine the place, frequency, time and procedure for notice of regular meetings.

(d) *Quorum.* A majority of the number of directors shall constitute a quorum for the transaction of business at any meeting of the board of directors. The act of the majority of the directors present at a meeting at which a quorum is present shall be the act of the board of directors, unless a greater number is prescribed by regulation of the Office.

(e) *Vacancies.* Any vacancy occurring in the board of directors may be filled by the affirmative vote of a majority of the remaining directors although less than a quorum of the board of directors. A director elected to fill a vacancy shall be elected to serve only until the next election of directors by the shareholders. Any directorship to be filled by reason of an increase in the number of directors may be filled by election by the board of directors for a term of office continuing only until the next election of directors by the shareholders.

(f) *Removal or resignation of directors.* (1) At a meeting of shareholders called expressly for that purpose, any director may be removed only for cause, as defined in § 563.39 of this chapter, by a vote of the holders of a majority of the shares then entitled to vote at an election of directors. Associations may provide for procedures regarding resignations in the bylaws.

(2) If less than the entire board is to be removed, no one of the directors may be removed if the votes cast against the removal would be sufficient to elect a director if then cumulatively voted at an election of the class of directors of which such director is a part.

(3) Whenever the holders of the shares of any class are entitled to elect one or more directors by the provisions of the charter or supplemental sections thereto, the provisions of this section shall apply, in respect to the removal of a director or directors so elected, to the vote of the holders of the outstanding shares of that class and not to the vote of the outstanding shares as a whole.

(g) *Executive and other committees.* The board of directors, by resolution adopted by a majority of the full board, may designate from among its members an executive committee and one or more other committees each of which, to the extent provided in the resolution or bylaws of the association, shall have and may exercise all of the authority of the board of directors, except no committee shall have the authority of the board of directors with reference to: the declaration of dividends; the amendment of the charter or bylaws of the association; recommending to the stockholders a plan of merger, consolidation, or conversion; the sale, lease, or other disposition of all, or substantially all, of the property and assets of the association otherwise than in the usual and regular course of its business; a voluntary dissolution of the association; a revocation of any of the foregoing; or the approval of a transaction in which any member of the executive committee, directly or indirectly, has any material beneficial interest. The designation of any committee and the delegation of authority thereto shall not operate to relieve the board of directors, or any director, of any responsibility imposed by law or regulation.

(h) *Notice of special meetings.* Written notice of at least 24 hours regarding any special meeting of the board of directors or of any committee designated thereby shall be given to each director in accordance with the bylaws, although such notice may be waived by the director. The attendance of a director at a meeting shall constitute a waiver of notice of such meeting, except where a director attends a meeting for the express purpose of objecting to the transaction of any business because the meeting is not lawfully called or convened. Neither the business to be transacted at, nor the purpose of, any meeting need be specified in the notice or waiver of notice of such meeting. The bylaws may provide for telephonic participation at a meeting.

(i) *Action without a meeting.* Any action required or permitted to be taken by the board of directors at a meeting may be taken without a meeting if a consent in writing, setting forth the actions so taken, shall be signed by all of the directors.

(j) *Presumption of assent.* A director of the association who is present at a meeting of the board of directors at which action on any association matter is taken shall be presumed to have assented to the action taken unless his or her dissent or abstention shall be entered in the minutes of the meeting or unless a written dissent to such action shall be filed with the person acting as the secretary of the meeting before the adjournment thereof or shall be forwarded by registered mail to the secretary of the association within five days after the date on which a copy of the minutes of the meeting is received. Such right to dissent shall not apply to a director who voted in favor of such action.

(k) *Age limitation on directors.* A Federal association may provide a bylaw on age limitation for directors. Bylaws on age limitations must comply with all Federal laws, rules and regulations.

[54 FR 49523, Nov. 30, 1989, as amended at 58 FR 4312, Jan. 14, 1993; 61 FR 64020, Dec. 3, 1996; 62 FR 66262, Dec. 18, 1997]

§ 552.6-2 Officers.

(a) *Positions.* The officers of the association shall be a president, one or more vice presidents, a secretary, and a treasurer or comptroller, each of whom shall be elected by the board of directors. The board of directors may also designate the chairman of the board as an officer. The offices of the secretary and treasurer or comptroller may be held by the same person and the vice president may also be either the secretary or the treasurer or comptroller. The board of directors may designate one or more vice presidents as executive vice president or senior vice president. The board of directors may also elect or authorize the appointment of such other officers as the business of the association may require. The officers shall have such authority and perform such duties as the board of directors may from time to time authorize or determine. In the absence of action by the board of directors, the officers shall have such powers and duties as generally pertain to their respective offices.

(b) *Removal.* Any officer may be removed by the board of directors whenever in its judgment the best interests of the association will be served thereby; but such removal, other than for cause, shall be without prejudice to the contractual rights, if any, of the person so removed. Employment contracts shall conform with § 563.39 of this chapter.

(c) *Age limitation on officers.* A Federal association may provide a bylaw on age limitation for officers. Bylaws on age limitations must comply with all Federal laws, rules, and regulations.

[54 FR 49523, Nov. 30, 1989, as amended at 56 FR 59866, Nov. 26, 1991; 60 FR 66869, Dec. 27, 1995; 61 FR 64020, Dec. 3, 1996]

§ 552.6-3 Certificates for shares and their transfer.

(a) *Certificates for shares.* Certificates representing shares of capital stock of the association shall be in such form as shall be determined by the board of directors and approved by the OTS. The certificates shall be signed by the chief executive officer or by any other officer of the association authorized by the board of directors, attested by the secretary or an assistant secretary, and sealed with the corporate seal or a facsimile thereof. The signatures of such officers upon a certificate may be facsimiles if the certificate is manually signed on behalf of a transfer agent or a registrar other than the association itself or one of its employees. Each certificate for shares of capital stock shall be consecutively numbered or otherwise identified. The name and address of the person to whom the shares are issued, with the number of shares and date of issue, shall be entered on the stock transfer books of the association. All certificates surrendered to the association for transfer shall be cancelled and no new certificate shall be issued until the former certificate for a like number of shares shall have been surrendered and cancelled, except that in the case of a lost or destroyed certificate a new certificate may be issued upon such terms and indemnity to the association as the board of directors may prescribe.

(b) *Transfer of shares.* Transfer of shares of capital stock of the association shall be made only on its stock transfer books. Authority for such transfer shall be given only by the holder of record or by a legal representative, who shall furnish proper evidence of such authority, or by an attorney authorized by a duly executed power of attorney and filed with the association. The transfer shall be made only on surrender for cancellation of the certificate for the shares. The person in whose name shares of capital stock stand on the books of the association shall be deemed by the association to be the owner for all purposes.

[54 FR 49523, Nov. 30, 1989, as amended at 55 FR 13514, Apr. 11, 1990; 57 FR 14343, Apr. 20, 1992]

§ 552.6-4 [Reserved]

§ 552.9 [Reserved]

§ 552.10 Annual reports to stockholders.

A Federal stock association not wholly-owned by a holding company shall, within 130 days after the end of its fiscal year, mail to each of its stockholders entitled to vote at its annual meeting an annual report containing financial statements that satisfy the requirements of rule 14a–3 under the Securities Exchange Act of 1934. (17 CFR 240.14a–3). Concurrently with such mailing a certification of such mailing signed by the chairman of the board, the president or a vice president of the association, together with copies of the report, shall be transmitted by the association to the OTS.

[57 FR 14343, Apr. 20, 1992, as amended at 62 FR 66262, Dec. 18, 1997]

§ 552.11 Books and records.

(a) Each Federal stock association shall keep correct and complete books and records of account; shall keep minutes of the proceedings of its stockholders, board of directors, and committees of directors; and shall keep at its home office or at the office of its transfer agent or registrar, a record of its stockholders, giving the names and addresses of all stockholders, and the number, class and series, if any, of the shares held by each.

(b) Any stockholder or group of stockholders of a Federal stock association, holding of record the number of voting shares of such association specified below, upon making written demand stating a proper purpose, shall have the right to examine, in person or by agent or attorney, at any reasonable time or times, nonconfidential portions of its books and records of account, minutes and record of stockholders and to make extracts therefrom. Such right of examination is limited to a stockholder or group of stockholders holding of record:

(1) Voting shares having a cost of not less than $100,000 or constituting not less than one percent of the total outstanding voting shares, provided in either case such stockholder or group of stockholders have held of record such voting shares for a period of at least six months before making such written demand, or

(2) Not less than five percent of the total outstanding voting shares.

No stockholder or group of stockholders of a Federal stock association shall have any other right under this section or common law to examine its books and records of account, minutes and record of stockholders, except as provided in its bylaws with respect to inspection of a list of stockholders.

(c) The right to examination authorized by paragraph (b) of this section and the right to inspect the list of stockholders provided by a Federal stock association's bylaws may be denied to any stockholder or group of stockholders upon the refusal of any such stockholder or group of stockholders to furnish such association, its transfer agent or registrar an affidavit that such examination or inspection is not desired for any purpose which is in the interest of a business or object other than the business of the association, that such stockholder has not within the five years preceding the date of the affidavit sold or offered for sale, and does not now intend to sell or offer for sale, any list of stockholders of the association or of any other corporation, and that such stockholder has not within said five-year period aided or abetted any other person in procuring any list of stockholders for purposes of selling or offering for sale such list.

(d) Notwithstanding any provision of this section or common law, no stockholder or group of stockholders shall have the right to obtain, inspect or copy any portion of any books or records of a Federal stock association containing:

(1) A list of depositors in or borrowers from such association;

(2) Their addresses;

(3) Individual deposit or loan balances or records; or

(4) Any data from which such information could be reasonably constructed.

[54 FR 49523, Nov. 30, 1989, as amended at 61 FR 64020, Dec. 3, 1996]

§ 552.12 [Reserved]

§ 552.13 Combinations involving Federal stock associations.

(a) *Scope and authority.* Federal stock associations may enter into combinations only in accordance with the provisions of this section, section 18(c) of the Federal Deposit Insurance Act, sections 5(d)(3)(A) and 10(s) of the Home Owners' Loan Act, and § 563.22 of this part.

(b) *Definitions.* The following definitions apply to §§ 552.13 and 552.14 of this part:

(1) *Combination.* A merger or consolidation with another depository institution, or an acquisition of all or substantially all of the assets or assumption of all or substantially all of the liabilities of a depository institution by another depository institution. *Combine* means to be a constituent institution in a combination.

(2) *Consolidation.* Fusion of two or more depository institutions into a newly-created depository institution.

(3) *Constituent institution.* Resulting, disappearing, acquiring, or transferring depository institution in a combination.

(4) *Depository institution* means any commercial bank (including a private bank), a savings bank, a trust company, a savings and loan association, a building and loan association, a homestead association, a cooperative bank, an industrial bank or a credit union, chartered in the United States and having its principal office located in the United States.

(5) *Disappearing institution.* A depository institution whose corporate existence does not continue after a combination.

(6) *Merger.* Uniting two or more depository institutions by the transfer of all property rights and franchises to the resulting depository institution, which retains its corporate identity.

(7) *Mutual savings association.* Any savings association organized in a form not requiring non-withdrawable stock under Federal or State law.

(8) *Resulting institution.* The depository institution whose corporate existence continues after a combination.

(9) *Savings association* has the same meaning as defined in § 561.43 of this chapter.

(10) *State.* Includes the District of Columbia, Commonwealth of Puerto Rico, and States, territories, and possessions of the United States.

(11) *Stock association.* Any savings association organized in a form requiring non-withdrawable stock.

(c) *Forms of combination.* A Federal stock association may combine with any depository institution, provided that:

(1) The combination is in compliance with, and receives all approvals required under, any applicable statutes and regulations;

(2) Any resulting Federal savings association meets the requirements for Federal Home Loan Bank membership and insurance of accounts;

(3) Any resulting Federal savings association conforms within the time prescribed by the OTS to the requirements of sections 5(c) and 10(m) of the Home Owners' Loan Act; and

(4) If any constituent savings association is a mutual savings association, the resulting institution shall be mutually held, unless:

(i) The transaction involves a supervisory merger;

(ii) The transaction is approved under part 563b of this chapter;

(iii) The transaction involves an interim Federal stock association or an interim State stock savings association; or

(iv) The transaction involves a transfer in the context of a mutual holding company reorganization under section 10(o) of the Home Owners' Loan Act.

(d) *Combinations.* Prior written notification to, notice to, or prior written approval of, the Office pursuant to § 563.22 of this chapter is required for every combination. In the case of applications and notices pursuant to § 563.22 (a) or (c), the Office shall apply the criteria set out in § 563.22 of this chapter and shall impose any conditions it deems necessary or appropriate to ensure compliance with those criteria and the requirements of this chapter.

(e) *Approval of the board of directors.* Before filing a notice or application for any combination involving a Federal

§ 552.13

stock association, the combination shall be approved:

(1) By a two-thirds vote of the entire board of each constituent Federal savings association; and

(2) As required by other applicable Federal or state law, for other constituent institutions.

(f) *Combination agreement.* All terms, conditions, agreements or understandings, or other provisions with respect to a combination involving a Federal savings association shall be set forth fully in a written combination agreement. The combination agreement shall state:

(1) That the combination shall not be effective unless and until:

(i) The combination receives any necessary approval from the Office pursuant to § 563.22 (a) or (c);

(ii) In the case of a transaction requiring a notification pursuant to § 563.22(b), notification has been provided to the OTS; or

(iii) In the case of a transaction requiring a notice pursuant to § 563.22(c), the notice has been filed, and the appropriate period of time has passed or the OTS has advised the parties that it will not disapprove the transaction;

(2) Which constituent institution is to be the resulting institution;

(3) The name of the resulting institution;

(4) The location of the home office and any other offices of the resulting institution;

(5) The terms and conditions of the combination and the method of effectuation;

(6) Any charter amendments, or the new charter in the combination;

(7) The basis upon which the savings accounts of the resulting institution shall be issued;

(8) If a Federal association is the resulting institution, the number, names, residence addresses, and terms of directors;

(9) The effect upon and assumption of any liquidation account of a disappearing institution by the resulting institution; and

(10) Such other provisions, agreements, or understandings as relate to the combination.

(g) [Reserved]

(h) *Approval by stockholders*—(1) *General rule.* Except as otherwise provided in this section, an affirmative vote of two-thirds of the outstanding voting stock of any constituent Federal savings association shall be required for approval of the combination agreement. If any class of shares is entitled to vote as a class pursuant to § 552.4 of this part, an affirmative vote of a majority of the shares of each voting class and two-thirds of the total voting shares shall be required. The required vote shall be taken at a meeting of the savings association.

(2) *General exception.* Stockholders of the resulting Federal stock association need not authorize a combination agreement if:

(i) It does not involve an interim Federal savings association or an interim state savings association;

(ii) The association's charter is not changed;

(iii) Each share of stock outstanding immediately prior to the effective date of the combination is to be an identical outstanding share or a treasury share of the resulting Federal stock association after such effective date; and

(iv) Either:

(A) No shares of voting stock of the resulting Federal stock association and no securities convertible into such stock are to be issued or delivered under the plan of combination, or

(B) The authorized unissued shares or the treasury shares of voting stock of the resulting Federal stock association to be issued or delivered under the plan of combination, plus those initially issuable upon conversion of any securities to be issued or delivered under such plan, do not exceed 15% of the total shares of voting stock of such association outstanding immediately prior to the effective date of the combination.

(3) *Exceptions for certain combinations involving an interim association.* Stockholders of a Federal stock association need not authorize by a two-thirds affirmative vote combinations involving an interim Federal savings association or interim state savings association when the resulting Federal stock association is acquired pursuant to § 574.7(a)(2) of this chapter. In those cases, an affirmative vote of 50 percent

of the shares of the outstanding voting stock of the Federal stock association plus one affirmative vote shall be required. If any class of shares is entitled to vote as a class pursuant to § 552.4 of this part, an affirmative vote of 50 percent of the shares of each voting class plus one affirmative vote shall be required. The required votes shall be taken at a meeting of the association.

(i) *Disclosure.* The OTS may require, in connection with a combination under this section, such disclosure of information as the OTS deems necessary or desirable for the protection of investors in any of the constituent associations.

(j) *Articles of combination.* (1) Following stockholder approval of any combination in which a Federal savings association is the resulting institution, articles of combination shall be executed in duplicate by each constituent institution, by its chief executive officer or executive vice president and by its secretary or an assistant secretary, and verified by one of the officers of each institution signing such articles, and shall set forth:

(i) The plan of combination;

(ii) The number of shares outstanding in each depository institution; and

(iii) The number of shares in each depository institution voted for and against such plan.

(2) Both sets of articles of combination shall be filed with the Office. If the Office determines that such articles conform to the requirements of this section, the Office shall endorse the articles and return one set to the resulting institution.

(k) *Effective date.* No combination under this section shall be effective until receipt of any approvals required by the Office. The effective date of a combination in which the resulting institution is a Federal stock association shall be the date of consummation of the transaction or such other later date specified on the endorsement of the articles of combination by the Office. If a disappearing institution combining under this section is a Federal stock association, its charter shall be deemed to be cancelled as of the effective date of the combination and such charter must be surrendered to the Office as soon as practicable after the effective date.

(l) *Mergers and consolidations: transfer of assets and liabilities to the resulting institution.* Upon the effective date of a merger or consolidation under this section, if the resulting institution is a Federal savings association, all assets and property (real, personal and mixed, tangible and intangible, choses in action, rights, and credits) then owned by each constituent institution or which would inure to any of them, shall, immediately by operation of law and without any conveyance, transfer, or further action, become the property of the resulting Federal savings association. The resulting Federal savings association shall be deemed to be a continuation of the entity of each constituent institution, the rights and obligations of which shall succeed to such rights and obligations and the duties and liabilities connected therewith, subject to the Home Owners' Loan Act and other applicable statutes.

[54 FR 49523, Nov. 30, 1989, as amended at 57 FR 14343, Apr. 20, 1992; 59 FR 44623, Aug. 30, 1994; 71 FR 19811, Apr. 18, 2006]

§ 552.14 Dissenter and appraisal rights.

(a) *Right to demand payment of fair or appraised value.* Except as provided in paragraph (b) of this section, any stockholder of a Federal stock association combining in accordance with § 552.13 of this part shall have the right to demand payment of the fair or appraised value of his stock: *Provided,* That such stockholder has not voted in favor of the combination and complies with the provisions of paragraph (c) of this section.

(b) *Exceptions.* No stockholder required to accept only qualified consideration for his or her stock shall have the right under this section to demand payment of the stock's fair or appraised value, if such stock was listed on a national securities exchange or quoted on the National Association of Securities Dealers' Automated Quotation System ("NASDAQ") on the date of the meeting at which the combination was acted upon or stockholder action is not required for a combination made pursuant to § 552.13(h)(2) of this part. "Qualified consideration"

§ 552.14

means cash, shares of stock of any association or corporation which at the effective date of the combination will be listed on a national securities exchange or quoted on NASDAQ, or any combination of such shares of stock and cash.

(c) *Procedure*—(1) *Notice.* Each constituent Federal stock association shall notify all stockholders entitled to rights under this section, not less than twenty days prior to the meeting at which the combination agreement is to be submitted for stockholder approval, of the right to demand payment of appraised value of shares, and shall include in such notice a copy of this section. Such written notice shall be mailed to stockholders of record and may be part of management's proxy solicitation for such meeting.

(2) *Demand for appraisal and payment.* Each stockholder electing to make a demand under this section shall deliver to the Federal stock association, before voting on the combination, a writing identifying himself or herself and stating his or her intention thereby to demand appraisal of and payment for his or her shares. Such demand must be in addition to and separate from any proxy or vote against the combination by the stockholder.

(3) *Notification of effective date and written offer.* Within ten days after the effective date of the combination, the resulting association shall:

(i) Give written notice by mail to stockholders of constituent Federal stock associations who have complied with the provisions of paragraph (c)(2) of this section and have not voted in favor of the combination, of the effective date of the combination;

(ii) Make a written offer to each stockholder to pay for dissenting shares at a specified price deemed by the resulting association to be the fair value thereof; and

(iii) Inform them that, within sixty days of such date, the respective requirements of paragraphs (c)(5) and (c)(6) of this section (set out in the notice) must be satisfied.

The notice and offer shall be accompanied by a balance sheet and statement of income of the association the shares of which the dissenting stockholder holds, for a fiscal year ending not more than sixteen months before the date of notice and offer, together with the latest available interim financial statements.

(4) *Acceptance of offer.* If within sixty days of the effective date of the combination the fair value is agreed upon between the resulting association and any stockholder who has complied with the provisions of paragraph (c)(2) of this section, payment therefor shall be made within ninety days of the effective date of the combination.

(5) *Petition to be filed if offer not accepted.* If within sixty days of the effective date of the combination the resulting association and any stockholder who has complied with the provisions of paragraph (c)(2) of this section do not agree as to the fair value, then any such stockholder may file a petition with the Office, with a copy by registered or certified mail to the resulting association, demanding a determination of the fair market value of the stock of all such stockholders. A stockholder entitled to file a petition under this section who fails to file such petition within sixty days of the effective date of the combination shall be deemed to have accepted the terms offered under the combination.

(6) *Stock certificates to be noted.* Within sixty days of the effective date of the combination, each stockholder demanding appraisal and payment under this section shall submit to the transfer agent his certificates of stock for notation thereon that an appraisal and payment have been demanded with respect to such stock and that appraisal proceedings are pending. Any stockholder who fails to submit his or her stock certificates for such notation shall no longer be entitled to appraisal rights under this section and shall be deemed to have accepted the terms offered under the combination.

(7) *Withdrawal of demand.* Notwithstanding the foregoing, at any time within sixty days after the effective date of the combination, any stockholder shall have the right to withdraw his or her demand for appraisal and to accept the terms offered upon the combination.

(8) *Valuation and payment.* The Director shall, as he or she may elect, either

Office of Thrift Supervision, Treasury § 555.100

appoint one or more independent persons or direct appropriate staff of the Office to appraise the shares to determine their fair market value, as of the effective date of the combination, exclusive of any element of value arising from the accomplishment or expectation of the combination. Appropriate staff of the Office shall review and provide an opinion on appraisals prepared by independent persons as to the suitability of the appraisal methodology and the adequacy of the analysis and supportive data. The Director after consideration of the appraisal report and the advice of the appropriate staff shall, if he or she concurs in the valuation of the shares, direct payment by the resulting association of the appraised fair market value of the shares, upon surrender of the certificates representing such stock. Payment shall be made, together with interest from the effective date of the combination, at a rate deemed equitable by the Director.

(9) *Costs and expenses.* The costs and expenses of any proceeding under this section may be apportioned and assessed by the Director as he or she may deem equitable against all or some of the parties. In making this determination the Director shall consider whether any party has acted arbitrarily, vexatiously, or not in good faith in respect to the rights provided by this section.

(10) *Voting and distribution.* Any stockholder who has demanded appraisal rights as provided in paragraph (c)(2) of this section shall thereafter neither be entitled to vote such stock for any purpose nor be entitled to the payment of dividends or other distributions on the stock (except dividends or other distribution payable to, or a vote to be taken by stockholders of record at a date which is on or prior to, the effective date of the combination): *Provided,* That if any stockholder becomes unentitled to appraisal and payment of appraised value with respect to such stock and accepts or is deemed to have accepted the terms offered upon the combination, such stockholder shall thereupon be entitled to vote and receive the distributions described above.

(11) *Status.* Shares of the resulting association into which shares of the stockholders demanding appraisal rights would have been converted or exchanged, had they assented to the combination, shall have the status of authorized and unissued shares of the resulting association.

§ 552.15 Supervisory combinations.

Notwithstanding the foregoing provisions of this part, the Director of the Office may waive or deem inapplicable any provision of § 552.13 or § 552.14 of this part if he or she determines that grounds exist, or may imminently exist, for appointment of a conservator or receiver for an association under subsection 5(d) of the Home Owners' Loan Act.

§ 552.16 Effect of subsequent charter or bylaw change.

Notwithstanding any subsequent change to its charter or bylaws, the authority of a Federal stock association to engage in any transaction shall be determined only by the association's charter or bylaws then in effect.

PART 555—ELECTRONIC OPERATIONS

Sec.
555.100 What does this part do?

Subpart A—Authority of Federal Savings Associations To Conduct Electronic Operations

555.200 How may I use or participate with others to use electronic means and facilities?
555.210 What precautions must I take?

Subpart B—Requirements Applicable to All Savings Associations

555.300 Must I inform OTS before I use electronic means or facilities?
555.310 How do I notify OTS?

AUTHORITY: 12 U.S.C. 1462a, 1463, 1464.

SOURCE: 63 FR 65682, Nov. 30, 1998, unless otherwise noted.

§ 555.100 What does this part do?

Subpart A of this part describes how a Federal savings association may provide products and services through electronic means and facilities. Subpart B of this part contains requirements applicable to all savings associations.

Subpart A—Authority of Federal Savings Associations To Conduct Electronic Operations

§ 555.200 How may I use or participate with others to use electronic means and facilities?

(a) *General.* A Federal savings association ("you") may use, or participate with others to use, electronic means or facilities to perform any function, or provide any product or service, as part of an authorized activity. Electronic means or facilities include, but are not limited to, automated teller machines, automated loan machines, personal computers, the Internet, the World Wide Web, telephones, and other similar electronic devices.

(b) *Other.* To optimize the use of your resources, you may market and sell, or participate with others to market and sell, electronic capacities and by-products to third-parties, if you acquired or developed these capacities and by-products in good faith as part of providing financial services.

§ 555.210 What precautions must I take?

If you use electronic means and facilities under this subpart, your management must:

(a) Identify, assess, and mitigate potential risks and establish prudent internal controls; and

(b) Implement security measures designed to ensure secure operations. Such measures must be adequate to:

(1) Prevent unauthorized access to your records and your customers' records;

(2) Prevent financial fraud through the use of electronic means or facilities; and

(3) Comply with applicable security devices requirements of part 568 of this chapter.

Subpart B—Requirements Applicable to All Savings Associations

§ 555.300 Must I inform OTS before I use electronic means or facilities?

(a) *General.* A savings association ("you") are not required to inform OTS before you use electronic means or facilities, except as provided in paragraphs (b) and (c) of this section. However, OTS encourages you to consult with your Regional Office before you engage in any activities using electronic means or facilities.

(b) *Activities requiring advance notice.* You must file a written notice as described in § 555.310 before you establish a transactional web site. A transactional web site is an Internet site that enables users to conduct financial transactions such as accessing an account, obtaining an account balance, transferring funds, processing bill payments, opening an account, applying for or obtaining a loan, or purchasing other authorized products or services.

(c) *Other procedures.* If the OTS Regional Office informs you of any supervisory or compliance concerns that may affect your use of electronic means or facilities, you must follow any procedures it imposes in writing.

§ 555.310 How do I notify OTS?

(a) *Notice requirement.* You must file a written notice with the appropriate Regional Office listed at § 516.40(a) of this chapter at least 30 days before you establish a transactional website. The notice must do three things:

(1) Describe the transactional web site.

(2) Indicate the date the transactional web site will become operational.

(3) List a contact familiar with the deployment, operation, and security of the transactional web site.

(b) *Transition provision.* If you established a transactional web site after the date of your last regular onsite OTS safety and soundness examination but before January 1, 1999, you must file a notice describing your activity by February 1, 1999.

[63 FR 65682, Nov. 30, 1998, as amended at 66 FR 13006, Mar. 2, 2001]

PART 557—DEPOSITS

Subpart A—General

Sec.
557.1 What does this part do?

Office of Thrift Supervision, Treasury § 557.13

Subpart B—Deposit Activities of Federal Savings Associations

557.10 What authorities govern the issuance of deposit accounts by a federal savings association?
557.11 To what extent does Federal law preempt deposit-related State laws?
557.12 What are some examples of preempted state laws affecting deposits?
557.13 What State laws affecting deposits are not preempted?
557.14 What interest rate may I pay on savings accounts?
557.15 Who owns a deposit account?

Subpart C—Deposit Activities of All Savings Associations

557.20 What records should I maintain on deposit activities?

AUTHORITY: 12 U.S.C. 1462a, 1463, 1464.

SOURCE: 62 FR 54764, Oct. 22, 1997, unless otherwise noted.

Subpart A—General

§ 557.1 What does this part do?

This part applies to the deposit activities of savings associations. If you are a federal savings association, subpart B of this part applies to your deposit activities. Subpart C of this part applies to the deposit activities of all federal and state-chartered savings associations.

Subpart B—Deposit Activities of Federal Savings Associations

§ 557.10 What authorities govern the issuance of deposit accounts by a federal savings association?

A federal savings association ("you") may raise funds through accounts and may issue evidence of accounts under section 5(b)(1) of the HOLA (12 U.S.C. 1464(b)(1)), your charter, and this part. Additionally, 12 CFR parts 204 and 230 apply to your deposit activities.

§ 557.11 To what extent does Federal law preempt deposit-related State laws?

(a) Under sections 4(a), 5(a), and 5(b) of the HOLA, 12 U.S.C. 1463(a), 1464(a), and 1464(b), OTS is authorized to promulgate regulations that preempt state laws affecting the operations of federal savings associations when appropriate to:

(1) Facilitate the safe and sound operations of federal savings associations;
(2) Enable federal savings associations to operate according to the best thrift institutions practices in the United States; or
(3) Further other purposes of HOLA.

(b) To further these purposes without undue regulatory duplication and burden, OTS hereby occupies the entire field of federal savings associations' deposit-related regulations. OTS intends to give federal savings associations maximum flexibility to exercise deposit-related powers according to a uniform federal scheme of regulation. Federal savings associations may exercise deposit-related powers as authorized under federal law, including this part, without regard to state laws purporting to regulate or otherwise affect deposit activities, except to the extent provided in § 557.13. State law includes any statute, regulation, ruling, order, or judicial decision.

[62 FR 54764, Oct. 22, 1997, as amended at 63 FR 71212, Dec. 24, 1998; 64 FR 69184, Dec. 10, 1999; 67 FR 78152, Dec. 23, 2002]

§ 557.12 What are some examples of preempted state laws affecting deposits?

The OTS preempts state laws that purport to impose requirements governing the following:

(a) Abandoned and dormant accounts;
(b) Checking accounts;
(c) Disclosure requirements;
(d) Funds availability;
(e) Savings account orders of withdrawal;
(f) Service charges and fees;
(g) State licensing or registration requirements; and
(h) Special purpose savings services.

§ 557.13 What State laws affecting deposits are not preempted?

(a) The OTS has not preempted the following types of state law, to the extent that the law only incidentally affects your deposit-related activities or is otherwise consistent with the purposes of § 557.11:

(1) Contract and commercial law;
(2) Tort law; and
(3) Criminal law.

§ 557.14

(b) The OTS will not preempt any other state law if the OTS, upon review, finds that the law:
(1) Furthers a vital state interest; and
(2) Either only incidentally affects your deposit-related activities or is not otherwise contrary to the purposes expressed in § 557.11.

§ 557.14 What interest rate may I pay on savings accounts?

(a) You may pay interest at any rate or anticipated rate of return on savings accounts, either in deposit or in share form, as provided in your charter and the account's terms.
(b) You may pay fixed or variable rates. If you pay a variable rate, you must base it on a schedule, index, or formula that you specify in the account's terms.

§ 557.15 Who owns a deposit account?

You may treat the holder of record as the account owner, even if you receive contrary notice, until you transfer the account on your records.

Subpart C—Deposit Activities of All Savings Associations

§ 557.20 What records should I maintain on deposit activities?

All federal and state chartered savings associations ("you") should establish and maintain deposit documentation practices and records that demonstrate that you appropriately administer and monitor deposit-related activities. Your records should adequately evidence ownership, balances, and all transactions involving each account. You may maintain records on deposit activities in any format that is consistent with standard business practices.

PART 558—POSSESSION BY CONSERVATORS AND RECEIVERS FOR FEDERAL AND STATE SAVINGS ASSOCIATIONS

Sec.
558.1 Procedure upon taking possession.
558.2 Notice of appointment.

AUTHORITY: 12 U.S.C. 1462, 1462a, 1463, 1464, 1467a.

§ 558.1 Procedure upon taking possession.

(a) The conservator or receiver for a Federal or state savings association shall take possession of the savings association by taking possession of the principal office of the Federal or state savings association in accordance with the terms of the Director's appointment.

(b) Upon taking possession, the conservator or receiver shall immediately:
(1) Take possession of the savings association's books, records and assets.
(2) Notify in writing, served personally or by registered mail or telegraph, all persons and entities that the conservator or receiver knows to be holding or in possession of assets of the savings association, that the conservator or receiver has succeeded to all rights, titles, powers and privileges of the savings associations.
(3) File with the Corporate Secretary a statement that possession was taken, including the time of the taking, which statement shall be conclusive evidence thereof.
(4) Post a notice on the door of the principal and other offices of the savings association in the form prescribed by the Director of the OTS.
(5) By operation of law and without any conveyance or other instrument, act or deed, succeed to the rights, titles, powers and privileges of the savings association, and to the rights, powers, and privileges of its stockholders, members, accountholders, depositors, officers, and directors. No stockholder, member, accountholder, depositor, officer or director shall thereafter have or exercise any right, power, or privilege, or act in connection with any of the savings association's assets or property.

[58 FR 4312, Jan. 14, 1993, as amended at 59 FR 53571, Oct. 25, 1994; 73 FR 18, Jan. 2, 2008]

§ 558.2 Notice of appointment.

(a) When the Director of OTS issues an order for the appointment of a conservator or receiver, the Director will designate the persons or entities whose employees or agents must, before the conservator or receiver takes possession of the savings association:

(1) Give notice of the appointment to any officer or employee who is present in and appears to be in charge at the principal office of the savings association as determined by OTS.

(2) Serve a copy of the order for the appointment upon the savings association or upon the conservator by:

(i) Leaving a certified copy of the order of appointment at the principal office of the savings association as determined by OTS; or

(ii) Handing a certified copy of the order of appointment to the previous conservator of the savings association, or to the officer or employee of the savings association, or to the previous conservator who is present in and appears to be in charge at the principal office of the savings association as determined by OTS.

(3) File with the Secretary of OTS a statement that includes the date and time that notice of the appointment was given and service of the order of appointment was made.

(b) If the Director of OTS appoints a conservator or receiver under this part, OTS will immediately file a notice of the appointment for publication in the FEDERAL REGISTER.

[73 FR 18, Jan. 2, 2008]

PART 559—SUBORDINATE ORGANIZATIONS

Sec.
559.1 What does this part cover?
559.2 Definitions.

Subpart A—Regulations Applicable to Federal Savings Associations

559.3 What are the characteristics of, and what requirements apply to, subordinate organizations of Federal savings associations?
559.4 What activities are preapproved for service corporations?
559.5 How much may a savings association invest in service corporations or lower-tier entities?

Subpart B—Regulations Applicable to All Savings Associations

559.10 How must separate corporate identities be maintained?
559.11 What notices are required to establish or acquire a new subsidiary or engage in new activities through an existing subsidiary?
559.12 How may a subsidiary of a savings association issue securities?
559.13 How may a savings association exercise its salvage power in connection with its service corporation or lower-tier entities?

AUTHORITY: 12 U.S.C. 1462, 1462a, 1463, 1464, 1828.

SOURCE: 61 FR 66571, Dec. 18, 1996, unless otherwise noted.

§ 559.1 What does this part cover?

(a) OTS is issuing this part 559 pursuant to its general rulemaking and supervisory authority under the Home Owners' Loan Act, 12 U.S.C. 1462 *et seq.*, and its specific authority under section 18(m) of the Federal Deposit Insurance Act, 12 U.S.C. 1828(m). Subpart A of this part 559 applies to subordinate organizations of federal savings associations. Subpart B of this part applies to subordinate organizations of all savings associations. OTS may, at any time, limit a savings association's investment in any of these entities, or may limit or refuse to permit any activities of any of these entities for supervisory, legal, or safety and soundness reasons.

(b) Notices under this part are applications for purposes of statutory and regulatory references to "applications." Any conditions that OTS imposes in approving any application are enforceable as a condition imposed in writing by the OTS in connection with the granting of a request by a savings association within the meaning of 12 U.S.C. 1818(b) or 1818(i).

§ 559.2 Definitions.

For purposes of this part:

Control has the same meaning as in part 574 of this chapter.

GAAP-consolidated subsidiary means an entity in which a savings association has a direct or indirect ownership interest and whose assets are consolidated with those of the savings association for purposes of reporting under Generally Accepted Accounting Principles (GAAP). Generally, these are entities in which a savings association has a majority ownership interest.

Lower-tier entity includes any company in which an operating subsidiary or a service corporation has a direct or indirect ownership interest.

§ 559.3

Operating subsidiary means any entity that satisfies all of the requirements for an operating subsidiary set forth in § 559.3 of this part and that is designated by the parent savings association as an operating subsidiary pursuant to § 559.3 of this part. More than 50% of the voting shares of an operating subsidiary must be owned, directly or indirectly, by a federal savings association and no other person or entity may exercise effective operating control. An operating subsidiary may only engage in activities permissible for a federal savings association.

Ownership interest means any equity interest in a business organization, including stock, limited or general partnership interests, or shares in a limited liability company.

Service corporation means any entity that satisfies all of the requirements for service corporations in 12 U.S.C. 1464(c)(4)(B) and § 559.3 of this part and that is designated by the investing savings association as a service corporation pursuant to § 559.3 of this part. A service corporation must be organized under the laws of the state where the federal savings association's home office is located, may only be owned by savings associations with home offices in that state, and may engage in the activities identified in §§ 559.3(e)(2) and 559.4 of this part.

Subordinate organization means any corporation, partnership, business trust, association, joint venture, pool, syndicate, or other similar business organization in which a savings association has a direct or indirect ownership interest, unless that ownership interest qualifies as a pass-through investment pursuant to § 560.32 of this chapter and is so designated by the investing savings association.

Subsidiary means any subordinate organization directly or indirectly controlled by a savings association.

Subpart A—Regulations Applicable to Federal Savings Associations

§ 559.3 What are the characteristics of, and what requirements apply to, subordinate organizations of Federal savings associations?

A federal savings association ("you") that meets the requirements of this section, as detailed in the following chart, may establish, or obtain an interest in an operating subsidiary or a service corporation. For ease of reference, this section cross-references other regulations in this chapter affecting operating subsidiaries and service corporations. You should refer to those regulations for the details of how they apply. The chart also discusses the regulations that may apply to lower-tier entities in which you have an indirect ownership interest through your operating subsidiary or service corporation. The chart follows:

	Operating subsidiary	Service corporation
(a) How may a federal savings association ("you") establish an operating subsidiary or a service corporation?	(1) You must file a notice satisfying § 559.11. Any finance subsidiary that existed on January 1, 1997 is deemed an operating subsidiary without further action on your part.	(2) You must file a notice satisfying § 559.11. Depending upon your condition and the activities in which the service corporation will engage, § 559.3(e)(2) may require you to file an application.
(b) Who may be an owner?	(1) Anyone may have an ownership interest in an operating subsidiary.	(2) Only savings associations with home offices in the state where you have your home office may have an ownership interest in any service corporation in which you invest.
(c) What ownership requirements apply?	(1) You must own, directly or indirectly, more than 50% of the voting shares of the operating subsidiary. No one else may exercise effective operating control.	(2) You are not required to have any particular percentage ownership interest and need not have control of the service corporation.
(d) What geographic restrictions apply?	(1) An operating subsidiary may be organized in any geographic location.	(2) A service corporation must be organized in the state where your home office is located.

Office of Thrift Supervision, Treasury § 559.3

	Operating subsidiary	Service corporation
(e) What activities are permissible?	(1) After you have notified OTS in accordance with § 559.11, an operating subsidiary may engage in any activity that you may conduct directly. You may hold another insured depository institution as an operating subsidiary.	(2)(i) If you are eligible for expedited treatment under § 516.5 of this chapter, and notify OTS as required by § 559.11, your service corporation may engage in the preapproved activities listed in § 559.4. You may request OTS approval for your service corporation to engage in any other activity reasonably related to the activities of financial institutions by filing an application in accordance with standard treatment processing procedures at part 516, subparts A and E of this chapter. (ii) If you are subject to standard treatment under § 516.5 of this chapter, and notify OTS as required by § 559.11, your service corporation may engage in any activity that you may conduct directly except taking deposits. You may request OTS approval for your service corporation to engage in any other activity reasonably related to the activities of financial institutions, including the activities set forth in § 559.4(b)–(j), by filing an application in accordance with standard treatment processing procedures at part 516, subparts A and E of this chapter.
(f) May the operating subsidiary or service corporation invest in lower-tier entities?	(1)(i) An operating subsidiary may itself hold an operating subsidiary. Part 559 applies equally to a lower-tier operating subsidiary. In applying the regulations in this part, the investing operating subsidiary should substitute "investing operating subsidiary" wherever the part uses "you" or "savings association." (ii) An operating subsidiary may also invest in other types of lower-tier entities. These entities must comply with all of the requirements of this part 559 that apply to service corporations except for paragraphs (b)(2) and (d)(2) of this section.	(2) A service corporation may invest in all types of lower-tier entities as long as the lower-tier entity is engaged solely in activities that are permissible for a service corporation. All of the requirements of this part apply to such entities except for paragraphs (b)(2) and (d)(2) of this section.
(g) How much may a federal savings association invest?	(1) There are no limits on the amount you may invest in your operating subsidiaries, either separately or in the aggregate.	(2) Section 559.5 limits your aggregate investments in service corporations and indicates when your investments (both debt and equity) in lower-tier entities must be aggregated with your investments in service corporations.
(h) Do federal statutes and regulations that apply to the savings association apply?	(1) Unless otherwise specifically provided by statute, regulation, or OTS policy, all federal statutes and regulations apply to operating subsidiaries in the same manner as they apply to you. You and your operating subsidiary are generally consolidated and treated as a unit for statutory and regulatory purposes.	(2) (i) If the federal statute or regulation specifically refers to "service corporation," it applies to all service corporations, even if you do not control the service corporation or it is not a GAAP-consolidated subsidiary. (ii) If the federal statute or regulation refers to "subsidiary," it applies only to service corporations that you directly or indirectly control.
(i) Do the investment limits that apply to federal savings associations (HOLA section 5(c) and part 560 of this chapter) apply?	(1) Your assets and those of your operating subsidiary are aggregated when calculating investment limitations.	(2) Your service corporation's assets are not subject to the same investment limitations that apply to you. The investment activities of your service corporation are governed by paragraph (e)(2) of this section and § 559.4.
(j) How does the capital regulation (part 567 of this chapter) apply?	(1) Your assets and those of your operating subsidiary are consolidated for all capital purposes.	(2) The capital treatment of a service corporation depends upon whether it is an includable subsidiary. That determination is based upon factors set forth in part 567 of this chapter, including your percentage ownership of the service corporation and the activities in which the service corporation engages. Both debt and equity investments in service corporations that are GAAP-consolidated subsidiaries are considered investments in subsidiaries for purposes of the capital regulation, regardless of the authority under which they are made.

§ 559.3

	Operating subsidiary	Service corporation
(k) How does the loans-to-one-borrower (LTOB) regulation (§ 560.93 of this chapter) apply?	(1) The LTOB regulation does not apply to loans from you to your operating subsidiary or loans from your operating subsidiary to you. Other loans made by your operating subsidiary are aggregated with your loans for LTOB purposes.	(2) The LTOB regulation does not apply to loans from you to your service corporation or from your service corporation to you. However, § 559.5 imposes restrictions on the amount of loans you may make to certain service corporations. Loans made by a service corporation that you control to entities other than you or your subordinate organizations are aggregated with your loans for LTOB purposes.
(l) How do the transactions with affiliates (TWA) regulations (§ 563.41 of this chapter) apply?	(1) Section 563.41 of this chapter explains how TWA applies. Generally, an operating subsidiary is not an affiliate, unless it is a depository institution; is directly controlled by another affiliate of the savings association or by shareholders that control the savings association; or is an employee stock option plan, trust, or similar organization that exists for the benefit of shareholders, partners, members, or employees of the savings association or an affiliate. A non-affiliate operating subsidiary is treated as a part of the savings association and its transactions with affiliates of the savings association are aggregated with those of the savings association	(2) Section 563.41 of this chapter explains how TWA applies. Generally, a service corporation is not an affiliate, unless it is a depository institution; is directly controlled by another affiliate of the savings association or by shareholders that control the savings association; or is an employee stock option plan, trust, or similar organization that exists for the benefit of shareholders, partners, members, or employees of the savings association or an affiliate. If a savings association directly or indirectly controls a service corporation and the service corporation is not otherwise an affiliate under § 563.41 of this chapter, the service corporation is treated as a part of the savings association and its transactions with affiliates of the savings association are aggregated with those of the savings association.
(m) How does the Qualified Thrift Lender (QTL) (12 U.S.C. 1467a(m)) test apply?	(1) Under 12 U.S.C. 1467a(m)(5), you may determine whether to consolidate the assets of a particular operating subsidiary for purposes of calculating your qualified thrift investments. If the operating subsidiary's assets are not consolidated with yours for that purpose, your investment in the operating subsidiary will be considered in calculating your qualified thrift investments.	(2) Under 12 U.S.C. 1467a(m)(5), you may determine whether to consolidate the assets of a particular service corporation for purposes of calculating your qualified thrift investments. If a service corporation's assets are not consolidated with yours for that purpose, your investment in the service corporation will be considered in calculating your qualified thrift investments.
(n) Does state law apply?	(1) State law applies to operating subsidiaries only to the extent it applies to you.	(2) State law applies to service corporations regardless of whether it applies to you, except where there is a conflict with federal law.
(o) May OTS conduct examinations?	(1) An operating subsidiary is subject to examination by OTS.	(2) A service corporation is subject to examination by OTS.
(p) What must be done to redesignate an operating subsidiary as a service corporation or a service corporation as an operating subsidiary?	(1) Before redesignating an operating subsidiary as a service corporation, you should consult with the OTS Regional Director for the Region in which your home office is located. You must maintain adequate internal records, available for examination by OTS, demonstrating that the redesignated service corporation meets all of the applicable requirements of this part and that your board of directors has approved the redesignation.	(2) Before redesignating a service corporation as an operating subsidiary, you should consult with the OTS Regional Director for the Region in which your home office is located. You must maintain adequate internal records, available for examination by OTS, demonstrating that the redesignated operating subsidiary meets all of the applicable requirements of this part and that your board of directors has approved the redesignation.
(q) What are the consequences of failing to comply with the requirements of this part?	(1) If an operating subsidiary, or any lower-tier entity in which the operating subsidiary invests pursuant to paragraph (f)(1) of this section fails to meet any of the requirements of this section, you must notify OTS. Unless otherwise advised by OTS, if the company cannot comply within 90 days with all of the requirements for either an operating subsidiary or a service corporation under this section, or any other investment authorized by 12 U.S.C. 1464(c) or part 560 of this chapter, you must promptly dispose of your investment.	(2) If a service corporation, or any lower-tier entity in which the service corporation invests pursuant to paragraph (f)(2) of this section, fails to meet any of the requirements of this section, you must notify OTS. Unless otherwise advised by OTS, if the company cannot comply within 90 days with all of the requirements for either an operating subsidiary or a service corporation under this section, or any other investment authorized by 12 U.S.C. 1464(c) or part 560 of this chapter, you must promptly dispose of your investment.

Office of Thrift Supervision, Treasury § 559.4

[61 FR 66571, Dec. 18, 1996, as amended at 62 FR 66262, Dec. 18, 1997; 63 FR 65683, Nov. 30, 1998; 66 FR 13006, Mar. 2, 2001; 67 FR 77916, Dec. 20, 2002; 67 FR 78152, Dec. 23, 2002; 68 FR 57796, Oct. 7, 2003]

§ 559.4 What activities are preapproved for service corporations?

This section sets forth the activities that have been preapproved for service corporations. Section 559.3(e)(2) of this part sets forth the procedures for engaging in a broader scope of activities on a case-by-case basis. You should read these two sections together to determine whether you must file a notice with OTS under § 559.11 of this part, or whether you must file an application under part 516 of this chapter and receive prior written OTS approval for your service corporation to engage in a particular activity. To the extent permitted by § 559.3(e)(2) of this part, a service corporation may engage in the following activities:

(a) Any activity that all federal savings associations may conduct directly, except taking deposits.

(b) Business and professional services. The following services are preapproved for service corporations only when they are limited to financial documents or financial clients or are generally finance-related:

(1) Accounting or internal audit;
(2) Advertising, marketing research and other marketing;
(3) Clerical;
(4) Consulting;
(5) Courier;
(6) Data processing;
(7) Data storage facilities operation and related services;
(8) Office supplies, furniture, and equipment purchasing and distribution;
(9) Personnel benefit program development or administration;
(10) Printing and selling forms that require Magnetic Ink Character Recognition (MICR) encoding;
(11) Relocation of personnel;
(12) Research studies and surveys;
(13) Software development and systems integration; and
(14) Remote service unit operation, leasing, ownership or establishment.

(c) Credit-related activities.
(1) Abstracting;
(2) Acquiring and leasing personal property;
(3) Appraising;
(4) Collection agency;
(5) Credit analysis;
(6) Check or credit card guaranty and verification;
(7) Escrow agent or trustee (under deeds of trust, including executing and deliverance of conveyances, reconveyances and transfers of title); and
(8) Loan inspection.

(d) Consumer services.
(1) Financial advice or consulting;
(2) Foreign currency exchange;
(3) Home ownership counseling;
(4) Income tax return preparation;
(5) Postal services;
(6) Stored value instrument sales;
(7) Welfare benefit distribution;
(8) Check printing and related services; and
(9) Remote service unit operation, leasing, ownership, or establishment.

(e) Real estate related services.
(1) Acquiring real estate for prompt development or subdivision, for construction of improvements, for resale or leasing to others for such construction, or for use as manufactured home sites, in accordance with a prudent program of property development;

(2) Acquiring improved real estate or manufactured homes to be held for rental or resale, for remodeling, renovating, or demolishing and rebuilding for sale or rental, or to be used for offices and related facilities of a stockholder of the service corporation;

(3) Maintaining and managing real estate; and

(4) Real estate brokerage for property owned by a savings association that owns capital stock of the service corporation, the service corporation, or a lower-tier entity in which the service corporation invests.

(f) Securities activities, liquidity management, and coins.

(1) Execution of transactions in securities on an agency or riskless principal basis solely upon the order and for the account of customers or the provision of investment advice. The service corporation must register with the Securities and Exchange Commission and State securities regulators, as

165

required by applicable Federal and State law and regulations.

(2) Liquidity management;

(3) Issuing notes, bonds, debentures, or other obligations or securities;

(4) Purchase or sale of coins issued by the U.S. Treasury.

(g) *Investments.* (1) Tax-exempt bonds used to finance residential real property for family units;

(2) Tax-exempt obligations of public housing agencies used to finance housing projects with rental assistance subsidies;

(3) Small business investment companies and new markets venture capital companies licensed by the U.S. Small Business Administration;

(4) Rural business investment companies; and

(5) Investing in savings accounts of an investing thrift.

(h) Community development and charitable activities:

(1) Investments in governmentally insured, guaranteed, subsidized or otherwise sponsored programs for housing, small farms, or businesses that are local in character;

(2) Investments designed primarily to promote the public welfare, including the welfare of low- and moderate-income communities or families (such as providing housing, services, or jobs);

(3) Investments in low-income housing tax credit and new markets tax credit projects and entities authorized by statute (e.g., community development financial institutions) to promote community, inner city, and community development purposes; and

(4) Establishing a corporation that is recognized by the Internal Revenue Service as organized for charitable purposes under 26 U.S.C. 501(c)(3) of the Internal Revenue Code and making a reasonable contribution to capitalize it, *provided* that the corporation engages exclusively in activities designed to promote the well-being of communities in which the owners of the service corporation operate.

(i) Activities conducted on behalf of a customer on an other than "as principal" basis.

(j) Activities reasonably incident to those listed in paragraphs (a) through (i) of this section if the service corporation engages in those activities.

[61 FR 66571, Dec. 18, 1996, as amended by 66 FR 13007, Mar. 2, 2001; 66 FR 65824, Dec. 21, 2001; 69 FR 68249, Nov. 24, 2004; 70 FR 76675, Dec. 28, 2005]

§ 559.5 How much may a savings association invest in service corporations or lower-tier entities?

The amount that a federal savings association ("you") may invest in a service corporation or any lower-tier entity depends upon several factors. These include your total assets, your capital, the purpose of the investment, and your ownership interest in the service corporation or entity.

(a) Under section 5(c)(4)(B) of the HOLA, you may invest up to 3% of your assets in the capital stock, obligations, and other securities of service corporations. Any investment you make under this paragraph that would cause your investment, in the aggregate, to exceed 2% of your assets must serve primarily community, inner city, or community development purposes. You must designate the investments serving those purposes, which include:

(1) Investments in governmentally insured, guaranteed, subsidized or otherwise sponsored programs for housing, small farms, or businesses that are local in character;

(2) Investments for the preservation or revitalization of either urban or rural communities;

(3) Investments designed to meet the community development needs of, and primarily benefit, low- and moderate-income communities; or

(4) Other community, inner city, or community development-related investments approved by OTS.

(b) In addition to the amounts you may invest under paragraph (a) of this section, and to the extent that you have authority under other provisions of section 5(c) of the HOLA and part 560 of this chapter, and available capacity within any applicable investment limits, you may make loans to any service corporation and any lower-tier entity, subject to the following conditions:

(1) You and your GAAP-consolidated subsidiaries may, in the aggregate, make loans of up to 15% of your total capital, as described in part 567 of this

Office of Thrift Supervision, Treasury § 559.12

chapter to each subordinate organization that does not qualify as a GAAP-consolidated subsidiary. All loans made under this paragraph (b)(1) may not, in the aggregate, exceed 50% of your total capital, as described in part 567 of this chapter.

(2) The Regional Director may limit the amount of loans to a GAAP-consolidated subsidiary, or may adjust the limits set forth in paragraph (b)(1) of this section where safety and soundness considerations warrant such action.

(c) For purposes of this section, the terms "loans" and "obligations" include all loans and other debt instruments (except accounts payable incurred in the ordinary course of business and paid within 60 days) and all guarantees or take-out commitments of such loans or debt instruments.

[61 FR 66571, Dec. 18, 1996, as amended at 72 FR 69438, Dec. 7, 2007]

Subpart B—Regulations Applicable to All Savings Associations

§ 559.10 How must separate corporate identities be maintained?

(a) Each savings association and subordinate organization thereof must be operated in a manner that demonstrates to the public that each maintains a separate corporate existence. Each must operate so that:

(1) Their respective business transactions, accounts, and records are not intermingled;

(2) Each observes the formalities of their separate corporate procedures;

(3) Each is adequately financed as a separate unit in light of normal obligations reasonably foreseeable in a business of its size and character;

(4) Each is held out to the public as a separate enterprise; and

(5) Unless the parent savings association has guaranteed a loan to the subordinate organization, all borrowings by the subordinate organization indicate that the parent is not liable.

(b) OTS regulations that apply both to savings associations and subordinate organizations shall not be construed as requiring a savings association and its subordinate organizations to operate as a single entity.

§ 559.11 What notices are required to establish or acquire a new subsidiary or engage in new activities through an existing subsidiary?

When required by section 18(m) of the Federal Deposit Insurance Act, a savings association ("you") must file a notice ("Notice") under part 516, subpart A of this chapter at least 30 days before establishing or acquiring a subsidiary or engaging in new activities in a subsidiary. The Notice must contain all of the information the Federal Deposit Insurance Corporation (FDIC) requires under 12 CFR 362.15. Providing OTS with a copy of the notice you file with the FDIC will satisfy this requirement. If OTS notifies you within 30 days that the Notice presents supervisory concerns, or raises significant issues of law or policy, you must apply for and receive OTS's prior written approval under the standard treatment processing procedures at part 516, subpart A and E of this chapter before establishing or acquiring the subsidiary or engaging in new activities in the subsidiary.

[61 FR 66571, Dec. 18, 1996, as amended at 64 FR 69185, Dec. 10, 1999; 66 FR 13007, Mar. 2, 2001]

§ 559.12 How may a subsidiary of a savings association issue securities?

(a) A subsidiary may issue, either directly or through a third party intermediary, any securities that its parent savings association ("you") may issue. The subsidiary must not state or imply that the securities it issues are covered by federal deposit insurance. A subsidiary may not issue any security the payment, maturity, or redemption of which may be accelerated upon the condition that you are insolvent or have been placed into receivership.

(b) You must file a notice with OTS in accordance with § 559.11 of this part at least 30 days before your first issuance of any securities through an existing subsidiary or in conjunction with establishing or acquiring a new subsidiary. If OTS notifies you within 30 days that the notice presents supervisory concerns or raises significant

§ 559.13

issues of law or policy, you must receive OTS's prior written approval before issuing securities through your subsidiary.

(c) For as long as any securities are outstanding, you must maintain all records generated through each securities issuance in the ordinary course of business, including a copy of any prospectus, offering circular, or similar document concerning such issuance, and make such records available for examination by OTS. Such records must include, but are not limited to:

(1) The amount of your assets or liabilities (including any guarantees you make with respect to the securities issuance) that have been transferred or made available to the subsidiary; the percentage that such amount represents of the current book value of your assets on an unconsolidated basis; and the current book value of all such assets of the subsidiary;

(2) The terms of any guarantee(s) issued by you or any third party;

(3) A description of the securities the subsidiary issued;

(4) The net proceeds from the issuance of securities (or the pro rata portion of the net proceeds from securities issued through a jointly owned subsidiary); the gross proceeds of the securities issuance; and the market value of assets collateralizing the securities issuance (any assets of the subsidiary, including any guarantees of its securities issuance you have made);

(5) The interest or dividend rates and yields, or the range thereof, and the frequency of payments on the subsidiary's securities;

(6) The minimum denomination of the subsidiary's securities; and

(7) Where the subsidiary marketed or intends to market the securities.

[61 FR 66571, Dec. 18, 1996, as amended at 69 FR 68249, Nov. 24, 2004]

§ 559.13 How may a savings association exercise its salvage power in connection with a service corporation or lower-tier entities?

(a) In accordance with this section, a savings association ("you") may exercise your salvage power to make a contribution or a loan (including a guarantee of a loan made by any other person) to your service corporation or lower-tier entity ("salvage investment") that exceeds the maximum amount otherwise permitted under law or regulation. You must notify OTS at least 30 days before making such a salvage investment. This notice must demonstrate that:

(1) The salvage investment protects your interest in the service corporation or lower-tier entity;

(2) The salvage investment is consistent with safety and soundness; and

(3) You considered alternatives to the salvage investment and determined that such alternatives would not adequately satisfy paragraphs (a)(1) and (a)(2) of this section.

(b) If OTS notifies you within 30 days that the Notice presents supervisory concerns, or raises significant issues of law or policy, you must apply for and receive OTS's prior written approval under the standard treatment processing procedures at part 516, subparts A and E of this chapter before making a salvage investment.

(c) If your service corporation or lower-tier entity is a GAAP-consolidated subsidiary, your salvage investment under this section will be considered an investment in a subsidiary for purposes of part 567 of this chapter.

[61 FR 66571, Dec. 18, 1996, as amended at 66 FR 13007, Mar. 2, 2001]

PART 560—LENDING AND INVESTMENT

Sec.
560.1 General.
560.2 Applicability of law.
560.3 Definitions.

Subpart A—Lending and Investment Powers for Federal Savings Associations

560.30 General lending and investment powers of Federal savings associations.
560.31 Election regarding categorization of loans or investments and related calculations.
560.32 Pass-through investments.
560.33 Late charges.
560.34 Prepayments.
560.35 Adjustments to home loans.
560.36 De minimis investments.
560.37 Real estate for office and related facilities.
560.40 Commercial paper and corporate debt securities.
560.41 Leasing.

Office of Thrift Supervision, Treasury § 560.2

560.42 State and local government obligations.
560.43 Foreign assistance investments.
560.50 Letters of credit and other independent undertakings—authority.
560.60 Suretyship and guaranty.

Subpart B—Lending and Investment Provisions Applicable to all Savings Associations

560.93 Lending limitations.
560.100 Real estate lending standards; purpose and scope.
560.101 Real estate lending standards.
560.110 Most favored lender usury preemption.
560.120 Letters of credit and other independent undertakings to pay against documents.
560.121 Investment in State housing corporations.
560.130 Prohibition on loan procurement fees.
560.160 Asset classification.
560.170 Records for lending transactions.
560.172 Re-evaluation of real estate owned.

Subpart C—Alternative Mortgage Transactions

560.210 Disclosures for variable rate transactions.
560.220 Alternative Mortgage Transaction Parity Act.

AUTHORITY: 12 U.S.C. 1462, 1462a, 1463, 1464, 1467a, 1701j–3, 1828, 3803, 3806; 42 U.S.C. 4106.

SOURCE: 61 FR 50971, Sept. 30, 1996, unless otherwise noted.

§ 560.1 General.

(a) *Authority and scope.* This part is being issued by OTS under its general rulemaking and supervisory authority under the Home Owners' Loan Act (HOLA), 12 U.S.C. 1462 *et seq.* Subpart A of this part sets forth the lending and investment powers of Federal savings associations. Subpart B of this part contains safety-and-soundness based lending and investment provisions applicable to all savings associations. Subpart C of this part addresses alternative mortgages and applies to all savings associations.

(b) *General lending standards.* Each savings association is expected to conduct its lending and investment activities prudently. Each association should use lending and investment standards that are consistent with safety and soundness, ensure adequate portfolio diversification and are appropriate for the size and condition of the institution, the nature and scope of its operations, and conditions in its lending market. Each association should adequately monitor the condition of its portfolio and the adequacy of any collateral securing its loans.

§ 560.2 Applicability of law.

(a) *Occupation of field.* Pursuant to sections 4(a) and 5(a) of the HOLA, 12 U.S.C. 1463(a), 1464(a), OTS is authorized to promulgate regulations that preempt state laws affecting the operations of federal savings associations when deemed appropriate to facilitate the safe and sound operation of federal savings associations, to enable federal savings associations to conduct their operations in accordance with the best practices of thrift institutions in the United States, or to further other purposes of the HOLA. To enhance safety and soundness and to enable federal savings associations to conduct their operations in accordance with best practices (by efficiently delivering low-cost credit to the public free from undue regulatory duplication and burden), OTS hereby occupies the entire field of lending regulation for federal savings associations. OTS intends to give federal savings associations maximum flexibility to exercise their lending powers in accordance with a uniform federal scheme of regulation. Accordingly, federal savings associations may extend credit as authorized under federal law, including this part, without regard to state laws purporting to regulate or otherwise affect their credit activities, except to the extent provided in paragraph (c) of this section or § 560.110 of this part. For purposes of this section, "state law" includes any state statute, regulation, ruling, order or judicial decision.

(b) *Illustrative examples.* Except as provided in § 560.110 of this part, the types of state laws preempted by paragraph (a) of this section include, without limitation, state laws purporting to impose requirements regarding:

(1) Licensing, registration, filings, or reports by creditors;

(2) The ability of a creditor to require or obtain private mortgage insurance, insurance for other collateral, or other credit enhancements;

§ 560.3

(3) Loan-to-value ratios;
(4) The terms of credit, including amortization of loans and the deferral and capitalization of interest and adjustments to the interest rate, balance, payments due, or term to maturity of the loan, including the circumstances under which a loan may be called due and payable upon the passage of time or a specified event external to the loan;
(5) Loan-related fees, including without limitation, initial charges, late charges, prepayment penalties, servicing fees, and overlimit fees;
(6) Escrow accounts, impound accounts, and similar accounts;
(7) Security property, including leaseholds;
(8) Access to and use of credit reports;
(9) Disclosure and advertising, including laws requiring specific statements, information, or other content to be included in credit application forms, credit solicitations, billing statements, credit contracts, or other credit-related documents and laws requiring creditors to supply copies of credit reports to borrowers or applicants;
(10) Processing, origination, servicing, sale or purchase of, or investment or participation in, mortgages;
(11) Disbursements and repayments;
(12) Usury and interest rate ceilings to the extent provided in 12 U.S.C. 1735f-7a and part 590 of this chapter and 12 U.S.C. 1463(g) and § 560.110 of this part; and
(13) Due-on-sale clauses to the extent provided in 12 U.S.C. 1701j-3 and part 591 of this chapter.

(c) *State laws that are not preempted.* State laws of the following types are not preempted to the extent that they only incidentally affect the lending operations of Federal savings associations or are otherwise consistent with the purposes of paragraph (a) of this section:

(1) Contract and commercial law;
(2) Real property law;
(3) Homestead laws specified in 12 U.S.C. 1462a(f);
(4) Tort law;
(5) Criminal law; and
(6) Any other law that OTS, upon review, finds:

(i) Furthers a vital state interest; and
(ii) Either has only an incidental effect on lending operations or is not otherwise contrary to the purposes expressed in paragraph (a) of this section.

§ 560.3 Definitions.

For purposes of this part and any determination under 12 U.S.C. 1467a(m):

Consumer loans include loans for personal, family, or household purposes and loans reasonably incident thereto, and may be made as either open-end or closed-end consumer credit (as defined at 12 CFR 226.2(a) (10) and (20)). Consumer loans do not include credit extended in connection with credit card loans, bona fide overdraft loans, and other loans that the savings association has designated as made under investment or lending authority other than section 5(c)(2)(D) of the HOLA.

Credit card is any card, plate, coupon book, or other single credit device that may be used from time to time to obtain credit.

Credit card account is a credit account established in conjunction with the issuance of, or the extension of credit through, a credit card. This term includes loans made to consolidate credit card debt, including credit card debt held by other lenders, and participation certificates, securities and similar instruments secured by credit card receivables.

Home loans include any loans made on the security of a home (including a dwelling unit in a multi-family residential property such as a condominium or a cooperative), combinations of homes and business property (*i.e.*, a home used in part for business), farm residences, and combinations of farm residences and commercial farm real estate.

Loan commitment includes a loan in process, a letter of credit, or any other commitment to extend credit.

Real estate loan, for purposes of this part, is a loan for which the savings association substantially relies upon a security interest in real estate given by the borrower as a condition of making the loan. A loan is made on the security of real estate if:

Office of Thrift Supervision, Treasury § 560.30

(1) The security property is real estate pursuant to the law of the state in which the property is located;

(2) The security interest of the Federal savings association may be enforced as a real estate mortgage or its equivalent pursuant to the law of the state in which the property is located;

(3) The security property is capable of separate appraisal; and

(4) With regard to a security property that is a leasehold or other interest for a period of years, the term of the interest extends, or is subject to extension or renewal at the option of the Federal savings association for a term of at least five years following the maturity of the loan.

Small business includes a small business concern or entity as defined by section 3(a) of the Small Business Act, 15 U.S.C. 632(a), and implemented by the regulations of the Small Business Administration at 13 CFR Part 121.

Small business loans and *loans to small businesses* include any loan to a small business as defined in this section; or a loan that does not exceed $2 million (including a group of loans to one borrower) and is for commercial, corporate, business, or agricultural purposes.

[61 FR 50971, Sept. 30, 1996, as amended at 61 FR 60184, Nov. 27, 1996; 62 FR 15825, Apr. 3, 1997; 64 FR 46565, Aug. 26, 1999; 66 FR 65825, Dec. 21, 2001]

Subpart A—Lending and Investment Powers for Federal Savings Associations

§ 560.30 General lending and investment powers of Federal savings associations.

Pursuant to section 5(c) of the Home Owners' Loan Act ("HOLA"), 12 U.S.C. 1464(c), a Federal savings association may make, invest in, purchase, sell, participate in, or otherwise deal in (including brokerage or warehousing) all loans and investments allowed under section 5(c) of the HOLA including, without limitation, the following loans, extensions of credit, and investments, subject to the limitations indicated and any such terms, conditions, or limitations as may be prescribed from time to time by OTS by policy directive, order, or regulation:

LENDING AND INVESTMENT POWERS CHART

Category	Statutory authorization [1]	Statutory investment limitations (Endnotes contain applicable regulatory limitations)
Bankers' bank stock	5(c)(4)(E)	Same terms as applicable to national banks.
Business development credit corporations	5(c)(4)(A)	The lesser of .5% of total outstanding loans or $250,000.
Commercial loans	5(c)(2)(A)	20% of total assets, provided that amounts in excess of 10% of total assets may be used only for small business loans.
Commercial paper and corporate debt securities	5(c)(2)(D)	Up to 35% of total assets. [2,3]
Community development loans and equity investments	5(c)(3)(A)	5% of total assets, provided equity investments do not exceed 2% of total assets. [4]
Construction loans without security	5(c)(3)(C)	In the aggregate, the greater of total capital or 5% of total assets.
Consumer loans	5(c)(2)(D)	Up to 35% of total assets. [2,5]
Credit card loans or loans made through credit card accounts.	5(c)(1)(T)	None. [6]
Deposits in insured depository institutions	5(c)(1)(G)	None. [6]
Education loans	5(c)(1)(U)	None. [6]
Federal government and government-sponsored enterprise securities and instruments.	5(c)(1)(C), 5(c)(1)(D), 5(c)(1)(E), 5(c)(1)(F).	None. [6]
Finance leasing	5(c)(1)(B), 5(c)(2)(A), 5(c)(2)(B), 5(c)(2)(D).	Based on purpose and property financed. [7]
Foreign assistance investments	5(c)(4)(C)	1% of total assets. [8]
General leasing	5(c)(2)(C)	10% of assets. [7]
Home improvement loans	5(c)(1)(J)	None. [6]
Home (residential) loans [9]	5(c)(1)(B)	None. [6,10]
HUD-insured or guaranteed investments	5(c)(1)(O)	None. [6]
Insured loans	5(c)(1)(I), 5(c)(1)(K)	None. [6]
Liquidity investments	5(c)(1)(M)	None. [6]
Loans secured by deposit accounts	5(c)(1)(A)	None. [6,11]
Loans to financial institutions, brokers, and dealers.	5(c)(1)(L)	None. [6,12]
Manufactured home loans	5(c)(1)(J)	None. [6,13]

LENDING AND INVESTMENT POWERS CHART—Continued

Category	Statutory authorization [1]	Statutory investment limitations (Endnotes contain applicable regulatory limitations)
Mortgage-backed securities	5(c)(1)(R)	None. [6]
National Housing Partnership Corporation and related partnerships and joint ventures.	5(c)(1)(N)	None. [6]
New markets venture capital companies	5(c)(4)(F)	5% of total capital.
Nonconforming loans	5(c)(3)(B)	5% of total assets.
Nonresidential real property loans	5(c)(2)(B)	400% of total capital. [14]
Open-end management investment companies [15]	5(c)(1)(Q)	None. [6]
Rural business investment companies	7 U.S.C. 2009cc–9	Five percent of total capital.
Service corporations	5(c)(4)(B)	3% of total assets, as long as any amounts in excess of 2% of total assets further community, inner city, or community development purposes. [16]
Small business investment companies	15 U.S.C. 682(b)(2)	5% of total capital.
Small-business-related securities	5(c)(1)(S)	None. [6]
State and local government obligations	5(c)(1)(H)	None for general obligations. Per issuer limitation of 10% of capital for other obligations. [6,17]
State housing corporations	5(c)(1)(P)	None. [6,18]
Transaction account loans, including overdrafts	5(c)(1)(A)	None. [6,19]

ENDNOTES

1. All references are to section 5 of the Home Owners' Loan Act (12 U.S.C. 1464) unless otherwise indicated.

2. For purposes of determining a Federal savings association's percentage of assets limitation, investment in commercial paper and corporate debt securities must be aggregated with the Federal savings association's investment in consumer loans.

3. A Federal savings association may invest in commercial paper and corporate debt securities, which includes corporate debt securities convertible into stock, subject to the provisions of § 560.40 of this part. Amounts in excess of 30% of assets, in the aggregate, may be invested only in obligations purchased by the association directly from the original obligor and for which no finder's or referral fees have been paid.

4. The 2% of assets limitation is a sublimit for investments within the overall 5% of assets limitation on community development loans and investments. The qualitative standards for such loans and investments are set forth in HOLA section 5(c)(3)(A) (formerly 5(c)(3)(B), as explained in an opinion of the OTS Chief Counsel dated May 10, 1995 (available at www.ots.treas.gov)).

5. Amounts in excess of 30% of assets, in the aggregate, may be invested only in loans made by the association directly to the original obligor and for which no finder's or referral fees have been paid. A Federal savings association may include loans to dealers in consumer goods to finance inventory and floor planning in the total investment made under this section.

6. While there is no statutory limit on certain categories of loans and investments, including credit card loans, home improvement loans, education loans, and deposit account loans, OTS may establish an individual limit on such loans or investments if the association's concentration in such loans or investments presents a safety and soundness concern.

7. A Federal savings association may engage in leasing activities subject to the provisions of § 560.41 of this part.

8. This 1% of assets limitation applies to the aggregate outstanding investments made under the Foreign Assistance Act and in the capital of the Inter-American Savings and Loan Bank. Such investments may be made subject to the provisions of § 560.43 of this part.

9. A home (or residential) loan includes loans secured by one-to-four family dwellings, multi-family residential property, and loans secured by a unit or units of a condominium or housing cooperative.

10. A Federal savings association may make home loans subject to the provisions of §§ 560.33, 560.34, and 560.35 of this part.

11. Loans secured by savings accounts and other time deposits may be made without limitation, provided the Federal savings association obtains a lien on, or a pledge of, such accounts. Such loans may not exceed the withdrawable amount of the account.

12. A Federal savings association may only invest in these loans if they are secured by obligations of, or by obligations fully guaranteed as to principal and interest by, the United States or any of its agencies or instrumentalities, the borrower is a financial institution insured by the Federal Deposit Insurance Corporation or is a broker or dealer registered with the Securities and Exchange Commission, and the market value of the securities for each loan at least equals the amount of the loan at the time it is made.

Office of Thrift Supervision, Treasury § 560.32

13. If the wheels and axles of the manufactured home have been removed and it is permanently affixed to a foundation, a loan secured by a combination of a manufactured home and developed residential lot on which it sits may be treated as a home loan.

14. Without regard to any limitations of this part, a Federal savings association may make or invest in the fully insured or guaranteed portion of nonresidential real estate loans insured or guaranteed by the Economic Development Administration, the Farmers Home Administration, or the Small Business Administration. Unguaranteed portions of guaranteed loans must be aggregated with uninsured loans when determining an association's compliance with the 400% of capital limitation for other real estate loans.

15. This authority is limited to investments in open-end management investment companies that are registered with the Securities and Exchange Commission under the Investment Company Act of 1940. The portfolio of the investment company must be restricted by the company's investment policy (changeable only if authorized by shareholder vote) solely to investments that a Federal savings association may, without limitation as to percentage of assets, invest in, sell, redeem, hold, or otherwise deal in. Separate and apart from this authority, a Federal savings association may make pass-through investments to the extent authorized by § 560.32 of this part.

16. A Federal savings association may invest in service corporations subject to the provisions of part 559 of this chapter.

17. This category includes obligations issued by any state, territory, or possession of the United States or political subdivision thereof (including any agency, corporation, or instrumentality of a state or political subdivision), subject to § 560.42 of this part.

18. A Federal savings association may invest in state housing corporations subject to the provisions of § 560.121 of this part.

19. Payments on accounts in excess of the account balance (overdrafts) on commercial deposit or transaction accounts shall be considered commercial loans for purposes of determining the association's percentage of assets limitation.

[66 FR 65825, Dec. 21, 2001, as amended at 68 FR 75109, Dec. 30, 2003; 70 FR 76675, Dec. 28, 2005]

§ 560.31 Election regarding categorization of loans or investments and related calculations.

(a) If a loan or other investment is authorized under more than one section of the HOLA, as amended, or this part, a Federal savings association may designate under which section the loan or investment has been made. Such a loan or investment may be apportioned among appropriate categories, and may be moved, in whole or part, from one category to another. A loan commitment shall be counted as an investment and included in total assets of a Federal savings association for purposes of calculating compliance with HOLA section 5(c)'s investment limitations only to the extent that funds have been advanced and not repaid pursuant to the commitment.

(b) Loans or portions of loans sold to a third party shall be included in the calculation of a percentage-of-assets or percentage-of-capital investment limitation only to the extent they are sold with recourse.

(c) A Federal savings association may make a loan secured by an assignment of loans to the extent that it could, under applicable law and regulations, make or purchase the underlying assigned loans.

§ 560.32 Pass-through investments.

(a) A federal savings association ("you") may make pass-through investments. A pass-through investment occurs when you invest in an entity ("company") that engages only in activities that you may conduct directly and the investment meets the requirements of this section. If an investment is authorized under both this section and some other provision of law, you may designate under which authority or authorities the investment is made. When making a pass-through investment, you must comply with all the statutes and regulations that would apply if you were engaging in the activity directly. For example, your proportionate share of the company's assets will be aggregated with the assets you hold directly in calculating investment limits (*e.g.*, no more than 400% of total capital may be invested in nonresidential real property loans).

(b) You may make a pass-through investment without prior notice to OTS if all of the following conditions are met:

(1) You do not invest more than 15% of your total capital in one company;

(2) The book value of your aggregate pass-through investments does not exceed 50% of your total capital after making the investment;

§ 560.33

(3) Your investment would not give you direct or indirect control of the company;

(4) Your liability is limited to the amount of your investment; and

(5) The company falls into one of the following categories:

(i) A limited partnership;
(ii) An open-end mutual fund;
(iii) A closed-end investment trust;
(iv) A limited liability company; or
(v) An entity in which you are investing primarily to use the company's services (*e.g.*, data processing).

(c) If you want to make other pass-through investments, you must provide OTS with 30 days' advance notice. If within that 30-day period OTS notifies you that an investment presents supervisory, legal, or safety and soundness concerns, you must apply for and receive OTS prior written approval under the standard treatment processing procedures at part 516, subparts A and E of this chapter before making the investment. Notices under this section are deemed to be applications for purposes of statutory and regulatory references to "applications." Any conditions that OTS imposes on any pass-through investment shall be enforceable as a condition imposed in writing by the OTS in connection with the granting of a request by a savings association within the meaning of 12 U.S.C. 1818(b) or 1818(i).

[61 FR 66578, Dec. 18, 1996, as amended at 66 FR 13007, Mar. 2, 2001]

§ 560.33 Late charges.

A Federal savings association may include in a home loan contract a provision authorizing the imposition of a late charge with respect to the payment of any delinquent periodic payment. With respect to any loan made after July 31, 1976, on the security of a home occupied or to be occupied by the borrower, no late charge, regardless of form, shall be assessed or collected by a Federal savings association, unless any billing, coupon, or notice the Federal savings association may provide regarding installment payments due on the loan discloses the date after which the charge may be assessed. A Federal savings association may not impose a late charge more than one time for late payment of the same installment, and any installment payment made by the borrower shall be applied to the longest outstanding installment due. A Federal savings association shall not assess a late charge as to any payment received by it within fifteen days after the due date of such payment. No form of such late charge permitted by this paragraph shall be considered as interest to the Federal savings association and the Federal savings association shall not deduct late charges from the regular periodic installment payments on the loan, but must collect them as such from the borrower.

§ 560.34 Prepayments.

Any prepayment on a real estate loan must be applied directly to reduce the principal balance on the loan unless the loan contract or the borrower specifies otherwise. Subject to the terms of the loan contract, a Federal savings association may impose a fee for any prepayment of a loan.

§ 560.35 Adjustments to home loans.

(a) For any home loan secured by borrower-occupied property, or property to be occupied by the borrower, adjustments to the interest rate, payment, balance, or term to maturity must comply with the limitations of this section and the disclosure and notice requirements of § 560.210 of this part.

(b) Adjustments to the interest rate shall correspond directly to the movement of an index satisfying the requirements of paragraph (d) of this section. A Federal savings association also may increase the interest rate pursuant to a formula or schedule that specifies the amount of the increase, the time at which it may be made, and which is set forth in the loan contract. A Federal savings association may decrease the interest rate at any time.

(c) Adjustments to the payment and the loan balance that do not reflect an interest-rate adjustment may be made if:

(1) The adjustments reflect a change in an index that may be used pursuant to paragraph (d) of this section;

(2) In the case of a payment adjustment, the adjustment reflects a change in the loan balance or is made pursuant

Office of Thrift Supervision, Treasury § 560.40

to a formula, or to a schedule specifying the percentage or dollar change in the payment as set forth in the loan contract; or

(3) In the case of an open-end line-of-credit loan, the adjustment reflects an advance taken by the borrower under the line-of-credit and is permitted by the loan contract.

(d)(1) Any index used must be readily available and independently verifiable. If set forth in the loan contract, an association may use any combination of indices, a moving average of index values, or more than one index during the term of a loan.

(2) Except as provided in paragraph (d)(3) of this section, any index used must be a national or regional index.

(3) A Federal savings association may use an index not satisfying the requirements of paragraph (d)(2) of this section 30 days after filing a notice unless, within that 30-day period, OTS has notified the association that the notice presents supervisory concerns or raises significant issues of law or policy. If OTS notifies the association of such concerns or issues, the Federal savings association may not use such an index unless it applies for and receives OTS's prior written approval under the standard treatment processing procedures at part 516, subparts A and E of this chapter.

[61 FR 50971, Sept. 30, 1996, as amended at 66 FR 13007, Mar. 2, 2001]

§ 560.36 De minimis investments.

A Federal savings association may invest in the aggregate up to the greater of 1% of its total capital or $250,000 in community development investments of the type permitted for a national bank under 12 CFR part 24.

[66 FR 65826, Dec. 21, 2001]

§ 560.37 Real estate for office and related facilities.

A federal savings association may invest in real estate (improved or unimproved) to be used for office and related facilities of the association, or for such office and related facilities and for rental or sale, if such investment is made and maintained under a prudent program of property acquisition to meet the federal savings association's present needs or its reasonable future needs for office and related facilities. A federal savings association may not make an investment that would cause the outstanding book value of all such investments (including investments under § 559.4(e)(2) of this chapter) to exceed its total capital.

[61 FR 66579, Dec. 18, 1996]

§ 560.40 Commercial paper and corporate debt securities.

Pursuant to HOLA section 5(c)(2)(D), a Federal savings association may invest in, sell, or hold commercial paper and corporate debt securities subject to the provisions of this section.

(a) *Limitations.* (1) Commercial paper must be:

(i) As of the date of purchase, rated in either one of the two highest categories by at least two nationally recognized investment ratings services as shown by the most recently published rating made of such investments; or

(ii) If unrated, guaranteed by a company having outstanding paper that is rated as provided in paragraph (a)(1)(i) of this section.

(2) Corporate debt securities must be:

(i) Securities that may be sold with reasonable promptness at a price that corresponds reasonably to their fair value; and

(ii) Rated in one of the four highest categories as to the portion of the security in which the association is investing by a nationally recognized investment ratings service at its most recently published rating before the date of purchase of the security.

(3) A Federal savings association's total investment in the commercial paper and corporate debt securities of any one issuer, or issued by any one person or entity affiliated with such issuer, together with other loans, shall not exceed the general lending limitations contained in § 560.93(c) of this part.

(4) Investments in corporate debt securities convertible into stock are subject to the following additional limitations:

(i) The purchase of securities convertible into stock at the option of the issuer is prohibited;

(ii) At the time of purchase, the cost of such securities must be written

175

§ 560.41

down to an amount that represents the investment value of the securities considered independently of the conversion feature; and

(iii) Federal savings associations are prohibited from exercising the conversion feature.

(5) A Federal savings association shall maintain information in its files adequate to demonstrate that it has exercised prudent judgment in making investments under this section.

(b) Notwithstanding the limitations contained in this section, the Office may permit investment in corporate debt securities of another savings association in connection with the purchase or sale of a branch office or in connection with a supervisory merger or acquisition.

(c) *Underwriting.* Before committing to acquire any investment security, a Federal savings association must determine whether the investment is safe and sound and suitable for the association. The Federal savings association must consider, as appropriate, the interest rate, credit, liquidity, price, transaction, and other risks associated with the investment activity. The Federal savings association must also determine that the issuer has adequate resources and the willingness to provide for all required payments on its obligations in a timely manner.

[61 FR 50971, Sept. 30, 1996, as amended at 66 FR 65826, Dec. 21, 2001]

§ 560.41 Leasing.

(a) *Permissible activities.* Subject to the limitations of this section, a Federal savings association may engage in leasing activities. These activities include becoming the legal or beneficial owner of tangible personal property or real property for the purpose of leasing such property, obtaining an assignment of a lessor's interest in a lease of such property, and incurring obligations incidental to its position as the legal or beneficial owner and lessor of the leased property.

(b) *Definitions.* For the purposes of this section:

(1) The term *net lease* means a lease under which the Federal savings association will not, directly or indirectly, provide or be obligated to provide for:

(i) The servicing, repair or maintenance of the leased property during the lease term;

(ii) The purchasing of parts and accessories for the leased property, except that improvements and additions to the leased property may be leased to the lessee upon its request in accordance with the full-payout requirements of paragraph (c)(2)(i) of this section;

(iii) The loan of replacement or substitute property while the leased property is being serviced;

(iv) The purchasing of insurance for the lessee, except where the lessee has failed to discharge a contractual obligation to purchase or maintain insurance; or

(v) The renewal of any license, registration, or filing for the property unless such action by the Federal savings association is necessary to protect its interest as an owner or financier of the property.

(2) The term *full-payout lease* means a lease transaction in which any unguaranteed portion of the estimated residual value relied on by the association to yield the return of its full investment in the leased property, plus the estimated cost of financing the property over the term of the lease, does not exceed 25% of the original cost of the property to the lessor. In general, a lease will qualify as a full-payout lease if the scheduled payments provide at least 75% of the principal and interest payments that a lessor would receive if the finance lease were structured as a market-rate loan.

(3) The term *realization of investment* means that a Federal savings association that enters into a lease financing transaction must reasonably expect to realize the return of its full investment in the leased property, plus the estimated cost of financing the property over the term of the lease from:

(i) Rentals;

(ii) Estimated tax benefits, if any; and

(iii) The estimated residual value of the property at the expiration of the term of the lease.

(c) *Finance leasing*—(1) *Investment limits.* A Federal savings association may exercise its authority under HOLA sections 5(c)(1)(B) (residential real estate loans), 5(c)(2)(A) (commercial, business, corporate or agricultural loans), 5(c)(2)(B) (nonresidential real estate loans), and 5(c)(2)(D) (consumer loans) by conducting leasing activities that are the functional equivalent of loans made under those HOLA sections. These activities are commonly referred to as financing leases. Such financing leases are subject to the same investment limits that apply to loans made under those sections. For example, a financing lease of tangible personal property made to a natural person for personal, family or household purposes is subject to all limitations applicable to the amount of a Federal savings association's investment in consumer loans. A financing lease made for commercial, corporate, business, or agricultural purposes is subject to all limitations applicable to the amount of a Federal savings association's investment in commercial loans. A financing lease of residential or nonresidential real property is subject to all limitations applicable to the amount of a Federal savings association's investment in these types of real estate loans.

(2) *Functional equivalent of lending.* To qualify as the functional equivalent of a loan:

(i) The lease must be a net, full-payout lease representing a non-cancelable obligation of the lessee, notwithstanding the possible early termination of the lease;

(ii) The portion of the estimated residual value of the property relied upon by the lessor to satisfy the requirements of a full-payout lease must be reasonable in light of the nature of the leased property and all relevant circumstances so that realization of the lessor's full investment plus the cost of financing the property depends primarily on the creditworthiness of the lessee, and not on the residual market value of the leased property; and

(iii) At the termination of a financing lease, either by expiration or default, property acquired must be liquidated or released on a net basis as soon as practicable. Any property held in anticipation of re-leasing must be reevaluated and recorded at the lower of fair market value or book value.

(d) *General leasing.* Pursuant to section 5(c)(2)(C) of the HOLA, a Federal savings association may invest in tangible personal property, including vehicles, manufactured homes, machinery, equipment, or furniture, for the purpose of leasing that property. In contrast to financing leases, lease investments made under this authority need not be the functional equivalent of loans.

(e) *Leasing salvage powers.* If, in good faith, a Federal savings association believes that there has been an unanticipated change in conditions that threatens its financial position by significantly increasing its exposure to loss, it may:

(1) As the owner and lessor, take reasonable and appropriate action to salvage or protect the value of the property or its interest arising under the lease;

(2) As the assignee of a lessor's interest in a lease, become the owner and lessor of the leased property pursuant to its contractual right, or take any reasonable and appropriate action to salvage or protect the value of the property or its interest arising under the lease; or

(3) Include any provisions in a lease, or make any additional agreements, to protect its financial position or investment in the circumstances set forth in paragraphs (e)(1) and (e)(2) of this section.

§ 560.42 State and local government obligations.

(a) *What limitations apply?* Pursuant to HOLA section 5(c)(1)(H), a Federal savings association ("you") may invest in obligations issued by any state, territory, possession, or political subdivision thereof ("governmental entity"), subject to appropriate underwriting and the following conditions:

	Aggregate limitation	Per-issuer limitation
(1) General obligations	None	None.
(2) Other obligations of a governmental entity (*e.g.*, revenue bonds) that hold one of the four highest investment grade ratings by a nationally recognized rating agency or that are nonrated but of investment quality.	None	10% of total capital.

177

§ 560.43

	Aggregate limitation	Per-issuer limitation
(3) Obligations of a governmental entity that do not qualify under any other paragraph but are approved by your Regional Director.	As approved by your Regional Director	10% of total capital.

(b) *What is a political subdivision?* *Political subdivision* means a county, city, town, or other municipal corporation, a public authority, or a publicly-owned entity that is an instrumentality of a state or a municipal corporation.

(c) *What is a general obligation of a state or political subdivision?* A *general obligation* is an obligation that is guaranteed by the full faith and credit of a state or political subdivision that has the power to tax. Indirect payments, such as through a special fund, may qualify as general obligations if a state or political subdivision with taxing authority has unconditionally agreed to provide funds to cover payments.

(d) *What is appropriate underwriting for this type of investment?* In the case of a security rated in one of the four highest investment grades by a nationally recognized rating agency, your assessment of the obligor's credit quality may be based, in part, on reliable rating agency estimates of the obligor's performance. For all other securities, you must perform your own detailed analysis of credit quality. In doing so, you must consider, as appropriate, the interest rate, credit, liquidity, price, transaction, and other risks associated with the investment activity and determine that such investment is appropriate for your institution. You must also determine that the obligor has adequate resources and willingness to provide for all required payments on its obligations in a timely manner.

[66 FR 65826, Dec. 21, 2001]

§ 560.43 Foreign assistance investments.

Pursuant to HOLA section 5(c)(4)(C), a Federal savings association may make foreign assistance investments in an aggregate amount not to exceed one percent of its assets, subject to the following conditions:

(a) For any investment made under the Foreign Assistance Act, the loan agreement shall specify what constitutes an event of default, and provide that upon default in payment of principal or interest under such agreement, the entire amount of outstanding indebtedness thereunder shall become immediately due and payable, at the lender's option. Additionally, the contract of guarantee shall cover 100% of any loss of investment thereunder, except for any portion of the loan arising out of fraud or misrepresentation for which the party seeking payment is responsible, and provide that the guarantor shall pay for any such loss in U.S. dollars within a specified reasonable time after the date of application for payment.

(b) To make any investments in the share capital and capital reserve of the Inter-American Savings and Loan Bank, a Federal savings association must be adequately capitalized and have adequate allowances for loan and lease losses. The Federal savings association's aggregate investment in such capital or capital reserve, including the amount of any obligations undertaken to provide said Bank with reserve capital in the future (call-able capital), must not, as a result of such investment, exceed the lesser of one-quarter of 1% of its assets or $100,000.

§ 560.50 Letters of credit and other independent undertakings—authority.

A Federal savings association may issue letters of credit and may issue such other independent undertakings as are approved by OTS, subject to the restrictions in § 560.120.

[64 FR 46565, Aug. 26, 1999]

§ 560.60 Suretyship and guaranty.

Pursuant to section 5(b)(2) of the HOLA, a Federal savings association may enter into a repayable suretyship or guaranty agreement, subject to the conditions in this section.

(a) *What is a suretyship or guaranty agreement?* Under a suretyship, a Federal savings association is bound with its principal to pay or perform an obligation to a third person. Under a guaranty agreement, a Federal savings association agrees to satisfy the obligation of the principal only if the principal fails to pay or perform.

(b) *What requirements apply to suretyship and guaranty agreements under this section?* A Federal savings association may enter into a suretyship or guaranty agreement under this section, subject to each of the following requirements:

(1) The Federal savings association must limit its obligations under the agreement to a fixed dollar amount and a specified duration.

(2) The Federal savings association's performance under the agreement must create an authorized loan or other investment.

(3) The Federal savings association must treat its obligation under the agreement as a loan to the principal for purposes of §§ 560.93 and 563.43 of this chapter.

(4) The Federal savings association must take and maintain a perfected security interest in collateral sufficient to cover its total obligation under the agreement.

(c) *What collateral is sufficient?* (1) The Federal savings association must take and maintain a perfected security interest in real estate or marketable securities equal to at least 110 percent of its obligation under the agreement, except as provided in paragraph (c)(2) of this section.

(i) If the collateral is real estate, the Federal savings association must establish the value by a signed appraisal or evaluation in accordance with part 564 of this chapter. In determining the value of the collateral, the Federal savings association must factor in the value of any existing senior mortgages, liens or other encumbrances on the property, except those held by the principal to the suretyship or guaranty agreement.

(ii) If the collateral is marketable securities, the Federal savings association must be authorized to invest in that security taken as collateral. The Federal savings association must ensure that the value of the security is 110 percent of the obligation at all times during the term of agreement.

(2) The Federal savings association may take and maintain a perfected security interest in collateral which is at all times equal to at least 100 percent of its obligation, if the collateral is:

(i) Cash;

(ii) Obligations of the United States or its agencies;

(iii) Obligations fully guaranteed by the United States or its agencies as to principal and interest; or

(iv) Notes, drafts, or bills of exchange or bankers' acceptances that are eligible for rediscount or purchase by a Federal Reserve Bank.

[64 FR 46565, Aug. 26, 1999]

Subpart B—Lending and Investment Provisions Applicable to all Savings Associations

§ 560.93 Lending limitations.

(a) *Scope.* This section applies to all loans and extensions of credit to third parties made by a savings association and its subsidiaries. This section does not apply to loans made by a savings association or a GAAP-consolidated subsidiary to subordinate organizations or affiliates of the savings association. The terms *subsidiary, GAAP-consolidated subsidiary,* and *subordinate organization* have the same meanings as specified in § 559.2 of this chapter. The term *affiliate* has the same meaning as specified in § 563.41 of this chapter.

(b) *Definitions.* In applying these lending limitations, savings associations shall apply the definitions and interpretations promulgated by the Office of the Comptroller of the Currency consistent with 12 U.S.C. 84. See 12 CFR part 32. In applying these definitions, pursuant to 12 U.S.C. 1464, savings associations shall use the terms *savings association, savings associations,* and *savings association's* in place of the terms *national bank* and *bank, banks, and bank's,* respectively. For purposes of this section:

(1) The term *one borrower* has the same meaning as the term *person* set forth at 12 CFR part 32. It also includes, in addition to the definition cited therein, a *financial institution* as defined at § 561.19 of this chapter.

(2) The term *company* means a corporation, partnership, business trust,

§ 560.93

association, or similar organization and, unless specifically excluded, the term *company* includes a *savings association* and a *bank*.

(3) *Contractual commitment to advance funds* has the meaning set forth in 12 CFR part 32.

(4) *Loans and extensions of credit* has the meaning set forth in 12 CFR part 32, and includes investments in commercial paper and corporate debt securities. The Office expressly reserves its authority to deem other arrangements that are, in substance, *loans and extensions of credit* to be encompassed by this term.

(5) The term *loans* as used in the phrase *Loans to one borrower to finance the sale of real property acquired in satisfaction of debts previously contracted for in good faith* does not include an association's taking of a purchase money mortgage note from the purchaser *provided that:*

(i) No new funds are advanced by the association to the borrower; and

(ii) The association is not placed in a more detrimental position as a result of the sale.

(6) [Reserved]

(7) *Readily marketable collateral* has the meaning set forth in 12 CFR part 32.

(8) *Residential housing units* has the same meaning as the term *residential real estate* set forth in § 541.23 of this chapter. The term *to develop* includes the various phases necessary to produce housing units as an end product, to include: acquisition, development and construction; development and construction; construction; rehabilitation; or conversion. The term *domestic* includes units within the fifty states, the District of Columbia, Puerto Rico, the Virgin Islands, Guam, and the Pacific Islands.

(9) *Single family dwelling unit* has the meaning set forth in § 541.25 of this chapter.

(10) A *standby letter of credit* has the meaning set forth in 12 CFR part 32.

(11) *Unimpaired capital and unimpaired surplus* means—

(i) A savings association's core capital and supplementary capital included in its total capital under part 567 of this chapter; plus

(ii) The balance of a savings association's allowance for loan and lease losses not included in supplementary capital under part 567 of this chapter; plus

(iii) The amount of a savings association's loans to, investments in, and advances to subsidiaries not included in calculating core capital under part 567 of this chapter.

(c) *General limitation.* Section 5200 of the Revised Statutes (12 U.S.C. 84) shall apply to savings associations in the same manner and to the same extent as it applies to national banks. This statutory provision and lending limit regulations and interpretations promulgated by the Office of the Comptroller of the Currency pursuant to a rulemaking conducted in accordance with the provisions of the Administrative Procedure Act, 5 U.S.C. 553 et seq. (including the regulations appearing at 12 CFR part 32) shall apply to savings associations in the same manner and to the same extent as these provisions apply to national banks:

(1) The total loans and extensions of credit by a savings association to one borrower outstanding at one time and not fully secured, as determined in the same manner as determined under 12 U.S.C. 84(a)(2), by collateral having a market value at least equal to the amount of the loan or extension of credit shall not exceed 15 percent of the unimpaired capital and unimpaired surplus of the association.

(2) The total loans and extensions of credit by a savings association to one borrower outstanding at one time and fully secured by readily marketable collateral having a market value, as determined by reliable and continuously available price quotations, at least equal to the amount of the funds outstanding shall not exceed 10 per centum of the unimpaired capital and unimpaired surplus of the association. This limitation shall be separate from and in addition to the limitation contained in paragraph (c)(1) of this section.

(d) *Exceptions to the general limitation*—(1) *$500,000 exception.* If a savings association's aggregate lending limitation calculated under paragraphs (c)(1) and (c)(2) of this section is less than

Office of Thrift Supervision, Treasury § 560.93

$500,000, notwithstanding this aggregate limitation in paragraphs (c)(1) and (c)(2) of this section, such savings association may have total loans and extensions of credit, for any purpose, to one borrower outstanding at one time not to exceed $500,000.

(2) *Statutory exceptions.* The exceptions to the lending limits set forth in 12 U.S.C. 84 and 12 CFR part 32 are applicable to savings associations in the same manner and to the extent as they apply to national banks.

(3) *Loans to develop domestic residential housing units.* Subject to paragraph (d)(4) of this section, a savings association may make loans to one borrower to develop domestic residential housing units, not to exceed the lesser of $30,000,000 or 30 percent of the savings association's unimpaired capital and unimpaired surplus, including all amounts loaned under the authority of the General Limitation set forth under paragraphs (c)(1) and (c)(2) of this section, *provided that:*

(i) The final purchase price of each single family dwelling unit the development of which is financed under this paragraph (d)(3) does not exceed $500,000;

(ii) The savings association is, and continues to be, in compliance with its capital requirements under part 567 of this chapter.

(iii) OTS permits, subject to conditions it may impose, the savings association to use the higher limit set forth under this paragraph (d)(3). A savings association that meets the requirements of paragraphs (d)(3)(i), (ii), (iv) and (v) of this section and that meets the requirements for "expedited treatment" under § 516.5 of this chapter may use the higher limit set forth under this paragraph (d)(3) if the savings association has filed a notice with OTS that it intends to use the higher limit at least 30 days prior to the proposed use. A savings association that meets the requirements of paragraphs (d)(3)(i), (ii), (iv), and (v) of this section and that meets the requirements for "standard treatment" under § 516.5 of this chapter may use the higher limit set forth under this paragraph (d)(3) if the savings association has filed an application with OTS and OTS has approved the use the higher limit;

(iv) Loans made under this paragraph (d)(3) to all borrowers do not, in aggregate, exceed 150 percent of the savings association's unimpaired capital and unimpaired surplus; and

(v) Such loans comply with the applicable loan-to-value requirements that apply to Federal savings associations.

(4) The authority of a savings association to make a loan or extension of credit under the exception in paragraph (d)(3) of this section ceases immediately upon the association's failure to comply with any one of the requirements set forth in paragraph (d)(3) of this section or any condition(s) set forth in a Director's order under paragraph (d)(3)(iii) of this section.

(5) Notwithstanding the limit set forth in paragraphs (c)(1) and (c)(2) of this section, a savings association may invest up to 10 percent of unimpaired capital and unimpaired surplus in the obligations of one issuer evidenced by:

(i) Commercial paper rated, as of the date of purchase, as shown by the most recently published rating by at least two nationally recognized investment rating services in the highest category; or

(ii) Corporate debt securities that may be sold with reasonable promptness at a price that corresponds reasonably to their fair value, and that are rated in one of the two highest categories by a nationally recognized investment rating service in its most recently published ratings before the date of purchase of the security.

(e) *Loans to finance the sale of REO.* A savings association's loans to one borrower to finance the sale of real property acquired in satisfaction of debts previously contracted for in good faith shall not, when aggregated with all other loans to such borrower, exceed the General Limitation in paragraph (c)(1) of this section.

(f) *Calculating compliance and recordkeeping.* (1) The amount of an association's unimpaired capital and unimpaired surplus pursuant to paragraph (b)(11) of this section shall be calculated as of the association's most recent periodic report required to be filed with OTS prior to the date of granting or purchasing the loan or otherwise creating the obligation to repay funds, unless the association knows, or

181

§ 560.93

has reason to know, based on transactions or events actually completed, that such level has changed significantly, upward or downward, subsequent to filing of such report.

(2) If a savings association or subsidiary thereof makes a loan or extension of credit to any one borrower, as defined in paragraph (b)(1) of this section, in an amount that, when added to the total balances of all outstanding loans owed to such association and its subsidiary by such borrower, exceeds the greater of $500,000 or 5 percent of unimpaired capital and unimpaired surplus, the records of such association or its subsidiary with respect to such loan shall include documentation showing that such loan was made within the limitations of paragraphs (c) and (d) of this section; for the purpose of such documentation such association or subsidiary may require, and may accept in good faith, a certification by the borrower identifying the persons, entities, and interests described in the definition of one borrower in paragraph (b)(1) of this section.

(g) [Reserved]

(h) *More stringent restrictions.* The Director may impose more stringent restrictions on a savings association's loans to one borrower if the Director determines that such restrictions are necessary to protect the safety and soundness of the savings association.

APPENDIX TO § 560.93—INTERPRETATIONS

Section 560.93–100 Interrelation of General Limitation With Exception for Loans To Develop Domestic Residential Housing Units

1. The § 560.93(d)(3) exception for loans to one person to develop domestic residential housing units is characterized in the regulation as an "alternative" limit. This exceptional $30,000,000 or 30 percent limitation does not operate *in addition to* the 15 percent General Limitation or the 10 percent additional amount an association may loan to one borrower secured by readily marketable collateral, but serves as the uppermost limitation on a savings association's lending to any one person once an association employs this exception. An example will illustrate the Office's interpretation of the application of this rule:

Example: Savings Associations A's lending limitation as calculated under the 15 percent General Limitation is $800,000. If Association A lends Y $800,000 for commercial purposes, Association A cannot lend Y *an additional*

12 CFR Ch. V (1–1–12 Edition)

$1,600,000, or 30 percent of capital and surplus, to develop residential housing units under the paragraph (d)(3) exception. The (d)(3) exception operates as the uppermost limitation on all lending to one borrower (for associations that may employ this exception) *and includes any amounts loaned to the same borrower under the General Limitation.* Association A, therefore, may lend only an additional $800,000 to Y, provided the paragraph (d)(3) prerequisites have been met. The amount loaned under the authority of the General Limitation ($800,000), when added to the amount loaned under the exception ($800,000), yields a sum that does not exceed the 30 percent uppermost limitation ($1,600,000).

2. This result does not change even if the facts are altered to assume that some or all of the $800,000 amount of lending permissible under the General Limitation's 15 percent basket is not used, or is devoted to the development of domestic residential housing units.

In other words, using the above example, if Association A lends Y $400,000 for commercial purposes and $300,000 for residential purposes—both of which would be permitted under the Association's $800,000 General Limitation—Association A's remaining permissible lending to Y would be: first, an additional $100,000 under the General Limitation, and then another $800,000 to develop domestic residential housing units if the Association meets the paragraph (d)(3) prerequisites. (The latter is $800,000 because in no event may the total lending to Y exceed 30 percent of unimpaired capital and unimpaired surplus). If Association A did not lend Y the remaining $100,000 permissible under the General Limitation, its permissible loans to develop domestic residential housing units under paragraph (d)(3) would be $900,000 instead of $800,000 (the total loans to Y would still equal $1,600,000).

3. In short, under the paragraph (d)(3) exception, the 30 percent or $30,000,000 limit will always operate as the uppermost limitation, unless of course the association does not avail itself of the exception and merely relies upon its General Limitation.

Section 560.93–101 Interrelationship Between the General Limitation and the 150 Percent Aggregate Limit on Loans to all Borrowers To Develop Domestic Residential Housing Units

1. The Office has already received numerous questions regarding the allocation of loans between the different lending limit "baskets," *i.e.,* the 15 percent General Limitation basket and the 30 percent Residential Development basket. In general, the inquiries concern the manner in which an association may "move" a loan from the General

182

Office of Thrift Supervision, Treasury §560.101

Limitation basket to the Residential Development basket. The following example is intended to provide guidance:

Example: Association A's General Limitation under section 5(u)(1) is $15 million. In January, Association A makes a $10 million loan to Borrower to develop domestic residential housing units. At the time the loan was made, Association A had not received approval under a Director order to avail itself of the residential development exception to lending limits. Therefore, the $10 million loan is made under Association A's General Limitation.

2. In June, Association A receives authorization to lend under the Residential Development exception. In July, Association A lends $3 million to Borrower to develop domestic residential housing units. In August, Borrower seeks an additional $12 million commercial loan from Association A. Association A cannot make the loan to Borrower, however, because it already has an outstanding $10 million loan to Borrower that counts against Association A's General Limitation of $15 million. Thus, Association A may lend only up to an additional $5 million to Borrower under the General Limitation.

3. However, Association A may be able to reallocate the $10 million loan it made to Borrower in January to its Residential Development basket provided that: (1) Association A has obtained authority under a Director's order to avail itself of the additional lending authority for residential development and maintains compliance with all prerequisites to such lending authority; (2) the original $10 million loan made in January constitutes a loan to develop domestic residential housing units as defined; and (3) the housing unit(s) constructed with the funds from the January loan remain in a stage of "development" at the time Association A reallocates the loan to the domestic residential housing basket. The project must be in a stage of acquisition, development, construction, rehabilitation, or conversion in order for the loan to be reallocated.

4. If Association A is able to reallocate the $10 million loan made to Borrower in January to its Residential Development basket, it may make the $12 million commercial loan requested by Borrower in August. Once the January loan is reallocated to the Residential Development basket, however, the $10 million loan counts towards Association's 150 percent aggregate limitation on loans to all borrowers under the residential development basket (section 5(u)(2)(A)(ii)(IV)).

5. If Association A reallocates the January loan to its domestic residential housing basket and makes an additional $12 million commercial loan to Borrower, Association A's totals under the respective limitations would be: $12 million under the General Limitation; and $13 million under the Residential Development limitation. The full $13 million residential development loan counts toward Association A's aggregate 150 percent limitation.

[61 FR 50976, Sept. 30, 1996, as amended at 61 FR 66579, Dec. 18, 1996; 62 FR 66262, Dec. 18, 1997; 66 FR 13007, Mar. 2, 2001; 69 FR 76602, Dec. 22, 2004]

§560.100 Real estate lending standards; purpose and scope.

This section, and §560.101 of this subpart, issued pursuant to section 304 of the Federal Deposit Insurance Corporation Improvement Act of 1991, 12 U.S.C. 1828(o), prescribe standards for real estate lending to be used by savings associations and all their includable subsidiaries, as defined in 12 CFR 567.1, over which the savings associations exercise control, in adopting internal real estate lending policies.

[61 FR 50971, Sept. 30, 1996, as amended at 62 FR 66262, Dec. 18, 1997]

§560.101 Real estate lending standards.

(a) Each savings association shall adopt and maintain written policies that establish appropriate limits and standards for extensions of credit that are secured by liens on or interests in real estate, or that are made for the purpose of financing permanent improvements to real estate.

(b)(1) Real estate lending policies adopted pursuant to this section must:

(i) Be consistent with safe and sound banking practices;

(ii) Be appropriate to the size of the institution and the nature and scope of its operations; and

(iii) Be reviewed and approved by the savings association's board of directors at least annually.

(2) The lending policies must establish:

(i) Loan portfolio diversification standards;

(ii) Prudent underwriting standards, including loan-to-value limits, that are clear and measurable;

(iii) Loan administration procedures for the savings association's real estate portfolio; and

(iv) Documentation, approval, and reporting requirements to monitor compliance with the savings association's real estate lending policies.

183

(c) Each savings association must monitor conditions in the real estate market in its lending area to ensure that its real estate lending policies continue to be appropriate for current market conditions.

(d) The real estate lending policies adopted pursuant to this section should reflect consideration of the Interagency Guidelines for Real Estate Lending Policies established by the Federal bank and thrift supervisory agencies.

APPENDIX TO §560.101—INTERAGENCY GUIDELINES FOR REAL ESTATE LENDING POLICIES

The agencies' regulations require that each insured depository institution adopt and maintain a written policy that establishes appropriate limits and standards for all extensions of credit that are secured by liens on or interests in real estate or made for the purpose of financing the construction of a building or other improvements.[1] These guidelines are intended to assist institutions in the formulation and maintenance of a real estate lending policy that is appropriate to the size of the institution and the nature and scope of its individual operations, as well as satisfies the requirements of the regulation. Each institution's policies must be comprehensive, and consistent with safe and sound lending practices, and must ensure that the institution operates within limits and according to standards that are reviewed and approved at least annually by the board of directors. Real estate lending is an integral part of many institutions' business plans and, when undertaken in a prudent manner, will not be subject to examiner criticism.

LOAN PORTFOLIO MANAGEMENT CONSIDERATIONS

The lending policy should contain a general outline of the scope and distribution of the institution's credit facilities and the manner in which real estate loans are made, serviced, and collected. In particular, the institution's policies on real estate lending should:

• Identify the geographic areas in which the institution will consider lending.
• Establish a loan portfolio diversification policy and set limits for real estate loans by type and geographic market (e.g., limits on higher risk loans).

---

[1] The agencies have adopted a uniform rule on real estate lending. See 12 CFR Part 365 (FDIC); 12 CFR Part 208, Subpart C (FRB); 12 CFR Part 34, Subpart D (OCC); and 12 CFR 560.100–560.101 (OTS).

• Identify appropriate terms and conditions by type of real estate loan.
• Establish loan origination and approval procedures, both generally and by size and type of loan.
• Establish prudent underwriting standards that are clear and measurable, including loan-to-value limits, that are consistent with these supervisory guidelines.
• Establish review and approval procedures for exception loans, including loans with loan-to-value percentages in excess of supervisory limits.
• Establish loan administration procedures, including documentation, disbursement, collateral inspection, collection, and loan review.
• Establish real estate appraisal and evaluation programs.
• Require that management monitor the loan portfolio and provide timely and adequate reports to the board of directors.

The institution should consider both internal and external factors in the formulation of its loan policies and strategic plan. Factors that should be considered include:

• The size and financial condition of the institution.
• The expertise and size of the lending staff.
• The need to avoid undue concentrations of risk.
• Compliance with all real estate related laws and regulations, including the Community Reinvestment Act, anti-discrimination laws, and for savings associations, the Qualified Thrift Lender test.
• Market conditions.

The institution should monitor conditions in the real estate markets in its lending area so that it can react quickly to changes in market conditions that are relevant to its lending decisions. Market supply and demand factors that should be considered include:

• Demographic indicators, including population and employment trends.
• Zoning requirements.
• Current and projected vacancy, construction, and absorption rates.
• Current and projected lease terms, rental rates, and sales prices, including concessions.
• Current and projected operating expenses for different types of projects.
• Economic indicators, including trends and diversification of the lending area.
• Valuation trends, including discount and direct capitalization rates.

UNDERWRITING STANDARDS

Prudently underwritten real estate loans should reflect all relevant credit factors, including:

• The capacity of the borrower, or income from the underlying property, to adequately service the debt.

Office of Thrift Supervision, Treasury § 560.101

- The value of the mortgaged property.
- The overall creditworthiness of the borrower.
- The level of equity invested in the property.
- Any secondary sources of repayment.
- Any additional collateral or credit enhancements (such as guarantees, mortgage insurance or takeout commitments).

The lending policies should reflect the level of risk that is acceptable to the board of directors and provide clear and measurable underwriting standards that enable the institution's lending staff to evaluate these credit factors. The underwriting standards should address:

- The maximum loan amount by type of property.
- Maximum loan maturities by type of property.
- Amortization schedules.
- Pricing structure for different types of real estate loans.
- Loan-to-value limits by type of property. For development and construction projects, and completed commercial properties, the policy should also establish, commensurate with the size and type of the project or property:
- Requirements for feasibility studies and sensitivity and risk analyses (*e.g.*, sensitivity of income projections to changes in economic variables such as interest rates, vacancy rates, or operating expenses).
- Minimum requirements for initial investment and maintenance of hard equity by the borrower (*e.g.*, cash or unencumbered investment in the underlying property).
- Minimum standards for net worth, cash flow, and debt service coverage of the borrower or underlying property.
- Standards for the acceptability of and limits on non-amortizing loans.
- Standards for the acceptability of and limits on the use of interest reserves.
- Pre-leasing and pre-sale requirements for income-producing property.
- Pre-sale and minimum unit release requirements for non-income-producing property loans.
- Limits on partial recourse or non-recourse loans and requirements for guarantor support.
- Requirements for takeout commitments.
- Minimum covenants for loan agreements.

LOAN ADMINISTRATION

The institution should also establish loan administration procedures for its real estate portfolio that address:

- Documentation, including:
Type and frequency of financial statements, including requirements for verification of information provided by the borrower;

Type and frequency of collateral evaluations (appraisals and other estimates of value).
- Loan closing and disbursement.
- Payment processing.
- Escrow administration.
- Collateral administration.
- Loan payoffs.
- Collections and foreclosure, including:
Delinquency follow-up procedures;
Foreclosure timing;
Extensions and other forms of forbearance;
Acceptance of deeds in lieu of foreclosure.
- Claims processing (*e.g.*, seeking recovery on a defaulted loan covered by a government guaranty or insurance program).
- Servicing and participation agreements.

SUPERVISORY LOAN-TO-VALUE LIMITS

Institutions should establish their own internal loan-to-value limits for real estate loans. These internal limits should not exceed the following supervisory limits:

Loan category	Loan-to-value limit (percent)
Raw land	65
Land development	75
Construction:	
Commercial, multifamily,[1] and other non-residential	80
1- to 4-family residential	85
Improved property	85
Owner-occupied 1- to 4-family and home equity	([2])

[1] Multifamily construction includes condominiums and co-operatives.
[2] A loan-to-value limit has not been established for permanent mortgage or home equity loans on owner-occupied, 1- to 4-family residential property. However, for any such loan with a loan-to-value ratio that equals or exceeds 90 percent at origination, an institution should require appropriate credit enhancement in the form of either mortgage insurance or readily marketable collateral.

The supervisory loan-to-value limits should be applied to the underlying property that collateralizes the loan. For loans that fund multiple phases of the same real estate project (e.g., a loan for both land development and construction of an office building), the appropriate loan-to-value limit is the limit applicable to the final phase of the project funded by the loan; however, loan disbursements should not exceed actual development or construction outlays. In situations where a loan is fully cross-collateralized by two or more properties or is secured by a collateral pool of two or more properties, the appropriate maximum loan amount under supervisory loan-to-value limits is the sum of the value of each property, less senior liens, multiplied by the appropriate loan-to-value limit for each property. To ensure that collateral margins remain within the supervisory limits, lenders should redetermine conformity whenever collateral substitutions are made to the collateral pool.

In establishing internal loan-to-value limits, each lender is expected to carefully consider the institution-specific and market factors listed under "Loan Portfolio Management Considerations," as well as any other relevant factors, such as the particular subcategory or type of loan. For any subcategory of loans that exhibits greater credit risk than the overall category, a lender should consider the establishment of an internal loan-to-value limit for that subcategory that is lower than the limit for the overall category.

The loan-to-value ratio is only one of several pertinent credit factors to be considered when underwriting a real estate loan. Other credit factors to be taken into account are highlighted in the "Underwriting Standards" section above. Because of these other factors, the establishment of these supervisory limits should not be interpreted to mean that loans at these levels will automatically be considered sound.

LOANS IN EXCESS OF THE SUPERVISORY LOAN-TO-VALUE LIMITS

The agencies recognize that appropriate loan-to-value limits vary not only among categories of real estate loans but also among individual loans. Therefore, it may be appropriate in individual cases to originate or purchase loans with loan-to-value ratios in excess of the supervisory loan-to-value limits, based on the support provided by other credit factors. Such loans should be identified in the institutions' records, and their aggregate amount reported at least quarterly to the institution's board of directors. (See additional reporting requirements described under "Exceptions to the General Policy.") The aggregate amount of all loans in excess of the supervisory loan-to-value limits should not exceed 100 percent of total capital.[2] Moreover, within the aggregate limit, total loans for all commercial, agricultural, multifamily or other non-1-to- 4 family residential properties should not exceed 30 percent of total capital. An institution will come under increased supervisory scrutiny as the total of such loans approaches these levels.

In determining the aggregate amount of such loans, institutions should: (a) Include all loans secured by the same property if any one of those loans exceeds the supervisory loan-to-value limits; and (b) include the recourse obligation of any such loan sold with recourse. Conversely, a loan should no longer be reported to the directors as part of aggregate totals when reduction in principal or senior liens, or additional contribution of collateral or equity (e.g., improvements to the real property securing the loan), bring the loan-to-value ratio into compliance with supervisory limits.

EXCLUDED TRANSACTIONS

The agencies also recognize that there are a number of lending situations in which other factors significantly outweigh the need to apply the supervisory loan-to-value limits.

These include:

• Loans guaranteed or insured by the U.S. government or its agencies, provided that the amount of the guaranty or insurance is at least equal to the portion of the loan that exceeds the supervisory loan-to-value limit.

• Loans backed by the full faith and credit of a state government, provided that the amount of the assurance is at least equal to the portion of the loan that exceeds the supervisory loan-to-value limit.

• Loans guaranteed or insured by a state, municipal or local government, or an agency thereof, provided that the amount of the guaranty or insurance is at least equal to the portion of the loan that exceeds the supervisory loan-to-value limit, and provided that the lender has determined that the guarantor or insurer has the financial capacity and willingness to perform under the terms of the guaranty or insurance agreement.

• Loans that are to be sold promptly after origination, without recourse, to a financially responsible third party.

• Loans that are renewed, refinanced, or restructured without the advancement of new funds or an increase in the line of credit (except for reasonable closing costs), or loans that are renewed, refinanced, or restructured in connection with a workout situation, either with or without the advancement of new funds, where consistent with safe and sound banking practices and part of a clearly defined and well-documented program to achieve orderly liquidation of the debt, reduce risk of loss, or maximize recovery on the loan.

• Loans that facilitate the sale of real estate acquired by the lender in the ordinary course of collecting a debt previously contracted in good faith.

• Loans for which a lien on or interest in real property is taken as additional collateral through an abundance of caution by the lender (e.g., the institution takes a blanket lien on all or substantially all of the assets of the borrower, and the value of the real property is low relative to the aggregate value of all other collateral).

---

[2] For the state member banks, the term "total capital" means "total risk-based capital" as defined in Appendix A to 12 CFR Part 208. For insured state non-member banks, "total capital" refers to that term described in table I of Appendix A to 12 CFR Part 325. For national banks, the term "total capital" is defined at 12 CFR 3.2(e). For savings associations, the term "total capital" as described in part 567 of this chapter.

Office of Thrift Supervision, Treasury § 560.101

- Loans, such as working capital loans, where the lender does not rely principally on real estate as security and the extension of credit is not used to acquire, develop, or construct permanent improvements on real property.
- Loans for the purpose of financing permanent improvements to real property, but not secured by the property, if such security interest is not required by prudent underwriting practice.

EXCEPTIONS TO THE GENERAL LENDING POLICY

Some provision should be made for the consideration of loan requests from creditworthy borrowers whose credit needs do not fit within the institution's general lending policy. An institution may provide for prudently underwritten exceptions to its lending policies, including loan-to-value limits, on a loan-by-loan basis. However, any exceptions from the supervisory loan-to-value limits should conform to the aggregate limits on such loans discussed above.

The board of directors is responsible for establishing standards for the review and approval of exception loans. Each institution should establish an appropriate internal process for the review and approval of loans that do not conform to its own internal policy standards. The approval of any such loan should be supported by a written justification that clearly sets forth all of the relevant credit factors that support the underwriting decision. The justification and approval documents for such loans should be maintained as a part of the permanent loan file. Each institution should monitor compliance with its real estate lending policy and individually report exception loans of a significant size to its board of directors.

SUPERVISORY REVIEW OF REAL ESTATE LENDING POLICIES AND PRACTICES

The real estate lending policies of institutions will be evaluated by examiners during the course of their examinations to determine if the policies are consistent with safe and sound lending practices, these guidelines, and the requirements of the regulation. In evaluating the adequacy of the institution's real estate lending policies and practices, examiners will take into consideration the following factors:
- The nature and scope of the institution's real estate lending activities.
- The size and financial condition of the institution.
- The quality of the institution's management and internal controls.
- The expertise and size of the lending and loan administration staff.
- Market conditions.

Lending policy exception reports will also be reviewed by examiners during the course of their examinations to determine whether the institutions' exceptions are adequately documented and appropriate in light of all of the relevant credit considerations. An excessive volume of exceptions to an institution's real estate lending policy may signal a weakening of its underwriting practices, or may suggest a need to revise the loan policy.

DEFINITIONS

For the purposes of these Guidelines:

Construction loan means an extension of credit for the purpose of erecting or rehabilitating buildings or other structures, including any infrastructure necessary for development.

Extension of credit or loan means:
(1) The total amount of any loan, line of credit, or other legally binding lending commitment with respect to real property; and
(2) The total amount, based on the amount of consideration paid, of any loan, line of credit, or other legally binding lending commitment acquired by a lender by purchase, assignment, or otherwise.

Improved property loan means an extension of credit secured by one of the following types of real property:
(1) Farmland, ranchland or timberland committed to ongoing management and agricultural production;
(2) 1- to 4-family residential property that is not owner-occupied;
(3) Residential property containing five or more individual dwelling units;
(4) Completed commercial property; or
(5) Other income-producing property that has been completed and is available for occupancy and use, except income-producing owner-occupied 1- to 4-family residential property.

Land development loan means an extension of credit for the purpose of improving unimproved real property prior to the erection of structures. The improvement of unimproved real property may include the laying or placement of sewers, water pipes, utility cables, streets, and other infrastructure necessary for future development.

Loan origination means the time of inception of the obligation to extend credit (i.e., when the last event or prerequisite, controllable by the lender, occurs causing the lender to become legally bound to fund an extension of credit).

Loan-to-value or *loan-to-value ratio* means the percentage or ratio that is derived at the time of loan origination by dividing an extension of credit by the total value of the property(ies) securing or being improved by the extension of credit plus the amount of any readily marketable collateral and other acceptable collateral that secures the extension of credit. The total amount of all senior liens on or interests in such property(ies) should be included in determining the loan-to-value ratio. When mortgage insurance or collateral is used in the calculation of the

§ 560.110

loan-to-value ratio, and such credit enhancement is later released or replaced, the loan-to-value ratio should be recalculated.

Other acceptable collateral means any collateral in which the lender has a perfected security interest, that has a quantifiable value, and is accepted by the lender in accordance with safe and sound lending practices. Other acceptable collateral should be appropriately discounted by the lender consistent with the lender's usual practices for making loans secured by such collateral. Other acceptable collateral includes, among other items, unconditional irrevocable standby letters of credit for the benefit of the lender.

Owner-occupied, when used in conjunction with the term *1- to 4-family residential property* means that the owner of the underlying real property occupies at least one unit of the real property as a principal residence of the owner.

Readily marketable collateral means insured deposits, financial instruments, and bullion in which the lender has a perfected interest. Financial instruments and bullion must be salable under ordinary circumstances with reasonable promptness at a fair market value determined by quotations based on actual transactions, on an auction or similarly available daily bid and ask price market. Readily marketable collateral should be appropriately discounted by the lender consistent with the lender's usual practices for making loans secured by such collateral.

Value means an opinion or estimate, set forth in an appraisal or evaluation, whichever may be appropriate, of the market value of real property, prepared in accordance with the agency's appraisal regulations and guidance. For loans to purchase an existing property, the term "value" means the lesser of the actual acquisition cost or the estimate of value.

1- to 4-family residential property means property containing fewer than five individual dwelling units, including manufactured homes permanently affixed to the underlying property (when deemed to be real property under state law).

[61 FR 50971, Sept. 30, 1996, as amended at 66 FR 65821, Dec. 21, 2001; 72 FR 69438, Dec. 7, 2007]

§ 560.110 Most favored lender usury preemption.

(a) *Definition.* The term "interest" as used in 12 U.S.C. 1463(g) includes any payment compensating a creditor or prospective creditor for an extension of credit, making available of a line of credit, or any default or breach by a borrower of a condition upon which credit was extended. It includes, among other things, the following fees connected with credit extension or availability: numerical periodic rates, late fees, not sufficient funds (NSF) fees, overlimit fees, annual fees, cash advance fees, and membership fees. It does not ordinarily include appraisal fees, premiums and commissions attributable to insurance guaranteeing repayment of any extension of credit, finders' fees, fees for document preparation or notarization, or fees incurred to obtain credit reports.

(b) *Authority.* A savings association located in a state may charge interest at the maximum rate permitted to any state-chartered or licensed lending institution by the law of that state. If state law permits different interest charges on specified classes of loans, a federal savings association making such loans is subject only to the provisions of state law relating to that class of loans that are material to the determination of the permitted interest. For example, a federal savings association may lawfully charge the highest rate permitted to be charged by a state-licensed small loan company, without being so licensed, but subject to state law limitations on the size of loans made by small loan companies. Except as provided in this paragraph, the applicability of state law to Federal savings associations shall be determined in accordance with § 560.2 of this part. State supervisors determine the degree to which state-chartered savings associations must comply with state laws other than those imposing restrictions on interest, as defined in paragraph (a) of this section.

(c) *Effect on state definitions of interest.* The Federal definition of the term "interest" in paragraph (a) of this section does not change how interest is defined by the individual states (nor how the state definition of interest is used) solely for purposes of state law. For example, if late fees are not "interest" under state law where a savings association is located but state law permits its most favored lender to charge late fees, then a savings association located in that state may charge late fees to its intrastate customers. The savings association may also charge late fees to its interstate customers because the fees are interest under the Federal definition of interest

Office of Thrift Supervision, Treasury **§ 560.120**

and an allowable charge under state law where the savings association is located. However, the late fees would not be treated as interest for purposes of evaluating compliance with state usury limitations because state law excludes late fees when calculating the maximum interest that lending institutions may charge under those limitations.

§ 560.120 Letters of credit and other independent undertakings to pay against documents.

(a) *General authority.* A savings association may issue and commit to issue letters of credit within the scope of applicable laws or rules of practice recognized by law. It may also issue other independent undertakings within the scope of such laws or rules of practice recognized by law, that have been approved by OTS (approved undertaking).[1] Under such letters of credit and approved undertakings, the savings association's obligation to honor depends upon the presentation of specified documents and not upon nondocumentary conditions or resolution of questions of fact or law at issue between the account party and the beneficiary. A savings association may also confirm or otherwise undertake to honor or purchase specified documents upon their presentation under another person's independent undertaking within the scope of such laws or rules.

(b) *Safety and soundness considerations*—(1) *Terms.* As a matter of safe and sound banking practice, savings associations that issue letters of credit or approved undertakings should not be exposed to undue risk. At a minimum, savings associations should consider the following:

(i) The independent character of the letter of credit or approved undertaking should be apparent from its terms (such as terms that subject it to laws or rules providing for its independent character);

(ii) The letter of credit or approved undertaking should be limited in amount;

(iii) The letter of credit or approved undertaking should:

(A) Be limited in duration; or

(B) Permit the savings association to terminate the letter of credit or approved undertaking, either on a periodic basis (consistent with the savings association's ability to make any necessary credit assessments) or at will upon either notice or payment to the beneficiary; or

(C) Entitle the savings association to cash collateral from the account party on demand (with a right to accelerate the customer's obligations, as appropriate); and

(iv) The savings association either should be fully collateralized or have a post-honor right of reimbursement from its customer or from another issuer of a letter of credit or an independent undertaking. Alternatively, if the savings association's undertaking is to purchase documents of title, securities, or other valuable documents, it should obtain a first priority right to realize on the documents if the savings association is not otherwise to be reimbursed.

(2) *Additional considerations in special circumstances.* Certain letters of credit and approved undertakings require particular protections against credit, operational, and market risk:

(i) In the event that the undertaking is to honor by delivery of an item of value other than money, the savings association should ensure that market fluctuations that affect the value of the item will not cause the savings association to assume undue market risk;

(ii) In the event that the undertaking provides for automatic renewal, the

---

[1] Samples of laws or rules of practice applicable to letters of credit and other independent undertakings include, but are not limited to: the applicable version of Article 5 of the Uniform Commercial Code (UCC) (1962, as amended 1990) or revised Article 5 of the UCC (as amended 1995) (available from West Publishing Co., 1/800/328–4880); the Uniform Customs and Practice for Documentary Credits (International Chamber of Commerce (ICC) Publication No. 500) (available from ICC Publishing, Inc., 212/206–1150; the United Nations Convention on Independent Guarantees and Standby Letters of Credit (adopted by the U.N. General Assembly in 1995 and signed by the U.S. in 1997) (available from the U.N. Commission on International Trade Law, 212/963–5353); and the Uniform Rules for Bank-to-Bank Reimbursements Under Documentary Credits (ICC Publication No. 525) (available from ICC Publishing, Inc., 212/206–1150).

§ 560.121

terms for renewal should allow the savings association to make any necessary credit assessment prior to renewal;

(iii) In the event that a savings association issues an undertaking for its own account, the underlying transaction for which it is issued must be within the savings association's authority and comply with any safety and soundness requirements applicable to that transaction.

(3) *Operational expertise.* The savings association should possess operational expertise that is commensurate with the sophistication of its letter of credit or independent undertaking activities.

(4) *Documentation.* The savings association must accurately reflect its letters of credit or approved undertakings in its records, including any acceptance or deferred payment or other absolute obligation arising out of its contingent undertaking.

[61 FR 50971, Sept. 30, 1996, as amended at 64 FR 46565, Aug. 26, 1999]

§ 560.121 Investment in State housing corporations.

(a) Any savings association to the extent it has legal authority to do so, may make investments in, commitments to invest in, loans to, or commitments to lend to any state housing corporation; provided, that such obligations or loans are secured directly, or indirectly through a fiduciary, by a first lien on improved real estate which is insured under the National Housing Act, as amended, and that in the event of default, the holder of such obligations or loans has the right directly, or indirectly through a fiduciary, to subject to the satisfaction of such obligations or loans the real estate described in the first lien, or the insurance proceeds.

(b) Any savings association that is adequately capitalized may, to the extent it has legal authority to do so, invest in obligations (including loans) of, or issued by, any state housing corporation incorporated in the state in which such savings association has its home or a branch office; provided (except with respect to loans), that:

(1) The obligations are rated in one of the four highest grades as shown by the most recently published rating made of such obligations by a nationally recognized rating service; or

(2) The obligations, if not rated, are approved by the Office. The aggregate outstanding direct investment in obligations under paragraph (b) of this section shall not exceed the amount of the savings association's total capital.

(c) Each state housing corporation in which a savings association invests under the authority of paragraph (b) of this section shall agree, before accepting any such investment (including any loan or loan commitment), to make available at any time to the Office such information as the Office may consider to be necessary to ensure that investments are properly made under this section.

§ 560.130 Prohibition on loan procurement fees.

If you are a director, officer, or other natural person having the power to direct the management or policies of a savings association, you must not receive, directly or indirectly, any commission, fee, or other compensation in connection with the procurement of any loan made by the savings association or a subsidiary of the savings association.

[61 FR 60178, Nov. 27, 1996]

§ 560.160 Asset classification.

(a)(1) Each savings association must evaluate and classify its assets on a regular basis in a manner consistent with, or reconcilable to, the asset classification system used by OTS in its Thrift Activities Handbook (Available at the address of Washington Headquarters Office at § 516.40(b) of this chapter).

(2) In connection with the examination of a savings association or its affiliates, OTS examiners may identify problem assets and classify them, if appropriate. The association must recognize such examiner classifications in its subsequent reports to OTS.

(b) Based on the evaluation and classification of its assets, each savings association shall establish adequate valuation allowances or charge-offs, as appropriate, consistent with generally accepted accounting principles and the

Office of Thrift Supervision, Treasury

practices of the federal banking agencies.

[61 FR 50971, Sept. 30, 1996, as amended at 66 FR 13007, Mar. 2, 2001]

§ 560.170 Records for lending transactions.

In establishing and maintaining its records pursuant to § 563.170 of this chapter, each savings association and service corporation should establish and maintain loan documentation practices that:

(a) Ensure that the institution can make an informed lending decision and can assess risk on an ongoing basis;

(b) Identify the purpose and all sources of repayment for each loan, and assess the ability of the borrower(s) and any guarantor(s) to repay the indebtedness in a timely manner;

(c) Ensure that any claims against a borrower, guarantor, security holders, and collateral are legally enforceable;

(d) Demonstrate appropriate administration and monitoring of its loans; and

(e) Take into account the size and complexity of its loans.

§ 560.172 Re-evaluation of real estate owned.

A savings association shall appraise each parcel of real estate owned at the earlier of in-substance foreclosure or at the time of the savings association's acquisition of such property, and at such times thereafter as dictated by prudent management policy; such appraisals shall be consistent with the requirements of part 564 of this chapter. The Regional Director or his or her designee may require subsequent appraisals if, in his or her discretion, such subsequent appraisal is necessary under the particular circumstances. The foregoing requirement shall not apply to any parcel of real estate that is sold and reacquired less than 12 months subsequent to the most recent appraisal made pursuant to this part. A dated, signed copy of each report of appraisal made pursuant to any provisions of this part shall be retained in the savings association's records.

Subpart C—Alternative Mortgage Transactions

§ 560.210 Disclosures for variable rate transactions.

A savings association must provide the initial disclosures described at 12 CFR 226.19(b) and the adjustment notices described at 12 CFR 226.20(c) for variable rate transactions, as described in those regulations. The OTS administers and enforces those provisions for savings associations.

[63 FR 38463, July 17, 1998]

§ 560.220 Alternative Mortgage Transaction Parity Act.

(a) *Applicable housing creditors.* A housing creditor that is not a commercial bank, a credit union, or a federal savings association, may make an alternative mortgage transaction as defined at 12 U.S.C. 3802(1), by following the regulations identified in paragraph (b) of this section, notwithstanding any state constitution, law, or regulation. *See* 12 U.S.C. 3803.

(b) *Applicable regulations.* OTS identifies §§ 560.35 and 560.210 as appropriate and applicable for state housing creditors. All other OTS regulations are not identified, and are inappropriate and inapplicable for state housing creditors. State housing creditors engaged in credit sales should read the term "loan" as "credit sale" wherever applicable in applying these regulations.

[67 FR 60554, Sept. 26, 2002]

PART 561—DEFINITIONS FOR REGULATIONS AFFECTING ALL SAVINGS ASSOCIATIONS

Sec.
561.1 General.
561.2 Account.
561.3 Accountholder.
561.4 Affiliate.
561.5 Affiliated person.
561.6 Audit period.
561.7–561.8 [Reserved]
561.9 Certificate account.
561.12 Consumer credit.
561.14 Controlling person.
561.15 Corporation.
561.16 Demand accounts.
561.18 Director.
561.19 Financial institution.
561.24 Immediate family.

§ 561.1

561.26 Land loan.
561.27 Low-rent housing.
561.28 Money Market Deposit Accounts.
561.29 Negotiable Order of Withdrawal Accounts.
561.30 Nonresidential construction loan.
561.31 Nonwithdrawable account.
561.33 Note account.
561.34 Office.
561.35 Officer.
561.37 Parent company; subsidiary.
561.38 Political subdivision.
561.39 Principal office.
561.40 Public unit.
561.41 [Reserved]
561.42 Savings account.
561.43 Savings association.
561.44 Security.
561.45 Service corporation.
561.49 [Reserved]
561.50 State.
561.51 Subordinated debt security.
561.52 Tax and loan account.
561.53 United States Treasury General Account.
561.54 United States Treasury Time Deposit Open Account.
561.55 With recourse.

AUTHORITY: 12 U.S.C. 1462, 1462a, 1463, 1464, 1467a.

SOURCE: 54 FR 49545, Nov. 30, 1989, unless otherwise noted.

§ 561.1 When do the definitions in this part apply?

The definitions in this part and in 12 CFR part 541 apply throughout this chapter, unless another definition is specifically provided.

[67 FR 78152, Dec. 23, 2002]

§ 561.2 Account.

The term *account* means any savings account, demand account, certificate account, tax and loan account, note account, United States Treasury general account or United States Treasury time deposit-open account, whether in the form of a deposit or a share, held by an accountholder in a savings association.

§ 561.3 Accountholder.

The term *accountholder* means the holder of an account or accounts in a savings association insured by the Deposit Insurance Fund. The term does not include the holder of any subordinated debt security or any mortgage-backed bond issued by the savings association.

[54 FR 49545, Nov. 30, 1989, as amended at 71 FR 19811, Apr. 18, 2006]

§ 561.4 Affiliate.

The term *affiliate* of a savings association, unless otherwise defined, means any corporation, business trust, association, or other similar organization:

(a) Of which a savings association, directly or indirectly, owns or controls either a majority of the voting shares or more than 50 percentum of the number of shares voted for the election of its directors, trustees, or other persons exercising similar functions at the preceding election, or controls in any manner the election of a majority of its directors, trustees, or other persons exercising similar functions; or

(b) Of which control is held, directly or indirectly through stock ownership or in any other manner, by the shareholders of a savings association who own or control either a majority of the shares of such savings association or more than 50 per centum of the number of shares voted for the election of directors of such savings association at the preceding election, or by trustees for the benefit of the shareholders of any such savings association; or

(c) Of which a majority of its directors, trustees, or other persons exercising similar functions are directors of any one savings association.

§ 561.5 Affiliated person.

The term *affiliated person* of a savings association means the following:

(a) A director, officer, or controlling person of such association;

(b) A spouse of a director, officer, or controlling person of such association;

(c) A member of the immediate family of a director, officer, or controlling person of such association, who has the same home as such person or who is a director or officer of any subsidiary of such association or of any holding company affiliate of such association;

(d) Any corporation or organization (other than the savings association or a corporation or organization through which the savings association operates) of which a director, officer or the controlling person of such association:

(1) Is chief executive officer, chief financial officer, or a person performing similar functions;

(2) Is a general partner;

(3) Is a limited partner who, directly or indirectly either alone or with his or her spouse and the members of his or her immediate family who are also affiliated persons of the association, owns an interest of 10 percent or more in the partnership (based on the value of his or her contribution) or who, directly or indirectly with other directors, officers, and controlling persons of such association and their spouses and their immediate family members who are also affiliated persons of the association, owns an interest of 25 percent or more in the partnership; or

(4) Directly or indirectly either alone or with his or her spouse and the members of his or her immediate family who are also affiliated persons of the association, owns or controls 10 percent or more of any class of equity securities or owns or controls, with other directors, officers, and controlling persons of such association and their spouses and their immediate family members who are also affiliated persons of the association, 25 percent or more of any class of equity securities; and

(5) Any trust or other estate in which a director, officer, or controlling person of such association or the spouse of such person has a substantial beneficial interest or as to which such person or his or her spouse serves as trustee or in a similar fiduciary capacity.

[59 FR 18476, Apr. 19, 1994]

§ 561.6 Audit period.

The *audit period* of a savings association means the twelve month period (or other period in the case of a change in audit period) covered by the annual audit conducted to satisfy § 563.170.

§§ 561.7–561.8 [Reserved]

§ 561.9 Certificate account.

The term *certificate account* means a savings account evidenced by a certificate that must be held for a fixed or minimum term.

§ 561.12 Consumer credit.

The term *consumer credit* means credit extended to a natural person for personal, family, or household purposes, including loans secured by liens on real estate and chattel liens secured by mobile homes and leases of personal property to consumers that may be considered the functional equivalent of loans on personal security: *Provided,* the savings association relies substantially upon other factors, such as the general credit standing of the borrower, guaranties, or security other than the real estate or mobile home, as the primary security for the loan. Appropriate evidence to demonstrate justification for such reliance should be retained in a savings association's files. Among the types of credit included within this term are consumer loans; educational loans; unsecured loans for real property alteration, repair or improvement, or for the equipping of real property; loans in the nature of overdraft protection; and credit extended in connection with credit cards.

§ 561.14 Controlling person.

The term *controlling person* of a savings association means any person or entity which, either directly or indirectly, or acting in concert with one or more other persons or entities, owns, controls, or holds with power to vote, or holds proxies representing, ten percent or more of the voting shares or rights of such savings association; or controls in any manner the election or appointment of a majority of the directors of such savings association. However, a director of a savings association will not be deemed to be a controlling person of such savings association based upon his or her voting, or acting in concert with other directors in voting, proxies:

(a) Obtained in connection with an annual solicitation of proxies, or

(b) Obtained from savings account holders and borrowers if such proxies are voted as directed by a majority vote of the entire board of directors of such association, or of a committee of such directors if such committee's composition and authority are controlled by a majority vote of the entire board and if its authority is revocable by such a majority.

§ 561.15 Corporation.

The terms *Corporation* and *FDIC* mean the Federal Deposit Insurance Corporation.

§ 561.16 Demand accounts.

The term *demand accounts* means non-interest-bearing demand deposits that are subject to check or to withdrawal or transfer on negotiable or transferable order to the savings association and that are permitted to be issued by statute, regulation, or otherwise and are payable on demand.

[54 FR 49545, Nov. 30, 1989, as amended at 58 FR 4313, Jan. 14, 1993; 62 FR 54765, Oct. 22, 1997; 70 FR 76676, Dec. 28, 2005]

§ 561.18 Director.

(a) The term *director* means any director, trustee, or other person performing similar functions with respect to any organization whether incorporated or unincorporated. Such term does not include an advisory director, honorary director, director emeritus, or similar person, unless the person is otherwise performing functions similar to those of a director.

(b) The term *Director* means the Director of the Office of Thrift Supervision as established in section 3 of the Act.

§ 561.19 Financial institution.

The term *financial institution* has the same meaning as the term *depository institution* set forth in 12 U.S.C. 1813(c)(1).

§ 561.24 Immediate family.

The term *immediate family* of any natural person means the following (whether by the full or half blood or by adoption):

(a) Such person's spouse, father, mother, children, brothers, sisters, and grandchildren;

(b) The father, mother, brothers, and sisters of such person's spouse; and

(c) The spouse of a child, brother, or sister of such person.

§ 561.26 Land loan.

The term *land loan* means a loan:

(a) Secured by real estate upon which all facilities and improvements have been completely installed, as required by local regulations and practices, so that it is entirely prepared for the erection of structures;

(b) To finance the purchase of land and the accomplishment of all improvements required to convert it to developed building lots; or

(c) Secured by land upon which there is no structure.

§ 561.27 Low-rent housing.

The term *low-rent housing* means real estate which is, or which is being constructed, remodeled, rehabilitated, modernized, or renovated to be, the subject of an annual contributions contract for low-rent housing under the provisions of the United States Housing Act of 1937, as amended.

§ 561.28 Money Market Deposit Accounts.

(a) Money Market Deposit Accounts (*MMDAs*) offered by Federal savings associations in accordance with 12 U.S.C. 1464(b)(1) and by state-chartered savings associations in accordance with applicable state law are savings accounts on which interest may be paid if issued subject to the following limitations:

(1) The savings association shall reserve the right to require at least seven days' notice prior to withdrawal or transfer of any funds in the account; and

(2)(i) The depositor is authorized by the savings association to make no more than six transfers per calendar month or statement cycle (or similar period) of at least four weeks by means of preauthorized, automatic, telephonic, or data transmission agreement, order, or instruction to another account of the depositor at the same savings association to the savings association itself, or to a third party.

(ii) Savings associations may permit holders of MMDAs to make unlimited transfers for the purpose of repaying loans (except overdraft loans on the depositor's demand account) and associated expenses at the same savings association (as originator or servicer), to make unlimited transfers of funds from this account to another account of the same depositor at the same savings association or to make unlimited payments directly to the depositor from the account when such transfers or payments are made by mail, messenger, automated teller machine, or in person, or when such payments are made by telephone (via check mailed to the depositor).

(3) In order to ensure that no more than the number of transfers specified in paragraph (a)(2)(i) of this section are made, a savings association must either:

(i) Prevent transfers of funds in excess of the limitations; or

(ii) Adopt procedures to monitor those transfers on an after-the-fact basis and contact customers who exceed the limits on more than an occasional basis. For customers who continue to violate those limits after being contacted by the depository savings association the depository savings association must either place funds in another account that the depositor is eligible to maintain or take away the account's transfer and draft capacities.

(iii) Insured savings association at their option, may use on a consistent basis either the date on a check or the date it is paid in determining whether the transfer limitations within the specified interval are exceeded.

(b) Federal savings associations may offer MMDAs to any depositor, and state-chartered savings associations may offer MMDAs to any depositor not inconsistent with applicable state law.

[54 FR 49545, Nov. 30, 1989, as amended at 75 FR 33502, June 14, 2010]

§ 561.29 Negotiable Order of Withdrawal Accounts.

(a) Negotiable Order of Withdrawal (*NOW*) accounts are savings accounts authorized by 12 U.S.C. 1832 on which the savings association reserves the right to require at least seven days' notice prior to withdrawal or transfer of any funds in the account.

(b) For purposes of 12 U.S.C. 1832:

(1) An organization shall be deemed "operated primarily for religious, philanthropic, charitable, educational, or other similar purposes and * * * not * * * for profit" if it is described in sections 501(c)(3) through (13), 501(c)(19), or 528 of the Internal Revenue Code; and

(2) The funds of a sole proprietorship or unincorporated business owned by a husband and wife shall be deemed beneficially owned by "one or more individuals."

§ 561.30 Nonresidential construction loan.

The term *nonresidential construction loan* means a loan for construction of other than one or more dwelling units.

§ 561.31 Nonwithdrawable account.

The term *nonwithdrawable account* means an account which by the terms of the contract of the accountholder with the savings association or by provisions of state law cannot be paid to the accountholder until all liabilities, including other classes of share liability of the savings association have been fully liquidated and paid upon the winding up of the savings association is referred to as a *nonwithdrawable account*.

§ 561.33 Note account.

The term *note account* means a note, subject to the right of immediate call, evidencing funds held by depositories electing the note option under applicable United States Treasury Department regulations. Note accounts are not savings accounts or savings deposits.

§ 561.34 Office.

The term *Office* means the Office as established in section 3 of the Act or any official duly authorized to act on its behalf. Where appropriate in context, it also refers to the Federal Home Loan Bank Board and the Federal Savings and Loan Insurance Corporation as predecessor agencies to the Office.

§ 561.35 Officer.

The term *Officer* means the president, any vice-president (but not an assistant vice-president, second vice-president, or other vice president having authority similar to an assistant or second vice-president), the secretary, the treasurer, the comptroller, and any other person performing similar functions with respect to any organization whether incorporated or unincorporated. The term *officer* also includes the chairman of the board of directors if the chairman is authorized by the charter or by-laws of the organization

§ 561.37

to participate in its operating management or if the chairman in fact participates in such management.

§ 561.37 Parent company; subsidiary.

The terms *parent company* and *subsidiary* have the meanings given to them by §§ 583.15 and 583.23 of this chapter, respectively.

§ 561.38 Political subdivision.

The term *political subdivision* includes any subdivision of a public unit, any principal department of such public unit:

(a) The creation of which subdivision or department has been expressly authorized by state statute,

(b) To which some functions of government have been delegated by state statute, and

(c) To which funds have been allocated by statute or ordinance for its exclusive use and control. It also includes drainage, irrigation, navigation, improvement, levee, sanitary, school or power districts and bridge or port authorities and other special districts created by state statute or compacts between the states. Excluded from the term are subordinate or nonautonomous divisions, agencies or boards within principal departments.

§ 561.39 Principal office.

The term *principal office* means the home office of a savings association established as such in conformity with the laws under which the savings association is organized.

§ 561.40 Public unit.

The term *public unit* means the United States, any state of the United States, the District of Columbia, any territory of the United States, Puerto Rico, the Virgin Islands, any county, any municipality or any political subdivision thereof.

§ 561.41 [Reserved]

§ 561.42 Savings account.

The term *savings account* means any withdrawable account, except a demand account as defined in § 561.16 of this chapter, a tax and loan account, a note account, a United States Treasury general account, or a United States Treasury time deposit-open account.

[54 FR 49545, Nov. 30, 1989, as amended at 62 FR 54765, Oct. 22, 1997]

§ 561.43 Savings association.

The term *savings association* means a savings association as defined in section 3 of the Federal Deposit Insurance Act, the deposits of which are insured by the Corporation. It includes a Federal savings association or Federal savings bank, chartered under section 5 of the Act, or a building and loan, savings and loan, or homestead association, or a cooperative bank (other than a cooperative bank which is a State bank as defined in section 3(a)(2) of the Federal Deposit Insurance Act) organized and operating according to the laws of the State in which it is chartered or organized, or a corporation (other than a bank as defined in section 3(a)(1) of the Federal Deposit Insurance Act) that the Board of Directors of the Federal Deposit Insurance Corporation and the Director of the Office of Thrift Supervision jointly determine to be operating substantially in the same manner as a savings association.

§ 561.44 Security.

The term *security* means any non-withdrawable account, note, stock, treasury stock, bond, debenture, evidence of indebtedness, certificate of interest or participation in any profit-sharing agreement, collateral-trust certificate, preorganization certificate or subscription, transferable share, investment contract, voting-trust certificate, or, in general, any interest or instrument commonly known as a *security*, or any certificate of interest or participation in, temporary or interim certificate for, receipt for, guarantee of, or warrant or right to subscribe to or purchase, any of the foregoing, except that a *security* shall not include an account or deposit insured by the Federal Deposit Insurance Corporation.

§ 561.45 Service corporation.

The term *service corporation* means any corporation, the majority of the capital stock of which is owned by one or more savings associations and which engages, directly or indirectly, in any activities similar to activities which may be engaged in by a service corporation in which a Federal savings association may invest under part 559 of this chapter.

[54 FR 49545, Nov. 30, 1989, as amended at 62 FR 66262, Dec. 18, 1997]

§ 561.50 State.

The term *State* means a State, the District of Columbia, Guam, Puerto Rico, and the Virgin Islands of the United States.

§ 561.51 Subordinated debt security.

The term *subordinated debt security* means any unsecured note, debenture, or other debt security issued by a savings association and subordinated on liquidation to all claims having the same priority as account holders or any higher priority.

§ 561.52 Tax and loan account.

The term *tax and loan account* means an account, the balance of which is subject to the right of immediate withdrawal, established for receipt of payments of Federal taxes and certain United States obligations. Such accounts are not savings accounts or savings deposits.

§ 561.53 United States Treasury General Account.

The term *United States Treasury General Account* means an account maintained in the name of the United States Treasury the balance of which is subject to the right of immediate withdrawal, except in the case of the closure of the member, and in which a zero balance may be maintained. Such accounts are not savings accounts or savings deposits.

§ 561.54 United States Treasury Time Deposit Open Account.

The term *United States Treasury Time Deposit Open Account* means a non-interest-bearing account maintained in the name of the United States Treasury which may not be withdrawn prior to the expiration of 30 days' written notice from the United States Treasury, or such other period of notice as the Treasury may require. Such accounts are not savings accounts or savings deposits.

§ 561.55 With recourse.

(a) The term *with recourse* means, in connection with the sale of a loan or a participation interest in a loan, an agreement or arrangement under which the purchaser is to be entitled to receive from the seller a sum of money or thing of value, whether tangible or intangible (including any substitution), upon default in payment of any loan involved or any part thereof or to withhold or to have withheld from the seller a sum of money or anything of value by way of security against default. The recourse liability resulting from a sale with recourse shall be the total book value of any loan sold with recourse less:

(1) The amount of any insurance or guarantee against loss in the event of default provided by a third party,

(2) The amount of any loss to be borne by the purchaser in the event of default, and

(3) The amount of any loss resulting from a recourse obligation entered on the books and records of the savings association.

(b) The term *with recourse* does not include loans or interests therein where the agreement of sale provides for the savings association directly or indirectly

(1) To hold or retain a subordinate interest in a specified percentage of the loans or interests; or

(2) To guarantee against loss up to a specified percentage of the loans or interests, which specified percentage shall not exceed ten percent of the outstanding balance of the loans or interests at the time of sale: *Provided*, That the savings association designates adequate reserves for the subordinate interest or guarantee.

(c) This definition does not apply for purposes of determining the capital adequacy requirements under part 567 of this chapter.

[54 FR 49545, Nov. 30, 1989, as amended at 57 FR 33437, July 29, 1992]

PART 562—REGULATORY REPORTING STANDARDS

Sec.
562.1 Regulatory reporting requirements.
562.2 Regulatory reports.

§ 562.1

562.4 Audit of savings associations and savings association holding companies.

AUTHORITY: 12 U.S.C. 1463.

SOURCE: 57 FR 40090, Sept. 2, 1992, unless otherwise noted.

§ 562.1 Regulatory reporting requirements.

(a) *Authority and scope.* This part is issued by the Office of Thrift Supervision (OTS) pursuant to section 4(b) and 4(c) of the Home Owners' Loan Act (HOLA). It applies to all savings associations regulated by the OTS.

(b) *Records and reports—general*—(1) *Records.* Each savings association and its affiliates shall maintain accurate and complete records of all business transactions. Such records shall support and be readily reconcilable to any regulatory reports submitted to the OTS and financial reports prepared in accordance with GAAP. The records shall be maintained in the United States and be readily accessible for examination and other supervisory purposes within 5 business days upon request by the OTS, at a location acceptable to the OTS.

(2) *Reports.* For purposes of examination by and regulatory reports to the OTS and compliance with this chapter, all savings associations shall use such forms and follow such regulatory reporting requirements as the OTS may require by regulation or otherwise.

§ 562.2 Regulatory reports.

(a) *Definition and scope.* This section applies to all regulatory reports, as defined herein. A regulatory report is any report that the OTS prepares, or is submitted to, or is used by the OTS, to determine compliance with its rules and regulations, and to evaluate the safe and sound condition and operation of savings associations. The Report of Examination and the Thrift Financial Report (TFR) are examples of regulatory reports. Regulatory reports are regulatory documents, not accounting documents.

(b) *Regulatory reporting requirements*—(1) *General.* The instructions to regulatory reports are referred to as "regulatory reporting requirements." Regulatory reporting requirements include, but are not limited to, the accounting instructions provided in the TFR, guidance contained in OTS regulations, bulletins, and examination handbooks, and safe and sound practices. Regulatory reporting requirements are not limited to the minimum requirements under generally accepted accounting principles (GAAP) because of the special supervisory, regulatory, and economic policy needs served by such reports. Regulatory reporting by savings associations that purports to comply with GAAP shall incorporate the GAAP that best reflects the underlying economic substance of the transaction at issue. Regulatory reporting requirements shall, at a minimum:

(i) Incorporate GAAP whenever GAAP is the referenced accounting instruction for regulatory reports to the Federal banking agencies;

(ii) Incorporate safe and sound practices contained in OTS regulations, bulletins, examination handbooks and instructions to regulatory reports. Such safety and soundness requirements shall be no less stringent than those applied by the Comptroller of the Currency for national banks; and

(iii) Incorporate additional safety and soundness requirements more stringent than GAAP, as the Director may prescribe.

(2) *Exceptions.* Regulatory reporting requirements that are not consistent with GAAP, if any, are not required to be reflected in audited financial statements, including financial statements contained in securities filings submitted to the OTS pursuant to the Securities and Exchange Act of 1934 or parts 563b, 563d, or 563g of this chapter.

(3) *Compliance.* When the OTS determines that a savings association's regulatory reports did not conform to regulatory reporting requirements in previous reporting periods, the association shall correct its regulatory reports in accordance with the directions of the OTS.

§ 562.4 Audit of savings associations and savings association holding companies.

(a) *General.* The OTS may require, at any time, an independent audit of the financial statements of, or the application of procedures agreed upon by the OTS to a savings association, savings and loan holding company, or affiliate

Office of Thrift Supervision, Treasury

(as defined by 12 CFR 563.41) by qualified independent public accountants when needed for any safety and soundness reason identified by the Director.

(b) *Audits required for safety and soundness purposes.* The OTS requires an independent audit for safety and soundness purposes:

(1) If a savings association has received a composite rating of 3, 4 or 5, as defined at § 516.5(c) of this chapter; or

(2) If, as of the beginning of its fiscal year, a savings and loan holding company controls savings association subsidiary(ies) with aggregate consolidated assets of $500 million or more.

(c) *Procedures.* (1) When the OTS requires an independent audit because such an audit is needed for safety and soundness purposes, the Director shall determine whether the audit was conducted and filed in a manner satisfactory to the OTS.

(2) The Director may waive the independent audit requirement described at paragraph (b)(1) of this section, if the Director determines that an audit would not provide further information on safety and soundness issues relevant to the examination rating.

(3) When the OTS requires the application of procedures agreed upon by the OTS for safety and soundness purposes, the Director shall identify the procedures to be performed. The Director shall also determine whether the agreed upon procedures were conducted and filed in a manner satisfactory to the OTS.

(d) *Qualifications for independent public accountants.* The audit shall be conducted by an independent public accountant who:

(1) Is registered or licensed to practice as a public accountant, and is in good standing, under the laws of the state or other political subdivision of the United States in which the savings association's or holding company's principal office is located;

(2) Agrees in the engagement letter to provide the OTS with access to and copies of any work papers, policies, and procedures relating to the services performed;

(3)(i) Is in compliance with the American Institute of Certified Public Accountants' (AICPA) Code of Professional Conduct; and

(ii) Meets the independence requirements and interpretations of the Securities and Exchange Commission and its staff; and

(4) Has received, or is enrolled in, a peer review program that meets guidelines acceptable to the OTS.

(e) *Voluntary audits.* When a savings association, savings and loan holding company, or affiliate (as defined by 12 CFR 563.41) obtains an independent audit voluntarily, it must be performed by an independent public accountant who satisfies the requirements of paragraphs (d)(1), (d)(2), and (d)(3)(i) of this section.

[59 FR 60304, Nov. 23, 1994, as amended at 62 FR 3780, Jan. 27, 1997; 66 FR 13007, Mar. 2, 2001; 67 FR 70531, Nov. 25, 2002; 67 FR 77917, December 20, 2002]

PART 563—SAVINGS ASSOCIATIONS—OPERATIONS

Subpart A—Accounts

Sec.
563.1 Chartering documents.
563.4 [Reserved]
563.5 Securities: Statement of non-insurance.

Subpart B—Operation and Structure

563.22 Merger, consolidation, purchase or sale of assets, or assumption of liabilities.
563.27 Advertising.
563.33 Directors, officers, and employees.
563.36 Tying restriction exception.
563.39 Employment contracts.
563.41 Transactions with affiliates.
563.43 Loans by savings associations to their executive officers, directors and principal shareholders.
563.47 Pension plans.

Subpart C—Securities and Borrowings

563.74 Mutual capital certificates.
563.76 Offers and sales of securities at an office of a savings association.
563.80 Borrowing limitations.
563.81 Inclusion of subordinated debt securities and mandatorily redeemable preferred stock as supplementary capital.

Subpart D—Registration of Residential Mortgage Loan Originators

563.101 Authority, purpose, and scope.
563.102 Definitions.
563.103 Registration of mortgage loan originators.

§ 563.1

563.104 Policies and procedures.
563.105 Use of unique identifier.
APPENDIX A TO SUBPART D OF PART 563—EXAMPLES OF MORTGAGE LOAN ORIGINATOR ACTIVITIES

Subpart E—Capital Distributions

563.140 What does this subpart cover?
563.141 What is a capital distribution?
563.142 What other definitions apply to this subpart?
563.143 Must I file with OTS?
563.144 How do I file with the OTS?
563.145 May I combine my notice or application with other notices or applications?
563.146 Will the OTS permit my capital distribution?

Subpart F—Financial Management Policies

563.161 Management and financial policies.
563.170 Examinations and audits; appraisals; establishment and maintenance of records.
563.171 Frequency of safety and soundness examination.
563.172 Financial derivatives.
563.176 Interest-rate-risk-management procedures.
563.177 Procedures for monitoring Bank Secrecy Act (BSA) compliance.

Subpart G—Reporting and Bonding

563.180 Suspicious Activity Reports and other reports and statements.
563.190 Bonds for directors, officers, employees, and agents; form of and amount of bonds.
563.191 Bonds for agents.
563.200 Conflicts of interest.
563.201 Corporate opportunity.

Subpart H—Notice of Change of Director or Senior Executive Officer

563.550 What does this subpart do?
563.555 What definitions apply to this subpart?
563.560 Who must give prior notice?
563.565 What procedures govern the filing of my notice?
563.570 What information must I include in my notice?
563.575 What procedures govern OTS review of my notice for completeness?
563.580 What standards and procedures will govern OTS review of the substance of my notice?
563.585 When may a proposed director or senior executive officer begin service?
563.590 When will the OTS waive the prior notice requirement?

AUTHORITY: 12 U.S.C. 375b, 1462, 1462a, 1463, 1464, 1467a, 1468, 1817, 1820, 1828, 1831o, 3806, 5101 et seq.; 31 U.S.C. 5318; 42 U.S.C. 4106.

12 CFR Ch. V (1–1–12 Edition)

SOURCE: 54 FR 49552, Nov. 30, 1989, unless otherwise noted.

Subpart A—Accounts

§ 563.1 Chartering documents.

(a) *Submission for approval.* Any de novo savings association prior to commencing operations shall file its charter and bylaws with the OTS for approval, together with a certification that such charter and bylaws are permissible under all applicable laws, rules and regulations.

(b) *Availability of chartering documents.* Each savings association shall cause a true copy of its charter and bylaws and all amendments thereto to be available to accountholders at all times in each office of the savings association, and shall upon request deliver to any accountholders a copy of such charter and bylaws or amendments thereto.

[57 FR 14344, Apr. 20, 1992]

§ 563.4 [Reserved]

§ 563.5 Securities: Statement of non-insurance.

Every security issued by a savings association must include in its provisions a clear statement that the security is not insured by the Federal Deposit Insurance Corporation.

Subpart B—Operation and Structure

§ 563.22 Merger, consolidation, purchase or sale of assets, or assumption of liabilities.

(a) No savings association may, without application to and approval by the Office:

(1) Combine with any insured depository institution, if the acquiring or resulting institution is to be a savings association; or

(2) Assume liability to pay any deposit made in, any insured depository institution.

(b)(1) No savings association may, without notifying the Office, as provided in paragraph (h)(1) of this section:

(i) Combine with another insured depository institution where a savings

Office of Thrift Supervision, Treasury §563.22

association is not the resulting institution; or

(ii) In the case of a savings association that meets the conditions for expedited treatment under §516.5 of this chapter, convert, directly or indirectly, to a national or state bank.

(2) A savings association that does not meet the conditions for expedited treatment under §516.5 of this chapter may not, directly or indirectly, convert to a national or state bank without prior application to and approval of OTS, as provided in paragraph (h)(2)(ii) of this section.

(c) No savings association may make any transfer (excluding transfers subject to paragraphs (a) or (b) of this section) without notice or application to the Office, as provided in paragraph (h)(2) of this section. For purposes of this paragraph, the term "transfer" means purchases or sales of assets or liabilities in bulk not made in the ordinary course of business including, but not limited to, transfers of assets or savings account liabilities, purchases of assets, and assumptions of deposit accounts or other liabilities, and combinations with a depository institution other than an insured depository institution.

(d)(1) In determining whether to confer approval for a transaction under paragraphs (a), (b)(2), or (c) of this section, the Office shall take into account the following:

(i) The capital level of any resulting savings association;

(ii) The financial and managerial resources of the constituent institutions;

(iii) The future prospects of the constituent institutions;

(iv) The convenience and needs of the communities to be served;

(v) The conformity of the transaction to applicable law, regulation, and supervisory policies;

(vi) Factors relating to the fairness of and disclosure concerning the transaction, including, but not limited to:

(A) *Equitable treatment.* The transaction should be equitable to all concerned—savings account holders, borrowers, creditors and stockholders (if any) of each savings association—giving proper recognition of and protection to their respective legal rights and interests. The transaction will be closely reviewed for fairness where the transaction does not appear to be the result of arms' length bargaining or, in the case of a stock savings association, where controlling stockholders are receiving different consideration from other stockholders. No finder's or similar fee should be paid to any officer, director, or controlling person of a savings association which is a party to the transaction.

(B) *Full disclosure.* The filing should make full disclosure of all written or oral agreements or understandings by which any person or company will receive, directly or indirectly, any money, property, service, release of pledges made, or other thing of value, whether tangible or intangible, in connection with the transaction.

(C) *Compensation to officers.* Compensation, including deferred compensation, to officers, directors and controlling persons of the disappearing savings association by the resulting institution or an affiliate thereof should not be in excess of a reasonable amount, and should be commensurate with their duties and responsibilities. The filing should fully justify the compensation to be paid to such persons. The transaction will be particularly scrutinized where any of such persons is to receive a material increase in compensation above that paid by the disappearing savings association prior to the commencement of negotiations regarding the proposed transaction. An increase in compensation in excess of the greater of 15% or $10,000 gives rise to presumptions of unreasonableness and sale of control. In the case of such an increase, evidence sufficient to rebut such presumptions should be submitted.

(D) *Advisory boards.* Advisory board members should be elected for a term not exceeding one year. No advisory board fees should be paid to salaried officers or employees of the resulting savings association. The filing should describe and justify the duties and responsibilities and any compensation paid to any advisory board of the resulting savings association that consists of officers, directors or controlling persons of the disappearing institution, particularly if the disappearing

§ 563.22

institution experienced significant supervisory problems prior to the transaction. No advisory board fees should exceed the director fees paid by the resulting savings association. Advisory board fees that are in excess of 115 percent of the director fees paid by the disappearing savings association prior to commencement of negotiations regarding the transaction give rise to presumptions of unreasonableness and sale of control unless sufficient evidence to rebut such presumptions is submitted. Rebuttal evidence is not required if:

(1) The advisory board fees do not exceed the fee that advisory board members of the resulting institution receive for each monthly meeting attended or $150, whichever is greater; or

(2) The advisory board fees do not exceed $100 per meeting attended for disappearing savings associations with assets greater than $10,000,000 or $50 per meeting attended for disappearing savings associations with assets of $10,000,000 or less, based on a schedule of 12 meetings per year.

(E) The accounting and tax treatment of the transaction; and

(F) Fees paid and professional services rendered in connection with the transaction.

(2) In conferring approval of a transaction under paragraph (a) of this section, the Office also will consider the competitive impact of the transaction, including whether:

(i) The transaction would result in a monopoly, or would be in furtherance of any monopoly or conspiracy to monopolize or to attempt to monopolize the savings association business in any part of the United States; or

(ii) The effect of the transaction on any section of the country may be substantially to lessen competition, or tend to create a monopoly, or in any other manner would be in restraint of trade, unless the Office finds that the anticompetitive effects of the proposed transaction are clearly outweighed in the public interest by the probable effect of the transaction in meeting the convenience and needs of the communities to be served.

(3) Applications and notices filed under this section shall be upon forms prescribed by the Office.

(4) Applications filed under paragraph (a) of this section must be processed in accordance with the time frames set forth in §§ 516.210 through 516.290 of this chapter, provided that the period for review may be extended only if the Office determines that the applicant has failed to furnish all requested information or that the information submitted is substantially inaccurate, in which case the review period may be extended for up to 30 days.

(e)(1) The following procedures apply to applications described in paragraph (a) of this section, unless OTS finds that it must act immediately to prevent the probable default of one of the depository institutions involved:

(i) The applicant must publish a public notice of the application in accordance with the procedures in subpart B of part 516 of this chapter. In addition to the initial publication, the applicant must also publish on a weekly basis during the public comment period.

(ii) Commenters may submit comments on an application in accordance with the procedures in subpart C of part 516 of this chapter. The public comment period is 30 calendar days after the date of publication of the initial public notice. However, if OTS has advised the Attorney General that an emergency exists requiring expeditious action, the public comment period is 10 calendar days after the date of publication of the initial public notice.

(iii) OTS may arrange a meeting in accordance with the procedures in subpart D of part 516 of this chapter.

(iv) OTS will request the Attorney General, the Office of the Comptroller of the Currency, the Board of Governors of the Federal Reserve System, and the Federal Deposit Insurance Corporation to provide reports on the competitive impacts involved in the transaction.

(v) OTS will immediately notify the Attorney General of the approval of the transaction. The applicant may not consummate the transaction before the date established under 12 U.S.C. 1828(c)(6).

(2) For applications described in § 563.22, certain savings associations described below must provide affected accountholders with a notice of a proposed account transfer and an option of

Office of Thrift Supervision, Treasury § 563.22

retaining the account in the transferring savings association. The notice must allow affected accountholders at least 30 days to consider whether to retain their accounts in the transferring savings association. The following savings associations must provide the notices:

(i) A savings association transferring account liabilities to an institution the accounts of which are not insured by the Deposit Insurance Fund or the National Credit Union Share Insurance Fund; and

(ii) Any mutual savings association transferring account liabilities to a stock form depository institution.

(f) *Automatic approvals by the Office.* Applications filed pursuant to paragraph (a) of this section shall be deemed to be approved automatically by the Office 30 calendar days after the Office sends written notice to the applicant that the application is complete, unless:

(1) The acquiring savings association does not meet the criteria for expedited treatment under § 516.5 of this chapter;

(2) The OTS recommends the imposition of non-standard conditions prior to approving the application;

(3) The OTS suspends the applicable processing time frames under § 516.190 of this chapter;

(4) The OTS raises objections to the transaction;

(5) The resulting savings association would be one of the 3 largest depository institutions competing in the relevant geographic area where before the transaction there were 5 or fewer depository institutions, the resulting savings association would have 25 percent or more of the total deposits held by depository institutions in the relevant geographic area, and the share of total deposits would have increased by 5 percent or more;

(6) The resulting savings association would be one of the 2 largest depository institutions competing in the relevant geographic area where before the transaction there were 6 to 11 depository institutions the resulting savings association would have 30 percent or more of the total deposits held by depositing institutions in the relevant geographic area, and the share of total deposits would have increased by 10 percent or more;

(7) The resulting savings association would be one of the 2 largest depository institutions competing in the relevant geographic area where before the transaction there were 12 or more depository institutions, the resulting savings association would have 35 percent or more of the total deposits held by the depository institutions in the relevant geographic area, and the share of total deposits would have increased by 15 percent or more;

(8) The Herfindahl-Hirschman Index (HHI) in the relevant geographic area was more than 1800 before the transaction, and the increase in the HHI used by the transaction would be 50 or more;

(9) In a transaction involving potential competition, the OTS determines that the acquiring savings association is one of three or fewer potential entrants into the relevant geographic area;

(10) The acquiring savings association has assets of $1 billion or more and proposes to acquire assets of $1 billion or more;

(11) The savings association that will be the resulting savings association in the transaction has a composite Community Reinvestment Act rating of less than satisfactory, or is otherwise seriously deficient with respect to the Office's nondiscrimination regulations and the deficiencies have not been resolved to the satisfaction of the OTS;

(12) The transaction involves any supervisory or assistance agreement with the Office, the Resolution Trust Corporation, or the Federal Deposit Insurance Corporation;

(13) The transaction is part of a conversion under part 563b of this chapter;

(14) The transaction raises a significant issue of law or policy; or

(15) The transaction is opposed by any constituent institution or contested by a competing acquiror.

(g) *Definitions.* (1) The terms used in this section shall have the same meaning as set forth in § 552.13(b) of this chapter.

(2) *Insured depository institution. Insured depository institution* has the same meaning as defined in section 3(c)(2) of the Federal Deposit Insurance Act.

§ 563.27

(3) With regard to paragraph (f) of this section, the term *relevant geographic area* is used as a substitute for *relevant geographic market*, which means the area within which the competitive effects of a merger or other combination may be evaluated. The relevant geographic area shall be delineated as a county or similar political subdivision, an area smaller than a county, or an aggregation of counties within which the merging or combining insured depository institutions compete. In addition, the Office may consider commuting patterns, newspaper and other advertising activities, or other factors as the Office deems relevant.

(h) *Special requirements and procedures for transactions under paragraphs (b) and (c) of this section*—(1) *Certain transactions with no surviving savings association.* The Office must be notified of any transaction under paragraph (b)(1) of this section. Such notification must be submitted to the OTS at least 30 days prior to the effective date of the transaction, but not later than the date on which an application relating to the proposed transaction is filed with the primary regulator of the resulting institution; the Office may, upon request or on its own initiative, shorten the 30-day prior notification requirement. Notifications under this paragraph must demonstrate compliance with applicable stockholder or accountholder approval requirements. Where the savings association submitting the notification maintains a liquidation account established pursuant to part 563b of this chapter, the notification must state that the resulting institution will assume such liquidation account.

The notification may be in the form of either a letter describing the material features of the transaction or a copy of a filing made with another Federal or state regulatory agency seeking approval from that agency for the transaction under the Bank Merger Act or other applicable statute. If the action contemplated by the notification is not completed within one year after the Office's receipt of the notification, a new notification must be submitted to the Office.

(2) *Other transfer transactions*—(i) *Expedited treatment.* A notice in conformity with § 516.25(a) of this chapter may be submitted to OTS under § 516.40 of this chapter for any transaction under paragraph (c) of this section, provided all constituent savings associations meet the conditions for expedited treatment under § 516.5 of this chapter. Notices submitted under this paragraph must be deemed approved automatically by OTS 30 days after receipt, unless OTS advises the applicant in writing prior to the expiration of such period that the proposed transaction may not be consummated without OTS's approval of an application under paragraphs (h)(2)(ii) or (h)(2)(iii) of this section.

(ii) *Standard treatment.* An application in conformity with § 516.25(b) of this chapter and paragraph (d) of this section must be submitted to OTS under § 516.40 by each savings association participating in a transaction under paragraph (b)(2) or (c) of this section, where any constituent savings association does not meet the conditions for expedited treatment under § 516.5 of this chapter. Applications under this paragraph must be processed in accordance with the procedures in part 516, subparts A and E of this chapter.

[54 FR 49552, Nov. 30, 1989, as amended at 55 FR 13514, Apr. 11, 1990; 57 FR 14344, Apr. 20, 1992; 59 FR 44624, Aug. 30, 1994; 59 FR 66159, Dec. 23, 1994; 62 FR 64146, Dec. 4, 1997; 66 FR 13007, Mar. 2, 2001; 69 FR 68250, Nov. 24, 2004; 71 FR 19811, Apr. 18, 2006]

§ 563.27 Advertising.

No savings association shall use advertising (which includes print or broadcast media, displays or signs, stationery, and all other promotional materials), or make any representation which is inaccurate in any particular or which in any way misrepresents its services, contracts, investments, or financial condition.

[54 FR 49552, Nov. 30, 1989, as amended at 58 FR 4313, Jan. 14, 1993]

§ 563.33 Directors, officers, and employees.

(a) *Directors*—(1) *Requirements.* The composition of the board of directors of a savings association must be in accordance with the following requirements:

(i) A majority of the directors must not be salaried officers or employees of the savings association or of any subsidiary or (except in the case of a savings association having 80% or more of any class of voting shares owned by a holding company) any holding company affiliate thereof.

(ii) Not more than two of the directors may be members of the same immediate family.

(iii) Not more than one director may be an attorney with a particular law firm.

(2) *Prospective application.* In the case of an association whose board of directors does not conform with any requirement set forth in paragraph (a)(1) of this section as of October 5, 1983, this paragraph (a) shall not prohibit the uninterrupted service, including re-election and re-appointment, of any person serving on the board of directors at that date.

(b) [Reserved]

[54 FR 49552, Nov. 30, 1989, as amended at 58 FR 4313, Jan. 14, 1993]

§ 563.36 Tying restriction exception.

(a) *Safe harbor for combined-balance discounts.* A savings and loan holding company or any savings association or any affiliate of either may vary the consideration for any product or package of products based on a customer's maintaining a combined minimum balance in certain products specified by the company varying the consideration (eligible products), if:

(1) That company (if it is a savings association) or a savings association affiliate of that company (if it is not a savings association) offers deposits, and all such deposits are eligible products; and

(2) Balances in deposits count at least as much as non-deposit products toward the minimum balance.

(b) *Limitations on exception.* This exception shall terminate upon a finding by the OTS that the arrangement is resulting in anti-competitive practices. The eligibility of a savings and loan holding company or savings association or affiliate of either to operate under this exception shall terminate upon a finding by the OTS that its exercise of this authority is resulting in anti-competitive practices.

[61 FR 60184, Nov. 27, 1996]

§ 563.39 Employment contracts.

(a) *General.* A savings association may enter into an employment contract with its officers and other employees only in accordance with the requirements of this section. All employment contracts shall be in writing and shall be approved specifically by an association's board of directors. An association shall not enter into an employment contract with any of its officers or other employees if such contract would constitute an unsafe or unsound practice. The making of such an employment contract would be an unsafe or unsound practice if such contract could lead to material financial loss or damage to the association or could interfere materially with the exercise by the members of its board of directors of their duty or discretion provided by law, charter, bylaw or regulation as to the employment or termination of employment of an officer or employee of the association. This may occur, depending upon the circumstances of the case, where an employment contract provides for an excessive term.

(b) *Required provisions.* Each employment contract shall provide that:

(1) The association's board of directors may terminate the officer or employee's employment at any time, but any termination by the association's board of directors other than termination for cause, shall not prejudice the officer or employee's right to compensation or other benefits under the contract. The officer or employee shall have no right to receive compensation or other benefits for any period after termination for cause. Termination for cause shall include termination because of the officer or employee's personal dishonesty, incompetence, willful misconduct, breach of fiduciary duty involving personal profit, intentional failure to perform stated duties, willful violation of any law, rule, or regulation (other than traffic violations or similar offenses) or final cease-and-desist order, or material breach of any provision of the contract.

(2) If the officer or employee is suspended and/or temporarily prohibited from participating in the conduct of the association's affairs by a notice served under section 8 (e)(3) or (g)(1) of

§ 563.41

Federal Deposit Insurance Act (12 U.S.C. 1818 (e)(3) and (g)(1)) the association's obligations under the contract shall be suspended as of the date of service unless stayed by appropriate proceedings. If the charges in the notice are dismissed, the association may in its discretion (i) pay the officer or employee all or part of the compensation withheld while its contract obligations were suspended, and (ii) reinstate (in whole or in part) any of its obligations which were suspended.

(3) If the officer or employee is removed and/or permanently prohibited from participating in the conduct of the association's affairs by an order issued under section 8 (e)(4) or (g)(1) of the Federal Deposit Insurance Act (12 U.S.C. 1818 (e)(4) or (g)(1)), all obligations of the association under the contract shall terminate as of the effective date of the order, but vested rights of the contracting parties shall not be affected.

(4) If the savings association is in default (as defined in section 3(x)(1) of the Federal Deposit Insurance Act), all obligations under the contract shall terminate as of the date of default, but this paragraph (b)(4) shall not affect any vested rights of the contracting parties: *Provided,* that this paragraph (b)(4) need not be included in an employment contract if prior written approval is secured from the Director or his or her designee.

(5) All obligations under the contract shall be terminated, except to the extent determined that continuation of the contract is necessary for the continued operation of the association

(i) By the Director or his or her designee, at the time the Federal Deposit Insurance Corporation or Resolution Trust Corporation enters into an agreement to provide assistance to or on behalf of the association under the authority contained in 13(c) of the Federal Deposit Insurance Act; or

12 CFR Ch. V (1–1–12 Edition)

(ii) By the Director or his or her designee, at the time the Director or his or her designee approves a supervisory merger to resolve problems related to operation of the association or when the association is determined by the Director to be in an unsafe or unsound condition.

Any rights of the parties that have already vested, however, shall not be affected by such action.

§ 563.41 Transactions with affiliates.

(a) *Scope.* (1) This section implements section 11(a) of the Home Owners' Loan Act (12 U.S.C. 1468(a)). Section 11(a) applies sections 23A and 23B of the FRA (12 U.S.C. 371c and 371c1) to every savings association in the same manner and to the same extent as if the association were a member bank; prohibits certain types of transactions with affiliates; and authorizes OTS to impose additional restrictions on a savings association's transactions with affiliates.

(2) For the purposes of this section, "savings association" is defined at section 3 of the Federal Deposit Insurance Act (12 U.S.C. 1813), and also includes any savings bank or any cooperative bank that is a savings association under 12 U.S.C. 1467a(l). A non-affiliate subsidiary of a savings association as described in paragraph (b)(11) of this section is treated as part of the savings association.

(b) *Sections 23A and 23B of the FRA/ Regulation W.* A savings association must comply with sections 23A and 23B of the Federal Reserve Act and the implementing regulations at 12 CFR part 223 (Regulation W) as if it were a member bank, except as described in the following chart. In addition, a savings association should read all references to "the Board" or "appropriate federal banking agency" to refer only to "OTS," except for references at 12 CFR 223.2(a)(9)(iv), 223.3(h), 223.3(z), 223.14(c)(4), 223.43, and 223.55.

Provision of Regulation W	Application
(1) 12 CFR 223.1—Authority, purpose, and scope	Does not apply. Section 563.41(a) addresses these matters.
(2) 12 CFR 223.2(a)(8)—"Affiliate" includes a financial subsidiary.	Does not apply. Savings association subsidiaries do not meet the statutory definition of financial subsidiary.
(3) 12 CFR 223.2(a)(12)—Determination that "affiliate" includes other types of companies.	Read to include the following statement: "Affiliate also includes any company that OTS determines, by order or regulation, to present a risk to the safety and soundness of the savings association."

206

Office of Thrift Supervision, Treasury § 563.41

Provision of Regulation W	Application
(4) 12 CFR 223.2(b)(1)(ii)—"Affiliate" includes a subsidiary that is a financial subsidiary.	Does not apply. Savings association subsidiaries do not meet the statutory definition of financial subsidiary.
(5) 12 CFR 223.3(d)—Definition of "capital stock and surplus."	Does not apply. Capital stock and surplus means "unimpaired capital and unimpaired surplus," as defined in 12 CFR 560.93(b)(11).
(6) 12 CFR 223.3(h)(1)—Section 23A covered transactions include an extension of credit to the affiliate.	Read to incorporate § 563.41(c)(1), which prohibits loans or extensions of credit to an affiliate, unless the affiliate is engaged only in the activities described at 12 U.S.C. 1467a(c)(2)(F)(i), as defined in § 584.2–2 of this chapter.
(7) 12 CFR 223.3(h)(2)—Section 23A covered transactions include a purchase of or investment in securities issued by an affiliate.	Read to incorporate § 563.41(c)(2), which prohibits purchases and investments in securities issued by an affiliate, other than with respect to shares of a subsidiary.
(8) 12 CFR 223.3(k)—Definition of "depository institution."	Read to include the following statement: "For the purposes of this definition, a non-affiliate subsidiary of a savings association is treated as part of the depository institution."
(9) 12 CFR 223.3(p)—Definition of "financial subsidiary."	Does not apply. Savings association subsidiaries do not meet the statutory definition of financial subsidiary.
(10) 12 CFR 223.3(w)—Definition of "member bank."	Read to include the following statement: "Member bank also includes a savings association. For purposes of this definition, a non-affiliate subsidiary of a savings association is treated as part of the savings association."
(11) 12 CFR 223.3(aa)—Definition of "operating subsidiary."	Does not apply. Other OTS regulations include a conflicting definition of this same term. Instead, OTS uses the phrase "non-affiliate subsidiary." A non-affiliate subsidiary is a subsidiary of a savings association other than a subsidiary described at 12 CFR 223.2(b)(1)(i), (iii) through (v).
(12) 12 CFR 223.3(ii)—Definition of "subsidiary."	Read to include the following statement: "A subsidiary of a savings association means a company that is controlled by the savings association."
(13) 12 CFR 223.3(kk)—Definition of "well capitalized."	Read to include the following statement: "For a savings and loan holding company, however, well-capitalized means that the holding company significantly exceeds OTS expectations for the amount of capital needed to adequately support the holding company's risk profile, as determined by OTS on a case-by-case basis."
(14) 12 CFR 223.31—Application of section 23A to an acquisition of an affiliate that becomes an operating subsidiary.	Read to refer to "a non-affiliate subsidiary" instead of "operating subsidiary."
(15) 12 CFR 223.32—Rules that apply to financial subsidiaries of a bank.	Does not apply. Savings association subsidiaries do not meet the statutory definition of financial subsidiary.
(16) 12 CFR 223.42(f)(2)—Exemption for purchasing certain marketable securities.	Read to refer to "Thrift Financial Report" instead of "Call Report." References to "state member bank" are unchanged.
(17) 12 CFR 223.42(g)(2)—Exemption for purchasing municipal securities.	Read to refer to "Thrift Financial Report" instead of "Call Report." References to "state member bank" are unchanged.
(18) 12 CFR 223.61—Application of sections 23A and 23B to U.S. branches and agencies of foreign banks.	Does not apply to savings associations or their subsidiaries.

(c) *Additional prohibitions and restrictions.* A savings association must comply with the additional prohibitions and restrictions in this paragraph. Except as described in paragraph (b) of this section, the definitions in 12 CFR part 223 apply to these additional prohibitions and restrictions.

(1) *Loans and extensions of credit.* (i) A savings association may not make a loan or other extension of credit to an affiliate, unless the affiliate is solely engaged in the activities described at 12 U.S.C. 1467a(c)(2)(F)(i), as defined in § 584.2–2 of this chapter. A loan or extension of credit to a third party is not prohibited merely because proceeds of the transaction are used for the benefit of, or are transferred to, an affiliate.

(ii) If OTS determines that a particular transaction is, in substance, a loan or extension of credit to an affiliate that is engaged in activities other than those described at 12 U.S.C. 1467a(c)(2)(F)(i), as defined in § 584.2–2 of this chapter, or OTS has other supervisory concerns concerning the transaction, OTS may inform the savings association that the transaction is prohibited under this paragraph (c)(1), and require the savings association to divest the loan, unwind the transaction, or take other appropriate action.

(2) *Purchases or investments in securities.* A savings association may not purchase or invest in securities issued by any affiliate other than with respect to shares of a subsidiary. For the purposes

§ 563.43

of this paragraph (c)(2), subsidiary includes a bank and a savings association.

(3) *Recordkeeping.* A savings association must make and retain records that reflect, in reasonable detail, all transactions between the savings association and its affiliates and any other person to the extent that the proceeds of a transaction are used for the benefit of, or transferred to, an affiliate. At a minimum, these records must:

(i) Identify the affiliate;

(ii) Specify the dollar amount of the transaction and demonstrate that this amount is within the quantitative limits in 12 CFR 223.11 and 223.12, or that the transaction is not subject to those limits;

(iii) Indicate whether the transaction involves a low-quality asset;

(iv) Identify the type and amount of any collateral involved in the transaction and demonstrate that this collateral meets the requirements in 12 CFR 223.14 or that the transaction is not subject to those requirements;

(v) Demonstrate that the transaction complies with 12 CFR part 223, subpart F or that the transaction is not subject to those requirements;

(vi) Demonstrate that all loans and extensions of credit to affiliates comply with paragraph (c)(1) of this section; and

(vii) Be readily accessible for examination and supervisory purposes.

(4) *Notice requirement.* (i) OTS may require a savings association to notify the agency before the savings association may engage in a transaction with an affiliate or a subsidiary (other than exempt transactions under 12 CFR part 223). OTS may impose this requirement if:

(A) The savings association is in troubled condition as defined at § 563.555 of this part;

(B) The savings association does not meet its regulatory capital requirements;

(C) The savings association commenced *de novo* operations within the past two years;

(D) OTS approved an application or notice under 12 CFR part 574 involving the savings association or its holding company within the past two years;

(E) The savings association entered into a consent to merge or a supervisory agreement within the past two years; or

(F) OTS or another banking agency initiated a formal enforcement proceeding against the savings association and the proceeding is pending.

(ii) OTS must notify the savings association in writing that it has imposed the notice requirement and must identify the circumstance listed in paragraph (c)(4)(i) of this section that supports the imposition of the notice requirement.

(iii) If OTS has imposed the notice requirement under this paragraph, a savings association must provide a written notice to OTS at least 30 days before the savings association may enter into a transaction with an affiliate or a subsidiary. The written notice must include a full description of the transaction. If OTS does not object during the 30-day period, the savings association may proceed with the proposed transaction.

[68 FR 57797, Oct. 7, 2003, as amended at 68 FR 75110, Dec. 30, 2003]

§ 563.43 Loans by savings associations to their executive officers, directors and principal shareholders.

Pursuant to 12 U.S.C. 1463(a) and 1468, a savings association, its subsidiaries and its insiders (as defined) shall be subject to the restrictions contained in the Federal Reserve Board's Regulation O (12 CFR part 215), in the same manner and to the same extent as if the association were a bank and a member bank of the Federal Reserve System, except that:

(a) Such provisions shall be administered and enforced by the OTS;

(b) References to the term "bank holding company" shall be deemed to refer to "savings and loan holding company";

(c) References to "report of condition filed under 12 U.S.C. 1817(a)(3)" shall be deemed to refer to "Thrift Financial Report";

(d) The term *subsidiary* includes a savings association that is controlled by a company (including for this purpose an insured depository institution) that is a savings and loan holding company. A company has control over a saving association if it: directly or indirectly, or acting through one or more other persons owns, controls, or has the power to vote 25 percent or more of any class of voting securities; or would be deemed to control the company under § 574.4(a) of this chapter or presumed to control the company under § 574.4(b) of this chapter, and in the latter case, control has not been rebutted. Notwithstanding any other provision of this section, no company shall be deemed to own or control another by virtue of its ownership or control of shares in a fiduciary capacity. When used to refer to a subsidiary of a savings association, the term *subsidiary* means a "subsidiary" that is controlled by the savings association within the meaning of 12 CFR part 574 of this chapter.

(e) References to the Reserve Bank or the Comptroller shall be deemed to include the Director of OTS; and

(f) References to the term "unimpaired capital and unimpaired surplus" shall be deemed to refer to "unimpaired capital and unimpaired surplus" as defined at § 560.93(b)(11) of this part.

[57 FR 45980, Oct. 6, 1992, as amended at 59 FR 53571, Oct. 25, 1994; 60 FR 66869, Dec. 27, 1995; 67 FR 77918, Dec. 20, 2002; 68 FR 57798, Oct. 7, 2003; 69 FR 76602, Dec. 22, 2004; 73 FR 18, Jan. 2, 2008]

§ 563.47 Pension plans.

(a) *General.* No savings association or service corporation thereof shall sponsor an employee pension plan which, because of unreasonable costs or any other reason, could lead to material financial loss or damage to the sponsor. For purposes of this section, an employee pension plan is defined in section 3(2) of the Employee Retirement Income Security Act of 1974, as amended. The prospective obligation or liability of a plan sponsor to each plan participant shall be stated in or determinable from the plan, and, for a defined benefit plan, shall also be based upon an actuarial estimate of future experience under the plan.

(b) *Funding.* Actuarial cost methods permitted under the Employee Retirement Income Security Act of 1974 and the Internal Revenue Code of 1954, as amended, shall be used to determine plan funding.

(c) *Plan amendment.* A plan may be amended to provide reasonable annual cost-of-living increases to retired participants: *Provided*, That

(1) Any such increase shall be for a period and amount determined by the sponsor's board of directors, but in no event shall it exceed the annual increase in the Consumer Price Index published by the Bureau of Labor Statistics; and

(2) No increase shall be granted unless (i) anticipated charges to net income for future periods have first been found by such board of directors to be reasonable and are documented by appropriate resolution and supporting analysis; and (ii) the increase will not reduce the association's regulatory capital below its regulatory capital requirement.

(d) *Termination.* The plan shall permit the sponsor's board of directors and its successors to terminate such plan. Notice of intent to terminate shall be filed with the OTS at least 60 days prior to the proposed termination date.

(e) *Records.* Each savings association or service corporation maintaining a plan not subject to recordkeeping and reporting requirements of the Employee Retirement Income Security Act of 1974, and the Internal Revenue Code of 1954, as amended, shall establish and maintain records containing the following:

(1) Plan description;

(2) Schedule of participants and beneficiaries;

(3) Schedule of participants and beneficiaries' rights and obligations;

(4) Plan's financial statements; and

(5) Except for defined contribution plans, an opinion signed by an enrolled actuary (as defined by the Employee Retirement Income Security Act of 1974) affirming that actuarial assumptions in the aggregate are reasonable, take into account the plan's experience and expectations, and represent the actuary's best estimate of the plan's projected experiences.

[59 FR 66159, Dec. 23, 1994]

Subpart C—Securities and Borrowings

§ 563.74 Mutual capital certificates.

(a) *General.* No savings association that is in the mutual form shall issue mutual capital certificates pursuant to this section or amend the terms of such certificates unless it has obtained written approval of the Office. No approval shall be granted unless the proposed issuance of the mutual capital certificates and the form and manner of filing of the application are in accordance with the provisions of this section.

(b) *Eligibility Requirements.* The Office will consider and process an application for approval of the issuance of mutual capital certificates pursuant to this section only if the issuance is authorized by applicable law and regulation and is not inconsistent with any provision of the applicant's charter, constitution or bylaws.

(c) *Application form; supporting information.* An application for approval of the issuance of mutual capital certificates pursuant to this section shall be in the form prescribed by the Office. Such application and instructions may be obtained from the OTS. Information and exhibits shall be furnished in support of the application in accordance with such instructions, setting forth all of the terms and provisions relating to the proposed issue and showing that all of the requirements of this section have been or will be met.

(d) *Charter amendment.* No application for approval of the issuance of mutual capital certificates pursuant to this section may be filed unless the amendment to the mutual association's charter, constitution or bylaws or other actions conferring such authority shall have been approved pursuant to the procedures and requirements set forth in the mutual association's charter, constitution or bylaws, or as may otherwise be required by applicable law.

(e) *Filing requirements.* The application for issuance of mutual capital certificates shall be publicly filed with the OTS.

(f) *Supervisory objection.* No application or approval of the issuance of mutual capital certificates pursuant to this section shall be approved if, in the opinion of the Office, the policies, condition, or operation of the applicant afford a basis for supervisory objection to the application.

(g) *Limitation on offering period.* Following the date of the approval of the application by the Office, the association shall have an offering period of not more than one year in which to complete the sale of the mutual capital certificates issued pursuant to this section. The Office may in its discretion extend such offering period if a written request showing good cause for such extension is filed with it not later than 30 days before the expiration of such offering period or any extension thereof.

(h) *Reports.* Within 30 days after completion of the sale of mutual capital certificates issued pursuant to this section, the association shall transmit to the OTS a written report stating the total dollar amount of securities sold, and the amount of net proceeds received by the association, and within 90 days it shall transmit a written report stating the number of purchasers.

(i) *Requirements as to mutual capital certificates*—(1) *Form of certificate.* Each mutual capital certificate and any governing agreement evidencing a mutual capital certificate issued by an association pursuant to this section:

(i) Shall bear on its face, in bold-face type, the following legend: "This security is not a savings account or a deposit and it is not insured by the United States or any agency or fund of the United States"; and

(ii) Shall clearly state that the certificate is subject to the requirements of § 563.74(i)(2).

(2) *Legal requirements.* Mutual capital certificates issued pursuant to this section shall:

(i) Be subordinate to all claims against the association having the same priority as savings accounts, savings certificates, debt obligations or any higher priority;

(ii) Not be eligible for use as collateral for any loan made by the issuing association;

(iii) Constitute a claim in liquidation not exceeding the face value plus accrued dividends of the certificates, on the general reserves, surplus and undivided profits of the association remaining after the payment in full of all savings accounts, savings certificates and debt obligations;

(iv) Be entitled to the payment of dividends, which may be fixed, variable, participating, or cumulative, or any combination thereof, only if, when and as declared by the association's board of directors out of funds legally available for that purpose, provided that no dividend may be declared or paid without the approval of the Office if such payment would cause the association to fail to meet its regulatory capital requirements under part 567 of this chapter, and provided further that no dividend may be paid if such payment would constitute a violation of 12 U.S.C. 1828(b);

(v) Not be redeemable, except: (A) Where the dollar weighted average term of each issue of mutual capital certificates to be redeemed is seven years or more and redemption is to be made pursuant to a redemption schedule; (B) in the event of a merger, consolidation or reorganization approved by the Office; or (C) where the funds for redemption are raised by the issuance of mutual capital certificates approved pursuant to this section, or in conjunction with the issuance of capital stock pursuant to part 563b of this chapter: *Provided*, that mandatory redemption shall not be required; that mutual capital certificates shall not be redeemable on the demand or at the option of the holder; and that mutual capital certificates shall not receive, benefit from, be credited with or otherwise be entitled to or due payments in or for redemption if such payments would cause the association to fail to meet its regulatory capital requirements under part 567 of this chapter; *And Provided further*, for the purposes of this paragraph (i)(2)(v), the "dollar weighted average term" of an issue of mutual capital certificates shall be the sum of the products calculated for each year that the mutual capital certificates in the issue have been redeemed or are scheduled to be redeemed. Each product shall be calculated by multiplying the number of years of each mutual capital certificate of a given term by a fraction, the numerator of which shall be the total dollar amount of each mutual capital certificate in the issue with the same term and the denominator of which shall be the total dollar amount of mutual capital certificates in the entire issue;

(vi) Not have preemptive rights;

(vii) Not have voting rights, except that an association may provide for voting rights if:

(A) The savings association fails to pay dividends for a minimum of three consecutive dividend periods, and then the holders of the class or classes of mutual capital certificates granted such voting rights, and voting as a single class, with one vote for each outstanding certificate, may elect by a majority vote a maximum of one-third of the association's board of directors, the directors so elected to serve until the next annual meeting of the association succeeding the payment of all current and past dividends;

(B) Any merger, consolidation, or reorganization (except in a supervisory case) is sought to be authorized, where the issuing association is not the survivor, provided that the regulatory capital of the resulting association available for payment of any class of mutual capital certificate on liquidation is less than the regulatory capital available for such class prior to the merger, consolidation, or reorganization;

(C) Action is sought to be authorized which would create any class of mutual capital certificates having a preference or priority over an outstanding class or classes of mutual capital certificates;

(D) Any action is sought to be authorized which would adversely change the specific terms of any class of mutual capital certificates;

(E) Action is sought to be authorized which would increase the number of a class of mutual capital certificates, or the number of a class of mutual capital certificates ranking prior to or on parity with another class of mutual capital certificates; or

(F) Action is sought which would authorize the issuance of an additional class or classes of mutual capital certificates without the association having met specific financial standards;

(viii) Not constitute an obligation of the association and shall confer no

§ 563.76   12 CFR Ch. V (1-1-12 Edition)

rights which would give rise to any claim of or action for default;

(ix) Not be convertible into any account, security, or interest, except that mutual capital certificates may be surrendered in exchange for preferred stock issued in connection with the conversion of the issuing savings association to the stock form pursuant to part 563b of this chapter, provided that the preferred stock shall have substantially the same voting rights, designations, preferences and relative, participating optional, or other special rights, and qualifications, limitations, and restrictions, as the mutual capital certificates exchanged for the preferred stock.

(x) Provide for charging of losses after the exhaustion of all other items in the regulatory capital account.

[54 FR 49552, Nov. 30, 1989, as amended at 55 FR 13515, Apr. 11, 1990; 57 FR 14345, Apr. 20, 1992; 59 FR 66159, Dec. 23, 1994; 72 FR 69438, Dec. 7, 2007]

§ 563.76 Offers and sales of securities at an office of a savings association.

(a) A saving association may not offer or sell debt or equity securities issued by the association or an affiliate of the association at an office of the association; except that equity securities issued by the association or an affiliate in connection with the association's conversion from the mutual to stock form of organization in a conversion approved pursuant to part 563b of this chapter may be offered and sold at the association's offices: *Provided,* That:

(1) The Regional Director does not object on supervisory grounds that the offer and sale of the securities at the offices of the association;

(2) No commissions, bonuses, or comparable payments are paid to any employee of the savings association or its affiliates or to any other person in connection with the sale of securities at an office of a savings association; except that compensation and commissions consistent with industry norms may be paid to securities personnel of registered broker-dealers;

(3) No offers or sales are made by tellers or at the teller counter, or by comparable persons at comparable locations;

(4) Sales activity is conducted in a segregated or separately identifiable area of the savings association's offices apart from the area accessible to the general public for the purposes of making or withdrawing deposits;

(5) Offers and sales are made only by regular, full-time employees of the savings association or by securities personnel who are subject to supervision by a registered broker-dealer;

(6) An acknowledgment, in the form set forth in paragraph (c) of this section, is signed by any customer to whom the security is sold in the savings association's offices prior to the sale of any such securities;

(7) A legend that the security is not a deposit or account and is not federally insured or guaranteed appears conspicuously on the security and in all offering documents and advertisements for the securities; the legend must state in bold or other prominent type at least as large as other textual type in the document that "This security is not a deposit or account and is not federally insured or guaranteed"; and

(8) The savings association will be in compliance with its current capital requirements upon completion of the conversion stock offering.

(b) Securities sales practices, advertisements, and other sales literature used in connection with offers and sales of securities by savings associations shall be subject to § 563g.10 of this chapter.

(c) Offers and sales of securities of a savings association or its affiliates in any office of the savings association must use a one-page, unambiguous, certification in substantially the following form:

FORM OF CERTIFICATION

I ACKNOWLEDGE THAT THIS SECURITY IS NOT A DEPOSIT OR ACCOUNT AND IS NOT FEDERALLY INSURED, AND IS NOT GUARANTEED BY [*insert name of savings association*] OR BY THE FEDERAL GOVERNMENT.

If anyone asserts that this security is federally insured or guaranteed, or is as safe as an insured deposit, I should call the Office of Thrift Supervision Regional Director [insert Regional Director's name and telephone number with area code].

I further certify that, before purchasing the [*description of security being offered*] of

212

Office of Thrift Supervision, Treasury § 563.81

[*name of issuer, name of savings association and affiliation to issuer (if different)*], I received an offering circular.

The offering circular that I received contains disclosure concerning the nature of the security being offered and describes the risks involved in the investment, including:

[*List briefly the principal risks involved and cross reference certain specified pages of the offering circular where a more complete description of the risks is made.*]

Signature: _____
Date: _____

(d) For purposes of this section, an "office" of an association means any premises used by the association that are identified to the public through advertising or signage using the association's name, trade name, or logo.

[57 FR 46088, Oct. 7, 1992]

§ 563.80 Borrowing limitations.

(a) *General.* Except as the Office otherwise may permit by advice in writing, a savings association may borrow only in accordance with the provisions of this section.

(b) *Amount of borrowing.* A savings association may borrow up to the amount authorized by the laws under which the savings association operates.

(c) *Security.* An association may give security for borrowings subject to any requirements imposed by the Office or the FDIC regarding notice of default on borrowings and any FDIC right of first refusal to purchase collateral.

(d) *Required statement for all securities evidencing outside borrowings.* Each security shall bear on its face, in a prominent place, the following legend:

This security is not a savings account or a deposit and it is not insured by the United States or any agency or fund of the United States.

(e) *Filing requirements for outside borrowings with maturities in excess of one year.* (1) Unless the savings association meets its capital requirement under part 567 of this chapter, it shall, at least ten business days prior to issuance, file with the Regional Director or his or her designee a notice of intent to issue securities evidencing such borrowings. Such notice shall contain a summary of the items of the security, including:

(i) Principal amount of the securities;

(ii) Anticipated interest rate range and price range at which the securities are to be sold;

(iii) Minimum denomination;

(iv) Stated and average effective maturity;

(v) Mandatory and optional prepayment provisions;

(vi) Description, amount, and maintenance of collateral if any;

(vii) Trustee provisions if any;

(viii) Events of default and remedies of default;

(ix) Any provisions which restrict, conditionally or otherwise, the operations of the association.

(2) The OTS shall have 10 business days after receipt of such filing to object to the issuance of such securities. The OTS shall object if the terms or covenants of the proposed issue place unreasonable burdens on, or control over, the operations of the association. If no objection is taken, the savings association shall have 120 calendar days within which to issue such securities.

(f) *Note accounts.* For purposes of this section, note accounts are not borrowings.

[54 FR 49552, Nov. 30, 1989, as amended at 55 FR 7300, Mar. 1, 1990; 55 FR 13515, Apr. 11, 1990; 57 FR 14345, Apr. 20, 1992; 57 FR 33438, July 29, 1992]

§ 563.81 Inclusion of subordinated debt securities and mandatorily redeemable preferred stock as supplementary capital.

(a) *Scope.* A savings association must comply with this section in order to include subordinated debt securities or mandatorily redeemable preferred stock ("covered securities") in supplementary capital (tier 2 capital) under part 567 of this chapter. If a savings association does not include covered securities in supplementary capital, it is not required to comply with this section.

(b) *Application and notice procedures.* (1) A savings association must file an application or notice under 12 CFR part 516, subpart A seeking OTS approval of, or non-objection to, the inclusion of covered securities in supplementary capital. The savings association may file its application or notice before or after it issues covered securities, but may not include covered securities in supplementary capital until OTS approves the application or does not object to the notice.

(2) A savings association must also comply with the securities offering rules at 12 CFR part 563g by filing an offering circular for a proposed issuance of covered securities, unless the offering qualifies for an exemption under that part.

(c) *Securities requirements.* To be included in supplementary capital, covered securities must meet the following requirements:

(1) *Form.* (i) Each certificate evidencing a covered security must:

(A) Bear the following legend on its face, in bold type: "This security is *not* a savings account or deposit and it is *not* insured by the United States or any agency or fund of the United States;"

(B) State that the security is subordinated on liquidation, as to principal, interest, and premium, to all claims against the savings association that have the same priority as savings accounts or a higher priority;

(C) State that the security is not secured by the savings association's assets or the assets of any affiliate of the savings association, as defined in 12 CFR 583.2;

(D) State that the security is not eligible collateral for a loan by the savings association;

(E) State the prohibition on the payment of dividends or interest at 12 U.S.C. 1828(b) and, in the case of subordinated debt securities, state the prohibition on the payment of principal and interest at 12 U.S.C. 1831o(h);

(F) For subordinated debt securities, state or refer to a document stating the terms under which the savings association may prepay the obligation; and

(G) State or refer to a document stating that the savings association must obtain OTS approval before the voluntarily prepayment of principal on subordinated debt securities, the acceleration of payment of principal on subordinated debt securities, or the voluntarily redemption of mandatorily redeemable preferred stock (other than scheduled redemptions), if the savings association is undercapitalized, significantly undercapitalized, or critically undercapitalized as described in §565.4(b) of this chapter, fails to meet the regulatory capital requirements at 12 CFR part 567, or would fail to meet any of these standards following the payment.

(ii) A savings association must include such additional statements as OTS may prescribe for certificates, purchase agreements, indentures, and other related documents. OTS will prescribe the text of these additional statements in its Application Processing Handbook.

(2) *Maturity requirements.* Covered securities must have an original weighted average maturity or original weighted average period to required redemption of at least five years.

(3) *Mandatory prepayment.* Subordinated debt securities and related documents may not provide events of default or contain other provisions that could result in a mandatory prepayment of principal, other than events of default that:

(i) Arise from the savings association's failure to make timely payment of interest or principal;

(ii) Arise from its failure to comply with reasonable financial, operating, and maintenance covenants of a type that are customarily included in indentures for publicly offered debt securities; or

(iii) Relate to bankruptcy, insolvency, receivership, or similar events.

(4) *Indenture.* (i) Except as provided in paragraph (c)(4)(ii) of this section, a savings association must use an indenture for subordinated debt securities. If the aggregate amount of subordinated debt securities publicly offered (excluding sales in a non-public offering as defined in 12 CFR 563g.4) and sold in any consecutive 12-month or 36-month period exceeds $5,000,000 or $10,000,000 respectively (or such lesser amount that the Securities and Exchange Commission shall establish by rule or regulation under 15 U.S.C. 77ddd), the indenture must provide for the appointment of a trustee other than the savings association or an affiliate of the savings association (as defined at 12 CFR 583.2) and for collective enforcement of the security holders' rights and remedies.

(ii) A savings association is not required to use an indenture if the subordinated debt securities are sold only to

Office of Thrift Supervision, Treasury § 563.81

accredited investors, as that term is defined in 15 U.S.C. 77d(6). A savings association must have an indenture that meets the requirements of paragraph (c)(4)(i) of this section in place before any debt securities for which an exemption from the indenture requirement is claimed, are transferred any non-accredited investor. If a savings association relies on this exemption from the indenture requirement, it must place a legend on the debt securities indicating that an indenture must be in place before the debt securities are transferred to any non-accredited investor.

(d) *OTS review.* (1) OTS will review notices and applications under 12 CFR part 516, subpart E.

(2) In reviewing notices and applications under this section, OTS will consider whether:

(i) The issuance of the covered securities is authorized under applicable laws and regulations and is consistent with the savings association's charter and bylaws.

(ii) The savings association is at least adequately capitalized under §565.4(b) of this chapter and meets the regulatory capital requirements at part 567 of this chapter.

(iii) The savings association is or will be able to service the covered securities.

(iv) The covered securities are consistent with the requirements of this section.

(v) The covered securities and related transactions sufficiently transfer risk from the Deposit Insurance Fund.

(vi) OTS has no objection to the issuance based on the savings association's overall policies, condition, and operations.

(3) OTS approval or non-objection is conditioned upon no material changes to the information disclosed in the application or notice submitted to OTS. OTS may impose such additional requirements or conditions as it may deem necessary to protect purchasers, the savings association, OTS, or the Deposit Insurance Fund.

(e) *Amendments.* If a savings association amends the covered securities or related documents following the completion of OTS review, it must obtain OTS approval or non-objection under this section before it may include the amended securities in supplementary capital.

(f) *Sale of covered securities.* The savings association must complete the sale of covered securities within one year after OTS approval or non-objection under this section. A savings association may request an extension of the offering period by filing a written request with OTS. The savings association must demonstrate good cause for the extension and file the request at least 30 days before the expiration of the offering period or any extension of the offering period.

(g) *Reports.* A savings association must file the following information with OTS within 30 days after the savings association completes the sale of covered securities includable as supplementary capital. If the savings association filed its application or notice following the completion of the sale, it must submit this information with its application or notice:

(1) A written report indicating the number of purchasers, the total dollar amount of securities sold, the net proceeds received by the savings association from the issuance, and the amount of covered securities, net of all expenses, to be included as supplementary capital;

(2) Three copies of an executed form of the securities and a copy of any related documents governing the issuance or administration of the securities; and

(3) A certification by the appropriate executive officer indicating that the savings association complied with all applicable laws and regulations in connection with the offering, issuance, and sale of the securities.

[72 FR 1927, Jan. 17, 2007, as amended at 72 FR 69438, Dec. 7, 2007]

Subpart D—Registration of Residential Mortgage Loan Originators

SOURCE: 75 FR 44696, July 28, 2010, unless otherwise noted.

§ 563.101 Authority, purpose, and scope.

(a) *Authority.* This subpart is issued pursuant to the Secure and Fair Enforcement for Mortgage Licensing Act of 2008, title V of the Housing and Economic Recovery Act of 2008 (S.A.F.E. Act) (Pub. L. 110–289, 122 Stat. 2654, 12 U.S.C. 5101 et seq.).

(b) *Purpose.* This subpart implements the S.A.F.E. Act's Federal registration requirement for mortgage loan originators. The S.A.F.E. Act provides that the objectives of this registration include aggregating and improving the flow of information to and between regulators; providing increased accountability and tracking of mortgage loan originators; enhancing consumer protections; supporting anti-fraud measures; and providing consumers with easily accessible information at no charge regarding the employment history of, and publicly adjudicated disciplinary and enforcement actions against, mortgage loan originators.

(c) *Scope*—(1) *In general.* This subpart applies to savings associations, their operating subsidiaries (collectively referred to in this subpart as savings associations), and their employees who act as mortgage loan originators.

(2) *De minimis exception.* (i) This subpart and the requirements of 12 U.S.C. 5103(a)(1)(A) and (2) of the S.A.F.E. Act do not apply to any employee of a savings association who has never been registered or licensed through the Registry as a mortgage loan originator if during the past 12 months the employee acted as a mortgage loan originator for 5 or fewer residential mortgage loans.

(ii) Prior to engaging in mortgage loan origination activity that exceeds the exception limit in paragraph (c)(2)(i) of this section, a savings association employee must register with the Registry pursuant to this subpart.

(iii) *Evasion.* Savings associations are prohibited from engaging in any act or practice to evade the limits of the *de minimis* exception set forth in paragraph (c)(2)(i) of this section.

§ 563.102 Definitions.

For purposes of this subpart D, the following definitions apply:

(a) *Annual renewal period* means November 1 through December 31 of each year.

(b)(1) *Mortgage loan originator*[1] means an individual who:

(i) Takes a residential mortgage loan application; and

(ii) Offers or negotiates terms of a residential mortgage loan for compensation or gain.

(2) The term *mortgage loan originator* does not include:

(i) An individual who performs purely administrative or clerical tasks on behalf of an individual who is described in paragraph (b)(1) of this section;

(ii) An individual who only performs real estate brokerage activities (as defined in 12 U.S.C. 5102(3)(D)) and is licensed or registered as a real estate broker in accordance with applicable State law, unless the individual is compensated by a lender, a mortgage broker, or other mortgage loan originator or by any agent of such lender, mortgage broker, or other mortgage loan originator, and meets the definition of mortgage loan originator in paragraph (b)(1) of this section; or

(iii) An individual or entity solely involved in extensions of credit related to timeshare plans, as that term is defined in 11 U.S.C. 101(53D).

(3) *Administrative or clerical tasks* means the receipt, collection, and distribution of information common for the processing or underwriting of a loan in the residential mortgage industry and communication with a consumer to obtain information necessary for the processing or underwriting of a residential mortgage loan.

(c) *Nationwide Mortgage Licensing System and Registry* or *Registry* means the system developed and maintained by the Conference of State Bank Supervisors and the American Association of Residential Mortgage Regulators for the State licensing and registration of State-licensed mortgage loan originators and the registration of mortgage loan originators pursuant to 12 U.S.C. 5107.

(d) *Registered mortgage loan originator* or *registrant* means any individual who:

---

[1] Appendix A of this subpart provides examples of activities that would, and would not, cause an employee to fall within this definition of mortgage loan originator.

Office of Thrift Supervision, Treasury § 563.103

(1) Meets the definition of mortgage loan originator and is an employee of a savings association; and

(2) Is registered pursuant to this subpart with, and maintains a unique identifier through, the Registry.

(e) *Residential mortgage loan* means any loan primarily for personal, family, or household use that is secured by a mortgage, deed of trust, or other equivalent consensual security interest on a dwelling (as defined in section 103(v) of the Truth in Lending Act, 15 U.S.C. 1602(v)) or residential real estate upon which is constructed or intended to be constructed a dwelling, and includes refinancings, reverse mortgages, home equity lines of credit and other first and additional lien loans that meet the qualifications listed in this definition.

(f) *Unique identifier* means a number or other identifier that:

(1) Permanently identifies a registered mortgage loan originator;

(2) Is assigned by protocols established by the Nationwide Mortgage Licensing System and Registry, the Federal banking agencies, and the Farm Credit Administration to facilitate:

(i) Electronic tracking of mortgage loan originators; and

(ii) Uniform identification of, and public access to, the employment history of and the publicly adjudicated disciplinary and enforcement actions against mortgage loan originators; and

(3) Must not be used for purposes other than those set forth under the S.A.F.E. Act.

§ 563.103 Registration of mortgage loan originators.

(a) *Registration requirement*—(1) *Employee registration.* Each employee of a savings association who acts as a mortgage loan originator must register with the Registry, obtain a unique identifier, and maintain this registration in accordance with the requirements of this subpart. Any such employee who is not in compliance with the registration and unique identifier requirements set forth in this subpart is in violation of the S.A.F.E. Act and this subpart.

(2) *Savings association requirement*—(i) *In general.* A savings association that employs one or more individuals who act as a residential mortgage loan originator must require each such employee to register with the Registry, maintain this registration, and obtain a unique identifier in accordance with the requirements of this subpart.

(ii) *Prohibition.* A savings association must not permit an employee of the association who is subject to the registration requirements of this subpart to act as a mortgage loan originator for the association unless such employee is registered with the Registry pursuant to this subpart.

(3) *Implementation period for initial registration.* An employee of a savings association who is a mortgage loan originator must complete an initial registration with the Registry pursuant to this subpart within 180 days from the date that the OTS provides in a public notice that the Registry is accepting registrations.

(4) *Employees previously registered or licensed through the Registry*—(i) *In general.* If an employee of a savings association was registered or licensed through, and obtained a unique identifier from, the Registry and has maintained this registration or license before the employee of the association becomes subject to this subpart at this association, then the registration requirements of the S.A.F.E. Act and this subpart are deemed to be met, provided that:

(A) The employment information in paragraphs (d)(1)(i)(C) and (d)(1)(ii) of this section is updated and the requirements of paragraph (d)(2) of this section are met;

(B) New fingerprints of the employee are submitted to the Registry for a background check, as required by paragraph (d)(1)(ix) of this section, unless the employee has fingerprints on file with the Registry that are less than 3 years old;

(C) The savings association information required in paragraphs (e)(1)(i) (to the extent the association has not previously met these requirements) and (e)(2)(i) of this section is submitted to the Registry; and

(D) The registration is maintained pursuant to paragraphs (b) and (e)(1)(ii) of this section, as of the date that the employee becomes subject to this subpart.

§ 563.103

(ii) *Rule for certain acquisitions, mergers, or reorganizations.* When registered or licensed mortgage loan originators become savings association employees as a result of an acquisition, merger, or reorganization, only the requirements of paragraphs (a)(4)(i)(A), (C), and (D) of this section must be met, and these requirements must be met within 60 days from the effective date of the acquisition, merger, or reorganization.

(b) *Maintaining registration.* (1) A mortgage loan originator who is registered with the Registry pursuant to paragraph (a) of this section must:

(i) Except as provided in paragraph (b)(3) of this section, renew the registration during the annual renewal period, confirming the responses set forth in paragraphs (d)(1)(i) through (viii) of this section remain accurate and complete, and updating this information, as appropriate; and

(ii) Update the registration within 30 days of any of the following events:

(A) A change in the name of the registrant;

(B) The registrant ceases to be an employee of the savings association; or

(C) The information required under paragraphs (d)(1)(iii) through (viii) of this section becomes inaccurate, incomplete, or out-of-date.

(2) A registered mortgage loan originator must maintain his or her registration, unless the individual is no longer engaged in the activity of a mortgage loan originator.

(3) The annual registration renewal requirement set forth in paragraph (b)(1) of this section does not apply to a registered mortgage loan originator who has completed his or her registration with the Registry pursuant to paragraph (a)(1) of this section less than 6 months prior to the end of the annual renewal period.

(c) *Effective dates*—(1) *Registration.* A registration pursuant to paragraph (a)(1) of this section is effective on the date the Registry transmits notification to the registrant that the registrant is registered.

(2) *Renewals or updates.* A renewal or update pursuant to paragraph (b) of this section is effective on the date the Registry transmits notification to the registrant that the registration has been renewed or updated.

(d) *Required employee information*—(1) *In general.* For purposes of the registration required by this section, a savings association must require each employee who is a mortgage loan originator to submit to the Registry, or must submit on behalf of the employee, the following categories of information, to the extent this information is collected by the Registry:

(i) Identifying information, including the employee's:

(A) Name and any other names used;

(B) Home address and contact information;

(C) Principal business location address and business contact information;

(D) Social security number;

(E) Gender; and

(F) Date and place of birth;

(ii) Financial services-related employment history for the 10 years prior to the date of registration or renewal, including the date the employee became an employee of the savings association;

(iii) Convictions of any criminal offense involving dishonesty, breach of trust, or money laundering against the employee or organizations controlled by the employee, or agreements to enter into a pretrial diversion or similar program in connection with the prosecution for such offense(s);

(iv) Civil judicial actions against the employee in connection with financial services-related activities, dismissals with settlements, or judicial findings that the employee violated financial services-related statutes or regulations, except for actions dismissed without a settlement agreement;

(v) Actions or orders by a State or Federal regulatory agency or foreign financial regulatory authority that:

(A) Found the employee to have made a false statement or omission or been dishonest, unfair or unethical; to have been involved in a violation of a financial services-related regulation or statute; or to have been a cause of a financial services-related business having its authorization to do business denied, suspended, revoked, or restricted;

(B) Are entered against the employee in connection with a financial services-related activity;

Office of Thrift Supervision, Treasury § 563.103

(C) Denied, suspended, or revoked the employee's registration or license to engage in a financial services-related activity; disciplined the employee or otherwise by order prevented the employee from associating with a financial services-related business or restricted the employee's activities; or

(D) Barred the employee from association with an entity or its officers regulated by the agency or authority or from engaging in a financial services-related business;

(vi) Final orders issued by a State or Federal regulatory agency or foreign financial regulatory authority based on violations of any law or regulation that prohibits fraudulent, manipulative, or deceptive conduct;

(vii) Revocation or suspension of the employee's authorization to act as an attorney, accountant, or State or Federal contractor;

(viii) Customer-initiated financial services-related arbitration or civil action against the employee that required action, including settlements, or which resulted in a judgment; and

(ix) Fingerprints of the employee, in digital form if practicable, and any appropriate identifying information for submission to the Federal Bureau of Investigation and any governmental agency or entity authorized to receive such information in connection with a State and national criminal history background check; however, fingerprints provided to the Registry that are less than 3 years old may be used to satisfy this requirement.

(2) *Employee authorizations and attestation.* An employee registering as a mortgage loan originator or renewing or updating his or her registration under this subpart, and not the employing savings association or other employees of the savings association, must:

(i) Authorize the Registry and the employing institution to obtain information related to sanctions or findings in any administrative, civil, or criminal action, to which the employee is a party, made by any governmental jurisdiction;

(ii) Attest to the correctness of all information required by paragraph (d) of this section, whether submitted by the employee or on behalf of the employee by the employing savings association; and

(iii) Authorize the Registry to make available to the public information required by paragraphs (d)(1)(i)(A) and (C), and (d)(1)(ii) through (viii) of this section.

(3) *Submission of information.* A savings association may identify one or more employees of the association who may submit the information required by paragraph (d)(1) of this section to the Registry on behalf of the association's employees provided that this individual, and any employee delegated such authority, does not act as a mortgage loan originator, consistent with paragraph (e)(1)(i)(F) of this section. In addition, a savings association may submit to the Registry some or all of the information required by paragraphs (d)(1) and (e)(2) of this section for multiple employees in bulk through batch processing in a format to be specified by the Registry, to the extent such batch processing is made available by the Registry.

(e) *Required savings association information.* A savings association must submit the following categories of information to the Registry:

(1) *Savings association record.* (i) In connection with the registration of one or more mortgage loan originators:

(A) Name, main office address, and business contact information;

(B) Internal Revenue Service Employer Tax Identification Number (EIN);

(C) Research Statistics Supervision and Discount (RSSD) number, as issued by the Board of Governors of the Federal Reserve System;

(D) Identification of its primary Federal regulator;

(E) Name(s) and contact information of the individual(s) with authority to act as the savings association's primary point of contact for the Registry;

(F) Name(s) and contact information of the individual(s) with authority to enter the information required by paragraphs (d)(1) and (e) of this section to the Registry and who may delegate this authority to other individuals. For the purpose of providing information required by paragraph (e) of this section, this individual and their delegates must not act as mortgage loan

§ 563.104

originators unless the savings association has 10 or fewer full time or equivalent employees and is not a subsidiary; and

(G) If a subsidiary of a savings association, indication that it is a subsidiary and the RSSD number of the parent association.

(ii) *Attestation.* The individual(s) identified in paragraphs (e)(1)(i)(E) and (F) of this section must comply with Registry protocols to verify their identity and must attest that they have the authority to enter data on behalf of the savings association, that the information provided to the Registry pursuant to this paragraph (e) is correct, and that the savings association will keep the information required by this paragraph (e) current and will file accurate supplementary information on a timely basis.

(iii) A savings association must update the information required by this paragraph (e) of this section within 30 days of the date that this information becomes inaccurate.

(iv) A savings association must renew the information required by paragraph (e) of this section on an annual basis.

(2) *Employee information.* In connection with the registration of each employee who acts as a mortgage loan originator:

(i) After the information required by paragraph (d) of this section has been submitted to the Registry, confirmation that it employs the registrant; and

(ii) Within 30 days of the date the registrant ceases to be an employee of the savings association, notification that it no longer employs the registrant and the date the registrant ceased being an employee.

§ 563.104 Policies and procedures.

A savings association that employs one or more mortgage loan originators must adopt and follow written policies and procedures designed to assure compliance with this subpart. These policies and procedures must be appropriate to the nature, size, complexity, and scope of the mortgage lending activities of the savings association, and apply only to those employees acting within the scope of their employment at the association. At a minimum, these policies and procedures must:

(a) Establish a process for identifying which employees of the savings association are required to be registered mortgage loan originators;

(b) Require that all employees of the savings association who are mortgage loan originators be informed of the registration requirements of the S.A.F.E. Act and this subpart and be instructed on how to comply with such requirements and procedures;

(c) Establish procedures to comply with the unique identifier requirements in § 563.105;

(d) Establish reasonable procedures for confirming the adequacy and accuracy of employee registrations, including updates and renewals, by comparisons with its own records;

(e) Establish reasonable procedures and tracking systems for monitoring compliance with registration and renewal requirements and procedures;

(f) Provide for independent testing for compliance with this subpart to be conducted at least annually by savings association personnel or by an outside party;

(g) Provide for appropriate action in the case of any employee who fails to comply with the registration requirements of the S.A.F.E. Act, this subpart, or the savings association's related policies and procedures, including prohibiting such employees from acting as mortgage loan originators or other appropriate disciplinary actions;

(h) Establish a process for reviewing employee criminal history background reports received pursuant to this subpart, taking appropriate action consistent with applicable Federal law, including section 19 of the Federal Deposit Insurance Act (12 U.S.C. 1829) and implementing regulations with respect to these reports, and maintaining records of these reports and actions taken with respect to applicable employees; and

(i) Establish procedures designed to ensure that any third party with which the savings association has arrangements related to mortgage loan origination has policies and procedures to

Office of Thrift Supervision, Treasury

comply with the S.A.F.E. Act, including appropriate licensing and/or registration of individuals acting as mortgage loan originators.

§ 563.105 Use of unique identifier.

(a) The savings association shall make the unique identifier(s) of its registered mortgage loan originator(s) available to consumers in a manner and method practicable to the institution.

(b) A registered mortgage loan originator shall provide his or her unique identifier to a consumer:

(1) Upon request;

(2) Before acting as a mortgage loan originator; and

(3) Through the originator's initial written communication with a consumer, if any, whether on paper or electronically.

APPENDIX A TO SUBPART D OF PART 563—EXAMPLES OF MORTGAGE LOAN ORIGINATOR ACTIVITIES

This Appendix provides examples to aid in the understanding of activities that would cause an employee of a savings association to fall within or outside the definition of mortgage loan originator. The examples in this Appendix are not all inclusive. They illustrate only the issue described and do not illustrate any other issues that may arise under this subpart. For purposes of the examples below, the term "loan" refers to a residential mortgage loan.

(a) *Taking a loan application.* The following examples illustrate when an employee takes, or does not take, a loan application.

(1) Taking an application includes: receiving information provided in connection with a request for a loan to be used to determine whether the consumer qualifies for a loan, even if the employee:

(i) Has received the consumer's information indirectly in order to make an offer or negotiate a loan;

(ii) Is not responsible for verifying information;

(iii) Is inputting information into an online application or other automated system on behalf of the consumer; or

(iv) Is not engaged in approval of the loan, including determining whether the consumer qualifies for the loan.

(2) Taking an application does not include any of the following activities performed solely or in combination:

(i) Contacting a consumer to verify the information in the loan application by obtaining documentation, such as tax returns or payroll receipts;

(ii) Receiving a loan application through the mail and forwarding it, without review, to loan approval personnel;

(iii) Assisting a consumer who is filling out an application by clarifying what type of information is necessary for the application or otherwise explaining the qualifications or criteria necessary to obtain a loan product;

(iv) Describing the steps that a consumer would need to take to provide information to be used to determine whether the consumer qualifies for a loan or otherwise explaining the loan application process;

(v) In response to an inquiry regarding a prequalified offer that a consumer has received from a savings association, collecting only basic identifying information about the consumer and forwarding the consumer to a mortgage loan originator; or

(vi) Receiving information in connection with a modification to the terms of an existing loan to a borrower as part of the savings association's loss mitigation efforts when the borrower is reasonably likely to default.

(b) *Offering or negotiating terms of a loan.* The following examples are designed to illustrate when an employee offers or negotiates terms of a loan, and conversely, what does not constitute offering or negotiating terms of a loan.

(1) Offering or negotiating the terms of a loan includes:

(i) Presenting a loan offer to a consumer for acceptance, either verbally or in writing, including, but not limited to, providing a disclosure of the loan terms after application under the Truth in Lending Act, even if:

(A) Further verification of information is necessary;

(B) The offer is conditional;

(C) Other individuals must complete the loan process; or

(D) Only the rate approved by the savings association's loan approval mechanism function for a specific loan product is communicated without authority to negotiate the rate.

(ii) Responding to a consumer's request for a lower rate or lower points on a pending loan application by presenting to the consumer a revised loan offer, either verbally or in writing, that includes a lower interest rate or lower points than the original offer.

(2) Offering or negotiating terms of a loan does not include solely or in combination:

(i) Providing general explanations or descriptions in response to consumer queries regarding qualification for a specific loan product, such as explaining loan terminology (*i.e.,* debt-to-income ratio); lending policies (*i.e.,* the loan-to-value ratio policy of the savings association); or product-related services;

(ii) In response to a consumer's request, informing a consumer of the loan rates that are publicly available, such as on the savings association's Web site, for specific types of

§ 563.140

loan products without communicating to the consumer whether qualifications are met for that loan product;

(iii) Collecting information about a consumer in order to provide the consumer with information on loan products for which the consumer generally may qualify, without presenting a specific loan offer to the consumer for acceptance, either verbally or in writing;

(iv) Arranging the loan closing or other aspects of the loan process, including communicating with a consumer about those arrangements, provided that communication with the consumer only verifies loan terms already offered or negotiated;

(v) Providing a consumer with information unrelated to loan terms, such as the best days of the month for scheduling loan closings at the savings association;

(vi) Making an underwriting decision about whether the consumer qualifies for a loan;

(vii) Explaining or describing the steps or process that a consumer would need to take in order to obtain a loan offer, including qualifications or criteria that would need to be met without providing guidance specific to that consumer's circumstances; or

(viii) Communicating on behalf of a mortgage loan originator that a written offer, including disclosures provided pursuant to the Truth in Lending Act, has been sent to a consumer without providing any details of that offer.

(c) *Offering or negotiating a loan for compensation or gain.* The following examples illustrate when an employee does or does not offer or negotiate terms of a loan "for compensation or gain."

(1) Offering or negotiating terms of a loan for compensation or gain includes engaging in any of the activities in paragraph (b)(1) of this Appendix in the course of carrying out employment duties, even if the employee does not receive a referral fee or commission or other special compensation for the loan.

(2) Offering or negotiating terms of a loan for compensation or gain does not include engaging in a seller-financed transaction for the employee's personal property that does not involve the savings association.

Subpart E—Capital Distributions

SOURCE: 64 FR 2809, Jan. 19, 1999, unless otherwise noted.

§ 563.140 What does this subpart cover?

This subpart applies to all capital distributions by a savings association ("you").

§ 563.141 What is a capital distribution?

A capital distribution is:

(a) A distribution of cash or other property to your owners made on account of their ownership, but excludes:

(1) Any dividend consisting only of your shares or rights to purchase your shares; or

(2) If you are a mutual savings association, any payment that you are required to make under the terms of a deposit instrument and any other amount paid on deposits that the OTS determines is not a distribution for the purposes of this section;

(b) Your payment to repurchase, redeem, retire or otherwise acquire any of your shares or other ownership interests, any payment to repurchase, redeem, retire, or otherwise acquire debt instruments included in your total capital under part 567 of this chapter, and any extension of credit to finance an affiliate's acquisition of your shares or interests;

(c) Any direct or indirect payment of cash or other property to owners or affiliates made in connection with a corporate restructuring. This includes your payment of cash or property to shareholders of another association or to shareholders of its holding company to acquire ownership in that association, other than by a distribution of shares;

(d) Any other distribution charged against your capital accounts if you would not be well capitalized, as set forth in § 565.4(b)(1) of this chapter, following the distribution; and

(e) Any transaction that the OTS or the Corporation determines, by order or regulation, to be in substance a distribution of capital.

[64 FR 2809, Jan. 19, 1999, as amended at 72 FR 69438, Dec. 7, 2007]

§ 563.142 What other definitions apply to this subpart?

The following definitions apply to this subpart:

Affiliate means an affiliate, as defined under § 563.41(b) of this part.

Capital means total capital, as computed under part 567 of this chapter.

Net income means your net income computed in accordance with generally accepted accounting principles.

Office of Thrift Supervision, Treasury § 563.144

Retained net income means your net income for a specified period less total capital distributions declared in that period.

Shares means common and preferred stock, and any options, warrants, or other rights for the acquisition of such stock. The term "share" also includes convertible securities upon their conversion into common or preferred stock. The term does not include convertible debt securities prior to their conversion into common or preferred stock or other securities that are not equity securities at the time of a capital distribution.

[64 FR 2809, Jan. 19, 1999, as amended at 72 FR 69438, Dec. 7, 2007]

§ 563.143 Must I file with OTS?

Whether and what you must file with the OTS depends on whether you and your proposed capital distribution fall within certain criteria.

(a) *Application required.*

If:	Then you:
(1) You are not eligible for expedited treatment under § 516.5 of this chapter.	Must file an application with the OTS.
(2) The total amount of all of your capital distributions (including the proposed capital distribution) for the applicable calendar year exceeds your net income for that year to date plus your retained net income for the preceding two years.	Must file an application with the OTS.
(3) You would not be at least adequately capitalized, as set forth in § 565.4(b)(2) of this chapter, following the distribution.	Must file an application with the OTS.
(4) Your proposed capital distribution would violate a prohibition contained in any applicable statute, regulation, or agreement between you and the OTS (or the Corporation), or violate a condition imposed on you in an OTS-approved application or notice.	Must file an application with the OTS.

(b) *Notice required.*

If you are not required to file an application under paragraph (a) of this section, but:	Then you:
(1) You would not be well capitalized, as set forth under § 565.4(b)(1), following the distribution.	Must file a notice with the OTS.
(2) Your proposed capital distribution would reduce the amount of or retire any part of your common or preferred stock or retire any part of debt instruments such as notes or debentures included in capital under part 567 of this chapter (other than regular payments required under a debt instrument approved under § 563.81).	Must file a notice with the OTS.
(3) You are a subsidiary of a savings and loan holding company ...	Must file a notice with the OTS.

(c) *No prior notice required.*

If neither you nor your proposed capital distribution meet any of the criteria listed in paragraphs (a) and (b) of this section.	Then you do not need to file a notice or an application with the OTS before making a capital distribution.

[64 FR 2809, Jan. 19, 1999, as amended at 66 FR 13008, Mar. 2, 2001]

§ 563.144 How do I file with the OTS?

(a) *Contents.* Your notice or application must:

(1) Be in narrative form.

(2) Include all relevant information concerning the proposed capital distribution, including the amount, timing, and type of distribution.

(3) Demonstrate compliance with § 563.146.

(b) *Schedules.* Your notice or application may include a schedule proposing

223

§ 563.145

capital distributions over a specified period, not to exceed 12 months.

(c) *Timing.* You must file your notice or application at least 30 days before the proposed declaration of dividend or approval of the proposed capital distribution by your board of directors.

§ 563.145 May I combine my notice or application with other notices or applications?

You may combine the notice or application required under § 563.143 with any other notice or application, if the capital distribution is a part of, or is proposed in connection with, another transaction requiring a notice or application under this chapter. If you submit a combined filing, you must:

(a) State that the related notice or application is intended to serve as a notice or application under this subpart; and

(b) Submit the notice or application in a timely manner.

§ 563.146 Will the OTS permit my capital distribution?

The OTS will review your notice or application under the review procedures in 12 CFR part 516, subpart E. The OTS may disapprove your notice or deny your application filed under § 563.143, in whole or in part, if the OTS makes any of the following determinations.

(a) You will be undercapitalized, significantly undercapitalized, or critically undercapitalized as set forth in § 565.4(b) of this chapter, following the capital distribution. If so, the OTS will determine if your capital distribution is permitted under 12 U.S.C. 1831o(d)(1)(B).

(b) Your proposed capital distribution raises safety or soundness concerns.

(c) Your proposed capital distribution violates a prohibition contained in any statute, regulation, agreement between you and the OTS (or the Corporation), or a condition imposed on you in an OTS-approved application or notice. If so, the OTS will determine whether it may permit your capital distribution notwithstanding the prohibition or condition.

[64 FR 2809, Jan. 19, 1999, as amended at 67 FR 78152, Dec. 23, 2002]

Subpart F—Financial Management Policies

§ 563.161 Management and financial policies.

(a)(1) For the protection of depositors and other savings associations, each savings association and each service corporation must be well managed and operate safely and soundly. Each also must pursue financial policies that are safe and consistent with economical home financing and the purposes of savings associations. In implementing this section, OTS will consider that service corporations may be authorized to engage in activities that involve a higher degree of risk than activities permitted to savings associations.

(2) As part of meeting its requirements under paragraph (a)(1) of this section, each savings association and service corporation must maintain sufficient liquidity to ensure its safe and sound operation.

(b) Compensation to officers, directors, and employees of each savings association and its service corporations shall not be in excess of that which is reasonable and commensurate with their duties and responsibilities. Former officers, directors, and employees of savings association or its service corporation who regularly perform services therefor under consulting contracts are employees thereof for purposes of this paragraph (b).

[54 FR 49552, Nov. 30, 1989, as amended at 66 FR 15017, Mar. 15, 2001]

§ 563.170 Examinations and audits; appraisals; establishment and maintenance of records.

(a) *Examinations and audits.* Each savings association and affiliate thereof shall be examined periodically, and may be examined at any time, by the Office, with appraisals when deemed advisable, in accordance with general policies from time to time established by the Office. The costs, as computed by the Office, of any examinations made by it, including office analysis, overhead, per diem, travel expense, other supervision by the Office, and other indirect costs, shall be paid by the savings associations examined, except that in the case of service corporations of Federal savings associations the cost of examinations, as determined by the Office, shall be paid by the service corporations. Payments shall be made in accordance with a schedule of annual assessments based upon each savings association's total assets and of rates for examiner time in amounts determined by the Office.

(b) *Appraisals.* (1) Unless otherwise ordered by the Office, appraisal of real estate by the Office in connection with any examination or audit of a savings association, affiliate, or service corporation shall be made by an appraiser, or by appraisers, selected by the Office's Regional Director of the Region in which such savings association is located. The cost of such appraisal shall promptly be paid by such savings association, affiliate, or service corporation direct to such appraiser or appraisers upon receipt by the savings association, affiliate, or service corporation of a statement of such cost as approved by such Regional Director. A copy of the report of each appraisal made by the Office pursuant to any of the foregoing provisions of this section shall be furnished to the savings association, affiliate, or service corporation, as appropriate within a reasonable time, not to exceed 90 days, following the completion of such appraisals and the filing of a report thereof by the appraiser, or appraisers, with such Regional Director.

(2) The Office may obtain at any time, at its expense, such appraisals of any of the assets, including the security therefor, of a savings association, affiliate, or service corporation as the Office deems appropriate.

(c) *Establishment and maintenance of records.* To enable the Office to examine savings associations and affiliates and audit savings associations, affiliates, and service corporations pursuant to the provisions of paragraph (a) of this section, each savings association, affiliate, and service corporation shall establish and maintain such accounting and other records as will provide an accurate and complete record of all business it transacts. This includes, without limitation, establishing and maintaining such other records as are required by statute or any other regulation to which the savings association, affiliate, or service corporation is subject. The documents, files, and other material or property comprising said records shall at all times be available for such examination and audit wherever any of said records, documents, files, material, or property may be.

(d) *Change in location of records.* A savings association shall not transfer the location of any of its general accounting or control records, or the maintenance thereof, from its home office to a branch or service office, or from a branch or service office to its home office or to another branch or service office unless prior to the date of transfer its board of directors has:

(1) By resolution authorized the transfer or maintenance and;

(2) Sent a certified copy of the resolution to the Regional Director of the OTS Region in which the principal office of the savings association is located.

(e) *Use of data processing services for maintenance of records.* A savings association which determines to maintain any of its records by means of data processing services shall so notify the Regional Director of the Region in which the principal office of such savings association is located, in writing, at least 90 days prior to the date on which such maintenance of records will begin. Such notification shall include identification of the records to be maintained by data processing services and a statement as to the location at which such records will be maintained. Any contract, agreement, or arrangement made by a savings association pursuant to which data processing services are to be performed for such savings association shall be in writing and shall expressly provide that the records to be maintained by such services shall at all times be available for examination and audit.

[54 FR 49552, Nov. 30, 1989, as amended at 55 FR 34547, Aug. 23, 1990; 57 FR 14335, Apr. 20, 1992; 57 FR 40092, Sept. 2, 1992; 58 FR 28348, May 13, 1993; 59 FR 29502, June 7, 1994; 59 FR 53571, Oct. 25, 1994; 59 FR 60304, Nov. 23, 1994; 60 FR 66718, Dec. 26, 1995; 61 FR 50984, Sept. 30, 1996]

§ 563.171 Frequency of safety and soundness examination.

(a) *General.* The OTS examines savings associations pursuant to authority conferred by 12 U.S.C. 1463 and the requirements of 12 U.S.C. 1820(d). The OTS is required to conduct a full-scope, on-site examination of every savings association at least once during each 12-month period.

(b) *18-month rule for certain small institutions.* The OTS may conduct a full-scope, on-site examination of a savings association at least once during each 18-month period, rather than each 12-month period as provided in paragraph (a) of this section, if the following conditions are satisfied:

(1) The savings association has total assets of less than $500 million;

(2) The savings association is well capitalized as defined in § 565.4 of this chapter;

(3) At its most recent examination, the OTS—

(i) Assigned the savings association a rating of 1 or 2 for management as part of the savings association's composite rating under the Uniform Financial Institutions Rating System (commonly referred to as CAMELS), and

(ii) Determined that the savings association was in outstanding or good condition, that is, it received a composite rating, as defined in § 516.5(c) of this chapter, of 1 or 2;

(4) The savings association currently is not subject to a formal enforcement proceeding or order by the OTS or the FDIC; and

(5) No person acquired control of the savings association during the preceding 12-month period in which a full-scope, on-site examination would have been required but for this section.

(c) *Authority to conduct more frequent examinations.* This section does not limit the authority of the OTS to examine any savings association as frequently as the agency deems necessary.

[63 FR 16381, Apr. 2, 1998, as amended at 64 FR 69185, Dec. 10, 1999; 66 FR 13008, Mar. 2, 2001; 72 FR 17803, Apr. 10, 2007]

§ 563.172 Financial derivatives.

(a) *What is a financial derivative?* A financial derivative is a financial contract whose value depends on the value of one or more underlying assets, indices, or reference rates. The most common types of financial derivatives are futures, forward commitments, options, and swaps. A mortgage derivative security, such as a collateralized mortgage obligation or a real estate mortgage investment conduit, is not a financial derivative under this section.

(b) *May I engage in transactions involving financial derivatives?* (1) If you are a Federal savings association, you may engage in a transaction involving a financial derivative if you are authorized to invest in the assets underlying the financial derivative, the transaction is safe and sound, and you otherwise meet the requirements in this section.

(2) If you are a state-chartered savings association, you may engage in a transaction involving a financial derivative if your charter or applicable State law authorizes you to engage in such transactions, the transaction is safe and sound, and you otherwise meet the requirements in this section.

(3) In general, if you engage in a transaction involving a financial derivative, you should do so to reduce your risk exposure.

(c) *What are my board of directors' responsibilities with respect to financial derivatives?* (1) Your board of directors is responsible for effective oversight of financial derivatives activities.

(2) Before you may engage in any transaction involving a financial derivative, your board of directors must establish written policies and procedures governing authorized financial derivatives. Your board of directors should review Thrift Bulletin 13a, "Management of Interest Rate Risk, Investment Securities, and Derivatives Activities," and other applicable agency guidance on establishing a sound risk management program.

(3) Your board of directors must periodically review:

(i) Compliance with the policies and procedures established under paragraph (c)(2) of this section; and

(ii) The adequacy of these policies and procedures to ensure that they continue to be appropriate to the nature and scope of your operations and existing market conditions.

(4) Your board of directors must ensure that management establishes an adequate system of internal controls

Office of Thrift Supervision, Treasury § 563.177

for transactions involving financial derivatives.

(d) *What are management's responsibilities with respect to financial derivatives?* (1) Management is responsible for daily oversight and management of financial derivatives activities. Management must implement the policies and procedures established by the board of directors and must establish a system of internal controls. This system of internal controls should, at a minimum, provide for periodic reporting to the board of directors and management, segregation of duties, and internal review procedures.

(2) Management must ensure that financial derivatives activities are conducted in a safe and sound manner and should review Thrift Bulletin 13a, "Management of Interest Rate Risk, Investment Securities, and Derivatives Activities" (available at the address listed at § 516.1 of this chapter), and other applicable agency guidance on implementing a sound risk management program.

(e) *What records must I keep on financial derivative transactions?* You must maintain records adequate to demonstrate compliance with this section and with your board of directors' policies and procedures on financial derivatives.

[63 FR 66349, Dec. 1, 1998]

§ 563.176 Interest-rate-risk-management procedures.

Savings associations shall take the following actions:

(a) The board of directors or a committee thereof shall review the savings association's interest-rate-risk exposure and devise a policy for the savings association's management of that risk.

(b) The board of directors shall formerly adopt a policy for the management of interest-rate risk. The management of the savings association shall establish guidelines and procedures to ensure that the board's policy is successfully implemented.

(c) The management of the savings association shall periodically report to the board of directors regarding implementation of the savings association's policy for interest-rate-risk management and shall make that information available upon request to the Office.

(d) The savings association's board of directors shall review the results of operations at least quarterly and shall make such adjustments as it considers necessary and appropriate to the policy for interest-rate-risk management, including adjustments to the authorized acceptable level of interest-rate risk.

[54 FR 49552, Nov. 30, 1989, as amended at 58 FR 45813, Aug. 31, 1993; 59 FR 53571, Oct. 25, 1994]

§ 563.177 Procedures for monitoring Bank Secrecy Act (BSA) compliance.

(a) *Purpose.* The purpose of this regulation is to require savings associations (as defined by § 561.43 of this chapter) to establish and maintain procedures reasonably designed to assure and monitor compliance with the requirements of subchapter II of chapter 53 of title 31, United States Code, and the implementing regulations promulgated thereunder by the U.S. Department of Treasury, 31 CFR part 103.

(b) *Establishment of a BSA compliance program*—(1) *Program requirement.* Each savings association shall develop and provide for the continued administration of a program reasonably designed to assure and monitor compliance with the recordkeeping and reporting requirements set forth in subchapter II of chapter 53 of title 31, United States Code and the implementing regulations issued by the Department of the Treasury at 31 CFR part 103. The compliance program must be written, approved by the savings association's board of directors, and reflected in the minutes of the savings association.

(2) *Customer identification program.* Each savings association is subject to the requirements of 31 U.S.C. 5318(l) and the implementing regulation jointly promulgated by the OTS and the Department of the Treasury at 31 CFR 103.121, which require a customer identification program to be implemented as part of the BSA compliance program required under this section.

(c) *Contents of compliance program.* The compliance program shall, at a minimum:

(1) Provide for a system of internal controls to assure ongoing compliance;

(2) Provide for independent testing for compliance to be conducted by a

savings association's in-house personnel or by an outside party;

(3) Designate individual(s) responsible for coordinating and monitoring day-to-day compliance; and

(4) Provide training for appropriate personnel.

(Approved by the Office of Management and Budget under control number 3068–0530)

[54 FR 49552, Nov. 30, 1989, as amended at 68 FR 25112, May 9, 2003]

Subpart G—Reporting and Bonding

§ 563.180 Suspicious Activity Reports and other reports and statements.

(a) *Periodic reports.* Each savings association and service corporation thereof shall make such periodic or other reports of its affairs in such manner and on such forms as the Office may prescribe. The Office may provide that reports filed by savings associations or service corporations to meet the requirements of other regulations also satisfy requirements imposed under this section.

(b) *False or misleading statements or omissions.* No savings association or director, officer, agent, employee, affiliated person, or other person participating in the conduct of the affairs of such association nor any person filing or seeking approval of any application shall knowingly:

(1) Make any written or oral statement to the Office or to an agent, representative or employee of the Office that is false or misleading with respect to any material fact or omits to state a material fact concerning any matter within the jurisdiction of the Office; or

(2) Make any such statement or omission to a person or organization auditing a savings association or otherwise preparing or reviewing its financial statements concerning the accounts, assets, management condition, ownership, safety, or soundness, or other affairs of the association.

(c) *Notifications of loss and reports of increase in deductible amount of bond.* A savings association maintaining bond coverage as required by § 563.190 of this part shall promptly notify its bond company and file a proof of loss under the procedures provided by its bond, concerning any covered losses greater than twice the deductible amount.

(d) *Suspicious Activity Reports*—(1) *Purpose and scope.* This paragraph (d) ensures that savings associations and service corporations file a Suspicious Activity Report when they detect a known or suspected violation of Federal law or a suspicious transaction related to a money laundering activity or a violation of the Bank Secrecy Act.

(2) *Definitions.* For the purposes of this paragraph (d):

(i) *FinCEN* means the Financial Crimes Enforcement Network of the Department of the Treasury.

(ii) *Institution-affiliated party* means any institution-affiliated party as that term is defined in sections 3(u) and 8(b)(9) of the Federal Deposit Insurance Act (12 U.S.C. 1813(u) and 1818(b)(9)).

(iii) *SAR* means a Suspicious Activity Report.

(3) *SARs required.* A savings association or service corporation shall file a SAR with the appropriate Federal law enforcement agencies and the Department of the Treasury on the form prescribed by the OTS and in accordance with the form's instructions, by sending a completed SAR to FinCEN in the following circumstances:

(i) *Insider abuse involving any amount.* Whenever the savings association or service corporation detects any known or suspected Federal criminal violation, or pattern of criminal violations, committed or attempted against the savings association or service corporation or involving a transaction or transactions conducted through the savings association or service corporation, where the savings association or service corporation believes that it was either an actual or potential victim of a criminal violation, or series of criminal violations, or that it was used to facilitate a criminal transaction, and it has a substantial basis for identifying one of its directors, officers, employees, agents or other institution-affiliated parties as having committed or aided in the commission of a criminal act, regardless of the amount involved in the violation.

(ii) *Violations aggregating $5,000 or more where a suspect can be identified.* Whenever the savings association or service corporation detects any known or suspected Federal criminal violation, or pattern of criminal violations, committed or attempted against the savings association or service corporation or involving a transaction or transactions conducted through the savings association or service corporation and involving or aggregating $5,000 or more in funds or other assets, where the savings association or service corporation believes that it was either an actual or potential victim of a criminal violation or series of criminal violations, or that it was used to facilitate a criminal transaction, and it has a substantial basis for identifying a possible suspect or group of suspects. If it is determined prior to filing this report that the identified suspect or group of suspects has used an alias, then information regarding the true identity of the suspect or group of suspects, as well as alias identifiers, such as drivers' license or social security numbers, addresses and telephone numbers, must be reported.

(iii) *Violations aggregating $25,000 or more regardless of potential suspects.* Whenever the savings association or service corporation detects any known or suspected Federal criminal violation, or pattern of criminal violations, committed or attempted against the savings association or service corporation or involving a transaction or transactions conducted through the savings association or service corporation and involving or aggregating $25,000 or more in funds or other assets, where the savings association or service corporation believes that it was either an actual or potential victim of a criminal violation or series of criminal violations, or that it was used to facilitate a criminal transaction, even though there is no substantial basis for identifying a possible suspect or group of suspects.

(iv) *Transactions aggregating $5,000 or more that involve potential money laundering or violations of the Bank Secrecy Act.* Any transaction (which for purposes of this paragraph (d)(3)(iv) means a deposit, withdrawal, transfer between accounts, exchange of currency, loan, extension of credit, purchase or sale of any stock, bond, certificate of deposit, or other monetary instrument or investment security, or any other payment, transfer, or delivery by, through, or to a financial institution, by whatever means effected) conducted or attempted by, at or through the savings association or service corporation and involving or aggregating $5,000 or more in funds or other assets, if the savings association or service corporation knows, suspects, or has reason to suspect that:

(A) The transaction involves funds derived from illegal activities or is intended or conducted in order to hide or disguise funds or assets derived from illegal activities (including, without limitation, the ownership, nature, source, location, or control of such funds or assets) as part of a plan to violate or evade any law or regulation or to avoid any transaction reporting requirement under Federal law;

(B) The transaction is designed to evade any regulations promulgated under the Bank Secrecy Act; or

(C) The transaction has no business or apparent lawful purpose or is not the sort in which the particular customer would normally be expected to engage, and the institution knows of no reasonable explanation for the transaction after examining the available facts, including the background and possible purpose of the transaction.

(4) *Service corporations.* When a service corporation is required to file a SAR under paragraph (d)(3) of this section, either the service corporation or a savings association that wholly or partially owns the service corporation may file the SAR.

(5) *Time for reporting.* A savings association or service corporation is required to file a SAR no later than 30 calendar days after the date of initial detection of facts that may constitute a basis for filing a SAR. If no suspect was identified on the date of detection of the incident requiring the filing, a savings association or service corporation may delay filing a SAR for an additional 30 calendar days to identify a suspect. In no case shall reporting be delayed more than 60 calendar days after the date of initial detection of a reportable transaction. In situations involving violations requiring immediate attention, such as when a reportable violation is ongoing, the savings

§ 563.180

association or service corporation shall immediately notify, by telephone, an appropriate law enforcement authority and the OTS in addition to filing a timely SAR.

(6) *Reports to state and local authorities.* A savings association or service corporation is encouraged to file a copy of the SAR with state and local law enforcement agencies where appropriate.

(7) *Exception.* A savings association or service corporation need not file a SAR for a robbery or burglary committed or attempted that is reported to appropriate law enforcement authorities.

(8) *Retention of records.* A savings association or service corporation shall maintain a copy of any SAR filed and the original or business record equivalent of any supporting documentation for a period of five years from the date of the filing of the SAR. Supporting documentation shall be identified and maintained by the savings association or service corporation as such, and shall be deemed to have been filed with the SAR. A savings association or service corporation shall make all supporting documentation available to appropriate law enforcement agencies upon request. A savings association or service corporation shall make all supporting documentation available to OTS, FinCEN, or any Federal, State, or local law enforcement agency, or any Federal regulatory authority that examines the savings association or service corporation for compliance with the Bank Secrecy Act, or any State regulatory authority administering a State law that requires the savings association or service corporation to comply with the Bank Secrecy Act or otherwise authorizes the State authority to ensure that the institution complies with the Bank Secrecy Act, upon request.

(9) *Notification to board of directors*—(i) *Generally.* Whenever a savings association (or a service corporation in which the savings association has an ownership interest) files a SAR pursuant to this paragraph (d), the management of the savings association or service corporation shall promptly notify its board of directors, or a committee of directors or executive officers designated by the board of directors to receive notice.

(ii) *Suspect is a director or executive officer.* If the savings association or service corporation files a SAR pursuant to this paragraph (d) and the suspect is a director or executive officer, the savings association or service corporation may not notify the suspect, pursuant to 31 U.S.C. 5318(g)(2), but shall notify all directors who are not suspects.

(10) *Compliance.* Failure to file a SAR in accordance with this section and the instructions may subject the savings association or service corporation, its directors, officers, employees, agents, or other institution-affiliated parties to supervisory action.

(11) *Obtaining SARs.* A savings association or service corporation may obtain SARs and the instructions from the appropriate OTS Regional Office listed in § 516.40(a) of this chapter.

(12) *Confidentiality of SARs.* A SAR, and any information that would reveal the existence of a SAR, are confidential, and shall not be disclosed except as authorized in this paragraph (d)(12).

(i) *Prohibition on disclosure by savings associations or service corporations.* (A) *General rule.* No savings association or service corporation, and no director, officer, employee, or agent of a savings association or service corporation, shall disclose a SAR or any information that would reveal the existence of a SAR. Any savings association or service corporation, and any director, officer, employee, or agent of any savings association or service corporation that is subpoenaed or otherwise requested to disclose a SAR, or any information that would reveal the existence of a SAR, shall decline to produce the SAR or such information, citing this section and 31 U.S.C. 5318(g)(2)(A)(i), and shall notify the following of any such request and the response thereto:

(A) Deputy Chief Counsel, Litigation Division, Office of Thrift Supervision; and

(B) The Financial Crimes Enforcement Network (FinCEN).

(ii) *Rules of construction.* Provided that no person involved in any reported suspicious transaction is notified that the transaction has been reported, paragraph (d)(1) of this section shall not be construed as prohibiting:

(A) The disclosure by a savings association or service corporation, or any

230

Office of Thrift Supervision, Treasury § 563.180

director, officer, employee or agent of a savings association or service corporation of:

(1) A SAR, or any information that would reveal the existence of a SAR, to FinCEN or OTS, or any Federal, State, or local law enforcement agency; or any Federal regulatory authority that examines the savings association or service corporation for compliance with the Bank Secrecy Act, or any State regulatory authority administering a State law that requires compliance with the Bank Secrecy Act or otherwise authorizes the State authority to ensure that the institution complies with the Bank Secrecy Act; or

(2) The underlying facts, transactions, and documents upon which a SAR is based, including, but not limited to, disclosures:

(i) To another financial institution, or any director, officer, employee or agent of a financial institution, for the preparation of a joint SAR; or

(ii) In connection with certain employment references or termination notices, to the full extent authorized in 31 U.S.C. 5318(g)(2)(B); or

(B) The sharing by a savings association or service corporation, or any director, officer, employee, or agent of a savings association or service corporation, of a SAR, or any information that would reveal the existence of a SAR, within the corporate organizational structure of the savings association or service corporation, for purposes consistent with Title II of the Bank Secrecy Act as determined by regulation or in guidance.

(iii) *Prohibition on disclosure by OTS.* The OTS will not, and no officer, employee or agent of OTS, shall disclose a SAR, or any information that would reveal the existence of a SAR, except as necessary to fulfill official duties consistent with Title II of the Bank Secrecy Act. For purposes of this section, "official duties" shall not include the disclosure of a SAR, or any information that would reveal the existence of a SAR, in response to a request for use in a private legal proceeding or in response to a request for disclosure of non-public information under 12 CFR 510.5.

(iv) *Limitation on liability.* A savings association or service corporation and any director, officer, employee or agent of a savings association or service corporation that makes a voluntary disclosure of any possible violation of law or regulation to a government agency or makes a disclosure pursuant to this section or any other authority, including a disclosure made jointly with another institution, shall be protected from liability for any such disclosure, or for failure to provide notice of such disclosure to any person identified in the disclosure, or both, to the full extent provided by 31 U.S.C. 5318(g)(3).

(13) *Safe harbor.* The safe harbor provision of 31 U.S.C. 5318(g), which exempts any financial institution that makes a disclosure of any possible violation of law or regulation from liability under any law or regulation of the United States, or any constitution, law or regulation of any state or political subdivision, covers all reports of suspected or known criminal violations and suspicious activities to law enforcement and financial institution supervisory authorities, including supporting documentation, regardless of whether such reports are filed pursuant to this paragraph (d), or are filed on a voluntary basis.

(e) *Adjustable-rate mortgage indices—* (1) *Reporting obligation.* Upon the request of a Federal Home Loan Bank, all savings associations within the jurisdiction of that Federal Home Loan Bank shall report the data items set forth in paragraph (e)(2) of this section for the Federal Home Loan Bank to use in calculating and publishing an adjustable-rate mortgage index.

(2) *Data to be reported.* For purposes of paragraph (e)(1) of this section, the term "data items" means the data items previously collected from the monthly Thrift Financial Report and such data items as may be altered, amended, or substituted by the requesting Federal Home Loan Bank.

(3) *Applicable indices.* For the purpose of this reporting requirement, the term "adjustable-rate mortgage index" means any of the adjustable-rate mortgage indices calculated and published by a Federal Home Loan Bank or the

§ 563.190

Federal Home Loan Bank Board on or before August 9, 1989.

[54 FR 49552, Nov. 30, 1989, as amended at 56 FR 29566, June 28, 1991; 56 FR 32474, July 16, 1991; 57 FR 61251, Dec. 24, 1992; 59 FR 66159, Dec. 23, 1994; 61 FR 6105, Feb. 16, 1996; 66 FR 13008, Mar. 2, 2001; 68 FR 75110, Dec. 30, 2003; 75 FR 75592, Dec. 3, 2010]

§ 563.190 Bonds for directors, officers, employees, and agents; form of and amount of bonds.

(a) Each savings association shall maintain fidelity bond coverage. The bond shall cover each director, officer, employee, and agent who has control over or access to cash, securities, or other property of the savings association.

(b) The amount of coverage to be required for each savings association shall be determined by the association's management, based on its assessment of the level that would be safe and sound in view of the association's potential exposure to risk; provided, such determination shall be subject to approval by the association's board of directors.

(c) Each savings association may maintain bond coverage in addition to that provided by the insurance underwriter industry's standard forms, through the use of endorsements, riders, or other forms of supplemental coverage, if, in the judgment of the association's board of directors, additional coverage is warranted.

(d) The board of directors of each savings association shall formally approve the association's bond coverage. In deciding whether to approve the bond coverage, the board shall review the adequacy of the standard coverage and the need for supplemental coverage. Documentation of the board's approval shall be included as a part of the minutes of the meeting at which the board approves coverage. Additionally, the board of directors shall review the association's bond coverage at least annually to assess the continuing adequacy of coverage.

[57 FR 12698, Apr. 13, 1992]

§ 563.191 Bonds for agents.

In lieu of the bond provided in § 563.190 of this part in the case of agents appointed by a savings association, a fidelity bond may be provided in an amount at least twice the average monthly collections of such agents, provided such agents shall be required to make settlement with the savings association at least monthly, and provided such bond is approved by the board of directors of the savings association. No bond need be obtained for any agent that is a financial institution insured by the Federal Deposit Insurance Corporation.

§ 563.200 Conflicts of interest.

If you are a director, officer, or employee of a savings association, or have the power to direct its management or policies, or otherwise owe a fiduciary duty to a savings association:

(a) You must not advance your own personal or business interests, or those of others with whom you have a personal or business relationship, at the expense of the savings association; and

(b) You must, if you have an interest in a matter or transaction before the board of directors:

(1) Disclose to the board all material nonprivileged information relevant to the board's decision on the matter or transaction, including:

(i) The existence, nature and extent of your interests; and

(ii) The facts known to you as to the matter or transaction under consideration;

(2) Refrain from participating in the board's discussion of the matter or transaction; and

(3) Recuse yourself from voting on the matter or transaction (if you are a director).

[61 FR 60178, Nov. 27, 1996]

§ 563.201 Corporate opportunity.

(a) If you are a director or officer of a savings association, or have the power to direct its management or policies, or otherwise owe a fiduciary duty to a savings association, you must not take advantage of corporate opportunities belonging to the savings association.

(b) A corporate opportunity belongs to a savings association if:

(1) The opportunity is within the corporate powers of the savings association or a subsidiary of the savings association; and

Office of Thrift Supervision, Treasury § 563.560

(2) The opportunity is of present or potential practical advantage to the savings association, either directly or through its subsidiary.

(c) OTS will not deem you to have taken advantage of a corporate opportunity belonging to the savings association if a disinterested and independent majority of the savings association's board of directors, after receiving a full and fair presentation of the matter, rejected the opportunity as a matter of sound business judgment.

[61 FR 60179, Nov. 27, 1996]

Subpart H—Notice of Change of Director or Senior Executive Officer

Source: 63 FR 51274, Sept. 25, 1998, unless otherwise noted.

§ 563.550 What does this subpart do?

This subpart implements 12 U.S.C. 1831i, which requires certain savings associations and savings and loan holding companies to notify the OTS before appointing or employing directors and senior executive officers.

§ 563.555 What definitions apply to this subpart?

The following definitions apply to this subpart:

Director means an individual who serves on the board of directors of a savings association or savings and loan holding company. This term does not include an advisory director who:

(1) Is not elected by the shareholders;

(2) Is not authorized to vote on any matters before the board of directors or any committee of the board of directors;

(3) Provides only general policy advice to the board of directors or any committee of the board of directors; and

(4) Has not been identified by the OTS in writing as an individual who performs the functions of a director, or who exercises significant influence over, or participates in, major policymaking decisions of the board of directors.

Senior executive officer means an individual who holds the title or performs the function of one or more of the following positions (without regard to title, salary, or compensation): president, chief executive officer, chief operating officer, chief financial officer, chief lending officer, or chief investment officer. *Senior executive officer* also includes any other person identified by the OTS in writing as an individual who exercises significant influence over, or participates in, major policymaking decisions, whether or not hired as an employee.

Troubled condition means:

(1) A savings association that has a composite rating of 4 or 5, as composite rating is defined in §516.5(c) of this chapter.

(2) A savings and loan holding company that has an unsatisfactory rating under the OTS's holding company rating system, or that is informed in writing by the OTS that it has an adverse effect on its subsidiary savings association;

(3) A savings association or savings and loan holding company that is subject to a capital directive, a cease-and-desist order, a consent order, a formal written agreement, or a prompt corrective action directive relating to the safety and soundness or financial viability of the savings association, unless otherwise informed in writing by the OTS; or

(4) A savings association or savings and loan holding company that is informed in writing by the OTS that it is in troubled condition based on information available to the OTS.

[63 FR 51274, Sept. 25, 1998, as amended by 66 FR 13008, Mar. 2, 2001]

§ 563.560 Who must give prior notice?

(a) *Savings association or savings and loan holding company.* Except as provided under §563.590, you must notify the OTS at least 30 days before adding or replacing any member of your board of directors, employing any person as a senior executive officer, or changing the responsibilities of any senior executive officer so that the person would assume a different senior executive position if:

(1) You are a savings association and at least one of the following circumstances apply:

§ 563.565

(i) You do not comply with all minimum capital requirements under part 567 of this chapter;
(ii) You are in troubled condition; or
(iii) The OTS has notified you, in connection with its review of a capital restoration plan required under section 38 of the Federal Deposit Insurance Act or part 565 of this chapter or otherwise, that a notice is required under this subpart; or
(2) You are a savings and loan holding company and you are in troubled condition.

(b) *Notice by individual.* If you are an individual seeking election to the board of directors of a savings association or savings and loan holding company described in paragraph (a) of this section, and have not been nominated by management, you must either provide the prior notice required under paragraph (a) of this section or follow the process under § 563.590(b).

§ 563.565 What procedures govern the filing of my notice?

The procedures found in part 516, subpart A of this chapter govern the filing of your notice under § 563.560.

[66 FR 13009, Mar. 2, 2001]

§ 563.570 What information must I include in my notice?

(a) *Content requirements.* Your notice must include:

(1) The information required under 12 U.S.C. 1817(j)(6)(A), and the information prescribed in the Interagency Notice of Change in Director or Senior Executive Officer and the Interagency Biographical and Financial Report which are available from OTS headquarters at the address in part 516 of this chapter; or from any OTS regional office;

(2) Legible fingerprints of the proposed director or senior executive officer. You are not required to file fingerprints if, within three years prior to the date of submission of the notice, the proposed director or senior executive officer provided legible fingerprints as part of a notice filed with the OTS under 12 U.S.C. 1831i; and

(3) Such other information required by the OTS.

(b) *Modification of content requirements.* The OTS may require or accept other information in place of the content requirements in paragraph (a) of this section.

§ 563.575 What procedures govern OTS review of my notice for completeness?

The OTS will first review your notice to determine whether it is complete.

(a) If your notice is complete, the OTS will notify you in writing of the date that the OTS received the complete notice.

(b) If your notice is not complete, the OTS will notify you in writing what additional information you need to submit, why we need the information, and when you must submit it. You must, within the specified time period, provide additional information or request that the OTS suspend processing of the notice. If you fail to act within the specified time period, the OTS may treat the notice as withdrawn or may review the application based on the information provided.

§ 563.580 What standards and procedures will govern OTS review of the substance of my notice?

The OTS will disapprove a notice if, pursuant to the standard set forth in 12 U.S.C. 1831i(e), the OTS finds that the competence, experience, character, or integrity of the proposed director or senior executive officer indicates that it would not be in the best interests of the depositors of the savings association or of the public to permit the individual to be employed by, or associated with, the savings association or savings and loan holding company. If the OTS disapproves a notice, it will issue a written notice that explains why the OTS disapproved the notice. The OTS will send the notice to the savings association or savings and loan holding company and the individual.

§ 563.585 When may a proposed director or senior executive officer begin service?

(a) A proposed director or senior executive officer may begin service 30 days after the date the OTS receives all required information, unless:

(1) The OTS notifies you that it has disapproved the notice; or

(2) The OTS extends the 30-day period for an additional period not to exceed

60 days. If the OTS extends the 30-day period, it will notify you in writing that the period has been extended, and will state the reason for the extension. The proposed director or senior executive officer may begin service upon expiration of the extended period, unless the OTS notifies you that it has disapproved the notice during the extended period.

(b) Notwithstanding paragraph (a) of this section, a proposed director or senior executive officer may begin service after the OTS notifies you, in writing, of its intention not to disapprove the notice.

§ 563.590 When will the OTS waive the prior notice requirement?

(a) *Waiver request.* (1) An individual may serve as a director or senior executive officer before filing a notice under this subpart if the OTS issues a written finding that:

(i) Delay would threaten the safety or soundness of the savings association;

(ii) Delay would not be in the public interest; or

(iii) Other extraordinary circumstances exist that justify waiver of prior notice.

(2) If the OTS grants a waiver, you must file a notice under this subpart within the time period specified by the OTS.

(b) *Automatic waiver.* An individual may serve as a director before filing a notice under this subpart, if the individual was not nominated by management and the individual submits a notice under this subpart within seven days after election as a director.

(c) *Subsequent OTS action.* The OTS may disapprove a notice within 30 days after the OTS issues a waiver under paragraph (a) of this section or within 30 days after the election of an individual who has filed a notice and is serving pursuant to an automatic waiver under paragraph (b) of this section.

PART 563b—CONVERSIONS FROM MUTUAL TO STOCK FORM

Sec.
563b.5 What does this part do?
563b.10 May I form a holding company as part of my conversion?
563b.15 May I form a charitable organization as part of my conversion?
563b.20 May I acquire another insured stock depository institution as part of my conversion?
563b.25 What definitions apply to this part?

Subpart A—Standard Conversions

PRIOR TO CONVERSION

563b.100 What must I do before a conversion?
563b.105 What information must I include in my business plan?
563b.110 Who must review my business plan?
563b.115 How will OTS review my business plan?
563b.120 May I discuss my plans to convert with others?

PLAN OF CONVERSION

563b.125 Must my board of directors adopt a plan of conversion?
563b.130 What must I include in my plan of conversion?
563b.135 How do I notify my members that my board of directors approved a plan of conversion?
563b.140 May I amend my plan of conversion?

FILING REQUIREMENTS

563b.150 What must I include in my application for conversion?
563b.155 How do I file my application for conversion?
563b.160 May I keep portions of my application for conversion confidential?
563b.165 How do I amend my application for conversion?

NOTICE OF FILING OF APPLICATION AND COMMENT PROCESS

563b.180 How do I notify the public that I filed an application for conversion?
563b.185 How may a person comment on my application for conversion?

OTS REVIEW OF THE APPLICATION FOR CONVERSION

563b.200 What actions may OTS take on my application?
563b.205 May a court review OTS's final action on my conversion?

VOTE BY MEMBERS

563b.225 Must I submit the plan of conversion to my members for approval?
563b.230 Who is eligible to vote?
563b.235 How must I notify my members of the meeting?
563b.240 What must I submit to OTS after the members' meeting?

Pt. 563b

Proxy Solicitation

563b.250 Who must comply with these proxy solicitation provisions?
563b.255 What must the form of proxy include?
563b.260 May I use previously executed proxies?
563b.265 How may I use proxies executed under this part?
563b.270 What must I include in my proxy statement?
563b.275 How do I file revised proxy materials?
563b.280 Must I mail a member's proxy solicitation material?
563b.285 What solicitations are prohibited?
563b.290 What will OTS do if a solicitation violates these prohibitions?
563b.295 Will OTS require me to re-solicit proxies?

Offering Circular

563b.300 What must happen before OTS declares my offering circular effective?
563b.305 When may I distribute the offering circular?
563b.310 When must I file a post-effective amendment to the offering circular?

Offers and Sales of Stock

563b.320 Who has priority to purchase my conversion shares?
563b.325 When may I offer to sell my conversion shares?
563b.330 How do I price my conversion shares?
563b.335 How do I sell my conversion shares?
563b.340 What sales practices are prohibited?
563b.345 How may a subscriber pay for my conversion shares?
563b.350 Must I pay interest on payments for conversion shares?
563b.355 What subscription rights must I give to each eligible account holder and each supplemental eligible account holder?
563b.360 Are my officers, directors, and their associates eligible account holders?
563b.365 May other voting members purchase conversion shares in the conversion?
563b.370 Does OTS limit the aggregate purchases by officers, directors, and their associates?
563b.375 How do I allocate my conversion shares if my shares are oversubscribed?
563b.380 May my employee stock ownership plan purchase conversion shares?
563b.385 May I impose any purchase limitations?
563b.390 Must I provide a purchase preference to persons in my local community?
563b.395 What other conditions apply when I offer conversion shares in a community offering, a public offering, or both?

Completion of the Offering

563b.400 When must I complete the sale of my stock?
563b.405 How do I extend the offering period?

Completion of the Conversion

563b.420 When must I complete my conversion?
563b.425 Who may terminate the conversion?
563b.430 What happens to my old charter?
563b.435 What happens to my corporate existence after conversion?
563b.440 What voting rights must I provide to stockholders after the conversion?
563b.445 What must I provide my savings account holders?

Liquidation Account

563b.450 What is a liquidation account?
563b.455 What is the initial balance of the liquidation account?
563b.460 How do I determine the initial balances of liquidation sub-accounts?
563b.465 Do account holders retain any voting rights based on their liquidation sub-accounts?
563b.470 Must I adjust liquidation sub-accounts?
563b.475 What is a liquidation?
563b.480 Does the liquidation account affect my net worth?
563b.485 What provision must I include in my new federal charter?

Post-Conversion

563b.500 What management stock benefit plans may I implement?
563b.505 May my directors, officers, and their associates freely trade shares?
563b.510 May I repurchase shares after conversion?
563b.515 What information must I provide to OTS before I repurchase my shares?
563b.520 May I declare or pay dividends after I convert?
563b.525 Who may acquire my shares after I convert?
563b.530 What other requirements apply after I convert?

Contributions to Charitable Organizations

563b.550 May I donate conversion shares or conversion proceeds to a charitable organization?
563b.555 How do my members approve a charitable contribution?
563b.560 How much may I contribute to a charitable organization?

Office of Thrift Supervision, Treasury

563b.565 What must the charitable organization include in its organizational documents?
563b.570 How do I address conflicts of interest involving my directors?
563b.575 What other requirements apply to charitable organizations?

Subpart B—Voluntary Supervisory Conversions

563b.600 What does this subpart do?
563b.605 How may I conduct a voluntary supervisory conversion?
563b.610 Do my members have rights in a voluntary supervisory conversion?

Eligibility

563b.625 When is a savings association eligible for a voluntary supervisory conversion?
563b.630 When is a state-chartered savings bank eligible for a voluntary supervisory conversion?

Plan of Supervisory Conversion

563b.650 What must I include in my plan of voluntary supervisory conversion?

Voluntary Supervisory Conversion Application

563b.660 What must I include in my voluntary supervisory conversion application?

OTS Review of the Voluntary Supervisory Conversion Application

563b.670 Will OTS approve my voluntary supervisory conversion application?
563b.675 What conditions will OTS impose on an approval?

Offers and Sales of Stock

563b.680 How do I sell my shares?

Post-Conversion

563b.690 Who may not acquire additional shares after the voluntary supervisory conversion?

AUTHORITY: 12 U.S.C. 1462, 1462a, 1463, 1464, 1467a, 2901; 15 U.S.C. 78c, 78l, 78m, 78n, 78w.

SOURCE: 67 FR 52020, Aug. 9, 2002, unless otherwise noted.

§ 563b.5 What does this part do?

(a) *General.* This part governs how a savings association ("you") may convert from the mutual to the stock form of ownership. Subpart A of this part governs standard mutual-to-stock conversions. Subpart B of this part governs voluntary supervisory mutual-to-stock conversions. This part supersedes all inconsistent charter and bylaw provisions of federal savings associations converting to stock form.

(b) *Prescribed forms.* You must use the forms prescribed under this part and provide such information as OTS may require under the forms by regulation or otherwise. The forms required under this part include: Form AC (Application for Conversion); Form PS (Proxy Statement); Form OC (Offering Circular); and Form OF (Order Form).

(c) *Waivers.* OTS may waive any requirement of this part or a provision in any prescribed form. To obtain a waiver, you must file a written request with OTS that:

(1) Specifies the requirement(s) or provision(s) you want OTS to waive;

(2) Demonstrates that the waiver is equitable; is not detrimental to you, your account holders, or other savings associations; and is not contrary to the public interest; and

(3) Includes an opinion of counsel demonstrating that applicable law does not conflict with the requirement or provision.

§ 563b.10 May I form a holding company as part of my conversion?

You may convert to the stock form of ownership as part of a transaction where you organize a holding company to acquire all of your shares upon their issuance. In such a transaction, your holding company will offer rights to purchase its shares instead of your shares. All of the requirements of subpart A generally apply to the holding company as they apply to the savings association. Section 574.6 of this chapter contains OTS's holding company application requirements.

§ 563b.15 May I form a charitable organization as part of my conversion?

When you convert to the stock form, you may form a charitable organization. Your contributions to the charitable organization are governed by the requirements of §§ 563b.550 through 563b.575.

§ 563b.20 May I acquire another insured stock depository institution as part of my conversion?

When you convert to stock form, you may acquire for cash or stock another

§ 563b.25

insured depository institution that is already in the stock form of ownership.

§ 563b.25 What definitions apply to this part?

The following definitions apply to this part and the forms prescribed under this part:

Acting in concert has the same meaning as in § 574.2(c) of this chapter. The rebuttable presumptions of § 574.4(d) of this chapter, other than §§ 574.4(d)(1) and (d)(2) of this chapter, apply to the share purchase limitations at §§ 563b.355 through 563b.395.

Affiliate of, or a person *affiliated with*, a specified person is a person that directly or indirectly, through one or more intermediaries, controls, is controlled by, or is under common control with the specified person.

Associate of a person is:

(1) A corporation or organization (other than you or your majority-owned subsidiaries), if the person is a senior officer or partner, or beneficially owns, directly or indirectly, 10 percent or more of any class of equity securities of the corporation or organization.

(2) A trust or other estate, if the person has a substantial beneficial interest in the trust or estate or is a trustee or fiduciary of the trust or estate. For purposes of §§ 563b.370, 563b.380, 563b.385, 563b.390, 563b.395 and 563b.505, a person who has a substantial beneficial interest in your tax-qualified or non-tax-qualified employee stock benefit plan, or who is a trustee or a fiduciary of the plan, is not an associate of the plan. For the purposes of § 563b.370, your tax-qualified employee stock benefit plan is not an associate of a person.

(3) Any person who is related by blood or marriage to such person and:

(i) Who lives in the same home as the person; or

(ii) Who is your director or senior officer, or a director or senior officer of your holding company or your subsidiary.

Association members or *members* are persons who, under applicable law, are eligible to vote at the meeting on conversion.

Control (including *controlling*, *controlled by*, and *under common control with*) means the direct or indirect power to direct or exercise a controlling influence over the management and policies of a person, whether through the ownership of voting securities, by contract, or otherwise as described in part 574 of this chapter.

Eligibility record date is the date for determining eligible account holders. The eligibility record date must be at least one year before the date your board of directors adopts the plan of conversion.

Eligible account holders are any persons holding qualifying deposits on the eligibility record date.

IRS is the Internal Revenue Service.

Local community includes:

(1) Every county, parish, or similar governmental subdivision in which you have a home or branch office;

(2) Each county's, parish's, or subdivision's metropolitan statistical area;

(3) All zip code areas in your Community Reinvestment Act assessment area; and

(4) Any other area or category you set out in your plan of conversion, as approved by OTS.

Offer, offer to sell, or *offer for sale* is an attempt or offer to dispose of, or a solicitation of an offer to buy, a security or interest in a security for value. Preliminary negotiations or agreements with an underwriter, or among underwriters who are or will be in privity of contract with you, are not offers, offers to sell, or offers for sale.

Person is an individual, a corporation, a partnership, an association, a joint-stock company, a limited liability company, a trust, an unincorporated organization, or a government or political subdivision of a government.

Proxy soliciting material includes a proxy statement, form of proxy, or other written or oral communication regarding the conversion.

Purchase or *buy* includes every contract to acquire a security or interest in a security for value.

Qualifying deposit is the total balance in an account holder's savings accounts at the close of business on the eligibility or supplemental eligibility record date. Your plan of conversion

238

Office of Thrift Supervision, Treasury

§ 563b.105

may provide that only savings accounts with total deposit balances of $50 or more will qualify.

Sale or *sell* includes every contract to dispose of a security or interest in a security for value. An exchange of securities in a merger or acquisition approved by OTS is not a sale.

Savings account is any withdrawable account as defined in § 561.42 of this chapter, including a demand account as defined in § 561.16 of this chapter.

Solicitation and *solicit* is a request for a proxy, whether or not accompanied by or included in a form of proxy; a request to execute, not execute, or revoke a proxy; or the furnishing of a form of proxy or other communication reasonably calculated to cause your members to procure, withhold, or revoke a proxy. Solicitation or solicit does not include providing a form of proxy at the unsolicited request of a member, the acts required to mail communications for members, or ministerial acts performed on behalf of a person soliciting a proxy.

Subscription offering is the offering of shares through nontransferable subscription rights to:

(1) Eligible account holders under § 563b.355;

(2) Tax-qualified employee stock ownership plans under § 563b.380;

(3) Supplemental eligible account holders under § 563b.355; and

(4) Other voting members under § 563b.365.

Supplemental eligibility record date is the date for determining supplemental eligible account holders. The supplemental eligibility record date is the last day of the calendar quarter before OTS approves your conversion and will only occur if OTS has not approved your conversion within 15 months after the eligibility record date.

Supplemental eligible account holders are any persons, except your officers, directors, and their associates, holding qualifying deposits on the supplemental eligibility record date.

Tax-qualified employee stock benefit plan is any defined benefit plan or defined contribution plan, such as an employee stock ownership plan, stock bonus plan, profit-sharing plan, or other plan, and a related trust, that is qualified under sec. 401 of the Internal Revenue Code (26 U.S.C. 401).

Underwriter is any person who purchases any securities from you with a view to distributing the securities, offers or sells securities for you in connection with the securities' distribution, or participates or has a direct or indirect participation in the direct or indirect underwriting of any such undertaking. Underwriter does not include a person whose interest is limited to a usual and customary distributor's or seller's commission from an underwriter or dealer.

Subpart A—Standard Conversions

PRIOR TO CONVERSION

§ 563b.100 What must I do before a conversion?

(a) Your board, or a subcommittee of your board, must meet with OTS before you pass your plan of conversion. The meeting may occur at OTS or your offices at your option. At that meeting you must provide OTS with a written strategic plan that outlines the objectives of the proposed conversion and the intended use of the conversion proceeds.

(b) You should also consult with OTS before you file your application for conversion. OTS will discuss the information that you must include in the application for conversion, general issues that you may confront in the conversion process, and any other pertinent issues.

§ 563b.105 What information must I include in my business plan?

(a) Prior to filing an application for conversion, you must adopt a business plan reflecting your intended plans for deployment of the proposed conversion proceeds. Your business plan is required, under § 563b.150, to be included in your conversion application. At a minimum, your business plan must address:

(1) Your projected operations and activities for three years following the conversion. You must describe how you will deploy the conversion proceeds at the converted savings association (and holding company, if applicable), what

239

§ 563b.110

opportunities are available to reasonably achieve your planned deployment of conversion proceeds in your proposed market areas, and how your deployment will provide a reasonable return on investment commensurate with investment risk, investor expectations, and industry norms, by the final year of the business plan. You must include three years of projected financial statements. The business plan must provide that the converted savings association must retain at least 50 percent of the net conversion proceeds. OTS may require that a larger percentage of proceeds remain in the institution.

(2) Your plan for deploying conversion proceeds to meet credit and lending needs in your proposed market areas. OTS strongly discourages business plans that provide for a substantial investment in mortgage securities or other securities, except as an interim measure to facilitate orderly, prudent deployment of proceeds during the three years following the conversion, or as part of a properly managed leverage strategy.

(3) The risks associated with your plan for deployment of conversion proceeds, and the effect of this plan on management resources, staffing, and facilities.

(4) The expertise of your management and board of directors, or that you have planned for adequate staffing and controls to prudently manage the growth, expansion, new investment, and other operations and activities proposed in your business plan.

(b) You may not project returns of capital or special dividends in any part of the business plan. A newly converted company may not plan on stock repurchases in the first year of the business plan.

§ 563b.110 Who must review my business plan?

(a) Your chief executive officer and members of the board of directors must review, and at least two-thirds of your board of directors must approve, the business plan.

(b) Your chief executive officer and at least two-thirds of the board of directors must certify that the business plan accurately reflects the intended plans for deployment of conversion proceeds, and that any new initiatives reflected in the business plan are reasonably achievable. You must submit these certifications with your business plan, as part of your conversion application under § 563b.150.

§ 563b.115 How will OTS review my business plan?

(a) OTS will review your business plan to determine that it demonstrates a safe and sound deployment of conversion proceeds, as part of its review of your conversion application. In making its determination, OTS will consider how you have addressed the applicable factors of § 563b.105. No single factor will be determinative. OTS will review every case on its merits.

(b) You must file your business plan with the Regional Office. OTS may request additional information, if necessary, to support its determination under paragraph (a) of this section. You must file your business plan as a confidential exhibit to the Form AC.

(c) If OTS approves your application for conversion and you complete your conversion, you must operate within the parameters of your business plan. You must obtain the prior written approval of the Regional Director for any material deviations from your business plan.

§ 563b.120 May I discuss my plans to convert with others?

(a) You may discuss information about your conversion with individuals that you authorize to prepare documents for your conversion.

(b) Except as permitted under paragraph (a) of this section, you must keep all information about your conversion confidential until your board of directors adopts your plan of conversion.

(c) If you violate this section, OTS may require you to take remedial action. For example, OTS may require you to take any or all of the following actions:

(1) Publicly announce that you are considering a conversion;

(2) Set an eligibility record date acceptable to OTS;

Office of Thrift Supervision, Treasury § 563b.135

(3) Limit the subscription rights of any person who violates or aids a violation of this section; or

(4) Take any other action to assure that your conversion is fair and equitable.

PLAN OF CONVERSION

§ 563b.125 Must my board of directors adopt a plan of conversion?

Prior to filing an application for conversion, your board of directors must adopt a plan of conversion that conforms to §§ 563b.320 through 563b.485 and 563b.505. Your board of directors must adopt the plan by at least a two-thirds vote. Your plan of conversion is required, under § 563b.150, to be included in your conversion application.

§ 563b.130 What must I include in my plan of conversion?

You must include the information included in §§ 563b.320 through 563b.485 and 563b.505 in your plan of conversion. OTS may require you to delete or revise any provision in your plan of conversion if OTS determines the provision is inequitable; is detrimental to you, your account holders, or other savings associations; or is contrary to public interest.

§ 563b.135 How do I notify my members that my board of directors approved a plan of conversion?

(a) *Notice.* You must promptly notify your members that your board of directors adopted a plan of conversion and that a copy of the plan is available for the members' inspection in your home office and in your branch offices. You must mail a letter to each member or publish a notice in the local newspaper in every local community where you have an office. You may also issue a press release. OTS may require broader publication, if necessary, to ensure adequate notice to your members.

(b) *Contents of notice.* You may include any of the following statements and descriptions in your letter, notice, or press release.

(1) Your board of directors adopted a proposed plan to convert from a mutual to a stock savings institution.

(2) You will send your members a proxy statement with detailed information on the proposed conversion before you convene a members' meeting to vote on the conversion.

(3) Your members will have an opportunity to approve or disapprove the proposed conversion at a meeting. At least a majority of the eligible votes must approve the conversion.

(4) You will not vote existing proxies to approve or disapprove the conversion. You will solicit new proxies for voting on the proposed conversion.

(5) OTS, and in the case of a state-chartered savings association, the appropriate state regulator, must approve the conversion before the conversion will be effective. Your members will have an opportunity to file written comments, including objections and materials supporting the objections, with OTS.

(6) The IRS must issue a favorable tax ruling, or a tax expert must issue an appropriate tax opinion, on the tax consequences of your conversion before OTS will approve the conversion. The ruling or opinion must indicate the conversion will be a tax-free reorganization.

(7) OTS, and in the case of a state-chartered savings association, the appropriate state regulator, might not approve the conversion, and the IRS or a tax expert might not issue a favorable tax ruling or tax opinion.

(8) Savings account holders will continue to hold accounts in the converted savings association with the same dollar amounts, rates of return, and general terms as existing deposits. FDIC will continue to insure the accounts.

(9) Your conversion will not affect borrowers' loans, including the amount, rate, maturity, security, and other contractual terms.

(10) Your business of accepting deposits and making loans will continue without interruption.

(11) Your current management and staff will continue to conduct current services for depositors and borrowers under current policies and in existing offices.

(12) You may continue to be a member of the Federal Home Loan Bank System.

(13) You may substantively amend your proposed plan of conversion before the members' meeting.

§ 563b.140

(14) You may terminate the proposed conversion.

(15) After OTS, and in the case of a state-chartered savings association, the appropriate state regulator, approves the proposed conversion, you will send proxy materials providing additional information. After you send proxy materials, members may telephone or write to you with additional questions.

(16) The proposed record date for determining the eligible account holders who are entitled to receive subscription rights to purchase your shares.

(17) A brief description of the circumstances under which supplemental eligible account holders will receive subscription rights to purchase your shares.

(18) A brief description of how voting members may participate in the conversion.

(19) A brief description of how directors, officers, and employees will participate in the conversion.

(20) A brief description of the proposed plan of conversion.

(21) The par value (if any) and approximate number of shares you will issue and sell in the conversion.

(c) *Other requirements.* (1) You may not solicit proxies, provide financial statements, describe the benefits of conversion, or estimate the value of your shares upon conversion in the letter, notice, or press release.

(2) If you respond to inquiries about the conversion, you may address only the matters listed in paragraph (b) of this section.

§ 563b.140 May I amend my plan of conversion?

You may amend your plan of conversion before you solicit proxies. After you solicit proxies, you may amend your plan of conversion only if OTS concurs.

FILING REQUIREMENTS

§ 563b.150 What must I include in my application for conversion?

(a) Your application for conversion must include all of the following information.

(1) Your plan of conversion.

(2) Pricing materials meeting the requirements of § 563b.200(b).

(3) Proxy soliciting materials under § 563b.270, including:

(i) A preliminary proxy statement with signed financial statements;

(ii) A form of proxy meeting the requirements of § 563b.255; and

(iii) Any additional proxy soliciting materials, including press releases, personal solicitation instructions, radio or television scripts that you plan to use or furnish to your members, and a legal opinion indicating that any marketing materials comply with all applicable securities laws.

(4) An offering circular described in § 563b.300.

(5) The documents and information required by Form AC. You may obtain Form AC from OTS Washington and Regional Offices (see § 516.40 of this chapter) and OTS's website (*www.ots.treas.gov*).

(6) Where indicated, written consents, signed and dated, of any accountant, attorney, investment banker, appraiser, or other professional who prepared, reviewed, passed upon, or certified any statement, report, or valuation for use. *See* Form AC, instruction B(7).

(7) Your business plan, submitted as a separately bound, confidential exhibit. *See* § 563b.160.

(8) Any additional information OTS requests.

(b) OTS will not accept for filing, and will return, any application for conversion that is improperly executed, materially deficient, substantially incomplete, or that provides for unreasonable conversion expenses.

§ 563b.155 How do I file my application for conversion?

You must file seven copies of your application for conversion on Form AC. You must file the original and three conformed copies with the Applications Filing Room in Washington, and three conformed copies with the appropriate Regional Office at the addresses in § 516.40 of this chapter.

§ 563b.160 May I keep portions of my application for conversion confidential?

(a) OTS makes all filings under this part available to the public, but may keep portions of your application for

Office of Thrift Supervision, Treasury § 563b.200

conversion confidential under paragraph (b) of this section.

(b) You may request OTS to keep portions of your application confidential. To do so, you must separately bind and clearly designate as "confidential" any portion of your application for conversion that you deem confidential. You must provide a written statement specifying the grounds supporting your request for confidentiality. OTS will not treat as confidential the portion of your application describing how you plan to meet your Community Reinvestment Act (CRA) objectives. The CRA portion of your application may not incorporate by reference information contained in the confidential portion of your application.

(c) OTS will determine whether confidential information must be made available to the public under 5 U.S.C. 552 and part 505 of this chapter. OTS will advise you before it makes information you designated as "confidential" available to the public.

§ 563b.165 How do I amend my application for conversion?

To amend your application for conversion, you must:

(a) File an amendment with an appropriate facing sheet;

(b) Number each amendment consecutively;

(c) Respond to all issues raised by OTS; and

(d) Demonstrate that the amendment conforms to all applicable regulations.

NOTICE OF FILING OF APPLICATION AND COMMENT PROCESS

§ 563b.180 How do I notify the public that I filed an application for conversion?

(a) You must publish a public notice of the application in accordance with the procedures in subpart B of part 516 of this chapter. You must simultaneously prominently post the notice in your home office and all branch offices.

(b) Promptly after publication, you must file four copies of any public notice and an affidavit of publication from each publisher. You must file the original and one copy with the Applications Filing Room in Washington, and two copies with the appropriate Regional Office at the addresses in § 516.40 of this chapter.

(c) If OTS does not accept your application for conversion under § 563b.200 and requires you to file a new application, you must publish and post a new notice and allow an additional 30 days for comment.

[69 FR 68250, Nov. 24, 2004]

§ 563b.185 How may a person comment on my application for conversion?

Commenters may submit comments on your application in accordance with the procedures in subpart C of part 516 of this chapter. A commenter must file the original and one copy of any comments with the Applications Filing Room in Washington and two copies with the appropriate Regional Office at the addresses in § 516.40 of this chapter.

[69 FR 68250, Nov. 24, 2004]

OTS REVIEW OF THE APPLICATION FOR CONVERSION

§ 563b.200 What actions may OTS take on my application?

(a) OTS may approve your application for conversion only if:

(1) Your conversion complies with this part;

(2) You will meet your regulatory capital requirements under part 567 of this chapter after the conversion; and

(3) Your conversion will not result in a taxable reorganization under the Internal Revenue Code of 1986, as amended.

(b) OTS will review the appraisal required by § 563b.150(a)(2) in determining whether to approve your application. OTS will review the appraisal under the following requirements.

(1) Independent persons experienced and expert in corporate appraisal, and acceptable to OTS, must prepare the appraisal report.

(2) An affiliate of the appraiser may serve as an underwriter or selling agent, if you ensure that the appraiser is separate from the underwriter or selling agent affiliate and the underwriter or selling agent affiliate does not make recommendations or affect the appraisal.

(3) The appraiser may not receive any fee in connection with the conversion other than for appraisal services.

§ 563b.205

(4) The appraisal report must include a complete and detailed description of the elements of the appraisal, a justification for the appraisal methodology, and sufficient support for the conclusions.

(5) If the appraisal is based on a capitalization of your pro forma income, it must indicate the basis for determining the income to be derived from the sale of shares, and demonstrate that the earnings multiple used is appropriate, including future earnings growth assumptions.

(6) If the appraisal is based on a comparison of your shares with outstanding shares of existing stock associations, the existing stock associations must be reasonably comparable in size, market area, competitive conditions, risk profile, profit history, and expected future earnings.

(7) OTS may decline to process the application for conversion and deem it materially deficient or substantially incomplete if the initial appraisal report is materially deficient or substantially incomplete.

(8) You may not represent or imply that OTS approved the appraisal.

(c) OTS will review your compliance record under part 563e of this chapter and your business plan to determine how you will serve the convenience and needs of your communities after the conversion.

(1) Based on this review, OTS may approve your application, deny your application, or approve your application on the condition that you will improve your CRA performance or that you will address the particular credit or lending needs of the communities that you will serve.

(2) OTS may deny your application if your business plan does not demonstrate that your proposed use of conversion proceeds will help you to meet the credit and lending needs of the communities that you will serve.

(d) OTS may request that you amend your application if further explanation is necessary, material is missing, or material must be corrected.

(e) OTS will deny your application if the application does not meet the requirements of this subpart, unless OTS waives the requirement under § 563b.5(c).

§ 563b.205 May a court review OTS's final action on my conversion?

(a) Any person aggrieved by OTS's final action on your application for conversion may ask the court of appeals of the United States for the circuit in which the principal office or residence of such person is located, or the U.S. Court of Appeals for the District of Columbia Circuit, to review the action under 12 U.S.C. 1464(i)(2)(B).

(b) To obtain court review of the action, this statute requires the aggrieved person to file a written petition requesting that the court modify, terminate, or set aside the final OTS action. The aggrieved person must file the petition with the court within the later of 30 days after OTS publishes notice of OTS's final action in the FEDERAL REGISTER or 30 days after you mail the proxy statement to your members under § 563b.235.

VOTE BY MEMBERS

§ 563b.225 Must I submit the plan of conversion to my members for approval?

(a) After OTS approves your plan of conversion, you must submit your plan of conversion to your members for approval. You must obtain this approval at a meeting of your members, which may be a special or annual meeting, unless you are a state-chartered savings association and state law requires you to obtain approval at an annual meeting.

(b) Your members must approve your plan of conversion by a majority of the total outstanding votes, unless you are a state-chartered savings association and state law prescribes a higher percentage.

(c) Your members may vote in person or by proxy.

(d) You may notify eligible account holders or supplemental eligible account holders who are not voting members of your proposed conversion. You may include only the information in § 563b.135 in your notice.

§ 563b.230 Who is eligible to vote?

You determine members' eligibility to vote by setting a voting record date. You must set a voting record date that is not more than 60 days nor less than

Office of Thrift Supervision, Treasury § 563b.255

20 days before your meeting, unless you are a state-chartered savings association and state law requires a different voting record date.

§ 563b.235 How must I notify my members of the meeting?

(a) You must notify your members of the meeting to consider your conversion by sending the members a proxy statement authorized by OTS.

(b) You must notify your members 20 to 45 days before your meeting, unless you are a state-chartered savings association and state law requires a different notice period.

(c) You must also notify each beneficial holder of an account held in a fiduciary capacity:

(1) If you are a federal association and the name of the beneficial holder is disclosed on your records; or

(2) If you are a state-chartered association and the beneficial holder possesses voting rights under state law.

§ 563b.240 What must I submit to OTS after the members' meeting?

(a) Promptly after the members' meeting, you must file all of the following information with OTS:

(1) A certified copy of each adopted resolution on the conversion.

(2) The total votes eligible to be cast.

(3) The total votes represented in person or by proxy.

(4) The total votes cast in favor of and against each matter.

(5) The percentage of votes necessary to approve each matter.

(6) An opinion of counsel that you conducted the members' meeting in compliance with all applicable state or federal laws and regulations.

(b) Promptly after completion of the conversion, you must submit an opinion of counsel that you complied with all laws applicable to the conversion.

PROXY SOLICITATION

§ 563b.250 Who must comply with these proxy solicitation provisions?

(a) You must comply with these proxy solicitation provisions when you provide proxy solicitation material to members for the meeting to vote on your plan of conversion.

(b) Your members must comply with these proxy solicitation provisions when they provide proxy solicitation materials to members for the meeting to vote on your conversion, pursuant to § 563b.280, except where:

(1) The member solicits 50 people or fewer and does not solicit proxies on your behalf; or

(2) The member solicits proxies through newspaper advertisements after your board of directors adopts the plan of conversion. Any newspaper advertisements may include only the following information:

(i) Your name;

(ii) The reason for the advertisement;

(iii) The proposal or proposals to be voted upon;

(iv) Where a member may obtain a copy of the proxy solicitation material; and

(v) A request for your members to vote at the meeting.

§ 563b.255 What must the form of proxy include?

The form of proxy must include all of the following:

(a) A statement in bold face type stating that management is soliciting the proxy.

(b) Blank spaces where the member must date and sign the proxy.

(c) Clear and impartial identification of each matter or group of related matters that members will vote upon. You must include any proposed charitable contribution as an item to be voted on separately.

(d) The phrase "Revocable Proxy" in bold face type (at least 18 point).

(e) A description of any charter or state law requirement that restricts or conditions votes by proxy.

(f) An acknowledgment that the member received a proxy statement before he or she signed the form of proxy.

(g) The date, time, and the place of the meeting, when available.

(h) A way for the member to specify by ballot whether he or she approves or disapproves of each matter that members will vote upon.

(i) A statement that management will vote the proxy in accordance with the member's specifications.

(j) A statement in bold face type indicating how management will vote the proxy if the member does not specify a choice for a matter.

245

§ 563b.260 May I use previously executed proxies?

You may not use previously executed proxies for the plan of conversion vote. If members consider your plan of conversion at an annual meeting, you may vote proxies obtained through other proxy solicitations only on matters not related to your plan of conversion.

§ 563b.265 How may I use proxies executed under this part?

You may vote a proxy obtained under this part on matters that are incidental to the conduct of the meeting. You may not vote a proxy obtained under this subpart at any meeting other than the meeting (or any adjournment of the meeting) to vote on your plan of conversion.

§ 563b.270 What must I include in my proxy statement?

(a) *Content requirements.* You must prepare your proxy statement in compliance with this part and Form PS. You may obtain Form PS from OTS Washington and Regional Offices (see § 516.40 of this chapter) and OTS's website (*http://www.ots.treas.gov*).

(b) *Other requirements.* (1) OTS will review your proxy solicitation material when it reviews the application for conversion and will authorize the use of proxy solicitation material.

(2) You must provide an authorized written proxy statement to your members before or at the same time you provide any other soliciting material. You must mail authorized proxy solicitation material to your members within ten days after OTS authorizes the solicitation.

§ 563b.275 How do I file revised proxy materials?

(a) You must file revised proxy materials as an amendment to your application for conversion. See § 563b.155 for where to file.

(b) To revise your proxy solicitation materials, you must file:

(1) Seven copies of your revised proxy materials as required by Form PS;

(2) Seven copies of your revised form of proxy, if applicable; and

(3) Seven copies of any additional proxy solicitation material subject to § 563b.270.

(c) You must mark four of the seven required copies to clearly indicate changes from the prior filing.

(d) You must file seven definitive copies of all proxy solicitation material, in the form in which you furnish the material to your members. You must file no later than the date that you send or give the proxy solicitation material to your members. You must indicate the date that you will release the materials.

(e) Unless OTS requests you to do so, you do not have to file copies of replies to inquiries from your members or copies of communications that merely request members to sign and return proxy forms.

§ 563b.280 Must I mail a member's proxy solicitation material?

(a) You must mail the member's authorized proxy solicitation material if:

(1) Your board of directors adopted a plan of conversion;

(2) A member requests in writing that you mail the proxy solicitation material;

(3) OTS has authorized the member's proxy solicitation; and

(4) The member agrees to defray your reasonable expenses.

(b) As soon as practicable after you receive a request under paragraph (a) of this section, you must mail or otherwise furnish the following information to the member:

(1) The approximate number of members that you solicited or will solicit, or the approximate number of members of any group of account holders that the member designates; and

(2) The estimated cost of mailing the proxy solicitation material for the member.

(c) You must mail authorized proxy solicitation material to the designated members promptly after the member furnishes the materials, envelopes (or other containers), and postage (or payment for postage) to you.

(d) You are not responsible for the content of a member's proxy solicitation material.

(e) A member may furnish other members its own proxy solicitation material, authorized by OTS, subject to the rules in this section.

Office of Thrift Supervision, Treasury

§ 563b.310

§ 563b.285 What solicitations are prohibited?

(a) *False or misleading statements.* (1) No one may use proxy solicitation material for the members' meeting if the material contains any statement which, considering the time and the circumstances of the statement:

(i) Is false or misleading with respect to any material fact;

(ii) Omits any material fact that is necessary to make the statements not false or misleading; or

(iii) Omits any material fact that is necessary to correct a statement in an earlier communication that has become false or misleading.

(2) No one may represent or imply that OTS determined that the proxy solicitation material is accurate, complete, not false or not misleading, or passed upon the merits of or approved any proposal.

(b) *Other prohibited solicitations.* No person may solicit:

(1) An undated or post-dated proxy;

(2) A proxy that states it will be dated after the date it is signed by a member;

(3) A proxy that is not revocable at will by the member; or

(4) A proxy that is part of another document or instrument.

§ 563b.290 What will OTS do if a solicitation violates these prohibitions?

(a) If a solicitation violates § 563b.285, OTS may require remedial measures, including:

(1) Correction of the violation by a retraction and a new solicitation;

(2) Rescheduling the members' meeting; or

(3) Any other actions necessary to ensure a fair vote.

(b) OTS may also bring an enforcement action against the violator.

§ 563b.295 Will OTS require me to resolicit proxies?

If you amend your application for conversion, OTS may require you to resolicit proxies for your members' meeting as a condition of approval of the amendment.

OFFERING CIRCULAR

§ 563b.300 What must happen before OTS declares my offering circular effective?

(a) You must prepare and file your offering circular with OTS in compliance with this part and Form OC and, where applicable, part 563g of this chapter. Section 563b.155 governs where to file your offering circular. You may obtain Form OC from OTS Washington and Regional Offices (see § 516.40 of this chapter) and OTS's website (*http://www.ots.treas.gov).*

(b) You must condition your stock offering upon member approval of your plan of conversion.

(c) OTS will review the Form OC and may comment on the included disclosures and financial statements.

(d) You must file seven copies of each revised offering circular, final offering circular, and any post-effective amendment to the final offering circular.

(e) OTS will not approve the adequacy or accuracy of the offering circular or the disclosures.

(f) After you satisfactorily address OTS's concerns, you must request OTS to declare your Form OC effective for a time period. The time period may not exceed the maximum time period for the completion of the sale of all of your shares under § 563b.400.

§ 563b.305 When may I distribute the offering circular?

(a) You may distribute a preliminary offering circular at the same time as or after you mail the proxy statement to your members.

(b) You may not distribute an offering circular until OTS declares it effective. You must distribute the offering circular in accordance with this part.

(c) You must distribute your offering circular to persons listed in your plan of conversion within 10 days after OTS declares it effective.

§ 563b.310 When must I file a post-effective amendment to the offering circular?

(a) You must file a post-effective amendment to the offering circular with OTS when a material event or change of circumstance occurs.

(b) After OTS declares the post-effective amendment effective, you must

247

§ 563b.320

immediately deliver the amendment to each person who subscribed for or ordered shares in the offering.

(c) Your post-effective amendment must indicate that each person may increase, decrease, or rescind their subscription or order.

(d) The post-effective offering period must remain open no less than 10 days nor more than 20 days, unless OTS approves a longer rescission period.

OFFERS AND SALES OF STOCK

§ 563b.320 Who has priority to purchase my conversion shares?

You must offer to sell your shares in the following order:
(a) Eligible account holders.
(b) Tax-qualified employee stock ownership plans.
(c) Supplemental eligible account holders.
(d) Other voting members who have subscription rights.
(e) Your community, your community and the general public, or the general public.

§ 563b.325 When may I offer to sell my conversion shares?

(a) You may offer to sell your conversion shares after OTS approves your conversion, authorizes your proxy statement, and declares your offering circular effective.

(b) The offer may commence at the same time you start the proxy solicitation of your members.

§ 563b.330 How do I price my conversion shares?

(a) You must sell your conversion shares at a uniform price per share and at a total price that is equal to the estimated pro forma market value of your shares after you convert.

(b) The maximum price must be no more than 15 percent above the midpoint of the estimated price range in your offering circular.

(c) The minimum price must be no more than 15 percent below the midpoint of the estimated price range in your offering circular.

(d) If OTS permits, you may increase the maximum price of conversion shares sold. The maximum price, as adjusted, must be no more than 15 percent above the maximum price computed under paragraph (b) of this section.

(e) The maximum price must be between $5 and $50 per share.

(f) You must include the estimated price in any preliminary offering circular.

§ 563b.335 How do I sell my conversion shares?

(a) You must distribute order forms to all eligible account holders, supplemental eligible account holders, and other voting members to enable them to subscribe for the conversion shares they are permitted under the plan of conversion. You may either send the order forms with your offering circular or after you distribute your offering circular.

(b) You may sell your conversion shares in a community offering, a public offering, or both. You may begin the community offering, the public offering, or both at any time during the subscription offering or upon conclusion of the subscription offering.

(c) You may pay underwriting commissions (including underwriting discounts). OTS may object to the payment of unreasonable commissions. You may reimburse an underwriter for accountable expenses in a subscription offering if the public offering is limited. If no public offering occurs, you may pay an underwriter a consulting fee. OTS may object to the payment of unreasonable consulting fees.

(d) If you conduct the community offering, the public offering, or both at the same time as the subscription offering, you must fill all subscription orders first.

(e) You must prepare your order form in compliance with this part and Form OF. You may obtain Form OF from OTS Washington and Regional Offices (see § 516.40 of this chapter) and OTS's website (*http://www.ots.treas.gov*).

§ 563b.340 What sales practices are prohibited?

(a) In connection with offers, sales, or purchases of conversion shares under this part, you and your directors, officers, agents, or employees may not:

(1) Employ any device, scheme, or artifice to defraud;

Office of Thrift Supervision, Treasury § 563b.355

(2) Obtain money or property by means of any untrue statement of a material fact or any omission of a material fact necessary to make the statements, in light of the circumstances under which they were made, not misleading; or

(3) Engage in any act, transaction, practice, or course of business that operates or would operate as a fraud or deceit upon a purchaser or seller.

(b) During your conversion, no person may:

(1) Transfer, or enter into any agreement or understanding to transfer, the legal or beneficial ownership of subscription rights for your conversion shares or the underlying securities to the account of another;

(2) Make any offer, or any announcement of an offer, to purchase any of your conversion shares from anyone but you; or

(3) Knowingly acquire more than the maximum purchase allowable under your plan of conversion.

(c) The restrictions in paragraphs (b)(1) and (b)(2) of this section do not apply to offers for more than 10 percent of any class of conversion shares by:

(1) An underwriter or a selling group, acting on your behalf, that makes the offer with a view toward public resale; or

(2) One or more of your tax-qualified employee stock ownership plans so long as the plan or plans do not beneficially own more than 25 percent of any class of your equity securities in the aggregate.

(d) If any person is found to have violated the restrictions in paragraphs (b)(1) and (b)(2) of this section, they may face prosecution or other legal action.

§ 563b.345 How may a subscriber pay for my conversion shares?

(a) A subscriber may purchase conversion shares with cash, by a withdrawal from a savings account, or a withdrawal from a certificate of deposit. If a subscriber purchases shares by a withdrawal from a certificate of deposit, you may not assess a penalty for the withdrawal.

(b) You may not extend credit to any person to purchase your conversion shares.

§ 563b.350 Must I pay interest on payments for conversion shares?

(a) You must pay interest from the date you receive a payment for conversion shares until the date you complete or terminate the conversion. You must pay interest at no less than your passbook rate for amounts paid in cash, check, or money order.

(b) If a subscriber withdraws money from a savings account to purchase conversion shares, you must pay interest on the payment until you complete or terminate the conversion as if the withdrawn amount remained in the account.

(c) If a depositor fails to maintain the applicable minimum balance requirement because he or she withdraws money from a certificate of deposit to purchase conversion shares, you may cancel the certificate and pay interest at no less than your passbook rate on any remaining balance.

§ 563b.355 What subscription rights must I give to each eligible account holder and each supplemental eligible account holder?

(a) You must give each eligible account holder subscription rights to purchase conversion shares in an amount equal to the greater of:

(1) The maximum purchase limitation established for the community offering or the public offering under § 563b.395;

(2) One-tenth of one percent of the total stock offering; or

(3) Fifteen times the following number: The total number of conversion shares that you will issue, multiplied by the following fraction. The numerator is the total qualifying deposit of the eligible account holder. The denominator is the total qualifying deposits of all eligible account holders. You must round down the product of this multiplied fraction to the next whole number.

(b) You must give subscription rights to purchase shares to each supplemental eligible account holder in the same amount as described in paragraph (a) of this section, except that you must compute the fraction described in

§ 563b.360

paragraph (a)(3) of this section as follows: The numerator is the total qualifying deposit of the supplemental eligible account holder. The denominator is the total qualifying deposits of all supplemental eligible account holders.

§ 563b.360 Are my officers, directors, and their associates eligible account holders?

Your officers, directors, and their associates may be eligible account holders. However, if an officer, director, or his or her associate receives subscription rights based on increased deposits in the year before the eligibility record date, you must subordinate subscription rights for these deposits to subscription rights exercised by other eligible account holders.

§ 563b.365 May other voting members purchase conversion shares in the conversion?

(a) You must give rights to purchase your conversion shares in the conversion to voting members who are neither eligible account holders nor supplemental eligible account holders. You must allocate rights to each voting member that are equal to the greater of:

(1) The maximum purchase limitation established for the community offering and the public offering under § 563b.395; or

(2) One-tenth of one percent of the total stock offering.

(b) You must subordinate the voting members' rights to the rights of eligible account holders, tax-qualified employee stock ownership plans, and supplemental eligible account holders.

§ 563b.370 Does OTS limit the aggregate purchases by officers, directors, and their associates?

(a) When you convert, your officers, directors, and their associates may not purchase, in the aggregate, more than the following percentage of your total stock offering:

Institution size	Officer and director purchases (percent)
$50,000,000 or less	35
$50,000,001–100,000,000	34
$100,000,001–150,000,000	33
$150,000,001–200,000,000	32
$200,000,001–250,000,000	31
$250,000,001–300,000,000	30

Institution size	Officer and director purchases (percent)
$300,000,001–350,000,000	29
$350,000,001–400,000,000	28
$400,000,001–450,000,000	27
$450,000,001–500,000,000	26
Over $500,000,000	25

(b) The purchase limitations in this section do not apply to shares held in tax-qualified employee stock benefit plans that are attributable to your officers, directors, and their associates.

§ 563b.375 How do I allocate my conversion shares if my shares are oversubscribed?

(a) If your conversion shares are oversubscribed by your eligible account holders, you must allocate shares among the eligible account holders so that each, to the extent possible, may purchase 100 shares.

(b) If your conversion shares are oversubscribed by your supplemental eligible account holders, you must allocate shares among the supplemental eligible account holders so that each, to the extent possible, may purchase 100 shares.

(c) If a person is an eligible account holder and a supplemental eligible account holder, you must include the eligible account holder's allocation in determining the number of conversion shares that you may allocate to the person as a supplemental eligible account holder.

(d) For conversion shares that you do not allocate under paragraphs (a) and (b) of this section, you must allocate the shares among the eligible or supplemental eligible account holders equitably, based on the amounts of qualifying deposits. You must describe this method of allocation in your plan of conversion.

(e) If shares remain after you have allocated shares as provided in paragraphs (a) and (b) of this section, and if your voting members oversubscribe, you must allocate your conversion shares among those members equitably. You must describe the method of allocation in your plan of conversion.

§ 563b.380 May my employee stock ownership plan purchase conversion shares?

(a) Your tax-qualified employee stock ownership plan may purchase up to 10 percent of the total offering of your conversion shares.

(b) If OTS approves a revised stock valuation range as described in § 563b.330(e), and the final conversion stock valuation range exceeds the former maximum stock offering range, you may allocate conversion shares to your tax-qualified employee stock ownership plan, up to the 10 percent limit in paragraph (a) of this section.

(c) If your tax-qualified employee stock ownership plan is not able to or chooses not to purchase stock in the offering, it may, with prior OTS approval and appropriate disclosure in your offering circular, purchase stock in the open market, or purchase authorized but unissued conversion shares.

(d) You may include stock contributed to a charitable organization in the conversion in the calculation of the total offering of conversion shares under paragraphs (a) and (b) of this section, unless OTS objects on supervisory grounds.

§ 563b.385 May I impose any purchase limitations?

(a) You may limit the number of shares that any person, group of associated persons, or persons otherwise acting in concert, may subscribe to up to five percent of the total stock sold.

(b) If you set a limit of five percent under paragraph (a) of this section, you may modify that limit with OTS approval to provide that any person, group of associated persons, or persons otherwise acting in concert subscribing for five percent, may purchase between five and ten percent as long as the aggregate amount that the subscribers purchase does not exceed 10 percent of the total stock offering.

(c) You may require persons exercising subscription rights to purchase a minimum number of conversion shares. The minimum number of shares must equal the lesser of the number of shares obtained by a $500 subscription or 25 shares.

(d) In setting purchase limitations under this section, you may not aggregate conversion shares attributed to a person in your tax-qualified employee stock ownership plan with shares purchased directly by, or otherwise attributable to, that person.

[67 FR 52020, Aug. 9, 2002, as amended at 72 FR 35149, June 27, 2007]

§ 563b.390 Must I provide a purchase preference to persons in my local community?

(a) In your subscription offering, you may give a purchase preference to eligible account holders, supplemental eligible account holders, and voting members residing in your local community.

(b) In your community offering, you must give a purchase preference to natural persons residing in your local community.

§ 563b.395 What other conditions apply when I offer conversion shares in a community offering, a public offering, or both?

(a) You must offer and sell your stock to achieve a widespread distribution of the stock.

(b) If you offer shares in a community offering, a public offering, or both, you must first fill orders for your stock up to a maximum of two percent of the conversion stock on a basis that will promote a widespread distribution of stock. You must allocate any remaining shares on an equal number of shares per order basis until you fill all orders.

COMPLETION OF THE OFFERING

§ 563b.400 When must I complete the sale of my stock?

You must complete all sales of your stock within 45 calendar days after the last day of the subscription period, unless the offering is extended under § 563b.405.

§ 563b.405 How do I extend the offering period?

(a) You must request, in writing, an extension of any offering period.

(b) OTS may grant extensions of time to sell your shares. OTS will not grant

§ 563b.420

any single extension of more than 90 days.

(c) If OTS grants your request for an extension of time, you must provide a post-effective amendment to the offering circular under § 563b.310 to each person who subscribed for or ordered stock. Your amendment must indicate that OTS extended the offering period and that each person who subscribed for or ordered stock may increase, decrease, or rescind their subscription or order within the time remaining in the extension period.

COMPLETION OF THE CONVERSION

§ 563b.420 When must I complete my conversion?

(a) In your plan of conversion, you must set a date by which the conversion must be completed. This date must not be more than 24 months from the date that your members approve the plan of conversion. The date, once set, may not be extended by you or by OTS. You must terminate the conversion if it is not completed by that date.

(b) Your conversion is complete on the date that you accept the offers for your stock.

§ 563b.425 Who may terminate the conversion?

(a) Your members may terminate the conversion by failing to approve the conversion at your members' meeting.

(b) You may terminate the conversion before your members' meeting.

(c) You may terminate the conversion after the members' meeting only if OTS concurs.

§ 563b.430 What happens to my old charter?

(a) If you are a federally chartered mutual savings association or savings bank, and you convert to a federally chartered stock savings association or savings bank, you must apply to OTS to amend your charter and bylaws consistent with part 552 of this chapter, as part of your application for conversion. You may only include OTS pre-approved anti-takeover provisions in your amended charter and bylaws. *See* 12 CFR 552.4(b)(8).

(b) If you are a federally chartered mutual savings association or savings bank and you convert to a state-chartered stock savings association under this part, you must surrender your federal charter to OTS for cancellation promptly after the state issues your charter. You must promptly file a copy of your new state stock charter with OTS.

(c) If you are a state-chartered mutual savings association or savings bank, and you convert to a federally chartered stock savings association or savings bank, you must apply to OTS for a new charter and bylaws consistent with part 552 of this chapter. You may only include OTS pre-approved anti-takeover provisions in your charter and bylaws. See 12 CFR 552.4(b)(8).

(d) Your new or amended charter must require you to establish and maintain a liquidation account for eligible and supplemental eligible account holders under § 563b.450.

§ 563b.435 What happens to my corporate existence after conversion?

Your corporate existence will continue following your conversion, unless you convert to a state-chartered stock savings association and state law prescribes otherwise.

§ 563b.440 What voting rights must I provide to stockholders after the conversion?

You must provide your stockholders with exclusive voting rights, except as provided in § 563b.445(c).

§ 563b.445 What must I provide my savings account holders?

(a) You must provide each savings account holder, without payment, a withdrawable savings account or accounts in the same amount and under the same terms and conditions as their accounts before your conversion.

(b) You must provide a liquidation account for each eligible and supplemental eligible account holder under § 563b.450.

(c) If you are a state-chartered savings association and state law requires you to provide voting rights to savings account holders or borrowers, your charter must:

(1) Limit these voting rights to the minimum required by state law; and

Office of Thrift Supervision, Treasury

(2) Require you to solicit proxies from the savings account holders and borrowers in the same manner that you solicit proxies from your stockholders.

LIQUIDATION ACCOUNT

§ 563b.450 What is a liquidation account?

(a) A liquidation account represents the potential interest of eligible account holders and supplemental eligible account holders in your net worth at the time of conversion. You must maintain a sub-account to reflect the interest of each account holder.

(b) Before you may provide a liquidation distribution to common stockholders, you must give a liquidation distribution to those eligible account holders and supplemental eligible account holders who hold savings accounts from the time of conversion until liquidation.

(c) You may not record the liquidation account in your financial statements. You must disclose the liquidation account in the footnotes to your financial statements.

§ 563b.455 What is the initial balance of the liquidation account?

The initial balance of the liquidation account is your net worth in the statement of financial condition included in the final offering circular.

§ 563b.460 How do I determine the initial balances of liquidation sub-accounts?

(a)(1) You determine the initial sub-account balance for a savings account held by an eligible account holder by multiplying the initial balance of the liquidation account by the following fraction: The numerator is the qualifying deposit in the savings account expressed in dollars on the eligibility record date. The denominator is total qualifying deposits of all eligible account holders on that date.

(2) You determine the initial sub-account balance for a savings account held by a supplemental eligible account holder by multiplying the initial balance of the liquidation account by the following fraction: The numerator is the qualifying deposit in the savings account expressed in dollars on the supplemental eligibility record date. The denominator is total qualifying deposits of all supplemental eligible account holders on that date.

(3) If an account holder holds a savings account on the eligibility record date and a separate savings account on the supplemental eligibility record date, you must compute separate sub-accounts for the qualifying deposits in the savings account on each record date.

(b) You may not increase the initial sub-account balances. You must decrease the initial balance under § 563b.470 as depositors reduce or close their accounts.

§ 563b.465 Do account holders retain any voting rights based on their liquidation sub-accounts?

Eligible account holders or supplemental eligible account holders do not retain any voting rights based on their liquidation sub-accounts.

§ 563b.470 Must I adjust liquidation sub-accounts?

(a)(1) You must reduce the balance of an eligible account holder's or supplemental eligible account holder's sub-account if the deposit balance in the account holder's savings account at the close of business on any annual closing date, which for purposes of this section is your fiscal year end, after the relevant eligibility record dates is less than:

(i) The deposit balance in the account holder's savings account at the close of business on any other annual closing date after the relevant eligibility record date; or

(ii) The qualifying deposits in the account holder's savings account on the relevant eligibility record date.

(2) The reduction must be proportionate to the reduction in the deposit balance.

(b) If you reduce the balance of a liquidation sub-account, you may not subsequently increase it if the deposit balance increases.

(c) You are not required to adjust the liquidation account and sub-account balances at each annual closing date if you maintain sufficient records to make the computations if a liquidation subsequently occurs.

§ 563b.475

(d) You must maintain the liquidation sub-account for each account holder as long as the account holder maintains an account with the same social security number.

(e) If there is a complete liquidation, you must provide each account holder with a liquidation distribution in the amount of the sub-account balance.

§ 563b.475 What is a liquidation?

(a) A liquidation is a sale of your assets and settlement of your liabilities with the intent to cease operations and close. Upon liquidation, you must return your charter to the governmental agency that issued it. The government agency must cancel your charter.

(b) A merger, consolidation, or similar combination or transaction with another depository institution, is not a liquidation. If you are involved in such a transaction, the surviving institution must assume the liquidation account.

§ 563b.480 Does the liquidation account affect my net worth?

The liquidation account does not affect your net worth.

§ 563b.485 What provision must I include in my new federal charter?

If you convert to federal stock form, you must include the following provision in your new charter: "Liquidation Account. Under OTS regulations, the association must establish and maintain a liquidation account for the benefit of its savings account holders as of _____. If the association undergoes a complete liquidation, it must comply with OTS regulations with respect to the amount and priorities on liquidation of each of the savings account holder's interests in the liquidation account. A savings account holder's interest in the liquidation account does not entitle the savings account holder to any voting rights."

POST-CONVERSION

§ 563b.500 What management stock benefit plans may I implement?

(a) During the 12 months after your conversion, you may implement a stock option plan (Option Plan), an employee stock ownership plan or other tax-qualified employee stock benefit plan (collectively, ESOP), and a management recognition plan (MRP), provided you meet all of the following requirements.

(1) You disclose the plans in your proxy statement and offering circular and indicate in your offering circular that there will be a separate shareholder vote on the Option Plan and the MRP at least six months after the conversion. No shareholder vote is required to implement the ESOP. Your ESOP must be tax-qualified.

(2) Your Option Plan does not encompass more than ten percent of the number of shares that you issued in the conversion.

(3)(i) Your ESOP and MRP do not encompass, in the aggregate, more than ten percent of the number of shares that you issued in the conversion. If you have tangible capital of ten percent or more following the conversion, OTS may permit your ESOP and MRP to encompass, in the aggregate, up to 12 percent of the number of shares issued in the conversion; and

(ii) Your MRP does not encompass more than three percent of the number of shares that you issued in the conversion. If you have tangible capital of ten percent or more after the conversion, OTS may permit your MRP to encompass up to four percent of the number of shares that you issued in the conversion.

(4) No individual receives more than 25 percent of the shares under any plan.

(5) Your directors who are not your officers do not receive more than five percent of the shares of your MRP or Option Plan individually, or 30 percent of any such plan in the aggregate.

(6) Your shareholders approve each of the Option Plan and the MRP by a majority of the total votes eligible to be cast at a duly called meeting before you establish or implement the plan. You may not hold this meeting until six months after your conversion.

(7) When you distribute proxies or related material to shareholders in connection with the vote on a plan, you state that the plan complies with OTS regulations and that OTS does not endorse or approve the plan in any way. You may not make any written or oral representations to the contrary.

(8) You do not grant stock options at less than the market price at the time of grant.

(9) You do not fund the Option Plan or the MRP at the time of the conversion.

(10) Your plan does not begin to vest earlier than one year after shareholders approve the plan, and does not vest at a rate exceeding 20 percent per year.

(11) Your plan permits accelerated vesting only for disability or death, or if you undergo a change of control.

(12) Your plan provides that your executive officers or directors must exercise or forfeit their options in the event the institution becomes critically undercapitalized (as defined in §565.4 of this chapter), is subject to OTS enforcement action, or receives a capital directive under §565.7 of this chapter.

(13) You file a copy of the proposed Option Plan or MRP with OTS and certify to OTS that the plan approved by the shareholders is the same plan that you filed with, and disclosed in, the proxy materials distributed to shareholders in connection with the vote on the plan.

(14) You file the plan and the certification with OTS within five calendar days after your shareholders approve the plan.

(b) You may provide dividend equivalent rights or dividend adjustment rights to allow for stock splits or other adjustments to your stock in your ESOP, MRP, and Option Plan.

(c) The restrictions in paragraph (a) of this section do not apply to plans implemented more than 12 months after the conversion, provided that materials pertaining to any shareholder vote regarding such plans are not distributed within the 12 months after the conversion. If a plan adopted in conformity with paragraph (a) of this section is amended more than 12 months following your conversion, your shareholders must ratify any material deviations to the requirements in paragraph (a).

[72 FR 35149, June 27, 2007]

§ 563b.505 May my directors, officers, and their associates freely trade shares?

(a) Directors and officers who purchase conversion shares may not sell the shares for one year after the date of purchase, except that in the event of the death of the officer or director, the successor in interest may sell the shares.

(b) You must include notice of the restriction described in paragraph (a) of this section on each certificate of stock that a director or officer purchases during the conversion or receives in connection with a stock dividend, stock split, or otherwise with respect to such restricted shares.

(c) You must instruct your stock transfer agent about the transfer restrictions in this section.

(d) For three years after you convert, your officers, directors, and their associates may purchase your stock only from a broker or dealer registered with the Securities and Exchange Commission. However, your officers, directors, and their associates may engage in a negotiated transaction involving more than one percent of your outstanding stock, and may purchase stock through any of your management or employee stock benefit plans.

§ 563b.510 May I repurchase shares after conversion?

(a) You may not repurchase your shares in the first year after the conversion except:

(1) In extraordinary circumstances, you may make open market repurchases of up to five percent of your outstanding stock in the first year after the conversion if you file a notice under §563b.515(a) and OTS does not disapprove your repurchase. OTS will not approve such repurchases unless the repurchase meets the standards in §563b.515(c), and the repurchase is consistent with paragraph (c) of this section.

(2) You may repurchase qualifying shares of a director or conduct an OTS approved repurchase pursuant to an offer made to all shareholders of your association.

§ 563b.515

(3) Repurchases to fund management recognition plans that have been ratified by shareholders do not count toward the repurchase limitations in this section. Repurchases in the first year to fund such plans require prior written notification to OTS.

(4) Purchases to fund tax qualified employee stock benefit plans do not count toward the repurchase limitations in this section.

(b) After the first year, you may repurchase your shares, subject to all other applicable regulatory and supervisory restrictions and paragraph (c) of this section.

(c) All stock repurchases are subject to the following restrictions.

(1) You may not repurchase your shares if the repurchase will reduce your regulatory capital below the amount required for your liquidation account under § 563b.450. You must comply with the capital distribution requirements at part 563, subpart E of this chapter.

(2) The restrictions on share repurchases apply to a charitable organization under § 563b.550. You must aggregate purchases of shares by the charitable organization with your repurchases.

§ 563b.515 What information must I provide to OTS before I repurchase my shares?

(a) To repurchase stock in the first year following conversion, other than repurchases under § 563b.510(a)(3) or (a)(4), you must file a written notice with the OTS. You must provide the following information:

(1) Your proposed repurchase program;

(2) The effect of the repurchases on your regulatory capital; and

(3) The purpose of the repurchases and, if applicable, an explanation of the extraordinary circumstances necessitating the repurchases.

(b) You must file your notice with your Regional Director, with a copy to the Applications Filing Room, at least ten days before you begin your repurchase program.

(c) You may not repurchase your shares if OTS objects to your repurchase program. OTS will not object to your repurchase program if:

(1) Your repurchase program will not adversely affect your financial condition;

(2) You submit sufficient information to evaluate your proposed repurchases;

(3) You demonstrate extraordinary circumstances and a compelling and valid business purpose for the share repurchases; and

(4) Your repurchase program would not be contrary to other applicable regulations.

§ 563b.520 May I declare or pay dividends after I convert?

You may declare or pay a dividend on your shares after you convert if:

(a) The dividend will not reduce your regulatory capital below the amount required for your liquidation account under § 563b.450;

(b) You comply with all capital requirements under part 567 of this chapter after you declare or pay dividends;

(c) You comply with the capital distribution requirements under part 563, subpart E, of this chapter; and

(d) You do not return any capital, other than ordinary dividends, to purchasers during the term of the business plan submitted with the conversion.

§ 563b.525 Who may acquire my shares after I convert?

(a) For three years after you convert, no person may, directly or indirectly, acquire or offer to acquire the beneficial ownership of more than ten percent of any class of your equity securities without OTS's prior written approval. If a person violates this prohibition, you may not permit the person to vote shares in excess of ten percent, and may not count the shares in excess of ten percent in any shareholder vote.

(b) A person acquires beneficial ownership of more than ten percent of a class of shares when he or she holds any combination of your stock or revocable or irrevocable proxies under circumstances that give rise to a conclusive control determination or rebuttable control determination under §§ 574.4(a) and (b) of this chapter. OTS will presume that a person has acquired shares if the acquiror entered into a binding written agreement for the transfer of shares. For purposes of this section, an offer is made when it is communicated. An offer does not include non-binding expressions of understanding or letters of intent regarding the terms of a potential acquisition.

(c) Notwithstanding the restrictions in this section:

(1) Paragraphs (a) and (b) of this section do not apply to any offer with a view toward public resale made exclusively to you, to the underwriters, or to a selling group acting on your behalf.

(2) Unless OTS objects in writing, any person may offer or announce an offer to acquire up to one percent of any class of shares. In computing the one percent limit, the person must include all of his or her acquisitions of the same class of shares during the prior 12 months.

(3) A corporation whose ownership is, or will be, substantially the same as your ownership may acquire or offer to acquire more than ten percent of your common stock, if it makes the offer or acquisition more than one year after you convert.

(4) One or more of your tax-qualified employee stock benefit plans may acquire your shares, if the plan or plans do not beneficially own more than 25 percent of any class of your shares in the aggregate.

(5) An acquiror does not have to file a separate application to obtain OTS approval under paragraph (a) of this section, if the acquiror files an application under part 574 of this chapter that specifically addresses the criteria listed under paragraph (d) of this section and you do not oppose the proposed acquisition.

(d) OTS may deny an application under paragraph (a) of this section if the proposed acquisition:

(1) Is contrary to the purposes of this part;

(2) Is manipulative or deceptive;

(3) Subverts the fairness of the conversion;

(4) Is likely to injure you;

(5) Is inconsistent with your plan to meet the credit and lending needs of your proposed market area;

(6) Otherwise violates laws or regulations; or

(7) Does not prudently deploy your conversion proceeds.

§ 563b.530 What other requirements apply after I convert?

After you convert, you must:

(a) Promptly register your shares under the Securities Exchange Act of 1934 (15 U.S.C. 78a–78jj, as amended). You may not deregister the shares for three years.

(b) Encourage and assist a market maker to establish and to maintain a market for your shares. A market maker for a security is a dealer who:

(1) Regularly publishes bona fide competitive bid and offer quotations for the security in a recognized interdealer quotation system;

(2) Furnishes bona fide competitive bid and offer quotations for the security on request; or

(3) May effect transactions for the security in reasonable quantities at quoted prices with other brokers or dealers.

(c) Use your best efforts to list your shares on a national or regional securities exchange or on the National Association of Securities Dealers Automated Quotation system.

(d) File all post-conversion reports that OTS requires.

CONTRIBUTIONS TO CHARITABLE ORGANIZATIONS

§ 563b.550 May I donate conversion shares or conversion proceeds to a charitable organization?

You may contribute some of your conversion shares or proceeds to a charitable organization if:

(a) Your plan of conversion provides for the proposed contribution;

(b) Your members approve the proposed contribution; and

(c) The IRS either has approved, or approves within two years after formation, the charitable organization as a tax-exempt charitable organization under the Internal Revenue Code.

§ 563b.555 How do my members approve a charitable contribution?

At the meeting to consider your conversion, your members must separately approve by at least a majority of the total eligible votes, a contribution of conversion shares or proceeds. If you are in mutual holding company form and adding a charitable contribution as part of a second step stock conversion, you must also have your minority shareholders separately approve the charitable contribution by a majority of their total eligible votes.

§ 563b.560 How much may I contribute to a charitable organization?

You may contribute a reasonable amount of conversion shares or proceeds to a charitable organization, if your contribution will not exceed limits for charitable deductions under the Internal Revenue Code and OTS does not object on supervisory grounds. If you are a well-capitalized savings association, OTS generally will not object if you contribute an aggregate amount of eight percent or less of the conversion shares or proceeds.

§ 563b.565 What must the charitable organization include in its organizational documents?

The charitable organization's charter (or trust agreement) and gift instrument must provide that:

(a) The charitable organization's primary purpose is to serve and make grants in your local community;

(b) As long as the charitable organization controls shares, it must vote those shares in the same ratio as all other shares voted on each proposal considered by your shareholders;

(c) For at least five years after its organization, one seat on the charitable organization's board of directors (or board of trustees) is reserved for an independent director (or trustee) from your local community. This director may not be your officer, director, or employee, or your affiliate's officer, director, or employee, and should have experience with local community charitable organizations and grant making; and

(d) For at least five years after its organization, one seat on the charitable organization's board of directors (or board of trustees) is reserved for a director from your board of directors or the board of directors of an acquiror or resulting institution in the event of a merger or acquisition of your organization.

§ 563b.570 How do I address conflicts of interest involving my directors?

(a) A person who is your director, officer, or employee, or a person who has the power to direct your management or policies, or otherwise owes a fiduciary duty to you (for example, holding company directors) and who will serve as an officer, director, or employee of the charitable organization, is subject to § 563.200 of this chapter. *See* Form AC (Exhibit 9) for further information on operating plans and conflict of interest plans.

(b) Before your board of directors may adopt a plan of conversion that includes a charitable organization, you must identify your directors that will serve on the charitable organization's board. These directors may not participate in your board's discussions concerning contributions to the charitable organization, and may not vote on the matter.

§ 563b.575 What other requirements apply to charitable organizations?

(a) The charitable organization's charter (or trust agreement) and the gift instrument for the contribution must provide that:

(1) OTS may examine the charitable organization at the charitable organization's expense;

(2) The charitable organization must comply with all supervisory directives that OTS imposes;

(3) The charitable organization must annually provide OTS with a copy of the annual report that the charitable organization submitted to the IRS;

(4) The charitable organization must operate according to written policies adopted by its board of directors (or board of trustees), including a conflict of interest policy; and

(5) The charitable organization may not engage in self-dealing, and must comply with all laws necessary to maintain its tax-exempt status under the Internal Revenue Code.

(b) You must include the following legend in the stock certificates of shares that you contribute to the charitable organization or that the charitable organization otherwise acquires: "The board of directors must consider the shares that this stock certificate represents as voted in the same ratio as all other shares voted on each proposal considered by the shareholders, as long as the shares are controlled by the charitable organization."

(c) As long as the charitable organization controls shares, you must consider those shares as voted in the same ratio as all of the shares voted on each proposal considered by your shareholders.

(d) After you complete your stock offering, you must submit four executed copies of the following documents to the OTS Applications Filing Room in Washington, and three executed copies to the OTS Regional Office: the charitable organization's charter and bylaws (or trust agreement), operating plan (within six months after your stock offering), conflict of interest policy, and the gift instrument for your contributions of either stock or cash to the charitable organization.

Subpart B—Voluntary Supervisory Conversions

§ 563b.600 What does this subpart do?

(a) You must comply with this subpart to engage in a voluntary supervisory conversion. This subpart applies to all voluntary supervisory conversions under secs. 5(i)(1), (i)(2), and (p) of the Home Owners' Loan Act (HOLA), 12 U.S.C. 1464(i)(1), (i)(2), and (p).

(b) Subpart A of this part also applies to a voluntary supervisory conversion, unless a requirement is clearly inapplicable.

§ 563b.605 How may I conduct a voluntary supervisory conversion?

(a) You may sell your shares or the shares of a holding company to the public under the requirements of subpart A of this part.

(b) You may convert to stock form by merging into an interim federal-or state-chartered stock association.

(c) You may sell your shares directly to an acquiror, who may be a person, company, depository institution, or depository institution holding company.

(d) You may merge or consolidate with an existing or newly created depository institution. The merger or consolidation must be authorized by, and is subject to, other applicable laws and regulations.

§ 563b.610 Do my members have rights in a voluntary supervisory conversion?

Your members do not have the right to approve or participate in a voluntary supervisory conversion, and will not have any legal or beneficial ownership interests in the converted association, unless OTS provides otherwise. Your members may have interests in a liquidation account, if one is established.

ELIGIBILITY

§ 563b.625 When is a savings association eligible for a voluntary supervisory conversion?

(a) If you are an insured savings association, you may be eligible to convert under this subpart if:

(1) You are significantly undercapitalized (or you are undercapitalized and a standard conversion that would make you adequately capitalized is not feasible) and you will be a viable entity following the conversion;

(2) Severe financial conditions threaten your stability and a conversion is likely to improve your financial condition;

(3) FDIC will assist you under section 13 of the Federal Deposit Insurance Act, 12 U.S.C. 1823; or

(4) You are in receivership and a conversion will assist you.

(b) You will be a viable entity following the conversion if you satisfy all of the following:

(1) You will be adequately capitalized as a result of the conversion;

(2) You, your proposed conversion, and your acquiror(s) comply with applicable supervisory policies;

(3) The transaction is in your best interest, and the best interest of the Deposit Insurance Fund and the public; and

(4) The transaction will not injure or be detrimental to you, the Deposit Insurance Fund, or the public interest.

[67 FR 52020, Aug. 9, 2002, as amended at 71 FR 19611, Apr. 18, 2006]

§ 563b.630 When is a state-chartered savings bank eligible for a voluntary supervisory conversion?

If you are a state-chartered savings bank you may be eligible to convert to

§ 563b.650

a federal stock savings bank under this subpart if:

(a) FDIC certifies under section 5(o)(2)(C) of the HOLA that severe financial conditions threaten your stability and that the voluntary supervisory conversion is likely to improve your financial condition, and OTS concurs with this certification; or

(b) You meet the following conditions:

(1) Your liabilities exceed your assets, as calculated under generally accepted accounting principles, assuming you are a going concern; and

(2) You will issue a sufficient amount of permanent capital stock to meet your applicable FDIC capital requirement immediately upon completion of the conversion, or FDIC determines that you will achieve an acceptable capital level within an acceptable time period.

[67 FR 52020, Aug. 9, 2002, as amended at 71 FR 19811, Apr. 18, 2006]

PLAN OF SUPERVISORY CONVERSION

§ 563b.650 What must I include in my plan of voluntary supervisory conversion?

A majority of your board of directors must adopt a plan of voluntary supervisory conversion. You must include all of the following information in your plan of voluntary supervisory conversion.

(a) Your name and address.

(b) The name, address, date and place of birth, and social security number of each proposed purchaser of conversion shares and a description of that purchaser's relationship to you.

(c) The title, per-unit par value, number, and per-unit and aggregate offering price of shares that you will issue.

(d) The number and percentage of shares that each investor will purchase.

(e) The aggregate number and percentage of shares that each director, officer, and any affiliates or associates of the director or officer will purchase.

(f) A description of any liquidation account.

(g) Certified copies of all resolutions of your board of directors relating to the conversion.

VOLUNTARY SUPERVISORY CONVERSION APPLICATION

§ 563b.660 What must I include in my voluntary supervisory conversion application?

You must include all of the following information and documents in a voluntary supervisory conversion application to OTS under this subpart:

(a) *Eligibility.* (1) Evidence establishing that you meet the eligibility requirements under §§ 563b.625 or 563b.630.

(2) An opinion of qualified, independent counsel or an independent, certified public accountant regarding the tax consequences of the conversion, or an IRS ruling indicating that the transaction qualifies as a tax-free reorganization.

(3) An opinion of independent counsel indicating that applicable state law authorizes the voluntary supervisory conversion, if you are a state-chartered savings association converting to state stock form.

(b) *Plan of conversion.* A plan of voluntary supervisory conversion that complies with § 563b.650.

(c) *Business plan.* A business plan that complies with § 563b.105, when required by OTS.

(d) *Financial data.* (1) Your most recent audited financial statements and Thrift Financial Report. You must explain how your current capital levels make you eligible to engage in a voluntary supervisory conversion under §§ 563b.625 or 563b.630.

(2) A description of your estimated conversion expenses.

(3) Evidence supporting the value of any non-cash asset contributions. Appraisals must be acceptable to OTS and the non-cash asset must meet all other OTS policy guidelines. See Thrift Activities Handbook Section 110 for guidelines at OTS's website (*www.ots.treas.gov*).

(4) Pro forma financial statements that reflect the effects of the transaction. You must identify your tangible, core, and risk-based capital levels and show the adjustments necessary to compute the capital levels. You must prepare your pro forma statements in conformance with OTS regulations and policy.

Office of Thrift Supervision, Treasury § 563b.675

(e) *Proposed documents.* (1) Your proposed charter and bylaws.

(2) Your proposed stock certificate form.

(f) *Agreements.* (1) A copy of any agreements between you and proposed purchasers.

(2) A copy and description of all existing and proposed employment contracts. You must describe the term, salary, and severance provisions of the contract, the identity and background of the officer or employee to be employed, and the amount of any conversion shares to be purchased by the officer or employee or his or her affiliates or associates.

(g) *Related applications.* (1) All filings required under the securities offering rules of parts 563b and 563g of this chapter.

(2) Any required Holding Company Act application, Control Act notice, or rebuttal submission under part 574 of this chapter, including prior-conduct certifications under Regulatory Bulletin 20.

(3) A subordinated debt application, if applicable.

(4) Applications for permission to organize a stock association and for approval of a merger, if applicable, and a copy of any application for Federal Home Loan Bank membership or FDIC insurance of accounts, if applicable.

(5) A statement describing any other applications required under federal or state banking laws for all transactions related to your conversion, copies of all dispositive documents issued by regulatory authorities relating to the applications, and, if requested by OTS, copies of the applications and related documents.

(h) *Waiver request.* A description of any of the features of your application that do not conform to the requirements of this subpart, including any request for waiver of these requirements.

OTS REVIEW OF THE VOLUNTARY SUPERVISORY CONVERSION APPLICATION

§ 563b.670 Will OTS approve my voluntary supervisory conversion application?

OTS will generally approve your application to engage in a voluntary supervisory conversion unless it determines:

(a) You do not meet the eligibility requirements for a voluntary supervisory conversion under §§ 563b.625 or 563b.630 or because the proceeds from the sale of your conversion stock, less the expenses of the conversion, would be insufficient to satisfy any applicable viability requirement;

(b) The transaction is detrimental to or would cause potential injury to you or the Deposit Insurance Fund or is contrary to the public interest;

(c) You or your acquiror, or the controlling parties or directors and officers of you or your acquiror, have engaged in unsafe or unsound practices in connection with the voluntary supervisory conversion; or

(d) You fail to justify an employment contract incidental to the conversion, or the employment contract will be an unsafe or unsound practice or represent a sale of control. In a voluntary supervisory conversion, OTS generally will not approve employment contracts of more than one year for your existing management.

[67 FR 52020, Aug. 9, 2002, as amended at 71 FR 19812, Apr. 18, 2006]

§ 563b.675 What conditions will OTS impose on an approval?

(a) OTS will condition approval of a voluntary supervisory conversion application on all of the following.

(1) You must complete the conversion stock sale within three months after OTS approves your application. OTS may grant an extension for good cause.

(2) You must comply with all filing requirements of parts 563b and 563g of this chapter.

(3) You must submit an opinion of independent legal counsel indicating that the sale of your shares complies with all applicable state securities law requirements.

(4) You must comply with all applicable laws, rules, and regulations.

(5) You must satisfy any other requirements or conditions OTS may impose.

(b) OTS may condition approval of a voluntary supervisory conversion application on either of the following:

261

§ 563b.680

(1) You must satisfy any conditions and restrictions OTS imposes to prevent unsafe or unsound practices, to protect the Deposit Insurance Fund and the public interest, and to prevent potential injury or detriment to you before and after the conversion. OTS may impose these conditions and restrictions on you (before and after the conversion), your acquiror, controlling parties, or directors and officers of you or your acquiror; or

(2) You must infuse a larger amount of capital, if necessary, for safety and soundness reasons.

[67 FR 52020, Aug. 9, 2002, as amended at 71 FR 19812, Apr. 18, 2006]

OFFERS AND SALES OF STOCK

§ 563b.680 How do I sell my shares?

If you convert under this subpart, you must offer and sell your shares under part 563g of this chapter.

POST-CONVERSION

§ 563b.690 Who may not acquire additional shares after the voluntary supervisory conversion?

For three years after the completion of a voluntary supervisory conversion, neither you nor your controlling shareholder(s) may acquire shares from minority shareholders without OTS's prior approval.

PART 563c—ACCOUNTING REQUIREMENTS

Subpart A—Form and Content of Financial Statements

Sec.
563c.1 Form and content of financial statements.
563c.2 Definitions.
563c.3 Qualification of public accountant.
563c.4 Condensed financial information [Parent only].

Subpart B [Reserved]

Subpart C—Financial Statement Presentation

563c.101 Application of this subpart.
563c.102 Financial statement presentation.

AUTHORITY: 12 U.S.C. 1462a, 1463, 1464; 15 U.S.C. 78c(b), 78m, 78n, 78w.

SOURCE: 54 FR 49627, Nov. 30, 1989, unless otherwise noted.

Subpart A—Form and Content of Financial Statements

§ 563c.1 Form and content of financial statements.

(a) This subpart A states the requirements as to form and content of financial statements included by a savings association in the following documents. However, the Office's regulations governing the applicable documents specify the actual financial statements that are to be included in that document.

(1) Any proxy statement or offering circular required to be used in connection with a conversion under part 563b of this chapter.

(2) Any offering circular or nonpublic offering materials required to be used in connection with an offer or sale of securities under part 563g of this chapter.

(3) Any filing under the Securities Exchange Act of 1934, 15 U.S.C. 78a *et seq.*, made pursuant to the requirements of part 563d of this chapter.

(b) Except as otherwise provided by the Office by rule, regulation, or order made specifically applicable to financial statements governed by this section, financial statements shall:

(1) Be prepared and presented in accordance with generally accepted accounting principles;

(2) Comply with subpart C of this part;

(3) Consistent with the provisions of this subpart, comply with articles 1, 2, 3, 4, 10, and 11 of Regulation S-X adopted by the Securities and Exchange Commission (17 CFR 210.1–210.4, 210.10, and 210.11).

(4) Be audited, when required, by an independent auditor in accordance with the standards imposed by the American Institute of Certified Public Accountants.

(c) The term "financial statements" includes all notes to the statements and related schedules.

§ 563c.2 Definitions.

(See also 17 CFR 210.1–02.)

Office of Thrift Supervision, Treasury § 563c.4

(a) *Registrant.* The term "registrant" means an applicant, a savings association, or any other person required to prepare financial statements in accordance with this subpart.

(b) *Significant subsidiary.* The term "significant subsidiary" means a subsidiary, including its subsidiaries, which meets any of the following conditions:

(1) The association's and its other subsidiaries' investments in and advances to the subsidiary exceed 10 percent of the total assets of the association and its subsidiaries consolidated as of the end of the most recently completed fiscal year (for purposes of determining whether financial statements of a business acquired or to be acquired in a business combination accounted for as a pooling of interests are required pursuant to 17 CFR 210.3-05, this condition is also met when the number of common shares exchanged by the association exceeds 10 percent of its total common shares outstanding at the date the combination is initiated); or

(2) The association's and its other subsidiaries' proportionate share of the total assets (after intercompany eliminations) of the subsidiary exceeds 10 percent of the total assets of the association and its subsidiaries consolidated as of the end of the most recently completed fiscal year; or

(3) The association's and its other subsidiaries' equity in the income from continuing operations before income taxes, extraordinary items, and cumulative effect of a change in accounting principle of the subsidiary exceeds 10 percent of such income of the association and its subsidiaries consolidated for the most recently completed fiscal year.

COMPUTATIONAL NOTE: For purposes of making the prescribed income test the following guidance should be applied:

1. When a loss has been incurred by either the parent or its consolidated subsidiaries or the tested subsidiary, but not both, the equity in the income or loss of the tested subsidiary should be excluded from the income of the association and its subsidiaries consolidated for purposes of the computation.

2. If income of the association and its subsidiaries consolidated for the most recent fiscal year is at least 10 percent lower than the average of the income for the last five fiscal years, such average income should be substituted for purposes of the computation. Any loss years should be omitted for purposes of computing average income.

§ 563c.3 Qualification of public accountant.

(See also 17 CFR 210.2-01.)

The term "qualified public accountant" means a certified public accountant or licensed public accountant certified or licensed by a regulatory authority of a State or other political subdivision of the United States who is in good standing as such under the laws of the jurisdiction where the home office of the registrant to be audited is located. Any person or firm who is suspended from practice before the Securities and Exchange Commission or other governmental agency is not a "qualified public accountant" for purposes of this section.

[54 FR 49627, Nov. 30, 1989, as amended at 60 FR 66718, Dec. 26, 1995]

§ 563c.4 Condensed financial information [Parent only].

(a) The information prescribed by Schedule III required by section IV of § 563c.102 of this part shall be presented in a note to the financial statements when the restricted net assets (17 CFR 210.4-08(e)(3)) of consolidated subsidiaries exceed 25 percent of consolidated net assets as of the end of the most recently completed fiscal year. The investment in and indebtedness of and to association subsidiaries shall be stated separately in the condensed balance sheet from amounts for other subsidiaries; and the amount of cash dividends paid to the parent association for each of the last three years by association subsidiaries shall be stated separately in the condensed income statement from amounts for other subsidiaries.

(b) For purposes of the above test, restricted net assets of consolidated subsidiaries shall mean that amount of the association's proportionate share of net assets of consolidated subsidiaries (after intercompany eliminations) which as of the end of the most recent year may not be transferred to the parent company by subsidiaries in the form of loans, advances, or cash dividends without the consent of a third

§ 563c.101

party (*i.e.*, lender, regulatory agency, foreign government, etc.).

(c) Where restrictions on the amount of funds which may be loaned or advanced differ from the amount restricted as to transfer in the form of cash dividends, the amount least restrictive to the subsidiary shall be used. Redeemable preferred stocks (See item I (22) in § 563c.102) and minority interest (See item I (21) in § 563c.102) shall be deducted in computing net assets for purposes of this test.

Subpart B [Reserved]

Subpart C—Financial Statement Presentation

§ 563c.101 Application of this subpart.

This subpart contains rules pertaining to the form and content of financial statements included as part of:

(a) A conversion application under part 563b, including financial statements in proxy statements and offering circulars,

(b) A filing under the Securities Exchange Act of 1934, 15 U.S.C. 78a *et seq.*, and

(c) Any offering circular required to be used in connection with the issuance of mutual capital certificates under § 563.74 and debt securities under § 563.80 and § 563.81 of this chapter.

[54 FR 49627, Nov. 30, 1989, as amended at 65 FR 16305, Mar. 28, 2000]

§ 563c.102 Financial statement presentation.

This section specifies the various line items which should appear on the face of the financial statements governed by this subpart C and additional disclosures which should be included with the financial statements in related notes.

I. BALANCE SHEET

Balance sheets shall comply with the following provisions:

Assets

1. *Cash and amounts due from depository institutions.* (a) The amounts in this caption should include noninterest-bearing deposits with depository institutions.

(b) State in a note the amount and terms of any deposits in depository institutions held as compensating balances against long- or short-term borrowing arrangements. This disclosure should include the provisions of any restrictions as to withdrawal or usage. Restrictions may include legally restricted deposits held as compensating balances against short-term borrowing arrangements, contracts entered into with others, or company statements of intention with regard to particular deposits; however, time deposits and short-term certificates of deposits are not generally included in legally restricted deposits. In cases where compensating balance arrangements exist but are not agreements which legally restrict the use of cash amounts shown on the balance sheet, describe in the notes to the financial statements these arrangements and the amount involved, if determinable, for the most recent audited balance sheet required and for any subsequent unaudited balance sheet required. Compensating balances that are maintained under an agreement to ensure future credit availability shall be disclosed in the notes to the financial statements along with the amount and terms of the agreement.

(c) Checks outstanding in excess of an applicant's book balance in a demand deposit account shall be shown as a liability.

2. *Interest-bearing deposits in other banks.*

3. *Federal funds sold and securities purchased under resale agreements or similar arrangements.* These amounts should be presented, *i.e.*, gross and not netted against Federal funds purchased and securities sold under agreement to repurchase, as reported in caption 15.

4. *Trading account assets.* Include securities considered to be held for trading purposes.

5. *Other short-term investments.*

6. *Investment securities.* (a) Include securities considered to be held for investment purposes. Disclose the aggregate book value of investment securities as the line item on the balance sheet; and also show on the face of the balance sheet the aggregate market value at the balance sheet date. The aggregate amounts should include securities pledged, loaned, or sold under repurchase agreements and similar arrangements. Borrowed securities and securities purchased under resale agreements or similar arrangements should be excluded.

(b) Disclose in a note the carrying value and market value of securities of (i) the U.S. Treasury and other U.S. Government agencies and corporations; (ii) states of the U.S. and political subdivisions thereof; and (iii) other securities.

7. *Assets held for sale.* Investments in assets considered to be held for sale purposes should be reported separately in the statement of financial condition.

8. *Loans.* (a) Disclose separately: (i) Total loans (including financing type leases), (ii)

Office of Thrift Supervision, Treasury § 563c.102

allowance for loan losses, (iii) unearned income on installment loans, (iv) discount on loans purchased, and (v) loans in process.

(b) State on the balance sheet or in a note the amount of loans in each of the following categories: (i) Real estate mortgage; (ii) real estate construction; (iii) installment; and (iv) commercial, financial, and agricultural.

(c)(i) Include under the real estate mortgage category loans payable in monthly, quarterly, or other periodic installments and secured by developed income property and/or personal residences.

(ii) Include under the real estate construction category loans secured by real estate which are made for the purpose of financing construction of real estate and land development projects.

(iii) Include under the installment category loans to individuals generally repayable in monthly installments. This category shall include, but not be limited to, credit card and related activities, individual automobile loans, other installment loans, mobile home loans, and residential repair and modernization loans.

(iv) Include under the commercial, financial, and agricultural category all loans not included in another category. This category shall include, but not be limited to, loans to real estate investment trusts, mortgage companies, banks, and other financial institutions; loans for carrying securities; and loans for agricultural purposes. Do not include loans secured primarily by developed real estate.

(d) State separately any other loan category regardless of relative size if necessary to reflect any unusual risk concentration.

(e) Unearned income on installment loans shall be shown and deducted separately from total loans.

(f) Unamortized discounts on purchased loans shall be deducted separately from total loans.

(g) Loans in process shall be deducted separately from total loans.

(h) A series of categories other than those specified in item (b) of paragraph 8. may be used to present details of loans if considered a more appropriate presentation. The categories specified in item (b) of paragraph 8. should be considered the minimum categories that may be presented.

(i) For each period for which an income statement is presented, disclose in a note the total dollar amount of loans being serviced by the association for the benefit of others.

(j)(i)(A) As of each balance sheet date, disclose in a note the aggregate dollar amount of loans (exclusive of loans to any such persons which in the aggregate do not exceed $60,000 during the last year) made by the association or any of its subsidiaries to directors, executive officers, or principal holders of equity securities (17 CFR 210.1–02) of the association or any of its significant subsidiaries (17 CFR 210.1–02) or to any associate of such persons. For the latest fiscal year, an analysis of activity with respect to such aggregate loans to related parties should be provided. The analysis should include at the beginning of the period new loans, repayments, and other changes. (Other changes, if significant, should be explained.)

(B) This disclosure need not be furnished when the aggregate amount of such loans at the balance sheet date (or with respect to the latest fiscal year, the maximum amount outstanding during the period) does not exceed 5 percent of stockholders' equity at the balance sheet date.

(ii) If a significant portion of the aggregate amount of loans outstanding at the end of the fiscal year disclosed pursuant to item (i)(A) of this paragraph (j) relates to nonaccrual, past due, restructured, and potential problem loans (see Securities and Exchange Commission's Securities Act Industry Guide 3, section III.C.), so state and disclose the aggregate amount of such loans along with such other information necessary to an understanding of the effects of the transactions on the financial statements.

(iii) Notwithstanding the aggregate disclosure called for by paragraph (j)(i) of this balance sheet caption 8, if any loans were not made in the ordinary course of business during any period for which an income statement is required to be filed, provide an appropriate description of each such loan (see 17 CFR 210.9–03.7(e)(3)).

(iv) For purposes only of Balance Sheet item 8(j), the following definitions shall apply:

(A) *Associate* used to indicate a relationship with any person means (1) any corporation, venture, or organization of which such person is a general partner or is, directly or indirectly, the beneficial owner of 10 percent or more of any class of equity securities; (2) any trust or other estate in which such person has a substantial beneficial interest or for which such person serves as trustee or in a similar capacity; and (3) any member of the immediate family of any of the foregoing persons.

(B) *Executive officer* means the president, any vice president in charge of a principal business unit, division, or function (such as loans, investments, operations, administration, or finance), and any other officer or person who performs similar policy-making functions.

(C) *Immediate family* with regard to a person means such person's spouse, parents, children, siblings, mother- and father-in-law, sons- and daughters-in-law, and brothers- and sisters-in-law.

(D) *Ordinary course of business* with regard to loans means those loans which were made on substantially the same terms, including interest rate and collateral, as those prevailing at the same time for comparable transactions with unrelated persons and did not involve more than the normal risk of collectibility or present other unfavorable features.

(k) For each period for which an income statement is presented, furnish in a note a statement of changes in the allowance for loan losses, showing balances at beginning and end of the period, provision charged to income, recoveries of amounts previously charged off, and losses charged to the allowance.

9. *Premises and equipment.*

10. *Real estate owned.* State, parenthetically or otherwise:

(a) The amount of real estate owned by class as described in item (b) of paragraph 10. and the basis for determining that amount; and

(b) A description of each class of real estate owned (i) acquired by foreclosure or by deed in lieu of foreclosure, (ii) in judgment and subject to redemption, or (iii) acquired for development or resale. Show separately any accumulated depreciation or valuation allowances. Disclose the policies regarding, and amounts of, capitalized costs, including interest.

11. *Investment in joint ventures.* In a note, present summarized aggregate financial statements for investments in real estate or other joint ventures which individually (a) are 20 percent or more owned by the association or any of its subsidiaries, or (b) have liabilities (including contingent liabilities) to the parent exceeding 10 percent of the parent's regulatory capital. If an allowance for real estate losses subsequent to acquisition is maintained, the amount shall be disclosed, deducted from the other real estate owned, and a statement of changes in the allowance showing balances at beginning and end of period should be included. Provision charged to income and losses charged to the allowance account shall be furnished for each period for which an income statement is filed.

12. *Other assets.* (a) Disclose separately on the balance sheet or in a note thereto any of the following assets or any other asset the amount of which exceeds 30 percent of stockholders' equity. The remaining assets may be shown as one amount.

(i) *Accrued interest receivable.* State separately those amounts relating to loans and those amounts relating to investments.

(ii) Excess of cost over assets acquired (net of amortization).

(b) State in a note (i) amounts representing investments in affiliates and investments in other persons which are accounted for by the equity method, and (ii) indebtedness of affiliates and other persons, the investments in which are accounted for by the equity method. State the basis of determining the amounts reported under paragraph (b)(i).

13. *Total assets.*

LIABILITIES, AND STOCKHOLDERS' EQUITY

14. *Deposits.* (a) Disclose separately on the balance sheet or in a note the amounts in the following categories of interest-bearing and noninterest-bearing deposits: (i) NOW account and MMDA deposits, (ii) savings deposits, and (iii) time deposits.

(b) Include under the savings-deposits category interest-bearing deposits without specified maturity or contractual provisions requiring advance notice of intention to withdraw funds. Include deposits for which an association may require at its option written notice of intended withdrawal not less than 14 days in advance.

(c) Include under the time-deposits category deposits subject to provisions specifying maturity or other withdrawal conditions such as time certificates of deposits, open account time deposits, and deposits accumulated for the payment of personal loans.

(d) Include accrued interest or dividends, if appropriate.

15. *Short-term borrowings.* (a) State separately, here or in a note, the amounts payable for (i) Federal funds purchased and securities sold under agreements to repurchase, (ii) commercial paper, and (iii) other short-term borrowings.

(b) Federal funds purchased and sales of securities under repurchase agreements shall be reported gross and not netted against sales of Federal funds and purchase of securities under resale agreements.

(c) Include as securities sold under agreements to repurchase all transactions of this type regardless of (i) whether they are called simultaneous purchases and sales, buybacks, turnarounds, overnight transactions, delayed deliveries, or other terms signifying the same substantive transaction, and (ii) whether the transactions are with the same or different institutions, if the purpose of the transactions is to repurchase identical or similar securities.

(d) The amount and terms (including commitment fees and the conditions under which lines may be withdrawn) of unused lines of credit for short-term financing shall be disclosed, if significant, in the notes to the financial statements. The amount of these lines of credit which support a commercial paper borrowing arrangement or similar arrangements shall be separately identified.

16. *Advance payments by borrowers for taxes and insurance.*

17. *Other liabilities.* Disclose separately on the balance sheet or in a note any of the following liabilities or any other items which are individually in excess of 30 percent of stockholders' equity (except that amounts in excess of 5 percent of stockholders' equity should be disclosed with respect to item (d)). The remaining items may be shown as one amount.

Office of Thrift Supervision, Treasury § 563c.102

(a) Income taxes payable.

(b) Deferred income taxes.

(c) Indebtedness to affiliate and other persons the investment in which is accounted for by the equity method.

(d) Indebtedness to directors, executive officers, and principal holders of equity securities of the registrant or any of its significant subsidiaries. (The guidance in balance sheet caption "8(j)" shall be used to identify related parties for purposes of this disclosure.)

18. *Bonds, mortgages, and similar debt.* (a) Include bonds, Federal Home Loan Bank advances, capital notes, debentures, mortgages, and similar debt.

(b) For each issue or type of obligation state in a note:

(i) The general character of each type of debt, including: (A) The rate of interest, (B) the date of maturity, or, if maturing serially, a brief indication of the serial maturities, such as "maturing serially from 1980 to 1990," (C) if the payment of principal or interest is contingent, an appropriate indication of such contingency, (D) a brief indication of priority, and (E) if convertible, the basis. For amounts owed to related parties see 17 CFR 210.4–08(k).

(ii) The amount and terms (including commitment fees and the conditions under which commitments may be withdrawn) of unused commitments for long-term financing arrangements that, if used, would be disclosed under this caption shall be disclosed in the notes to the financial statements, if significant.

(c) State in the notes with appropriate explanations (i) the title and amount of each issue of debt of a subsidiary included in item (a) of paragraph 18 which has not been assumed or guaranteed by the association, and (ii) any liens on premises of a subsidiary or its consolidated subsidiaries which have not been assumed by the subsidiary or its consolidated subsidiaries.

19. *Deferred credits.* State separately those items which exceed 30 percent of stockholders' equity.

20. *Commitments and contingent liabilities.* Total commitments to fund loans should be disclosed. The dollar amounts and terms of other than floating market-rate commitments should also be disclosed.

21. *Minority interest in consolidated subsidiaries.*

22. *Preferred stock subject to mandatory redemption requirements or the redemption of which is outside the control of the issuer.* (a) Include under this caption amounts applicable to any class of stock which has any of the following characteristics: (i) it is redeemable at a fixed or determinable price on a fixed or determinable date or dates, whether by operation of a sinking fund or otherwise; (ii) it is redeemable at the option of the holder; or (iii) it has conditions for redemption which are not solely within the control of the issuer, such as stock which must be redeemed out of future earnings. Amounts attributable to preferred stock which is not redeemable or is redeemable solely at the option of the issuer shall be included under caption 23 unless it meets one or more of the above criteria.

(b) State on the face of the balance sheet the title, carrying amount, and redemption amount of each issue. (If there is more than one issue, these amounts may be aggregated on the face of the balance sheet and details concerning each issue may be presented in the note required by item (c) of paragraph 22.) Show also the dollar amount of any shares subscribed for but unissued, and show the deduction of subscriptions receivable therefrom. If the carrying value is different from the redemption amount, describe the accounting treatment for such difference in the note required by item (c) of paragraph 22. Also state in this note or on the face of the balance sheet, for each issue, the number of shares authorized and the number of shares issued or outstanding, as appropriate. (See 17 CFR 210.4–07.)

(c) State in a separate note captioned "Redeemable Preferred Stock" (i) a general description of each issue, including its redemption features (*e.g.,* sinking fund, at option of holders, out of future earnings) and the rights, if any, of holders in the event of default, including the effect, if any, on junior securities in the event a required dividend, sinking fund, or other redemption payment(s) is not made, (ii) the combined aggregate amount of redemption requirements for all issues each year for the five years following the date of the latest balance sheet, and (iii) the changes in each issue for each period for which an income statement is required to be presented. (See also 17 CFR 210.4–08(d).

(d) Securities reported under this caption are not to be included under a general heading "stockholders' equity" or combined in a total with items described in captions 23, 24 or 25, which follow.

23. *Preferred stock which is not redeemable or is redeemed solely at the option of the issuer.* State on the face of the balance sheet, or, if more than one issue is outstanding, state in a note, the title of each issue and the dollar amount thereof. Show also the dollar amount of any shares subscribed for but unissued, and show the deduction of subscriptions receivable. State on the face of the balance sheet or in a note, for each issue, the number of shares authorized and the number of shares issued or outstanding, as appropriate. (See 17 CFR 210.4–07.) Show in a note or separate statement the changes in each class of preferred shares reported under this caption for each period for which an income statement is required to be presented. (See also 17 CFR 210.4–08(d).)

24. *Common stock.* For each class of common shares state, on the face of the balance sheet, the number of shares issued or outstanding, as appropriate (see 17 CFR 210.4–07), and the dollar amount thereof. If convertible, this fact should be indicated on the face of the balance sheet. For each class of common stock state, on the face of the balance sheet or in a note, the title of the issue, the number of shares authorized, and, if convertible, the basis for conversion (see also 17 CFR 210.4–08(d).) Show also the dollar amount of any common stock subscribed for but unissued, and show the deduction of subscriptions receivable. Show in a note or statement the changes in each class of common stock for each period for which an income statement is required to be presented.

25. *Other stockholders' equity.* (a) Separate captions shall be shown on the face of the balance sheet for (i) additional paid-in capital, (ii) other additional capital, and (iii) retained earnings, both (A) restricted and (B) unrestricted. (See 17 CFR 210.4–08(e).) Additional paid-in capital and other additional capital may be combined with the stock caption to which it applies, if appropriate. State whether or not the association is in compliance with the Federal regulatory capital requirements (and state requirements where applicable). Also include the dollar amount of those regulatory capital requirements and the amount by which the association exceeds or fails to meet those requirements.

(b) For a period of at least 10 years subsequent to the effective date of a quasi-reorganization, any description of retained earnings shall indicate the point in time from which the new retained earnings dates, and for a period of at least three years shall indicate, on the face of the balance sheet, the total amount of the deficit eliminated.

(c) Changes in stockholders' equity shall be disclosed in accordance with the requirements of 17 CFR 210.3–04.

26. *Total liabilities and stockholders' equity.*

II. INCOME STATEMENT

Income statements shall comply with the following provisions:

1. *Interest and fees on loans.* (a) Include interest, service charges, and fees which are related to or are an adjustment of the loan interest yield.

(b) Current amortization of premiums on mortgages or other loans shall be deducted from interest on loans, and current accretion of discount on such items shall be added to interest on loans.

(c) Discounts and other deferred amounts which are related to or are an adjustment of the loan interest yield shall be amortized into income using the interest (level yield) method.

2. *Interest and dividends on investment securities.* Include accretion of discount on securities and deduct amortization of premiums on securities.

3. *Trading account interest.* Include interest from securities carried in a dealer trading account or accounts that are held principally for resale to customers.

4. *Other interest income.* Include interest on short-term investments (Federal funds sold and securities purchased under agreements to resell) and interest on bank deposits.

5. *Total interest income.*

6. *Interest on deposits.* Include interest on all deposits. On the income statement or in a note, state separately, in the same categories as those specified for deposits at balance sheet caption 14(a), the interest on those deposits. Early withdrawal penalties should be netted against interest on deposits and, if material, disclosed on the income statement.

7. *Interest on short-term borrowings.* Include interest on borrowed funds, including Federal funds purchased, securities sold under agreements to repurchase, commercial paper, and other short-term borrowings.

8. *Interest on long-term borrowings.* Include interest on bonds, capital notes, debentures, mortgages on association premises, capitalized leases, and similar debt.

9. *Total interest expense.*

10. *Net interest income.*

11. *Provision for loan losses.*

12. *Net interest income after provision for loan losses.*

13. *Other income.* Disclose separately any of the following amounts, or any other item of other income, which exceeds 1 percent of the aggregate of total interest income and other income. The remaining amount may be shown as one amount, except for investment securities gains or losses which shall be shown separately regardless of size.

(a) Commissions and fees from fiduciary activities.

(b) Fees for other services to customers.

(c) Commissions, fees, and markups on securities underwriting and other securities activities.

(d) Profit or loss on transactions in investment securities.

(e) Equity in earnings of unconsolidated subsidiaries and 50-percent- or less-owned persons.

(f) Gains or losses on disposition of investments in securities of subsidiaries and 50-percent- or less-owned persons.

(g) Profit or loss from real estate operations.

(h) Other fees related to loan originations or commitments not included in income statement caption 1.

The remaining other income may be shown in one amount.

(i) Investment securities gains or losses. The method followed in determining the cost of investments sold (*e.g.*, "average cost,"

Office of Thrift Supervision, Treasury § 563c.102

"first-in, first-out," or "identified certificate") and related income taxes shall be disclosed.

14. *Other expenses.* Disclose separately any of the following amounts, or any other item of other expense, which exceeds 1 percent of the aggregate of total interest income and other income. The remaining amounts may be shown as one amount.

(a) Salaries and employee benefits.
(b) Net occupancy expense of premises.
(c) Net cost of operations of other real estate (including provisions for real estate losses, rental income, and gains and losses on sales of real estate).
(d) Minority interest in income of consolidated subsidiaries.
(e) Goodwill amortization.

15. *Other income and expenses.* State separately material events or transactions that are unusual in nature or occur infrequently, but not both, and therefore do not meet both criteria for classification as an extraordinary item. Examples of items which would be reported separately are gain or loss from the sale of premises and equipment, provision for loss on real estate owned, or provision for gain or loss on the sale of loans.

16. *Income or losses before income tax expense.*

17. *Income tax expense.* The information required by 17 CFR 210.4–08(h) should be disclosed.

18. *Income or loss before extraordinary items effects of changes in accounting principles.*

19. *Extraordinary items, less applicable tax.*

20. *Cumulative effects of changes in accounting principles.*

21. *Net income or loss.*

22. *Earnings-per-share data.*

23. *Conversion footnote.* If the association is an applicant for conversion from a mutual to a stock association or has converted within the last three years, describe in a note the general terms of the conversion and restrictions on the operations of the association imposed by the conversion. Also, state the amount of net proceeds received from the conversion and costs associated with the conversion.

24. *Mergers and acquisitions.* For the period in which a business combination occurs and is accounted for by the purchase method of accounting, in addition to those disclosures required by Accounting Principles Board Opinion No. 16, the association shall make those disclosures as noted below for all combinations involving significant acquisitions. (A significant acquisition is defined for this purpose to be one in which the assets of the acquired association, or group of associations, exceed 10 percent of the assets of the consolidated association at the end of the most recent period being reported upon.)

(a) Amounts and descriptions of discounts and premiums related to recording the aggregate interest-bearing assets and liabilities at their fair market value. The disclosure should also include the methods of amortization or accretion and the estimated remaining lives.

(b) The net effect on net income before taxes of the amortization and accretion of discounts, premiums, and intangible assets related to the purchase accounting transaction(s). For subsequent periods, the association shall disclose the remaining total unamortized or unaccreted amounts of discounts, premiums, and intangible assets as of the date of the most recent balance sheet presented. In addition, the association shall disclose the net effect on net income before taxes of the amortization and accretion of discounts, premiums, and intangible assets related to prior business combinations accounted for by the purchase method of accounting. Such disclosures need not be made if the total amounts of discounts, premiums, or intangible assets do not exceed 30 percent of stockholders' equity as of the date of the most recent balance sheet presented.

III. STATEMENT OF CASH FLOWS

The amounts shown in this statement should be those items which materially enhance the reader's understanding of the association's business. For example, gains from sales of loans should be segregated from sales of mortgage-backed securities and other securities, if material, proceeds from principal repayments and maturities from loans and mortgage-backed securities should be segregated from proceeds from sales of loans and mortgage-backed securities, purchases of loans, mortgage-backed securities and other securities should be segregated, if material. Additional guidance may be found in the FASB's Statement of Financial Accounting Standards No. 95 Statement of Cash Flows.

IV. SCHEDULES REQUIRED TO BE FILED

The following schedules, which should be examined by an independent accountant, shall be filed unless the required information is not applicable or is presented in the related financial statements:

(1) *Schedule I—Indebtedness of and to related parties—Not Current.* For each period for which an income statement is required, the following schedule should be filed in support of the amounts required to be reported by balance sheet items 8(j) and 17(c) unless such aggregate amount does not exceed 5 percent of stockholders' equity at either the beginning or the end of the period:

§ 563c.102

INDEBTEDNESS OF AND TO RELATED PARTIES—NOT CURRENT

	Indebtedness of—			
Name of person [1]	Balance at beginning	Additions [2]	Deductions [3]	Balance at end
A	B	C	D	E

INDEBTEDNESS OF AND TO RELATED PARTIES—NOT CURRENT

	Indebtedness to—			
Name of person [1]	Balance at beginning	Additions [2]	Deductions [3]	Balance at end
A	F	G	H	I

[1] The persons named shall be grouped as in the related schedule required for investments in related parties. The information called for shall be shown separately for any persons whose investments were shown separately in such related schedule.

[2] For each person named in column A, explain in a note the nature and purpose of any increase during the period that is in excess of 10 percent of the related balance at either the beginning or end of the period.

[3] If deduction was other than a receipt or disbursement of cash, explain.

(2) *Schedule II—Guarantees of securities of other issuers.* The following schedule should be filed as of the date of the most recently audited balance sheet with respect to any guarantees of securities of other issuers by the person for which the statements are being filed:

GUARANTEES OF SECURITIES OF OTHER ISSUERS [1]

Col. A. Name of issuer of securities guaranteed by person for which statement is filed	Col. B. Title of issue of each class of securities guaranteed	Col. C. Total amount guaranteed and outstanding [2]	Col. D. Amount owned by person or persons for which statement is filed

GUARANTEES OF SECURITIES OF OTHER ISSUERS [1]

Col. A. Name of issuer of securities guaranteed by person for which statement is filed	Col. E. Amount in treasury of issuer of securities guaranteed	Col. F. Nature of guarantee [3]	Col. G. Nature of any default by issue of securities guaranteed in principal, interest, sinking fund or redemption provisions, or payment of dividends [4]

[1] Indicate in a note to the most recent schedule being filed for a particular person or group any significant changes since the date of the related balance sheet. If this schedule is filed in support of consolidated or combined statements, there shall be set forth guarantees by any person included in the consolidation or combination, except that such guarantees of securities which are included in the consolidated or combined balance sheet need not be set forth.

[2] Indicate any amounts included in column C which are included also in column D or E.

[3] There need be made only a brief statement of the nature of the guarantee, such as "Guarantee of principal and interest," or "Guarantee of dividends." If the guarantee is of interest or dividends, state the annual aggregate amount of interest or dividends so guaranteed.

[4] Only a brief statement as to any such defaults need be made.

(3) *Schedule III—Condensed financial information.* The following schedule shall be filed as of the dates and for the periods specified in the schedule.

Condensed Financial Information

[Parent only]

[Association may determine disclosure based on information provided in footnotes below]

(a) Provide condensed financial information as to financial position, changes in financial position, and results of operations of the association as of the same dates and for the same periods for which audited consolidated financial statements are required. The financial information required need not be presented in greater detail than is required for condensed statement by 17 CFR 210.10-01(a) (2), (3), (4). Detailed footnote disclosure which would normally be included with complete financial statements may be omitted with the exception of disclosure regarding material contingencies, long-term obligations, and guarantees. Description of significant provisions of the association's long-term obligations, mandatory dividend, or redemption requirements of redeemable stocks, and guarantees of the association shall be provided along with a 5-year schedule of maturities of debt. If the material contingencies, long-term obligations, redeemable stock requirements, and guarantees of the association have been separately disclosed in the consolidated statements, they need not be repeated in this schedule.

(b) Disclose separately the amount of cash dividends paid to the association for each of the last three fiscal years by consolidated subsidiaries, unconsolidated subsidiaries,

Office of Thrift Supervision, Treasury § 563d.2

and 50-percent- or less-owned persons accounted for by the equity method, respectively.

[54 FR 49627, Nov. 30, 1989, as amended at 57 FR 26990, June 17, 1992]

PART 563d—SECURITIES OF SAVINGS ASSOCIATIONS

Subpart A—Regulations

Sec.
563d.1 Requirements under certain sections of the Securities Exchange Act of 1934.
563d.2 Mailing requirements for securities filings.
563d.3b-6 Liability for certain statements by savings associations.
563d.210 Form and content of financial statements.

Subpart B—Interpretations

563d.801 Application of this subpart.
563d.802 Description of business.

AUTHORITY: 12 U.S.C. 1462a, 1463, 1464; 15 U.S.C. 78c(b), 78l, 78m, 78w, 78d-1.

SOURCE: 54 FR 49634, Nov. 30, 1989, unless otherwise noted.

Subpart A—Regulations

§ 563d.1 Requirements under certain sections of the Securities Exchange Act of 1934.

In respect to any securities issued by savings associations, the powers, functions, and duties vested in the Securities and Exchange Commission (the "Commission") to administer and enforce sections 12, 13, 14(a), 14(c), 14(d), 14(f), and 16 of the Securities Exchange Act of 1934 (the "Act") are vested in the Office. The rules, regulations and forms prescribed by the Commission pursuant to those sections or applicable in connection with obligations imposed by those sections, shall apply to securities issued by savings associations, except as otherwise provided in this part. The term "Commission" as used in those rules and regulations shall with respect to securities issued by savings associations be deemed to refer to the Office unless the context otherwise requires. All filings with respect to securities issued by savings associations required by those rules and regulations to be made with the Commission shall be made with the Business Transactions Division, Chief Counsel's Office, Office of Thrift Supervision, 1700 G Street, NW., Washington, DC 20552, by submitting such filings to the Securities Filing Desk at the above address, except as noted in § 563d.2 of this part. Except to the extent otherwise specifically provided by the Office in the application fee schedule published in the Thrift Bulletin pursuant to 12 CFR part 502, all filing fees specified by the Commission's rules shall be paid to the Office. If, after the Office reviews a Form 10-K, Form 10-Q, Schedule 13D or Schedule 13G and determines that the filing is materially deficient such that the Office requires that an amendment be filed to correct the deficiency, then, upon the filing of the amendment to the Form 10-K, Form 10-Q, Schedule 13D or Schedule 13G, as the case may be, the filer shall pay an additional filing fee to the Office, in the amount specified by the Office in the application fee schedule published in the Thrift Bulletin pursuant to 12 CFR part 502.

[54 FR 49634 Nov. 30, 1989, as amended at 55 FR 34531, Aug. 23, 1990; 60 FR 66718, Dec. 26, 1995; 61 FR 65179, Dec. 11, 1996; 66 FR 65821, Dec. 21, 2001]

§ 563d.2 Mailing requirements for securities filings.

Any savings association or other party required to file reports with the Business Transactions Division, as set forth in § 563d.1 of this part, shall file one of the required number of copies with the Regional Office of the Region in which the association is located or in the case of an association located in more than one Region, the Region where the association's home office is located. Such copies shall be marked to the attention of the Regional Director. The originally-signed copy and all remaining copies of each filing shall be sent to the Business Transactions Division by submitting such filings to the Securities Filing Desk at the address specified in § 563d.1 of this part. Copies sent to the Regional Offices shall be mailed on the same day as the original and remaining copies are forwarded to the Business Transactions Division.

[55 FR 3041, Jan. 30, 1990, as amended at 60 FR 66718, Dec. 26, 1995; 66 FR 65821, Dec. 21, 2001]

§ 563d.3b-6 Liability for certain statements by savings associations.

This section replaces adherence to 17 CFR 240.3b-6 and applies as follows:

(a) A statement within the coverage of paragraph (b) of this section which is made by or on behalf of an issuer or by an outside reviewer retained by the issuer shall be deemed not to be a fraudulent statement (as defined in paragraph (d) of this section), unless it is shown that such statement was made or reaffirmed without a reasonable basis or was disclosed other than in good faith.

(b) This section applies to the following statements:

(1) A forward-looking statement (as defined in paragraph (c) of this section) made in a proxy statement or offering circular filed with the Office under part 563b of this chapter; in a registration statement filed with the Office under the Act on Form 10 (17 CFR 249.210); in part I of a quarterly report filed with the Office on Form 10-Q (17 CFR 241.308a); in an annual report to shareholders meeting the requirements of § 563d.1 of this part, particularly 17 CFR 240.14a-3 (b) and (c) or 17 CFR 240.14c-3 (a) and (b) under the Act; in a statement reaffirming such forward-looking statement subsequent to the date the document was filed or the annual report was made publicly available; or a forward-looking statement made prior to the date the document was filed or the date the annual report was made publicly available if such statement is reaffirmed in a filed document or annual report made publicly available within a reasonable time after the making of such forward-looking statement: *Provided*, That

(i) At the time such statements are made or reaffirmed, either:

(A) The issuer is subject to the reporting requirements of section 13(a) or 15(d) of the Act and has complied with the requirements of 17 CFR 240.13a-1 or 240.15d-1 thereunder, if applicable, to file its most recent annual report on Form 10-K; or

(B) If the issuer is not subject to the reporting requirements of section 13(a) or 15(d) of the Act, the statements are made either in a registration statement filed under the Securities Act of 1933 or pursuant to section 12 (b) or (g) of the Act, or in a proxy statement or offering circular filed with the Office under part 563b of this chapter if such statements are reaffirmed in a registration statement under the Act on Form 10, filed with the Office within 180 days of the savings association's conversion, and

(ii) The statements are not made by or on behalf of an issuer that is an investment company registered under the Investment Company Act of 1940;

(2) Information (i) relating to the effects of changing prices on the business enterprise presented voluntarily or pursuant to item 303 of Regulation S-K (17 CFR 229.303), management's discussion and analysis of financial condition and results of operations, or item 302 of Regulation S-K (17 CFR 229.302), supplementary financial information, and (ii) disclosed in a document filed with the Office or in an annual report to shareholders meeting the requirements of 17 CFR 240.14a-3 (b) and (c) or 17 CFR 240.14c-3 (a) and (b) under the Act: *Provided*, That such information included in a proxy statement or offering circular filed pursuant to part 563b of this chapter shall be reaffirmed in a registration statement under the Act on Form 10 filed with the Office within 180 days of the association's conversion.

(c) For purposes of this section, the term "forward-looking statement" shall mean and shall be limited to:

(1) A statement containing a projection of revenues, income (loss), earnings (loss) per share, capital expenditures, dividends, capital structure, or other financial items;

(2) A statement of management's plans and objectives for future operations;

(3) A statement of future economic performance contained in management's discussion and analysis of financial condition and results of operations pursuant to item 303 of Regulation S-K; or

(4) A statement of the assumptions underlying or relating to any of the statements described in paragraph (c)(1), (c)(2), or (c)(3) of this section.

(d) For purposes of this section, the term "fraudulent statement" shall mean a statement which is an untrue statement of a material fact, a statement false or misleading with respect to any material fact, an omission to state a material fact necessary to make a statement not misleading, or which constitutes the employment of a manipulative, deceptive, or fraudulent device, contrivance, scheme, transaction, act, practice, course of business, or an artifice to defraud, as those terms are used in the Securities Act of 1933 or the rules or regulations promulgated thereunder.

§ 563d.210 Form and content of financial statements.

The financial statements required to be contained in filings with the Office under the Act are as set out in the applicable form and Regulation S-X, 17 CFR part 210. Those financial statements, however, shall conform as to form and content to the requirements of § 563c.1 of this chapter.

Subpart B—Interpretations

§ 563d.801 Application of this subpart.

This subpart contains interpretations pertaining to the requirements of the Act and the rules and regulations thereunder as applied to savings associations by the Office.

§ 563d.802 Description of business.

(a) This section applies to the description-of-business portion of:

(1) Registration statements filed on Form 10 (item 1) (17 CFR 249.210),

(2) Proxy and information statements relating to mergers, consolidations, acquisitions, and similar matters (item 14 of Schedule 14A and item 1 of Schedule 14C) (17 CFR 240.14a–101 and 240.14c–101), and

(3) Annual reports filed on Form 10 K (item 7) (17 CFR 249.310).

(b) The description of business should conform to the description of business required by item 7 of Form PS under part 563b of this chapter.

(c) No repetitive disclosure is required by virtue of similar requirements in item 7 of Form PS and items 301 and 303 of Regulation S-K (17 CFR 229.301, 303). However, there should be included appropriate disclosure which arises by virtue of the registrant being a stock savings association. For example, the table regarding return on equity and assets, item 7(d)(5), should include a line item for "dividend payout ratio (dividends declared per share divided by net income per share)."

PART 563e—COMMUNITY REINVESTMENT

Subpart A—General

Sec.
563e.11 Authority, purposes, and scope.
563e.12 Definitions.

Subpart B—Standards for Assessing Performance

563e.21 Performance tests, standards, and ratings, in general.
563e.22 Lending test.
563e.23 Investment test.
563e.24 Service test.
563e.25 Community development test for wholesale or limited purpose savings associations.
563e.26 Small savings association performance standards.
563e.27 Strategic plan.
563e.28 Assigned ratings.
563e.29 Effect of CRA performance on applications.

Subpart C—Records, Reporting, and Disclosure Requirements

563e.41 Assessment area delineation.
563e.42 Data collection, reporting, and disclosure.
563e.43 Content and availability of public file.
563e.44 Public notice by savings associations.
563e.45 Publication of planned examination schedule.

APPENDIX A TO PART 563e—RATINGS
APPENDIX B TO PART 563e—CRA NOTICE

AUTHORITY: 12 U.S.C. 1462a, 1463, 1464, 1467a, 1814, 1816, 1828(c), and 2901 through 2908.

SOURCE: 54 FR 49635, Nov. 30, 1989, unless otherwise noted.

Subpart A—General

SOURCE: 60 FR 22212, May 4, 1995, unless otherwise noted.

§ 563e.11 Authority, purposes, and scope.

(a) *Authority and OMB control number*—(1) *Authority.* This part is issued under the Community Reinvestment Act of 1977 (CRA), as amended (12 U.S.C. 2901 *et seq.*); section 5, as amended, and sections 3, 4, and 10, as added,

§ 563e.12

of the Home Owners' Loan Act of 1933 (12 U.S.C. 1462a, 1463, 1464, and 1467a); and sections 4, 6, and 18(c), as amended of the Federal Deposit Insurance Act (12 U.S.C. 1814, 1816, 1828(c)).

(2) *OMB control number.* The information collection requirements contained in this part were approved by the Office of Management and Budget under the provisions of 44 U.S.C. 3501 *et seq.* and have been assigned OMB control number 1550–0012.

(b) *Purposes.* In enacting the CRA, the Congress required each appropriate Federal financial supervisory agency to assess an institution's record of helping to meet the credit needs of the local communities in which the institution is chartered, consistent with the safe and sound operation of the institution, and to take this record into account in the agency's evaluation of an application for a deposit facility by the institution. This part is intended to carry out the purposes of the CRA by:

(1) Establishing the framework and criteria by which the OTS assesses a savings association's record of helping to meet the credit needs of its entire community, including low- and moderate-income neighborhoods, consistent with the safe and sound operation of the savings association; and

(2) Providing that the OTS takes that record into account in considering certain applications.

(c) *Scope*—(1) *General.* This part applies to all savings associations except as provided in paragraph (c)(2) of this section.

(2) *Certain special purpose savings associations.* This part does not apply to special purpose savings associations that do not perform commercial or retail banking services by granting credit to the public in the ordinary course of business, other than as incident to their specialized operations. These associations include banker's banks, as defined in 12 U.S.C. 24 (Seventh), and associations that engage only in one or more of the following activities: providing cash management controlled disbursement services or serving as correspondent associations, trust companies, or clearing agents.

[60 FR 22212, May 4, 1995, as amended at 62 FR 67708, Dec. 30, 1997]

§ 563e.12 Definitions.

For purposes of this part, the following definitions apply:

(a) *Affiliate* means any company that controls, is controlled by, or is under common control with another company. The term "control" has the meaning given to that term in 12 U.S.C. 1841(a)(2), and a company is under common control with another company if both companies are directly or indirectly controlled by the same company.

(b) *Area median income* means:

(1) The median family income for the MSA, if a person or geography is located in an MSA, or for the metropolitan division, if a person or geography is located in an MSA that has been subdivided into metropolitan divisions; or

(2) The statewide nonmetropolitan median family income, if a person or geography is located outside an MSA.

(c) *Assessment area* means a geographic area delineated in accordance with § 563e.41.

(d) *Automated teller machine (ATM)* means an automated, unstaffed banking facility owned or operated by, or operated exclusively for, the savings association at which deposits are received, cash dispersed, or money lent.

(e) [Reserved]

(f) *Branch* means a staffed banking facility authorized as a branch, whether shared or unshared, including, for example, a mini-branch in a grocery store or a branch operated in conjunction with any other local business or nonprofit organization.

(g) *Community development* means:

(1) Affordable housing (including multifamily rental housing) for low or moderate-income individuals;

(2) Community services targeted to low- or moderate-income individuals;

(3) Activities that promote economic development by financing businesses or farms that meet the size eligibility standards of the Small Business Administration's Development Company or Small Business Investment Company programs (13 CFR 121.301) or have gross annual revenues of $1 million or less;

(4) Activities that revitalize or stabilize—

(i) Low- or moderate-income geographies;

(ii) Designated disaster areas; or

(iii) Distressed or underserved, nonmetropolitan middle-income geographies designated by OTS based on—

(A) Rates of poverty, unemployment, and population loss; or

(B) Population size, density, and dispersion. Activities revitalize and stabilize geographies designated based on population size, density, and dispersion if they help to meet essential community needs, including needs of low- and moderate-income individuals; or

(5) Loans, investments, and services that—

(i) Support, enable or facilitate projects or activities that meet the "eligible uses" criteria described in Section 2301(c) of the Housing and Economic Recovery Act of 2008 (HERA), Public Law 110–289, 122 Stat. 2654, as amended, and are conducted in designated target areas identified in plans approved by the United States Department of Housing and Urban Development in accordance with the Neighborhood Stabilization Program (NSP);

(ii) Are provided no later than two years after the last date funds appropriated for the NSP are required to be spent by grantees; and

(iii) Benefit low-, moderate-, and middle-income individuals and geographies in the savings association's assessment area(s) or areas outside the savings association's assessment area(s) provided the savings association has adequately addressed the community development needs of its assessment area(s).

(h) *Community development loan* means a loan that:

(1) Has as its primary purpose community development; and

(2) Except in the case of a wholesale or limited purpose savings association:

(i) Has not been reported or collected by the savings association or an affiliate for consideration in the savings association's assessment as a home mortgage, small business, small farm, or consumer loan, unless it is a multifamily dwelling loan (as described in appendix A to part 203 of this title); and

(ii) Benefits the savings association's assessment area(s) or a broader statewide or regional area that includes the savings association's assessment area(s).

(i) *Community development service* means a service that:

(1) Has as its primary purpose community development;

(2) Is related to the provision of financial services; and

(3) Has not been considered in the evaluation of the savings association's retail banking services under § 563e.24(d).

(j) *Consumer loan* means a loan to one or more individuals for household, family, or other personal expenditures. A consumer loan does not include a home mortgage, small business, or small farm loan. Consumer loans include the following categories of loans:

(1) *Motor vehicle loan,* which is a consumer loan extended for the purchase of and secured by a motor vehicle;

(2) *Credit card loan,* which is a line of credit for household, family, or other personal expenditures that is accessed by a borrower's use of a "credit card," as this term is defined in § 226.2 of this title;

(3) *Home equity loan,* which is a consumer loan secured by a residence of the borrower;

(4) *Other secured consumer loan,* which is a secured consumer loan that is not included in one of the other categories of consumer loans; and

(5) *Other unsecured consumer loan,* which is an unsecured consumer loan that is not included in one of the other categories of consumer loans.

(k) *Geography* means a census tract delineated by the United States Bureau of the Census in the most recent decennial census.

(l) *Home mortgage loan* means a "home improvement loan," "home purchase loan," or a "refinancing" as defined in § 203.2 of this title.

(m) *Income level* includes:

(1) *Low-income,* which means an individual income that is less than 50 percent of the area median income or a median family income that is less than 50 percent in the case of a geography.

(2) *Moderate-income,* which means an individual income that is at least 50 percent and less than 80 percent of the area median income or a median family income that is at least 50 and less

than 80 percent in the case of a geography.

(3) *Middle-income,* which means an individual income that is at least 80 percent and less than 120 percent of the area median income or a median family income that is at least 80 and less than 120 percent in the case of a geography.

(4) *Upper-income,* which means an individual income that is 120 percent or more of the area median income or a median family income that is 120 percent or more in the case of a geography.

(n) *Limited purpose savings association* means a savings association that offers only a narrow product line (such as credit card or motor vehicle loans) to a regional or broader market and for which a designation as a limited purpose savings association is in effect, in accordance with § 563e.25(b).

(o) *Loan location.* A loan is located as follows:

(1) A consumer loan is located in the geography where the borrower resides;

(2) A home mortgage loan is located in the geography where the property to which the loan relates is located; and

(3) A small business or small farm loan is located in the geography where the main business facility or farm is located or where the loan proceeds otherwise will be applied, as indicated by the borrower.

(p) *Loan production office* means a staffed facility, other than a branch, that is open to the public and that provides lending-related services, such as loan information and applications.

(q) *Metropolitan division* means a metropolitan division as defined by the Director of the Office of Management and Budget.

(r) *MSA* means a metropolitan statistical area as defined by the Director of the Office of Management and Budget.

(s) *Nonmetropolitan area* means any area that is not located in an MSA.

(t) *Qualified investment* means a lawful investment, deposit, membership share, or grant that has as its primary purpose community development.

(u) *Small savings association*—(1) *Definition. Small savings association* means a savings association that, as of December 31 of either of the prior two calendar years, had assets of less than $1.122 billion. *Intermediate small savings association* means a small savings association with assets of at least $280 million as of December 31 of both of the prior two calendar years and less than $1.122 billion as of December 31 of either of the prior two calendar years.

(2) *Adjustment.* The dollar figures in paragraph (u)(1) of this section shall be adjusted annually and published by the OTS, based on the year-to-year change in the average of the Consumer Price Index for Urban Wage Earners and Clerical Workers, not seasonally adjusted, for each twelve-month period ending in November, with rounding to the nearest million.

(v) *Small business loan* means a loan included in "loans to small businesses" as defined in the instructions for preparation of the Thrift Financial Report.

(w) *Small farm loan* means a loan included in "loans to small farms" as defined in the instructions for preparation of the Thrift Financial Report.

(x) *Wholesale savings association* means a savings association that is not in the business of extending home mortgage, small business, small farm, or consumer loans to retail customers, and for which a designation as a wholesale savings association is in effect, in accordance with § 563e.25(b).

[60 FR 22212, May 4, 1995, as amended at 60 FR 66050, Dec. 20, 1995; 61 FR 21364, May 10, 1996; 69 FR 41188, July 8, 2004; 69 FR 51161, Aug. 18, 2004; 71 FR 18618, Apr. 12, 2006; 72 FR 13435, Mar. 22, 2007; 72 FR 72573, Dec. 21, 2007; 73 FR 78155, Dec. 22, 2008; 74 FR 68664, Dec. 29, 2009; 75 FR 82219, Dec. 30, 2010; 75 FR 79286, Dec. 20, 2010]

Subpart B—Standards for Assessing Performance

SOURCE: 60 FR 22213, May 4, 1995, unless otherwise noted.

§ 563e.21 Performance tests, standards, and ratings, in general.

(a) *Performance tests and standards.* The OTS assesses the CRA performance of a savings association in an examination as follows:

(1) *Lending, investment, and service tests.* The OTS applies the lending, investment, and service tests, as provided in §§ 563e.22 through 563e.24, in

evaluating the performance of a savings association, except as provided in paragraphs (a)(2), (a)(3), and (a)(4) of this section.

(2) *Community development test for wholesale or limited purpose savings associations.* The OTS applies the community development test for a wholesale or limited purpose savings association, as provided in § 563e.25, except as provided in paragraph (a)(4) of this section.

(3) *Small savings association performance standards.* The OTS applies the small savings association performance standards as provided in § 563e.26 in evaluating the performance of a small savings association or a savings association that was a small savings association during the prior calendar year, unless the savings association elects to be assessed as provided in paragraphs (a)(1), (a)(2), or (a)(4) of this section. The savings association may elect to be assessed as provided in paragraph (a)(1) of this section only if it collects and reports the data required for other savings associations under § 563e.42.

(4) *Strategic plan.* The OTS evaluates the performance of a savings association under a strategic plan if the savings association submits, and the OTS approves, a strategic plan as provided in § 563e.27.

(b) *Performance context.* The OTS applies the tests and standards in paragraph (a) of this section and also considers whether to approve a proposed strategic plan in the context of:

(1) Demographic data on median income levels, distribution of household income, nature of housing stock, housing costs, and other relevant data pertaining to a savings association's assessment area(s);

(2) Any information about lending, investment, and service opportunities in the savings association's assessment area(s) maintained by the savings association or obtained from community organizations, state, local, and tribal governments, economic development agencies, or other sources;

(3) The savings association's product offerings and business strategy as determined from data provided by the savings association;

(4) Institutional capacity and constraints, including the size and financial condition of the savings association, the economic climate (national, regional, and local), safety and soundness limitations, and any other factors that significantly affect the savings association's ability to provide lending, investments, or services in its assessment area(s);

(5) The savings association's past performance and the performance of similarly situated lenders;

(6) The savings association's public file, as described in § 563e.43, and any written comments about the savings association's CRA performance submitted to the savings association or the OTS; and

(7) Any other information deemed relevant by the OTS.

(c) *Assigned ratings.* The OTS assigns to a savings association one of the following four ratings pursuant to § 563e.28 and Appendix A of this part: "outstanding"; "satisfactory"; "needs to improve"; or "substantial noncompliance," as provided in 12 U.S.C. 2906(b)(2). The rating assigned by the OTS reflects the savings association's record of helping to meet the credit needs of its entire community, including low- and moderate-income neighborhoods, consistent with the safe and sound operation of the savings association.

(d) *Safe and sound operations.* This part and the CRA do not require a savings association to make loans or investments or to provide services that are inconsistent with safe and sound operations. To the contrary, the OTS anticipates savings associations can meet the standards of this part with safe and sound loans, investments, and services on which the savings associations expect to make a profit. Savings associations are permitted and encouraged to develop and apply flexible underwriting standards for loans that benefit low- or moderate-income geographies or individuals, only if consistent with safe and sound operations.

(e) *Low-cost education loans provided to low-income borrowers.* In assessing and taking into account the record of a savings association under this part, the OTS considers, as a factor, low-cost education loans originated by the savings association to borrowers, particularly in its assessment area(s), who

§ 563e.22

have an individual income that is less than 50 percent of the area median income. For purposes of this paragraph, "low-cost education loans" means any education loan, as defined in section 140(a)(7) of the Truth in Lending Act (15 U.S.C. 1650(a)(7)) (including a loan under a state or local education loan program), originated by the savings association for a student at an "institution of higher education," as that term is generally defined in sections 101 and 102 of the Higher Education Act of 1965 (20 U.S.C. 1001 and 1002) and the implementing regulations published by the U.S. Department of Education, with interest rates and fees no greater than those of comparable education loans offered directly by the U.S. Department of Education. Such rates and fees are specified in section 455 of the Higher Education Act of 1965 (20 U.S.C. 1087e).

(f) *Activities in cooperation with minority- or women-owned financial institutions and low-income credit unions.* In assessing and taking into account the record of a nonminority-owned and nonwomen-owned savings association under this part, the OTS considers as a factor capital investment, loan participation, and other ventures undertaken by the savings association in cooperation with minority- and women-owned financial institutions and low-income credit unions. Such activities must help meet the credit needs of local communities in which the minority- and women-owned financial institutions and low-income credit unions are chartered. To be considered, such activities need not also benefit the savings association's assessment area(s) or the broader statewide or regional area that includes the savings association's assessment area(s).

[60 FR 22213, May 4, 1995, as amended at 70 FR 10030, Mar. 2, 2005; 72 FR 13435, Mar. 22, 2007; 75 FR 61045, Oct. 4, 2010]

§ 563e.22 Lending test.

(a) *Scope of test.* (1) The lending test evaluates a savings association's record of helping to meet the credit needs of its assessment area(s) through its lending activities by considering a savings association's home mortgage, small business, small farm, and community development lending. If consumer lending constitutes a substantial majority of a savings association's business, the OTS will evaluate the savings association's consumer lending in one or more of the following categories: motor vehicle, credit card, home equity, other secured, and other unsecured loans. In addition, at a savings association's option, the OTS will evaluate one or more categories of consumer lending, if the savings association has collected and maintained, as required in § 563e.42(c)(1), the data for each category that the savings association elects to have the OTS evaluate.

(2) The OTS considers originations and purchases of loans. The OTS will also consider any other loan data the savings association may choose to provide, including data on loans outstanding, commitments and letters of credit.

(3) A savings association may ask the OTS to consider loans originated or purchased by consortia in which the savings association participates or by third parties in which the savings association has invested only if the loans meet the definition of community development loans and only in accordance with paragraph (d) of this section. The OTS will not consider these loans under any criterion of the lending test except the community development lending criterion.

(b) *Performance criteria.* The OTS evaluates a savings association's lending performance pursuant to the following criteria:

(1) *Lending activity.* The number and amount of the savings association's home mortgage, small business, small farm, and consumer loans, if applicable, in the savings association's assessment area(s);

(2) *Geographic distribution.* The geographic distribution of the savings association's home mortgage, small business, small farm, and consumer loans, if applicable, based on the loan location, including:

(i) The proportion of the savings association's lending in the savings association's assessment area(s);

(ii) The dispersion of lending in the savings association's assessment area(s); and

(iii) The number and amount of loans in low-, moderate-, middle-, and upper-income geographies in the savings association's assessment area(s);

(3) *Borrower characteristics.* The distribution, particularly in the savings association's assessment area(s), of the savings association's home mortgage, small business, small farm, and consumer loans, if applicable, based on borrower characteristics, including the number and amount of:

(i) Home mortgage loans to low-, moderate-, middle-, and upper-income individuals;

(ii) Small business and small farm loans to businesses and farms with gross annual revenues of $1 million or less;

(iii) Small business and small farm loans by loan amount at origination; and

(iv) Consumer loans, if applicable, to low-, moderate-, middle-, and upper-income individuals;

(4) *Community development lending.* The savings association's community development lending, including the number and amount of community development loans, and their complexity and innovativeness; and

(5) *Innovative or flexible lending practices.* The savings association's use of innovative or flexible lending practices in a safe and sound manner to address the credit needs of low- or moderate-income individuals or geographies.

(c) *Affiliate lending.* (1) At a savings association's option, the OTS will consider loans by an affiliate of the savings association, if the savings association provides data on the affiliate's loans pursuant to § 563e.42.

(2) The OTS considers affiliate lending subject to the following constraints:

(i) No affiliate may claim a loan origination or loan purchase if another institution claims the same loan origination or purchase; and

(ii) If a savings association elects to have the OTS consider loans within a particular lending category made by one or more of the savings association's affiliates in a particular assessment area, the savings association shall elect to have the OTS consider, in accordance with paragraph (c)(1) of this section, all the loans within that lending category in that particular assessment area made by all of the savings association's affiliates.

(3) The OTS does not consider affiliate lending in assessing a savings association's performance under paragraph (b)(2)(i) of this section.

(d) *Lending by a consortium or a third party.* Community development loans originated or purchased by a consortium in which the savings association participates or by a third party in which the savings association has invested:

(1) Will be considered, at the savings association's option, if the savings association reports the data pertaining to these loans under § 563e.42(b)(2); and

(2) May be allocated among participants or investors, as they choose, for purposes of the lending test, except that no participant or investor:

(i) May claim a loan origination or loan purchase if another participant or investor claims the same loan origination or purchase; or

(ii) May claim loans accounting for more than its percentage share (based on the level of its participation or investment) of the total loans originated by the consortium or third party.

(e) *Lending performance rating.* The OTS rates a savings association's lending performance as provided in Appendix A of this part.

§ 563e.23 Investment test.

(a) *Scope of test.* The investment test evaluates a savings association's record of helping to meet the credit needs of its assessment area(s) through qualified investments that benefit its assessment area(s) or a broader statewide or regional area that includes the savings association's assessment area(s).

(b) *Exclusion.* Activities considered under the lending or service tests may not be considered under the investment test.

(c) *Affiliate investment.* At a savings association's option, the OTS will consider, in its assessment of a savings association's investment performance, a qualified investment made by an affiliate of the savings association, if the qualified investment is not claimed by any other institution.

(d) *Disposition of branch premises.* Donating, selling on favorable terms, or

279

§ 563e.24

making available on a rent-free basis a branch of the savings association that is located in a predominantly minority neighborhood to a minority depository institution or women's depository institution (as these terms are defined in 12 U.S.C. 2907(b)) will be considered as a qualified investment.

(e) *Performance criteria.* The OTS evaluates the investment performance of a savings association pursuant to the following criteria:

(1) The dollar amount of qualified investments;

(2) The innovativeness or complexity of qualified investments;

(3) The responsiveness of qualified investments to credit and community development needs; and

(4) The degree to which the qualified investments are not routinely provided by private investors.

(f) *Investment performance rating.* The OTS rates a savings association's investment performance as provided in Appendix A of this part.

§ 563e.24 Service test.

(a) *Scope of test.* The service test evaluates a savings association's record of helping to meet the credit needs of its assessment area(s) by analyzing both the availability and effectiveness of a savings association's systems for delivering retail banking services and the extent and innovativeness of its community development services.

(b) *Area(s) benefitted.* Community development services must benefit a savings association's assessment area(s) or a broader statewide or regional area that includes the savings association's assessment area(s).

(c) *Affiliate service.* At a savings association's option, the OTS will consider, in its assessment of a savings association's service performance, a community development service provided by an affiliate of the savings association, if the community development service is not claimed by any other institution.

(d) *Performance criteria—retail banking services.* The OTS evaluates the availability and effectiveness of a savings association's systems for delivering retail banking services, pursuant to the following criteria:

(1) The current distribution of the savings association's branches among low-, moderate-, middle-, and upper-income geographies;

(2) In the context of its current distribution of the savings association's branches, the savings association's record of opening and closing branches, particularly branches located in low- or moderate-income geographies or primarily serving low- or moderate-income individuals;

(3) The availability and effectiveness of alternative systems for delivering retail banking services (*e.g.,* ATMs, ATMs not owned or operated by or exclusively for the savings association, banking by telephone or computer, loan production offices, and bank-at-work or bank-by-mail programs) in low- and moderate-income geographies and to low- and moderate-income individuals; and

(4) The range of services provided in low-, moderate-, middle-, and upper-income geographies and the degree to which the services are tailored to meet the needs of those geographies.

(e) *Performance criteria—community development services.* The OTS evaluates community development services pursuant to the following criteria:

(1) The extent to which the savings association provides community development services; and

(2) The innovativeness and responsiveness of community development services.

(f) *Service performance rating.* The OTS rates a savings association's service performance as provided in Appendix A of this part.

§ 563e.25 Community development test for wholesale or limited purpose savings associations.

(a) *Scope of test.* The OTS assesses a wholesale or limited purpose savings association's record of helping to meet the credit needs of its assessment area(s) under the community development test through its community development lending, qualified investments, or community development services.

(b) *Designation as a wholesale or limited purpose savings association.* In order to receive a designation as a wholesale or limited purpose savings association, a savings association shall file a request, in writing, with the OTS, at least three months prior to the proposed effective date of the designation. If the OTS approves the designation, it remains in effect until the savings association requests revocation of the designation or until one year after the OTS notifies the savings association that the OTS has revoked the designation on its own initiative.

(c) *Performance criteria.* The OTS evaluates the community development performance of a wholesale or limited purpose savings association pursuant to the following criteria:

(1) The number and amount of community development loans (including originations and purchases of loans and other community development loan data provided by the savings association, such as data on loans outstanding, commitments, and letters of credit), qualified investments, or community development services;

(2) The use of innovative or complex qualified investments, community development loans, or community development services and the extent to which the investments are not routinely provided by private investors; and

(3) The savings association's responsiveness to credit and community development needs.

(d) *Indirect activities.* At a savings association's option, the OTS will consider in its community development performance assessment:

(1) Qualified investments or community development services provided by an affiliate of the savings association, if the investments or services are not claimed by any other institution; and

(2) Community development lending by affiliates, consortia and third parties, subject to the requirements and limitations in § 563e.22 (c) and (d).

(e) *Benefit to assessment area(s)*—(1) *Benefit inside assessment area(s).* The OTS considers all qualified investments, community development loans, and community development services that benefit areas within the savings association's assessment area(s) or a broader statewide or regional area that includes the savings association's assessment area(s).

(2) *Benefit outside assessment area(s).* The OTS considers the qualified investments, community development loans, and community development services that benefit areas outside the savings association's assessment area(s), if the savings association has adequately addressed the needs of its assessment area(s).

(f) *Community development performance rating.* The OTS rates a savings association's community development performance as provided in Appendix A of this part.

§ 563e.26 Small savings association performance standards.

(a) *Performance criteria*—(1) *Small savings associations that are not intermediate small savings associations.* The OTS evaluates the record of a small savings association that is not, or that was not during the prior calendar year, an intermediate small savings association, of helping to meet the credit needs of its assessment area(s) pursuant to the criteria set forth in paragraph (b) of this section.

(2) *Intermediate small savings associations.* The OTS evaluates the record of a small savings association that is, or that was during the prior calendar year, an intermediate small savings association, of helping to meet the credit needs of its assessment area(s) pursuant to the criteria set forth in paragraphs (b) and (c) of this section.

(b) *Lending test.* A small savings association's lending performance is evaluated pursuant to the following criteria:

(1) The savings association's loan-to-deposit ratio, adjusted for seasonal variation, and, as appropriate, other lending-related activities, such as loan originations for sale to the secondary markets, community development loans, or qualified investments;

(2) The percentage of loans and, as appropriate, other lending-related activities located in the savings association's assessment area(s);

(3) The savings association's record of lending to and, as appropriate, engaging in other lending-related activities for borrowers of different income levels and businesses and farms of different sizes;

(4) The geographic distribution of the savings association's loans; and

§ 563e.27

(5) The savings association's record of taking action, if warranted, in response to written complaints about its performance in helping to meet credit needs in its assessment area(s).

(c) *Community development test.* An intermediate small savings association's community development performance also is evaluated pursuant to the following criteria:

(1) The number and amount of community development loans;

(2) The number and amount of qualified investments;

(3) The extent to which the savings association provides community development services; and

(4) The savings association's responsiveness through such activities to community development lending, investment, and services needs.

(d) *Small savings association performance rating.* The OTS rates the performance of a savings association evaluated under this section as provided in Appendix A of this part.

[72 FR 13435, Mar. 22, 2007, as amended at 72 FR 72573, Dec. 21, 2007]

§ 563e.27 Strategic plan.

(a) *Alternative election.* The OTS will assess a savings association's record of helping to meet the credit needs of its assessment area(s) under a strategic plan if:

(1) The savings association has submitted the plan to the OTS as provided for in this section;

(2) The OTS has approved the plan;

(3) The plan is in effect; and

(4) The savings association has been operating under an approved plan for at least one year.

(b) *Data reporting.* The OTS's approval of a plan does not affect the savings association's obligation, if any, to report data as required by § 563e.42.

(c) *Plans in general*—(1) *Term.* A plan may have a term of no more than five years, and any multi-year plan must include annual interim measurable goals under which the OTS will evaluate the savings association's performance.

(2) *Multiple assessment areas.* A savings association with more than one assessment area may prepare a single plan for all of its assessment areas or one or more plans for one or more of its assessment areas.

(3) *Treatment of affiliates.* Affiliated institutions may prepare a joint plan if the plan provides measurable goals for each institution. Activities may be allocated among institutions at the institutions' option, provided that the same activities are not considered for more than one institution.

(d) *Public participation in plan development.* Before submitting a plan to the OTS for approval, a savings association shall:

(1) Informally seek suggestions from members of the public in its assessment area(s) covered by the plan while developing the plan;

(2) Once the savings association has developed a plan, formally solicit public comment on the plan for at least 30 days by publishing notice in at least one newspaper of general circulation in each assessment area covered by the plan; and

(3) During the period of formal public comment, make copies of the plan available for review by the public at no cost at all offices of the savings association in any assessment area covered by the plan and provide copies of the plan upon request for a reasonable fee to cover copying and mailing, if applicable.

(e) *Submission of plan.* The savings association shall submit its plan to the OTS at least three months prior to the proposed effective date of the plan. The savings association shall also submit with its plan a description of its informal efforts to seek suggestions from members of the public, any written public comment received, and, if the plan was revised in light of the comment received, the initial plan as released for public comment.

(f) *Plan content*—(1) *Measurable goals.* (i) A savings association shall specify in its plan measurable goals for helping to meet the credit needs of each assessment area covered by the plan, particularly the needs of low- and moderate-income geographies and low- and moderate-income individuals, through lending, investment, and services, as appropriate.

(ii) A savings association shall address in its plan all three performance categories and, unless the savings association has been designated as a wholesale or limited purpose savings association, shall emphasize lending and lending-related activities. Nevertheless, a different emphasis, including a focus on one or more performance categories, may be appropriate if responsive to the characteristics and credit needs of its assessment area(s), considering public comment and the savings association's capacity and constraints, product offerings, and business strategy.

(2) *Confidential information.* A savings association may submit additional information to the OTS on a confidential basis, but the goals stated in the plan must be sufficiently specific to enable the public and the OTS to judge the merits of the plan.

(3) *Satisfactory and outstanding goals.* A savings association shall specify in its plan measurable goals that constitute "satisfactory" performance. A plan may specify measurable goals that constitute "outstanding" performance. If a savings association submits, and the OTS approves, both "satisfactory" and "outstanding" performance goals, the OTS will consider the savings association eligible for an "outstanding" performance rating.

(4) *Election if satisfactory goals not substantially met.* A savings association may elect in its plan that, if the savings association fails to meet substantially its plan goals for a satisfactory rating, the OTS will evaluate the savings association's performance under the lending, investment, and service tests, the community development test, or the small savings association performance standards, as appropriate.

(g) *Plan approval*—(1) *Timing.* The OTS will act upon a plan within 60 calendar days after the OTS receives the complete plan and other material required under paragraph (e) of this section. If the OTS fails to act within this time period, the plan shall be deemed approved unless the OTS extends the review period for good cause.

(2) *Public participation.* In evaluating the plan's goals, the OTS considers the public's involvement in formulating the plan, written public comment on the plan, and any response by the savings association to public comment on the plan.

(3) *Criteria for evaluating plan.* The OTS evaluates a plan's measurable goals using the following criteria, as appropriate:

(i) The extent and breadth of lending or lending-related activities, including, as appropriate, the distribution of loans among different geographies, businesses and farms of different sizes, and individuals of different income levels, the extent of community development lending, and the use of innovative or flexible lending practices to address credit needs;

(ii) The amount and innovativeness, complexity, and responsiveness of the savings association's qualified investments; and

(iii) The availability and effectiveness of the savings association's systems for delivering retail banking services and the extent and innovativeness of the savings association's community development services.

(h) *Plan amendment.* During the term of a plan, a savings association may request the OTS to approve an amendment to the plan on grounds that there has been a material change in circumstances. The savings association shall develop an amendment to a previously approved plan in accordance with the public participation requirements of paragraph (d) of this section.

(i) *Plan assessment.* The OTS approves the goals and assesses performance under a plan as provided for in Appendix A of this part.

[60 FR 22216, May 4, 1995, as amended at 60 FR 66050, Dec. 20, 1995; 69 FR 41188, July 8, 2004]

§ 563e.28 Assigned ratings.

(a) *Ratings in general.* Subject to paragraphs (b) and(c) of this section, the OTS assigns to a savings association a rating of "outstanding," "satisfactory," "needs to improve," or "substantial noncompliance" based on the savings association's performance under the lending, investment and service tests, the community development test, the small savings association performance standards, or an approved strategic plan, as applicable.

(b) *Lending, investment, and service tests.* The OTS assigns a rating for a savings association assessed under the lending, investment, and service tests

§ 563e.29

in accordance with the following principles:

(1) A savings association that receives an "outstanding" rating on the lending test receives an assigned rating of at least "satisfactory";

(2) A savings association that receives an "outstanding" rating on both the service test and the investment test and a rating of at least "high satisfactory" on the lending test receives an assigned rating of "outstanding"; and

(3) No savings association may receive an assigned rating of "satisfactory" or higher unless it receives a rating of at least "low satisfactory" on the lending test.

(c) *Effect of evidence of discriminatory or other illegal credit practices.* (1) The OTS's evaluation of a savings association's CRA performance is adversely affected by evidence of discriminatory or other illegal credit practices in any geography by the savings association or in any assessment area by any affiliate whose loans have been considered as part of the savings association's lending performance. In connection with any type of lending activity described in § 563e.22(a), evidence of discriminatory or other credit practices that violate an applicable law, rule, or regulation includes, but is not limited to:

(i) Discrimination against applicants on a prohibited basis in violation, for example, of the Equal Credit Opportunity Act or the Fair Housing Act;

(ii) Violations of the Home Ownership and Equity Protection Act;

(iii) Violations of section 5 of the Federal Trade Commission Act;

(iv) Violations of section 8 of the Real Estate Settlement Procedures Act; and

(v) Violations of the Truth in Lending Act provisions regarding a consumer's right of rescission.

(2) In determining the effect of evidence of practices described in paragraph (c)(1) of this section on the savings association's assigned rating, the OTS considers the nature, extent, and strength of the evidence of the practices; the policies and procedures that the savings association (or affiliate, as applicable) has in place to prevent the practices; any corrective action that the savings association (or affiliate, as applicable) has taken or has committed to take, including voluntary corrective action resulting from self-assessment; and any other relevant information.

[60 FR 22213, May 4, 1995, as amended at 70 FR 10030, Mar. 2, 2005; 72 FR 13435, Mar. 22, 2007; 72 FR 19110, Apr. 17, 2007]

§ 563e.29 Effect of CRA performance on applications.

(a) *CRA performance.* Among other factors, the OTS takes into account the record of performance under the CRA of each applicant savings association, and for applications under section 10(e) of the Home Owners' Loan Act (12 U.S.C. 1467a(e)), of each proposed subsidiary savings association, in considering an application for:

(1) The establishment of a domestic branch or other facility that would be authorized to take deposits;

(2) The relocation of the main office or a branch;

(3) The merger or consolidation with or the acquisition of the assets or assumption of the liabilities of an insured depository institution requiring OTS approval under the Bank Merger Act (12 U.S.C. 1828(c));

(4) A Federal thrift charter; and

(5) Acquisitions subject to section 10(e) of the Home Owners' Loan Act (12 U.S.C. 1467a(e)).

(b) *Charter application.* An applicant for a Federal thrift charter shall submit with its application a description of how it will meet its CRA objectives. The OTS takes the description into account in considering the application and may deny or condition approval on that basis.

(c) *Interested parties.* The OTS takes into account any views expressed by interested parties that are submitted in accordance with the applicable comment procedures in considering CRA performance in an application listed in paragraphs (a) and (b) of this section.

(d) *Denial or conditional approval of application.* A savings association's record of performance may be the basis for denying or conditioning approval of an application listed in paragraph (a) of this section.

(e) *Insured depository institution.* For purposes of this section, the term "insured depository institution" has the meaning given to that term in 12 U.S.C. 1813.

Subpart C—Records, Reporting, and Disclosure Requirements

SOURCE: 60 FR 22217, May 4, 1995, unless otherwise noted.

§ 563e.41 Assessment area delineation.

(a) *In general.* A savings association shall delineate one or more assessment areas within which the OTS evaluates the savings association's record of helping to meet the credit needs of its community. The OTS does not evaluate the savings association's delineation of its assessment area(s) as a separate performance criterion, but the OTS reviews the delineation for compliance with the requirements of this section.

(b) *Geographic area(s) for wholesale or limited purpose savings associations.* The assessment area(s) for a wholesale or limited purpose savings association must consist generally of one or more MSAs or metropolitan divisions (using the MSA or metropolitan division boundaries that were in effect as of January 1 of the calendar year in which the delineation is made) or one or more contiguous political subdivisions, such as counties, cities, or towns, in which the savings association has its main office, branches, and deposit-taking ATMs.

(c) *Geographic area(s) for other savings associations.* The assessment area(s) for a savings association other than a wholesale or limited purpose savings association must:

(1) Consist generally of one or more MSAs or metropolitan divisions (using the MSA or metropolitan division boundaries that were in effect as of January 1 of the calendar year in which the delineation is made) or one or more contiguous political subdivisions, such as counties, cities, or towns; and

(2) Include the geographies in which the savings association has its main office, its branches, and its deposit-taking ATMs, as well as the surrounding geographies in which the savings association has originated or purchased a substantial portion of its loans (including home mortgage loans, small business and small farm loans, and any other loans the savings association chooses, such as those consumer loans on which the savings association elects to have its performance assessed).

(d) *Adjustments to geographic area(s).* A savings association may adjust the boundaries of its assessment area(s) to include only the portion of a political subdivision that it reasonably can be expected to serve. An adjustment is particularly appropriate in the case of an assessment area that otherwise would be extremely large, of unusual configuration, or divided by significant geographic barriers.

(e) *Limitations on the delineation of an assessment area.* Each savings association's assessment area(s):

(1) Must consist only of whole geographies;

(2) May not reflect illegal discrimination;

(3) May not arbitrarily exclude low- or moderate-income geographies, taking into account the savings association's size and financial condition; and

(4) May not extend substantially beyond an MSA boundary or beyond a state boundary unless the assessment area is located in a multistate MSA. If a savings association serves a geographic area that extends substantially beyond a state boundary, the savings association shall delineate separate assessment areas for the areas in each state. If a savings association serves a geographic area that extends substantially beyond an MSA boundary, the savings association shall delineate separate assessment areas for the areas inside and outside the MSA.

(f) *Savings associations serving military personnel.* Notwithstanding the requirements of this section, a savings association whose business predominantly consists of serving the needs of military personnel or their dependents who are not located within a defined geographic area may delineate its entire deposit customer base as its assessment area.

(g) *Use of assessment area(s).* The OTS uses the assessment area(s) delineated by a savings association in its evaluation of the savings association's CRA performance unless the OTS determines that the assessment area(s) do

§ 563e.42

not comply with the requirements of this section.

[60 FR 22217, May 4, 1995, as amended at 69 FR 41188, July 8, 2004]

§ 563e.42 Data collection, reporting, and disclosure.

(a) *Loan information required to be collected and maintained.* A savings association, except a small savings association, shall collect, and maintain in machine readable form (as prescribed by the OTS) until the completion of its next CRA examination, the following data for each small business or small farm loan originated or purchased by the savings association:

(1) A unique number or alpha-numeric symbol that can be used to identify the relevant loan file;

(2) The loan amount at origination;

(3) The loan location; and

(4) An indicator whether the loan was to a business or farm with gross annual revenues of $1 million or less.

(b) *Loan information required to be reported.* A savings association, except a small savings association or a savings association that was a small savings association during the prior calendar year, shall report annually by March 1 to the OTS in machine readable form (as prescribed by the OTS) the following data for the prior calendar year:

(1) *Small business and small farm loan data.* For each geography in which the savings association originated or purchased a small business or small farm loan, the aggregate number and amount of loans:

(i) With an amount at origination of $100,000 or less;

(ii) With amount at origination of more than $100,000 but less than or equal to $250,000;

(iii) With an amount at origination of more than $250,000; and

(iv) To businesses and farms with gross annual revenues of $1 million or less (using the revenues that the savings association considered in making its credit decision);

(2) *Community development loan data.* The aggregate number and aggregate amount of community development loans originated or purchased; and

(3) *Home mortgage loans.* If the savings association is subject to reporting under part 203 of this title, the location of each home mortgage loan application, origination, or purchase outside the MSAs in which the savings association has a home or branch office (or outside any MSA) in accordance with the requirements of part 203 of this title.

(c) *Optional data collection and maintenance*—(1) *Consumer loans.* A savings association may collect and maintain in machine readable form (as prescribed by the OTS) data for consumer loans originated or purchased by the savings association for consideration under the lending test. A savings association may maintain data for one or more of the following categories of consumer loans: motor vehicle, credit card, home equity, other secured, and other unsecured. If the savings association maintains data for loans in a certain category, it shall maintain data for all loans originated or purchased within that category. The savings association shall maintain data separately for each category, including for each loan:

(i) A unique number or alpha-numeric symbol that can be used to identify the relevant loan file;

(ii) The loan amount at origination or purchase;

(iii) The loan location; and

(iv) The gross annual income of the borrower that the savings association considered in making its credit decision.

(2) *Other loan data.* At its option, a savings association may provide other information concerning its lending performance, including additional loan distribution data.

(d) *Data on affiliate lending.* A savings association that elects to have the OTS consider loans by an affiliate, for purposes of the lending or community development test or an approved strategic plan, shall collect, maintain, and report for those loans the data that the savings association would have collected, maintained, and reported pursuant to paragraphs (a), (b), and (c) of this section had the loans been originated or purchased by the savings association. For home mortgage loans, the savings association shall also be prepared to identify the home mortgage loans reported under part 203 of this title by the affiliate.

Office of Thrift Supervision, Treasury § 563e.42

(e) *Data on lending by a consortium or a third-party.* A savings association that elects to have the OTS consider community development loans by a consortium or third party, for purposes of the lending or community development tests or an approved strategic plan, shall report for those loans the data that the savings association would have reported under paragraph (b)(2) of this section had the loans been originated or purchased by the savings association.

(f) *Small savings associations electing evaluation under the lending, investment, and service tests.* A savings association that qualifies for evaluation under the small savings association performance standards but elects evaluation under the lending, investment, and service tests shall collect, maintain, and report the data required for other savings associations pursuant to paragraphs (a) and (b) of this section.

(g) *Assessment area data.* A savings association, except a small savings association or a savings association that was a small savings association during the prior calendar year, shall collect and report to the OTS by March 1 of each year a list for each assessment area showing the geographies within the area.

(h) *CRA Disclosure Statement.* The OTS prepares annually for each savings association that reports data pursuant to this section a CRA Disclosure Statement that contains, on a state-by-state basis:

(1) For each county (and for each assessment area smaller than a county) with a population of 500,000 persons or fewer in which the savings association reported a small business or small farm loan:

(i) The number and amount of small business and small farm loans reported as originated or purchased located in low-, moderate-, middle-, and upper-income geographies;

(ii) A list grouping each geography according to whether the geography is low-, moderate-, middle-, or upper-income;

(iii) A list showing each geography in which the savings association reported a small business or small farm loan; and

(iv) The number and amount of small business and small farm loans to businesses and farms with gross annual revenues of $1 million or less;

(2) For each county (and for each assessment area smaller than a county) with a population in excess of 500,000 persons in which the savings association reported a small business or small farm loan:

(i) The number and amount of small business and small farm loans reported as originated or purchased located in geographies with median income relative to the area median income of less than 10 percent, 10 or more but less than 20 percent, 20 or more but less than 30 percent, 30 or more but less than 40 percent, 40 or more but less than 50 percent, 50 or more but less than 60 percent, 60 or more but less than 70 percent, 70 or more but less than 80 percent, 80 or more but less than 90 percent, 90 or more but less than 100 percent, 100 or more but less than 110 percent, 110 or more but less than 120 percent, and 120 percent or more;

(ii) A list grouping each geography in the county or assessment area according to whether the median income in the geography relative to the area median income is less than 10 percent, 10 or more but less than 20 percent, 20 or more but less than 30 percent, 30 or more but less than 40 percent, 40 or more but less than 50 percent, 50 or more but less than 60 percent, 60 or more but less than 70 percent, 70 or more but less than 80 percent, 80 or more but less than 90 percent, 90 or more but less than 100 percent, 100 or more but less than 110 percent, 110 or more but less than 120 percent, and 120 percent or more;

(iii) A list showing each geography in which the savings association reported a small business or small farm loan; and

(iv) The number and amount of small business and small farm loans to businesses and farms with gross annual revenues of $1 million or less;

(3) The number and amount of small business and small farm loans located inside each assessment area reported by the savings association and the number and amount of small business and small farm loans located outside

§ 563e.43

the assessment area(s) reported by the savings association; and

(4) The number and amount of community development loans reported as originated or purchased.

(i) *Aggregate disclosure statements.* The OTS, in conjunction with the Board of Governors of the Federal Reserve System, the Federal Deposit Insurance Corporation, and the Office of the Comptroller of the Currency, prepares annually, for each MSA or metropolitan division (including an MSA or metropolitan division that crosses a state boundary) and the nonmetropolitan portion of each state, an aggregate disclosure statement of small business and small farm lending by all institutions subject to reporting under this part or parts 25, 228, or 345 of this title. These disclosure statements indicate, for each geography, the number and amount of all small business and small farm loans originated or purchased by reporting institutions, except that the OTS may adjust the form of the disclosure if necessary, because of special circumstances, to protect the privacy of a borrower or the competitive position of an institution.

(j) *Central data depositories.* The OTS makes the aggregate disclosure statements, described in paragraph (i) of this section, and the individual savings association CRA Disclosure Statements, described in paragraph (h) of this section, available to the public at central data depositories. The OTS publishes a list of the depositories at which the statements are available.

[60 FR 22217, May 4, 1995, as amended at 69 FR 41189, July 8, 2004]

§ 563e.43 Content and availability of public file.

(a) *Information available to the public.* A savings association shall maintain a public file that includes the following information:

(1) All written comments received from the public for the current year and each of the prior two calendar years that specifically relate to the savings association's performance in helping to meet community credit needs, and any response to the comments by the savings association, if neither the comments nor the responses contain statements that reflect adversely on the good name or reputation of any persons other than the savings association or publication of which would violate specific provisions of law;

(2) A copy of the public section of the savings association's most recent CRA Performance Evaluation prepared by the OTS. The savings association shall place this copy in the public file within 30 business days after its receipt from the OTS;

(3) A list of the savings association's branches, their street addresses, and geographies;

(4) A list of branches opened or closed by the savings association during the current year and each of the prior two calendar years, their street addresses, and geographies;

(5) A list of services (including hours of operation, available loan and deposit products, and transaction fees) generally offered at the savings association's branches and descriptions of material differences in the availability or cost of services at particular branches, if any. At its option, a savings association may include information regarding the availability of alternative systems for delivering retail banking services (*e.g.*, ATMs, ATMs not owned or operated by or exclusively for the savings association, banking by telephone or computer, loan production offices, and bank-at-work or bank-by-mail programs);

(6) A map of each assessment area showing the boundaries of the area and identifying the geographies contained within the area, either on the map or in a separate list; and

(7) Any other information the savings association chooses.

(b) *Additional information available to the public*—(1) *Savings associations other than small savings associations.* A savings association, except a small savings association or a savings association that was a small savings association during the prior calendar year, shall include in its public file the following information pertaining to the savings association and its affiliates, if applicable, for each of the prior two calendar years:

(i) If the savings association has elected to have one or more categories of its consumer loans considered under

Office of Thrift Supervision, Treasury § 563e.44

the lending test, for each of these categories, the number and amount of loans:

(A) To low-, moderate-, middle-, and upper-income individuals;

(B) Located in low-, moderate-, middle-, and upper-income census tracts; and

(C) Located inside the savings association's assessment area(s) and outside the savings association's assessment area(s); and

(ii) The savings association's CRA Disclosure Statement. The savings association shall place the statement in the public file within three business days of its receipt from the OTS.

(2) *Savings associations required to report Home Mortgage Disclosure Act (HMDA) data.* A savings association required to report home mortgage loan data pursuant to part 203 of this title shall include in its public file a copy of the HMDA Disclosure Statement provided by the Federal Financial Institutions Examination Council pertaining to the savings association for each of the prior two calendar years. In addition, a savings association that elected to have the OTS consider the mortgage lending of an affiliate for any of these years shall include in its public file the affiliate's HMDA Disclosure Statement for those years. The savings association shall place the statement(s) in the public file within three business days after its receipt.

(3) *Small savings associations.* A small savings association or a savings association that was a small savings association during the prior calendar year shall include in its public file:

(i) The savings association's loan-to-deposit ratio for each quarter of the prior calendar year and, at its option, additional data on its loan-to-deposit ratio; and

(ii) The information required for other savings associations by paragraph (b)(1) of this section, if the savings association has elected to be evaluated under the lending, investment, and service tests.

(4) *Savings associations with strategic plans.* A savings association that has been approved to be assessed under a strategic plan shall include in its public file a copy of that plan. A savings association need not include information submitted to the OTS on a confidential basis in conjunction with the plan.

(5) *Savings associations with less than satisfactory ratings.* A savings association that received a less than satisfactory rating during its most recent examination shall include in its public file a description of its current efforts to improve its performance in helping to meet the credit needs of its entire community. The savings association shall update the description quarterly.

(c) *Location of public information.* A savings association shall make available to the public for inspection upon request and at no cost the information required in this section as follows:

(1) At the main office and, if an interstate savings association, at one branch office in each state, all information in the public file; and

(2) At each branch:

(i) A copy of the public section of the savings association's most recent CRA Performance Evaluation and a list of services provided by the branch; and

(ii) Within five calendar days of the request, all the information in the public file relating to the assessment area in which the branch is located.

(d) *Copies.* Upon request, a savings association shall provide copies, either on paper or in another form acceptable to the person making the request, of the information in its public file. The savings association may charge a reasonable fee not to exceed the cost of copying and mailing (if applicable).

(e) *Updating.* Except as otherwise provided in this section, a savings association shall ensure that the information required by this section is current as of April 1 of each year.

§ 563e.44 Public notice by savings associations.

A savings association shall provide in the public lobby of its main office and each of its branches the appropriate public notice set forth in Appendix B of this part. Only a branch of a savings association having more than one assessment area shall include the bracketed material in the notice for branch offices. Only a savings association that is an affiliate of a holding company shall include the last two sentences of the notices.

§ 563e.45 Publication of planned examination schedule.

The OTS publishes at least 30 days in advance of the beginning of each calendar quarter a list of savings associations scheduled for CRA examinations in that quarter.

APPENDIX A TO PART 563e—RATINGS

(a) *Ratings in general.* (1) In assigning a rating, the OTS evaluates a savings association's performance under the applicable performance criteria in this part, in accordance with §§ 563e.21 and 563e.28. This includes consideration of low-cost education loans provided to low-income borrowers and activities in cooperation with minority- or women-owned financial institutions and low-income credit unions, as well as adjustments on the basis of evidence of discriminatory or other illegal credit practices.

(2) A savings association's performance need not fit each aspect of a particular rating profile in order to receive that rating, and exceptionally strong performance with respect to some aspects may compensate for weak performance in others. The savings association's overall performance, however, must be consistent with safe and sound banking practices and generally with the appropriate rating profile as follows.

(b) *Savings associations evaluated under the lending, investment, and service tests*—(1) *Lending performance rating.* The OTS assigns each savings association's lending performance one of the five following ratings.

(i) *Outstanding.* The OTS rates a savings association's lending performance "outstanding" if, in general, it demonstrates:

(A) Excellent responsiveness to credit needs in its assessment area(s), taking into account the number and amount of home mortgage, small business, small farm, and consumer loans, if applicable, in its assessment area(s);

(B) A substantial majority of its loans are made in its assessment area(s);

(C) An excellent geographic distribution of loans in its assessment area(s);

(D) An excellent distribution, particularly in its assessment area(s), of loans among individuals of different income levels and businesses (including farms) of different sizes, given the product lines offered by the savings association;

(E) An excellent record of serving the credit needs of highly economically disadvantaged areas in its assessment area(s), low-income individuals, or businesses (including farms) with gross annual revenues of $1 million or less, consistent with safe and sound operations;

(F) Extensive use of innovative or flexible lending practices in a safe and sound manner to address the credit needs of low- or moderate-income individuals or geographies; and

(G) It is a leader in making community development loans.

(ii) *High satisfactory.* The OTS rates a savings association's lending performance "high satisfactory" if, in general, it demonstrates:

(A) Good responsiveness to credit needs in its assessment area, taking into account the number and amount of home mortgage, small business, small farm, and consumer loans, if applicable, in its assessment area(s);

(B) A high percentage of its loans are made in its assessment area(s);

(C) A good geographic distribution of loans in its assessment area(s);

(D) A good distribution, particularly in its assessment area(s), of loans among individuals of different income levels and businesses (including farms) of different sizes, given the product lines offered by the savings association;

(E) A good record of serving the credit needs of highly economically disadvantaged areas in its assessment area(s), low-income individuals, or businesses (including farms) with gross annual revenues of $1 million or less, consistent with safe and sound operations;

(F) Use of innovative or flexible lending practices in a safe and sound manner to address the credit needs of low- or moderate-income individuals or geographies; and

(G) It has made a relatively high level of community development loans.

(iii) *Low satisfactory.* The OTS rates a savings association's lending performance "low satisfactory" if, in general, it demonstrates:

(A) Adequate responsiveness to credit needs in its assessment area(s), taking into account the number and amount of home mortgage, small business, small farm, and consumer loans, if applicable, in its assessment area(s);

(B) An adequate percentage of its loans are made in its assessment area(s);

(C) An adequate geographic distribution of loans in its assessment area(s);

(D) An adequate distribution, particularly in its assessment area(s), of loans among individuals of different income levels and businesses (including farms) of different sizes, given the product lines offered by the savings association;

(E) An adequate record of serving the credit needs of highly economically disadvantaged areas in its assessment area(s), low-income individuals, or businesses (including farms) with gross annual revenues of $1 million or less, consistent with safe and sound operations;

(F) Limited use of innovative or flexible lending practices in a safe and sound manner to address the credit needs of low- or moderate-income individuals or geographies; and

(G) It has made an adequate level of community development loans.

Office of Thrift Supervision, Treasury

(iv) *Needs to improve.* The OTS rates a savings association's lending performance "needs to improve" if, in general, it demonstrates:

(A) Poor responsiveness to credit needs in its assessment area(s), taking into account the number and amount of home mortgage, small business, small farm, and consumer loans, if applicable, in its assessment area(s);

(B) A small percentage of its loans are made in its assessment area(s);

(C) A poor geographic distribution of loans, particularly to low- or moderate-income geographies, in its assessment area(s);

(D) A poor distribution, particularly in its assessment area(s), of loans among individuals of different income levels and businesses (including farms) of different sizes, given the product lines offered by the savings association;

(E) A poor record of serving the credit needs of highly economically disadvantaged areas in its assessment area(s), low-income individuals, or businesses (including farms) with gross annual revenues of $1 million or less, consistent with safe and sound operations;

(F) Little use of innovative or flexible lending practices in a safe and sound manner to address the credit needs of low- or moderate-income individuals or geographies; and

(G) It has made a low level of community development loans.

(v) *Substantial noncompliance.* The OTS rates a savings association's lending performance as being in "substantial noncompliance" if, in general, it demonstrates:

(A) A very poor responsiveness to credit needs in its assessment area(s), taking into account the number and amount of home mortgage, small business, small farm, and consumer loans, if applicable, in its assessment area(s);

(B) A very small percentage of its loans are made in its assessment area(s);

(C) A very poor geographic distribution of loans, particularly to low- or moderate-income geographies, in its assessment area(s);

(D) A very poor distribution, particularly in its assessment area(s), of loans among individuals of different income levels and businesses (including farms) of different sizes, given the product lines offered by the savings association;

(E) A very poor record of serving the credit needs of highly economically disadvantaged areas in its assessment area(s), low-income individuals, or businesses (including farms) with gross annual revenues of $1 million or less, consistent with safe and sound operations;

(F) No use of innovative or flexible lending practices in a safe and sound manner to address the credit needs of low- or moderate-income individuals or geographies; and

(G) It has made few, if any, community development loans.

(2) *Investment performance rating.* The OTS assigns each savings association's investment performance one of the five following ratings.

(i) *Outstanding.* The OTS rates a savings association's investment performance "outstanding" if, in general, it demonstrates:

(A) An excellent level of qualified investments, particularly those that are not routinely provided by private investors, often in a leadership position;

(B) Extensive use of innovative or complex qualified investments; and

(C) Excellent responsiveness to credit and community development needs.

(ii) *High satisfactory.* The OTS rates a savings association's investment performance "high satisfactory" if, in general, it demonstrates:

(A) A significant level of qualified investments, particularly those that are not routinely provided by private investors, occasionally in a leadership position;

(B) Significant use of innovative or complex qualified investments; and

(C) Good responsiveness to credit and community development needs.

(iii) *Low satisfactory.* The OTS rates a savings association's investment performance "low satisfactory" if, in general, it demonstrates:

(A) An adequate level of qualified investments, particularly those that are not routinely provided by private investors, although rarely in a leadership position;

(B) Occasional use of innovative or complex qualified investments; and

(C) Adequate responsiveness to credit and community development needs.

(iv) *Needs to improve.* The OTS rates a savings association's investment performance "needs to improve" if, in general, it demonstrates:

(A) A poor level of qualified investments, particularly those that are not routinely provided by private investors;

(B) Rare use of innovative or complex qualified investments; and

(C) Poor responsiveness to credit and community development needs.

(v) *Substantial noncompliance.* The OTS rates a savings association's investment performance as being in "substantial noncompliance" if, in general, it demonstrates:

(A) Few, if any, qualified investments, particularly those that are not routinely provided by private investors;

(B) No use of innovative or complex qualified investments; and

(C) Very poor responsiveness to credit and community development needs.

(3) *Service performance rating.* The OTS assigns each savings association's service performance one of the five following ratings.

Pt. 563e, App. A

(i) *Outstanding.* The OTS rates a savings association's service performance "outstanding" if, in general, the savings association demonstrates:

(A) Its service delivery systems are readily accessible to geographies and individuals of different income levels in its assessment area(s);

(B) To the extent changes have been made, its record of opening and closing branches has improved the accessibility of its delivery systems, particularly in low- or moderate-income geographies or to low- or moderate-income individuals;

(C) Its services (including, where appropriate, business hours) are tailored to the convenience and needs of its assessment area(s), particularly low- or moderate-income geographies or low- or moderate-income individuals; and

(D) It is a leader in providing community development services.

(ii) *High satisfactory.* The OTS rates a savings association's service performance "high satisfactory" if, in general, the savings association demonstrates:

(A) Its service delivery systems are accessible to geographies and individuals of different income levels in its assessment area(s);

(B) To the extent changes have been made, its record of opening and closing branches has not adversely affected the accessibility of its delivery systems, particularly in low- and moderate-income geographies and to low- and moderate-income individuals;

(C) Its services (including, where appropriate, business hours) do not vary in a way that inconveniences its assessment area(s), particularly low- and moderate-income geographies and low- and moderate-income individuals; and

(D) It provides a relatively high level of community development services.

(iii) *Low satisfactory.* The OTS rates a savings association's service performance "low satisfactory" if, in general, the savings association demonstrates:

(A) Its service delivery systems are reasonably accessible to geographies and individuals of different income levels in its assessment area(s);

(B) To the extent changes have been made, its record of opening and closing branches has generally not adversely affected the accessibility of its delivery systems, particularly in low- and moderate-income geographies and to low- and moderate-income individuals;

(C) Its services (including, where appropriate, business hours) do not vary in a way that inconveniences its assessment area(s), particularly low- and moderate-income geographies and low- and moderate-income individuals; and

(D) It provides an adequate level of community development services.

(iv) *Needs to improve.* The OTS rates a savings association's service performance "needs to improve" if, in general, the savings association demonstrates:

(A) Its service delivery systems are unreasonably inaccessible to portions of its assessment area(s), particularly to low- or moderate-income geographies or to low- or moderate-income individuals;

(B) To the extent changes have been made, its record of opening and closing branches has adversely affected the accessibility of its delivery systems, particularly in low- or moderate-income geographies or to low- or moderate-income individuals;

(C) Its services (including, where appropriate, business hours) vary in a way that inconveniences its assessment area(s), particularly low- or moderate-income geographies or low- or moderate-income individuals; and

(D) It provides a limited level of community development services.

(v) *Substantial noncompliance.* The OTS rates a savings association's service performance as being in "substantial noncompliance" if, in general, the savings association demonstrates:

(A) Its service delivery systems are unreasonably inaccessible to significant portions of its assessment area(s), particularly to low- or moderate-income geographies or to low- or moderate-income individuals;

(B) To the extent changes have been made, its record of opening and closing branches has significantly adversely affected the accessibility of its delivery systems, particularly in low- or moderate-income geographies or to low- or moderate-income individuals;

(C) Its services (including, where appropriate, business hours) vary in a way that significantly inconveniences its assessment area(s), particularly low- or moderate-income geographies or low- or moderate-income individuals; and

(D) It provides few, if any, community development services.

(c) *Wholesale or limited purpose savings associations.* The OTS assigns each wholesale or limited purpose savings association's community development performance one of the four following ratings.

(1) *Outstanding.* The OTS rates a wholesale or limited purpose savings association's community development performance "outstanding" if, in general, it demonstrates:

(i) A high level of community development loans, community development services, or qualified investments, particularly investments that are not routinely provided by private investors;

(ii) Extensive use of innovative or complex qualified investments, community development loans, or community development services; and

Office of Thrift Supervision, Treasury

Pt. 563e, App. A

(iii) Excellent responsiveness to credit and community development needs in its assessment area(s).

(2) *Satisfactory.* The OTS rates a wholesale or limited purpose savings association's community development performance "satisfactory" if, in general, it demonstrates:

(i) An adequate level of community development loans, community development services, or qualified investments, particularly investments that are not routinely provided by private investors;

(ii) Occasional use of innovative or complex qualified investments, community development loans, or community development services; and

(iii) Adequate responsiveness to credit and community development needs in its assessment area(s).

(3) *Needs to improve.* The OTS rates a wholesale or limited purpose savings association's community development performance as "needs to improve" if, in general, it demonstrates:

(i) A poor level of community development loans, community development services, or qualified investments, particularly investments that are not routinely provided by private investors;

(ii) Rare use of innovative or complex qualified investments, community development loans, or community development services; and

(iii) Poor responsiveness to credit and community development needs in its assessment area(s).

(4) *Substantial noncompliance.* The OTS rates a wholesale or limited purpose savings association's community development performance in "substantial noncompliance" if, in general, it demonstrates:

(i) Few, if any, community development loans, community development services, or qualified investments, particularly investments that are not routinely provided by private investors;

(ii) No use of innovative or complex qualified investments, community development loans, or community development services; and

(iii) Very poor responsiveness to credit and community development needs in its assessment area(s).

(d) *Savings associations evaluated under the small savings association performance standards.*—(1) *Lending test ratings.* (i) *Eligibility for a satisfactory lending test rating.* The OTS rates a small savings association's lending performance "satisfactory" if, in general, the savings association demonstrates:

(A) A reasonable loan-to-deposit ratio (considering seasonal variations) given the savings association's size, financial condition, the credit needs of its assessment area(s), and taking into account, as appropriate, other lending-related activities such as loan originations for sale to the secondary markets and community development loans and qualified investments;

(B) A majority of its loans and, as appropriate, other lending-related activities, are in its assessment area;

(C) A distribution of loans to and, as appropriate, other lending-related activities for individuals of different income levels (including low- and moderate-income individuals) and businesses and farms of different sizes that is reasonable given the demographics of the savings association's assessment area(s);

(D) A record of taking appropriate action, when warranted, in response to written complaints, if any, about the savings association's performance in helping to meet the credit needs of its assessment area(s); and

(E) A reasonable geographic distribution of loans given the savings association's assessment area(s).

(ii) *Eligibility for an "outstanding" lending test rating.* A small savings association that meets each of the standards for a "satisfactory" rating under this paragraph and exceeds some or all of those standards may warrant consideration for a lending test rating of "outstanding."

(iii) *Needs to improve or substantial noncompliance ratings.* A small savings association may also receive a lending test rating of "needs to improve" or "substantial noncompliance" depending on the degree to which its performance has failed to meet the standard for a "satisfactory" rating.

(2) *Community development test ratings for intermediate small savings associations*—(i) *Eligibility for a satisfactory community development test rating.* The OTS rates an intermediate small savings association's community development performance "satisfactory" if the savings association demonstrates adequate responsiveness to the community development needs of its assessment area(s) through community development loans, qualified investments, and community development services. The adequacy of the savings association's response will depend on its capacity for such community development activities, its assessment area's need for such community development activities, and the availability of such opportunities for community development in the savings association's assessment area(s).

(ii) *Eligibility for an outstanding community development test rating.* The OTS rates an intermediate small savings association's community development performance "outstanding" if the savings association demonstrates excellent responsiveness to community development needs in its assessment area(s) through community development loans, qualified investments, and community development services, as appropriate, considering the savings association's capacity and

293

the need and availability of such opportunities for community development in the savings association's assessment area(s).

(iii) *Needs to improve or substantial noncompliance ratings.* An intermediate small savings association may also receive a community development test rating of "needs to improve" or "substantial noncompliance" depending on the degree to which its performance has failed to meet the standards for a "satisfactory" rating.

(3) *Overall rating*—(i) *Eligibility for a satisfactory overall rating.* No intermediate small savings association may receive an assigned overall rating of "satisfactory" unless it receives a rating of at least "satisfactory" on both the lending test and the community development test.

(ii) *Eligibility for an outstanding overall rating.* (A) An intermediate small savings association that receives an "outstanding" rating on one test and at least "satisfactory" on the other test may receive an assigned overall rating of "outstanding."

(B) A small savings association that is not an intermediate small savings association that meets each of the standards for a "satisfactory" rating under the lending test and exceeds some or all of those standards may warrant consideration for an overall rating of "outstanding." In assessing whether a savings association's performance is "outstanding," the OTS considers the extent to which the savings association exceeds each of the performance standards for a "satisfactory" rating and its performance in making qualified investments and its performance in providing branches and other services and delivery systems that enhance credit availability in its assessment area(s).

(iii) *Needs to improve or substantial noncompliance overall ratings.* A small savings association may also receive a rating of "needs to improve" or "substantial noncompliance" depending on the degree to which its performance has failed to meet the standards for a "satisfactory" rating.

(e) *Strategic plan assessment and rating*—(1) *Satisfactory goals.* The OTS approves as "satisfactory" measurable goals that adequately help to meet the credit needs of the savings association's assessment area(s).

(2) *Outstanding goals.* If the plan identifies a separate group of measurable goals that substantially exceed the levels approved as "satisfactory," the OTS will approve those goals as "outstanding."

(3) *Rating.* The OTS assesses the performance of a savings association operating under an approved plan to determine if the savings association has met its plan goals:

(i) If the savings association substantially achieves its plan goals for a satisfactory rating, the OTS will rate the savings association's performance under the plan as "satisfactory."

(ii) If the savings association exceeds its plan goals for a satisfactory rating and substantially achieves its plan goals for an outstanding rating, the OTS will rate the savings association's performance under the plan as "outstanding."

(iii) If the savings association fails to meet substantially its plan goals for a satisfactory rating, OTS will rate the savings association as either "needs to improve" or "substantial noncompliance," depending on the extent to which it falls short of its plan goals, unless the savings association elected in its plan to be rated otherwise, as provided in §563e.27(f)(4).

[60 FR 22220, May 4, 1995, as amended at 67 FR 78152, Dec. 23, 2002; 72 FR 13435, Mar. 22, 2007; 72 FR 19110, Apr. 17, 2007; 75 FR 61046, Oct. 4, 2010]

APPENDIX B TO PART 563e—CRA NOTICE

(a) *Notice for main offices and, if an interstate savings association, one branch office in each state.*

COMMUNITY REINVESTMENT ACT NOTICE

Under the Federal Community Reinvestment Act (CRA), the Office of Thrift Supervision (OTS) evaluates our record of helping to meet the credit needs of this community consistent with safe and sound operations. The OTS also takes this record into account when deciding on certain applications submitted by us.

Your involvement is encouraged.

You are entitled to certain information about our operations and our performance under the CRA, including, for example, information about our branches, such as their location and services provided at them; the public section of our most recent CRA Performance Evaluation, prepared by the OTS; and comments received from the public relating to our performance in helping to meet community credit needs, as well as our responses to those comments. You may review this information today.

At least 30 days before the beginning of each quarter, the OTS publishes a nationwide list of the savings associations that are scheduled for CRA examination in that quarter. This list is available from the Regional Director (address). You may send written comments about our performance in helping to meet community credit needs to (name and address of official at savings association) and OTS (address). Your letter, together with any response by us, will be considered by the OTS in evaluating our CRA performance and may be made public.

You may ask to look at any comments received by the Regional Director. You may also request from the Regional Director an announcement of our applications covered by the CRA filed with the OTS. We are an affiliate of (name of holding company), a savings and loan holding company. You may request from the Regional Director an announcement of applications covered by the CRA filed by savings and loan holding companies.

(b) *Notice for branch offices.*

COMMUNITY REINVESTMENT ACT NOTICE

Under the Federal Community Reinvestment Act (CRA), the Office of Thrift Supervision (OTS) evaluates our record of helping to meet the credit needs of this community consistent with safe and sound operations. The OTS also takes this record into account when deciding on certain applications submitted by us.

Your involvement is encouraged.

You are entitled to certain information about our operations and our performance under the CRA. You may review today the public section of our most recent CRA evaluation, prepared by the OTS, and a list of services provided at this branch. You may also have access to the following additional information, which we will make available to you at this branch within five calendar days after you make a request to us: (1) A map showing the assessment area containing this branch, which is the area in which the OTS evaluates our CRA performance in this community; (2) information about our branches in this assessment area; (3) a list of services we provide at those locations; (4) data on our lending performance in this assessment area; and (5) copies of all written comments received by us that specifically relate to our CRA performance in this assessment area, and any responses we have made to those comments. If we are operating under an approved strategic plan, you may also have access to a copy of the plan.

[If you would like to review information about our CRA performance in other communities served by us, the public file for our entire savings association is available at (name of office located in state), located at (address).]

At least 30 days before the beginning of each quarter, the OTS publishes a nationwide list of the savings associations that are scheduled for CRA examination in that quarter. This list is available from the Regional Director (address). You may send written comments about our performance in helping to meet community credit needs to (name and address of official at savings association) and the Regional Director (address). Your letter, together with any response by us, will be considered by the OTS in evaluating our CRA performance and may be made public.

You may ask to look at any comments received by the Regional Director. You may also request from the Regional Director an announcement of our applications covered by the CRA filed with the OTS. We are an affiliate of (name of holding company), a savings and loan holding company. You may request from the Regional Director an announcement of applications covered by the CRA filed by savings and loan holding companies.

[60 FR 22223, May 4, 1995]

PART 563f—MANAGEMENT OFFICIAL INTERLOCKS

Sec.
563f.1 Authority, purpose, and scope.
563f.2 Definitions.
563f.3 Prohibitions.
563f.4 Interlocking relationships permitted by statute.
563f.5 Small market share exemption.
563f.6 General exemption.
563f.7 Change in circumstances.
563f.8 Enforcement.
563f.9 Interlocking relationships permitted pursuant to Federal Deposit Insurance Act.

AUTHORITY: 12 U.S.C. 3201–3208.

SOURCE: 61 FR 40308, Aug. 2, 1996, unless otherwise noted.

§ 563f.1 Authority, purpose, and scope.

(a) *Authority.* This part is issued under the provisions of the Depository Institution Management Interlocks Act (Interlocks Act) (12 U.S.C. 3201 *et seq.*), as amended.

(b) *Purpose.* The purpose of the Interlocks Act and this part is to foster competition by generally prohibiting a management official from serving two nonaffiliated depository organizations in situations where the management interlock likely would have an anticompetitive effect.

(c) *Scope.* This part applies to management officials of savings associations, savings and loan holding companies, and affiliates of either.

§ 563f.2 Definitions.

For purposes of this part, the following definitions apply:

(a) *Affiliate.* (1) The term *affiliate* has the meaning given in section 202 of the Interlocks Act (12 U.S.C. 3201). For purposes of that section 202, shares held by an individual include shares held by members of his or her immediate family. "Immediate family" means spouse, mother, father, child, grandchild, sister, brother, or any of their spouses, whether or not any of their shares are held in trust.

(2) For purposes of section 202(3)(B) of the Interlocks Act (12 U.S.C. 3201(3)(B)), an affiliate relationship involving a savings association or savings and loan holding company based on common ownership does not exist if the OTS determines, after giving the affected persons the opportunity to respond, that the asserted affiliation was established in order to avoid the prohibitions of the Interlocks Act and does not represent a true commonality of interest between the depository organizations. In making this determination, the OTS considers, among other things, whether a person, including members of his or her immediate family, whose shares are necessary to constitute the group owns a nominal percentage of the shares of one of the organizations and the percentage is substantially disproportionate to that person's ownership of shares in the other organization.

(b) *Area median income* means:

(1) The median family income for the metropolitan statistical area (MSA), if a depository organization is located in an MSA; or

(2) The statewide nonmetropolitan median family income, if a depository organization is located outside an MSA.

(c) *Community* means a city, town, or village, and contiguous or adjacent cities, towns, or villages.

(d) *Contiguous or adjacent cities, towns, or villages* means cities, towns, or villages whose borders touch each other or whose borders are within 10 road miles of each other at their closest points. The property line of an office located in an unincorporated city, town, or village is the boundary line of that city, town, or village for the purpose of this definition.

(e) *Depository holding company* means a bank holding company or a savings and loan holding company (as more fully defined in section 202 of the Interlocks Act (12 U.S.C. 3201)) having its principal office located in the United States.

(f) *Depository institution* means a commercial bank (including a private bank), a savings bank, a trust company, a savings and loan association, a building and loan association, a homestead association, a cooperative bank, an industrial bank, or a credit union, chartered under the laws of the United States and having a principal office located in the United States. Additionally, a United States office, including a branch or agency, of a foreign commercial bank is a depository institution.

(g) *Depository institution affiliate* means a depository institution that is an affiliate of a depository organization.

(h) *Depository organization* means a depository institution or a depository holding company.

(i) *Low- and moderate-income areas* means census tracts (or, if an area is not in a census tract, block numbering areas delineated by the United States Bureau of the Census) where the median family income is less than 100 percent of the area median income.

(j) *Management official.* (1) The term *management official* means:

(i) A director;

(ii) An advisory or honorary director of a depository institution with total assets of $100 million or more;

(iii) A senior executive officer as that term is defined in §563.555 of this chapter;

(iv) A branch manager;

(v) A trustee of a depository organization under the control of trustees; and

(vi) Any person who has a representative or nominee serving in any of the capacities in this paragraph (j)(1).

(2) The term *management official* does not include:

(i) A person whose management functions relate exclusively to the business of retail merchandising or manufacturing;

(ii) A person whose management functions relate principally to the business outside the United States of a foreign commercial bank; or

(iii) A person described in the provisos of section 202(4) of the Interlocks Act (12 U.S.C. 3201(4)) (referring to an officer of a State-chartered savings bank, cooperative bank, or trust company that neither makes real estate mortgage loans nor accepts savings).

(k) *Office* means a principal or branch office of a depository institution located in the United States. *Office* does not include a representative office of a foreign commercial bank, an electronic terminal, or a loan production office.

(l) *Person* means a natural person, corporation, or other business entity.

(m) *Relevant metropolitan statistical area (RMSA)* means an MSA, a primary MSA, or a consolidated MSA that is not comprised of designated Primary MSAs to the extent that these terms are defined and applied by the Office of Management and Budget.

(n) *Representative or nominee* means a natural person who serves as a management official and has an obligation to act on behalf of another person with respect to management responsibilities. The OTS will find that a person has an obligation to act on behalf of another person only if the first person has an agreement, express or implied, to act on behalf of the second person with respect to management responsibilities. The OTS will determine, after giving the affected persons an opportunity to respond, whether a person is a *representative or nominee*.

(o) *Savings association* means:

(1) Any Federal savings association (as defined in section 3(b)(2) of the Federal Deposit Insurance Act (12 U.S.C. 1813(b)(2));

(2) Any state savings association (as defined in section 3(b)(3) of the Federal Deposit Insurance Act (12 U.S.C. 1813(b)(3)) the deposits of which are insured by the Federal Deposit Insurance Corporation; and

(3) Any corporation (other than a bank as defined in section 3(a)(1) of the Federal Deposit Insurance Act (12 U.S.C. 1813(a)(1)) the deposits of which are insured by the Federal Deposit Insurance Corporation, that the Board of Directors of the Federal Deposit Insurance Corporation and the Director of the Office of Thrift Supervision jointly determine to be operating in substantially the same manner as a savings association.

(p) *Total assets.* (1) The term *total assets* means assets measured on a consolidated basis and reported in the most recent fiscal year-end Consolidated Report of Condition and Income.

(2) The term *total assets* does not include:

(i) Assets of a diversified savings and loan holding company as defined by section 10(a)(1)(F) of the Home Owners' Loan Act (12 U.S.C. 1467a(a)(1)(F)) other than the assets of its depository institution affiliate;

(ii) Assets of a bank holding company that is exempt from the prohibitions of section 4 of the Bank Holding Company Act of 1956 pursuant to an order issued under section 4(d) of that Act (12 U.S.C. 1843(d)) other than the assets of its depository institution affiliate; or

(iii) Assets of offices of a foreign commercial bank other than the assets of its United States branch or agency.

(q) *United States* means the United States of America, any State or territory of the United States of America, the District of Columbia, Puerto Rico, Guam, American Samoa, and the Virgin Islands.

[61 FR 40308, Aug. 2, 1996, as amended at 63 FR 51275, Sept. 25, 1998; 64 FR 51680, Sept. 24, 1999; 72 FR 1276, Jan. 11, 2007]

§ 563f.3 Prohibitions.

(a) *Community.* A management official of a depository organization may not serve at the same time as a management official of an unaffiliated depository organization if the depository organizations in question (or a depository institution affiliate thereof) have offices in the same community.

(b) *RMSA.* A management official of a depository organization may not serve at the same time as a management official of an unaffiliated depository organization if the depository organizations in question (or a depository institution affiliate thereof) have offices in the same RMSA and each depository organization has total assets of $50 million or more.

(c) *Major assets.* A management official of a depository organization with total assets exceeding $2.5 billion (or any affiliate of such an organization) may not serve at the same time as a management official of an unaffiliated depository organization with total assets exceeding $1.5 billion (or any affiliate of such an organization), regardless of the location of the two depository organizations. The OTS will adjust these thresholds, as necessary, based on the year-to-year change in the average of the Consumer Price Index for the Urban Wage Earners and Clerical Workers, not seasonally adjusted,

§ 563f.4

with rounding to the nearest $100 million. The OTS will announce the revised thresholds by publishing a final rule without notice and comment in the FEDERAL REGISTER.

[61 FR 40308, Aug. 2, 1996, as amended at 64 FR 51680, Sept. 24, 1999; 72 FR 1276, Jan. 11, 2007]

§ 563f.4 Interlocking relationships permitted by statute.

The prohibitions of § 563f.3 do not apply in the case of any one or more of the following organizations or to a subsidiary thereof:

(a) A depository organization that has been placed formally in liquidation, or which is in the hands of a receiver, conservator, or other official exercising a similar function;

(b) A corporation operating under section 25 or section 25A of the Federal Reserve Act (12 U.S.C. 601 et seq. and 12 U.S.C. 611 et seq., respectively) (Edge Corporations and Agreement Corporations);

(c) A credit union being served by a management official of another credit union;

(d) A depository organization that does not do business within the United States except as an incident to its activities outside the United States;

(e) A State-chartered savings and loan guaranty corporation;

(f) A Federal Home Loan Bank or any other bank organized solely to serve depository institutions (a bankers' bank) or solely for the purpose of providing securities clearing services and services related thereto for depository institutions and securities companies;

(g) A depository organization that is closed or is in danger of closing as determined by the appropriate Federal depository institutions regulatory agency and is acquired by another depository organization. This exemption lasts for five years, beginning on the date the depository organization is acquired;

(h)(1) A diversified savings and loan holding company (as defined in section 10(a)(1)(F) of the Home Owners' Loan Act (12 U.S.C. 1467a(a)(1)(F)) with respect to the service of a director of such company who also is a director of an unaffiliated depository organization if:

(i) Both the diversified savings and loan holding company and the unaffiliated depository organization notify their appropriate Federal depository institutions regulatory agency at least 60 days before the dual service is proposed to begin; and

(ii) The appropriate regulatory agency does not disapprove the dual service before the end of the 60-day period.

(2) The OTS may disapprove a notice of proposed service if it finds that:

(i) The service cannot be structured or limited so as to preclude an anticompetitive effect in financial services in any part of the United States;

(ii) The service would lead to substantial conflicts of interest or unsafe or unsound practices; or

(iii) The notificant failed to furnish all the information required by the OTS.

(3) The OTS may require that any interlock permitted under this paragraph (h) be terminated if a change in circumstances occurs with respect to one of the interlocked depository organizations that would have provided a basis for disapproval of the interlock during the notice period; and

(i) Any savings association or any savings and loan holding company (as defined in section 10(a)(1)(D) of the Home Owners' Loan Act) which has issued stock in connection with a qualified stock issuance pursuant to section 10(q) of such Act, except that this paragraph (i) shall apply only with regard to service by a single management official of such savings association or holding company, or any subsidiary of such savings association or holding company, by a single management official of the savings and loan holding company which purchased the stock issued in connection with such qualified stock issuance, and shall apply only when the OTS has determined that such service is consistent with the purposes of the Interlocks Act and the Home Owners' Loan Act.

§ 563f.5 Small market share exemption.

(a) *Exemption.* A management interlock that is prohibited by § 563f.3 is permissible, if:

(1) The interlock is not prohibited by § 563f.3(c); and

Office of Thrift Supervision, Treasury § 563f.8

(2) The depository organizations (and their depository institution affiliates) hold, in the aggregate, no more than 20 percent of the deposits in each RMSA or community in which both depository organizations (or their depository institution affiliates) have offices. The amount of deposits shall be determined by reference to the most recent annual Summary of Deposits published by the FDIC for the RMSA or community.

(b) *Confirmation and records.* Each depository organization must maintain records sufficient to support its determination of eligibility for the exemption under paragraph (a) of this section, and must reconfirm that determination on an annual basis.

[64 FR 51680, Sept. 24, 1999]

§ 563f.6 General exemption.

(a) *Exemption.* The OTS may by agency order exempt an interlock from the prohibitions in § 563f.3 if the OTS finds that the interlock would not result in a monopoly or substantial lessening of competition and would not present safety and soundness concerns. A depository organization may apply to OTS for an exemption under part 516, subpart E, of this chapter.

(b) *Presumptions.* In reviewing an application for an exemption under this section, the OTS will apply a rebuttable presumption that an interlock will not result in a monopoly or substantial lessening of competition if the depository organization seeking to add a management official:

(1) Primarily serves low- and moderate-income areas;

(2) Is controlled or managed by persons who are members of a minority group, or women;

(3) Is a depository institution that or has been chartered for less than two years; or

(4) Is deemed to be in "troubled condition" as defined in § 563.555 of this chapter.

(c) *Duration.* Unless a shorter expiration period is provided in the OTS approval, an exemption permitted by paragraph (a) of this section may continue so long as it does not result in a monopoly or substantial lessening of competition, or is unsafe or unsound. If the OTS grants an interlock exemption in reliance upon a presumption under paragraph (b) of this section, the interlock may continue for three years, unless otherwise provided by the OTS in writing.

[64 FR 51680, Sept. 24, 1999, as amended at 66 FR 13009, Mar. 2, 2001]

§ 563f.7 Change in circumstances.

(a) *Termination.* A management official shall terminate his or her service or apply for an exemption if a change in circumstances causes the service to become prohibited. A change in circumstances may include an increase in asset size of an organization, a change in the delineation of the RMSA or community, the establishment of an office, an increase in the aggregate deposits of the depository organization, or an acquisition, merger, consolidation, or reorganization of the ownership structure of a depository organization that causes a previously permissible interlock to become prohibited.

(b) *Transition period.* A management official described in paragraph (a) of this section may continue to serve the depository organization involved in the interlock for 15 months following the date of the change in circumstances. The OTS may shorten this period under appropriate circumstances.

[61 FR 40308, Aug. 2, 1996, as amended at 64 FR 51681, Sept. 24, 1999]

§ 563f.8 Enforcement.

Except as provided in this section, the OTS administers and enforces the Interlocks Act with respect to savings associations, savings and loan holding companies, and affiliates of either, and may refer any case of a prohibited interlocking relationship involving these entities to the Attorney General of the United States to enforce compliance with the Interlocks Act and this part. If an affiliate of a savings association or savings and loan holding company is subject to the primary regulation of another Federal depository organization supervisory agency, then the OTS does not administer and enforce the Interlocks Act with respect to that affiliate.

§ 563f.9 Interlocking relationships permitted pursuant to Federal Deposit Insurance Act.

A management official or prospective management official of a depository organization may enter into an otherwise prohibited interlocking relationship with another depository organization for a period of up to 10 years if such relationship is approved by the Federal Deposit Insurance Corporation pursuant to section 13(k)(1)(A)(v) of the Federal Deposit Insurance Act, as amended (12 U.S.C. 1823(k)(1)(A)(v)).

PART 563g—SECURITIES OFFERINGS

Sec.
563g.1 Definitions.
563g.2 Offering circular requirement.
563g.3 Exemptions.
563g.4 Non-public offering.
563g.5 Filing and signature requirements.
563g.6 Effective date.
563g.7 Form, content, and accounting.
563g.8 Use of the offering circular.
563g.9 Escrow requirement.
563g.10 Unsafe or unsound practices.
563g.11 Withdrawal or abandonment.
563g.12 Securities sale report.
563g.13 Public disclosure and confidential treatment.
563g.14 Waiver.
563g.15 Requests for interpretive advice or waiver.
563g.16 Delayed or continuous offering and sale of securities.
563g.17 Sales of securities at an office of a savings association.
563g.18 Current and periodic reports.
563g.19 Approval of the security.
563g.20 Form for securities sale report.
563g.21 Filing of copies of offering circulars in certain exempt offerings.

AUTHORITY: 12 U.S.C. 1462a, 1463, 1464; 15 U.S.C. 78c(b), 78*l*, 78m, 78n, 78p, 78w.

SOURCE: 54 FR 49641, Nov. 30, 1989, unless otherwise noted.

§ 563g.1 Definitions.

(a) For purposes of this part, the following definitions apply:

(1) *Accredited investor* means the same as in Commission Rule 501(a) (17 CFR 230.501(a)) under the Securities Act, and includes any savings association.

(2) *Commission* means the Securities and Exchange Commission.

(3) *Dividend or interest reinvestment plan* means a plan which is offered solely to existing security holders of the savings association which allows such persons to reinvest dividends or interest paid to them on securities issued by the savings association, and which also may allow additional cash amounts to be contributed by the participants in the plan, provided that the securities to be issued are newly issued, or are purchased for the account of plan participants, at prices not in excess of current market prices at the time of purchase, or at prices not in excess of an amount determined in accordance with a pricing formula specified in the plan and based upon average or current market prices at the time of purchase.

(4) *Employee benefit plan* means any purchase, savings, option, rights, bonus, ownership, appreciation, profit sharing, thrift, incentive, pension or similar plan solely for officers, directors or employees.

(5) *Exchange Act* means the Securities Exchange Act of 1934 (15 U.S.C. 78a–78jj).

(6) *Filing date* means the date on which a document is actually received during business hours, 9:00 a.m. to 5:00 p.m. Eastern Standard Time, by the Chief Counsel, Business Transactions Division, Office of Thrift Supervision, 1700 G Street, NW., Washington, DC 20552. However if the last date on which a document can be accepted falls on a Saturday, Sunday, or holiday, such document may be filed on the next business day.

(7) *Issuer* means a savings association which issues or proposes to issue any security.

(8) *Offer; Sale* or *sell.* For purposes of this part, the term *offer, offer to sell,* or *offer for sale* shall include every attempt or offer to dispose of, or solicitation of an offer to buy, a security or interest in a security, for value. However, these terms shall not include preliminary negotiations or agreements between an issuer and any underwriter or among underwriters who are or are to be in privity of contract with the issuer. *Sale* and *sell* includes every contract to sell or otherwise dispose of a security or interest in a security for value. Every offer or sale of a warrant or right to purchase or subscribe to another security of the same or another issuer, as well as every sale or offer of a security which gives the holder a

300

Office of Thrift Supervision, Treasury § 563g.1

present or future right or privilege to convert the security into another security of the same or another issuer, includes an offer and sale of the other security only at the time of the offer or sale of the warrant or right or convertible security; but neither the exercise of the right to purchase or subscribe or to convert nor the issuance of securities pursuant thereto is an offer or sale.

(9) *Person* means the same as in § 563b.25 of this chapter, and includes a savings association.

(10) *Purchase* and *buy* mean the same as in § 563b.25 of this chapter.

(11) *Savings association* has the same meaning as in part 561 of this chapter, and includes a federally-chartered savings association in organization under this chapter, and a state-chartered savings association in organization which is granted conditional approval of insurance of accounts by the Federal Deposit Insurance Corporation. In addition, for purposes of § 563g.2 of this part, *savings association* includes any underwriter participating in the distribution of securities of a savings association.

(12) *Securities Act* means the Securities Act of 1933 (15 U.S.C. 77a–77aa).

(13) *Security* means any nonwithdrawable account, note, stock, treasury stock, bond, debenture, evidence of indebtedness, certificate of interest or participation in any profit-sharing agreement, collateral-trust certificate, preorganization or subscription, transferable share, investment contract, voting trust certificate or, in general, any interest or instrument commonly known as a *security*, or any certificate of interest or participation in, temporary or interim certificate for, receipt for, guarantee of, or warrant or right to subscribe to or purchase any of the foregoing, except that a *security* shall not include an account insured, in whole or in part, by the Federal Deposit Insurance Corporation.

(14) *Underwriter* means any person who has purchased from an issuer with a view to, or offers or sells for an issuer in connection with, the distribution of any security, or participates or has a participation in the direct or indirect underwriting of any such undertaking; but such term shall not include a person whose interest is limited to a commission from an underwriter or dealer not in excess of the usual and customary distributors' or sellers' commission and such term shall also not include any person who has continually held the securities being transferred for a period of two (2) consecutive years provided that the securities sold in any one (1) transaction shall be less than ten percent (10%) of the issued and outstanding securities of the same class. The following shall apply for the purpose of determining the period securities have been held:

(i) *Stock dividends, splits and recapitalizations.* Securities acquired from the issuer as a dividend or pursuant to a stock split, reverse split or recapitalization shall be deemed to have been acquired at the same time as the securities on which the dividend or, if more than one, the initial dividend was paid, the securities involved in the split or reverse split, or the securities surrendered in connection with the recapitalization.

(ii) *Conversions.* If the securities sold were acquired from the issuer for consideration consisting solely of other securities of the same issuer surrendered for conversion, the securities so acquired shall be deemed to have been acquired at the same time as the securities surrendered for conversion.

(iii) *Contingent issuance of securities.* Securities acquired as a contingent payment of the purchase price of an equity interest in a business, or the assets of a business, sold to the issuer or an affiliate of the issuer shall be deemed to have been acquired at the time of such sale if the issuer was then committed to issue the securities subject only to conditions other than the payment of further consideration for such securities. An agreement entered into in connection with any such purchase to remain in the employment of, or not to compete with, the issuer or affiliate or the rendering of services pursuant to such agreement shall not be deemed to be the payment of further consideration for such securities.

(iv) *Pledged securities.* Securities which are *bona fide* pledged by any person other than the issuer when sold by the pledgee, or by a purchaser, after a default in the obligation secured by the

§ 563g.2

pledge, shall be deemed to have been acquired when they were acquired by the pledgor, except that if the securities were pledged without recourse they shall be deemed to have been acquired by the pledgee at the time of the pledge or by the purchaser at the time of purchase.

(v) *Gifts of securities.* Securities acquired from any person, other than the issuer, by gift shall be deemed to have been acquired by the donee when they were acquired by the donor.

(vi) *Trusts.* Securities acquired from the settler of a trust by the trust or acquired from the trust by the beneficiaries thereof shall be deemed to have been acquired when they were acquired by the settler.

(vii) *Estates.* Securities held by the estate of a deceased person or acquired from such an estate by the beneficiaries thereof shall be deemed to have been acquired when they were acquired by the deceased person, except that no holding period is required if the estate is not an affiliate of the issuer or if the securities are sold by a beneficiary of the estate who is not such an affiliate.

(viii) *Exchange transactions.* A person receiving securities in a transaction involving an exchange of the securities of one issuer for securities of another issuer shall be deemed to have acquired the securities received when such person acquired the securities exchanged.

(b) A term not defined in this part but defined in another part of this chapter, when used in this part, shall have the meanings given in such other part, unless the context otherwise requires.

(c) When used in the rules, regulations, or forms of the Commission referred to in this part, the term *Commission* shall be deemed to refer to the Office, the term *registrant* shall be deemed to refer to an issuer defined in this part, and the term *registration statement* or *prospectus* shall be deemed to refer to an offering circular filed under this part, unless the context otherwise requires.

[54 FR 49641, Nov. 30, 1989, as amended at 62 FR 54765, Oct. 22, 1997; 68 FR 75110, Dec. 30, 2003]

§ 563g.2 Offering circular requirement.

(a) *General.* No savings association shall offer or sell, directly or indirectly, any security issued by it unless:

(1) The offer or sale is accompanied or preceded by an offering circular which includes the information required by this part and which has been filed and declared effective pursuant to this part; or

(2) An exemption is available under this part.

(b) *Communications not deemed an offer.* The following communications shall not be deemed an offer under this section:

(1) Prior to filing an offering circular, any notice of a proposed offering which satisfies the requirements of Commission Rule 135 (17 CFR 230.135) under the Securities Act;

(2) Subsequent to filing an offering circular, any notice circular, advertisement, letter, or other communication published or transmitted to any person which satisfies the requirements of Commission Rule 134 (17 CFR 230.134) under the Securities Act; and

(3) Oral offers of securities covered by an offering circular made after filing the offering circular with the Office.

(c) *Preliminary offering circular.* Notwithstanding paragraph (a) of this section, a preliminary offering circular may be used for an offer of any security prior to the effective date of the offering circular if:

(1) The preliminary offering circular has been filed pursuant to this part;

(2) The preliminary offering circular includes the information required by this part, except for the omission of information relating to offering price, discounts or commissions, amount of proceeds, conversion rates, call prices, or other matters dependent on the offering price; and

(3) The offering circular declared effective by the Office is furnished to the purchaser prior to, or simultaneously with, the sale of any such security.

§ 563g.3 Exemptions.

The offering circular requirement of § 563g.2 of this part shall not apply to an issuer's offer or sale of securities:

(a) [Reserved]

(b) Exempt from registration under either section 3(a) or section 4 of the

Office of Thrift Supervision, Treasury § 563g.4

Securities Act, but only by reason of an exemption other than section 3(a)(5) (for regulated savings associations), and section 3(a)(11) (for intrastate offerings) of the Securities Act;

(c) In a conversion from the mutual to the stock form of organization pursuant to part 563b of this chapter, except for a supervisory conversion undertaken pursuant to subpart C of part 563b of this chapter;

(d) In a non-public offering which satisfies the requirements of § 563g.4 of this part;

(e) That are debt securities issued in denominations of $100,000 or more, which are fully collateralized by cash, any security issued, or guaranteed as to principal and interest, by the United States, the Federal Home Loan Mortgage Corporation, Federal National Mortgage Association, Government National Mortgage Association or by interests in mortgage notes secured by real property;

(f) Distributed exclusively abroad to foreign nationals: *Provided*, That (1) the offering is made subject to safeguards reasonably designed to preclude distribution or redistribution of the securities within, or to nationals of, the United States, and (2) such safeguards include, without limitation, measures that would be sufficient to ensure that registration of the securities would not be required if the securities were not exempt under the Securities Act; or

(g) To its officers, directors or employees pursuant to an employee benefit plan or a dividend or interest reinvestment plan, and provided that any such plan has been approved by the majority of shareholders present in person or by proxy at an annual or special meeting of the shareholders of the savings association.

[54 FR 49641, Nov. 30, 1989, as amended at 65 FR 16305, Mar. 28, 2000]

§ 563g.4 Non-public offering.

Offers and sales of securities by an issuer that satisfy the conditions of paragraph (a) or (b) of this section and the requirements of paragraphs (c) and (d) of this section shall be deemed to be transactions not involving any public offering within the meaning of section 4(2) of the Securities Act and §§ 563g.3(b) and 563g.3(d) of this part. However, an issuer shall not be deemed to be not in compliance with the provisions of this section solely by reason of making an untimely filing of the notice required to be filed by paragraph (c) of this section so long as the notice is actually filed and all other conditions and requirements of this section are satisfied.

(a) *Regulation D.* The offer and sale of all securities in the transaction satisfies the Commission's Regulation D (17 CFR 230.501–230.506), except for the notice requirements of Commission Rule 503 (17 CFR 230.503) and the limitations on resale in Commission Rule 502(d) (17 CFR 230.502(d)).

(b) *Sales to 35 persons.* The offer and sale of all securities in the transaction satisfies each of the following conditions:

(1) Sales of the security are not made to more than 35 persons during the offering period, as determined under the integration provisions of Commission Rule 502(a) (17 CFR 230.502(a)). The number of purchasers referred to above is exclusive of any accredited investor, officer, director or affiliate of the issuer. For purposes of paragraph (b) of this section, a husband and wife (together with any custodian or trustee acting for the account of their minor children) are counted as one person and a partnership, corporation or other organization which was not specifically formed for the purpose of purchasing the security offered in reliance upon this exemption, is counted as one person.

(2) All purchasers either have a preexisting personal or business relationship with the issuer or any of its officers, directors or controlling persons, or by reason of their business or financial experience or the business or financial experience of their professional advisors who are unaffiliated with and who are not compensated by the issuer or any affiliate or selling agent of the issuer, directly or indirectly, could reasonably be assumed to have the capacity to protect their own interests in connection with the transaction.

(3) Each purchaser represents that the purchaser is purchasing for the purchaser's own account (or a trust account if the purchaser is a trustee) and

§ 563g.5

not with a view to or for sale in connection with any distribution of the security.

(4) The offer and sale of the security is not accomplished by the publication of any advertisement.

(c) *Filing of notice of sales.* Within 30 days after the first sale of the securities, every six months after the first sale of the securities and not later than 30 days after the last sale of securities in an offering pursuant to this section, the issuer, shall file with the Office a report describing the results of the sale of securities as required by § 563g.12(b) of this part.

(d) *Limitation on resale.* The issuer shall exercise reasonable care to assure that the purchasers of the securities are not underwriters within the meaning of § 563g.1(a)(14) of this part, which reasonable care shall include, but not be limited to, the following:

(1) Reasonable inquiry to determine if the purchaser is acquiring the securities for the purchaser or for other persons;

(2) Written disclosure to each purchaser prior to the sale that the securities are not offered by an offering circular filed with, and declared effective by, the Office pursuant to § 563g.2 of this part, but instead are being sold in reliance upon the exemption from the offering circular requirement provided for by this section; and

(3) Placement of a legend on the certificate, or other document evidencing the securities, indicating that the securities have not been offered by an offering circular filed with, and declared effective by, the Office and that due care should be taken to ensure that the seller of the securities is not an underwriter within the meaning of § 563g.1(a)(14) of this part.

§ 563g.5 Filing and signature requirements.

(a) *Procedures.* An offering circular, amendment, notice, report, or other document required by this part shall, unless otherwise indicated, be filed in accordance with the requirements of §§ 563b.115(a), 563b.150(a)(6), 563b.155, 563b.180(b), and Form AC, General Instruction B, of this chapter.

(b) *Number of copies.* (1) Unless otherwise required, any filing under this part shall include nine copies of the document to be filed with the Business Transactions Division, Chief Counsel's Office, as follows:

(i) Seven copies, which shall include one manually signed copy with exhibits, three conformed copies with exhibits, and three conformed copies without exhibits, to the Securities Filing Desk, Office of Thrift Supervision, 1700 G Street, NW., Washington, DC 20552; and

(ii) Two copies, which shall include one manually signed copy with exhibits and one conformed copy, without exhibits, to the Regional Director.

(2) Within five days after the effective date of an offering circular or the commencement of a public offering after the effective date, whichever occurs later, nine copies of the offering circular used shall be filed with OTS, as follows: seven copies to the Securities Filing Desk, Office of Thrift Supervision, 1700 G Street, NW., Washington, DC 20552, and two copies to the Regional Director.

(3) After the effective date of an offering circular, an offering circular which varies from the form previously filed shall not be used, unless it includes only non-material supplemental or additional information and until 10 copies have been filed with the Office in the manner required.

(c) *Signature.* (1) Any offering circular, amendment, or consent filed with the Office pursuant to this part shall include an attached manually signed signature page which authorizes the filing and has been signed by:

(i) The issuer, by its duly authorized representative;

(ii) The issuer's principal executive officer;

(iii) The issuer's principal financial officer;

(iv) The issuer's principal accounting officer; and

(v) At least a majority of the issuer's directors.

(2) Any other document filed pursuant to this part shall be signed by a person authorized to do so.

(3) At least *one copy* of every document filed pursuant to this part shall be manually signed, and every copy of a document filed shall:

Office of Thrift Supervision, Treasury § 563g.7

(i) Have the name of each person who signs typed or printed beneath the signature;

(ii) State the capacity or capacities in which the signature is provided;

(iii) Provide the name of each director of the issuer, if a majority of directors is required to sign the document; and

(iv) With regard to any copies not manually signed, bear typed or printed signatures.

[54 FR 49641, Nov. 30, 1989, as amended at 60 FR 66869, Dec. 27, 1995; 66 FR 65821, Dec. 21, 2001; 68 FR 75110, Dec. 30, 2003]

§ 563g.6 Effective date.

(a) Except as provided for in paragraph (d) of this section, an offering circular filed by a savings association shall be deemed to be automatically declared effective by the Office on the twentieth day after filing or on such earlier date as the Office may determine for good cause shown.

(b) If any amendment is filed prior to the effective date, the offering circular shall be deemed to have been filed when such amendment was filed.

(c) The period until automatic effectiveness under this section shall be stated at the bottom of the facing page of the Form OC or any amendment.

(d) The effectiveness will be delayed if a duly authorized amendment, telegram confirmed in writing, or letter states that the effective date is delayed until a further amendment is filed specifically stating that the offering circular will become effective in accordance with this section.

(e) An amendment filed after the effective date of the offering circular shall become effective on such date as the Office may determine.

(f) If it appears to the Office at any time that the offering circular includes any untrue statement of a material fact or omits to state any material fact required to be stated therein or necessary to make the statements therein not misleading, then the Office may pursue any remedy it is authorized to pursue under section 5(d) of the Home Owners' Loan Act of 1933, as amended (12 U.S.C. 1464(d)) or section 8 of the Federal Deposit Insurance Act, as amended (12 U.S.C. 1818), including, but not limited to, institution of cease-and-desist proceedings.

§ 563g.7 Form, content, and accounting.

(a) *Form and content.* Any offering circular or amendment filed pursuant to this part shall:

(1) Be filed under cover of Form OC, which is under part 563b of this chapter;

(2) Comply with the requirements of Items 3 and 4 of Form OC and the requirements of all items of the form for registration (17 CFR part 239) that the issuer would be eligible to use were it required to register the securities under the Securities Act;

(3) Comply with all item requirements of the Form S-1 (17 CFR part 239) for registration under the Securities Act, if the association issuing the securities is not in compliance with the Office's regulatory capital requirements during the time the offering is made;

(4) Where a form specifies that the information required by an item in the Commission's Regulation S-K (17 CFR part 229) should be furnished, include such information and all of the information required by Item 7 of Form PS, which is under part 563b of this chapter;

(5) Include after the facing page of the Form OC a cross-reference sheet listing each item requirement of the form for registration under the Securities Act and indicate for each item the applicable heading or subheading in the offering circular under which the required information is disclosed;

(6) Include in part II of the Form OC the applicable undertakings required by the form for registration under the Securities Act;

(7) If the issuer has not previously been required to file reports pursuant to section 13(a) of the Exchange Act or § 563g.18 of this part, include in part II of Form OC the following undertaking: "The issuer hereby undertakes, in connection with any distribution of the offering circular, to have a preliminary or effective offering circular including the information required by this part distributed to all persons expected to be mailed confirmations of sale not less than 48 hours prior to the time

305

§ 563g.8

such confirmations are expected to be mailed;''

(8) In offerings involving the issuance of options, warrants, subscription rights or conversion rights within the meaning of § 563g.1(a)(8) of this part, include in part II of Form OC an undertaking to provide a copy of the issuer's most recent audited financial statements to persons exercising such options, warrants or rights promptly upon receiving written notification of the exercise thereof;

(9) Include as supplemental information and not as part of the Form OC and only with respect to *de novo* offerings, a copy of the application for permission to organize as submitted to the Office for federally-chartered associations, or a copy of the application for insurance of accounts as submitted to the Federal Deposit Insurance Corporation for state-chartered associations; and

(10) In addition to the information expressly required to be included by this section, there shall be added such further material information, if any, as may be necessary to make the required statements, in light of the circumstances under which they are made, not misleading.

(b) *Accounting requirements.* To be declared effective an offering circular or amendment shall satisfy the accounting requirements in subpart A of part 563c of this chapter.

§ 563g.8 Use of the offering circular.

(a) An offering circular or amendment declared effective by the Office shall not be used more than nine months after the effective date, unless the information contained therein is as of a date not more than 16 months prior to such use.

(b) An offering circular filed under § 563g.5(b)(3) of this part shall not extend the period for which an effective offering circular or amendment may be used under paragraph (c) of this section.

(c) If any event arises, or change in fact occurs, after the effective date and such event or change in fact, individually or in the aggregate, results in the offering circular containing any untrue statement of material fact, or omitting to state a material fact necessary in order to make statements made in the offering circular not misleading under the circumstances, then no offering circular, which has been declared effective under this part, shall be used until an amendment reflecting such event or change in fact has been filed with, and declared effective by, the Office.

§ 563g.9 Escrow requirement.

(a) Any funds received in an offering which is offered and sold on a best efforts all-or-none condition or with a minimum-maximum amount to be sold shall be held in an escrow or similar separate account until such time as all of the securities are sold with respect to a best efforts all-or-none offering or the stated minimum amount of securities are sold in a minimum-maximum offering.

(b) If the amount of securities required to be sold under escrow conditions in paragraph (a) of this section are not sold within the time period for the offering as disclosed in the offering circular, all funds in the escrow account shall be promptly refunded unless the Office otherwise approves an extension of the offering period upon a showing of good cause and provided that the extension is consistent with the public interest and the protection of investors.

§ 563g.10 Unsafe or unsound practices.

(a) No person shall directly or indirectly,

(1) Employ any device, scheme or artifice to defraud,

(2) Make any untrue statement of a material fact or omit to state a material fact necessary in order to make statements made, in light of the circumstances under which they were made, not misleading, or

(3) Engage in any act, practice, or course of business which operates as a fraud or deceit upon any person, in connection with the purchase or sale of any security of a savings association.

(b) Violations of this section shall constitute an unsafe or unsound practice within the meaning of section (3)(a) of the Home Owners' Loan Act of 1933, as amended, 12 U.S.C. 1462a(a), and section 8 of the Federal Deposit Insurance Act, as amended, 12 U.S.C. 1818.

Office of Thrift Supervision, Treasury § 563g.14

(c) Nothing in this section shall be construed as a limitation on the applicability of section 10(b) of the Exchange Act (15 U.S.C. 78j(b)) or Rule 10b–5 promulgated thereunder (17 CFR 240.10b–5).

§ 563g.11 Withdrawal or abandonment.

(a) Any offering circular, amendment, or exhibit may be withdrawn prior to the effective date. A withdrawal shall be signed and state the grounds upon which it is made. Any document withdrawn will not be removed from the files of the Office, but will be marked "Withdrawn upon the request of the issuer on (date)."

(b) When an offering circular or amendment has been on file with the Office for a period of nine months and has not become effective, the Office may, in its discretion, determine whether the filing has been abandoned, after notifying the issuer that the filing is out of date and must either be amended to comply with the applicable requirements of this part or be withdrawn within 30 days after the date of such notice. When a filing is abandoned, the filing will not be removed from the files of the Office, but will be marked "Declared abandoned by the Office on (date)."

§ 563g.12 Securities sale report.

(a) Within 30 days after the first sale of the securities, every six months after such 30 day period and not later than 30 days after the later of the last sale of securities in an offering pursuant to § 563g.2 of this part or the application of the proceeds therefrom, the issuer shall file with the Office a report describing the results of the sale of the securities and the application of the proceeds, which shall include all of the information required by Form G–12 set forth at § 563g.20 of this part and shall also include the following:

(1) The name, address, and docket number of the issuer;

(2) The title, number, aggregate and per-unit offering price of the securities sold;

(3) The aggregate and per-unit dollar amounts of actual itemized expenses, discounts or commissions, and other fees;

(4) The aggregate and per-unit dollar amounts of the net proceeds raised, and the use of proceeds therefrom; and

(5) The number of purchasers of each class of securities sold and the number of owners of record of each class of the issuer's equity securities after the issuance of the securities or termination of the offer.

(b) Within 30 days after the first sale of the securities, every six months after the first sale of the securities and not later than 30 days after the last sale of securities in an offering pursuant to § 563g.4 of this part, the issuer shall file with the Office a report describing the results of the sale of securities, which shall include all of the information required by Form G–12 set forth at § 563g.20 of this part, and shall also include the following:

(1) All of the information required by paragraph (a) of this section; and

(2) A detailed statement of the factual and legal grounds for the exemption claimed.

§ 563g.13 Public disclosure and confidential treatment.

(a) Any offering circular, amendment, exhibit, notice, or report filed pursuant to this part will be publicly available. Any other related documents will be treated in accordance with the provisions of the Freedom of Information Act (5 U.S.C. 552), the Privacy Act of 1974 (5 U.S.C. 552a), and parts 503 and 505 of this chapter.

(b) Any requests for confidential treatment of information in a document required to be filed under this part shall be made as required under Commission Rule 24b–2 (17 CFR 240.24b–2) under the Exchange Act.

§ 563g.14 Waiver.

(a) The Office may waive any requirement of this part, or any required information:

(1) Determined to be unnecessary by the Office;

(2) In connection with a transaction approved by the Office for supervisory reasons, or

(3) Where a provision of this part conflicts with a requirement of applicable state law.

(b) Any condition, stipulation or provision binding any person acquiring a security issued by a savings association which seeks to waive compliance with any provision of this part shall be void, unless approved by the Office.

§ 563g.15 Requests for interpretive advice or waiver.

Any requests to the Office for interpretive advice or a waiver with respect to any provision of this part shall satisfy the following requirements:

(a) A copy of the request, including any attachments, shall be filed with the Chief Counsel, Corporate and Securities Division;

(b) The provisions of this part to which the request relates, the participants in the proposed transaction, and the reasons for the request, shall be specifically identified or described; and

(c) The request shall include a legal opinion as to each legal issue raised and an accounting opinion as to each accounting issue raised.

§ 563g.16 Delayed or continuous offering and sale of securities.

Any offer or sale of securities under § 563g.2 of this part may be made on a continuous or delayed basis in the future, if:

(a) The securities would satisfy all of the eligibility requirements of the Commission's Rule 415, 17 CFR 230.415; and

(b) The association issuing the securities is in compliance with the Office's regulatory capital requirements during the time the offering is made.

§ 563g.17 Sales of securities at an office of a savings association.

Sales of securities of a savings association or its affiliates at an office of a savings association may only be made in accordance with the provisions of 12 CFR 563.76.

[57 FR 46088, Oct. 7, 1992]

§ 563g.18 Current and periodic reports.

(a) Each savings association which files an offering circular which becomes effective pursuant to this part, after such effective date, shall file with the Office periodic and current reports on Forms 8–K, 10–Q and 10–K as may be required by section 13 of the Exchange Act (15 U.S.C. 78m) as if the securities sold by such offering circular were securities registered pursuant to section 12 of the Exchange Act (15 U.S.C. 78l). The duty to file periodic and current reports under this section shall be automatically suspended if and so long as any issue of securities of the savings association is registered pursuant to section 12 of the Exchange Act (15 U.S.C. 78l). The duty to file under this section shall also be automatically suspended as to any fiscal year, other than the fiscal year within which such offering circular became effective, if, at the beginning of such fiscal year, the securities of each class to which the offering circular relates are held of record by less than three hundred persons and upon the filing of a Form 15.

(b) For purposes of registering securities under section 12(b) or 12(g) of the Exchange Act, an issuer subject to the reporting requirements of paragraph (a) of this section may use the Commission's registration statement on Form 10 or Form 8–A or 8–B as applicable.

[54 FR 49641, Nov. 30, 1989, as amended at 66 FR 65821, Dec. 21, 2001]

§ 563g.19 Approval of the security.

Any securities of a savings association which are not exempt under this part and are offered or sold pursuant to an offering circular which becomes effective under this part, are deemed to be approved as to form and terms for purposes of § 563.3 of this chapter.

[54 FR 49641, Nov. 30, 1989, as amended at 67 FR 78153, Dec. 23, 2002]

§ 563g.20 Form for securities sale report.

OFFICE OF THRIFT SUPERVISION, 1700 G STREET, NW., WASHINGTON, DC 20552

[Form G–12]

Securities Sale Report Pursuant to § 563g.12

OTS No. _____
Issuer's Name: _____
Address: _____
If in organization, state the date of FDIC certification of insurance of accounts: _____
State the title, number, aggregate and per-unit offering price of the securities sold: _____

State the aggregate and per-unit dollar amounts of actual itemized offering expenses, discounts, commissions, and other fees: _____

State the aggregate and per-unit dollar amounts of the net proceeds raised: _____

Describe the use of proceeds. If unknown, provide reasonable estimates of the dollar amount allocated to each purpose for which the proceeds will be used: _____

State the number of purchasers of each class of securities sold and the number of owners of record of each class of the issuer's equity securities at the close or termination of the offering: _____

For a non-public offering, also state the factual and legal grounds for the exemption claimed (attach additional pages if necessary): _____

For a non-public offering, all offering materials used should be listed: _____

Person to Contact: _____
Telephone No.: _____

This issuer has duly caused this securities sale report to be signed on its behalf by the undersigned person.

Date of securities sale report _____
Issuer: _____
Signature: _____
Name: _____
Title: _____

Instruction: Print the name and title of the signing representative under his or her signature. Ten copies of the securities sale report should be filed, including one copy manually signed, as required under 12 CFR 563g.5.

Attention

Intentional misstatements or omissions of fact constitute violations of Federal law (See 18 U.S.C. 1001 and 12 CFR 563.180(b)).

§ 563g.21 Filing of copies of offering circulars in certain exempt offerings.

A copy of the offering circular, or similar document, if any, used in connection with an offering exempt from the offering circular requirement of § 563g.2 by reason of § 563g.3(e) or § 563g.4 of this part shall be mailed to the Office within 30 days after the first sale of such securities. Such copy of the offering circular, or similar document, is solely for the information of the Office and shall not be deemed to be "filed" with the Office pursuant to § 563g.2 of this part. The mailing to the Office of such offering circular, or similar document, shall not be a pre-condition of the applicable exemption from the offering circular requirements of § 563g.2 of this part.

PART 564—APPRAISALS

Sec.
564.1 Authority, purpose, and scope.
564.2 Definitions.
564.3 Appraisals required; transactions requiring a State certified or licensed appraiser.
564.4 Minimum appraisal standards.
564.5 Appraiser independence.
564.6 Professional association membership; competency.
564.7 Enforcement.
564.8 Appraisal policies and practices of savings associations and subsidiaries.

AUTHORITY: 12 U.S.C. 1462, 1462a, 1463, 1464, 1828(m), 3331 et seq.

§ 564.1 Authority, purpose, and scope.

(a) *Authority.* This part is issued by the Office of Thrift Supervision ("OTS") under title XI of the Financial Institutions Reform, Recovery, and Enforcement Act of 1989 ("FIRREA") (Pub. L. 101–73, 103 Stat. 183, 511 (1989)), 12 U.S.C. 3301 et seq., and the Home Owners' Loan Act ("HOLA"), 12 U.S.C. 1461 et seq., as amended by FIRREA.

(b) *Purpose and scope.* (1) Title XI provides protection for federal financial and public policy interests in real estate related transactions by requiring real estate appraisals used in connection with federally related transactions to be performed in writing, in accordance with uniform standards, by appraisers whose competency has been demonstrated and whose professional conduct will be subject to effective supervision. This part implements the requirements of title XI and applies to all federally related transactions entered into by the OTS or by institutions regulated by the OTS ("regulated institutions").

(2) This part: (i) Identifies which real estate-related financial transactions require the services of an appraiser;

(ii) Prescribes which categories of federally related transactions shall be appraised by a State certified appraiser and which by a State licensed appraiser; and

(iii) Prescribes minimum standards for the performance of real estate appraisals in connection with federally related transactions under the jurisdiction of the OTS.

[55 FR 34547, Aug. 23, 1990]

§ 564.2 Definitions.

(a) *Appraisal* means a written statement independently and impartially prepared by a qualified appraiser setting forth an opinion as to the market value of an adequately described property as of a specific date(s), supported by the presentation and analysis of relevant market information.

(b) *Appraisal Foundation* means the Appraisal Foundation established on November 30, 1987, as a not-for-profit corporation under the laws of Illinois.

(c) *Appraisal Subcommittee* means the Appraisal Subcommittee of the Federal Financial Institution Examination Council.

(d) *Business loan* means a loan or extension of credit to any corporation, general or limited partnership, business trust, joint venture, pool, syndicate, sole proprietorship, or other business entity.

(e) *Complex 1-to-4 family residential property appraisal* means one in which the property to be appraised, the form of ownership, or market conditions are atypical.

(f) *Federally related transaction* means any real estate-related financial transaction entered into on or after August 9, 1990, that:

(1) The OTS or any regulated institution engages in or contracts for; and

(2) Requires the services of an appraiser.

(g) *Market value* means the most probable price which a property should bring in a competitive and open market under all conditions requisite to a fair sale, the buyer and seller each acting prudently and knowledgeably, and assuming the price is not affected by undue stimulus. Implicit in this definition is the consummation of a sale as of a specified date and the passing of title from seller to buyer under conditions whereby:

(1) Buyer and seller are typically motivated;

(2) Both parties are well informed or well advised, and acting in what they consider their own best interests;

(3) A reasonable time is allowed for exposure in the open market;

(4) Payment is made in terms of cash in U.S. dollars or in terms of financial arrangements comparable thereto; and

(5) The price represents the normal consideration for the property sold unaffected by special or creative financing or sales concessions granted by anyone associated with the sale.

(h) *Real estate* or *real property* means an identified parcel or tract of land, with improvements, and includes easements, rights of way, undivided or future interests, or similar rights in a tract of land, but does not include mineral rights, timber rights, growing crops, water rights, or similar interests severable from the land when the transaction does not involve the associated parcel or tract of land.

(i) *Real estate-related financial transaction* means any transaction involving:

(1) The sale, lease, purchase, investment in or exchange of real property, including interests in property, or the financing thereof; or

(2) The refinancing of real property or interests in real property; or

(3) The use of real property or interests in property as security for a loan or investment, including mortgage-backed securities.

(j) *State certified appraiser* means any individual who has satisfied the requirements for certification in a State or territory whose criteria for certification as a real estate appraiser currently meet the minimum criteria for certification issued by the Appraiser Qualifications Board of the Appraisal Foundation. No individual shall be a State certified appraiser unless such individual has achieved a passing grade upon a suitable examination administered by a State or territory that is consistent with and equivalent to the Uniform State Certification Examination issued or endorsed by the Appraiser Qualifications Board of the National Foundation. In addition, the Appraisal Subcommittee must not have issued a finding that the policies, practices, or procedures of the State or territory are inconsistent with title XI of FIRREA. The OTS may, from time to time, impose additional qualification criteria for certified appraisers performing appraisals in connection with federally related transactions within its jurisdiction.

(k) *State licensed appraiser* means any individual who has satisfied the requirements for licensing in a State or territory where the licensing procedures comply with title XI of FIRREA and where the Appraisal Subcommittee has not issued a finding that the policies, practices, or procedures of the State or territory are inconsistent with title XI. The OTS may, from time to time, impose additional qualification criteria for licensed appraisers performing appraisals in connection with federally related transactions within its jurisdiction.

(l) *Tract development* means a project of five units or more that is constructed or is to be constructed as a single development.

(m) *Transaction value* means:

(1) For loans or other extensions of credit, the amount of the loan or extension of credit;

(2) For sales, leases, purchases, and investments in or exchanges of real property, the market value of the real property interest involved; and

(3) For the pooling of loans or interests in real property for resale or purchase, the amount of the loan or market value of the real property calculated with respect to each such loan or interest in real property.

[55 FR 34547, Aug. 23, 1990, as amended at 57 FR 12705, Apr. 13, 1992; 59 FR 29502, June 7, 1994]

§ 564.3 Appraisals required; transactions requiring a State certified or licensed appraiser.

(a) *Appraisals required.* An appraisal performed by a State certified or licensed appraiser is required for all real estate-related financial transactions except those in which:

(1) The transaction value is $250,000 or less;

(2) A lien on real estate has been taken as collateral in an abundance of caution;

(3) The transaction is not secured by real estate;

(4) A lien on real estate has been taken for purposes other than the real estate's value;

(5) The transaction is a business loan that:

(i) Has a transaction value of $1 million or less; and

(ii) Is not dependent on the sale of, or rental income derived from, real estate as the primary source of repayment;

(6) A lease of real estate is entered into, unless the lease is the economic equivalent of a purchase or sale of the leased real estate;

(7) The transaction involves an existing extension of credit at the lending institution, provided that:

(i) There has been no obvious and material change in market conditions or physical aspects of the property that threatens the adequacy of the institution's real estate collateral protection after the transaction, even with the advancement of new monies; or

(ii) There is no advancement of new monies, other than funds necessary to cover reasonable closing costs;

(8) The transaction involves the purchase, sale, investment in, exchange of, or extension of credit secured by, a loan or interest in a loan, pooled loans, or interests in real property, including mortgaged-backed securities, and each loan or interest in a loan, pooled loan, or real property interest met OTS regulatory requirements for appraisals at the time of origination;

(9) The transaction is wholly or partially insured or guaranteed by a United States government agency or United States government sponsored agency;

(10) The transaction either:

(i) Qualifies for sale to a United States government agency or United States government sponsored agency; or

(ii) Involves a residential real estate transaction in which the appraisal conforms to the Federal National Mortgage Association or Federal Home Loan Mortgage Corporation appraisal standards applicable to that category of real estate;

(11) The regulated institution is acting in a fiduciary capacity and is not required to obtain an appraisal under other law; or

(12) The OTS determines that the services of an appraiser are not necessary in order to protect Federal financial and public policy interests in real estate-related financial transactions or to protect the safety and soundness of the institution.

§ 564.4

(b) *Evaluations required.* For a transaction that does not require the services of a State certified or licensed appraiser under paragraph (a)(1), (a)(5) or (a)(7) of this section, the institution shall obtain an appropriate evaluation of real property collateral that is consistent with safe and sound banking practices.

(c) *Appraisals to address safety and soundness concerns.* The OTS reserves the right to require an appraisal under this part whenever the agency believes it is necessary to address safety and soundness concerns.

(d) *Transactions requiring a State certified appraiser*—(1) *All transactions of $1,000,000 or more.* All federally related transactions having a transaction value of $1,000,000 or more shall require an appraisal prepared by a State certified appraiser.

(2) *Nonresidential and residential (other than 1-to-4 family) transactions of $250,000 or more.* All federally related transactions having a transaction value of $250,000 or more, other than those involving appraisals of 1-to-4 family residential properties, shall require an appraisal prepared by a State certified appraiser.

(3) *Complex residential transactions of $250,000 or more.* All complex 1-to-4 family residential property appraisals rendered in connection with federally related transactions shall require a State certified appraiser if the transaction value is $250,000 or more. A regulated institution may presume that appraisals of 1-to-4 family residential properties are not complex, unless the institution has readily available information that a given appraisal will be complex. The regulated institution shall be responsible for making the final determination of whether the appraisal is complex. If during the course of the appraisal a licensed appraiser identifies factors that would result in the property, form of ownership, or market conditions being considered atypical, then either:

(i) The regulated institution may ask the licensed appraiser to complete the appraisal and have a certified appraiser approve and co-sign the appraisal; or

(ii) The institution may engage a certified appraiser to complete the appraisal.

(e) *Transactions requiring either a State certified or licensed appraiser.* All appraisals for federally related transactions not requiring the services of a State certified appraiser shall be prepared by either a State certified appraiser or a State licensed appraiser.

(f) *Effective date.* Savings associations are required to use State certified or licensed appraisers as set forth in this part no later than December 31, 1992.

[55 FR 34548, Aug. 23, 1990, as amended at 57 FR 12705, Apr. 13, 1992; 59 FR 29502, June 7, 1994]

§ 564.4 Minimum appraisal standards.

For federally related transactions, all appraisals shall, at a minimum:

(a) Conform to generally accepted appraisal standards as evidenced by the Uniform Standards of Professional Appraisal Practice (USPAP) promulgated by the Appraisal Standards Board of the Appraisal Foundation, 1029 Vermont Ave., NW., Washington, DC 20005, unless principles of safe and sound banking require compliance with stricter standards;

(b) Be written and contain sufficient information and analysis to support the institution's decision to engage in the transaction;

(c) Analyze and report appropriate deductions and discounts for proposed construction or renovation, partially leased buildings, non-market lease terms, and tract developments with unsold units;

(d) Be based upon the definition of market value as set forth in this part; and

(e) Be performed by State licensed or certified appraisers in accordance with requirements set forth in this part.

[59 FR 29503, June 7, 1994]

§ 564.5 Appraiser independence.

(a) *Staff appraisers.* If an appraisal is prepared by a staff appraiser, that appraiser must be independent of the lending, investment, and collection functions and not involved, except as an appraiser, in the federally related transaction, and have no direct or indirect interest, financial or otherwise, in the property. If the only qualified persons available to perform an appraisal are involved in the lending, investment, or collection functions of the regulated institution, the regulated institution shall take appropriate steps to ensure that the appraisers exercise independent judgment and that the appraisal is adequate. Such steps include, but are not limited to, prohibiting an individual from performing an appraisal in connection with federally related transactions in which the appraiser is otherwise involved and prohibiting directors and officers from participating in any vote or approval involving assets on which they performed an appraisal.

(b) *Fee appraisers.* (1) If an appraisal is prepared by a fee appraiser, the appraiser shall be engaged directly by the regulated institution or its agent, and have no direct or indirect interest, financial or otherwise, in the property or the transaction.

(2) A regulated institution also may accept an appraisal that was prepared by an appraiser engaged directly by another financial services institution, if:

(i) The appraiser has no direct or indirect interest, financial or otherwise, in the property or the transaction; and

(ii) The regulated institution determines that the appraisal conforms to the requirements of this part and is otherwise acceptable.

[55 FR 34549, Aug. 23, 1990, as amended at 59 FR 29503, June 7, 1994]

§ 564.6 Professional association membership; competency.

(a) *Membership in appraisal organizations.* A State certified appraiser or a State licensed appraiser may not be excluded from consideration for an assignment for a federally related transaction solely by virtue of membership or lack of membership in any particular appraisal organization.

(b) *Competency.* All staff and fee appraisers performing appraisals in connection with federally related transactions must be State certified or licensed, as appropriate. However, a State certified or licensed appraiser may not be considered competent solely by virtue of being certified or licensed. Any determination of competency shall be based upon the individual's experience and educational background as they relate to the particular appraisal assignment for which he or she is being considered.

[55 FR 34549, Aug. 23, 1990]

§ 564.7 Enforcement.

Institutions and institution-affiliated parties, including staff appraisers and fee appraisers, who violate this part may be subject to removal and/or prohibition orders, cease and desist orders, and the imposition of civil money penalties pursuant to the Federal Deposit Insurance Act, 12 U.S.C. 1811 *et seq.*, as amended, or other applicable law.

[55 FR 34549, Aug. 23, 1990]

§ 564.8 Appraisal policies and practices of savings associations and subsidiaries.

(a) *Introduction.* The soundness of a savings association's mortgage loans and real estate investments, and those of its service corporation(s), depends to a great extent upon the adequacy of the loan underwriting used to support these transactions. An appraisal standard is one of several critical components of a sound underwriting policy because appraisal reports contain estimates of the value of collateral held or assets owned. This section sets forth the responsibilities of management to develop, implement, and maintain appraisal standards in determining compliance with the appraisal requirements of § 563.170 of this chapter.

(b) *Definition.* For purposes of this section, management means: the directors and officers of a savings association, or service corporation of such savings association, as those terms are defined in §§ 561.18 and 561.35 of this chapter respectively.

(c) *Responsibilities of management.* An appraisal is a critical component of the loan underwriting or real estate investment decision. Therefore, management shall develop, implement, and maintain appraisal policies to ensure that appraisals reflect professional competence and to facilitate the reporting of estimates of market value upon which savings associations may rely to make lending decisions. To achieve these results:

(1) Management shall develop written appraisal policies, subject to formal adoption by the savings association's

board of directors, that it shall implement in consultation with other appropriate personnel. These policies shall ensure that adequate appraisals are obtained and proper appraisal procedures are followed consistent with the requirements of this part 564.

(2) Management shall develop and adopt guidelines and institute procedures pertaining to the hiring of appraisers to perform appraisal services for the savings association consistent with the requirements of this part 564. These guidelines shall set forth specific factors to be considered by management including, but not limited to, an appraiser's State certification or licensing, professional education, and type of experience. An appraiser's membership in professional appraisal organizations may be considered consistent with the requirements of § 564.6

(3) Management shall review on an annual basis the performance of all approved appraisers used within the preceding 12-month period for compliance with (i) the savings association's appraisal policies and procedures; and (ii) the reasonableness of the value estimates reported.

(d) *Exemptions.* The requirements of § 564.4(b) through (d) shall not apply with respect to appraisals on nonresidential properties prepared on form reports approved by the Office and completed in accordance with the applicable instructional booklet.

[54 FR 49552, Nov. 30, 1989. Redesignated and amended at 55 FR 34549, Aug. 23, 1990; 55 FR 43440, Oct. 29, 1990; 59 FR 29503, June 7, 1994; 59 FR 53571, Oct. 25, 1994; 73 FR 18, Jan. 2, 2008]

PART 565—PROMPT CORRECTIVE ACTION

Sec.
565.1 Authority, purpose, scope, other supervisory authority, and disclosure of capital categories.
565.2 Definitions.
565.3 Notice of capital category.
565.4 Capital measures and capital category definitions.
565.5 Capital restoration plans.
565.6 Mandatory and discretionary supervisory actions under section 38.
565.7 Directives to take prompt corrective action.
565.8 Procedures for reclassifying a savings association based on criteria other than capital.
565.9 Order to dismiss a director or senior executive officer.
565.10 Enforcement of directives.

AUTHORITY: 12 U.S.C. 1831o.

SOURCE: 57 FR 44903, Sept. 29, 1992, unless otherwise noted.

§ 565.1 Authority, purpose, scope, other supervisory authority, and disclosure of capital categories.

(a) *Authority.* This part is issued by the OTS pursuant to section 38 (section 38) of the Federal Deposit Insurance Act (FDI Act) as added by section 131 of the Federal Deposit Insurance Corporation Improvement Act of 1991 (Pub. L. 102–242, 105 Stat. 2236 (1991)) (12 U.S.C. 1831o).

(b) *Purpose.* Section 38 of the FDI Act establishes a framework of supervisory actions for insured depository institutions that are not adequately capitalized. The principal purpose of this part is to define, for savings associations, the capital measures and capital levels that are used for determining the supervisory actions authorized under section 38 of the FDI Act. This part also establishes procedures for submission and review of capital restoration plans and for issuance and review of directives and orders pursuant to section 38.

(c) *Scope.* This part implements the provisions of section 38 of the FDI Act as they apply to savings associations. Certain of these provisions also apply to officers, directors and employees of savings associations. Other provisions apply to any company that controls a savings association and to the affiliates of a savings association.

(d) *Other supervisory authority.* Neither section 38 nor this part in any way limits the authority of the OTS under any other provision of law to take supervisory actions to address unsafe or unsound practices, deficient capital levels, violations of law, unsafe or unsound conditions, or other practices. Action under section 38 of the FDI Act and this part may be taken independently of, in conjunction with, or in addition to any other enforcement action available to the OTS, including issuance of cease and desist orders, capital directives, approval or denial of

Office of Thrift Supervision, Treasury § 565.2

applications or notices, assessment of civil money penalties, or any other actions authorized by law.

(e) *Disclosure of capital categories.* The assignment of a savings association under this part within a particular capital category is for purposes of implementing and applying the provisions of section 38. Unless permitted by the OTS or otherwise required by law, no savings association may state in any advertisement or promotional material its capital category under this subpart or that the OTS or any other federal banking agency has assigned the savings association to a particular category.

§ 565.2 Definitions.

For purposes of this part, except as modified in this section or unless the context otherwise requires, the terms used in this part have the same meanings as set forth in sections 38 and 3 of the FDI Act.

(a)(1) *Control* has the same meaning assigned to it in section 2 of the Bank Holding Company Act (12 U.S.C. 1841), and the term "controlled" shall be construed consistently with the term "control."

(2) *Exclusion for fiduciary ownership.* No insured depository institution or company controls another insured depository institution or company by virtue of its ownership or control of shares in a fiduciary capacity. Shares shall not be deemed to have been acquired in a fiduciary capacity if the acquiring insured depository institution or company has sole discretionary authority to exercise voting rights with respect thereto.

(3) *Exclusion for debts previously contracted.* No insured depository institution or company controls another insured depository institution or company by virtue of its ownership or control of shares acquired in securing or collecting a debt previously contracted in good faith, until two years after the date of acquisition. The two-year period may be extended at the discretion of the appropriate federal banking agency for up to three one-year periods.

(b) *Controlling person* means any person having control of an insured depository institution and any company controlled by that person.

(c) *Leverage ratio* means the ratio of Tier 1 capital to adjusted total assets, as calculated in accordance with part 567 of this chapter.

(d) *Management fee* means any payment of money or provision of any other thing of value to a company or individual for the provision of management services or advice to the savings association or related overhead expenses, including payments related to supervisory, executive, managerial or policymaking functions, other than compensation to an individual in the individual's capacity as an officer or employee of the savings association.

(e) *Risk-weighted assets* means total risk-weighted assets, as calculated in accordance with part 567 of this chapter.

(f) *Tangible equity* means the amount of a savings association's core capital as computed in part 567 of this chapter plus the amount of its outstanding cumulative perpetual preferred stock (including related surplus), minus intangible assets as defined in § 567.1 of this chapter, except mortgage servicing assets to the extent they are includable under § 567.12. Non-mortgage servicing assets that have not been previously deducted in calculating core capital are deducted.

(g) *Tier 1 capital* means the amount of core capital as defined in part 567 of this chapter.

(h) *Tier 1 risk-based capital ratio* means the ratio of Tier 1 capital to risk-weighted assets, as calculated in accordance with part 567 of this chapter.

(i) *Total assets,* for purposes of § 565.4(b)(5), means adjusted total assets as calculated in accordance with part 567 of this chapter, minus intangible assets as provided in the definition of tangible equity.

(j) *Total risk-based capital ratio* means the ratio of total capital to risk-weighted assets, as calculated in accordance with part 567 of this chapter.

[57 FR 44903, Sept. 29, 1992, as amended at 60 FR 39232, Aug. 1, 1995; 62 FR 66263, Dec. 18, 1997; 63 FR 42678, Aug. 10, 1998; 73 FR 79607, Dec. 30, 2008]

§ 565.3 Notice of capital category.

(a) *Effective date of determination of capital category.* A savings association shall be deemed to be within a given capital category for purposes of section 38 of the FDI Act and this part as of the date the savings association is notified of, or is deemed to have notice of, its capital category, pursuant to paragraph (b) of this section.

(b) *Notice of capital category.* A savings association shall be deemed to have been notified of its capital levels and its capital category as of the most recent date:

(1) A Thrift Financial Report (TFR) is required to be filed with the OTS;

(2) A final report of examination is delivered to the savings association; or

(3) Written notice is provided by the OTS to the savings association of its capital category for purposes of section 38 of the FDI Act and this part or that the savings association's capital category has changed as provided in paragraph (c) of this section or § 565.4(c).

(c) *Adjustments to reported capital levels and category*—(1) *Notice of adjustment by savings association.* A savings association shall provide the OTS with written notice that an adjustment to the savings association's capital category may have occurred no later than 15 calendar days following the date that any material event has occurred that would cause the savings association to be placed in a lower capital category from the category assigned to the savings association for purposes of section 38 and this part on the basis of the savings association's most recent TFR or report of examination.

(2) *Determination by the OTS to change capital category.* After receiving notice pursuant to paragraph (c)(1) of this section, the OTS shall determine whether to change the capital category of the savings association and shall notify the savings association of the OTS's determination.

§ 565.4 Capital measures and capital category definitions.

(a) *Capital measures.* For purposes of section 38 and this part, the relevant capital measures shall be:

(1) The total risk-based capital ratio;

(2) The Tier 1 risk-based capital ratio; and

(3) The leverage ratio.

(b) *Capital categories.* For purposes of section 38 and this part, a savings association shall be deemed to be:

(1) *Well capitalized* if the savings association:

(i) Has a total risk-based capital ratio of 10.0 percent or greater; and

(ii) Has a Tier 1 risk-based capital ratio of 6.0 percent or greater; and

(iii) Has a leverage ratio of 5.0 percent or greater; and

(iv) Is not subject to any written agreement, order, capital directive, or prompt corrective action directive issued by OTS under section 8 of the FDI Act, the International Lending Supervision Act of 1983 (12 U.S.C. 3907), the Home Owners' Loan Act (12 U.S.C. 1464(t)(6)(A)(ii)), or section 38 of the FDI Act, or any regulation thereunder, to meet and maintain a specific capital level for any capital measure.

(2) *Adequately capitalized* if the savings association:

(i) Has a total risk-based capital ratio of 8.0 percent or greater; and

(ii) Has a Tier 1 risk-based capital ratio of 4.0 percent or greater; and

(iii) Has:

(A) A leverage ratio of 4.0 percent or greater; or

(B) A leverage ratio of 3.0 percent or greater if the savings association is assigned a composite rating of 1, as composite rating is defined in § 516.5(c) of this chapter; and

(iv) Does not meet the definition of a *well capitalized* savings association.

(3) *Undercapitalized* if the savings association:

(i) Has a total risk-based capital ratio that is less than 8.0 percent; or

(ii) Has a Tier 1 risk-based capital ratio that is less than 4.0 percent; or

(iii) (A) Except as provided in paragraph (b)(3)(iii) (B) of this section, has a leverage ratio that is less than 4.0 percent; or

(B) Has a leverage ratio that is less than 3.0 percent if the savings association is assigned a composite rating of 1, as composite rating is defined in § 516.5(c) of this chapter.

(4) *Significantly undercapitalized* if the savings association has:

(i) A total risk-based capital ratio that is less than 6.0 percent; or

(ii) A Tier 1 risk-based capital ratio that is less than 3.0 percent; or

(iii) A leverage ratio that is less than 3.0 percent.

(5) *Critically undercapitalized* if the savings association has a ratio of tangible equity to total assets that is equal to or less than 2.0 percent.

(c) *Reclassification based on supervisory criteria other than capital.* The OTS may reclassify a well capitalized savings association as adequately capitalized and may require an adequately capitalized or undercapitalized savings association to comply with certain mandatory or discretionary supervisory actions as if the savings association were in the next lower capital category (except that the OTS may not reclassify a significantly undercapitalized savings association as critically undercapitalized) (each of these actions are hereinafter referred to generally as "reclassifications") in the following circumstances:

(1) *Unsafe or unsound condition.* The OTS has determined, after notice and opportunity for hearing pursuant to § 565.8(a) of this part, that the savings association is in an unsafe or unsound condition; or

(2) *Unsafe or unsound practice.* The OTS has determined, after notice and an opportunity for hearing pursuant to § 565.8(a) of this part, that the savings association received a less-than-satisfactory rating for any rating category (other than in a rating category specifically addressing capital adequacy) under the Uniform Financial Institutions Rating System,[1] or an equivalent rating under a comparable rating system adopted by the OTS; and has not corrected the conditions that served as the basis for the less than satisfactory rating. Ratings under this paragraph (c)(2) refer to the most recent ratings (as determined either on-site or off-site by the most recent examination) of which the savings association has been notified in writing.

[57 FR 44903, Sept. 29, 1992, as amended at 62 FR 3781, Jan. 27, 1997; 66 FR 13009, Mar. 2, 2001; 66 FR 65821, Dec. 21, 2001]

---

[1] Copies are available at the address specified in § 516.40 of this chapter.

§ 565.5 **Capital restoration plans.**

(a) *Schedule for filing plan*—(1) *In general.* A savings association shall file a written capital restoration plan with the appropriate Regional Office within 45 days of the date that the savings association receives notice or is deemed to have notice that the savings association is undercapitalized, significantly undercapitalized, or critically undercapitalized, unless the OTS notifies the savings association in writing that the plan is to be filed within a different period. An adequately capitalized savings association that has been required pursuant to § 565.4(c) to comply with supervisory actions as if the savings association were undercapitalized is not required to submit a capital restoration plan solely by virtue of the reclassification.

(2) *Additional capital restoration plans.* Notwithstanding paragraph (a)(1) of this section, a savings association that has already submitted and is operating under a capital restoration plan approved under section 38 and this part is not required to submit an additional capital restoration plan based on a revised calculation of its capital measures or a reclassification of the institution under § 565.4(c) unless the OTS notifies the savings association that it must submit a new or revised capital plan. A savings association that is notified that it must submit a new or revised capital restoration plan shall file the plan in writing with the appropriate Regional Office within 45 days of receiving such notice, unless the OTS notifies the savings association in writing that the plan is to be filed within a different period.

(b) *Contents of plan.* All financial data submitted in connection with a capital restoration plan shall be prepared in accordance with the instructions provided on the TFR, unless the OTS instructs otherwise. The capital restoration plan shall include all of the information required to be filed under section 38(e)(2) of the FDI Act. A savings association that is required to submit a capital restoration plan as the result of a reclassification of the savings association pursuant to § 565.4(c) of this part shall include a description of the steps the savings association will take

§ 565.5

to correct the unsafe or unsound condition or practice. No plan shall be accepted unless it includes any performance guarantee described in section 38(e)(2)(C) of the FDI Act by each company that controls the savings association.

(c) *Review of capital restoration plans.* Within 60 days after receiving a capital restoration plan under this part, the OTS shall provide written notice to the savings association of whether the plan has been approved. The OTS may extend the time within which notice regarding approval of a plan shall be provided.

(d) *Disapproval of capital plan.* If a capital restoration plan is not approved by the OTS, the savings association shall submit a revised capital restoration plan, when directed to do so, within the time specified by the OTS. Upon receiving notice that its capital restoration plan has not been approved, any undercapitalized savings association (as defined in § 565.4(b)(3) of this part) shall be subject to all of the provisions of section 38 and this part applicable to significantly undercapitalized institutions. These provisions shall be applicable until such time as a new or revised capital restoration plan submitted by the savings association has been approved by the OTS.

(e) *Failure to submit a capital restoration plan.* A savings association that is undercapitalized (as defined in § 565.4(b)(3) of this part) and that fails to submit a written capital restoration plan within the period provided in this section shall, upon the expiration of that period, be subject to all of the provisions of section 38 and this part applicable to significantly undercapitalized institutions.

(f) *Failure to implement a capital restoration plan.* Any undercapitalized savings association that fails in any material respect to implement a capital restoration plan shall be subject to all of the provisions of section 38 and this part applicable to significantly undercapitalized institutions.

(g) *Amendment of capital plan.* A savings association that has filed an approved capital restoration plan may, after prior written notice to and approval by the OTS, amend the plan to reflect a change in circumstance. Until such time as a proposed amendment has been approved, the savings association shall implement the capital restoration plan as approved prior to the proposed amendment.

(h) *Notice to FDIC.* Within 45 days of the effective date of OTS approval of a capital restoration plan, or any amendment to a capital restoration plan, the OTS shall provide a copy of the plan or amendment to the FDIC.

(i) *Performance guarantee by companies that control a savings association*—(1) *Limitation on liability*—(i) *Amount limitation.* The aggregate liability under the guarantee provided under section 38 and this part for all companies that control a specific savings association that is required to submit a capital restoration plan under this part shall be limited to the lesser of:

(A) An amount equal to 5.0 percent of the savings association's total assets at the time the savings association was notified or deemed to have notice that the savings association was undercapitalized; or

(B) The amount necessary to restore the relevant capital measures of the savings association to the levels required for the savings association to be classified as adequately capitalized, as those capital measures and levels are defined at the time that the savings association initially fails to comply with a capital restoration plan under this part.

(ii) *Limit on duration.* The guarantee and limit of liability under section 38 and this part shall expire after the OTS notifies the savings association that it has remained adequately capitalized for each of four consecutive calendar quarters. The expiration or fulfillment by a company of a guarantee of a capital restoration plan shall not limit the liability of the company under any guarantee required or provided in connection with any capital restoration plan filed by the same savings association after expiration of the first guarantee.

(iii) *Collection on guarantee.* Each company that controls a given savings association shall be jointly and severally liable for the guarantee for such savings association as required under section 38 and this part, and the OTS may require and collect payment of the

Office of Thrift Supervision, Treasury § 565.6

full amount of that guarantee from any or all of the companies issuing the guarantee.

(2) *Failure to provide guarantee.* In the event that a savings association that is controlled by any company submits a capital restoration plan that does not contain the guarantee required under section 38(e)(2) of the FDI Act, the savings association shall, upon submission of the plan, be subject to the provisions of section 38 and this part that are applicable to savings associations that have not submitted an acceptable capital restoration plan.

(3) *Failure to perform guarantee.* Failure by any company that controls a savings association to perform fully its guarantee of any capital plan shall constitute a material failure to implement the plan for purposes of section 38(f) of the FDI Act. Upon such failure, the savings association shall be subject to the provisions of section 38 and this part that are applicable to savings associations that have failed in a material respect to implement a capital restoration plan.

§ 565.6 Mandatory and discretionary supervisory actions under section 38.

(a) *Mandatory supervisory actions*—(1) *Provisions applicable to all savings associations.* All savings associations are subject to the restrictions contained in section 38(d) of the FDI Act on payment of capital distributions and management fees.

(2) *Provisions applicable to undercapitalized, significantly undercapitalized, and critically undercapitalized savings associations.* Immediately upon receiving notice or being deemed to have notice, as provided in § 565.3 or § 565.5 of this part, that the savings association is undercapitalized, significantly undercapitalized, or critically undercapitalized, the savings association shall become subject to the provisions of section 38 of the FDI Act:

(i) Restricting payment of capital distributions and management fees (section 38(d));

(ii) Requiring that the OTS monitor the condition of the savings association (section 38(e)(1));

(iii) Requiring submission of a capital restoration plan within the schedule established in this part (section 38(e)(2));

(iv) Restricting the growth of the savings association's assets (section 38(e)(3)); and

(v) Requiring prior approval of certain expansion proposals (section 38(e)(4)).

(3) *Additional provisions applicable to significantly undercapitalized, and critically undercapitalized savings associations.* In addition to the provisions of section 38 of the FDI Act described in paragraph (a)(2) of this section, immediately upon receiving notice or being deemed to have notice, as provided in § 565.3 or § 565.5 of this part, that the savings association is significantly undercapitalized, or critically undercapitalized, or that the savings association is subject to the provisions applicable to institutions that are significantly undercapitalized because the savings association failed to submit or implement in any material respect an acceptable capital restoration plan, the savings association shall become subject to the provisions of section 38 of the FDI Act that restrict compensation paid to senior executive officers of the institution (section 38(f)(4)).

(4) *Additional provisions applicable to critically undercapitalized savings associations.* In addition to the provisions of section 38 of the FDI Act described in paragraphs (a)(2) and (a)(3) of this section, immediately upon receiving notice or being deemed to have notice, as provided in § 565.3 of this part, that the savings association is critically undercapitalized, the savings association shall become subject to the provisions of section 38 of the FDI Act:

(i) Restricting the activities of the savings association (section 38(h)(1)); and

(ii) Restricting payments on subordinated debt of the savings association (section 38(h)(2)).

(b) *Discretionary supervisory actions.* In taking any action under section 38 that is within the OTS's discretion to take in connection with: A savings association that is deemed to be undercapitalized, significantly undercapitalized or critically undercapitalized, or has been reclassified as undercapitalized, or significantly undercapitalized; an officer or director of such savings

§ 565.7

association; or a company that controls such savings association, the OTS shall follow the procedures for issuing directives under §§ 565.7 and 565.9 of this part unless otherwise provided in section 38 or this part.

§ 565.7 Directives to take prompt corrective action.

(a) *Notice of intent to issue a directive*—(1) *In general.* The OTS shall provide an undercapitalized, significantly undercapitalized, or critically undercapitalized savings association or, where appropriate, any company that controls the savings association, prior written notice of the OTS's intention to issue a directive requiring such savings association or company to take actions or to follow proscriptions described in section 38 that are within the OTS's discretion to require or impose under section 38 of the FDI Act, including sections 38(e)(5), (f)(2), (f)(3), or (f)(5). The savings association shall have such time to respond to a proposed directive as provided by the OTS under paragraph (c) of this section.

(2) *Immediate issuance of final directive.* If the OTS finds it necessary in order to carry out the purposes of section 38 of the FDI Act, the OTS may, without providing the notice prescribed in paragraph (a)(1) of this section, issue a directive requiring a savings association or any company that controls a savings association immediately to take actions or to follow proscriptions described in section 38 that are within the OTS's discretion to require or impose under section 38 of the FDI Act, including section 38(e)(5), (f)(2), (f)(3), or (f)(5). A savings association or company that is subject to such an immediately effective directive may submit a written appeal of the directive to the OTS. Such an appeal must be received by the OTS within 14 calendar days of the issuance of the directive, unless the OTS permits a longer period. The OTS shall consider any such appeal, if filed in a timely matter, within 60 days of receiving the appeal. During such period of review, the directive shall remain in effect unless the OTS, in its sole discretion, stays the effectiveness of the directive.

(b) *Contents of notice.* A notice of intention to issue a directive shall include:

(1) A statement of the savings association's capital measures and capital levels;

(2) A description of the restrictions, prohibitions or affirmative actions that the OTS proposes to impose or require;

(3) The proposed date when such restrictions or prohibitions would be effective or the proposed date for completion of such affirmative actions; and

(4) The date by which the savings association or company subject to the directive may file with the OTS a written response to the notice.

(c) *Response to notice*—(1) *Time for response.* A savings association or company may file a written response to a notice of intent to issue a directive within the time period set by the OTS. The date shall be at least 14 calendar days from the date of the notice unless the OTS determines that a shorter period is appropriate in light of the financial condition of the savings association or other relevant circumstances.

(2) *Content of response.* The response should include:

(i) An explanation why the action proposed by the OTS is not an appropriate exercise of discretion under section 38;

(ii) Any recommended modification of the proposed directive; and

(iii) Any other relevant information, mitigating circumstances, documentation, or other evidence in support of the position of the savings association or company regarding the proposed directive.

(d) *OTS consideration of response.* After considering the response, the OTS may:

(1) Issue the directive as proposed or in modified form;

(2) Determine not to issue the directive and so notify the savings association or company; or

(3) Seek additional information or clarification of the response from the savings association or company, or any other relevant source.

(e) *Failure to file response.* Failure by a savings association or company to file with the OTS, within the specified time period, a written response to a proposed directive shall constitute a waiver of the opportunity to respond and shall constitute consent to the issuance of the directive.

(f) *Request for modification or rescission of directive.* Any savings association or company that is subject to a directive under this part may, upon a change in circumstances, request in writing that the OTS reconsider the terms of the directive, and may propose that the directive be rescinded or modified. Unless otherwise ordered by the OTS, the directive shall continue in place while such request is pending before the OTS.

§ 565.8 Procedures for reclassifying a savings association based on criteria other than capital.

(a) *Reclassification based on unsafe or unsound condition or practice*—(1) *Issuance of notice of proposed reclassification*—(i) *Grounds for reclassification.* (A) Pursuant to § 565.4(c) of this part, the OTS may reclassify a well capitalized savings association as adequately capitalized or subject an adequately capitalized or undercapitalized institution to the supervisory actions applicable to the next lower capital category if:

(*1*) The OTS determines that the savings association is in unsafe or unsound condition; or

(*2*) The OTS deems the savings association to be engaged in an unsafe or unsound practice and not to have corrected the deficiency.

(B) Any action pursuant to this paragraph (a)(1)(i) shall hereinafter be referred to as "reclassification."

(ii) *Prior notice to institution.* Prior to taking action pursuant to § 565.4(c)(1), the OTS shall issue and serve on the savings association a written notice of the OTS's intention to reclassify the savings association.

(2) *Contents of notice.* A notice of intention to reclassify a savings association based on unsafe or unsound condition shall include:

(i) A statement of the savings association's capital measures and capital levels and the category to which the savings association would be reclassified;

(ii) The reasons for reclassification of the savings association;

(iii) The date by which the savings association subject to the notice of reclassification may file with the OTS a written appeal of the proposed reclassification and a request for a hearing, which shall be at least 14 calendar days from the date of service of the notice unless the OTS determines that a shorter period is appropriate in light of the financial condition of the savings association or other relevant circumstances.

(3) *Response to notice of proposed reclassification.* A savings association may file a written response to a notice of proposed reclassification within the time period set by the OTS. The response should include:

(i) An explanation of why the savings association is not in unsafe or unsound condition or otherwise should not be reclassified; and

(ii) Any other relevant information, mitigating circumstances, documentation, or other evidence in support of the position of the savings association or company regarding the reclassification.

(4) *Failure to file response.* Failure by a savings association to file, within the specified time period, a written response with the OTS to a notice of proposed reclassification shall constitute a waiver of the opportunity to respond and shall constitute consent to the reclassification.

(5) *Request for hearing and presentation of oral testimony or witnesses.* The response may include a request for an informal hearing before the OTS or its designee under this section. If the savings association desires to present oral testimony or witnesses at the hearing, the savings association shall include a request to do so with the request for an informal hearing. A request to present oral testimony or witnesses shall specify the names of the witnesses and the general nature of their expected testimony. Failure to request a hearing shall constitute a waiver of any right to a hearing, and failure to request the opportunity to present oral testimony or witnesses shall constitute a waiver of any right to present oral testimony or witnesses.

(6) *Order for informal hearing.* Upon receipt of a timely written request that includes a request for a hearing, the

§ 565.9

OTS shall issue an order directing an informal hearing to commence no later than 30 days after receipt of the request, unless the OTS allows further time at the request of the savings association. The hearing shall be held in Washington, DC or at such other place as may be designated by the OTS, before a presiding officer(s) designated by the OTS to conduct the hearing.

(7) *Hearing procedures.* (i) The savings association shall have the right to introduce relevant written materials and to present oral argument at the hearing. The savings association may introduce oral testimony and present witnesses only if expressly authorized by the OTS or the presiding officer(s). Neither the provisions of the Administrative Procedure Act (5 U.S.C. 554–557) governing adjudications required by statute to be determined on the record nor part 509 of this chapter apply to an informal hearing under this section unless the OTS orders that such procedures shall apply.

(ii) The informal hearing shall be recorded and a transcript furnished to the savings association upon request and payment of the cost thereof. Witnesses need not be sworn, unless specifically requested by a party or the presiding officer(s). The presiding officer(s) may ask questions of any witness.

(iii) The presiding officer(s) may order that the hearing be continued for a reasonable period (normally five business days) following completion of oral testimony or argument to allow additional written submissions to the hearing record.

(8) *Recommendation of presiding officers.* Within 20 calendar days following the date the hearing and the record on the proceeding are closed, the presiding officer(s) shall make a recommendation to the OTS on the reclassification.

(9) *Time for decision.* Not later than 60 calendar days after the date the record is closed or the date of the response in a case where no hearing was requested, the OTS will decide whether to reclassify the savings association and notify the savings association of the OTS's decision.

(b) *Request for rescission of reclassification.* Any savings association that has been reclassified under this section, may, upon a change in circumstances, request in writing that the OTS reconsider the reclassification, and may propose that the reclassification be rescinded and that any directives issued in connection with the reclassification be modified, rescinded, or removed. Unless otherwise ordered by the OTS, the savings association shall remain subject to the reclassification and to any directives issued in connection with that reclassification while such request is pending before the OTS.

§ 565.9 Order to dismiss a director or senior executive officer.

(a) *Service of notice.* When the OTS issues and serves a directive on a savings association pursuant to section 565.7 requiring the savings association to dismiss any director or senior executive officer under section 38(f)(2)(F)(ii) of the FDI Act, the OTS shall also serve a copy of the directive, or the relevant portions of the directive where appropriate, upon the person to be dismissed.

(b) *Response to directive*—(1) *Request for reinstatement.* A director or senior executive officer who has been served with a directive under paragraph (a) of this section (Respondent) may file a written request for reinstatement. The request for reinstatement shall be filed within 10 calendar days of the receipt of the directive by the Respondent, unless further time is allowed by the OTS at the request of the Respondent.

(2) *Contents of request; informal hearing.* The request for reinstatement should include reasons why the Respondent should be reinstated, and may include a request for an informal hearing before the OTS or its designee under this section. If the Respondent desires to present oral testimony or witnesses at the hearing, the Respondent shall include a request to do so with the request for an informal hearing. The request to present oral testimony or witnesses shall specify the names of the witnesses and the general nature of their expected testimony. Failure to request a hearing shall constitute a waiver of any right to a hearing and failure to request the opportunity to present oral testimony or witnesses shall constitute a waiver of

any right or opportunity to present oral testimony or witnesses.

(3) *Effective date.* Unless otherwise ordered by the OTS, the dismissal shall remain in effect while a request for reinstatement is pending.

(c) *Order for informal hearing.* Upon receipt of a timely written request from a Respondent for an informal hearing on the portion of a directive requiring a savings association to dismiss from office any director or senior executive officer, the OTS shall issue an order directing an informal hearing to commence no later than 30 days after receipt of the request, unless the Respondent requests a later date. The hearing shall be held in Washington, DC, or at such other place as may be designated by the OTS, before a presiding officer(s) designated by the OTS to conduct the hearing.

(d) *Hearing procedures.* (1) A Respondent may appear at the hearing personally or through counsel. A Respondent shall have the right to introduce relevant written materials and to present oral argument. A Respondent may introduce oral testimony and present witnesses only if expressly authorized by the OTS or the presiding officer(s). Neither the provisions of the Administrative Procedure Act governing adjudications required by statute to be determined on the record nor part 509 of this chapter apply to an informal hearing under this section unless the OTS orders that such procedures shall apply.

(2) The informal hearing shall be recorded and a transcript furnished to the Respondent upon request and payment of the cost thereof. Witnesses need not be sworn, unless specifically requested by a party or the presiding officer(s). The presiding officer(s) may ask questions of any witness.

(3) The presiding officer(s) may order that the hearing be continued for a reasonable period (normally five business days) following completion of oral testimony or argument to allow additional written submissions to the hearing record.

(e) *Standard for review.* A Respondent shall bear the burden of demonstrating that his or her continued employment by or service with the savings association would materially strengthen the savings association's ability:

(1) To become adequately capitalized, to the extent that the directive was issued as a result of the savings association's capital level or failure to submit or implement a capital restoration plan; and

(2) To correct the unsafe or unsound condition or unsafe or unsound practice, to the extent that the directive was issued as a result of classification of the savings association based on supervisory criteria other than capital, pursuant to section 38(g) of the FDI Act.

(f) *Recommendation of presiding officers.* Within 20 calendar days following the date the hearing and the record on the proceeding are closed, the presiding officer(s) shall make a recommendation to the OTS concerning the Respondent's request for reinstatement with the savings association.

(g) *Time for decision.* Not later than 60 calendar days after the date the record is closed or the date of the response in a case where no hearing has been requested, the OTS shall grant or deny the request for reinstatement and notify the Respondent of the OTS's decision. If the OTS denies the request for reinstatement, the OTS shall set forth in the notification the reasons for the OTS's action.

[57 FR 44903, Sept. 29, 1992, as amended at 60 FR 66719, Dec. 26, 1995]

§ 565.10 Enforcement of directives.

(a) *Judicial remedies.* Whenever a savings association or company that controls a savings association fails to comply with a directive issued under section 38, the OTS may seek enforcement of the directive in the appropriate United States district court pursuant to section 8(i)(1) of the FDI Act.

(b) *Administrative remedies*—(1) *Failure to comply with directive.* Pursuant to section 8(i)(2)(A) of the FDI Act, the OTS may assess a civil money penalty against any savings association or company that controls a savings association that violates or otherwise fails to comply with any final directive issued under section 38 and against any institution-affiliated party who participates in such violation or noncompliance.

(2) *Failure to implement capital restoration plan.* The failure of a savings association to implement a capital restoration plan required under section 38, or this part, or the failure of a company having control of a savings association to fulfill a guarantee of a capital restoration plan made pursuant to section 38(e)(2) of the FDI Act shall subject the savings association or company to the assessment of civil money penalties pursuant to section 8(i)(2)(A) of the FDI Act.

(c) *Other enforcement action.* In addition to the actions described in paragraphs (a) and (b) of this section, the OTS may seek enforcement of the provisions of section 38 or this part through any other judicial or administrative proceeding authorized by law.

PART 567—CAPITAL

Sec.

Subpart A—Scope

567.0 Scope.

Subpart B—Regulatory Captial Requirements

567.1 Definitions.
567.2 Minimum regulatory capital requirement.
567.3 Individual minimum capital requirements.
567.4 Capital directives.
567.5 Components of capital.
567.6 Risk-based capital credit risk-weight categories.
567.8 Leverage ratio.
567.9 Tangible capital requirement.
567.10 Consequences of failure to meet capital requirements.
567.11 Reservation of authority.
567.12 Purchased credit card relationships, servicing assets, intangible assets (other than purchased credit card relationships and servicing assets), credit-enhancing interest-only strips, and deferred tax assets.
567.14–567.19 [Reserved]
APPENDICES A–B TO PART 567 [RESERVED]
APPENDIX C TO PART 567—RISK-BASED CAPITAL REQUIREMENTS—INTERNAL-RATINGS-BASED AND ADVANCED MEASUREMENT APPROACHES

AUTHORITY: 12 U.S.C. 1462, 1462a, 1463, 1464, 1467a, 1828 (note).

SOURCE: 54 FR 49649, Nov. 30, 1989, unless otherwise noted.

Subpart A—Scope

§ 567.0 Scope.

(a) This part prescribes the minimum regulatory capital requirements for savings associations. Subpart B of this part applies to all savings associations, except as described in paragraph (b) of this section.

(b)(1) A savings association that uses Appendix C of this part must comply with the minimum qualifying criteria for internal risk measurement and management processes for calculating risk-based capital requirements, utilize the methodologies for calculating risk-based capital requirements, and make the required disclosures described in that appendix.

(2) Subpart B of this part does not apply to the computation of risk-based capital requirements by a savings association that uses Appendix C of this part. However, these savings associations:

(i) Must compute the components of capital under § 567.5, subject to the modifications in sections 11 and 12 of Appendix C of this part.

(ii) Must meet the leverage ratio requirement at §§ 567.2(a)(2) and 567.8 with tier 1 capital, as computed under sections 11 and 12 of Appendix C of this part.

(iii) Must meet the tangible capital requirement described at §§ 567.2(a)(3) and 567.9.

(iv) Are subject to §§ 567.3 (individual minimum capital requirement), 567.4 (capital directives); and 567.10 (consequences of failure to meet capital requirements).

(v) Are subject to the reservations of authority at § 567.11, which supplement the reservations of authority at section 1 of Appendix C of this part.

(c) *Optional transition provisions related to the implementation of consolidation requirements under FAS 167*—(1) *Scope, applicability, and purpose.* The section provides optional transition provisions for a savings association that is required for financial and regulatory reporting purposes, as a result of its implementation of Statement of Financial Accounting Standards No. 167, Amendments to FASB Interpretation No. 46(R) (referred to in this section as FAS 167), to consolidate certain

Office of Thrift Supervision, Treasury § 567.0

variable interest entities (VIEs) as defined under United States generally accepted accounting principles (GAAP). These transition provisions apply through the end of the fourth quarter following the date of a savings association's implementation of FAS 167 (implementation date).

(2) *Exclusion period*—(i) *Exclusion of risk-weighted assets for first and second quarters.* For the first two quarters, after the implementation date (exclusion period), including for the two calendar quarter-end regulatory report dates within those quarters, a savings association may exclude from risk-weighted assets:

(A) Subject to the limitations in paragraph (c)(4) of this section, assets held by a VIE, provided that the following conditions are met:

(*1*) The VIE existed prior to the implementation date;

(*2*) The savings association did not consolidate the VIE on its balance sheet for calendar quarter-end regulatory report dates prior to the implementation date;

(*3*) The savings association must consolidate the VIE on its balance sheet beginning as of the implementation date as a result of its implementation of FAS 167; and

(*4*) The savings association excludes all assets held by VIEs described in paragraphs (c)(2)(i)(A)(*1*) through (*3*) of this section.

(B) Subject to the limitations in paragraph (c)(4) of this section, assets held by a VIE that is a consolidated asset-backed commercial paper (ABCP) program, provided that the following conditions are met:

(*1*) The savings association is the sponsor of the ABCP program;

(*2*) Prior to the implementation date, the savings association consolidated the VIE onto its balance sheet under GAAP and excluded the VIE's assets from the savings association's risk-weighted assets; and

(*3*) The savings association chooses to exclude all assets held by ABCP program VIEs described in paragraphs (c)(2)(i)(B)(i) and (ii) of this section.

(ii) *Risk-weighted assets during exclusion period.* During the exclusion period, including the two calendar quarter-end regulatory report dates within the exclusion period, a savings association adopting the optional provisions of paragraph (c)(2) of this section must calculate risk-weighted assets for its contractual exposures to the VIEs referenced in paragraph (c)(2)(i) on the implementation date and include this calculated amount in its risk-weighted assets. Such contractual exposures may include direct-credit substitutes, recourse obligations, residual interests, liquidity facilities, and loans.

(iii) *Inclusion of Allowance for Loan and Lease Losses (ALLL) in tier 2 capital for the first and second quarters.* During the exclusion period, including for the two calendar quarter-end regulatory report dates within the exclusion period, a savings association that excludes VIE assets from risk-weighted assets pursuant to paragraph (c)(2)(i) of this section may include in tier 2 capital the full amount of the allowance for loan and lease losses (ALLL) calculated as of the implementation date that is attributable to the assets it excludes pursuant to paragraph (c)(2)(i) of this section (inclusion amount). The amount of ALLL includable in tier 2 capital in accordance with this paragraph shall not be subject to the limitations set forth at § 567.5(b)(4).

(3) *Phase-in period*—(i) *Exclusion amount.* For purposes of this paragraph, exclusion amount is defined as the amount of risk-weighted assets excluded in paragraph (c)(2)(i) of this section as of the implementation date.

(ii) *Risk-weighted assets for the third and fourth quarters.* A savings association that excludes assets of consolidated VIEs from risk-weighted assets pursuant to paragraph (c)(2)(i) of this section may, for the third and fourth quarters, after the implementation date (phase-in period), including for the two calendar quarter-end regulatory report dates within those quarters exclude from risk-weighted assets 50 percent of the exclusion amount, provided that the savings association may not include in risk-weighted assets pursuant to this paragraph an amount less than the aggregate risk-weighted assets calculated pursuant to paragraph (b)(2)(ii) of this section.

(iii) *Inclusion of ALLL in Tier 2 capital for the third and fourth quarters.* A savings association that excludes assets of

325

§ 567.1

consolidated VIEs from risk-weighted assets pursuant to paragraph (c)(3)(ii) of this section may, for the phase-in period, include in tier 2 capital 50 percent of the inclusion amount it included in tier 2 capital during the exclusion period, notwithstanding the limit on including ALLL in tier 2 capital in § 567.5(b)(4).

(4) *Implicit recourse limitation.* Notwithstanding any other provision in § 567.0(c), assets held by a VIE to which a savings association has provided recourse through credit enhancement beyond any contractual obligation to support assets it has sold may not be excluded from risk-weighted assets.

[72 FR 69438, Dec. 7, 2007, as amended at 75 FR 4652, Jan. 28, 2010]

Subpart B—Regulatory Capital Requirements

§ 567.1 Definitions.

For the purposes of this subpart:

Adjusted total assets. The term *adjusted total assets* means:

(1) A savings association's total assets as that term is defined in this section;

(2) Plus

(i) The prorated assets of any includable subsidiary in which the savings association has a minority ownership interest that is not consolidated under generally accepted accounting principles; and

(ii) The remaining goodwill (FSLIC Capital Contributions) resulting from prior regulatory accounting practices as provided in the definition of *qualifying supervisory goodwill* in this section;

(3) Minus

(i) Assets not included in the applicable capital standard except for those subject to paragraphs (3)(ii) and (3)(iii) of this definition;

(ii) Investments in any includable subsidiary in which a savings association has a minority interest;

(iii) Investments in any subsidiary subject to consolidation under paragraph (2)(ii) of this definition; and

(iv) For purposes of determining core capital, qualifying supervisory goodwill.

Asset-backed commercial paper program. The term *asset-backed commercial paper program* (ABCP program) means a program that primarily issues commercial paper that has received a credit rating from an NRSRO and that is backed by assets or other exposures held in a bankruptcy-remote special purpose entity. The term *sponsor* of an ABCP program means a savings association that:

(1) Establishes an ABCP program;

(2) Approves the sellers permitted to participate in an ABCP program;

(3) Approves the asset pools to be purchased by an ABCP program; or

(4) Administers the ABCP program by monitoring the assets, arranging for debt placement, compiling monthly reports, or ensuring compliance with the program documents and with the program's credit and investment policy.

Cash items in the process of collection. The term *cash items in the process of collection* means checks or drafts in the process of collection that are drawn on another depository institution, including a central bank, and that are payable immediately upon presentation; U.S. Government checks that are drawn on the United States Treasury or any other U.S. Government or Government-sponsored agency and that are payable immediately upon presentation; broker's security drafts and commodity or bill-of-lading drafts payable immediately upon presentation; and unposted debits.

Commitment. The term *commitment* means any arrangement that obligates a savings association to:

(1) Purchase loans or securities;

(2) Extend credit in the form of loans or leases, participations in loans or leases, overdraft facilities, revolving credit facilities, home equity lines of credit, eligible ABCP liquidity facilities, or similar transactions.

Common stockholders' equity. The term *common stockholders' equity* means common stock, common stock surplus, retained earnings, and adjustments for the cumulative effect of foreign currency translation, less net unrealized losses on available-for-sale equity securities with readily determinable fair values.

Conditional guarantee. The term *conditional guarantee* means a contingent obligation of the United States Government or its agencies, the validity of which to the beneficiary is dependent upon some affirmative action—*e.g.*, servicing requirements—on the part of the beneficiary of the guarantee or a third party.

Credit derivative. The term *credit derivative* means a contract that allows one party (the protection purchaser) to transfer the credit risk of an asset or off-balance sheet credit exposure to another party (the protection provider). The value of a credit derivative is dependent, at least in part, on the credit performance of a "referenced asset."

Credit-enhancing interest-only strip. (1) The term *credit-enhancing interest-only strip* means an on-balance sheet asset that, in form or in substance:

(i) Represents the contractual right to receive some or all of the interest due on transferred assets; and

(ii) Exposes the savings association to credit risk directly or indirectly associated with the transferred assets that exceeds its *pro rata* share of the savings association's claim on the assets whether through subordination provisions or other credit enhancement techniques.

(2) OTS reserves the right to identify other cash flows or related interests as a credit-enhancing interest-only strip. In determining whether a particular interest cash flow functions as a credit-enhancing interest-only strip, OTS will consider the economic substance of the transaction.

Credit-enhancing representations and warranties. (1) The term *credit-enhancing representations and warranties* means representations and warranties that are made or assumed in connection with a transfer of assets (including loan servicing assets) and that obligate a savings association to protect investors from losses arising from credit risk in the assets transferred or loans serviced.

(2) Credit-enhancing representations and warranties include promises to protect a party from losses resulting from the default or nonperformance of another party or from an insufficiency in the value of the collateral.

(3) Credit-enhancing representations and warranties do not include:

(i) Early-default clauses and similar warranties that permit the return of, or premium refund clauses covering, qualifying mortgage loans for a period not to exceed 120 days from the date of transfer. These warranties may cover only those loans that were originated within one year of the date of the transfer;

(ii) Premium refund clauses covering assets guaranteed, in whole or in part, by the United States government, a United States government agency, or a United States government-sponsored enterprise, provided the premium refund clause is for a period not to exceed 120 days from the date of transfer; or

(iii) Warranties that permit the return of assets in instances of fraud, misrepresentation or incomplete documentation.

Depository institution. The term *domestic depository institution* means a financial institution that engages in the business of banking; that is recognized as a bank by the bank supervisory or monetary authorities of the country of its incorporation and the country of its principal banking operations; that receives deposits to a substantial extent in the regular course of business; and that has the power to accept demand deposits. In the United States, this definition encompasses all federally insured offices of commercial banks, mutual and stock savings banks, savings or building and loan associations (stock and mutual), cooperative banks, credit unions, and international banking facilities of domestic depository institutions. Bank holding companies and savings and loan holding companies are excluded from this definition. For the purposes of assigning risk weights, the differentiation between OECD depository institutions and non-OECD depository institutions is based on the country of incorporation. Claims on branches and agencies of foreign banks located in the United States are to be categorized on the basis of the parent bank's country of incorporation.

Direct credit substitute. The term *direct credit substitute* means an arrangement in which a savings association assumes, in form or in substance, credit risk associated with an on-or off-balance sheet asset or exposure that was not previously owned by the savings association (third-party asset) and the

§ 567.1

risk assumed by the savings association exceeds the *pro rata* share of the savings association's interest in the third-party asset. If a savings association has no claim on the third-party asset, then the savings association's assumption of any credit risk is a direct credit substitute. Direct credit substitutes include:

(1) Financial standby letters of credit that support financial claims on a third party that exceed a savings association's *pro rata* share in the financial claim;

(2) Guarantees, surety arrangements, credit derivatives, and similar instruments backing financial claims that exceed a savings association's *pro rata* share in the financial claim;

(3) Purchased subordinated interests that absorb more than their *pro rata* share of losses from the underlying assets;

(4) Credit derivative contracts under which the savings association assumes more than its *pro rata* share of credit risk on a third-party asset or exposure;

(5) Loans or lines of credit that provide credit enhancement for the financial obligations of a third party;

(6) Purchased loan servicing assets if the servicer is responsible for credit losses or if the servicer makes or assumes credit-enhancing representations and warranties with respect to the loans serviced. Servicer cash advances as defined in this section are not direct credit substitutes;

(7) Clean-up calls on third party assets. However, clean-up calls that are 10 percent or less of the original pool balance and that are exercisable at the option of the savings association are not direct credit substitutes; and

(8) Liquidity facilities that provide support to asset-backed commercial paper (other than eligible ABCP liquidity facilities).

Eligible ABCP liquidity facility. The term *eligible ABCP liquidity facility* means a liquidity facility that supports asset-backed commercial paper, in form or in substance, and that meets the following criteria:

(1)(i) At the time of the draw, the liquidity facility must be subject to an asset quality test that precludes funding against assets that are 90 days or more past due or in default; and

12 CFR Ch. V (1-1-12 Edition)

(ii) If the assets that the liquidity facility is required to fund against are assets or exposures that have received a credit rating by a NRSRO at the time the inception of the facility, the facility can be used to fund only those assets or exposures that are rated investment grade by an NRSRO at the time of funding; or

(2) If the assets that are funded under the liquidity facility do not meet the criteria described in paragraph (1) of this definition, the assets must be guaranteed, conditionally or unconditionally, by the United States Government, its agencies, or the central government of an OECD country.

Eligible savings association. (1) The term *eligible savings association* means a savings association with respect to which the Director of the Office of Thrift Supervision has determined, on the basis of information available at the time, that:

(i) The savings association's management appears to be competent;

(ii) The savings association, as certified by its Board of Directors, is in substantial compliance with all applicable statutes, regulations, orders and written agreements and directives; and

(iii) The savings association's management, as certified by its Board of Directors, has not engaged in insider dealing, speculative practices, or any other activities that have or may jeopardize the association's safety and soundness or contributed to impairing the association's capital.

(2) Savings associations, for purposes of this paragraph, will be deemed to be eligible unless the Director makes a determination otherwise or notifies the savings association of its intent to conduct either an informal or formal examination to determine eligibility and provides written notification thereof to the savings association.

Equity investments. (1) The term *equity investments* includes investments in equity securities and real property that would be considered an equity investment under generally accepted accounting principles.

(2)(i) The term *equity securities* means any:

(A) Stock, certificate of interest of participation in any profit-sharing agreement, collateral trust certificate

328

Office of Thrift Supervision, Treasury §567.1

or subscription, preorganization certificate or subscription, transferable share, investment contract, or voting trust certificate; or

(B) In general, any interest or instrument commonly known as an equity security; or

(C) Loans having profit sharing features which generally accepted accounting principles would reclassify as equity securities; or

(D) Any security immediately convertible at the option of the holder without payment of substantial additional consideration into such a security; or

(E) Any security carrying any warrant or right to subscribe to or purchase such a security; or

(F) Any certificate of interest or participation in, temporary or Interim certificate for, or receipt for any of the foregoing or any partnership interest; or

(G) Investments in equity securities and loans or advances to and guarantees issued on behalf of partnerships or joint ventures in which a savings association holds an interest in real property under generally accepted accounting principles.

(ii) The term *equity securities* does not include investments in a subsidiary as that term is defined in this section, equity investments that are permissible for national banks, ownership interests in pools of assets that are risk-weighted in accordance with §567.6(a)(1)(vi) of this part, or the stock of Federal Home Loan Banks or Federal Reserve Banks.

(3) For purposes of this part, the term *equity investments in real property* does not include interests in real property that are primarily used or intended to be used by the savings association, its subsidiaries, or its affiliates as offices or related facilities for the conduct of its business.

(4) In addition, for purposes of this part, the term *equity investments in real property* does not include interests in real property that are acquired in satisfaction of a debt previously contracted in good faith or acquired in sales under judgments, decrees, or mortgages held by the savings association, provided that the property is not intended to be held for real estate investment purposes but is expected to be disposed of within five years or a longer period approved by the Office.

Exchange rate contracts. The term *exchange rate contracts* includes cross-currency interest rate swaps; forward foreign exchange rate contracts; currency options purchased; and any similar instrument that, in the opinion of the Office, may give rise to similar risks.

Face amount. The term *face amount* means the notational principal, or face value, amount of an off-balance sheet item or the amortized cost of an on-balance sheet asset.

Financial asset. The term *financial asset* means cash or other monetary instrument, evidence of debt, evidence of an ownership interest in an entity, or a contract that conveys a right to receive or exchange cash or another financial instrument from another party.

Financial standby letter of credit. The term *financial standby letter of credit* means a letter of credit or similar arrangement that represents an irrevocable obligation to a third-party beneficiary:

(1) To repay money borrowed by, or advanced to, or for the account of, a second party (the account party); or

(2) To make payment on behalf of the account party, in the event that the account party fails to fulfill its obligation to the beneficiary.

Includable subsidiary. The term *includable subsidiary* means a subsidiary of a savings association that is:

(1) Engaged solely in activities not impermissible for a national bank;

(2) Engaged in activities not permissible for a national bank, but only if acting solely as agent for its customers and such agency position is clearly documented in the savings association's files;

(3) Engaged solely in mortgage-banking activities;

(4)(i) Itself an insured depository institution or a company the sole investment of which is an insured depository institution, and

(ii) Was acquired by the parent savings association prior to May 1, 1989; or

(5) A subsidiary of any Federal savings association existing as a Federal savings association on August 9, 1989 that

329

§ 567.1

(i) Was chartered prior to October 15, 1982, as a savings bank or a cooperative bank under State law, or

(ii) Acquired its principal assets from an association that was chartered prior to October 15, 1982, as a savings bank or a cooperative bank under State law.

Intangible assets. The term *intangible assets* means assets considered to be intangible assets under generally accepted accounting principles. These assets include, but are not limited to, goodwill, core deposit premiums, purchased credit card relationships, favorable leaseholds, and servicing assets (mortgage and non-mortgage). Interest-only strips receivable and other nonsecurity financial instruments are not intangible assets under this definition.

Interest-rate contracts. The term *interest-rate contracts* includes single currency interest-rate swaps; basis swaps; forward rate agreements; interest-rate options purchased; forward forward deposits accepted; and any other instrument that, in the opinion of the Office, may give rise to similar risks, including when-issued securities.

Liquidity facility. The term *liquidity facility* means a legally binding commitment to provide liquidity support to asset-backed commercial paper by lending to, or purchasing assets from any structure, program or conduit in the event that funds are required to repay maturing asset-backed commercial paper.

Mortgage-related securities. The term *mortgage-related securities* means any mortgage-related qualifying securities under section 3(a)(41) of the Securities Exchange Act of 1934, 15 U.S.C. 78c(a)(41), *Provided,* That the rating requirements of that section shall not be considered for purposes of this definition.

Nationally recognized statistical rating organization (NRSRO). The term *nationally recognized statistical rating organization* means an entity recognized by the Division of Market Regulation of the Securities and Exchange Commission (Commission) as a nationally recognized statistical rating organization for various purposes, including the Commission's uniform net capital requirements for brokers and dealers.

OECD-based country. The term *OECD-based country* means a member of that grouping of countries that are full members of the Organization for Economic Cooperation and Development (OECD) plus countries that have concluded special lending arrangements with the International Monetary Fund (IMF) associated with the IMF's General Arrangements to Borrow. This term excludes any country that has rescheduled its external sovereign debt within the previous five years. A rescheduling of external sovereign debt generally would include any renegotiation of terms arising from a country's inability or unwillingness to meet its external debt service obligations, but generally would not include renegotiations of debt in the normal course of business, such as a renegotiation to allow the borrower to take advantage of a decline in interest rates or other change in market conditions.

Original maturity. The term *original maturity* means, with respect to a commitment, the earliest date after a commitment is made on which the commitment is scheduled to expire (*i.e.,* it will reach its stated maturity and cease to be binding on either party), *Provided,* That either:

(i) The commitment is not subject to extension or renewal and will actually expire on its stated expiration date; or

(ii) If the commitment is subject to extension or renewal beyond its stated expiration date, the stated expiration date will be deemed the original maturity only if the extension or renewal must be based upon terms and conditions independently negotiated in good faith with the customer at the time of the extension or renewal and upon a new, *bona fide* credit analysis utilizing current information on financial condition and trends.

Performance-based standby letter of credit. The term *performance-based standby letter of credit* means any letter of credit, or similar arrangement, however named or described, which represents an irrevocable obligation to the beneficiary on the part of the issuer to make payment on account of any default by a third party in the performance of a nonfinancial or commercial

Office of Thrift Supervision, Treasury § 567.1

obligation. Such letters of credit include arrangements backing subcontractors' and suppliers' performance, labor and materials contracts, and construction bids.

Perpetual preferred stock. The term *perpetual preferred stock* means preferred stock without a fixed maturity date that cannot be redeemed at the option of the holder, and that has no other provisions that will require future redemption of the issue. For purposes of these instruments, preferred stock that can be redeemed at the option of the holder is deemed to have an "original maturity" of the earliest possible date on which it may be so redeemed. Cumulative perpetual preferred stock is preferred stock where the dividends accumulate from one period to the next. Noncumulative perpetual preferred stock is preferred stock where the unpaid dividends are not carried over to subsequent dividend periods.

Problem institution. The term *problem institution* means a savings association that, at the time of its acquisition, merger, purchase of assets or other business combination with or by another savings association:

(1) Was subject to special regulatory controls by its primary Federal or state regulatory authority;

(2) Posed particular supervisory concerns to its primary Federal or state regulatory authority; or

(3) Failed to meet its regulatory capital requirement immediately before the transaction.

Prorated assets. The term *prorated assets* means the total assets (as determined in the most recently available GAAP report but in no event more than one year old) of a subsidiary (including those subsidiaries where the savings association has a minority interest) multiplied by the savings association's percentage of ownership of that subsidiary.

Qualifying mortgage loan. (1) The term *qualifying mortgage loan* means a loan that:

(i) Is fully secured by a first lien on a one-to four-family residential property;

(ii) Is underwritten in accordance with prudent underwriting standards, including standards relating the ratio of the loan amount to the value of the property (LTV ratio). See Appendix to 12 CFR 560.101. A nonqualifying mortgage loan that is paid down to an appropriate LTV ratio (calculated using value at origination) may become a qualifying loan if it meets all other requirements of this definition;

(iii) Maintains an appropriate LTV ratio based on the amortized principal balance of the loan; and

(iv) Is performing and is not more than 90 days past due.

(2) If a savings association holds the first and junior lien(s) on a residential property and no other party holds an intervening lien, the transaction is treated as a single loan secured by a first lien for the purposes of determining the LTV ratio and the appropriate risk weight under § 567.6(a).

(3) A loan to an individual borrower for the construction of the borrower's home may be included as a qualifying mortgage loan.

(4) A loan that meets the requirements of this section prior to modification on a permanent or trial basis under the U.S. Department of Treasury's Home Affordable Mortgage Program may be included as a *qualifying mortgage loan*, so long as the loan is not 90 days or more past due.

Qualifying multifamily mortgage loan. (1) The term *qualifying multifamily mortgage loan* means a loan secured by a first lien on multifamily residential properties consisting of 5 or more dwelling units, provided that:

(i) The amortization of principal and interest occurs over a period of not more than 30 years;

(ii) The original minimum maturity for repayment of principal on the loan is not less than seven years;

(iii) When considering the loan for placement in a lower risk-weight category, all principal and interest payments have been made on a timely basis in accordance with its terms for the preceding year;

(iv) The loan is performing and not 90 days or more past due;

(v) The loan is made by the savings association in accordance with prudent underwriting standards; and

(vi) If the interest rate on the loan does not change over the term of the loan:

331

§ 567.1

(A) The current loan balance amount does not exceed 80 percent of the value of the property securing the loan; and

(B) For the property's most recent fiscal year, the ratio of annual net operating income generated by the property (before payment of any debt service on the loan) to annual debt service on the loan is not less than 120 percent, or in the case of cooperative or other not-for-profit housing projects, the property generates sufficient cash flows to provide comparable protection to the institution; or

(vii) If the interest rate on the loan changes over the term of the loan:

(A) The current loan balance amount does not exceed 75 percent of the value of the property securing the loan; and

(B) For the property's most recent fiscal year, the ratio of annual net operating income generated by the property (before payment of any debt service on the loan) to annual debt service on the loan is not less than 115 percent, or in the case of cooperative or other not-for-profit housing projects, the property generates sufficient cash flows to provide comparable protection to the institution.

(2) The term *qualifying multifamily mortgage loan* also includes a multifamily mortgage loan that on March 18, 1994 was a first mortgage loan on an existing property consisting of 5–36 dwelling units with an initial loan-to-value ratio of not more than 80% where an average annual occupancy rate of 80% or more of total units had existed for at least one year, and continues to meet these criteria.

(3) For purposes of paragraphs (1) (vi) and (vii) of this definition, the term *value of the property* means, at origination of a loan to purchase a multifamily property: the lower of the purchase price or the amount of the initial appraisal, or if appropriate, the initial evaluation. In cases not involving the purchase of a multifamily loan, the *value of the property* is determined by the most current appraisal, or if appropriate, the most current evaluation.

(4) In cases where a borrower refinances a loan on an existing property, as an alternative to paragraphs (1) (iii), (vi), and (vii) of this definition:

(i) All principal and interest payments on the loan being refinanced have been made on a timely basis in accordance with the terms of that loan for the preceding year; and

(ii) The net income on the property for the preceding year would support timely principal and interest payments on the new loan in accordance with the applicable debt service requirement.

Qualifying residential construction loan. (1) The term *qualifying residential construction loan*, also referred to as a residential bridge loan, means a loan made in accordance with sound lending principles satisfying the following criteria:

(i) The builder must have substantial project equity in the home construction project;

(ii) The residence being constructed must be a 1–4 family residence sold to a home purchaser;

(iii) The lending savings association must obtain sufficient documentation from a permanent lender (which may be the construction lender) demonstrating that:

(A) The home buyer intends to purchase the residence; and

(B) Has the ability to obtain a permanent qualifying mortgage loan sufficient to purchase the residence;

(iv) The home purchaser must have made a substantial earnest money deposit;

(v) The construction loan must not exceed 80 percent of the sales price of the residence;

(vi) The construction loan must be secured by a first lien on the lot, residence under construction, and other improvements;

(vii) The lending thrift must retain sufficient undisbursed loan funds throughout the construction period to ensure project completion;

(viii) The builder must incur a significant percentage of direct costs (*i.e.*, the actual costs of land, labor, and material) before any drawdown on the loan;

(ix) If at any time during the life of the construction loan any of the criteria of this rule are no longer satisfied, the association must immediately recategorize the loan at a 100 percent risk-weight and must accurately report the loan in the association's next quarterly Thrift Financial Report;

Office of Thrift Supervision, Treasury § 567.1

(x) The home purchaser must intend that the home will be owner-occupied;

(xi) The home purchaser(s) must be an individual(s), not a partnership, joint venture, trust corporation, or any other entity (including an entity acting as a sole proprietorship) that is purchasing the home(s) for speculative purposes; and

(xii) The loan must be performing and not more than 90 days past due.

(2) The documentation for each loan and home sale must be sufficient to demonstrate compliance with the criteria in paragraph (1) of this definition. The OTS retains the discretion to determine that any loans not meeting sound lending principles must be placed in a higher risk-weight category. The OTS also reserves the discretion to modify these criteria on a case-by-case basis provided that any such modifications are not inconsistent with the safety and soundness objectives of this definition.

Qualifying securities firm. The term *qualifying securities firm* means:

(1) A securities firm incorporated in the United States that is a broker-dealer that is registered with the Securities and Exchange Commission (SEC) and that complies with the SEC's net capital regulations (17 CFR 240.15c3(1)); and

(2) A securities firm incorporated in any other OECD-based country, if the savings association is able to demonstrate that the securities firm is subject to consolidated supervision and regulation (covering its subsidiaries, but not necessarily its parent organizations) comparable to that imposed on depository institutions in OECD countries. Such regulation must include risk-based capital requirements comparable to those imposed on depository institutions under the Accord on International Convergence of Capital Measurement and Capital Standards (1988, as amended in 1998).

Qualifying supervisory goodwill. The term *qualifying supervisory goodwill* means, for eligible savings associations:

(1) Any unamortized goodwill (FSLIC Capital Contributions, as reported in the September 30, 1989 Thrift Financial Report) that existed on April 12, 1989 resulting from prior regulatory accounting practices less any amortization that would have occurred subsequent to April 12, 1989 through the current reporting period where the amortization is calculated on a straight line basis over the shorter of 20 years, or the remaining period for amortization in effect on April 12, 1989 for regulatory accounting practices; plus

(2) The lesser of:

(i) Supervisory goodwill as defined in this section that is included in goodwill that is reflected in the current reporting period under generally accepted accounting principles ("GAAP"); or

(ii)(A) Supervisory goodwill as defined in this section that is included in goodwill that is reflected in the current reporting period under GAAP;

(B) Plus any amortization of the goodwill in paragraph (2)(ii)(A) of this definition that occurred subsequent to April 12, 1989 for GAAP reporting purposes;

(C) Minus the amortization of the goodwill in paragraph (2)(ii)(A) of this definition through the current reporting period that results when the goodwill is amortized subsequent to April 12, 1989 on a straightline basis over the shorter of—

(*1*) 20 years; or

(*2*) The remaining period for amortization in effect on April 12, 1989 under regulatory accounting practices.

Reciprocal holdings of depository institution instruments. The term *reciprocal holdings of depository institution instruments* means cross-holdings or other formal or informal arrangements in which two or more depository institutions swap, exchange, or otherwise agree to hold each other's capital instruments. This definition does not include holdings of capital instruments issued by other depository institutions that were taken in satisfaction of debts previously contracted, provided that the reporting savings association has not held such instruments for more than five years or a longer period approved by the Office.

Recourse. The term *recourse* means a savings association's retention, in form or in substance, of any credit risk directly or indirectly associated with an asset it has sold (in accordance with generally accepted accounting principles) that exceeds a *pro rata* share of

§ 567.1

that savings association's claim on the asset. If a savings association has no claim on an asset it has sold, then the retention of any credit risk is recourse. A recourse obligation typically arises when a savings association transfers assets in a sale and retains an explicit obligation to repurchase assets or to absorb losses due to a default on the payment of principal or interest or any other deficiency in the performance of the underlying obligor or some other party. Recourse may also exist implicitly if a savings association provides credit enhancement beyond any contractual obligation to support assets it has sold. Recourse obligations include:

(1) Credit-enhancing representations and warranties made on transferred assets;

(2) Loan servicing assets retained pursuant to an agreement under which the savings association will be responsible for losses associated with the loans serviced. Servicer cash advances as defined in this section are not recourse obligations;

(3) Retained subordinated interests that absorb more than their *pro rata* share of losses from the underlying assets;

(4) Assets sold under an agreement to repurchase, if the assets are not already included on the balance sheet;

(5) Loan strips sold without contractual recourse where the maturity of the transferred portion of the loan is shorter than the maturity of the commitment under which the loan is drawn;

(6) Credit derivatives that absorb more than the savings association's pro rata share of losses from the transferred assets;

(7) Clean-up calls on assets the savings association has sold. However, clean-up calls that are 10 percent or less of the original pool balance and that are exercisable at the option of the savings association are not recourse arrangements; and

(8) Liquidity facilities that provide support to asset-backed commercial paper (other than eligible ABCP liquidity facilities).

Replacement cost. The term *replacement cost* means, with respect to interest rate and exchange-rate contracts, the loss that would be incurred in the event of a counterparty default, as measured by the net cost of replacing the contract at the current market value. If default would result in a theoretical profit, the replacement value is considered to be zero. This mark-to-market process must incorporate changes in both interest rates and counterparty credit quality.

Residential properties. The term *residential properties* means houses, condominiums, cooperative units, and manufactured homes. This definition does not include boats or motor homes, even if used as a primary residence, or timeshare properties.

Residual characteristics. The term *residual characteristics* means interests similar to a multi-class pay-through obligation representing the excess cash flow generated from mortgage collateral over the amount required for the issue's debt service and ongoing administrative expenses or interests presenting similar degrees of interest-rate/prepayment risk and principal loss risks.

Residual interest. (1) The term *residual interest* means any on-balance sheet asset that:

(i) Represents an interest (including a beneficial interest) created by a transfer that qualifies as a sale (in accordance with generally accepted accounting principles) of financial assets, whether through a securitization or otherwise; and

(ii) Exposes a savings association to credit risk directly or indirectly associated with the transferred asset that exceeds a *pro rata* share of that savings association's claim on the asset, whether through subordination provisions or other credit enhancement techniques.

(2) Residual interests generally include credit-enhancing interest-only strips, spread accounts, cash collateral accounts, retained subordinated interests (and other forms of overcollateralization), and similar assets that function as a credit enhancement.

(3) Residual interests further include those exposures that, in substance, cause the savings association to retain the credit risk of an asset or exposure that had qualified as a residual interest before it was sold.

Office of Thrift Supervision, Treasury § 567.1

(4) Residual interests generally do not include assets purchased from a third party. However, a credit-enhancing interest-only strip that is acquired in any asset transfer is a residual interest.

Risk participation. The term *risk participation* means a participation in which the originating party remains liable to the beneficiary for the full amount of an obligation (*e.g.*, a direct credit substitute), notwithstanding that another party has acquired a participation in that obligation.

Risk-weighted assets. The term *risk-weighted assets* means the sum total of risk-weighted on-balance sheet assets and the total of risk-weighted off-balance sheet credit equivalent amounts. These assets are calculated in accordance with § 567.6 of this part.

Securitization. The term *securitization* means the pooling and repackaging by a special purpose entity of assets or other credit exposures that can be sold to investors. *Securitization* includes transactions that create stratified credit risk positions whose performance is dependent upon an underlying pool of credit exposures, including loans and commitments.

Servicer cash advance. The term *servicer cash advance* means funds that a residential mortgage servicer advances to ensure an uninterrupted flow of payments, including advances made to cover foreclosure costs or other expenses to facilitate the timely collection of the loan. A servicer cash advance is not a recourse obligation or a direct credit substitute if:

(1) The servicer is entitled to full reimbursement and this right is not subordinated to other claims on the cash flows from the underlying asset pool; or

(2) For any one loan, the servicer's obligation to make nonreimbursable advances is contractually limited to an insignificant amount of the outstanding principal amount on that loan.

State. The term *State* means any one of the several states of the United States of America, the District of Columbia, Puerto Rico, and the territories and possessions of the United States.

Structured financing program. The term *structured financing program* means a program where receivable interests and asset-or mortgage-backed securities issued by multiple participants are purchased by a special purpose entity that repackages those exposures into securities that can be sold to investors. Structured financing programs allocate credit risk, generally, between the participants and credit enhancement provided to the program.

Subsidiary. The term *subsidiary* means any corporation, partnership, business trust, joint venture, association or similar organization in which a savings association directly or indirectly holds an ownership interest and the assets of which are consolidated with those of the savings association for purposes of reporting under Generally Accepted Accounting Principles (GAAP). Generally, these are majority-owned subsidiaries.[1] This definition does not include ownership interests that were taken in satisfaction of debts previously contracted, provided that the reporting association has not held the interest for more than five years or a longer period approved by the OTS.

Supervisory goodwill. The term *supervisory goodwill* means goodwill[2] resulting from the acquisition, merger, consolidation, purchase of assets, or other business combination (if such transaction occurred on or before April 12, 1989) of

(1) A savings association where the fair market value of assets was less than the fair market value of liabilities at the acquisition date; or

(2) A problem institution.

Tier 1 capital. The term *Tier 1 capital* means core capital as computed in accordance with § 567.5(a) of this part.

---

[1] The OTS reserves the right to review a savings association's investment in a subsidiary on a case-by-case basis. If the OTS determines that such investment is more appropriately treated as an equity security or an ownership interest in a subsidiary, it will make such determination regardless of the percentage of ownership held by the savings association.

[2] Goodwill that has been written off of an association's balance sheet for its GAAP financial statements or Thrift Financial Report cannot be counted as supervisory goodwill.

§ 567.2

Tier 2 capital. The term *Tier 2 capital* means supplementary capital as computed in accordance with § 567.5 of this part.

Total assets. The term *total assets* means total assets as would be required to be reported for consolidated entities on period-end reports filed with the Office in accordance with generally accepted accounting principles.

Traded position. The term *traded position* means a position retained, assumed, or issued in connection with a securitization that is rated by a NRSRO, where there is a reasonable expectation that, in the near future, the rating will be relied upon by:

(1) Unaffiliated investors to purchase the security; or

(2) An unaffiliated third party to enter into a transaction involving the position, such as a purchase, loan, or repurchase agreement.

Unconditionally cancelable. The term *unconditionally cancelable* means, with respect to a commitment-type lending arrangement, that the savings association may, at any time, with or without cause, refuse to advance funds or extend credit under the facility. In the case of home equity lines of credit, the savings association is deemed able to unconditionally cancel the commitment if it can, at its option, prohibit additional extensions of credit, reduce the line, and terminate the commitment to the full extent permitted by relevant Federal law.

United States Government or its agencies. The term *United States Government or its agencies* means an instrumentality of the U.S. Government whose debt obligations are fully and explicitly guaranteed as to the timely payment of principal and interest by the full faith and credit of the United States Government.

United States Government-sponsored agency or corporation. The term *United States Government-sponsored agency or corporation* means an agency or corporation originally established or chartered to serve public purposes specified by the United States Congress but whose obligations are not explicitly guaranteed by the full faith and credit of the United States Government.

[54 FR 49649, Nov. 30, 1989]

EDITORIAL NOTE: For FEDERAL REGISTER citations affecting § 567.1, see the List of CFR Sections Affected, which appears in the Finding Aids section of the printed volume and at *www.fdsys.gov*.

§ 567.2 Minimum regulatory capital requirement.

(a) To meet its regulatory capital requirement a savings association must satisfy each of the following capital standards:

(1) *Risk-based capital requirement.* (i) A savings association's minimum risk-based capital requirement shall be an amount equal to 8% of its risk-weighted assets as measured under § 567.6 of this part.

(ii) A savings association may not use supplementary capital to satisfy this requirement in an amount greater than 100% of its core capital as defined in § 567.5 of this part.

(2) *Leverage ratio requirement.* (i) A savings association's minimum leverage ratio requirement shall be the amount set forth in § 567.8 of this part.

(ii) A savings association must satisfy this requirement with core capital as defined in § 567.5(a) of this part.

(3) *Tangible capital requirement.* (i) A savings association's minimum tangible capital requirement shall be the amount set forth in § 567.9 of this part.

(ii) A savings association must satisfy this requirement with tangible capital as defined in § 567.9 of this part in an amount not less than 1.5% of its adjusted total assets.

(b) [Reserved]

(c) Savings associations are expected to maintain compliance with all of these standards at all times.

[54 FR 49649, Nov. 30, 1989, as amended at 57 FR 33440, July 29, 1992; 58 FR 45813, Aug. 31, 1993; 62 FR 66263, Dec. 18, 1997; 64 FR 10201, Mar 2, 1999; 66 FR 59663, Nov. 29, 2001]

§ 567.3 Individual minimum capital requirements.

(a) *Purpose and scope.* The rules and procedures specified in this section apply to the establishment of an individual minimum capital requirement for a savings association that varies from the risk-based capital requirement, the leverage ratio requirement or the tangible capital requirement that would otherwise apply to the savings association under this part.

Office of Thrift Supervision, Treasury § 567.3

(b) *Appropriate considerations for establishing individual minimum capital requirements.* Minimum capital levels higher than the risk-based capital requirement, the leverage ratio requirement or the tangible capital requirement required under this part may be appropriate for individual savings associations. Increased individual minimum capital requirements may be established upon a determination that the savings association's capital is or may become inadequate in view of its circumstances. For example, higher capital levels may be appropriate for:

(1) A savings association receiving special supervisory attention;

(2) A savings association that has or is expected to have losses resulting in capital inadequacy;

(3) A savings association that has a high degree of exposure to interest rate risk, prepayment risk, credit risk, concentration of credit risk, certain risks arising from nontraditional activities, or similar risks; or a high proportion of off-balance sheet risk, especially standby letters of credit;

(4) A savings association that has poor liquidity or cash flow;

(5) A savings association growing, either internally or through acquisitions, at such a rate that supervisory problems are presented that are not dealt with adequately by other Office regulations or other guidance;

(6) A savings association that may be adversely affected by the activities or condition of its holding company, affiliate(s), subsidiaries, or other persons or savings associations with which it has significant business relationships, including concentrations of credit;

(7) A savings association with a portfolio reflecting weak credit quality or a significant likelihood of financial loss, or that has loans in nonperforming status or on which borrowers fail to comply with repayment terms;

(8) A savings association that has inadequate underwriting policies, standards, or procedures for its loans and investments; or

(9) A savings association that has a record of operational losses that exceeds the average of other, similarly situated savings associations; has management deficiencies, including failure to adequately monitor and control financial and operating risks, particularly the risks presented by concentrations of credit and nontraditional activities; or has a poor record of supervisory compliance.

(c) *Standards for determination of appropriate individual minimum capital requirements.* The appropriate minimum capital level for an individual savings association cannot be determined solely through the application of a rigid mathematical formula or wholly objective criteria. The decision is necessarily based, in part, on subjective judgment grounded in agency expertise. The factors to be considered in the determination will vary in each case and may include, for example:

(1) The conditions or circumstances leading to the determination that a higher minimum capital requirement is appropriate or necessary for the savings association;

(2) The exigency of those circumstances or potential problems;

(3) The overall condition, management strength, and future prospects of the savings association and, if applicable, its holding company, subsidiaries, and affiliates;

(4) The savings association's liquidity, capital and other indicators of financial stability, particularly as compared with those of similarly situated savings associations; and

(5) The policies and practices of the savings association's directors, officers, and senior management as well as the internal control and internal audit systems for implementation of such adopted policies and practices.

(d) *Procedures*—(1) *Notification.* When the OTS determines that a minimum capital requirement is necessary or appropriate for a particular savings association, it shall notify the savings association in writing of its proposed individual minimum capital requirement; the schedule for compliance with the new requirement; and the specific causes for determining that the higher individual minimum capital requirement is necessary or appropriate for the savings association. The OTS shall forward the notifying letter to the appropriate state supervisor if a state-chartered savings association would be subject to an individual minimum capital requirement.

337

§ 567.4

(2) *Response.* (i) The response shall include any information that the savings association wants the OTS to consider in deciding whether to establish or to amend an individual minimum capital requirement for the savings association, what the individual capital requirement should be, and, if applicable, what compliance schedule is appropriate for achieving the required capital level. The responses of the savings association and appropriate state supervisor must be in writing and must be delivered to the OTS within 30 days after the date on which the notification was received. Such response must be filed in accordance with §§ 516.30 and 516.40 of this chapter. The OTS may extend the time period for good cause. The time period for response by the insured savings association may be shortened for good cause:

(A) When, in the opinion of the OTS, the condition of the savings association so requires, and the OTS informs the savings association of the shortened response period in the notice;

(B) With the consent of the savings association; or

(C) When the savings association already has advised the OTS that it cannot or will not achieve its applicable minimum capital requirement.

(ii) Failure to respond within 30 days, or such other time period as may be specified by the OTS, may constitute a waiver of any objections to the proposed individual minimum capital requirement or to the schedule for complying with it, unless the OTS has provided an extension of the response period for good cause.

(3) *Decision.* After expiration of the response period, the OTS shall decide whether or not he believes the proposed individual minimum capital requirement should be established for the savings association, or whether that proposed requirement should be adopted in modified form, based on a review of the savings association's response and other relevant information. The OTS's decision shall address comments received within the response period from the savings association and the appropriate state supervisor (if a state-chartered savings association is involved) and shall state the level of capital required, the schedule for compliance with this requirement, and any specific remedial action the savings association could take to eliminate the need for continued applicability of the individual minimum capital requirement. The OTS shall provide the savings association and the appropriate state supervisor (if a state-chartered savings association is involved) with a written decision on the individual minimum capital requirement, addressing the substantive comments made by the savings association and setting forth the decision and the basis for that decision. Upon receipt of this decision by the savings association, the individual minimum capital requirement becomes effective and binding upon the savings association. This decision represents final agency action.

(4) *Failure to comply.* Failure to satisfy an individual minimum capital requirement, or to meet any required incremental additions to capital under a schedule for compliance with such an individual minimum capital requirement, shall constitute a legal basis for issuing a capital directive pursuant to § 567.4 of this part.

(5) *Change in circumstances.* If, after a decision is made under paragraph (d)(3) of this section, there is a change in the circumstances affecting the savings association's capital adequacy or its ability to reach its required minimum capital level by the specified date, OTS may amend the individual minimum capital requirement or the savings association's schedule for such compliance. The OTS may decline to consider a savings association's request for such changes that are not based on a significant change in circumstances or that are repetitive or frivolous. Pending the OTS's reexamination of the original decision, that original decision and any compliance schedule established thereunder shall continue in full force and effect.

[54 FR 49649, Nov. 30, 1989, as amended at 55 FR 13516, Apr. 11, 1990; 57 FR 14335, 14348, Apr. 20, 1992; 59 FR 64564, Dec. 15, 1994; 60 FR 66719, Dec. 26, 1995; 66 FR 13009, Mar. 2, 2001; 72 FR 69438, Apr. 1, 2007]

§ 567.4 Capital directives.

(a) *Issuance of a Capital Directive*—(1) *Purpose.* In addition to any other action authorized by law, the Office, may

Office of Thrift Supervision, Treasury § 567.4

issue a capital directive to a savings association that does not have an amount of capital satisfying its minimum capital requirement. Issuance of such a capital directive may be based on a savings association's noncompliance with the risk-based capital requirement, the leverage ratio requirement, the tangible capital requirement, or individual minimum capital requirement established under this part, by a written agreement under 12 U.S.C. 1464(s), or as a condition for approval of an application. A capital directive may order a savings association to:

(i) Achieve its minimum capital requirement by a specified date;

(ii) Adhere to the compliance schedule for achieving its individual minimum capital requirement;

(iii) Submit and adhere to a capital plan acceptable to the Office describing the means and a time schedule by which the savings association shall reach its required capital level;

(iv) Take other action, including but not limited to, reducing the savings association's assets or its rate of liability growth, or imposing restrictions on the savings association's payment of dividends, in order to cause the savings association to reach its required capital level;

(v) Take any action authorized under § 567.10(e); or

(vi) Take a combination of any of these actions.

A capital directive issued under this section, including a plan submitted pursuant to a capital directive, is enforceable under 12 U.S.C. 1818 in the same manner and to the same extent as an effective and outstanding cease and desist order which has become final under 12 U.S.C. 1818.

(2) *Notice of intent to issue capital directive.* The OTS will determine whether to initiate the process of issuing a capital directive. The OTS will notify a savings association in writing by registered mail of its intention to issue a capital directive. If a state-chartered savings association is involved, the OTS will also notify and solicit comment from the appropriate state supervisor. The notice will state:

(i) The reasons for issuance of the capital directive and

(ii) The proposed contents of the capital directive.

(3) *Response to notice of intent.* (i) A savings association may respond to the notice of intent by submitting its own compliance plan, or may propose an alternative plan. The response should also include any information that the savings association wishes the OTS to consider in deciding whether to issue a capital directive. The appropriate state supervisor may also submit a response. These responses must be in writing and be delivered within 30 days after the receipt of the notices. Such responses must be filed in accordance with §§ 516.30 and 516.40 of this chapter. In its discretion, the Office may extend the time period for the response for good cause. The Office may, for good cause, shorten the 30-day time period for response by the insured savings assocation:

(A) When, in the opinion of the Office, the condition of the savings association so requires, and the Office informs the savings association of the shortened response period in the notice;

(B) With the consent of the savings association; or

(C) When the savings association already has advised the Office that it cannot or will not achieve its applicable minimum capital requirement.

(ii) Failure to respond within 30 days of receipt, or such other time period as may be specified by the Office, may constitute a waiver of any objections to the capital directive unless the Office grants an extension of the time period for good cause.

(4) *Decision.* After the closing date of the savings association's response period, or upon receipt of the savings association's response, if earlier, the Office shall consider the savings association's response and may seek additional information or clarification of the response. Thereafter, the Office will determine whether or not to issue a capital directive and, if one is to be issued, whether it should be as originally proposed or in modified form.

(5) *Service and effectiveness.* (i) Upon issuance, a capital directive will be served upon the savings association. It will include or be accompanied by a statement of reasons for its issuance

§ 567.5

and shall address the responses received during the response period.

(ii) A capital directive shall become effective upon the expiration of 30 days after service upon the savings association, unless the Office determines that a shorter effective period is necessary either on account of the public interest or in order to achieve the capital directive's purpose. If the savings association has consented to issuance of the capital directive, it may become effective immediately. A capital directive shall remain in effect and enforceable unless, and then only to the extent that, it is stayed, modified, or terminated by the Office.

(6) *Change in circumstances.* Upon a change in circumstances, a savings association may submit a request to the OTS to reconsider the terms of the capital directive or consider changes in the savings association's capital plan issued under a directive for the savings association to achieve its minimum capital requirement. If the OTS believes such a change is warranted, the OTS may modify the savings association's capital requirement or may refuse to make such modification if it determines that there are not significant changes in circumstances. Pending a decision on reconsideration, the capital directive and capital plan shall continue in full force and effect.

(b) *Relation to other administrative actions.* The Office—

(1) May consider a savings association's progress in adhering to any capital plan required under this section whenever such savings association or any affiliate of such savings association (including any company which controls such savings association) seeks approval for any proposal that would have the effect of diverting earnings, diminishing capital, or otherwise impeding such savings association's progress in meeting its minimum capital requirement; and

(2) May disapprove any proposal referred to in paragraph (b)(1) of this section if the Office determines that the proposal would adversely affect the ability of the savings association on a current or pro forma basis to satisfy its capital requirement.

[54 FR 49649, Nov. 30, 1989, as amended at 55 FR 13517, Apr. 11, 1990; 57 FR 14335, Apr. 20, 1992; 57 FR 33440, July 29, 1992; 60 FR 66719, Dec. 26, 1995; 66 FR 13009, Mar. 2, 2001; 72 FR 69439, Dec. 7, 2007]

§ 567.5 Components of capital.

(a) *Core Capital.* (1) The following elements,[3] less the amount of any deductions pursuant to paragraph (a)(2) of this section, comprise a savings association's core capital:

(i) Common stockholders' equity (including retained earnings);

(ii) Noncumulative perpetual preferred stock and related surplus;[4]

(iii) Minority interests in the equity accounts of the subsidiaries that are fully consolidated.

(iv) Nonwithdrawable accounts and pledged deposits of mutual savings associations (excluding any treasury shares held by the savings association) meeting the criteria of regulations and memoranda of the Office to the extent that such accounts or deposits have no fixed maturity date, cannot be withdrawn at the option of the accountholder, and do not earn interest that carries over to subsequent periods;

(v) The remaining goodwill (FSLIC Capital Contributions) resulting from prior regulatory accounting practices as provided in paragraph (1) of the definition for *qualifying supervisory goodwill* in § 567.1 of this part.

(2) *Deductions from core capital.* (i) Intangible assets, as defined in § 567.1 of this part, are deducted from assets and

---

[3] Stock issues where the dividend is reset periodically based on current market conditions and the savings associations's current credit rating, including but not limited to, auction rate, money market or remarketable preferred stock, are assigned to supplementary capital, regardless of cumulative or noncumulative characteristics.

[4] Stock issued by subsidiaries that may not be counted by the parent savings association on the Thrift Financial Report, likewise shall not be considered in calculating capital. For example, preferred stock issued by a savings association or a subsidiary that is, in effect, collateralized by assets of the savings association or one of its subsidiaries shall not be included in capital. Similarly, common stock with mandatorily redeemable provisions is not includable in core capital.

Office of Thrift Supervision, Treasury § 567.5

capital in computing core capital, except as otherwise provided by § 567.12 of this part.

(ii) Servicing assets that are not includable in core capital pursuant to § 567.12 of this part are deducted from assets and capital in computing core capital.

(iii) Credit-enhancing interest-only strips that are not includable in core capital under § 567.12 of this part are deducted from assets and capital in computing core capital.

(iv) Investments, both equity and debt, in subsidiaries that are not includable subsidiaries (including those subsidiaries where the savings association has a minority ownership interest) are deducted from assets and, thus core capital except as provided in paragraphs (a)(2)(v) and (a)(2)(vi) of this section.

(v) If a savings association has any investments (both debt and equity) in one or more subsidiaries engaged as of April 12, 1989 and continuing to be engaged in any activity that would not fall within the scope of activities in which includable subsidiaries may engage, it must deduct such investments from assets and, thus, core capital in accordance with this paragraph (a)(2)(v). The savings association must first deduct from assets and, thus, core capital the amount by which any investments in such subsidiary(ies) exceed the amount of such investments held by the savings association as of April 12, 1989. Next the savings association must deduct from assets and, thus, core capital the lesser of:

(A) The savings association's investments in and extensions of credit to the subsidiary as of April 12, 1989; or

(B) The savings association's investments in and extensions of credit to the subsidiary on the date as of which the savings association's capital is being determined.

(vi) If a savings association holds a subsidiary (either directly or through a subsidiary) that is itself a domestic depository institution, the Office may, in its sole discretion upon determining that the amount of core capital that would be required would be higher if the assets and liabilities of such subsidiary were consolidated with those of the parent savings association than the amount that would be required if the parent savings association's investment were deducted pursuant to paragraphs (a)(2)(iv) and (a)(2)(v) of this section, consolidate the assets and liabilities of that subsidiary with those of the parent savings association in calculating the capital adequacy of the parent savings association, regardless of whether the subsidiary would otherwise be an includable subsidiary as defined in § 567.1 of this part.

(vii) Deferred tax assets that are not includable in core capital pursuant to § 567.12 of this part are deducted from assets and capital in computing core capital.

(b) *Supplementary Capital.* Supplementary capital counts towards a savings association's total capital up to a maximum of 100% of the savings association's core capital. The following elements comprise a savings association's supplementary capital:

(1) *Permanent Capital Instruments.* (i) Cumulative perpetual preferred stock and other perpetual preferred stock[5] issued pursuant to regulations and memoranda of the Office;

(ii) Mutual capital certificates issued pursuant to regulations and memoranda of the Office;

(iii) Nonwithdrawable accounts and pledged deposits (excluding any treasury shares held by the savings association) meeting the criteria of 12 CFR 561.42 to the extent that such instruments are not included in core capital under paragraph (a) of this section;

(iv) Perpetual subordinated debt issued pursuant to regulations and memoranda of the Office; and

(v) Mandatory convertible subordinated debt (capital notes) issued pursuant to regulations and memoranda of the Office.

(2) *Maturing Capital Instruments.* (i) Subordinated debt issued pursuant to regulations and memoranda of the Office;

---

[5] Preferred stock issued by subsidiaries that may not be counted by the parent savings association on the Thrift Financial Report likewise may not be considered in calculating capital. Preferred stock issued by a savings association or a subsidiary that is, in effect, collateralized by assets of the savings association or one of its subsidiaries may not be included in capital.

§ 567.5

(ii) Intermediate-term preferred stock issued pursuant to regulations and memoranda of the Office and any related surplus:

(iii) Mandatory convertible subordinated debt (commitment notes) issued pursuant to regulations and memoranda of the Office; and

(iv) Mandatorily redeemable preferred stock that was issued before July 23, 1985 or issued pursuant to regulations and memoranda of the Office and approved in writing by the FSLIC for inclusion as regulatory capital before or after issuance.

(3) *Transition rules for maturing capital instruments*—(i) *Maturing capital instruments issued on or before November 7, 1989.* All maturing capital instruments issued on or before November 7, 1989, are includable in supplementary capital to the extent such instruments were includable in capital pursuant to the regulations of the OTS in effect as of that date, including any applicable amortization schedules. With the prior approval of the OTS, a savings association may include maturing capital instruments issued on or before November 7, 1989, in supplementary capital in accordance with the treatment set forth in paragraph (b)(3)(ii) of this section.

Years to maturity of outstanding subordinated debt	Percent included in supplementary capital
Greater than or equal to 7	100
Less than 7 but greater than or equal to 6	86
Less than 6 but greater than or equal to 5	71
Less than 5 but greater than or equal to 4	57
Less than 4 but greater than or equal to 3	43
Less than 3 but greater than or equal to 2	29
Less than 2 but greater than or equal to 1	14
Less than 1	0

(ii) *Maturing capital instruments issued after November 7, 1989.* A savings association issuing maturing capital instruments after November 7, 1989, may choose, subject to paragraph (b)(3)(ii)(C) of this section, to include such instruments pursuant to either paragraph (b)(3)(ii)(A) or (b)(3)(ii)(B) of this section.

(A) At the beginning of each of the last five years of the life of the maturing capital instrument, the amount that is eligible to be included as supplementary capital is reduced by 20%

12 CFR Ch. V (1-1-12 Edition)

of the original amount of that instrument (net of redemptions).[6]

(B) Only the aggregate amount of maturing capital instruments that mature in any one year during the seven years immediately prior to an instrument's maturity that does not exceed 20% of an institution's capital will qualify as supplementary capital.

(C) Once a savings association selects either paragraph (b)(3)(ii)(A) or (b)(3)(ii)(B) of this section for the issuance of a maturing capital instrument, it must continue to elect that option for all subsequent issuances of maturing capital instruments for as long as there is a balance outstanding of such post-November 7, 1989 issuances. Only when such issuances have all been repaid and the savings association has no balance of such issuances outstanding may the savings association elect the other option.

(4) *Allowance for loan and lease losses.* Allowance for loan and lease losses established under OTS regulations and memoranda to a maximum of 1.25 percent of risk-weighted assets.[7]

(5) *Unrealized gains on equity securities.* Up to 45 percent of unrealized gains on available-for-sale equity securities with readily determinable fair

---

[6] Capital instruments may be redeemed prior to maturity and without the prior approval of the Office, as long as the instruments are redeemed with the proceeds of, or replaced by, a like amount of a similar or higher quality capital instrument. However, the Office must be notified in writing at least 30 days in advance of such redemption.

[7] The amount of the allowance for loan and lease losses that may be included in capital is based on a percentage of risk-weighted assets. The gross sum of risk-weighted assets used in this calculation includes all risk-weighted assets, with the exception of assets required to be deducted under § 567.6 in establishing risk-weighted assets. "Excess reserves for loan and lease losses" is defined as assets required to be deducted from capital under § 567.5(a)(2). A savings association may deduct excess reserves for loan and lease losses from the gross sum of risk-weighted assets (i.e., risk-weighted assets including allowance for loan and lease losses) in computing the denominator of the risk-based capital standard. Thus, a savings association will exclude the same amount of excess allowance for loan and lease losses from both the numerator and the denominator of the risk-based capital ratio.

Office of Thrift Supervision, Treasury § 567.6

values may be included in supplementary capital. Unrealized gains are unrealized holding gains, net of unrealized holding losses, before income taxes, calculated as the amount, if any, by which fair value exceeds historical cost. The OTS may disallow such inclusion in the calculation of supplementary capital if the Office determines that the equity securities are not prudently valued.

(c) *Total capital.* (1) A savings association's total capital equals the sum of its core capital and supplementary capital (to the extent that such supplementary capital does not exceed 100% of its core capital).

(2) The following assets, in addition to assets required to be deducted elsewhere in calculating core capital, are deducted from assets for purposes of determining total capital:

(i) Reciprocal holdings of depository institution capital instruments; and

(ii) All equity investments.

[54 FR 49649, Nov. 30, 1989]

EDITORIAL NOTE: For FEDERAL REGISTER citations affecting § 567.5, see the List of CFR Sections Affected, which appears in the Finding Aids section of the printed volume and at *www.fdsys.gov.*

§ 567.6 Risk-based capital credit risk-weight categories.

(a) *Risk-weighted assets.* Risk-weighted assets equal risk-weighted on-balance sheet assets (computed under paragraph (a)(1) of this section), plus risk-weighted off-balance sheet activities (computed under paragraph (a)(2) of this section), plus risk-weighted recourse obligations, direct credit substitutes, and certain other positions (computed under paragraph (b) of this section). Assets not included (*i.e.,* deducted from capital) for purposes of calculating capital under § 567.5 are not included in calculating risk-weighted assets.

(1) *On-balance sheet assets.* Except as provided in paragraph (b) of this section, risk-weighted on-balance sheet assets are computed by multiplying the on-balance sheet asset amounts times the appropriate risk-weight categories. The risk-weight categories are:

(i) *Zero percent Risk Weight (Category 1).* (A) Cash, including domestic and foreign currency owned and held in all offices of a savings association or in transit. Any foreign currency held by a savings association must be converted into U.S. dollar equivalents;

(B) Securities issued by and other direct claims on the U.S. Government or its agencies (to the extent such securities or claims are unconditionally backed by the full faith and credit of the United States Government) or the central government of an OECD country;

(C) Notes and obligations issued by either the Federal Savings and Loan Insurance Corporation or the Federal Deposit Insurance Corporation and backed by the full faith and credit of the United States Government;

(D) Deposit reserves at, claims on, and balances due from Federal Reserve Banks;

(E) The book value of paid-in Federal Reserve Bank stock;

(F) That portion of assets that is fully covered against capital loss and/or yield maintenance agreements by the Federal Savings and Loan Insurance Corporation or any successor agency.

(G) That portion of assets directly and unconditionally guaranteed by the United States Government or its agencies, or the central government of an OECD country.

(H) Claims on, and claims guaranteed by, a qualifying securities firm that are collateralized by cash on deposit in the savings association or by securities issued or guaranteed by the United States Government or its agencies, or the central government of an OECD country. To be eligible for this risk weight, the savings association must maintain a positive margin of collateral on the claim on a daily basis, taking into account any change in a savings association's exposure to the obligor or counterparty under the claim in relation to the market value of the collateral held in support of the claim.

(ii) *20 percent Risk Weight (Category 2).* (A) Cash items in the process of collection;

(B) That portion of assets collateralized by the current market value of securities issued or guaranteed by the United States government or its agencies, or the central government of an OECD country;

(C) That portion of assets conditionally guaranteed by the United States Government or its agencies, or the central government of an OECD country;

(D) Securities (not including equity securities) issued by and other claims on the U.S. Government or its agencies which are not backed by the full faith and credit of the United States Government;

(E) Securities (not including equity securities) issued by, or other direct claims on, United States Government-sponsored agencies;

(F) That portion of assets guaranteed by United States Government-sponsored agencies;

(G) That portion of assets collateralized by the current market value of securities issued or guaranteed by United States Government-sponsored agencies;

(H) Claims on, and claims guaranteed by, a qualifying securities firm, subject to the following conditions:

(*1*) A qualifying securities firm must have a long-term issuer credit rating, or a rating on at least one issue of long-term unsecured debt, from a NRSRO. The rating must be in one of the three highest investment grade categories used by the NRSRO. If two or more NRSROs assign ratings to the qualifying securities firm, the savings association must use the lowest rating to determine whether the rating requirement of this paragraph is met. A qualifying securities firm may rely on the rating of its parent consolidated company, if the parent consolidated company guarantees the claim.

(*2*) A collateralized claim on a qualifying securities firm does not have to comply with the rating requirements under paragraph (a)(1)(ii)(H)(*1*) of this section if the claim arises under a contract that:

(*i*) Is a reverse repurchase/repurchase agreement or securities lending/borrowing transaction executed using standard industry documentation;

(*ii*) Is collateralized by debt or equity securities that are liquid and readily marketable;

(*iii*) Is marked-to-market daily;

(*iv*) Is subject to a daily margin maintenance requirement under the standard industry documentation; and

(*v*) Can be liquidated, terminated or accelerated immediately in bankruptcy or similar proceeding, and the security or collateral agreement will not be stayed or avoided under applicable law of the relevant jurisdiction. For example, a claim is exempt from the automatic stay in bankruptcy in the United States if it arises under a securities contract or a repurchase agreement subject to section 555 or 559 of the Bankruptcy Code (11 U.S.C. 555 or 559), a qualified financial contract under section 11(e)(8) of the Federal Deposit Insurance Act (12 U.S.C. 1821(e)(8)), or a netting contract between or among financial institutions under sections 401–407 of the Federal Deposit Insurance Corporation Improvement Act of 1991 (12 U.S.C. 4401–4407), or Regulation EE (12 CFR part 231).

(*3*) If the securities firm uses the claim to satisfy its applicable capital requirements, the claim is not eligible for a risk weight under this paragraph (a)(1)(ii)(H);

(I) Claims representing general obligations of any public-sector entity in an OECD country, and that portion of any claims guaranteed by any such public-sector entity;

(J) Bonds issued by the Financing Corporation or the Resolution Funding Corporation;

(K) Balances due from and all claims on domestic depository institutions. This includes demand deposits and other transaction accounts, savings deposits and time certificates of deposit, federal funds sold, loans to other depository institutions, including overdrafts and term federal funds, holdings of the savings association's own discounted acceptances for which the account party is a depository institution, holdings of bankers acceptances of other institutions and securities issued by depository institutions, except those that qualify as capital;

(L) The book value of paid-in Federal Home Loan Bank stock;

(M) Deposit reserves at, claims on and balances due from the Federal Home Loan Banks;

(N) Assets collateralized by cash held in a segregated deposit account by the reporting savings association;

(O) Claims on, or guaranteed by, official multilateral lending institutions

Office of Thrift Supervision, Treasury § 567.6

or regional development institutions in which the United States Government is a shareholder or contributing member;[8]

(P) That portion of assets collateralized by the current market value of securities issued by official multilateral lending institutions or regional development institutions in which the United States Government is a shareholder or contributing member.

(Q) All claims on depository institutions incorporated in an OECD country, and all assets backed by the full faith and credit of depository institutions incorporated in an OECD country. This includes the credit equivalent amount of participations in commitments and standby letters of credit sold to other depository institutions incorporated in an OECD country, but only if the originating bank remains liable to the customer or beneficiary for the full amount of the commitment or standby letter of credit. Also included in this category are the credit equivalent amounts of risk participations in bankers' acceptances conveyed to other depository institutions incorporated in an OECD country. However, bank-issued securities that qualify as capital of the issuing bank are not included in this risk category;

(R) Claims on, or guaranteed by depository institutions other than the central bank, incorporated in a non-OECD country, with a remaining maturity of one year or less;

(S) That portion of local currency claims conditionally guaranteed by central governments of non-OECD countries, to the extent the savings association has local currency liabilities in that country.

(iii) *50 percent Risk Weight (Category 3)*. (A) Revenue bonds issued by any public-sector entity in an OECD country for which the underlying obligor is a public- sector entity, but which are repayable solely from the revenues generated from the project financed through the issuance of the obligations;

(B) Qualifying mortgage loans and qualifying multifamily mortgage loans;

(C) Privately-issued mortgage-backed securities (*i.e.*, those that do not carry the guarantee of a government or government sponsored entity) representing an interest in qualifying mortgage loans or qualifying multifamily mortgage loans. If the security is backed by qualifying multifamily mortgage loans, the savings association must receive timely payments of principal and interest in accordance with the terms of the security. Payments will generally be considered timely if they are not 30 days past due;

(D) Qualifying residential construction loans as defined in § 567.1 of this part.

(iv) *100 percent Risk Weight (Category 4)*. All assets not specified above or deducted from calculations of capital pursuant to § 567.5 of this part, including, but not limited to:

(A) Consumer loans;

(B) Commercial loans;

(C) Home equity loans;

(D) Non-qualifying mortgage loans;

(E) Non-qualifying multifamily mortgage loans;

(F) Residential construction loans;

(G) Land loans;

(H) Nonresidential construction loans;

(I) Obligations issued by any state or any political subdivision thereof for the benefit of a private party or enterprise where that party or enterprise, rather than the issuing state or political subdivision, is responsible for the timely payment of principal and interest on the obligations, *e.g.*, industrial development bonds;

(J) Debt securities not otherwise described in this section;

(K) Investments in fixed assets and premises;

(L) Certain nonsecurity financial instruments including servicing assets and intangible assets includable in core capital under § 567.12 of this part;

(M) Interest-only strips receivable, other than credit-enhancing interest-only strips;

(N)–(O) [Reserved]

---

[8] These institutions include, but are not limited to, the International Bank for Reconstruction and Development (World Bank), the Inter-American Development Bank, the Asian Development Bank, the African Development Bank, the European Investments Bank, the International Monetary Fund and the Bank for International Settlements.

§ 567.6

(P) That portion of equity investments not deducted pursuant to § 567.5 of this part;

(Q) The prorated assets of subsidiaries (except for the assets of includable, fully consolidated subsidiaries) to the extent such assets are included in adjusted total assets;

(R) All repossessed assets or assets that are more than 90 days past due; and

(S) Equity investments that the Office determines have the same risk characteristics as foreclosed real estate by the savings association;

(T) Equity investments permissible for a national bank.

(v) [Reserved]

(vi) *Indirect ownership interests in pools of assets.* Assets representing an indirect holding of a pool of assets, e.g., mutual funds, are assigned to risk-weight categories under this section based upon the risk weight that would be assigned to the assets in the portfolio of the pool. An investment in shares of a mutual fund whose portfolio consists primarily of various securities or money market instruments that, if held separately, would be assigned to different risk-weight categories, generally is assigned to the risk-weight category appropriate to the highest risk-weighted asset that the fund is permitted to hold in accordance with the investment objectives set forth in its prospectus. The savings association may, at its option, assign the investment on a pro rata basis to different risk-weight categories according to the investment limits in its prospectus. In no case will an investment in shares in any such fund be assigned to a total risk weight less than 20 percent. If the savings association chooses to assign investments on a pro rata basis, and the sum of the investment limits of assets in the fund's prospectus exceeds 100 percent, the savings association must assign the highest pro rata amounts of its total investment to the higher risk categories. If, in order to maintain a necessary degree of short-term liquidity, a fund is permitted to hold an insignificant amount of its assets in short-term, highly liquid securities of superior credit quality that do not qualify for a preferential risk weight, such securities will generally be disregarded in determining the risk-weight category into which the savings association's holding in the overall fund should be assigned. The prudent use of hedging instruments by a mutual fund to reduce the risk of its assets will not increase the risk weighting of the mutual fund investment. For example, the use of hedging instruments by a mutual fund to reduce the interest rate risk of its government bond portfolio will not increase the risk weight of that fund above the 20 percent category. Nonetheless, if the fund engages in any activities that appear speculative in nature or has any other characteristics that are inconsistent with the preferential risk-weighting assigned to the fund's assets, holdings in the fund will be assigned to the 100 percent risk-weight category.

(2) *Off-balance sheet items.* Except as provided in paragraph (b) of this section, risk-weighted off-balance sheet items are determined by the following two-step process. First, the face amount of the off-balance sheet item must be multiplied by the appropriate credit conversion factor listed in this paragraph (a)(2). This calculation translates the face amount of an off-balance sheet exposure into an on-balance sheet credit-equivalent amount. Second, the credit-equivalent amount must be assigned to the appropriate risk-weight category using the criteria regarding obligors, guarantors, and collateral listed in paragraph (a)(1) of this section, *provided* that the maximum risk weight assigned to the credit-equivalent amount of an interest-rate or exchange-rate contract is 50 percent. The following are the credit conversion factors and the off-balance sheet items to which they apply.

(i) *100 percent credit conversion factor (Group A).*

(A) [Reserved]

(B) Risk participations purchased in bankers' acceptances;

(C) [Reserved]

(D) Forward agreements and other contingent obligations with a certain draw down, e.g., legally binding agreements to purchase assets at a specified future date. On the date an institution enters into a forward agreement or similar obligation, it should convert

Office of Thrift Supervision, Treasury § 567.6

the principal amount of the assets to be purchased at 100 percent as of that date and then assign this amount to the risk-weight category appropriate to the obligor or guarantor of the item, or the nature of the collateral;

(E) Indemnification of customers whose securities the savings association has lent as agent. If the customer is not indemnified against loss by the savings association, the transaction is excluded from the risk-based capital calculation. When a savings association lends its own securities, the transaction is treated as a loan. When a savings association lends its own securities or is acting as agent, agrees to indemnify a customer, the transaction is assigned to the risk weight appropriate to the obligor or collateral that is delivered to the lending or indemnifying institution or to an independent custodian acting on their behalf.

(ii) *50 percent credit conversion factor (Group B).* (A) Transaction-related contingencies, including, among other things, performance bonds and performance-based standby letters of credit related to a particular transaction;

(B) Unused portions of commitments (including home equity lines of credit and eligible ABCP liquidity facilities) with an original maturity exceeding one year except those listed in paragraph (a)(2)(v) of this section. For eligible ABCP liquidity facilities, the resulting credit equivalent amount is assigned to the risk category appropriate to the assets to be funded by the liquidity facility based on the assets or the obligor, after considering any collateral or guarantees, or external credit ratings under paragraph (b)(3) of this section, if applicable; and

(C) Revolving underwriting facilities, note issuance facilities, and similar arrangements pursuant to which the savings association's customer can issue short-term debt obligations in its own name, but for which the savings association has a legally binding commitment to either:

(*1*) Purchase the obligations the customer is unable to sell by a stated date; or

(*2*) Advance funds to its customer, if the obligations cannot be sold.

(iii) *20 percent credit conversion factor (Group C).* Trade-related contingencies, *i.e.,* short-term, self-liquidating instruments used to finance the movement of goods and collateralized by the underlying shipment. A commercial letter of credit is an example of such an instrument.

(iv) *10 percent credit conversion factor (Group D).* Unused portions of eligible ABCP liquidity facilities with an original maturity of one year or less. The resulting credit equivalent amount is assigned to the risk category appropriate to the assets to be funded by the liquidity facility based on the assets or the obligor, after considering any collateral or guarantees, or external credit ratings under paragraph (b)(3) of this section, if applicable;

(v) *Zero percent credit conversion factor (Group E).* (A) Unused portions of commitments with an original maturity of one year or less, except for eligible ABCP liquidity facilities;

(B) Unused commitments with an original maturity greater than one year, if they are unconditionally cancelable at any time at the option of the savings association and the savings association has the contractual right to make, and in fact does make, either:

(*1*) A separate credit decision based upon the borrower's current financial condition before each drawing under the lending facility; or

(*2*) An annual (or more frequent) credit review based upon the borrower's current financial condition to determine whether or not the lending facility should be continued; and

(C) The unused portion of retail credit card lines or other related plans that are unconditionally cancelable by the savings association in accordance with applicable law.

(vi) *Off-balance sheet contracts; interest-rate and foreign exchange rate contracts (Group F)*—(A) *Calculation of credit equivalent amounts.* The credit equivalent amount of an off-balance sheet interest rate or foreign exchange rate contract that is not subject to a qualifying bilateral netting contract in accordance with paragraph (a)(2)(vi)(B) of this section is equal to the sum of the current credit exposure, *i.e.,* the replacement cost of the contract, and the potential future credit exposure of the off-balance sheet rate contract. The calculation of credit equivalent

347

amounts is measured in U.S. dollars, regardless of the currency or currencies specified in the off-balance sheet rate contract.

(*1*) *Current credit exposure.* The current credit exposure of an off-balance sheet rate contract is determined by the mark-to-market value of the contract. If the mark-to-market value is positive, then the current credit exposure equals that mark-to-market value. If the mark-to-market value is zero or negative, then the current exposure is zero. In determining its current credit exposure for multiple off-balance sheet rate contracts executed with a single counterparty, a savings association may net positive and negative mark-to-market values of off-balance sheet rate contracts if subject to a bilateral netting contract as provided in paragraph (a)(2)(vi)(B) of this section.

(*2*) *Potential future credit exposure.* The potential future credit exposure of an off-balance sheet rate contract, including a contract with a negative mark-to-market value, is estimated by multiplying the notional principal[9] by a credit conversion factor. Savings associations, subject to examiner review, should use the effective rather than the apparent or stated notional amount in this calculation. The conversion factors are:[10]

Remaining maturity	Interest rate contracts (percents)	Foreign exchange rate contracts (percents)
One year or less	0.0	1.0
Over one year	0.5	5.0

(B) *Off-balance sheet rate contracts subject to bilateral netting contracts.* In determining its current credit exposure for multiple off-balance sheet rate contracts executed with a single counterparty, a savings association may net off-balance sheet rate contracts subject to a bilateral netting contract by offsetting positive and negative mark-to-market values, provided that:

(*1*) The bilateral netting contract is in writing;

(*2*) The bilateral netting contract creates a single legal obligation for all individual off-balance sheet rate contracts covered by the bilateral netting contract. In effect, the bilateral netting contract provides that the savings association has a single claim or obligation either to receive or pay only the net amount of the sum of the positive and negative mark-to-market values on the individual off-balance sheet rate contracts covered by the bilateral netting contract. The single legal obligation for the net amount is operative in the event that a counterparty, or a counterparty to whom the bilateral netting contract has been validly assigned, fails to perform due to any of the following events: default, insolvency, bankruptcy, or other similar circumstances;

(*3*) The savings association obtains a written and reasoned legal opinion(s) representing, with a high degree of certainty, that in the event of a legal challenge, including one resulting from default, insolvency, bankruptcy or similar circumstances, the relevant court and administrative authorities would find the savings association's exposure to be the net amount under:

(*i*) The law of the jurisdiction in which the counterparty is chartered or the equivalent location in the case of noncorporate entities, and if a branch of the counterparty is involved, then also under the law of the jurisdiction in which the branch is located;

(*ii*) The law that governs the individual off-balance sheet rate contracts covered by the bilateral netting contract; and

(*iii*) The law that governs the bilateral netting contract;

(*4*) The savings association establishes and maintains procedures to monitor possible changes in relevant law and to ensure that the bilateral netting contract continues to satisfy the requirements of this section; and

---

[9] For purposes of calculating potential future credit exposure for foreign exchange contracts and other similar contracts, in which notional principal is equivalent to cash flows, total notional principal is defined as the net receipts to each party falling due on each value date in each currency.

[10] No potential future credit exposure is calculated for single currency interest rate swaps in which payments are made based upon two floating rate indices, so-called floating/floating or basis swaps; the credit equivalent amount is measured solely on the basis of the current credit exposure.

Office of Thrift Supervision, Treasury § 567.6

(5) The savings association maintains in its files documentation adequate to support the netting of an off-balance sheet rate contract.[11]

(C) *Walkaway clause.* A bilateral netting contract that contains a walkaway clause is not eligible for netting for purposes of calculating the current credit exposure amount. The term "walkaway clause" means a provision in a bilateral netting contract that permits a nondefaulting counterparty to make a lower payment than it would make otherwise under the bilateral netting contract, or no payment at all, to a defaulter or the estate of a defaulter, even if the defaulter or the estate of the defaulter is a net creditor under the bilateral netting contract.

(D) *Risk weighting.* Once the savings association determines the credit equivalent amount for an off-balance sheet rate contract, that amount is assigned to the risk-weight category appropriate to the counterparty, or, if relevant, to the nature of any collateral or guarantee. Collateral held against a netting contract is not recognized for capital purposes unless it is legally available for all contracts included in the netting contract. However, the maximum risk weight for the credit equivalent amount of such off-balance sheet rate contracts is 50 percent.

(E) *Exceptions.* The following off-balance sheet rate contracts are not subject to the above calculation, and therefore, are not part of the denominator of a savings association's risk-based capital ratio:

(1) A foreign exchange rate contract with an original maturity of 14 calendar days or less; and

(2) Any interest rate or foreign exchange rate contract that is traded on an exchange requiring the daily payment of any variations in the market value of the contract.

(3) If a savings association has multiple overlapping exposures (such as a program-wide credit enhancement and a liquidity facility) to an ABCP program that is not consolidated for risk-based capital purposes, the savings association is not required to hold duplicative risk-based capital under this part against the overlapping position. Instead, the savings association should apply to the overlapping position the applicable risk-based capital treatment that results in the highest capital charge.

(b) *Recourse obligations, direct credit substitutes, and certain other positions*—(1) *In general.* Except as otherwise permitted in this paragraph (b), to determine the risk-weighted asset amount for a recourse obligation or a direct credit substitute (but not a residual interest):

(i) Multiply the full amount of the credit-enhanced assets for which the savings association directly or indirectly retains or assumes credit risk by a 100 percent conversion factor. (For a direct credit substitute that is an on-balance sheet asset (e.g., a purchased subordinated security), a savings association must use the amount of the direct credit substitute and the full amount of the asset its supports, *i.e.*, all the more senior positions in the structure); and

(ii) Assign this credit equivalent amount to the risk-weight category appropriate to the obligor in the underlying transaction, after considering any associated guarantees or collateral. Paragraph (a)(1) of this section lists the risk-weight categories.

(2) *Residual interests.* Except as otherwise permitted under this paragraph (b), a savings association must maintain risk-based capital for residual interests as follows:

(i) *Credit-enhancing interest-only strips.* After applying the concentration limit under § 567.12(e)(2) of this part, a saving association must maintain risk-

---

[11] By netting individual off-balance sheet rate contracts for the purpose of calculating its credit equivalent amount, a savings association represents that documentation adequate to support the netting of an off-balance sheet rate contract is in the savings association's files and available for inspection by the OTS. Upon determination by the OTS that a savings association's files are inadequate or that a bilateral netting contract may not be legally enforceable under any one of the bodies of law described in paragraphs (a)(2)(vi)(B)(3) (i) through (iii) of this section, the underlying individual off-balance sheet rate contracts may not be netted for the purposes of this section.

§ 567.6

based capital for a credit-enhancing interest-only strip equal to the remaining amount of the strip (net of any existing associated deferred tax liability), even if the amount of risk-based capital that must be maintained exceeds the full risk-based capital requirement for the assets transferred. Transactions that, in substance, result in the retention of credit risk associated with a transferred credit-enhancing interest-only strip are treated as if the strip was retained by the savings association and was not transferred.

(ii) *Other residual interests.* A saving association must maintain risk-based capital for a residual interest (excluding a credit-enhancing interest-only strip) equal to the face amount of the residual interest (net of any existing associated deferred tax liability), even if the amount of risk-based capital that must be maintained exceeds the full risk-based capital requirement for the assets transferred. Transactions that, in substance, result in the retention of credit risk associated with a transferred residual interest are treated as if the residual interest was retained by the savings association and was not transferred.

(iii) *Residual interests and other recourse obligations.* Where a savings association holds a residual interest (including a credit-enhancing interest-only strip) and another recourse obligation in connection with the same transfer of assets, the savings association must maintain risk-based capital equal to the greater of:

(A) The risk-based capital requirement for the residual interest as calculated under paragraph (b)(2)(i) through (ii) of this section; or

(B) The full risk-based capital requirement for the assets transferred, subject to the low-level recourse rules under paragraph (b)(7) of this section.

(3) *Ratings-based approach*—(i) *Calculation.* A savings association may calculate the risk-weighted asset amount for an eligible position described in paragraph (b)(3)(ii) of this section by multiplying the face amount of the position by the appropriate risk weight determined in accordance with Table A or B of this section.

NOTE: Stripped mortgage-backed securities or other similar instruments, such as interest-only and principal-only strips, that are not credit enhancing must be assigned to the 100% risk-weight category.

TABLE A

Long term rating category	Risk weight (In percent)
Highest or second highest investment grade	20
Third highest investment grade	50
Lowest investment grade	100
One category below investment grade	200

TABLE B

Short term rating category	Risk weight (In percent)
Highest investment grade	20
Second highest investment grade	50
Lowest investment grade	100

(ii) *Eligibility*—(A) *Traded positions.* A position is eligible for the treatment described in paragraph (b)(3)(i) of this section, if:

(*1*) The position is a recourse obligation, direct credit substitute, residual interest, or asset- or mortgage-backed security and is not a credit-enhancing interest-only strip;

(*2*) The position is a traded position; and

(*3*) The NRSRO has rated a long term position as one grade below investment grade or better or a short term position as investment grade. If two or more NRSROs assign ratings to a traded position, the savings association must use the lowest rating to determine the appropriate risk-weight category under paragraph (b)(3)(i) of this section.

(B) *Non-traded positions.* A position that is not traded is eligible for the treatment described in paragraph (b)(3)(i) of this section if:

(*1*) The position is a recourse obligation, direct credit substitute, residual interest, or asset- or mortgage-backed security extended in connection with a securitization and is not a credit-enhancing interest-only strip;

(*2*) More than one NRSRO rate the position;

(*3*) All of the NRSROs that provide a rating rate a long term position as one grade below investment grade or better or a short term position as investment grade. If the NRSROs assign different ratings to the position, the savings association must use the lowest rating to determine the appropriate risk-weight category under paragraph (b)(3)(i) of this section;

(4) The NRSROs base their ratings on the same criteria that they use to rate securities that are traded positions; and

(5) The ratings are publicly available.

(C) *Unrated senior positions.* If a recourse obligation, direct credit substitute, residual interest, or asset- or mortgage-backed security is not rated by an NRSRO, but is senior or preferred in all features to a traded position (including collateralization and maturity), the savings association may risk-weight the face amount of the senior position under paragraph (b)(3)(i) of this section, based on the rating of the traded position, subject to supervisory guidance. The savings association must satisfy OTS that this treatment is appropriate. This paragraph (b)(3)(i)(C) applies only if the traded position provides substantive credit support to the unrated position until the unrated position matures.

(4) *Certain positions that are not rated by NRSROs*—(i) *Calculation.* A savings association may calculate the risk-weighted asset amount for eligible position described in paragraph (b)(4)(ii) of this section based on the savings association's determination of the credit rating of the position. To risk-weight the asset, the savings association must multiply the face amount of the position by the appropriate risk weight determined in accordance with Table C of this section.

TABLE C

Rating category	Risk weight (In percent)
Investment grade	100
One category below investment grade	200

(ii) *Eligibility.* A position extended in connection with a securitization is eligible for the treatment described in paragraph (b)(4)(i) of this section if it is not rated by an NRSRO, is not a residual interest, and meets the one of the three alternative standards described in paragraph (b)(4)(ii)(A), (B), or (C) below of this section:

(A) *Position rated internally.* A direct credit substitute, but not a purchased credit-enhancing interest-only strip, is eligible for the treatment described under paragraph (b)(4)(i) of this section, if the position is assumed in connection with an asset-backed commercial paper program sponsored by the savings association. Before it may rely on an internal credit risk rating system, the saving association must demonstrate to OTS's satisfaction that the system is adequate. Adequate internal credit risk rating systems typically:

(1) Are an integral part of the savings association's risk management system that explicitly incorporates the full range of risks arising from the savings association's participation in securitization activities;

(2) Link internal credit ratings to measurable outcomes, such as the probability that the position will experience any loss, the expected loss on the position in the event of default, and the degree of variance in losses in the event of default on that position;

(3) Separately consider the risk associated with the underlying loans or borrowers, and the risk associated with the structure of the particular securitization transaction;

(4) Identify gradations of risk among "pass" assets and other risk positions;

(5) Use clear, explicit criteria to classify assets into each internal rating grade, including subjective factors;

(6) Employ independent credit risk management or loan review personnel to assign or review the credit risk ratings;

(7) Include an internal audit procedure to periodically verify that internal risk ratings are assigned in accordance with the savings association's established criteria;

(8) Monitor the performance of the assigned internal credit risk ratings over time to determine the appropriateness of the initial credit risk rating assignment, and adjust individual credit risk ratings or the overall internal credit risk rating system, as needed; and

(9) Make credit risk rating assumptions that are consistent with, or more conservative than, the credit risk rating assumptions and methodologies of NRSROs.

(B) *Program ratings.* (1) A recourse obligation or direct credit substitute, but not a residual interest, is eligible for the treatment described in paragraph

§ 567.6

(b)(4)(i) of this section, if the position is retained or assumed in connection with a structured finance program and an NRSRO has reviewed the terms of the program and stated a rating for positions associated with the program. If the program has options for different combinations of assets, standards, internal or external credit enhancements and other relevant factors, and the NRSRO specifies ranges of rating categories to them, the savings association may apply the rating category applicable to the option that corresponds to the savings association's position.

(2) To rely on a program rating, the savings association must demonstrate to OTS's satisfaction that the credit risk rating assigned to the program meets the same standards generally used by NRSROs for rating traded positions. The savings association must also demonstrate to OTS's satisfaction that the criteria underlying the assignments for the program are satisfied by the particular position.

(3) If a savings association participates in a securitization sponsored by another party, OTS may authorize the savings association to use this approach based on a program rating obtained by the sponsor of the program.

(C) *Computer program.* A recourse obligation or direct credit substitute, but not a residual interest, is eligible for the treatment described in paragraph (b)(4)(i) of this section, if the position is extended in connection with a structured financing program and the savings association uses an acceptable credit assessment computer program to determine the rating of the position. An NRSRO must have developed the computer program and the savings association must demonstrate to OTS's satisfaction that the ratings under the program correspond credibly and reliably with the rating of traded positions.

(5) *Alternative capital computation for small business obligations*—(i) *Definitions.* For the purposes of this paragraph (b)(5):

(A) *Qualified savings association* means a savings association that:

(*1*) Is well capitalized as defined in § 565.4 of this chapter without applying the capital treatment described in this paragraph (b)(5); or

(*2*) Is adequately capitalized as defined in § 565.4 of this chapter without applying the capital treatment described in this paragraph (b)(5) and has received written permission from the OTS to apply that capital treatment.

(B) *Small business* means a business that meets the criteria for a small business concern established by the Small Business Administration in 13 CFR 121 pursuant to 15 U.S.C. 632.

(ii) *Capital requirement.* Notwithstanding any other provision of this paragraph (b), with respect to a transfer of a small business loan or lease of personal property with recourse that is a sale under generally accepted accounting principles, a qualified savings association may elect to include only the amount of its recourse in its risk-weighted assets. To qualify for this election, the savings association must establish and maintain a reserve under generally accepted accounting principles sufficient to meet the reasonable estimated liability of the savings association under the recourse obligation.

(iii) *Aggregate amount of recourse.* The total outstanding amount of recourse retained by a qualified savings association with respect to transfers of small business loans and leases of personal property and included in the risk-weighted assets of the savings association as described in paragraph (b)(5)(ii) of this section, may not exceed 15 percent of the association's total capital computed under § 567.5(c).

(iv) *Savings association that ceases to be a qualified savings association or that exceeds aggregate limits.* If a savings association ceases to be a qualified savings association or exceeds the aggregate limit described in paragraph (b)(5)(iii) of this section, the savings association may continue to apply the capital treatment described in paragraph (b)(5)(ii) of this section to transfers of small business loans and leases of personal property that occurred when the association was a qualified savings association and did not exceed the limit.

(v) *Prompt corrective action not affected.* (A) A savings association shall compute its capital without regard to this paragraph (b)(5) of this section for purposes of prompt corrective action

Office of Thrift Supervision, Treasury § 567.6

(12 U.S.C. 1831o), unless the savings association is adequately or well capitalized without applying the capital treatment described in this paragraph (b)(5) and would be well capitalized after applying that capital treatment.

(B) A savings association shall compute its capital requirement without regard to this paragraph (b)(5) for the purposes of applying 12 U.S.C. 1831o(g), regardless of the association's capital level.

(6) *Risk participations and syndications of direct credit substitutes.* A savings association must calculate the risk-weighted asset amount for a risk participation in, or syndication of, a direct credit substitute as follows:

(i) If a savings association conveys a risk participation in a direct credit substitute, the savings association must convert the full amount of the assets that are supported by the direct credit substitute to a credit equivalent amount using a 100 percent conversion factor. The savings association must assign the *pro rata* share of the credit equivalent amount that was conveyed through the risk participation to the lower of: The risk-weight category appropriate to the obligor in the underlying transaction, after considering any associated guarantees or collateral; or the risk-weight category appropriate to the party acquiring the participation. The savings association must assign the *pro rata* share of the credit equivalent amount that was not participated out to the risk-weight category appropriate to the obligor, after considering any associated guarantees or collateral.

(ii) If a savings association acquires a risk participation in a direct credit substitute, the savings association must multiply its *pro rata* share of the direct credit substitute by the full amount of the assets that are supported by the direct credit substitute, and convert this amount to a credit equivalent amount using a 100 percent conversion factor. The savings association must assign the resulting credit equivalent amount to the risk-weight category appropriate to the obligor in the underlying transaction, after considering any associated guarantees or collateral.

(iii) If the savings association holds a direct credit substitute in the form of a syndication where each savings association or other participant is obligated only for its *pro rata* share of the risk and there is no recourse to the originating party, the savings association must calculate the credit equivalent amount by multiplying only its *pro rata* share of the assets supported by the direct credit substitute by a 100 percent conversion factor. The savings association must assign the resulting credit equivalent amount to the risk-weight category appropriate to the obligor in the underlying transaction after considering any associated guarantees or collateral.

(7) *Limitations on risk-based capital requirements*—(i) *Low-level exposure rule.* If the maximum contractual exposure to loss retained or assumed by a savings association is less than the effective risk-based capital requirement, as determined in accordance with this paragraph (b), for the assets supported by the savings association's position, the risk-based capital requirement is limited to the savings association's contractual exposure less any recourse liability account established in accordance with generally accepted accounting principles. This limitation does not apply when a savings association provides credit enhancement beyond any contractual obligation to support assets it has sold.

(ii) *Mortgage-related securities or participation certificates retained in a mortgage loan swap.* If a savings association holds a mortgage-related security or a participation certificate as a result of a mortgage loan swap with recourse, it must hold risk-based capital to support the recourse obligation and that percentage of the mortgage-related security or participation certificate that is not covered by the recourse obligation. The total amount of risk-based capital required for the security (or certificate) and the recourse obligation is limited to the risk-based capital requirement for the underlying loans, calculated as if the savings association continued to hold these loans as an on-balance sheet asset.

(iii) *Related on-balance sheet assets.* If an asset is included in the calculation of the risk-based capital requirement

353

§ 567.8

under this paragraph (b) and also appears as an asset on the savings association's balance sheet, the savings association must risk-weight the asset only under this paragraph (b), except in the case of loan servicing assets and similar arrangements with embedded recourse obligations or direct credit substitutes. In that case, the savings association must separately risk-weight the on-balance sheet servicing asset and the related recourse obligations and direct credit substitutes under this section, and incorporate these amounts into the risk-based capital calculation.

(8) *Obligations of subsidiaries.* If a savings association retains a recourse obligation or assumes a direct credit substitute on the obligation of a subsidiary that is not an includable subsidiary, and the recourse obligation or direct credit substitute is an equity or debt investment in that subsidiary under generally accepted accounting principles, the face amount of the recourse obligation or direct credit substitute is deducted for capital under §§ 567.5(a)(2) and 567.9(c). All other recourse obligations and direct credit substitutes retained or assumed by a savings association on the obligations of an entity in which the savings association has an equity investment are risk-weighted in accordance with this paragraph (b).

[54 FR 49649, Nov. 30, 1989]

EDITORIAL NOTE: For FEDERAL REGISTER citations affecting § 567.6, see the List of CFR Sections Affected, which appears in the Finding Aids section of the printed volume and at *www.fdsys.gov.*

§ 567.8 Leverage ratio.

(a) The minimum leverage capital requirement for a savings association assigned a composite rating of 1, as defined in § 516.3 of this chapter, shall consist of a ratio of core capital to adjusted total assets of 3 percent. These generally are strong associations that are not anticipating or experiencing significant growth and have well-diversified risks, including no undue interest rate risk exposure, excellent asset quality, high liquidity, and good earnings.

(b) For all savings associations not meeting the conditions set forth in paragraph (a) of this section, the minimum leverage capital requirement shall consist of a ratio of core capital to adjusted total assets of 4 percent. Higher capital ratios may be required if warranted by the particular circumstances or risk profiles of an individual savings association. In all cases, savings associations should hold capital commensurate with the level and nature of all risks, including the volume and severity of problem loans, to which they are exposed.

[64 FR 10201, Mar. 2, 1999]

§ 567.9 Tangible capital requirement.

(a) Savings associations shall have and maintain tangible capital in an amount equal to at least 1.5% of adjusted total assets.

(b) The following elements, less the amount of any deductions pursuant to paragraph (c) of this section, comprise a savings association's tangible capital:

(1) Common stockholders' equity (including retained earnings);

(2) Noncumulative perpetual preferred stock and related earnings;

(3) Nonwithdrawable accounts and pledged deposits that would qualify as core capital under § 567.5 of this part; and

(4) Minority interests in the equity accounts of fully consolidated subsidiaries.

(c) *Deductions from tangible capital.* In calculating tangible capital, a savings association must deduct from assets, and, thus, from capital:

(1) Intangible assets (as defined in § 567.1) except for mortgage servicing assets to the extent they are includable in tangible capital under § 567.12, and credit enhancing interest-only strips and deferred tax assets not includable in tangible capital under § 567.12.

(2) Investments, both equity and debt, in subsidiaries that are not includable subsidiaries (including those subsidiaries where the savings association has a minority ownership interest), except as provided in paragraphs (c)(3) and (c)(4) of this section.

(3) If a savings association has any investments (both debt and equity) in one or more subsidiary(ies) engaged as of April 12, 1989 and continuing to be engaged in any activity that would not

fall within the scope of activities in which includable subsidiaries may engage, it must deduct such investments from assets and, thus, tangible capital in accordance with this paragraph (c)(3). The savings association must first deduct from assets and, thus, capital the amount by which any investments in such a subsidiary(ies) exceed the amount of such investments held by the savings association as of April 12, 1989. Next, the savings association must deduct from assets and, thus, tangible capital the lesser of:

(i) The savings association's investments in and extensions of credit to the subsidiary as of April 12, 1989; or

(ii) The savings association's investments in and extensions of credit to the subsidiary on the date as of which the savings association's capital is being determined.

(4) If a savings association holds a subsidiary (either directly or through a subsidiary) that is itself a domestic depository institution the Office may, in its sole discretion upon determining that the amount of tangible capital that would be required would be higher if the assets and liabilities of such subsidiary were consolidated with those of the parent savings association than the amount that would be required if the parent savings association's investment were deducted pursuant to paragraphs (c)(2) and (c)(3) of this section, consolidate the assets and liabilities of that subsidiary with those of the parent savings association in calculating the capital adequacy of the parent savings association, regardless of whether the subsidiary would otherwise be an includable subsidiary as defined in § 507.1 of this part.

[54 FR 49649, Nov. 30, 1989, as amended at 57 FR 33441, July 29, 1992; 59 FR 4788, Feb. 2, 1994; 60 FR 39232, Aug. 1, 1995; 62 FR 66264, Dec. 18, 1997; 63 FR 42678, Aug. 10, 1998; 66 FR 59666, Nov. 29, 2001; 73 FR 79607, Dec. 30, 2008]

§ 567.10 Consequences of failure to meet capital requirements.

(a) *Capital plans.* (1) [Reserved]

(2) The Director shall require any savings association not in compliance with capital standards to submit a capital plan that:

(i) Addresses the savings association's need for increased capital;

(ii) Describes the manner in which the savings association will increase capital so as to achieve compliance with capital standards;

(iii) Specifies types and levels of activities in which the savings association will engage;

(iv) Requires any increase in assets to be accompanied by increase in tangible capital not less in percentage amount than the leverage limit then applicable;

(v) Requires any increase in assets to be accompanied by an increase in capital not less in percentage amount than required under the risk-based capital standard then applicable; and

(vi) Is acceptable to the Director.

(3) To be acceptable to the Director under this section, a plan must, in addition to satisfying all of the requirements set forth in paragraphs (a)(2)(i) through (a)(2)(v) of this section, contain a certification that while the plan is under review by the Office, the savings association will not, without the prior written approval of the Regional Director:

(i) Grow beyond net interest credited;

(ii) Make any capital distributions; or

(iii) Act inconsistently with any other limitations on activities established by statute, regulation or by the Office in supervisory guidance for savings associations not meeting capital standards.

(4) If the plan submitted to the Director under paragraph (a)(2) of this section is not approved by the Office, the savings association shall immediately and without any further action, be subject to the following restrictions:

(i) It may not increase its assets beyond the amount held on the day it receives written notice of the Director's disapproval of the plan; and

(ii) It must comply with any other restrictions or limitations set forth in the written notice of the Director's disapproval of the plan.

(b) On or after January 1, 1991, the Director shall:

(1) Prohibit any asset growth by any savings association not in compliance with capital standards, *except* as provided in paragraph (d) of this section; and

(2) Require any savings association not in compliance with capital standards to comply with a capital directive issued by the Director which may include the restrictions contained in paragraph (e) of this section and any other restrictions the Director determines appropriate.

(c) A savings association that wishes to obtain an exemption from the sanctions provided in paragraph (b)(2) of this section must file a request for exemption with the Regional Director. Such request must include a capital plan that satisfies the requirements of paragraph (a)(2) of this section.

(d) The Director may permit any savings association that is subject to paragraph (b) of this section to increase its assets in an amount not exceeding the amount of net interest credited to the savings association's deposit liabilities, if:

(1) The savings association obtains the Director's prior approval;

(2) Any increase in assets is accompanied by an increase in tangible capital in an amount not less than 3% of the increase in assets;

(3) Any increase in assets is accompanied by an increase in capital not less in percentage amount than required under the risk-based capital standards then applicable;

(4) Any increase in assets is invested in low-risk assets; and

(5) The savings association's ratio of core capital to total assets is not less than the ratio existing on January 1, 1991.

(e) If a savings association fails to meet the risk-based capital requirement, the leverage ratio requirement, or the tangible capital requirement established under this part, the Director may, through enforcement proceedings or otherwise, require such savings association to take one or more of the following corrective actions:

(1) Increase the amount of its regulatory capital to a specified level or levels;

(2) Convene a meeting or meetings with the Office's supervision staff for the purpose of accomplishing the objectives of this section;

(3) Reduce the rate of earnings that may be paid on savings accounts;

(4) Limit the receipt of deposits to those made to existing accounts;

(5) Cease or limit the issuance of new accounts of any or all classes or categories, except in exchange for existing accounts;

(6) Cease or limit lending or the making of a particular type or category of loan;

(7) Cease or limit the purchase of loans or the making of specified other investments;

(8) Limit operational expenditures to specified levels;

(9) Increase liquid assets and maintain such increased liquidity at specified levels; or

(10) Take such other action or actions as the Director may deem necessary or appropriate for the safety and soundness of the savings association, or depositors or investors in the savings association.

(f) The Director shall treat as an unsafe and unsound practice any material failure by a savings association to comply with any plan, regulation, written agreement undertaken under this section or order or directive issued to comply with the requirements of this part.

[54 FR 49649, Nov. 30, 1989, as amended at 57 FR 33441, July 29, 1992; 60 FR 66720, Dec. 26, 1995; 72 FR 69439, Dec. 7, 2007]

§ 567.11 Reservation of authority.

(a) *Transactions for purposes of evasion.* The Director or the Regional Director for the region in which a savings association is located may disregard any transaction entered into primarily for the purpose of reducing the minimum required amount of regulatory capital or otherwise evading the requirements of this part.

(b) *Average versus period-end figures.* The Office reserves the right to require a savings association to compute its capital ratios on the basis of average, rather than period-end, assets when the Office determines appropriate to carry out the purposes of this part.

(c)(1) *Reservation of authority.* Notwithstanding the definitions of core and supplementary capital in § 567.5 of this part, OTS may find that a particular type of purchased intangible asset or capital instrument constitutes

Office of Thrift Supervision, Treasury §567.12

or may constitute core or supplementary capital, and may permit one or more savings associations to include all or a portion of such intangible asset or funds obtained through such capital instrument as core or supplementary capital, permanently or on a temporary basis, for the purposes of compliance with this part or for any other purposes. Similarly, the Office may find that a particular asset or core or supplementary capital component has characteristics or terms that diminish its contribution to a savings association's ability to absorb losses, and the Office may require the discounting or deduction of such asset or component from the computation of core, supplementary, or total capital.

(2) Notwithstanding §567.6 of this part, OTS will look to the substance of a transaction and may find that the assigned risk weight for any asset, or credit equivalent amount or credit conversion factor for any off-balance sheet item does not appropriately reflect the risks imposed on the savings association. OTS may require the savings association to apply another risk-weight, credit equivalent amount, or credit conversion factor that OTS deems appropriate.

(3) OTS may find that the capital treatment for an exposure to a transaction not subject to consolidation on the savings association's balance sheet does not appropriately reflect the risks imposed on the savings association. Accordingly, OTS may require the savings association to treat the transaction as if it were consolidated on the savings association's balance sheet. OTS will look to the substance of and risk associated with the transaction as well as other relevant factors in determining whether to require such treatment and in calculating risk based capital as OTS deems appropriate.

(4) If this part does not specifically assign a risk weight, credit equivalent amount, or credit conversion factor, OTS may assign any risk weight, credit equivalent amount, or credit conversion factor that it deems appropriate. In making this determination, OTS will consider the risks associated with the asset or off-balance sheet item as well as other relevant factors.

(d) In making a determination under this paragraph (c) of this section, the OTS will notify the savings association of the determination and solicit a response from the savings association. After review of the response by the savings association, the OTS shall issue a final supervisory decision regarding the determination made under paragraph (c) of this section.

[54 FR 49649, Nov. 30, 1989, as amended at 57 FR 33441, July 29, 1992; 66 FR 59666, Nov. 29, 2001; 75 FR 4652, Jan. 28, 2010]

§567.12 Purchased credit card relationships, servicing assets, intangible assets (other than purchased credit card relationships and servicing assets), credit-enhancing interest-only strips, and deferred tax assets.

(a) *Scope.* This section prescribes the maximum amount of purchased credit card relationships, serving assets, intangible assets (other than purchased credit card relationships and servicing assets), credit-enhancing interest-only strips, and deferred tax assets that savings associations may include in calculating tangible and core capital.

(b) *Computation of core and tangible capital.* (1) Purchased credit card relationships may be included (that is, not deducted) in computing core capital in accordance with the restrictions in this section, but must be deducted in computing tangible capital.

(2) In accordance with the restrictions in this section, mortgage servicing assets may be included in computing core and tangible capital and nonmortgage servicing assets may be included in core capital.

(3) Intangible assets, as defined in §567.1 of this part, other than purchased credit card relationships described in paragraph (b)(1) of this section, servicing assets described in paragraph (b)(2) of this section, and core deposit intangibles described in paragraph (g)(3) of this section, are deducted in computing tangible and core capital, subject to paragraph (e)(3)(ii) of this section.

(4) Credit-enhancing interest-only strips may be included (that is not deducted) in computing core capital subject to the restrictions of this section, and may be included in tangible capital in the same amount.

357

§ 567.12

(5) Deferred tax assets may be included (that is not deducted) in computing core capital subject to the restrictions of paragraph (h) of this section, and may be included in tangible capital in the same amount.

(c) *Market valuations.* The OTS reserves the authority to require any savings association to perform an independent market valuation of assets subject to this section on a case-by-case basis or through the issuance of policy guidance. An independent market valuation, if required, shall be conducted in accordance with any policy guidance issued by the OTS. A required valuation shall include adjustments for any significant changes in original valuation assumptions, including changes in prepayment estimates or attrition rates. The valuation shall determine the current fair value of assets subject to this section. This independent market valuation may be conducted by an independent valuation expert evaluating the reasonableness of the internal calculations and assumptions used by the association in conducting its internal analysis. The association shall calculate an estimated fair value for assets subject to this section at least quarterly regardless of whether an independent valuation expert is required to perform an independent market valuation

(d) *Value limitation.* For purposes of calculating core capital under this part (but not for financial statement purposes), purchased credit card relationships and servicing assets must be valued at the lesser of:

(1) 90 percent of their fair value determined in accordance with paragraph (c) of this section; or

(2) 100 percent of their remaining unamortized book value determined in accordance with the instructions for the Thrift Financial Report.

(e) *Core capital limitations*—(1) *Servicing assets and purchased credit card relationships.* (i) The maximum aggregate amount of servicing assets and purchased credit card relationships that may be included in core capital is limited to the lesser of:

(A) 100 percent of the amount of core capital; or

(B) The amount of servicing assets and purchased credit card relationships

12 CFR Ch. V (1-1-12 Edition)

determined in accordance with paragraph (d) of this section.

(ii) In addition to the aggregate limitation in paragraph (e)(1)(i) of this section, a sublimit applies to purchased credit card relationships and non mortgage-related serving assets. The maximum allowable amount of these two types of assets combined is limited to the lesser of:

(A) 25 percent the amount of core capital; and

(B) The amount of purchased credit card relationships and non mortgage-related servicing assets determined in accordance with paragraph (d) of this section.

(2) *Credit-enhancing interest-only strips.* The maximum aggregate amount of credit-enhancing interest-only strips that may be included in core capital is limited to 25 percent of the amount of core capital. Purchased and retained credit-enhancing interest-only strips, on a non-tax adjusted basis, are included in the total amount that is used for purposes of determining whether a savings association exceeds the core capital limit.

(3) *Computation.* (i) For purposes of computing the limits and sublimits in paragraphs (e) and (h) of this section, core capital is computed before the deduction of disallowed servicing assets, disallowed purchased credit card relationships, disallowed credit-enhancing interest-only strips (purchased and retained), and disallowed deferred tax assets.

(ii) A savings association may elect to deduct the following items on a basis net of deferred tax liabilities:

(A) Disallowed servicing assets;

(B) Goodwill such that only the net amount must be deducted from Tier 1 capital;

(C) Disallowed credit-enhancing interest only strips (both purchased and retained); and

(D) Other intangible assets arising from non-taxable business combinations. A deferred tax liability that is specifically related to an intangible asset (other than purchased credit card relationships) arising from a non-taxable business combination may be netted against this intangible asset. The net amount of the intangible asset must be deducted from Tier 1 capital.

358

Office of Thrift Supervision, Treasury § 567.12

(iii) Deferred tax liabilities that are netted in accordance with paragraph (e)(3)(ii) of this section cannot also be netted against deferred tax assets when determining the amount of deferred tax assets that are dependent upon future taxable income.

(f) *Tangible capital limitation.* The maximum amount of mortgage servicing assets that may be included in tangible capital shall be the same amount includable in core capital in accordance with the limitations set by paragraph (e) of this section. All non-mortgage servicing assets are deducted in computing tangible capital.

(g) *Exemption for certain subsidiaries—* (1) *Exemption standard.* An association holding purchased mortgage servicing rights in separately capitalized, non-includable subsidiaries may submit an application for approval by the OTS for an exemption from the deductions and limitations set forth in this section. The deductions and limitations will apply to such purchased mortgage servicing rights, however, if the OTS determines that:

(i) The thrift and subsidiary are not conducting activities on an arm's length basis; or

(ii) The exemption is not consistent with the association's safe and sound operation.

(2) *Applicable requirements.* If the OTS determines to grant or to permit the continuation of an exemption under paragraph (h)(1) of this section, the association receiving the exemption must ensure the following:

(i) The association's investments in, and extensions of credit to, the subsidiary are deducted from capital when calculating capital under this part;

(ii) Extensions of credit and other transactions with the subsidiary are conducted in compliance with the rules for covered transactions with affiliates set forth in sections 23A and 23B of the Federal Reserve Act, as applied to thrifts; and

(iii) Any contracts entered into by the subsidiary include a written disclosure indicating that the subsidiary is not a bank or savings association; the subsidiary is an organization separate and apart from any bank or savings association; and the obligations of the subsidiary are not backed or guaranteed by any bank or savings association and are not insured by the FDIC.

(h) *Treatment of deferred tax assets.* For purposes of calculating Tier 1 capital under this part (but not for financial statement purposes) deferred tax assets are subject to the conditions, limitations, and restrictions described in this section.

(1) Tier 1 capital limitations. (i) The maximum allowable amount of deferred tax assets net of any valuation allowance that are dependent upon future taxable income will be limited to the lesser of:

(A) The amount of deferred tax assets that are dependent upon future taxable income that is expected to be realized within one year of the calendar quarter-end date, based on a projected future taxable income for that year; or

(B) Ten percent of the amount of Tier 1 capital that exists before the deduction of any disallowed servicing assets, any disallowed purchased credit card relationships, any disallowed credit-enhancing interest-only strips, and any disallowed deferred tax assets.

(ii) For purposes of this limitation, all existing temporary differences should be assumed to fully reverse at the calendar quarter-end date. The recorded amount of deferred tax assets that are dependent upon future taxable income, net of any valuation allowance for deferred tax assets, in excess of this limitation will be deducted from assets and from equity capital for purposes of determining Tier 1 capital under this part. The amount of deferred tax assets that can be realized from taxes paid in prior carryback years and from the reversal of existing taxable temporary differences generally would not be deducted from assets and from equity capital.

(iii) Notwithstanding paragraph (h)(1)(B)(ii) of this section, the amount of carryback potential that may be considered in calculating the amount of deferred tax assets that a savings association that is part of a consolidated group (for tax purposes) may include in Tier 1 capital may not exceed the amount which the association could reasonably expect to have refunded by its parent.

(2) *Projected future taxable income.* Projected future taxable income should

§§ 567.14–567.19

not include net operating loss carryforwards to be used within one year of the most recent calendar quarter-end date or the amount of existing temporary differences expected to reverse within that year. Projected future taxable income should include the estimated effect of tax planning strategies that are expected to be implemented to realize tax carryforwards that will otherwise expire during that year. Future taxable income projections for the current fiscal year (adjusted for any significant changes that have occurred or are expected to occur) may be used when applying the capital limit at an interim calendar quarter-end date rather than preparing a new projection each quarter.

(3) *Unrealized holding gains and losses on available-for-sale debt securities.* The deferred tax effects of any unrealized holding gains and losses on available-for-sale debt securities may be excluded from the determination of the amount of deferred tax assets that are dependent upon future taxable income and the calculation of the maximum allowable amount of such assets. If these deferred tax effects are excluded, this treatment must be followed consistently over time.

[59 FR 4788, Feb. 2, 1994, as amended at 60 FR 39232, Aug. 1, 1995; 62 FR 66264, Dec. 18, 1997; 63 FR 42678, Aug. 10, 1998; 66 FR 59666, Nov. 29, 2001; 73 FR 19, Jan. 2, 2008; 73 FR 79607, Dec. 30, 2008]

§§ 567.14–567.19 [Reserved]

APPENDIXES A–B [RESERVED]

APPENDIX C TO PART 567—RISK-BASED CAPITAL REQUIREMENTS—INTERNAL-RATINGS-BASED AND ADVANCED MEASUREMENT APPROACHES

Part I General Provisions
  Section 1 Purpose, Applicability, Reservation of Authority, and Principle of Conservatism
  Section 2 Definitions
  Section 3 Minimum Risk-Based Capital Requirements
Part II Qualifying Capital
  Section 11 Additional Deductions
  Section 12 Deductions and Limitations Not Required
  Section 13 Eligible Credit Reserves
Part III Qualification
  Section 21 Qualification Process
  Section 22 Qualification Requirements
  Section 23 Ongoing Qualification
  Section 24 Merger and Acquisition Transitional Arrangements
Part IV Risk-Weighted Assets for General Credit Risk
  Section 31 Mechanics for Calculating Total Wholesale and Retail Risk-Weighted Assets
  Section 32 Counterparty Credit Risk of Repo-Style Transactions, Eligible Margin Loans, and OTC Derivative Contracts
  Section 33 Guarantees and Credit Derivatives: PD Substitution and LGD Adjustment Approaches
  Section 34 Guarantees and Credit Derivatives: Double Default Treatment
  Section 35 Risk-Based Capital Requirement for Unsettled Transactions
Part V Risk-Weighted Assets for Securitization Exposures
  Section 41 Operational Criteria for Recognizing the Transfer of Risk
  Section 42 Risk-Based Capital Requirement for Securitization Exposures
  Section 43 Ratings-Based Approach (RBA)
  Section 44 Internal Assessment Approach (IAA)
  Section 45 Supervisory Formula Approach (SFA)
  Section 46 Recognition of Credit Risk Mitigants for Securitization Exposures
  Section 47 Risk-Based Capital Requirement for Early Amortization Provisions
Part VI Risk-Weighted Assets for Equity Exposures
  Section 51 Introduction and Exposure Measurement
  Section 52 Simple Risk Weight Approach (SRWA)
  Section 53 Internal Models Approach (IMA)
  Section 54 Equity Exposures to Investment Funds
  Section 55 Equity Derivative Contracts
Part VII Risk-Weighted Assets for Operational Risk
  Section 61 Qualification Requirements for Incorporation of Operational Risk Mitigants
  Section 62 Mechanics of Risk-Weighted Asset Calculation
Part VIII Disclosure
  Section 71 Disclosure Requirements
Part IX—Transition Provisions
  Section 81—Optional Transition Provisions Related to the Implementation of Consolidation Requirements Under FAS 167

PART I. GENERAL PROVISIONS

Section 1. Purpose, Applicability, Reservation of Authority, and Principle of Conservatism

(a) *Purpose.* This appendix establishes:

(1) Minimum qualifying criteria for savings associations using savings association-specific internal risk measurement and management processes for calculating risk-based capital requirements;

Office of Thrift Supervision, Treasury   Pt. 567, App. C

(2) Methodologies for such savings associations to calculate their risk-based capital requirements; and

(3) Public disclosure requirements for such savings associations.

(b) *Applicability.* (1) This appendix applies to a savings association that:

(i) Has consolidated assets, as reported on the most recent year-end Thrift Financial Report (TFR) equal to $250 billion or more;

(ii) Has consolidated total on-balance sheet foreign exposure at the most recent year-end equal to $10 billion or more (where total on-balance sheet foreign exposure equals total cross-border claims less claims with head office or guarantor located in another country plus redistributed guaranteed amounts to the country of head office or guarantor plus local country claims on local residents plus revaluation gains on foreign exchange and derivative products, calculated in accordance with the Federal Financial Institutions Examination Council (FFIEC) 009 Country Exposure Report);

(iii) Is a subsidiary of a depository institution that uses 12 CFR part 3, appendix C, 12 CFR part 208, appendix F, 12 CFR part 325, appendix D, or 12 CFR part 567, appendix C, to calculate its risk-based capital requirements; or

(iv) Is a subsidiary of a bank holding company that uses 12 CFR part 225, appendix G, to calculate its risk-based capital requirements.

(2) Any savings association may elect to use this appendix to calculate its risk-based capital requirements.

(3) A savings association that is subject to this appendix must use this appendix unless the OTS determines in writing that application of this appendix is not appropriate in light of the savings association's asset size, level of complexity, risk profile, or scope of operations. In making a determination under this paragraph, the OTS will apply notice and response procedures in the same manner and to the same extent as the notice and response procedures in § 567.3(d).

(c) *Reservation of authority*—(1) *Additional capital in the aggregate.* The OTS may require a savings association to hold an amount of capital greater than otherwise required under this appendix if the OTS determines that the savings association's risk-based capital requirement under this appendix is not commensurate with the savings association's credit, market, operational, or other risks. In making a determination under this paragraph, the OTS will apply notice and response procedures in the same manner and to the same extent as the notice and response procedures in § 567.3(d).

(2) *Specific risk-weighted asset amounts.* (i) If the OTS determines that the risk-weighted asset amount calculated under this appendix by the savings association for one or more exposures is not commensurate with the risks associated with those exposures, the OTS may require the savings association to assign a different risk-weighted asset amount to the exposures, to assign different risk parameters to the exposures (if the exposures are wholesale or retail exposures), or to use different model assumptions for the exposures (if relevant), all as specified by the OTS.

(ii) If the OTS determines that the risk-weighted asset amount for operational risk produced by the savings association under this appendix is not commensurate with the operational risks of the savings association, the OTS may require the savings association to assign a different risk-weighted asset amount for operational risk, to change elements of its operational risk analytical framework, including distributional and dependence assumptions, or to make other changes to the savings association's operational risk management processes, data and assessment systems, or quantification systems, all as specified by the OTS.

(3) *Regulatory capital treatment of unconsolidated entities.* OTS may find that the capital treatment for an exposure to a transaction not subject to consolidation on the savings association's balance sheet does not appropriately reflect the risks imposed on the savings association. Accordingly, OTS may require the savings association to treat the transaction as if it were consolidated on the savings association's balance sheet. OTS will look to the substance of and risk associated with the transaction as well as other relevant factors in determining whether to require such treatment and in calculating risk-based capital as OTS deems appropriate.

(4) *Other supervisory authority.* Nothing in this appendix limits the authority of the OTS under any other provision of law or regulation to take supervisory or enforcement action, including action to address unsafe or unsound practices or conditions, deficient capital levels, or violations of law.

(d) *Principle of conservatism.* Notwithstanding the requirements of this appendix, a savings association may choose not to apply a provision of this appendix to one or more exposures, provided that:

(1) The savings association can demonstrate on an ongoing basis to the satisfaction of the OTS that not applying the provision would, in all circumstances, unambiguously generate a risk-based capital requirement for each such exposure greater than that which would otherwise be required under this appendix;

(2) The savings association appropriately manages the risk of each such exposure;

(3) The savings association notifies the OTS in writing prior to applying this principle to each such exposure; and

(4) The exposures to which the savings association applies this principle are not, in

the aggregate, material to the savings association.

Section 2. Definitions

Advanced internal ratings-based (IRB) systems means a savings association's internal risk rating and segmentation system; risk parameter quantification system; data management and maintenance system; and control, oversight, and validation system for credit risk of wholesale and retail exposures.

Advanced systems means a savings association's advanced IRB systems, operational risk management processes, operational risk data and assessment systems, operational risk quantification systems, and, to the extent the savings association uses the following systems, the internal models methodology, double default excessive correlation detection process, IMA for equity exposures, and IAA for securitization exposures to ABCP programs.

Affiliate with respect to a company means any company that controls, is controlled by, or is under common control with, the company.

Applicable external rating means:
(1) With respect to an exposure that has multiple external ratings assigned by NRSROs, the lowest solicited external rating assigned to the exposure by any NRSRO; and
(2) With respect to an exposure that has a single external rating assigned by an NRSRO, the external rating assigned to the exposure by the NRSRO.

Applicable inferred rating means:
(1) With respect to an exposure that has multiple inferred ratings, the lowest inferred rating based on a solicited external rating; and
(2) With respect to an exposure that has a single inferred rating, the inferred rating.

Asset-backed commercial paper (ABCP) program means a program that primarily issues commercial paper that:
(1) Has an external rating; and
(2) Is backed by underlying exposures held in a bankruptcy-remote SPE.

Asset-backed commercial paper (ABCP) program sponsor means a savings association that:
(1) Establishes an ABCP program;
(2) Approves the sellers permitted to participate in an ABCP program;
(3) Approves the exposures to be purchased by an ABCP program; or
(4) Administers the ABCP program by monitoring the underlying exposures, underwriting or otherwise arranging for the placement of debt or other obligations issued by the program, compiling monthly reports, or ensuring compliance with the program documents and with the program's credit and investment policy.

Backtesting means the comparison of a savings association's internal estimates with actual outcomes during a sample period not used in model development. In this context, backtesting is one form of out-of-sample testing.

Bank holding company is defined in section 2 of the Bank Holding Company Act (12 U.S.C. 1841).

Benchmarking means the comparison of a savings association's internal estimates with relevant internal and external data or with estimates based on other estimation techniques.

Business environment and internal control factors means the indicators of a savings association's operational risk profile that reflect a current and forward-looking assessment of the savings association's underlying business risk factors and internal control environment.

Carrying value means, with respect to an asset, the value of the asset on the balance sheet of the savings association, determined in accordance with GAAP.

Clean-up call means a contractual provision that permits an originating savings association or servicer to call securitization exposures before their stated maturity or call date. See also *eligible clean-up call*.

Commodity derivative contract means a commodity-linked swap, purchased commodity-linked option, forward commodity-linked contract, or any other instrument linked to commodities that gives rise to similar counterparty credit risks.

Company means a corporation, partnership, limited liability company, depository institution, business trust, special purpose entity, association, or similar organization.

Control. A person or company *controls* a company if it:
(1) Owns, controls, or holds with power to vote 25 percent or more of a class of voting securities of the company; or
(2) Consolidates the company for financial reporting purposes.

Controlled early amortization provision means an early amortization provision that meets all the following conditions:
(1) The originating savings association has appropriate policies and procedures to ensure that it has sufficient capital and liquidity available in the event of an early amortization;
(2) Throughout the duration of the securitization (including the early amortization period), there is the same pro rata sharing of interest, principal, expenses, losses, fees, recoveries, and other cash flows from the underlying exposures based on the originating savings association's and the investors' relative shares of the underlying exposures outstanding measured on a consistent monthly basis;
(3) The amortization period is sufficient for at least 90 percent of the total underlying exposures outstanding at the beginning of the early amortization period to be repaid or recognized as in default; and

Office of Thrift Supervision, Treasury   Pt. 567, App. C

(4) The schedule for repayment of investor principal is not more rapid than would be allowed by straight-line amortization over an 18-month period.

Credit derivative means a financial contract executed under standard industry credit derivative documentation that allows one party (the protection purchaser) to transfer the credit risk of one or more exposures (reference exposure) to another party (the protection provider). See also *eligible credit derivative*.

Credit-enhancing interest-only strip (CEIO) means an on-balance sheet asset that, in form or in substance:

(1) Represents a contractual right to receive some or all of the interest and no more than a minimal amount of principal due on the underlying exposures of a securitization; and

(2) Exposes the holder to credit risk directly or indirectly associated with the underlying exposures that exceeds a pro rata share of the holder's claim on the underlying exposures, whether through subordination provisions or other credit-enhancement techniques.

Credit-enhancing representations and warranties means representations and warranties that are made or assumed in connection with a transfer of underlying exposures (including loan servicing assets) and that obligate a savings association to protect another party from losses arising from the credit risk of the underlying exposures. Credit-enhancing representations and warranties include provisions to protect a party from losses resulting from the default or nonperformance of the obligors of the underlying exposures or from an insufficiency in the value of the collateral backing the underlying exposures. Credit-enhancing representations and warranties do not include:

(1) Early default clauses and similar warranties that permit the return of, or premium refund clauses that cover, first-lien residential mortgage exposures for a period not to exceed 120 days from the date of transfer, provided that the date of transfer is within one year of origination of the residential mortgage exposure;

(2) Premium refund clauses that cover underlying exposures guaranteed, in whole or in part, by the U.S. government, a U.S. government agency, or a U.S. government sponsored enterprise, provided that the clauses are for a period not to exceed 120 days from the date of transfer; or

(3) Warranties that permit the return of underlying exposures in instances of misrepresentation, fraud, or incomplete documentation.

Credit risk mitigant means collateral, a credit derivative, or a guarantee.

Credit-risk-weighted assets means 1.06 multiplied by the sum of:

(1) Total wholesale and retail risk-weighted assets;

(2) Risk-weighted assets for securitization exposures; and

(3) Risk-weighted assets for equity exposures.

Current exposure means, with respect to a netting set, the larger of zero or the market value of a transaction or portfolio of transactions within the netting set that would be lost upon default of the counterparty, assuming no recovery on the value of the transactions. Current exposure is also called replacement cost.

Default—(1) *Retail.* (i) A retail exposure of a savings association is in default if:

(A) The exposure is 180 days past due, in the case of a residential mortgage exposure or revolving exposure;

(B) The exposure is 120 days past due, in the case of all other retail exposures; or

(C) The savings association has taken a full or partial charge-off, write-down of principal, or material negative fair value adjustment of principal on the exposure for credit-related reasons.

(ii) Notwithstanding paragraph (1)(i) of this definition, for a retail exposure held by a non-U.S. subsidiary of the savings association that is subject to an internal ratings-based approach to capital adequacy consistent with the Basel Committee on Banking Supervision's "International Convergence of Capital Measurement and Capital Standards: A Revised Framework" in a non-U.S. jurisdiction, the savings association may elect to use the definition of default that is used in that jurisdiction, provided that the savings association has obtained prior approval from the OTS to use the definition of default in that jurisdiction.

(iii) A retail exposure in default remains in default until the savings association has reasonable assurance of repayment and performance for all contractual principal and interest payments on the exposure.

(2) *Wholesale.* (i) A savings association's wholesale obligor is in default if:

(A) The savings association determines that the obligor is unlikely to pay its credit obligations to the savings association in full, without recourse by the savings association to actions such as realizing collateral (if held); or

(B) The obligor is past due more than 90 days on any material credit obligation(s) to the savings association.[1]

(ii) An obligor in default remains in default until the savings association has reasonable assurance of repayment and performance for all contractual principal and interest payments on all exposures of the savings

---

[1] Overdrafts are past due once the obligor has breached an advised limit or been advised of a limit smaller than the current outstanding balance.

363

association to the obligor (other than exposures that have been fully written-down or charged-off).

Dependence means a measure of the association among operational losses across and within units of measure.

Depository institution is defined in section 3 of the Federal Deposit Insurance Act (12 U.S.C. 1813).

Derivative contract means a financial contract whose value is derived from the values of one or more underlying assets, reference rates, or indices of asset values or reference rates. Derivative contracts include interest rate derivative contracts, exchange rate derivative contracts, equity derivative contracts, commodity derivative contracts, credit derivatives, and any other instrument that poses similar counterparty credit risks. Derivative contracts also include unsettled securities, commodities, and foreign exchange transactions with a contractual settlement or delivery lag that is longer than the lesser of the market standard for the particular instrument or five business days.

Early amortization provision means a provision in the documentation governing a securitization that, when triggered, causes investors in the securitization exposures to be repaid before the original stated maturity of the securitization exposures, unless the provision:

(1) Is triggered solely by events not directly related to the performance of the underlying exposures or the originating savings association (such as material changes in tax laws or regulations); or

(2) Leaves investors fully exposed to future draws by obligors on the underlying exposures even after the provision is triggered.

Economic downturn conditions means, with respect to an exposure held by the savings association, those conditions in which the aggregate default rates for that exposure's wholesale or retail exposure subcategory (or subdivision of such subcategory selected by the savings association) in the exposure's national jurisdiction (or subdivision of such jurisdiction selected by the savings association) are significantly higher than average.

Effective maturity (M) of a wholesale exposure means:

(1) For wholesale exposures other than repo-style transactions, eligible margin loans, and OTC derivative contracts described in paragraph (2) or (3) of this definition:

(i) The weighted-average remaining maturity (measured in years, whole or fractional) of the expected contractual cash flows from the exposure, using the undiscounted amounts of the cash flows as weights; or

(ii) The nominal remaining maturity (measured in years, whole or fractional) of the exposure.

(2) For repo-style transactions, eligible margin loans, and OTC derivative contracts subject to a qualifying master netting agreement for which the savings association does not apply the internal models approach in paragraph (d) of section 32 of this appendix, the weighted-average remaining maturity (measured in years, whole or fractional) of the individual transactions subject to the qualifying master netting agreement, with the weight of each individual transaction set equal to the notional amount of the transaction.

(3) For repo-style transactions, eligible margin loans, and OTC derivative contracts for which the savings association applies the internal models approach in paragraph (d) of section 32 of this appendix, the value determined in paragraph (d)(4) of section 32 of this appendix.

Effective notional amount means, for an eligible guarantee or eligible credit derivative, the lesser of the contractual notional amount of the credit risk mitigant and the EAD of the hedged exposure, multiplied by the percentage coverage of the credit risk mitigant. For example, the effective notional amount of an eligible guarantee that covers, on a pro rata basis, 40 percent of any losses on a $100 bond would be $40.

Eligible clean-up call means a clean-up call that:

(1) Is exercisable solely at the discretion of the originating savings association or servicer;

(2) Is not structured to avoid allocating losses to securitization exposures held by investors or otherwise structured to provide credit enhancement to the securitization; and

(3) (i) For a traditional securitization, is only exercisable when 10 percent or less of the principal amount of the underlying exposures or securitization exposures (determined as of the inception of the securitization) is outstanding; or

(ii) For a synthetic securitization, is only exercisable when 10 percent or less of the principal amount of the reference portfolio of underlying exposures (determined as of the inception of the securitization) is outstanding.

Eligible credit derivative means a credit derivative in the form of a credit default swap, n^{th}-to-default swap, total return swap, or any other form of credit derivative approved by the OTS, provided that:

(1) The contract meets the requirements of an eligible guarantee and has been confirmed by the protection purchaser and the protection provider;

(2) Any assignment of the contract has been confirmed by all relevant parties;

(3) If the credit derivative is a credit default swap or n^{th}-to-default swap, the contract includes the following credit events:

(i) Failure to pay any amount due under the terms of the reference exposure, subject

Office of Thrift Supervision, Treasury
Pt. 567, App. C

to any applicable minimal payment threshold that is consistent with standard market practice and with a grace period that is closely in line with the grace period of the reference exposure; and

(ii) Bankruptcy, insolvency, or inability of the obligor on the reference exposure to pay its debts, or its failure or admission in writing of its inability generally to pay its debts as they become due, and similar events;

(4) The terms and conditions dictating the manner in which the contract is to be settled are incorporated into the contract;

(5) If the contract allows for cash settlement, the contract incorporates a robust valuation process to estimate loss reliably and specifies a reasonable period for obtaining post-credit event valuations of the reference exposure;

(6) If the contract requires the protection purchaser to transfer an exposure to the protection provider at settlement, the terms of at least one of the exposures that is permitted to be transferred under the contract provides that any required consent to transfer may not be unreasonably withheld;

(7) If the credit derivative is a credit default swap or n^{th}-to-default swap, the contract clearly identifies the parties responsible for determining whether a credit event has occurred, specifies that this determination is not the sole responsibility of the protection provider, and gives the protection purchaser the right to notify the protection provider of the occurrence of a credit event; and

(8) If the credit derivative is a total return swap and the savings association records net payments received on the swap as net income, the savings association records offsetting deterioration in the value of the hedged exposure (either through reductions in fair value or by an addition to reserves).

Eligible credit reserves means all general allowances that have been established through a charge against earnings to absorb credit losses associated with on- or off-balance sheet wholesale and retail exposures, including the allowance for loan and lease losses (ALLL) associated with such exposures but excluding specific reserves created against recognized losses.

Eligible double default guarantor, with respect to a guarantee or credit derivative obtained by a savings association, means:

(1) *U.S.-based entities.* A depository institution, a bank holding company, a savings and loan holding company (as defined in 12 U.S.C. 1467a) provided all or substantially all of the holding company's activities are permissible for a financial holding company under 12 U.S.C. 1843(k), a securities broker or dealer registered with the SEC under the Securities Exchange Act of 1934 (15 U.S.C. 78o *et seq.*), or an insurance company in the business of providing credit protection (such as a monoline bond insurer or re-insurer) that is subject to supervision by a State insurance regulator, if:

(i) At the time the guarantor issued the guarantee or credit derivative or at any time thereafter, the savings association assigned a PD to the guarantor's rating grade that was equal to or lower than the PD associated with a long-term external rating in the third-highest investment-grade rating category; and

(ii) The savings association currently assigns a PD to the guarantor's rating grade that is equal to or lower than the PD associated with a long-term external rating in the lowest investment-grade rating category; or

(2) *Non-U.S.-based entities.* A foreign bank (as defined in §211.2 of the Federal Reserve Board's Regulation K (12 CFR 211.2)), a non-U.S.-based securities firm, or a non-U.S.-based insurance company in the business of providing credit protection, if:

(i) The savings association demonstrates that the guarantor is subject to consolidated supervision and regulation comparable to that imposed on U.S. depository institutions, securities broker-dealers, or insurance companies (as the case may be), or has issued and outstanding an unsecured long-term debt security without credit enhancement that has a long-term applicable external rating of at least investment grade;

(ii) At the time the guarantor issued the guarantee or credit derivative or at any time thereafter, the savings association assigned a PD to the guarantor's rating grade that was equal to or lower than the PD associated with a long-term external rating in the third-highest investment-grade rating category; and

(iii) The savings association currently assigns a PD to the guarantor's rating grade that is equal to or lower than the PD associated with a long-term external rating in the lowest investment-grade rating category.

Eligible guarantee means a guarantee that:

(1) Is written and unconditional;

(2) Covers all or a pro rata portion of all contractual payments of the obligor on the reference exposure;

(3) Gives the beneficiary a direct claim against the protection provider;

(4) Is not unilaterally cancelable by the protection provider for reasons other than the breach of the contract by the beneficiary;

(5) Is legally enforceable against the protection provider in a jurisdiction where the protection provider has sufficient assets against which a judgment may be attached and enforced;

(6) Requires the protection provider to make payment to the beneficiary on the occurrence of a default (as defined in the guarantee) of the obligor on the reference exposure in a timely manner without the beneficiary first having to take legal actions to pursue the obligor for payment;

(7) Does not increase the beneficiary's cost of credit protection on the guarantee in response to deterioration in the credit quality of the reference exposure; and

(8) Is not provided by an affiliate of the savings association, unless the affiliate is an insured depository institution, bank, securities broker or dealer, or insurance company that:

(i) Does not control the savings association; and

(ii) Is subject to consolidated supervision and regulation comparable to that imposed on U.S. depository institutions, securities broker-dealers, or insurance companies (as the case may be).

Eligible margin loan means an extension of credit where:

(1) The extension of credit is collateralized exclusively by liquid and readily marketable debt or equity securities, gold, or conforming residential mortgages;

(2) The collateral is marked to market daily, and the transaction is subject to daily margin maintenance requirements;

(3) The extension of credit is conducted under an agreement that provides the savings association the right to accelerate and terminate the extension of credit and to liquidate or set off collateral promptly upon an event of default (including upon an event of bankruptcy, insolvency, or similar proceeding) of the counterparty, provided that, in any such case, any exercise of rights under the agreement will not be stayed or avoided under applicable law in the relevant jurisdictions;[2] and

(4) The savings association has conducted sufficient legal review to conclude with a well-founded basis (and maintains sufficient written documentation of that legal review) that the agreement meets the requirements of paragraph (3) of this definition and is legal, valid, binding, and enforceable under applicable law in the relevant jurisdictions.

Eligible operational risk offsets means amounts, not to exceed expected operational loss, that:

(1) Are generated by internal business practices to absorb highly predictable and reasonably stable operational losses, including reserves calculated consistent with GAAP; and

(2) Are available to cover expected operational losses with a high degree of certainty over a one-year horizon.

Eligible purchased wholesale exposure means a purchased wholesale exposure that:

(1) The savings association or securitization SPE purchased from an unaffiliated seller and did not directly or indirectly originate;

(2) Was generated on an arm's-length basis between the seller and the obligor (intercompany accounts receivable and receivables subject to contra-accounts between firms that buy and sell to each other do not satisfy this criterion);

(3) Provides the savings association or securitization SPE with a claim on all proceeds from the exposure or a pro rata interest in the proceeds from the exposure;

(4) Has an M of less than one year; and

(5) When consolidated by obligor, does not represent a concentrated exposure relative to the portfolio of purchased wholesale exposures.

Eligible securitization guarantor means:

(1) A sovereign entity, the Bank for International Settlements, the International Monetary Fund, the European Central Bank, the European Commission, a Federal Home Loan Bank, Federal Agricultural Mortgage Corporation (Farmer Mac), a multilateral development bank, a depository institution, a bank holding company, a savings and loan holding company (as defined in 12 U.S.C. 1467a) provided all or substantially all of the holding company's activities are permissible for a financial holding company under 12 U.S.C. 1843(k), a foreign bank (as defined in § 211.2 of the Federal Reserve Board's Regulation K (12 CFR 211.2)), or a securities firm;

(2) Any other entity (other than a securitization SPE) that has issued and outstanding an unsecured long-term debt security without credit enhancement that has a long-term applicable external rating in one of the three highest investment-grade rating categories; or

(3) Any other entity (other than a securitization SPE) that has a PD assigned by the savings association that is lower than or equal to the PD associated with a long-term external rating in the third highest investment-grade rating category.

Eligible servicer cash advance facility means a servicer cash advance facility in which:

(1) The servicer is entitled to full reimbursement of advances, except that a servicer may be obligated to make non-reimbursable advances for a particular underlying exposure if any such advance is contractually limited to an insignificant amount of the outstanding principal balance of that exposure;

(2) The servicer's right to reimbursement is senior in right of payment to all other

---

[2] This requirement is met where all transactions under the agreement are (i) executed under U.S. law and (ii) constitute "securities contracts" under section 555 of the Bankruptcy Code (11 U.S.C. 555), qualified financial contracts under section 11(e)(8) of the Federal Deposit Insurance Act (12 U.S.C. 1821(e)(8)), or netting contracts between or among financial institutions under sections 401–407 of the Federal Deposit Insurance Corporation Improvement Act of 1991 (12 U.S.C. 4401–4407) or the Federal Reserve Board's Regulation EE (12 CFR part 231).

Office of Thrift Supervision, Treasury

claims on the cash flows from the underlying exposures of the securitization; and

(3) The servicer has no legal obligation to, and does not, make advances to the securitization if the servicer concludes the advances are unlikely to be repaid.

Equity derivative contract means an equity-linked swap, purchased equity-linked option, forward equity-linked contract, or any other instrument linked to equities that gives rise to similar counterparty credit risks.

Equity exposure means:

(1) A security or instrument (whether voting or non-voting) that represents a direct or indirect ownership interest in, and is a residual claim on, the assets and income of a company, unless:

(i) The issuing company is consolidated with the savings association under GAAP;

(ii) The savings association is required to deduct the ownership interest from tier 1 or tier 2 capital under this appendix;

(iii) The ownership interest incorporates a payment or other similar obligation on the part of the issuing company (such as an obligation to make periodic payments); or

(iv) The ownership interest is a securitization exposure;

(2) A security or instrument that is mandatorily convertible into a security or instrument described in paragraph (1) of this definition;

(3) An option or warrant that is exercisable for a security or instrument described in paragraph (1) of this definition; or

(4) Any other security or instrument (other than a securitization exposure) to the extent the return on the security or instrument is based on the performance of a security or instrument described in paragraph (1) of this definition.

Excess spread for a period means:

(1) Gross finance charge collections and other income received by a securitization SPE (including market interchange fees) over a period minus interest paid to the holders of the securitization exposures, servicing fees, charge-offs, and other senior trust or similar expenses of the SPE over the period; divided by

(2) The principal balance of the underlying exposures at the end of the period.

Exchange rate derivative contract means a cross-currency interest rate swap, forward foreign-exchange contract, currency option purchased, or any other instrument linked to exchange rates that gives rise to similar counterparty credit risks.

Excluded mortgage exposure means any one-to four-family residential pre-sold construction loan for a residence for which the purchase contract is cancelled that would receive a 100 percent risk weight under section 618(a)(2) of the Resolution Trust Corporation Refinancing, Restructuring, and Improvement Act and under 12 CFR 567.1 (definition

Pt. 567, App. C

of "qualifying residential construction loan") and 12 CFR 567.6(a)(1)(iv).

Expected credit loss (ECL) means:

(1) For a wholesale exposure to a non-defaulted obligor or segment of non-defaulted retail exposures that is carried at fair value with gains and losses flowing through earnings or that is classified as held-for-sale and is carried at the lower of cost or fair value with losses flowing through earnings, zero.

(2) For all other wholesale exposures to non-defaulted obligors or segments of non-defaulted retail exposures, the product of PD times LGD times EAD for the exposure or segment.

(3) For a wholesale exposure to a defaulted obligor or segment of defaulted retail exposures, the savings association's impairment estimate for allowance purposes for the exposure or segment.

(4) Total ECL is the sum of expected credit losses for all wholesale and retail exposures other than exposures for which the savings association has applied the double default treatment in section 34 of this appendix.

Expected exposure (EE) means the expected value of the probability distribution of non-negative credit risk exposures to a counterparty at any specified future date before the maturity date of the longest term transaction in the netting set. Any negative market values in the probability distribution of market values to a counterparty at a specified future date are set to zero to convert the probability distribution of market values to the probability distribution of credit risk exposures.

Expected operational loss (EOL) means the expected value of the distribution of potential aggregate operational losses, as generated by the savings association's operational risk quantification system using a one-year horizon.

Expected positive exposure (EPE) means the weighted average over time of expected (non-negative) exposures to a counterparty where the weights are the proportion of the time interval that an individual expected exposure represents. When calculating risk-based capital requirements, the average is taken over a one-year horizon.

Exposure at default (EAD). (1) For the on-balance sheet component of a wholesale exposure or segment of retail exposures (other than an OTC derivative contract, or a repo-style transaction, or eligible margin loan for which the savings association determines EAD under section 32 of this appendix), EAD means:

(i) If the exposure or segment is a security classified as available-for-sale, the savings associations carrying value (including net accrued but unpaid interest and fees) for the exposure or segment less any unrealized gains on the exposure or segment and plus any unrealized losses on the exposure or segment; or

367

(ii) If the exposure or segment is not a security classified as available-for-sale, the savings association's carrying value (including net accrued but unpaid interest and fees) for the exposure or segment.

(2) For the off-balance sheet component of a wholesale exposure or segment of retail exposures (other than an OTC derivative contract, or a repo-style transaction or eligible margin loan for which the savings association determines EAD under section 32 of this appendix) in the form of a loan commitment, line of credit, trade-related letter of credit, or transaction-related contingency, EAD means the savings association's best estimate of net additions to the outstanding amount owed the savings association, including estimated future additional draws of principal and accrued but unpaid interest and fees, that are likely to occur over a one-year horizon assuming the wholesale exposure or the retail exposures in the segment were to go into default. This estimate of net additions must reflect what would be expected during economic downturn conditions. Trade-related letters of credit are short-term, self-liquidating instruments that are used to finance the movement of goods and are collateralized by the underlying goods. Transaction-related contingencies relate to a particular transaction and include, among other things, performance bonds and performance-based letters of credit.

(3) For the off-balance sheet component of a wholesale exposure or segment of retail exposures (other than an OTC derivative contract, or a repo-style transaction or eligible margin loan for which the savings association determines EAD under section 32 of this appendix) in the form of anything other than a loan commitment, line of credit, trade-related letter of credit, or transaction-related contingency, EAD means the notional amount of the exposure or segment.

(4) EAD for OTC derivative contracts is calculated as described in section 32 of this appendix. A savings association also may determine EAD for repo-style transactions and eligible margin loans as described in section 32 of this appendix.

(5) For wholesale or retail exposures in which only the drawn balance has been securitized, the savings association must reflect its share of the exposures' undrawn balances in EAD. Undrawn balances of revolving exposures for which the drawn balances have been securitized must be allocated between the seller's and investors' interests on a pro rata basis, based on the proportions of the seller's and investors' shares of the securitized drawn balances.

Exposure category means any of the wholesale, retail, securitization, or equity exposure categories.

External operational loss event data means, with respect to a savings association, gross operational loss amounts, dates, recoveries, and relevant causal information for operational loss events occurring at organizations other than the savings association.

External rating means a credit rating that is assigned by an NRSRO to an exposure, provided:

(1) The credit rating fully reflects the entire amount of credit risk with regard to all payments owed to the holder of the exposure. If a holder is owed principal and interest on an exposure, the credit rating must fully reflect the credit risk associated with timely repayment of principal and interest. If a holder is owed only principal on an exposure, the credit rating must fully reflect only the credit risk associated with timely repayment of principal; and

(2) The credit rating is published in an accessible form and is or will be included in the transition matrices made publicly available by the NRSRO that summarize the historical performance of positions rated by the NRSRO.

Financial collateral means collateral:

(1) In the form of:

(i) Cash on deposit with the savings association (including cash held for the savings association by a third-party custodian or trustee);

(ii) Gold bullion;

(iii) Long-term debt securities that have an applicable external rating of one category below investment grade or higher;

(iv) Short-term debt instruments that have an applicable external rating of at least investment grade;

(v) Equity securities that are publicly traded;

(vi) Convertible bonds that are publicly traded;

(vii) Money market mutual fund shares and other mutual fund shares if a price for the shares is publicly quoted daily; or

(viii) Conforming residential mortgages; and

(2) In which the savings association has a perfected, first priority security interest or, outside of the United States, the legal equivalent thereof (with the exception of cash on deposit and notwithstanding the prior security interest of any custodial agent).

GAAP means generally accepted accounting principles as used in the United States.

Gain-on-sale means an increase in the equity capital (as reported on Schedule SC of the Thrift Financial Report) of a savings association that results from a securitization (other than an increase in equity capital that results from the savings association's receipt of cash in connection with the securitization).

Guarantee means a financial guarantee, letter of credit, insurance, or other similar financial instrument (other than a credit derivative) that allows one party (beneficiary) to transfer the credit risk of one or more specific exposures (reference exposure) to another party (protection provider). See also *eligible guarantee*.

High volatility commercial real estate (HVCRE) exposure means a credit facility that finances or has financed the acquisition, development, or construction (ADC) of real property, unless the facility finances:

(1) One- to four-family residential properties; or

(2) Commercial real estate projects in which:

(i) The loan-to-value ratio is less than or equal to the applicable maximum supervisory loan-to-value ratio in the OTS's real estate lending standards at 12 CFR 560.100–560.101;

(ii) The borrower has contributed capital to the project in the form of cash or unencumbered readily marketable assets (or has paid development expenses out-of-pocket) of at least 15 percent of the real estate's appraised "as completed" value; and

(iii) The borrower contributed the amount of capital required by paragraph (2)(ii) of this definition before the savings association advances funds under the credit facility, and the capital contributed by the borrower, or internally generated by the project, is contractually required to remain in the project throughout the life of the project. The life of a project concludes only when the credit facility is converted to permanent financing or is sold or paid in full. Permanent financing may be provided by the savings association that provided the ADC facility as long as the permanent financing is subject to the savings association's underwriting criteria for long-term mortgage loans.

Inferred rating. A securitization exposure has an *inferred rating* equal to the external rating referenced in paragraph (2)(i) of this definition if:

(1) The securitization exposure does not have an external rating; and

(2) Another securitization exposure issued by the same issuer and secured by the same underlying exposures:

(i) Has an external rating;

(ii) Is subordinated in all respects to the unrated securitization exposure;

(iii) Does not benefit from any credit enhancement that is not available to the unrated securitization exposure; and

(iv) Has an effective remaining maturity that is equal to or longer than that of the unrated securitization exposure.

Interest rate derivative contract means a single-currency interest rate swap, basis swap, forward rate agreement, purchased interest rate option, when-issued securities, or any other instrument linked to interest rates that gives rise to similar counterparty credit risks.

Internal operational loss event data means, with respect to a savings association, gross operational loss amounts, dates, recoveries, and relevant causal information for operational loss events occurring at the savings association.

Investing savings association means, with respect to a securitization, a savings association that assumes the credit risk of a securitization exposure (other than an originating savings association) of the securitization). In the typical synthetic securitization, the investing savings association sells credit protection on a pool of underlying exposures to the originating savings association.

Investment fund means a company:

(1) All or substantially all of the assets of which are financial assets; and

(2) That has no material liabilities.

Investors' interest EAD means, with respect to a securitization, the EAD of the underlying exposures multiplied by the ratio of:

(1) The total amount of securitization exposures issued by the securitization SPE to investors; divided by

(2) The outstanding principal amount of underlying exposures.

Loss given default (LGD) means:

(1) For a wholesale exposure, the greatest of:

(i) Zero;

(ii) The savings association's empirically based best estimate of the long-run default-weighted average economic loss, per dollar of EAD, the savings association would expect to incur if the obligor (or a typical obligor in the loss severity grade assigned by the savings association to the exposure) were to default within a one-year horizon over a mix of economic conditions, including economic downturn conditions; or

(iii) The savings association's empirically based best estimate of the economic loss, per dollar of EAD, the savings association would expect to incur if the obligor (or a typical obligor in the loss severity grade assigned by the savings association to the exposure) were to default within a one-year horizon during economic downturn conditions.

(2) For a segment of retail exposures, the greatest of:

(i) Zero;

(ii) The savings association's empirically based best estimate of the long-run default-weighted average economic loss, per dollar of EAD, the savings association would expect to incur if the exposures in the segment were to default within a one-year horizon over a mix of economic conditions, including economic downturn conditions; or

(iii) The savings association's empirically based best estimate of the economic loss, per dollar of EAD, the savings association would expect to incur if the exposures in the segment were to default within a one-year horizon during economic downturn conditions.

(3) The economic loss on an exposure in the event of default is all material credit-related losses on the exposure (including accrued but

unpaid interest or fees, losses on the sale of collateral, direct workout costs, and an appropriate allocation of indirect workout costs). Where positive or negative cash flows on a wholesale exposure to a defaulted obligor or a defaulted retail exposure (including proceeds from the sale of collateral, workout costs, additional extensions of credit to facilitate repayment of the exposure, and draw-downs of unused credit lines) occur after the date of default, the economic loss must reflect the net present value of cash flows as of the default date using a discount rate appropriate to the risk of the defaulted exposure.

Main index means the Standard & Poor's 500 Index, the FTSE All-World Index, and any other index for which the savings association can demonstrate to the satisfaction of the OTS that the equities represented in the index have comparable liquidity, depth of market, and size of bid-ask spreads as equities in the Standard & Poor's 500 Index and FTSE All-World Index.

Multilateral development bank means the International Bank for Reconstruction and Development, the International Finance Corporation, the Inter-American Development Bank, the Asian Development Bank, the African Development Bank, the European Bank for Reconstruction and Development, the European Investment Bank, the European Investment Fund, the Nordic Investment Bank, the Caribbean Development Bank, the Islamic Development Bank, the Council of Europe Development Bank, and any other multilateral lending institution or regional development bank in which the U.S. government is a shareholder or contributing member or which the OTS determines poses comparable credit risk.

Nationally recognized statistical rating organization (NRSRO) means an entity registered with the SEC as a nationally recognized statistical rating organization under section 15E of the Securities Exchange Act of 1934 (15 U.S.C. 78o–7).

Netting set means a group of transactions with a single counterparty that are subject to a qualifying master netting agreement or qualifying cross-product master netting agreement. For purposes of the internal models methodology in paragraph (d) of section 32 of this appendix, each transaction that is not subject to such a master netting agreement is its own netting set.

Nth-to-default credit derivative means a credit derivative that provides credit protection only for the nth-defaulting reference exposure in a group of reference exposures.

Obligor means the legal entity or natural person contractually obligated on a wholesale exposure, except that a savings association may treat the following exposures as having separate obligors:

(1) Exposures to the same legal entity or natural person denominated in different currencies;

(2) (i) An income-producing real estate exposure for which all or substantially all of the repayment of the exposure is reliant on the cash flows of the real estate serving as collateral for the exposure; the savings association, in economic substance, does not have recourse to the borrower beyond the real estate collateral; and no cross-default or cross-acceleration clauses are in place other than clauses obtained solely out of an abundance of caution; and

(ii) Other credit exposures to the same legal entity or natural person; and

(3) (i) A wholesale exposure authorized under section 364 of the U.S. Bankruptcy Code (11 U.S.C. 364) to a legal entity or natural person who is a debtor-in-possession for purposes of Chapter 11 of the Bankruptcy Code; and

(ii) Other credit exposures to the same legal entity or natural person.

Operational loss means a loss (excluding insurance or tax effects) resulting from an operational loss event. Operational loss includes all expenses associated with an operational loss event except for opportunity costs, forgone revenue, and costs related to risk management and control enhancements implemented to prevent future operational losses.

Operational loss event means an event that results in loss and is associated with any of the following seven operational loss event type categories:

(1) Internal fraud, which means the operational loss event type category that comprises operational losses resulting from an act involving at least one internal party of a type intended to defraud, misappropriate property, or circumvent regulations, the law, or company policy, excluding diversity- and discrimination-type events.

(2) External fraud, which means the operational loss event type category that comprises operational losses resulting from an act by a third party of a type intended to defraud, misappropriate property, or circumvent the law. Retail credit card losses arising from non-contractual, third-party initiated fraud (for example, identity theft) are external fraud operational losses. All other third-party initiated credit losses are to be treated as credit risk losses.

(3) Employment practices and workplace safety, which means the operational loss event type category that comprises operational losses resulting from an act inconsistent with employment, health, or safety laws or agreements, payment of personal injury claims, or payment arising from diversity- and discrimination-type events.

(4) Clients, products, and business practices, which means the operational loss

Office of Thrift Supervision, Treasury Pt. 567, App. C

event type category that comprises operational losses resulting from the nature or design of a product or from an unintentional or negligent failure to meet a professional obligation to specific clients (including fiduciary and suitability requirements).

(5) Damage to physical assets, which means the operational loss event type category that comprises operational losses resulting from the loss of or damage to physical assets from natural disaster or other events.

(6) Business disruption and system failures, which means the operational loss event type category that comprises operational losses resulting from disruption of business or system failures.

(7) Execution, delivery, and process management, which means the operational loss event type category that comprises operational losses resulting from failed transaction processing or process management or losses arising from relations with trade counterparties and vendors.

Operational risk means the risk of loss resulting from inadequate or failed internal processes, people, and systems or from external events (including legal risk but excluding strategic and reputational risk).

Operational risk exposure means the 99.9th percentile of the distribution of potential aggregate operational losses, as generated by the savings association's operational risk quantification system over a one-year horizon (and not incorporating eligible operational risk offsets or qualifying operational risk mitigants).

Originating savings association, with respect to a securitization, means a savings association that:
(1) Directly or indirectly originated or securitized the underlying exposures included in the securitization; or
(2) Serves as an ABCP program sponsor to the securitization.

Other retail exposure means an exposure (other than a securitization exposure, an equity exposure, a residential mortgage exposure, an excluded mortgage exposure, a qualifying revolving exposure, or the residual value portion of a lease exposure) that is managed as part of a segment of exposures with homogeneous risk characteristics, not on an individual-exposure basis, and is either:
(1) An exposure to an individual for non-business purposes; or
(2) An exposure to an individual or company for business purposes if the savings association's consolidated business credit exposure to the individual or company is $1 million or less.

Over-the-counter (OTC) derivative contract means a derivative contract that is not traded on an exchange that requires the daily receipt and payment of cash-variation margin.

Probability of default (PD) means:

(1) For a wholesale exposure to a non-defaulted obligor, the savings association's empirically based best estimate of the long-run average one-year default rate for the rating grade assigned by the savings association to the obligor, capturing the average default experience for obligors in the rating grade over a mix of economic conditions (including economic downturn conditions) sufficient to provide a reasonable estimate of the average one-year default rate over the economic cycle for the rating grade.

(2) For a segment of non-defaulted retail exposures, the savings association's empirically based best estimate of the long-run average one-year default rate for the exposures in the segment, capturing the average default experience for exposures in the segment over a mix of economic conditions (including economic downturn conditions) sufficient to provide a reasonable estimate of the average one-year default rate over the economic cycle for the segment and adjusted upward as appropriate for segments for which seasoning effects are material. For purposes of this definition, a segment for which seasoning effects are material is a segment where there is a material relationship between the time since origination of exposures within the segment and the savings association's best estimate of the long-run average one-year default rate for the exposures in the segment.

(3) For a wholesale exposure to a defaulted obligor or segment of defaulted retail exposures, 100 percent.

Protection amount (P) means, with respect to an exposure hedged by an eligible guarantee or eligible credit derivative, the effective notional amount of the guarantee or credit derivative, reduced to reflect any currency mismatch, maturity mismatch, or lack of restructuring coverage (as provided in section 33 of this appendix).

Publicly traded means traded on:
(1) Any exchange registered with the SEC as a national securities exchange under section 6 of the Securities Exchange Act of 1934 (15 U.S.C. 78f); or
(2) Any non-U.S.-based securities exchange that:
(i) Is registered with, or approved by, a national securities regulatory authority; and
(ii) Provides a liquid, two-way market for the instrument in question, meaning that there are enough independent bona fide offers to buy and sell so that a sales price reasonably related to the last sales price or current bona fide competitive bid and offer quotations can be determined promptly and a trade can be settled at such a price within five business days.

Qualifying central counterparty means a counterparty (for example, a clearinghouse) that:

(1) Facilitates trades between counterparties in one or more financial markets by either guaranteeing trades or novating contracts;

(2) Requires all participants in its arrangements to be fully collateralized on a daily basis; and

(3) The savings association demonstrates to the satisfaction of the OTS is in sound financial condition and is subject to effective oversight by a national supervisory authority.

Qualifying cross-product master netting agreement means a qualifying master netting agreement that provides for termination and close-out netting across multiple types of financial transactions or qualifying master netting agreements in the event of a counterparty's default, provided that:

(1) The underlying financial transactions are OTC derivative contracts, eligible margin loans, or repo-style transactions; and

(2) The savings association obtains a written legal opinion verifying the validity and enforceability of the agreement under applicable law of the relevant jurisdictions if the counterparty fails to perform upon an event of default, including upon an event of bankruptcy, insolvency, or similar proceeding.

Qualifying master netting agreement means any written, legally enforceable bilateral agreement, provided that:

(1) The agreement creates a single legal obligation for all individual transactions covered by the agreement upon an event of default, including bankruptcy, insolvency, or similar proceeding, of the counterparty;

(2) The agreement provides the savings association the right to accelerate, terminate, and close-out on a net basis all transactions under the agreement and to liquidate or set off collateral promptly upon an event of default, including upon an event of bankruptcy, insolvency, or similar proceeding, of the counterparty, provided that, in any such case, any exercise of rights under the agreement will not be stayed or avoided under applicable law in the relevant jurisdictions;

(3) The savings association has conducted sufficient legal review to conclude with a well-founded basis (and maintains sufficient written documentation of that legal review) that:

(i) The agreement meets the requirements of paragraph (2) of this definition; and

(ii) In the event of a legal challenge (including one resulting from default or from bankruptcy, insolvency, or similar proceeding) the relevant court and administrative authorities would find the agreement to be legal, valid, binding, and enforceable under the law of the relevant jurisdictions; and

(4) The savings association establishes and maintains procedures to monitor possible changes in relevant law and to ensure that the agreement continues to satisfy the requirements of this definition; and

(5) The agreement does not contain a walkaway clause (that is, a provision that permits a non-defaulting counterparty to make a lower payment than it would make otherwise under the agreement, or no payment at all, to a defaulter or the estate of a defaulter, even if the defaulter or the estate of the defaulter is a net creditor under the agreement).

Qualifying revolving exposure (QRE) means an exposure (other than a securitization exposure or equity exposure) to an individual that is managed as part of a segment of exposures with homogeneous risk characteristics, not on an individual-exposure basis, and:

(1) Is revolving (that is, the amount outstanding fluctuates, determined largely by the borrower's decision to borrow and repay, up to a pre-established maximum amount);

(2) Is unsecured and unconditionally cancelable by the savings association to the fullest extent permitted by Federal law; and

(3) Has a maximum exposure amount (drawn plus undrawn) of up to $100,000.

Repo-style transaction means a repurchase or reverse repurchase transaction, or a securities borrowing or securities lending transaction, including a transaction in which the savings association acts as agent for a customer and indemnifies the customer against loss, provided that:

(1) The transaction is based solely on liquid and readily marketable securities, cash, gold, or conforming residential mortgages;

(2) The transaction is marked-to-market daily and subject to daily margin maintenance requirements;

(3)(i) The transaction is a "securities contract" or "repurchase agreement" under section 555 or 559, respectively, of the Bankruptcy Code (11 U.S.C. 555 or 559), a qualified financial contract under section 11(e)(8) of the Federal Deposit Insurance Act (12 U.S.C. 1821(e)(8)), or a netting contract between or among financial institutions under sections 401–407 of the Federal Deposit Insurance Corporation Improvement Act of 1991 (12 U.S.C. 4401–4407) or the Federal Reserve Board's Regulation EE (12 CFR part 231); or

(ii) If the transaction does not meet the criteria set forth in paragraph (3)(i) of this definition, then either:

(A) The transaction is executed under an agreement that provides the savings association the right to accelerate, terminate, and close-out the transaction on a net basis and to liquidate or set off collateral promptly upon an event of default (including upon an event of bankruptcy, insolvency, or similar proceeding) of the counterparty, provided that, in any such case, any exercise of rights under the agreement will not be stayed or avoided under applicable law in the relevant jurisdictions; or

(B) The transaction is:

Office of Thrift Supervision, Treasury   Pt. 567, App. C

(1) Either overnight or unconditionally cancelable at any time by the savings association; and

(2) Executed under an agreement that provides the savings association the right to accelerate, terminate, and close-out the transaction on a net basis and to liquidate or set off collateral promptly upon an event of counterparty default; and

(4) The savings association has conducted sufficient legal review to conclude with a well-founded basis (and maintains sufficient written documentation of that legal review) that the agreement meets the requirements of paragraph (3) of this definition and is legal, valid, binding, and enforceable under applicable law in the relevant jurisdictions.

Residential mortgage exposure means an exposure (other than a securitization exposure, equity exposure, or excluded mortgage exposure) that is managed as part of a segment of exposures with homogeneous risk characteristics, not on an individual-exposure basis, and is:

(1) An exposure that is primarily secured by a first or subsequent lien on one- to four-family residential property; or

(2) An exposure with an original and outstanding amount of $1 million or less that is primarily secured by a first or subsequent lien on residential property that is not one to four family.

Retail exposure means a residential mortgage exposure, a qualifying revolving exposure, or an other retail exposure.

Retail exposure subcategory means the residential mortgage exposure, qualifying revolving exposure, or other retail exposure subcategory.

Risk parameter means a variable used in determining risk-based capital requirements for wholesale and retail exposures, specifically probability of default (PD), loss given default (LGD), exposure at default (EAD), or effective maturity (M).

Scenario analysis means a systematic process of obtaining expert opinions from business managers and risk management experts to derive reasoned assessments of the likelihood and loss impact of plausible high-severity operational losses. Scenario analysis may include the well-reasoned evaluation and use of external operational loss event data, adjusted as appropriate to ensure relevance to a savings association's operational risk profile and control structure.

SEC means the U.S. Securities and Exchange Commission.

Securitization means a traditional securitization or a synthetic securitization.

Securitization exposure means an on-balance sheet or off-balance sheet credit exposure that arises from a traditional or synthetic securitization (including credit-enhancing representations and warranties).

Securitization special purpose entity (securitization SPE) means a corporation, trust, or other entity organized for the specific purpose of holding underlying exposures of a securitization; the activities of which are limited to those appropriate to accomplish this purpose, and the structure of which is intended to isolate the underlying exposures held by the entity from the credit risk of the seller of the underlying exposures to the entity.

Senior securitization exposure means a securitization exposure that has a first priority claim on the cash flows from the underlying exposures. When determining whether a securitization exposure has a first priority claim on the cash flows from the underlying exposures, a savings association is not required to consider amounts due under interest rate or currency derivative contracts, fees due, or other similar payments. Both the most senior commercial paper issued by an ABCP program and a liquidity facility that supports the ABCP program may be senior securitization exposures if the liquidity facility provider's right to reimbursement of the drawn amounts is senior to all claims on the cash flows from the underlying exposures except amounts due under interest rate or currency derivative contracts, fees due, or other similar payments.

Servicer cash advance facility means a facility under which the servicer of the underlying exposures of a securitization may advance cash to ensure an uninterrupted flow of payments to investors in the securitization, including advances made to cover foreclosure costs or other expenses to facilitate the timely collection of the underlying exposures. See also *eligible servicer cash advance facility*.

Sovereign entity means a central government (including the U.S. government) or an agency, department, ministry, or central bank of a central government.

Sovereign exposure means:

(1) A direct exposure to a sovereign entity; or

(2) An exposure directly and unconditionally backed by the full faith and credit of a sovereign entity.

Subsidiary means, with respect to a company, a company controlled by that company.

Synthetic securitization means a transaction in which:

(1) All or a portion of the credit risk of one or more underlying exposures is transferred to one or more third parties through the use of one or more credit derivatives or guarantees (other than a guarantee that transfers only the credit risk of an individual retail exposure);

(2) The credit risk associated with the underlying exposures has been separated into at least two tranches reflecting different levels of seniority;

(3) Performance of the securitization exposures depends upon the performance of the underlying exposures; and

(4) All or substantially all of the underlying exposures are financial exposures (such as loans, commitments, credit derivatives, guarantees, receivables, asset-backed securities, mortgage-backed securities, other debt securities, or equity securities).

Tier 1 capital is defined in subpart B of part 567, as modified in part II of this appendix.

Tier 2 capital is defined in subpart B of part 567, as modified in part II of this appendix.

Total qualifying capital means the sum of tier 1 capital and tier 2 capital, after all deductions required in this appendix.

Total risk-weighted assets means:

(1) The sum of:

(i) Credit risk-weighted assets; and

(ii) Risk-weighted assets for operational risk; minus

(2) Excess eligible credit reserves not included in tier 2 capital.

Total wholesale and retail risk-weighted assets means the sum of risk-weighted assets for wholesale exposures to non-defaulted obligors and segments of non-defaulted retail exposures; risk-weighted assets for wholesale exposures to defaulted obligors and segments of defaulted retail exposures; risk-weighted assets for assets not defined by an exposure category; and risk-weighted assets for non-material portfolios of exposures (all as determined in section 31 of this appendix) and risk-weighted assets for unsettled transactions (as determined in section 35 of this appendix) minus the amounts deducted from capital pursuant to subpart B of part 567 (excluding those deductions reversed in section 12 of this appendix).

Traditional securitization means a transaction in which:

(1) All or a portion of the credit risk of one or more underlying exposures is transferred to one or more third parties other than through the use of credit derivatives or guarantees;

(2) The credit risk associated with the underlying exposures has been separated into at least two tranches reflecting different levels of seniority;

(3) Performance of the securitization exposures depends upon the performance of the underlying exposures;

(4) All or substantially all of the underlying exposures are financial exposures (such as loans, commitments, credit derivatives, guarantees, receivables, asset-backed securities, mortgage-backed securities, other debt securities, or equity securities);

(5) The underlying exposures are not owned by an operating company;

(6) The underlying exposures are not owned by a small business investment company described in section 302 of the Small Business Investment Act of 1958 (15 U.S.C. 682); and

(7) The underlying exposures are not owned by a firm an investment in which is designed primarily to promote community welfare, including the welfare of low- and moderate-income communities or families, such as by providing services or jobs.

(8) The OTS may determine that a transaction in which the underlying exposures are owned by an investment firm that exercises substantially unfettered control over the size and composition of its assets, liabilities, and off-balance sheet exposures is not a traditional securitization based on the transaction's leverage, risk profile, or economic substance.

(9) The OTS may deem a transaction that meets the definition of a traditional securitization, notwithstanding paragraph (5), (6), or (7) of this definition, to be a traditional securitization based on the transaction's leverage, risk profile, or economic substance.

Tranche means all securitization exposures associated with a securitization that have the same seniority level.

Underlying exposures means one or more exposures that have been securitized in a securitization transaction.

Unexpected operational loss (UOL) means the difference between the savings association's operational risk exposure and the savings association's expected operational loss.

Unit of measure means the level (for example, organizational unit or operational loss event type) at which the savings association's operational risk quantification system generates a separate distribution of potential operational losses.

Value-at-Risk (VaR) means the estimate of the maximum amount that the value of one or more exposures could decline due to market price or rate movements during a fixed holding period within a stated confidence interval.

Wholesale exposure means a credit exposure to a company, natural person, sovereign entity, or governmental entity (other than a securitization exposure, retail exposure, excluded mortgage exposure, or equity exposure). Examples of a wholesale exposure include:

(1) A non-tranched guarantee issued by a savings association on behalf of a company;

(2) A repo-style transaction entered into by a savings association with a company and any other transaction in which a savings association posts collateral to a company and faces counterparty credit risk;

(3) An exposure that a savings association treats as a covered position under any applicable market risk rule for which there is a counterparty credit risk capital requirement;

(4) A sale of corporate loans by a savings association to a third party in which the savings association retains full recourse;

Office of Thrift Supervision, Treasury

Pt. 567, App. C

(5) An OTC derivative contract entered into by a savings association with a company;

(6) An exposure to an individual that is not managed by a savings association as part of a segment of exposures with homogeneous risk characteristics; and

(7) A commercial lease.

Wholesale exposure subcategory means the HVCRE or non-HVCRE wholesale exposure subcategory.

Section 3. Minimum Risk-Based Capital Requirements

(a) Except as modified by paragraph (c) of this section or by section 23 of this appendix, each savings association must meet a minimum ratio of:

(1) Total qualifying capital to total risk-weighted assets of 8.0 percent; and

(2) Tier 1 capital to total risk-weighted assets of 4.0 percent.

(b) Each savings association must hold capital commensurate with the level and nature of all risks to which the savings association is exposed.

(c) When a savings association subject to any applicable market risk rule calculates its risk-based capital requirements under this appendix, the savings association must also refer to any applicable market risk rule for supplemental rules to calculate risk-based capital requirements adjusted for market risk.

PART II. QUALIFYING CAPITAL

Section 11. Additional Deductions

(a) *General.* A savings association that uses this appendix must make the same deductions from its tier 1 capital and tier 2 capital required in subpart B of part 567, except that:

(1) A savings association is not required to deduct certain equity investments and CEIOs (as provided in section 12 of this appendix); and

(2) A savings association also must make the deductions from capital required by paragraphs (b) and (c) of this section.

(b) *Deductions from tier 1 capital.* A savings association must deduct from tier 1 capital any gain-on-sale associated with a securitization exposure as provided in paragraph (a) of section 41 and paragraphs (a)(1), (c), (g)(1), and (h)(1) of section 42 of this appendix.

(c) *Deductions from tier 1 and tier 2 capital.* A savings association must deduct the exposures specified in paragraphs (c)(1) through (c)(7) in this section 50 percent from tier 1 capital and 50 percent from tier 2 capital. If the amount deductible from tier 2 capital exceeds the savings association's actual tier 2 capital, however, the savings association must deduct the excess from tier 1 capital.

(1) *Credit-enhancing interest-only strips (CEIOs).* In accordance with paragraphs (a)(1) and (c) of section 42 of this appendix, any CEIO that does not constitute gain-on-sale.

(2) *Non-qualifying securitization exposures.* In accordance with paragraphs (a)(4) and (c) of section 42 of this appendix, any securitization exposure that does not qualify for the Ratings-Based Approach, the Internal Assessment Approach, or the Supervisory Formula Approach under sections 43, 44, and 45 of this appendix, respectively.

(3) *Securitizations of non-IRB exposures.* In accordance with paragraphs (c) and (g)(4) of section 42 of this appendix, certain exposures to a securitization any underlying exposure of which is not a wholesale exposure, retail exposure, securitization exposure, or equity exposure.

(4) *Low-rated securitization exposures.* In accordance with section 43 and paragraph (c) of section 42 of this appendix, any securitization exposure that qualifies for and must be deducted under the Ratings-Based Approach.

(5) *High-risk securitization exposures subject to the Supervisory Formula Approach.* In accordance with paragraphs (b) and (c) of section 45 of this appendix and paragraph (c) of section 42 of this appendix, certain high-risk securitization exposures (or portions thereof) that qualify for the Supervisory Formula Approach.

(6) *Eligible credit reserves shortfall.* In accordance with paragraph (a)(1) of section 13 of this appendix, any eligible credit reserves shortfall.

(7) *Certain failed capital markets transactions.* In accordance with paragraph (e)(3) of section 35 of this appendix, the savings association's exposure on certain failed capital markets transactions.

Section 12. Deductions and Limitations Not Required

(a) *Deduction of CEIOs.* A savings association is not required to make the deduction from capital for CEIOs in 12 CFR 567.5(a)(2)(iii) and 567.12(e).

(b) *Deduction for certain equity investments.* A savings association is not required to deduct equity securities from capital under 12 CFR 567.5(c)(2)(ii). However, it must continue to deduct equity investments in real estate under that section. See 12 CFR 567.1, which defines equity investments, including equity securities and equity investments in real estate.

Section 13. Eligible Credit Reserves

(a) *Comparison of eligible credit reserves to expected credit losses*—(1) *Shortfall of eligible credit reserves.* If a savings association's eligible credit reserves are less than the savings association's total expected credit losses, the savings association must deduct the shortfall amount 50 percent from tier 1 capital and 50 percent from tier 2 capital. If the amount deductible from tier 2 capital exceeds the savings association's actual tier 2 capital, the savings association must deduct the excess amount from tier 1 capital.

(2) *Excess eligible credit reserves.* If a savings association's eligible credit reserves exceed the savings association's total expected credit losses, the savings association may include the excess amount in tier 2 capital to the extent that the excess amount does not exceed 0.6 percent of the savings association's credit-risk-weighted assets.

(b) *Treatment of allowance for loan and lease losses.* Regardless of any provision in subpart B of part 567, the ALLL is included in tier 2 capital only to the extent provided in paragraph (a)(2) of this section and in section 24 of this appendix.

PART III. QUALIFICATION

Section 21. Qualification Process

(a) *Timing.* (1) A savings association that is described in paragraph (b)(1) of section 1 of this appendix must adopt a written implementation plan no later than six months after the later of April 1, 2008, or the date the savings association meets a criterion in that section. The implementation plan must incorporate an explicit first floor period start date no later than 36 months after the later of April 1, 2008, or the date the savings association meets at least one criterion under paragraph (b)(1) of section 1 of this appendix. The OTS may extend the first floor period start date.

(2) A savings association that elects to be subject to this appendix under paragraph (b)(2) of section 1 of this appendix must adopt a written implementation plan.

(b) *Implementation plan.* (1) The savings association's implementation plan must address in detail how the savings association complies, or plans to comply, with the qualification requirements in section 22 of this appendix. The savings association also must maintain a comprehensive and sound planning and governance process to oversee the implementation efforts described in the plan. At a minimum, the plan must:

(i) Comprehensively address the qualification requirements in section 22 of this appendix for the savings association and each consolidated subsidiary (U.S. and foreign-based) of the savings association with respect to all portfolios and exposures of the savings association and each of its consolidated subsidiaries;

(ii) Justify and support any proposed temporary or permanent exclusion of business lines, portfolios, or exposures from application of the advanced approaches in this appendix (which business lines, portfolios, and exposures must be, in the aggregate, immaterial to the savings association);

(iii) Include the savings association's self-assessment of:

(A) The savings association's current status in meeting the qualification requirements in section 22 of this appendix; and

(B) The consistency of the savings association's current practices with the OTS's supervisory guidance on the qualification requirements;

(iv) Based on the savings association's self-assessment, identify and describe the areas in which the savings association proposes to undertake additional work to comply with the qualification requirements in section 22 of this appendix or to improve the consistency of the savings association's current practices with the OTS's supervisory guidance on the qualification requirements (gap analysis);

(v) Describe what specific actions the savings association will take to address the areas identified in the gap analysis required by paragraph (b)(1)(iv) of this section;

(vi) Identify objective, measurable milestones, including delivery dates and a date when the savings association's implementation of the methodologies described in this appendix will be fully operational;

(vii) Describe resources that have been budgeted and are available to implement the plan; and

(viii) Receive approval of the savings association's board of directors.

(2) The savings association must submit the implementation plan, together with a copy of the minutes of the board of directors' approval, to the OTS at least 60 days before the savings association proposes to begin its parallel run, unless the OTS waives prior notice.

(c) *Parallel run.* Before determining its risk-based capital requirements under this appendix and following adoption of the implementation plan, the savings association must conduct a satisfactory parallel run. A satisfactory parallel run is a period of no less than four consecutive calendar quarters during which the savings association complies with the qualification requirements in section 22 of this appendix to the satisfaction of the OTS. During the parallel run, the savings association must report to the OTS on a calendar quarterly basis its risk-based capital ratios using subpart B of part 567 and the risk-based capital requirements described in this appendix. During this period, the savings association is subject to subpart B of part 567.

(d) *Approval to calculate risk-based capital requirements under this appendix.* The OTS will notify the savings association of the date that the savings association may begin its first floor period if the OTS determines that:

(1) The savings association fully complies with all the qualification requirements in section 22 of this appendix;

Office of Thrift Supervision, Treasury   Pt. 567, App. C

(2) The savings association has conducted a satisfactory parallel run under paragraph (c) of this section; and

(3) The savings association has an adequate process to ensure ongoing compliance with the qualification requirements in section 22 of this appendix.

(e) *Transitional floor periods.* Following a satisfactory parallel run, a savings association is subject to three transitional floor periods.

(1) *Risk-based capital ratios during the transitional floor periods*—(i) *Tier 1 risk-based capital ratio.* During a savings association's transitional floor periods, the savings association's tier 1 risk-based capital ratio is equal to the lower of:

(A) The savings association's floor-adjusted tier 1 risk-based capital ratio; or

(B) The savings association's advanced approaches tier 1 risk-based capital ratio.

(ii) *Total risk-based capital ratio.* During a savings association's transitional floor periods, the savings association's total risk-based capital ratio is equal to the lower of:

(A) The savings association's floor-adjusted total risk-based capital ratio; or

(B) The savings association's advanced approaches total risk-based capital ratio.

(2) *Floor-adjusted risk-based capital ratios.* (i) A savings association's floor-adjusted tier 1 risk-based capital ratio during a transitional floor period is equal to the savings association's tier 1 capital as calculated under subpart B of part 567, divided by the product of:

(A) The savings association's total risk-weighted assets as calculated under subpart B of part 567; and

(B) The appropriate transitional floor percentage in Table 1.

(ii) A savings association's floor-adjusted total risk-based capital ratio during a transitional floor period is equal to the sum of the savings association's tier 1 and tier 2 capital as calculated under subpart B of part 567, divided by the product of:

(A) The savings association's total risk-weighted assets as calculated under subpart B of part 567; and

(B) The appropriate transitional floor percentage in Table 1.

(iii) A savings association that meets the criteria in paragraph (b)(1) or (b)(2) of section 1 of this appendix as of April 1, 2008, must use subpart B of part 567 during the parallel run and as the basis for its transitional floors.

TABLE 1—TRANSITIONAL FLOORS

Transitional floor period	Transitional floor percentage
First floor period	95 percent.
Second floor period	90 percent.
Third floor period	85 percent.

(3) *Advanced approaches risk-based capital ratios.* (i) A savings association's advanced approaches tier 1 risk-based capital ratio equals the savings association's tier 1 risk-based capital ratio as calculated under this appendix (other than this section on transitional floor periods).

(ii) A savings association's advanced approaches total risk-based capital ratio equals the savings association's total risk-based capital ratio as calculated under this appendix (other than this section on transitional floor periods).

(4) *Reporting.* During the transitional floor periods, a savings association must report to the OTS on a calendar quarterly basis both floor-adjusted risk-based capital ratios and both advanced approaches risk-based capital ratios.

(5) *Exiting a transitional floor period.* A savings association may not exit a transitional floor period until the savings association has spent a minimum of four consecutive calendar quarters in the period and the OTS has determined that the savings association may exit the floor period. The OTS's determination will be based on an assessment of the savings association's ongoing compliance with the qualification requirements in section 22 of this appendix.

(6) *Interagency study.* After the end of the second transition year (2010), the Federal banking agencies will publish a study that evaluates the advanced approaches to determine if there are any material deficiencies. For any primary Federal supervisor to authorize any institution to exit the third transitional floor period, the study must determine that there are no such material deficiencies that cannot be addressed by then-existing tools, or, if such deficiencies are found, they are first remedied by changes to this appendix. Notwithstanding the preceding sentence, a primary Federal supervisor that disagrees with the finding of material deficiency may not authorize any institution under its jurisdiction to exit the third transitional floor period unless it provides a public report explaining its reasoning.

Section 22. Qualification Requirements

(a) *Process and systems requirements.* (1) A savings association must have a rigorous process for assessing its overall capital adequacy in relation to its risk profile and a comprehensive strategy for maintaining an appropriate level of capital.

(2) The systems and processes used by a savings association for risk-based capital purposes under this appendix must be consistent with the savings association's internal risk management processes and management information reporting systems.

(3) Each savings association must have an appropriate infrastructure with risk measurement and management processes that meet the qualification requirements of this section and are appropriate given the savings

association's size and level of complexity. Regardless of whether the systems and models that generate the risk parameters necessary for calculating a savings association's risk-based capital requirements are located at any affiliate of the savings association, the savings association itself must ensure that the risk parameters and reference data used to determine its risk-based capital requirements are representative of its own credit risk and operational risk exposures.

(b) *Risk rating and segmentation systems for wholesale and retail exposures.* (1) A savings association must have an internal risk rating and segmentation system that accurately and reliably differentiates among degrees of credit risk for the savings association's wholesale and retail exposures.

(2) For wholesale exposures:

(i) A savings association must have an internal risk rating system that accurately and reliably assigns each obligor to a single rating grade (reflecting the obligor's likelihood of default). A savings association may elect, however, not to assign to a rating grade an obligor to whom the savings association extends credit based solely on the financial strength of a guarantor, provided that all of the savings association's exposures to the obligor are fully covered by eligible guarantees, the savings association applies the PD substitution approach in paragraph (c)(1) of section 33 of this appendix to all exposures to that obligor, and the savings association immediately assigns the obligor to a rating grade if a guarantee can no longer be recognized under this appendix. The savings association's wholesale obligor rating system must have at least seven discrete rating grades for non-defaulted obligors and at least one rating grade for defaulted obligors.

(ii) Unless the savings association has chosen to directly assign LGD estimates to each wholesale exposure, the savings association must have an internal risk rating system that accurately and reliably assigns each wholesale exposure to a loss severity rating grade (reflecting the savings association's estimate of the LGD of the exposure). A savings association employing loss severity rating grades must have a sufficiently granular loss severity grading system to avoid grouping together exposures with widely ranging LGDs.

(3) For retail exposures, a savings association must have an internal system that groups retail exposures into the appropriate retail exposure subcategory, groups the retail exposures in each retail exposure subcategory into separate segments with homogeneous risk characteristics, and assigns accurate and reliable PD and LGD estimates for each segment on a consistent basis. The savings association's system must identify and group in separate segments by subcategories exposures identified in paragraphs (c)(2)(ii) and (iii) of section 31 of this appendix.

(4) The savings association's internal risk rating policy for wholesale exposures must describe the savings association's rating philosophy (that is, must describe how wholesale obligor rating assignments are affected by the savings association's choice of the range of economic, business, and industry conditions that are considered in the obligor rating process).

(5) The savings association's internal risk rating system for wholesale exposures must provide for the review and update (as appropriate) of each obligor rating and (if applicable) each loss severity rating whenever the savings association receives new material information, but no less frequently than annually. The savings association's retail exposure segmentation system must provide for the review and update (as appropriate) of assignments of retail exposures to segments whenever the savings association receives new material information, but generally no less frequently than quarterly.

(c) *Quantification of risk parameters for wholesale and retail exposures.* (1) The savings association must have a comprehensive risk parameter quantification process that produces accurate, timely, and reliable estimates of the risk parameters for the savings association's wholesale and retail exposures.

(2) Data used to estimate the risk parameters must be relevant to the savings association's actual wholesale and retail exposures, and of sufficient quality to support the determination of risk-based capital requirements for the exposures.

(3) The savings association's risk parameter quantification process must produce appropriately conservative risk parameter estimates where the savings association has limited relevant data, and any adjustments that are part of the quantification process must not result in a pattern of bias toward lower risk parameter estimates.

(4) The savings association's risk parameter estimation process should not rely on the possibility of U.S. government financial assistance, except for the financial assistance that the U.S. government has a legally binding commitment to provide.

(5) Where the savings association's quantifications of LGD directly or indirectly incorporate estimates of the effectiveness of its credit risk management practices in reducing its exposure to troubled obligors prior to default, the savings association must support such estimates with empirical analysis showing that the estimates are consistent with its historical experience in dealing with such exposures during economic downturn conditions.

(6) PD estimates for wholesale obligors and retail segments must be based on at least five years of default data. LGD estimates for wholesale exposures must be based on at

Office of Thrift Supervision, Treasury   Pt. 567, App. C

least seven years of loss severity data, and LGD estimates for retail segments must be based on at least five years of loss severity data. EAD estimates for wholesale exposures must be based on at least seven years of exposure amount data, and EAD estimates for retail segments must be based on at least five years of exposure amount data.

(7) Default, loss severity, and exposure amount data must include periods of economic downturn conditions, or the savings association must adjust its estimates of risk parameters to compensate for the lack of data from periods of economic downturn conditions.

(8) The savings association's PD, LGD, and EAD estimates must be based on the definition of default in this appendix.

(9) The savings association must review and update (as appropriate) its risk parameters and its risk parameter quantification process at least annually.

(10) The savings association must at least annually conduct a comprehensive review and analysis of reference data to determine relevance of reference data to the savings association's exposures, quality of reference data to support PD, LGD, and EAD estimates, and consistency of reference data to the definition of default contained in this appendix.

(d) *Counterparty credit risk model.* A savings association must obtain the prior written approval of the OTS under section 32 of this appendix to use the internal models methodology for counterparty credit risk.

(e) *Double default treatment.* A savings association must obtain the prior written approval of the OTS under section 34 of this appendix to use the double default treatment.

(f) *Securitization exposures.* A savings association must obtain the prior written approval of the OTS under section 44 of this appendix to use the Internal Assessment Approach for securitization exposures to ABCP programs.

(g) *Equity exposures model.* A savings association must obtain the prior written approval of the OTS under section 53 of this appendix to use the Internal Models Approach for equity exposures.

(h) *Operational risk*—(1) *Operational risk management processes.* A savings association must:

(i) Have an operational risk management function that:

(A) Is independent of business line management; and

(B) Is responsible for designing, implementing, and overseeing the savings association's operational risk data and assessment systems, operational risk quantification systems, and related processes;

(ii) Have and document a process (which must capture business environment and internal control factors affecting the savings association's operational risk profile) to identify, measure, monitor, and control operational risk in savings association products, activities, processes, and systems; and

(iii) Report operational risk exposures, operational loss events, and other relevant operational risk information to business unit management, senior management, and the board of directors (or a designated committee of the board).

(2) *Operational risk data and assessment systems.* A savings association must have operational risk data and assessment systems that capture operational risks to which the savings association is exposed. The savings association's operational risk data and assessment systems must:

(i) Be structured in a manner consistent with the savings association's current business activities, risk profile, technological processes, and risk management processes; and

(ii) Include credible, transparent, systematic, and verifiable processes that incorporate the following elements on an ongoing basis:

(A) *Internal operational loss event data.* The savings association must have a systematic process for capturing and using internal operational loss event data in its operational risk data and assessment systems.

(*1*) The savings association's operational risk data and assessment systems must include a historical observation period of at least five years for internal operational loss event data (or such shorter period approved by the OTS to address transitional situations, such as integrating a new business line).

(*2*) The savings association must be able to map its internal operational loss event data into the seven operational loss event type categories.

(*3*) The savings association may refrain from collecting internal operational loss event data for individual operational losses below established dollar threshold amounts if the savings association can demonstrate to the satisfaction of the OTS that the thresholds are reasonable, do not exclude important internal operational loss event data, and permit the savings association to capture substantially all the dollar value of the savings association's operational losses.

(B) *External operational loss event data.* The savings association must have a systematic process for determining its methodologies for incorporating external operational loss event data into its operational risk data and assessment systems.

(C) *Scenario analysis.* The savings association must have a systematic process for determining its methodologies for incorporating scenario analysis into its operational risk data and assessment systems.

(D) *Business environment and internal control factors.* The savings association must incorporate business environment and internal

379

control factors into its operational risk data and assessment systems. The savings association must also periodically compare the results of its prior business environment and internal control factor assessments against its actual operational losses incurred in the intervening period.

(3) *Operational risk quantification systems.* (i) The savings association's operational risk quantification systems:

(A) Must generate estimates of the savings association's operational risk exposure using its operational risk data and assessment systems;

(B) Must employ a unit of measure that is appropriate for the savings association's range of business activities and the variety of operational loss events to which it is exposed, and that does not combine business activities or operational loss events with demonstrably different risk profiles within the same loss distribution;

(C) Must include a credible, transparent, systematic, and verifiable approach for weighting each of the four elements, described in paragraph (h)(2)(ii) of this section, that a savings association is required to incorporate into its operational risk data and assessment systems;

(D) May use internal estimates of dependence among operational losses across and within units of measure if the savings association can demonstrate to the satisfaction of the OTS that its process for estimating dependence is sound, robust to a variety of scenarios, and implemented with integrity, and allows for the uncertainty surrounding the estimates. If the savings association has not made such a demonstration, it must sum operational risk exposure estimates across units of measure to calculate its total operational risk exposure; and

(E) Must be reviewed and updated (as appropriate) whenever the savings association becomes aware of information that may have a material effect on the savings association's estimate of operational risk exposure, but the review and update must occur no less frequently than annually.

(ii) With the prior written approval of the OTS, a savings association may generate an estimate of its operational risk exposure using an alternative approach to that specified in paragraph (h)(3)(i) of this section. A savings association proposing to use such an alternative operational risk quantification system must submit a proposal to the OTS. In determining whether to approve a savings association's proposal to use an alternative operational risk quantification system, the OTS will consider the following principles:

(A) Use of the alternative operational risk quantification system will be allowed only on an exception basis, considering the size, complexity, and risk profile of the savings association;

(B) The savings association must demonstrate that its estimate of its operational risk exposure generated under the alternative operational risk quantification system is appropriate and can be supported empirically; and

(C) A savings association must not use an allocation of operational risk capital requirements that includes entities other than depository institutions or the benefits of diversification across entities.

(i) *Data management and maintenance.* (1) A savings association must have data management and maintenance systems that adequately support all aspects of its advanced systems and the timely and accurate reporting of risk-based capital requirements.

(2) A savings association must retain data using an electronic format that allows timely retrieval of data for analysis, validation, reporting, and disclosure purposes.

(3) A savings association must retain sufficient data elements related to key risk drivers to permit adequate monitoring, validation, and refinement of its advanced systems.

(j) *Control, oversight, and validation mechanisms.* (1) The savings association's senior management must ensure that all components of the savings association's advanced systems function effectively and comply with the qualification requirements in this section.

(2) The savings association's board of directors (or a designated committee of the board) must at least annually review the effectiveness of, and approve, the savings association's advanced systems.

(3) A savings association must have an effective system of controls and oversight that:

(i) Ensures ongoing compliance with the qualification requirements in this section;

(ii) Maintains the integrity, reliability, and accuracy of the savings association's advanced systems; and

(iii) Includes adequate governance and project management processes.

(4) The savings association must validate, on an ongoing basis, its advanced systems. The savings association's validation process must be independent of the advanced systems' development, implementation, and operation, or the validation process must be subjected to an independent review of its adequacy and effectiveness. Validation must include:

(i) An evaluation of the conceptual soundness of (including developmental evidence supporting) the advanced systems;

(ii) An ongoing monitoring process that includes verification of processes and benchmarking; and

(iii) An outcomes analysis process that includes back-testing.

Office of Thrift Supervision, Treasury

Pt. 567, App. C

(5) The savings association must have an internal audit function independent of business-line management that at least annually assesses the effectiveness of the controls supporting the savings association's advanced systems and reports its findings to the savings association's board of directors (or a committee thereof).

(6) The savings association must periodically stress test its advanced systems. The stress testing must include a consideration of how economic cycles, especially downturns, affect risk-based capital requirements (including migration across rating grades and segments and the credit risk mitigation benefits of double default treatment).

(k) *Documentation.* The savings association must adequately document all material aspects of its advanced systems.

Section 23. Ongoing Qualification

(a) *Changes to advanced systems.* A savings association must meet all the qualification requirements in section 22 of this appendix on an ongoing basis. A savings association must notify the OTS when the savings association makes any change to an advanced system that would result in a material change in the savings association's risk-weighted asset amount for an exposure type, or when the savings association makes any significant change to its modeling assumptions.

(b) *Failure to comply with qualification requirements.* (1) If the OTS determines that a savings association that uses this appendix and has conducted a satisfactory parallel run fails to comply with the qualification requirements in section 22 of this appendix, the OTS will notify the savings association in writing of the savings association's failure to comply.

(2) The savings association must establish and submit a plan satisfactory to the OTS to return to compliance with the qualification requirements.

(3) In addition, if the OTS determines that the savings association's risk-based capital requirements are not commensurate with the savings association's credit, market, operational, or other risks, the OTS may require such a savings association to calculate its risk-based capital requirements:

(i) Under subpart B of part 567; or

(ii) Under this appendix with any modifications provided by the OTS.

Section 24. Merger and Acquisition Transitional Arrangements

(a) *Mergers and acquisitions of companies without advanced systems.* If a savings association merges with or acquires a company that does not calculate its risk-based capital requirements using advanced systems, the savings association may use subpart B of part 567 to determine the risk-weighted asset amounts for, and deductions from capital associated with, the merged or acquired company's exposures for up to 24 months after the calendar quarter during which the merger or acquisition consummates. The OTS may extend this transition period for up to an additional 12 months. Within 90 days of consummating the merger or acquisition, the savings association must submit to the OTS an implementation plan for using its advanced systems for the acquired company. During the period when subpart A of this part applies to the merged or acquired company, any ALLL associated with the merged or acquired company's exposures may be included in the savings association's tier 2 capital up to 1.25 percent of the acquired company's risk-weighted assets. All general allowances of the merged or acquired company must be excluded from the savings association's eligible credit reserves. In addition, the risk-weighted assets of the merged or acquired company are not included in the savings association's credit-risk-weighted assets but are included in total risk-weighted assets. If a savings association relies on this paragraph, the savings association must disclose publicly the amounts of risk-weighted assets and qualifying capital calculated under this appendix for the acquiring savings association and under subpart B of part 567 for the acquired company.

(b) *Mergers and acquisitions of companies with advanced systems*—(1) If a savings association merges with or acquires a company that calculates its risk-based capital requirements using advanced systems, the savings association may use the acquired company's advanced systems to determine the risk-weighted asset amounts for, and deductions from capital associated with, the merged or acquired company's exposures for up to 24 months after the calendar quarter during which the acquisition or merger consummates. The OTS may extend this transition period for up to an additional 12 months. Within 90 days of consummating the merger or acquisition, the savings association must submit to the OTS an implementation plan for using its advanced systems for the merged or acquired company.

(2) If the acquiring savings association is not subject to the advanced approaches in this appendix at the time of acquisition or merger, during the period when subpart B of part 567 apply to the acquiring savings association, the ALLL associated with the exposures of the merged or acquired company may not be directly included in tier 2 capital. Rather, any excess eligible credit reserves associated with the merged or acquired company's exposures may be included in the savings association's tier 2 capital up to 0.6 percent of the credit-risk-weighted assets associated with those exposures.

PART IV. RISK-WEIGHTED ASSETS FOR GENERAL CREDIT RISK

Section 31. Mechanics for Calculating Total Wholesale and Retail Risk-Weighted Assets

(a) *Overview.* A savings association must calculate its total wholesale and retail risk-weighted asset amount in four distinct phases:

(1) Phase 1—categorization of exposures;

(2) Phase 2—assignment of wholesale obligors and exposures to rating grades and segmentation of retail exposures;

(3) Phase 3—assignment of risk parameters to wholesale exposures and segments of retail exposures; and

(4) Phase 4—calculation of risk-weighted asset amounts.

(b) *Phase 1—Categorization.* The savings association must determine which of its exposures are wholesale exposures, retail exposures, securitization exposures, or equity exposures. The savings association must categorize each retail exposure as a residential mortgage exposure, a QRE, or an other retail exposure. The savings association must identify which wholesale exposures are HVCRE exposures, sovereign exposures, OTC derivative contracts, repo-style transactions, eligible margin loans, eligible purchased wholesale exposures, unsettled transactions to which section 35 of this appendix applies, and eligible guarantees or eligible credit derivatives that are used as credit risk mitigants. The savings association must identify any on-balance sheet asset that does not meet the definition of a wholesale, retail, equity, or securitization exposure, as well as any non-material portfolio of exposures described in paragraph (e)(4) of this section.

(c) *Phase 2—Assignment of wholesale obligors and exposures to rating grades and retail exposures to segments—*(1) *Assignment of wholesale obligors and exposures to rating grades.*

(i) The savings association must assign each obligor of a wholesale exposure to a single obligor rating grade and must assign each wholesale exposure to which it does not directly assign an LGD estimate to a loss severity rating grade.

(ii) The savings association must identify which of its wholesale obligors are in default.

(2) *Segmentation of retail exposures.* (i) The savings association must group the retail exposures in each retail subcategory into segments that have homogeneous risk characteristics.

(ii) The savings association must identify which of its retail exposures are in default. The savings association must segment defaulted retail exposures separately from non-defaulted retail exposures.

(iii) If the savings association determines the EAD for eligible margin loans using the approach in paragraph (b) of section 32 of this appendix, the savings association must identify which of its retail exposures are eligible margin loans for which the savings association uses this EAD approach and must segment such eligible margin loans separately from other retail exposures.

(3) *Eligible purchased wholesale exposures.* A savings association may group its eligible purchased wholesale exposures into segments that have homogeneous risk characteristics. A savings association must use the wholesale exposure formula in Table 2 in this section to determine the risk-based capital requirement for each segment of eligible purchased wholesale exposures.

(d) *Phase 3—Assignment of risk parameters to wholesale exposures and segments of retail exposures—*(1) *Quantification process.* Subject to the limitations in this paragraph (d), the savings association must:

(i) Associate a PD with each wholesale obligor rating grade;

(ii) Associate an LGD with each wholesale loss severity rating grade or assign an LGD to each wholesale exposure;

(iii) Assign an EAD and M to each wholesale exposure; and

(iv) Assign a PD, LGD, and EAD to each segment of retail exposures.

(2) *Floor on PD assignment.* The PD for each wholesale obligor or retail segment may not be less than 0.03 percent, except for exposures to or directly and unconditionally guaranteed by a sovereign entity, the Bank for International Settlements, the International Monetary Fund, the European Commission, the European Central Bank, or a multilateral development bank, to which the savings association assigns a rating grade associated with a PD of less than 0.03 percent.

(3) *Floor on LGD estimation.* The LGD for each segment of residential mortgage exposures (other than segments of residential mortgage exposures for which all or substantially all of the principal of each exposure is directly and unconditionally guaranteed by the full faith and credit of a sovereign entity) may not be less than 10 percent.

(4) *Eligible purchased wholesale exposures.* A savings association must assign a PD, LGD, EAD, and M to each segment of eligible purchased wholesale exposures. If the savings association can estimate ECL (but not PD or LGD) for a segment of eligible purchased wholesale exposures, the savings association must assume that the LGD of the segment equals 100 percent and that the PD of the segment equals ECL divided by EAD. The estimated ECL must be calculated for the exposures without regard to any assumption of recourse or guarantees from the seller or other parties.

(5) *Credit risk mitigation—credit derivatives, guarantees, and collateral.* (i) A savings association may take into account the risk reducing effects of eligible guarantees and eligible credit derivatives in support of a

Office of Thrift Supervision, Treasury

wholesale exposure by applying the PD substitution or LGD adjustment treatment to the exposure as provided in section 33 of this appendix or, if applicable, applying double default treatment to the exposure as provided in section 34 of this appendix. A savings association may decide separately for each wholesale exposure that qualifies for the double default treatment under section 34 of this appendix whether to apply the double default treatment or to use the PD substitution or LGD adjustment treatment without recognizing double default effects.

(ii) A savings association may take into account the risk reducing effects of guarantees and credit derivatives in support of retail exposures in a segment when quantifying the PD and LGD of the segment.

(iii) Except as provided in paragraph (d)(6) of this section, a savings association may take into account the risk reducing effects of collateral in support of a wholesale exposure when quantifying the LGD of the exposure and may take into account the risk reducing effects of collateral in support of retail exposures when quantifying the PD and LGD of the segment.

(6) *EAD for OTC derivative contracts, repo-style transactions, and eligible margin loans.* (i) A savings association must calculate its EAD for an OTC derivative contract as provided in paragraphs (c) and (d) of section 32 of this appendix. A savings association may take into account the risk-reducing effects of financial collateral in support of a repo-style transaction or eligible margin loan and of any collateral in support of a repo-style transaction that is included in the savings association's VaR-based measure under any applicable market risk rule through an adjustment to EAD as provided in paragraphs (b) and (d) of section 32 of this appendix. A savings association that takes collateral into account through such an adjustment to EAD under section 32 of this appendix may not reflect such collateral in LGD.

(ii) A savings association may attribute an EAD of zero to:

(A) Derivative contracts that are publicly traded on an exchange that requires the daily receipt and payment of cash-variation margin;

(B) Derivative contracts and repo-style transactions that are outstanding with a qualifying central counterparty (but not for those transactions that a qualifying central counterparty has rejected); and

(C) Credit risk exposures to a qualifying central counterparty in the form of clearing deposits and posted collateral that arise from transactions described in paragraph (d)(6)(ii)(B) of this section.

(7) *Effective maturity.* An exposure's M must be no greater than five years and no less than one year, except that an exposure's M must be no less than one day if the exposure has an original maturity of less than one year and is not part of a savings association's ongoing financing of the obligor. An exposure is not part of a savings association's ongoing financing of the obligor if the savings association:

(i) Has a legal and practical ability not to renew or roll over the exposure in the event of credit deterioration of the obligor;

(ii) Makes an independent credit decision at the inception of the exposure and at every renewal or roll over; and

(iii) Has no substantial commercial incentive to continue its credit relationship with the obligor in the event of credit deterioration of the obligor.

(e) *Phase 4—Calculation of risk-weighted assets*—(1) *Non-defaulted exposures.* (i) A savings association must calculate the dollar risk-based capital requirement for each of its wholesale exposures to a non-defaulted obligor (except eligible guarantees and eligible credit derivatives that hedge another wholesale exposure and exposures to which the savings association applies the double default treatment in section 34 of this appendix) and segments of non-defaulted retail exposures by inserting the assigned risk parameters for the wholesale obligor and exposure or retail segment into the appropriate risk-based capital formula specified in Table 2 and multiplying the output of the formula (K) by the EAD of the exposure or segment. Alternatively, a savings association may apply a 300 percent risk weight to the EAD of an eligible margin loan if the savings association is not able to meet the agencies' requirements for estimation of PD and LGD for the margin loan.

Table 2 – IRB Risk-Based Capital Formulas for Wholesale Exposures to Non-Defaulted Obligors and Segments of Non-Defaulted Retail Exposures[1]

Retail	Capital Requirement (K) Non-Defaulted Exposures	$K = \left[LGD \times N\left(\dfrac{N^{-1}(PD) + \sqrt{R} \times N^{-1}(0.999)}{\sqrt{1-R}} \right) - (LGD \times PD) \right]$
Retail	Correlation Factor (R)	For residential mortgage exposures: $R = 0.15$
Retail	Correlation Factor (R)	For qualifying revolving exposures: $R = 0.04$
Retail	Correlation Factor (R)	For other retail exposures: $R = 0.03 + 0.13 \times e^{-35 \times PD}$
Wholesale	Capital Requirement (K) Non-Defaulted Exposures	$K = \left[LGD \times N\left(\dfrac{N^{-1}(PD) + \sqrt{R} \times N^{-1}(0.999)}{\sqrt{1-R}} \right) - (LGD \times PD) \right] \times \left(\dfrac{1 + (M - 2.5) \times b}{1 - 1.5 \times b} \right)$
Wholesale	Correlation Factor (R)	For HVCRE exposures: $R = 0.12 + 0.18 \times e^{-50 \times PD}$ For wholesale exposures other than HVCRE exposures: $R = 0.12 + 0.12 \times e^{-50 \times PD}$
Wholesale	Maturity Adjustment (b)	$b = (0.11852 - 0.05478 \times \ln(PD))^2$

[1] N(.) means the cumulative distribution function for a standard normal random variable. N^{-1}(.) means the inverse cumulative distribution function for a standard normal random variable. The symbol e refers to the base of the natural logarithms, and the function ln(.) refers to the natural logarithm of the expression within parentheses. The formulas apply when PD is greater than zero. If PD equals zero, the capital requirement K is set equal to zero.

(ii) The sum of all the dollar risk-based capital requirements for each wholesale exposure to a non-defaulted obligor and segment of non-defaulted retail exposures calculated in paragraph (e)(1)(i) of this section and in paragraph (e) of section 34 of this appendix equals the total dollar risk-based capital requirement for those exposures and segments.

(iii) The aggregate risk-weighted asset amount for wholesale exposures to non-defaulted obligors and segments of non-defaulted retail exposures equals the total dollar risk-based capital requirement calculated in paragraph (e)(1)(ii) of this section multiplied by 12.5.

(2) *Wholesale exposures to defaulted obligors and segments of defaulted retail exposures.* (i) The dollar risk-based capital requirement for each wholesale exposure to a defaulted obligor equals 0.08 multiplied by the EAD of the exposure.

(ii) The dollar risk-based capital requirement for a segment of defaulted retail exposures equals 0.08 multiplied by the EAD of the segment.

(iii) The sum of all the dollar risk-based capital requirements for each wholesale exposure to a defaulted obligor calculated in paragraph (e)(2)(i) of this section plus the dollar risk-based capital requirements for each segment of defaulted retail exposures

Office of Thrift Supervision, Treasury Pt. 567, App. C

calculated in paragraph (e)(2)(ii) of this section equals the total dollar risk-based capital requirement for those exposures and segments.

(iv) The aggregate risk-weighted asset amount for wholesale exposures to defaulted obligors and segments of defaulted retail exposures equals the total dollar risk-based capital requirement calculated in paragraph (e)(2)(iii) of this section multiplied by 12.5.

(3) *Assets not included in a defined exposure category.* (i) A savings association may assign a risk-weighted asset amount of zero to cash owned and held in all offices of the savings association or in transit and for gold bullion held in the savings association's own vaults, or held in another savings association's vaults on an allocated basis, to the extent the gold bullion assets are offset by gold bullion liabilities.

(ii) The risk-weighted asset amount for the residual value of a retail lease exposure equals such residual value.

(iii) The risk-weighted asset amount for any other on-balance-sheet asset that does not meet the definition of a wholesale, retail, securitization, or equity exposure equals the carrying value of the asset.

(4) *Non-material portfolios of exposures.* The risk-weighted asset amount of a portfolio of exposures for which the savings association has demonstrated to the OTS's satisfaction that the portfolio (when combined with all other portfolios of exposures that the savings association seeks to treat under this paragraph) is not material to the savings association is the sum of the carrying values of on-balance sheet exposures plus the notional amounts of off-balance sheet exposures in the portfolio. For purposes of this paragraph (e)(4), the notional amount of an OTC derivative contract that is not a credit derivative is the EAD of the derivative as calculated in section 32 of this appendix.

Section 32. Counterparty Credit Risk of Repo-Style Transactions, Eligible Margin Loans, and OTC Derivative Contracts

(a) *In General.* (1) This section describes two methodologies—a collateral haircut approach and an internal models methodology—that a savings association may use instead of an LGD estimation methodology to recognize the benefits of financial collateral in mitigating the counterparty credit risk of repo-style transactions, eligible margin loans, collateralized OTC derivative contracts, and single product netting sets of such transactions and to recognize the benefits of any collateral in mitigating the counterparty credit risk of repo-style transactions that are included in a savings association's VaR-based measure under any applicable market risk rule. A third methodology, the simple VaR methodology, is available for single product netting sets of repo-style transactions and eligible margin loans.

(2) This section also describes the methodology for calculating EAD for an OTC derivative contract or a set of OTC derivative contracts subject to a qualifying master netting agreement. A savings association also may use the internal models methodology to estimate EAD for qualifying cross-product master netting agreements.

(3) A savings association may only use the standard supervisory haircut approach with a minimum 10-business-day holding period to recognize in EAD the benefits of conforming residential mortgage collateral that secures repo-style transactions (other than repo-style transactions included in the savings association's VaR-based measure under any applicable market risk rule), eligible margin loans, and OTC derivative contracts.

(4) A savings association may use any combination of the three methodologies for collateral recognition; however, it must use the same methodology for similar exposures.

(b) *EAD for eligible margin loans and repo-style transactions*—(1) *General.* A savings association may recognize the credit risk mitigation benefits of financial collateral that secures an eligible margin loan, repo-style transaction, or single-product netting set of such transactions by factoring the collateral into its LGD estimates for the exposure. Alternatively, a savings association may estimate an unsecured LGD for the exposure, as well as for any repo-style transaction that is included in the savings association's VaR-based measure under any applicable market risk rule, and determine the EAD of the exposure using:

(i) The collateral haircut approach described in paragraph (b)(2) of this section;

(ii) For netting sets only, the simple VaR methodology described in paragraph (b)(3) of this section; or

(iii) The internal models methodology described in paragraph (d) of this section.

(2) *Collateral haircut approach*—(i) *EAD equation.* A savings association may determine EAD for an eligible margin loan, repo-style transaction, or netting set by setting EAD equal to max {0, [(ΣE − ΣC) + Σ(Es × Hs) + Σ(Efx × Hfx)]}, where:

(A) ΣE equals the value of the exposure (the sum of the current market values of all instruments, gold, and cash the savings association has lent, sold subject to repurchase, or posted as collateral to the counterparty under the transaction (or netting set);

(B) ΣC equals the value of the collateral (the sum of the current market values of all instruments, gold, and cash the savings association has borrowed, purchased subject to resale, or taken as collateral from the counterparty under the transaction (or netting set));

(C) Es equals the absolute value of the net position in a given instrument or in gold

385

(where the net position in a given instrument or in gold equals the sum of the current market values of the instrument or gold the savings association has lent, sold subject to repurchase, or posted as collateral to the counterparty minus the sum of the current market values of that same instrument or gold the savings association has borrowed, purchased subject to resale, or taken as collateral from the counterparty);

(D) Hs equals the market price volatility haircut appropriate to the instrument or gold referenced in Es;

(E) Efx equals the absolute value of the net position of instruments and cash in a currency that is different from the settlement currency (where the net position in a given currency equals the sum of the current market values of any instruments or cash in the currency the savings association has lent, sold subject to repurchase, or posted as collateral to the counterparty minus the sum of the current market values of any instruments or cash in the currency the savings association has borrowed, purchased subject to resale, or taken as collateral from the counterparty); and

(F) Hfx equals the haircut appropriate to the mismatch between the currency referenced in Efx and the settlement currency.

(ii) *Standard supervisory haircuts.* (A) Under the standard supervisory haircuts approach:

(*1*) A savings association must use the haircuts for market price volatility (Hs) in Table 3, as adjusted in certain circumstances as provided in paragraph (b)(2)(ii)(A)(*3*) and (*4*) of this section;

TABLE 3—STANDARD SUPERVISORY MARKET PRICE VOLATILITY HAIRCUTS [1]

Applicable external rating grade category for debt securities	Residual maturity for debt securities	Issuers exempt from the 3 basis point floor	Other issuers
Two highest investment-grade rating categories for long-term ratings/highest investment-grade rating category for short-term ratings.	≤ 1 year >1 year, ≤ 5 years > 5 years	0.005 0.02 0.04	0.01 0.04 0.08
Two lowest investment-grade rating categories for both short- and long-term ratings.	≤ 1 year > 1 year, ≤ 5 years > 5 years	0.01 0.03 0.06	0.02 0.06 0.12
One rating category below investment grade	All	0.15	0.25
Main index equities (including convertible bonds) and gold		0.15	
Other publicly traded equities (including convertible bonds), conforming residential mortgages, and nonfinancial collateral.		0.25	
Mutual funds		Highest haircut applicable to any security in which the fund can invest.	
Cash on deposit with the savings association (including a certificate of deposit issued by the savings association).		0	

[1] The market price volatility haircuts in Table 3 are based on a ten-business-day holding period.

(*2*) For currency mismatches, a savings association must use a haircut for foreign exchange rate volatility (Hfx) of 8 percent, as adjusted in certain circumstances as provided in paragraph (b)(2)(ii)(A)(*3*) and (*4*) of this section.

(*3*) For repo-style transactions, a savings association may multiply the supervisory haircuts provided in paragraphs (b)(2)(ii)(A)(*1*) and (*2*) of this section by the square root of ½ (which equals 0.707107).

(*4*) A savings association must adjust the supervisory haircuts upward on the basis of a holding period longer than ten business days (for eligible margin loans) or five business days (for repo-style transactions) where and as appropriate to take into account the illiquidity of an instrument.

(iii) *Own internal estimates for haircuts.* With the prior written approval of the OTS, a savings association may calculate haircuts (Hs and Hfx) using its own internal estimates of the volatilities of market prices and foreign exchange rates.

(A) To receive OTS approval to use its own internal estimates, a savings association must satisfy the following minimum quantitative standards:

(*1*) A savings association must use a 99th percentile one-tailed confidence interval.

(*2*) The minimum holding period for a repo-style transaction is five business days and for an eligible margin loan is ten business days. When a savings association calculates an own-estimates haircut on a T_N-day holding period, which is different from the minimum holding period for the transaction type, the applicable haircut (H_M) is calculated using the following square root of time formula:

Office of Thrift Supervision, Treasury Pt. 567, App. C

$$H_M = H_N \sqrt{\frac{T_M}{T_N}}, \text{ where}$$

(i) T_M equals 5 for repo-style transactions and 10 for eligible margin loans;
(ii) T_N equals the holding period used by the savings association to derive H_N; and
(iii) H_N equals the haircut based on the holding period T_N.

(3) A savings association must adjust holding periods upwards where and as appropriate to take into account the illiquidity of an instrument.

(4) The historical observation period must be at least one year.

(5) A savings association must update its data sets and recompute haircuts no less frequently than quarterly and must also reassess data sets and haircuts whenever market prices change materially.

(B) With respect to debt securities that have an applicable external rating of investment grade, a savings association may calculate haircuts for categories of securities. For a category of securities, the savings association must calculate the haircut on the basis of internal volatility estimates for securities in that category that are representative of the securities in that category that the savings association has lent, sold subject to repurchase, posted as collateral, borrowed, purchased subject to resale, or taken as collateral. In determining relevant categories, the savings association must at a minimum take into account:

(1) The type of issuer of the security;
(2) The applicable external rating of the security;
(3) The maturity of the security; and
(4) The interest rate sensitivity of the security.

(C) With respect to debt securities that have an applicable external rating of below investment grade and equity securities, a savings association must calculate a separate haircut for each individual security.

(D) Where an exposure or collateral (whether in the form of cash or securities) is denominated in a currency that differs from the settlement currency, the savings association must calculate a separate currency mismatch haircut for its net position in each mismatched currency based on estimated volatilities of foreign exchange rates between the mismatched currency and the settlement currency.

(E) A savings association's own estimates of market price and foreign exchange rate volatilities may not take into account the correlations among securities and foreign exchange rates on either the exposure or collateral side of a transaction (or netting set) or the correlations among securities and foreign exchange rates between the exposure and collateral sides of the transaction (or netting set).

(3) *Simple VaR methodology.* With the prior written approval of the OTS, a savings association may estimate EAD for a netting set using a VaR model that meets the requirements in paragraph (b)(3)(iii) of this section. In such event, the savings association must set EAD equal to max {0, [(ΣE—ΣC) + PFE]}, where:

(i) ΣE equals the value of the exposure (the sum of the current market values of all instruments, gold, and cash the savings association has lent, sold subject to repurchase, or posted as collateral to the counterparty under the netting set);

(ii) ΣC equals the value of the collateral (the sum of the current market values of all instruments, gold, and cash the savings association has borrowed, purchased subject to resale, or taken as collateral from the counterparty under the netting set); and

(iii) PFE (potential future exposure) equals the savings association's empirically based best estimate of the 99th percentile, one-tailed confidence interval for an increase in the value of (ΣE—ΣC) over a five-business-day holding period for repo-style transactions or over a ten-business-day holding period for eligible margin loans using a minimum one-year historical observation period of price data representing the instruments that the savings association has lent, sold subject to repurchase, posted as collateral, borrowed, purchased subject to resale, or taken as collateral. The savings association must validate its VaR model, including by establishing and maintaining a rigorous and regular back-testing regime.

(c) *EAD for OTC derivative contracts.* (1) A savings association must determine the EAD for an OTC derivative contract that is not subject to a qualifying master netting agreement using the current exposure methodology in paragraph (c)(5) of this section or using the internal models methodology described in paragraph (d) of this section.

(2) A savings association must determine the EAD for multiple OTC derivative contracts that are subject to a qualifying master netting agreement using the current exposure methodology in paragraph (c)(6) of this section or using the internal models methodology described in paragraph (d) of this section.

(3) *Counterparty credit risk for credit derivatives.* Notwithstanding the above, (i) A savings association that purchases a credit derivative that is recognized under section 33 or 34 of this appendix as a credit risk mitigant for an exposure that is not a covered position under any applicable market risk rule need not compute a separate counterparty credit risk capital requirement under this section so long as the savings association does so consistently for all such credit derivatives and either includes all or

excludes all such credit derivatives that are subject to a master netting agreement from any measure used to determine counterparty credit risk exposure to all relevant counterparties for risk-based capital purposes.

(ii) A savings association that is the protection provider in a credit derivative must treat the credit derivative as a wholesale exposure to the reference obligor and need not compute a counterparty credit risk capital requirement for the credit derivative under this section, so long as it does so consistently for all such credit derivatives and either includes all or excludes all such credit derivatives that are subject to a master netting agreement from any measure used to determine counterparty credit risk exposure to all relevant counterparties for risk-based capital purposes (unless the savings association is treating the credit derivative as a covered position under any applicable market risk rule, in which case the savings association must compute a supplemental counterparty credit risk capital requirement under this section).

(4) *Counterparty credit risk for equity derivatives.* A savings association must treat an equity derivative contract as an equity exposure and compute a risk-weighted asset amount for the equity derivative contract under part VI (unless the savings association is treating the contract as a covered position under any applicable market risk rule). In addition, if the savings association is treating the contract as a covered position under any applicable market risk rule and in certain other cases described in section 55 of this appendix, the savings association must also calculate a risk-based capital requirement for the counterparty credit risk of an equity derivative contract under this part.

(5) *Single OTC derivative contract.* Except as modified by paragraph (c)(7) of this section, the EAD for a single OTC derivative contract that is not subject to a qualifying master netting agreement is equal to the sum of the savings association's current credit exposure and potential future credit exposure (PFE) on the derivative contract.

(i) *Current credit exposure.* The current credit exposure for a single OTC derivative contract is the greater of the mark-to-market value of the derivative contract or zero.

(ii) *PFE.* The PFE for a single OTC derivative contract, including an OTC derivative contract with a negative mark-to-market value, is calculated by multiplying the notional principal amount of the derivative contract by the appropriate conversion factor in Table 4. For purposes of calculating either the PFE under this paragraph or the gross PFE under paragraph (c)(6) of this section for exchange rate contracts and other similar contracts in which the notional principal amount is equivalent to the cash flows, notional principal amount is the net receipts to each party falling due on each value date in each currency. For any OTC derivative contract that does not fall within one of the specified categories in Table 4, the PFE must be calculated using the "other" conversion factors. A savings association must use an OTC derivative contract's effective notional principal amount (that is, its apparent or stated notional principal amount multiplied by any multiplier in the OTC derivative contract) rather than its apparent or stated notional principal amount in calculating PFE. PFE of the protection provider of a credit derivative is capped at the net present value of the amount of unpaid premiums.

TABLE 4—CONVERSION FACTOR MATRIX FOR OTC DERIVATIVE CONTRACTS [1]

Remaining maturity [2]	Interest rate	Foreign exchange rate and gold	Credit (investment-grade reference obligor) [3]	Credit (non-investment-grade reference obligor)	Equity	Precious metals (except gold)	Other
One year or less	0.00	0.01	0.05	0.10	0.06	0.07	0.10
Over one to five years	0.005	0.05	0.05	0.10	0.08	0.07	0.12
Over five years	0.015	0.075	0.05	0.10	0.10	0.08	0.15

[1] For an OTC derivative contract with multiple exchanges of principal, the conversion factor is multiplied by the number of remaining payments in the derivative contract.

[2] For an OTC derivative contract that is structured such that on specified dates any outstanding exposure is settled and the terms are reset so that the market value of the contract is zero, the remaining maturity equals the time until the next reset date. For an interest rate derivative contract with a remaining maturity of greater than one year that meets these criteria, the minimum conversion factor is 0.005.

[3] A savings association must use the column labeled "Credit (investment-grade reference obligor)" for a credit derivative whose reference obligor has an outstanding unsecured long-term debt security without credit enhancement that has a long-term applicable external rating of at least investment grade. A savings association must use the column labeled "Credit (non-investment-grade reference obligor)" for all other credit derivatives.

(6) *Multiple OTC derivative contracts subject to a qualifying master netting agreement.* Except as modified by paragraph (c)(7) of this section, the EAD for multiple OTC derivative contracts subject to a qualifying master netting agreement is equal to the sum of the net current credit exposure and the adjusted sum of the PFE exposure for all OTC derivative contracts subject to the qualifying master netting agreement.

(i) *Net current credit exposure.* The net current credit exposure is the greater of:

Office of Thrift Supervision, Treasury Pt. 567, App. C

(A) The net sum of all positive and negative mark-to-market values of the individual OTC derivative contracts subject to the qualifying master netting agreement; or

(B) zero.

(ii) *Adjusted sum of the PFE.* The adjusted sum of the PFE, Anet, is calculated as Anet = (0.4×Agross)+(0.6×NGR×Agross), where:

(A) Agross = the gross PFE (that is, the sum of the PFE amounts (as determined under paragraph (c)(5)(ii) of this section) for each individual OTC derivative contract subject to the qualifying master netting agreement); and

(B) NGR = the net to gross ratio (that is, the ratio of the net current credit exposure to the gross current credit exposure). In calculating the NGR, the gross current credit exposure equals the sum of the positive current credit exposures (as determined under paragraph (c)(5)(i) of this section) of all individual OTC derivative contracts subject to the qualifying master netting agreement.

(7) *Collateralized OTC derivative contracts.* A savings association may recognize the credit risk mitigation benefits of financial collateral that secures an OTC derivative contract or single-product netting set of OTC derivatives by factoring the collateral into its LGD estimates for the contract or netting set. Alternatively, a savings association may recognize the credit risk mitigation benefits of financial collateral that secures such a contract or netting set that is marked to market on a daily basis and subject to a daily margin maintenance requirement by estimating an unsecured LGD for the contract or netting set and adjusting the EAD calculated under paragraph (c)(5) or (c)(6) of this section using the collateral haircut approach in paragraph (b)(2) of this section. The savings association must substitute the EAD calculated under paragraph (c)(5) or (c)(6) of this section for ΣE in the equation in paragraph (b)(2)(i) of this section and must use a ten-business-day minimum holding period ($T_M = 10$).

(d) *Internal models methodology.* (1) With prior written approval from the OTS, a savings association may use the internal models methodology in this paragraph (d) to determine EAD for counterparty credit risk for OTC derivative contracts (collateralized or uncollateralized) and single-product netting sets thereof, for eligible margin loans and single-product netting sets thereof, and for repo-style transactions and single-product netting sets thereof. A savings association that uses the internal models methodology for a particular transaction type (OTC derivative contracts, eligible margin loans, or repo-style transactions) must use the internal models methodology for all transactions of that transaction type. A savings association may choose to use the internal models methodology for one or two of these three types of exposures and not the other types. A savings association may also use the internal models methodology for OTC derivative contracts, eligible margin loans, and repo-style transactions subject to a qualifying cross-product netting agreement if:

(i) The savings association effectively integrates the risk mitigating effects of cross-product netting into its risk management and other information technology systems; and

(ii) The savings association obtains the prior written approval of the OTS. A savings association that uses the internal models methodology for a transaction type must receive approval from the OTS to cease using the methodology for that transaction type or to make a material change to its internal model.

(2) Under the internal models methodology, a savings association uses an internal model to estimate the expected exposure (EE) for a netting set and then calculates EAD based on that EE.

(i) The savings association must use its internal model's probability distribution for changes in the market value of a netting set that are attributable to changes in market variables to determine EE.

(ii) Under the internal models methodology, EAD = α × effective EPE, or, subject to OTS approval as provided in paragraph (d)(7), a more conservative measure of EAD.

$$\text{(A) EffectiveEPE}_{t_k} = \sum_{k=1}^{n} \text{EffectiveEE}_{t_k} \times \Delta t_k$$

(that is, effective EPE is the time-weighted average of effective EE where the weights are the proportion that an individual effective EE represents in a one-year time interval) where:

(1) Effective EE_{t_k} = max (Effective $EE_{t_{k-1}}$, EE_{t_k}) (that is, for a specific date$_{t_k}$, effective EE is the greater of EE at that date or the effective EE at the previous date); and

(2) t_k represents the kth future time period in the model and there are n time periods represented in the model over the first year; and

(B) α = 1.4 except as provided in paragraph (d)(6), or when the OTS has determined that the savings association must set α higher based on the savings association's specific characteristics of counterparty credit risk.

(iii) A savings association may include financial collateral currently posted by the counterparty as collateral (but may not include other forms of collateral) when calculating EE.

(iv) If a savings association hedges some or all of the counterparty credit risk associated with a netting set using an eligible credit derivative, the savings association may take the reduction in exposure to the counterparty into account when estimating EE. If the savings association recognizes this reduction in exposure to the counterparty in

389

its estimate of EE, it must also use its internal model to estimate a separate EAD for the savings association's exposure to the protection provider of the credit derivative.

(3) To obtain OTS approval to calculate the distributions of exposures upon which the EAD calculation is based, the savings association must demonstrate to the satisfaction of the OTS that it has been using for at least one year an internal model that broadly meets the following minimum standards, with which the savings association must maintain compliance:

(i) The model must have the systems capability to estimate the expected exposure to the counterparty on a daily basis (but is not expected to estimate or report expected exposure on a daily basis).

(ii) The model must estimate expected exposure at enough future dates to reflect accurately all the future cash flows of contracts in the netting set.

(iii) The model must account for the possible non-normality of the exposure distribution, where appropriate.

(iv) The savings association must measure, monitor, and control current counterparty exposure and the exposure to the counterparty over the whole life of all contracts in the netting set.

(v) The savings association must be able to measure and manage current exposures gross and net of collateral held, where appropriate. The savings association must estimate expected exposures for OTC derivative contracts both with and without the effect of collateral agreements.

(vi) The savings association must have procedures to identify, monitor, and control specific wrong-way risk throughout the life of an exposure. Wrong-way risk in this context is the risk that future exposure to a counterparty will be high when the counterparty's probability of default is also high.

(vii) The model must use current market data to compute current exposures. When estimating model parameters based on historical data, at least three years of historical data that cover a wide range of economic conditions must be used and must be updated quarterly or more frequently if market conditions warrant. The savings association should consider using model parameters based on forward-looking measures, where appropriate.

(viii) A savings association must subject its internal model to an initial validation and annual model review process. The model review should consider whether the inputs and risk factors, as well as the model outputs, are appropriate.

(4) *Maturity.* (i) If the remaining maturity of the exposure or the longest-dated contract in the netting set is greater than one year, the savings association must set M for the exposure or netting set equal to the lower of five years or M(EPE),[3] where:

(A) $$\dot{M}(EPE) = 1 + \frac{\sum_{t_k > 1\,year}^{maturity} EE_k \times \Delta t_k \times df_k}{\sum_{k=1}^{t_k \leq 1\,year} \textit{effectiveEE}_k \times \Delta t_k \times df_k}$$

(B) df_k is the risk-free discount factor for future time period t_k; and

(C) $\Delta t_k = t_k - t_{k-1}$.

(ii) If the remaining maturity of the exposure or the longest-dated contract in the netting set is one year or less, the savings association must set M for the exposure or netting set equal to one year, except as provided in paragraph (d)(7) of section 31 of this appendix.

(5) *Collateral agreements.* A savings association may capture the effect on EAD of a collateral agreement that requires receipt of collateral when exposure to the counterparty increases but may not capture the effect on EAD of a collateral agreement that requires

---

[3] Alternatively, a savings association that uses an internal model to calculate a one-sided credit valuation adjustment may use the effective credit duration estimated by the model as M(EPE) in place of the formula in paragraph (d)(4).

Office of Thrift Supervision, Treasury   Pt. 567, App. C

receipt of collateral when counterparty credit quality deteriorates. For this purpose, a collateral agreement means a legal contract that specifies the time when, and circumstances under which, the counterparty is required to pledge collateral to the savings association for a single financial contract or for all financial contracts in a netting set and confers upon the savings association a perfected, first priority security interest (notwithstanding the prior security interest of any custodial agent), or the legal equivalent thereof, in the collateral posted by the counterparty under the agreement. This security interest must provide the savings association with a right to close out the financial positions and liquidate the collateral upon an event of default of, or failure to perform by, the counterparty under the collateral agreement. A contract would not satisfy this requirement if the savings association's exercise of rights under the agreement may be stayed or avoided under applicable law in the relevant jurisdictions. Two methods are available to capture the effect of a collateral agreement:

(i) With prior written approval from the OTS, a savings association may include the effect of a collateral agreement within its internal model used to calculate EAD. The savings association may set EAD equal to the expected exposure at the end of the margin period of risk. The margin period of risk means, with respect to a netting set subject to a collateral agreement, the time period from the most recent exchange of collateral with a counterparty until the next required exchange of collateral plus the period of time required to sell and realize the proceeds of the least liquid collateral that can be delivered under the terms of the collateral agreement and, where applicable, the period of time required to re-hedge the resulting market risk, upon the default of the counterparty. The minimum margin period of risk is five business days for repo-style transactions and ten business days for other transactions when liquid financial collateral is posted under a daily margin maintenance requirement. This period should be extended to cover any additional time between margin calls; any potential closeout difficulties; any delays in selling collateral, particularly if the collateral is illiquid; and any impediments to prompt re-hedging of any market risk.

(ii) A savings association that can model EPE without collateral agreements but cannot achieve the higher level of modeling sophistication to model EPE with collateral agreements can set effective EPE for a collateralized netting set equal to the lesser of:

(A) The threshold, defined as the exposure amount at which the counterparty is required to post collateral under the collateral agreement, if the threshold is positive, plus an add-on that reflects the potential increase in exposure of the netting set over the margin period of risk. The add-on is computed as the expected increase in the netting set's exposure beginning from current exposure of zero over the margin period of risk. The margin period of risk must be at least five business days for netting sets consisting only of repo-style transactions subject to daily re-margining and daily marking-to-market, and ten business days for all other netting sets; or

(B) Effective EPE without a collateral agreement.

(6) *Own estimate of alpha.* With prior written approval of the OTS, a savings association may calculate alpha as the ratio of economic capital from a full simulation of counterparty exposure across counterparties that incorporates a joint simulation of market and credit risk factors (numerator) and economic capital based on EPE (denominator), subject to a floor of 1.2. For purposes of this calculation, economic capital is the unexpected losses for all counterparty credit risks measured at a 99.9 percent confidence level over a one-year horizon. To receive approval, the savings association must meet the following minimum standards to the satisfaction of the OTS:

(i) The savings association's own estimate of alpha must capture in the numerator the effects of:

(A) The material sources of stochastic dependency of distributions of market values of transactions or portfolios of transactions across counterparties;

(B) Volatilities and correlations of market risk factors used in the joint simulation, which must be related to the credit risk factor used in the simulation to reflect potential increases in volatility or correlation in an economic downturn, where appropriate; and

(C) The granularity of exposures (that is, the effect of a concentration in the proportion of each counterparty's exposure that is driven by a particular risk factor).

(ii) The savings association must assess the potential model uncertainty in its estimates of alpha.

(iii) The savings association must calculate the numerator and denominator of alpha in a consistent fashion with respect to modeling methodology, parameter specifications, and portfolio composition.

(iv) The savings association must review and adjust as appropriate its estimates of the numerator and denominator of alpha on at least a quarterly basis and more frequently when the composition of the portfolio varies over time.

(7) *Other measures of counterparty exposure.* With prior written approval of the OTS, a savings association may set EAD equal to a

measure of counterparty credit risk exposure, such as peak EAD, that is more conservative than an alpha of 1.4 (or higher under the terms of paragraph (d)(2)(ii)(B) of this section) times EPE for every counterparty whose EAD will be measured under the alternative measure of counterparty exposure. The savings association must demonstrate the conservatism of the measure of counterparty credit risk exposure used for EAD. For material portfolios of new OTC derivative products, the savings association may assume that the current exposure methodology in paragraphs (c)(5) and (c)(6) of this section meets the conservatism requirement of this paragraph for a period not to exceed 180 days. For immaterial portfolios of OTC derivative contracts, the savings association generally may assume that the current exposure methodology in paragraphs (c)(5) and (c)(6) of this section meets the conservatism requirement of this paragraph.

Section 33. Guarantees and Credit Derivatives: PD Substitution and LGD Adjustment Approaches

(a) *Scope.* (1) This section applies to wholesale exposures for which:

(i) Credit risk is fully covered by an eligible guarantee or eligible credit derivative; or

(ii) Credit risk is covered on a pro rata basis (that is, on a basis in which the savings association and the protection provider share losses proportionately) by an eligible guarantee or eligible credit derivative.

(2) Wholesale exposures on which there is a tranching of credit risk (reflecting at least two different levels of seniority) are securitization exposures subject to the securitization framework in part V.

(3) A savings association may elect to recognize the credit risk mitigation benefits of an eligible guarantee or eligible credit derivative covering an exposure described in paragraph (a)(1) of this section by using the PD substitution approach or the LGD adjustment approach in paragraph (c) of this section or, if the transaction qualifies, using the double default treatment in section 34 of this appendix. A savings association's PD and LGD for the hedged exposure may not be lower than the PD and LGD floors described in paragraphs (d)(2) and (d)(3) of section 31 of this appendix.

(4) If multiple eligible guarantees or eligible credit derivatives cover a single exposure described in paragraph (a)(1) of this section, a savings association may treat the hedged exposure as multiple separate exposures each covered by a single eligible guarantee or eligible credit derivative and may calculate a separate risk-based capital requirement for each separate exposure as described in paragraph (a)(3) of this section.

(5) If a single eligible guarantee or eligible credit derivative covers multiple hedged wholesale exposures described in paragraph (a)(1) of this section, a savings association must treat each hedged exposure as covered by a separate eligible guarantee or eligible credit derivative and must calculate a separate risk-based capital requirement for each exposure as described in paragraph (a)(3) of this section.

(6) A savings association must use the same risk parameters for calculating ECL as it uses for calculating the risk-based capital requirement for the exposure.

(b) *Rules of recognition.* (1) A savings association may only recognize the credit risk mitigation benefits of eligible guarantees and eligible credit derivatives.

(2) A savings association may only recognize the credit risk mitigation benefits of an eligible credit derivative to hedge an exposure that is different from the credit derivative's reference exposure used for determining the derivative's cash settlement value, deliverable obligation, or occurrence of a credit event if:

(i) The reference exposure ranks pari passu (that is, equally) with or is junior to the hedged exposure; and

(ii) The reference exposure and the hedged exposure are exposures to the same legal entity, and legally enforceable cross-default or cross-acceleration clauses are in place to assure payments under the credit derivative are triggered when the obligor fails to pay under the terms of the hedged exposure.

(c) *Risk parameters for hedged exposures*—(1) *PD substitution approach*—(i) *Full coverage.* If an eligible guarantee or eligible credit derivative meets the conditions in paragraphs (a) and (b) of this section and the protection amount (P) of the guarantee or credit derivative is greater than or equal to the EAD of the hedged exposure, a savings association may recognize the guarantee or credit derivative in determining the savings association's risk-based capital requirement for the hedged exposure by substituting the PD associated with the rating grade of the protection provider for the PD associated with the rating grade of the obligor in the risk-based capital formula applicable to the guarantee or credit derivative in Table 2 and using the appropriate LGD as described in paragraph (c)(1)(iii) of this section. If the savings association determines that full substitution of the protection provider's PD leads to an inappropriate degree of risk mitigation, savings association may substitute a higher PD than that of the protection provider.

(ii) *Partial coverage.* If an eligible guarantee or eligible credit derivative meets the conditions in paragraphs (a) and (b) of this section and the protection amount (P) of the guarantee or credit derivative is less than the EAD of the hedged exposure, the savings association must treat the hedged exposure as two separate exposures (protected and unprotected) in order to recognize the credit risk mitigation benefit of the guarantee or credit derivative.

(A) The savings association must calculate its risk-based capital requirement for the protected exposure under section 31 of this appendix, where PD is the protection provider's PD, LGD is determined under paragraph (c)(1)(iii) of this section, and EAD is P. If the savings association determines that full substitution leads to an inappropriate degree of risk mitigation, the savings association may use a higher PD than that of the protection provider.

(B) The savings association must calculate its risk-based capital requirement for the unprotected exposure under section 31 of this appendix, where PD is the obligor's PD, LGD is the hedged exposure's LGD (not adjusted to reflect the guarantee or credit derivative), and EAD is the EAD of the original hedged exposure minus P.

(C) The treatment in this paragraph (c)(1)(ii) is applicable when the credit risk of a wholesale exposure is covered on a partial pro rata basis or when an adjustment is made to the effective notional amount of the guarantee or credit derivative under paragraph (d), (e), or (f) of this section.

(iii) *LGD of hedged exposures.* The LGD of a hedged exposure under the PD substitution approach is equal to:

(A) The lower of the LGD of the hedged exposure (not adjusted to reflect the guarantee or credit derivative) and the LGD of the guarantee or credit derivative, if the guarantee or credit derivative provides the savings association with the option to receive immediate payout upon triggering the protection; or

(B) The LGD of the guarantee or credit derivative, if the guarantee or credit derivative does not provide the savings association with the option to receive immediate payout upon triggering the protection.

(2) *LGD adjustment approach*—(i) *Full coverage.* If an eligible guarantee or eligible credit derivative meets the conditions in paragraphs (a) and (b) of this section and the protection amount (P) of the guarantee or credit derivative is greater than or equal to the EAD of the hedged exposure, the savings association's risk-based capital requirement for the hedged exposure is the greater of:

(A) The risk-based capital requirement for the exposure as calculated under section 31 of this appendix, with the LGD of the exposure adjusted to reflect the guarantee or credit derivative; or

(B) The risk-based capital requirement for a direct exposure to the protection provider as calculated under section 31 of this appendix, using the PD for the protection provider, the LGD for the guarantee or credit derivative, and an EAD equal to the EAD of the hedged exposure.

(ii) *Partial coverage.* If an eligible guarantee or eligible credit derivative meets the conditions in paragraphs (a) and (b) of this section and the protection amount (P) of the guarantee or credit derivative is less than the EAD of the hedged exposure, the savings association must treat the hedged exposure as two separate exposures (protected and unprotected) in order to recognize the credit risk mitigation benefit of the guarantee or credit derivative.

(A) The savings association's risk-based capital requirement for the protected exposure would be the greater of:

(*1*) The risk-based capital requirement for the protected exposure as calculated under section 31 of this appendix, with the LGD of the exposure adjusted to reflect the guarantee or credit derivative and EAD set equal to P; or

(*2*) The risk-based capital requirement for a direct exposure to the guarantor as calculated under section 31 of this appendix, using the PD for the protection provider, the LGD for the guarantee or credit derivative, and an EAD set equal to P.

(B) The savings association must calculate its risk-based capital requirement for the unprotected exposure under section 31 of this appendix, where PD is the obligor's PD, LGD is the hedged exposure's LGD (not adjusted to reflect the guarantee or credit derivative), and EAD is the EAD of the original hedged exposure minus P.

(3) *M of hedged exposures.* The M of the hedged exposure is the same as the M of the exposure if it were unhedged.

(d) *Maturity mismatch.* (1) A savings association that recognizes an eligible guarantee or eligible credit derivative in determining its risk-based capital requirement for a hedged exposure must adjust the effective notional amount of the credit risk mitigant to reflect any maturity mismatch between the hedged exposure and the credit risk mitigant.

(2) A maturity mismatch occurs when the residual maturity of a credit risk mitigant is less than that of the hedged exposure(s).

(3) The residual maturity of a hedged exposure is the longest possible remaining time before the obligor is scheduled to fulfill its obligation on the exposure. If a credit risk mitigant has embedded options that may reduce its term, the savings association (protection purchaser) must use the shortest possible residual maturity for the credit risk mitigant. If a call is at the discretion of the protection provider, the residual maturity of the credit risk mitigant is at the first call date. If the call is at the discretion of the savings association (protection purchaser), but the terms of the arrangement at origination of the credit risk mitigant contain a positive incentive for the savings association to call the transaction before contractual maturity, the remaining time to the first call date is the residual maturity of the credit risk mitigant. For example, where there is

a step-up in cost in conjunction with a call feature or where the effective cost of protection increases over time even if credit quality remains the same or improves, the residual maturity of the credit risk mitigant will be the remaining time to the first call.

(4) A credit risk mitigant with a maturity mismatch may be recognized only if its original maturity is greater than or equal to one year and its residual maturity is greater than three months.

(5) When a maturity mismatch exists, the savings association must apply the following adjustment to the effective notional amount of the credit risk mitigant: $Pm = E \times (t - 0.25)/(T - 0.25)$, where:

(i) Pm = effective notional amount of the credit risk mitigant, adjusted for maturity mismatch;

(ii) E = effective notional amount of the credit risk mitigant;

(iii) t = the lesser of T or the residual maturity of the credit risk mitigant, expressed in years; and

(iv) T = the lesser of five or the residual maturity of the hedged exposure, expressed in years.

(e) *Credit derivatives without restructuring as a credit event.* If a savings association recognizes an eligible credit derivative that does not include as a credit event a restructuring of the hedged exposure involving forgiveness or postponement of principal, interest, or fees that results in a credit loss event (that is, a charge-off, specific provision, or other similar debit to the profit and loss account), the savings association must apply the following adjustment to the effective notional amount of the credit derivative: $Pr = Pm \times 0.60$, where:

(1) Pr = effective notional amount of the credit risk mitigant, adjusted for lack of restructuring event (and maturity mismatch, if applicable); and

(2) Pm = effective notional amount of the credit risk mitigant adjusted for maturity mismatch (if applicable).

(f) *Currency mismatch.* (1) If a savings association recognizes an eligible guarantee or eligible credit derivative that is denominated in a currency different from that in which the hedged exposure is denominated, the savings association must apply the following formula to the effective notional amount of the guarantee or credit derivative: $Pc = Pr \times (1 - H_{FX})$, where:

(i) Pc = effective notional amount of the credit risk mitigant, adjusted for currency mismatch (and maturity mismatch and lack of restructuring event, if applicable);

(ii) Pr = effective notional amount of the credit risk mitigant (adjusted for maturity mismatch and lack of restructuring event, if applicable); and

(iii) H_{FX} = haircut appropriate for the currency mismatch between the credit risk mitigant and the hedged exposure.

(2) A savings association must set H_{FX} equal to 8 percent unless it qualifies for the use of and uses its own internal estimates of foreign exchange volatility based on a ten-business-day holding period and daily marking-to-market and remargining. A savings association qualifies for the use of its own internal estimates of foreign exchange volatility if it qualifies for:

(i) The own-estimates haircuts in paragraph (b)(2)(iii) of section 32 of this appendix;

(ii) The simple VaR methodology in paragraph (b)(3) of section 32 of this appendix; or

(iii) The internal models methodology in paragraph (d) of section 32 of this appendix.

(3) A savings association must adjust H_{FX} calculated in paragraph (f)(2) of this section upward if the savings association revalues the guarantee or credit derivative less frequently than once every ten business days using the square root of time formula provided in paragraph (b)(2)(iii)(A)(2) of section 32 of this appendix.

Section 34. Guarantees and Credit Derivatives: Double Default Treatment

(a) *Eligibility and operational criteria for double default treatment.* A savings association may recognize the credit risk mitigation benefits of a guarantee or credit derivative covering an exposure described in paragraph (a)(1) of section 33 of this appendix by applying the double default treatment in this section if all the following criteria are satisfied.

(1) The hedged exposure is fully covered or covered on a pro rata basis by:

(i) An eligible guarantee issued by an eligible double default guarantor; or

(ii) An eligible credit derivative that meets the requirements of paragraph (b)(2) of section 33 of this appendix and is issued by an eligible double default guarantor.

(2) The guarantee or credit derivative is:

(i) An uncollateralized guarantee or uncollateralized credit derivative (for example, a credit default swap) that provides protection with respect to a single reference obligor; or

(ii) An nth-to-default credit derivative (subject to the requirements of paragraph (m) of section 42 of this appendix).

(3) The hedged exposure is a wholesale exposure (other than a sovereign exposure).

(4) The obligor of the hedged exposure is not:

(i) An eligible double default guarantor or an affiliate of an eligible double default guarantor; or

(ii) An affiliate of the guarantor.

(5) The savings association does not recognize any credit risk mitigation benefits of the guarantee or credit derivative for the hedged exposure other than through application of the double default treatment as provided in this section.

(6) The savings association has implemented a process (which has received the

prior, written approval of the OTS) to detect excessive correlation between the creditworthiness of the obligor of the hedged exposure and the protection provider. If excessive correlation is present, the savings association may not use the double default treatment for the hedged exposure.

(b) *Full coverage.* If the transaction meets the criteria in paragraph (a) of this section and the protection amount (P) of the guarantee or credit derivative is at least equal to the EAD of the hedged exposure, the savings association may determine its risk-weighted asset amount for the hedged exposure under paragraph (e) of this section.

(c) *Partial coverage.* If the transaction meets the criteria in paragraph (a) of this section and the protection amount (P) of the guarantee or credit derivative is less than the EAD of the hedged exposure, the savings association must treat the hedged exposure as two separate exposures (protected and unprotected) in order to recognize double default treatment on the protected portion of the exposure.

(1) For the protected exposure, the savings association must set EAD equal to P and calculate its risk-weighted asset amount as provided in paragraph (e) of this section.

(2) For the unprotected exposure, the savings association must set EAD equal to the EAD of the original exposure minus P and then calculate its risk-weighted asset amount as provided in section 31 of this appendix.

(d) *Mismatches.* For any hedged exposure to which a savings association applies double default treatment, the savings association must make applicable adjustments to the protection amount as required in paragraphs (d), (e), and (f) of section 33 of this appendix.

(e) *The double default dollar risk-based capital requirement.* The dollar risk-based capital requirement for a hedged exposure to which a savings association has applied double default treatment is K_{DD} multiplied by the EAD of the exposure. K_{DD} is calculated according to the following formula: $K_{DD} = K_o \times (0.15 + 160 \times PD_g)$,

Where:

(1)

$$K_O = LGD_g \times \left[N\left(\frac{N^{-1}(PD_o) + N^{-1}(0.999)\sqrt{\rho_{os}}}{\sqrt{1-\rho_{os}}} \right) - PD_o \right] \times \left[\frac{1+(M-2.5)\times b}{1-1.5\times b} \right]$$

(2) PD_g = PD of the protection provider.
(3) PD_o = PD of the obligor of the hedged exposure.
(4) LGD_g = (i) The lower of the LGD of the hedged exposure (not adjusted to reflect the guarantee or credit derivative) and the LGD of the guarantee or credit derivative, if the guarantee or credit derivative provides the savings association with the option to receive immediate payout on triggering the protection; or
(ii) The LGD of the guarantee or credit derivative, if the guarantee or credit derivative does not provide the savings association with the option to receive immediate payout on triggering the protection.
(5) ρ_{os} (asset value correlation of the obligor) is calculated according to the appropriate formula for (R) provided in Table 2 in section 31 of this appendix, with PD equal to PD_o.
(6) b (maturity adjustment coefficient) is calculated according to the formula for b provided in Table 2 in section 31 of this appendix, with PD equal to the lesser of PD_o and PD_g.
(7) M (maturity) is the effective maturity of the guarantee or credit derivative, which may not be less than one year or greater than five years.

Section 35. Risk-Based Capital Requirement for Unsettled Transactions

(a) *Definitions.* For purposes of this section:
(1) *Delivery-versus-payment (DvP) transaction* means a securities or commodities transaction in which the buyer is obligated to make payment only if the seller has made delivery of the securities or commodities and the seller is obligated to deliver the securities or commodities only if the buyer has made payment.
(2) *Payment-versus-payment (PvP) transaction* means a foreign exchange transaction in which each counterparty is obligated to make a final transfer of one or more currencies only if the other counterparty has made a final transfer of one or more currencies.
(3) *Normal settlement period.* A transaction has a *normal settlement period* if the contractual settlement period for the transaction is equal to or less than the market standard for the instrument underlying the transaction and equal to or less than five business days.
(4) *Positive current exposure.* The positive current exposure of a savings association for a transaction is the difference between the transaction value at the agreed settlement price and the current market price of the transaction, if the difference results in a

credit exposure of the savings association to the counterparty.

(b) *Scope.* This section applies to all transactions involving securities, foreign exchange instruments, and commodities that have a risk of delayed settlement or delivery. This section does not apply to:

(1) Transactions accepted by a qualifying central counterparty that are subject to daily marking-to-market and daily receipt and payment of variation margin;

(2) Repo-style transactions, including unsettled repo-style transactions (which are addressed in sections 31 and 32 of this appendix);

(3) One-way cash payments on OTC derivative contracts (which are addressed in sections 31 and 32 of this appendix); or

(4) Transactions with a contractual settlement period that is longer than the normal settlement period (which are treated as OTC derivative contracts and addressed in sections 31 and 32 of this appendix).

(c) *System-wide failures.* In the case of a system-wide failure of a settlement or clearing system, the OTS may waive risk-based capital requirements for unsettled and failed transactions until the situation is rectified.

(d) *Delivery-versus-payment (DvP) and payment-versus-payment (PvP) transactions.* A savings association must hold risk-based capital against any DvP or PvP transaction with a normal settlement period if the savings association's counterparty has not made delivery or payment within five business days after the settlement date. The savings association must determine its risk-weighted asset amount for such a transaction by multiplying the positive current exposure of the transaction for the savings association by the appropriate risk weight in Table 5.

TABLE 5—RISK WEIGHTS FOR UNSETTLED DvP AND PvP TRANSACTIONS

Number of business days after contractual settlement date	Risk weight to be applied to positive current exposure (percent)
From 5 to 15	100
From 16 to 30	625
From 31 to 45	937.5
46 or more	1,250

(e) *Non-DvP/non-PvP (non-delivery-versus-payment/non-payment-versus-payment) transactions.* (1) A savings association must hold risk-based capital against any non-DvP/non-PvP transaction with a normal settlement period if the savings association has delivered cash, securities, commodities, or currencies to its counterparty but has not received its corresponding deliverables by the end of the same business day. The savings association must continue to hold risk-based capital against the transaction until the savings association has received its corresponding deliverables.

(2) From the business day after the savings association has made its delivery until five business days after the counterparty delivery is due, the savings association must calculate its risk-based capital requirement for the transaction by treating the current market value of the deliverables owed to the savings association as a wholesale exposure.

(i) A savings association may assign an obligor rating to a counterparty for which it is not otherwise required under this appendix to assign an obligor rating on the basis of the applicable external rating of any outstanding unsecured long-term debt security without credit enhancement issued by the counterparty.

(ii) A savings association may use a 45 percent LGD for the transaction rather than estimating LGD for the transaction provided the savings association uses the 45 percent LGD for all transactions described in paragraphs (e)(1) and (e)(2) of this section.

(iii) A savings association may use a 100 percent risk weight for the transaction provided the savings association uses this risk weight for all transactions described in paragraphs (e)(1) and (e)(2) of this section.

(3) If the savings association has not received its deliverables by the fifth business day after the counterparty delivery was due, the savings association must deduct the current market value of the deliverables owed to the savings association 50 percent from tier 1 capital and 50 percent from tier 2 capital.

(f) *Total risk-weighted assets for unsettled transactions.* Total risk-weighted assets for unsettled transactions is the sum of the risk-weighted asset amounts of all DvP, PvP, and non-DvP/non-PvP transactions.

PART V. RISK-WEIGHTED ASSETS FOR SECURITIZATION EXPOSURES

Section 41. Operational Criteria for Recognizing the Transfer of Risk

(a) *Operational criteria for traditional securitizations.* A savings association that transfers exposures it has originated or purchased to a securitization SPE or other third party in connection with a traditional securitization may exclude the exposures from the calculation of its risk-weighted assets only if each of the conditions in this paragraph (a) is satisfied. A savings association that meets these conditions must hold risk-based capital against any securitization exposures it retains in connection with the securitization. A savings association that fails to meet these conditions must hold risk-based capital against the transferred exposures as if they had not been securitized and must deduct from tier 1 capital any after-tax gain-on-sale resulting from the transaction. The conditions are:

Office of Thrift Supervision, Treasury

(1) The transfer is considered a sale under GAAP;

(2) The savings association has transferred to third parties credit risk associated with the underlying exposures; and

(3) Any clean-up calls relating to the securitization are eligible clean-up calls.

(b) *Operational criteria for synthetic securitizations.* For synthetic securitizations, a savings association may recognize for risk-based capital purposes the use of a credit risk mitigant to hedge underlying exposures only if each of the conditions in this paragraph (b) is satisfied. A savings association that fails to meet these conditions must hold risk-based capital against the underlying exposures as if they had not been synthetically securitized. The conditions are:

(1) The credit risk mitigant is financial collateral, an eligible credit derivative from an eligible securitization guarantor or an eligible guarantee from an eligible securitization guarantor;

(2) The savings association transfers credit risk associated with the underlying exposures to third parties, and the terms and conditions in the credit risk mitigants employed do not include provisions that:

(i) Allow for the termination of the credit protection due to deterioration in the credit quality of the underlying exposures;

(ii) Require the savings association to alter or replace the underlying exposures to improve the credit quality of the pool of underlying exposures;

(iii) Increase the savings association's cost of credit protection in response to deterioration in the credit quality of the underlying exposures;

(iv) Increase the yield payable to parties other than the savings association in response to a deterioration in the credit quality of the underlying exposures; or

(v) Provide for increases in a retained first loss position or credit enhancement provided by the savings association after the inception of the securitization;

(3) The savings association obtains a well-reasoned opinion from legal counsel that confirms the enforceability of the credit risk mitigant in all relevant jurisdictions; and

(4) Any clean-up calls relating to the securitization are eligible clean-up calls.

Section 42. Risk-Based Capital Requirement for Securitization Exposures

(a) *Hierarchy of approaches.* Except as provided elsewhere in this section:

(1) A savings association must deduct from tier 1 capital any after-tax gain-on-sale resulting from a securitization and must deduct from total capital in accordance with paragraph (c) of this section the portion of any CEIO that does not constitute gain-on-sale.

(2) If a securitization exposure does not require deduction under paragraph (a)(1) of this section and qualifies for the Ratings-Based Approach in section 43 of this appendix, a savings association must apply the Ratings-Based Approach to the exposure.

(3) If a securitization exposure does not require deduction under paragraph (a)(1) of this section and does not qualify for the Ratings-Based Approach, the savings association may either apply the Internal Assessment Approach in section 44 of this appendix to the exposure (if the savings association, the exposure, and the relevant ABCP program qualify for the Internal Assessment Approach) or the Supervisory Formula Approach in section 45 of this appendix to the exposure (if the savings association and the exposure qualify for the Supervisory Formula Approach).

(4) If a securitization exposure does not require deduction under paragraph (a)(1) of this section and does not qualify for the Ratings-Based Approach, the Internal Assessment Approach, or the Supervisory Formula Approach, the savings association must deduct the exposure from total capital in accordance with paragraph (c) of this section.

(5) If a securitization exposure is an OTC derivative contract (other than a credit derivative) that has a first priority claim on the cash flows from the underlying exposures (notwithstanding amounts due under interest rate or currency derivative contracts, fees due, or other similar payments), with approval of the OTS, a savings association may choose to set the risk-weighted asset amount of the exposure equal to the amount of the exposure as determined in paragraph (e) of this section rather than apply the hierarchy of approaches described in paragraphs (a) (1) through (4) of this section.

(b) *Total risk-weighted assets for securitization exposures.* A savings association's total risk-weighted assets for securitization exposures is equal to the sum of its risk-weighted assets calculated using the Ratings-Based Approach in section 43 of this appendix, the Internal Assessment Approach in section 44 of this appendix, and the Supervisory Formula Approach in section 45 of this appendix, and its risk-weighted assets amount for early amortization provisions calculated in section 47 of this appendix.

(c) *Deductions.* (1) If a savings association must deduct a securitization exposure from total capital, the savings association must take the deduction 50 percent from tier 1 capital and 50 percent from tier 2 capital. If the amount deductible from tier 2 capital exceeds the savings association's tier 2 capital, the savings association must deduct the excess from tier 1 capital.

(2) A savings association may calculate any deduction from tier 1 capital and tier 2 capital for a securitization exposure net of any deferred tax liabilities associated with the securitization exposure.

(d) *Maximum risk-based capital requirement.* Regardless of any other provisions of this part, unless one or more underlying exposures does not meet the definition of a wholesale, retail, securitization, or equity exposure, the total risk-based capital requirement for all securitization exposures held by a single savings association associated with a single securitization (including any risk-based capital requirements that relate to an early amortization provision of the securitization but excluding any risk-based capital requirements that relate to the savings association's gain-on-sale or CEIOs associated with the securitization) may not exceed the sum of:

(1) The savings association's total risk-based capital requirement for the underlying exposures as if the savings association directly held the underlying exposures; and

(2) The total ECL of the underlying exposures.

(e) *Amount of a securitization exposure.* (1) The amount of an on-balance sheet securitization exposure that is not a repo-style transaction, eligible margin loan, or OTC derivative contract (other than a credit derivative) is:

(i) The savings association's carrying value minus any unrealized gains and plus any unrealized losses on the exposure, if the exposure is a security classified as available-for-sale; or

(ii) The savings association's carrying value, if the exposure is not a security classified as available-for-sale.

(2) The amount of an off-balance sheet securitization exposure that is not an OTC derivative contract (other than a credit derivative) is the notional amount of the exposure. For an off-balance-sheet securitization exposure to an ABCP program, such as a liquidity facility, the notional amount may be reduced to the maximum potential amount that the savings association could be required to fund given the ABCP program's current underlying assets (calculated without regard to the current credit quality of those assets).

(3) The amount of a securitization exposure that is a repo-style transaction, eligible margin loan, or OTC derivative contract (other than a credit derivative) is the EAD of the exposure as calculated in section 32 of this appendix.

(f) *Overlapping exposures.* If a savings association has multiple securitization exposures that provide duplicative coverage of the underlying exposures of a securitization (such as when a savings association provides a program-wide credit enhancement and multiple pool-specific liquidity facilities to an ABCP program), the savings association is not required to hold duplicative risk-based capital against the overlapping position. Instead, the savings association may apply to the overlapping position the applicable risk-based capital treatment that results in the highest risk-based capital requirement.

(g) *Securitizations of non-IRB exposures.* If a savings association has a securitization exposure where any underlying exposure is not a wholesale exposure, retail exposure, securitization exposure, or equity exposure, the savings association must:

(1) If the savings association is an originating savings association, deduct from tier 1 capital any after-tax gain-on-sale resulting from the securitization and deduct from total capital in accordance with paragraph (c) of this section the portion of any CEIO that does not constitute gain-on-sale;

(2) If the securitization exposure does not require deduction under paragraph (g)(1), apply the RBA in section 43 of this appendix to the securitization exposure if the exposure qualifies for the RBA;

(3) If the securitization exposure does not require deduction under paragraph (g)(1) and does not qualify for the RBA, apply the IAA in section 44 of this appendix to the exposure (if the savings association, the exposure, and the relevant ABCP program qualify for the IAA); and

(4) If the securitization exposure does not require deduction under paragraph (g)(1) and does not qualify for the RBA or the IAA, deduct the exposure from total capital in accordance with paragraph (c) of this section.

(h) *Implicit support.* If a savings association provides support to a securitization in excess of the savings association's contractual obligation to provide credit support to the securitization (implicit support):

(1) The savings association must hold regulatory capital against all of the underlying exposures associated with the securitization as if the exposures had not been securitized and must deduct from tier 1 capital any after-tax gain-on-sale resulting from the securitization; and

(2) The savings association must disclose publicly:

(i) That it has provided implicit support to the securitization; and

(ii) The regulatory capital impact to the savings association of providing such implicit support.

(i) *Eligible servicer cash advance facilities.* Regardless of any other provisions of this part, a savings association is not required to hold risk-based capital against the undrawn portion of an eligible servicer cash advance facility.

(j) *Interest-only mortgage-backed securities.* Regardless of any other provisions of this part, the risk weight for a non-credit-enhancing interest-only mortgage-backed security may not be less than 100 percent.

Office of Thrift Supervision, Treasury   Pt. 567, App. C

(k) *Small-business loans and leases on personal property transferred with recourse.* (1) Regardless of any other provisions of this appendix, a savings association that has transferred small-business loans and leases on personal property (small-business obligations) with recourse must include in risk-weighted assets only the contractual amount of retained recourse if all the following conditions are met:

(i) The transaction is a sale under GAAP.

(ii) The savings association establishes and maintains, pursuant to GAAP, a non-capital reserve sufficient to meet the savings association's reasonably estimated liability under the recourse arrangement.

(iii) The loans and leases are to businesses that meet the criteria for a small-business concern established by the Small Business Administration under section 3(a) of the Small Business Act (15 U.S.C. 632).

(iv) The savings association is well capitalized, as defined in the OTS's prompt corrective action regulation at 12 CFR part 565. For purposes of determining whether a savings association is well capitalized for purposes of this paragraph, the savings association's capital ratios must be calculated without regard to the capital treatment for transfers of small-business obligations with recourse specified in paragraph (k)(1) of this section.

(2) The total outstanding amount of recourse retained by a savings association on transfers of small-business obligations receiving the capital treatment specified in paragraph (k)(1) of this section cannot exceed 15 percent of the savings association's total qualifying capital.

(3) If a savings association ceases to be well capitalized or exceeds the 15 percent capital limitation, the preferential capital treatment specified in paragraph (k)(1) of this section will continue to apply to any transfers of small-business obligations with recourse that occurred during the time that the savings association was well capitalized and did not exceed the capital limit.

(4) The risk-based capital ratios of the savings association must be calculated without regard to the capital treatment for transfers of small-business obligations with recourse specified in paragraph (k)(1) of this section as provided in 12 CFR 567.6(b)(5)(v).

(1) N^{th}-*to-default credit derivatives*—(1) *First-to-default credit derivatives*—(i) *Protection purchaser.* A savings association that obtains credit protection on a group of underlying exposures through a first-to-default credit derivative must determine its risk-based capital requirement for the underlying exposures as if the savings association synthetically securitized the underlying exposure with the lowest risk-based capital requirement and had obtained no credit risk mitigant on the other underlying exposures.

(ii) *Protection provider.* A savings association that provides credit protection on a group of underlying exposures through a first-to-default credit derivative must determine its risk-weighted asset amount for the derivative by applying the RBA in section 43 of this appendix (if the derivative qualifies for the RBA) or, if the derivative does not qualify for the RBA, by setting its risk-weighted asset amount for the derivative equal to the product of:

(A) The protection amount of the derivative;

(B) 12.5; and

(C) The sum of the risk-based capital requirements of the individual underlying exposures, up to a maximum of 100 percent.

(2) *Second-or-subsequent-to-default credit derivatives*—(i) *Protection purchaser.* (A) A savings association that obtains credit protection on a group of underlying exposures through a nth-to-default credit derivative (other than a first-to-default credit derivative) may recognize the credit risk mitigation benefits of the derivative only if:

(*1*) The savings association also has obtained credit protection on the same underlying exposures in the form of first-through-(n-1)-to-default credit derivatives; or

(*2*) If n-1 of the underlying exposures have already defaulted.

(B) If a savings association satisfies the requirements of paragraph (m)(2)(i)(A) of this section, the savings association must determine its risk-based capital requirement for the underlying exposures as if the savings association had only synthetically securitized the underlying exposure with the nth lowest risk-based capital requirement and had obtained no credit risk mitigant on the other underlying exposures.

(ii) *Protection provider.* A savings association that provides credit protection on a group of underlying exposures through a nth-to-default credit derivative (other than a first-to-default credit derivative) must determine its risk-weighted asset amount for the derivative by applying the RBA in section 43 of this appendix (if the derivative qualifies for the RBA) or, if the derivative does not qualify for the RBA, by setting its risk-weighted asset amount for the derivative equal to the product of:

(A) The protection amount of the derivative;

(B) 12.5; and

(C) The sum of the risk-based capital requirements of the individual underlying exposures (excluding the n-1 underlying exposures with the lowest risk-based capital requirements), up to a maximum of 100 percent.

Section 43. Ratings-Based Approach (RBA)

(a) *Eligibility requirements for use of the RBA*—(1) *Originating savings association.* An originating savings association must use the RBA to calculate its risk-based capital requirement for a securitization exposure if the exposure has two or more external ratings or inferred ratings (and may not use the RBA if the exposure has fewer than two external ratings or inferred ratings).

(2) *Investing savings association.* An investing savings association must use the RBA to calculate its risk-based capital requirement for a securitization exposure if the exposure has one or more external or inferred ratings (and may not use the RBA if the exposure has no external or inferred rating).

(b) *Ratings-based approach.* (1) A savings association must determine the risk-weighted asset amount for a securitization exposure by multiplying the amount of the exposure (as defined in paragraph (e) of section 42 of this appendix) by the appropriate risk weight provided in Table 6 and Table 7.

(2) A savings association must apply the risk weights in Table 6 when the securitization exposure's applicable external or applicable inferred rating represents a long-term credit rating, and must apply the risk weights in Table 7 when the securitization exposure's applicable external or applicable inferred rating represents a short-term credit rating.

(i) A savings association must apply the risk weights in column 1 of Table 6 or Table 7 to the securitization exposure if:

(A) N (as calculated under paragraph (e)(6) of section 45 of this appendix) is six or more (for purposes of this section only, if the notional number of underlying exposures is 25 or more or if all of the underlying exposures are retail exposures, a savings association may assume that N is six or more unless the savings association knows or has reason to know that N is less than six); and

(B) The securitization exposure is a senior securitization exposure.

(ii) A savings association must apply the risk weights in column 3 of Table 6 or Table 7 to the securitization exposure if N is less than six, regardless of the seniority of the securitization exposure.

(iii) Otherwise, a savings association must apply the risk weights in column 2 of Table 6 or Table 7.

TABLE 6—LONG-TERM CREDIT RATING RISK WEIGHTS UNDER RBA AND IAA

Applicable external or inferred rating (Illustrative rating example)	Column 1 Risk weights for senior securitization exposures backed by granular pools	Column 2 Risk weights for non-senior securitization exposures backed by granular pools	Column 3 Risk weights for securitization exposures backed by non-granular pools
Highest investment grade (for example, AAA)	7%	12%	20%
Second highest investment grade (for example, AA)	8%	15%	25%
Third-highest investment grade—positive designation (for example, A+)	10%	18%	35%
Third-highest investment grade (for example, A)	12%	20%	
Third-highest investment grade—negative designation (for example, A−)	20%	35%	
Lowest investment grade—positive designation (for example, BBB+)	35%	50%	
Lowest investment grade (for example, BBB)	60%	75%	
Lowest investment grade—negative designation (for example, BBB−)	100%		
One category below investment grade—positive designation (for example, BB+)	250%		
One category below investment grade (for example, BB)	425%		
One category below investment grade—negative designation (for example, BB−)	650%		
More than one category below investment grade	Deduction from tier 1 and tier 2 capital.		

TABLE 7—SHORT-TERM CREDIT RATING RISK WEIGHTS UNDER RBA AND IAA

Applicable external or inferred rating (Illustrative rating example)	Column 1 Risk weights for senior securitization exposures backed by granular pools	Column 2 Risk weights for non-senior securitization exposures backed by granular pools	Column 3 Risk weights for securitization exposures backed by non-granular pools
Highest investment grade (for example, A1)	7%	12%	20%
Second highest investment grade (for example, A2)	12%	20%	35%
Third highest investment grade (for example, A3)	60%	75%	75%
All other ratings	Deduction from tier 1 and tier 2 capital.		

Office of Thrift Supervision, Treasury   **Pt. 567, App. C**

Section 44. Internal Assessment Approach (IAA)

(a) *Eligibility requirements.* A savings association may apply the IAA to calculate the risk-weighted asset amount for a securitization exposure that the savings association has to an ABCP program (such as a liquidity facility or credit enhancement) if the savings association, the ABCP program, and the exposure qualify for use of the IAA.

(1) *Savings association qualification criteria.* A savings association qualifies for use of the IAA if the savings association has received the prior written approval of the OTS. To receive such approval, the savings association must demonstrate to the OTS's satisfaction that the savings association's internal assessment process meets the following criteria:

(i) The savings association's internal credit assessments of securitization exposures must be based on publicly available rating criteria used by an NRSRO.

(ii) The savings association's internal credit assessments of securitization exposures used for risk-based capital purposes must be consistent with those used in the savings association's internal risk management process, management information reporting systems, and capital adequacy assessment process.

(iii) The savings association's internal credit assessment process must have sufficient granularity to identify gradations of risk. Each of the savings association's internal credit assessment categories must correspond to an external rating of an NRSRO.

(iv) The savings association's internal credit assessment process, particularly the stress test factors for determining credit enhancement requirements, must be at least as conservative as the most conservative of the publicly available rating criteria of the NRSROs that have provided external ratings to the commercial paper issued by the ABCP program.

(A) Where the commercial paper issued by an ABCP program has an external rating from two or more NRSROs and the different NRSROs' benchmark stress factors require different levels of credit enhancement to achieve the same external rating equivalent, the savings association must apply the NRSRO stress factor that requires the highest level of credit enhancement.

(B) If any NRSRO that provides an external rating to the ABCP program's commercial paper changes its methodology (including stress factors), the savings association must evaluate whether to revise its internal assessment process.

(v) The savings association must have an effective system of controls and oversight that ensures compliance with these operational requirements and maintains the integrity and accuracy of the internal credit assessments. The savings association must have an internal audit function independent from the ABCP program business line and internal credit assessment process that assesses at least annually whether the controls over the internal credit assessment process function as intended.

(vi) The savings association must review and update each internal credit assessment whenever new material information is available, but no less frequently than annually.

(vii) The savings association must validate its internal credit assessment process on an ongoing basis and at least annually.

(2) *ABCP-program qualification criteria.* An ABCP program qualifies for use of the IAA if all commercial paper issued by the ABCP program has an external rating.

(3) *Exposure qualification criteria.* A securitization exposure qualifies for use of the IAA if the exposure meets the following criteria:

(i) The savings association initially rated the exposure at least the equivalent of investment grade.

(ii) The ABCP program has robust credit and investment guidelines (that is, underwriting standards) for the exposures underlying the securitization exposure.

(iii) The ABCP program performs a detailed credit analysis of the sellers of the exposures underlying the securitization exposure.

(iv) The ABCP program's underwriting policy for the exposures underlying the securitization exposure establishes minimum asset eligibility criteria that include the prohibition of the purchase of assets that are significantly past due or of assets that are defaulted (that is, assets that have been charged off or written down by the seller prior to being placed into the ABCP program or assets that would be charged off or written down under the program's governing contracts), as well as limitations on concentration to individual obligors or geographic areas and the tenor of the assets to be purchased.

(v) The aggregate estimate of loss on the exposures underlying the securitization exposure considers all sources of potential risk, such as credit and dilution risk.

(vi) Where relevant, the ABCP program incorporates structural features into each purchase of exposures underlying the securitization exposure to mitigate potential credit deterioration of the underlying exposures. Such features may include wind-down triggers specific to a pool of underlying exposures.

(b) *Mechanics.* A savings association that elects to use the IAA to calculate the risk-based capital requirement for any securitization exposure must use the IAA to calculate the risk-based capital requirements for all securitization exposures that qualify for the IAA approach. Under the IAA, a savings association must map its internal assessment of such a securitization exposure to an equivalent external rating from an NRSRO. Under the IAA, a savings association must determine the risk-weighted asset amount for such a securitization exposure by multiplying the amount of the exposure (as defined in paragraph (e) of section 42 of this appendix) by the appropriate risk weight in Table 6 and Table 7 in paragraph (b) of section 43 of this appendix.

Section 45. Supervisory Formula Approach (SFA)

(a) *Eligibility requirements.* A savings association may use the SFA to determine its risk-based capital requirement for a securitization exposure only if the savings association can calculate on an ongoing basis each of the SFA parameters in paragraph (e) of this section.

(b) *Mechanics.* Under the SFA, a securitization exposure incurs a deduction from total capital (as described in paragraph (c) of section 42 of this appendix) and/or an SFA risk-based capital requirement, as determined in paragraph (c) of this section. The risk-weighted asset amount for the securitization exposure equals the SFA risk-based capital requirement for the exposure multiplied by 12.5.

(c) *The SFA risk-based capital requirement.* (1) If K_{IRB} is greater than or equal to L + T, the entire exposure must be deducted from total capital.

(2) If K_{IRB} is less than or equal to L, the exposure's SFA risk-based capital requirement is UE multiplied by TP multiplied by the greater of:

(i) 0.0056 * T; or

(ii) S[L + T] − S[L].

(3) If K_{IRB} is greater than L and less than L + T, the savings association must deduct from total capital an amount equal to UE*TP*(K_{IRB} − L), and the exposure's SFA risk-based capital requirement is UE multiplied by TP multiplied by the greater of:

(i) 0.0056 * (T − (K_{IRB} − L)); or

(ii) S[L + T] − S[K_{IRB}].

(d) *The supervisory formula:*

Office of Thrift Supervision, Treasury — Pt. 567, App. C

$$(1)\ S[Y] = \begin{cases} Y & \text{when } Y \leq K_{IRB} \\ K_{IRB} + K[Y] - K[K_{IRB}] + \dfrac{d \cdot K_{IRB}}{20}(1 - e^{\frac{20 \cdot (K_{IRB} - Y)}{K_{IRB}}}) & \text{when } Y > K_{IRB} \end{cases}$$

$$(2)\ K[Y] = (1-h) \cdot \left[(1 - \beta[Y; a, b]) \cdot Y + \beta[Y; a+1, b] \cdot c\right]$$

$$(3)\ h = \left(1 - \dfrac{K_{IRB}}{EWALGD}\right)^N$$

$$(4)\ a = g \cdot c$$

$$(5)\ b = g \cdot (1 - c)$$

$$(6)\ c = \dfrac{K_{IRB}}{1 - h}$$

$$(7)\ g = \dfrac{(1 - c) \cdot c}{f} - 1$$

$$(8)\ f = \dfrac{v + K_{IRB}^2}{1 - h} - c^2 + \dfrac{(1 - K_{IRB}) \cdot K_{IRB} - v}{(1 - h) \cdot 1000}$$

$$(9)\ v = K_{IRB} \cdot \dfrac{(EWALGD - K_{IRB}) + .25 \cdot (1 - EWALGD)}{N}$$

$$(10)\ d = 1 - (1 - h) \cdot (1 - \beta[K_{IRB}; a, b]).$$

(11) In these expressions, β[Y; a, b] refers to the cumulative beta distribution with parameters a and b evaluated at Y. In the case where N = 1 and EWALGD = 100 percent, S[Y] in formula (1) must be calculated with K[Y] set equal to the product of K$_{IRB}$ and Y, and d set equal to 1 − K$_{IRB}$.

(e) *SFA parameters*—(1) *Amount of the underlying exposures (UE).* UE is the EAD of any underlying exposures that are wholesale and retail exposures (including the amount of any funded spread accounts, cash collateral accounts, and other similar funded credit enhancements) plus the amount of any underlying exposures that are securitization exposures (as defined in paragraph (e) of section 42 of this appendix) plus the adjusted carrying value of any underlying exposures that are equity exposures (as defined in paragraph (b) of section 51 of this appendix).

(2) *Tranche percentage (TP).* TP is the ratio of the amount of the savings association's

securitization exposure to the amount of the tranche that contains the securitization exposure.

(3) *Capital requirement on underlying exposures (K_{IRB})*. (i) K_{IRB} is the ratio of:

(A) The sum of the risk-based capital requirements for the underlying exposures plus the expected credit losses of the underlying exposures (as determined under this appendix as if the underlying exposures were directly held by the savings association); to

(B) UE.

(ii) The calculation of K_{IRB} must reflect the effects of any credit risk mitigant applied to the underlying exposures (either to an individual underlying exposure, to a group of underlying exposures, or to the entire pool of underlying exposures).

(iii) All assets related to the securitization are treated as underlying exposures, including assets in a reserve account (such as a cash collateral account).

(4) *Credit enhancement level (L)*. (i) L is the ratio of:

(A) The amount of all securitization exposures subordinated to the tranche that contains the savings association's securitization exposure; to

(B) UE.

(ii) A savings association must determine L before considering the effects of any tranche-specific credit enhancements.

(iii) Any gain-on-sale or CEIO associated with the securitization may not be included in L.

(iv) Any reserve account funded by accumulated cash flows from the underlying exposures that is subordinated to the tranche that contains the savings association's securitization exposure may be included in the numerator and denominator of L to the extent cash has accumulated in the account. Unfunded reserve accounts (that is, reserve accounts that are to be funded from future cash flows from the underlying exposures) may not be included in the calculation of L.

(v) In some cases, the purchase price of receivables will reflect a discount that provides credit enhancement (for example, first loss protection) for all or certain tranches of the securitization. When this arises, L should be calculated inclusive of this discount if the discount provides credit enhancement for the securitization exposure.

(5) *Thickness of tranche (T)*. T is the ratio of:

(i) The amount of the tranche that contains the savings association's securitization exposure; to

(ii) UE.

(6) *Effective number of exposures (N)*. (i) Unless the savings association elects to use the formula provided in paragraph (f) of this section,

$$N = \frac{(\sum_i EAD_i)^2}{\sum_i EAD_i^2}$$

where EAD_i represents the EAD associated with the ith instrument in the pool of underlying exposures.

(ii) Multiple exposures to one obligor must be treated as a single underlying exposure.

(iii) In the case of a re-securitization (that is, a securitization in which some or all of the underlying exposures are themselves securitization exposures), the savings association must treat each underlying exposure as a single underlying exposure and must not look through to the originally securitized underlying exposures.

(7) *Exposure-weighted average loss given default (EWALGD)*. EWALGD is calculated as:

$$EWALGD = \frac{\sum_i LGD_i \cdot EAD_i}{\sum_i EAD_i}$$

where LGD_i represents the average LGD associated with all exposures to the ith obligor. In the case of a re-securitization, an LGD of 100 percent must be assumed for the underlying exposures that are themselves securitization exposures.

(f) *Simplified method for computing N and EWALGD*. (1) If all underlying exposures of a securitization are retail exposures, a savings association may apply the SFA using the following simplifications:

(i) h = 0; and

(ii) v = 0.

(2) Under the conditions in paragraphs (f)(3) and (f)(4) of this section, a savings association may employ a simplified method for calculating N and EWALGD.

(3) If C_1 is no more than 0.03, a savings association may set EWALGD = 0.50 if none of the underlying exposures is a securitization exposure or EWALGD = 1 if one or more of the underlying exposures is a securitization exposure, and may set N equal to the following amount:

404

Office of Thrift Supervision, Treasury

Pt. 567, App. C

$$N = \frac{1}{C_1 C_m + \left(\frac{C_m - C_1}{m-1}\right) \max(1 - mC_1, 0)}$$

where:

(i) C_m is the ratio of the sum of the amounts of the 'm' largest underlying exposures to UE; and

(ii) The level of m is to be selected by the savings association.

(4) Alternatively, if only C_1 is available and C_1 is no more than 0.03, the savings association may set EWALGD = 0.50 if none of the underlying exposures is a securitization exposure or EWALGD = 1 if one or more of the underlying exposures is a securitization exposure and may set $N = 1/C_1$.

Section 46. Recognition of Credit Risk Mitigants for Securitization Exposures

(a) *General.* An originating savings association that has obtained a credit risk mitigant to hedge its securitization exposure to a synthetic or traditional securitization that satisfies the operational criteria in section 41 of this appendix may recognize the credit risk mitigant, but only as provided in this section. An investing savings association that has obtained a credit risk mitigant to hedge a securitization exposure may recognize the credit risk mitigant, but only as provided in this section. A savings association that has used the RBA in section 43 of this appendix or the IAA in section 44 of this appendix to calculate its risk-based capital requirement for a securitization exposure whose external or inferred rating (or equivalent internal rating under the IAA) reflects the benefits of a credit risk mitigant provided to the associated securitization or that supports some or all of the underlying exposures may not use the credit risk mitigation rules in this section to further reduce its risk-based capital requirement for the exposure to reflect that credit risk mitigant.

(b) *Collateral*—(1) *Rules of recognition.* A savings association may recognize financial collateral in determining the savings association's risk-based capital requirement for a securitization exposure (other than a repo-style transaction, an eligible margin loan, or an OTC derivative contract for which the savings association has reflected collateral in its determination of exposure amount under section 32 of this appendix) as follows. The savings association's risk-based capital requirement for the collateralized securitization exposure is equal to the risk-based capital requirement for the securitization exposure as calculated under the RBA in section 43 of this appendix or under the SFA in section 45 of this appendix multiplied by the ratio of adjusted exposure amount (SE*) to original exposure amount (SE), where:

(i) SE* = max {0, [SE—C x (1 – Hs – Hfx)]};

(ii) SE = the amount of the securitization exposure calculated under paragraph (e) of section 42 of this appendix;

(iii) C = the current market value of the collateral;

(iv) Hs = the haircut appropriate to the collateral type; and

(v) Hfx=the haircut appropriate for any currency mismatch between the collateral and the exposure.

(2) *Mixed collateral.* Where the collateral is a basket of different asset types or a basket of assets denominated in different currencies, the haircut on the basket will be

$$H = \sum_i a_i H_i,$$

where a_i is the current market value of the asset in the basket divided by the current market value of all assets in the basket and H_i is the haircut applicable to that asset.

(3) *Standard supervisory haircuts.* Unless a savings association qualifies for use of and uses own-estimates haircuts in paragraph (b)(4) of this section:

(i) A savings association must use the collateral type haircuts (Hs) in Table 3;

(ii) A savings association must use a currency mismatch haircut (Hfx) of 8 percent if the exposure and the collateral are denominated in different currencies;

(iii) A savings association must multiply the supervisory haircuts obtained in paragraphs (b)(3)(i) and (ii) by the square root of 6.5 (which equals 2.549510); and

(iv) A savings association must adjust the supervisory haircuts upward on the basis of a holding period longer than 65 business days where and as appropriate to take into account the illiquidity of the collateral.

(4) *Own estimates for haircuts.* With the prior written approval of the OTS, a savings association may calculate haircuts using its own internal estimates of market price volatility and foreign exchange volatility, subject to paragraph (b)(2)(iii) of section 32 of this appendix. The minimum holding period (TM) for securitization exposures is 65 business days.

405

(c) *Guarantees and credit derivatives*—(1) *Limitations on recognition.* A savings association may only recognize an eligible guarantee or eligible credit derivative provided by an eligible securitization guarantor in determining the savings association's risk-based capital requirement for a securitization exposure.

(2) *ECL for securitization exposures.* When a savings association recognizes an eligible guarantee or eligible credit derivative provided by an eligible securitization guarantor in determining the savings association's risk-based capital requirement for a securitization exposure, the savings association must also:

(i) Calculate ECL for the protected portion of the exposure using the same risk parameters that it uses for calculating the risk-weighted asset amount of the exposure as described in paragraph (c)(3) of this section; and

(ii) Add the exposure's ECL to the savings association's total ECL.

(3) *Rules of recognition.* A savings association may recognize an eligible guarantee or eligible credit derivative provided by an eligible securitization guarantor in determining the savings association's risk-based capital requirement for the securitization exposure as follows:

(i) *Full coverage.* If the protection amount of the eligible guarantee or eligible credit derivative equals or exceeds the amount of the securitization exposure, the savings association may set the risk-weighted asset amount for the securitization exposure equal to the risk-weighted asset amount for a direct exposure to the eligible securitization guarantor (as determined in the wholesale risk weight function described in section 31 of this appendix), using the savings association's PD for the guarantor, the savings association's LGD for the guarantee or credit derivative, and an EAD equal to the amount of the securitization exposure (as determined in paragraph (e) of section 42 of this appendix).

(ii) *Partial coverage.* If the protection amount of the eligible guarantee or eligible credit derivative is less than the amount of the securitization exposure, the savings association may set the risk-weighted asset amount for the securitization exposure equal to the sum of:

(A) *Covered portion.* The risk-weighted asset amount for a direct exposure to the eligible securitization guarantor (as determined in the wholesale risk weight function described in section 31 of this appendix), using the savings association's PD for the guarantor, the savings association's LGD for the guarantee or credit derivative, and an EAD equal to the protection amount of the credit risk mitigant; and

(B) *Uncovered portion.* (1) 1.0 minus the ratio of the protection amount of the eligible guarantee or eligible credit derivative to the amount of the securitization exposure); multiplied by

(2) The risk-weighted asset amount for the securitization exposure without the credit risk mitigant (as determined in sections 42–45 of this appendix).

(4) *Mismatches.* The savings association must make applicable adjustments to the protection amount as required in paragraphs (d), (e), and (f) of section 33 of this appendix for any hedged securitization exposure and any more senior securitization exposure that benefits from the hedge. In the context of a synthetic securitization, when an eligible guarantee or eligible credit derivative covers multiple hedged exposures that have different residual maturities, the savings association must use the longest residual maturity of any of the hedged exposures as the residual maturity of all the hedged exposures.

Section 47. Risk-Based Capital Requirement for Early Amortization Provisions

(a) *General.* (1) An originating savings association must hold risk-based capital against the sum of the originating savings association's interest and the investors' interest in a securitization that:

(i) Includes one or more underlying exposures in which the borrower is permitted to vary the drawn amount within an agreed limit under a line of credit; and

(ii) Contains an early amortization provision.

(2) For securitizations described in paragraph (a)(1) of this section, an originating savings association must calculate the risk-based capital requirement for the originating savings association's interest under sections 42–45 of this appendix, and the risk-based capital requirement for the investors' interest under paragraph (b) of this section.

(b) *Risk-weighted asset amount for investors' interest.* The originating savings association's risk-weighted asset amount for the investors' interest in the securitization is equal to the product of the following 5 quantities:

(1) The investors' interest EAD;

(2) The appropriate conversion factor in paragraph (c) of this section;

(3) K_{IRB} (as defined in paragraph (e)(3) of section 45 of this appendix);

(4) 12.5; and

(5) The proportion of the underlying exposures in which the borrower is permitted to vary the drawn amount within an agreed limit under a line of credit.

(c) *Conversion factor.* (1) (i) Except as provided in paragraph (c)(2) of this section, to calculate the appropriate conversion factor, a savings association must use Table 8 for a securitization that contains a controlled early amortization provision and must use Table 9 for a securitization that contains a non-controlled early amortization provision. In circumstances where a securitization contains a mix of retail and nonretail exposures or a mix of committed and uncommitted exposures, a savings association may take a pro rata approach to determining the conversion factor for the securitization's early amortization provision. If a pro rata approach is not feasible, a savings association must treat the mixed securitization as a securitization of nonretail exposures if a single underlying exposure is a nonretail exposure and must treat the mixed securitization as a securitization of committed exposures if a single underlying exposure is a committed exposure.

(ii) To find the appropriate conversion factor in the tables, a savings association must divide the three-month average annualized excess spread of the securitization by the excess spread trapping point in the securitization structure. In securitizations that do not require excess spread to be trapped, or that specify trapping points based primarily on performance measures other than the three-month average annualized excess spread, the excess spread trapping point is 4.5 percent.

TABLE 8—CONTROLLED EARLY AMORTIZATION PROVISIONS

	Uncommitted	Committed
Retail Credit Lines	Three-month average annualized excess spread Conversion Factor (CF) 133.33% of trapping point or more, 0% CF. less than 133.33% to 100% of trapping point, 1% CF. less than 100% to 75% of trapping point, 2% CF. less than 75% to 50% of trapping point, 10% CF. less than 50% to 25% of trapping point, 20% CF. less than 25% of trapping point, 40% CF.	90% CF
Non-retail Credit Lines	90% CF	90% CF

TABLE 9—NON-CONTROLLED EARLY AMORTIZATION PROVISIONS

	Uncommitted	Committed
Retail Credit Lines	Three-month average annualized excess spread Conversion Factor (CF) 133.33% of trapping point or more, 0% CF. less than 133.33% to 100% of trapping point, 5% CF. less than 100% to 75% of trapping point, 15% CF. less than 75% to 50% of trapping point, 50% CF. less than 50% of trapping point, 100% CF.	100% CF
Non-retail Credit Lines	100% CF	100% CF

(2) For a securitization for which all or substantially all of the underlying exposures are residential mortgage exposures, a savings association may calculate the appropriate conversion factor using paragraph (c)(1) of this section or may use a conversion factor of 10 percent. If the savings association chooses to use a conversion factor of 10 percent, it must use that conversion factor for all securitizations for which all or substantially all of the underlying exposures are residential mortgage exposures.

PART VI. RISK-WEIGHTED ASSETS FOR EQUITY EXPOSURES

Section 51. Introduction and Exposure Measurement

(a) *General.* To calculate its risk-weighted asset amounts for equity exposures that are not equity exposures to investment funds, a savings association may apply either the Simple Risk Weight Approach (SRWA) in section 52 of this appendix or, if it qualifies to do so, the Internal Models Approach (IMA) in section 53 of this appendix. A savings association must use the look-through approaches in section 54 of this appendix to calculate its risk-weighted asset amounts for equity exposures to investment funds.

(b) *Adjusted carrying value.* For purposes of this part, the adjusted carrying value of an equity exposure is:

(1) For the on-balance sheet component of an equity exposure, the savings association's carrying value of the exposure reduced by any unrealized gains on the exposure that are reflected in such carrying value but excluded from the savings association's tier 1 and tier 2 capital; and

(2) For the off-balance sheet component of an equity exposure, the effective notional principal amount of the exposure, the size of which is equivalent to a hypothetical on-balance sheet position in the underlying equity instrument that would evidence the same change in fair value (measured in dollars) for a given small change in the price of the underlying equity instrument, minus the adjusted carrying value of the on-balance sheet component of the exposure as calculated in paragraph (b)(1) of this section. For unfunded equity commitments that are unconditional, the effective notional principal amount is

the notional amount of the commitment. For unfunded equity commitments that are conditional, the effective notional principal amount is the savings association's best estimate of the amount that would be funded under economic downturn conditions.

Section 52. Simple Risk Weight Approach (SRWA)

(a) *General.* Under the SRWA, a savings association's aggregate risk-weighted asset amount for its equity exposures is equal to the sum of the risk-weighted asset amounts for each of the savings association's individual equity exposures (other than equity exposures to an investment fund) as determined in this section and the risk-weighted asset amounts for each of the savings association's individual equity exposures to an investment fund as determined in section 54 of this appendix.

(b) *SRWA computation for individual equity exposures.* A savings association must determine the risk-weighted asset amount for an individual equity exposure (other than an equity exposure to an investment fund) by multiplying the adjusted carrying value of the equity exposure or the effective portion and ineffective portion of a hedge pair (as defined in paragraph (c) of this section) by the lowest applicable risk weight in this paragraph (b).

(1) *0 percent risk weight equity exposures.* An equity exposure to an entity whose credit exposures are exempt from the 0.03 percent PD floor in paragraph (d)(2) of section 31 of this appendix is assigned a 0 percent risk weight.

(2) *20 percent risk weight equity exposures.* An equity exposure to a Federal Home Loan Bank or Farmer Mac is assigned a 20 percent risk weight.

(3) *100 percent risk weight equity exposures.* The following equity exposures are assigned a 100 percent risk weight:

(i) An equity exposure that is designed primarily to promote community welfare, including the welfare of low- and moderate-income communities or families, such as by providing services or jobs, excluding equity exposures to an unconsolidated small business investment company and equity exposures held through a consolidated small business investment company described in section 302 of the Small Business Investment Act of 1958 (15 U.S.C. 682).

(ii) *Effective portion of hedge pairs.* The effective portion of a hedge pair.

(iii) *Non-significant equity exposures.* Equity exposures, excluding exposures to an investment firm that would meet the definition of a traditional securitization were it not for the OTS's application of paragraph (8) of that definition and has greater than immaterial leverage, to the extent that the aggregate adjusted carrying value of the exposures does not exceed 10 percent of the savings association's tier 1 capital plus tier 2 capital.

(A) To compute the aggregate adjusted carrying value of a savings association's equity exposures for purposes of this paragraph (b)(3)(iii), the savings association may exclude equity exposures described in paragraphs (b)(1), (b)(2), (b)(3)(i), and (b)(3)(ii) of this section, the equity exposure in a hedge pair with the smaller adjusted carrying value, and a proportion of each equity exposure to an investment fund equal to the proportion of the assets of the investment fund that are not equity exposures or that meet the criterion of paragraph (b)(3)(i) of this section. If a savings association does not know the actual holdings of the investment fund, the savings association may calculate the proportion of the assets of the fund that are not equity exposures based on the terms of the prospectus, partnership agreement, or similar contract that defines the fund's permissible investments. If the sum of the investment limits for all exposure classes within the fund exceeds 100 percent, the savings association must assume for purposes of this paragraph (b)(3)(iii) that the investment fund invests to the maximum extent possible in equity exposures.

(B) When determining which of a savings association's equity exposures qualify for a 100 percent risk weight under this paragraph, a savings association first must include equity exposures to unconsolidated small business investment companies or held through consolidated small business investment companies described in section 302 of the Small Business Investment Act of 1958 (15 U.S.C. 682), then must include publicly traded equity exposures (including those held indirectly through investment funds), and then must include non-publicly traded equity exposures (including those held indirectly through investment funds).

(4) *300 percent risk weight equity exposures.* A publicly traded equity exposure (other than an equity exposure described in paragraph (b)(6) of this section and including the ineffective portion of a hedge pair) is assigned a 300 percent risk weight.

(5) *400 percent risk weight equity exposures.* An equity exposure (other than an equity exposure described in paragraph (b)(6) of this section) that is not publicly traded is assigned a 400 percent risk weight.

(6) *600 percent risk weight equity exposures.* An equity exposure to an investment firm that:

(i) Would meet the definition of a traditional securitization were it not for the OTS's application of paragraph (8) of that definition; and

(ii) Has greater than immaterial leverage is assigned a 600 percent risk weight.

(c) *Hedge transactions*—(1) *Hedge pair.* A hedge pair is two equity exposures that form an effective hedge so long as each equity exposure is publicly traded or has a return that

Office of Thrift Supervision, Treasury   Pt. 567, App. C

is primarily based on a publicly traded equity exposure.

(2) *Effective hedge.* Two equity exposures form an effective hedge if the exposures either have the same remaining maturity or each has a remaining maturity of at least three months; the hedge relationship is formally documented in a prospective manner (that is, before the savings association acquires at least one of the equity exposures); the documentation specifies the measure of effectiveness (E) the savings association will use for the hedge relationship throughout the life of the transaction; and the hedge relationship has an E greater than or equal to 0.8. A savings association must measure E at least quarterly and must use one of three alternative measures of E:

(i) Under the dollar-offset method of measuring effectiveness, the savings association must determine the ratio of value change (RVC). The RVC is the ratio of the cumulative sum of the periodic changes in value of one equity exposure to the cumulative sum of the periodic changes in the value of the other equity exposure. If RVC is positive, the hedge is not effective and E equals 0. If RVC is negative and greater than or equal to −1 (that is, between zero and −1), then E equals the absolute value of RVC. If RVC is negative and less than −1, then E equals 2 plus RVC.

(ii) Under the variability-reduction method of measuring effectiveness:

$$E = 1 - \frac{\sum_{t=1}^{T}(X_t - X_{t-1})^2}{\sum_{t=1}^{T}(A_t - A_{t-1})^2}, \text{ where}$$

(A) $X_t = A_t - B_t$;
(B) A_t = the value at time t of one exposure in a hedge pair; and
(C) B_t = the value at time t of the other exposure in a hedge pair.

(iii) Under the regression method of measuring effectiveness, E equals the coefficient of determination of a regression in which the change in value of one exposure in a hedge pair is the dependent variable and the change in value of the other exposure in a hedge pair is the independent variable. However, if the estimated regression coefficient is positive, then the value of E is zero.

(3) The effective portion of a hedge pair is E multiplied by the greater of the adjusted carrying values of the equity exposures forming a hedge pair.

(4) The ineffective portion of a hedge pair is (1−E) multiplied by the greater of the adjusted carrying values of the equity exposures forming a hedge pair.

Section 53. Internal Models Approach (IMA)

(a) *General.* A savings association may calculate its risk-weighted asset amount for equity exposures using the IMA by modeling publicly traded and non-publicly traded equity exposures (in accordance with paragraph (c) of this section) or by modeling only publicly traded equity exposures (in accordance with paragraph (d) of this section).

(b) *Qualifying criteria.* To qualify to use the IMA to calculate risk-based capital requirements for equity exposures, a savings association must receive prior written approval from the OTS. To receive such approval, the savings association must demonstrate to the OTS's satisfaction that the savings association meets the following criteria:

(1) The savings association must have one or more models that:

(i) Assess the potential decline in value of its modeled equity exposures;

(ii) Are commensurate with the size, complexity, and composition of the savings association's modeled equity exposures; and

(iii) Adequately capture both general market risk and idiosyncratic risk.

(2) The savings association's model must produce an estimate of potential losses for its modeled equity exposures that is no less than the estimate of potential losses produced by a VaR methodology employing a 99.0 percent, one-tailed confidence interval of the distribution of quarterly returns for a benchmark portfolio of equity exposures comparable to the savings association's modeled equity exposures using a long-term sample period.

(3) The number of risk factors and exposures in the sample and the data period used for quantification in the savings association's model and benchmarking exercise must be sufficient to provide confidence in the accuracy and robustness of the savings association's estimates.

(4) The savings association's model and benchmarking process must incorporate data that are relevant in representing the risk profile of the savings association's modeled

Pt. 567, App. C

equity exposures, and must include data from at least one equity market cycle containing adverse market movements relevant to the risk profile of the savings association's modeled equity exposures. In addition, the savings association's benchmarking exercise must be based on daily market prices for the benchmark portfolio. If the savings association's model uses a scenario methodology, the savings association must demonstrate that the model produces a conservative estimate of potential losses on the savings association's modeled equity exposures over a relevant long-term market cycle. If the savings association employs risk factor models, the savings association must demonstrate through empirical analysis the appropriateness of the risk factors used.

(5) The savings association must be able to demonstrate, using theoretical arguments and empirical evidence, that any proxies used in the modeling process are comparable to the savings association's modeled equity exposures and that the savings association has made appropriate adjustments for differences. The savings association must derive any proxies for its modeled equity exposures and benchmark portfolio using historical market data that are relevant to the savings association's modeled equity exposures and benchmark portfolio (or, where not, must use appropriately adjusted data), and such proxies must be robust estimates of the risk of the savings association's modeled equity exposures.

(c) *Risk-weighted assets calculation for a savings association modeling publicly traded and non-publicly traded equity exposures.* If a savings association models publicly traded and non-publicly traded equity exposures, the savings association's aggregate risk-weighted asset amount for its equity exposures is equal to the sum of:

(1) The risk-weighted asset amount of each equity exposure that qualifies for a 0 percent, 20 percent, or 100 percent risk weight under paragraphs (b)(1) through (b)(3)(i) of section 52 (as determined under section 52 of this appendix) and each equity exposure to an investment fund (as determined under section 54 of this appendix); and

(2) The greater of:

(i) The estimate of potential losses on the savings association's equity exposures (other than equity exposures referenced in paragraph (c)(1) of this section) generated by the savings association's internal equity exposure model multiplied by 12.5; or

(ii) The sum of:

(A) 200 percent multiplied by the aggregate adjusted carrying value of the savings association's publicly traded equity exposures that do not belong to a hedge pair, do not qualify for a 0 percent, 20 percent, or 100 percent risk weight under paragraphs (b)(1) through (b)(3)(i) of section 52 of this appen-

12 CFR Ch. V (1-1-12 Edition)

dix, and are not equity exposures to an investment fund;

(B) 200 percent multiplied by the aggregate ineffective portion of all hedge pairs; and

(C) 300 percent multiplied by the aggregate adjusted carrying value of the savings association's equity exposures that are not publicly traded, do not qualify for a 0 percent, 20 percent, or 100 percent risk weight under paragraphs (b)(1) through (b)(3)(i) of section 52 of this appendix, and are not equity exposures to an investment fund.

(d) *Risk-weighted assets calculation for a savings association using the IMA only for publicly traded equity exposures.* If a savings association models only publicly traded equity exposures, the savings association's aggregate risk-weighted asset amount for its equity exposures is equal to the sum of:

(1) The risk-weighted asset amount of each equity exposure that qualifies for a 0 percent, 20 percent, or 100 percent risk weight under paragraphs (b)(1) through (b)(3)(i) of section 52 (as determined under section 52 of this appendix), each equity exposure that qualifies for a 400 percent risk weight under paragraph (b)(5) of section 52 or a 600 percent risk weight under paragraph (b)(6) of section 52 (as determined under section 52 of this appendix), and each equity exposure to an investment fund (as determined under section 54 of this appendix); and

(2) The greater of:

(i) The estimate of potential losses on the savings association's equity exposures (other than equity exposures referenced in paragraph (d)(1) of this section) generated by the savings association's internal equity exposure model multiplied by 12.5; or

(ii) The sum of:

(A) 200 percent multiplied by the aggregate adjusted carrying value of the savings association's publicly traded equity exposures that do not belong to a hedge pair, do not qualify for a 0 percent, 20 percent, or 100 percent risk weight under paragraphs (b)(1) through (b)(3)(i) of section 52 of this appendix, and are not equity exposures to an investment fund; and

(B) 200 percent multiplied by the aggregate ineffective portion of all hedge pairs.

Section 54. Equity Exposures to Investment Funds

(a) *Available approaches.* (1) Unless the exposure meets the requirements for a community development equity exposure in paragraph (b)(3)(i) of section 52 of this appendix, a savings association must determine the risk-weighted asset amount of an equity exposure to an investment fund under the Full Look-Through Approach in paragraph (b) of this section, the Simple Modified Look-Through Approach in paragraph (c) of this section, the Alternative Modified Look-Through Approach in paragraph (d) of this section, or, if the investment fund qualifies

410

Office of Thrift Supervision, Treasury **Pt. 567, App. C**

for the Money Market Fund Approach, the Money Market Fund Approach in paragraph (e) of this section.

(2) The risk-weighted asset amount of an equity exposure to an investment fund that meets the requirements for a community development equity exposure in paragraph (b)(3)(i) of section 52 of this appendix is its adjusted carrying value.

(3) If an equity exposure to an investment fund is part of a hedge pair and the savings association does not use the Full Look-Through Approach, the savings association may use the ineffective portion of the hedge pair as determined under paragraph (c) of section 52 of this appendix as the adjusted carrying value for the equity exposure to the investment fund. The risk-weighted asset amount of the effective portion of the hedge pair is equal to its adjusted carrying value.

(b) *Full Look-Through Approach.* A savings association that is able to calculate a risk-weighted asset amount for its proportional ownership share of each exposure held by the investment fund (as calculated under this appendix as if the proportional ownership share of each exposure were held directly by the savings association) may either:

(1) Set the risk-weighted asset amount of the savings association's exposure to the fund equal to the product of:

(i) The aggregate risk-weighted asset amounts of the exposures held by the fund as if they were held directly by the savings association; and

(ii) The savings association's proportional ownership share of the fund; or

(2) Include the savings association's proportional ownership share of each exposure held by the fund in the savings association's IMA.

(c) *Simple Modified Look-Through Approach.* Under this approach, the risk-weighted asset amount for a savings association's equity exposure to an investment fund equals the adjusted carrying value of the equity exposure multiplied by the highest risk weight in Table 10 that applies to any exposure the fund is permitted to hold under its prospectus, partnership agreement, or similar contract that defines the fund's permissible investments (excluding derivative contracts that are used for hedging rather than speculative purposes and that do not constitute a material portion of the fund's exposures).

TABLE 10—MODIFIED LOOK-THROUGH APPROACHES FOR EQUITY EXPOSURES TO INVESTMENT FUNDS

Risk weight	Exposure class
0 percent	Sovereign exposures with a long-term applicable external rating in the highest investment-grade rating category and sovereign exposures of the United States.
20 percent	Non-sovereign exposures with a long-term applicable external rating in the highest or second-highest investment-grade rating category; exposures with a short-term applicable external rating in the highest investment-grade rating category; and exposures to, or guaranteed by, depository institutions, foreign banks (as defined in 12 CFR 211.2), or securities firms subject to consolidated supervision and regulation comparable to that imposed on U.S. securities broker-dealers that are repo-style transactions or bankers' acceptances.
50 percent	Exposures with a long-term applicable external rating in the third-highest investment-grade rating category or a short-term applicable external rating in the second-highest investment-grade rating category.
100 percent	Exposures with a long-term or short-term applicable external rating in the lowest investment-grade rating category.
200 percent	Exposures with a long-term applicable external rating one rating category below investment grade.
300 percent	Publicly traded equity exposures.
400 percent	Non-publicly traded equity exposures; exposures with a long-term applicable external rating two rating categories or more below investment grade; and exposures without an external rating (excluding publicly traded equity exposures).
1,250 percent	OTC derivative contracts and exposures that must be deducted from regulatory capital or receive a risk weight greater than 400 percent under this appendix.

(d) *Alternative Modified Look-Through Approach.* Under this approach, a savings association may assign the adjusted carrying value of an equity exposure to an investment fund on a pro rata basis to different risk weight categories in Table 10 based on the investment limits in the fund's prospectus, partnership agreement, or similar contract that defines the fund's permissible investments. The risk-weighted asset amount for the savings association's equity exposure to the investment fund equals the sum of each portion of the adjusted carrying value assigned to an exposure class multiplied by the applicable risk weight. If the sum of the investment limits for exposure classes within the fund exceeds 100 percent, the savings association must assume that the fund invests to the maximum extent permitted under its investment limits in the exposure class with the highest risk weight under Table 10, and continues to make investments in order of the exposure class with the next highest risk weight under Table 10 until the maximum total investment level is reached. If more than one exposure class applies to an exposure, the savings association must use the highest applicable risk weight. A savings association may exclude derivative contracts held by the fund that are used for hedging rather than for speculative purposes and do not constitute a material portion of the fund's exposures.

(e) *Money Market Fund Approach.* The risk-weighted asset amount for a savings association's equity exposure to an investment fund that is a money market fund subject to 17 CFR 270.2a–7 and that has an applicable external rating in the highest investment-grade rating category equals the adjusted carrying value of the equity exposure multiplied by 7 percent.

Section 55. Equity Derivative Contracts

Under the IMA, in addition to holding risk-based capital against an equity derivative contract under this part, a savings association must hold risk-based capital against the counterparty credit risk in the equity derivative contract by also treating the equity derivative contract as a wholesale exposure and computing a supplemental risk-weighted asset amount for the contract under part IV. Under the SRWA, a savings association may choose not to hold risk-based capital against the counterparty credit risk of equity derivative contracts, as long as it does so for all such contracts. Where the equity derivative contracts are subject to a qualified master netting agreement, a savings association using the SRWA must either include all or exclude all of the contracts from any measure used to determine counterparty credit risk exposure.

PART VII. RISK-WEIGHTED ASSETS FOR OPERATIONAL RISK

Section 61. Qualification Requirements for Incorporation of Operational Risk Mitigants

(a) *Qualification to use operational risk mitigants.* A savings association may adjust its estimate of operational risk exposure to reflect qualifying operational risk mitigants if:

(1) The savings association's operational risk quantification system is able to generate an estimate of the savings association's operational risk exposure (which does not incorporate qualifying operational risk mitigants) and an estimate of the savings association's operational risk exposure adjusted to incorporate qualifying operational risk mitigants; and

(2) The savings association's methodology for incorporating the effects of insurance, if the savings association uses insurance as an operational risk mitigant, captures through appropriate discounts to the amount of risk mitigation:

(i) The residual term of the policy, where less than one year;

(ii) The cancellation terms of the policy, where less than one year;

(iii) The policy's timeliness of payment;

(iv) The uncertainty of payment by the provider of the policy; and

(v) Mismatches in coverage between the policy and the hedged operational loss event.

(b) *Qualifying operational risk mitigants.* Qualifying operational risk mitigants are:

(1) Insurance that:

(i) Is provided by an unaffiliated company that has a claims payment ability that is rated in one of the three highest rating categories by a NRSRO;

(ii) Has an initial term of at least one year and a residual term of more than 90 days;

(iii) Has a minimum notice period for cancellation by the provider of 90 days;

(iv) Has no exclusions or limitations based upon regulatory action or for the receiver or liquidator of a failed depository institution; and

(v) Is explicitly mapped to a potential operational loss event; and

(2) Operational risk mitigants other than insurance for which the OTS has given prior written approval. In evaluating an operational risk mitigant other than insurance, the OTS will consider whether the operational risk mitigant covers potential operational losses in a manner equivalent to holding regulatory capital.

Section 62. Mechanics of Risk-Weighted Asset Calculation

(a) If a savings association does not qualify to use or does not have qualifying operational risk mitigants, the savings association's dollar risk-based capital requirement for operational risk is its operational risk exposure minus eligible operational risk offsets (if any).

(b) If a savings association qualifies to use operational risk mitigants and has qualifying operational risk mitigants, the savings association's dollar risk-based capital requirement for operational risk is the greater of:

(1) The savings association's operational risk exposure adjusted for qualifying operational risk mitigants minus eligible operational risk offsets (if any); or

(2) 0.8 multiplied by the difference between:

(i) The savings association's operational risk exposure; and

(ii) Eligible operational risk offsets (if any).

(c) The savings association's risk-weighted asset amount for operational risk equals the savings association's dollar risk-based capital requirement for operational risk determined under paragraph (a) or (b) of this section multiplied by 12.5.

PART VIII. DISCLOSURE

Section 71. Disclosure Requirements

(a) Each savings association must publicly disclose each quarter its total and tier 1 risk-based capital ratios and their components (that is, tier 1 capital, tier 2 capital, total qualifying capital, and total risk-weighted assets).[4]

(b) A savings association must comply with paragraph (c) of section 71 of this appendix unless it is a consolidated subsidiary of a depository institution or bank holding company that is subject to these requirements.

(c)(1) Each consolidated savings association described in paragraph (b) of this section that is not a subsidiary of a non-U.S. banking organization that is subject to comparable public disclosure requirements in its home jurisdiction and has successfully completed its parallel run must provide timely public disclosures each calendar quarter of the information in tables 11.1–11.11 below. If a significant change occurs, such that the most recent reported amounts are no longer reflective of the savings association's capital adequacy and risk profile, then a brief discussion of this change and its likely impact must be provided as soon as practicable thereafter. Qualitative disclosures that typically do not change each quarter (for example, a general summary of the savings association's risk management objectives and policies, reporting system, and definitions) may be disclosed annually, provided any significant changes to these are disclosed in the interim. Management is encouraged to provide all of the disclosures required by this appendix in one place on the savings association's public Web site.[5] The savings association must make these disclosures publicly available for each of the last three years (twelve quarters) or such shorter period since it began its first floor period.

(2) Each savings association is required to have a formal disclosure policy approved by the board of directors that addresses its approach for determining the disclosures it makes. The policy must address the associated internal controls and disclosure controls and procedures. The board of directors and senior management are responsible for establishing and maintaining an effective internal control structure over financial reporting, including the disclosures required by this appendix, and must ensure that appropriate review of the disclosures takes place. One or more senior officers of the savings association must attest that the disclosures required by this appendix meet the requirements of this appendix.

(3) If a savings association believes that disclosure of specific commercial or financial information would prejudice seriously its position by making public information that is either proprietary or confidential in nature, the savings association need not disclose those specific items, but must disclose more general information about the subject matter of the requirement, together with the fact that, and the reason why, the specific items of information have not been disclosed.

TABLE 11.1—SCOPE OF APPLICATION

Qualitative Disclosures	(a) The name of the top corporate entity in the group to which the appendix applies.
	(b) An outline of differences in the basis of consolidation for accounting and regulatory purposes, with a brief description of the entities[6] within the group that are fully consolidated; that are deconsolidated and deducted; for which the regulatory capital requirement is deducted; and that are neither consolidated nor deducted (for example, where the investment is risk-weighted).
	(c) Any restrictions, or other major impediments, on transfer of funds or regulatory capital within the group.
Quantitative Disclosures	(d) The aggregate amount of surplus capital of insurance subsidiaries (whether deducted or subjected to an alternative method) included in the regulatory capital of the consolidated group.
	(e) The aggregate amount by which actual regulatory capital is less than the minimum regulatory capital requirement in all subsidiaries with regulatory capital requirements and the name(s) of the subsidiaries with such deficiencies.

[6] Entities include securities, insurance and other financial subsidiaries, commercial subsidiaries (where permitted), and significant minority equity investments in insurance, financial and commercial entities.

TABLE 11.2—CAPITAL STRUCTURE

Qualitative Disclosures	(a) Summary information on the terms and conditions of the main features of all capital instruments, especially in the case of innovative, complex or hybrid capital instruments.
Quantitative Disclosures	(b) The amount of tier 1 capital, with separate disclosure of:

---

[4] Other public disclosure requirements continue to apply—for example, Federal securities law and regulatory reporting requirements.

[5] Alternatively, a savings association may provide the disclosures in more than one place, as some of them may be included in public financial reports (for example, in Management's Discussion and Analysis included in SEC filings) or other regulatory reports. The savings association must provide a summary table on its public Web site that specifically indicates where all the disclosures may be found (for example, regulatory report schedules, page numbers in annual reports).

TABLE 11.2—CAPITAL STRUCTURE—Continued

	• Common stock/surplus; • Retained earnings; • Minority interests in the equity of subsidiaries; • Regulatory calculation differences deducted from tier 1 capital;thnsp;[7] and • Other amounts deducted from tier 1 capital, including goodwill and certain intangibles. (c) The total amount of tier 2 capital. (d) Other deductions from capital.[8] (e) Total eligible capital.

[7] Representing 50 percent of the amount, if any, by which total expected credit losses as calculated within the IRB approach exceed eligible credit reserves, which must be deducted from tier 1 capital.

[8] Including 50 percent of the amount, if any, by which total expected credit losses as calculated within the IRB approach exceed eligible credit reserves, which must be deducted from tier 2 capital.

TABLE 11.3—CAPITAL ADEQUACY

Qualitative disclosures	(a) A summary discussion of the savings association's approach to assessing the adequacy of its capital to support current and future activities.

Quantitative disclosures	(b) Risk-weighted assets for credit risk from:
	• Wholesale exposures;
	• Residential mortgage exposures;
	• Qualifying revolving exposures;
	• Other retail exposures;
	• Securitization exposures;
	• Equity exposures
	   • Equity exposures subject to the simple risk weight approach; and
	   • Equity exposures subject to the internal models approach.
	(c) Risk-weighted assets for market risk as calculated under any applicable market risk rule:[9]
	• Standardized approach for specific risk; and
	• Internal models approach for specific risk.
	(d) Risk-weighted assets for operational risk.
	(e) Total and tier 1 risk-based capital ratios:[10]
	• For the top consolidated group; and
	• For each DI subsidiary.

[9] Risk-weighted assets determined under any applicable market risk rule are to be disclosed only for the approaches used.
[10] Total risk-weighted assets should also be disclosed.

GENERAL QUALITATIVE DISCLOSURE REQUIREMENT

For each separate risk area described in tables 11.4 through 11.11, the savings association must describe its risk management objectives and policies, including:

• strategies and processes;
• the structure and organization of the relevant risk management function;
• the scope and nature of risk reporting and/or measurement systems;
• policies for hedging and/or mitigating risk and strategies and processes for monitoring the continuing effectiveness of hedges/mitigants.

TABLE 11.4 [11]—CREDIT RISK: GENERAL DISCLOSURES

Qualitative Disclosures	(a) The general qualitative disclosure requirement with respect to credit risk (excluding counterparty credit risk disclosed in accordance with Table 11.6), including: • Definitions of past due and impaired (for accounting purposes); • Description of approaches followed for allowances, including statistical methods used where applicable; and • Discussion of the savings association's credit risk management policy.
Quantitative Disclosures	(b) Total credit risk exposures and average credit risk exposures, after accounting offsets in accordance with GAAP,[12] and without taking into account the effects of credit risk mitigation techniques (for example, collateral and netting), over the period broken down by major types of credit exposure.[13] (c) Geographic[14] distribution of exposures, broken down in significant areas by major types of credit exposure. (d) Industry or counterparty type distribution of exposures, broken down by major types of credit exposure. (e) Remaining contractual maturity breakdown (for example, one year or less) of the whole portfolio, broken down by major types of credit exposure. (f) By major industry or counterparty type: • Amount of impaired loans; • Amount of past due loans;[15] • Allowances; and • Charge-offs during the period.

Office of Thrift Supervision, Treasury
Pt. 567, App. C

TABLE 11.4[11]—CREDIT RISK: GENERAL DISCLOSURES—Continued

	(g) Amount of impaired loans and, if available, the amount of past due loans broken down by significant geographic areas including, if practical, the amounts of allowances related to each geographical area.[16]
	(h) Reconciliation of changes in the allowance for loan and lease losses.[17]

[11] Table 4 does not include equity exposures.
[12] For example, FASB Interpretations 39 and 41.
[13] For example, savings associations could apply a breakdown similar to that used for accounting purposes. Such a breakdown might, for instance, be (a) loans, off-balance sheet commitments, and other non-derivative off-balance sheet exposures, (b) debt securities, and (c) OTC derivatives.
[14] Geographical areas may comprise individual countries, groups of countries, or regions within countries. A savings association might choose to define the geographical areas based on the way the company's portfolio is geographically managed. The criteria used to allocate the loans to geographical areas must be specified.
[15] A savings association is encouraged also to provide an analysis of the aging of past-due loans.
[16] The portion of general allowance that is not allocated to a geographical area should be disclosed separately.
[17] The reconciliation should include the following: a description of the allowance; the opening balance of the allowance; charge-offs taken against the allowance during the period; amounts provided (or reversed) for estimated probable loan losses during the period; any other adjustments (for example, exchange rate differences, business combinations, acquisitions and disposals of subsidiaries), including transfers between allowances; and the closing balance of the allowance. Charge-offs and recoveries that have been recorded directly to the income statement should be disclosed separately.

TABLE 11.5—CREDIT RISK: DISCLOSURES FOR PORTFOLIOS SUBJECT TO IRB RISK-BASED CAPITAL FORMULAS

Qualitative disclosures	(a) Explanation and review of the:
	• Structure of internal rating systems and relation between internal and external ratings;
	• Use of risk parameter estimates other than for regulatory capital purposes;
	• Process for managing and recognizing credit risk mitigation (see table 11.7); and
	• Control mechanisms for the rating system, including discussion of independence, accountability, and rating systems review.
	(b) Description of the internal ratings process, provided separately for the following:
	• Wholesale category;
	• Retail subcategories;
	  • Residential mortgage exposures;
	  • Qualifying revolving exposures; and
	  • Other retail exposures.
	For each category and subcategory the description should include:
	• The types of exposure included in the category/subcategories; and
	• The definitions, methods and data for estimation and validation of PD, LGD, and EAD, including assumptions employed in the derivation of these variables.[18]

Quantitative disclosures: risk assessment.	(c) For wholesale exposures, present the following information across a sufficient number of PD grades (including default) to allow for a meaningful differentiation of credit risk:[19] • Total EAD;[20] • Exposure-weighted average LGD (percentage); • Exposure-weighted average risk weight; and • Amount of undrawn commitments and exposure-weighted average EAD for wholesale exposures. For each retail subcategory, present the disclosures outlined above across a sufficient number of segments to allow for a meaningful differentiation of credit risk.
Quantitative disclosures: historical results.	(d) Actual losses in the preceding period for each category and subcategory and how this differs from past experience. A discussion of the factors that impacted the loss experience in the preceding period—for example, has the savings association experienced higher than average default rates, loss rates or EADs. (e) Savings association's estimates compared against actual outcomes over a longer period.[21] At a minimum, this should include information on estimates of losses against actual losses in the wholesale category and each retail subcategory over a period sufficient to allow for a meaningful assessment of the performance of the internal rating processes for each category/subcategory.[22] Where appropriate, the savings association should further decompose this to provide analysis of PD, LGD, and EAD outcomes against estimates provided in the quantitative risk assessment disclosures above.[23]

[18] This disclosure does not require a detailed description of the model in full—it should provide the reader with a broad overview of the model approach, describing definitions of the variables and methods for estimating and validating those variables set out in the quantitative risk disclosures below. This should be done for each of the four category/subcategories. The savings association should disclose any significant differences in approach to estimating these variables within each category/subcategories.
[19] The PD, LGD and EAD disclosures in Table 11.5(c) should reflect the effects of collateral, qualifying master netting agreements, eligible guarantees and eligible credit derivatives as defined in part I. Disclosure of each PD grade should include the exposure-weighted average PD for each grade. Where a savings association aggregates PD grades for the purposes of disclosure, this should be a representative breakdown of the distribution of PD grades used for regulatory capital purposes.
[20] Outstanding loans and EAD on undrawn commitments can be presented on a combined basis for these disclosures.
[21] These disclosures are a way of further informing the reader about the reliability of the information provided in the "quantitative disclosures: risk assessment" over the long run. The disclosures are requirements from year-end 2010; in the meantime, early adoption is encouraged. The phased implementation is to allow a savings association sufficient time to build up a longer run of data that will make these disclosures meaningful.
[22] This regulation is not prescriptive about the period used for this assessment. Upon implementation, it might be expected that a savings association would provide these disclosures for as long a run of data as possible—for example, if a savings association has 10 years of data, it might choose to disclose the average default rates for each PD grade over that 10-year period. Annual amounts need not be disclosed.

[23] A savings association should provide this further decomposition where it will allow users greater insight into the reliability of the estimates provided in the "quantitative disclosures: risk assessment." In particular, it should provide this information where there are material differences between its estimates of PD, LGD or EAD compared to actual outcomes over the long run. The savings association should also provide explanations for such differences.

TABLE 11.6—GENERAL DISCLOSURE FOR COUNTERPARTY CREDIT RISK OF OTC DERIVATIVE CONTRACTS, REPO-STYLE TRANSACTIONS, AND ELIGIBLE MARGIN LOANS

Qualitative Disclosures	(a) The general qualitative disclosure requirement with respect to OTC derivatives, eligible margin loans, and repo-style transactions, including: • Discussion of methodology used to assign economic capital and credit limits for counterparty credit exposures; • Discussion of policies for securing collateral, valuing and managing collateral, and establishing credit reserves; • Discussion of the primary types of collateral taken; • Discussion of policies with respect to wrong-way risk exposures; and • Discussion of the impact of the amount of collateral the savings association would have to provide if the savings association were to receive a credit rating downgrade.
Quantitative Disclosures	(b) Gross positive fair value of contracts, netting benefits, netted current credit exposure, collateral held (including type, for example, cash, government securities), and net unsecured credit exposure.[24] Also report measures for EAD used for regulatory capital for these transactions, the notional value of credit derivative hedges purchased for counterparty credit risk protection, and, for savings associations not using the internal models methodology in section 32(d) of this appendix, the distribution of current credit exposure by types of credit exposure.[25] (c) Notional amount of purchased and sold credit derivatives, segregated between use for the savings association's own credit portfolio and for its intermediation activities, including the distribution of the credit derivative products used, broken down further by protection bought and sold within each product group. (d) The estimate of alpha if the savings association has received supervisory approval to estimate alpha.

[24] Net unsecured credit exposure is the credit exposure after considering the benefits from legally enforceable netting agreements and collateral arrangements, without taking into account haircuts for price volatility, liquidity, etc.
[25] This may include interest rate derivative contracts, foreign exchange derivative contracts, equity derivative contracts, credit derivatives, commodity or other derivative contracts, repo-style transactions, and eligible margin loans.

TABLE 11.7—CREDIT RISK MITIGATION [26,27,28]

Qualitative Disclosures	(a) The general qualitative disclosure requirement with respect to credit risk mitigation including: • Policies and processes for, and an indication of the extent to which the savings association uses, on- and off-balance sheet netting; • Policies and processes for collateral valuation and management; • A description of the main types of collateral taken by the savings association; • The main types of guarantors/credit derivative counterparties and their creditworthiness; and • Information about (market or credit) risk concentrations within the mitigation taken.
Quantitative Disclosures	(b) For each separately disclosed portfolio, the total exposure (after, where applicable, on-or off-balance sheet netting) that is covered by guarantees/credit derivatives.

[26] At a minimum, a savings associagtion must provide the disclosures in Table 11.7 in relation to credit risk mitigation that has been recognized for the purposes of reducing capital requirements under this appendix. Where relevant, savings associations are encouraged to give further information about mitigants that have not been recognized for that purpose.
[27] Credit derivatives that are treated, for the purposes of this appendix, as synthetic securitization exposures should be excluded from the credit risk mitigation disclosures and included within those relating to securitization.
[28] Counterparty credit risk-related exposures disclosed pursuant to Table 11.6 should be excluded from the credit risk mitigation disclosures in Table 11.7.

TABLE 11.8—SECURITIZATION

Qualitative Disclosures	(a) The general qualitative disclosure requirement with respect to securitization (including synthetics), including a discussion of: • The savings association's objectives relating to securitization activity, including the extent to which these activities transfer credit risk of the underlying exposures away from the savings association to other entities; • The roles played by the savings association in the securitization process[29] and an indication of the extent of the savings association's involvement in each of them; and • The regulatory capital approaches (for example, RBA, IAA and SFA) that the savings association follows for its securitization activities. (b) Summary of the savings association's accounting policies for securitization activities, including: • Whether the transactions are treated as sales or financings; • Recognition of gain-on-sale; • Key assumptions for valuing retained interests, including any significant changes since the last reporting period and the impact of such changes; and • Treatment of synthetic securitizations.

Office of Thrift Supervision, Treasury
Pt. 567, App. C

TABLE 11.8—SECURITIZATION—Continued

Quantitative Disclosures	(c) Names of NRSROs used for securitizations and the types of securitization exposure for which each agency is used. (d) The total outstanding exposures securitized by the savings association in securitizations that meet the operational criteria in section 41 of this appendix (broken down into traditional/synthetic), by underlying exposure type. [30] [31] [32] (e) For exposures securitized by the savings association in securitizations that meet the operational criteria in Section 41 of this appendix: • Amount of securitized assets that are impaired/past due; and • Losses recognized by the savings association during the current period [33] broken down by exposure type. (f) Aggregate amount of securitization exposures broken down by underlying exposure type. (g) Aggregate amount of securitization exposures and the associated IRB capital requirements for these exposures broken down into a meaningful number of risk weight bands. Exposures that have been deducted from capital should be disclosed separately by type of underlying asset. (h) For securitizations subject to the early amortization treatment, the following items by underlying asset type for securitized facilities: • The aggregate drawn exposures attributed to the seller's and investors' interests; and • The aggregate IRB capital charges incurred by the savings association against the investors' shares of drawn balances and undrawn lines. (i) Summary of current year's securitization activity, including the amount of exposures securitized (by exposure type), and recognized gain or loss on sale by asset type.

[29] For example: originator, investor, servicer, provider of credit enhancement, sponsor of asset backed commercial paper facility, liquidity provider, or swap provider.
[30] Underlying exposure types may include, for example, one- to four-family residential loans, home equity lines, credit card receivables, and auto loans.
[31] Securitization transactions in which the originating savings association does not retain any securitization exposure should be shown separately but need only be reported for the year of inception.
[32] Where relevant, a savings association is encouraged to differentiate between exposures resulting from activities in which they act only as sponsors, and exposures that result from all other savings association securitization activities.
[33] For example, charge-offs/allowances (if the assets remain on the savings association's balance sheet) or write-downs of I/O strips and other residual interests.

TABLE 11.9—OPERATIONAL RISK

Qualitative Disclosures	(a) The general qualitative disclosure requirement for operational risk. (b) Description of the AMA, including a discussion of relevant internal and external factors considered in the savings association's measurement approach. (c) A description of the use of insurance for the purpose of mitigating operational risk.

TABLE 11.10—EQUITIES NOT SUBJECT TO MARKET RISK RULE

Qualitative Disclosures	(a) The general qualitative disclosure requirement with respect to equity risk, including: • Differentiation between holdings on which capital gains are expected and those held for other objectives, including for relationship and strategic reasons; and • Discussion of important policies covering the valuation of and accounting for equity holdings in the banking book. This includes the accounting techniques and valuation methodologies used, including key assumptions and practices affecting valuation as well as significant changes in these practices.
Quantitative Disclosures	(b) Value disclosed in the balance sheet of investments, as well as the fair value of those investments; for quoted securities, a comparison to publicly-quoted share values where the share price is materially different from fair value. (c) The types and nature of investments, including the amount that is: • Publicly traded; and • Non-publicly traded. (d) The cumulative realized gains (losses) arising from sales and liquidations in the reporting period. (e) • Total unrealized gains (losses) [34] • Total latent revaluation gains (losses) [35] • Any amounts of the above included in tier 1 and/or tier 2 capital. (f) Capital requirements broken down by appropriate equity groupings, consistent with the savings association's methodology, as well as the aggregate amounts and the type of equity investments subject to any supervisory transition regarding regulatory capital requirements. [36]

[34] Unrealized gains (losses) recognized in the balance sheet but not through earnings.

³⁵ Unrealized gains (losses) not recognized either in the balance sheet or through earnings.
³⁶ This disclosure should include a breakdown of equities that are subject to the 0 percent, 20 percent, 100 percent, 300 percent, 400 percent, and 600 percent risk weights, as applicable.

TABLE 11.11—INTEREST RATE RISK FOR NON-TRADING ACTIVITIES

Qualitative Disclosures	(a) The general qualitative disclosure requirement, including the nature of interest rate risk for non-trading activities and key assumptions, including assumptions regarding loan prepayments and behavior of non-maturity deposits, and frequency of measurement of interest rate risk for non-trading activities.
Quantitative Disclosures	(b) The increase (decline) in earnings or economic value (or relevant measure used by management) for upward and downward rate shocks according to management's method for measuring interest rate risk for non-trading activities, broken down by currency (as appropriate).

PART IX—TRANSITION PROVISIONS

Section 81—Optional Transition Provisions Related to the Implementation of Consolidation Requirements Under FAS 167

(a) *Scope, applicability, and purpose.* This section 81 provides optional transition provisions for a savings association that is required for financial and regulatory reporting purposes, as a result of its implementation of Statement of Financial Accounting Standards No. 167, *Amendments to FASB Interpretation No. 46(R)* (FAS 167), to consolidate certain variable interest entities (VIEs) as defined under GAAP. These transition provisions apply through the end of the fourth quarter following the date of a savings association's implementation of FAS 167 (implementation date).

(b) *Exclusion period.*

(1) *Exclusion of risk-weighted assets for the first and second quarters.* For the first two quarters after the implementation date (exclusion period), including for the two calendar quarter-end regulatory report dates within those quarters, a savings association may exclude from risk-weighted assets:

(i) Subject to the limitations in paragraph (d) of section 81, assets held by a VIE, provided that the following conditions are met:

(A) The VIE existed prior to the implementation date,

(B) The savings association did not consolidate the VIE on its balance sheet for calendar quarter-end regulatory report dates prior to the implementation date,

(C) The savings association must consolidate the VIE on its balance sheet beginning as of the implementation date as a result of its implementation of FAS 167, and

(D) The savings association excludes all assets held by VIEs described in paragraphs (b)(1)(i)(A) through (C) of this section 81; and

(ii) Subject to the limitations in paragraph (d) of this section 81, assets held by a VIE that is a consolidated ABCP program, provided that the following conditions are met:

(A) The savings association is the sponsor of the ABCP program,

(B) Prior to the implementation date, the savings association consolidated the VIE onto its balance sheet under GAAP and excluded the VIE's assets from the savings association's risk-weighted assets, and

(C) The savings association chooses to exclude all assets held by ABCP program VIEs described in paragraphs (b)(1)(ii)(A) and (B) of this section 81.

(2) *Risk-weighted assets during exclusion period.* During the exclusion period, including for the two calendar quarter-end regulatory report dates within the exclusion period, a savings association adopting the optional provisions in paragraph (b) of this section must calculate risk-weighted assets for its contractual exposures to the VIEs referenced in paragraph (b)(1) of this section 81 on the implementation date and include this calculated amount in risk-weighted assets. Such contractual exposures may include direct-credit substitutes, recourse obligations, residual interests, liquidity facilities, and loans.

(3) *Inclusion of ALLL in tier 2 capital for the first and second quarters.* During the exclusion period, including for the two calendar quarter-end regulatory report dates within the exclusion period, a savings association that excludes VIE assets from risk-weighted assets pursuant to paragraph (b)(1) of this section 81 may include in tier 2 capital the full amount of the ALLL calculated as of the implementation date that is attributable to the assets it excludes pursuant to paragraph (b)(1) of this section 81 (inclusion amount). The amount of ALLL includable in tier 2 capital in accordance with this paragraph shall not be subject to the limitations set forth in section 13(A)(2) and 13(b) of this Appendix.

(c) *Phase-in period.*

(1) *Exclusion amount.* For purposes of this paragraph (c), exclusion amount is defined as the amount of risk-weighted assets excluded in paragraph (b)(1) of this section as of the implementation date.

(2) *Risk-weighted assets for the third and fourth quarters.* A savings association that excludes assets of consolidated VIEs from risk-weighted assets pursuant to paragraph (b)(1) of this section may, for the third and fourth quarters after the implementation date (phase-in period), including for the two

Office of Thrift Supervision, Treasury

§ 568.3

calendar quarter-end regulatory report dates within those quarters, exclude from risk-weighted assets 50 percent of the exclusion amount, provided that the savings association may not include in risk-weighted assets pursuant to this paragraph an amount less than the aggregate risk-weighted assets calculated pursuant to paragraph (b)(2) of this section 81.

(3) *Inclusion of ALLL in tier 2 capital for the third and fourth quarters.* A savings association that excludes assets of consolidated VIEs from risk-weighted assets pursuant to paragraph (c)(2) of this section may, for the phase-in period, include in tier 2 capital 50 percent of the inclusion amount it included in tier 2 capital, during the exclusion period, notwithstanding the limit on including ALLL in tier 2 capital in section 13(a)(2) and 13(b) of this Appendix.

(d) *Implicit recourse limitation.* Notwithstanding any other provision in this section 81, assets held by a VIE to which the savings association has provided recourse through credit enhancement beyond any contractual obligation to support assets it has sold may not be excluded from risk-weighted assets.

[72 FR 69396, 69439, Dec. 7, 2007; 73 FR 21690, Apr. 22, 2008, as amended at 75 FR 4653, Jan. 28, 2010]

PART 568—SECURITY PROCEDURES

Sec.
568.1 Authority, purpose, and scope.
568.2 Designation of security officer.
568.3 Security program.
568.4 Report.
568.5 Protection of customer information.

AUTHORITY: 12 U.S.C. 1462a, 1463, 1464, 1467a, 1828, 1831p-1, 1881–1884; 15 U.S.C. 1681s and 1681w; 15 U.S.C. 6801 and 6805(b)(1).

SOURCE: 56 FR 29566, June 28, 1991, unless otherwise noted.

§ 568.1 Authority, purpose, and scope.

(a) This part is issued by the Office of Thrift Supervision (OTS) under section 3 of the Bank Protection Act of 1968 (12 U.S.C 1882), sections 501 and 505(b)(1) of the Gramm-Leach-Bliley Act (15 U.S.C. 6801 and 6805(b)(1)), and sections 621 and 628 of the Fair Credit Reporting Act (15 U.S.C. 1681s and 1681w). This part is applicable to savings associations. It requires each savings association to adopt appropriate security procedures to discourage robberies, burglaries, and larcenies and to assist in the identification and prosecution of persons who commit such acts. Section 568.5 of this part is applicable to savings associations and their subsidiaries (except brokers, dealers, persons providing insurance, investment companies, and investment advisers). Section 568.5 of this part requires covered institutions to establish and implement appropriate administrative, technical, and physical safeguards to protect the security, confidentiality, and integrity of customer information.

(b) It is the responsibility of an association's board of directors to comply with this regulation and ensure that a written security program for the association's main office and branches is developed and implemented.

[56 FR 29566, June 28, 1991, as amended at 66 FR 8639, Feb. 1, 2001; 69 FR 77620, Dec. 28, 2004]

§ 568.2 Designation of security officer.

Within 30 days after the effective date of insurance of accounts, the board of directors of each savings association shall designate a security officer who shall have the authority, subject to the approval of the board of directors, to develop, within a reasonable time but no later than 180 days, and to administer a written security program for each of the association's offices.

§ 568.3 Security program.

(a) *Contents of security program.* The security program shall:

(1) Establish procedures for opening and closing for business and for the safekeeping of all currency, negotiable securities, and similar valuables at all times;

(2) Establish procedures that will assist in identifying persons committing crimes against the association and that will preserve evidence that may aid in their identification and prosecution. Such procedures may include, but are not limited to:

(i) Maintaining a camera that records activity in the office;

(ii) Using identification devices, such as prerecorded serial-numbered bills, or chemical and electronic devices; and

(iii) Retaining a record of any robbery, burglary, or larceny committed against the association;

(3) Provide for initial and periodic training of officers and employees in their responsibilities under the security program and in proper employee

419

§ 568.4

conduct during and after a burglary, robbery, or larceny; and

(4) Provide for selecting, testing, operating and maintaining appropriate security devices, as specified in paragraph (b) of this section.

(b) *Security devices.* Each savings association shall have, at a minimum, the following security devices:

(1) A means of protecting cash and other liquid assets, such as a vault, safe, or other secure space;

(2) A lighting system for illuminating, during the hours of darkness, the area around the vault, if the vault is visible from outside the office;

(3) Tamper-resistant locks on exterior doors and exterior windows that may be opened;

(4) An alarm system or other appropriate device for promptly notifying the nearest responsible law enforcement officers of an attempted or perpetrated robbery or burglary; and

(5) Such other devices as the security officer determines to be appropriate, taking into consideration:

(i) The incidence of crimes against financial institutions in the area;

(ii) The amount of currency and other valuables exposed to robbery, burglary, or larceny;

(iii) The distance of the office from the nearest responsible law enforcement officers;

(iv) The cost of the security devices;

(v) Other security measures in effect at the office; and

(vi) The physical characteristics of the structure of the office and its surroundings.

§ 568.4 Report.

The security officer for each savings association shall report at least annually to the association's board of directors on the implementation, administration, and effectiveness of the security program.

§ 568.5 Protection of customer information.

Savings associations and their subsidiaries (except brokers, dealers, persons providing insurance, investment companies, and investment advisers) must comply with the Interagency Guidelines Establishing Information Security Standards set forth in appendix B to part 570 of this chapter. Supplement A to appendix B to part 570 of this chapter provides interpretive guidance.

[70 FR 32229, June 2, 2005]

PART 569—PROXIES

Sec.
569.1 Definitions.
569.2 Form of proxies.
569.3 Holders of proxies.
569.4 Proxy soliciting material.

AUTHORITY: Sec. 2, 48 Stat. 128, as amended (12 U.S.C. 1462); sec. 3, as added by sec. 301, 103 Stat. 278 (12 U.S.C. 1462a); sec. 4, as added by sec. 301, 103 Stat. 280 (12 U.S.C. 1463).

SOURCE: 54 FR 49665, Nov. 30, 1989, unless otherwise noted.

§ 569.1 Definitions.

As used in this part:

(a) *Security holder.* The term *security holder* means any person having the right to vote in the affairs of a savings association by virtue of:

(1) Ownership of any security of the association or

(2) Any indebtedness to the association.

For purposes of this part, the term *security holder* shall include any account holder having the right to vote in the affairs of a mutual savings association.

(b) *Person.* The term *person* includes, in addition to natural persons, corporations, partnerships, pension funds, profit-sharing funds, trusts, and any other group of associated persons of whatever nature.

(c) *Proxy.* The term *proxy* includes every form of authorization by which a person is, or may be deemed to be, designated to act for the security holder in the exercise of his or her voting rights in the affairs of a savings association. Such an authorization may take the form of failure to dissent or object.

(d) *Solicit; solicitation.* The terms *solicit* and *solicitation* refer to:

(1) Any request for a proxy whether or not accompanied by or included in a form of proxy;

(2) Any request to execute, not execute, or revoke a proxy; or

(3) The furnishing of a form of proxy or other communication to security

Office of Thrift Supervision, Treasury §570.1

holders under circumstances reasonably calculated to result in the procurement, withholding, or revocation of a proxy.

The terms do not apply, however, to the furnishing of a form of proxy to a security holder upon the request of such security holder or to the performance by any person of ministerial acts on behalf of a person soliciting a proxy.

§ 569.2 Form of proxies.

Every form of proxy shall conform to the following requirements:

(a) The proxy shall be revocable at will by the person giving it. The power to revoke may not be conditioned on any event or occurrence or be otherwise limited; except that, in the case of a proxy relating to capital stock if such proxy is coupled with an interest, states such fact on its face, and is valid under the laws of the State in which it is to be exercised, such proxy may be made irrevocable to the extent permitted by such State law.

(b) The proxy may not be part of any other document or instrument (such as an account card).

(c) The proxy shall be clearly labeled "Revocable Proxy" in boldface type (at least as large as 18 point).

§ 569.3 Holders of proxies.

No proxy of a mutual savings association with a term greater than eleven months or solicited at the expense of the association may designate as holder anyone other than the board of directors [trustees] as a whole, or a committee appointed by a majority of such board.

§ 569.4 Proxy soliciting material.

No solicitation of a proxy shall be made by means of any statement, form of proxy, notice of meeting, or other communication, written or oral, which:

(a) Solicits any undated or postdated proxy;

(b) Solicits any proxy that provides that it shall be deemed to be dated as of any date subsequent to the date on which it is signed by the security holder; or

(c)(1) Contains any statement that is false or misleading with respect to any material fact, or

(2) Omits to state any material fact:

(i) Necessary in order to make the statements therein not false or misleading or

(ii) Necessary to correct any statement in any earlier communication with respect to the solicitation of a proxy for the same meeting or subject matter that has subsequently become false or misleading.

PART 570—SAFETY AND SOUNDNESS GUIDELINES AND COMPLIANCE PROCEDURES

Sec.
570.1 Authority, purpose, scope and preservation of existing authority.
570.2 Determination and notification of failure to meet safety and soundness standards and request for compliance plan.
570.3 Filing of safety and soundness compliance plan.
570.4 Issuance of orders to correct deficiencies and to take or refrain from taking other actions.
570.5 Enforcement of orders.
APPENDIX A TO PART 570—INTERAGENCY GUIDELINES ESTABLISHING STANDARDS FOR SAFETY AND SOUNDNESS
APPENDIX B TO PART 570—INTERAGENCY GUIDELINES ESTABLISHING INFORMATION SECURITY STANDARDS

AUTHORITY: 12 U.S.C. 1462a, 1463, 1464, 1467a, 1828, 1831p–1, 1881–1884; 15 U.S.C. 1681s and 1681w; 15 U.S.C. 6801 and 6805(b)(1).

SOURCE: 60 FR 35686, July 10, 1995, unless otherwise noted.

§ 570.1 Authority, purpose, scope and preservation of existing authority.

(a) *Authority.* This part and the Guidelines in Appendices A and B to this part are issued by the OTS under section 39 (section 39) of the Federal Deposit Insurance Act (FDI Act) (12 U.S.C. 1831p–1) as added by section 132 of the Federal Deposit Insurance Corporation Improvement Act of 1991 (FDICIA) (Pub. L. 102–242, 105 Stat. 2236 (1991)), and as amended by section 956 of the Housing and Community Development Act of 1992 (Pub. L. 102–550, 106 Stat. 3895 (1992)), and as amended by section 318 of the Community Development Banking Act of 1994 (Pub. L. 103–325, 108 Stat. 2160 (1994)). Appendix B to this part is further issued under sections 501(b) and 505 of the Gramm-Leach-Bliley Act (Pub. L. 106–102, 113 Stat. 1338 (1999)).

§ 570.2

(b) *Purpose.* Section 39 of the FDI Act requires the OTS to establish safety and soundness standards. Pursuant to section 39, a savings association may be required to submit a compliance plan if it is not in compliance with a safety and soundness standard established by guideline under section 39 (a) or (b). An enforceable order under section 8 of the FDI Act may be issued if, after being notified that it is in violation of a safety and soundness standard prescribed under section 39, the savings association fails to submit an acceptable compliance plan or fails in any material respect to implement an accepted plan. This part establishes procedures for submission and review of safety and soundness compliance plans and for issuance and review of orders pursuant to section 39. Interagency Guidelines Establishing Standards for Safety and Soundness pursuant to section 39 of the FDI Act are set forth in Appendix A to this part. Interagency Guidelines Establishing Information Security Standards are set forth in appendix B to this part.

(c) *Scope.* This part and the Interagency Guidelines Establishing Standards for Safety and Soundness as set forth at appendix A to this part and the Interagency Guidelines Establishing Information Security Standards at appendix B to this part implement the provisions of section 39 of the FDI Act as they apply to savings associations.

(d) *Preservation of existing authority.* Neither section 39 of the FDI Act nor this part in any way limits the authority of the OTS under any other provision of law to take supervisory actions to address unsafe or unsound practices, violations of law, unsafe or unsound conditions, or other practices. Action under section 39 and this part may be taken independently of, in conjunction with, or in addition to any other enforcement action available to the OTS.

[60 FR 35686, July 10, 1995, as amended at 63 FR 55488, Oct. 15, 1998; 64 FR 66708, Nov. 29, 1999; 66 FR 8639, Feb. 1, 2001; 69 FR 76603, Dec. 22, 2004; 69 FR 77620, Dec. 28, 2004]

§ 570.2 Determination and notification of failure to meet safety and soundness standards and request for compliance plan.

(a) *Determination.* OTS may, based upon an examination, inspection, or any other information that becomes available to OTS, determine that a savings association has failed to satisfy the safety and soundness standards contained in the Interagency Guidelines Establishing Standards for Safety and Soundness as set forth in appendix A to this part or the Interagency Guidelines Establishing Information Security Standards as set forth in appendix B to this part.

(b) *Request for compliance plan.* If the OTS determines that a savings association has failed to meet a safety and soundness standard pursuant to paragraph (a) of this section, the OTS may request by letter or through a report of examination, the submission of a compliance plan. The savings association shall be deemed to have notice of the request three days after mailing or delivery of the letter or report of examination by the OTS.

[60 FR 35686, July 10, 1995, as amended at 63 FR 55489, Oct. 15, 1998; 66 FR 8639, Feb. 1, 2001; 69 FR 77620, Dec. 28, 2004]

§ 570.3 Filing of safety and soundness compliance plan.

(a) *Schedule for filing compliance plan*—(1) *In general.* A savings association shall file a written safety and soundness compliance plan with the OTS within 30 days of receiving a request for a compliance plan pursuant to § 570.2(b), unless the OTS notifies the savings association in writing that the plan is to be filed within a different period.

(2) *Other plans.* If a savings association is obligated to file, or is currently operating under, a capital restoration plan submitted pursuant to section 38 of the FDI Act (12 U.S.C. 1831o), a cease-and-desist order entered into pursuant to section 8 of the FDI Act, a formal or informal agreement, or a response to a report of examination, it may, with the permission of the OTS, submit a compliance plan under this section as part of that plan, order, agreement, or response, subject to the

Office of Thrift Supervision, Treasury § 570.4

deadline provided in paragraph (a)(1) of this section.

(b) *Contents of plan.* The compliance plan shall include a description of the steps the savings association will take to correct the deficiency and the time within which those steps will be taken.

(c) *Review of safety and soundness compliance plans.* Within 30 days after receiving a safety and soundness compliance plan under this subpart, the OTS shall provide written notice to the savings association of whether the plan has been approved or seek additional information from the savings association regarding the plan. The OTS may extend the time within which notice regarding approval of a plan will be provided.

(d) *Failure to submit or implement a compliance plan.* If a savings association fails to submit an acceptable plan within the time specified by the OTS or fails in any material respect to implement a compliance plan, then the OTS shall, by order, require the savings association to correct the deficiency and may take further actions provided in section 39(e)(2)(B) of the FDI Act. Pursuant to section 39(e)(3), the OTS may be required to take certain actions if the savings association commenced operations or experienced a change in control within the previous 24-month period, or the savings association experienced extraordinary growth during the previous 18-month period.

(e) *Amendment of compliance plan.* A savings association that has filed an approved compliance plan may, after prior written notice to and approval by the OTS, amend the plan to reflect a change in circumstance. Until such time as a proposed amendment has been approved, the savings association shall implement the compliance plan as previously approved.

§ 570.4 Issuance of orders to correct deficiencies and to take or refrain from taking other actions.

(a) *Notice of intent to issue order*—(1) *In general.* The OTS shall provide a savings association prior written notice of the OTS's intention to issue an order requiring the savings association to correct a safety and soundness deficiency or to take or refrain from taking other actions pursuant to section 39 of the FDI Act. The savings association shall have such time to respond to a proposed order as provided by the OTS under paragraph (c) of this section.

(2) *Immediate issuance of final order.* If the OTS finds it necessary in order to carry out the purposes of section 39 of the FDI Act, the OTS may, without providing the notice prescribed in paragraph (a)(1) of this section, issue an order requiring a savings association immediately to take actions to correct a safety and soundness deficiency or to take or refrain from taking other actions pursuant to section 39. A savings association that is subject to such an immediately effective order may submit a written appeal of the order to the OTS. Such an appeal must be received by the OTS within 14 calendar days of the issuance of the order, unless the OTS permits a longer period. The OTS shall consider any such appeal, if filed in a timely manner, within 60 days of receiving the appeal. During such period of review, the order shall remain in effect unless the OTS, in its sole discretion, stays the effectiveness of the order.

(b) *Contents of notice.* A notice of intent to issue an order shall include:

(1) A statement of the safety and soundness deficiency or deficiencies that have been identified at the savings association;

(2) A description of any restrictions, prohibitions, or affirmative actions that the OTS proposes to impose or require;

(3) The proposed date when such restrictions or prohibitions would be effective or the proposed date for completion of any required action; and

(4) The date by which the savings association subject to the order may file with the OTS a written response to the notice.

(c) *Response to notice*—(1) *Time for response.* A savings association may file a written response to a notice of intent to issue an order within the time period set by the OTS. Such a response must be received by the OTS within 14 calendar days from the date of the notice unless the OTS determines that a different period is appropriate in light

§ 570.5

of the safety and soundness of the savings association or other relevant circumstances.

(2) *Contents of response.* The response should include:

(i) An explanation why the action proposed by the OTS is not an appropriate exercise of discretion under section 39 of the FDI Act;

(ii) Any recommended modification of the proposed order; and

(iii) Any other relevant information, mitigating circumstances, documentation, or other evidence in support of the position of the savings association regarding the proposed order.

(d) *OTS consideration of response.* After considering the response, the OTS may:

(1) Issue the order as proposed or in modified form;

(2) Determine not to issue the order and so notify the savings association; or

(3) Seek additional information or clarification of the response from the savings association, or any other relevant source.

(e) *Failure to file response.* Failure by a savings association to file with the OTS, within the specified time period, a written response to a proposed order shall constitute a waiver of the opportunity to respond and shall constitute consent to the issuance of the order.

(f) *Request for modification or rescission of order.* Any savings association that is subject to an order under this subpart may, upon a change in circumstances, request in writing that the OTS reconsider the terms of the order, and may propose that the order be rescinded or modified. Unless otherwise ordered by the OTS, the order shall continue in place while such request is pending before the OTS.

§ 570.5 Enforcement of orders.

(a) *Judicial remedies.* Whenever a savings association fails to comply with an order issued under section 39 of the FDI Act, the OTS may seek enforcement of the order in the appropriate United States district court pursuant to section 8(i)(1) of the FDI Act.

(b) *Administrative remedies.* Pursuant to section 8(i)(2)(A) of the FDI Act, the OTS may assess a civil money penalty against any savings association that violates or otherwise fails to comply with any final order issued under section 39 and against any savings association-affiliated party who participates in such violation or noncompliance.

(c) *Other enforcement action.* In addition to the actions described in paragraphs (a) and (b) of this section, the OTS may seek enforcement of the provisions of section 39 of the FDI Act or this part through any other judicial or administrative proceeding authorized by law.

APPENDIX A TO PART 570—INTERAGENCY GUIDELINES ESTABLISHING STANDARDS FOR SAFETY AND SOUNDNESS

I. Introduction

A. Preservation of existing authority.
B. Definitions.

II. Operational and Managerial Standards

A. Internal controls and information systems.
B. Internal audit system.
C. Loan documentation.
D. Credit underwriting.
E. Interest rate exposure.
F. Asset growth.
G. Asset quality.
H. Earnings.
I. Compensation, fees and benefits.

III. Prohibition on Compensation That Constitutes an Unsafe and Unsound Practice

A. Excessive compensation.
B. Compensation leading to material financial loss.

I. Introduction

i. Section 39 of the Federal Deposit Insurance Act[1] (FDI Act) requires each Federal banking agency (collectively, the agencies) to establish certain safety and soundness standards by regulation or by guideline for all insured depository institutions. Under section 39, the agencies must establish three types of standards: (1) Operational and managerial standards; (2) compensation standards; and (3) such standards relating to asset

---

[1] Section 39 of the Federal Deposit Insurance Act (12 U.S.C. 1831p–1) was added by section 132 of the Federal Deposit Insurance Corporation Improvement Act of 1991 (FDICIA), Pub. L. 102–242, 105 Stat. 2236 (1991), and amended by section 956 of the Housing and Community Development Act of 1992, Pub. L. 102–550, 106 Stat. 3895 (1992) and section 318 of the Riegle Community Development and Regulatory Improvement Act of 1994, Pub. L. 103–325, 108 Stat. 2160 (1994).

Office of Thrift Supervision, Treasury

Pt. 570, App. A

quality, earnings, and stock valuation as they determine to be appropriate.

ii. Section 39(a) requires the agencies to establish operational and managerial standards relating to: (1) Internal controls, information systems and internal audit systems, in accordance with section 36 of the FDI Act (12 U.S.C. 1831m); (2) loan documentation; (3) credit underwriting; (4) interest rate exposure; (5) asset growth; and (6) compensation, fees, and benefits, in accordance with subsection (c) of section 39. Section 39(b) requires the agencies to establish standards relating to asset quality, earnings, and stock valuation that the agencies determine to be appropriate.

iii. Section 39(c) requires the agencies to establish standards prohibiting as an unsafe and unsound practice any compensatory arrangement that would provide any executive officer, employee, director, or principal shareholder of the institution with excessive compensation, fees or benefits and any compensatory arrangement that could lead to material financial loss to an institution. Section 39(c) also requires that the agencies establish standards that specify when compensation is excessive.

iv. If an agency determines that an institution fails to meet any standard established by guideline under subsection (a) or (b) of section 39, the agency may require the institution to submit to the agency an acceptable plan to achieve compliance with the standard. In the event that an institution fails to submit an acceptable plan within the time allowed by the agency or fails in any material respect to implement an accepted plan, the agency must, by order, require the institution to correct the deficiency. The agency may, and in some cases must, take other supervisory actions until the deficiency has been corrected.

v. The agencies have adopted amendments to their rules and regulations to establish deadlines for submission and review of compliance plans.[2]

vi. The following Guidelines set out the safety and soundness standards that the agencies use to identify and address problems at insured depository institutions before capital becomes impaired. The agencies believe that the standards adopted in these Guidelines serve this end without dictating how institutions must be managed and operated. These standards are designed to identify potential safety and soundness concerns and ensure that action is taken to address those concerns before they pose a risk to the Deposit Insurance Fund.

A. Preservation of Existing Authority

Neither section 39 nor these Guidelines in any way limits the authority of the agencies to address unsafe or unsound practices, violations of law, unsafe or unsound conditions, or other practices. Action under section 39 and these Guidelines may be taken independently of, in conjunction with, or in addition to any other enforcement action available to the agencies. Nothing in these Guidelines limits the authority of the FDIC pursuant to section 38(i)(2)(F) of the FDI Act (12 U.S.C. 1831(o)) and Part 325 of Title 12 of the Code of Federal Regulations.

B. Definitions

1. *In general.* For purposes of these Guidelines, except as modified in the Guidelines or unless the context otherwise requires, the terms used have the same meanings as set forth in sections 3 and 39 of the FDI Act (12 U.S.C. 1813 and 1831p-1).

2. *Board of directors,* in the case of a state-licensed insured branch of a foreign bank and in the case of a federal branch of a foreign bank, means the managing official in charge of the insured foreign branch.

3. *Compensation* means all direct and indirect payments or benefits, both cash and non-cash, granted to or for the benefit of any executive officer, employee, director, or principal shareholder, including but not limited to payments or benefits derived from an employment contract, compensation or benefit agreement, fee arrangement, perquisite, stock option plan, postemployment benefit, or other compensatory arrangement.

4. *Director* shall have the meaning described in 12 CFR 215.2(c).[3]

5. *Executive officer* shall have the meaning described in 12 CFR 215.2(d).[4]

6. *Principal shareholder* shall have the meaning described in 12 CFR 215.2(l).[5]

II. Operational and Managerial Standards

A. Internal controls and information systems.

An institution should have internal controls and information systems that are appropriate to the size of the institution and the

---

[2] For the Office of the Comptroller of the Currency, these regulations appear at 12 CFR Part 30; for the Board of Governors of the Federal Reserve System, these regulations appear at 12 CFR Part 263; for the Federal Deposit Insurance Corporation, these regulations appear at 12 CFR Part 308, subpart R, and for the Office of Thrift Supervision, these regulations appear at 12 CFR Part 570.

[3] In applying these definitions for savings associations, pursuant to 12 U.S.C. 1464, savings associations shall use the terms "savings association" and "insured savings association" in place of the terms "member bank" and "insured bank."

[4] See footnote 3 in section I.B.4. of this appendix.

[5] See footnote 3 in section I.B.4. of this appendix.

nature, scope and risk of its activities and that provide for:

1. An organizational structure that establishes clear lines of authority and responsibility for monitoring adherence to established policies;
2. Effective risk assessment;
3. Timely and accurate financial, operational and regulatory reports;
4. Adequate procedures to safeguard and manage assets; and
5. Compliance with applicable laws and regulations.

B. *Internal audit system.* An institution should have an internal audit system that is appropriate to the size of the institution and the nature and scope of its activities and that provides for:

1. Adequate monitoring of the system of internal controls through an internal audit function. For an institution whose size, complexity or scope of operations does not warrant a full scale internal audit function, a system of independent reviews of key internal controls may be used;
2. Independence and objectivity;
3. Qualified persons;
4. Adequate testing and review of information systems;
5. Adequate documentation of tests and findings and any corrective actions;
6. Verification and review of management actions to address material weaknesses; and
7. Review by the institution's audit committee or board of directors of the effectiveness of the internal audit systems.

C. *Loan documentation.* An institution should establish and maintain loan documentation practices that:

1. Enable the institution to make an informed lending decision and to assess risk, as necessary, on an ongoing basis;
2. Identify the purpose of a loan and the source of repayment, and assess the ability of the borrower to repay the indebtedness in a timely manner;
3. Ensure that any claim against a borrower is legally enforceable;
4. Demonstrate appropriate administration and monitoring of a loan; and
5. Take account of the size and complexity of a loan.

D. *Credit underwriting.* An institution should establish and maintain prudent credit underwriting practices that:

1. Are commensurate with the types of loans the institution will make and consider the terms and conditions under which they will be made;
2. Consider the nature of the markets in which loans will be made;
3. Provide for consideration, prior to credit commitment, of the borrower's overall financial condition and resources, the financial responsibility of any guarantor, the nature and value of any underlying collateral, and the borrower's character and willingness to repay as agreed;
4. Establish a system of independent, ongoing credit review and appropriate communication to management and to the board of directors;
5. Take adequate account of concentration of credit risk; and
6. Are appropriate to the size of the institution and the nature and scope of its activities.

E. *Interest rate exposure.* An institution should:

1. Manage interest rate risk in a manner that is appropriate to the size of the institution and the complexity of its assets and liabilities; and
2. Provide for periodic reporting to management and the board of directors regarding interest rate risk with adequate information for management and the board of directors to assess the level of risk.

F. *Asset growth.* An institution's asset growth should be prudent and consider:

1. The source, volatility and use of the funds that support asset growth;
2. Any increase in credit risk or interest rate risk as a result of growth; and
3. The effect of growth on the institution's capital.

G. *Asset quality.* An insured depository institution should establish and maintain a system that is commensurate with the institution's size and the nature and scope of its operations to identify problem assets and prevent deterioration in those assets. The institution should:

1. Conduct periodic asset quality reviews to identify problem assets;
2. Estimate the inherent losses in those assets and establish reserves that are sufficient to absorb estimated losses;
3. Compare problem asset totals to capital;
4. Take appropriate corrective action to resolve problem assets;
5. Consider the size and potential risks of material asset concentrations; and
6. Provide periodic asset reports with adequate information for management and the board of directors to assess the level of asset risk.

H. *Earnings.* An insured depository institution should establish and maintain a system that is commensurate with the institution's size and the nature and scope of its operations to evaluate and monitor earnings and ensure that earnings are sufficient to maintain adequate capital and reserves. The institution should:

1. Compare recent earnings trends relative to equity, assets, or other commonly used benchmarks to the institution's historical results and those of its peers;
2. Evaluate the adequacy of earnings given the size, complexity, and risk profile of the institution's assets and operations;

Office of Thrift Supervision, Treasury Pt. 570, App. B

3. Assess the source, volatility, and sustainability of earnings, including the effect of nonrecurring or extraordinary income or expense;

4. Take steps to ensure that earnings are sufficient to maintain adequate capital and reserves after considering the institution's asset quality and growth rate; and

5. Provide periodic earnings reports with adequate information for management and the board of directors to assess earnings performance.

I. *Compensation, fees and benefits.* An institution should maintain safeguards to prevent the payment of compensation, fees, and benefits that are excessive or that could lead to material financial loss to the institution.

III. Prohibition on Compensation That Constitutes an Unsafe and Unsound Practice

A. Excessive Compensation

Excessive compensation is prohibited as an unsafe and unsound practice. Compensation shall be considered excessive when amounts paid are unreasonable or disproportionate to the services performed by an executive officer, employee, director, or principal shareholder, considering the following:

1. The combined value of all cash and non-cash benefits provided to the individual;

2. The compensation history of the individual and other individuals with comparable expertise at the institution;

3. The financial condition of the institution;

4. Comparable compensation practices at comparable institutions, based upon such factors as asset size, geographic location, and the complexity of the loan portfolio or other assets;

5. For postemployment benefits, the projected total cost and benefit to the institution;

6. Any connection between the individual and any fraudulent act or omission, breach of trust or fiduciary duty, or insider abuse with regard to the institution; and

7. Any other factors the agencies determines to be relevant.

B. Compensation Leading to Material Financial Loss

Compensation that could lead to material financial loss to an institution is prohibited as an unsafe and unsound practice.

[60 FR 35678, 35687, July 10, 1995, as amended at 61 FR 43952, Aug. 27, 1996; 71 FR 19812, Apr. 18, 2006]

APPENDIX B TO PART 570—INTERAGENCY GUIDELINES ESTABLISHING INFORMATION SECURITY STANDARDS

TABLE OF CONTENTS

I. Introduction
  A. Scope
  B. Preservation of Existing Authority
  C. Definitions
II. Standards for Safeguarding Customer Information
  A. Information Security Program
  B. Objectives
III. Development and Implementation of Customer Information Security Program
  A. Involve the Board of Directors
  B. Assess Risk
  C. Manage and Control Risk
  D. Oversee Service Provider Arrangements
  E. Adjust the Program
  F. Report to the Board
  G. Implement the Standards

I. INTRODUCTION

The Interagency Guidelines Establishing Information Security Standards (Guidelines) set forth standards pursuant to section 39(a) of the Federal Deposit Insurance Act (12 U.S.C. 1831p–1), and sections 501 and 505(b) of the Gramm-Leach-Bliley Act (15 U.S.C. 6801 and 6805(b)). These Guidelines address standards for developing and implementing administrative, technical, and physical safeguards to protect the security, confidentiality, and integrity of customer information. These Guidelines also address standards with respect to the proper disposal of consumer information, pursuant to sections 621 and 628 of the Fair Credit Reporting Act (15 U.S.C. 1681s and 1681w).

A. *Scope.* The Guidelines apply to customer information maintained by or on behalf of entities over which OTS has authority. For purposes of this appendix, these entities are savings associations whose deposits are FDIC-insured and any subsidiaries of such savings associations, except brokers, dealers, persons providing insurance, investment companies, and investment advisers. This appendix refers to such entities as "you". These Guidelines also apply to the proper disposal of consumer information by or on behalf of such entities.

B. *Preservation of Existing Authority* Neither section 39 nor these Guidelines in any way limit OTS's authority to address unsafe or unsound practices, violations of law, unsafe or unsound conditions, or other practices. OTS may take action under section 39 and these Guidelines independently of, in conjunction with, or in addition to, any other enforcement action available to OTS.

C. *Definitions.* 1. Except as modified in the Guidelines, or unless the context otherwise requires, the terms used in these Guidelines have the same meanings as set forth in sections 3 and 39 of the Federal Deposit Insurance Act (12 U.S.C. 1813 and 1831p–1).

2. For purposes of the Guidelines, the following definitions apply:

Pt. 570, App. B

a. *Consumer information* means any record about an individual, whether in paper, electronic, or other form, that is a consumer report or is derived from a consumer report and that is maintained or otherwise possessed by you or on your behalf for a business purpose. Consumer information also means a compilation of such records. The term does not include any record that does not identify an individual.

i. *Examples.* (1) *Consumer information* includes:

(A) A consumer report that a savings association obtains;

(B) Information from a consumer report that you obtain from your affiliate after the consumer has been given a notice and has elected not to opt out of that sharing;

(C) Information from a consumer report that you obtain about an individual who applies for but does not receive a loan, including any loan sought by an individual for a business purpose;

(D) Information from a consumer report that you obtain about an individual who guarantees a loan (including a loan to a business entity); or

(E) Information from a consumer report that you obtain about an employee or prospective employee.

(2) *Consumer information* does not include:

(A) Aggregate information, such as the mean credit score, derived from a group of consumer reports; or

(B) Blind data, such as payment history on accounts that are not personally identifiable, that may be used for developing credit scoring models or for other purposes.

b. *Consumer report* has the same meaning as set forth in the Fair Credit Reporting Act, 15 U.S.C. 1681a(d).

c. *Customer* means any of your customers as defined in §573.3(h) of this chapter.

d. *Customer information* means any record containing nonpublic personal information, as defined in §573.3(n) of this chapter, about a customer, whether in paper, electronic, or other form, that you maintain or that is maintained on your behalf.

e. *Customer information systems* means any methods used to access, collect, store, use, transmit, protect, or dispose of customer information.

f. *Service provider* means any person or entity that maintains, processes, or otherwise is permitted access to customer information or consumer information, through its provision of services directly to you.

II. STANDARDS FOR INFORMATION SECURITY

A. *Information Security Program.* You shall implement a comprehensive written information security program that includes administrative, technical, and physical safeguards appropriate to your size and complexity and the nature and scope of your activities. While all parts of your organization are not required to implement a uniform set of policies, all elements of your information security program must be coordinated.

B. *Objectives.* Your information security program shall be designed to:

1. Ensure the security and confidentiality of customer information;

2. Protect against any anticipated threats or hazards to the security or integrity of such information;

3. Protect against unauthorized access to or use of such information that could result in substantial harm or inconvenience to any customer; and

4. Ensure the proper disposal of customer information and consumer information.

III. DEVELOPMENT AND IMPLEMENTATION OF INFORMATION SECURITY PROGRAM

A. *Involve the Board of Directors.* Your board of directors or an appropriate committee of the board shall:

1. Approve your written information security program; and

2. Oversee the development, implementation, and maintenance of your information security program, including assigning specific responsibility for its implementation and reviewing reports from management.

B. *Assess Risk.* You shall:

1. Identify reasonably foreseeable internal and external threats that could result in unauthorized disclosure, misuse, alteration, or destruction of customer information or customer information systems.

2. Assess the likelihood and potential damage of these threats, taking into consideration the sensitivity of customer information.

3. Assess the sufficiency of policies, procedures, customer information systems, and other arrangements in place to control risks.

C. *Manage and Control Risk.* You shall:

1. Design your information security program to control the identified risks, commensurate with the sensitivity of the information as well as the complexity and scope of your activities. You must consider whether the following security measures are appropriate for you and, if so, adopt those measures you conclude are appropriate:

a. Access controls on customer information systems, including controls to authenticate and permit access only to authorized individuals and controls to prevent employees from providing customer information to unauthorized individuals who may seek to obtain this information through fraudulent means.

b. Access restrictions at physical locations containing customer information, such as buildings, computer facilities, and records storage facilities to permit access only to authorized individuals;

Office of Thrift Supervision, Treasury

Pt. 570, App. B

c. Encryption of electronic customer information, including while in transit or in storage on networks or systems to which unauthorized individuals may have access;

d. Procedures designed to ensure that customer information system modifications are consistent with your information security program;

e. Dual control procedures, segregation of duties, and employee background checks for employees with responsibilities for or access to customer information;

f. Monitoring systems and procedures to detect actual and attempted attacks on or intrusions into customer information systems;

g. Response programs that specify actions for you to take when you suspect or detect that unauthorized individuals have gained access to customer information systems, including appropriate reports to regulatory and law enforcement agencies; and

h. Measures to protect against destruction, loss, or damage of customer information due to potential environmental hazards, such as fire and water damage or technological failures.

2. Train staff to implement your information security program.

3. Regularly test the key controls, systems and procedures of the information security program. The frequency and nature of such tests should be determined by your risk assessment. Tests should be conducted or reviewed by independent third parties or staff independent of those that develop or maintain the security programs.

4. Develop, implement, and maintain, as part of your information security program, appropriate measures to properly dispose of customer information and consumer information in accordance with each of the requirements in this paragraph III.

D. *Oversee Service Provider Arrangements.* You shall:

1. Exercise appropriate due diligence in selecting your service providers;

2. Require your service providers by contract to implement appropriate measures designed to meet the objectives of these Guidelines; and

3. Where indicated by your risk assessment, monitor your service providers to confirm that they have satisfied their obligations as required by paragraph D.2. As part of this monitoring, you should review audits, summaries of test results, or other equivalent evaluations of your service providers.

E. *Adjust the Program.* You shall monitor, evaluate, and adjust, as appropriate, the information security program in light of any relevant changes in technology, the sensitivity of your customer information, internal or external threats to information, and your own changing business arrangements, such as mergers and acquisitions, alliances and joint ventures, outsourcing arrangements, and changes to customer information systems.

F. *Report to the Board.* You shall report to your board or an appropriate committee of the board at least annually. This report should describe the overall status of the information security program and your compliance with these Guidelines. The reports should discuss material matters related to your program, addressing issues such as: risk assessment; risk management and control decisions; service provider arrangements; results of testing; security breaches or violations and management's responses; and recommendations for changes in the information security program.

G. *Implement the Standards.* 1. *Effective date.* You must implement an information security program pursuant to these Guidelines by July 1, 2001.

2. *Two-year grandfathering of agreements with service providers.* Until July 1, 2003, a contract that you have entered into with a service provider to perform services for you or functions on your behalf satisfies the provisions of paragraph III.D., even if the contract does not include a requirement that the servicer maintain the security and confidentiality of customer information, as long as you entered into the contract on or before March 5, 2001.

3. *Effective date for measures relating to the disposal of consumer information.* You must satisfy these Guidelines with respect to the proper disposal of consumer information by July 1, 2005.

4. *Exception for existing agreements with service providers relating to the disposal of consumer information.* Notwithstanding the requirement in paragraph III.G.3., your contracts with service providers that have access to consumer information and that may dispose of consumer information, entered into before July 1, 2005, must comply with the provisions of the Guidelines relating to the proper disposal of consumer information by July 1, 2006.

[60 FR 35086, July 10, 1995, as amended at 69 FR 77620, Dec. 28, 2004]

SUPPLEMENT A TO APPENDIX B TO PART 570—INTERAGENCY GUIDANCE ON RESPONSE PROGRAMS FOR UNAUTHORIZED ACCESS TO CUSTOMER INFORMATION AND CUSTOMER NOTICE

I. BACKGROUND

This Guidance[1] interprets section 501(b) of the Gramm-Leach-Bliley Act ("GLBA") and

---

[1] This Guidance is being jointly issued by the Board of Governors of the Federal Reserve System (Board), the Federal Deposit Insurance Corporation (FDIC), the Office of

Continued

the Interagency Guidelines Establishing Information Security Standards (the "Security Guidelines")[2] and describes response programs, including customer notification procedures, that a financial institution should develop and implement to address unauthorized access to or use of customer information that could result in substantial harm or inconvenience to a customer. The scope of, and definitions of terms used in, this Guidance are identical to those of the Security Guidelines. For example, the term "customer information" is the same term used in the Security Guidelines, and means any record containing nonpublic personal information about a customer, whether in paper, electronic, or other form, maintained by or on behalf of the institution.

A. Interagency Security Guidelines

Section 501(b) of the GLBA required the Agencies to establish appropriate standards for financial institutions subject to their jurisdiction that include administrative, technical, and physical safeguards, to protect the security and confidentiality of customer information. Accordingly, the Agencies issued Security Guidelines requiring every financial institution to have an information security program designed to:

1. Ensure the security and confidentiality of customer information;

2. Protect against any anticipated threats or hazards to the security or integrity of such information; and

3. Protect against unauthorized access to or use of such information that could result in substantial harm or inconvenience to any customer.

B. Risk Assessment and Controls

1. The Security Guidelines direct every financial institution to assess the following risks, among others, when developing its information security program:

a. Reasonably foreseeable internal and external threats that could result in unauthorized disclosure, misuse, alteration, or destruction of customer information or customer information systems;

b. The likelihood and potential damage of threats, taking into consideration the sensitivity of customer information; and

c. The sufficiency of policies, procedures, customer information systems, and other arrangements in place to control risks.[3]

2. Following the assessment of these risks, the Security Guidelines require a financial institution to design a program to address the identified risks. The particular security measures an institution should adopt will depend upon the risks presented by the complexity and scope of its business. At a minimum, the financial institution is required to consider the specific security measures enumerated in the Security Guidelines,[4] and adopt those that are appropriate for the institution, including:

a. Access controls on customer information systems, including controls to authenticate and permit access only to authorized individuals and controls to prevent employees from providing customer information to unauthorized individuals who may seek to obtain this information through fraudulent means;

b. Background checks for employees with responsibilities for access to customer information; and

c. Response programs that specify actions to be taken when the financial institution suspects or detects that unauthorized individuals have gained access to customer information systems, including appropriate reports to regulatory and law enforcement agencies.[5]

C. Service Providers

The Security Guidelines direct every financial institution to require its service providers by contract to implement appropriate measures designed to protect against unauthorized access to or use of customer information that could result in substantial harm or inconvenience to any customer.[6]

II. RESPONSE PROGRAM

Millions of Americans, throughout the country, have been victims of identity theft.[7] Identity thieves misuse personal information they obtain from a number of

---

the Comptroller of the Currency (OCC), and the Office of Thrift Supervision (OTS).

[2] 12 CFR part 30, app. B (OCC); 12 CFR part 208, app. D–2 and part 225, app. F (Board); 12 CFR part 364, app. B (FDIC); and 12 CFR part 570, app. B (OTS). The "Interagency Guidelines Establishing Information Security Standards" were formerly known as "The Interagency Guidelines Establishing Standards for Safeguarding Customer Information."

[3] See Security Guidelines, III.B.
[4] See Security Guidelines, III.C.
[5] See Security Guidelines, III.C.
[6] See Security Guidelines, II.B. and III.D. Further, the Agencies note that, in addition to contractual obligations to a financial institution, a service provider may be required to implement its own comprehensive information security program in accordance with the Safeguards Rule promulgated by the Federal Trade Commission ("FTC"), 16 CFR part 314.
[7] The FTC estimates that nearly 10 million Americans discovered they were victims of some form of identity theft in 2002. See The Federal Trade Commission, *Identity Theft*

Office of Thrift Supervision, Treasury   Pt. 570, App. B

sources, including financial institutions, to perpetrate identity theft. Therefore, financial institutions should take preventative measures to safeguard customer information against attempts to gain unauthorized access to the information. For example, financial institutions should place access controls on customer information systems and conduct background checks for employees who are authorized to access customer information.[8] However, every financial institution should also develop and implement a risk-based response program to address incidents of unauthorized access to customer information in customer information systems[9] that occur nonetheless. A response program should be a key part of an institution's information security program.[10] The program should be appropriate to the size and complexity of the institution and the nature and scope of its activities.

In addition, each institution should be able to address incidents of unauthorized access to customer information in customer information systems maintained by its domestic and foreign service providers. Therefore, consistent with the obligations in the Guidelines that relate to these arrangements, and with existing guidance on this topic issued by the Agencies,[11] an institution's contract with its service provider should require the service provider to take appropriate actions to address incidents of unauthorized access to the financial institution's customer information, including notification to the institution as soon as possible of any such incident, to enable the institution to expeditiously implement its response program.

A. Components of a Response Program

1. At a minimum, an institution's response program should contain procedures for the following:

a. Assessing the nature and scope of an incident, and identifying what customer information systems and types of customer information have been accessed or misused;

b. Notifying its primary Federal regulator as soon as possible when the institution becomes aware of an incident involving unauthorized access to or use of *sensitive* customer information, as defined below;

c. Consistent with the Agencies' Suspicious Activity Report ("SAR") regulations,[12] notifying appropriate law enforcement authorities, in addition to filing a timely SAR in

---

Survey Report, (September 2003), available at *http://www.ftc.gov/os/2003/09/synovatereport.pdf.*

[8] Institutions should also conduct background checks of employees to ensure that the institution does not violate 12 U.S.C. 1829, which prohibits an institution from hiring an individual convicted of certain criminal offenses or who is subject to a prohibition order under 12 U.S.C. 1818(e)(6).

[9] Under the Guidelines, an institution's *customer information systems* consist of all of the methods used to access, collect, store, use, transmit, protect, or dispose of customer information, including the systems maintained by its service providers. *See* Security Guidelines, I.C.2.d (I.C.2.c for OTS).

[10] *See* FFIEC Information Technology Examination Handbook, Information Security Booklet, Dec. 2002 available at *http://www.ffiec.gov/ffiecinfobase/html_pages/infosec_book_frame.htm.* Federal Reserve SR 97–32, Sound Practice Guidance for Information Security for Networks, Dec. 4, 1997; OCC Bulletin 2000–14, "Infrastructure Threats—Intrusion Risks" (May 15, 2000), for additional guidance on preventing, detecting, and responding to intrusions into financial institution computer systems.

[11] *See* Federal Reserve SR Ltr. 00–04, Outsourcing of Information and Transaction Processing, Feb. 9, 2000; OCC Bulletin 2001–47, "Third-Party Relationships Risk Management Principles," Nov. 1, 2001; FDIC FIL 68–99, Risk Assessment Tools and Practices for Information System Security, July 7, 1999;

OTS Thrift Bulletin 82a, Third Party Arrangements, Sept. 1, 2004.

[12] An institution's obligation to file a SAR is set out in the Agencies' SAR regulations and Agency guidance. *See* 12 CFR 21.11 (national banks, Federal branches and agencies); 12 CFR 208.62 (State member banks); 12 CFR 211.5(k) (Edge and agreement corporations); 12 CFR 211.24(f) (uninsured State branches and agencies of foreign banks); 12 CFR 225.4(f) (bank holding companies and their nonbank subsidiaries); 12 CFR part 353 (State non-member banks); and 12 CFR 563.180 (savings associations). National banks must file SARs in connection with computer intrusions and other computer crimes. *See* OCC Bulletin 2000–14, "Infrastructure Threats—Intrusion Risks" (May 15, 2000); Advisory Letter 97–9, "Reporting Computer Related Crimes" (November 19, 1997) (general guidance still applicable though instructions for new SAR form published in 65 FR 1229, 1230 (January 7, 2000)). *See also* Federal Reserve SR 01–11, Identity Theft and Pretext Calling, Apr. 26, 2001; SR 97–28, Guidance Concerning Reporting of Computer Related Crimes by Financial Institutions, Nov. 6, 1997; FDIC FIL 48–2000, Suspicious Activity Reports, July 14, 2000; FIL 47–97, Preparation of Suspicious Activity Reports, May 6, 1997; OTS CEO Memorandum 139, Identity Theft and Pretext Calling, May 4, 2001; CEO Memorandum 126, New Suspicious Activity Report Form, July 5, 2000; *http://www.ots.treas.gov/BSA* (for the latest SAR form and filing instructions required by OTS as of July 1, 2003).

situations involving Federal criminal violations requiring immediate attention, such as when a reportable violation is ongoing;

d. Taking appropriate steps to contain and control the incident to prevent further unauthorized access to or use of customer information, for example, by monitoring, freezing, or closing affected accounts, while preserving records and other evidence;[13] and

e. Notifying customers when warranted.

2. Where an incident of unauthorized access to customer information involves customer information systems maintained by an institution's service providers, it is the responsibility of the financial institution to notify the institution's customers and regulator. However, an institution may authorize or contract with its service provider to notify the institution's customers or regulator on its behalf.

III. CUSTOMER NOTICE

Financial institutions have an affirmative duty to protect their customers' information against unauthorized access or use. Notifying customers of a security incident involving the unauthorized access or use of the customer's information in accordance with the standard set forth below is a key part of that duty. Timely notification of customers is important to manage an institution's reputation risk. Effective notice also may reduce an institution's legal risk, assist in maintaining good customer relations, and enable the institution's customers to take steps to protect themselves against the consequences of identity theft. When customer notification is warranted, an institution may not forgo notifying its customers of an incident because the institution believes that it may be potentially embarrassed or inconvenienced by doing so.

A. Standard for Providing Notice

When a financial institution becomes aware of an incident of unauthorized access to sensitive customer information, the institution should conduct a reasonable investigation to promptly determine the likelihood that the information has been or will be misused. If the institution determines that misuse of its information about a customer has occurred or is reasonably possible, it should notify the affected customer as soon as possible. Customer notice may be delayed if an appropriate law enforcement agency determines that notification will interfere with a criminal investigation and provides the institution with a written request for the delay. However, the institution should notify its customers as soon as notification will no longer interfere with the investigation.

1. Sensitive Customer Information

Under the Guidelines, an institution must protect against unauthorized access to or use of customer information that could result in substantial harm or inconvenience to any customer. Substantial harm or inconvenience is most likely to result from improper access to *sensitive customer information* because this type of information is most likely to be misused, as in the commission of identity theft. For purposes of this Guidance, *sensitive customer information* means a customer's name, address, or telephone number, in conjunction with the customer's social security number, driver's license number, account number, credit or debit card number, or a personal identification number or password that would permit access to the customer's account. *Sensitive customer information* also includes any combination of components of customer information that would allow someone to log onto or access the customer's account, such as user name and password or password and account number.

2. Affected Customers

If a financial institution, based upon its investigation, can determine from its logs or other data precisely which customers' information has been improperly accessed, it may limit notification to those customers with regard to whom the institution determines that misuse of their information has occurred or is reasonably possible. However, there may be situations where the institution determines that a group of files has been accessed improperly, but is unable to identify which specific customers' information has been accessed. If the circumstances of the unauthorized access lead the institution to determine that misuse of the information is reasonably possible, it should notify all customers in the group.

B. Content of Customer Notice

1. Customer notice should be given in a clear and conspicuous manner. The notice should describe the incident in general terms and the type of customer information that was the subject of unauthorized access or use. It also should generally describe what the institution has done to protect the customers' information from further unauthorized access. In addition, it should include a telephone number that customers can call for further information and assistance.[14] The notice also should remind customers of the

---

[13] *See* FFIEC Information Technology Examination Handbook, Information Security Booklet, Dec. 2002, pp. 68–74.

[14] The institution should, therefore, ensure that it has reasonable policies and procedures in place, including trained personnel, to respond appropriately to customer inquiries and requests for assistance.

need to remain vigilant over the next twelve to twenty-four months, and to promptly report incidents of suspected identity theft to the institution. The notice should include the following additional items, when appropriate:

a. A recommendation that the customer review account statements and immediately report any suspicious activity to the institution;

b. A description of fraud alerts and an explanation of how the customer may place a fraud alert in the customer's consumer reports to put the customer's creditors on notice that the customer may be a victim of fraud;

c. A recommendation that the customer periodically obtain credit reports from each nationwide credit reporting agency and have information relating to fraudulent transactions deleted;

d. An explanation of how the customer may obtain a credit report free of charge; and

e. Information about the availability of the FTC's online guidance regarding steps a consumer can take to protect against identity theft. The notice should encourage the customer to report any incidents of identity theft to the FTC, and should provide the FTC's Web site address and toll-free telephone number that customers may use to obtain the identity theft guidance and report suspected incidents of identity theft.[15]

2. The Agencies encourage financial institutions to notify the nationwide consumer reporting agencies prior to sending notices to a large number of customers that include contact information for the reporting agencies.

C. Delivery of Customer Notice

Customer notice should be delivered in any manner designed to ensure that a customer can reasonably be expected to receive it. For example, the institution may choose to contact all customers affected by telephone or by mail, or by electronic mail for those customers for whom it has a valid e-mail address and who have agreed to receive communications electronically.

[66 FR 8640, Feb. 1, 2001, as amended at 70 FR 15754, Mar. 29, 2005; 71 FR 5780, Feb. 3, 2006]

---

[15] Currently, the FTC Web site for the ID Theft brochure and the FTC Hotline phone number are *http://www.consumer.gov/idtheft* and 1-877-IDTHEFT. The institution may also refer customers to any materials developed pursuant to section 151(b) of the FACT Act (educational materials developed by the FTC to teach the public how to prevent identity theft).

PART 571—FAIR CREDIT REPORTING

Subpart A—General Provisions

Sec.
571.1 Purpose and scope.
571.2 Examples.
571.3 Definitions.

Subpart B [Reserved]

Subpart C—Affiliate Marketing

571.20 Coverage and definitions.
571.21 Affiliate marketing opt-out and exceptions.
571.22 Scope and duration of opt-out.
571.23 Contents of opt-out notice; consolidated and equivalent notices.
571.24 Reasonable opportunity to opt out.
571.25 Reasonable and simple methods of opting out.
571.26 Delivery of opt-out notices.
571.27 Renewal of opt-out.
571.28 Effective date, compliance date, and prospective application.

Subpart D—Medical Information

571.30 Obtaining or using medical information in connection with a determination of eligibility for credit.
571.31 Limits on redisclosure of information.
571.32 Sharing medical information with affiliates.

Subpart E—Duties of Furnishers of Information

571.40 Scope.
571.41 Definitions.
571.42 Reasonable policies and procedures concerning the accuracy and integrity of furnished information.
571.43 Direct disputes.

Subparts F–H [Reserved]

Subpart I—Duties of Users of Consumer Reports Regarding Address Discrepancies and Records Disposal

571.80–81 [Reserved]
571.82 Duties of users regarding address discrepancies.
571.83 Disposal of consumer information.

Subpart J to Part 571—Identity Theft Red Flags

571.90 Duties regarding the detection, prevention, and mitigation of identity theft.
571.91 Duties of card issuers regarding changes of address.

APPENDICES A–B TO PART 571 [RESERVED]

§ 571.1

APPENDIX C TO PART 571—MODEL FORMS FOR OPT-OUT NOTICES
APPENDIX D TO PART 571 [RESERVED]
APPENDIX E TO PART 571—INTERAGENCY GUIDELINES CONCERNING THE ACCURACY AND INTEGRITY OF INFORMATION FURNISHED TO CONSUMER REPORTING AGENCIES
APPENDICES F–I TO PART 571 [RESERVED]
APPENDIX J TO PART 571—INTERAGENCY GUIDELINES ON IDENTITY THEFT DETECTION, PREVENTION, AND MITIGATION

AUTHORITY: 12 U.S.C. 1462a, 1463, 1464, 1467a, 1828, 1831p–1, and 1881–1884; 15 U.S.C. 1681b, 1681c, 1681m, 1681s, 1681s–2, 1681s–3, 1681t, and 1681w; 15 U.S.C. 6801 and 6805; Sec. 214 Pub. L. 108–159, 117 Stat. 1952.

SOURCE: 69 FR 77621, Dec. 28, 2004, unless otherwise noted.

Subpart A—General Provisions

§ 571.1 Purpose and scope.

(a) *Purpose.* The purpose of this part is to establish standards regarding consumer report information. In addition, the purpose of this part is to specify the extent to which you may obtain, use, or share certain information. This part also contains a number of measures you must take to combat consumer fraud and related crimes, including identity theft.

(b) *Scope.* (1)–(2) [Reserved]

(3) The scope of Subpart C of this part is stated in § 571.20(a) of this part.

(4) The scope of Subpart D of this part is stated in §§ 571.30(a), 571.31(a), and 571.32(a) of this part.

(5) The scope of subpart E of this part is stated in § 571.40 of this part.

(6)–(8) [Reserved]

(9)(i) The scope of § 571.82 of Subpart I of this part is stated in § 571.82(a) of this part.

(ii) The scope of § 571.83 of Subpart I of this part is stated in § 571.83(a) of this part.

(10)(i) The scope of § 571.90 of Subpart J of this part is stated in § 571.90(a) of this part.

(ii) The scope of § 571.91 of Subpart J of this part is stated in § 571.91(a) of this part.

[69 FR 77621, Dec. 28, 2004, as amended at 70 FR 70689, Nov. 22, 2005; 72 FR 62972, Nov. 7, 2007; 72 FR 63764, Nov. 9, 2007; 74 FR 31520, July 1, 2009]

§ 571.2 Examples.

The examples in this part are not exclusive. Compliance with an example, to the extent applicable, constitutes compliance with this part. Examples in a paragraph illustrate only the issue described in the paragraph and do not illustrate any other issue that may arise in this part.

[70 FR 70689, Nov. 22, 2005]

§ 571.3 Definitions.

For purposes of this part, unless explicitly stated otherwise:

(a) *Act* means the Fair Credit Reporting Act (15 U.S.C. 1681 *et seq.*).

(b) *Affiliate* means any company that is related by common ownership or common corporate control with another company.

(c) [Reserved]

(d) *Company* means any corporation, limited liability company, business trust, general or limited partnership, association, or similar organization.

(e) *Consumer* means an individual.

(f)–(h) [Reserved]

(i) *Common ownership or common corporate control* means a relationship between two companies under which:

(1) One company has, with respect to the other company:

(i) Ownership, control, or power to vote 25 percent or more of the outstanding shares of any class of voting security of a company, directly or indirectly, or acting through one or more other persons;

(ii) Control in any manner over the election of a majority of the directors, trustees, or general partners (or individuals exercising similar functions) of a company; or

(iii) The power to exercise, directly or indirectly, a controlling influence over the management or policies of a company, as the OTS determines; or

(2) Any other person has, with respect to both companies, a relationship described in paragraphs (i)(1)(i) through (i)(1)(iii) of this section.

(j) [Reserved]

(k) *Medical information* means:

(1) Information or data, whether oral or recorded, in any form or medium, created by or derived from a health care provider or the consumer, that relates to—

Office of Thrift Supervision, Treasury § 571.20

(i) The past, present, or future physical, mental, or behavioral health or condition of an individual;

(ii) The provision of health care to an individual; or

(iii) The payment for the provision of health care to an individual.

(2) The term does not include:

(i) The age or gender of a consumer;

(ii) Demographic information about the consumer, including a consumer's residence address or e-mail address;

(iii) Any other information about a consumer that does not relate to the physical, mental, or behavioral health or condition of a consumer, including the existence or value of any insurance policy; or

(iv) Information that does not identify a specific consumer.

(l) *Person* means any individual, partnership, corporation, trust, estate cooperative, association, government or governmental subdivision or agency, or other entity.

[69 FR 77621, Dec. 28, 2004, as amended at 70 FR 70689, Nov. 22, 2005; 72 FR 63764, Nov. 9, 2007]

Subpart B [Reserved]

Subpart C—Affiliate Marketing

SOURCE: 72 FR 62972, Nov. 7, 2007, unless otherwise noted.

§ 571.20 Coverage and definitions.

(a) *Coverage.* Subpart C of this part applies to savings associations whose deposits are insured by the Federal Deposit Insurance Corporation or, in accordance with § 559.3(h)(1) of this chapter, federal savings association operating subsidiaries that are not functionally regulated within the meaning of section 5(c)(5) of the Bank Holding Company Act of 1956, as amended (12 U.S.C. 1844(c)(5)).

(b) *Definitions.* For purposes of this subpart:

(1) *Clear and conspicuous.* The term "clear and conspicuous" means reasonably understandable and designed to call attention to the nature and significance of the information presented.

(2) *Concise.* (i) *In general.* The term "concise" means a reasonably brief expression or statement.

(ii) *Combination with other required disclosures.* A notice required by this subpart may be concise even if it is combined with other disclosures required or authorized by federal or state law.

(3) *Eligibility information.* The term "eligibility information" means any information the communication of which would be a consumer report if the exclusions from the definition of "consumer report" in section 603(d)(2)(A) of the Act did not apply. Eligibility information does not include aggregate or blind data that does not contain personal identifiers such as account numbers, names, or addresses.

(4) *Pre-existing business relationship.* (i) *In general.* The term "pre-existing business relationship" means a relationship between a person, or a person's licensed agent, and a consumer based on—

(A) A financial contract between the person and the consumer which is in force on the date on which the consumer is sent a solicitation covered by this subpart;

(B) The purchase, rental, or lease by the consumer of the person's goods or services, or a financial transaction (including holding an active account or a policy in force or having another continuing relationship) between the consumer and the person, during the 18-month period immediately preceding the date on which the consumer is sent a solicitation covered by this subpart; or

(C) An inquiry or application by the consumer regarding a product or service offered by that person during the three-month period immediately preceding the date on which the consumer is sent a solicitation covered by this subpart.

(ii) *Examples of pre-existing business relationships.* (A) If a consumer has a time deposit account, such as a certificate of deposit, at a depository institution that is currently in force, the depository institution has a pre-existing business relationship with the consumer and can use eligibility information it receives from its affiliates to make solicitations to the consumer about its products or services.

(B) If a consumer obtained a certificate of deposit from a depository institution, but did not renew the certificate at maturity, the depository institution has a pre-existing business relationship with the consumer and can use eligibility information it receives from its affiliates to make solicitations to the consumer about its products or services for 18 months after the date of maturity of the certificate of deposit.

(C) If a consumer obtains a mortgage, the mortgage lender has a pre-existing business relationship with the consumer. If the mortgage lender sells the consumer's entire loan to an investor, the mortgage lender has a pre-existing business relationship with the consumer and can use eligibility information it receives from its affiliates to make solicitations to the consumer about its products or services for 18 months after the date it sells the loan, and the investor has a pre-existing business relationship with the consumer upon purchasing the loan. If, however, the mortgage lender sells a fractional interest in the consumer's loan to an investor but also retains an ownership interest in the loan, the mortgage lender continues to have a pre-existing business relationship with the consumer, but the investor does not have a pre-existing business relationship with the consumer. If the mortgage lender retains ownership of the loan, but sells ownership of the servicing rights to the consumer's loan, the mortgage lender continues to have a pre-existing business relationship with the consumer. The purchaser of the servicing rights also has a pre-existing business relationship with the consumer as of the date it purchases ownership of the servicing rights, but only if it collects payments from or otherwise deals directly with the consumer on a continuing basis.

(D) If a consumer applies to a depository institution for a product or service that it offers, but does not obtain a product or service from or enter into a financial contract or transaction with the institution, the depository institution has a pre-existing business relationship with the consumer and can therefore use eligibility information it receives from an affiliate to make solicitations to the consumer about its products or services for three months after the date of the application.

(E) If a consumer makes a telephone inquiry to a depository institution about its products or services and provides contact information to the institution, but does not obtain a product or service from or enter into a financial contract or transaction with the institution, the depository institution has a pre-existing business relationship with the consumer and can therefore use eligibility information it receives from an affiliate to make solicitations to the consumer about its products or services for three months after the date of the inquiry.

(F) If a consumer makes an inquiry to a depository institution by e-mail about its products or services, but does not obtain a product or service from or enter into a financial contract or transaction with the institution, the depository institution has a pre-existing business relationship with the consumer and can therefore use eligibility information it receives from an affiliate to make solicitations to the consumer about its products or services for three months after the date of the inquiry.

(G) If a consumer has an existing relationship with a depository institution that is part of a group of affiliated companies, makes a telephone call to the centralized call center for the group of affiliated companies to inquire about products or services offered by the insurance affiliate, and provides contact information to the call center, the call constitutes an inquiry to the insurance affiliate that offers those products or services. The insurance affiliate has a pre-existing business relationship with the consumer and can therefore use eligibility information it receives from its affiliated depository institution to make solicitations to the consumer about its products or services for three months after the date of the inquiry.

(iii) *Examples where no pre-existing business relationship is created.* (A) If a consumer makes a telephone call to a centralized call center for a group of affiliated companies to inquire about the consumer's existing account at a depository institution, the call does

Office of Thrift Supervision, Treasury

§ 571.21

not constitute an inquiry to any affiliate other than the depository institution that holds the consumer's account and does not establish a pre-existing business relationship between the consumer and any affiliate of the account-holding depository institution.

(B) If a consumer who has a deposit account with a depository institution makes a telephone call to an affiliate of the institution to ask about the affiliate's retail locations and hours, but does not make an inquiry about the affiliate's products or services, the call does not constitute an inquiry and does not establish a pre-existing business relationship between the consumer and the affiliate. Also, the affiliate's capture of the consumer's telephone number does not constitute an inquiry and does not establish a pre-existing business relationship between the consumer and the affiliate.

(C) If a consumer makes a telephone call to a depository institution in response to an advertisement that offers a free promotional item to consumers who call a toll-free number, but the advertisement does not indicate that the depository institution's products or services will be marketed to consumers who call in response, the call does not create a pre-existing business relationship between the consumer and the depository institution because the consumer has not made an inquiry about a product or service offered by the institution, but has merely responded to an offer for a free promotional item.

(5) *Solicitation.* (i) *In general.* The term "solicitation" means the marketing of a product or service initiated by a person to a particular consumer that is—

(A) Based on eligibility information communicated to that person by its affiliate as described in this subpart; and

(B) Intended to encourage the consumer to purchase or obtain such product or service.

(ii) *Exclusion of marketing directed at the general public.* A solicitation does not include marketing communications that are directed at the general public. For example, television, general circulation magazine, and billboard advertisements do not constitute solicitations, even if those communications are intended to encourage consumers to purchase products and services from the person initiating the communications.

(iii) *Examples of solicitations.* A solicitation would include, for example, a telemarketing call, direct mail, e-mail, or other form of marketing communication directed to a particular consumer that is based on eligibility information received from an affiliate.

(6) *You* means a person described in paragraph (a) of this section.

§ 571.21 Affiliate marketing opt-out and exceptions.

(a) *Initial notice and opt-out requirement.* (1) *In general.* You may not use eligibility information about a consumer that you receive from an affiliate to make a solicitation for marketing purposes to the consumer, unless—

(i) It is clearly and conspicuously disclosed to the consumer in writing or, if the consumer agrees, electronically, in a concise notice that you may use eligibility information about that consumer received from an affiliate to make solicitations for marketing purposes to the consumer;

(ii) The consumer is provided a reasonable opportunity and a reasonable and simple method to "opt out," or prohibit you from using eligibility information to make solicitations for marketing purposes to the consumer; and

(iii) The consumer has not opted out.

(2) *Example.* A consumer has a homeowner's insurance policy with an insurance company. The insurance company furnishes eligibility information about the consumer to its affiliated depository institution. Based on that eligibility information, the depository institution wants to make a solicitation to the consumer about its home equity loan products. The depository institution does not have a pre-existing business relationship with the consumer and none of the other exceptions apply. The depository institution is prohibited from using eligibility information received from its insurance affiliate to make solicitations to the consumer about its home equity loan products unless the consumer is given a notice and opportunity to opt out and the consumer does not opt out.

437

§571.21

(3) *Affiliates who may provide the notice.* The notice required by this paragraph must be provided:

(i) By an affiliate that has or has previously had a pre-existing business relationship with the consumer; or

(ii) As part of a joint notice from two or more members of an affiliated group of companies, provided that at least one of the affiliates on the joint notice has or has previously had a pre-existing business relationship with the consumer.

(b) *Making solicitations*—(1) *In general.* For purposes of this subpart, you make a solicitation for marketing purposes if—

(i) You receive eligibility information from an affiliate;

(ii) You use that eligibility information to do one or more of the following:

(A) Identify the consumer or type of consumer to receive a solicitation;

(B) Establish criteria used to select the consumer to receive a solicitation; or

(C) Decide which of your products or services to market to the consumer or tailor your solicitation to that consumer; and

(iii) As a result of your use of the eligibility information, the consumer is provided a solicitation.

(2) *Receiving eligibility information from an affiliate, including through a common database.* You may receive eligibility information from an affiliate in various ways, including when the affiliate places that information into a common database that you may access.

(3) *Receipt or use of eligibility information by your service provider.* Except as provided in paragraph (b)(5) of this section, you receive or use an affiliate's eligibility information if a service provider acting on your behalf (whether an affiliate or a nonaffiliated third party) receives or uses that information in the manner described in paragraphs (b)(1)(i) or (b)(1)(ii) of this section. All relevant facts and circumstances will determine whether a person is acting as your service provider when it receives or uses an affiliate's eligibility information in connection with marketing your products and services.

(4) *Use by an affiliate of its own eligibility information.* Unless you have used eligibility information that you receive from an affiliate in the manner described in paragraph (b)(1)(ii) of this section, you do not make a solicitation subject to this subpart if your affiliate:

(i) Uses its own eligibility information that it obtained in connection with a pre-existing business relationship it has or had with the consumer to market your products or services to the consumer; or

(ii) Directs its service provider to use the affiliate's own eligibility information that it obtained in connection with a pre-existing business relationship it has or had with the consumer to market your products or services to the consumer, and you do not communicate directly with the service provider regarding that use.

(5) *Use of eligibility information by a service provider.* (i) *In general.* You do not make a solicitation subject to Subpart C of this part if a service provider (including an affiliated or third-party service provider that maintains or accesses a common database that you may access) receives eligibility information from your affiliate that your affiliate obtained in connection with a pre-existing business relationship it has or had with the consumer and uses that eligibility information to market your products or services to the consumer, so long as—

(A) Your affiliate controls access to and use of its eligibility information by the service provider (including the right to establish the specific terms and conditions under which the service provider may use such information to market your products or services);

(B) Your affiliate establishes specific terms and conditions under which the service provider may access and use the affiliate's eligibility information to market your products and services (or those of affiliates generally) to the consumer, such as the identity of the affiliated companies whose products or services may be marketed to the consumer by the service provider, the types of products or services of affiliated companies that may be marketed, and the number of times the consumer may receive marketing materials, and periodically evaluates the service provider's compliance with those terms and conditions;

(C) Your affiliate requires the service provider to implement reasonable policies and procedures designed to ensure that the service provider uses the affiliate's eligibility information in accordance with the terms and conditions established by the affiliate relating to the marketing of your products or services;

(D) Your affiliate is identified on or with the marketing materials provided to the consumer; and

(E) You do not directly use your affiliate's eligibility information in the manner described in paragraph (b)(1)(ii) of this section.

(ii) *Writing requirements.* (A) The requirements of paragraphs (b)(5)(i)(A) and (C) of this section must be set forth in a written agreement between your affiliate and the service provider; and

(B) The specific terms and conditions established by your affiliate as provided in paragraph (b)(5)(i)(B) of this section must be set forth in writing.

(6) *Examples of making solicitations.* (i) A consumer has a deposit account with a depository institution, which is affiliated with an insurance company. The insurance company receives eligibility information about the consumer from the depository institution. The insurance company uses that eligibility information to identify the consumer to receive a solicitation about insurance products, and, as a result, the insurance company provides a solicitation to the consumer about its insurance products. Pursuant to paragraph (b)(1) of this section, the insurance company has made a solicitation to the consumer.

(ii) The same facts as in the example in paragraph (b)(6)(i) of this section, except that after using the eligibility information to identify the consumer to receive a solicitation about insurance products, the insurance company asks the depository institution to send the solicitation to the consumer and the depository institution does so. Pursuant to paragraph (b)(1) of this section, the insurance company has made a solicitation to the consumer because it used eligibility information about the consumer that it received from an affiliate to identify the consumer to receive a solicitation about its products or services, and, as a result, a solicitation was provided to the consumer about the insurance company's products.

(iii) The same facts as in the example in paragraph (b)(6)(i) of this section, except that eligibility information about consumers that have deposit accounts with the depository institution is placed into a common database that all members of the affiliated group of companies may independently access and use. Without using the depository institution's eligibility information, the insurance company develops selection criteria and provides those criteria, marketing materials, and related instructions to the depository institution. The depository institution reviews eligibility information about its own consumers using the selection criteria provided by the insurance company to determine which consumers should receive the insurance company's marketing materials and sends marketing materials about the insurance company's products to those consumers. Even though the insurance company has received eligibility information through the common database as provided in paragraph (b)(2) of this section, it did not use that information to identify consumers or establish selection criteria; instead, the depository institution used its own eligibility information. Therefore, pursuant to paragraph (b)(4)(i) of this section, the insurance company has not made a solicitation to the consumer.

(iv) The same facts as in the example in paragraph (b)(6)(iii) of this section, except that the depository institution provides the insurance company's criteria to the depository institution's service provider and directs the service provider to use the depository institution's eligibility information to identify depository institution consumers who meet the criteria and to send the insurance company's marketing materials to those consumers. The insurance company does not communicate directly with the service provider regarding the use of the depository institution's information to market its products to the depository institution's consumers. Pursuant to paragraph (b)(4)(ii) of this section, the insurance

§ 571.21

company has not made a solicitation to the consumer.

(v) An affiliated group of companies includes a depository institution, an insurance company, and a service provider. Each affiliate in the group places information about its consumers into a common database. The service provider has access to all information in the common database. The depository institution controls access to and use of its eligibility information by the service provider. This control is set forth in a written agreement between the depository institution and the service provider. The written agreement also requires the service provider to establish reasonable policies and procedures designed to ensure that the service provider uses the depository institution's eligibility information in accordance with specific terms and conditions established by the depository institution relating to the marketing of the products and services of all affiliates, including the insurance company. In a separate written communication, the depository institution specifies the terms and conditions under which the service provider may use the depository institution's eligibility information to market the insurance company's products and services to the depository institution's consumers. The specific terms and conditions are: A list of affiliated companies (including the insurance company) whose products or services may be marketed to the depository institution's consumers by the service provider; the specific products or types of products that may be marketed to the depository institution's consumers by the service provider; the categories of eligibility information that may be used by the service provider in marketing products or services to the depository institution's consumers; the types or categories of the depository institution's consumers to whom the service provider may market products or services of depository institution affiliates; the number and/or types of marketing communications that the service provider may send to the depository institution's consumers; and the length of time during which the service provider may market the products or services of the depository institution's affiliates

12 CFR Ch. V (1-1-12 Edition)

to its consumers. The depository institution periodically evaluates the service provider's compliance with these terms and conditions. The insurance company asks the service provider to market insurance products to certain consumers who have deposit accounts with the depository institution. Without using the depository institution's eligibility information, the insurance company develops selection criteria and provides those criteria, marketing materials, and related instructions to the service provider. The service provider uses the depository institution's eligibility information from the common database to identify the depository institution's consumers to whom insurance products will be marketed. When the insurance company's marketing materials are provided to the identified consumers, the name of the depository institution is displayed on the insurance marketing materials, an introductory letter that accompanies the marketing materials, an account statement that accompanies the marketing materials, or the envelope containing the marketing materials. The requirements of paragraph (b)(5) of this section have been satisfied, and the insurance company has not made a solicitation to the consumer.

(vi) The same facts as in the example in paragraph (b)(6)(v) of this section, except that the terms and conditions permit the service provider to use the depository institution's eligibility information to market the products and services of other affiliates to the depository institution's consumers whenever the service provider deems it appropriate to do so. The service provider uses the depository institution's eligibility information in accordance with the discretion afforded to it by the terms and conditions. Because the terms and conditions are not specific, the requirements of paragraph (b)(5) of this section have not been satisfied.

(c) *Exceptions.* The provisions of this subpart do not apply to you if you use eligibility information that you receive from an affiliate:

(1) To make a solicitation for marketing purposes to a consumer with whom you have a pre-existing business relationship;

Office of Thrift Supervision, Treasury § 571.21

(2) To facilitate communications to an individual for whose benefit you provide employee benefit or other services pursuant to a contract with an employer related to and arising out of the current employment relationship or status of the individual as a participant or beneficiary of an employee benefit plan;

(3) To perform services on behalf of an affiliate, except that this subparagraph shall not be construed as permitting you to send solicitations on behalf of an affiliate if the affiliate would not be permitted to send the solicitation as a result of the election of the consumer to opt out under this subpart;

(4) In response to a communication about your products or services initiated by the consumer;

(5) In response to an authorization or request by the consumer to receive solicitations; or

(6) If your compliance with this subpart would prevent you from complying with any provision of State insurance laws pertaining to unfair discrimination in any State in which you are lawfully doing business.

(d) *Examples of exceptions*—(1) *Example of the pre-existing business relationship exception.* A consumer has a deposit account with a depository institution. The consumer also has a relationship with the depository institution's securities affiliate for management of the consumer's securities portfolio. The depository institution receives eligibility information about the consumer from its securities affiliate and uses that information to make a solicitation to the consumer about the depository institution's wealth management services. The depository institution may make this solicitation even if the consumer has not been given a notice and opportunity to opt out because the depository institution has a pre-existing business relationship with the consumer.

(2) *Examples of service provider exception.* (i) A consumer has an insurance policy issued by an insurance company. The insurance company furnishes eligibility information about the consumer to its affiliated depository institution. Based on that eligibility information, the depository institution wants to make a solicitation to the consumer about its deposit products. The depository institution does not have a pre-existing business relationship with the consumer and none of the other exceptions in paragraph (c) of this section apply. The consumer has been given an opt-out notice and has elected to opt out of receiving such solicitations. The depository institution asks a service provider to send the solicitation to the consumer on its behalf. The service provider may not send the solicitation on behalf of the depository institution because, as a result of the consumer's opt-out election, the depository institution is not permitted to make the solicitation.

(ii) The same facts as in paragraph (d)(2)(i) of this section, except the consumer has been given an opt-out notice, but has not elected to opt out. The depository institution asks a service provider to send the solicitation to the consumer on its behalf. The service provider may send the solicitation on behalf of the depository institution because, as a result of the consumer's not opting out, the depository institution is permitted to make the solicitation.

(3) *Examples of consumer-initiated communications.* (i) A consumer who has a deposit account with a depository institution initiates a communication with the depository institution's credit card affiliate to request information about a credit card. The credit card affiliate may use eligibility information about the consumer it obtains from the depository institution or any other affiliate to make solicitations regarding credit card products in response to the consumer-initiated communication.

(ii) A consumer who has a deposit account with a depository institution contacts the institution to request information about how to save and invest for a child's college education without specifying the type of product in which the consumer may be interested. Information about a range of different products or services offered by the depository institution and one or more affiliates of the institution may be responsive to that communication. Such products or services may include the following: Mutual funds offered by the

§ 571.21

institution's mutual fund affiliate; section 529 plans offered by the institution, its mutual fund affiliate, or another securities affiliate; or trust services offered by a different financial institution in the affiliated group. Any affiliate offering investment products or services that would be responsive to the consumer's request for information about saving and investing for a child's college education may use eligibility information to make solicitations to the consumer in response to this communication.

(iii) A credit card issuer makes a marketing call to the consumer without using eligibility information received from an affiliate. The issuer leaves a voice-mail message that invites the consumer to call a toll-free number to apply for the issuer's credit card. If the consumer calls the toll-free number to inquire about the credit card, the call is a consumer-initiated communication about a product or service and the credit card issuer may now use eligibility information it receives from its affiliates to make solicitations to the consumer.

(iv) A consumer calls a depository institution to ask about retail locations and hours, but does not request information about products or services. The institution may not use eligibility information it receives from an affiliate to make solicitations to the consumer about its products or services because the consumer-initiated communication does not relate to the depository institution's products or services. Thus, the use of eligibility information received from an affiliate would not be responsive to the communication and the exception does not apply.

(v) A consumer calls a depository institution to ask about retail locations and hours. The customer service representative asks the consumer if there is a particular product or service about which the consumer is seeking information. The consumer responds that the consumer wants to stop in and find out about certificates of deposit. The customer service representative offers to provide that information by telephone and mail additional information and application materials to the consumer. The consumer agrees and provides or confirms contact information

12 CFR Ch. V (1-1-12 Edition)

for receipt of the materials to be mailed. The depository institution may use eligibility information it receives from an affiliate to make solicitations to the consumer about certificates of deposit because such solicitations would respond to the consumer-initiated communication about products or services.

(4) *Examples of consumer authorization or request for solicitations.* (i) A consumer who obtains a mortgage from a mortgage lender authorizes or requests information about homeowner's insurance offered by the mortgage lender's insurance affiliate. Such authorization or request, whether given to the mortgage lender or to the insurance affiliate, would permit the insurance affiliate to use eligibility information about the consumer it obtains from the mortgage lender or any other affiliate to make solicitations to the consumer about homeowner's insurance.

(ii) A consumer completes an online application to apply for a credit card from a credit card issuer. The issuer's online application contains a blank check box that the consumer may check to authorize or request information from the credit card issuer's affiliates. The consumer checks the box. The consumer has authorized or requested solicitations from the card issuer's affiliates.

(iii) A consumer completes an online application to apply for a credit card from a credit card issuer. The issuer's online application contains a pre-selected check box indicating that the consumer authorizes or requests information from the issuer's affiliates. The consumer does not deselect the check box. The consumer has not authorized or requested solicitations from the card issuer's affiliates.

(iv) The terms and conditions of a credit card account agreement contain preprinted boilerplate language stating that by applying to open an account the consumer authorizes or requests to receive solicitations from the credit card issuer's affiliates. The consumer has not authorized or requested solicitations from the card issuer's affiliates.

(e) *Relation to affiliate-sharing notice and opt-out.* Nothing in this subpart limits the responsibility of a person to comply with the notice and opt-out provisions of section 603(d)(2)(A)(iii) of the Act where applicable.

§ 571.22 Scope and duration of opt-out.

(a) *Scope of opt-out*—(1) *In general.* Except as otherwise provided in this section, the consumer's election to opt out prohibits any affiliate covered by the opt-out notice from using eligibility information received from another affiliate as described in the notice to make solicitations to the consumer.

(2) *Continuing relationship*—(i) *In general.* If the consumer establishes a continuing relationship with you or your affiliate, an opt-out notice may apply to eligibility information obtained in connection with—

(A) A single continuing relationship or multiple continuing relationships that the consumer establishes with you or your affiliates, including continuing relationships established subsequent to delivery of the opt-out notice, so long as the notice adequately describes the continuing relationships covered by the opt-out; or

(B) Any other transaction between the consumer and you or your affiliates as described in the notice.

(ii) *Examples of continuing relationships.* A consumer has a continuing relationship with you or your affiliate if the consumer—

(A) Opens a deposit or investment account with you or your affiliate;

(B) Obtains a loan for which you or your affiliate owns the servicing rights;

(C) Purchases an insurance product from you or your affiliate;

(D) Holds an investment product through you or your affiliate, such as when you act or your affiliate acts as a custodian for securities or for assets in an individual retirement arrangement;

(E) Enters into an agreement or understanding with you or your affiliate whereby you or your affiliate undertakes to arrange or broker a home mortgage loan for the consumer;

(F) Enters into a lease of personal property with you or your affiliate; or

(G) Obtains financial, investment, or economic advisory services from you or your affiliate for a fee.

(3) *No continuing relationship*—(i) *In general.* If there is no continuing relationship between a consumer and you or your affiliate, and you or your affiliate obtain eligibility information about a consumer in connection with a transaction with the consumer, such as an isolated transaction or a credit application that is denied, an opt-out notice provided to the consumer only applies to eligibility information obtained in connection with that transaction.

(ii) *Examples of isolated transactions.* An isolated transaction occurs if—

(A) The consumer uses your or your affiliate's ATM to withdraw cash from an account at another financial institution; or

(B) You or your affiliate sells the consumer a cashier's check or money order, airline tickets, travel insurance, or traveler's checks in isolated transactions.

(4) *Menu of alternatives.* A consumer may be given the opportunity to choose from a menu of alternatives when electing to prohibit solicitations, such as by electing to prohibit solicitations from certain types of affiliates covered by the opt-out notice but not other types of affiliates covered by the notice, electing to prohibit solicitations based on certain types of eligibility information but not other types of eligibility information, or electing to prohibit solicitations by certain methods of delivery but not other methods of delivery. However, one of the alternatives must allow the consumer to prohibit all solicitations from all of the affiliates that are covered by the notice.

(5) *Special rule for a notice following termination of all continuing relationships*—(i) *In general.* A consumer must be given a new opt-out notice if, after all continuing relationships with you or your affiliate(s) are terminated, the consumer subsequently establishes another continuing relationship with you or your affiliate(s) and the consumer's eligibility information is to be used to make a solicitation. The new opt-out notice must apply, at a minimum, to eligibility information obtained in connection with the new continuing relationship. Consistent with paragraph (b) of this section, the consumer's decision

§ 571.23

not to opt out after receiving the new opt-out notice would not override a prior opt-out election by the consumer that applies to eligibility information obtained in connection with a terminated relationship, regardless of whether the new opt-out notice applies to eligibility information obtained in connection with the terminated relationship.

(ii) *Example.* A consumer has a checking account with a depository institution that is part of an affiliated group. The consumer closes the checking account. One year after closing the checking account, the consumer opens a savings account with the same depository institution. The consumer must be given a new notice and opportunity to opt out before the depository institution's affiliates may make solicitations to the consumer using eligibility information obtained by the depository institution in connection with the new savings account relationship, regardless of whether the consumer opted out in connection with the checking account.

(b) *Duration of opt-out.* The election of a consumer to opt out must be effective for a period of at least five years (the "opt-out period") beginning when the consumer's opt-out election is received and implemented, unless the consumer subsequently revokes the opt-out in writing or, if the consumer agrees, electronically. An opt-out period of more than five years may be established, including an opt-out period that does not expire unless revoked by the consumer.

(c) *Time of opt-out.* A consumer may opt out at any time.

§ 571.23 Contents of opt-out notice; consolidated and equivalent notices.

(a) *Contents of opt-out notice*—(1) *In general.* A notice must be clear, conspicuous, and concise, and must accurately disclose:

(i) The name of the affiliate(s) providing the notice. If the notice is provided jointly by multiple affiliates and each affiliate shares a common name, such as "ABC," then the notice may indicate that it is being provided by multiple companies with the ABC name or multiple companies in the ABC group or family of companies, for example, by stating that the notice is provided by "all of the ABC companies," "the ABC banking, credit card, insurance, and securities companies," or by listing the name of each affiliate providing the notice. But if the affiliates providing the joint notice do not all share a common name, then the notice must either separately identify each affiliate by name or identify each of the common names used by those affiliates, for example, by stating that the notice is provided by "all of the ABC and XYZ companies" or by "the ABC banking and credit card companies and the XYZ insurance companies";

(ii) A list of the affiliates or types of affiliates whose use of eligibility information is covered by the notice, which may include companies that become affiliates after the notice is provided to the consumer. If each affiliate covered by the notice shares a common name, such as "ABC," then the notice may indicate that it applies to multiple companies with the ABC name or multiple companies in the ABC group or family of companies, for example, by stating that the notice is provided by "all of the ABC companies," "the ABC banking, credit card, insurance, and securities companies," or by listing the name of each affiliate providing the notice. But if the affiliates covered by the notice do not all share a common name, then the notice must either separately identify each covered affiliate by name or identify each of the common names used by those affiliates, for example, by stating that the notice applies to "all of the ABC and XYZ companies" or to "the ABC banking and credit card companies and the XYZ insurance companies";

(iii) A general description of the types of eligibility information that may be used to make solicitations to the consumer;

(iv) That the consumer may elect to limit the use of eligibility information to make solicitations to the consumer;

(v) That the consumer's election will apply for the specified period of time stated in the notice and, if applicable, that the consumer will be allowed to renew the election once that period expires;

Office of Thrift Supervision, Treasury § 571.24

(vi) If the notice is provided to consumers who may have previously opted out, such as if a notice is provided to consumers annually, that the consumer who has chosen to limit solicitations does not need to act again until the consumer receives a renewal notice; and

(vii) A reasonable and simple method for the consumer to opt out.

(2) *Joint relationships.* (i) If two or more consumers jointly obtain a product or service, a single opt-out notice may be provided to the joint consumers. Any of the joint consumers may exercise the right to opt out.

(ii) The opt-out notice must explain how an opt-out direction by a joint consumer will be treated. An opt-out direction by a joint consumer may be treated as applying to all of the associated joint consumers, or each joint consumer may be permitted to opt-out separately. If each joint consumer is permitted to opt out separately, one of the joint consumers must be permitted to opt out on behalf of all of the joint consumers and the joint consumers must be permitted to exercise their separate rights to opt out in a single response.

(iii) It is impermissible to require *all* joint consumers to opt out before implementing *any* opt-out direction.

(3) *Alternative contents.* If the consumer is afforded a broader right to opt out of receiving marketing than is required by this subpart, the requirements of this section may be satisfied by providing the consumer with a clear, conspicuous, and concise notice that accurately discloses the consumer's opt-out rights.

(4) *Model notices.* Model notices are provided in appendix C of this part.

(b) *Coordinated and consolidated notices.* A notice required by this subpart may be coordinated and consolidated with any other notice or disclosure required to be issued under any other provision of law by the entity providing the notice, including but not limited to the notice described in section 603(d)(2)(A)(iii) of the Act and the Gramm-Leach-Bliley Act privacy notice.

(c) *Equivalent notices.* A notice or other disclosure that is equivalent to the notice required by this subpart, and that is provided to a consumer together with disclosures required by any other provision of law, satisfies the requirements of this section.

§ 571.24 **Reasonable opportunity to opt out.**

(a) *In general.* You must not use eligibility information about a consumer that you receive from an affiliate to make a solicitation to the consumer about your products or services, unless the consumer is provided a reasonable opportunity to opt out, as required by § 571.21(a)(1)(ii) of this part.

(b) *Examples of a reasonable opportunity to opt out.* The consumer is given a reasonable opportunity to opt out if:

(1) *By mail.* The opt-out notice is mailed to the consumer. The consumer is given 30 days from the date the notice is mailed to elect to opt out by any reasonable means.

(2) *By electronic means.* (i) The opt-out notice is provided electronically to the consumer, such as by posting the notice at an Internet Web site at which the consumer has obtained a product or service. The consumer acknowledges receipt of the electronic notice. The consumer is given 30 days after the date the consumer acknowledges receipt to elect to opt out by any reasonable means.

(ii) The opt-out notice is provided to the consumer by e-mail where the consumer has agreed to receive disclosures by e-mail from the person sending the notice. The consumer is given 30 days after the e-mail is sent to elect to opt out by any reasonable means.

(3) *At the time of an electronic transaction.* The opt-out notice is provided to the consumer at the time of an electronic transaction, such as a transaction conducted on an Internet Web site. The consumer is required to decide, as a necessary part of proceeding with the transaction, whether to opt out before completing the transaction. There is a simple process that the consumer may use to opt out at that time using the same mechanism through which the transaction is conducted.

(4) *At the time of an in-person transaction.* The opt-out notice is provided to the consumer in writing at the time

§ 571.25

of an in-person transaction. The consumer is required to decide, as a necessary part of proceeding with the transaction, whether to opt out before completing the transaction, and is not permitted to complete the transaction without making a choice. There is a simple process that the consumer may use during the course of the in-person transaction to opt out, such as completing a form that requires consumers to write a "yes" or "no" to indicate their opt-out preference or that requires the consumer to check one of two blank check boxes—one that allows consumers to indicate that they want to opt out and one that allows consumers to indicate that they do not want to opt out.

(5) *By including in a privacy notice.* The opt-out notice is included in a Gramm-Leach-Bliley Act privacy notice. The consumer is allowed to exercise the opt-out within a reasonable period of time and in the same manner as the opt-out under that privacy notice.

§ 571.25 Reasonable and simple methods of opting out.

(a) *In general.* You must not use eligibility information about a consumer that you receive from an affiliate to make a solicitation to the consumer about your products or services, unless the consumer is provided a reasonable and simple method to opt out, as required by § 571.21(a)(1)(ii) of this part.

(b) *Examples.* (1) *Reasonable and simple opt-out methods.* Reasonable and simple methods for exercising the opt-out right include—

(i) Designating a check-off box in a prominent position on the opt-out form;

(ii) Including a reply form and a self-addressed envelope together with the opt-out notice;

(iii) Providing an electronic means to opt out, such as a form that can be electronically mailed or processed at an Internet Web site, if the consumer agrees to the electronic delivery of information;

(iv) Providing a toll-free telephone number that consumers may call to opt out; or

(v) Allowing consumers to exercise all of their opt-out rights described in a consolidated opt-out notice that includes the privacy opt-out under the Gramm-Leach-Bliley Act (15 U.S.C. 6801 et seq.), the affiliate sharing opt-out under the Act, and the affiliate marketing opt-out under the Act, by a single method, such as by calling a single toll-free telephone number.

(2) *Opt-out methods that are not reasonable and simple.* Reasonable and simple methods for exercising an opt-out right *do not* include—

(i) Requiring the consumer to write his or her own letter;

(ii) Requiring the consumer to call or write to obtain a form for opting out, rather than including the form with the opt-out notice;

(iii) Requiring the consumer who receives the opt-out notice in electronic form only, such as through posting at an Internet Web site, to opt out solely by paper mail or by visiting a different Web site without providing a link to that site.

(c) *Specific opt-out means.* Each consumer may be required to opt out through a specific means, as long as that means is reasonable and simple for that consumer.

§ 571.26 Delivery of opt-out notices.

(a) *In general.* The opt-out notice must be provided so that each consumer can reasonably be expected to receive actual notice. For opt-out notices provided electronically, the notice may be provided in compliance with either the electronic disclosure provisions in this subpart or the provisions in section 101 of the Electronic Signatures in Global and National Commerce Act, 15 U.S.C. 7001 *et seq.*

(b) *Examples of reasonable expectation of actual notice.* A consumer may reasonably be expected to receive actual notice if the affiliate providing the notice:

(1) Hand-delivers a printed copy of the notice to the consumer;

(2) Mails a printed copy of the notice to the last known mailing address of the consumer;

(3) Provides a notice by e-mail to a consumer who has agreed to receive electronic disclosures by e-mail from the affiliate providing the notice; or

Office of Thrift Supervision, Treasury § 571.27

(4) Posts the notice on the Internet Web site at which the consumer obtained a product or service electronically and requires the consumer to acknowledge receipt of the notice.

(c) *Examples of no reasonable expectation of actual notice.* A consumer may not reasonably be expected to receive actual notice if the affiliate providing the notice:

(1) Only posts the notice on a sign in a branch or office or generally publishes the notice in a newspaper;

(2) Sends the notice via e-mail to a consumer who has not agreed to receive electronic disclosures by e-mail from the affiliate providing the notice; or

(3) Posts the notice on an Internet Web site without requiring the consumer to acknowledge receipt of the notice.

§ 571.27 Renewal of opt-out.

(a) *Renewal notice and opt-out requirement.* (1) *In general.* After the opt-out period expires, you may not make solicitations based on eligibility information you receive from an affiliate to a consumer who previously opted out, unless:

(i) The consumer has been given a renewal notice that complies with the requirements of this section and §§ 571.24 through 571.26 of this part, and a reasonable opportunity and a reasonable and simple method to renew the opt-out, and the consumer does not renew the opt-out; or

(ii) An exception in § 571.21(c) of this part applies.

(2) *Renewal period.* Each opt-out renewal must be effective for a period of at least five years as provided in § 571.22(b) of this part.

(3) *Affiliates who may provide the notice.* The notice required by this paragraph must be provided:

(i) By the affiliate that provided the previous opt-out notice, or its successor; or

(ii) As part of a joint renewal notice from two or more members of an affiliated group of companies, or their successors, that jointly provided the previous opt-out notice.

(b) *Contents of renewal notice.* The renewal notice must be clear, conspicuous, and concise, and must accurately disclose:

(1) The name of the affiliate(s) providing the notice. If the notice is provided jointly by multiple affiliates and each affiliate shares a common name, such as "ABC," then the notice may indicate that it is being provided by multiple companies with the ABC name or multiple companies in the ABC group or family of companies, for example, by stating that the notice is provided by "all of the ABC companies," "the ABC banking, credit card, insurance, and securities companies," or by listing the name of each affiliate providing the notice. But if the affiliates providing the joint notice do not all share a common name, then the notice must either separately identify each affiliate by name or identify each of the common names used by those affiliates, for example, by stating that the notice is provided by "all of the ABC and XYZ companies" or by "the ABC banking and credit card companies and the XYZ insurance companies";

(2) A list of the affiliates or types of affiliates whose use of eligibility information is covered by the notice, which may include companies that become affiliates after the notice is provided to the consumer. If each affiliate covered by the notice shares a common name, such as "ABC," then the notice may indicate that it applies to multiple companies with the ABC name or multiple companies in the ABC group or family of companies, for example, by stating that the notice is provided by "all of the ABC companies," "the ABC banking, credit card, insurance, and securities companies," or by listing the name of each affiliate providing the notice. But if the affiliates covered by the notice do not all share a common name, then the notice must either separately identify each covered affiliate by name or identify each of the common names used by those affiliates, for example, by stating that the notice applies to "all of the ABC and XYZ companies" or to "the ABC banking and credit card companies and the XYZ insurance companies";

(3) A general description of the types of eligibility information that may be

§ 571.28

used to make solicitations to the consumer;

(4) That the consumer previously elected to limit the use of certain information to make solicitations to the consumer;

(5) That the consumer's election has expired or is about to expire;

(6) That the consumer may elect to renew the consumer's previous election;

(7) If applicable, that the consumer's election to renew will apply for the specified period of time stated in the notice and that the consumer will be allowed to renew the election once that period expires; and

(8) A reasonable and simple method for the consumer to opt out.

(c) *Timing of the renewal notice.* (1) *In general.* A renewal notice may be provided to the consumer either—

(i) A reasonable period of time before the expiration of the opt-out period; or

(ii) Any time after the expiration of the opt-out period but before solicitations that would have been prohibited by the expired opt-out are made to the consumer.

(2) *Combination with annual privacy notice.* If you provide an annual privacy notice under the Gramm-Leach-Bliley Act, 15 U.S.C. 6801 *et seq.*, providing a renewal notice with the last annual privacy notice provided to the consumer before expiration of the opt-out period is a reasonable period of time before expiration of the opt-out in all cases.

(d) *No effect on opt-out period.* An opt-out period may not be shortened by sending a renewal notice to the consumer before expiration of the opt-out period, even if the consumer does not renew the opt-out.

§ 571.28 Effective date, compliance date, and prospective application.

(a) *Effective date.* This subpart is effective January 1, 2008.

(b) *Mandatory compliance date.* Compliance with this subpart is required not later than October 1, 2008.

(c) *Prospective application.* The provisions of this subpart shall not prohibit you from using eligibility information that you receive from an affiliate to make solicitations to a consumer if you receive such information prior to October 1, 2008. For purposes of this section, you are deemed to receive eligibility information when such information is placed into a common database and is accessible by you.

Subpart D—Medical Information

SOURCE: 70 FR 70689, Nov. 22, 2005, unless otherwise noted.

§ 571.30 Obtaining or using medical information in connection with a determination of eligibility for credit.

(a) *Scope.* This section applies to:

(1) Any of the following that participates as a creditor in a transaction—

(i) A savings association;

(ii) A subsidiary owned in whole or in part by a savings association;

(iii) A savings and loan holding company;

(iv) A subsidiary of a savings and loan holding company other than a bank or subsidiary of a bank; or

(v) A service corporation owned in whole or in part by a savings association; or

(2) Any other person that participates as a creditor in a transaction involving a person described in paragraph (a)(1) of this section.

(b) *General prohibition on obtaining or using medical information*—(1) *In general.* A creditor may not obtain or use medical information pertaining to a consumer in connection with any determination of the consumer's eligibility, or continued eligibility, for credit, except as provided in this section.

(2) *Definitions.* (i) *Credit* has the same meaning as in section 702 of the Equal Credit Opportunity Act, 15 U.S.C. 1691a.

(ii) *Creditor* has the same meaning as in section 702 of the Equal Credit Opportunity Act, 15 U.S.C. 1691a.

(iii) *Eligibility, or continued eligibility, for credit* means the consumer's qualification or fitness to receive, or continue to receive, credit, including the terms on which credit is offered. The term does not include:

(A) Any determination of the consumer's qualification or fitness for employment, insurance (other than a credit insurance product), or other non-credit products or services;

(B) Authorizing, processing, or documenting a payment or transaction on

Office of Thrift Supervision, Treasury §571.30

behalf of the consumer in a manner that does not involve a determination of the consumer's eligibility, or continued eligibility, for credit; or

(C) Maintaining or servicing the consumer's account in a manner that does not involve a determination of the consumer's eligibility, or continued eligibility, for credit.

(c) *Rule of construction for obtaining and using unsolicited medical information*—(1) *In general.* A creditor does not obtain medical information in violation of the prohibition if it receives medical information pertaining to a consumer in connection with any determination of the consumer's eligibility, or continued eligibility, for credit without specifically requesting medical information.

(2) *Use of unsolicited medical information.* A creditor that receives unsolicited medical information in the manner described in paragraph (c)(1) of this section may use that information in connection with any determination of the consumer's eligibility, or continued eligibility, for credit to the extent the creditor can rely on at least one of the exceptions in § 571.30(d) or (e).

(3) *Examples.* A creditor does not obtain medical information in violation of the prohibition if, for example:

(i) In response to a general question regarding a consumer's debts or expenses, the creditor receives information that the consumer owes a debt to a hospital;

(ii) In a conversation with the creditor's loan officer, the consumer informs the creditor that the consumer has a particular medical condition; or

(iii) In connection with a consumer's application for an extension of credit, the creditor requests a consumer report from a consumer reporting agency and receives medical information in the consumer report furnished by the agency even though the creditor did not specifically request medical information from the consumer reporting agency.

(d) *Financial information exception for obtaining and using medical information*—(1) *In general.* A creditor may obtain and use medical information pertaining to a consumer in connection with any determination of the consumer's eligibility, or continued eligibility, for credit so long as:

(i) The information is the type of information routinely used in making credit eligibility determinations, such as information relating to debts, expenses, income, benefits, assets, collateral, or the purpose of the loan, including the use of proceeds;

(ii) The creditor uses the medical information in a manner and to an extent that is no less favorable than it would use comparable information that is not medical information in a credit transaction; and

(iii) The creditor does not take the consumer's physical, mental, or behavioral health, condition or history, type of treatment, or prognosis into account as part of any such determination.

(2) *Examples.* (i) *Examples of the types of information routinely used in making credit eligibility determinations.* Paragraph (d)(1)(i) of this section permits a creditor, for example, to obtain and use information about:

(A) The dollar amount, repayment terms, repayment history, and similar information regarding medical debts to calculate, measure, or verify the repayment ability of the consumer, the use of proceeds, or the terms for granting credit;

(B) The value, condition, and lien status of a medical device that may serve as collateral to secure a loan;

(C) The dollar amount and continued eligibility for disability income, workers' compensation income, or other benefits related to health or a medical condition that is relied on as a source of repayment; or

(D) The identity of creditors to whom outstanding medical debts are owed in connection with an application for credit, including but not limited to, a transaction involving the consolidation of medical debts.

(ii) *Examples of uses of medical information consistent with the exception.* (A) A consumer includes on an application for credit information about two $20,000 debts. One debt is to a hospital; the other debt is to a retailer. The creditor contacts the hospital and the retailer to verify the amount and payment status of the debts. The creditor learns that both debts are more than 90 days past due. Any two debts of this size

§ 571.30

that are more than 90 days past due would disqualify the consumer under the creditor's established underwriting criteria. The creditor denies the application on the basis that the consumer has a poor repayment history on outstanding debts. The creditor has used medical information in a manner and to an extent no less favorable than it would use comparable non-medical information.

(B) A consumer indicates on an application for a $200,000 mortgage loan that she receives $15,000 in long-term disability income each year from her former employer and has no other income. Annual income of $15,000, regardless of source, would not be sufficient to support the requested amount of credit. The creditor denies the application on the basis that the projected debt-to-income ratio of the consumer does not meet the creditor's underwriting criteria. The creditor has used medical information in a manner and to an extent that is no less favorable than it would use comparable non-medical information.

(C) A consumer includes on an application for a $10,000 home equity loan that he has a $50,000 debt to a medical facility that specializes in treating a potentially terminal disease. The creditor contacts the medical facility to verify the debt and obtain the repayment history and current status of the loan. The creditor learns that the debt is current. The applicant meets the income and other requirements of the creditor's underwriting guidelines. The creditor grants the application. The creditor has used medical information in accordance with the exception.

(iii) *Examples of uses of medical information inconsistent with the exception.* (A) A consumer applies for $25,000 of credit and includes on the application information about a $50,000 debt to a hospital. The creditor contacts the hospital to verify the amount and payment status of the debt, and learns that the debt is current and that the consumer has no delinquencies in her repayment history. If the existing debt were instead owed to a retail department store, the creditor would approve the application and extend credit based on the amount and repayment history of the outstanding debt. The creditor, however, denies the application because the consumer is indebted to a hospital. The creditor has used medical information, here the identity of the medical creditor, in a manner and to an extent that is less favorable than it would use comparable non-medical information.

(B) A consumer meets with a loan officer of a creditor to apply for a mortgage loan. While filling out the loan application, the consumer informs the loan officer orally that she has a potentially terminal disease. The consumer meets the creditor's established requirements for the requested mortgage loan. The loan officer recommends to the credit committee that the consumer be denied credit because the consumer has that disease. The credit committee follows the loan officer's recommendation and denies the application because the consumer has a potentially terminal disease. The creditor has used medical information in a manner inconsistent with the exception by taking into account the consumer's physical, mental, or behavioral health, condition, or history, type of treatment, or prognosis as part of a determination of eligibility or continued eligibility for credit.

(C) A consumer who has an apparent medical condition, such as a consumer who uses a wheelchair or an oxygen tank, meets with a loan officer to apply for a home equity loan. The consumer meets the creditor's established requirements for the requested home equity loan and the creditor typically does not require consumers to obtain a debt cancellation contract, debt suspension agreement, or credit insurance product in connection with such loans. However, based on the consumer's apparent medical condition, the loan officer recommends to the credit committee that credit be extended to the consumer only if the consumer obtains a debt cancellation contract, debt suspension agreement, or credit insurance product from a nonaffiliated third party. The credit committee agrees with the loan officer's recommendation. The loan officer informs the consumer that the consumer must obtain a debt cancellation contract, debt suspension agreement, or credit insurance product from a nonaffiliated third

Office of Thrift Supervision, Treasury § 571.30

party to qualify for the loan. The consumer obtains one of these products and the creditor approves the loan. The creditor has used medical information in a manner inconsistent with the exception by taking into account the consumer's physical, mental, or behavioral health, condition, or history, type of treatment, or prognosis in setting conditions on the consumer's eligibility for credit.

(e) *Specific exceptions for obtaining and using medical information*—(1) *In general.* A creditor may obtain and use medical information pertaining to a consumer in connection with any determination of the consumer's eligibility, or continued eligibility, for credit—

(i) To determine whether the use of a power of attorney or legal representative that is triggered by a medical condition or event is necessary and appropriate or whether the consumer has the legal capacity to contract when a person seeks to exercise a power of attorney or act as legal representative for a consumer based on an asserted medical condition or event;

(ii) To comply with applicable requirements of local, state, or federal laws;

(iii) To determine, at the consumer's request, whether the consumer qualifies for a legally permissible special credit program or credit-related assistance program that is—

(A) Designed to meet the special needs of consumers with medical conditions; and

(B) Established and administered pursuant to a written plan that—

(*1*) Identifies the class of persons that the program is designed to benefit; and

(*2*) Sets forth the procedures and standards for extending credit or providing other credit-related assistance under the program;

(iv) To the extent necessary for purposes of fraud prevention or detection;

(v) In the case of credit for the purpose of financing medical products or services, to determine and verify the medical purpose of a loan and the use of proceeds;

(vi) Consistent with safe and sound practices, if the consumer or the consumer's legal representative specifically requests that the creditor use medical information in determining the consumer's eligibility, or continued eligibility, for credit, to accommodate the consumer's particular circumstances, and such request is documented by the creditor;

(vii) Consistent with safe and sound practices, to determine whether the provisions of a forbearance practice or program that is triggered by a medical condition or event apply to a consumer;

(viii) To determine the consumer's eligibility for, the triggering of, or the reactivation of a debt cancellation contract or debt suspension agreement if a medical condition or event is a triggering event for the provision of benefits under the contract or agreement; or

(ix) To determine the consumer's eligibility for, the triggering of, or the reactivation of a credit insurance product if a medical condition or event is a triggering event for the provision of benefits under the product.

(2) *Example of determining eligibility for a special credit program or credit assistance program.* A not-for-profit organization establishes a credit assistance program pursuant to a written plan that is designed to assist disabled veterans in purchasing homes by subsidizing the down payment for the home purchase mortgage loans of qualifying veterans. The organization works through mortgage lenders and requires mortgage lenders to obtain medical information about the disability of any consumer that seeks to qualify for the program, use that information to verify the consumer's eligibility for the program, and forward that information to the organization. A consumer who is a veteran applies to a creditor for a home purchase mortgage loan. The creditor informs the consumer about the credit assistance program for disabled veterans and the consumer seeks to qualify for the program. Assuming that the program complies with all applicable law, including applicable fair lending laws, the creditor may obtain and use medical information about the medical condition and disability, if any, of the consumer to determine whether the consumer qualifies for the credit assistance program.

(3) *Examples of verifying the medical purpose of the loan or the use of proceeds.*

451

(i) If a consumer applies for $10,000 of credit for the purpose of financing vision correction surgery, the creditor may verify with the surgeon that the procedure will be performed. If the surgeon reports that surgery will not be performed on the consumer, the creditor may use that medical information to deny the consumer's application for credit, because the loan would not be used for the stated purpose.

(ii) If a consumer applies for $10,000 of credit for the purpose of financing cosmetic surgery, the creditor may confirm the cost of the procedure with the surgeon. If the surgeon reports that the cost of the procedure is $5,000, the creditor may use that medical information to offer the consumer only $5,000 of credit.

(iii) A creditor has an established medical loan program for financing particular elective surgical procedures. The creditor receives a loan application from a consumer requesting $10,000 of credit under the established loan program for an elective surgical procedure. The consumer indicates on the application that the purpose of the loan is to finance an elective surgical procedure not eligible for funding under the guidelines of the established loan program. The creditor may deny the consumer's application because the purpose of the loan is not for a particular procedure funded by the established loan program.

(4) *Examples of obtaining and using medical information at the request of the consumer.* (i) If a consumer applies for a loan and specifically requests that the creditor consider the consumer's medical disability at the relevant time as an explanation for adverse payment history information in his credit report, the creditor may consider such medical information in evaluating the consumer's willingness and ability to repay the requested loan to accommodate the consumer's particular circumstances, consistent with safe and sound practices. The creditor may also decline to consider such medical information to accommodate the consumer, but may evaluate the consumer's application in accordance with its otherwise applicable underwriting criteria. The creditor may not deny the consumer's application or otherwise treat the consumer less favorably because the consumer specifically requested a medical accommodation, if the creditor would have extended the credit or treated the consumer more favorably under the creditor's otherwise applicable underwriting criteria.

(ii) If a consumer applies for a loan by telephone and explains that his income has been and will continue to be interrupted on account of a medical condition and that he expects to repay the loan by liquidating assets, the creditor may, but is not required to, evaluate the application using the sale of assets as the primary source of repayment, consistent with safe and sound practices, provided that the creditor documents the consumer's request by recording the oral conversation or making a notation of the request in the consumer's file.

(iii) If a consumer applies for a loan and the application form provides a space where the consumer may provide any other information or special circumstances, whether medical or non-medical, that the consumer would like the creditor to consider in evaluating the consumer's application, the creditor may use medical information provided by the consumer in that space on that application to accommodate the consumer's application for credit, consistent with safe and sound practices, or may disregard that information.

(iv) If a consumer specifically requests that the creditor use medical information in determining the consumer's eligibility, or continued eligibility, for credit and provides the creditor with medical information for that purpose, and the creditor determines that it needs additional information regarding the consumer's circumstances, the creditor may request, obtain, and use additional medical information about the consumer as necessary to verify the information provided by the consumer or to determine whether to make an accommodation for the consumer. The consumer may decline to provide additional information, withdraw the request for an accommodation, and have the application considered under the creditor's otherwise applicable underwriting criteria.

(v) If a consumer completes and signs a credit application that is not for medical purpose credit and the application contains boilerplate language that routinely requests medical information from the consumer or that indicates that by applying for credit the consumer authorizes or consents to the creditor obtaining and using medical information in connection with a determination of the consumer's eligibility, or continued eligibility, for credit, the consumer has not specifically requested that the creditor obtain and use medical information to accommodate the consumer's particular circumstances.

(5) *Example of a forbearance practice or program.* After an appropriate safety and soundness review, a creditor institutes a program that allows consumers who are or will be hospitalized to defer payments as needed for up to three months, without penalty, if the credit account has been open for more than one year and has not previously been in default, and the consumer provides confirming documentation at an appropriate time. A consumer is hospitalized and does not pay her bill for a particular month. This consumer has had a credit account with the creditor for more than one year and has not previously been in default. The creditor attempts to contact the consumer and speaks with the consumer's spouse, who is not the consumer's legal representative. The spouse informs the creditor that the consumer is hospitalized and is unable to pay the bill at that time. The creditor defers payments for up to three months, without penalty, for the hospitalized consumer and sends the consumer a letter confirming this practice and the date on which the next payment will be due. The creditor has obtained and used medical information to determine whether the provisions of a medically-triggered forbearance practice or program apply to a consumer.

§ 571.31 Limits on redisclosure of information.

(a) *Scope.* This section applies to savings associations and federal savings association operating subsidiaries.

(b) *Limits on redisclosure.* If a person described in paragraph (a) of this section receives medical information about a consumer from a consumer reporting agency or its affiliate, the person must not disclose that information to any other person, except as necessary to carry out the purpose for which the information was initially disclosed, or as otherwise permitted by statute, regulation, or order.

§ 571.32 Sharing medical information with affiliates.

(a) *Scope.* This section applies to savings associations and federal savings association operating subsidiaries.

(b) *In general.* The exclusions from the term "consumer report" in section 603(d)(2) of the Act that allow the sharing of information with affiliates do not apply if a person described in paragraph (a) of this section communicates to an affiliate:

(1) Medical information;

(2) An individualized list or description based on the payment transactions of the consumer for medical products or services; or

(3) An aggregate list of identified consumers based on payment transactions for medical products or services.

(c) *Exceptions.* A person described in paragraph (a) of this section may rely on the exclusions from the term "consumer report" in section 603(d)(2) of the Act to communicate the information in paragraph (b) of this section to an affiliate:

(1) In connection with the business of insurance or annuities (including the activities described in section 18B of the model Privacy of Consumer Financial and Health Information Regulation issued by the National Association of Insurance Commissioners, as in effect on January 1, 2003);

(2) For any purpose permitted without authorization under the regulations promulgated by the Department of Health and Human Services pursuant to the Health Insurance Portability and Accountability Act of 1996 (HIPAA);

(3) For any purpose referred to in section 1179 of HIPAA;

(4) For any purpose described in section 502(e) of the Gramm-Leach-Bliley Act;

(5) In connection with a determination of the consumer's eligibility, or

§ 571.40

continued eligibility, for credit consistent with § 571.30; or

(6) As otherwise permitted by order of the OTS.

Subpart E—Duties of Furnishers of Information

SOURCE: 74 FR 31520, July 1, 2009, unless otherwise noted.

§ 571.40 Scope.

Subpart E of this part applies to savings associations whose deposits are insured by the Federal Deposit Insurance Corporation or, in accordance with § 559.3(h)(1) of this chapter, Federal savings association operating subsidiaries that are not functionally regulated within the meaning of section 5(c)(5) of the Bank Holding Company Act of 1956, as amended (12 U.S.C. 1844(c)(5)).

§ 571.41 Definitions.

For purposes of this subpart and Appendix E of this part, the following definitions apply:

(a) *Accuracy* means that information that a furnisher provides to a consumer reporting agency about an account or other relationship with the consumer correctly:

(1) Reflects the terms of and liability for the account or other relationship;

(2) Reflects the consumer's performance and other conduct with respect to the account or other relationship; and

(3) Identifies the appropriate consumer.

(b) *Direct dispute* means a dispute submitted directly to a furnisher (including a furnisher that is a debt collector) by a consumer concerning the accuracy of any information contained in a consumer report and pertaining to an account or other relationship that the furnisher has or had with the consumer.

(c) *Furnisher* means an entity that furnishes information relating to consumers to one or more consumer reporting agencies for inclusion in a consumer report. An entity is not a furnisher when it:

(1) Provides information to a consumer reporting agency solely to obtain a consumer report in accordance with sections 604(a) and (f) of the Fair Credit Reporting Act;

(2) Is acting as a "consumer reporting agency" as defined in section 603(f) of the Fair Credit Reporting Act;

(3) Is a consumer to whom the furnished information pertains; or

(4) Is a neighbor, friend, or associate of the consumer, or another individual with whom the consumer is acquainted or who may have knowledge about the consumer, and who provides information about the consumer's character, general reputation, personal characteristics, or mode of living in response to a specific request from a consumer reporting agency.

(d) *Identity theft* has the same meaning as in 16 CFR 603.2(a).

(e) *Integrity* means that information that a furnisher provides to a consumer reporting agency about an account or other relationship with the consumer:

(1) Is substantiated by the furnisher's records at the time it is furnished;

(2) Is furnished in a form and manner that is designed to minimize the likelihood that the information may be incorrectly reflected in a consumer report; and

(3) Includes the information in the furnisher's possession about the account or other relationship that OTS has:

(i) Determined that the absence of which would likely be materially misleading in evaluating a consumer's creditworthiness, credit standing, credit capacity, character, general reputation, personal characteristics, or mode of living; and

(ii) Listed in section I.(b)(2)(iii) of Appendix E of this part.

§ 571.42 Reasonable policies and procedures concerning the accuracy and integrity of furnished information.

(a) *Policies and procedures.* Each furnisher must establish and implement reasonable written policies and procedures regarding the accuracy and integrity of the information relating to consumers that it furnishes to a consumer reporting agency. The policies and procedures must be appropriate to the nature, size, complexity, and scope of each furnisher's activities.

(b) *Guidelines.* Each furnisher must consider the guidelines in Appendix E of this part in developing its policies

Office of Thrift Supervision, Treasury

§ 571.43

and procedures required by this section, and incorporate those guidelines that are appropriate.

(c) *Reviewing and updating policies and procedures.* Each furnisher must review its policies and procedures required by this section periodically and update them as necessary to ensure their continued effectiveness.

§ 571.43 Direct disputes.

(a) *General rule.* Except as otherwise provided in this section, a furnisher must conduct a reasonable investigation of a direct dispute if it relates to:

(1) The consumer's liability for a credit account or other debt with the furnisher, such as direct disputes relating to whether there is or has been identity theft or fraud against the consumer, whether there is individual or joint liability on an account, or whether the consumer is an authorized user of a credit account;

(2) The terms of a credit account or other debt with the furnisher, such as direct disputes relating to the type of account, principal balance, scheduled payment amount on an account, or the amount of the credit limit on an open-end account;

(3) The consumer's performance or other conduct concerning an account or other relationship with the furnisher, such as direct disputes relating to the current payment status, high balance, date a payment was made, the amount of a payment made, or the date an account was opened or closed; or

(4) Any other information contained in a consumer report regarding an account or other relationship with the furnisher that bears on the consumer's creditworthiness, credit standing, credit capacity, character, general reputation, personal characteristics, or mode of living.

(b) *Exceptions.* The requirements of paragraph (a) of this section do not apply to a furnisher if:

(1) The direct dispute relates to:

(i) The consumer's identifying information (other than a direct dispute relating to a consumer's liability for a credit account or other debt with the furnisher, as provided in paragraph (a)(1) of this section) such as name(s), date of birth, Social Security number, telephone number(s), or address(es);

(ii) The identity of past or present employers;

(iii) Inquiries or requests for a consumer report;

(iv) Information derived from public records, such as judgments, bankruptcies, liens, and other legal matters (unless provided by a furnisher with an account or other relationship with the consumer);

(v) Information related to fraud alerts or active duty alerts; or

(vi) Information provided to a consumer reporting agency by another furnisher; or

(2) The furnisher has a reasonable belief that the direct dispute is submitted by, is prepared on behalf of the consumer by, or is submitted on a form supplied to the consumer by, a credit repair organization, as defined in 15 U.S.C. 1679a(3), or an entity that would be a credit repair organization, but for 15 U.S.C. 1679a(3)(B)(i).

(c) *Direct dispute address.* A furnisher is required to investigate a direct dispute only if a consumer submits a dispute notice to the furnisher at:

(1) The address of a furnisher provided by a furnisher and set forth on a consumer report relating to the consumer;

(2) An address clearly and conspicuously specified by the furnisher for submitting direct disputes that is provided to the consumer in writing or electronically (if the consumer has agreed to the electronic delivery of information from the furnisher); or

(3) Any business address of the furnisher if the furnisher has not so specified and provided an address for submitting direct disputes under paragraphs (c)(1) or (2) of this section.

(d) *Direct dispute notice contents.* A dispute notice must include:

(1) Sufficient information to identify the account or other relationship that is in dispute, such as an account number and the name, address, and telephone number of the consumer, if applicable;

(2) The specific information that the consumer is disputing and an explanation of the basis for the dispute; and

(3) All supporting documentation or other information reasonably required by the furnisher to substantiate the

basis of the dispute. This documentation may include, for example: A copy of the relevant portion of the consumer report that contains the allegedly inaccurate information; a police report; a fraud or identity theft affidavit; a court order; or account statements.

(e) *Duty of furnisher after receiving a direct dispute notice.* After receiving a dispute notice from a consumer pursuant to paragraphs (c) and (d) of this section, the furnisher must:

(1) Conduct a reasonable investigation with respect to the disputed information;

(2) Review all relevant information provided by the consumer with the dispute notice;

(3) Complete its investigation of the dispute and report the results of the investigation to the consumer before the expiration of the period under section 611(a)(1) of the Fair Credit Reporting Act (15 U.S.C. 1681i(a)(1)) within which a consumer reporting agency would be required to complete its action if the consumer had elected to dispute the information under that section; and

(4) If the investigation finds that the information reported was inaccurate, promptly notify each consumer reporting agency to which the furnisher provided inaccurate information of that determination and provide to the consumer reporting agency any correction to that information that is necessary to make the information provided by the furnisher accurate.

(f) *Frivolous or irrelevant disputes.* (1) A furnisher is not required to investigate a direct dispute if the furnisher has reasonably determined that the dispute is frivolous or irrelevant. A dispute qualifies as frivolous or irrelevant if:

(i) The consumer did not provide sufficient information to investigate the disputed information as required by paragraph (d) of this section;

(ii) The direct dispute is substantially the same as a dispute previously submitted by or on behalf of the consumer, either directly to the furnisher or through a consumer reporting agency, with respect to which the furnisher has already satisfied the applicable requirements of the Act or this section; provided, however, that a direct dispute is not substantially the same as a dispute previously submitted if the dispute includes information listed in paragraph (d) of this section that had not previously been provided to the furnisher; or

(iii) The furnisher is not required to investigate the direct dispute because one or more of the exceptions listed in paragraph (b) of this section applies.

(2) *Notice of determination.* Upon making a determination that a dispute is frivolous or irrelevant, the furnisher must notify the consumer of the determination not later than five business days after making the determination, by mail or, if authorized by the consumer for that purpose, by any other means available to the furnisher.

(3) *Contents of notice of determination that a dispute is frivolous or irrelevant.* A notice of determination that a dispute is frivolous or irrelevant must include the reasons for such determination and identify any information required to investigate the disputed information, which notice may consist of a standardized form describing the general nature of such information.

Subparts F–H [Reserved]

Subpart I—Duties of Users of Consumer Reports Regarding Address Discrepancies and Records Disposal

§§ 571.80–570.81 [Reserved]

§ 571.82 Duties of users regarding address discrepancies.

(a) *Scope.* This section applies to a user of consumer reports (user) that receives a notice of address discrepancy from a consumer reporting agency described in 15 U.S.C. 1681a(p), and that is a savings association whose deposits are insured by the Federal Deposit Insurance Corporation or, in accordance with § 559.3(h)(1) of this chapter, a federal savings association operating subsidiary that is not functionally regulated within the meaning of section 5(c)(5) of the Bank Holding Company Act of 1956, as amended (12 U.S.C. 1844(c)(5)).

(b) *Definition.* For purposes of this section, a *notice of address discrepancy* means a notice sent to a user by a consumer reporting agency described in 15

Office of Thrift Supervision, Treasury § 571.83

U.S.C. 1681a(p) pursuant to 15 U.S.C. 1681c(h)(1), that informs the user of a substantial difference between the address for the consumer that the user provided to request the consumer report and the address(es) in the agency's file for the consumer.

(c) *Reasonable belief*—(1) *Requirement to form a reasonable belief.* A user must develop and implement reasonable policies and procedures designed to enable the user to form a reasonable belief that a consumer report relates to the consumer about whom it has requested the report, when the user receives a notice of address discrepancy.

(2) *Examples of reasonable policies and procedures.* (i) Comparing the information in the consumer report provided by the consumer reporting agency with information the user:

(A) Obtains and uses to verify the consumer's identity in accordance with the requirements of the Customer Identification Program (CIP) rules implementing 31 U.S.C. 5318(l) (31 CFR 103.121);

(B) Maintains in its own records, such as applications, change of address notifications, other customer account records, or retained CIP documentation; or

(C) Obtains from third-party sources; or

(ii) Verifying the information in the consumer report provided by the consumer reporting agency with the consumer.

(d) *Consumer's address*—(1) *Requirement to furnish consumer's address to a consumer reporting agency.* A user must develop and implement reasonable policies and procedures for furnishing an address for the consumer that the user has reasonably confirmed is accurate to the consumer reporting agency described in 15 U.S.C. 1681a(p) from whom it received the notice of address discrepancy when the user:

(i) Can form a reasonable belief that the consumer report relates to the consumer about whom the user requested the report;

(ii) Establishes a continuing relationship with the consumer; and

(iii) Regularly and in the ordinary course of business furnishes information to the consumer reporting agency from which the notice of address discrepancy relating to the consumer was obtained.

(2) *Examples of confirmation methods.* The user may reasonably confirm an address is accurate by:

(i) Verifying the address with the consumer about whom it has requested the report;

(ii) Reviewing its own records to verify the address of the consumer;

(iii) Verifying the address through third-party sources; or

(iv) Using other reasonable means.

(3) *Timing.* The policies and procedures developed in accordance with paragraph (d)(1) of this section must provide that the user will furnish the consumer's address that the user has reasonably confirmed is accurate to the consumer reporting agency described in 15 U.S.C. 1681a(p) as part of the information it regularly furnishes for the reporting period in which it establishes a relationship with the consumer.

[72 FR 63764, Nov. 9, 2007, as amended at 74 FR 22643, May 14, 2009]

§ 571.83 Disposal of consumer information.

(a) *Scope.* This section applies to savings associations whose deposits are insured by the Federal Deposit Insurance Corporation and federal savings association operating subsidiaries in accordance with § 559.3(h)(1) of this chapter (defined as "you").

(b) *In general.* You must properly dispose of any consumer information that you maintain or otherwise possess in accordance with the Interagency Guidelines Establishing Information Security Standards, as set forth in appendix B to part 570, to the extent that you are covered by the scope of the Guidelines.

(c) *Rule of construction.* Nothing in this section shall be construed to:

(1) Require you to maintain or destroy any record pertaining to a consumer that is not imposed under any other law; or

(2) Alter or affect any requirement imposed under any other provision of law to maintain or destroy such a record.

[69 FR 77621, Dec. 28, 2004, as amended at 72 FR 63764, Nov. 9, 2007]

Subpart J—Identity Theft Red Flags

SOURCE: 72 FR 63765, Nov. 9, 2007, unless otherwise noted.

§ 571.90 Duties regarding the detection, prevention, and mitigation of identity theft.

(a) *Scope.* This section applies to a financial institution or creditor that is a savings association whose deposits are insured by the Federal Deposit Insurance Corporation or, in accordance with § 559.3(h)(1) of this chapter, a federal savings association operating subsidiary that is not functionally regulated within the meaning of section 5(c)(5) of the Bank Holding Company Act of 1956, as amended (12 U.S.C. 1844(c)(5)).

(b) *Definitions.* For purposes of this section and appendix J, the following definitions apply:

(1) *Account* means a continuing relationship established by a person with a financial institution or creditor to obtain a product or service for personal, family, household or business purposes. Account includes:

(i) An extension of credit, such as the purchase of property or services involving a deferred payment; and

(ii) A deposit account.

(2) The term *board of directors* includes:

(i) In the case of a branch or agency of a foreign bank, the managing official in charge of the branch or agency; and

(ii) In the case of any other creditor that does not have a board of directors, a designated employee at the level of senior management.

(3) *Covered account* means:

(i) An account that a financial institution or creditor offers or maintains, primarily for personal, family, or household purposes, that involves or is designed to permit multiple payments or transactions, such as a credit card account, mortgage loan, automobile loan, margin account, cell phone account, utility account, checking account, or savings account; and

(ii) Any other account that the financial institution or creditor offers or maintains for which there is a reasonably foreseeable risk to customers or to the safety and soundness of the financial institution or creditor from identity theft, including financial, operational, compliance, reputation, or litigation risks.

(4) *Credit* has the same meaning as in 15 U.S.C. 1681a(r)(5).

(5) *Creditor* has the same meaning as in 15 U.S.C. 1681a(r)(5), and includes lenders such as banks, finance companies, automobile dealers, mortgage brokers, utility companies, and telecommunications companies.

(6) *Customer* means a person that has a covered account with a financial institution or creditor.

(7) *Financial institution* has the same meaning as in 15 U.S.C. 1681a(t).

(8) *Identity theft* has the same meaning as in 16 CFR 603.2(a).

(9) *Red Flag* means a pattern, practice, or specific activity that indicates the possible existence of identity theft.

(10) *Service provider* means a person that provides a service directly to the financial institution or creditor.

(c) *Periodic Identification of Covered Accounts.* Each financial institution or creditor must periodically determine whether it offers or maintains covered accounts. As a part of this determination, a financial institution or creditor must conduct a risk assessment to determine whether it offers or maintains covered accounts described in paragraph (b)(3)(ii) of this section, taking into consideration:

(1) The methods it provides to open its accounts;

(2) The methods it provides to access its accounts; and

(3) Its previous experiences with identity theft.

(d) *Establishment of an Identity Theft Prevention Program*—(1) *Program requirement.* Each financial institution or creditor that offers or maintains one or more covered accounts must develop and implement a written Identity Theft Prevention Program (Program) that is designed to detect, prevent, and mitigate identity theft in connection with the opening of a covered account or any existing covered account. The Program must be appropriate to the size and complexity of the financial institution or creditor and the nature and scope of its activities.

Office of Thrift Supervision, Treasury § 571.91

(2) *Elements of the Program.* The Program must include reasonable policies and procedures to:

(i) Identify relevant Red Flags for the covered accounts that the financial institution or creditor offers or maintains, and incorporate those Red Flags into its Program;

(ii) Detect Red Flags that have been incorporated into the Program of the financial institution or creditor;

(iii) Respond appropriately to any Red Flags that are detected pursuant to paragraph (d)(2)(ii) of this section to prevent and mitigate identity theft; and

(iv) Ensure the Program (including the Red Flags determined to be relevant) is updated periodically, to reflect changes in risks to customers and to the safety and soundness of the financial institution or creditor from identity theft.

(e) *Administration of the Program.* Each financial institution or creditor that is required to implement a Program must provide for the continued administration of the Program and must:

(1) Obtain approval of the initial written Program from either its board of directors or an appropriate committee of the board of directors;

(2) Involve the board of directors, an appropriate committee thereof, or a designated employee at the level of senior management in the oversight, development, implementation and administration of the Program;

(3) Train staff, as necessary, to effectively implement the Program; and

(4) Exercise appropriate and effective oversight of service provider arrangements.

(f) *Guidelines.* Each financial institution or creditor that is required to implement a Program must consider the guidelines in appendix J of this part and include in its Program those guidelines that are appropriate.

§ 571.91 Duties of card issuers regarding changes of address.

(a) *Scope.* This section applies to an issuer of a debit or credit card (card issuer) that is a savings association whose deposits are insured by the Federal Deposit Insurance Corporation or, in accordance with § 559.3(h)(1) of this chapter, a federal savings association operating subsidiary that is not functionally regulated within the meaning of section 5(c)(5) of the Bank Holding Company Act of 1956, as amended (12 U.S.C. 1844(c)(5)).

(b) *Definitions.* For purposes of this section:

(1) *Cardholder* means a consumer who has been issued a credit or debit card.

(2) *Clear and conspicuous* means reasonably understandable and designed to call attention to the nature and significance of the information presented.

(c) *Address validation requirements.* A card issuer must establish and implement reasonable policies and procedures to assess the validity of a change of address if it receives notification of a change of address for a consumer's debit or credit card account and, within a short period of time afterwards (during at least the first 30 days after it receives such notification), the card issuer receives a request for an additional or replacement card for the same account. Under these circumstances, the card issuer may not issue an additional or replacement card, until, in accordance with its reasonable policies and procedures and for the purpose of assessing the validity of the change of address, the card issuer:

(1)(i) Notifies the cardholder of the request:

(A) At the cardholder's former address; or

(B) By any other means of communication that the card issuer and the cardholder have previously agreed to use; and

(ii) Provides to the cardholder a reasonable means of promptly reporting incorrect address changes; or

(2) Otherwise assesses the validity of the change of address in accordance with the policies and procedures the card issuer has established pursuant to § 571.90 of this part.

(d) *Alternative timing of address validation.* A card issuer may satisfy the requirements of paragraph (c) of this section if it validates an address pursuant to the methods in paragraph (c)(1) or (c)(2) of this section when it receives an address change notification, before it receives a request for an additional or replacement card.

Pt. 571, App. C

(e) *Form of notice.* Any written or electronic notice that the card issuer provides under this paragraph must be clear and conspicuous and provided separately from its regular correspondence with the cardholder.

APPENDIXES A–B TO PART 571 [RESERVED]

APPENDIX C TO PART 571—MODEL FORMS FOR OPT-OUT NOTICES

a. Although use of the model forms is not required, use of the model forms in this Appendix (as applicable) complies with the requirement in section 624 of the Act for clear, conspicuous, and concise notices.

b. Certain changes may be made to the language or format of the model forms without losing the protection from liability afforded by use of the model forms. These changes may not be so extensive as to affect the substance, clarity, or meaningful sequence of the language in the model forms. Persons making such extensive revisions will lose the safe harbor that this Appendix provides. Acceptable changes include, for example:

1. Rearranging the order of the references to "your income," "your account history," and "your credit score."

2. Substituting other types of information for "income," "account history," or "credit score" for accuracy, such as "payment history," "credit history," "payoff status," or "claims history."

3. Substituting a clearer and more accurate description of the affiliates providing or covered by the notice for phrases such as "the [ABC] group of companies," including without limitation a statement that the entity providing the notice recently purchased the consumer's account.

4. Substituting other types of affiliates covered by the notice for "credit card," "insurance," or "securities" affiliates.

5. Omitting items that are not accurate or applicable. For example, if a person does not limit the duration of the opt-out period, the notice may omit information about the renewal notice.

6. Adding a statement informing consumers how much time they have to opt out before shared eligibility information may be used to make solicitations to them.

7. Adding a statement that the consumer may exercise the right to opt out at any time.

8. Adding the following statement, if accurate: "If you previously opted out, you do not need to do so again."

9. Providing a place on the form for the consumer to fill in identifying information, such as his or her name and address.

10. Adding disclosures regarding the treatment of opt-outs by joint consumers to comply with §571.23(a)(2) of this part.

C–1 Model Form for Initial Opt-out Notice (Single-Affiliate Notice)
C–2 Model Form for Initial Opt-out Notice (Joint Notice)
C–3 Model Form for Renewal Notice (Single-Affiliate Notice)
C–4 Model Form for Renewal Notice (Joint Notice)
C–5 Model Form for Voluntary "No Marketing" Notice
C–6 Model Form for Voluntary "No Marketing" Notice

C–1—Model Form for Initial Opt-out Notice (Single-Affiliate Notice)—[Your Choice To Limit Marketing]/[Marketing Opt-out]

• [Name of Affiliate] is providing this notice.

• [Optional: Federal law gives you the right to limit some but not all marketing from our affiliates. Federal law also requires us to give you this notice to tell you about your choice to limit marketing from our affiliates.]

• You may limit our affiliates in the [ABC] group of companies, such as our [credit card, insurance, and securities] affiliates, from marketing their products or services to you based on your personal information that we collect and share with them. This information includes your [income], your [account history with us], and your [credit score].

• Your choice to limit marketing offers from our affiliates will apply [until you tell us to change your choice]/[for x years from when you tell us your choice]/[for at least 5 years from when you tell us your choice]. [Include if the opt-out period expires.] Once that period expires, you will receive a renewal notice that will allow you to continue to limit marketing offers from our affiliates for [another x years]/[at least another 5 years].

• [Include, if applicable, in a subsequent notice, including an annual notice, for consumers who may have previously opted out.] If you have already made a choice to limit marketing offers from our affiliates, you do not need to act again until you receive the renewal notice.

To limit marketing offers, contact us [include all that apply]:

• By telephone: 1–877–###–####
• On the Web: *www.---.com*
• By mail: Check the box and complete the form below, and send the form to:

[Company name]
[Company address]

__Do not allow your affiliates to use my personal information to market to me.

Office of Thrift Supervision, Treasury Pt. 571, App. C

C-2—Model Form for Initial Opt-out Notice (Joint Notice)—[Your Choice To Limit Marketing]/[Marketing Opt-out]

• The [ABC group of companies] is providing this notice.

• [Optional: Federal law gives you the right to limit some but not all marketing from the [ABC] companies. Federal law also requires us to give you this notice to tell you about your choice to limit marketing from the [ABC] companies.]

• You may limit the [ABC] companies, such as the [ABC credit card, insurance, and securities] affiliates, from marketing their products or services to you based on your personal information that they receive from other [ABC] companies. This information includes your [income], your [account history], and your [credit score].

• Your choice to limit marketing offers from the [ABC] companies will apply [until you tell us to change your choice]/[for x years from when you tell us your choice]/[for at least 5 years from when you tell us your choice]. [Include if the opt-out period expires.] Once that period expires, you will receive a renewal notice that will allow you to continue to limit marketing offers from the [ABC] companies for [another x years]/[at least another 5 years].

• [Include, if applicable, in a subsequent notice, including an annual notice, for consumers who may have previously opted out.] If you have already made a choice to limit marketing offers from the [ABC] companies, you do not need to act again until you receive the renewal notice.

To limit marketing offers, contact us [include all that apply]:

• By telephone: 1–877–###–####
• On the Web: *www.---.com*
• By mail: Check the box and complete the form below, and send the form to:

[Company name]
[Company address]

__Do not allow any company [in the ABC group of companies] to use my personal information to market to me.

C-3—Model Form for Renewal Notice (Single-Affiliate Notice)—[Renewing Your Choice To Limit Marketing]/[Renewing Your Marketing Opt-out]

• [Name of Affiliate] is providing this notice.

• [Optional: Federal law gives you the right to limit some but not all marketing from our affiliates. Federal law also requires us to give you this notice to tell you about your choice to limit marketing from our affiliates.]

• You previously chose to limit our affiliates in the [ABC] group of companies, such as our [credit card, insurance, and securities] affiliates, from marketing their products or services to you based on your personal information that we share with them. This information includes your [income], your [account history with us], and your [credit score].

• Your choice has expired or is about to expire.

To renew your choice to limit marketing for [x] more years, contact us [include all that apply]:

• By telephone: 1–877–###–####
• On the Web: *www.---.com*
• By mail: Check the box and complete the form below, and send the form to:

[Company name]
[Company address]

__Renew my choice to limit marketing for [x] more years.

C-4—Model Form for Renewal Notice (Joint Notice)—[Renewing Your Choice To Limit Marketing]/[Renewing Your Marketing Opt-out]

• The [ABC group of companies] is providing this notice.

• [Optional: Federal law gives you the right to limit some but not all marketing from the [ABC] companies. Federal law also requires us to give you this notice to tell you about your choice to limit marketing from the [ABC] companies.]

• You previously chose to limit the [ABC] companies, such as the [ABC credit card, insurance, and securities] affiliates, from marketing their products or services to you based on your personal information that they receive from other ABC companies. This information includes your [income], your [account history], and your [credit score].

• Your choice has expired or is about to expire.

To renew your choice to limit marketing for [x] more years, contact us [include all that apply]:

• By telephone: 1–877–###–####
• On the Web: *www.---.com*
• By mail: Check the box and complete the form below, and send the form to:

[Company name]
[Company address]

__Renew my choice to limit marketing for [x] more years.

C-5—Model Form for Voluntary "No Marketing" Notice Your Choice To Stop Marketing

• [Name of Affiliate] is providing this notice.

• You may choose to stop all marketing from us and our affiliates.

• [Your choice to stop marketing from us and our affiliates will apply until you tell us to change your choice.]

To stop all marketing, contact us [include all that apply]:

• By telephone: 1–877–###–####
• On the Web: www.–.com

461

- By mail: Check the box and complete the form below, and send the form to:
[Company name]
[Company address]
__Do not market to me.

[72 FR 62980, Nov. 7, 2007, as amended at 74 FR 22643, May 14, 2009]

APPENDIX D TO PART 571 [RESERVED]

APPENDIX E TO PART 571—INTERAGENCY GUIDELINES CONCERNING THE ACCURACY AND INTEGRITY OF INFORMATION FURNISHED TO CONSUMER REPORTING AGENCIES

OTS encourages voluntary furnishing of information to consumer reporting agencies. Section 571.42 of this part requires each furnisher to establish and implement reasonable written policies and procedures concerning the accuracy and integrity of the information it furnishes to consumer reporting agencies. Under §571.42(b), a furnisher must consider the guidelines set forth below in developing its policies and procedures. In establishing these policies and procedures, a furnisher may include any of its existing policies and procedures that are relevant and appropriate. Section 571.42(c) requires each furnisher to review its policies and procedures periodically and update them as necessary to ensure their continued effectiveness.

I. NATURE, SCOPE, AND OBJECTIVES OF POLICIES AND PROCEDURES

(a) *Nature and Scope.* Section 571.42(a) of this part requires that a furnisher's policies and procedures be appropriate to the nature, size, complexity, and scope of the furnisher's activities. In developing its policies and procedures, a furnisher should consider, for example:

(1) The types of business activities in which the furnisher engages;

(2) The nature and frequency of the information the furnisher provides to consumer reporting agencies; and

(3) The technology used by the furnisher to furnish information to consumer reporting agencies.

(b) *Objectives.* A furnisher's policies and procedures should be reasonably designed to promote the following objectives:

(1) To furnish information about accounts or other relationships with a consumer that is accurate, such that the furnished information:

(i) Identifies the appropriate consumer;

(ii) Reflects the terms of and liability for those accounts or other relationships; and

(iii) Reflects the consumer's performance and other conduct with respect to the account or other relationship;

(2) To furnish information about accounts or other relationships with a consumer that has integrity, such that the furnished information:

(i) Is substantiated by the furnisher's records at the time it is furnished;

(ii) Is furnished in a form and manner that is designed to minimize the likelihood that the information may be incorrectly reflected in a consumer report; thus, the furnished information should:

(A) Include appropriate identifying information about the consumer to whom it pertains; and

(B) Be furnished in a standardized and clearly understandable form and manner and with a date specifying the time period to which the information pertains; and

(iii) Includes the credit limit, if applicable and in the furnisher's possession;

(3) To conduct reasonable investigations of consumer disputes and take appropriate actions based on the outcome of such investigations; and

(4) To update the information it furnishes as necessary to reflect the current status of the consumer's account or other relationship, including, for example:

(i) Any transfer of an account (*e.g.*, by sale or assignment for collection) to a third party; and

(ii) Any cure of the consumer's failure to abide by the terms of the account or other relationship.

II. ESTABLISHING AND IMPLEMENTING POLICIES AND PROCEDURES

In establishing and implementing its policies and procedures, a furnisher should:

(a) Identify practices or activities of the furnisher that can compromise the accuracy or integrity of information furnished to consumer reporting agencies, such as by:

(1) Reviewing its existing practices and activities, including the technological means and other methods it uses to furnish information to consumer reporting agencies and the frequency and timing of its furnishing of information;

(2) Reviewing its historical records relating to accuracy or integrity or to disputes; reviewing other information relating to the accuracy or integrity of information provided by the furnisher to consumer reporting agencies; and considering the types of errors, omissions, or other problems that may have affected the accuracy or integrity of information it has furnished about consumers to consumer reporting agencies;

(3) Considering any feedback received from consumer reporting agencies, consumers, or other appropriate parties;

(4) Obtaining feedback from the furnisher's staff; and

Office of Thrift Supervision, Treasury   **Pt. 571, App. J**

(5) Considering the potential impact of the furnisher's policies and procedures on consumers.

(b) Evaluate the effectiveness of existing policies and procedures of the furnisher regarding the accuracy and integrity of information furnished to consumer reporting agencies; consider whether new, additional, or different policies and procedures are necessary; and consider whether implementation of existing policies and procedures should be modified to enhance the accuracy and integrity of information about consumers furnished to consumer reporting agencies.

(c) Evaluate the effectiveness of specific methods (including technological means) the furnisher uses to provide information to consumer reporting agencies; how those methods may affect the accuracy and integrity of the information it provides to consumer reporting agencies; and whether new, additional, or different methods (including technological means) should be used to provide information to consumer reporting agencies to enhance the accuracy and integrity of that information.

III. SPECIFIC COMPONENTS OF POLICIES AND PROCEDURES

In developing its policies and procedures, a furnisher should address the following, as appropriate:

(a) Establishing and implementing a system for furnishing information about consumers to consumer reporting agencies that is appropriate to the nature, size, complexity, and scope of the furnisher's business operations.

(b) Using standard data reporting formats and standard procedures for compiling and furnishing data, where feasible, such as the electronic transmission of information about consumers to consumer reporting agencies.

(c) Maintaining records for a reasonable period of time, not less than any applicable recordkeeping requirement, in order to substantiate the accuracy of any information about consumers it furnishes that is subject to a direct dispute.

(d) Establishing and implementing appropriate internal controls regarding the accuracy and integrity of information about consumers furnished to consumer reporting agencies, such as by implementing standard procedures and verifying random samples of information provided to consumer reporting agencies.

(e) Training staff that participates in activities related to the furnishing of information about consumers to consumer reporting agencies to implement the policies and procedures.

(f) Providing for appropriate and effective oversight of relevant service providers whose activities may affect the accuracy or integrity of information about consumers furnished to consumer reporting agencies to ensure compliance with the policies and procedures.

(g) Furnishing information about consumers to consumer reporting agencies following mergers, portfolio acquisitions or sales, or other acquisitions or transfers of accounts or other obligations in a manner that prevents re-aging of information, duplicative reporting, or other problems that may similarly affect the accuracy or integrity of the information furnished.

(h) Deleting, updating, and correcting information in the furnisher's records, as appropriate, to avoid furnishing inaccurate information.

(i) Conducting reasonable investigations of disputes.

(j) Designing technological and other means of communication with consumer reporting agencies to prevent duplicative reporting of accounts, erroneous association of information with the wrong consumer(s), and other occurrences that may compromise the accuracy or integrity of information provided to consumer reporting agencies.

(k) Providing consumer reporting agencies with sufficient identifying information in the furnisher's possession about each consumer about whom information is furnished to enable the consumer reporting agency properly to identify the consumer.

(l) Conducting a periodic evaluation of its own practices, consumer reporting agency practices of which the furnisher is aware, investigations of disputed information, corrections of inaccurate information, means of communication, and other factors that may affect the accuracy or integrity of information furnished to consumer reporting agencies.

(m) Complying with applicable requirements under the Fair Credit Reporting Act and its implementing regulations.

[74 FR 31521, July 1, 2009]

APPENDICES F–I TO PART 571
[RESERVED]

APPENDIX J TO PART 571—INTERAGENCY GUIDELINES ON IDENTITY THEFT DETECTION, PREVENTION, AND MITIGATION

Section 571.90 of this part requires each financial institution and creditor that offers or maintains one or more covered accounts, as defined in §571.90(b)(3) of this part, to develop and provide for the continued administration of a written Program to detect, prevent, and mitigate identity theft in connection with the opening of a covered account or any existing covered account. These guidelines are intended to assist financial institutions and creditors in the formulation and maintenance of a Program that satisfies the requirements of § 571.90 of this part.

I. The Program

In designing its Program, a financial institution or creditor may incorporate, as appropriate, its existing policies, procedures, and other arrangements that control reasonably foreseeable risks to customers or to the safety and soundness of the financial institution or creditor from identity theft.

II. Identifying Relevant Red Flags

(a) *Risk Factors.* A financial institution or creditor should consider the following factors in identifying relevant Red Flags for covered accounts, as appropriate:

(1) The types of covered accounts it offers or maintains;

(2) The methods it provides to open its covered accounts;

(3) The methods it provides to access its covered accounts; and

(4) Its previous experiences with identity theft.

(b) *Sources of Red Flags.* Financial institutions and creditors should incorporate relevant Red Flags from sources such as:

(1) Incidents of identity theft that the financial institution or creditor has experienced;

(2) Methods of identity theft that the financial institution or creditor has identified that reflect changes in identity theft risks; and

(3) Applicable supervisory guidance.

(c) *Categories of Red Flags.* The Program should include relevant Red Flags from the following categories, as appropriate. Examples of Red Flags from each of these categories are appended as Supplement A to this Appendix J.

(1) Alerts, notifications, or other warnings received from consumer reporting agencies or service providers, such as fraud detection services;

(2) The presentation of suspicious documents;

(3) The presentation of suspicious personal identifying information, such as a suspicious address change;

(4) The unusual use of, or other suspicious activity related to, a covered account; and

(5) Notice from customers, victims of identity theft, law enforcement authorities, or other persons regarding possible identity theft in connection with covered accounts held by the financial institution or creditor.

III. Detecting Red Flags

The Program's policies and procedures should address the detection of Red Flags in connection with the opening of covered accounts and existing covered accounts, such as by:

(a) Obtaining identifying information about, and verifying the identity of, a person opening a covered account, for example, using the policies and procedures regarding identification and verification set forth in the Customer Identification Program rules implementing 31 U.S.C. 5318(l) (31 CFR 103.121); and

(b) Authenticating customers, monitoring transactions, and verifying the validity of change of address requests, in the case of existing covered accounts.

IV. Preventing and Mitigating Identity Theft

The Program's policies and procedures should provide for appropriate responses to the Red Flags the financial institution or creditor has detected that are commensurate with the degree of risk posed. In determining an appropriate response, a financial institution or creditor should consider aggravating factors that may heighten the risk of identity theft, such as a data security incident that results in unauthorized access to a customer's account records held by the financial institution, creditor, or third party, or notice that a customer has provided information related to a covered account held by the financial institution or creditor to someone fraudulently claiming to represent the financial institution or creditor or to a fraudulent website. Appropriate responses may include the following:

(a) Monitoring a covered account for evidence of identity theft;

(b) Contacting the customer;

(c) Changing any passwords, security codes, or other security devices that permit access to a covered account;

(d) Reopening a covered account with a new account number;

(e) Not opening a new covered account;

(f) Closing an existing covered account;

(g) Not attempting to collect on a covered account or not selling a covered account to a debt collector;

(h) Notifying law enforcement; or

(i) Determining that no response is warranted under the particular circumstances.

V. Updating the Program

Financial institutions and creditors should update the Program (including the Red Flags determined to be relevant) periodically, to reflect changes in risks to customers or to the safety and soundness of the financial institution or creditor from identity theft, based on factors such as:

(a) The experiences of the financial institution or creditor with identity theft;

(b) Changes in methods of identity theft;

(c) Changes in methods to detect, prevent, and mitigate identity theft;

(d) Changes in the types of accounts that the financial institution or creditor offers or maintains; and

(e) Changes in the business arrangements of the financial institution or creditor, including mergers, acquisitions, alliances, joint ventures, and service provider arrangements.

VI. Methods for Administering the Program

(a) *Oversight of Program.* Oversight by the board of directors, an appropriate committee of the board, or a designated employee at the level of senior management should include:

(1) Assigning specific responsibility for the Program's implementation;

(2) Reviewing reports prepared by staff regarding compliance by the financial institution or creditor with § 571.90 of this part; and

(3) Approving material changes to the Program as necessary to address changing identity theft risks.

(b) *Reports.* (1) *In general.* Staff of the financial institution or creditor responsible for development, implementation, and administration of its Program should report to the board of directors, an appropriate committee of the board, or a designated employee at the level of senior management, at least annually, on compliance by the financial institution or creditor with § 571.90 of this part.

(2) *Contents of report.* The report should address material matters related to the Program and evaluate issues such as: the effectiveness of the policies and procedures of the financial institution or creditor in addressing the risk of identity theft in connection with the opening of covered accounts and with respect to existing covered accounts; service provider arrangements; significant incidents involving identity theft and management's response; and recommendations for material changes to the Program.

(c) *Oversight of service provider arrangements.* Whenever a financial institution or creditor engages a service provider to perform an activity in connection with one or more covered accounts the financial institution or creditor should take steps to ensure that the activity of the service provider is conducted in accordance with reasonable policies and procedures designed to detect, prevent, and mitigate the risk of identity theft. For example, a financial institution or creditor could require the service provider by contract to have policies and procedures to detect relevant Red Flags that may arise in the performance of the service provider's activities, and either report the Red Flags to the financial institution or creditor, or to take appropriate steps to prevent or mitigate identity theft.

VII. Other Applicable Legal Requirements

Financial institutions and creditors should be mindful of other related legal requirements that may be applicable, such as:

(a) For financial institutions and creditors that are subject to 31 U.S.C. 5318(g), filing a Suspicious Activity Report in accordance with applicable law and regulation;

(b) Implementing any requirements under 15 U.S.C. 1681c-1(h) regarding the circumstances under which credit may be extended when the financial institution or creditor detects a fraud or active duty alert;

(c) Implementing any requirements for furnishers of information to consumer reporting agencies under 15 U.S.C. 1681s-2, for example, to correct or update inaccurate or incomplete information, and to not report information that the furnisher has reasonable cause to believe is inaccurate; and

(d) Complying with the prohibitions in 15 U.S.C. 1681m on the sale, transfer, and placement for collection of certain debts resulting from identity theft.

Supplement A to Appendix J

In addition to incorporating Red Flags from the sources recommended in section II.b. of the Guidelines in Appendix J of this part, each financial institution or creditor may consider incorporating into its Program, whether singly or in combination, Red Flags from the following illustrative examples in connection with covered accounts:

Alerts, Notifications or Warnings from a Consumer Reporting Agency

1. A fraud or active duty alert is included with a consumer report.

2. A consumer reporting agency provides a notice of credit freeze in response to a request for a consumer report.

3. A consumer reporting agency provides a notice of address discrepancy, as defined in § 571.82(b) of this part.

4. A consumer report indicates a pattern of activity that is inconsistent with the history and usual pattern of activity of an applicant or customer, such as:

a. A recent and significant increase in the volume of inquiries;

b. An unusual number of recently established credit relationships;

c. A material change in the use of credit, especially with respect to recently established credit relationships; or

d. An account that was closed for cause or identified for abuse of account privileges by a financial institution or creditor.

Suspicious Documents

5. Documents provided for identification appear to have been altered or forged.

6. The photograph or physical description on the identification is not consistent with the appearance of the applicant or customer presenting the identification.

7. Other information on the identification is not consistent with information provided by the person opening a new covered account or customer presenting the identification.

8. Other information on the identification is not consistent with readily accessible information that is on file with the financial institution or creditor, such as a signature card or a recent check.

9. An application appears to have been altered or forged, or gives the appearance of having been destroyed and reassembled.

Suspicious Personal Identifying Information

10. Personal identifying information provided is inconsistent when compared against external information sources used by the financial institution or creditor. For example:

a. The address does not match any address in the consumer report; or

b. The Social Security Number (SSN) has not been issued, or is listed on the Social Security Administration's Death Master File.

11. Personal identifying information provided by the customer is not consistent with other personal identifying information provided by the customer. For example, there is a lack of correlation between the SSN range and date of birth.

12. Personal identifying information provided is associated with known fraudulent activity as indicated by internal or third-party sources used by the financial institution or creditor. For example:

a. The address on an application is the same as the address provided on a fraudulent application; or

b. The phone number on an application is the same as the number provided on a fraudulent application.

13. Personal identifying information provided is of a type commonly associated with fraudulent activity as indicated by internal or third-party sources used by the financial institution or creditor. For example:

a. The address on an application is fictitious, a mail drop, or a prison; or

b. The phone number is invalid, or is associated with a pager or answering service.

14. The SSN provided is the same as that submitted by other persons opening an account or other customers.

15. The address or telephone number provided is the same as or similar to the address or telephone number submitted by an unusually large number of other persons opening accounts or by other customers.

16. The person opening the covered account or the customer fails to provide all required personal identifying information on an application or in response to notification that the application is incomplete.

17. Personal identifying information provided is not consistent with personal identifying information that is on file with the financial institution or creditor.

18. For financial institutions and creditors that use challenge questions, the person opening the covered account or the customer cannot provide authenticating information beyond that which generally would be available from a wallet or consumer report.

Unusual Use of, or Suspicious Activity Related to, the Covered Account

19. Shortly following the notice of a change of address for a covered account, the institution or creditor receives a request for a new, additional, or replacement card or a cell phone, or for the addition of authorized users on the account.

20. A new revolving credit account is used in a manner commonly associated with known patterns of fraud. For example:

a. The majority of available credit is used for cash advances or merchandise that is easily convertible to cash (e.g., electronics equipment or jewelry); or

b. The customer fails to make the first payment or makes an initial payment but no subsequent payments.

21. A covered account is used in a manner that is not consistent with established patterns of activity on the account. There is, for example:

a. Nonpayment when there is no history of late or missed payments;

b. A material increase in the use of available credit;

c. A material change in purchasing or spending patterns;

d. A material change in electronic fund transfer patterns in connection with a deposit account; or

e. A material change in telephone call patterns in connection with a cellular phone account.

22. A covered account that has been inactive for a reasonably lengthy period of time is used (taking into consideration the type of account, the expected pattern of usage and other relevant factors).

23. Mail sent to the customer is returned repeatedly as undeliverable although transactions continue to be conducted in connection with the customer's covered account.

24. The financial institution or creditor is notified that the customer is not receiving paper account statements.

25. The financial institution or creditor is notified of unauthorized charges or transactions in connection with a customer's covered account.

Notice from Customers, Victims of Identity Theft, Law Enforcement Authorities, or Other Persons Regarding Possible Identity Theft in Connection With Covered Accounts Held by the Financial Institution or Creditor

26. The financial institution or creditor is notified by a customer, a victim of identity theft, a law enforcement authority, or any other person that it has opened a fraudulent

account for a person engaged in identity theft.

[72 FR 63766, Nov. 9, 2007, as amended at 74 FR 22643, May 14, 2009]

PART 572—LOANS IN AREAS HAVING SPECIAL FLOOD HAZARDS

Sec.
572.1 Authority, purpose, and scope.
572.2 Definitions.
572.3 Requirement to purchase flood insurance where available.
572.4 Exemptions.
572.5 Escrow requirement.
572.6 Required use of standard flood hazard determination form.
572.7 Forced placement of flood insurance.
572.8 Determination fees.
572.9 Notice of special flood hazards and availability of Federal disaster relief assistance.
572.10 Notice of servicer's identity.

APPENDIX A TO PART 572—SAMPLE FORM OF NOTICE OF SPECIAL FLOOD HAZARDS AND AVAILABILITY OF FEDERAL DISASTER RELIEF ASSISTANCE

AUTHORITY: 12 U.S.C. 1462, 1462a, 1463, 1464; 42 U.S.C. 4012a, 4104a, 4104b, 4106, and 4128.

SOURCE: 61 FR 45709, Aug. 29, 1996, unless otherwise noted.

§ 572.1 Authority, purpose, and scope.

(a) *Authority.* This part is issued pursuant to 12 U.S.C. 1462, 1462a, 1463, 1464 and 42 U.S.C. 4012a, 4104a, 4104b, 4106, 4128.

(b) *Purpose.* The purpose of this part is to implement the requirements of the National Flood Insurance Act of 1968 and the Flood Disaster Protection Act of 1973, as amended (42 U.S.C. 4001–4129).

(c) *Scope.* This part, except for §§ 572.6 and 572.8, applies to loans secured by buildings or mobile homes located or to be located in areas determined by the Director of the Federal Emergency Management Agency to have special flood hazards. Sections 572.6 and 572.8 of this part apply to loans secured by buildings or mobile homes, regardless of location.

§ 572.2 Definitions.

(a) *Act* means the National Flood Insurance Act of 1968, as amended (42 U.S.C. 4001–4129).

(b) *Savings association* means, for purposes of this part, a savings association as that term is defined in 12 U.S.C. 1813(b)(1) and any subsidiaries or service corporations thereof.

(c) *Building* means a walled and roofed structure, other than a gas or liquid storage tank, that is principally above ground and affixed to a permanent site, and a walled and roofed structure while in the course of construction, alteration, or repair.

(d) *Community* means a State or a political subdivision of a State that has zoning and building code jurisdiction over a particular area having special flood hazards.

(e) *Designated loan* means a loan secured by a building or mobile home that is located or to be located in a special flood hazard area in which flood insurance is available under the Act.

(f) *Director of FEMA* means the Director of the Federal Emergency Management Agency.

(g) *Mobile home* means a structure, transportable in one or more sections, that is built on a permanent chassis and designed for use with or without a permanent foundation when attached to the required utilities. The term *mobile home* does not include a recreational vehicle. For purposes of this part, the term *mobile home* means a mobile home on a permanent foundation. The term *mobile home* includes a manufactured home as that term is used in the NFIP.

(h) *NFIP* means the National Flood Insurance Program authorized under the Act.

(i) *Residential improved real estate* means real estate upon which a home or other residential building is located or to be located.

(j) *Servicer* means the person responsible for:

(1) Receiving any scheduled, periodic payments from a borrower under the terms of a loan, including amounts for taxes, insurance premiums, and other charges with respect to the property securing the loan; and

(2) Making payments of principal and interest and any other payments from the amounts received from the borrower as may be required under the terms of the loan.

(k) *Special flood hazard area* means the land in the flood plain within a

§ 572.3

community having at least a one percent chance of flooding in any given year, as designated by the Director of FEMA.

(1) *Table funding* means a settlement at which a loan is funded by a contemporaneous advance of loan funds and an assignment of the loan to the person advancing the funds.

§ 572.3 **Requirement to purchase flood insurance where available.**

(a) *In general.* A savings association shall not make, increase, extend, or renew any designated loan unless the building or mobile home and any personal property securing the loan is covered by flood insurance for the term of the loan. The amount of insurance must be at least equal to the lesser of the outstanding principal balance of the designated loan or the maximum limit of coverage available for the particular type of property under the Act. Flood insurance coverage under the Act is limited to the overall value of the property securing the designated loan minus the value of the land on which the property is located.

(b) *Table funded loans.* A savings association that acquires a loan from a mortgage broker or other entity through table funding shall be considered to be making a loan for the purposes of this part.

§ 572.4 **Exemptions.**

The flood insurance requirement prescribed by § 572.3 does not apply with respect to:

(a) Any State-owned property covered under a policy of self-insurance satisfactory to the Director of FEMA, who publishes and periodically revises the list of States falling within this exemption; or

(b) Property securing any loan with an original principal balance of $5,000 or less and a repayment term of one year or less.

§ 572.5 **Escrow requirement.**

If a savings association requires the escrow of taxes, insurance premiums, fees, or any other charges for a loan secured by *residential* improved real estate or a mobile home that is made, increased, extended, or renewed on or after October 1, 1996, the savings association shall also require the escrow of all premiums and fees for any flood insurance required under § 572.3. The savings association, or a servicer acting on behalf of the savings association, shall deposit the flood insurance premiums on behalf of the borrower in an escrow account. This escrow account will be subject to escrow requirements adopted pursuant to section 10 of the Real Estate Settlement Procedures Act of 1974 (12 U.S.C. 2609) (RESPA), which generally limits the amount that may be maintained in escrow accounts for certain types of loans and requires escrow account statements for those accounts, only if the loan is otherwise subject to RESPA. Following receipt of a notice from the Director of FEMA or other provider of flood insurance that premiums are due, the savings association, or a servicer acting on behalf of the savings association, shall pay the amount owed to the insurance provider from the escrow account by the date when such premiums are due.

§ 572.6 **Required use of standard flood hazard determination form.**

(a) *Use of form.* A savings association shall use the standard flood hazard determination form developed by the Director of· FEMA when determining whether the building or mobile home offered as collateral security for a loan is or will be located in a special flood hazard area in which flood insurance is available under the Act. The standard flood hazard determination form may be used in a printed, computerized, or electronic manner. A savings association may obtain the standard flood hazard determination form from FEMA, P.O. Box 2012, Jessup, MD 20794–2012.

(b) *Retention of form.* A savings association shall retain a copy of the completed standard flood hazard determination form, in either hard copy or electronic form, for the period of time the savings association owns the loan.

[61 FR 45709, Aug. 29, 1996, as amended at 64 FR 69185, Dec. 10, 1999]

§ 572.7 **Forced placement of flood insurance.**

If a savings association, or a servicer acting on behalf of the savings association, determines at any time during

Office of Thrift Supervision, Treasury § 572.9

the term of a designated loan that the building or mobile home and any personal property securing the designated loan is not covered by flood insurance or is covered by flood insurance in an amount less than the amount required under § 572.3, then the savings association or its servicer shall notify the borrower that the borrower should obtain flood insurance, at the borrower's expense, in an amount at least equal to the amount required under § 572.3, for the remaining term of the loan. If the borrower fails to obtain flood insurance within 45 days after notification, then the savings association or its servicer shall purchase insurance on the borrower's behalf. The savings association or its servicer may charge the borrower for the cost of premiums and fees incurred in purchasing the insurance.

§ 572.8 Determination fees.

(a) *General.* Notwithstanding any Federal or State law other than the Flood Disaster Protection Act of 1973, as amended (42 U.S.C. 4001–4129), any savings association, or a servicer acting on behalf of the savings association, may charge a reasonable fee for determining whether the building or mobile home securing the loan is located or will be located in a special flood hazard area. A determination fee may also include, but is not limited to, a fee for life-of-loan monitoring.

(b) *Borrower fee.* The determination fee authorized by paragraph (a) of this section may be charged to the borrower if the determination:

(1) Is made in connection with a making, increasing, extending, or renewing of the loan that is initiated by the borrower;

(2) Reflects the Director of FEMA's revision or updating of floodplain areas or flood-risk zones;

(3) Reflects the Director of FEMA's publication of a notice or compendium that:

(i) Affects the area in which the building or mobile home securing the loan is located; or

(ii) By determination of the Director of FEMA, may reasonably require a determination whether the building or mobile home securing the loan is located in a special flood hazard area; or

(4) Results in the purchase of flood insurance coverage by the lender or its servicer on behalf of the borrower under § 572.7.

(c) *Purchaser or transferee fee.* The determination fee authorized by paragraph (a) of this section may be charged to the purchaser or transferee of a loan in the case of the sale or transfer of the loan.

§ 572.9 Notice of special flood hazards and availability of Federal disaster relief assistance.

(a) *Notice requirement.* When a savings association makes, increases, extends, or renews a loan secured by a building or a mobile home located or to be located in a special flood hazard area, the savings association shall mail or deliver a written notice to the borrower and to the servicer in all cases whether or not flood insurance is available under the Act for the collateral securing the loan.

(b) *Contents of notice.* The written notice must include the following information:

(1) A warning, in a form approved by the Director of FEMA, that the building or the mobile home is or will be located in a special flood hazard area;

(2) A description of the flood insurance purchase requirements set forth in section 102(b) of the Flood Disaster Protection Act of 1973, as amended (42 U.S.C. 4012a(b));

(3) A statement, where applicable, that flood insurance coverage is available under the NFIP and may also be available from private insurers; and

(4) A statement whether Federal disaster relief assistance may be available in the event of damage to the building or mobile home caused by flooding in a Federally-declared disaster.

(c) *Timing of notice.* The savings association shall provide the notice required by paragraph (a) of this section to the borrower within a reasonable time before the completion of the transaction, and to the servicer as promptly as practicable after the savings association provides notice to the borrower and in any event no later than the savings association provides other similar notices to the servicer concerning hazard insurance and taxes. Notice to the servicer may be made electronically or may take the form of a copy of the notice to the borrower.

(d) *Record of receipt.* The savings association shall retain a record of the receipt of the notices by the borrower and the servicer for the period of time the savings association owns the loan.

(e) *Alternate method of notice.* Instead of providing the notice to the borrower required by paragraph (a) of this section, a savings association may obtain satisfactory written assurance from a seller or lessor that, within a reasonable time before the completion of the sale or lease transaction, the seller or lessor has provided such notice to the purchaser or lessee. The savings association shall retain a record of the written assurance from the seller or lessor for the period of time the savings association owns the loan.

(f) *Use of prescribed form of notice.* A savings association will be considered to be in compliance with the requirement for notice to the borrower of this section by providing written notice to the borrower containing the language presented in appendix A to this part within a reasonable time before the completion of the transaction. The notice presented in appendix A to this part satisfies the borrower notice requirements of the Act.

§ 572.10 Notice of servicer's identity.

(a) *Notice requirement.* When a savings association makes, increases, extends, renews, sells, or transfers a loan secured by a building or mobile home located or to be located in a special flood hazard area, the savings association shall notify the Director of FEMA (or the Director's designee) in writing of the identity of the servicer of the loan. The Director of FEMA has designated the insurance provider to receive the savings association's notice of the servicer's identity. This notice may be provided electronically if electronic transmission is satisfactory to the Director of FEMA's designee.

(b) *Transfer of servicing rights.* The savings association shall notify the Director of FEMA (or the Director's designee) of any change in the servicer of a loan described in paragraph (a) of this section within 60 days after the effective date of the change. This notice may be provided electronically if electronic transmission is satisfactory to the Director of FEMA's designee. Upon any change in the servicing of a loan described in paragraph (a) of this section, the duty to provide notice under this paragraph (b) shall transfer to the transferee servicer.

APPENDIX A TO PART 572—SAMPLE FORM OF NOTICE OF SPECIAL FLOOD HAZARDS AND AVAILABILITY OF FEDERAL DISASTER RELIEF ASSISTANCE

We are giving you this notice to inform you that:

The building or mobile home securing the loan for which you have applied is or will be located in an area with special flood hazards. The area has been identified by the Director of the Federal Emergency Management Agency (FEMA) as a special flood hazard area using FEMA's *Flood Insurance Rate Map* or the *Flood Hazard Boundary Map* for the following community: _____. This area has at least a one percent (1%) chance of a flood equal to or exceeding the base flood elevation (a 100-year flood) in any given year. During the life of a 30-year mortgage loan the risk of a 100-year flood in a special flood hazard area is 26 percent (26%).

Federal law allows a lender and borrower jointly to request the Director of FEMA to review the determination of whether the property securing the loan is located in a special flood hazard area. If you would like to make such a request, please contact us for further information.

_____ The community in which the property securing the loan is located participates in the National Flood Insurance Program (NFIP). Federal law will not allow us to make you the loan that you have applied for if you do not purchase flood insurance. The flood insurance must be maintained for the life of the loan. If you fail to purchase or renew flood insurance on the property, Federal law authorizes and requires us to purchase the flood insurance for you at your expense.

• Flood insurance coverage under the NFIP may be purchased through an insurance agent who will obtain the policy either directly through the NFIP or through an insurance company that participates in the NFIP. Flood insurance also may be available from private insurers that do not participate in the NFIP.

• At a minimum, flood insurance purchased must cover *the lesser of:*

(1) the outstanding principal balance of the loan; *or*

(2) the maximum amount of coverage allowed for the type of property under the NFIP.

Office of Thrift Supervision, Treasury §573.1

Flood insurance coverage under the NFIP is limited to the overall value of the property securing the loan minus the value of the land on which the property is located.

• Federal disaster relief assistance (usually in the form of a low-interest loan) may be available for damages incurred in excess of your flood insurance if your community's participation in the NFIP is in accordance with NFIP requirements.

_____ Flood insurance coverage under the NFIP is not available for the property securing the loan because the community in which the property is located does not participate in the NFIP. In addition, if the non-participating community has been identified for at least one year as containing a special flood hazard area, properties located in the community will not be eligible for Federal disaster relief assistance in the event of a Federally-declared flood disaster.

PART 573—PRIVACY OF CONSUMER FINANCIAL INFORMATION

Sec.
573.1 Purpose and scope.
573.2 Model privacy form and examples
573.3 Definitions.

Subpart A—Privacy and Opt Out Notices

573.4 Initial privacy notice to consumers required.
573.5 Annual privacy notice to customers required.
573.6 Information to be included in privacy notices.
573.7 Form of opt out notice to consumers; opt out methods.
573.8 Revised privacy notices.
573.9 Delivering privacy and opt out notices.

Subpart B—Limits on Disclosures

573.10 Limitation on disclosure of nonpublic personal information to nonaffiliated third parties.
573.11 Limits on redisclosure and reuse of information.
573.12 Limits on sharing account number information for marketing purposes.

Subpart C—Exceptions

573.13 Exception to opt out requirements for service providers and joint marketing.
573.14 Exceptions to notice and opt out requirements for processing and servicing transactions.
573.15 Other exceptions to notice and opt out requirements.

Subpart D—Relation to Other Laws; Effective Date

573.16 Protection of Fair Credit Reporting Act.
573.17 Relation to State laws.
573.18 Effective date; transition rule.
APPENDIX A TO PART 573—MODEL PRIVACY FORM

AUTHORITY: 12 U.S.C. 1462a, 1463, 1464, 1828; 15 U.S.C. 6801 *et seq.*

SOURCE: 65 FR 35226, June 1, 2000, unless otherwise noted.

§573.1 Purpose and scope.

(a) *Purpose.* This part governs the treatment of nonpublic personal information about consumers by the financial institutions listed in paragraph (b) of this section. This part:

(1) Requires a financial institution to provide notice to customers about its privacy policies and practices;

(2) Describes the conditions under which a financial institution may disclose nonpublic personal information about consumers to nonaffiliated third parties; and

(3) Provides a method for consumers to prevent a financial institution from disclosing that information to most nonaffiliated third parties by "opting out" of that disclosure, subject to the exceptions in §§ 573.13, 573.14, and 573.15.

(b) *Scope.* (1) This part applies only to nonpublic personal information about individuals who obtain financial products or services primarily for personal, family, or household purposes from the institutions listed below. This part does not apply to information about companies or about individuals who obtain financial products or services for business, commercial, or agricultural purposes. This part applies to savings associations whose deposits are insured by the Federal Deposit Insurance Corporation, and any subsidiaries of such savings associations, but not subsidiaries that are brokers, dealers, persons providing insurance, investment companies, or investment advisers. This part refers to these entities as "you."

(2) Nothing in this part modifies, limits, or supersedes the standards governing individually identifiable health information promulgated by the Secretary of Health and Human Services under the authority of sections 262 and

§ 573.2

264 of the Health Insurance Portability and Accountability Act of 1996 (42 U.S.C. 1320d–1320d–8).

§ 573.2 Model privacy form and examples.

(a) *Model privacy form.* Use of the model privacy form in Appendix A of this part, consistent with the instructions in Appendix A, constitutes compliance with the notice content requirements of §§ 573.6 and 573.7 of this part, although use of the model privacy form is not required.

(b) *Examples.* The examples in this part are not exclusive. Compliance with an example, to the extent applicable, constitutes compliance with this part.

[74 FR 62945, Dec. 1, 2009]

§ 573.3 Definitions.

As used in this part, unless the context requires otherwise:

(a) *Affiliate* means any company that controls, is controlled by, or is under common control with another company.

(b)(1) *Clear and conspicuous* means that a notice is reasonably understandable and designed to call attention to the nature and significance of the information in the notice.

(2) *Examples*—(i) *Reasonably understandable.* You make your notice reasonably understandable if you:

(A) Present the information in the notice in clear, concise sentences, paragraphs, and sections;

(B) Use short explanatory sentences or bullet lists whenever possible;

(C) Use definite, concrete, everyday words and active voice whenever possible;

(D) Avoid multiple negatives;

(E) Avoid legal and highly technical business terminology whenever possible; and

(F) Avoid explanations that are imprecise and readily subject to different interpretations.

(ii) *Designed to call attention.* You design your notice to call attention to the nature and significance of the information in it if you:

(A) Use a plain-language heading to call attention to the notice;

(B) Use a typeface and type size that are easy to read;

(C) Provide wide margins and ample line spacing;

(D) Use boldface or italics for key words; and

(E) In a form that combines your notice with other information, use distinctive type size, style, and graphic devices, such as shading or sidebars, when you combine your notice with other information.

(iii) *Notices on web sites.* If you provide a notice on a web page, you design your notice to call attention to the nature and significance of the information in it if you use text or visual cues to encourage scrolling down the page if necessary to view the entire notice and ensure that other elements on the web site (such as text, graphics, hyperlinks, or sound) do not distract attention from the notice, and you either:

(A) Place the notice on a screen that consumers frequently access, such as a page on which transactions are conducted; or

(B) Place a link on a screen that consumers frequently access, such as a page on which transactions are conducted, that connects directly to the notice and is labeled appropriately to convey the importance, nature, and relevance of the notice.

(c) *Collect* means to obtain information that you organize or can retrieve by the name of an individual or by identifying number, symbol, or other identifying particular assigned to the individual, irrespective of the source of the underlying information.

(d) *Company* means any corporation, limited liability company, business trust, general or limited partnership, association, or similar organization.

(e)(1) *Consumer* means an individual who obtains or has obtained a financial product or service from you that is to be used primarily for personal, family, or household purposes, or that individual's legal representative.

(2) *Examples.* (i) An individual who applies to you for credit for personal, family, or household purposes is a consumer of a financial service, regardless of whether the credit is extended.

(ii) An individual who provides nonpublic personal information to you in order to obtain a determination about whether he or she may qualify for a loan to be used primarily for personal, family, or household purposes is a consumer of a financial service, regardless of whether the loan is extended.

(iii) An individual who provides nonpublic personal information to you in connection with obtaining or seeking to obtain financial, investment, or economic advisory services is a consumer regardless of whether you establish a continuing advisory relationship.

(iv) If you hold ownership or servicing rights to an individual's loan that is used primarily for personal, family, or household purposes, the individual is your consumer, even if you hold those rights in conjunction with one or more other institutions. (The individual is also a consumer with respect to the other financial institutions involved.) An individual who has a loan in which you have ownership or servicing rights is your consumer, even if you, or another institution with those rights, hire an agent to collect on the loan.

(v) An individual who is a consumer of another financial institution is not your consumer solely because you act as agent for, or provide processing or other services to, that financial institution.

(vi) An individual is not your consumer solely because he or she has designated you as trustee for a trust.

(vii) An individual is not your consumer solely because he or she is a beneficiary of a trust for which you are a trustee.

(viii) An individual is not your consumer solely because he or she is a participant or a beneficiary of an employee benefit plan that you sponsor or for which you act as a trustee or fiduciary.

(f) *Consumer reporting agency* has the same meaning as in section 603(f) of the Fair Credit Reporting Act (15 U.S.C. 1681a(f)).

(g) *Control* of a company means:

(1) Ownership, control, or power to vote 25 percent or more of the outstanding shares of any class of voting security of the company, directly or indirectly, or acting through one or more other persons;

(2) Control in any manner over the election of a majority of the directors, trustees, or general partners (or individuals exercising similar functions) of the company; or

(3) The power to exercise, directly or indirectly, a controlling influence over the management or policies of the company, as the OTS determines.

(h) *Customer* means a consumer who has a customer relationship with you.

(i)(1) *Customer relationship* means a continuing relationship between a consumer and you under which you provide one or more financial products or services to the consumer that are to be used primarily for personal, family, or household purposes.

(2) *Examples*—(i) *Continuing relationship.* A consumer has a continuing relationship with you if the consumer:

(A) Has a deposit or investment account with you;

(B) Obtains a loan from you;

(C) Has a loan for which you own the servicing rights;

(D) Purchases an insurance product from you;

(E) Holds an investment product through you, such as when you act as a custodian for securities or for assets in an Individual Retirement Arrangement;

(F) Enters into an agreement or understanding with you whereby you undertake to arrange or broker a home mortgage loan for the consumer;

(G) Enters into a lease of personal property with you; or

(H) Obtains financial, investment, or economic advisory services from you for a fee.

(ii) *No continuing relationship.* A consumer does not, however, have a continuing relationship with you if:

(A) The consumer obtains a financial product or service only in isolated transactions, such as using your ATM to withdraw cash from an account at another financial institution or purchasing a cashier's check or money order;

(B) You sell the consumer's loan and do not retain the rights to service that loan; or

(C) You sell the consumer airline tickets, travel insurance, or traveler's checks in isolated transactions.

(j) *Federal functional regulator* means:

(1) The Board of Governors of the Federal Reserve System;

(2) The Office of the Comptroller of the Currency;

§ 573.3

(3) The Board of Directors of the Federal Deposit Insurance Corporation;

(4) The Director of the Office of Thrift Supervision;

(5) The National Credit Union Administration Board; and

(6) The Securities and Exchange Commission.

(k)(1) *Financial institution* means any institution the business of which is engaging in activities that are financial in nature or incidental to such financial activities as described in section 4(k) of the Bank Holding Company Act of 1956 (12 U.S.C. 1843(k)).

(2) *Financial institution* does not include:

(i) Any person or entity with respect to any financial activity that is subject to the jurisdiction of the Commodity Futures Trading Commission under the Commodity Exchange Act (7 U.S.C. 1 *et seq.*);

(ii) The Federal Agricultural Mortgage Corporation or any entity chartered and operating under the Farm Credit Act of 1971 (12 U.S.C. 2001 *et seq.*); or

(iii) Institutions chartered by Congress specifically to engage in securitizations, secondary market sales (including sales of servicing rights), or similar transactions related to a transaction of a consumer, as long as such institutions do not sell or transfer nonpublic personal information to a nonaffiliated third party.

(l)(1) *Financial product or service* means any product or service that a financial holding company could offer by engaging in an activity that is financial in nature or incidental to such a financial activity under section 4(k) of the Bank Holding Company Act of 1956 (12 U.S.C. 1843(k)).

(2) *Financial service* includes your evaluation or brokerage of information that you collect in connection with a request or an application from a consumer for a financial product or service.

(m)(1) *Nonaffiliated third party* means any person except:

(i) Your affiliate; or

(ii) A person employed jointly by you and any company that is not your affiliate (but *nonaffiliated third party* includes the other company that jointly employs the person).

(2) *Nonaffiliated third party* includes any company that is an affiliate solely by virtue of your or your affiliate's direct or indirect ownership or control of the company in conducting merchant banking or investment banking activities of the type described in section 4(k)(4)(H) or insurance company investment activities of the type described in section 4(k)(4)(I) of the Bank Holding Company Act of 1956 (12 U.S.C. 1843(k)(4)(H) and (I)).

(n)(1) *Nonpublic personal information* means:

(i) Personally identifiable financial information; and

(ii) Any list, description, or other grouping of consumers (and publicly available information pertaining to them) that is derived using any personally identifiable financial information that is not publicly available.

(2) *Nonpublic personal information* does not include:

(i) Publicly available information, except as included on a list described in paragraph (n)(1)(ii) of this section; or

(ii) Any list, description, or other grouping of consumers (and publicly available information pertaining to them) that is derived without using any personally identifiable financial information that is not publicly available.

(3) *Examples of lists.* (i) Nonpublic personal information includes any list of individuals' names and street addresses that is derived in whole or in part using personally identifiable financial information that is not publicly available, such as account numbers.

(ii) Nonpublic personal information does not include any list of individuals' names and addresses that contains only publicly available information, is not derived in whole or in part using personally identifiable financial information that is not publicly available, and is not disclosed in a manner that indicates that any of the individuals on the list is a consumer of a financial institution.

(o)(1) *Personally identifiable financial information* means any information:

(i) A consumer provides to you to obtain a financial product or service from you;

(ii) About a consumer resulting from any transaction involving a financial

Office of Thrift Supervision, Treasury § 573.4

product or service between you and a consumer; or

(iii) You otherwise obtain about a consumer in connection with providing a financial product or service to that consumer.

(2) *Examples*—(i) *Information included.* Personally identifiable financial information includes:

(A) Information a consumer provides to you on an application to obtain a loan, credit card, or other financial product or service;

(B) Account balance information, payment history, overdraft history, and credit or debit card purchase information;

(C) The fact that an individual is or has been one of your customers or has obtained a financial product or service from you;

(D) Any information about your consumer if it is disclosed in a manner that indicates that the individual is or has been your consumer;

(E) Any information that a consumer provides to you or that you or your agent otherwise obtain in connection with collecting on a loan or servicing a loan;

(F) Any information you collect through an Internet "cookie" (an information collecting device from a web server); and

(G) Information from a consumer report.

(ii) *Information not included.* Personally identifiable financial information does not include:

(A) A list of names and addresses of customers of an entity that is not a financial institution; and

(B) Information that does not identify a consumer, such as aggregate information or blind data that does not contain personal identifiers such as account numbers, names, or addresses.

(p)(1) *Publicly available information* means any information that you have a reasonable basis to believe is lawfully made available to the general public from:

(i) Federal, State, or local government records;

(ii) Widely distributed media; or

(iii) Disclosures to the general public that are required to be made by Federal, State, or local law.

(2) *Reasonable basis.* You have a reasonable basis to believe that information is lawfully made available to the general public if you have taken steps to determine:

(i) That the information is of the type that is available to the general public; and

(ii) Whether an individual can direct that the information not be made available to the general public and, if so, that your consumer has not done so.

(3) *Examples*—(i) *Government records.* Publicly available information in government records includes information in government real estate records and security interest filings.

(ii) *Widely distributed media.* Publicly available information from widely distributed media includes information from a telephone book, a television or radio program, a newspaper, or a web site that is available to the general public on an unrestricted basis. A web site is not restricted merely because an Internet service provider or a site operator requires a fee or a password, so long as access is available to the general public.

(iii) *Reasonable basis.* (A) You have a reasonable basis to believe that mortgage information is lawfully made available to the general public if you have determined that the information is of the type included on the public record in the jurisdiction where the mortgage would be recorded.

(B) You have a reasonable basis to believe that an individual's telephone number is lawfully made available to the general public if you have located the telephone number in the telephone book or the consumer has informed you that the telephone number is not unlisted.

Subpart A—Privacy and Opt Out Notices

§ 573.4 Initial privacy notice to consumers required.

(a) *Initial notice requirement.* You must provide a clear and conspicuous notice that accurately reflects your privacy policies and practices to:

(1) *Customer.* An individual who becomes your customer, not later than

§ 573.4

when you establish a customer relationship, except as provided in paragraph (e) of this section; and

(2) *Consumer.* A consumer, before you disclose any nonpublic personal information about the consumer to any nonaffiliated third party, if you make such a disclosure other than as authorized by §§ 573.14 and 573.15.

(b) *When initial notice to a consumer is not required.* You are not required to provide an initial notice to a consumer under paragraph (a) of this section if:

(1) You do not disclose any nonpublic personal information about the consumer to any nonaffiliated third party, other than as authorized by §§ 573.14 and 573.15; and

(2) You do not have a customer relationship with the consumer.

(c) *When you establish a customer relationship*—(1) *General rule.* You establish a customer relationship when you and the consumer enter into a continuing relationship.

(2) *Special rule for loans.* You establish a customer relationship with a consumer when you originate a loan to the consumer for personal, family, or household purposes. If you subsequently transfer the servicing rights to that loan to another financial institution, the customer relationship transfers with the servicing rights.

(3)(i) *Examples of establishing customer relationship.* You establish a customer relationship when the consumer:

(A) Opens a credit card account with you;

(B) Executes the contract to open a deposit account with you, obtains credit from you, or purchases insurance from you;

(C) Agrees to obtain financial, economic, or investment advisory services from you for a fee; or

(D) Becomes your client for the purpose of your providing credit counseling or tax preparation services.

(ii) *Examples of loan rule.* You establish a customer relationship with a consumer who obtains a loan for personal, family, or household purposes when you:

(A) Originate the loan to the consumer; or

(B) Purchase the servicing rights to the consumer's loan.

(d) *Existing customers.* When an existing customer obtains a new financial product or service from you that is to be used primarily for personal, family, or household purposes, you satisfy the initial notice requirements of paragraph (a) of this section as follows:

(1) You may provide a revised privacy notice, under § 573.8, that covers the customer's new financial product or service; or

(2) If the initial, revised, or annual notice that you most recently provided to that customer was accurate with respect to the new financial product or service, you do not need to provide a new privacy notice under paragraph (a) of this section.

(e) *Exceptions to allow subsequent delivery of notice.* (1) You may provide the initial notice required by paragraph (a)(1) of this section within a reasonable time after you establish a customer relationship if:

(i) Establishing the customer relationship is not at the customer's election; or

(ii) Providing notice not later than when you establish a customer relationship would substantially delay the customer's transaction and the customer agrees to receive the notice at a later time.

(2) *Examples of exceptions*—(i) *Not at customer's election.* Establishing a customer relationship is not at the customer's election if you acquire a customer's deposit liability or the servicing rights to a customer's loan from another financial institution and the customer does not have a choice about your acquisition.

(ii) *Substantial delay of customer's transaction.* Providing notice not later than when you establish a customer relationship would substantially delay the customer's transaction when:

(A) You and the individual agree over the telephone to enter into a customer relationship involving prompt delivery of the financial product or service; or

(B) You establish a customer relationship with an individual under a program authorized by Title IV of the Higher Education Act of 1965 (20 U.S.C.

1070 et seq.) or similar student loan programs where loan proceeds are disbursed promptly without prior communication between you and the customer.

(iii) *No substantial delay of customer's transaction.* Providing notice not later than when you establish a customer relationship would not substantially delay the customer's transaction when the relationship is initiated in person at your office or through other means by which the customer may view the notice, such as on a web site.

(f) *Delivery.* When you are required to deliver an initial privacy notice by this section, you must deliver it according to § 573.9. If you use a short-form initial notice for non-customers according to § 573.6(d), you may deliver your privacy notice according to § 573.6(d)(3).

§ 573.5 Annual privacy notice to customers required.

(a)(1) *General rule.* You must provide a clear and conspicuous notice to customers that accurately reflects your privacy policies and practices not less than annually during the continuation of the customer relationship. *Annually* means at least once in any period of 12 consecutive months during which that relationship exists. You may define the 12-consecutive-month period, but you must apply it to the customer on a consistent basis.

(2) *Example.* You provide a notice annually if you define the 12-consecutive-month period as a calendar year and provide the annual notice to the customer once in each calendar year following the calendar year in which you provided the initial notice. For example, if a customer opens an account on any day of year 1, you must provide an annual notice to that customer by December 31 of year 2.

(b)(1) *Termination of customer relationship.* You are not required to provide an annual notice to a former customer.

(2) *Examples.* Your customer becomes a former customer when:

(i) In the case of a deposit account, the account is inactive under your policies;

(ii) In the case of a closed-end loan, the customer pays the loan in full, you charge off the loan, or you sell the loan without retaining servicing rights;

(iii) In the case of a credit card relationship or other open-end credit relationship, you no longer provide any statements or notices to the customer concerning that relationship or you sell the credit card receivables without retaining servicing rights; or

(iv) You have not communicated with the customer about the relationship for a period of 12 consecutive months, other than to provide annual privacy notices or promotional material.

(c) *Special rule for loans.* If you do not have a customer relationship with a consumer under the special rule for loans in § 573.4(c)(2), then you need not provide an annual notice to that consumer under this section.

(d) *Delivery.* When you are required to deliver an annual privacy notice by this section, you must deliver it according to § 573.9.

§ 573.6 Information to be included in privacy notices.

(a) *General rule.* The initial, annual, and revised privacy notices that you provide under §§ 573.4, 573.5, 573.8 must include each of the following items of information, in addition to any other information you wish to provide, that applies to you and to the consumers to whom you send your privacy notice:

(1) The categories of nonpublic personal information that you collect;

(2) The categories of nonpublic personal information that you disclose;

(3) The categories of affiliates and nonaffiliated third parties to whom you disclose nonpublic personal information, other than those parties to whom you disclose information under §§ 573.14 and 573.15;

(4) The categories of nonpublic personal information about your former customers that you disclose and the categories of affiliates and nonaffiliated third parties to whom you disclose nonpublic personal information about your former customers, other than those parties to whom you disclose information under §§ 573.14 and 573.15;

(5) If you disclose nonpublic personal information to a nonaffiliated third party under § 573.13 (and no other exception in § 573.14 or 573.15 applies to that disclosure), a separate statement of the categories of information you

§ 573.6

disclose and the categories of third parties with whom you have contracted;

(6) An explanation of the consumer's right under § 573.10(a) to opt out of the disclosure of nonpublic personal information to nonaffiliated third parties, including the method(s) by which the consumer may exercise that right at that time;

(7) Any disclosures that you make under section 603(d)(2)(A)(iii) of the Fair Credit Reporting Act (15 U.S.C. 1681a(d)(2)(A)(iii)) (that is, notices regarding the ability to opt out of disclosures of information among affiliates);

(8) Your policies and practices with respect to protecting the confidentiality and security of nonpublic personal information; and

(9) Any disclosure that you make under paragraph (b) of this section.

(b) *Description of nonaffiliated third parties subject to exceptions.* If you disclose nonpublic personal information to third parties as authorized under §§ 573.14 and 573.15, you are not required to list those exceptions in the initial or annual privacy notices required by §§ 573.4 and 573.5. When describing the categories with respect to those parties, it is sufficient to state that you make disclosures to other nonaffiliated companies:

(1) For your everyday business purposes, such as [include all that apply] to process transactions, maintain account(s), respond to court orders and legal investigations, or report to credit bureaus; or

(2) As permitted by law.

(c) *Examples*—(1) *Categories of nonpublic personal information that you collect.* You satisfy the requirement to categorize the nonpublic personal information that you collect if you list the following categories, as applicable:

(i) Information from the consumer;

(ii) Information about the consumer's transactions with you or your affiliates;

(iii) Information about the consumer's transactions with nonaffiliated third parties; and

(iv) Information from a consumer reporting agency.

(2) *Categories of nonpublic personal information you disclose.* (i) You satisfy the requirement to categorize the nonpublic personal information that you

12 CFR Ch. V (1–1–12 Edition)

disclose if you list the categories described in paragraph (c)(1) of this section, as applicable, and a few examples to illustrate the types of information in each category.

(ii) If you reserve the right to disclose all of the nonpublic personal information about consumers that you collect, you may simply state that fact without describing the categories or examples of the nonpublic personal information you disclose.

(3) *Categories of affiliates and nonaffiliated third parties to whom you disclose.* You satisfy the requirement to categorize the affiliates and nonaffiliated third parties to whom you disclose nonpublic personal information if you list the following categories, as applicable, and a few examples to illustrate the types of third parties in each category.

(i) Financial service providers;

(ii) Non-financial companies; and

(iii) Others.

(4) *Disclosures under exception for service providers and joint marketers.* If you disclose nonpublic personal information under the exception in § 573.13 to a nonaffiliated third party to market products or services that you offer alone or jointly with another financial institution, you satisfy the disclosure requirement of paragraph (a)(5) of this section if you:

(i) List the categories of nonpublic personal information you disclose, using the same categories and examples you used to meet the requirements of paragraph (a)(2) of this section, as applicable; and

(ii) State whether the third party is:

(A) A service provider that performs marketing services on your behalf or on behalf of you and another financial institution; or

(B) A financial institution with whom you have a joint marketing agreement.

(5) *Simplified notices.* If you do not disclose, and do not wish to reserve the right to disclose, nonpublic personal information about customers or former customers to affiliates or nonaffiliated third parties except as authorized under §§ 573.14 and 573.15, you may simply state that fact, in addition to the information you must provide under

478

paragraphs (a)(1), (a)(8), (a)(9), and (b) of this section.

(6) *Confidentiality and security.* You describe your policies and practices with respect to protecting the confidentiality and security of nonpublic personal information if you do both of the following:

(i) Describe in general terms who is authorized to have access to the information; and

(ii) State whether you have security practices and procedures in place to ensure the confidentiality of the information in accordance with your policy. You are not required to describe technical information about the safeguards you use.

(d) *Short-form initial notice with opt out notice for non-customers.* (1) You may satisfy the initial notice requirements in §§ 573.4(a)(2), 573.7(b), and 573.7(c) for a consumer who is not a customer by providing a short-form initial notice at the same time as you deliver an opt out notice as required in § 573.7.

(2) A short-form initial notice must:

(i) Be clear and conspicuous;

(ii) State that your privacy notice is available upon request; and

(iii) Explain a reasonable means by which the consumer may obtain that notice.

(3) You must deliver your short-form initial notice according to § 573.9. You are not required to deliver your privacy notice with your short-form initial notice. You instead may simply provide the consumer a reasonable means to obtain your privacy notice. If a consumer who receives your short-form notice requests your privacy notice, you must deliver your privacy notice according to § 573.9.

(4) *Examples of obtaining privacy notice.* You provide a reasonable means by which a consumer may obtain a copy of your privacy notice if you:

(i) Provide a toll-free telephone number that the consumer may call to request the notice; or

(ii) For a consumer who conducts business in person at your office, maintain copies of the notice on hand that you provide to the consumer immediately upon request.

(e) *Future disclosures.* Your notice may include:

(1) Categories of nonpublic personal information that you reserve the right to disclose in the future, but do not currently disclose; and

(2) Categories of affiliates or non-affiliated third parties to whom you reserve the right in the future to disclose, but to whom you do not currently disclose, nonpublic personal information.

(f) *Model privacy form.* Pursuant to § 573.2(a) of this part, a model privacy form that meets the notice content requirements of this section is included in Appendix A of this part.

[65 FR 35226, June 1, 2000, as amended at 74 FR 62945, Dec. 1, 2009]

§ 573.7 **Form of opt out notice to consumers; opt out methods.**

(a)(1) *Form of opt out notice.* If you are required to provide an opt out notice under § 573.10(a), you must provide a clear and conspicuous notice to each of your consumers that accurately explains the right to opt out under that section. The notice must state:

(i) That you disclose or reserve the right to disclose nonpublic personal information about your consumer to a nonaffiliated third party;

(ii) That the consumer has the right to opt out of that disclosure; and

(iii) A reasonable means by which the consumer may exercise the opt out right.

(2) *Examples*—(i) *Adequate opt out notice.* You provide adequate notice that the consumer can opt out of the disclosure of nonpublic personal information to a nonaffiliated third party if you:

(A) Identify all of the categories of nonpublic personal information that you disclose or reserve the right to disclose, and all of the categories of nonaffiliated third parties to which you disclose the information, as described in § 573.6(a)(2) and (3), and state that the consumer can opt out of the disclosure of that information; and

(B) Identify the financial products or services that the consumer obtains from you, either singly or jointly, to which the opt out direction would apply.

(ii) *Reasonable opt out means.* You provide a reasonable means to exercise an opt out right if you:

§ 573.7

(A) Designate check-off boxes in a prominent position on the relevant forms with the opt out notice;

(B) Include a reply form together with the opt out notice;

(C) Provide an electronic means to opt out, such as a form that can be sent via electronic mail or a process at your web site, if the consumer agrees to the electronic delivery of information; or

(D) Provide a toll-free telephone number that consumers may call to opt out.

(iii) *Unreasonable opt out means.* You *do not* provide a reasonable means of opting out if:

(A) The only means of opting out is for the consumer to write his or her own letter to exercise that opt out right; or

(B) The only means of opting out as described in any notice subsequent to the initial notice is to use a check-off box that you provided with the initial notice but did not include with the subsequent notice.

(iv) *Specific opt out means.* You may require each consumer to opt out through a specific means, as long as that means is reasonable for that consumer.

(b) *Same form as initial notice permitted.* You may provide the opt out notice together with or on the same written or electronic form as the initial notice you provide in accordance with § 573.4.

(c) *Initial notice required when opt out notice delivered subsequent to initial notice.* If you provide the opt out notice later than required for the initial notice in accordance with § 573.4, you must also include a copy of the initial notice with the opt out notice in writing or, if the consumer agrees, electronically.

(d) *Joint relationships.* (1) If two or more consumers jointly obtain a financial product or service from you, you may provide a single opt out notice. Your opt out notice must explain how you will treat an opt out direction by a joint consumer (as explained in paragraph (d)(5) of this section).

(2) Any of the joint consumers may exercise the right to opt out. You may either:

(i) Treat an opt out direction by a joint consumer as applying to all of the associated joint consumers; or

(ii) Permit each joint consumer to opt out separately.

(3) If you permit each joint consumer to opt out separately, you must permit one of the joint consumers to opt out on behalf of all of the joint consumers.

(4) You may not require *all* joint consumers to opt out before you implement *any* opt out direction.

(5) *Example.* If John and Mary have a joint checking account with you and arrange for you to send statements to John's address, you may do any of the following, but you must explain in your opt out notice which opt out policy you will follow:

(i) Send a single opt out notice to John's address, but you must accept an opt out direction from either John or Mary.

(ii) Treat an opt out direction by either John or Mary as applying to the entire account. If you do so, and John opts out, you may not require Mary to opt out as well before implementing John's opt out direction.

(iii) Permit John and Mary to make different opt out directions. If you do so:

(A) You must permit John and Mary to opt out for each other;

(B) If both opt out, you must permit both to notify you in a single response (such as on a form or through a telephone call); and

(C) If John opts out and Mary does not, you may only disclose nonpublic personal information about Mary, but not about John and not about John and Mary jointly.

(e) *Time to comply with opt out.* You must comply with a consumer's opt out direction as soon as reasonably practicable after you receive it.

(f) *Continuing right to opt out.* A consumer may exercise the right to opt out at any time.

(g) *Duration of consumer's opt out direction.* (1) A consumer's direction to opt out under this section is effective until the consumer revokes it in writing or, if the consumer agrees, electronically.

Office of Thrift Supervision, Treasury § 573.9

(2) When a customer relationship terminates, the customer's opt out direction continues to apply to the nonpublic personal information that you collected during or related to that relationship. If the individual subsequently establishes a new customer relationship with you, the opt out direction that applied to the former relationship does not apply to the new relationship.

(h) *Delivery.* When you are required to deliver an opt out notice by this section, you must deliver it according to § 573.9.

(i) *Model privacy form.* Pursuant to § 573.2(a) of this part, a model privacy form that meets the notice content requirements of this section is included in Appendix A of this part.

[65 FR 35226, June 1, 2000, as amended at 74 FR 62946, Dec. 1, 2009]

§ 573.8 Revised privacy notices.

(a) *General rule.* Except as otherwise authorized in this part, you must not, directly or through any affiliate, disclose any nonpublic personal information about a consumer to a nonaffiliated third party other than as described in the initial notice that you provided to that consumer under § 573.4, unless:

(1) You have provided to the consumer a clear and conspicuous revised notice that accurately describes your policies and practices;

(2) You have provided to the consumer a new opt out notice;

(3) You have given the consumer a reasonable opportunity, before you disclose the information to the nonaffiliated third party, to opt out of the disclosure; and

(4) The consumer does not opt out.

(b) *Examples.* (1) Except as otherwise permitted by §§ 573.13, 573.14, and 573.15, you must provide a revised notice before you:

(i) Disclose a new category of nonpublic personal information to any nonaffiliated third party;

(ii) Disclose nonpublic personal information to a new category of nonaffiliated third party; or

(iii) Disclose nonpublic personal information about a former customer to a nonaffiliated third party, if that former customer has not had the opportunity to exercise an opt out right regarding that disclosure.

(2) A revised notice is not required if you disclose nonpublic personal information to a new nonaffiliated third party that you adequately described in your prior notice.

(c) *Delivery.* When you are required to deliver a revised privacy notice by this section, you must deliver it according to § 573.9.

§ 573.9 Delivering privacy and opt out notices.

(a) *How to provide notices.* You must provide any privacy notices and opt out notices, including short-form initial notices, that this part requires so that each consumer can reasonably be expected to receive actual notice in writing or, if the consumer agrees, electronically.

(b)(1) *Examples of reasonable expectation of actual notice.* You may reasonably expect that a consumer will receive actual notice if you:

(i) Hand-deliver a printed copy of the notice to the consumer;

(ii) Mail a printed copy of the notice to the last known address of the consumer;

(iii) For the consumer who conducts transactions electronically, post the notice on the electronic site and require the consumer to acknowledge receipt of the notice as a necessary step to obtaining a particular financial product or service;

(iv) For an isolated transaction with the consumer, such as an ATM transaction, post the notice on the ATM screen and require the consumer to acknowledge receipt of the notice as a necessary step to obtaining the particular financial product or service.

(2) *Examples of unreasonable expectation of actual notice.* You may *not,* however, reasonably expect that a consumer will receive actual notice of your privacy policies and practices if you:

(i) Only post a sign in your branch or office or generally publish advertisements of your privacy policies and practices;

(ii) Send the notice via electronic mail to a consumer who does not obtain a financial product or service from you electronically.

481

§ 573.10

(c) *Annual notices only.* You may reasonably expect that a customer will receive actual notice of your annual privacy notice if:

(1) The customer uses your web site to access financial products and services electronically and agrees to receive notices at the web site, and you post your current privacy notice continuously in a clear and conspicuous manner on the web site; or

(2) The customer has requested that you refrain from sending any information regarding the customer relationship, and your current privacy notice remains available to the customer upon request.

(d) *Oral description of notice insufficient.* You may not provide any notice required by this part solely by orally explaining the notice, either in person or over the telephone.

(e) *Retention or accessibility of notices for customers.* (1) For customers only, you must provide the initial notice required by § 573.4(a)(1), the annual notice required by § 573.5(a), and the revised notice required by § 573.8 so that the customer can retain them or obtain them later in writing or, if the customer agrees, electronically.

(2) *Examples of retention or accessibility.* You provide a privacy notice to the customer so that the customer can retain it or obtain it later if you:

(i) Hand-deliver a printed copy of the notice to the customer;

(ii) Mail a printed copy of the notice to the last known address of the customer; or

(iii) Make your current privacy notice available on a web site (or a link to another web site) for the customer who obtains a financial product or service electronically and agrees to receive the notice at the web site.

(f) *Joint notice with other financial institutions.* You may provide a joint notice from you and one or more of your affiliates or other financial institutions, as identified in the notice, as long as the notice is accurate with respect to you and the other institutions.

(g) *Joint relationships.* If two or more consumers jointly obtain a financial product or service from you, you may satisfy the initial, annual, and revised notice requirements of §§ 573.4(a), 573.5(a), and 573.8(a), respectively, by providing one notice to those consumers jointly.

Subpart B—Limits on Disclosures

§ 573.10 Limits on disclosure of nonpublic personal information to nonaffiliated third parties.

(a)(1) *Conditions for disclosure.* Except as otherwise authorized in this part, you may not, directly or through any affiliate, disclose any nonpublic personal information about a consumer to a nonaffiliated third party unless:

(i) You have provided to the consumer an initial notice as required under § 573.4;

(ii) You have provided to the consumer an opt out notice as required in § 573.7;

(iii) You have given the consumer a reasonable opportunity, before you disclose the information to the nonaffiliated third party, to opt out of the disclosure; and

(iv) The consumer does not opt out.

(2) *Opt out definition.* Opt out means a direction by the consumer that you not disclose nonpublic personal information about that consumer to a nonaffiliated third party, other than as permitted by §§ 573.13, 573.14, and 573.15.

(3) *Examples of reasonable opportunity to opt out.* You provide a consumer with a reasonable opportunity to opt out if:

(i) *By mail.* You mail the notices required in paragraph (a)(1) of this section to the consumer and allow the consumer to opt out by mailing a form, calling a toll-free telephone number, or any other reasonable means within 30 days from the date you mailed the notices.

(ii) *By electronic means.* A customer opens an on-line account with you and agrees to receive the notices required in paragraph (a)(1) of this section electronically, and you allow the customer to opt out by any reasonable means within 30 days after the date that the customer acknowledges receipt of the notices in conjunction with opening the account.

(iii) *Isolated transaction with consumer.* For an isolated transaction, such as the purchase of a cashier's check by a consumer, you provide the consumer with a reasonable opportunity to opt out if you provide the notices required in paragraph (a)(1) of this section at the time of the transaction and request that the consumer decide, as a necessary part of the transaction, whether to opt out before completing the transaction.

(b) *Application of opt out to all consumers and all nonpublic personal information.* (1) You must comply with this section, regardless of whether you and the consumer have established a customer relationship.

(2) Unless you comply with this section, you may not, directly or through any affiliate, disclose any nonpublic personal information about a consumer that you have collected, regardless of whether you collected it before or after receiving the direction to opt out from the consumer.

(c) *Partial opt out.* You may allow a consumer to select certain nonpublic personal information or certain nonaffiliated third parties with respect to which the consumer wishes to opt out.

§ 573.11 Limits on redisclosure and reuse of information.

(a)(1) *Information you receive under an exception.* If you receive nonpublic personal information from a nonaffiliated financial institution under an exception in § 573.14 or 573.15 of this part, your disclosure and use of that information is limited as follows:

(i) You may disclose the information to the affiliates of the financial institution from which you received the information;

(ii) You may disclose the information to your affiliates, but your affiliates may, in turn, disclose and use the information only to the extent that you may disclose and use the information; and

(iii) You may disclose and use the information pursuant to an exception in § 573.14 or 573.15 in the ordinary course of business to carry out the activity covered by the exception under which you received the information.

(2) *Example.* If you receive a customer list from a nonaffiliated financial institution in order to provide account processing services under the exception in § 573.14(a), you may disclose that information under any exception in § 573.14 or 573.15 in the ordinary course of business in order to provide those services. For example, you could disclose the information in response to a properly authorized subpoena or to your attorneys, accountants, and auditors. You could not disclose that information to a third party for marketing purposes or use that information for your own marketing purposes.

(b)(1) *Information you receive outside of an exception.* If you receive nonpublic personal information from a nonaffiliated financial institution other than under an exception in § 573.14 or 573.15 of this part, you may disclose the information only:

(i) To the affiliates of the financial institution from which you received the information;

(ii) To your affiliates, but your affiliates may, in turn, disclose the information only to the extent that you can disclose the information; and

(iii) To any other person, if the disclosure would be lawful if made directly to that person by the financial institution from which you received the information.

(2) *Example.* If you obtain a customer list from a nonaffiliated financial institution outside of the exceptions in § 573.14 and 573.15:

(i) You may use that list for your own purposes; and

(ii) You may disclose that list to another nonaffiliated third party only if the financial institution from which you purchased the list could have lawfully disclosed the list to that third party. That is, you may disclose the list in accordance with the privacy policy of the financial institution from which you received the list, as limited by the opt out direction of each consumer whose nonpublic personal information you intend to disclose, and you may disclose the list in accordance with an exception in § 573.14 or 573.15, such as to your attorneys or accountants.

(c) *Information you disclose under an exception.* If you disclose nonpublic personal information to a nonaffiliated third party under an exception in § 573.14 or 573.15 of this part, the third party may disclose and use that information only as follows:

§ 573.12

(1) The third party may disclose the information to your affiliates;

(2) The third party may disclose the information to its affiliates, but its affiliates may, in turn, disclose and use the information only to the extent that the third party may disclose and use the information; and

(3) The third party may disclose and use the information pursuant to an exception in § 573.14 or 573.15 in the ordinary course of business to carry out the activity covered by the exception under which it received the information.

(d) *Information you disclose outside of an exception.* If you disclose nonpublic personal information to a nonaffiliated third party other than under an exception in § 573.14 or 573.15 of this part, the third party may disclose the information only:

(1) To your affiliates;

(2) To its affiliates, but its affiliates, in turn, may disclose the information only to the extent the third party can disclose the information; and

(3) To any other person, if the disclosure would be lawful if you made it directly to that person.

§ 573.12 Limits on sharing account number information for marketing purposes.

(a) *General prohibition on disclosure of account numbers.* You must not, directly or through an affiliate, disclose, other than to a consumer reporting agency, an account number or similar form of access number or access code for a consumer's credit card account, deposit account, or transaction account to any nonaffiliated third party for use in telemarketing, direct mail marketing, or other marketing through electronic mail to the consumer.

(b) *Exceptions.* Paragraph (a) of this section does not apply if you disclose an account number or similar form of access number or access code:

(1) To your agent or service provider solely in order to perform marketing for your own products or services, as long as the agent or service provider is not authorized to directly initiate charges to the account; or

(2) To a participant in a private label credit card program or an affinity or similar program where the participants in the program are identified to the customer when the customer enters into the program.

(c) *Examples*—(1) *Account number.* An account number, or similar form of access number or access code, does not include a number or code in an encrypted form, as long as you do not provide the recipient with a means to decode the number or code.

(2) *Transaction account.* A transaction account is an account other than a deposit account or a credit card account. A transaction account does not include an account to which third parties cannot initiate charges.

Subpart C—Exceptions

§ 573.13 Exception to opt out requirements for service providers and joint marketing.

(a) *General rule.* (1) The opt out requirements in §§ 573.7 and 573.10 do not apply when you provide nonpublic personal information to a nonaffiliated third party to perform services for you or functions on your behalf, if you:

(i) Provide the initial notice in accordance with § 573.4; and

(ii) Enter into a contractual agreement with the third party that prohibits the third party from disclosing or using the information other than to carry out the purposes for which you disclosed the information, including use under an exception in § 573.14 or 573.15 in the ordinary course of business to carry out those purposes.

(2) *Example.* If you disclose nonpublic personal information under this section to a financial institution with which you perform joint marketing, your contractual agreement with that institution meets the requirements of paragraph (a)(1)(ii) of this section if it prohibits the institution from disclosing or using the nonpublic personal information except as necessary to carry out the joint marketing or under an exception in § 573.14 or 573.15 in the ordinary course of business to carry out that joint marketing.

(b) *Service may include joint marketing.* The services a nonaffiliated third party performs for you under paragraph (a) of this section may include marketing of

Office of Thrift Supervision, Treasury § 573.15

your own products or services or marketing of financial products or services offered pursuant to joint agreements between you and one or more financial institutions.

(c) *Definition of joint agreement.* For purposes of this section, *joint agreement* means a written contract pursuant to which you and one or more financial institutions jointly offer, endorse, or sponsor a financial product or service.

§ 573.14 Exceptions to notice and opt out requirements for processing and servicing transactions.

(a) *Exceptions for processing transactions at consumer's request.* The requirements for initial notice in § 573.4(a)(2), for the opt out in §§ 573.7 and 573.10, and for service providers and joint marketing in § 573.13 do not apply if you disclose nonpublic personal information as necessary to effect, administer, or enforce a transaction that a consumer requests or authorizes, or in connection with:

(1) Servicing or processing a financial product or service that a consumer requests or authorizes;

(2) Maintaining or servicing the consumer's account with you, or with another entity as part of a private label credit card program or other extension of credit on behalf of such entity; or

(3) A proposed or actual securitization, secondary market sale (including sales of servicing rights), or similar transaction related to a transaction of the consumer.

(b) *Necessary to effect, administer, or enforce a transaction* means that the disclosure is:

(1) Required, or is one of the lawful or appropriate methods, to enforce your rights or the rights of other persons engaged in carrying out the financial transaction or providing the product or service; or

(2) Required, or is a usual, appropriate or acceptable method:

(i) To carry out the transaction or the product or service business of which the transaction is a part, and record, service, or maintain the consumer's account in the ordinary course of providing the financial service or financial product;

(ii) To administer or service benefits or claims relating to the transaction or the product or service business of which it is a part;

(iii) To provide a confirmation, statement, or other record of the transaction, or information on the status or value of the financial service or financial product to the consumer or the consumer's agent or broker;

(iv) To accrue or recognize incentives or bonuses associated with the transaction that are provided by you or any other party;

(v) To underwrite insurance at the consumer's request or for reinsurance purposes, or for any of the following purposes as they relate to a consumer's insurance: account administration, reporting, investigating, or preventing fraud or material misrepresentation, processing premium payments, processing insurance claims, administering insurance benefits (including utilization review activities), participating in research projects, or as otherwise required or specifically permitted by Federal or State law;

(vi) In connection with:

(A) The authorization, settlement, billing, processing, clearing, transferring, reconciling or collection of amounts charged, debited, or otherwise paid using a debit, credit, or other payment card, check, or account number, or by other payment means;

(B) The transfer of receivables, accounts, or interests therein; or

(C) The audit of debit, credit, or other payment information.

§ 573.15 Other exceptions to notice and opt out requirements.

(a) *Exceptions to opt out requirements.* The requirements for initial notice in § 573.4(a)(2), for the opt out in §§ 573.7 and 573.10, and for service providers and joint marketing in § 573.13 do not apply when you disclose nonpublic personal information:

(1) With the consent or at the direction of the consumer, provided that the consumer has not revoked the consent or direction;

(2)(i) To protect the confidentiality or security of your records pertaining to the consumer, service, product, or transaction;

(ii) To protect against or prevent actual or potential fraud, unauthorized transactions, claims, or other liability;

(iii) For required institutional risk control or for resolving consumer disputes or inquiries;

(iv) To persons holding a legal or beneficial interest relating to the consumer; or

(v) To persons acting in a fiduciary or representative capacity on behalf of the consumer;

(3) To provide information to insurance rate advisory organizations, guaranty funds or agencies, agencies that are rating you, persons that are assessing your compliance with industry standards, and your attorneys, accountants, and auditors;

(4) To the extent specifically permitted or required under other provisions of law and in accordance with the Right to Financial Privacy Act of 1978 (12 U.S.C. 3401 et seq.), to law enforcement agencies (including a federal functional regulator, the Secretary of the Treasury, with respect to 31 U.S.C. Chapter 53, Subchapter II (Records and Reports on Monetary Instruments and Transactions) and 12 U.S.C. Chapter 21 (Financial Recordkeeping), a State insurance authority, with respect to any person domiciled in that insurance authority's State that is engaged in providing insurance, and the Federal Trade Commission), self-regulatory organizations, or for an investigation on a matter related to public safety;

(5)(i) To a consumer reporting agency in accordance with the Fair Credit Reporting Act (15 U.S.C. 1681 et seq.), or

(ii) From a consumer report reported by a consumer reporting agency;

(6) In connection with a proposed or actual sale, merger, transfer, or exchange of all or a portion of a business or operating unit if the disclosure of nonpublic personal information concerns solely consumers of such business or unit; or

(7)(i) To comply with Federal, State, or local laws, rules and other applicable legal requirements;

(ii) To comply with a properly authorized civil, criminal, or regulatory investigation, or subpoena or summons by Federal, State, or local authorities; or

(iii) To respond to judicial process or government regulatory authorities having jurisdiction over you for examination, compliance, or other purposes as authorized by law.

(b) *Examples of consent and revocation of consent.* (1) A consumer may specifically consent to your disclosure to a nonaffiliated insurance company of the fact that the consumer has applied to you for a mortgage so that the insurance company can offer homeowner's insurance to the consumer.

(2) A consumer may revoke consent by subsequently exercising the right to opt out of future disclosures of nonpublic personal information as permitted under § 573.7(f).

[65 FR 35226, June 1, 2000, as amended at 66 FR 65822, Dec. 21, 2001]

Subpart D—Relation to Other Laws; Effective Date

§ 573.16 Protection of Fair Credit Reporting Act.

Nothing in this part shall be construed to modify, limit, or supersede the operation of the Fair Credit Reporting Act (15 U.S.C. 1681 et seq.), and no inference shall be drawn on the basis of the provisions of this part regarding whether information is transaction or experience information under section 603 of that Act.

§ 573.17 Relation to State laws.

(a) *In general.* This part shall not be construed as superseding, altering, or affecting any statute, regulation, order, or interpretation in effect in any State, except to the extent that such State statute, regulation, order, or interpretation is inconsistent with the provisions of this part, and then only to the extent of the inconsistency.

(b) *Greater protection under State law.* For purposes of this section, a State statute, regulation, order, or interpretation is not inconsistent with the provisions of this part if the protection such statute, regulation, order, or interpretation affords any consumer is greater than the protection provided under this part, as determined by the Federal Trade Commission, after consultation with the OTS, on the Federal Trade Commission's own motion, or upon the petition of any interested party.

§ 573.18 Effective date; transition rule.

(a) *Effective date.* This part is effective November 13, 2000. In order to provide sufficient time for you to establish policies and systems to comply with the requirements of this part, the OTS has extended the time for compliance with this part until July 1, 2001.

(b)(1) *Notice requirement for consumers who are your customers on the compliance date.* By July 1, 2001, you must have provided an initial notice, as required by § 573.4, to consumers who are your customers on July 1, 2001.

(2) *Example.* You provide an initial notice to consumers who are your customers on July 1, 2001, if, by that date, you have established a system for providing an initial notice to all new customers and have mailed the initial notice to all your existing customers.

(c) *Two-year grandfathering of service agreements.* Until July 1, 2002, a contract that you have entered into with a nonaffiliated third party to perform services for you or functions on your behalf satisfies the provisions of § 573.13(a)(1)(ii) of this part, even if the contract does not include a requirement that the third party maintain the confidentiality of nonpublic personal information, as long as you entered into the contract on or before July 1, 2000.

Pt. 573, App. A   12 CFR Ch. V (1-1-12 Edition)

APPENDIX A TO PART 573—MODEL PRIVACY FORM

A. The Model Privacy Form

Version 1: Model Form With No Opt-Out.

Rev. [insert date]

FACTS	WHAT DOES [NAME OF FINANCIAL INSTITUTION] DO WITH YOUR PERSONAL INFORMATION?
Why?	Financial companies choose how they share your personal information. Federal law gives consumers the right to limit some but not all sharing. Federal law also requires us to tell you how we collect, share, and protect your personal information. Please read this notice carefully to understand what we do.
What?	The types of personal information we collect and share depend on the product or service you have with us. This information can include: ■ Social Security number and [income] ■ [account balances] and [payment history] ■ [credit history] and [credit scores] When you are *no longer* our customer, we continue to share your information as described in this notice.
How?	All financial companies need to share customers' personal information to run their everyday business. In the section below, we list the reasons financial companies can share their customers' personal information; the reasons [name of financial institution] chooses to share; and whether you can limit this sharing.

Reasons we can share your personal information	Does [name of financial institution] share?	Can you limit this sharing?
For our everyday business purposes— such as to process your transactions, maintain your account(s), respond to court orders and legal investigations, or report to credit bureaus		
For our marketing purposes— to offer our products and services to you		
For joint marketing with other financial companies		
For our affiliates' everyday business purposes— information about your transactions and experiences		
For our affiliates' everyday business purposes— information about your creditworthiness		
For our affiliates to market to you		
For nonaffiliates to market to you		

Questions?	Call [phone number] or go to [website]

488

Page 2

Who we are

Who is providing this notice?	[insert]

What we do

How does [name of financial institution] protect my personal information?	To protect your personal information from unauthorized access and use, we use security measures that comply with federal law. These measures include computer safeguards and secured files and buildings. [insert]
How does [name of financial institution] collect my personal information?	We collect your personal information, for example, when you ■ [open an account] or [deposit money] ■ [pay your bills] or [apply for a loan] ■ [use your credit or debit card] [We also collect your personal information from other companies.] OR [We also collect your personal information from others, such as credit bureaus, affiliates, or other companies.]
Why can't I limit all sharing?	Federal law gives you the right to limit only ■ sharing for affiliates' everyday business purposes—information about your creditworthiness ■ affiliates from using your information to market to you ■ sharing for nonaffiliates to market to you State laws and individual companies may give you additional rights to limit sharing. [See below for more on your rights under state law.]

Definitions

Affiliates	Companies related by common ownership or control. They can be financial and nonfinancial companies. ■ [affiliate information]
Nonaffiliates	Companies not related by common ownership or control. They can be financial and nonfinancial companies. ■ [nonaffiliate information]
Joint marketing	A formal agreement between nonaffiliated financial companies that together market financial products or services to you. ■ [joint marketing information]

Other important information

[insert other important information]

Pt. 573, App. A

12 CFR Ch. V (1-1-12 Edition)

Version 2: Model Form with Opt-Out by Telephone and/or Online.

Rev. [insert date]

FACTS	WHAT DOES [NAME OF FINANCIAL INSTITUTION] DO WITH YOUR PERSONAL INFORMATION?
Why?	Financial companies choose how they share your personal information. Federal law gives consumers the right to limit some but not all sharing. Federal law also requires us to tell you how we collect, share, and protect your personal information. Please read this notice carefully to understand what we do.
What?	The types of personal information we collect and share depend on the product or service you have with us. This information can include: ■ Social Security number and [income] ■ [account balances] and [payment history] ■ [credit history] and [credit scores]
How?	All financial companies need to share customers' personal information to run their everyday business. In the section below, we list the reasons financial companies can share their customers' personal information; the reasons [name of financial institution] chooses to share; and whether you can limit this sharing.

Reasons we can share your personal information	Does [name of financial institution] share?	Can you limit this sharing?
For our everyday business purposes— such as to process your transactions, maintain your account(s), respond to court orders and legal investigations, or report to credit bureaus		
For our marketing purposes— to offer our products and services to you		
For joint marketing with other financial companies		
For our affiliates' everyday business purposes— information about your transactions and experiences		
For our affiliates' everyday business purposes— information about your creditworthiness		
For our affiliates to market to you		
For nonaffiliates to market to you		

To limit our sharing	■ Call [phone number]—our menu will prompt you through your choice(s) or ■ Visit us online: [website] Please note: If you are a *new* customer, we can begin sharing your information [30] days from the date we sent this notice. When you are *no longer* our customer, we continue to share your information as described in this notice. However, you can contact us at any time to limit our sharing.
Questions?	Call [phone number] or go to [website]

490

Office of Thrift Supervision, Treasury

Pt. 573, App. A

Page 2

Who we are	
Who is providing this notice?	[insert]

What we do	
How does [name of financial institution] protect my personal information?	To protect your personal information from unauthorized access and use, we use security measures that comply with federal law. These measures include computer safeguards and secured files and buildings. [insert]
How does [name of financial institution] collect my personal information?	We collect your personal information, for example, when you • [open an account] or [deposit money] • [pay your bills] or [apply for a loan] • [use your credit or debit card] [We also collect your personal information from other companies.] OR [We also collect your personal information from others, such as credit bureaus, affiliates, or other companies.]
Why can't I limit all sharing?	Federal law gives you the right to limit only • sharing for affiliates' everyday business purposes—information about your creditworthiness • affiliates from using your information to market to you • sharing for nonaffiliates to market to you State laws and individual companies may give you additional rights to limit sharing. [See below for more on your rights under state law.]
What happens when I limit sharing for an account I hold jointly with someone else?	[Your choices will apply to everyone on your account.] OR [Your choices will apply to everyone on your account—unless you tell us otherwise.]

Definitions	
Affiliates	Companies related by common ownership or control. They can be financial and nonfinancial companies. • [affiliate information]
Nonaffiliates	Companies not related by common ownership or control. They can be financial and nonfinancial companies. • [nonaffiliate information]
Joint marketing	A formal agreement between nonaffiliated financial companies that together market financial products or services to you. • [joint marketing information]

Other important information
[insert other important information]

Pt. 573, App. A   12 CFR Ch. V (1-1-12 Edition)

Version 3: Model Form with Mail-In Opt-Out Form.

Rev. [insert date]

FACTS	WHAT DOES [NAME OF FINANCIAL INSTITUTION] DO WITH YOUR PERSONAL INFORMATION?
Why?	Financial companies choose how they share your personal information. Federal law gives consumers the right to limit some but not all sharing. Federal law also requires us to tell you how we collect, share, and protect your personal information. Please read this notice carefully to understand what we do.
What?	The types of personal information we collect and share depend on the product or service you have with us. This information can include: ■ Social Security number and [income] ■ [account balances] and [payment history] ■ [credit history] and [credit scores]
How?	All financial companies need to share customers' personal information to run their everyday business. In the section below, we list the reasons financial companies can share their customers' personal information; the reasons [name of financial institution] chooses to share; and whether you can limit this sharing.

Reasons we can share your personal information	Does [name of financial institution] share?	Can you limit this sharing?
For our everyday business purposes— such as to process your transactions, maintain your account(s), respond to court orders and legal investigations, or report to credit bureaus		
For our marketing purposes— to offer our products and services to you		
For joint marketing with other financial companies		
For our affiliates' everyday business purposes— information about your transactions and experiences		
For our affiliates' everyday business purposes— information about your creditworthiness		
For our affiliates to market to you		
For nonaffiliates to market to you		

To limit our sharing	■ Call [phone number]—our menu will prompt you through your choice(s) ■ Visit us online: [website] or ■ Mail the form below **Please note:** If you are a new customer, we can begin sharing your information [30] days from the date we sent this notice. When you are no longer our customer, we continue to share your information as described in this notice. However, you can contact us at any time to limit our sharing.
Questions?	Call [phone number] or go to [website]

✂-----

Mail-in Form		
Leave Blank OR [If you have a joint account, your choice(s) will apply to everyone on your account unless you mark below. ☐ Apply my choices only to me]	Mark any/all you want to limit: ☐ Do not share information about my creditworthiness with your affiliates for their everyday business purposes. ☐ Do not allow your affiliates to use my personal information to market to me. ☐ Do not share my personal information with nonaffiliates to market their products and services to me.	
	Name	Mail to:
	Address	[Name of Financial Institution]
	City, State, Zip	[Address 1] [Address2] [City], [ST] [ZIP]

Office of Thrift Supervision, Treasury — Pt. 573, App. A

Page 2

Who we are

Who is providing this notice?	[insert]

What we do

How does [name of financial institution] protect my personal information?	To protect your personal information from unauthorized access and use, we use security measures that comply with federal law. These measures include computer safeguards and secured files and buildings. [insert]
How does [name of financial institution] collect my personal information?	We collect your personal information, for example, when you - [open an account] or [deposit money] - [pay your bills] or [apply for a loan] - [use your credit or debit card] [We also collect your personal information from other companies.] OR [We also collect your personal information from others, such as credit bureaus, affiliates, or other companies.]
Why can't I limit all sharing?	Federal law gives you the right to limit only - sharing for affiliates' everyday business purposes—information about your creditworthiness - affiliates from using your information to market to you - sharing for nonaffiliates to market to you State laws and individual companies may give you additional rights to limit sharing. [See below for more on your rights under state law.]
What happens when I limit sharing for an account I hold jointly with someone else?	[Your choices will apply to everyone on your account.] OR [Your choices will apply to everyone on your account — unless you tell us otherwise.]

Definitions

Affiliates	Companies related by common ownership or control. They can be financial and nonfinancial companies. - [affiliate information]
Nonaffiliates	Companies not related by common ownership or control. They can be financial and nonfinancial companies. - [nonaffiliate information]
Joint marketing	A formal agreement between nonaffiliated financial companies that together market financial products or services to you. - [joint marketing information]

Other important information

[insert other important information]

Version 4. Optional Mail-in Form.

Leave Blank OR [If you have a joint account, your choice(s) will apply to everyone on your account unless you mark below. ☐ Apply my choices only to me]	Mark any/all you want to limit: ☐ Do not share information about my creditworthiness with your affiliates for their everyday business purposes. ☐ Do not allow your affiliates to use my personal information to market to me. ☐ Do not share my personal information with nonaffiliates to market their products and services to me.
	Name
	Address
	City, State, Zip

Mail To: [Name of Financial Institution], [Address 1] [Address 2], [City], [ST] [ZIP]

B. General Instructions

1. How the Model Privacy Form Is Used

(a) The model form may be used, at the option of a financial institution, including a group of financial institutions that use a common privacy notice, to meet the content requirements of the privacy notice and opt-out notice set forth in §§ 573.6 and 573.7 of this part.

(b) The model form is a standardized form, including page layout, content, format, style, pagination, and shading. Institutions seeking to obtain the safe harbor through use of the model form may modify it only as described in these Instructions.

(c) Note that disclosure of certain information, such as assets, income, and information from a consumer reporting agency, may give rise to obligations under the Fair Credit Reporting Act [15 U.S.C. 1681–1681x] (FCRA), such as a requirement to permit a consumer to opt out of disclosures to affiliates or designation as a consumer reporting agency if disclosures are made to nonaffiliated third parties.

(d) The word "customer" may be replaced by the word "member" whenever it appears in the model form, as appropriate.

2. The Contents of the Model Privacy Form

The model form consists of two pages, which may be printed on both sides of a single sheet of paper, or may appear on two separate pages. Where an institution provides a long list of institutions at the end of the model form in accordance with Instruction C.3(a)(1), or provides additional information in accordance with Instruction C.3(c), and such list or additional information exceeds the space available on page two of the model form, such list or additional information may extend to a third page.

(a) *Page One.* The first page consists of the following components:

(1) Date last revised (upper right-hand corner).

(2) Title.

(3) Key frame (Why?, What?, How?).

(4) Disclosure table ("Reasons we can share your personal information").

(5) "To limit our sharing" box, as needed, for the financial institution's opt-out information.

(6) "Questions" box, for customer service contact information.

(7) Mail-in opt-out form, as needed.

(b) *Page Two.* The second page consists of the following components:

(1) Heading (Page 2).

(2) Frequently Asked Questions ("Who we are" and "What we do").

(3) Definitions.

(4) "Other important information" box, as needed.

3. The Format of the Model Privacy Form

The format of the model form may be modified only as described below.

(a) *Easily readable type font.* Financial institutions that use the model form must use an easily readable type font. While a number of factors together produce easily readable type font, institutions are required to use a minimum of 10-point font (unless otherwise expressly permitted in these Instructions) and sufficient spacing between the lines of type.

(b) *Logo.* A financial institution may include a corporate logo on any page of the notice, so long as it does not interfere with the

Office of Thrift Supervision, Treasury

Pt. 573, App. A

readability of the model form or the space constraints of each page.

(c) *Page size and orientation.* Each page of the model form must be printed on paper in portrait orientation, the size of which must be sufficient to meet the layout and minimum font size requirements, with sufficient white space on the top, bottom, and sides of the content.

(d) *Color.* The model form must be printed on white or light color paper (such as cream) with black or other contrasting ink color. Spot color may be used to achieve visual interest, so long as the color contrast is distinctive and the color does not detract from the readability of the model form. Logos may also be printed in color.

(e) *Languages.* The model form may be translated into languages other than English.

C. Information Required in the Model Privacy Form

The information in the model form may be modified only as described below:

1. Name of the Institution or Group of Affiliated Institutions Providing the Notice

Insert the name of the financial institution providing the notice or a common identity of affiliated institutions jointly providing the notice on the form wherever [name of financial institution] appears.

2. Page One

(a) *Last revised date.* The financial institution must insert in the upper right-hand corner the date on which the notice was last revised. The information shall appear in minimum 8-point font as "rev. [month/year]" using either the name or number of the month, such as "rev. July 2009" or "rev. 7/09".

(b) *General instructions for the "What?" box.*

(1) The bulleted list identifies the types of personal information that the institution collects and shares. All institutions must use the term "Social Security number" in the first bullet.

(2) Institutions must use five (5) of the following terms to complete the bulleted list: Income; account balances; payment history; transaction history; transaction or loss history; credit history; credit scores; assets; investment experience; credit-based insurance scores; insurance claim history; medical information; overdraft history; purchase history; account transactions; risk tolerance; medical-related debts; credit card or other debt; mortgage rates and payments; retirement assets; checking account information; employment information; wire transfer instructions.

(c) *General instructions for the disclosure table.* The left column lists reasons for sharing or using personal information. Each reason correlates to a specific legal provision described in paragraph C.2(d) of this Instruction. In the middle column, each institution must provide a "Yes" or "No" response that accurately reflects its information sharing policies and practices with respect to the reason listed on the left. In the right column, each institution must provide in each box one of the following three (3) responses, as applicable, that reflects whether a consumer can limit such sharing: "Yes" if it is required to or voluntarily provides an opt-out; "No" if it does not provide an opt-out; or "We don't share" if it answers "No" in the middle column. Only the sixth row ("For our affiliates to market to you") may be omitted at the option of the institution. *See* paragraph C.2(d)(6) of this Instruction.

(d) *Specific disclosures and corresponding legal provisions.*

(1) *For our everyday business purposes.* This reason incorporates sharing information under §§ 573.14 and 573.15 and with service providers pursuant to § 573.13 of this part other than the purposes specified in paragraphs C.2(d)(2) or C.2(d)(3) of these Instructions.

(2) *For our marketing purposes.* This reason incorporates sharing information with service providers by an institution for its own marketing pursuant to § 573.13 of this part. An institution that shares for this reason may choose to provide an opt-out.

(3) *For joint marketing with other financial companies.* This reason incorporates sharing information under joint marketing agreements between two or more financial institutions and with any service provider used in connection with such agreements pursuant to § 573.13 of this part. An institution that shares for this reason may choose to provide an opt-out.

(4) *For our affiliates' everyday business purposes—information about transactions and experiences.* This reason incorporates sharing information specified in sections 603(d)(2)(A)(i) and (ii) of the FCRA. An institution that shares for this reason may choose to provide an opt-out.

(5) *For our affiliates' everyday business purposes—information about creditworthiness.* This reason incorporates sharing information pursuant to section 603(d)(2)(A)(iii) of the FCRA. An institution that shares for this reason must provide an opt-out.

(6) *For our affiliates to market to you.* This reason incorporates sharing information specified in section 624 of the FCRA. This reason may be omitted from the disclosure table when: The institution does not have affiliates (or does not disclose personal information to its affiliates); the institution's affiliates do not use personal information in a manner that requires an opt-out; or the institution provides the affiliate marketing notice separately. Institutions that include

this reason must provide an opt-out of indefinite duration. An institution that is required to provide an affiliate marketing opt-out, but does not include that opt-out in the model form under this part, must comply with section 624 of the FCRA and 12 CFR part 571, subpart C, with respect to the initial notice and opt-out and any subsequent renewal notice and opt-out. An institution not required to provide an opt-out under this subparagraph may elect to include this reason in the model form.

(7) *For nonaffiliates to market to you.* This reason incorporates sharing described in §§ 573.7 and 573.10(a) of this part. An institution that shares personal information for this reason must provide an opt-out.

(e) *To limit our sharing:* A financial institution must include this section of the model form *only* if it provides an opt-out. The word "choice" may be written in either the singular or plural, as appropriate. Institutions must select one or more of the applicable opt-out methods described: Telephone, such as by a toll-free number; a Web site; or use of a mail-in opt-out form. Institutions may include the words "toll-free" before telephone, as appropriate. An institution that allows consumers to opt out online must provide either a specific Web address that takes consumers directly to the opt-out page or a general Web address that provides a clear and conspicuous direct link to the opt-out page. The opt-out choices made available to the consumer who contacts the institution through these methods must correspond accurately to the "Yes" responses in the third column of the disclosure table. In the part titled "Please note," institutions may insert a number that is 30 or greater in the space marked "[30]." Instructions on voluntary or state privacy law opt-out information are in paragraph C.2(g)(5) of these Instructions.

(f) *Questions box.* Customer service contact information must be inserted as appropriate, where [phone number] or [Web site] appear. Institutions may elect to provide either a phone number, such as a toll-free number, or a Web address, or both. Institutions may include the words "toll-free" before the telephone number, as appropriate.

(g) *Mail-in opt-out form.* Financial institutions must include this mail-in form *only* if they state in the "To limit our sharing" box that consumers can opt out by mail. The mail-in form must provide opt-out options that correspond accurately to the "Yes" responses in the third column in the disclosure table. Institutions that require customers to provide only name and address may omit the section identified as "[account #]." Institutions that require additional or different information, such as a random opt-out number or a truncated account number, to implement an opt-out election should modify the "[account #]" reference accordingly. This includes institutions that require customers with multiple accounts to identify each account to which the opt-out should apply. An institution must enter its opt-out mailing address: in the far right of this form (*see* version 3); or below the form (*see* version 4). The reverse side of the mail-in opt-out form must not include any content of the model form.

(1) *Joint accountholder.* Only institutions that provide their joint accountholders the choice to opt out for only one accountholder, in accordance with paragraph C.3(a)(5) of these Instructions, must include in the far left column of the mail-in form the following statement: "If you have a joint account, your choice(s) will apply to everyone on your account unless you mark below. ☐ Apply my choice(s) only to me." The word "choice" may be written in either the singular or plural, as appropriate. Financial institutions that provide insurance products or services, provide this option, and elect to use the model form may substitute the word "policy" for "account" in this statement. Institutions that do not provide this option may eliminate this left column from the mail-in form.

(2) *FCRA Section 603(d)(2)(A)(iii) opt-out.* If the institution shares personal information pursuant to section 603(d)(2)(A)(iii) of the FCRA, it must include in the mail-in opt-out form the following statement: "☐ Do not share information about my creditworthiness with your affiliates for their everyday business purposes."

(3) *FCRA Section 624 opt-out.* If the institution incorporates section 624 of the FCRA in accord with paragraph C.2(d)(6) of these Instructions, it must include in the mail-in opt-out form the following statement: "☐ Do not allow your affiliates to use my personal information to market to me."

(4) *Nonaffiliate opt-out.* If the financial institution shares personal information pursuant to § 573.10(a) of this part, it must include in the mail-in opt-out form the following statement: "☐ Do not share my personal information with nonaffiliates to market their products and services to me."

(5) *Additional opt-outs.* Financial institutions that use the disclosure table to provide opt-out options beyond those required by Federal law must provide those opt-outs in this section of the model form. A financial institution that chooses to offer an opt-out for its own marketing in the mail-in opt-out form must include one of the two following statements: "☐ Do not share my personal information to market to me." *or* "☐ Do not use my personal information to market to me." A financial institution that chooses to offer an opt-out for joint marketing must include the following statement: "☐ Do not share my personal information with other financial institutions to jointly market to me."

Office of Thrift Supervision, Treasury Pt. 573, App. A

(h) *Barcodes.* A financial institution may elect to include a barcode and/or "tagline" (an internal identifier) in 6-point font at the bottom of page one, as needed for information internal to the institution, so long as these do not interfere with the clarity or text of the form.

3. Page Two

(a) *General Instructions for the Questions.* Certain of the Questions may be customized as follows:

(1) *"Who is providing this notice?"* This question may be omitted where only one financial institution provides the model form and that institution is clearly identified in the title on page one. Two or more financial institutions that jointly provide the model form must use this question to identify themselves as required by §573.9(f) of this part. Where the list of institutions exceeds four (4) lines, the institution must describe in the response to this question the general types of institutions jointly providing the notice and must separately identify those institutions, in minimum 8-point font, directly following the "Other important information" box, or, if that box is not included in the institution's form, directly following the "Definitions." The list may appear in a multi-column format.

(2) *"How does [name of financial institution] protect my personal information?"* The financial institution may only provide additional information pertaining to its safeguards practices following the designated response to this question. Such information may include information about the institution's use of cookies or other measures it uses to safeguard personal information. Institutions are limited to a maximum of 30 additional words.

(3) *"How does [name of financial institution] collect my personal information?"* Institutions must use five (5) of the following terms to complete the bulleted list for this question: Open an account; deposit money; pay your bills; apply for a loan; use your credit or debit card; seek financial or tax advice; apply for insurance; pay insurance premiums; file an insurance claim; seek advice about your investments; buy securities from us; sell securities to us; direct us to buy securities; direct us to sell your securities; make deposits or withdrawals from your account; enter into an investment advisory contract; give us your income information; provide employment information; give us your employment history; tell us about your investment or retirement portfolio; tell us about your investment or retirement earnings; apply for financing; apply for a lease; provide account information; give us your contact information; pay us by check; give us your wage statements; provide your mortgage information; make a wire transfer; tell us who receives the money; tell us where to send the money; show your government-issued ID; show your driver's license; order a commodity futures or option trade. Institutions that collect personal information from their affiliates and/or credit bureaus must include after the bulleted list the following statement: "We also collect your personal information from others, such as credit bureaus, affiliates, or other companies." Institutions that do not collect personal information from their affiliates or credit bureaus but do collect information from other companies must include the following statement instead: "We also collect your personal information from other companies." Only institutions that do not collect any personal information from affiliates, credit bureaus, or other companies can omit both statements.

(4) *"Why can't I limit all sharing?"* Institutions that describe state privacy law provisions in the "Other important information" box must use the bracketed sentence: "See below for more on your rights under state law." Other institutions must omit this sentence.

(5) *"What happens when I limit sharing for an account I hold jointly with someone else?"* Only financial institutions that provide opt-out options must use this question. Other institutions must omit this question. Institutions must choose one of the following two statements to respond to this question: "Your choices will apply to everyone on your account." or "Your choices will apply to everyone on your account—unless you tell us otherwise." Financial institutions that provide insurance products or services and elect to use the model form may substitute the word "policy" for "account" in these statements.

(b) *General Instructions for the Definitions.* The financial institution must customize the space below the responses to the three definitions in this section. This specific information must be in italicized lettering to set off the information from the standardized definitions.

(1) *Affiliates.* As required by §573.6(a)(3) of this part, where [affiliate information] appears, the financial institution must:

(i) If it has no affiliates, state: "[name of financial institution] has no affiliates;"

(ii) If it has affiliates but does not share personal information, state: "[name of financial institution] does not share with our affiliates"; or

(iii) If it shares with its affiliates, state, as applicable: "Our affiliates include companies with a [common corporate identity of financial institution] name; financial companies such as [insert illustrative list of companies]; non-financial companies, such as [insert illustrative list of companies]; and others, such as [insert illustrative list]."

(2) *Nonaffiliates.* As required by §573.6(c)(3) of this part, where [nonaffiliate information] appears, the financial institution must:

(i) If it does not share with nonaffiliated third parties, state: "*[name of financial institution] does not share with nonaffiliates so they can market to you*"; or

(ii) If it shares with nonaffiliated third parties, state, as applicable: "*Nonaffiliates we share with can include [list categories of companies such as mortgage companies, insurance companies, direct marketing companies, and nonprofit organizations].*"

(3) *Joint Marketing.* As required by §573.13 of this part, where *[joint marketing]* appears, the financial institution must:

(i) If it does not engage in joint marketing, state: "*[name of financial institution] doesn't jointly market*"; or

(ii) If it shares personal information for joint marketing, state, as applicable: "*Our joint marketing partners include [list categories of companies such as credit card companies].*"

(c) *General instructions for the "Other important information" box.* This box is optional. The space provided for information in this box is not limited. Only the following types of information can appear in this box.

(1) State and/or international privacy law information; and/or

(2) Acknowledgment of receipt form.

[74 FR 62946, Dec. 1, 2009]

PART 574—ACQUISITION OF CONTROL OF SAVINGS ASSOCIATIONS

Sec.
574.1 Scope of part.
574.2 Definitions.
574.3 Acquisition of control of savings associations.
574.4 Control.
574.5 Certifications of ownership.
574.6 Procedural requirements.
574.7 Determination by the OTS.
574.8 Qualified stock issuances by undercapitalized savings associations or holding companies.
574.100 Rebuttal of control agreement.

AUTHORITY: 12 U.S.C. 1467a, 1817, 1831i.

SOURCE: 54 FR 49690, Nov. 30, 1989, unless otherwise noted.

§574.1 Scope of part.

The purpose of this part is to implement the provisions of the Change in Bank Control Act, 12 U.S.C.1817(j) ("Control Act"), and the Savings and Loan Holding Company Act, 12 U.S.C. 1467a ("Holding Company Act"), relating to acquisitions and changes in control of savings associations that are organized in stock form and savings and loan holding companies thereof.

[61 FR 60184, Nov. 27, 1996]

§574.2 Definitions.

As used in this part and in the forms under this part, the following definitions apply, unless the context otherwise requires:

(a) *Acquire* when used in connection with the acquisition of stock of a savings association means obtaining ownership, control, power to vote, or sole power of disposition of stock, directly or indirectly or through one or more transactions or subsidiaries, through purchase, assignment, transfer, exchange, succession, or other means, including:

(1) An increase in percentage ownership resulting from a redemption, repurchase, reverse stock split or a similar transaction involving other securities of the same class, and

(2) The acquisition of stock by a group of persons and/or companies acting in concert which shall be deemed to occur upon formation of such group: *Provided,* That an investment advisor shall not be deemed to acquire the voting stock of its advisee if the advisor:

(i) Votes the stock only upon instruction from the beneficial owner, and

(ii) Does not provide the beneficial owner with advice concerning the voting of such stock.

(b) *Acquiror* means a person or company.

(c) *Acting in concert* means: (1) Knowing participation in a joint activity or interdependent conscious parallel action towards a common goal whether or not pursuant to an express agreement, or

(2) A combination or pooling of voting or other interests in the securities of an issuer for a common purpose pursuant to any contract, understanding, relationship, agreement or other arrangement, whether written or otherwise.

(3) A person or company which acts in concert with another person or company ("other party") shall also be deemed to be acting in concert with any person or company who is also acting in concert with that other party, except that any tax-qualified employee stock benefit plan as defined in §563b.25

of this chapter will not be deemed to be acting in concert with its trustee or a person who serves in a similar capacity solely for the purpose of determining whether stock held by the trustee and stock held by the plan will be aggregated.

(d) *Affiliate* means any person or company which controls, is controlled by or is under common control with a person, savings association or company.

(e) [Reserved]

(f) *Company* means any corporation, partnership, trust, association, joint venture, pool, syndicate, unincorporated organization, joint-stock company or similar organization, as defined in paragraph (r) of this section; but a company does not include:

(1) The Federal Deposit Insurance Corporation, the Resolution Trust Corporation, the Office of Thrift Supervision, or any Federal Home Loan Bank, or

(2) Any company the majority of shares of which is owned by:

(i) The United States or any State,

(ii) An officer of the United States or any State in his or her official capacity, or

(iii) An instrumentality of the United States or any State.

(g) *Controlling shareholder* means any person who directly or indirectly or acting in concert with one or more persons or companies, or together with members of his or her immediate family, owns, controls, or holds with power to vote 10 percent or more of the voting stock of a company or controls in any manner the election or appointment of a majority of the company's board of directors.

(h) *Director* means the Director of the Office of Thrift Supervision.

(i) [Reserved]

(j) *Immediate family* means a person's spouse, father, mother, children, brothers, sisters and grandchildren; the father, mother, brothers, and sisters of the person's spouse; and the spouse of the person's child, brother or sister.

(k) *Management official* means any president, chief executive officer, chief operating officer, vice president, director, partner, or trustee, or any other person who performs or has a representative or nominee performing similar policymaking functions, including executive officers of principal business units or divisions or subsidiaries who perform policymaking functions, for a savings association or a company, whether or not incorporated.

(l) *Office* means the Office of Thrift Supervision.

(m) *Person* means an individual or a group of individuals acting in concert who do not constitute a "company" as defined in paragraph (f) of this section.

(n) *Repealed Control Act* means the Change in Savings and Loan Control Act, 12 U.S.C. 1730(q), as in effect immediately prior to its repeal by the Financial Institutions Reform, Recovery, and Enforcement Act of 1989.

(o) [Reserved]

(p) *Savings Association* means a Federal savings and loan association or a Federal savings bank chartered under section 5 of the Home Owners' Loan Act, a building and loan, savings and loan or homestead association or a cooperative bank (other than a cooperative bank described in 12 U.S.C. 1813(a)(2)) the deposits of which are insured by the Federal Deposit Insurance Corporation, and any corporation (other than a bank) the deposits of which are insured by the Federal Deposit Insurance Corporation that the Office and the Federal Deposit Insurance Corporation jointly determine to be operating in substantially the same manner as a savings association, and shall include any savings bank or any cooperative bank which is deemed by the Office to be a savings association under 12 U.S.C. 1467a(1), and any savings and loan holding company as defined in paragraph (q) of this section.

(q) *Savings and loan holding company* means any company that directly or indirectly controls a savings association, but does not include:

(1) Any company by virtue of its ownership or control of voting stock of a savings association acquired in connection with the underwriting of securities if such stock is held only for such period of time (not exceeding 120 days unless extended by the Office) as will permit the sale thereof on a reasonable basis; and

(2) Any trust (other than a pension, profit-sharing, stockholders', voting, or business trust) which controls a savings association if such trust by its

§ 574.2

terms must terminate within 25 years or not later than 21 years and 10 months after the death of individuals living on the effective date of the trust, and:

(i) Was in existence and in control of a savings association on June 26, 1967, or

(ii) Is a testamentary trust; and

(3) A bank holding company that is registered under, and subject to, the Bank Holding Company Act of 1956, or any company directly or indirectly controlled by such company (other than a savings association).

(r) *Similar organization* for purposes of paragraph (f) of this section means a combination of parties with the potential for or practical likelihood of continuing rather than temporary existence, where the parties thereto have knowingly and voluntarily associated for a common purpose pursuant to identifiable and binding relationships which govern the parties with respect to either:

(1) The transferability and voting of any stock or other indicia of participation in another entity, or

(2) Achievement of a common or shared objective, such as to collectively manage or control another entity.

(s) *Stock* means common or preferred stock, general or limited partnership shares or interests, or similar interests.

(t) *Uninsured institution* means any financial institution the deposits of which are not insured by the Federal Deposit Insurance Corporation.

(u)(1) *Voting stock* means common or preferred stock, general or limited partnership shares or interests, or similar interests if the shares or interests, by statute, charter or in any manner, entitle the holder:

(i) To vote for or to select directors, trustees, or partners (or persons exercising similar functions of the issuing savings association or company); or

(ii) To vote or to direct the conduct of the operations or other significant policies of the issuer:

(2) Notwithstanding anything in paragraph (u)(1) of this section, preferred stock, limited partnership shares or interests, or similar interests are not "voting stock" if:

12 CFR Ch. V (1-1-12 Edition)

(i) Voting rights associated with the stock, shares or interests are limited solely to the type customarily provided by statute with regard to matters that would significantly and adversely affect the rights or preference of the stock, security or other interest, such as the issuance of additional amounts or classes of senior securities, the modification of the terms of the stock, security or interest, the dissolution of the issuer, or the payment of dividends by the issuer when preferred dividends are in arrears;

(ii) The stock, shares or interests represent an essentially passive investment or financing device and do not otherwise provide the holder with control over the issuer; and

(iii) The stock, shares or interests do not at the time entitle the holder, by statute, charter, or otherwise, to select or to vote for the selection of directors, trustees, or partners (or persons exercising similar functions) of the issuer;

(3) Notwithstanding anything in paragraphs (u)(1) and (u)(2) of this section, "voting stock" shall be deemed to include stock and other securities that, upon transfer or otherwise, are convertible into voting stock or exercisable to acquire voting stock where the holder of the stock, convertible security or right to acquire voting stock has the preponderant economic risk in the underlying voting stock. Securities immediately convertible into voting stock at the option of the holder without payment of additional consideration shall be deemed to constitute the voting stock into which they are convertible; other convertible securities and rights to acquire voting stock shall not be deemed to vest the holder with the preponderant economic risk in the underlying voting stock if the holder has paid less than 50 percent of the consideration required to directly acquire the voting stock and has no other economic interest in the underlying voting stock. For purposes of calculating the percentage of voting stock held by a particular acquiror, stock or other securities convertible into voting stock or exercisable to acquire voting stock which are deemed voting stock under this paragraph (u)(3) shall be included in calculating the amount of voting stock held by the acquiror and

500

Office of Thrift Supervision, Treasury § 574.3

the total amount of stock outstanding only to the extent of the voting stock obtainable by such acquiror by such conversion or exercise of rights.

[54 FR 49690, Nov. 30, 1989, as amended at 60 FR 66720, Dec. 26, 1995; 61 FR 60184, Nov. 27, 1996; 71 FR 19812, Apr. 18, 2006; 73 FR 19, Jan. 2, 2008]

§ 574.3 Acquisition of control of savings associations.

(a) *Acquisition by a company or certain persons.* Unless a transaction is exempt under paragraph (c) of this section, or exempt from prior approval under paragraph (d) of this section, no company or any director or officer of a savings and loan holding company, or any individual who owns, controls, or holds with power to vote (or holds proxies representing) more than 25 percent of the voting stock of a savings and loan holding company, shall acquire control, as defined in § 574.4 (a) and (b) of this part, of a savings association except upon receipt of the written approval of the Office.

(b) *Acquisition by a person.* Unless a transaction is exempt under paragraph (c) of this section, or exempt from prior notice under paragraph (d) of this section, no person (other than certain persons affiliated with a savings and loan holding company who are subject to paragraph (a) of this section), shall acquire control, as defined in § 574.4 (a) and (b) of this part, of a savings association until written notice has been provided to the Office and (1) the Office indicates in writing its intent not to disapprove the proposed acquisition or (2) 60 days (or such period of time as the Office may specify if the review period has been extended under § 574.6(c)(3) of this part) have passed since receipt of a notice deemed sufficient under § 574.6(c)(2). Notwithstanding the forgoing, acquisitions by persons by means of a merger with an interim association are not subject to this part, but shall be subject to approval under § 563.22, and either § 552.13 or applicable state law.

(c) *Exempt transactions.* (1) The following transactions are exempt from the application requirements of paragraph (a) of this section:

(i) Control of a savings association acquired by devise under the terms of a will creating a trust which is excluded from the definition of savings and loan holding company under § 574.2(q) of this part;

(ii) Control of a savings association acquired in connection with a reorganization that involves solely the acquisition of control of that association by a newly formed company that is controlled by the same acquirors that controlled the savings association for the immediately preceding three years, and entails no other transactions, such as an assumption of the acquirors' debt by the newly formed company: *Provided,* that the acquirors have filed with the Office an H–(e)4 notification as provided in section 574.6 of this part and the OTS does not object to the acquisition within 30 days of the filing date;

(iii) Control of a savings association acquired by a bank holding company that is registered under and subject to, the Bank Holding Company Act of 1956, or any company controlled by such bank holding company;

(iv) Control of a savings association acquired solely as a result of (A) a pledge or hypothecation of stock to secure a loan contracted for in good faith or (B) the liquidation of a loan contracted for in good faith, in either case where such loan was made in the ordinary course of the business of the lender: *Provided, further,* That acquisition of control pursuant to such pledge, hypothecation or liquidation is reported to the Office within 30 days, and *Provided, further,* That the acquiror shall not retain such control for more than one year from the date on which such control was acquired; however, the Office may, upon application by an acquiror, extend such one-year period from year to year, for an additional period of time not exceeding three years, if the Office finds such extension is warranted and would not be detrimental to the public interest;

(v) Control of a savings association acquired through a percentage increase in stock ownership following a *pro rata* stock dividend or stock split, if the proportional interests of the recipients remain substantially the same;

(vi) Acquisition of additional stock after approval under § 574.7 of this part, or any predecessor provision, has been

501

§ 574.3

received: *Provided,* That such acquisition is consistent with any conditions imposed in connection with such approval and with the representations made by the acquiror in its application;

(vii) Acquisitions of up to twenty-five percent (25%) of a class of stock by a tax-qualified employee stock benefit plan as defined in § 563b.25; and

(viii) Acquisitions of up to 15 percent of the voting stock of any savings association by a savings and loan holding company (other than a bank holding company) in connection with a qualified stock issuance if such acquisition is approved by the Office pursuant to § 574.8(a).

(2) The following transactions are exempt from the notice requirements of paragraph (b) of this section:

(i) Transactions which are exempt pursuant to paragraphs (c)(1)(iii), (c)(1)(iv), (c)(1)(v), and (c)(1)(vi) of this section;

(ii) Transactions for which approval is required under paragraph (a) of this section;

(iii) Transactions for which approval is required under part 546 or § 552.13 and § 563.22 of this chapter;

(iv) Transactions for which a change of control notice must be submitted to the Board of Governors of the Federal Reserve System pursuant to the Change in Bank Control Act, 12 U.S.C. 1817(j);

(v) Acquisition of additional stock of a savings association by any person who:

(A) Has held power to vote 25 percent or more of any class of voting stock in such association continuously since March 9, 1979; or

(B) Has maintained control of the savings association continuously since acquiring control in compliance with the Control Act (or the Repealed Control Act) and the Office's regulations thereunder then in effect: *Provided,* That such acquisition is consistent with any conditions imposed in connection with such acquisition of control and with the representations made by the acquiror in its notice; and

(vi) Acquisitions of stock of a *de novo* federal savings association in connection with the organization of such association: *Provided,* That the Office has considered the financial and managerial resources of the acquiror in granting the association its federal savings association charter; and additional acquisitions of stock of such association, and *further provided,* that the acquisitions are consistent with any conditions imposed in connection with the approval of the association's charter and with representations made by the acquiror in its application for a federal savings association charter, and that the Regional Director has no supervisory objection to the acquiror's additional acquisitions.

(3) An acquiror that would be considered to be in control of a savings association pursuant to § 574.4 of this part on December 26, 1985, shall not be subject to this § 574.3 unless the acquiror acquires additional stock of the savings association or obtains a control factor with respect to such association after December 26, 1985: *Provided,* That an acquiror shall not be deemed to have acquired control of a savings association on the basis of actions taken prior to December 26, 1985, or on the basis of actions taken after December 26, 1985, if such actions are pursuant to and consistent with a materially complete application under the Holding Company Act or notice under the Repealed Control Act filed prior to December 26, 1985, if such acquisition is made pursuant to an application approved under the Holding Company Act or a notice under the Repealed Control Act that was not disapproved.

(d) *Transactions exempt from prior approval or notice.* (1) Subject to the conditions set forth in paragraph (d)(2) of this section, the following transactions are exempt from prior approval and prior notice under § 574.3: *Provided,* That the timing of the transaction was not within the control of the acquiror.

(i) Control of a savings association acquired through *bona fide* gift;

(ii) Control of a savings association acquired through liquidation of a loan contracted in good faith where the loan was not made in the ordinary course of business of the lender;

(iii) Control of a savings association acquired through a percentage increase in ownership following a stock split or redemption that was not *pro rata;*

Office of Thrift Supervision, Treasury § 574.4

(iv) Control determined pursuant to § 574.4 (a) or (b) as a result of actions by third parties that are not within the control of the acquiror;

(v) Control of a savings association acquired through testate or intestate succession: *Provided,* That the acquiror transmits written notification of the acquisition to the Office within 60 days of the acquisition and provides such additional information as the Office may specifically request.

(2) The exemptions provided by paragraphs (d)(1)(i) through (d)(1)(iv) of this section are subject to the following conditions:

(i) The acquiror shall file an application, notice or rebuttal, as appropriate, with the Office within 90 days of acquisition of control;

(ii) The acquiror shall not take any action to direct the management or policies of the savings association or which are designed to effect a change in the business plan of the savings association other than voting on matters that may be presented to stockholders by management of the savings association until the Office has acted favorably upon the acquiror's application or notice, and the Office may require that the acquiror take such steps as the Office deems necessary to insure that control is not exercised; and

(iii) If the Office disapproves the acquiror's application or notice, the acquiror shall divest such portion of the stock held by the acquiror so as to cause the acquiror not to be determined to be in control of the savings association under § 574.4 of this part, within one year or such shorter period of time and in the manner that the Office may order.

(e) *Prohibited acquisitions.* No acquisition shall be approved by the Office pursuant to § 574.3(a) which would result in the formation by any company, through one or more subsidiaries or through one or more transactions, of a multiple savings and loan holding company controlling savings associations in more than one state where the acquisition causes a savings association to become an affiliate of another savings association with which it was not previously affiliated unless:

(1) Such company, or a savings association subsidiary of such company, is authorized to acquire control of a savings association subsidiary, or to operate a home or branch office, in the additional state or states pursuant to section 13(k) of the Federal Deposit Insurance Act, 12 U.S.C. 1823(k) (or section 408(m) of the National Housing Act as in effect immediately prior to enactment of the Financial Institutions Reform, Recovery and Enforcement Act of 1989);

(2) Such company controls a savings association subsidiary which operated a home or branch office in the additional state or states as of March 5, 1987; or

(3) The statute laws of the state in which the savings association, control of which is to be acquired, is located are such that a savings association chartered by such state could be acquired by a savings association chartered by the state where the acquiring savings association or savings and loan holding company is located (or by a holding company that controls such a state chartered savings association), and such statute laws specifically authorize such an acquisition by language to that effect and not merely by implication.

[54 FR 49690, Nov. 30, 1989, as amended at 57 FR 14348, Apr. 20, 1992; 60 FR 66720, Dec. 26, 1995; 61 FR 60184, Nov. 27, 1996; 67 FR 52035, Aug. 9, 2002]

§ 574.4 Control.

(a) *Conclusive control.* (1) An acquiror shall be deemed to have acquired control of a savings association, other than a savings and loan holding company, if the acquiror directly or indirectly, through one or more subsidiaries or transactions or acting in concert with one or more persons or companies:

(i) Acquires more than 25 percent of any class of voting stock of the savings association;

(ii) Acquires irrevocable proxies representing more than 25 percent of any class of voting stock of the savings association;

(iii) Acquires any combination of voting stock and irrevocable proxies representing more than 25 percent of any class of voting stock of a savings association; or

§ 574.4

(iv) Controls in any manner the election of a majority of the directors of the savings association.

(2) An acquiror shall be deemed to have acquired control of a company, including a savings and loan holding company, if the acquiror directly or indirectly, or through one or more subsidiaries or transactions or acting in concert with one or more persons or companies:

(i) Acquires more than 25 percent of any class of voting stock of the company;

(ii) Acquires irrevocable proxies representing more than 25 percent of any class of voting stock of the company;

(iii) Acquires any combination of voting stock and irrevocable proxies representing more than 25 percent of any class of voting stock of a savings association;

(iv) Controls in any manner the election of a majority of the directors or trustees of a company;

(v) Is a general partner of a company;

(vi) Has contributed more than 25 percent of the capital of the company; or

(vii) Is a trustee of a trust.

(3) A company shall be deemed to control a savings association if the Office finds, after notice and opportunity for hearing, that the company has the power directly or indirectly, to exercise a controlling influence over the management or policies of the savings association.

(4) A person shall be deemed to control a savings association if the Office determines that such person has the power to direct the management or policies of the savings association.

(b) *Rebuttable control determinations.* (1) Except as provided in § 574.8, an acquiror shall be determined, subject to rebuttal, to have acquired control of a savings association, if the acquiror directly or indirectly, or through one or more subsidiaries or transactions or acting in concert with one or more persons or companies:

(i) Acquires more than 10 percent of any class of voting stock of the savings association and is subject to any control factor, as defined in paragraph (c) of this section;

(ii) Acquires more than 25 percent of any class of stock of the savings association and is subject to any control factor, as defined in paragraph (c) of this section.

(2) An acquiror shall be determined, subject to rebuttal, to have acquired control of a savings association, if the acquiror directly or indirectly, or through one or more subsidiaries or transactions or acting in concert with one or more persons or companies, holds any combination of voting stock and revocable and/or irrevocable proxies, representing more than 25 percent of any class of voting stock of a savings association, excluding such proxies held in connection with a solicitation by, or in opposition to, a solicitation on behalf of management of the savings association, but including a solicitation in connection with an election of directors, and such proxies would enable the acquiror to:

(i) Elect one-third or more of the savings association's board of directors, including nominees or representatives of the acquiror currently serving on such board;

(ii) Cause the savings association's stockholders to approve the acquisition or corporate reorganization of the savings association; or

(iii) Exert a continuing influence on a material aspect of the business operations of the savings association.

(c) *Control factors.* For purposes of paragraph (b)(1) of this section, the following constitute control factors. References to the acquiror include actions taken directly or indirectly, or through one or more subsidiaries or transactions or acting in concert with one or more persons or companies:

(1) The acquiror would be one of the two largest holders of any class of voting stock of the savings association.

(2) The acquiror would hold more than 25 percent of the total stockholders' equity of the savings association.

(3) The acquiror would hold more than 35 percent of the combined debt securities and stockholders' equity of the savings association.

(4) The acquiror is party to any agreement:

(i) Pursuant to which the acquiror possesses a material economic stake in the savings association resulting from a profit-sharing arrangement, use of

Office of Thrift Supervision, Treasury § 574.4

common names, facilities or personnel, or the provision of essential services to the savings association; or

(ii) That enables the acquiror to influence a material aspect of the management or policies of the savings association, other than agreements to which the savings association is a party where the restrictions are customary under the circumstances and in the case of an acquisition agreement, which apply only during the period when the acquiror is seeking the Office's approval to acquire the savings association, the agreement prohibits transactions between the acquiror and the savings association and their respective affiliates without approval by the Regional Director during the pendency of the application process, and the agreement contains no material forfeiture provisions applicable to the savings association in the event the acquisition is not approved or not approved by a specified date.

(5) The acquiror would have the ability, other than through the holding of revocable proxies, to direct the votes of more than 25 percent of a class of the savings association's voting stock or to vote more than 25 percent of a class of the savings association's voting stock in the future upon the occurrence of a future event.

(6) The acquiror would have the power to direct the disposition of more than 25 percent of a class of the savings association's voting stock in a manner other than a widely dispersed or public offering.

(7) The acquiror and/or the acquiror's representatives or nominees would constitute more than one member of the savings association's board of directors.

(8) The acquiror or a nominee or management official of the acquiror would serve as the chairman of the board of directors, chairman of the executive committee, chief executive officer, chief operating officer, chief financial officer or in any position with similar policymaking authority in the savings association.

(d) *Rebuttable presumptions of concerted action.* An acquiror will be presumed to be acting in concert with the following persons and companies:

(1) A company will be presumed to be acting in concert with a controlling shareholder, partner, trustee or management official of such company with respect to the acquisition of stock of a savings association, if

(i) Both the company and the person own stock in the savings association,

(ii) The company provides credit to the person to purchase the savings association's stock, or

(iii) The company pledges its assets or otherwise is instrumental in obtaining financing for the person to acquire stock of the savings association;

(2) A person will be presumed to be acting in concert with members of the person's immediate family;

(3) Persons will be presumed to be acting in concert with each other where

(i) Both own stock in a savings association and both are also management officials, controlling shareholders, partners, or trustees of another company, or

(ii) One person provides credit to another person or is instrumental in obtaining financing for another person to purchase stock of the savings association;

(4) A company controlling or controlled by another company and companies under common control will be presumed to be acting in concert;

(5) Persons or companies will be presumed to be acting in concert where they constitute a group under the beneficial ownership reporting rules under section 13 or the proxy rules under section 14 of the Securities Exchange Act of 1934, promulgated by the Securities and Exchange Commission.

(6) A person or company will be presumed to be acting in concert with any trust for which such person or company serves as trustee, except that a tax-qualified employee stock benefit plan as defined in § 563b.2(a)(39) shall not be presumed to be acting in concert with its trustee or person acting in a similar fiduciary capacity solely for the purposes of determining whether to combine the holdings of a plan and its trustee or fiduciary.

(7) Persons or companies will be presumed to be acting in concert with each other and with any other person

§ 574.4

or company with which they also are presumed to act in concert.

(e) *Procedures for rebuttal*—(1) *Rebuttal of control determination.* An acquiror attempting to rebut a determination of control that would arise under paragraph (b) of this section shall file a submission with the Office setting forth the facts and circumstances which support the acquiror's contention that no control relationship would exist if the acquiror acquires stock or obtains a control factor with respect to a savings association. The rebuttal must be filed and accepted in accordance with this section before the acquiror acquires such stock or control factor.

(i) An acquiror seeking to rebut the determination of control arising under paragraph (b)(1) of this section shall submit to the Office an executed agreement materially conforming to the agreement set forth at § 574.100 of this part. Unless agreed to by the Office in writing, no other agreement or filing shall be deemed to rebut the determination of control arising under paragraph (b)(1) of this section. If accepted by the Office, the acquiror shall furnish a copy of the executed agreement to the association to which the rebuttal pertains.

(ii) An acquiror seeking to rebut the determination of control with respect to holding of proxies arising under paragraph (b)(2) of this section shall be subject to the requirements of paragraph (e)(1) of this section, except that in the case of a rebuttal of the presumption of control arising under paragraph (b)(2) of this section, the Office may require the acquiror to furnish information in response to a specific request for information and depending upon the particular facts and circumstances, to provide an executed rebuttal agreement materially conforming to the agreement set forth at § 574.100 of this part, with any modifications deemed necessary by the Office.

(2) *Presumptions of concerted action.* An acquiror attempting to rebut the presumption of concerted action arising under paragraph (d) of this section shall file a submission with the Office setting forth facts and circumstances which clearly and convincingly demonstrate the acquiror's contention that no action in concert exists. Such a statement must be accompanied by an affidavit, in form and content satisfactory to the Office, executed by each person or company presumed to be acting in concert, stating that such person or company does not and shall not, without having made necessary filings and obtained approval or clearance thereof under the Holding Company Act or the Control Act, as applicable, have any agreements or understandings, written or tacit, with respect to the exercise of control, directly or indirectly, over the management or policies of the savings association, including agreements relating to voting, acquisition or disposition of the savings association's stock. The affidavit shall also recite that the signatory is aware that the filing of a false affidavit may subject the person or company to criminal sanctions, would constitute a violation of the Office's regulations at 12 CFR 563.180(b), and would be considered a "presumptive disqualifier" under 12 CFR 574.7(g)(1)(v).

(3) *Determination.* A rebuttal filed pursuant to paragraph (e) of this section shall not be deemed sufficient unless it includes all the information, agreements, and affidavits required by the Office and this part, as well as any additional relevant information as the Office may require by written request to the acquiror. Within 20 calendar days after proper filing of a rebuttal submission, the Office will provide written notification of its determination to accept or reject the submission; request additional information in connection with the submission; or return the submission to the acquiror as materially deficient. Within 15 calendar days after proper filing of any additional information furnished in response to a specific request by the Office, the Office shall notify the acquiror in writing as to whether the rebuttal is thereby deemed to be sufficient. If the Office fails to notify an acquiror within such time, the rebuttal shall be deemed to be accepted. The Office may reject any rebuttal which is inconsistent with facts and circumstances known to it or where the

Office of Thrift Supervision, Treasury

§ 574.6

rebuttal does not clearly and convincingly refute the rebuttable determination of control or presumption of action in concert, and may determine to reject a submission solely on such bases.

(f) *Safe harbor.* Notwithstanding any other provision of this section, where an acquiror has no intention to participate in or to seek to exercise control over a savings association's management or policies, the acquiror may seek to qualify for a safe harbor with respect to its ownership of stock of a savings association.

(1) In order to qualify for the safe harbor, an acquiror must submit a certification to the OTS that shall be signed by the acquiror or an authorized representative thereof and shall read as follows:

The undersigned makes this submission pursuant to § 574.4(f) of the regulations of the Office of Thrift Supervision ("Office") with respect to [name of savings association] and hereby certifies to the Office the following:

The undersigned is not in control of [name of savings association] under § 574.4(a);

The undersigned is not subject to any control factor as enumerated in § 574.4(c) with respect to the [name of savings association];

The undersigned will not solicit proxies relating to the voting stock of [name of savings association];

Before any change in status occurs that would bring the undersigned within the scope of § 574.4 (a) or (b), the undersigned will file and obtain approval of a rebuttal, notice or application, as appropriate.

The undersigned has not acquired stock of [name of savings association] for the purpose or effect of changing or influencing the control of [name of savings association] or in connection with or as a participant in any transaction having such purpose or effect.

(2) An acquiror claiming safe-harbor status may vote freely and dissent with respect to its own stock. Certifications provided for in this paragraph must be filed with OTS in accordance with §§ 516.30 and 516.40 of this chapter.

[54 FR 49690, Nov. 30, 1989, as amended at 57 FR 14349, Apr. 20, 1992; 60 FR 66720, Dec. 26, 1995; 66 FR 13009, Mar. 2, 2001]

§ 574.5 Certifications of ownership.

(a) *Acquisition of stock.* (1) Upon the acquisition of beneficial ownership that exceeds, in the aggregate, 10 percent of any class of stock of a savings association or additional stock above 10 percent of the stock of a savings association occurring after December 26, 1985, an acquiror shall file with the OTS a certification as described in this section.

(2) The certification filed pursuant to this section shall be signed by the acquiror or an authorized representative thereof and shall read as follows:

The undersigned is the beneficial owner of 10 percent or more of a class of stock of [name of savings association or holding company]. The undersigned is not in control of such association or company, as defined in 12 CFR 574.4(a), and is not subject to a rebuttable determination of control under § 574.4(b), and will take no action that would result in a determination of control or a rebuttable determination of control without first filing and obtaining approval of an application under the Savings and Loan Holding Company Act, 12 U.S.C. 1467a, or notice under the Change in Bank Control Act, 12 U.S.C. 1817(j), or filing and obtaining acceptance by the Office of Thrift Supervision of a rebuttal of the rebuttable determination of control.

(3) Notwithstanding anything contained in this paragraph (a), an acquiror is not required to file a certification if (i) the Office has approved the acquisition of the savings association or (ii) the acquiror has filed a materially complete application or notice pursuant to § 574.3 of this part.

(b) *Privacy.* All certifications filed under this § 574.5 shall be for the information of the Office in connection with its examination functions and shall be provided confidential treatment by the Office.

[54 FR 49690, Nov. 30, 1989, as amended at 57 FR 14349, Apr. 20, 1992; 59 FR 53571, Oct. 25, 1994]

§ 574.6 Procedural requirements.

(a) *Form of application or notice.* An application, notice, or informational filing required by § 574.3 of this part shall be filed on the Application/Information Filing H–(e) _____ form. (As specified in the form's instructions, the blank line following the H–(e) should be filled in by applicants with the appropriate "1", "1–S", "2", "3", or "4" depending on the type of application.) The specific application requirements for each type of filing are indicated on the form. An acquiror may request confidential treatment of portions of an

§ 574.6

application or notice only by complying with the requirements of paragraph (f) of this section. In the case of an application involving a merger (including a merger with an interim association) the Application/Information Filing H–(e) _____ form shall be used in lieu of an application that otherwise would be required for such merger under §§ 546.2, 552.13, and 563.22 of this chapter.

(1) *H–(e)1.* This application type shall be filed under § 574.3(a) of this part by a company, other than a savings and loan holding company, for approval to acquire direct or indirect control of one savings association.

(2) *H–(e)1–S.* This application type shall be filed under § 574.3(a) of this part by a savings association for approval to reorganize into a holding company structure, provided that the proposed transaction satisfies each of the conditions for automatic approval specified in § 574.7 (a)(2) and (a)(3) of this part.

(3) *H–(e)2.* (i) This application type shall be filed under § 574.3(a) of this part:

(A) By a savings and loan holding company for approval to acquire and hold separately one or more savings associations;

(B) By any other company for approval to acquire and hold separately more than one savings association;

(C) By a savings and loan holding company for approval of an acquisition of shares issued by a savings association in a qualified stock issuance pursuant to § 574.8 of this part; or

(D) By any director, officer, or any individual who owns, controls, or holds with power to vote (or holds proxies representing) more than 25 percent of the voting shares of a savings and loan holding company for approval of an acquisition of one or more savings associations.

(ii) The OTS may determine as a general matter or on a case-by-case basis not to require application information not relevant to transactions described in paragraphs (a)(3)(i) (C) and (D) of this section.

(4) *H–(e)3.* This application shall be used for all applications filed under § 574.3(a) of this part:

12 CFR Ch. V (1–1–12 Edition)

(i) By a savings and loan holding company for approval of acquisitions by a merger, consolidation, or purchase of assets of a savings association or uninsured institution or a savings and loan holding company; or

(ii) By any company for approval of acquisitions by a merger, consolidation, or purchase of assets of two or more savings associations.

(5) *H–(e)4.* This information filing shall be used to claim that a reorganization is exempt from prior written approval of the OTS under § 574.3(c)(1)(ii) of this part.

(6) *Notice Form 1393, parts A and B.* This form shall be used for all notices filed under § 574.3(b) of this part regarding the acquisition of control of a savings association by any person or persons not constituting a company except as provided in paragraph (a)(3) of this section.

(b) *Filing requirements*—(1) *Applications, notices, and rebuttals.* (i) Complete copies including exhibits and all other pertinent documents of applications, notices, and rebuttal submissions shall be filed with the Region in which the savings association or associations involved in the transaction have their home office or offices. Unsigned copies shall be conformed. Each copy shall include a summary of the proposed transaction.

(ii) Any person or company may amend an application, notice or rebuttal submission, or file additional information, upon request of the OTS or, in the case of the party filing an application, notice, or rebuttal, upon such party's own initiative.

(2) *H–(e)4 Information filing.* Any information filing required to be made to claim that a reorganization is exempt from prior written approval of the OTS under § 574.3(c)(1)(ii) of this part shall be clearly labeled "H–(e)4 Information Filing".

(c) *Sufficiency and waiver.* (1) Except as provided in § 574.6(c)(5), an application or notice filed pursuant to § 574.3 (a) or (b) shall not be deemed sufficient unless it includes all of the information required by the form prescribed by the Office and this part, including a complete description of the acquiror's proposed plan for acquisition of control

Office of Thrift Supervision, Treasury § 574.6

whether pursuant to one or more transactions, and any additional relevant information as the Office may require by written request to the applicant. Unless an application or notice specifically indicates otherwise, the application or notice shall be considered to pertain to acquisition of 100 percent of a savings association's voting stock. Where an application or notice pertains to a lesser amount of stock, the Office may condition its approval or non-disapproval to apply only to such amount, in which case additional acquisitions may be made only by amendment to the acquiror's application or notice and the Office's approval or non-disapproval thereof. Failure by an applicant to respond completely to a written request by the Office for additional information within 30 calendar days of the date of such request may be deemed to constitute withdrawal of the application, notice, or rebuttal filing or may be treated as grounds for denial of an application, issuance of a notice of disapproval of a notice, or rejection of a rebuttal.

(2) The period for the Office's review of any proposed acquisition will commence upon receipt by the Office of a notice or application deemed sufficient under paragraph (c)(1) of this section. The Office shall notify an acquiror in writing within 30 calendar days after proper filing of an application or notice as to whether an application or notice—

(i) Is sufficient;

(ii) Is insufficient, and what additional information is requested in order to render the application or notice sufficient; or

(iii) Is materially deficient and will not be processed. The Office shall also notify an acquiror in writing within 15 calendar days after proper filing of any additional information furnished in response to a specific request by the Office as to whether the application or notice is thereby deemed to be sufficient. If the Office fails to so notify an acquiror within such time, the application or notice shall be deemed to be sufficient as of the expiration of the applicable period.

(3) After additional information has been requested and supplied, the Office may request additional information only with respect to matters derived from or prompted by information already furnished, or information of a material nature that was not reasonably available from the acquiror, was concealed, or pertains to developments subsequent to the time of the Office's initial request for additional information. With regard to information of a material nature that was not reasonably available from the acquiror or was concealed at the time an application or notice was deemed to be sufficient or which pertains to developments subsequent to the time an application or notice was deemed to be sufficient, the Office, at its option, may request such additional information as it considers necessary, or may deem the application or notice not to be sufficient until such additional information is furnished and cause the review period to commence again in its entirety upon receipt of such additional information.

(i) The 60-day period for the Office's review of an application or notice deemed to be sufficient also may be extended by the Office for up to an additional 30 days.

(ii) The period for the Office's review of a notice may be further extended not to exceed two additional times for not more than 45 days each time if—

(A) The Office determines that any acquiring party has not furnished all the information required under this part;

(B) In the Office's judgment, any material information submitted is substantially inaccurate;

(C) The Office has been unable to complete an investigation of each acquiror because of any delay caused by, or the inadequate cooperation of, such acquiror; or

(D) The Office determines that additional time is needed to investigate and determine that no acquiring party has a record of failing to comply with the requirements of subchapter II of chapter 53 of title 31 of the United States Code.

(4) With respect to an H–(e)4 information filing, the Chief Counsel or his or her designee shall have 30 days after receipt of a filing deemed sufficient to

509

§ 574.6

disapprove the assertion that the company qualifies for the exemption provided in § 574.3(c)(1)(ii). After the expiration of such 30-day period without response from the Chief Counsel, the filing shall be deemed to be approved.

(5) The Office may waive any requirements of this paragraph (c) determined to be unnecessary by the Office, upon its own initiative, upon the written request of an acquiring person, or in a supervisory case.

(d) *Public notice.* (1) The acquiror must publish a public notice of an application under § 574.3(a) or § 574.8 of this chapter or a notice under § 574.3(b) of this chapter, in accordance with the procedures in subpart B of part 516 of this chapter. Promptly after publication, the acquiror must transmit copies of the public notice and the publisher's affidavit to OTS.

(2) The acquiror must provide a copy of the public notice to the savings association whose stock is sought to be acquired, and may provide a copy of the public notice to any other person who may have an interest in the application.

(3) OTS will notify the appropriate state supervisor and will notify persons whose requests for announcements, as described in 12 CFR part 563e, appendix B, have been received in time for the notification. OTS may also notify any other persons who may have an interest in the application or notice.

(e) *Submission of comments.* Commenters may submit comments on the application or notice in accordance with the procedures in subpart C of part 516 of this chapter.

(f) *Disclosure.* (1) Any application, notice, other filings, public comment, or portion thereof, made pursuant to this part for which confidential treatment is not requested in accordance with this paragraph (f), shall be immediately available to the public and not subject to the procedures set forth herein. Public disclosure shall be made of other portions of an application, notice, other filing or public comment in accordance with paragraph (f)(2) of this section, the provisions of the Freedom of Information Act (5 U.S.C. 552a) and parts 503 and 505 of this chapter. Applicants and other submitters should provide confidential and non-confidential versions of their filings, as described in § 574.6(f) (2) and (3) in order to facilitate this process.

(2) Any person who submits any information or causes or permits any information to be submitted to the Office pursuant to this part may request that the Office afford confidential treatment under the Freedom of Information Act to such information for reasons of personal privacy or business confidentiality, which shall include such information that would be deemed to result in the commencement of a tender offer under § 240.14d–2 of title 17 of the Code of Federal Regulations, or for any other reason permitted by Federal law. Such request for confidentiality must be made and justified in accordance with paragraph (f)(5) of this section at the time of filing, and must, to the extent practicable, identify with specificity the information for which confidential treatment may be available and not merely indicate portions of documents or entire documents in which such information is contained. Failure to specifically identify information for which confidential treatment is requested, failure to specifically justify the bases upon which confidentiality is claimed in accordance with paragraph (f)(5) of this section, or overbroad and indiscriminate claims for confidential treatment, may be bases for denial of the request. In addition, the filing party should take all steps reasonably necessary to ensure, as nearly as practicable, that at the time the information is first received by the Office (i) it is supplied segregated from information for which confidential treatment is not being requested, (ii) it is appropriately marked as confidential, and (iii) it is accompanied by a written request for confidential treatment which identifies with specificity the information as to which confidential treatment is requested. Any such request must be substantiated in accordance with paragraph (f)(5) of this section.

(3) All documents which contain information for which a request for confidential treatment is made or the appropriate segregable portions thereof shall be marked by the person submitting the records with a prominent stamp, typed legend, or other suitable

form of notice on each page or segregable portion of each page, stating "Confidential Treatment Requested by [name]." If such marking is impracticable under the circumstances, a cover sheet prominently marked "Confidential Treatment Requested by [name]" should be securely attached to each group of records submitted for which confidential treatment is requested. Each of the records transmitted in this manner should be individually marked with an identifying number and code so that they are separately identifiable.

(4) A determination as to the validity of any request for confidential treatment may be made when a request for disclosure of the information under the Freedom of Information Act is received, or at any time prior thereto. If the Office receives a request for the information under the Freedom of Information Act, OTS will advise the filing party before it discloses material for which confidential treatment has been requested.

(5) Substantiation of a request for confidential treatment shall consist of a statement setting forth, to the extent appropriate or necessary for the determination of the request for confidential treatment, the following information regarding the request:

(i) The reasons, concisely stated and referring to specific exemptive provisions of the Freedom of Information Act, why the information should be withheld from access under the Freedom of Information Act;

(ii) The applicability of any specific statutory or regulatory provisions which govern or may govern the treatment of the information;

(iii) The existence and applicability of any prior determination by the Office, other Federal agencies, or a court, concerning confidential treatment of the information;

(iv) The adverse consequences to a business enterprise, financial or otherwise, that would result from disclosure of confidential commercial or financial information, including any adverse effect on the business' competitive position;

(v) The measures taken by the business to protect the confidentiality of the commercial or financial information in question and of similar information, prior to, and after, its submission to the Office;

(vi) The ease or difficulty of a competitor's obtaining or compiling the commercial or financial information;

(vii) Whether commercial or financial information was voluntarily submitted to the Office, and, if so, whether and how disclosure of the information would tend to impede the availability of similar information to the Office;

(viii) The extent, if any, to which portions of the substantiation of the request for confidential treatment should be afforded confidential treatment;

(ix) The amount of time after the consummation of the proposed acquisition for which the information should remain confidential and a justification thereof;

(x) Such additional facts and such legal and other authorities as the requesting person may consider appropriate.

(6) Any person requesting access to an application, notice, other filing, or public comment made pursuant to this part for purposes of commenting on a pending submission may prominently label such request: "Request for Disclosure of Filing(s) Made Under part 574/Priority Treatment Requested."

(g) *Supervisory cases.* The provisions of paragraphs (d), (e) and (f) of this section may be waived by the Office in connection with a transaction approved by the Office for supervisory reasons.

(h) *Notification of State supervisor.* Upon receiving a notice relating to an acquisition of control of a state-chartered savings association, the Office shall forward a copy of the notice to the appropriate state savings and loan association supervisory agency, and shall allow 30 days within which the views and recommendations of such state supervisory agency may be submitted. The Office shall give due consideration to the views and recommendations of such state agency in determining whether to disapprove any proposed acquisition. Notwithstanding the provisions of this paragraph (h), if the Office determines that it must act immediately upon any notice of a proposed acquisition in order to prevent the default of the association involved

§ 574.7

in the proposed acquisition, the Office may dispense with the requirement of this paragraph (h) or, if a copy of the notice is forwarded to the state supervisory agency, the Office may request that the views and recommendations of such state supervisory agency be submitted immediately in any form or by any means acceptable to the Office.

(i) *Additional procedures for acquisitions involving mergers.* Acquisitions of control involving mergers (including mergers with an interim association) shall also be subject to the procedures set forth in § 563.22 of this chapter to the extent applicable, except as provided in paragraph (a) of this section.

(j) *Additional procedures for acquisitions of recently converted savings associations.* Applications, notices and rebuttals involving acquisitions of the stock of a recently converted savings association under § 563b.3(i)(3) of this chapter shall also address the criteria for approval set forth at § 563b.3(i)(5) of this chapter.

[54 FR 49690, Nov. 30, 1989, as amended at 55 FR 13517, Apr. 11, 1990; 57 FR 14349, Apr. 20, 1992; 59 FR 28470, June 2, 1994; 60 FR 66720, Dec. 26, 1995; 61 FR 65179, Dec. 11, 1996; 66 FR 13009, Mar. 2, 2001; 69 FR 68250, Nov. 24, 2004]

§ 574.7 Determination by the OTS.

(a) *Acquisition by a company.* (1) The Office shall approve an application by any company other than a savings and loan holding company to acquire control of one savings association unless it determines that the criteria set forth in paragraph (c) of this section are not met. Acquisitions involving mergers with an interim association shall also be subject to §§ 546.2, 552.13, and 563.22 of this chapter.

(2) Subject to compliance with the requirements of §§ 546.2, 552.13 and 563.22, as applicable, an application filed pursuant to § 574.6(a)(2) by a savings association solely for the purpose of obtaining approval for the creation of a savings and loan holding company by such savings association, and related applications for permission to organize an interim federal association, and for merger with such interim association, shall be deemed to be approved 45 calendar days after such applications are properly filed in accordance with the procedures set forth herein, unless, prior to such date:

(i) The Office has requested additional information of the applicant in writing;

(ii) Notified the applicant that the application is materially deficient and will not be processed; or

(iii) Denied the application prior to that time; provided that to be eligible for approval under this paragraph (a)(2):

(A) The holding company shall not be capitalized initially in an amount exceeding the amount the savings association is permitted to pay in dividends to its holding company as of the date of the reorganization pursuant to applicable regulations or, in the absence thereof, pursuant to the then current policy guidelines issued by the OTS;

(B) The creation of the savings and loan holding company by the association is the sole transaction contained in the application, and there are no other transactions requiring Office approval incident to the creation of the holding company (other than the creation of an interim association that will disappear upon consummation of the reorganization and the merger of the savings association with such interim association to effect the reorganization), and the holding company is not also seeking any regulatory waivers, regulatory forbearances, or resolution of legal or supervisory issues;

(C) The board of directors and executive officers of the holding company are composed of persons who, at the time of acquisition, are executive officers and directors of the association;

(D) The acquisition raises no significant issues of law or policy under then current Office policy;

(E) Prior to consummation of the reorganization transaction, the holding company shall enter into any dividend limitation, regulatory capital maintenance, or prenuptial agreement required by Office regulations, or in the absence thereof, required pursuant to policy guidelines issued by the OTS;

(F) The holding company shall furnish the following information in accordance with the specified time frames:

512

Office of Thrift Supervision, Treasury § 574.7

(1) On the business day prior to the date of consummation of the acquisition, the chief financial officers of the holding company and the savings association shall certify to the OTS in writing that no material adverse events or material adverse changes have occurred with respect to the financial condition or operations of the holding company or the savings association since the date of the financial statements submitted with the application;

(2) No later than thirty days from the date of consummation of the acquisition, the holding company shall file with the OTS a certification by legal counsel stating the effective date of the acquisition, the exact number of shares of stock of the savings association acquired by the holding company, and that the acquisition has been consummated in accordance with the provisions of all applicable laws and regulations and the application;

(3) No later than thirty days from the date of consummation of the acquisition, the holding company shall file with the OTS an opinion from its independent auditors certifying that the transaction was consummated in accordance with generally accepted accounting principles; and

(4) No later than thirty days from the date of consummation of the acquisition, the holding company shall file with the OTS a certification stating that the holding company will not cause the savings association to deviate materially from the business plan submitted in connection with the application, unless prior written approval from the OTS is obtained;

(G) In the event an interim association is utilized to facilitate the reorganization transaction, the resulting association shall, no later than 30 days from the date of consummation of the reorganization transaction, furnish a certification by legal counsel stating:

(1) The effective date of the merger involving the interim association and that the merger has been consummated in accordance with the Agreement and Plan of Reorganization or similar document pursuant to which the transaction was accomplished;

(2) The interim association has not opened for business;

(3) The merger was consummated within 120 calendar days of the date of approval: and

(4) After completion of the organization of the interim association, the board of directors of the interim association ratified the Agreement and Plan of Reorganization or similar document; and

(H) The proposed acquisition shall be consummated within 120 days after the application is automatically approved under this § 574.7(a)(2).

(3) To the extent that an association reorganizing into holding company form is subject to provisions relating to its mutual to stock conversion imposed by 12 CFR 563b.3(c)(9), (c)(17), (c)(18), (c)(19), (g)(1) or (i), such provisions shall be applicable to any holding company approved automatically pursuant to paragraph (a)(2) of this section.

(b) *Acquisition by a savings and loan holding company.* The Office shall not approve an acquisition by a savings and loan holding company to acquire control of a savings association, by any other company to acquire control of more than one savings association, by any director or officer of a savings and loan holding company, or any individual who owns, controls, or holds with power to vote (or holds proxies representing) more than 25 percent of the voting stock of a savings and loan holding company to acquire control of a savings association, or by a savings and loan holding company to acquire a qualified stock issuance by a savings association pursuant to § 574.8 of this part, except in accordance with paragraph (c) of this section. Before approving any such acquisition, except a transaction under section 13(k) of the Federal Deposit Insurance Act, the Office shall request from the Attorney General and consider any report rendered within 30 days of such request on the competitive factors involved. Acquisitions involving mergers (including mergers with an interim association) shall also be subject to §§ 546.2, 552.13, and 563.22 of this chapter.

(c) *Application criteria.* (1) The OTS may deny an application by a company or certain persons, described in paragraph (b) of this section, affiliated with a savings and loan holding company, to

513

§ 574.7

acquire control of a savings association, or by a savings and loan holding company to acquire a qualified stock issuance pursuant to § 574.8 of this part:

(i) If the OTS finds that the financial and managerial resources and future prospects of the acquiror and association involved would be detrimental to the association or the insurance risk of the Deposit Insurance Fund; or

(ii) If the acquiror fails or refuses to furnish information requested by the OTS.

(2) Consideration of the managerial resources of a company or savings association shall include consideration of the competence, experience, and integrity of the officers, directors, and controlling shareholders of the company or association. In connection with the applications filed pursuant to §§ 574.6 (a)(3) and 574.8 of this part, the OTS will also consider the convenience and needs of the community to be served. Moreover, the OTS shall not approve any proposed acquisition:

(i) Which would result in a monopoly, or which would be in furtherance of any combination or conspiracy to monopolize or to attempt to monopolize the savings and loan business in any part of the United States;

(ii) The effect of which on any section of the country may be substantially to lessen competition, or tend to create a monopoly, or which in any other manner would be in restraint of trade, unless the OTS finds that the anticompetitive effects of the proposed acquisition are clearly outweighed in the public interest by the probable effect of the acquisition in meeting the convenience and needs of the community to be served;

(iii) If the company fails to provide adequate assurances to the OTS that the company will make available to the OTS such information on the operations or activities of the company, and any affiliate of the company, as the OTS determines to be appropriate to determine and enforce compliance with the Home Owners' Loan Act; or

(iv) In the case of an application by a foreign bank, if the foreign bank is not subject to comprehensive supervision or regulation on a consolidated basis by the appropriate authorities in the home country of the foreign bank. For purposes of this paragraph (c)(2)(iv), "comprehensive supervision or regulation on a consolidated basis by the appropriate authorities" shall be determined using the standards set forth at 12 CFR 211.24(c)(1)(ii).

(d) *Notice criteria.* In making its determination whether to disapprove a notice, the Office may disapprove any proposed acquisition, if the Office determines that:

(1) The proposed acquisition of control would result in a monopoly or would be in furtherance of any combination or conspiracy to monopolize or to attempt to monopolize the banking business in any part of the United States;

(2) The effect of the proposed acquisition of control in any section of the country may be substantially to lessen competition or to tend to create a monopoly or the proposed acquisition of control would in any other manner be in restraint of trade, and the anticompetitive effects of the proposed acquisition of control are not clearly outweighed in the public interest by the probable effect of the transaction in meeting the convenience and needs of the community to be served;

(3) The financial condition of the acquiring person is such as might jeopardize the financial stability of the association or prejudice the interests of the depositors of the association;

(4) The competence, experience, or integrity of the acquiring person or any of the proposed management personnel indicates that it would not be in the interests of the depositors of the association, the Office, or the public to permit such person to control the association;

(5) The acquiring person fails or refuses to furnish information requested by the Office; or

(6) The Office determines that the proposed acquisition would have an adverse effect on the Deposit Insurance Fund.

(e) *Failure to disapprove a notice.* If, upon expiration of the 60-day review period of any notice deemed to be sufficient filed pursuant to § 574.6(c), or extension thereof, the Office has failed to disapprove such notice, the proposed acquisition may take place: *Provided,* That it is consummated within one

Office of Thrift Supervision, Treasury § 574.7

year and in accordance with the terms and representations in the notice and that there is no material change in circumstances prior to the acquisition.

(f) [Reserved]

(g) *Presumptive disqualifiers*—(1) *Integrity factors.* The following factors shall give rise to a rebuttable presumption that an acquiror may fail to satisfy the managerial resources and future prospects tests of paragraph (c) of this section or the integrity test of paragraph (d)(4) of this section:

(i) During the 10-year period immediately preceding filing of the application or notice, criminal, civil or administrative judgments, consents or orders, and any indictments, formal investigations, examinations, or civil or administrative proceedings (excluding routine or customary audits, inspections and investigations) that terminated in any agreements, undertakings, consents or orders, issued against, entered into by, or involving the acquiror or affiliates of the acquiror by any federal or state court, any department, agency, or commission of the U.S. Government, any state or municipality, any Federal Home Loan Bank, any self-regulatory trade or professional organization, or any foreign government or governmental entity, which involve:

(A) Fraud, moral turpitude, dishonesty, breach of trust or fiduciary duties, organized crime or racketeering;

(B) Violation of securities or commodities laws or regulations;

(C) Violation of depository institution laws or regulations;

(D) Violation of housing authority laws or regulations; or

(E) Violation of the rules, regulations, codes of conduct or ethics of a self-regulatory trade or professional organization;

(ii) Denial, or withdrawal after receipt of formal or informal notice of an intent to deny, by the acquiror or affiliates of the acquiror, of

(A) Any application relating to the organization of a financial institution,

(B) An application to acquire any financial institution or holding company thereof under the Holding Company Act or the Bank Holding Company Act or otherwise,

(C) A notice relating to a change in control of any of the foregoing under the Control Act or the Repealed Control Act; or

(D) An application or notice under a state holding company or change in control statute;

(iii) The acquiror or affiliates of the acquiror were placed in receivership or conservatorship during the preceding 10 years, or any management official of the acquiror was a management official or director (other than an official or director serving at the request of the Office, the Federal Deposit Insurance Corporation, the Resolution Trust Corporation, or the former Federal Savings and Loan Insurance Corporation) or controlling shareholder of a company or savings association that was placed into receivership, conservatorship, or a management consignment program, or was liquidated during his or her tenure or control or within two years thereafter;

(iv) Felony conviction of the acquiror, an affiliate of the acquiror or a management official of the acquiror or an affiliate of the acquiror;

(v) Knowingly making any written or oral statement to the Office or any predecessor agency (or its delegate) in connection with an application, notice or other filing under this part that is false or misleading with respect to a material fact or omits to state a material fact with respect to information furnished or requested in connection with such an application, notice or other filing;

(vi) Acquisition and retention at the time of submission of an application or notice, of stock in the savings association by the acquiror in violation of § 574.3 or its predecessor sections.

(2) *Financial factors.* The following shall give rise to a rebuttable presumption that an acquiror may fail to satisfy the financial-resources and future-prospects tests of paragraph (c) of this section, or the financial condition test of paragraph (d)(3) of this section:

(i) Liability for amounts of debt which, in the opinion of the Office, create excessive risks of default and pressure on the savings association to be acquired; or

(ii) Failure to furnish a business plan or furnishing a business plan projecting

515

§ 574.8

activities which are inconsistent with economical home financing.

[54 FR 49690, Nov. 30, 1989, as amended at 57 FR 14349, Apr. 20, 1992; 59 FR 28471, June 2, 1994; 59 FR 44627, Aug. 30, 1994; 60 FR 66720, Dec. 26, 1995; 71 FR 19812, Apr. 18, 2006]

§ 574.8 Qualified stock issuances by undercapitalized savings associations or holding companies.

(a) *Acquisitions by savings and loan holding companies.* No savings and loan holding company shall be deemed to control a savings association solely by reason of the purchase by such savings and loan holding company of shares issued by such savings association, or issued by any savings and loan holding company (other than a bank holding company) which controls such savings association, in connection with a qualified stock issuance if prior approval of such acquisition is granted by the Office under this § 574.8, unless the acquiring savings and loan holding company, directly or indirectly, or acting in concert with 1 or more other persons, or through 1 or more subsidiaries, owns, controls, or holds with power to vote, or holds proxies representing, more than 15 percent of the voting shares of such savings association or holding company.

(b) *Qualification.* For purposes of this section, any issuance of shares of stock shall be treated as a qualified stock issuance if the following conditions are met:

(1) The shares of stock are issued by—

(i) An undercapitalized savings association, which for purposes of this paragraph (b)(1)(i) shall mean any savings association—

(A) The assets of which exceed the liabilities of such association; and

(B) Which does not comply with one or more of the capital standards in effect under section 5(t) of the Home Owners' Loan Act; or

(ii) A savings and loan holding company which is not a bank holding company but which controls an undercapitalized savings association if, at the time of issuance, the savings and loan holding company is legally obligated to contribute the net proceeds from the issuance of such stock to the capital of an undercapitalized savings association subsidiary of such holding company.

(2) All shares of stock issued consist of previously unissued stock or treasury shares.

(3) All shares of stock issued are purchased by a savings and loan holding company that is registered, as of the date of purchase, with the Office in accordance with the provisions of section 10(b) of the Home Owners' Loan Act and the Office's regulations promulgated thereunder.

(4) Subject to paragraph (c) of this section, the Office approves the purchase of the shares of stock by the acquiring savings and loan holding company.

(5) The entire consideration for the stock issued is paid in cash by the acquiring savings and loan holding company.

(6) At the time of the stock issuance, each savings association subsidiary of the acquiring savings and loan holding company (other than an association acquired in a transaction pursuant to section 13(c) or 13(k) of the Federal Deposit Insurance Act, or section 408(m) of the National Housing Act, as in effect immediately prior to enactment of the Financial Institutions Reform, Recovery and Enforcement Act of 1989) has capital (after deducting any subordinated debt, intangible assets, and deferred, unamortized gains or losses) of not less than 6½ percent of the total assets of such savings association.

(7) Immediately after the stock issuance, the acquiring savings and loan holding company holds not more than 15 percent of the outstanding voting stock of the issuing undercapitalized savings association or savings and loan holding company.

(8) Not more than one of the directors of the issuing association or company is an officer, director, employee, or other representative of the acquiring company or any of its affiliates.

(9) Transactions between the savings association or savings and loan holding company that issues the shares pursuant to this section and the acquiring company and any of its affiliates shall be subject to the provisions of section 11 of the Home Owners' Loan Act and the Office's regulations promulgated thereunder.

Office of Thrift Supervision, Treasury § 574.100

(c) *Approval of acquisitions*—(1) *Criteria.* The Office, in deciding whether to approve or deny an application filed on the basis that it is a qualified stock issuance, shall apply the application criteria set forth in § 574.7(c) of this part, including the presumptive disqualifiers set forth in § 574.7(g) of this part.

(2) *Additional capital commitments not required.* The Office shall not disapprove any application for the purchase of stock in connection with a qualified stock issuance on the grounds that the acquiring savings and loan holding company has failed to undertake to make subsequent additional capital contributions to maintain the capital of the undercapitalized savings association at or above the minimum level required by the Office or any other Federal agency having jurisdiction.

(3) *Other conditions.* The Office shall impose such conditions on any approval of an application for the purchase of stock in connection with a qualified stock issuance as the Office determines to be appropriate, including—

(i) A requirement that any savings association subsidiary of the acquiring savings and loan holding company limit dividends paid to such holding company for such period of time as the Office may require; and

(ii) Such other conditions as the Office deems necessary or appropriate to prevent evasions of this section, including, but not limited to, requiring a rebuttal of control agreement in a form substantially similar to that appearing at § 574.100.

(4) *Application deemed approved if not disapproved within 90 days.* An application for approval of a purchase of stock in connection with a qualified stock issuance shall be deemed to have been approved by the Office if such application has not been disapproved by the Office before the end of the 90-day period beginning on the date such application has been deemed sufficient under this part.

(d) *No limitation on class of stock issued.* The shares of stock issued in connection with a qualified stock issuance may be shares of any class.

(e) *Application form.* A savings and loan holding company making application to acquire a qualified stock issuance pursuant to this § 574.8, shall use Form H-(e)2, as provided in § 574.6(a)(3).

§ 574.100 Rebuttal of control agreement.

AGREEMENT

Rebuttal of Rebuttable Determination Of Control Under Part 574

I. WHEREAS

A. [ ] is the owner of [ ] shares (the "Shares") of the [ ] stock (the "Stock") of [name and address of association], which Shares represent [ ] percent of a class of "voting stock" of [ ] as defined under the Acquisition of Control Regulations ("Regulations") of the Office of Thrift Supervision ("Office"), 12 CFR part 574 ("Voting Stock");

B. [ ] is a "savings association" within the meaning of the Regulations;

C. [ ] seeks to acquire additional shares of stock of [ ] ("Additional Shares"), such that [ ]'s ownership thereof will exceed 10 percent of a class of Voting Stock but will not exceed 25 percent of a class of Voting Stock of [ ]; [and/or] [ ] seeks to [ ], which would constitute the acquisition of a "control factor" as defined in the Regulations ("Control Factor");

D. [ ] does not seek to acquire the [Additional Shares or Control Factor] for the purpose or effect of changing the control of [ ] or in connection with or as a participant in any transaction having such purpose or effect;

E. The Regulations require a company or a person who intends to hold 10 percent or more but not in excess of 25 percent of any class of Voting Stock of a savings association or holding company thereof and that also would possess any of the Control Factors specified in the Regulations, to file and obtain approval of an application ("Application") under the Savings and Loan Holding Company Act ("Holding Company Act"), 12 U.S.C. 1467a, or file and obtain clearance of a notice ("Notice") under the Change in Control Act ("Control Act"), 12 U.S.C. 1817(j), prior to acquiring such amount of stock and a Control Factor unless the rebuttable determination of control has been rebutted.

F. Under the Regulations, [ ] would be determined to be in control, subject to rebuttal, of [ ] upon acquisition of the [Additional Shares or Control Factor];

G. [ ] has no intention to manage or control, directly or indirectly, [ ];

H. [ ] has filed on [ ], a written statement seeking to rebut the determination of control, attached hereto and incorporated by

§ 574.100   12 CFR Ch. V (1–1–12 Edition)

reference herein, (this submission referred to as the "Rebuttal");

I. In order to rebut the rebuttable determination of control, [ ] agrees to offer this Agreement as evidence that the acquisition of the [Additional Shares or Control Factor] as proposed would not constitute an acquisition of control under the Regulations.

II. The Office has determined, and hereby agrees, to act favorably on the Rebuttal, and in consideration of such a determination and agreement by the Office to act favorably on the Rebuttal, [ ] and any other existing, resulting or successor entities of [ ] agree with the Office that:

A. Unless [ ] shall have filed a Notice under the Control Act, or an Application under the Holding Company Act, as appropriate, and either shall have obtained approval of the Application or clearance of the Notice in accordance with the Regulations, [ ] will not, except as expressly permitted otherwise herein or pursuant to an amendment to this Rebuttal Agreement:

1. Seek or accept representation of more than one member of the board of directors of [insert name of association and any holding company thereof];

2. Have or seek to have any representative serve as the chairman of the board of directors, or chairman of an executive or similar committee of [insert name of association and any holding company thereof]'s board of directors or as president or chief executive officer of [insert name of association and any holding company thereof];

3. Engage in any intercompany transaction with [ ] or [ ]'s affiliates;

4. Propose a director in opposition to nominees proposed by the management of [insert name of association and any holding company thereof] for the board of directors of [insert name of association and any holding company thereof] other than as permitted in paragraph A–1;

5. Solicit proxies or participate in any solicitation of proxies with respect to any matter presented to the stockholders [ ] other than in support of, or in opposition to, a solicitation conducted on behalf of management of [ ];

6. Do any of the following, except as necessary solely in connection with [ ]'s performance of duties as a member of [ ]'s board of directors:

(a) Influence or attempt to influence in any respect the loan and credit decisions or policies of [ ], the pricing of services, any personnel decisions, the location of any offices, branching, the hours of operation or similar activities of [ ];

(b) Influence or attempt to influence the dividend policies and practices of [ ] or any decisions or policies of [ ] as to the offering or exchange of any securities;

(c) Seek to amend, or otherwise take action to change, the bylaws, articles of incorporation, or charter of [ ];

(d) Exercise, or attempt to exercise, directly or indirectly, control or a controlling influence over the management, policies or business operations of [ ]; or

(e) Seek or accept access to any non-public information concerning [ ].

B. [ ] is not a party to any agreement with [ ].

C. [ ] shall not assist, aid or abet any of [ ]'s affiliates or associates that are not parties to this Agreement to act, or act in concert with any person or persons, in a manner which is inconsistent with the terms hereof or which constitutes an attempt to evade the requirements of this Agreement.

D. Any amendment to this Agreement shall only be proposed in connection with an amended rebuttal filed by [ ] with the Office for its determination;

E. Prior to acquisition of any shares of "Voting Stock" of [ ] as defined in the Regulations in excess of the Additional Shares, any required filing will be made by [ ] under the Control Act or the Holding Company Act and either approval of the acquisition under the Holding Company Act shall be obtained from the Office or any Notice filed under the Control Act shall be cleared in accordance with the Regulations;

F. At any time during which 10 percent or more of any class of Voting Stock of [ ] is owned or controlled by [ ], no action which is inconsistent with the provisions of this Agreement shall be taken by [ ] until [ ] files and either obtains from the Office a favorable determination with respect to either an amended rebuttal, approval of an Application under the Holding Company Act, or clearance of a Notice under the Control Act, in accordance with the Regulations;

G. Where any amended rebuttal filed by [ ] is denied or disapproved, [ ] shall take no action which is inconsistent with the terms of this Agreement, except after either (1) reducing the amount of shares of Voting Stock of [ ] owned or controlled by [ ] to an amount under 10 percent of a class of Voting Stock, or immediately ceasing any other actions that give rise to a conclusive or rebuttable determination of control under the Regulations; or (2) filing a Notice under the Control Act, or an Application under the Holding Company Act, as appropriate, and either obtaining approval of the Application or clearance of the Notice, in accordance with the Regulations;

H. Where any Application or Notice filed by [ ] is disapproved, [ ] shall take no action which is inconsistent with the terms of this Agreement, except after reducing the amount of shares of Voting Stock of [ ] owned or controlled by [ ] to an amount under 10 percent of any class of Voting

518

Office of Thrift Supervision, Treasury § 575.1

Stock, or immediately ceasing any other actions that give rise to a conclusive or rebuttable determination of control under the Regulations;

I. Should circumstances beyond [ ]'s control result in [ ] being placed in a position to direct the management or policies of [ ], then [ ] shall either (1) promptly file an Application under the Holding Company Act or a Notice under the Control Act, as appropriate, and take no affirmative steps to enlarge that control pending either a final determination with respect to the Application or Notice, or (2) promptly reduce the amount of shares of [ ] Voting Stock owned or controlled by [ ] to an amount under 10 percent of any class of Voting Stock or immediately cease any actions that give rise to a conclusive or rebuttable determination of control under the Regulations;

J. By entering into this Agreement and by offering it for reliance in reaching a decision on the request to rebut the presumption of control under the Regulations, as long as 10 percent or more of any class of Voting Stock of [ ] is owned or controlled, directly or indirectly, by [ ], and [ ] possesses any Control Factor as defined in the Regulations, [ ] will submit to the jurisdiction of the Regulations, including (1) the filing of an amended rebuttal or Application or Notice for any proposed action which is prohibited by this Agreement, and (2) the provisions relating to a penalty for any person who willfully violates or with reckless disregard for the safety or soundness of a savings association participates in a violation of the [Holding Company Act or Control Act] and the Regulations thereunder, and any regulation or order issued by the Office.

K. Any violation of this Agreement shall be deemed to be a violation of the [Holding Company Act or Control Act] and the Regulations, and shall be subject to such remedies and procedures as are provided in the [Holding Company Act or Control Act] and the Regulations for a violation thereunder and in addition shall be subject to any such additional remedies and procedures as are provided under any other applicable statutes or regulations for a violation, willful or otherwise, of any agreement entered into with the Office.

III. This Agreement may be executed in one or more counterparts, each of which shall be deemed an original but all of which counterparts collectively shall constitute one instrument representing the Agreement among the parties thereto. It shall not be necessary that any one counterpart be signed by all of the parties hereto as long as each of the parties has signed at least one counterpart.

IV. This Agreement shall be interpreted in a manner consistent with the provisions of the Rules and Regulations of the Office.

V. This Agreement shall terminate upon (i) the approval by the Office of [ ]'s Application under the Holding Company Act or clearance by the Office of [ ]'s Notice under the Control Act to acquire [ ], and consummation of the transaction as described in such Application or Notice, (ii) the disposition by [ ] of a sufficient number of shares of [ ], or (iii) the taking of such other action that thereafter [ ] is not in control and would not be determined to be in control of [ ] under the Control Act, the Holding Company Act or the Regulations as in effect at that time.

VI. IN WITNESS THEREOF, the parties thereto have executed this Agreement by their duly authorized officer.

[Acquiror]
Office of Thrift Supervision.
Date: _____
By: _____

[54 FR 49690, Nov. 30, 1989, as amended at 63 FR 71213, Dec. 24, 1998]

PART 575—MUTUAL HOLDING COMPANIES

Sec.
575.1 Scope.
575.2 Definitions.
575.3 Mutual holding company reorganizations.
575.4 Grounds for disapproval of reorganizations.
575.5 Membership rights.
575.6 Contents of Reorganization Plans.
575.7 Issuances of stock by savings association subsidiaries of mutual holding companies.
575.8 Contents of Stock Issuance Plans.
575.9 Charters and bylaws for mutual holding companies and their savings association subsidiaries.
575.10 Acquisition and disposition of savings associations, savings and loan holding companies, and other corporations by mutual holding companies.
575.11 Operating restrictions.
575.12 Conversion or liquidation of mutual holding companies.
575.13 Procedural requirements.
575.14 Subsidiary holding companies.

AUTHORITY: 12 U.S.C. 1462, 1462a, 1463, 1464, 1467a, 1828, 2901.

SOURCE: 58 FR 44114, Aug. 19, 1993, unless otherwise noted.

§ 575.1 Scope.

(a) *Purpose.* The purpose of this part is to implement the mutual holding company provisions of the Savings and

§ 575.2

Loan Holding Company Act, 12 U.S.C. 1467a(o).

(b) *General.* Except as the OTS may otherwise determine, the provisions of this part shall exclusively govern the reorganization of mutual savings associations and any related stock issuances, and no mutual savings association shall reorganize to a mutual holding company or issue minority stock without the prior written approval of the OTS. The OTS may grant a waiver in writing from any requirement of this part for good cause shown.

[58 FR 44114, Aug. 19, 1993, as amended at 59 FR 61262, Nov. 30, 1994]

§ 575.2 Definitions.

As used in this part, the following definitions apply, unless specified elsewhere in this part:

(a) The terms *associate* and *tax-qualified employee stock benefit plan* have the meanings set forth in § 563b.25 of this chapter.

(b) The terms *acting in concert, affiliate, company, person,* and *savings association* have the meanings set forth in § 574.2 of this chapter.

(c) The term *acquiree association* means any savings association, other than a resulting association, that:

(1) Is acquired by a mutual holding company as part of, and concurrently with, a mutual holding company reorganization; and

(2) Is in the mutual form immediately prior to such acquisition.

(d) The term *control* has the same meaning as specified in § 574.4 of this chapter.

(e) The term *default* means any adjudication or other official determination of a court of competent jurisdiction or other public authority pursuant to which a conservator, receiver, or other legal custodian is appointed for a mutual holding company or savings association subsidiary of a mutual holding company.

(f) The term *insider* means any officer or director of a company or of any affiliate of such company, and any person acting in concert with any such officer or director.

(g) The term *member* means any depositor or borrower of a mutual savings association that is entitled, under the charter of the savings association, to vote on matters affecting the association, and any depositor or borrower of a savings association subsidiary of a mutual holding company that is entitled, under the charter of the mutual holding company, to vote on matters affecting the mutual holding company.

(h) The term *mutual holding company* means a mutual holding company organized under this part, and unless otherwise indicated, a subsidiary holding company controlled by a mutual holding company, organized under this part.

(i) The term *parent* has the same meaning as the term *parent company* specified at § 583.15 of this chapter.

(j) The term *Reorganization Notice* means a notice of a proposed mutual holding company reorganization that is in the form and contains the information required by the OTS.

(k) The term *Reorganization Plan* means a plan to reorganize into the mutual holding company format containing the information required by § 575.6 of this part.

(l) The term *reorganizing association* means a mutual savings association that proposes to reorganize to become a mutual holding company pursuant to this part.

(m) The term *resulting association* means a savings association in the stock form that is organized as a subsidiary of a reorganizing association to receive the substantial part of the assets and liabilities (including all deposit accounts) of the reorganizing association upon consummation of the reorganization.

(n) The term *stock* means common or preferred stock, or any other type of equity security, including (without limitation) warrants or options to acquire common or preferred stock, or other securities that are convertible into common or preferred stock.

(o) The term *Stock Issuance Plan* means a plan, submitted pursuant to § 575.7 and containing the information required by § 575.8, providing for the issuance of stock by:

(1) A savings association subsidiary of a mutual holding company; or

(2) A subsidiary holding company.

(p) The term *subsidiary* has the meaning specified at § 583.23 of this chapter.

Office of Thrift Supervision, Treasury § 575.4

(q) The term *subsidiary holding company* means a federally chartered stock holding company, controlled by a mutual holding company, that owns the stock of a savings association whose depositors have membership rights in the parent mutual holding company.

[58 FR 44114, Aug. 19, 1993, as amended at 60 FR 66720, Dec. 26, 1995; 61 FR 60184, Nov. 27, 1996; 63 FR 11365, Mar. 9, 1998; 67 FR 52035, Aug. 9, 2002]

§ 575.3 Mutual holding company reorganizations.

A mutual savings association may reorganize to become a mutual holding company, or join in a mutual holding company reorganization as an acquiree association, only upon satisfaction of the following conditions:

(a) A Reorganization Plan is approved by a majority of the board of directors of the reorganizing association and any acquiree association;

(b) A Reorganization Notice is filed with the OTS and either:

(1) The OTS has given written notice of its intent not to disapprove the proposed reorganization; or

(2) Sixty days have passed since OTS received the Reorganization Notice and deemed it complete under § 516.210 or § 516.220 of this chapter, and OTS has not:

(i) Given written notice that the proposed reorganization is disapproved; or

(ii) Extended for an additional 30 days the period during which disapproval may be issued;

(c) The Reorganization Plan is submitted to the members of the reorganizing association and any acquiree association pursuant to a proxy statement cleared in advance by the OTS and such Reorganization Plan is approved by a majority of the total votes of the members of each association eligible to be cast at a meeting held at the call of each association's directors in accordance with the procedures prescribed by each association's charter and bylaws; and

(d) All necessary regulatory approvals have been obtained and all conditions specified in § 575.9(c)(5) of this part or otherwise imposed by the OTS in connection with the issuance of a notice of intent not to disapprove under § 575.3(b)(1) of this part or by the OTS in connection with the granting of the approvals specified in this paragraph have been satisfied.

[58 FR 44114, Aug. 19, 1993, as amended at 66 FR 13009, Mar. 2, 2001]

§ 575.4 Grounds for disapproval of reorganizations.

(a) *Basic standards.* The OTS may disapprove a proposed mutual holding company reorganization pursuant to § 575.3(b) of this part if:

(1) Disapproval is necessary to prevent unsafe or unsound practices;

(2) The financial or managerial resources of the reorganizing association or any acquiree association warrant disapproval;

(3) The proposed capitalization of the mutual holding company fails to meet the requirements of paragraph (b) of this section;

(4) A stock issuance is proposed in connection with the reorganization pursuant to § 575.7 of this part that fails to meet the standards established by that section;

(5) The reorganizing association or any acquiree association fails to furnish the information required to be included in the Reorganization Notice or any other information requested by the OTS in connection with the proposed reorganization; or

(6) The proposed reorganization would violate any provision of law, including (without limitation) § 575.3 (a) and (c) of this part (regarding board of directors and membership approval) or § 575.5(a) of this part (regarding continuity of membership rights).

(b) *Capitalization.* (1) The OTS shall disapprove a proposal by a reorganizing association or any acquiree association to capitalize a mutual holding company in an amount in excess of a nominal amount if immediately following the reorganization, the resulting association or the acquiree association would fail to be "adequately capitalized" as defined under 12 CFR part 565.

(2) Proposals by reorganizing associations and acquiree associations to capitalize mutual holding companies shall also comply with any applicable statutes, and with regulations or written policies of the OTS governing capital distributions by savings associations in

§ 575.4

effect at the time of the reorganization. (Issuance by the OTS of a notice of intent not to disapprove a mutual holding company reorganization pursuant to § 575.3(b) of this part, or failure by the OTS to disapprove such a reorganization within the time prescribed in § 575.3(b) of this part, shall also be deemed to constitute OTS approval under any regulation or written policy of the OTS governing capital distributions by savings associations, if such approval is required, of the capitalization proposal set forth in the Reorganization Notice, subject to any conditions imposed by § 575.4(d)(2) of this part.)

(c) *Presumptive disqualifiers*—(1) *Managerial resources.* The factors specified in § 574.7 (g)(1)(i)–(g)(1)(vi) of this chapter shall give rise to a rebuttable presumption that the managerial resources test of paragraph (a)(2) of this section is not met. For this purpose, each place the term *acquiror* appears in § 574.7 (g)(1)(i)–(g)(1)(vi) of this chapter, it shall be read to mean the reorganizing association or any acquiree association, and the reference in § 574.7(g)(1)(v) of this chapter to filings under this part shall be deemed to include filings under either part 574 of this chapter or this part.

(2) *Safety and soundness and financial resources.* Failure by a reorganizing association and any acquiree association to submit a business plan in connection with a Reorganization Notice, or submission of a business plan that projects activities that are inconsistent with the credit and lending needs of your proposed market area or that fails to demonstrate that the capital of the mutual holding company will be deployed in a safe and sound manner, shall give rise to a rebuttable presumption that the safety and soundness and financial resources tests of paragraphs (a)(1) and (a)(2) of this section are not met.

(d) *Failure of the OTS to act on a Reorganization Notice within the prescribed time period.* A proposed reorganization that obtains regulatory clearance from the OTS due to the operation of § 575.3(b)(2) of this part may take place in the manner proposed, subject to the following conditions:

12 CFR Ch. V (1–1–12 Edition)

(1) The reorganization shall be consummated within one year of the date of the expiration of the OTS's review period under § 575.3(b)(2) of this part;

(2) The mutual holding company shall not be capitalized in an amount in excess of what is permissible under § 575.4(b) of this part;

(3) No request for regulatory waivers or forbearances shall be deemed granted;

(4) The following information shall be submitted within the specified time frames:

(i) On the business day prior to the date of the reorganization, the chief financial officers of the reorganizing association and any acquiree association shall certify to the OTS in writing that no material adverse events or material adverse changes have occurred with respect to the financial condition or operations of their respective associations since the date of the financial statements submitted with the Reorganization Notice;

(ii) No later than thirty days after the reorganization, the mutual holding company shall file with the OTS a certification by legal counsel stating the effective date of the reorganization, the exact number of shares of stock of the resulting association and any acquiree association acquired by the mutual holding company and by any other persons, and that the reorganization has been consummated in accordance with § 575.3 of this part and all other applicable laws and regulations and the Reorganization Notice;

(iii) No later than thirty days after the reorganization, the mutual holding company shall file with the OTS an opinion from its independent auditors certifying that the reorganization was consummated in accordance with generally accepted accounting principles; and

(iv) No later than thirty days after the reorganization, the mutual holding company shall file with the OTS a certification stating that the mutual holding company will not deviate materially, or cause its savings association subsidiaries to deviate materially, from the business plan submitted in connection with the Reorganization

Notice, unless prior written approval from the Regional Director is obtained.

[58 FR 44114, Aug. 19, 1993, as amended at 67 FR 52035, Aug. 9, 2002]

§ 575.5 Membership rights.

(a) *Depositors and borrowers of resulting associations, acquiree associations, and associations in mutual form when acquired.* The charter of a mutual holding company must:

(1) Confer upon existing and future depositors of the resulting association the same membership rights in the mutual holding company as were conferred upon depositors by the charter of the reorganizing association as in effect immediately prior to the reorganization;

(2) Confer upon existing and future depositors of any acquiree association or any association that is in the mutual form when acquired by the mutual holding company the same membership rights in the mutual holding company as were conferred upon depositors by the charter of the acquired association immediately prior to acquisition, *provided that* if the acquired association is merged into another association from which the mutual holding company draws members, the depositors of the acquired association shall receive the same membership rights as the depositors of the association into which the acquired association is merged;

(3) Confer upon the borrowers of the resulting association who are borrowers at the time of reorganization the same membership rights in the mutual holding company as were conferred upon them by the charter of the reorganizing association immediately prior to reorganization, but shall not confer any membership rights in connection with any borrowings made after the reorganization; and

(4) Confer upon the borrowers of any acquiree association or any association that is in the mutual form when acquired by the mutual holding company who are borrowers at the time of the acquisition the same membership rights in the mutual holding company as were conferred upon them by the charter of the acquired association immediately prior to acquisition, but shall not confer any membership rights in connection with any borrowings made after the acquisition, *provided that* if the acquired association is merged into another association from which the mutual holding company draws members, the borrowers of the acquired association shall instead receive the same grandfathered membership rights as the borrowers of the association into which the acquired association is merged received at the time that association became a subsidiary of the mutual holding company.

(b) *Depositors and borrowers of associations in the stock form when acquired.* A mutual holding company that acquires a savings association in the stock form, other than a resulting association or an acquiree association, shall not confer any membership rights upon the depositors and borrowers of such association, unless such association is merged into an association from which the mutual holding company draws members, in which case the depositors of the stock association shall receive the same membership rights as other depositors of the association into which the stock association is merged.

§ 575.6 Contents of Reorganization Plans.

Each Reorganization Plan shall contain a complete description of all significant terms of the proposed reorganization, shall attach and incorporate any Stock Issuance Plan proposed in connection with the Reorganization Plan, and shall:

(a) Provide for amendment of the charter and bylaws of the reorganizing association to read in the form of the charter and bylaws of a mutual holding company, and attach and incorporate such charter and bylaws;

(b) Provide for the organization of the resulting association, which shall be an interim federal or state savings association subsidiary of the reorganizing association, and attach and incorporate the proposed charter and bylaws of such association;

(c) If the reorganizing association proposes to form a subsidiary holding company, provide for the organization of a subsidiary holding company and attach and incorporate the proposed charter and bylaws of such subsidiary holding company.

§ 575.7

(d) Provide for amendment of the charter and bylaws of any acquiree association to read in the form of the charter and bylaws of a state or federal savings association in the stock form (as modified by § 575.9(b) of this part), and attach and incorporate such charter and bylaws;

(e) Provide that, upon consummation of the reorganization, substantially all of the assets and liabilities (including all savings accounts, demand accounts, tax and loan accounts, United States Treasury General Accounts, or United States Treasury Time Deposit Open Accounts, as defined in part 561 of this chapter) of the reorganizing association shall be transferred to the resulting association, which shall thereupon become an operating savings association subsidiary of the mutual holding company;

(f) Provide that all assets, rights, obligations, and liabilities of whatever nature of the reorganizing association that are not expressly retained by the mutual holding company shall be deemed transferred to the resulting association;

(g) Provide that each depositor in the reorganizing association or any acquiree association immediately prior to the reorganization shall upon consummation of the reorganization receive, without payment, an identical account in the resulting association or the acquiree association, as the case may be (Appropriate modifications should be made to this provision if savings associations are being merged as a part of the reorganization);

(h) Provide that the Reorganization Plan as adopted by the boards of directors of the reorganizing association and any acquiree association may be substantively amended by those boards of directors as a result of comments from regulatory authorities or otherwise prior to the solicitation of proxies from the members of the reorganizing association and any acquiree association to vote on the Reorganization Plan and at any time thereafter with the concurrence of the OTS; and that the reorganization may be terminated by the board of directors of the reorganizing association or any acquiree association at any time prior to the meeting of the members of the association called to consider the Reorganization Plan and at any time thereafter with the concurrence of the OTS;

(i) Provide that the Reorganization Plan shall be terminated if not completed within a specified period of time (The time period shall not be more than 24 months from the date upon which the members of the reorganizing association or the date upon which the members of any acquiree association, whichever is earlier, approve the Reorganization Plan and may not be extended by the reorganizing or acquiree association); and

(j) Provide that the expenses incurred in connection with the reorganization shall be reasonable.

[58 FR 44114, Aug. 19, 1993, as amended at 63 FR 11365, Mar. 9, 1998]

§ 575.7 Issuances of stock by savings association subsidiaries of mutual holding companies.

(a) *Requirements.* No savings association subsidiary of a mutual holding company (including any resulting association or acquiree association) may issue stock to persons other than its mutual holding company parent in connection with a mutual holding company reorganization, or at any time subsequent to the association's acquisition by the mutual holding company, unless the association obtains advance approval of each such issuance from the OTS. Issuance by the OTS of a notice of intent not to disapprove a mutual holding company reorganization pursuant to § 575.3(b) of this part, or failure by the OTS to disapprove such a reorganization within the time prescribed in § 575.3(b) of this part, shall be deemed to constitute approval of any stock issuance specifically applied for pursuant to this section in connection with the reorganization, unless otherwise specified by the OTS. The OTS shall approve any proposed issuance that meets each of the criteria set forth below in paragraphs (a)(1)–(a)(7) of this section.

(1) The proposed issuance is to be made pursuant to a Stock Issuance Plan that contains all the provisions required by § 575.8 of this part.

Office of Thrift Supervision, Treasury §575.7

(2) The Stock Issuance Plan is consistent with the terms of the association's charter (or any proposed amendments thereto), including terms governing the type and amount of stock that may be issued.

(3) The Stock Issuance Plan would provide the association, its mutual holding company parent, and any other savings association subsidiaries of the mutual holding company with fully sufficient capital and would not be inequitable or detrimental to the association or its mutual holding company parent or to members of the mutual holding company parent.

(4) The proposed price or price range of the stock to be issued is reasonable. (The OTS shall review the reasonableness of the proposed price or price range in accordance with paragraph (b) of this section.)

(5) The aggregate amount of outstanding common stock of the association owned or controlled by persons other than the association's mutual holding company parent at the close of the proposed issuance shall be less than 50% of the association's total outstanding common stock, unless the association was a stock association when acquired by the mutual holding company and is not a resulting association or an acquiree association, in which case the foregoing restriction shall not apply. Any amount of preferred stock may be issued by any savings association subsidiary of a mutual holding company to persons other than the association's mutual holding company, consistent with any other applicable laws and regulations.

(6) The association furnishes the information required by the OTS in connection with the proposed issuance.

(7) The proposed stock issuance would fail to meet the convenience and needs standard of §563b.200(c) of this chapter.

(8) The proposed issuance complies with all other applicable laws and regulations.

(9) Unless otherwise determined by the OTS, the limitations on the minimum and maximum amounts of the estimated price range required by §563b.330 of this chapter shall apply.

(b) *Related approvals.* Approval by the OTS of any stock issuance pursuant to this section shall also be deemed to constitute:

(1) Approval under §563.3 of this chapter of the form of stock certificate proposed to be utilized in connection with the stock issuance, provided such form was included in the application materials filed pursuant to this section; and

(2) Preliminary approval under §552.4 of this chapter and approval under §563.3 of this chapter of any charter or bylaw amendment required to authorize issuance of the stock, provided such amendment was proposed in the application materials filed pursuant to this section.

(c) *Offering restrictions.* (1) No representations may be made in any manner in connection with the offer or sale of any stock issued pursuant to this section that the price, price range or any other pricing information related to such stock issuance has been approved by the OTS or that the stock has been approved or disapproved by the OTS or that the OTS has endorsed the accuracy or adequacy of any securities offering documents disseminated in connection with such stock.

(2) The sale of minority stock of the reorganized stock savings association to be made under the minority stock issuance plan, including any sale in a public offering or direct community marketing, shall be completed as promptly as possible and within 45 calendar days after the last day of the subscription period, unless extended by the OTS.

(3) In the offer, sale, or purchase of stock issued pursuant to this section, no person shall:

(i) Employ any device, scheme, or artifice to defraud;

(ii) Make any untrue statement of a material fact or omit to state a material fact necessary in order to make the statements made, in the light of the circumstances under which they were made, not misleading; or

(iii) Engage in any act, practice, or course of business which operates or would operate as a fraud or deceit upon a purchaser or seller.

(4) Prior to the completion of a stock issuance pursuant to this section, no person shall transfer, or enter into any agreement or understanding to transfer, the legal or beneficial ownership of

the stock to be issued to any other person.

(5) Prior to the completion of a stock issuance pursuant to this section, no person shall make any offer, or any announcement of any offer, to purchase any stock to be issued, or knowingly acquire any stock in the issuance, in excess of the maximum purchase limitations established in the Stock Issuance Plan.

(6) All stock issuances pursuant to this section must:

(i) Comply with 12 CFR part 563g and, to the extent applicable, Form OC; and

(ii) Provide that the offering be structured in a manner similar to a standard conversion under 12 CFR part 563b, including the stock purchase priorities accorded members of the issuing association's mutual holding company, unless the association would qualify for a supervisory conversion if it were to undertake a conversion under 12 CFR part 563b; or demonstrates to the satisfaction of the OTS that a non-conforming issuance would be more beneficial to the association compared to a conforming offering, considering, in the aggregate, the effect of each on the association's financial and managerial resources and future prospects, the effect of the issuance upon the association, the insurance risk to the Deposit Insurance Fund, and the convenience and needs of the community to be served.

(7) Notwithstanding the restrictions in paragraph (d)(6)(ii) of this section, a savings association subsidiary of a mutual holding company may issue stock as part of a stock benefit plan to any insider, associate of an insider, or tax qualified or non-tax qualified employee stock benefit plan of the mutual holding company or subsidiary of the mutual holding company without including the purchase priorities of part 563b of this chapter.

(8) As part of a reorganization, a reasonable amount of shares or proceeds may be contributed to a charitable organization that complies with §§ 563b.550 to 563b.575 of this chapter, provided such contribution does not result in any taxes on excess business holdings under section 4943 of the Internal Revenue Code (26 U.S.C. 4943).

(d) *Procedural and substantive requirements.* The procedural and substantive requirements of 12 CFR part 563b shall apply to all mutual holding company stock issuances under this section, unless clearly inapplicable, as determined by OTS. For purposes of this paragraph (d), the term *conversion* as it appears in the provisions of Part 563b of this chapter shall refer to the stock issuance, and the term *converted* or *converting savings association* shall refer to the savings association undertaking the stock issuance.

[58 FR 44114, Aug. 19, 1993, as amended at 59 FR 22735, May 3, 1994; 67 FR 52035, Aug. 9, 2002; 67 FR 78153, Dec. 23, 2002; 68 FR 75110, Dec. 30, 2003; 71 FR 19812, Apr. 18, 2006; 72 FR 35150, June 27, 2007]

§ 575.8 Contents of Stock Issuance Plans.

(a) *Mandatory provisions.* Each of the provisions mandatory for all stock issuance plans under this paragraph shall be deemed regulatory requirements. Each Stock Issuance Plan shall contain a complete description of all significant terms of the proposed stock issuance (including the information specified in § 563b.650 of this chapter to the extent known), shall attach and incorporate the proposed form of stock certificate, the proposed stock order form, and any agreements or other documents defining the rights of the stockholders, and shall:

(1) Provide that the stock shall be sold at a total price equal to the estimated *pro forma* market value of such stock, based upon an independent valuation, as provided in § 575.7(b) of this part;

(2) Provide that the aggregate amount of outstanding common stock of the association owned or controlled by persons other than the association's mutual holding company parent at the close of the proposed issuance shall be less than fifty percent of the association's total outstanding common stock (This provision may be omitted if the proposed issuance will be conducted by an association that was in the stock form when acquired by its mutual holding company parent, provided the association is not a resulting association or an acquiree association);

Office of Thrift Supervision, Treasury § 575.8

(3) Provide that all employee stock ownership plans or other tax-qualified employee stock benefit plans (collectively, ESOPs) must not encompass, in the aggregate, more than either 4.9 percent of the outstanding shares of the savings association's common stock or 4.9 percent of the savings association's stockholders' equity at the close of the proposed issuance.

(4) Provide that all ESOPs and management recognition plans (MRPs) must not encompass, in the aggregate, more than either 4.9 percent of the outstanding shares of the savings association's common stock or 4.9 percent of the savings association's stockholders' equity at the close of the proposed issuance. However, if the savings association's tangible capital equals at least ten percent at the time of implementation of the plan, OTS may permit such ESOPs and MRPs to encompass, in the aggregate, up to 5.88 percent of the outstanding common stock or stockholders' equity at the close of the proposed issuance.

(5) Provide that all MRPs must not encompass, in the aggregate, more than either 1.47 percent of the common stock of the savings association or 1.47 percent of the savings association's stockholders' equity at the close of the proposed issuance. However, if the savings association's tangible capital is at least ten percent at the time of implementation of the plan, OTS may permit MRPs to encompass, in the aggregate, up to 1.96 percent of the outstanding shares of the savings association's common stock or 1.96 percent of the savings association's stockholders' equity at the close of the proposed issuance.

(6) Provide that all stock option plans (Option Plans) must not encompass, in the aggregate, more than either 4.9 percent of the savings association's outstanding common stock at the close of the proposed issuance or 4.9 percent of the savings association's stockholders' equity at the close of the proposed issuance.

(7) Provide that an ESOP, a MRP or an Option Plan modified or adopted no earlier than one year after the close of: the proposed issuance, or any subsequent issuance that is made in substantial conformity with the purchase priorities set forth in part 563b, may exceed the percentage limitations contained in paragraphs (a)(3) through (6) of this section (plan expansion), subject to the following two requirements. First, all common stock awarded in connection with any plan expansion must be acquired for such awards in the secondary market. Second, such acquisitions must begin no earlier than when such plan expansion is permitted to be made.

(8)(i) Provide that the aggregate amount of common stock that may be encompassed under all Option Plans and MRPs, or acquired by all insiders of the association and associates of insiders of the association, must not exceed the following percentages of common stock or stockholders' equity of the savings association, held by persons other than the savings association's mutual holding company parent at the close of the proposed issuance:

Institution size	Officer and director purchases (percent)
$ 50,000,000 or less	35
$ 50,000,001–100,000,000	34
$100,000,001–150,000,000	33
$150,000,001–200,000,000	32
$200,000,001–250,000,000	31
$250,000,001–300,000,000	30
$300,000,001–350,000,000	29
$350,000,001–400,000,000	28
$400,000,001–450,000,000	27
$450,000,001–500,000,000	26
Over $500,000,000	25

(ii) The percentage limitations contained in paragraph 8(i) may be exceeded provided that all stock acquired by insiders and associates of insiders or awarded under all MRPs and Option Plans in excess of those limitations is acquired in the secondary market. If acquired for such awards on the secondary market, such acquisitions must begin no earlier than one year after the close of the proposed issuance or any subsequent issuance that is made in substantial conformity with the purchase priorities set forth in Part 563b.

(iii) In calculating the number of shares held by insiders and their associates under this provision, shares awarded but not delivered under an ESOP, MRP, or Option Plan that are attributable to such persons shall not be counted as being acquired by such persons.

§ 575.8

(9) Provide that the amount of common stock that may be encompassed under all Option Plans and MRPs must not exceed, in the aggregate, 25 percent of the outstanding common stock held by persons other than the savings association's mutual holding company parent at the close of the proposed issuance.

(10) Provide that the issuance shall be conducted in compliance with 12 CFR part 563g and, to the extent applicable, Form OC;

(11) Provide that the sales price of the shares of stock to be sold in the issuance shall be a uniform price determined in accordance with § 575.7 of this part;

(12) Provide that, if at the close of the stock issuance the association has more than thirty-five shareholders of any class of stock, the association shall promptly register that class of stock pursuant to the Securities Exchange Act of 1934, as amended (15 U.S.C. 78a–78jj), and undertake not to deregister such stock for a period of three years thereafter;

(13) Provide that, if at the close of the stock issuance the association has more than one hundred shareholders of any class of stock, the association shall use its best efforts to:

(i) Encourage and assist a market maker to establish and maintain a market for that class of stock; and

(ii) List that class of stock on a national or regional securities exchange or on the NASDAQ quotation system;

(14) Provide that, for a period of three years following the proposed issuance, no insider of the association or his or her associates shall purchase, without the prior written approval of the OTS, any stock of the association except from a broker dealer registered with the Securities and Exchange Commission, except that the foregoing restriction shall not apply to:

(i) Negotiated transactions involving more than one percent of the outstanding stock in the class of stock; or

(ii) Purchases of stock made by and held by any tax-qualified or non-tax-qualified employee stock benefit plan of the association even if such stock is attributable to insiders of the association or their associates;

(15) Provide that stock purchased by insiders of the association and their associates in the proposed issuance shall not be sold for a period of at least one year following the date of purchase, except in the case of death of the insider or associate;

(16) Provide that, in connection with stock subject to restriction on sale for a period of time:

(i) Each certificate for such stock shall bear a legend giving appropriate notice of such restriction;

(ii) Appropriate instructions shall be issued to the association's transfer agent with respect to applicable restrictions on transfer of such stock; and

(iii) Any shares issued as a stock dividend, stock split, or otherwise with respect to any such restricted stock shall be subject to the same restrictions as apply to the restricted stock;

(17) Provide that the association will not offer or sell any of the stock proposed to be issued to any person whose purchase would be financed by funds loaned, directly or indirectly, to the person by the association;

(18) Provide that, if necessary, the association's charter will be amended to authorize issuance of the stock and attach and incorporate by reference the text of any such amendment;

(19) Provide that the expenses incurred in connection with the issuance shall be reasonable;

(20) Provide that the Stock Issuance Plan, if proposed as part of a Reorganization Plan, may be amended or terminated in the same manner as the Reorganization Plan. Otherwise, the Stock Issuance Plan shall provide that it may be substantively amended by the board of directors of the issuing association as a result of comments from regulatory authorities or otherwise prior to approval of the Plan by the OTS, and at any time thereafter with the concurrence of the OTS; and that the Stock Issuance Plan may be terminated by the board of directors at any time prior to approval of the Plan by the OTS, and at any time thereafter with the concurrence of the OTS;

(21) Provide that, unless an extension is granted by the OTS, the Stock Issuance Plan shall be terminated if not completed within 90 days of:

Office of Thrift Supervision, Treasury § 575.9

(i) The date of such approval; or

(ii) For stock issuances subject to the offering circular requirements of part 563g of this chapter, the date on which the offering circular was declared effective by the OTS; and

(22) Provide that the association may make scheduled discretionary contributions to a tax-qualified employee stock benefit plan provided such contributions do not cause the association to fail to meet any of its regulatory capital requirements.

(b) *Optional provisions.* A Stock Issuance Plan may:

(1) Provide that, in the event the proposed stock issuance is part of a Reorganization Plan, the stock offering may be commenced concurrently with or at any time after the mailing to the members of the reorganizing association and any acquiree association of any proxy statement(s) authorized for use by the OTS. The offering may be closed before the required membership vote(s), provided the offer and sale of the stock shall be conditioned upon the approval of the Reorganization Plan and Stock Issuance Plan by the members of the reorganizing association and any acquiree association;

(2) Provide that any insignificant residue of stock of the association not sold in the offering may be sold in such other manner as provided in the Stock Issuance Plan, with the OTS's approval;

(3) Provide that the association may issue and sell, in lieu of shares of its stock, units of securities consisting of stock and long-term warrants or other equity securities, in which event any reference in the provisions of this section and in §575.7 of this part to stock shall apply to such units of equity securities unless the context otherwise requires; or

(4) Provide that the association may reserve shares representing up to ten percent of the proposed offering for issuance in connection with an employee stock benefit plan.

(c) *Applicability of provisions of §563b.500(a) to minority stock issuances.* Notwithstanding §575.7(d) of this section, §563b.500(a)(2) and (3) do not apply to minority stock issuances, because the permissible sizes of ESOPs, MRPs, and Option Plans in minority stock issuances are subject to each of the requirements set forth at paragraphs (a)(3) through (a)(9) of this section. Section 563b.500, paragraphs (a)(4) through (14), apply for one year after the savings association engages in a minority stock issuance that is conducted in accordance with the purchase priorities set forth in part 563b. In addition to the shareholder vote requirement for Option Plans and MRPs set forth at §563b.500(a)(6), any Option Plans and MRPs put to a shareholder vote after a minority stock issuance that is conducted in accordance with the purchase priorities set forth in part 563b must be approved by a majority of the votes cast by stockholders other than the mutual holding company.

[58 FR 44114, Aug. 19, 1993, as amended at 67 FR 52035, Aug. 9, 2002; 72 FR 35150, June 27, 2007]

§ 575.9 Charters and bylaws for mutual holding companies and their savings association subsidiaries.

(a) *Charters and bylaws for mutual holding companies*—(1) *Charters.* The charter of a mutual holding company shall be in the form set forth in this paragraph (a)(1) and may include any of the additional provisions permitted pursuant to paragraph (a)(2) of this section.

CHARTER

Section 1: Corporate title. The name of the mutual holding company is ____ (the "Mutual Company").

Section 2: Duration. The duration of the Mutual Company is perpetual.

Section 3: Purpose and powers. The purpose of the Mutual Company is to pursue any or all of the lawful objectives of a federal mutual savings and loan holding company chartered under section 10(o) of the Home Owners' Loan Act, 12 U.S.C. 1467a(o), and to exercise all of the express, implied, and incidental powers conferred thereby and all acts amendatory thereof and supplemental thereto, subject to the Constitution and the laws of the United States as they are now in effect, or as they may hereafter be amended, and subject to all lawful and applicable rules, regulations, and orders of the Office of Thrift Supervision ("OTS").

Section 4: Capital. The Mutual Company shall have no capital stock.

Section 5: Members. [The content of this section 5 shall be identical to the content of the

529

§ 575.9

parallel section in the charter of the reorganizing association, with the following exceptions: (A) Any provisions conferring membership rights upon borrowers of the reorganizing association shall be eliminated and replaced with provisions grandfathering those rights in accordance with 12 CFR 575.5; and (B) appropriate changes shall be made to indicate that membership rights in the mutual holding company derive from deposit accounts in and, to the extent of any grandfather provisions, borrowings from the resulting association. Set forth below is an example of how section 5 should appear in the charter of a mutual holding company formed by a reorganizing association whose charter conforms to the model charter prescribed for federal mutual savings associations for calendar year 1989. Additional changes to this section 5 may be required whenever a mutual holding company reorganization involves an acquiree association, or a mutual holding company makes a post-reorganization acquisition of a mutual savings association, so as to preserve the membership rights of the members of the acquired association consistent with 12 CFR 575.5.]

All holders of the savings, demand, or other authorized accounts of _____ [insert the name of the resulting association] (the "Association") are members of the Mutual Company. With respect to all questions requiring action by the members of the Mutual Company, each holder of an account in the Association shall be permitted to cast one vote for each $100, or fraction thereof, of the withdrawal value of the member's account. In addition, borrowers from the Association as of _____ [insert the date of the reorganization or any earlier date as of which new borrowings ceased to result in membership rights] shall be entitled to one vote for the period of time during which such borrowings are in existence. [The foregoing sentence should be included only if the charter of the reorganizing association confers voting rights on any borrowers.] No member, however, shall cast more than one thousand votes. All accounts shall be nonassessable.

Section 6. Directors. The Mutual Company shall be under the direction of a board of directors. The authorized number of directors shall not be fewer than five nor more than fifteen, as fixed in the Mutual Company's by-laws, except that the number of directors may be decreased to a number less than five or increased to a number greater than fifteen with the prior approval of the Director of the Office or his or her delegate.

Section 7: Capital, surplus, and distribution of earnings. [The content of this section 7 shall be identical to the content of the parallel section in the charter of the reorganizing association, except for changes made to indicate that distribution rights in the mutual holding company derive from deposit accounts in the resulting association, any changes required to provide that the Director of the OTS shall be the approving authority in instances where the charter requires regulatory approval of distributions, and any other changes necessary to accommodate the mutual holding company format. Set forth below is an example of how section 7 should appear in the charter of a mutual holding company formed by a reorganizing association whose charter conforms to the model charter prescribed for federal mutual savings associations for calendar year 1989. Additional changes to this section 7 may be required whenever a mutual holding company reorganization involves an acquiree association, or a mutual holding company makes a post-reorganization acquisition of a mutual savings association, so as to preserve the membership rights of the members of the acquired association consistent with 12 CFR 575.5.]

The Mutual Company shall distribute net earnings to account holders of the Association on such basis and in accordance with such terms and conditions as may from time to time be authorized by the Director of the OTS, provided that the Mutual Company may establish minimum account balance requirements for account holders to be eligible for distributions of earnings.

All holders of accounts of the Association shall be entitled to equal distribution of the assets of the Mutual Company, *pro rata* to the value of their accounts in the Association, in the event of voluntary or involuntary liquidation, dissolution, or winding up of the Mutual Company.

Section 8. Amendment. Adoption of any preapproved charter amendment shall be effective after such preapproved amendment has been approved by the members at a legal meeting. Any other amendment, addition, change, or repeal of this charter must be approved by the Office prior to approval by the members at a legal meeting and shall be effective upon filing with the Office in accordance with regulatory procedures.

Attest: _____
    Secretary of the Association
By: _____
    President or Chief Executive Officer of the Association
Attest: _____
    Secretary of the Office of Thrift Supervision
By: _____
    Director of the Office of Thrift Supervision
Effective Date: _____

(2) *Charter amendments.* The rules and regulations set forth in § 544.2 of this chapter regarding charter amendments and reissuances of charters (including

Office of Thrift Supervision, Treasury § 575.9

delegations and filing instructions) shall be applicable to mutual holding companies to the same extent as if mutual holding companies were Federal mutual savings associations, except that, with respect to the pre-approved charter amendments set forth in § 544.2 of this chapter, §§ 544.2(b)(1) and (b)(3) of this chapter shall not apply to mutual holding companies, and mutual holding companies changing their corporate title pursuant to § 544.2(b)(2) of this chapter shall be required to comply with § 575.9(a)(3) of this part as well as § 543.1(b) of this chapter.

(3) *Corporate title.* The corporate title of each mutual holding company shall include the term "mutual" or the abbreviation "M.H.C."

(4) *Bylaws.* The rules and regulations set forth in § 544.5 of this chapter regarding bylaws (including their content, any amendments thereto, delegations, and filing instructions) shall be applicable to mutual holding companies to the same extent as if mutual holding companies were federal mutual savings associations. The model bylaws for Federal mutual savings associations set forth in the OTS Applications Processing Handbook shall also serve as the model bylaws for mutual holding companies, except that the term "association" each time it appears therein shall be replaced with the term "Mutual Company"; section 11(e) (extending leniency to borrowing members) and section 11(f) (rejection of applications for accounts or membership) shall be removed and the remaining paragraphs of section 12 redesignated accordingly.

(5) *Availability of charter and bylaws.* A mutual holding company shall make available to its members at all times in the offices of each subsidiary savings association from which the mutual holding company draws members a true copy of its charter and bylaws, including any amendments, and shall deliver such a copy to any member upon request. Mutual holding companies shall also be subject to the provisions of § 544.8 of this chapter.

(b) *Charters and bylaws of subsidiary savings associations of mutual holding companies.* Except as specified otherwise by the OTS in any notice of intent not to disapprove a mutual holding company reorganization or in any regulation or order, each subsidiary savings association of a mutual holding company shall be subject to the same rules and regulations regarding charters and bylaws as are applicable to stock savings associations that are chartered by the OTS, 12 CFR part 552, or by the appropriate state chartering authority, as the case may be, *provided* that the charter of each resulting association, each acquiree association, and each mutual savings association that is acquired by a mutual holding company shall contain the provision set forth below:

In any situation in which the priority of the accounts of the association is in controversy, all such accounts shall, to the extent of their withdrawable value, be debts of the association having at least as high a priority as the claims of general creditors of the association not having priority (other than any priority arising or resulting from consensual subordination) over other general creditors of the association.

(c) *Optional charter provision limiting minority stock ownership.* A federal resulting association or federal acquiree association that engages in its initial minority stock issuance after October 1, 2008 may, before it conducts its initial minority stock issuance, at the time of such minority stock issuance, or at any time during the five years following a minority stock issuance that such association conducts in accordance with the purchase priorities set forth in 12 CFR part 563b, include in its charter the following provision. For purposes of this charter provision, the definitions set forth at § 552.4(b)(8) of this chapter apply. This charter provision expires a maximum of five years from the date of the minority stock issuance. The federal resulting association or federal acquiree association may adopt the charter provision after a minority stock issuance only if it provided, in the offering materials related to its previous minority stock issuance or issuances, full disclosure of the possibility that the association might adopt such a charter provision.

Beneficial Ownership Limitation. No person may directly or indirectly offer to acquire or acquire the beneficial ownership of more than 10 percent of the outstanding stock of any class of voting stock of the association

§ 575.9

held by persons other than the association's mutual holding company. This limitation expires on [insert date within five years of minority stock issuance] and does not apply to a transaction in which an underwriter purchases stock in connection with a public offering, or the purchase of stock by an employee stock ownership plan or other tax-qualified employee stock benefit plan that is exempt from the approval requirements under § 574.3(c)(1)(vii) of the Office's regulations.

In the event a person acquires stock in violation of this section, all stock beneficially owned by such person in excess of 10 percent of the stock held by stockholders other than the mutual holding company shall be considered "excess shares" and shall not be counted as stock entitled to vote and shall not be voted by any person or counted as voting stock in connection with any matters submitted to the stockholders for a vote.

(d) *Approval of charters and bylaws of mutual holding companies and their savings association subsidiaries in connection with Reorganization Plans.* (1) Issuance by the OTS of a notice of intent not to disapprove a reorganization pursuant to § 575.3(b) of this part, or failure by the OTS to disapprove such a reorganization within the time prescribed in § 575.3(b) of this part, shall be deemed to constitute:

(i) Approval pursuant to § 575.3(d) of this part and this section for the reorganizing association to amend its charter and bylaws in their entirety to read in the form of the mutual holding company charter and bylaws proposed in the Reorganization Notice (as modified by any conditions imposed by the OTS in its notice of intent not to disapprove or paragraph (c)(2) of this section and subject to paragraph (c)(5) of this section);

(ii) If the Reorganization Plan provides that the resulting association is to be federally chartered, approval pursuant to 12 U.S.C. 1464 (a) and (e) and §§ 552.2-1 and 552.2-2 of this chapter of the organization of the resulting association and the proposed charter and bylaws of such association (as modified by any conditions imposed by the OTS in its notice of intent not to disapprove or by paragraph (c)(2) of this section and subject to paragraph (c)(5) of this section); and

(iii) If the Reorganization Plan provides that the acquiree association is to be federally chartered, approval pursuant to § 552.4 of this chapter of the amendment of the existing charter of the acquiree association in its entirety to read in the form of the proposed charter and bylaws of such association (as modified by any conditions imposed by the OTS in its notice of intent not to disapprove or paragraph (c)(2) of this section and subject to paragraph (c)(5) of this section).

(2) In the event the charter and bylaws of a mutual holding company and of any federally-chartered resulting association or acquiree association are approved pursuant to paragraph (c)(1) of this section due to failure of the OTS to disapprove a Reorganization Notice within the time prescribed in § 575.3(b) of this part, such approval shall be subject to the condition that such charter(s) and bylaws shall conform in every particular to the model charter(s) and bylaws for mutual holding companies and/or federal stock savings associations, as the case may be, as set forth in the OTS's regulations.

(3) Promptly after approval of the amendment of the charter of a reorganizing association to read in the form of a mutual holding company charter pursuant to paragraph (c)(1) of this section, the OTS shall issue an executed copy of such charter to the reorganizing association. Such charter shall not become effective until consummation of the Reorganization Plan, at which point in time it shall replace and nullify the charter of the reorganizing association. The charter of the reorganizing association shall be surrendered to the OTS within five days after consummation of the Reorganization Plan. If the Reorganization Plan is terminated for any reason, the charter of the mutual holding company shall become immediately null and void and shall be returned to the OTS within five days.

(4) Promptly after approval of any federal charter for a resulting association pursuant to paragraph (c)(1) of this section or approval of the amendment of any federal charter of an acquiree association pursuant to paragraph (c)(1) of this section, the OTS shall issue an executed copy of such charter(s) to the reorganizing association and/or the acquiree association, as the case may be.

Office of Thrift Supervision, Treasury

§ 575.10

(i) Prior to consummation of the Reorganization Plan, the resulting association (whether chartered under federal or state law) shall constitute an interim savings association subsidiary of the reorganizing association and shall not accept any deposits or engage in any other business activities except for those activities necessary to consummate the Reorganization Plan. If the Reorganization Plan is terminated for any reason, the charter of the resulting association shall immediately become null and void and, if the resulting association is federally chartered, the charter shall be returned to the OTS within five days.

(ii) Any amended charter issued to an acquiree association (whether by the OTS or the appropriate state authority) shall not become effective until consummation of the Reorganization Plan, at which point in time it shall replace and nullify the prior charter of the acquiree association. The prior charter of any federally-chartered acquiree association shall be surrendered to the OTS within five days after consummation of the Reorganization Plan. If the Reorganization Plan is terminated for any reason, the amended charter of the acquiree association shall become immediately null and void and, if the acquiree association is federally chartered, the amended charter shall be returned to the OTS within five days.

(5) Approval of the amendment of the charter and bylaws of the reorganizing association to read in the form of the charter and bylaws of a mutual holding company and of any acquiree association to read in the form of a stock association and approval of the organization of any resulting association and of its charter and bylaws pursuant to paragraph (c)(1) of this section shall be subject to any conditions subsequent that the OTS may impose in connection therewith or with its notice of intent not to disapprove the reorganization.

[58 FR 44114, Aug. 19, 1993, as amended at 61 FR 64021, Dec. 3, 1996; 62 FR 66264, Dec. 18, 1997; 73 FR 39219, July 9, 2008; 73 FR 76939, Dec. 18, 2008]

§ 575.10 Acquisition and disposition of savings associations, savings and loan holding companies, and other corporations by mutual holding companies.

(a) *Acquisitions*—(1) *Stock savings associations.* A mutual holding company may acquire control of a savings association that is in the stock form, provided the necessary approvals are obtained from the OTS, including (without limitation) approval pursuant to part 574 of this chapter and, if the acquisition involves a merger or transfer of assets or liabilities, approval pursuant to §§ 552.13, 563.22, and part 546 of this chapter, as appropriate.

(2) *Mutual savings associations.* A mutual holding company may acquire a savings association in the mutual form by merger of such association into any subsidiary savings association of such holding company from which the parent mutual holding company draws members or into an interim savings association subsidiary of the mutual holding company, provided:

(i) The proposed acquisition is approved by a majority of the board of directors of the mutual association;

(ii) The proposed acquisition is submitted to the mutual association's members pursuant to a proxy statement authorized for use by the OTS and such acquisition is approved by a majority of the total votes of the association's members eligible to be cast at a meeting held at the call of the association's directors in accordance with the procedures prescribed by the association's charter and bylaws;

(iii) The necessary approvals are obtained from the OTS, including (without limitation) approval pursuant to part 574 of this chapter and §§ 552.13, 563.22, and part 546 of this chapter, as appropriate, and any approvals required to form an interim association, to amend the charter and bylaws of the association being acquired, and/or to amend the charter and bylaws of the mutual holding company consistent with 575.6(a) of this part; and

(iv) The approval of the members of the mutual holding company is obtained, if the OTS advises the mutual holding company in writing that such approval will be required.

533

§ 575.10

(3) *Mutual holding companies.* A mutual holding company that is not a subsidiary holding company may acquire control of another mutual holding company, including a subsidiary holding company, by merging with or into such company, provided the necessary approvals are obtained from the OTS, including (without limitation) approval pursuant to part 574 of this chapter. The approval of the members of the mutual holding companies shall also be obtained if the OTS advises the mutual holding companies in writing that such approval will be required.

(4) *Stock holding companies.* A mutual holding company may acquire control of a savings and loan holding company in the stock form that is not a subsidiary holding company, provided the necessary approvals are obtained from the OTS, including (without limitation) approval pursuant to part 574 of this chapter. The acquired holding company may be held as a subsidiary of the mutual holding company or merged into the mutual holding company.

(5) *Non-controlling acquisitions of savings association stock.* A mutual holding company may acquire non-controlling amounts of the stock of savings associations and savings and loan holding companies subject to the restrictions imposed by 12 U.S.C. 1467a(e) and (q) and §§ 574.8 and 584.4 of this chapter.

(6) *Other corporations.* A mutual holding company may acquire control of, and make non-controlling investments in the stock of, any corporation other than a savings association or savings and loan holding company only if:

(i) (A) Such corporation is engaged exclusively in activities that are permissible for mutual holding companies pursuant to § 575.11(a) of this part; or

(B) It is lawful for the stock of such corporation to be purchased by a federal savings association under part 559 of this chapter or by a state savings association under the law of any state where any subsidiary savings association of the mutual holding company has its home office; and

(ii) Such corporation is not controlled, directly or indirectly, by a savings association subsidiary of the mutual holding company.

(b) *Dispositions.* (1) A mutual holding company shall provide written notice to the OTS at least 30 days prior to the effective date of any direct or indirect transfer of any of the stock that it holds in a subsidiary holding company, a resulting association, an acquiree association, or any subsidiary savings association that was in the mutual form when acquired by the mutual holding company, including stock transferred in connection with a pledge pursuant to § 575.11(b) or any transfer of all or a substantial portion of the assets or liabilities of any such subsidiary holding company or association. Any such disposition shall comply with the requirements of this part or with part 563b of this chapter, as appropriate, and with any other applicable statute or regulation including, without limitation, parts 546, 563 and 574 of this chapter.

(2) A mutual holding company may, subject to applicable laws and regulations, transfer any or all of the stock or cause or permit the transfer of any or all of the assets and liabilities of:

(i) Any subsidiary savings association that was in the stock form when acquired, provided such association is not a resulting association or an acquiree association;

(ii) Any subsidiary savings and loan holding company acquired pursuant to paragraph (a)(4) of this section; or

(iii) Any corporation other than a savings association or savings and loan holding company.

(3) A mutual holding company may, subject to applicable laws and regulations, transfer any stock acquired pursuant to paragraph (a)(5) of this section.

(4) No transfer authorized by this section may be made to any insider of the mutual holding company, any associate of an insider of the mutual holding company, or any tax-qualified or non-tax-qualified employee stock benefit plan of the mutual holding company unless the mutual holding company provides notice to the OTS at least 30 days prior to the effective date of the proposed transfer. This notice shall be in addition to any other application or notice required under applicable laws or regulations, including,

without limitation, this part and parts 563, 563b, 574 of this chapter.

[58 FR 44114, Aug. 19, 1993, as amended at 60 FR 66720, Dec. 26, 1995; 63 FR 11365, Mar. 9, 1998]

§ 575.11 Operating restrictions.

(a) *Activities restrictions.* A mutual holding company may engage in any business activity specified in 12 U.S.C. 1467a(c)(2) or (c)(9)(A)(ii). In addition, the business activities of subsidiaries of mutual holding companies may include the activities specified in § 575.10(a)(6) of this part. A mutual holding company or its subsidiaries may engage in the foregoing activities only upon compliance with the procedures specified in §§ 584.2–1(c) or 584.2–2(b) of this chapter.

(b) *Pledging stock.* (1) No mutual holding company may pledge the stock of its resulting association, an acquiree association, or any subsidiary savings association that was in the mutual form when acquired by the mutual holding company (or its parent mutual holding company), unless the proceeds of the loan secured by the pledge are infused into the association whose stock is pledged. No mutual holding company may pledge the stock of its subsidiary holding company unless the proceeds of the loan secured by the pledge are infused into any savings association subsidiary of the subsidiary holding company that is a resulting association, an acquiree association, or a subsidiary savings association that was in the mutual form when acquired by the subsidiary holding company (or its parent mutual holding company). In the event the subsidiary holding company has more than one savings association subsidiary, the loan proceeds shall, unless otherwise approved by the OTS, be infused in equal amounts to each savings association subsidiary. Any amount of the stock of such association or subsidiary holding company may be pledged for these purposes. Nothing in this paragraph (b)(1) shall be deemed to prohibit:

(i) The payment of dividends from a subsidiary savings association to its mutual holding company parent to the extent otherwise permissible; or

(ii) The payment of dividends from a subsidiary holding company to its mutual holding company parent to the extent otherwise permissible; or

(iii) A mutual holding company from pledging the stock of more than one savings association subsidiary provided that the stock pledged of each such subsidiary association is proportionate to the proceeds of the loan infused into each subsidiary association.

(2) Within 10 days after its pledge of stock pursuant to paragraph (b)(1) of this section, a mutual holding company shall provide written notice to the OTS regarding the terms of the transaction (including the amount of principal and interest, repayment terms, maturity date, the nature and amount of collateral, and the terms governing seizure of the collateral) and shall include in such notice a certification that the proceeds of the loan have been transferred to the subsidiary savings association whose stock (or the stock of its parent subsidiary holding company) has been pledged.

(3) Any mutual holding company that fails to make any payment on a loan secured by the pledge of stock pursuant to paragraph (b)(1) of this section on or before the date on which such payment is due shall, on the first day after such payment is due, provide written notice of nonpayment to the Regional Director.

(c) *Restrictions on stock repurchases.* (1) No subsidiary savings association of a mutual holding company that has any stockholders other than the association's mutual holding company and no subsidiary holding company that has any stockholders other than its parent mutual holding company may repurchase any share of stock within one year of its date of issuance (which may include the time period the shares issued by the savings association were outstanding if the subsidiary holding company was formed after the initial issuance by the savings association), unless the repurchase:

(i) Is in compliance with § 563b.510 of this chapter;

(ii) Is part of a general repurchase made on a pro rata basis pursuant to an offer approved by the OTS and made to all stockholders of the association or subsidiary holding company (except

§ 575.11

that the parent mutual holding company may be excluded from the repurchase with the OTS' approval);

(iii) Is limited to the repurchase of qualifying shares of a director; or

(iv) Is purchased in the open market by a tax-qualified or non-tax-qualified employee stock benefit plan of the savings association (or of a subsidiary holding company) in an amount reasonable and appropriate to fund such plan.

(2) No mutual holding company may purchase shares of its subsidiary savings association or subsidiary holding company within one year after a stock issuance, except if the purchase complies with § 563b.510 of this chapter. For purposes of this subsection, the reference in § 563b.510 of this chapter to five percent refers to minority shareholders.

(d) *Restrictions on waiver of dividends.* No mutual holding company may waive its right to receive any dividend declared by a subsidiary unless either:

(1) No insider of the mutual holding company, associate of an insider, or tax-qualified or non-tax-qualified employee stock benefit plan of the mutual holding company holds any share of stock in the class of stock to which the waiver would apply; or

(2) The mutual holding company provides the OTS with written notice of its intent to waive its right to receive dividends 30 days prior to the proposed date of payment of the dividend, and the OTS does not object. The OTS shall not object to a notice of intent to waive dividends if:

(i) The waiver would not be detrimental to the safe and sound operation of the savings association; and

(ii) The board of directors of the mutual holding company expressly determines that waiver of the dividend by the mutual holding company is consistent with the directors' fiduciary duties to the mutual members of such company. A dividend waiver notice shall include a copy of the resolution of the board of directors of the mutual holding company, in form and substance satisfactory to the OTS, together with any supporting materials relied upon by the board, concluding that the proposed dividend waiver is consistent with the board's fiduciary duties to the mutual members of the mutual holding company.

(3) The OTS will not consider waived dividends in determining an appropriate exchange ratio in the event of a full conversion to stock form.

(e) *Restrictions on issuance of stock to insiders.* A subsidiary of a mutual holding company that is not a savings association or subsidiary holding company may issue stock to any insider, associate of an insider or tax-qualified or non-tax-qualified employee stock benefit plan of the mutual holding company or any subsidiary of the mutual holding company, provided that such persons or plans provide written notice to the OTS at least 30 days prior to the stock issuance, and OTS does not object to the subsequent stock issuance. Subsidiary savings associations and subsidiary holding companies may issue stock to such persons only in accordance with § 575.7.

(f) *Restrictions on indemnification.* The provisions of § 545.121 of this chapter shall apply to mutual holding companies in the same manner as if they were federal savings associations.

(g) *Restrictions on employment contracts.* The provisions of § 563.39 of this chapter and any policies of the OTS thereunder shall apply to mutual holding companies in the same manner as if they were savings associations.

(h) *Applicability of rules governing savings and loan holding companies.* Except as expressly provided in this part, mutual holding companies shall be subject to the provisions of 12 U.S.C. 1467a and 3201 *et seq.* and parts 563e, 574, 583, and 584 of this chapter.

(i) *Separate vote for charitable organization contribution.* In a mutual holding company stock issuance, a separate vote of a majority of the outstanding shares of common stock held by stockholders other than the mutual holding company or subsidiary holding company must approve any charitable organization contribution.

[58 FR 44114, Aug. 19, 1993, as amended at 60 FR 66720, Dec. 26, 1995; 63 FR 11365, Mar. 9, 1998; 65 FR 43091, July 12, 2000; 67 FR 52036, Aug. 9, 2002]

Office of Thrift Supervision, Treasury § 575.13

§ 575.12 Conversion or liquidation of mutual holding companies.

(a) *Conversion*—(1) *Generally.* A mutual holding company may convert to the stock form in accordance with the rules and regulations set forth in part 563b of this chapter.

(2) Exchange of savings association stock. Any stock issued pursuant to § 575.7 by a subsidiary savings association or subsidiary holding company of a mutual holding company to persons other than the parent mutual holding company may be exchanged for the stock issued by the parent mutual holding company in connection with the conversion of the parent mutual holding company to stock form. The parent mutual holding company and the subsidiary holding company or savings association must demonstrate to the satisfaction of the OTS that the basis for the exchange is fair and reasonable.

(3) If a subsidiary holding company or subsidiary savings association has issued shares to an entity other than the mutual holding company, the conversion of the mutual holding company to stock form may not be consummated unless a majority of the shares issued to entities other than the mutual holding company vote in favor of the conversion. This requirement applies in addition to any otherwise required account holder or shareholder votes.

(b) *Involuntary liquidation.* (1) The OTS may file a petition with the federal bankruptcy courts requesting the liquidation of a mutual holding company pursuant to 12 U.S.C. 1467a(o)(9) and title 11, United States Code, upon the occurrence of any of the following events:

(i) The default of the resulting association, any acquiree association, or any subsidiary savings association of the mutual holding company that was in the mutual form when acquired by the mutual holding company;

(ii) The default of the parent mutual holding company or its subsidiary holding company; or

(iii) Foreclosure on any pledge by the mutual holding company of subsidiary savings association stock or subsidiary holding company stock pursuant to § 575.11(b).

(2) Except as provided in paragraph (b)(3) of this section, the net proceeds of any liquidation of any mutual holding company shall be transferred to the members of the mutual holding company or the stock holders of the subsidiary holding company in accordance with the charter of the mutual holding company or subsidiary holding company.

(3) If the FDIC incurs a loss as a result of the default of any savings association subsidiary of a mutual holding company and that mutual holding company is liquidated pursuant to paragraph (b)(1) of this section, the FDIC shall succeed to the membership interests of the depositors of such savings association in the mutual holding company, to the extent of the FDIC's loss.

(c) *Voluntary liquidation.* The provisions of § 546.4 of this chapter shall apply to mutual holding companies in the same manner as if they were federal savings associations.

[58 FR 44114, Aug. 19, 1993, as amended at 63 FR 11366, Mar. 9, 1998; 67 FR 52036, Aug. 9, 2002]

§ 575.13 Procedural requirements.

(a) *Proxies and proxy statements*—(1) *Solicitation of proxies.* The provisions of §§ 563b.225 to 563b.295 of this chapter shall apply to all solicitations of proxies by any person in connection with any membership vote required by this part. OTS must authorize all proxy materials used in connection with such solicitations. Proxy materials must be in the form and contain the information specified in §§ 563b.255 and 563b.270 of this chapter and Form PS, to the extent such information is relevant to the action that members are being asked to approve, with such additions, deletions, and other modifications as are necessary or appropriate under the disclosure standard set forth in § 563b.280 of this chapter. File proxies and proxy statements in accordance with § 563b.155 of this chapter and address them to the Business Transactions Division, Chief Counsel's Office, Office of Thrift Supervision, at the address set forth in § 516.40 of this chapter. For purposes of this paragraph (a)(1), the term *conversion,* as it appears in the provisions of part 563b of this chapter cited above in this paragraph

§ 575.13

(a)(1), refers to *the reorganization* or *the stock issuance*, as appropriate.

(2) *Additional proxy disclosure requirements.* In addition to all disclosure required by Form PS, all proxies requesting accountholder approval of a mutual holding company reorganization shall address in detail:

(i) The reasons for the reorganization, including the relative advantages and disadvantages of undertaking the transaction proposed instead of a standard conversion;

(ii) Whether management believes the reorganization is in the best interests of the association and its accountholders and the basis of that belief;

(iii) The fiduciary duties owed to accountholders by the association's officers and directors and why the reorganization is in accord with those duties and is otherwise equitable to the accountholders and the association;

(iv) Any compensation agreements that will be entered into by management in connection with the reorganization; and

(v) Whether the mutual holding company intends to waive dividends, the implications to accountholders, and the reasons such waivers are consistent with the fiduciary duties of the directors of the mutual holding company.

(3) *Nonconforming minority stock issuances.* Savings associations proposing non-conforming minority stock issuances pursuant to § 575.7(d)(6)(ii)(2) of this part must include in the proxy materials to accountholders seeking approval of a proposed reorganization an additional disclosure statement that serves as a cover sheet that clearly addresses:

(i) The consequences to accountholders of voting to approve a reorganization in which their subscription rights are prioritized differently and potentially eliminated; and

(ii) Any intent by the mutual holding company to waive dividends, and the implications to accountholders.

(4) *Use of "running" proxies.* A mutual savings association or mutual holding company may make use of any proxy conferring general authority to vote on any and all matters at any meeting of members, provided that the member granting such proxy has been furnished a proxy statement regarding the matters and the member does not grant a later-dated proxy to vote at the meeting at which the matter will be considered or attend such meeting and vote in person, and further provided that "running" proxies or similar proxies may not be used to vote for a mutual holding company reorganization, mutual-to-stock conversion undertaken either by a mutual savings association or a mutual holding company or any other material transaction. Subject to the limitations set forth in this paragraph, any proxy conferring on the board of directors or officers of a mutual savings association general authority to cast a member's votes on any and all matters presented to the members shall be deemed to cover the member's votes as a member of the mutual holding company and such authority shall be conferred on the board of directors or officers of a mutual holding company.

(b) *Applications under this part.* Except as provided in paragraph (c) of this section, any application, notice or certification required to be filed with OTS under this part must be filed in accordance with part 516, subpart A of this chapter.

(c) *Reorganization Notices and stock issuance applications*—(1) *Contents.* Each Reorganization Notice submitted to the OTS pursuant to § 575.3(b) of this part and each application for approval of the issuance of stock submitted to the OTS pursuant to § 575.7(a) of this part shall be in the form and contain the information specified by the OTS.

(2) *Filing instructions.* Any Reorganization Notice submitted under § 575.3(b) of this part must be filed in accordance with part 516, subpart A of this chapter. Any stock issuance application submitted pursuant to § 575.7(a) of this part shall be filed in accordance with § 563b.150 of this chapter.

(3) *Public notice, public comment, and meetings.* This part imposes no requirements regarding public notice, public comment, or meetings for mutual holding company reorganizations. However, mutual holding company reorganizations under this part are subject to applicable public notice, public comment, and meeting requirements under the Bank Merger Act regulations at

Office of Thrift Supervision, Treasury § 575.14

§ 563.22(e)(1) of this chapter and the Savings and Loan Holding Company Act regulations at § 574.6(d) and (e) of this chapter.

(d) *Amendments.* Any association or mutual holding company may amend any notice or application submitted pursuant to this part or file additional information with respect thereto upon request of the OTS or upon the association's or mutual holding company's own initiative.

(e) *Time-frames.* All Reorganization Notices and applications filed pursuant to this part must be processed in accordance with standard treatment processing procedures at part 516, subparts A and E. Any related approvals requested in connection with Reorganization Notices or applications for approval of stock issuances (including, without limitation, requests for approval to transfer assets to resulting associations, to acquire acquiree associations, and to organize resulting associations or interim associations, and requests for approval of charters, bylaws, and stock forms) shall be processed pursuant to the procedures specified in this section in conjunction with the Reorganization Notice or stock issuance application to which they pertain, rather than pursuant to any inconsistent procedures specified elsewhere in this chapter. The approval standards for all such related applications, however, shall remain unchanged. The review by OTS of proxy solicitation materials, including forms of proxy and proxy statements, and of any other materials used in connection with the issuance of stock under § 575.7 of this part must not be subject to the applications processing time-frames set forth in §§ 516.210 through 516.290 of this chapter.

(f) *Disclosure.* The rules governing disclosure of any notice or application submitted pursuant to this part, or any public comment submitted pursuant to paragraph (c) of this section, shall be the same as set forth in § 574.6(f) of this chapter for notices, applications, and public comments filed under part 574 of this chapter.

(g) [Reserved]

(h) *Appeals.* Any party aggrieved by a final action by the OTS which approves or disapproves any application or notice pursuant to this part 575 may obtain review of such action only by complying with 12 U.S.C. 1467a(j).

(i) *Federal preemption.* This part 575 preempts state law with regard to the creation and regulation of mutual holding companies.

[58 FR 44114, Aug. 19, 1993, as amended at 59 FR 22735, May 3, 1994; 59 FR 44627, Aug. 30, 1994; 59 FR 61262, Nov. 30, 1994; 66 FR 13010, Mar. 2, 2001; 67 FR 52036, Aug. 9, 2002; 69 FR 68251, Nov. 24, 2004]

§ 575.14 **Subsidiary holding companies.**

(a) *Subsidiary holding companies.* A mutual holding company may establish a subsidiary holding company as a direct subsidiary to hold 100% of the stock of its savings association subsidiary. The formation and operation of the subsidiary holding company may not be utilized as a means to evade or frustrate the purposes of this part 575 or part 563b of this chapter. The subsidiary holding company may be established either at the time of the initial mutual holding company reorganization or at a subsequent date, subject to the approval of the OTS.

(b) *Stock issuances.* For purposes of §§ 575.7 and 575.8, the subsidiary holding company shall be treated as a savings association issuing stock and shall be subject to the requirements of those sections. In the case of a stock issuance by a subsidiary holding company, the aggregate amount of outstanding common stock of the association owned or controlled by persons other than the subsidiary holding company's mutual holding company parent at the close of the proposed issuance shall be less than 50% of the subsidiary holding company's total outstanding common stock.

(c) *Charters and bylaws for subsidiary holding companies*—(1) *Charters.* The charter of a subsidiary holding company shall be in the form set forth in this paragraph (c)(1) and may include any of the additional provisions permitted pursuant to paragraph (c)(2) of this section. The form of the charter is as follows:

FEDERAL MHC SUBSIDIARY HOLDING COMPANY CHARTER

Section 1. Corporate title. The full corporate title of the MHC subsidiary holding company is XXX.

539

§ 575.14

Section 2. Domicile. The domicile of the MHC subsidiary holding company shall be in the city of _____, in the State of _____.

Section 3. Duration. The duration of the MHC subsidiary holding company is perpetual.

Section 4. Purpose and powers. The purpose of the MHC subsidiary holding company is to pursue any or all of the lawful objectives of a federal mutual holding company chartered under section 10(o) of the Home Owners' Loan Act, 12 U.S.C. 1467a(o), and to exercise all of the express, implied, and incidental powers conferred thereby and by all acts amendatory thereof and supplemental thereto, subject to the Constitution and laws of the United States as they are now in effect, or as they may hereafter be amended, and subject to all lawful and applicable rules, regulations, and orders of the Office of Thrift Supervision ("Office").

Section 5. Capital stock. The total number of shares of all classes of the capital stock that the MHC subsidiary holding company has the authority to issue is _____, all of which shall be common stock of par [or if no par is specified then shares shall have a stated] value of _____ per share. The shares may be issued from time to time as authorized by the board of directors without the approval of its shareholders, except as otherwise provided in this section 5 or to the extent that such approval is required by governing law, rule, or regulation. The consideration for the issuance of the shares shall be paid in full before their issuance and shall not be less than the par [or stated] value. Neither promissory notes nor future services shall constitute payment or part payment for the issuance of shares of the MHC subsidiary holding company. The consideration for the shares shall be cash, tangible or intangible property (to the extent direct investment in such property would be permitted to the MHC subsidiary holding company), labor, or services actually performed for the MHC subsidiary holding company, or any combination of the foregoing. In the absence of actual fraud in the transaction, the value of such property, labor, or services, as determined by the board of directors of the MHC subsidiary holding company, shall be conclusive. Upon payment of such consideration, such shares shall be deemed to be fully paid and nonassessable. In the case of a stock dividend, that part of the retained earnings of the MHC subsidiary holding company that is transferred to common stock or paid-in capital accounts upon the issuance of shares as a stock dividend shall be deemed to be the consideration for their issuance.

Except for shares issued in the initial organization of the MHC subsidiary holding company, no shares of capital stock (including shares issuable upon conversion, exchange, or exercise of other securities) shall be issued, directly or indirectly, to officers, directors, or controlling persons (except for shares issued to the parent mutual holding company) of the MHC subsidiary holding company other than as part of a general public offering or as qualifying shares to a director, unless the issuance or the plan under which they would be issued has been approved by a majority of the total votes eligible to be cast at a legal meeting.

The holders of the common stock shall exclusively possess all voting power. Each holder of shares of common stock shall be entitled to one vote for each share held by such holder, except as to the cumulation of votes for the election of directors, unless the charter provides that there shall be no such cumulative voting. Subject to any provision for a liquidation account, in the event of any liquidation, dissolution, or winding up of the MHC subsidiary holding company, the holders of the common stock shall be entitled, after payment or provision for payment of all debts and liabilities of the MHC subsidiary holding company, to receive the remaining assets of the MHC subsidiary holding company available for distribution, in cash or in kind. Each share of common stock shall have the same relative rights as and be identical in all respects with all the other shares of common stock.

Section 6. Preemptive rights. Holders of the capital stock of the MHC subsidiary holding company shall not be entitled to preemptive rights with respect to any shares of the MHC subsidiary holding company which may be issued.

Section 7. Directors. The MHC subsidiary holding company shall be under the direction of a board of directors. The authorized number of directors, as stated in the MHC subsidiary holding company's bylaws, shall not be fewer than five nor more than fifteen except when a greater or lesser number is approved by the Director of the Office, or his or her delegate.

Section 8. Amendment of charter. Except as provided in Section 5, no amendment, addition, alteration, change or repeal of this charter shall be made, unless such is proposed by the board of directors of the MHC subsidiary holding company, approved by the shareholders by a majority of the votes eligible to be cast at a legal meeting, unless a higher vote is otherwise required, and approved or preapproved by the Office.

Attest: _____
Secretary of the Subsidiary Holding Company
By: _____
President or Chief Executive Officer of the Subsidiary Holding Company
Attest: _____
Secretary of the Office of Thrift Supervision
By: _____
Director of the Office of Thrift Supervision

Office of Thrift Supervision, Treasury

Effective Date: _____

(2) *Charter amendments.* The rules and regulations set forth in § 552.4 of this chapter regarding charter amendments and reissuances of charters (including delegations and filing instructions) shall be applicable to subsidiary holding companies to the same extent as if the subsidiary holding companies were Federal stock savings associations, except that, with respect to the pre-approved charter amendments set forth in § 552.4 of this chapter, the reference to home office in § 552.4(b)(2) of this chapter shall be deemed to refer to the domicile of the subsidiary holding company and the requirements of § 545.95 of this chapter shall not apply to subsidiary holding companies.

(3) *Optional charter provision limiting minority stock ownership.* A subsidiary holding company that engages in its initial minority stock issuance after October 1, 2008 may, before it conducts its initial minority stock issuance, at the time it conducts its initial minority stock issuance, or at any time during the five years following a minority stock issuance that such subsidiary holding company conducts in accordance with the purchase priorities set forth in 12 CFR part 563b, include in its charter the provision set forth below. For purposes of this charter provision, the definitions set forth at § 552.4(b)(8) of this chapter apply. This charter provision expires a maximum of five years from the date of the minority stock issuance. The subsidiary holding company may adopt the charter provision after a minority stock issuance only if it provided, in the offering materials related to its previous minority stock issuance or issuances, full disclosure of the possibility that the association might adopt such a charter provision.

Beneficial Ownership Limitation. No person may directly or indirectly offer to acquire or acquire the beneficial ownership of more than 10 percent of the outstanding stock of any class of voting stock of the association held by persons other than the subsidiary holding company's mutual holding company parent. This limitation expires on [insert date within five years of minority stock issuance] and does not apply to a transaction in which an underwriter purchases stock in connection with a public offering, or the purchase of stock by an employee stock ownership plan or other tax-qualified employee stock benefit plan which is exempt from the approval requirements under § 574.3(c)(1)(vii) of the Office's regulations.

In the event a person acquires stock in violation of this section, all stock beneficially owned in excess of 10 percent shall be considered "excess stock" and shall not be counted as stock entitled to vote and shall not be voted by any person or counted as voting stock in connection with any matters submitted to the stockholders for a vote.

(4) *Bylaws.* The rules and regulations set forth in § 552.5 of this chapter regarding bylaws (including their content, any amendments thereto, delegations, and filing instructions) shall be applicable to subsidiary holding companies to the same extent as if subsidiary holding companies were federal stock savings associations. The model bylaws for Federal stock savings associations set forth in the OTS Applications Processing Handbook shall also serve as the model bylaws for subsidiary holding companies, except that the term "association" each time it appears therein shall be replaced with the term "Subsidiary Holding Company."

(5) *Annual reports and books and records.* The rules and regulations set forth in §§ 552.10 and 552.11 of this chapter regarding annual reports to stockholders and maintaining books and records shall be applicable to subsidiary holding companies to the same extent as if subsidiary holding companies were Federal stock savings associations.

[63 FR 11366, Mar. 9, 1998, as amended at 73 FR 39259, July 9, 2008; 73 FR 76891, Dec. 18, 2008]

PART 583—DEFINITIONS FOR REGULATIONS AFFECTING SAVINGS AND LOAN HOLDING COMPANIES

Sec.
583.1 Acquire.
583.2 Affiliate.
583.3 Bank.
583.4 Bank holding company.
583.5 [Reserved]
583.6 Company.
583.7 Control.
583.8 Corporation.
583.9 Director.
583.11 Diversified savings and loan holding company.
583.12 Multiple savings and loan holding company.

§ 583.1

583.13 Office.
583.14 Officer.
583.15 Parent company.
583.16 Person.
583.17 Qualified thrift lender.
583.18 Registrant.
583.19 [Reserved]
583.20 Savings and loan holding company.
583.21 Savings association.
583.22 State.
583.23 Subsidiary.
583.24 Uninsured institution.

AUTHORITY: 12 U.S.C. 1462, 1462a, 1463, 1464, 1467a, 1468.

SOURCE: 54 FR 49707, Nov. 30, 1989, unless otherwise noted.

§ 583.1 Acquire.

The term *acquire* means to acquire, directly or indirectly, ownership or control through an acquisition of shares, an acquisition of assets or assumption of liabilities, a merger or consolidation, or any similar transaction.

§ 583.2 Affiliate.

The term *affiliate* of a specified savings association means any person or company which controls, is controlled by, or is under common control with, such savings association.

§ 583.3 Bank.

The term *bank* means any national bank, state bank, state-chartered savings bank, cooperative bank, or industrial bank, the deposits of which are insured by the Deposit Insurance Fund.

[71 FR 19812, Apr. 18, 2006]

§ 583.4 Bank holding company.

The term *bank holding company* means any company which has control over any bank or over any company that is or becomes a bank holding company.

§ 583.5 [Reserved]

§ 583.6 Company.

The term *company* means any corporation, partnership, trust, joint-stock company, or similar organization, but does not include:
(a) The Federal Deposit Insurance Corporation,
(b) The Resolution Trust Corporation,
(c) Any Federal Home Loan Bank,
(d) The Office of Thrift Supervision, or
(e) Any company the majority of the shares of which is owned by
(1) The United States or any State,
(2) An officer of the United States or any State in his or her official capacity, or
(3) An instrumentality of the United States or any State.

§ 583.7 Control.

For purposes of this chapter, a person shall be deemed to have *control* of:

(a) A savings association if the person directly or indirectly or acting in concert with one or more other persons, or through one or more subsidiaries, owns, controls, or holds with power to vote, or holds proxies representing, more than 25 percent of the voting shares of such savings association, or controls in any manner the election of a majority of the directors of such association;

(b) Any other company if the person directly or indirectly or acting in concert with one or more other persons, or through one or more subsidiaries, owns, controls, or holds with power to vote, or holds proxies representing, more than 25 percent of the voting shares or rights of such other company, or controls in any manner the election or appointment of a majority of the directors or trustees of such other company, or is a general partner in or has contributed more than 25 percent of the capital of such other company;

(c) A trust if the person is a trustee thereof; or

(d) A savings association or any other company if the Office determines, after reasonable notice and opportunity for hearing, that such person directly or indirectly exercises a controlling influence over the management or policies of such association or other company.

§ 583.8 Corporation.

The term *Corporation* means the Federal Deposit Insurance Corporation.

§ 583.9 Director.

The term *director* as used in any document specified in part 584 of this

Office of Thrift Supervision, Treasury § 583.21

chapter means any director of a corporation or any individual who performs similar functions in respect of any company, including a trustee under a trust.

§ 583.11 Diversified savings and loan holding company.

The term *diversified savings and loan holding company* means any savings and loan holding company whose subsidiary savings association and related activities, as specified in 12 U.S.C. 1467a(c)(2), represented on either an actual or *pro forma* basis, less than 50 percent of its consolidated net worth at the close of its preceding fiscal year and of its consolidated net earnings for such fiscal year. For purposes of the foregoing, consolidated net worth and consolidated net earnings shall be determined in accordance with generally accepted accounting principles.

§ 583.12 Multiple savings and loan holding company.

The term *multiple savings and loan holding company* means any savings and loan holding company which directly or indirectly controls two or more savings associations.

§ 583.13 Office.

The term *Office* means the Office of Thrift Supervision.

§ 583.14 Officer.

The term *officer* as used in any document specified in part 584 of this chapter means the chairman of the board, president, vice president, treasurer, secretary, or comptroller of any company, or any other person who participates in its major policy decisions.

§ 583.15 Parent company.

The term *parent company* means any company which directly or indirectly controls any other company or companies.

§ 583.16 Person.

The term *person* means an individual or company.

§ 583.17 Qualified thrift lender.

The term *qualified thrift lender* means a financial institution that meets the appropriate qualified thrift lender test set forth in 12 U.S.C. 1467a(m).

[54 FR 49707, Nov. 30, 1989, as amended at 60 FR 66870, Dec. 27, 1995]

§ 583.18 Registrant.

The term *registrant* means a savings and loan holding company filing a registration statement with the Office pursuant to § 584.1 of this chapter.

§ 583.19 [Reserved]

§ 583.20 Savings and loan holding company.

The term *savings and loan holding company* means any company that directly or indirectly controls a savings association, but does not include:

(a) Any company by virtue of its ownership or control of voting stock of a savings association or a savings and loan holding company acquired in connection with the underwriting of securities if such stock is held only for such period of time (not exceeding 120 days unless extended by the Office) as will permit the sale thereof on a reasonable basis; and

(b) Any trust (other than a pension, profit-sharing, stockholders', voting or business trust) which directly or indirectly controls a savings association if such trust by its terms must terminate within 25 years or not later than 21 years and 10 months after the death of individuals living on the effective date of the trust, and:

(1) Was in existence and was directly or indirectly in control of a savings association on June 26, 1967, or

(2) Is a testamentary trust; and

(c) A bank holding company that is registered under, and subject to, the Bank Holding Company Act of 1956, or any company directly or indirectly controlled by such company (other than a savings association).

[54 FR 49707, Nov. 30, 1989, as amended at 61 FR 60185, Nov. 27, 1996]

§ 583.21 Savings association.

The term *savings association* means a Federal savings and loan association or a Federal savings bank chartered under section 5 of the Home Owners' Loan Act, a building and loan, savings and

§ 583.22

loan or homestead association or a cooperative bank (other than a cooperative bank described in 12 U.S.C. 1813(a)(2)) the deposits of which are insured by the Corporation, and any corporation (other than a bank) the deposits of which are insured by the Corporation that the Office and the Corporation jointly determine to be operating in substantially the same manner as a savings association, and shall include any savings bank or any cooperative bank which is deemed by the Office to be a savings association under 12 U.S.C. 1467a(1).

§ 583.22 State.

The term *State* includes the District of Columbia and the Commonwealth of Puerto Rico.

§ 583.23 Subsidiary.

The term *subsidiary* means any company which is owned or controlled directly or indirectly by a person, and includes any service corporation owned in whole or in part by a savings association, or a subsidiary of such service corporation.

§ 583.24 Uninsured institution.

The term *uninsured institution* means any depository institution the deposits of which are not insured by the Corporation.

PART 584—SAVINGS AND LOAN HOLDING COMPANIES

Sec.
584.1 Registration, examination and reports.
584.2 Prohibited activities.
584.2a Exempt savings and loan holding companies and grandfathered activities.
584.2-1 Prescribed services and activities of savings and loan holding companies.
584.2-2 Permissible bank holding company activities of savings and loan holding companies.
584.4 Certain acquisitions by savings and loan holding companies.
584.9 Prohibited acts.

AUTHORITY: 12 U.S.C. 1462, 1462a, 1463, 1464, 1467a, 1468.

SOURCE: 54 FR 49708, Nov. 30, 1989, unless otherwise noted.

§ 584.1 Registration, examination and reports.

(a) *Filing of registration statement and other reports*—(1) *Filing of registration statement.* Not later than 90 days after becoming a savings and loan holding company, each savings and loan holding company shall register with the OTS by filing a registration statement H–(b)10.

(2) *Filing of annual/current reports.* Each registered savings and loan holding company, including subsidiary savings and loan holding companies, shall file an annual/current report H–(b)11, except that such report need not be filed by a savings and loan holding company that is a trust (other than a business trust), secured creditor, or corporate trustee. The H–(b)11 report must be filed no later than 90 days after the close of the fiscal year. Quarterly filings must also be submitted on the H–(b)11 report within 45 days of the end of each quarter (except for the fourth quarter of the holding company's fiscal year) and should describe any material changes from the most recently filed H–(b)11 report or should indicate that no such changes have occurred. However, if material changes have occurred during the fourth quarter with respect to certain items described in the form instructions, an H–(b)11 report for such quarter must be filed within 45 days of the end of such quarter.

(3) *General.* Registration statements and annual/current reports are to be filed with the OTS in accordance with the instructions contained in each form. In addition, multiple savings and loan holding companies must file conformed copies with any area office that has supervisory authority over a subsidiary savings association. Copies of the forms to be used in submitting registration statements or annual/current reports may be obtained from any Regional Director, or designee.

(b) *Date of registration.* The date of registration of a savings and loan holding company shall be the date on which its registration statement is received by the Regional Director.

(c) *Extension of time for registration.* For timely and good cause shown, the Office may extend the time within

Office of Thrift Supervision, Treasury

§ 584.2

which a savings and loan holding company shall register.

(d) *Release from registration.* The Office may at any time, upon its own motion or upon application, release a registered savings and loan holding company from any registration theretofore made by such company, if the Office shall determine that such company no longer has control of any savings association.

(e) *Reports.* Each savings and loan holding company and each subsidiary thereof, other than a savings association, shall file with the OTS such reports as may be required by the OTS. Such reports shall be made under oath or otherwise, and shall be in such form and for such periods, as the OTS may prescribe. Each report shall contain information concerning the operations of such savings and loan holding company and its subsidiaries as the OTS may require.

(f) *Books and records.* Each savings and loan holding company shall maintain such books and records as may be prescribed by the Office.

(g) *Examinations.* Each savings and loan holding company and each subsidiary thereof shall be subject to such examinations as the Office may prescribe. The cost of such examinations (other than examinations of savings associations) shall be assessed against and paid by such holding company. Examination and other reports may be furnished by the Office to the appropriate State supervisory authority. The Office shall, to the extent deemed feasible, use for the purposes of this section reports filed with or examinations made by other Federal agencies or the appropriate State supervisory authority.

(h) *Appointment of agent.* The Office may require any savings and loan holding company, or persons connected therewith if it is not a corporation, to execute and file a prescribed form of irrevocable appointment of agent for service of process.

[54 FR 49708, Nov. 30, 1989, as amended at 55 FR 13517, Apr. 11, 1990; 57 FR 35458, Aug. 10, 1992; 60 FR 66720, Dec. 26, 1995]

§ 584.2 Prohibited activities.

(a) *Evasion of law or regulation.* No savings and loan holding company or subsidiary thereof which is not a savings association shall, for or on behalf of a subsidiary savings association, engage in any activity or render any services for the purpose or with the effect of evading any law or regulation applicable to such savings association.

(b) *Unrelated business activity.* No savings and loan holding company or subsidiary thereof that is not a savings association shall commence any business activity at any time, or continue any business activity after the end of the two-year period beginning on the date on which such company received approval to become a savings and loan holding company that is subject to the limitations of this paragraph (b), except (in either case) the following:

(1) Furnishing or performing management services for a savings association subsidiary of such company;

(2) Conducting an insurance agency or an escrow business;

(3) Holding, managing, or liquidating assets owned by or acquired from a subsidiary savings association of such company;

(4) Holding or managing properties used or occupied by a subsidiary savings association of such company;

(5) Acting as trustee under deed of trust;

(6) Any other activity: (i) That the Board of Governors of the Federal Reserve System has permitted for bank holding companies pursuant to regulations promulgated under section 4(c) of the Bank Holding Company Act; or

(ii) Is set forth in § 584.2-1 of this part, subject to the limitations therein; or

(7) In the case of a savings and loan holding company, purchasing, holding, or disposing of stock acquired in connection with a qualified stock issuance if prior approval for the acquisition of such stock by such savings and loan holding company is granted by the Office pursuant to § 574.8 of this chapter.

Notwithstanding the provisions of this paragraph (b), any savings and loan holding company that, between March 5, 1987 and August 10, 1987, received approval pursuant to 12 U.S.C. 1730a(e), as then in effect, to acquire control of a savings association shall not continue any business activity other than those

§ 584.2a

activities set forth in this paragraph (b) after August 10, 1987.

(c) *Treatment of certain holding companies.* If a director or officer of a savings and loan holding company, or an individual who owns, controls, or holds with the power to vote (or proxies representing) more than 25 percent of the voting shares of a savings and loan holding company, directly or indirectly controls more than one savings association, any savings and loan holding company controlled by such individual shall be subject to the activities limitations contained in paragraph (b) of this section, to the same extent such limitations apply to multiple savings and loan holding companies pursuant to §§ 584.2, 584.2a, 584.2-1 and 584.2-2 of this part.

[54 FR 49708, Nov. 30, 1989, as amended at 63 FR 71213, Dec. 24, 1998; 72 72238, Dec. 20, 2007]

§ 584.2a Exempt savings and loan holding companies and grandfathered activities.

(a) *Exempt savings and loan holding companies.* (1) The following savings and loan holding companies are exempt from the limitations of § 584.2(b) of this part:

(i) Any savings and loan holding company (or subsidiary of such company) that controls only one savings association, if the savings association subsidiary of such company is a qualified thrift lender as defined in § 583.17 of this chapter.

(ii) Any savings and loan holding company (or subsidiary thereof) that controls more than one savings association if all, or all but one of the savings association subsidiaries of such company were acquired pursuant to an acquisition under section 13(c) or 13(k) of the Federal Deposit Insurance Act, or section 408(m) of the National Housing Act, as in effect immediately prior to the date of enactment of the Financial Institutions Reform, Recovery and Enforcement Act of 1989, and all of the savings association subsidiaries of such company are qualified thrift lenders as defined in § 583.17 of this chapter.

(2) Any savings and loan holding company whose subsidiary savings association(s) fails to qualify as a qualified thrift lender pursuant to 12 U.S.C. 1467a(m) may not commence, or continue, any service or activity other than those permitted under § 584.2(b) of this part, except that, the Office may allow, for good cause shown, such company (or subsidiary of such company which is not a savings association) up to 3 years to comply with the limitations set forth in § 584.2(b) of this part: *Provided,* That effective August 9, 1990, any company that controls a savings association that should have become or ceases to be a qualified thrift lender, except a savings association that requalified as a qualified thrift lender pursuant to section 10(m)(3)(D) of the Home Owners' Loan Act, shall within one year after the date on which the savings association fails to qualify as a qualified thrift lender, register as and be deemed to be a bank holding company, subject to all of the provisions of the Bank Holding Company Act, section 8 of the Federal Deposit Insurance Act, and other statutes applicable to bank holding companies in the same manner and to the same extent as if the company were a bank holding company and the savings association were a bank, as those terms are defined in the Bank Holding Company Act.

(b) *Grandfathered activities for certain savings and loan holding companies.* Notwithstanding § 584.2(b) of this part and subject to paragraph (c) of this section, any savings and loan holding company that received approval prior to March 5, 1987 to acquire control of a savings association may engage, directly or indirectly or through any subsidiary (other than a subsidiary savings association of such company) in any activity in which it was lawfully engaged on March 5, 1987, *Provided,* That:

(1) The holding company does not, after August 10, 1987, acquire control of a bank or an additional savings association, other than a savings association acquired pursuant to section 13(c) or 13(k) of the Federal Deposit Insurance Act, or section 406(f) or 408(m) of the National Housing Act, as in effect immediately prior to the date of enactment of the Financial Institutions Reform, Recovery and Enforcement Act of 1989;

(2) Any savings association subsidiary of the holding company continues to qualify as a domestic building and loan association under section

Office of Thrift Supervision, Treasury § 584.2-1

7701(a)(19) of the Internal Revenue Code of 1986 after August 10, 1987;

(3) The holding company does not engage in any business activity other than those permitted under §584.2(b) of this part or in which it was engaged on March 5, 1987;

(4) Any savings association subsidiary of the holding company does not increase the number of locations from which such savings association conducts business after March 5, 1987, other than an increase due to a transaction under section 13(c) or 13(k) of the Federal Deposit Insurance Act, or under section 408(m) of the National Housing Act, as in effect immediately prior to the date of enactment of the Financial Institutions Reform, Recovery and Enforcement Act of 1989; and

(5) Any savings association subsidiary of the holding company does not permit any overdraft (including an intra-day overdraft) or incur any such overdraft in its account at a Federal Reserve bank, on behalf of an affiliate, unless such overdraft results from an inadvertent computer or accounting error that is beyond the control of both the savings association subsidiary and the affiliate.

(c) *Termination by the Office of grandfathered activities.* Notwithstanding the provisions of paragraph (b) of this section, the Office may, after opportunity for hearing, terminate any activity engaged in under paragraph (b) of this section upon determination that such action is necessary:

(1) To prevent conflicts of interest;

(2) To prevent unsafe or unsound practices; or

(3) To protect the public interest.

(d) *Foreign holding company.* Any savings and loan holding company organized under the laws of a foreign country as of June 1, 1984 (including any subsidiary thereof that is not a savings association) that controlled a single savings association on August 10, 1987, shall not be subject to the restrictions set forth in §584.2(b) of this part with respect to any activities of such holding company that are conducted exclusively in a foreign country.

[54 FR 49708, Nov. 30, 1989, as amended at 60 FR 66870, Dec. 27, 1995; 61 FR 60185, Nov. 27, 1996]

§ 584.2-1 Prescribed services and activities of savings and loan holding companies.

(a) *General.* For the purpose of §584.2(b)(6)(ii) of this part, the activities set forth in paragraph (b) of this section are, and were as of March 5, 1987, permissible services and activities for savings and loan holding companies or subsidiaries thereof that are neither savings associations nor service corporation subsidiaries of subsidiary savings associations. Services and activities of service corporation subsidiaries of savings and loan holding company subsidiary savings associations are prescribed by paragraph (d) of this section.

(b) *Prescribed services and activities.* Subject to the provisions of paragraph (c) of this section, a savings and loan holding company subject to restrictions on its activities pursuant to §584.2(b) of this part, or a subsidiary thereof which is neither a savings association nor a service corporation of a subsidiary savings association, may furnish or perform the following services and engage in the following activities to the extent that it has legal power to do so:

(1) Originating, purchasing, selling and servicing any of the following:

(i) Loans, and participation interests in loans, on a prudent basis and secured by real estate, including brokerage and warehousing of such real estate loans, except that such a company or subsidiary shall not invest in a loan secured by real estate as to which a subsidiary savings association of such company has a security interest;

(ii) Manufactured home chattel paper (written evidence of both a monetary obligation and a security interest of first priority in one or more manufactured homes, and any equipment installed or to be installed therein), including brokerage and warehousing of such chattel paper;

(iii) Loans, with or without security, for the altering, repairing, improving, equipping or furnishing of any residential real estate;

(iv) Educational loans; and

(v) Consumer loans, as defined in §560.3 of this chapter, *Provided,* That, no subsidiary savings association of such holding company or service corporation of such savings association

547

§ 584.2-1

shall engage directly or indirectly, in any transaction with any affiliate involving the purchase or sale, in whole or in part, of any consumer loan.

(2) Subject to the provisions of 12 U.S.C. 1468, furnishing or performing clerical accounting and internal audit services primarily for its affiliates;

(3) Subject to the provisions of 12 U.S.C. 1468, furnishing or performing the following services primarily for its affiliates, and for any savings association and service corporation subsidiary thereof, and for other multiple holding companies and affiliates thereof:

(i) Data processing;

(ii) Credit information, appraisals, construction loan inspections, and abstracting;

(iii) Development and administration of personnel benefit programs, including life insurance, health insurance, and pension or retirement plans;

(iv) Research, studies, and surveys;

(v) Purchase of office supplies, furniture and equipment;

(vi) Development and operation of storage facilities for microfilm or other duplicate records; and

(vii) Advertising and other services to procure and retain both savings accounts and loans;

(4) Acquisition of unimproved real estate lots, and acquisition of other unimproved real estate for the purpose of prompt development and subdivision, for:

(i) Construction of improvements,

(ii) Resale to others for such construction, or

(iii) Use as mobile home sites;

(5) Development, subdivision and construction of improvements on real estate acquired pursuant to paragraph (b)(4) of this section, for sale or rental;

(6) Acquisition of improved real estate and mobile homes to be held for rental;

(7) Acquisition of improved real estate for remodeling, rehabilitation, modernization, renovation, or demolition and rebuilding for sale or for rental;

(8) Maintenance and management of improved real estate;

(9) Underwriting or reinsuring contract of credit life or credit health and accident insurance in connection with extensions of credit by the savings and loan holding company or any of its subsidiaries, or extensions of credit by any savings association or service corporation subsidiary thereof, or any other savings and loan holding company or subsidiary thereof;

(10) Preparation of State and Federal tax returns for accountholders of or borrowers from (including immediate family members of such accountholders or borrowers but not including an accountholder or borrower which is a corporation operated for profit) an affiliated savings association;

(11) Purchase and sale of gold coins minted and issued by the United States Treasury pursuant to Pub. L. 99-185, 99 Stat. 1177 (1985), and activities reasonably incident thereto; and

(12) Any services or activities approved by order of the former Federal Savings and Loan Insurance Corporation prior to March 5, 1987, pursuant to its authority under section 408(c)(2)(F) of the National Housing Act, as in effect at the time.

(c) *Procedures for commencing services or activities.* (1) Before a savings and loan holding company subject to restrictions on its activities pursuant to § 584.2(b) of this part or a subsidiary thereof may commence performing or engaging in a service or activity prescribed by paragraph (b) of this section (other than purchase or sale of a government debt security), either *de novo* or by an acquisition of a going concern, it shall file a notice of intent to do so in a form prescribed by the OTS. The activity or service may be commenced unless, before the close of the period specified immediately below, the OTS finds that the activity or service proposed would not be, under the circumstances, a proper incident to the operations of savings associations or would be detrimental to the interests of savings account holders. The period for review shall be 30 calendar days after the date of receipt of such notice, in the case of a de novo entry, or 60 calendar days, in the case of an acquisition of a going concern.

(2) The Office may require a savings and loan holding company or subsidiary thereof which has commenced a service or activity pursuant to this section to modify or terminate, in whole

Office of Thrift Supervision, Treasury

§ 584.4

or in part, such service or activity as the Office finds necessary in order to ensure compliance with the provisions and purposes of this part and of section 10 of the Home Owners' Loan Act, as amended, or to prevent evasions thereof.

(3) Except as may be otherwise provided in a resolution by or on behalf of the Office in a particular case, a service or activity commenced pursuant to this section shall not be altered in any material respect from that described in the notice filed under paragraph (c)(1) of this section, unless before making such alteration notice of intent to do so is filed in compliance with the appropriate procedures of said paragraph (c)(1) of this section.

(d) *Service corporation subsidiaries of savings associations.* The Office hereby approves without application the furnishing or performing of such services or engaging in such activities as permitted by the Office pursuant to 12 CFR 545.74, as in effect on March 5, 1987, if such service or activity is conducted by a service corporation subsidiary of a subsidiary savings association of a savings and loan holding company and if such service corporation has legal power to do so.

[54 FR 49708, Nov. 30, 1989, as amended at 55 FR 13518, Apr. 11, 1990; 57 FR 14349, Apr. 20, 1992; 60 FR 66870, Dec. 27, 1995; 63 FR 71213, Dec. 24, 1998; 66 FR 15017, Mar. 15, 2001]

§ 584.2–2 Permissible bank holding company activities of savings and loan holding companies.

(a) *General.* For purposes of § 584.2(b)(6)(i) of this part, the services and activities permissible for bank holding companies pursuant to regulations that the Board of Governors of the Federal Reserve System has promulgated pursuant to section 4(c) of the Bank Holding Company Act are permissible for savings and loan holding companies, or subsidiaries thereof that are neither savings associations nor service corporation subsidiaries of subsidiary savings associations: *Provided,* That no savings and loan holding company shall commence any activity described in this paragraph (a) without the prior approval of this Office pursuant to paragraph (b) of this section, unless—

(1) The holding company received a rating of satisfactory or above prior to January 1, 2008, or a composite rating of "1" or "2" thereafter, in its most recent examination, and is not in a troubled condition as defined in § 563.555, and the holding company does not propose to commence the activity by an acquisition (in whole or in part) of a going concern; or

(2) The activity is permissible under authority other than section 10(c)(2)(F)(i) of the HOLA without prior notice or approval. Where an activity is within the scope of both § 584.2–1 of this part and this section, the procedures of § 584.2–1 of this part shall govern.

(b) *Procedures for applications.* Applications to commence any activity prescribed under paragraph (a) of this section shall be filed with the OTS. OTS must act upon such application under the guidelines in part 516, subpart E of this chapter.

(c) *Factors considered in acting on applications.* In evaluating an application filed under paragraph (b) of this section, the OTS shall consider whether the performance by the applicant of the activity can reasonably be expected to produce benefits to the public (such as greater convenience, increased competition, or gains in efficiency) that outweigh possible adverse effects (such as undue concentration of resources, decreased or unfair competition, conflicts of interest, or unsound financial practices). This consideration includes an evaluation of the financial and managerial resources of the applicant, including its subsidiaries, and of any company to be acquired, and the effect of the proposed transaction on those resources.

[54 FR 49708, Nov. 30, 1989, as amended at 55 FR 13518, Apr. 11, 1990; 57 FR 14349, Apr. 20, 1992; 60 FR 66720, Dec. 26, 1995; 63 FR 71213, Dec. 24, 1998; 66 FR 13010, Mar. 2, 2001; 72 FR 72238, Dec. 20, 2007]

§ 584.4 Certain acquisitions by savings and loan holding companies.

(a) *Acquisitions by a savings and loan holding company of more than five percent of a non-subsidiary savings association or savings and loan holding company.* No savings and loan holding company, directly or indirectly, or through one or more subsidiaries or through one or more transactions, shall, without prior written OTS approval, acquire by purchase or otherwise, or retain, more than five percent of the voting stock or shares of a savings association not a subsidiary, or of a savings and loan holding company not a subsidiary. A savings and loan holding company seeking approval of an acquisition under this section must file an application under 12 CFR part 516, subpart A. Applications filed under this section are subject to the publication, public comment, and meeting provisions of 12 CFR part 516, subparts B, C, and D. OTS will review applications filed under this section under the review standards set forth for savings and loan holding company applications in section 10(e)(2) of the HOLA, § 574.7(c) of this chapter, and § 563e.29(a) of this chapter.

(b) *Certain acquisitions by multiple savings and loan holding companies.* No multiple savings and loan holding company (other than a savings and loan holding company described in § 584.2a(a)(1)(ii) of this part) may, directly or indirectly, or through one or more subsidiaries or through one or more transactions, acquire or retain more than five percent of the voting shares of any company that is not a subsidiary that is engaged in any business activity other than those specified in § 584.2(b) of this part.

(c)(1) *Exception for certain acquisitions of voting shares of savings associations and savings and loan holding companies.* Paragraphs (a) and (b) of this section do not apply to voting shares of a savings association or of a savings and loan holding company—

(i) Held as a *bona fide* fiduciary (whether with or without the sole discretion to vote such shares);

(ii) Held temporarily pursuant to an underwriting commitment in the normal course of an underwriting business;

(iii) Held in an account solely for trading purposes or over which no control is held other than control of voting rights acquired in the normal course of a proxy solicitation;

(iv) Acquired in securing or collecting a debt previously contracted in good faith, for two years after the date of acquisition or for such additional time (not exceeding three years) as the Office may permit if, in the Office's judgment, such an extension would not be detrimental to the public interest;

(v) Acquired under section 13(k)(1)(A)(i) of the Federal Deposit Insurance Act (or section 408(m) of the National Housing Act as in effect immediately prior to the enactment of the Financial Institutions Reform, Recovery and Enforcement Act of 1989);

(vi) Held by any insurance companies as defined in section 2(a)(17) of the Investment Company Act of 1940: *Provided,* That all shares held by all insurance company affiliates of such savings association or savings and loan holding company may not, in the aggregate, exceed five percent of all outstanding shares or of the voting power of the savings association or savings and loan holding company, and such shares are not acquired or retained with a view to acquiring, exercising, or transferring control of the savings association or savings and loan holding company; and

(vii) Acquired pursuant to a qualified stock issuance if such a purchase is approved pursuant to § 574.8 of this chapter.

(2) The aggregate amount of shares held under this paragraph (c) (other than pursuant to paragraphs (c)(1)(i) through (iv) and (c)(1)(vi) may not exceed 15 percent of all outstanding shares or the voting power of a savings association or savings and loan holding company.

(d) *Acquisitions of uninsured institutions.* No savings and loan holding company may, directly or indirectly, or through one or more subsidiaries or through one or more transactions, acquire control of an uninsured institution or retain, for more than one year after the date any savings association subsidiary becomes uninsured, control of such association.

[72 FR 72238, Dec. 20, 2007]

§ 584.9 Prohibited acts.

(a) *Control of mutual savings association.* No savings and loan holding company or any subsidiary thereof, or any director, officer, or employee of a savings and loan holding company or subsidiary thereof, or person owning, controlling, or holding with power to vote, or holding proxies representing, more than 25 percent of the voting shares of such holding company or subsidiary, may hold, solicit, or exercise any proxies in respect of any voting rights in a mutual savings association.

(b) *Management interlocks.* No director or officer of a savings and loan holding company, or any person owning, controlling, or holding with power to vote, or holding proxies representing more than 25 percent of the voting shares of such holding company may acquire control of any savings association not a subsidiary of such savings and loan holding company, unless such acquisition is approved by the Office pursuant to § 574.3(a) of this chapter.

(c) *Convicted persons.* No individual who has been convicted of any criminal offense involving dishonesty or breach of trust may serve or act as a director, officer, or trustee of, or become a partner in, any savings and loan holding company, except with the prior written approval of the Office.

(d) *Applications for approval.* Applications for an approval under paragraph (c) of this section shall contain a full statement of the reasons in support thereof. Such applications shall be filed with the OTS.

[54 FR 49708, Nov. 30, 1989, as amended at 57 FR 14349, Apr. 20, 1992]

PART 585—PROHIBITED SERVICE AT SAVINGS AND LOAN HOLDING COMPANIES

Sec.
585.10 What does this part do?
585.20 What definitions apply to this part?

Subpart A—Prohibition

585.30 What actions are prohibited?
585.40 What convictions or agreements to enter into pre-trial diversions or similar programs are covered by this part?
585.50 What adjudications and offenses are not covered by this part?

Subpart B—Exemptions

585.100 Who is exempt from the prohibition under this part?
585.110 How do I apply for a case-by-case exemption?
585.120 What factors will OTS consider in reviewing my exemption application?
585.130 How will I know if my application is approved?
585.140 What procedures govern a hearing on my application?

AUTHORITY: 12 U.S.C. 1462, 1462a, 1463, 1464, 1467a, and 1829(e)

SOURCE: 72 FR 25955, May 8, 2007, unless otherwise noted.

§ 585.10 What does this part do?

This part implements section 19(e)(1) of the Federal Deposit Insurance Act (FDIA), which prohibits persons who have been convicted of certain criminal offenses or who have agreed to enter into a pre-trial diversion or similar program in connection with a prosecution for such criminal offenses from occupying various positions with a savings and loan holding company. This part also implements section 19(e)(2) of the FDIA, which permits the Director to provide exemptions, by regulation or order, from the application of the prohibition. This part provides an exemption for savings and loan holding company employees whose activities and responsibilities are limited solely to agriculture, forestry, retail merchandising, manufacturing, or public utilities operations, and a temporary exemption for certain persons who held positions with respect to a savings and loan holding company as of October 13, 2006. The part also describes procedures for applying for an OTS order granting a case-by-case exemption.

§ 585.20 What definitions apply to this part?

The following definitions apply to this part:

Institution-affiliated party is defined at 12 U.S.C. 1813(u), except that the phrase "savings and loan holding company" is substituted for "insured depository institution" each place that it appears in that definition.

Person means an individual and does not include a corporation, firm or other business entity.

Savings and loan holding company is defined at 12 CFR 583.20, but excludes a subsidiary of a savings and loan holding company that is not itself a savings and loan holding company.

Subpart A—Prohibition

§ 585.30 What actions are prohibited?

(a) *Person.* If a person was convicted of a criminal offense described in § 585.40, or agreed to enter into a pretrial diversion or similar program in connection with a prosecution for such a criminal offense, he or she may not:

(1) Become, or continue as, an institution-affiliated party with respect to any savings and loan holding company.

(2) Own or control, directly or indirectly, any savings and loan holding company. A person will own or control a savings and loan holding company if he or she owns or controls that company under 12 CFR part 574.

(3) Otherwise participate, directly or indirectly, in the conduct of the affairs of any savings and loan holding company.

(b) *Savings and loan holding company.* A savings and loan holding company may not permit any person described in paragraph (a) of this section to engage in any conduct or to continue any relationship prohibited under that paragraph.

§ 585.40 What convictions or agreements to enter into pre-trial diversions or similar programs are covered by this part?

(a) *Covered convictions and agreements.* Except as described in § 585.50, this part covers:

(1) Any conviction of a criminal offense involving dishonesty, breach of trust, or money laundering. Convictions do not cover arrests, pending cases not brought to trial, acquittals, convictions reversed on appeal, pardoned convictions, or expunged convictions.

(2) Any agreement to enter into a pretrial diversion or similar program in connection with a prosecution for a criminal offense involving dishonesty, breach of trust or money laundering. A pretrial diversion or similar program is a program involving a suspension or eventual dismissal of charges or of a criminal prosecution based upon an agreement for treatment, rehabilitation, restitution, or other non-criminal or non-punitive alternative.

(b) *Dishonesty or breach of trust.* A determination whether a criminal offense involves dishonesty or breach of trust is based on the statutory elements of the crime.

(1) "Dishonesty" means directly or indirectly to cheat or defraud, to cheat or defraud for monetary gain or its equivalent, or to wrongfully take property belonging to another in violation of any criminal statute. Dishonesty includes acts involving a want of integrity, lack of probity, or a disposition to distort, cheat, or act deceitfully or fraudulently, and may include crimes which federal, state or local laws define as dishonest.

(2) "Breach of trust" means a wrongful act, use, misappropriation, or omission with respect to any property or fund which has been committed to a person in a fiduciary or official capacity, or the misuse of one's official or fiduciary position to engage in a wrongful act, use, misappropriation, or omission.

§ 585.50 What adjudications and offenses are not covered by this part?

(a) *Youthful offender or juvenile delinquent.* This part does not cover any adjudication by a court against a person as:

(1) A youthful offender under any youthful offender law; or

(2) A juvenile delinquent by a court with jurisdiction over minors as defined by state law.

(b) *De minimis criminal offense.* This part does not cover *de minimis* criminal offenses. A criminal offense is *de minimis* if:

(1) The person has only one conviction or pretrial diversion or similar program of record;

(2) The offense was punishable by imprisonment for a term of less than one year, a fine of less than $1,000, or both, and the person did not serve time in jail;

(3) The conviction or program was entered at least five years before the date the person first held a position described in § 585.30(a); and

(4) The offense did not involve an insured depository institution, insured credit union, or other banking organization (including a savings and loan holding company, bank holding company, or financial holding company).

Office of Thrift Supervision, Treasury § 585.110

(5) The person must disclose the conviction or pretrial diversion or similar program to all insured depository institutions and other banking organizations the affairs of which he or she participates.

(6) The person must be covered by a fidelity bond to the same extent as others in similar positions with the savings and loan holding company.

Subpart B—Exemptions

§ 585.100 Who is exempt from the prohibition under this part?

(a) *Employees.* An employee of a savings and loan holding company is exempt from the prohibition in § 585.30, if all of the following conditions are met:

(1) The employee's responsibilities and activities are limited solely to agriculture, forestry, retail merchandising, manufacturing, or public utilities operations.

(2) The savings and loan holding company maintains a list of all policymaking positions and reviews this list annually.

(3) The employee's position does not appear on the savings and loan holding company's list of policymaking positions, and the employee does not, in fact, exercise any policymaking function with the savings and loan holding company.

(4) The employee:

(i) Is not an institution-affiliated party of the savings and loan holding company other than by virtue of the employment described in paragraph (a) of this section.

(ii) Does not own or control, directly or indirectly, the savings and loan holding company; and

(iii) Does not participate, directly or indirectly, in the conduct of the affairs of the savings and loan holding company.

(b) *Temporary exemption.* (1) Any prohibited person who was an institution-affiliated party with respect to a savings and loan holding company, who owned or controlled, directly or indirectly a savings and loan holding company, or who otherwise participated directly or indirectly in the conduct of the affairs of a savings and loan holding company on October 13, 2006, may continue to hold the position with the savings and loan holding company.

(2) This exemption expires on December 31, 2012, unless the savings and loan holding company or the person files an application seeking a case-by-case exemption for the person under § 585.110 by that date. If the savings and loan holding company or the person files such an application, the temporary exemption expires on:

(i) The date of issuance of an OTS order approving the application under § 585.130(a);

(ii) The expiration of the 20-day period for filing a request for hearing under § 585.130(b) provided there is no timely request for hearing following the issuance of an OTS order denying the application under that section;

(iii) The date that OTS denies a timely request for hearing under § 585.140(a) following the issuance of an OTS order denying the application under § 585.130(b);

(iv) The date that the Director issues a decision under § 585.140(d); or

(v) The date an applicant withdraws the application.

[72 FR 25955, May 8, 2007, as amended at 72 FR 50645, Sept. 4, 2007; 73 FR 10986, Feb. 29, 2008; 73 FR 30737, May 29, 2008; 73 FR 65258, Nov. 3, 2008; 74 FR 14458, Mar. 31, 2009; 74 FR 49792, Sept. 29, 2009; 75 FR 81377, Dec. 28, 2010]

§ 585.110 How do I apply for a case-by-case exemption?

(a) *Who may file.* (1) A savings and loan holding company or a person who was convicted of a criminal offense described in § 585.40 or who has agreed to enter into a pre-trial diversion or similar program in connection with a prosecution for such a criminal offense ("you") may file an application seeking an OTS order granting an exemption from the prohibitions in this part.

(2) You may seek an exemption only for a designated position (or positions) with respect to a named savings and loan holding company.

(3) You may not file an application less than one year after the latter of the date of OTS's denial of the same exemption under § 585.130(b), § 585.140(a)(2) or § 585.140(d).

(b) *Application and review procedures.* You may seek OTS approval by filing your application with OTS under the

§ 585.120

standard treatment described in 12 CFR part 516, subpart A of this chapter. OTS will review your application under 12 CFR part 516, subpart E of this chapter (excluding 12 CFR 516.270 and 516.280).

(c) *Prohibition pending OTS action.* Unless you are exempt under § 585.100(b), the prohibitions in § 585.30 continue to apply pending OTS action on your application.

§ 585.120 What factors will OTS consider in reviewing my application?

(a) *OTS review.* (1) In determining whether to approve an exemption application filed under § 585.110, OTS will consider the extent to which the position that is the subject of your application enables a person to:

(i) Participate in the major policy-making functions of the savings and loan holding company; or

(ii) Threaten the safety and soundness of any insured depository institution that is controlled by the savings and loan holding company, the interests of its depositors, or the public confidence in the insured depository institution.

(2) OTS will also consider whether you have demonstrated the person's fitness to hold the described position. Some positions may be approved without an extensive review of a person's fitness because the position does not enable a person to take the actions described in paragraph (a)(1) of this section.

(b) *Factors.* In making the determinations under paragraph (a) of this section, OTS will consider the following factors:

(1) The position;

(2) The amount of influence and control a person holding the position will be able to exercise over the affairs and operations of the savings and loan holding company and the insured depository institution;

(3) The ability of the management of the savings and loan holding company to supervise and control the activities of a person holding the position;

(4) The level of ownership that the person will have at the savings and loan holding company;

(5) The specific nature and circumstances of the criminal offense. The question whether a person who was convicted of a crime or who agreed to enter into a pretrial diversion or similar program for a crime was guilty of that crime is not relevant;

(6) Evidence of rehabilitation; and

(7) Any other relevant factor.

§ 585.130 How will I know if my application is approved?

(a) *Approval.* If OTS approves your application, OTS will issue an approval order. An approval order will include a summary of the relevant factors that OTS considered under § 585.120, will require fidelity bond coverage for the position to the same extent as similar positions with the SLHC. The approval order may include such other conditions as may be appropriate.

(b) *Denial.* If OTS denies your application, OTS will issue a denial order. The denial order will include the following written information:

(1) A summary of the relevant factors that OTS considered under § 585.120; and

(2) A statement indicating that you may file a written request demonstrating good cause for a hearing on the denial of your application, and that you must file this request with OTS within 20 days of the date of issuance of the order.

§ 585.140 What procedures govern a hearing on my application?

(a) *OTS review of hearing request.* OTS will review your hearing request to determine if you have demonstrated good cause for a hearing on your application. Within 30 days after the filing of a timely request for a hearing, OTS will notify you in writing of its decision to grant or deny the hearing request. If OTS grants your request for a hearing, it will order a hearing to be commenced within 60 days of the issuance of the notification. Upon the request of a party, the OTS may order a later hearing date.

(b) *Hearing procedures.* Hearing procedures are set out at 12 CFR part 509, subpart D of this chapter.

PART 590—PREEMPTION OF STATE USURY LAWS

Sec.
590.1 Authority, purpose, and scope.

Office of Thrift Supervision, Treasury

§ 590.2

590.2 Definitions.
590.3 Operation.
590.4 Federally-related residential manufactured housing loans—consumer protection provisions.
590.100 Status of Interpretations issued under Public Law 96-161.
590.101 State criminal usury statutes.

AUTHORITY: 12 U.S.C. 1735f-7a.

SOURCE: 54 FR 49715, Nov. 30, 1989, unless otherwise noted.

§ 590.1 Authority, purpose, and scope.

(a) *Authority.* This part contains regulations issued under section 501 of the Depository Institutions Deregulation and Monetary Control Act of 1980, Pub. L. 96-221, 94 Stat. 161.

(b) *Purpose and scope.* The purpose of this permanent preemption of state interest-rate ceilings applicable to Federally-related residential mortgage loans is to ensure that the availability of such loans is not impeded in states having restrictive interest limitations. This part applies to loans, mortages, credit sales, and advances, secured by first liens on residential real property, stock in residential cooperative housing corporations, or residential manufactured homes as defined in § 590.2 of this part.

§ 590.2 Definitions.

For the purposes of this part, the following definitions apply:

(a) *Loans* mean any loans, mortgages, credit sales, or advances.

(b) *Federally-related loans* include any loan:

(1) Made by any lender whose deposits or accounts are insured by any agency of the Federal government;

(2) Made by any lender regulated by any agency of the Federal government;

(3) Made by any lender approved by the Secretary of Housing and Urban Development for participation in any mortgage insurance program under the National Housing Act;

(4) Made in whole or in part by the Secretary of Housing and Urban Development; insured, guaranteed, supplemented, or assisted in any way by the Secretary or any officer or agency of the Federal government, or made under or in connection with a housing or urban development program administered by the Secretary, or a housing or related program administered by any other such officer or agency;

(5) Eligible for purchase by the Federal National Mortgage Association, the Government National Mortgage Association, or the Federal Home Loan Mortgage Corporation, or made by any financial institution from which the loan could be purchased by the Federal Home Loan Mortgage Corporation; or

(6) Made in whole or in part by any entity which:

(i) Regularly extends, or arranges for the extension of, credit payable by agreement in more than four installments or for which the payment of a finance charge is or may be required; and

(ii) Makes or invests in residential real property loans, including loans secured by first liens on residential manufactured homes that aggregate more than $1,000,000 per year; except that the latter requirement shall not apply to such an entity selling residential manufactured homes and providing financing for such sales through loans or credit sales secured by first liens on residential manufactured homes, if the entity has an arrangement to sell such loans or credit sales in whole or in part, or where such loans or credit sales are sold in whole or in part, to a lender or other institution otherwise included in this section.

(c) *Loans which are secured by first liens on real estate* means loans on the security of any instrument (whether a mortgage, deed of trust, or land contract) which makes the interest in real estate (whether in fee, or in a leasehold or subleasehold extending, or renewable, automatically or at the option of the holder or the lender, for a period of at least 5 years beyond the maturity of the loan) specific security for the payment of the obligation secured by the instrument: *Provided,* That the instrument is of such a nature that, in the event of default, the real estate described in the instrument could be subjected to the satisfaction of the obligation with the same priority as a first mortgage of a first deed of trust in the jurisdiction where the real estate is located.

(d) *Loans secured by first liens on stock in a residential cooperative housing corporation* means loans on the security of:

(1) A first security interest in stock or a membership certificate issued to a tenant stockholder or resident member by a cooperative housing organization; and

(2) An assignment of the borrower's interest in the proprietary lease or occupancy agreement issued by such organization.

(e) *Loans secured by first liens on residential manufactured homes* means a loan made pursuant to an agreement by which the party extending the credit acquires a security interest in the residential manufactured home which will have priority over any conflicting security interest.

(f) *Residential real property* means real estate improved or to be improved by a structure or structures designed primarily for dwelling, as opposed to commercial use.

(g) *Residential manufactured home* shall mean a manufactured home as defined in the National Manufactured Home Construction and Safety Standards Act, 42 U.S.C. 5402(6), which is or will be used as a residence.

(h) *State* means the several states, Puerto Rico, the District of Columbia, Guam, the Trust Territories of the Pacific Islands, the Northern Mariana Islands, and the Virgin Islands, except as provided in section 501(a)(2)(B) of the Depository Institutions Deregulation and Monetary Control Act of 1980, Pub. L. 96–221, 94 Stat. 161.

§ 590.3 Operation.

(a) The provisions of the constitution or law of any state expressly limiting the rate or amount of interest, discount points, finance charges, or other charges which may be charged, taken, received, or reserved shall not apply to any Federally-related loan:

(1) Made after March 31, 1980; and
(2) Secured by a first lien on:
 (i) Residential real property;
 (ii) Stock in a residential cooperative housing corporation when the loan is used to finance the acquisition of such stock; or
 (iii) A residential manufactured home: *Provided*, That the loan so secured contains the consumer safeguards required by § 590.4 of this part;

(b) The provisions of paragraph (a) of this section shall apply to loans made in any state on or before the date (after April 1, 1980 and prior to April 1, 1983) on which the state adopts a law or certifies that the voters of such state have voted in favor of any law, constitutional or otherwise, which states explicitly and by its terms that such state does not want the provisions of paragraph (a) of this section to apply with respect to loans made in such state, except that—

(1) The provisions of paragraph (a) of this section shall apply to any loan which is made after such date pursuant to a commitment therefore which was entered into during the period beginning on April 1, 1980, and ending on the date the state takes such action;

(2) The provisions of paragraph (a) of this section shall apply to any rollover of a loan which loan was made, or committed to be made, during the period beginning on April 1, 1980, and ending on the date the state takes such action, if the mortgage document or loan note provided that the interest rate to the original borrower could be changed through the use of such a rollover; and

(3) At any time after the date of adoption of these regulations, any state may adopt a provision of law placing limitations on discount points or such other charges on any loan described in this part.

(c) Nothing in this section preempts limitations in state laws on prepayment charges, attorneys' fees, late charges or other provisions designed to protect borrowers.

[54 FR 49715, Nov. 30, 1989, as amended at 66 FR 65822, Dec. 21, 2001]

§ 590.4 Federally-related residential manufactured housing loans—consumer protection provisions.

(a) *Definitions.* As used in this section:

(1) *Prepayment.* A "prepayment" occurs upon—

(i) Refinancing or consolidation of the indebtedness;

(ii) Actual prepayment of the indebtedness by the debtor, whether voluntarily or following acceleration of the payment obligation by the creditor; or

Office of Thrift Supervision, Treasury § 590.4

(iii) The entry of a judgment for the indebtedness in favor of the creditor.

(2) *Actuarial method*. The term *actuarial method* means the method of allocating payments made on a debt between the outstanding balance of the obligation and the finance charge pursuant to which a payment is applied first to the accumulated finance charge and any remainder is subtracted from, or any deficiency is added to, the outstanding balance of the obligation.

(3) *Precomputed Finance Charge*. The term *precomputed finance charge* means interest or a time/price differential as computed by the add-on or discount method. Precomputed finance charges do not include loan fees, points, finder's fees, or similar charges.

(4) *Creditor*. The term *creditor* means any entity covered by this part, including those which regularly extend or arrange for the extension of credit and assignees that are creditors under section 501(a)(1)(C)(v) of the Depository Institutions Deregulation and Monetary Control Act of 1980.

(b) *General*. (1) The provisions of the constitution or the laws of any state expressly limiting the rate or amount of interest, discount points, finance charges, or other charges which may be charged, taken, received, or reserved shall not apply to any loan, mortgage, credit sale, or advance which is secured by a first lien on a residential mobile home if a creditor covered by this part complies with the consumer protection regulations of this section.

(2) *Relation to state law*. (i) In making loans or credit sales subject to this section, creditors shall comply with state and Federal law in accordance with the following:

(A) *State law regulating matters not covered by this section*. When state law regulating matters not covered by this section is otherwise applicable to a loan or credit sale subject to this section, creditors shall comply with such state law provisions.

(B) *State law regulating matters covered by this section*. Creditors need comply only with the provisions of this section, unless the Office determines that an otherwise applicable state law regulating matters covered by this section provides greater protection to consumers. Such determinations shall be published in the FEDERAL REGISTER and shall operate prospectively.

(ii) Any interested party may petition the Office for a determination that state law requirements are more protective of consumers than the provisions of this section. Petitions shall be sent to: Secretary to the Office of Thrift Supervision, 1700 G Street, NW., Washington, DC 20552, and shall include:

(A) A copy of the state law to be considered;

(B) Copies of any relevant judicial, regulatory, or administrative interpretations of the state law; and

(C) An opinion or memorandum from the state Attorney General or other appropriate state official having primary enforcement responsibilities for the subject state law provision, indicating how the state law to be considered offers greater protection to consumers than the Office's regulation.

(c) *Refund of precomputed finance charge*. In the event the entire indebtedness is prepaid, the unearned portion of the precomputed finance charge shall be refunded to the debtor. This refund shall be in an amount not less than the amount which would be refunded if the unearned precomputed finance charge were calculated in accordance with the actuarial method, except that the debtor shall not be entitled to a refund which, is less than one dollar. The unearned portion of the precomputed finance charge is, at the option of the creditor, either:

(1) That portion of the precomputed finance charge which is allocable to all unexpired payment periods as originally scheduled, or if deferred, as deferred. A payment period shall be deemed unexpired if prepayment is made within 15 days after the payment period's scheduled due date. The unearned precomputed finance charge is the total of that which would have been earned for each such period had the loan not been precomputed, by applying to unpaid balances of principal, according to the actuarial method, an annual percentage rate based on those charges which are considered precomputed finance charges in this section, assuming that all payments were made as originally scheduled, or as deferred, if deferred. The creditor, at

§ 590.4

its option, may round this annual percentage rate to the nearest one-quarter of one percent; or

(2) The total precomputed finance charge less the earned precomputed finance charge. The earned precomputed finance charge shall be determined by applying an annual percentage rate based on the total precomputed finance charge (as that term is defined in this section), under the actuarial method, to the unpaid balances for the actual time those balances were unpaid up to the date of prepayment. If a late charge or deferral fee has been collected, it shall be treated as a payment.

(d) *Prepayment penalties.* A debtor may prepay in full or in part the unpaid balance of the loan at any time without penalty. The right to prepay shall be disclosed in the loan contract in type larger than that used for the body of the document.

(e) *Balloon payments*—(1) *Federal savings associations.* Federal savings association creditors may enter into agreements with debtors which provide for non-amortized and partially-amortized loans on residential manufactured homes, and such loans shall be governed by the provisions of this section and § 560.220 of this chapter.

(2) *Other creditors.* All other creditors may enter into agreements with debtors which provide for non-amortized and partially-amortized loans on residential manufactured homes to the extent authorized by applicable Federal or state law or regulation.

(f) *Late charges.* (1) No late charge may be assessed, imposed, or collected unless provided for by written contract between the creditor and debtor.

(2) To the extent that applicable state law does not provide for a longer period of time, no late charge may be collected on an installment which is paid in full on or before the 15th day after its scheduled or deferred due date even though an earlier maturing installment or a late charge on an earlier installment may not have been paid in full. For purposes of assessing late charges, payments received are deemed to be applied first to current installments.

(3) A late charge may be imposed only once on an installment; however,

12 CFR Ch. V (1-1-12 Edition)

no such charge may be collected for a late installment which has been deferred.

(4) To the extent that applicable state law does not provide for a lower charge or a longer grace period, a late charge on any installment not paid in full on or before the 15th day after its scheduled or deferred due date may not exceed five percent of the unpaid amount of the installment.

(5) If, at any time after imposition of a late charge, the lender provides the borrower with written notice regarding amounts claimed to be due but unpaid, the notice shall separately state the total of all late charges claimed.

(6) Interest after the final scheduled maturity date may not exceed the maximum rate otherwise allowable under State law for such contracts, and if such interest is charged, no separate late charge may be made on the final scheduled installment.

(g) *Deferral fees.* (1) With respect to mobile home credit transactions containing precomputed finance charges, agreements providing for deferral of all or part of one or more installments shall be in writing, signed by the parties, and

(i) Provide, to the extent that applicable state law does not provide for a lower charge, for a charge not exceeding one percent of each installment or part thereof for each month from the date when such installment was due to the date when it is agreed to become payable and proportionately for a part of each month, counting each day as 1/30th of a month;

(ii) Incorporate by reference the transaction to which the deferral applied;

(iii) Disclose each installment or part thereof in the amount to be deferred, the date or dates originally payable, and the date or dates agreed to become payable: and

(iv) Set forth the fact of the deferral charge, the dollar amount of the charge for each installment to be deferred, and the total dollar amount to be paid by the debtor for the privilege of deferring payment.

(2) No term of a writing executed by the debtor shall constitute authority for a creditor unilaterally to grant a

558

Office of Thrift Supervision, Treasury

§ 590.101

deferral with respect to which a charge is to be imposed or collected.

(3) The deferral period is that period of time in which no payment is required or made by reason of the deferral.

(4) Payments received with respect to deferred installments shall be deemed to be applied first to deferred installments.

(5) A charge may not be collected for the deferral of an installment or any part thereof if, with respect to that installment, a refinancing or consolidation agreement is concluded by the parties, or a late charge has been imposed or collected, unless such late charge is refunded to the borrower or credited to the deferral charge.

(h) *Notice before repossession, foreclosure, or acceleration.* (1) Except in the case of abandonment or other extreme circumstances, no action to repossess or foreclose, or to accelerate payment of the entire outstanding balance of the obligation, may be taken against the debtor until 30 days after the creditor sends the debtor a notice of default in the form set forth in paragraph (h)(2) of this section. Such notice shall be sent by registered or certified mail with return receipt requested. In the case of default on payments, the sum stated in the notice may only include payments in default and applicable late or deferral charges. If the debtor cures the default within 30 days of the postmark of the notice and subsequently defaults a second time, the creditor shall again give notice as described in this paragraph (h)(1). The debtor is not entitled to notice of default more than twice in any one-year period.

(2) The notice in the following form shall state the nature of the default, the action the debtor must take to cure the default, the creditor's intended actions upon failure of the debtor to cure the default, and the debtor's right to redeem under state law.

To:
Date: , 19

NOTICE OF DEFAULT AND RIGHT TO CURE DEFAULT

Name, address, and telephone number of creditor

Account number, if any

Brief identification of credit transaction

You are now in default on this credit transaction. You have a right to correct this default within 30 days from the postmarked date of this notice.

If you correct the default, you may continue with the contract as though you did not default. Your default consists of:

DESCRIBE DEFAULT ALLEGED

Cure of default: Within 30 days from the postmarked date of this notice, you may cure your default by (describe the acts necessary for cure, including, if applicable, the amount of payment required, including itemized delinquency or deferral charges).

Creditor's rights: If you do not correct your default in the time allowed, we may exercise our rights against you under the law by (describe action creditor intends to take).

If you have any questions, write (the creditor) at the above address or call (creditor's designated employee) at (telephone number) between the hours of   and   on (state days of week).

If this default was caused by your failure to make a payment or payments, and you want to pay by mail, please send a check or money order; do not send cash.

[54 FR 49715, Nov. 30, 1989, as amended at 61 FR 50984, Sept. 30, 1996; 67 FR 60554, Sept. 26, 2002]

§ 590.100 Status of Interpretations issued under Public Law 96–161.

The Office continues to adhere to the views expressed in the formal Interpretations issued under the authority of section 105(c) of Pub. L. 96–161, 93 Stat. 1233 (1979). These interpretations, which relate to the temporary preemption of state interest ceilings contained in Pub. L. 96–161, may be found at 45 FR 2840 (Jan. 15, 1980); 45 FR 6165 (Jan. 25, 1980); 45 FR 8000 (Feb. 6, 1980); 45 FR 15921 (Mar. 12, 1980).

§ 590.101 State criminal usury statutes.

(a) Section 501 provides that "the provisions of the constitution or laws of any state expressly limiting the rate or amount of interest, discount points, finance charges, or other charges shall not apply to any" federally-related loan secured by a first lien on residential real property, a residential manufactured home, or all the stock allocated to a dwelling unit in a residential housing cooperative. 12 U.S.C. 1735f–7 note (Supp. IV 1980). The question has arisen as to whether the federal statute preempts a state law which deems it a criminal offense to charge interest at a rate in excess of that specified in the state law.

(b) In the Office's view, section 501 preempts all state laws which expressly limit the rate or amount of interest chargeable on a federally-related residential first mortgage. It does not matter whether the statute in question imposes criminal or civil sanctions; section 501, by its terms, preempts "any" state law which imposes a ceiling on interest rates. The wording of the federal statute clearly expresses an intent to displace all direct state law restraints on interest. Any state law that conflicts with this Congressional purpose must yield.

PART 591—PREEMPTION OF STATE DUE-ON-SALE LAWS

Sec.
591.1 Authority, purpose, and scope.
591.2 Definitions.
591.3 Loans originated by Federal savings associations.
591.4 Loans originated by lenders other than Federal savings associations.
591.5 Limitations on exercise of due-on-sale clauses.
591.6 Interpretations.

AUTHORITY: 12 U.S.C. 1464 and 1701j-3.

SOURCE: 54 FR 49718, Nov. 30, 1989, unless otherwise noted.

§ 591.1 Authority, purpose, and scope.

(a) *Authority.* This part contains regulations issued under section 5 of the Home Owners' Loan Act of 1933, as amended, and under section 341 of the Garn-St Germain Depository Institutions Act of 1982, Pub. L. 97-320, 96 Stat. 1469, 1505-1507.

(b) *Purpose and scope.* The purpose of this permanent preemption of state prohibitions on the exercise of due-on-sale clauses by all lenders, whether federally- or state-chartered, is to reaffirm the authority of Federal savings associations to enforce due-on-sale clauses, and to confer on other lenders generally comparable authority with respect to the exercise of such clauses. This part applies to all real property loans, and all lenders making such loans, as those terms are defined in § 591.2 of this part.

§ 591.2 Definitions.

For the purposes of this part, the following definitions apply:

(a) *Assumed* includes transfers of real property subject to a real property loan by assumptions, installment land sales contracts, wraparound loans, contracts for deed, transfers subject to the mortgage or similar lien, and other like transfers. "Completed credit application" has the same meaning as completed application for credit as provided in § 202.2(f) of this title.

(b) *Due-on-sale clause* means a contract provision which authorizes the lender, at its option, to declare immediately due and payable sums secured by the lender's security instrument upon a sale of transfer of all or any part of the real property securing the loan without the lender's prior written consent. For purposes of this definition, a *sale or transfer* means the conveyance of real property of any right, title or interest therein, whether legal or equitable, whether voluntary or involuntary, by outright sale, deed, installment sale contract, land contract, contract for deed, leasehold interest with a term greater than three years, lease-option contract or any other method of conveyance of real property interests.

(c) *Federal savings association* has the same meaning as provided in § 541.11 of this chapter.

(d) *Federal credit union* means a credit union chartered under the Federal Credit Union Act.

(e) *Home* has the same meaning as provided in § 541.14 of this chapter.

(f) *Savings association* has the same meaning as provided in § 561.43 of this chapter.

(g) *Lender* means a person or government agency making a real property loan, including without limitation, individuals, Federal savings associations, state-chartered savings associations, national banks, state-chartered banks and state-chartered mutual savings banks, Federal credit unions, state-chartered credit unions, mortgage banks, insurance companies and finance companies which make real property loans, manufactured-home retailers who extend credit, agencies of the Federal government, any lender approved by the Secretary of Housing and

Office of Thrift Supervision, Treasury § 591.2

Urban Development for participation in any mortgage insurance program under the National Housing Act, and any assignee or transferee, in whole or part, of any such persons or agencies.

(h) *Loan secured by a lien on real property* means a loan on the security of any instrument (whether a mortgage, deed or trust, or land contract) which makes the interest in real property (whether in fee, or in a leasehold or subleasehold) specific security for the payment of the obligation secured by the instrument.

(i) *Loan secured by a lien on stock in a residential cooperative housing corporation* means a loan on the security of:

(1) A security interest in stock or a membership certificate issued to a tenant stockholder or resident member by a cooperative housing organization; and

(2) An assignment of the borrower's interest in the proprietary lease or occupancy agreement issued by such organization.

(j) *Loan secured by a lien on a residential manufactured home, whether real or personal property,* means a loan made pursuant to an agreement by which the party extending the credit acquires a security interest in the residential manufactured home.

(k) *Loan originated by* a Federal savings association or other lender means any loan for which the lender makes the first advance of credit thereunder, *Provided,* That such lender then held a beneficial interest in the loan, whether as to the whole loan or a portion thereof, and whether or not the loan is later held by or transferred to another lender.

(l) *Real property loan* means any loan, mortgage, advance or credit sale secured by a lien on real property, the stock or membership certificate allocated to a dwelling unit in a cooperative housing corporation, or a residential manufactured home, whether real or personal property.

(m) *Residential manufactured home* has the same meaning as provided in § 590.2(g) of this chapter.

(n) *Reverse mortgage* means an instrument that provides for one or more payments to a homeowner based on accumulated equity. The lender may make payment directly, through the purchase of an annuity through an insurance company, or in any other manner. The loan may be due either on a specific date or when a specified event occurs, such as the sale of the property or the death of the borrower.

(o) *State* means the several states, Puerto Rico, the District of Columbia, Guam, the Trust Territory of the Pacific Islands, the Northern Mariana Islands, the Virgin Islands, and American Samoa.

(p)(1) A *window-period loan* means a real property loan, not originated by a Federal savings association, which was made or assumed during a window-period created by state law and subject to that law, which loan was recorded, at the time of origination or assumption, before October 15, 1982, or within 60 days thereafter (December 14, 1982).

(2) The window-period begins on: (i) The date a state adopted a law (by means of a constitutional provision or statute) prohibiting the unrestricted exercise of due-on-sale clauses upon outright transfers of property securing loans subject to the state law creating the window-period, or the effective date of a constitutional or statutory provision so adopted, whichever is later; or

(ii) The date on which the highest court of the state rendered a decision prohibiting such unrestricted exercise (or if the highest court has not so decided, the date on which the next highest appellate court rendered a decision resulting in a final judgment which applies statewide), and ends on the earlier of the date such state law prohibition terminated under state law or October 15, 1982.

(3) Categories of state law which create window-periods by prohibiting the unrestricted exercise of due-on-sale clauses upon outright transfers of property securing loans subject to such state law restrictions include laws or judicial decisions which permit the lender to exercise its option under a due-on-sale clause only where:

(i) The lender's security interest or the likelihood of repayment is impaired; or

(ii) The lender is required to accept an assumption of the existing loan without an interest-rate change or with an interest-rate change below the

§ 591.3

market interest rate currently being offered by the lender on similar loans secured by similar property at the time of the transfer.

[54 FR 49718, Nov. 30, 1989, as amended at 67 FR 60554, Sept. 26, 2002]

§ 591.3 Loans originated by Federal savings associations.

(a) With regard to any real property loan originated or to be originated by a Federal savings association, as a matter of contract between it and the borrower, a Federal savings association continues to have the power to include a due-on-sale clause in its loan instrument.

(b) Except as otherwise provided in § 591.5 of this part with respect to any such loan made on the security of a home occupied or to be occupied by the borrower, exercise by any lender of a due-on-sale clause in a loan originated by a Federal savings association shall be exclusively governed by the terms of the loan contract, and all rights and remedies of the lender and borrower shall at all times be fixed and governed by that contract.

§ 591.4 Loans originated by lenders other than Federal savings associations.

(a) With regard to any real property loan originated by a lender other than a Federal savings association, as a matter of contract between it and the borrower, the lender has the power to include a due on sale clause in its loan instrument.

(b) Except as otherwise provided in paragraph (c) of this section and § 591.5 of this part, the exercise of due-on-sale clauses in loans originated by lenders other than Federal savings associations shall be governed exclusively by the terms of the loan contract, and all rights and remedies of the lender and the borrower shall be fixed and governed by that contract.

(c)(1) In the case of a window-period loan, the provisions of paragraph (b) of this section shall apply only in the case of a sale or transfer of the property subject to the real property loan and only if such sale or transfer occurs on or after October 15, 1985: *Provided*, That:

(i) With respect to real property loans originated in a state by lenders other than national banks, Federal savings associations, and Federal credit unions, a state may otherwise regulate such contracts by state law enacted prior to October 16, 1985, in which case paragraph (b) of this section shall apply only if such state law so provides; and

(ii) With respect to real property loans originated by national banks and Federal credit unions, the Comptroller of the Currency or the National Credit Union Administration Board, respectively, may otherwise regulate such contracts by regulations promulgated prior to October 16, 1985, in which case paragraph (b) of this section shall apply only if such regulation so provides.

(2) A lender may not exercise its options pursuant to a due-on-sale clause contained in a window-period loan in the case of a sale or transfer of property securing such loan where the sale or transfer occurred prior to October 15, 1982.

(d)(1) Prior to the sale or transfer of property securing a window-period loan subject to the provisions of paragraph (c) of this section.

(i) Any lender in the business of making real property loans may require any successor or transferee of the borrower to supply credit information customarily required by the lender in connection with credit applications, to complete its customary credit application, and to meet customary credit standards applied by such lender, at the date of sale or transfer, to the lender's similar loans secured by similar property.

(ii) Any lender not in the business of making loans may require any successor or transferee of the borrower to meet credit standards customarily applied by other similarly situated lenders or sellers in the geographic market within which the transaction occurs, for similar loans secured by similar property, prior to the lender's consent to the transfer.

(2) The lender may exercise a due-on-sale clause in a window-period loan if:

(i) The successor or transferee of the borrower fails to meet the lender's

Office of Thrift Supervision, Treasury § 591.5

credit standards as set forth in paragraphs (b)(1)(i) and (b)(1)(ii) of this section; or

(ii) Upon transfer of the security property and not later than fifteen days after written request by the lender, the successor or transferee of the borrower fails to provide information requested by the lender pursuant to paragraph (d)(1)(i) or (d)(1)(ii) of this section, to determine whether such successor or transferee of the borrower meets the lender's customary credit standards.

(3) The lender shall, within thirty days of receipt of a completed credit application and any other related information provided by the successor or transferee of the borrower, determine whether such successor or transferee meets the customary credit standards of the lender and provide written notice to the successor or transferee of its decision, and the reasons in the event of a disapproval. Failure of the lender to provide such notice shall preclude the lender from exercise of its due-on-sale clause upon the sale or transfer of the property securing the loan.

(4) The lender's right to exercise a due-on-sale clause pursuant to this paragraph (d)(4) is in addition to any other rights afforded the lender by state law regulating window-period loans with regard to the exercise of due-on-sale clauses and loan assumptions.

§ 591.5 Limitation on exercise of due-on-sale clauses.

(a) *General.* Except as provided in § 591.4 (c) and (d)(4) of this part, due-on-sale practices of Federal savings associations and other lenders shall be governed exclusively by the Office's regulations, in preemption of and without regard to any limitations imposed by state law on either their inclusion or exercise including, without limitation, state law prohibitions against restraints on alienation, prohibitions against penalties and forfeitures, equitable restrictions and state law dealing with equitable transfers.

(b) *Specific limitations.* With respect to any loan on the security of a home occupied or to be occupied by the borrower,

(1) A lender shall not (except with regard to a reverse mortgage) exercise its option pursuant to a due-on-sale clause upon:

(i) The creation of a lien or other encumbrance subordinate to the lender's security instrument which does not relate to a transfer of rights of occupancy in the property: *Provided,* That such lien or encumbrance is not created pursuant to a contract for deed;

(ii) The creation of a purchase-money security interest for household appliances;

(iii) A transfer by devise, descent, or operation of law on the death of a joint tenant or tenant by the entirety;

(iv) The granting of a leasehold interest which has a term of three years or less and which does not contain an option to purchase (that is, either a lease of more than three years or a lease with an option to purchase will allow the exercise of a due-on-sale clause);

(v) A transfer, in which the transferee is a person who occupies or will occupy the property, which is:

(A) A transfer to a relative resulting from the death of the borrower;

(B) A transfer where the spouse or child(ren) becomes an owner of the property; or

(C) A transfer resulting from a decree of dissolution of marriage, legal separation agreement, or from an incidental property settlement agreement by which the spouse becomes an owner of the property; or

(vi) A transfer into an inter vivos trust in which the borrower is and remains the beneficiary and occupant of the property, unless, as a condition precedent to such transfer, the borrower refuses to provide the lender with reasonable means acceptable to the lender by which the lender will be assured of timely notice of any subsequent transfer of the beneficial interest or change in occupancy.

(2) A lender shall not impose a prepayment penalty or equivalent fee when the lender or party acting on behalf of the lender

(i) Declares by written notice that the loan is due pursuant to a due-on-sale clause or

(ii) Commences a judicial or non-judicial foreclosure proceeding to enforce a due-on-sale clause or to seek payment in full as a result of invoking such clause.

(3) A lender shall not impose a prepayment penalty or equivalent fee when the lender or party acting on behalf of the lender fails to approve within 30 days the completed credit application of a qualified transferee of the security property to assume the loan in accordance with the terms of the loan, and thereafter the borrower transfers the security property to such transferee and prepays the loan in full within 120 days after receipt by the lender of the completed credit application. For purposes of this paragraph (b)(3), a *qualified transferee* is a person who qualifies for the loan under the lender's applicable underwriting standards and who occupies or will occupy the security property.

(4) A lender waives its option to exercise a due-on-sale clause as to a specific transfer if, before the transfer, the lender and the existing borrower's prospective successor in interest agree in writing that the successor in interest will be obligated under the terms of the loan and that interest on sums secured by the lender's security interest will be payable at a rate the lender shall request. Upon such agreement and resultant waiver, a lender shall release the existing borrower from all obligations under the loan instruments, and the lender is deemed to have made a new loan to the existing borrower's successor in interest. The waiver and release apply to all loans secured by homes occupied by borrowers made by a Federal savings association after July 31, 1976, and to all loans secured by homes occupied by borrowers made by other lenders after the effective date of this regulation.

(5) Nothing in paragraph (b)(1) of this section shall be construed to restrict a lender's right to enforce a due-on-sale clause upon the subsequent occurrence of any event which disqualifies a transfer for a previously-applicable exception under that paragraph (b)(1).

(c) *Policy considerations.* Paragraph (b) of this section does not prohibit a lender from requiring, as a condition to an assumption, continued maintenance of mortgage insurance by the existing borrower's successor in interest, whether by endorsement of the existing policy or by entrance into a new contract of insurance.

§ 591.6 Interpretations.

The Office periodically will publish Interpretations under section 341 of the Garn-St Germain Depository Institutions Act of 1982, Pub. L. 97–320, 96 Stat. 1469, 1505–1507, in the FEDERAL REGISTER in response to written requests sent to the Secretary, Office of Thrift Supervision, 1700 G Street, NW., Washington, DC 20552.

PARTS 592–599 [RESERVED]

FINDING AIDS

A list of CFR titles, subtitles, chapters, subchapters and parts and an alphabetical list of agencies publishing in the CFR are included in the CFR Index and Finding Aids volume to the Code of Federal Regulations which is published separately and revised annually.

Table of CFR Titles and Chapters
Alphabetical List of Agencies Appearing in the CFR
List of CFR Sections Affected

Table of CFR Titles and Chapters
(Revised as of January 1, 2012)

Title 1—General Provisions

I   Administrative Committee of the Federal Register (Parts 1—49)
II   Office of the Federal Register (Parts 50—299)
III   Administrative Conference of the United States (Parts 300—399)
IV   Miscellaneous Agencies (Parts 400—500)

Title 2—Grants and Agreements

SUBTITLE A—OFFICE OF MANAGEMENT AND BUDGET GUIDANCE FOR GRANTS AND AGREEMENTS

I   Office of Management and Budget Governmentwide Guidance for Grants and Agreements (Parts 2—199)
II   Office of Management and Budget Circulars and Guidance (200—299)

SUBTITLE B—FEDERAL AGENCY REGULATIONS FOR GRANTS AND AGREEMENTS

III   Department of Health and Human Services (Parts 300—399)
IV   Department of Agriculture (Parts 400—499)
VI   Department of State (Parts 600—699)
VII   Agency for International Development (Parts 700—799)
VIII   Department of Veterans Affairs (Parts 800—899)
IX   Department of Energy (Parts 900—999)
XI   Department of Defense (Parts 1100—1199)
XII   Department of Transportation (Parts 1200—1299)
XIII   Department of Commerce (Parts 1300—1399)
XIV   Department of the Interior (Parts 1400—1499)
XV   Environmental Protection Agency (Parts 1500—1599)
XVIII   National Aeronautics and Space Administration (Parts 1800—1899)
XX   United States Nuclear Regulatory Commission (Parts 2000—2099)
XXII   Corporation for National and Community Service (Parts 2200—2299)
XXIII   Social Security Administration (Parts 2300—2399)
XXIV   Housing and Urban Development (Parts 2400—2499)
XXV   National Science Foundation (Parts 2500—2599)
XXVI   National Archives and Records Administration (Parts 2600—2699)
XXVII   Small Business Administration (Parts 2700—2799)
XXVIII   Department of Justice (Parts 2800—2899)

Chap. **Title 2—Grants and Agreements—Continued**

- XXX   Department of Homeland Security (Parts 3000—3099)
- XXXI   Institute of Museum and Library Services (Parts 3100—3199)
- XXXII   National Endowment for the Arts (Parts 3200—3299)
- XXXIII   National Endowment for the Humanities (Parts 3300—3399)
- XXXV   Export-Import Bank of the United States (Parts 3500—3599)
- XXXVII   Peace Corps (Parts 3700—3799)
- LVIII   Election Assistance Commission (Parts 5800—5899)

Title 3—The President

- I   Executive Office of the President (Parts 100—199)

Title 4—Accounts

- I   Government Accountability Office (Parts 1—99)
- II   Recovery Accountability and Transparency Board (Parts 200—299)

Title 5—Administrative Personnel

- I   Office of Personnel Management (Parts 1—1199)
- II   Merit Systems Protection Board (Parts 1200—1299)
- III   Office of Management and Budget (Parts 1300—1399)
- V   The International Organizations Employees Loyalty Board (Parts 1500—1599)
- VI   Federal Retirement Thrift Investment Board (Parts 1600—1699)
- VIII   Office of Special Counsel (Parts 1800—1899)
- IX   Appalachian Regional Commission (Parts 1900—1999)
- XI   Armed Forces Retirement Home (Parts 2100—2199)
- XIV   Federal Labor Relations Authority, General Counsel of the Federal Labor Relations Authority and Federal Service Impasses Panel (Parts 2400—2499)
- XV   Office of Administration, Executive Office of the President (Parts 2500—2599)
- XVI   Office of Government Ethics (Parts 2600—2699)
- XXI   Department of the Treasury (Parts 3100—3199)
- XXII   Federal Deposit Insurance Corporation (Parts 3200—3299)
- XXIII   Department of Energy (Parts 3300—3399)
- XXIV   Federal Energy Regulatory Commission (Parts 3400—3499)
- XXV   Department of the Interior (Parts 3500—3599)
- XXVI   Department of Defense (Parts 3600— 3699)
- XXVIII   Department of Justice (Parts 3800—3899)
- XXIX   Federal Communications Commission (Parts 3900—3999)
- XXX   Farm Credit System Insurance Corporation (Parts 4000—4099)
- XXXI   Farm Credit Administration (Parts 4100—4199)
- XXXIII   Overseas Private Investment Corporation (Parts 4300—4399)

Title 5—Administrative Personnel—Continued

Chap.	
XXXIV	Securities and Exchange Commission (Parts 4400—4499)
XXXV	Office of Personnel Management (Parts 4500—4599)
XXXVII	Federal Election Commission (Parts 4700—4799)
XL	Interstate Commerce Commission (Parts 5000—5099)
XLI	Commodity Futures Trading Commission (Parts 5100—5199)
XLII	Department of Labor (Parts 5200—5299)
XLIII	National Science Foundation (Parts 5300—5399)
XLV	Department of Health and Human Services (Parts 5500—5599)
XLVI	Postal Rate Commission (Parts 5600—5699)
XLVII	Federal Trade Commission (Parts 5700—5799)
XLVIII	Nuclear Regulatory Commission (Parts 5800—5899)
XLIX	Federal Labor Relations Authority (Parts 5900—5999)
L	Department of Transportation (Parts 6000—6099)
LII	Export-Import Bank of the United States (Parts 6200—6299)
LIII	Department of Education (Parts 6300—6399)
LIV	Environmental Protection Agency (Parts 6400—6499)
LV	National Endowment for the Arts (Parts 6500—6599)
LVI	National Endowment for the Humanities (Parts 6600—6699)
LVII	General Services Administration (Parts 6700—6799)
LVIII	Board of Governors of the Federal Reserve System (Parts 6800—6899)
LIX	National Aeronautics and Space Administration (Parts 6900—6999)
LX	United States Postal Service (Parts 7000—7099)
LXI	National Labor Relations Board (Parts 7100—7199)
LXII	Equal Employment Opportunity Commission (Parts 7200—7299)
LXIII	Inter-American Foundation (Parts 7300—7399)
LXIV	Merit Systems Protection Board (Parts 7400—7499)
LXV	Department of Housing and Urban Development (Parts 7500—7599)
LXVI	National Archives and Records Administration (Parts 7600—7699)
LXVII	Institute of Museum and Library Services (Parts 7700—7799)
LXVIII	Commission on Civil Rights (Parts 7800—7899)
LXIX	Tennessee Valley Authority (Parts 7900—7999)
LXX	Court Services and Offender Supervision Agency for the District of Columbia (Parts 8000—8099)
LXXI	Consumer Product Safety Commission (Parts 8100—8199)
LXXIII	Department of Agriculture (Parts 8300—8399)
LXXIV	Federal Mine Safety and Health Review Commission (Parts 8400—8499)
LXXVI	Federal Retirement Thrift Investment Board (Parts 8600—8699)
LXXVII	Office of Management and Budget (Parts 8700—8799)
LXXX	Federal Housing Finance Agency (Parts 9000—9099)
LXXXII	Special Inspector General for Iraq Reconstruction (Parts 9200—9299)

Chap. **Title 5—Administrative Personnel—Continued**

XCVII Department of Homeland Security Human Resources Management System (Department of Homeland Security—Office of Personnel Management) (Parts 9700—9799)

Title 6—Domestic Security

I Department of Homeland Security, Office of the Secretary (Parts 1—99)

Title 7—Agriculture

SUBTITLE A—OFFICE OF THE SECRETARY OF AGRICULTURE (PARTS 0—26)

SUBTITLE B—REGULATIONS OF THE DEPARTMENT OF AGRICULTURE

I Agricultural Marketing Service (Standards, Inspections, Marketing Practices), Department of Agriculture (Parts 27—209)

II Food and Nutrition Service, Department of Agriculture (Parts 210—299)

III Animal and Plant Health Inspection Service, Department of Agriculture (Parts 300—399)

IV Federal Crop Insurance Corporation, Department of Agriculture (Parts 400—499)

V Agricultural Research Service, Department of Agriculture (Parts 500—599)

VI Natural Resources Conservation Service, Department of Agriculture (Parts 600—699)

VII Farm Service Agency, Department of Agriculture (Parts 700—799)

VIII Grain Inspection, Packers and Stockyards Administration (Federal Grain Inspection Service), Department of Agriculture (Parts 800—899)

IX Agricultural Marketing Service (Marketing Agreements and Orders; Fruits, Vegetables, Nuts), Department of Agriculture (Parts 900—999)

X Agricultural Marketing Service (Marketing Agreements and Orders; Milk), Department of Agriculture (Parts 1000—1199)

XI Agricultural Marketing Service (Marketing Agreements and Orders; Miscellaneous Commodities), Department of Agriculture (Parts 1200—1299)

XIV Commodity Credit Corporation, Department of Agriculture (Parts 1400—1499)

XV Foreign Agricultural Service, Department of Agriculture (Parts 1500—1599)

XVI Rural Telephone Bank, Department of Agriculture (Parts 1600—1699)

XVII Rural Utilities Service, Department of Agriculture (Parts 1700—1799)

XVIII Rural Housing Service, Rural Business-Cooperative Service, Rural Utilities Service, and Farm Service Agency, Department of Agriculture (Parts 1800—2099)

XX Local Television Loan Guarantee Board (Parts 2200—2299)

Title 7—Agriculture—Continued

Chap.	
XXV	Office of Advocacy and Outreach, Department of Agriculture (Parts 2500—2599)
XXVI	Office of Inspector General, Department of Agriculture (Parts 2600—2699)
XXVII	Office of Information Resources Management, Department of Agriculture (Parts 2700—2799)
XXVIII	Office of Operations, Department of Agriculture (Parts 2800—2899)
XXIX	Office of Energy Policy and New Uses, Department of Agriculture (Parts 2900—2999)
XXX	Office of the Chief Financial Officer, Department of Agriculture (Parts 3000—3099)
XXXI	Office of Environmental Quality, Department of Agriculture (Parts 3100—3199)
XXXII	Office of Procurement and Property Management, Department of Agriculture (Parts 3200—3299)
XXXIII	Office of Transportation, Department of Agriculture (Parts 3300—3399)
XXXIV	National Institute of Food and Agriculture (Parts 3400—3499)
XXXV	Rural Housing Service, Department of Agriculture (Parts 3500—3599)
XXXVI	National Agricultural Statistics Service, Department of Agriculture (Parts 3600—3699)
XXXVII	Economic Research Service, Department of Agriculture (Parts 3700—3799)
XXXVIII	World Agricultural Outlook Board, Department of Agriculture (Parts 3800—3899)
XLI	[Reserved]
XLII	Rural Business-Cooperative Service and Rural Utilities Service, Department of Agriculture (Parts 4200—4299)

Title 8—Aliens and Nationality

I	Department of Homeland Security (Immigration and Naturalization) (Parts 1—499)
V	Executive Office for Immigration Review, Department of Justice (Parts 1000—1399)

Title 9—Animals and Animal Products

I	Animal and Plant Health Inspection Service, Department of Agriculture (Parts 1—199)
II	Grain Inspection, Packers and Stockyards Administration (Packers and Stockyards Programs), Department of Agriculture (Parts 200—299)
III	Food Safety and Inspection Service, Department of Agriculture (Parts 300—599)

Title 10—Energy

Chap.
- I Nuclear Regulatory Commission (Parts 0—199)
- II Department of Energy (Parts 200—699)
- III Department of Energy (Parts 700—999)
- X Department of Energy (General Provisions) (Parts 1000—1099)
- XIII Nuclear Waste Technical Review Board (Parts 1300—1399)
- XVII Defense Nuclear Facilities Safety Board (Parts 1700—1799)
- XVIII Northeast Interstate Low-Level Radioactive Waste Commission (Parts 1800—1899)

Title 11—Federal Elections

- I Federal Election Commission (Parts 1—9099)
- II Election Assistance Commission (Parts 9400—9499)

Title 12—Banks and Banking

- I Comptroller of the Currency, Department of the Treasury (Parts 1—199)
- II Federal Reserve System (Parts 200—299)
- III Federal Deposit Insurance Corporation (Parts 300—399)
- IV Export-Import Bank of the United States (Parts 400—499)
- V Office of Thrift Supervision, Department of the Treasury (Parts 500—599)
- VI Farm Credit Administration (Parts 600—699)
- VII National Credit Union Administration (Parts 700—799)
- VIII Federal Financing Bank (Parts 800—899)
- IX Federal Housing Finance Board (Parts 900—999)
- X Bureau of Consumer Financial Protection (Parts 1000—1099)
- XI Federal Financial Institutions Examination Council (Parts 1100—1199)
- XII Federal Housing Finance Agency (Parts 1200—1299)
- XIII Financial Stability Oversight Council (Parts 1300—1399)
- XIV Farm Credit System Insurance Corporation (Parts 1400—1499)
- XV Department of the Treasury (Parts 1500—1599)
- XVI Office of Financial Research (Parts 1600—1699)
- XVII Office of Federal Housing Enterprise Oversight, Department of Housing and Urban Development (Parts 1700—1799)
- XVIII Community Development Financial Institutions Fund, Department of the Treasury (Parts 1800—1899)

Title 13—Business Credit and Assistance

- I Small Business Administration (Parts 1—199)
- III Economic Development Administration, Department of Commerce (Parts 300—399)
- IV Emergency Steel Guarantee Loan Board (Parts 400—499)
- V Emergency Oil and Gas Guaranteed Loan Board (Parts 500—599)

Title 14—Aeronautics and Space

Chap.
- I Federal Aviation Administration, Department of Transportation (Parts 1—199)
- II Office of the Secretary, Department of Transportation (Aviation Proceedings) (Parts 200—399)
- III Commercial Space Transportation, Federal Aviation Administration, Department of Transportation (Parts 400—1199)
- V National Aeronautics and Space Administration (Parts 1200—1299)
- VI Air Transportation System Stabilization (Parts 1300—1399)

Title 15—Commerce and Foreign Trade

SUBTITLE A—OFFICE OF THE SECRETARY OF COMMERCE (PARTS 0—29)

SUBTITLE B—REGULATIONS RELATING TO COMMERCE AND FOREIGN TRADE

- I Bureau of the Census, Department of Commerce (Parts 30—199)
- II National Institute of Standards and Technology, Department of Commerce (Parts 200—299)
- III International Trade Administration, Department of Commerce (Parts 300—399)
- IV Foreign-Trade Zones Board, Department of Commerce (Parts 400—499)
- VII Bureau of Industry and Security, Department of Commerce (Parts 700—799)
- VIII Bureau of Economic Analysis, Department of Commerce (Parts 800—899)
- IX National Oceanic and Atmospheric Administration, Department of Commerce (Parts 900—999)
- XI Technology Administration, Department of Commerce (Parts 1100—1199)
- XIII East-West Foreign Trade Board (Parts 1300—1399)
- XIV Minority Business Development Agency (Parts 1400—1499)

SUBTITLE C—REGULATIONS RELATING TO FOREIGN TRADE AGREEMENTS

- XX Office of the United States Trade Representative (Parts 2000—2099)

SUBTITLE D—REGULATIONS RELATING TO TELECOMMUNICATIONS AND INFORMATION

- XXIII National Telecommunications and Information Administration, Department of Commerce (Parts 2300—2399)

Title 16—Commercial Practices

- I Federal Trade Commission (Parts 0—999)
- II Consumer Product Safety Commission (Parts 1000—1799)

Title 17—Commodity and Securities Exchanges

Chap.

I   Commodity Futures Trading Commission (Parts 1—199)
II Securities and Exchange Commission (Parts 200—399)
IV Department of the Treasury (Parts 400—499)

Title 18—Conservation of Power and Water Resources

I   Federal Energy Regulatory Commission, Department of Energy (Parts 1—399)
III   Delaware River Basin Commission (Parts 400—499)
VI   Water Resources Council (Parts 700—799)
VIII Susquehanna River Basin Commission (Parts 800—899)
XIII Tennessee Valley Authority (Parts 1300—1399)

Title 19—Customs Duties

I   U.S. Customs and Border Protection, Department of Homeland Security; Department of the Treasury (Parts 0—199)
II   United States International Trade Commission (Parts 200—299)
III International Trade Administration, Department of Commerce (Parts 300—399)
IV   U.S. Immigration and Customs Enforcement, Department of Homeland Security (Parts 400—599)

Title 20—Employees' Benefits

I   Office of Workers' Compensation Programs, Department of Labor (Parts 1—199)
II   Railroad Retirement Board (Parts 200—399)
III   Social Security Administration (Parts 400—499)
IV   Employees' Compensation Appeals Board, Department of Labor (Parts 500—599)
V   Employment and Training Administration, Department of Labor (Parts 600—699)
VI   Office of Workers' Compensation Programs, Department of Labor (Parts 700—799)
VII   Benefits Review Board, Department of Labor (Parts 800—899)
VIII Joint Board for the Enrollment of Actuaries (Parts 900—999)
IX   Office of the Assistant Secretary for Veterans' Employment and Training Service, Department of Labor (Parts 1000—1099)

Title 21—Food and Drugs

I   Food and Drug Administration, Department of Health and Human Services (Parts 1—1299)
II   Drug Enforcement Administration, Department of Justice (Parts 1300—1399)
III Office of National Drug Control Policy (Parts 1400—1499)

Title 22—Foreign Relations

Chap.
- I Department of State (Parts 1—199)
- II Agency for International Development (Parts 200—299)
- III Peace Corps (Parts 300—399)
- IV International Joint Commission, United States and Canada (Parts 400—499)
- V Broadcasting Board of Governors (Parts 500—599)
- VII Overseas Private Investment Corporation (Parts 700—799)
- IX Foreign Service Grievance Board (Parts 900—999)
- X Inter-American Foundation (Parts 1000—1099)
- XI International Boundary and Water Commission, United States and Mexico, United States Section (Parts 1100—1199)
- XII United States International Development Cooperation Agency (Parts 1200—1299)
- XIII Millennium Challenge Corporation (Parts 1300—1399)
- XIV Foreign Service Labor Relations Board; Federal Labor Relations Authority; General Counsel of the Federal Labor Relations Authority; and the Foreign Service Impasse Disputes Panel (Parts 1400—1499)
- XV African Development Foundation (Parts 1500—1599)
- XVI Japan-United States Friendship Commission (Parts 1600—1699)
- XVII United States Institute of Peace (Parts 1700—1799)

Title 23—Highways

- I Federal Highway Administration, Department of Transportation (Parts 1—999)
- II National Highway Traffic Safety Administration and Federal Highway Administration, Department of Transportation (Parts 1200—1299)
- III National Highway Traffic Safety Administration, Department of Transportation (Parts 1300—1399)

Title 24—Housing and Urban Development

SUBTITLE A—OFFICE OF THE SECRETARY, DEPARTMENT OF HOUSING AND URBAN DEVELOPMENT (PARTS 0—99)

SUBTITLE B—REGULATIONS RELATING TO HOUSING AND URBAN DEVELOPMENT

- I Office of Assistant Secretary for Equal Opportunity, Department of Housing and Urban Development (Parts 100—199)
- II Office of Assistant Secretary for Housing-Federal Housing Commissioner, Department of Housing and Urban Development (Parts 200—299)
- III Government National Mortgage Association, Department of Housing and Urban Development (Parts 300—399)
- IV Office of Housing and Office of Multifamily Housing Assistance Restructuring, Department of Housing and Urban Development (Parts 400—499)

Title 24—Housing and Urban Development—Continued

Chap.

V   Office of Assistant Secretary for Community Planning and Development, Department of Housing and Urban Development (Parts 500—599)

VI   Office of Assistant Secretary for Community Planning and Development, Department of Housing and Urban Development (Parts 600—699) [Reserved]

VII   Office of the Secretary, Department of Housing and Urban Development (Housing Assistance Programs and Public and Indian Housing Programs) (Parts 700—799)

VIII   Office of the Assistant Secretary for Housing—Federal Housing Commissioner, Department of Housing and Urban Development (Section 8 Housing Assistance Programs, Section 202 Direct Loan Program, Section 202 Supportive Housing for the Elderly Program and Section 811 Supportive Housing for Persons With Disabilities Program) (Parts 800—899)

IX   Office of Assistant Secretary for Public and Indian Housing, Department of Housing and Urban Development (Parts 900—1699)

X   Office of Assistant Secretary for Housing—Federal Housing Commissioner, Department of Housing and Urban Development (Interstate Land Sales Registration Program) (Parts 1700—1799)

XII   Office of Inspector General, Department of Housing and Urban Development (Parts 2000—2099)

XV   Emergency Mortgage Insurance and Loan Programs, Department of Housing and Urban Development (Parts 2700—2799)

XX   Office of Assistant Secretary for Housing—Federal Housing Commissioner, Department of Housing and Urban Development (Parts 3200—3899)

XXIV   Board of Directors of the HOPE for Homeowners Program (Parts 4000—4099)

XXV   Neighborhood Reinvestment Corporation (Parts 4100—4199)

Title 25—Indians

I   Bureau of Indian Affairs, Department of the Interior (Parts 1—299)

II   Indian Arts and Crafts Board, Department of the Interior (Parts 300—399)

III   National Indian Gaming Commission, Department of the Interior (Parts 500—599)

IV   Office of Navajo and Hopi Indian Relocation (Parts 700—799)

V   Bureau of Indian Affairs, Department of the Interior, and Indian Health Service, Department of Health and Human Services (Part 900)

VI   Office of the Assistant Secretary-Indian Affairs, Department of the Interior (Parts 1000—1199)

VII   Office of the Special Trustee for American Indians, Department of the Interior (Parts 1200—1299)

Chap.

Title 26—Internal Revenue

I Internal Revenue Service, Department of the Treasury (Parts 1—End)

Title 27—Alcohol, Tobacco Products and Firearms

I Alcohol and Tobacco Tax and Trade Bureau, Department of the Treasury (Parts 1—399)
II Bureau of Alcohol, Tobacco, Firearms, and Explosives, Department of Justice (Parts 400—699)

Title 28—Judicial Administration

I Department of Justice (Parts 0—299)
III Federal Prison Industries, Inc., Department of Justice (Parts 300—399)
V Bureau of Prisons, Department of Justice (Parts 500—599)
VI Offices of Independent Counsel, Department of Justice (Parts 600—699)
VII Office of Independent Counsel (Parts 700—799)
VIII Court Services and Offender Supervision Agency for the District of Columbia (Parts 800—899)
IX National Crime Prevention and Privacy Compact Council (Parts 900—999)
XI Department of Justice and Department of State (Parts 1100—1199)

Title 29—Labor

SUBTITLE A—OFFICE OF THE SECRETARY OF LABOR (PARTS 0—99)
SUBTITLE B—REGULATIONS RELATING TO LABOR

I National Labor Relations Board (Parts 100—199)
II Office of Labor-Management Standards, Department of Labor (Parts 200—299)
III National Railroad Adjustment Board (Parts 300—399)
IV Office of Labor-Management Standards, Department of Labor (Parts 400—499)
V Wage and Hour Division, Department of Labor (Parts 500—899)
IX Construction Industry Collective Bargaining Commission (Parts 900—999)
X National Mediation Board (Parts 1200—1299)
XII Federal Mediation and Conciliation Service (Parts 1400—1499)
XIV Equal Employment Opportunity Commission (Parts 1600—1699)
XVII Occupational Safety and Health Administration, Department of Labor (Parts 1900—1999)
XX Occupational Safety and Health Review Commission (Parts 2200—2499)
XXV Employee Benefits Security Administration, Department of Labor (Parts 2500—2599)

Chap.
Title 29—Labor—Continued

XXVII   Federal Mine Safety and Health Review Commission (Parts 2700—2799)

XL   Pension Benefit Guaranty Corporation (Parts 4000—4999)

Title 30—Mineral Resources

I   Mine Safety and Health Administration, Department of Labor (Parts 1—199)

II   Bureau of Safety and Environmental Enforcement, Department of the Interior (Parts 200—299)

IV   Geological Survey, Department of the Interior (Parts 400—499)

V   Bureau of Ocean Energy Management, Department of the Interior (Parts 500—599)

VII   Office of Surface Mining Reclamation and Enforcement, Department of the Interior (Parts 700—999)

XII   Office of Natural Resources Revenue, Department of the Interior (Parts 1200—1299)

Title 31—Money and Finance: Treasury

SUBTITLE A—OFFICE OF THE SECRETARY OF THE TREASURY (PARTS 0—50)

SUBTITLE B—REGULATIONS RELATING TO MONEY AND FINANCE

I   Monetary Offices, Department of the Treasury (Parts 51—199)

II   Fiscal Service, Department of the Treasury (Parts 200—399)

IV   Secret Service, Department of the Treasury (Parts 400—499)

V   Office of Foreign Assets Control, Department of the Treasury (Parts 500—599)

VI   Bureau of Engraving and Printing, Department of the Treasury (Parts 600—699)

VII   Federal Law Enforcement Training Center, Department of the Treasury (Parts 700—799)

VIII   Office of International Investment, Department of the Treasury (Parts 800—899)

IX   Federal Claims Collection Standards (Department of the Treasury—Department of Justice) (Parts 900—999)

X   Financial Crimes Enforcement Network, Department of the Treasury (Parts 1000—1099)

Title 32—National Defense

SUBTITLE A—DEPARTMENT OF DEFENSE

I   Office of the Secretary of Defense (Parts 1—399)

V   Department of the Army (Parts 400—699)

VI   Department of the Navy (Parts 700—799)

VII   Department of the Air Force (Parts 800—1099)

SUBTITLE B—OTHER REGULATIONS RELATING TO NATIONAL DEFENSE

Title 32—National Defense—Continued

Chap.
- XII Defense Logistics Agency (Parts 1200—1299)
- XVI Selective Service System (Parts 1600—1699)
- XVII Office of the Director of National Intelligence (Parts 1700—1799)
- XVIII National Counterintelligence Center (Parts 1800—1899)
- XIX Central Intelligence Agency (Parts 1900—1999)
- XX Information Security Oversight Office, National Archives and Records Administration (Parts 2000—2099)
- XXI National Security Council (Parts 2100—2199)
- XXIV Office of Science and Technology Policy (Parts 2400—2499)
- XXVII Office for Micronesian Status Negotiations (Parts 2700—2799)
- XXVIII Office of the Vice President of the United States (Parts 2800—2899)

Title 33—Navigation and Navigable Waters

- I Coast Guard, Department of Homeland Security (Parts 1—199)
- II Corps of Engineers, Department of the Army (Parts 200—399)
- IV Saint Lawrence Seaway Development Corporation, Department of Transportation (Parts 400—499)

Title 34—Education

SUBTITLE A—OFFICE OF THE SECRETARY, DEPARTMENT OF EDUCATION (PARTS 1—99)

SUBTITLE B—REGULATIONS OF THE OFFICES OF THE DEPARTMENT OF EDUCATION

- I Office for Civil Rights, Department of Education (Parts 100—199)
- II Office of Elementary and Secondary Education, Department of Education (Parts 200—299)
- III Office of Special Education and Rehabilitative Services, Department of Education (Parts 300—399)
- IV Office of Vocational and Adult Education, Department of Education (Parts 400—499)
- V Office of Bilingual Education and Minority Languages Affairs, Department of Education (Parts 500—599)
- VI Office of Postsecondary Education, Department of Education (Parts 600—699)
- VII Office of Educational Research and Improvement, Department of Education [Reserved]
- XI National Institute for Literacy (Parts 1100—1199)

SUBTITLE C—REGULATIONS RELATING TO EDUCATION

- XII National Council on Disability (Parts 1200—1299)

Title 35 [Reserved]

Title 36—Parks, Forests, and Public Property

- I National Park Service, Department of the Interior (Parts 1—199)

Title 36—Parks, Forests, and Public Property—Continued

Chap.

II	Forest Service, Department of Agriculture (Parts 200—299)
III	Corps of Engineers, Department of the Army (Parts 300—399)
IV	American Battle Monuments Commission (Parts 400—499)
V	Smithsonian Institution (Parts 500—599)
VI	[Reserved]
VII	Library of Congress (Parts 700—799)
VIII	Advisory Council on Historic Preservation (Parts 800—899)
IX	Pennsylvania Avenue Development Corporation (Parts 900—999)
X	Presidio Trust (Parts 1000—1099)
XI	Architectural and Transportation Barriers Compliance Board (Parts 1100—1199)
XII	National Archives and Records Administration (Parts 1200—1299)
XV	Oklahoma City National Memorial Trust (Parts 1500—1599)
XVI	Morris K. Udall Scholarship and Excellence in National Environmental Policy Foundation (Parts 1600—1699)

Title 37—Patents, Trademarks, and Copyrights

I	United States Patent and Trademark Office, Department of Commerce (Parts 1—199)
II	Copyright Office, Library of Congress (Parts 200—299)
III	Copyright Royalty Board, Library of Congress (Parts 300—399)
IV	Assistant Secretary for Technology Policy, Department of Commerce (Parts 400—499)
V	Under Secretary for Technology, Department of Commerce (Parts 500—599)

Title 38—Pensions, Bonuses, and Veterans' Relief

I	Department of Veterans Affairs (Parts 0—99)
II	Armed Forces Retirement Home (Parts 200—299)

Title 39—Postal Service

I	United States Postal Service (Parts 1—999)
III	Postal Regulatory Commission (Parts 3000—3099)

Title 40—Protection of Environment

I	Environmental Protection Agency (Parts 1—1099)
IV	Environmental Protection Agency and Department of Justice (Parts 1400—1499)
V	Council on Environmental Quality (Parts 1500—1599)
VI	Chemical Safety and Hazard Investigation Board (Parts 1600—1699)
VII	Environmental Protection Agency and Department of Defense; Uniform National Discharge Standards for Vessels of the Armed Forces (Parts 1700—1799)

Title 41—Public Contracts and Property Management

Chap.

SUBTITLE A—FEDERAL PROCUREMENT REGULATIONS SYSTEM [NOTE]

SUBTITLE B—OTHER PROVISIONS RELATING TO PUBLIC CONTRACTS

50	Public Contracts, Department of Labor (Parts 50-1—50-999)
51	Committee for Purchase From People Who Are Blind or Severely Disabled (Parts 51-1—51-99)
60	Office of Federal Contract Compliance Programs, Equal Employment Opportunity, Department of Labor (Parts 60-1—60-999)
61	Office of the Assistant Secretary for Veterans' Employment and Training Service, Department of Labor (Parts 61-1—61-999)
62—100	[Reserved]

SUBTITLE C—FEDERAL PROPERTY MANAGEMENT REGULATIONS SYSTEM

101	Federal Property Management Regulations (Parts 101-1—101-99)
102	Federal Management Regulation (Parts 102-1—102-299)
103—104	[Reserved]
105	General Services Administration (Parts 105-1—105-999)
109	Department of Energy Property Management Regulations (Parts 109-1—109-99)
114	Department of the Interior (Parts 114-1—114-99)
115	Environmental Protection Agency (Parts 115-1—115-99)
128	Department of Justice (Parts 128-1—128-99)
129—200	[Reserved]

SUBTITLE D—OTHER PROVISIONS RELATING TO PROPERTY MANAGEMENT [RESERVED]

SUBTITLE E—FEDERAL INFORMATION RESOURCES MANAGEMENT REGULATIONS SYSTEM [RESERVED]

SUBTITLE F—FEDERAL TRAVEL REGULATION SYSTEM

300	General (Parts 300-1—300-99)
301	Temporary Duty (TDY) Travel Allowances (Parts 301-1—301-99)
302	Relocation Allowances (Parts 302-1—302-99)
303	Payment of Expenses Connected with the Death of Certain Employees (Part 303-1—303-99)
304	Payment of Travel Expenses from a Non-Federal Source (Parts 304-1—304-99)

Title 42—Public Health

I	Public Health Service, Department of Health and Human Services (Parts 1—199)
IV	Centers for Medicare & Medicaid Services, Department of Health and Human Services (Parts 400—599)
V	Office of Inspector General-Health Care, Department of Health and Human Services (Parts 1000—1999)

Chap.

Title 43—Public Lands: Interior

SUBTITLE A—OFFICE OF THE SECRETARY OF THE INTERIOR (PARTS 1—199)

SUBTITLE B—REGULATIONS RELATING TO PUBLIC LANDS

I   Bureau of Reclamation, Department of the Interior (Parts 200—599)

II   Bureau of Land Management, Department of the Interior (Parts 1000—9999)

III   Utah Reclamation Mitigation and Conservation Commission (Parts 10000—10099)

Title 44—Emergency Management and Assistance

I   Federal Emergency Management Agency, Department of Homeland Security (Parts 0—399)

IV   Department of Commerce and Department of Transportation (Parts 400—499)

Title 45—Public Welfare

SUBTITLE A—DEPARTMENT OF HEALTH AND HUMAN SERVICES (PARTS 1—199)

SUBTITLE B—REGULATIONS RELATING TO PUBLIC WELFARE

II   Office of Family Assistance (Assistance Programs), Administration for Children and Families, Department of Health and Human Services (Parts 200—299)

III   Office of Child Support Enforcement (Child Support Enforcement Program), Administration for Children and Families, Department of Health and Human Services (Parts 300—399)

IV   Office of Refugee Resettlement, Administration for Children and Families, Department of Health and Human Services (Parts 400—499)

V   Foreign Claims Settlement Commission of the United States, Department of Justice (Parts 500—599)

VI   National Science Foundation (Parts 600—699)

VII   Commission on Civil Rights (Parts 700—799)

VIII   Office of Personnel Management (Parts 800—899) [Reserved]

X   Office of Community Services, Administration for Children and Families, Department of Health and Human Services (Parts 1000—1099)

XI   National Foundation on the Arts and the Humanities (Parts 1100—1199)

XII   Corporation for National and Community Service (Parts 1200—1299)

XIII   Office of Human Development Services, Department of Health and Human Services (Parts 1300—1399)

XVI   Legal Services Corporation (Parts 1600—1699)

XVII   National Commission on Libraries and Information Science (Parts 1700—1799)

XVIII   Harry S. Truman Scholarship Foundation (Parts 1800—1899)

XXI   Commission on Fine Arts (Parts 2100—2199)

Title 45—Public Welfare—Continued

Chap.
XXIII Arctic Research Commission (Part 2301)
XXIV James Madison Memorial Fellowship Foundation (Parts 2400—2499)
XXV Corporation for National and Community Service (Parts 2500—2599)

Title 46—Shipping

I Coast Guard, Department of Homeland Security (Parts 1—199)
II Maritime Administration, Department of Transportation (Parts 200—399)
III Coast Guard (Great Lakes Pilotage), Department of Homeland Security (Parts 400—499)
IV Federal Maritime Commission (Parts 500—599)

Title 47—Telecommunication

I Federal Communications Commission (Parts 0—199)
II Office of Science and Technology Policy and National Security Council (Parts 200—299)
III National Telecommunications and Information Administration, Department of Commerce (Parts 300—399)
IV National Telecommunications and Information Administration, Department of Commerce, and National Highway Traffic Safety Administration, Department of Transportation (Parts 400—499)

Title 48—Federal Acquisition Regulations System

1 Federal Acquisition Regulation (Parts 1—99)
2 Defense Acquisition Regulations System, Department of Defense (Parts 200—299)
3 Health and Human Services (Parts 300—399)
4 Department of Agriculture (Parts 400—499)
5 General Services Administration (Parts 500—599)
6 Department of State (Parts 600—699)
7 Agency for International Development (Parts 700—799)
8 Department of Veterans Affairs (Parts 800—899)
9 Department of Energy (Parts 900—999)
10 Department of the Treasury (Parts 1000—1099)
12 Department of Transportation (Parts 1200—1299)
13 Department of Commerce (Parts 1300—1399)
14 Department of the Interior (Parts 1400—1499)
15 Environmental Protection Agency (Parts 1500—1599)
16 Office of Personnel Management, Federal Employees Health Benefits Acquisition Regulation (Parts 1600—1699)
17 Office of Personnel Management (Parts 1700—1799)

Title 48—Federal Acquisition Regulations System—Continued

Chap.

18 National Aeronautics and Space Administration (Parts 1800—1899)
19 Broadcasting Board of Governors (Parts 1900—1999)
20 Nuclear Regulatory Commission (Parts 2000—2099)
21 Office of Personnel Management, Federal Employees Group Life Insurance Federal Acquisition Regulation (Parts 2100—2199)
23 Social Security Administration (Parts 2300—2399)
24 Department of Housing and Urban Development (Parts 2400—2499)
25 National Science Foundation (Parts 2500—2599)
28 Department of Justice (Parts 2800—2899)
29 Department of Labor (Parts 2900—2999)
30 Department of Homeland Security, Homeland Security Acquisition Regulation (HSAR) (Parts 3000—3099)
34 Department of Education Acquisition Regulation (Parts 3400—3499)
51 Department of the Army Acquisition Regulations (Parts 5100—5199)
52 Department of the Navy Acquisition Regulations (Parts 5200—5299)
53 Department of the Air Force Federal Acquisition Regulation Supplement [Reserved]
54 Defense Logistics Agency, Department of Defense (Parts 5400—5499)
57 African Development Foundation (Parts 5700—5799)
61 Civilian Board of Contract Appeals, General Services Administration (Parts 6100—6199)
63 Department of Transportation Board of Contract Appeals (Parts 6300—6399)
99 Cost Accounting Standards Board, Office of Federal Procurement Policy, Office of Management and Budget (Parts 9900—9999)

Title 49—Transportation

SUBTITLE A—OFFICE OF THE SECRETARY OF TRANSPORTATION (PARTS 1—99)

SUBTITLE B—OTHER REGULATIONS RELATING TO TRANSPORTATION

I Pipeline and Hazardous Materials Safety Administration, Department of Transportation (Parts 100—199)
II Federal Railroad Administration, Department of Transportation (Parts 200—299)
III Federal Motor Carrier Safety Administration, Department of Transportation (Parts 300—399)
IV Coast Guard, Department of Homeland Security (Parts 400—499)
V National Highway Traffic Safety Administration, Department of Transportation (Parts 500—599)
VI Federal Transit Administration, Department of Transportation (Parts 600—699)

Title 49—Transportation—Continued

Chap.
VII National Railroad Passenger Corporation (AMTRAK) (Parts 700—799)
VIII National Transportation Safety Board (Parts 800—999)
X Surface Transportation Board, Department of Transportation (Parts 1000—1399)
XI Research and Innovative Technology Administration, Department of Transportation [Reserved]
XII Transportation Security Administration, Department of Homeland Security (Parts 1500—1699)

Title 50—Wildlife and Fisheries

I United States Fish and Wildlife Service, Department of the Interior (Parts 1—199)
II National Marine Fisheries Service, National Oceanic and Atmospheric Administration, Department of Commerce (Parts 200—299)
III International Fishing and Related Activities (Parts 300—399)
IV Joint Regulations (United States Fish and Wildlife Service, Department of the Interior and National Marine Fisheries Service, National Oceanic and Atmospheric Administration, Department of Commerce); Endangered Species Committee Regulations (Parts 400—499)
V Marine Mammal Commission (Parts 500—599)
VI Fishery Conservation and Management, National Oceanic and Atmospheric Administration, Department of Commerce (Parts 600—699)

CFR Index and Finding Aids

Subject/Agency Index
List of Agency Prepared Indexes
Parallel Tables of Statutory Authorities and Rules
List of CFR Titles, Chapters, Subchapters, and Parts
Alphabetical List of Agencies Appearing in the CFR

Alphabetical List of Agencies Appearing in the CFR
(Revised as of January 1, 2012)

Agency	CFR Title, Subtitle or Chapter
Administrative Committee of the Federal Register	1, I
Administrative Conference of the United States	1, III
Advisory Council on Historic Preservation	36, VIII
Advocacy and Outreach, Office of	7, XXV
African Development Foundation	22, XV
Federal Acquisition Regulation	48, 57
Agency for International Development	2, VII; 22, II
Federal Acquisition Regulation	48, 7
Agricultural Marketing Service	7, I, IX, X, XI
Agricultural Research Service	7, V
Agriculture Department	2, IV; 5, LXXIII
Advocacy and Outreach, Office of	7, XXV
Agricultural Marketing Service	7, I, IX, X, XI
Agricultural Research Service	7, V
Animal and Plant Health Inspection Service	7, III; 9, I
Chief Financial Officer, Office of	7, XXX
Commodity Credit Corporation	7, XIV
Economic Research Service	7, XXXVII
Energy Policy and New Uses, Office of	2, IX; 7, XXIX
Environmental Quality, Office of	7, XXXI
Farm Service Agency	7, VII, XVIII
Federal Acquisition Regulation	48, 4
Federal Crop Insurance Corporation	7, IV
Food and Nutrition Service	7, II
Food Safety and Inspection Service	9, III
Foreign Agricultural Service	7, XV
Forest Service	36, II
Grain Inspection, Packers and Stockyards Administration	7, VIII; 9, II
Information Resources Management, Office of	7, XXVII
Inspector General, Office of	7, XXVI
National Agricultural Library	7, XLI
National Agricultural Statistics Service	7, XXXVI
National Institute of Food and Agriculture	7, XXXIV
Natural Resources Conservation Service	7, VI
Operations, Office of	7, XXVIII
Procurement and Property Management, Office of	7, XXXII
Rural Business-Cooperative Service	7, XVIII, XLII, L
Rural Development Administration	7, XLII
Rural Housing Service	7, XVIII, XXXV, L
Rural Telephone Bank	7, XVI
Rural Utilities Service	7, XVII, XVIII, XLII, L
Secretary of Agriculture, Office of	7, Subtitle A
Transportation, Office of	7, XXXIII
World Agricultural Outlook Board	7, XXXVIII
Air Force Department	32, VII
Federal Acquisition Regulation Supplement	48, 53
Air Transportation Stabilization Board	14, VI
Alcohol and Tobacco Tax and Trade Bureau	27, I
Alcohol, Tobacco, Firearms, and Explosives, Bureau of	27, II
AMTRAK	49, VII
American Battle Monuments Commission	36, IV
American Indians, Office of the Special Trustee	25, VII
Animal and Plant Health Inspection Service	7, III; 9, I

587

Agency	CFR Title, Subtitle or Chapter
Appalachian Regional Commission	5, IX
Architectural and Transportation Barriers Compliance Board	36, XI
Arctic Research Commission	45, XXIII
Armed Forces Retirement Home	5, XI
Army Department	32, V
Engineers, Corps of	33, II; 36, III
Federal Acquisition Regulation	48, 51
Bilingual Education and Minority Languages Affairs, Office of	34, V
Blind or Severely Disabled, Committee for Purchase from People Who Are	41, 51
Broadcasting Board of Governors	22, V
Federal Acquisition Regulation	48, 19
Bureau of Ocean Energy Management, Regulation, and Enforcement	30, II
Census Bureau	15, I
Centers for Medicare & Medicaid Services	42, IV
Central Intelligence Agency	32, XIX
Chemical Safety and Hazardous Investigation Board	40, VI
Chief Financial Officer, Office of	7, XXX
Child Support Enforcement, Office of	45, III
Children and Families, Administration for	45, II, III, IV, X
Civil Rights, Commission on	5, LXVIII; 45, VII
Civil Rights, Office for	34, I
Court Services and Offender Supervision Agency for the District of Columbia	5, LXX
Coast Guard	33, I; 46, I; 49, IV
Coast Guard (Great Lakes Pilotage)	46, III
Commerce Department	2, XIII; 44, IV; 50, VI
Census Bureau	15, I
Economic Affairs, Under Secretary	37, V
Economic Analysis, Bureau of	15, VIII
Economic Development Administration	13, III
Emergency Management and Assistance	44, IV
Federal Acquisition Regulation	48, 13
Foreign-Trade Zones Board	15, IV
Industry and Security, Bureau of	15, VII
International Trade Administration	15, III; 19, III
National Institute of Standards and Technology	15, II
National Marine Fisheries Service	50, II, IV
National Oceanic and Atmospheric Administration	15, IX; 50, II, III, IV, VI
National Telecommunications and Information Administration	15, XXIII; 47, III, IV
National Weather Service	15, IX
Patent and Trademark Office, United States	37, I
Productivity, Technology and Innovation, Assistant Secretary for	37, IV
Secretary of Commerce, Office of	15, Subtitle A
Technology, Under Secretary for	37, V
Technology Administration	15, XI
Technology Policy, Assistant Secretary for	37, IV
Commercial Space Transportation	14, III
Commodity Credit Corporation	7, XIV
Commodity Futures Trading Commission	5, XLI; 17, I
Community Planning and Development, Office of Assistant Secretary for	24, V, VI
Community Services, Office of	45, X
Comptroller of the Currency	12, I
Construction Industry Collective Bargaining Commission	29, IX
Consumer Financial Protection Bureau	12, X
Consumer Product Safety Commission	5, LXXI; 16, II
Copyright Office	37, II
Copyright Royalty Board	37, III
Corporation for National and Community Service	2, XXII; 45, XII, XXV
Cost Accounting Standards Board	48, 99
Council on Environmental Quality	40, V
Court Services and Offender Supervision Agency for the District of Columbia	5, LXX; 28, VIII

Agency	CFR Title, Subtitle or Chapter
Customs and Border Protection	19, I
Defense Contract Audit Agency	32, I
Defense Department	2, XI; 5, XXVI; 32, Subtitle A; 40, VII
Advanced Research Projects Agency	32, I
Air Force Department	32, VII
Army Department	32, V; 33, II; 36, III, 48, 51
Defense Acquisition Regulations System	48, 2
Defense Intelligence Agency	32, I
Defense Logistics Agency	32, I, XII; 48, 54
Engineers, Corps of	33, II; 36, III
National Imagery and Mapping Agency	32, I
Navy Department	32, VI; 48, 52
Secretary of Defense, Office of	2, XI; 32, I
Defense Contract Audit Agency	32, I
Defense Intelligence Agency	32, I
Defense Logistics Agency	32, XII; 48, 54
Defense Nuclear Facilities Safety Board	10, XVII
Delaware River Basin Commission	18, III
District of Columbia, Court Services and Offender Supervision Agency for the	5, LXX; 28, VIII
Drug Enforcement Administration	21, II
East-West Foreign Trade Board	15, XIII
Economic Affairs, Under Secretary	37, V
Economic Analysis, Bureau of	15, VIII
Economic Development Administration	13, III
Economic Research Service	7, XXXVII
Education, Department of	5, LIII
Bilingual Education and Minority Languages Affairs, Office of	34, V
Civil Rights, Office for	34, I
Educational Research and Improvement, Office of	34, VII
Elementary and Secondary Education, Office of	34, II
Federal Acquisition Regulation	48, 34
Postsecondary Education, Office of	34, VI
Secretary of Education, Office of	34, Subtitle A
Special Education and Rehabilitative Services, Office of	34, III
Vocational and Adult Education, Office of	34, IV
Educational Research and Improvement, Office of	34, VII
Election Assistance Commission	2, LVIII; 11, II
Elementary and Secondary Education, Office of	34, II
Emergency Oil and Gas Guaranteed Loan Board	13, V
Emergency Steel Guarantee Loan Board	13, IV
Employee Benefits Security Administration	29, XXV
Employees' Compensation Appeals Board	20, IV
Employees Loyalty Board	5, V
Employment and Training Administration	20, V
Employment Standards Administration	20, VI
Endangered Species Committee	50, IV
Energy, Department of	2, IX; 5, XXIII; 10, II, III, X
Federal Acquisition Regulation	48, 9
Federal Energy Regulatory Commission	5, XXIV; 18, I
Property Management Regulations	41, 109
Energy, Office of	7, XXIX
Engineers, Corps of	33, II; 36, III
Engraving and Printing, Bureau of	31, VI
Environmental Protection Agency	2, XV; 5, LIV; 40, I, IV, VII
Federal Acquisition Regulation	48, 15
Property Management Regulations	41, 115
Environmental Quality, Office of	7, XXXI
Equal Employment Opportunity Commission	5, LXII; 29, XIV
Equal Opportunity, Office of Assistant Secretary for	24, I
Executive Office of the President	3, I
Administration, Office of	5, XV

Agency	CFR Title, Subtitle or Chapter
Environmental Quality, Council on	40, V
Management and Budget, Office of	2, Subtitle A; 5, III, LXXVII; 14, VI; 48, 99
National Drug Control Policy, Office of	21, III
National Security Council	32, XXI; 47, 2
Presidential Documents	3
Science and Technology Policy, Office of	32, XXIV; 47, II
Trade Representative, Office of the United States	15, XX
Export-Import Bank of the United States	2, XXXV; 5, LII; 12, IV
Family Assistance, Office of	45, II
Farm Credit Administration	5, XXXI; 12, VI
Farm Credit System Insurance Corporation	5, XXX; 12, XIV
Farm Service Agency	7, VII, XVIII
Federal Acquisition Regulation	48, 1
Federal Aviation Administration	14, I
Commercial Space Transportation	14, III
Federal Claims Collection Standards	31, IX
Federal Communications Commission	5, XXIX; 47, I
Federal Contract Compliance Programs, Office of	41, 60
Federal Crop Insurance Corporation	7, IV
Federal Deposit Insurance Corporation	5, XXII; 12, III
Federal Election Commission	5, XXXVII; 11, I
Federal Emergency Management Agency	44, I
Federal Employees Group Life Insurance Federal Acquisition Regulation	48, 21
Federal Employees Health Benefits Acquisition Regulation	48, 16
Federal Energy Regulatory Commission	5, XXIV; 18, I
Federal Financial Institutions Examination Council	12, XI
Federal Financing Bank	12, VIII
Federal Highway Administration	23, I, II
Federal Home Loan Mortgage Corporation	1, IV
Federal Housing Enterprise Oversight Office	12, XVII
Federal Housing Finance Agency	5, LXXX; 12, XII
Federal Housing Finance Board	12, IX
Federal Labor Relations Authority	5, XIV, XLIX; 22, XIV
Federal Law Enforcement Training Center	31, VII
Federal Management Regulation	41, 102
Federal Maritime Commission	46, IV
Federal Mediation and Conciliation Service	29, XII
Federal Mine Safety and Health Review Commission	5, LXXIV; 29, XXVII
Federal Motor Carrier Safety Administration	49, III
Federal Prison Industries, Inc.	28, III
Federal Procurement Policy Office	48, 99
Federal Property Management Regulations	41, 101
Federal Railroad Administration	49, II
Federal Register, Administrative Committee of	1, I
Federal Register, Office of	1, II
Federal Reserve System	12, II
Board of Governors	5, LVIII
Federal Retirement Thrift Investment Board	5, VI, LXXVI
Federal Service Impasses Panel	5, XIV
Federal Trade Commission	5, XLVII; 16, I
Federal Transit Administration	49, VI
Federal Travel Regulation System	41, Subtitle F
Financial Crimes Enforcement Network	31, X
Financial Research Office	12, XVI
Financial Stability Oversight Council	12, XIII
Fine Arts, Commission on	45, XXI
Fiscal Service	31, II
Fish and Wildlife Service, United States	50, I, IV
Food and Drug Administration	21, I
Food and Nutrition Service	7, II
Food Safety and Inspection Service	9, III
Foreign Agricultural Service	7, XV
Foreign Assets Control, Office of	31, V
Foreign Claims Settlement Commission of the United States	45, V
Foreign Service Grievance Board	22, IX

Agency	CFR Title, Subtitle or Chapter
Foreign Service Impasse Disputes Panel	22, XIV
Foreign Service Labor Relations Board	22, XIV
Foreign-Trade Zones Board	15, IV
Forest Service	36, II
General Services Administration	5, LVII; 41, 105
Contract Appeals, Board of	48, 61
Federal Acquisition Regulation	48, 5
Federal Management Regulation	41, 102
Federal Property Management Regulations	41, 101
Federal Travel Regulation System	41, Subtitle F
General	41, 300
Payment From a Non-Federal Source for Travel Expenses	41, 304
Payment of Expenses Connected With the Death of Certain Employees	41, 303
Relocation Allowances	41, 302
Temporary Duty (TDY) Travel Allowances	41, 301
Geological Survey	30, IV
Government Accountability Office	4, I
Government Ethics, Office of	5, XVI
Government National Mortgage Association	24, III
Grain Inspection, Packers and Stockyards Administration	7, VIII; 9, II
Harry S. Truman Scholarship Foundation	45, XVIII
Health and Human Services, Department of	2, III; 5, XLV; 45, Subtitle A,
Centers for Medicare & Medicaid Services	42, IV
Child Support Enforcement, Office of	45, III
Children and Families, Administration for	45, II, III, IV, X
Community Services, Office of	45, X
Family Assistance, Office of	45, II
Federal Acquisition Regulation	48, 3
Food and Drug Administration	21, I
Human Development Services, Office of	45, XIII
Indian Health Service	25, V
Inspector General (Health Care), Office of	42, V
Public Health Service	42, I
Refugee Resettlement, Office of	45, IV
Homeland Security, Department of	2, XXX; 6, I
Coast Guard	33, I; 46, I; 49, IV
Coast Guard (Great Lakes Pilotage)	46, III
Customs and Border Protection	19, I
Federal Emergency Management Agency	44, I
Human Resources Management and Labor Relations Systems	5, XCVII
Immigration and Customs Enforcement Bureau	19, IV
Immigration and Naturalization	8, I
Transportation Security Administration	49, XII
HOPE for Homeowners Program, Board of Directors of	24, XXIV
Housing and Urban Development, Department of	2, XXIV; 5, LXV; 24, Subtitle B
Community Planning and Development, Office of Assistant Secretary for	24, V, VI
Equal Opportunity, Office of Assistant Secretary for	24, I
Federal Acquisition Regulation	48, 24
Federal Housing Enterprise Oversight, Office of	12, XVII
Government National Mortgage Association	24, III
Housing—Federal Housing Commissioner, Office of Assistant Secretary for	24, II, VIII, X, XX
Housing, Office of, and Multifamily Housing Assistance Restructuring, Office of	24, IV
Inspector General, Office of	24, XII
Public and Indian Housing, Office of Assistant Secretary for	24, IX
Secretary, Office of	24, Subtitle A, VII
Housing—Federal Housing Commissioner, Office of Assistant Secretary for	24, II, VIII, X, XX
Housing, Office of, and Multifamily Housing Assistance Restructuring, Office of	24, IV
Human Development Services, Office of	45, XIII

Agency	CFR Title, Subtitle or Chapter
Immigration and Customs Enforcement Bureau	19, IV
Immigration and Naturalization	8, I
Immigration Review, Executive Office for	8, V
Independent Counsel, Office of	28, VII
Indian Affairs, Bureau of	25, I, V
Indian Affairs, Office of the Assistant Secretary	25, VI
Indian Arts and Crafts Board	25, II
Indian Health Service	25, V
Industry and Security, Bureau of	15, VII
Information Resources Management, Office of	7, XXVII
Information Security Oversight Office, National Archives and Records Administration	32, XX
Inspector General	
Agriculture Department	7, XXVI
Health and Human Services Department	42, V
Housing and Urban Development Department	24, XII, XV
Institute of Peace, United States	22, XVII
Inter-American Foundation	5, LXIII; 22, X
Interior Department	2, XIV
American Indians, Office of the Special Trustee	25, VII
Bureau of Ocean Energy Management, Regulation, and Enforcement	30, II
Endangered Species Committee	50, IV
Federal Acquisition Regulation	48, 14
Federal Property Management Regulations System	41, 114
Fish and Wildlife Service, United States	50, I, IV
Geological Survey	30, IV
Indian Affairs, Bureau of	25, I, V
Indian Affairs, Office of the Assistant Secretary	25, VI
Indian Arts and Crafts Board	25, II
Land Management, Bureau of	43, II
National Indian Gaming Commission	25, III
National Park Service	36, I
Natural Resource Revenue, Office of	30, XII
Ocean Energy Management, Bureau of	30, V
Reclamation, Bureau of	43, I
Secretary of the Interior, Office of	2, XIV; 43, Subtitle A
Surface Mining Reclamation and Enforcement, Office of	30, VII
Internal Revenue Service	26, I
International Boundary and Water Commission, United States and Mexico, United States Section	22, XI
International Development, United States Agency for	22, II
Federal Acquisition Regulation	48, 7
International Development Cooperation Agency, United States	22, XII
International Joint Commission, United States and Canada	22, IV
International Organizations Employees Loyalty Board	5, V
International Trade Administration	15, III; 19, III
International Trade Commission, United States	19, II
Interstate Commerce Commission	5, XL
Investment Security, Office of	31, VIII
James Madison Memorial Fellowship Foundation	45, XXIV
Japan–United States Friendship Commission	22, XVI
Joint Board for the Enrollment of Actuaries	20, VIII
Justice Department	2, XXVIII; 5, XXVIII; 28, I, XI; 40, IV
Alcohol, Tobacco, Firearms, and Explosives, Bureau of	27, II
Drug Enforcement Administration	21, II
Federal Acquisition Regulation	48, 28
Federal Claims Collection Standards	31, IX
Federal Prison Industries, Inc.	28, III
Foreign Claims Settlement Commission of the United States	45, V
Immigration Review, Executive Office for	8, V
Offices of Independent Counsel	28, VI
Prisons, Bureau of	28, V
Property Management Regulations	41, 128

Agency	CFR Title, Subtitle or Chapter
Labor Department	5, XLII
Employee Benefits Security Administration	29, XXV
Employees' Compensation Appeals Board	20, IV
Employment and Training Administration	20, V
Employment Standards Administration	20, VI
Federal Acquisition Regulation	48, 29
Federal Contract Compliance Programs, Office of	41, 60
Federal Procurement Regulations System	41, 50
Labor-Management Standards, Office of	29, II, IV
Mine Safety and Health Administration	30, I
Occupational Safety and Health Administration	29, XVII
Office of Workers' Compensation Programs	20, VII
Public Contracts	41, 50
Secretary of Labor, Office of	29, Subtitle A
Veterans' Employment and Training Service, Office of the Assistant Secretary for	41, 61; 20, IX
Wage and Hour Division	29, V
Workers' Compensation Programs, Office of	20, I
Labor-Management Standards, Office of	29, II, IV
Land Management, Bureau of	43, II
Legal Services Corporation	45, XVI
Library of Congress	36, VII
Copyright Office	37, II
Copyright Royalty Board	37, III
Local Television Loan Guarantee Board	7, XX
Management and Budget, Office of	5, III, LXXVII; 14, VI; 48, 99
Marine Mammal Commission	50, V
Maritime Administration	46, II
Merit Systems Protection Board	5, II, LXIV
Micronesian Status Negotiations, Office for	32, XXVII
Millennium Challenge Corporation	22, XIII
Mine Safety and Health Administration	30, I
Minority Business Development Agency	15, XIV
Miscellaneous Agencies	1, IV
Monetary Offices	31, I
Morris K. Udall Scholarship and Excellence in National Environmental Policy Foundation	36, XVI
Museum and Library Services, Institute of	2, XXXI
National Aeronautics and Space Administration	2, XVIII; 5, LIX; 14, V
Federal Acquisition Regulation	48, 18
National Agricultural Library	7, XLI
National Agricultural Statistics Service	7, XXXVI
National and Community Service, Corporation for	2, XXII; 45, XII, XXV
National Archives and Records Administration	2, XXVI; 5, LXVI; 36, XII
Information Security Oversight Office	32, XX
National Capital Planning Commission	1, IV
National Commission for Employment Policy	1, IV
National Commission on Libraries and Information Science	45, XVII
National Council on Disability	34, XII
National Counterintelligence Center	32, XVIII
National Credit Union Administration	12, VII
National Crime Prevention and Privacy Compact Council	28, IX
National Drug Control Policy, Office of	21, III
National Endowment for the Arts	2, XXXII
National Endowment for the Humanities	2, XXXIII
National Foundation on the Arts and the Humanities	45, XI
National Highway Traffic Safety Administration	23, II, III; 47, VI; 49, V
National Imagery and Mapping Agency	32, I
National Indian Gaming Commission	25, III
National Institute for Literacy	34, XI
National Institute of Food and Agriculture	7, XXXIV
National Institute of Standards and Technology	15, II
National Intelligence, Office of Director of	32, XVII
National Labor Relations Board	5, LXI; 29, I
National Marine Fisheries Service	50, II, IV

593

Agency	CFR Title, Subtitle or Chapter
National Mediation Board	29, X
National Oceanic and Atmospheric Administration	15, IX; 50, II, III, IV, VI
National Park Service	36, I
National Railroad Adjustment Board	29, III
National Railroad Passenger Corporation (AMTRAK)	49, VII
National Science Foundation	2, XXV; 5, XLIII; 45, VI
Federal Acquisition Regulation	48, 25
National Security Council	32, XXI
National Security Council and Office of Science and Technology Policy	47, II
National Telecommunications and Information Administration	15, XXIII; 47, III, IV
National Transportation Safety Board	49, VIII
Natural Resources Conservation Service	7, VI
Natural Resource Revenue, Office of	30, XII
Navajo and Hopi Indian Relocation, Office of	25, IV
Navy Department	32, VI
Federal Acquisition Regulation	48, 52
Neighborhood Reinvestment Corporation	24, XXV
Northeast Interstate Low-Level Radioactive Waste Commission	10, XVIII
Nuclear Regulatory Commission	2, XX; 5, XLVIII; 10, I
Federal Acquisition Regulation	48, 20
Occupational Safety and Health Administration	29, XVII
Occupational Safety and Health Review Commission	29, XX
Ocean Energy Management, Bureau of	30, V
Offices of Independent Counsel	28, VI
Office of Workers' Compensation Programs	20, VII
Oklahoma City National Memorial Trust	36, XV
Operations Office	7, XXVIII
Overseas Private Investment Corporation	5, XXXIII; 22, VII
Patent and Trademark Office, United States	37, I
Payment From a Non-Federal Source for Travel Expenses	41, 304
Payment of Expenses Connected With the Death of Certain Employees	41, 303
Peace Corps	2, XXXVII; 22, III
Pennsylvania Avenue Development Corporation	36, IX
Pension Benefit Guaranty Corporation	29, XL
Personnel Management, Office of	5, I, XXXV; 45, VIII
Human Resources Management and Labor Relations Systems, Department of Homeland Security	5, XCVII
Federal Acquisition Regulation	48, 17
Federal Employees Group Life Insurance Federal Acquisition Regulation	48, 21
Federal Employees Health Benefits Acquisition Regulation	48, 16
Pipeline and Hazardous Materials Safety Administration	49, I
Postal Regulatory Commission	5, XLVI; 39, III
Postal Service, United States	5, LX; 39, I
Postsecondary Education, Office of	34, VI
President's Commission on White House Fellowships	1, IV
Presidential Documents	3
Presidio Trust	36, X
Prisons, Bureau of	28, V
Procurement and Property Management, Office of	7, XXXII
Productivity, Technology and Innovation, Assistant Secretary	37, IV
Public Contracts, Department of Labor	41, 50
Public and Indian Housing, Office of Assistant Secretary for	24, IX
Public Health Service	42, I
Railroad Retirement Board	20, II
Reclamation, Bureau of	43, I
Recovery Accountability and Transparency Board	4, II
Refugee Resettlement, Office of	45, IV
Relocation Allowances	41, 302
Research and Innovative Technology Administration	49, XI
Rural Business-Cooperative Service	7, XVIII, XLII, L
Rural Development Administration	7, XLII

Agency	CFR Title, Subtitle or Chapter
Rural Housing Service	7, XVIII, XXXV, L
Rural Telephone Bank	7, XVI
Rural Utilities Service	7, XVII, XVIII, XLII, L
Saint Lawrence Seaway Development Corporation	33, IV
Science and Technology Policy, Office of	32, XXIV
Science and Technology Policy, Office of, and National Security Council	47, II
Secret Service	31, IV
Securities and Exchange Commission	5, XXXIV; 17, II
Selective Service System	32, XVI
Small Business Administration	2, XXVII; 13, I
Smithsonian Institution	36, V
Social Security Administration	2, XXIII; 20, III; 48, 23
Soldiers' and Airmen's Home, United States	5, XI
Special Counsel, Office of	5, VIII
Special Education and Rehabilitative Services, Office of	34, III
Special Inspector General for Iraq Reconstruction	5, LXXXVII
State Department	2, VI; 22, I; 28, XI
Federal Acquisition Regulation	48, 6
Surface Mining Reclamation and Enforcement, Office of	30, VII
Surface Transportation Board	49, X
Susquehanna River Basin Commission	18, VIII
Technology Administration	15, XI
Technology Policy, Assistant Secretary for	37, IV
Technology, Under Secretary for	37, V
Tennessee Valley Authority	5, LXIX; 18, XIII
Thrift Supervision Office, Department of the Treasury	12, V
Trade Representative, United States, Office of	15, XX
Transportation, Department of	2, XII; 5, L
Commercial Space Transportation	14, III
Contract Appeals, Board of	48, 63
Emergency Management and Assistance	44, IV
Federal Acquisition Regulation	48, 12
Federal Aviation Administration	14, I
Federal Highway Administration	23, I, II
Federal Motor Carrier Safety Administration	49, III
Federal Railroad Administration	49, II
Federal Transit Administration	49, VI
Maritime Administration	46, II
National Highway Traffic Safety Administration	23, II, III; 47, IV; 49, V
Pipeline and Hazardous Materials Safety Administration	49, I
Saint Lawrence Seaway Development Corporation	33, IV
Secretary of Transportation, Office of	14, II; 49, Subtitle A
Surface Transportation Board	49, X
Transportation Statistics Bureau	49, XI
Transportation, Office of	7, XXXIII
Transportation Security Administration	49, XII
Transportation Statistics Bureau	49, XI
Travel Allowances, Temporary Duty (TDY)	41, 301
Treasury Department	5, XXI; 12, XV; 17, IV; 31, IX
Alcohol and Tobacco Tax and Trade Bureau	27, I
Community Development Financial Institutions Fund	12, XVIII
Comptroller of the Currency	12, I
Customs and Border Protection	19, I
Engraving and Printing, Bureau of	31, VI
Federal Acquisition Regulation	48, 10
Federal Claims Collection Standards	31, IX
Federal Law Enforcement Training Center	31, VII
Financial Crimes Enforcement Network	31, X
Fiscal Service	31, II
Foreign Assets Control, Office of	31, V
Internal Revenue Service	26, I
Investment Security, Office of	31, VIII
Monetary Offices	31, I
Secret Service	31, IV
Secretary of the Treasury, Office of	31, Subtitle A

Agency	CFR Title, Subtitle or Chapter
Thrift Supervision, Office of	12, V
Truman, Harry S. Scholarship Foundation	45, XVIII
United States and Canada, International Joint Commission	22, IV
United States and Mexico, International Boundary and Water Commission, United States Section	22, XI
Utah Reclamation Mitigation and Conservation Commission	43, III
Veterans Affairs Department	2, VIII; 38, I
Federal Acquisition Regulation	48, 8
Veterans' Employment and Training Service, Office of the Assistant Secretary for	41, 61; 20, IX
Vice President of the United States, Office of	32, XXVIII
Vocational and Adult Education, Office of	34, IV
Wage and Hour Division	29, V
Water Resources Council	18, VI
Workers' Compensation Programs, Office of	20, I
World Agricultural Outlook Board	7, XXXVIII

List of CFR Sections Affected

All changes in this volume of the Code of Federal Regulations that were made by documents published in the FEDERAL REGISTER since January 1, 2001, are enumerated in the following list. Entries indicate the nature of the changes effected. Page numbers refer to FEDERAL REGISTER pages. The user should consult the entries for chapters and parts as well as sections for revisions.

For the period before January 1, 2001, see the "List of CFR Sections Affected, 1949–1963, 1964–1972, 1973–1985, and 1986–2000," published in 11 separate volumes.

2001

12 CFR — 66 FR Page

Chapter V
- 500 Heading revised.......................65819
- 502.20 Revised 33159
- 505.1 (b) amended 65819
- 505.2 Revised 65819
- 505.3 Amended 65819
- 505.4 Amended 65819
- 506.1 (b) table amended 65819
- 506.1 (b) amended; interim 15017
- Regulation at 66 FR 15017 confirmed......................................37407
- 516 Heading revised......................65820
- 516.1—516.3 (Subpart A) Removed 13000
- 516.1 Added 13000
- 516.5 Added 13000
- 516.10 Added 13000
- 516.15—516.47 (Subpart A) Added 13000
- 516.40 (a)(2) revised 65820
- 516.55 Added 13002
- 516.110 Amended 13003
- 516.120 Revised 13003
- 516.130 Revised 13003
- 516.140 Revised 13003
- 516.150 Revised 13003
- 516.185 Added 13003
- 516.190 Revised 13003
- 516.200—516.290 (Subpart E) Added 13003
- 517 Heading revised......................65820
- 517.6 (b) revised...........................13005
- 533 Added 2106
- 536 Regulation at 65 FR 75845 eff. date delayed 15345
- 541 Heading revised......................65820

12 CFR—Continued — 66 FR Page

Chapter V—Continued
- 543 Heading revised......................65820
- 543.9 (a) revised 13005
- 544 Heading revised......................65820
- 544.2 (c) amended 13005
- 544.5 (c)(1)(ii) revised 13006
  - (c)(1)(iii) revised 15020
- 545 Heading revised......................65820
- 545.92 (b) and (d)(2) revised; (f) amended 13006
- 545.92 (d)(2) revised 65820
- 545.93 Redesignated from 556.5 65820
- 546 Heading revised......................65820
- 550.80 Revised...............................13006
- 550.260 (b)(2) amended 13006
- 550.530 Amended 13006
- 552 Heading revised......................65820
- 552.2–6 Amended 13006
- Existing text designated as (a); (b) added 23154
- Regulation at 66 FR 37407 confirmed......................................37408
- 552.4 (d) amended 13006
- 552.5 (b)(1)(ii) revised 13006
  - (b)(1)(iii) revised 15020
- 555.310 (a) introductory text amended 13006
- 556 Removed..................................65820
- 556.5 Redesignated as 545.93..........65820
- 556.347 Revised 19854
- 559.3 (e)(2)(i) and (ii) amended 13006
- 559.4 Introductory text amended 13007
- Introductory text, (g)(3), (h)(2), (3) and (i) revised; (j) added.........65824
- 559.11 Amended............................13007
- 559.13 (b) revised..........................13007
- 560.3 Amended 65825

597

12 CFR—Continued

66 FR Page

Chapter V—Continued

- 560.30 Table amended; interim Regulation at 66 FR 15017 confirmed 15017, 15017
- Revised 65825
- 560.32 (c) amended 13007
- 560.35 (d)(3) revised 13007
- 560.36 Revised 65826
- 560.40 (a)(2)(ii) amended; (c) added 65826
- 560.42 Revised 65826
- 560.93 (d)(3)(iii) amended 13007
- 560.101 Appendix amended 65821
- 560.160 (a)(1) revised 13007
- 561 Heading revised 65821
- 562.4 (b)(1) revised 13007
- (c)(3) correctly added; CFR correction 33632
- 563 Heading revised 65821
- 563.22 (b)(1)(ii), (2), (d)(4), (f)(1) and (h)(2) revised 13007
- 563.41 (e)(2)(ii)(A) revised 13008
- 563.81 (a)(1), (2) and (c) amended 13008
- 563.143 Heading revised; (a)(1) amended 13008
- 563.161 (a) revised; interim Regulation at 66 FR 15017 confirmed 15017, 15017
- 563.171 (b)(4) revised 13008
- 563.180 (d)(11) revised 13008
- 563.183 (c)(1) revised 13008
- 563.555 Amended 13008
- 563.565 Revised 13009
- 563b.27 (e) footnote 1 amended 13009
- 563d.1 Amended 65821
- 563d.2 Amended 65821
- 563f.6 (a) amended 13009
- 563g.5 (b)(1) introductory text, (1)(i) and (2) revised 65821
- 563g.18 (a) amended 65821
- 565.4 (b)(2)(iii)(B), (3)(iii)(B) and (c)(2) note 1 amended 13009
- (b)(1)(iv) revised 65821
- 566 Removed; interim 15017
- Regulation at 66 FR 15017 confirmed 15017
- 567.1 Amended 59661
- 567.2 (a)(1)(i) revised 59663
- 567.3 (d)(2)(i) introductory text amended 13009
- (a)(2) correctly removed; CFR correction 33632
- 567.4 (a)(3)(i) amended 13009
- 567.5 (a)(2)(iii) added 59663

12 CFR—Continued

66 FR Page

Chapter V—Continued

- 567.6 (a) introductory text, (1), (ii)(R), (iii)(C), (iv)(J), (M), (2) introductory text, (i)(B) and (ii)(A) revised; (a)(1)(ii)(H), (iv)(N), (2)(i)(A), (C) and (3) removed; (b) added 59663
- 567.7 (f) revised 13009
- 567.9 (c)(1) revised 59666
- 567.11 (c) redesignated as (c)(1); (c)(2) and (3) added 59666
- 567.12 Heading, (a) and (e) revised; (b)(4) added 59667
- 568 Authority citation revised 8639
- Heading and authority citation revised 65821
- 568.1 (a) revised 8639
- 568.5 Added 8639
- 570 Heading revised 65821
- 570.1 (a) and (b) amended 8639
- 570.2 (a) revised 8639
- 570 Appendix B revised 8640
- 573.15 (a)(7)(ii) revised 65822
- 574.4 (f)(2) amended 13009
- 574.6 (f)(4) amended 13009
- 575.3 (b)(2) introductory text revised 13009
- 575.13 (a)(1), (b), (c)(2) and (e) amended 13010
- 583 Heading revised 65822
- 584.2-1 (a) and (c)(1) amended; interim 15017
- Regulation at 66 FR 15017 confirmed 15017
- 584.2-2 (b) amended 13010
- 590.3 (c) revised 65822

2002

12 CFR

67 FR Page

Chapter V

- 502.5 (a) revised 78151
- 505.2 Amended 78151
- 505.3 Revised 78151
- 505.4 Revised 78151
- 506.1 (b) table amended (OMB numbers) 76298, 78151
- (b) table amended (OMB numbers); interim; eff. 4-1-03 77916
- 516.40 (a)(2) revised 31726, 78151
- 516.220 (a) table corrected 3264
- 541.1 Revised 78152
- 545.74 (b)(2) revised 78152
- 550.20 Revised 76298
- 550.60 Amended 76298
- 550.70 Revised 76298
- 550.125 Added 76299

598

List of CFR Sections Affected

12 CFR—Continued
67 FR Page

Chapter V—Continued
- 550.130 Revised 76299
- 550.135 Added 76299
- 550.136 Added 76299
- 550.310 Amended 76299
- 550.580 Heading and introductory text revised; (c) removed 76299
- 550.600 Heading and introductory text revised 76299
- 551 Added 76299
- 557.11 (b) amended 78152
- 559.3 (1) revised; interim; eff. 4–1–03 77916
- (e)(2)(ii) amended 78152
- 560.220 Revised 60554
- Regulation at 67 FR 60554 eff. date delayed in part to 7–1–03 76304
- 561.1 Revised 78152
- 562 Technical correction 75809
- 562.4 (d)(3) and (e) revised; interim 70531
- (a) and (e) amended; interim; eff. 4–1–03 77917
- 563.41 Revised; interim; eff. 4–1–03 77917
- 563.42 Removed; interim; eff. 4–1–03 77918
- 563.43 (d) revised; interim; eff. 4–1–03 77918
- 563.146 Amended 78152
- 563b Revised 52020
- 563e Appendix A amended 78152
- 563g.19 Amended 78153
- 567 Technical correction 34991
- 567.1 Amended 16979, 31726
- 567.5 (b)(4) revised; (c)(2)(i) and (ii) amended; (c)(2)(iii) and (3) removed 31726
- 567.6 (a)(1)(i)(H) and (ii)(H) added 16980
- (a)(1)(iv)(G) and (H) revised 31726
- 567.7 Removed 31727
- 574 Authority citation revised 52035
- 574.3 (c)(1)(vii) amended 52035
- 575.2 (a) amended 52035
- 575.4 (c)(2) amended 52035
- 575.7 (a) heading and introductory text, (7), (b)(1), (2), (d)(6)(i) and (e) amended; (d)(7) and (8) added 52035
- (c)(1) and (2) amended 78153

12 CFR—Continued
67 FR Page

Chapter V—Continued
- 575.8 (a)(7) and (8) revised; (a)(9) through (21) redesignated as (a)(10) through (22); new (a)(9) added; (a) introductory text, (3) through (6) and new (10) amended 52035
- 575.11 (c)(1)(i), (2) and (e) amended; (i) added 52036
- 575.12 (a)(3) added 52036
- 575.13 (a)(1) revised; (c)(2) amended 52036
- 590.4 Heading and (f)(4) revised 60554
- 591 Authority citation revised 60554
- 591.2 (n) revised 60554

2003

12 CFR
68 FR Page

Chapter V
- 506 Technical correction 59997
- 506.1 (b) table amended 75109
- 513 Authority citation revised 48272
- 513.8 Added 48272
- 545.96 Amended; (a) revised 53025
- 550.70 Corrected 2108
- Table amended 75109
- 550.136 (a) amended 53026
- 559.3 Regulation at 67 FR 77916 confirmed; (1) revised 57796
- 560.30 Table amended 75109
- 562.4 Regulation at 67 FR 70531 confirmed 52832
- Regulation at 67 FR 77917 confirmed 57796
- 563 Authority citation revised 25112
- 563.41 Corrected 1218
- Regulation at 67 FR 77917 confirmed; revised 57797
- (b) introductory text amended 75110
- 563.42 Regulation at 67 FR 77918 confirmed 57796
- 563.43 Regulation at 67 FR 77918 confirmed; (d) and (e) revised 57798
- 563.177 Heading and (b) revised 25112
- 563.180 (c) amended 75110
- 563g.1 (a)(6), (9) and (10) amended 75110
- 563g.5 (a) amended 75110
- 567.1 Amended; interim 56536
- 567.5 (a)(1)(iii) revised; interim 56536
- 567.6 (a)(3) and (4) added; interim 56536
- 575.7 (d)(6)(i) amended 75110

599

2004

12 CFR
69 FR Page

Chapter V
- 502.5 (b) and (c) revised 30568
- 502.10—502.45 (Subpart A) Revised 30568
- 502.50 Revised 30571
- 502.75 (b) revised 30571
- 506.1 (b) table amended (OMB numbers); interim 68246
- (b) table amended (OMB numbers) 76602
- 509.103 (c) revised 64251
- 516.40 (a)(2) table amended 76602
- 516.70 Revised; interim 68246
- 516.120 (b) revised; interim 68247
- 516.140 Revised; interim 68247
- 516.150 Removed; interim 68247
- 516.160—516.190 (Subpart D) Revised; interim 68247
- 528.4 Introductory text revised; interim 68247
- 541.25 Revised 76602
- 543.2 (f) revised; interim 68247
- 544.2 (b)(3) revised; interim 68248
- 545.74 Removed; interim 68248
- 545.91 Revised; interim 68248
- 545.92 Revised; interim 68248
- 545.93 Revised; interim 68248
- 545.95 Revised; interim 68249
- 545.96 Revised; interim 68249
- 552.2–1 (a)(4) revised; interim 68249
- 552.4 (b)(2) revised; interim 68249
- 559.4 (f) revised; interim 68249
- 559.12 (d) removed; interim 68249
- 560.93 (b)(9) amended 76602
- 563.22 (e) revised; interim 68250
- 563.43 (f) amended 76602
- 563.181 Removed; interim 68250
- 563.183 Removed; interim 68250
- 563b.180 Revised; interim 68250
- 563b.185 Revised; interim 68250
- 563e.12 (f) removed; (g) through (p) and (r) through (v) redesignated as (f) through (o) and (s) through (w); new (q) and (r) added; (b)(1), new (j), (k) and (q) revised; interim 41188
- (t) revised 51161
- 563e.27 (g)(1) amended; interim 41188
- 563e.41 (b), (c)(1) and (e)(4) revised; interim 41188
- 563e.42 (i) revised; interim 41189
- 564 Note removed 76602
- 567.1 Amended 44924
- 567.5 (a)(1)(iii) amended; interim 22385

12 CFR—Continued
69 FR Page

Chapter V—Continued
- (a)(1)(iii) revised 44925
- 567.6 (a)(3)(iv) and (4)(ii) amended; interim 22385
- (a)(2)(iv) and (v) redesignated as (a)(2)(v) and (vi); (a)(2)(ii)(B), new (v)(A) and (3) revised; new (a)(2)(iv) added; new (a)(2)(vi) amended; (a)(4) removed 44925
- (a)(2)(v) revised 76602
- 567.13 Removed; interim 68250
- 568 Authority citation revised 77620
- 568 Heading revised; eff. 7-1-05 77620
- 568.1 (a) amended; eff. 7-1-05 77620
- 568.5 Revised; eff. 7-1-05 77620
- 570 Table of contents amended 76603
- Authority citation revised 77620
- 570.1 (c) revised 76603
- (b) and (c) amended; eff. 7-1-05 77620
- 570.2 (a) amended; eff. 7-1-05 77620
- 570 Appendix B amended; eff. 7-1-05 77620
- 571 Added; eff. 7-1-05 77621
- 574.6 (c)(2)(iii), (d) and (e) revised; interim 68250
- 575.13 (c)(3) and (f) revised; (c)(4) and (g) removed; interim 68251

2005

12 CFR
70 FR Page

Chapter V
- 506.1 Regulation at 69 FR 68246 confirmed 51586
- 507 Added 69640
- 509 Authority citation revised 69641
- 509.1 (f) amended; (g) redesignated as (h); new (g) added 69641
- 509.100 (a) revised; interim 10023
- 509.200—509.204 (Subpart C) Added; interim 10023
- 510.2 (b) amended 76675
- 516.70 Regulation at 69 FR 68246 confirmed 51586
- 516.120 Regulation at 69 FR 68247 confirmed 51586
- 516.140 Regulation at 69 FR 68247 confirmed 51586
- 516.150 Regulation at 69 FR 68247 confirmed 51586
- 516.160—516.190 (Subpart D) Regulation at 69 FR 68247 confirmed 51586
- 528.4 Regulation at 69 FR 68247 confirmed 51586
- 543.2 Regulation at 69 FR 68247 confirmed 51586

List of CFR Sections Affected

12 CFR—Continued
70 FR Page

Chapter V—Continued
544.2 Regulation at 69 FR 68248 confirmed...................................51586
545.74 Regulation at 69 FR 68248 confirmed...................................51586
545.91 Regulation at 69 FR 68248 confirmed...................................51586
545.92 Regulation at 69 FR 68248 confirmed...................................51586
545.93 Regulation at 69 FR 68248 confirmed; (b)(3)(iii) redesignated as (b)(3)(iv); new (b)(3)(iii) added........................51586
545.95 Regulation at 69 FR 68249 confirmed; heading revised; (b)(1)(iii) added........................51586
545.96 Regulation at 69 FR 68249 confirmed...................................51586
546.4 (a) and (b) amended..............76675
552.2-1 Regulation at 69 FR 68249 confirmed...................................51586
552.4 Regulation at 69 FR 68249 confirmed...................................51586
559.4 Regulation at 69 FR 68249 confirmed...................................51586
(g) revised......................................76675
559.12 Regulation at 69 FR 68249 confirmed...................................51586
560.30 Table amended....................76675
561.16 (a) designation and (b) removed; existing text amended...76676
563.22 Regulation at 69 FR 68250 confirmed...................................51586
563.181 Regulation at 69 FR 68250 confirmed...................................51586
563.183 Regulation at 69 FR 68250 confirmed...................................51586
563b.180 Regulation at 69 FR 68250 confirmed...................................51586
563b.185 Regulation at 69 FR 68250 confirmed...................................51586
563e.12 Regulation at 69 FR 41188 confirmed...................................15574
563e.21 (a)(1) revised....................10030
563e.27 Regulation at 69 FR 41188 confirmed...................................15574
563e.28 (a) amended; (d) added.......10030
563e.41 Regulation at 69 FR 41188 confirmed...................................15574
563e.42 Regulation at 69 FR 41189 confirmed...................................15574
564 Policy statement....................59987
567.6 (b)(5)(v)(B) amended.............76676
567.13 Regulation at 69 FR 68250 confirmed...................................51586

12 CFR—Continued
70 FR Page

Chapter V—Continued
568 Heading and authority citation revised.............................15754
568.5 Amended............................15754
Revised.......................................32229
570 Authority citation revised......15754
Appendix B amended....................15754
571 Authority citation revised.....33989, 70689
571.1 (b)(2) revised; interim; eff. 3-7-06...33989
Regulation at 70 FR 33989 eff. date delayed to 4-1-06...............70664
(b) revised; eff. 4-1-06..................70689
571.2 Added; interim; eff. 3-7-06......33989
Regulation at 70 FR 33989 eff. date delayed to 4-1-06...............70664
Added; eff. 4-1-06........................70689
Correctly revised........................75931
571.3 Introductory text, (a) through (n) revised; interim; eff. 3-7-06..................................33989
Regulation at 70 FR 33989 eff. date delayed to 4-1-06...............70664
Introductory text and (a) through (n) revised; eff. 4-1-06.
....70689
571.30—571.32 (Subpart D) Added; interim; eff. 3-7-06......................33990
Regulation at 70 FR 33990 eff. date delayed to 4-1-06...............70664
Added; eff. 4-1-06........................70689
Correctly revised........................75931
574.6 Regulation at 69 FR 68250 confirmed...................................51586
575.13 Regulation at 69 FR 68251 confirmed...................................51586

2006

12 CFR
71 FR Page

Chapter V
528.1 (b) revised............................19811
546.2 (a)(3) revised.......................19811
552.13 (a) and (c)(3) revised............19811
561.3 Amended..............................19811
561.7 Removed..............................19811
561.41 Removed............................19811
563.22 (d)(4) revised; (e)(2)(i) and (h)(2)(ii) amended; (h)(2)(iii) removed..19811
563.81 (b)(3), (f), (k)(3)(ii) and (5)(i) amended.....................................19811
563b.625 (b)(3) and (4) amended.......19811
563b.630 Heading revised; introductory text amended..............19811
563b.670 (b) amended....................19812

12 CFR—Continued

71 FR Page

Chapter V—Continued
563b.675 (b)(1) amended 19812
563e.12 (e) through (w) redesignated as (f) through (x); new (e) added; new (g)(4) revised 18618
570 Appendix B correctly amended 5780
Appendix A amended 19812
574.2 (e) and (o) removed 19812
574.7 (c)(1)(i) and (d)(6) amended 19812
575.7 (d)(6)(ii) amended 19812
583.3 Revised 19812
583.5 Removed 19812
583.19 Removed 19812

2007

12 CFR

72 FR Page

Chapter V
509 Authority citation revised 25955
509.1 (i) added; interim 25955
509.300—509.301 (Subpart D) Added; interim 25955
551.150 (a) amended; interim 30474
Regulation at 72 FR 30474 confirmed 62768
559.5 (b)(1) revised; eff. 4-1-08 69438
560.101 Appendix amended; eff. 4-1-08 69438
563.74 (i)(2)(iv) and (v) amended; eff. 4-1-08 69438
563.81 Revised 1927
(a) and (d)(2)(ii) amended; eff. 4-1-08 69438
563.141 (b) amended; eff. 4-1-08 69438
563.142 Amended; eff. 4-1-08 69438
563.171 (b) revised; interim 17803
Regulation at 72 FR 17803 confirmed 54349
563b.385 (a) amended 35149
563b.500 Revised 35149
563e.12 (u) revised 13435
(u)(1) correctly revised 72573
563e.21 (a)(1) amended 13435
563e.26 Revised 13435
(a)(1) heading correctly revised 72573
563e.28 (a) amended; (c) revised; (d) removed 13435
(c)(1) correctly amended 19110
563e Appendix A amended 13435
Appendix A correctly amended 19110
563f.2 (j)(1)(vi) amended; interim 1276

12 CFR—Continued

72 FR Page

Chapter V—Continued
Regulation at 72 FR 1276 confirmed 38755
563f.3 (b) amended; interim 1276
Regulation at 72 FR 1276 confirmed 38755
567.0 (Subpart A) Added; eff. 4-1-08 69438
567.1—567.12 Designated as Subpart B; heading added; eff. 4-1-08 69438
567.1 Introductory text revised; eff. 4-1-08 69438
567.3 (a), (b) introductory text and (d)(1) revised; eff. 4-1-08 69438
567.4 (a)(1) introductory text revised; eff. 4-1-08 69439
567.10 (e) introductory text revised; eff. 4-1-08 69439
567 Appendix C added and amended; eff. 4-1-08 69439
571 Authority citation revised 62972, 63764
571.1 (b)(3) added 62972
(b)(9) revised; (b)(10) added 63764
571.3 Introductory text revised; (o) removed 63764
571.20—571.28 (Subpart C) Added 62972
571.80—571.83 (Subpart I) Heading revised 63764
571.82 Added 63764
571.83 (a) and (b) redesignated as new (b) and (c); new (a) added 63764
571.90—571.91 (Subpart J) Added 63765
571 Appendix C added 62980
Appendix J added 63766
575.7 (a) and (b)(2) amended; (b)(1) and (3) removed; (b)(2), (c), (d) and (e) redesignated as (a)(9), (b), (c) and (d); new (d) revised 35150
575.8 (a)(3) through (9) revised; (c) added 35150
584 Heading revised; eff. 04/08 72238
Technical correction 73424
584.2 (b)(6)((i) revised; eff. 04/08 72238
584.2-2 (a) revised; eff. 04/08 72238
584.4 Revised; eff. 04/08 72238
585 Added; interim 25955
585.100 (b)(2) introductory text revised 50645

List of CFR Sections Affected

2008

12 CFR — 73 FR Page

Chapter V
509.103 (c) revised 63626
516.40 (a)(2) table revised 76939
558.1 (b)(1) and (2) removed; (b)(3) through (7) redesignated as new (b)(1) through (5) 18
558.2 Revised 18
559 Technical correction 21690
560 Technical correction 21690
563 Technical correction 21690
563.43 Introductory text amended 18
563e.12 (u)(1) revised 78155
564.8 (a) amended 18
565.2 (f) revised; eff. 1-29-09 79607
567 Technical correction 21690
Policy statement 44620
567.1 Amended; eff. 1-29-09 79607
567.5 (b)(1)(iv) and (v) removed; (b)(1)(vi) and (vii) redesignated as new (b)(1)(iv) and (v) 19
(a)(2)(vii) added; eff. 1-29-09 79607
567.9 (c)(1) revised; eff. 1-29-09 79607
567.12 (g) removed; (h) redesignated as new (g) 19
Heading, (a), (b)(3) and (e)(3) revised; (b)(5) and (h) added; eff. 1-29-09 79607
Appendix C corrected 21690
574.2 (c)(3) amended 19
575.9 (c) redesignated as (d); new (c) added 39219
(c) amended 76939
575.14 (c)(3) and (4) redesignated as (c)(4) and (5); new (c)(3) added 39219
(c)(3) amended 76939
585.100 (b)(2) introductory text amended 10986
(b)(2) introductory text revised 30737, 65258

2009

12 CFR — 74 FR Page

Chapter V
502.26 (a)(1) revised 68665
502.29 (a) revised 68665
535 Revised; eff. 7-1-10 5567
563e.11 (u)(1) revised 68664
567.1 Amended; interim 31167
Amended 60143
567.3 Second (d)(1) removed; CFR correction 67811
571 Authority citation revised 31520

12 CFR—Continued — 74 FR Page

Chapter V—Continued
571.1 (b)(5) added 31520
571.40—571.43 (Subpart E) Added 31520
571.82 (a), (b), (c)(2)(i)(A), (d)(1) and (3) amended 22643
571 Appendices C and J amended 22643
Appendix E added 31521
573.2 Revised 62945
573.6 (b) and (f) revised; (g) added; (g) removed eff. 1-1-12 62945
573.7 (i) added 62946
573 Appendix A redesignated as Appendix B; new Appendix A added 62946
Appendix B amended; Appendix B removed eff. 1-1-12 62955
585.100 (b)(2) introductory text revised 14458, 49792

2010

12 CFR — 75 FR Page

Chapter V
510.5 (a)(3)(ii), (iii), (d)(4)(i)(C) and (D) amended; (a)(3)(iv) and (d)(4)(i)(E) added; eff. 1-3-11 75586
535 Revised 23566
561.28 (a)(2)(i) revised 33502
563 Authority citation revised 44696
Technical correction 51623
563.101—563.105 (Subpart D) Added 44696
563.180 (d)(2)(iii), (3) introductory text and (12) revised; (d)(8) amended; eff. 1-3-11 75593
563e Authority citation revised 61045
563e.12 (g)(3) and (4)(iii)(B) amended; (g)(5) added; eff. 1-19-11 79286
(u)(1) revised 82219
563e.21 (e) and (f) added 61045
563e Appendix A amended 61046
567.0 (c) added 4652
567.5 (a)(1)(iii) revised 4652
567.6 (a)(3) revised 4652
567.11 (c)(3) redesignated as (c)(4); new (c)(3) and (d) added 4652
567 Appendix C amended 4653
585.100 (b)(2) introductory text revised 81377

603

2011

12 CFR

76 FR Page

Chapter V

563e.12 (u) heading and (1) corrected; CFR correction 20490